Garage Sale & Flea Market Annual

SIXTEENTH EDITION

CASHING IN ON
TODAY'S LUCRATIVE
COLLECTIBLES MARKET

CURRENT VALUES ON:

TODAY'S COLLECTIBLES
TOMORROW'S ANTIQUES

COLLECTOR BOOKS

A Division of Schroeder Publishing Co., Inc.

Front cover, top to bottom, left to right: Ceramic Arts Studio, figurine, Archibald, dragon, 8", $425.00. Ideal, Tiffany Taylor, 1974 – 1976, 19", $85.00. AMT, '62 Corvette Hardtop/Convertible, MIB, $55.00. Pflueger, Trory Minnow, 1902, 3⅞", $2,500.00 – 3,000.00. Hattie Carnegie, Christmas holly and berries earrings and brooch, 1970s, $45.00 – 65.00. CPC calendar, 1910, 9" x 12⁵⁄₁₆, $300.00. Precious Moments. It's So Much More Friendly with Two, 720019, $70.00. Satellite lunch box, steel with glass bottle, $140.00 – 150.00. McCoy, Harley Hog cookie jar, $325.00 – 375.00. Liberty Works, amber American Pioneer candlesticks, 6½", pair, $200.00.

Back cover, top to bottom, left to right: Made in Japan, dogs creamer and sugar set, 6½", $85.00 – 100.00. Mortens Studios, boxer, 4", $60.00 – 75.00. Breyer Animals, boxer, #66, $32.00. Handkerchief, Dogs by Rutherford, $15.00 – 20.00. Rookwood, beagle dogs bookends, 1929, 6", $400.00. Flue cover, profile of dog, 12" x 10", $80.00. Pilcher, compact, metal, leather, and composition, 1940s – 1950s, $65.00 – 85.00. Scottie dog pin, Lucite, 1950s, $55.00 – 65.00. Dell comic book, Old Yeller, #869, 1957, $30.00.

Cover design by Beth Summers
Book design by Heather Carvell, Beth Ray, Terri Hunter,
and Lisa Henderson

COLLECTOR BOOKS
P.O. Box 3009
Paducah, Kentucky 42002-3009

www.collectorbooks.com

Copyright © 2008 Schroeder Publishing Company

The current values in this book should be used only as a guide. They are not intended to set prices, which vary from one section of the country to another. Auction prices as well as dealer prices vary greatly and are affected by condition as well as demand. Neither the editors nor the publisher assumes responsibility for any losses that might be incurred as a result of consulting this guide.

Searching for a Publisher?

We are always looking for people knowledgeable within their fields. If you feel that there is a real need for a book on your collectible subject and have a large comprehensive collection, contact Collector Books.

A Word From the Editor

Garage sales, flea markets, auctions — gotta love 'em. If like us you're hooked on collecting, you'll be out there every weekend. What great fun! Though we seldom are able to add to our own collections, when we're shopping, our goal is to buy for resale anyway. Our small rural Indiana town has turned into an antique mecca — antique stores, specialty shops, and a mall literally line the streets on the downtown square. We have a couple of booths in the mall, and sales have been suprisingly brisk. Regarding garage sales, our mantra is 'Go early, go often, and go prepared.'

In this edition, we've tried to the best of our ability to give you accurate price evaluations. We all now that the market is soft right now and that values on many collectibles have leveled off and in many instances actually dropped. No one likes to think about their collection is loosing value, and we hate to report lower prices; but if this book is going to be at all helpful, it has to be honest. I'm sure the median age of today's collector has risen dramatically in the past 10 to 20 years, as many of the younger generation seem to have little or no interest in amassing 'things'; but there is still plenty of us around to keep things lively, and even some of the younger people, influenced no doubt by today's home decorating shows on HGT, are out and about searching for items ranging from old doors to convert to coffee tables, interesting mirrors for a wall arrangement, McCoy flowerpots for the kitchen windowsill, and mismatched silver-plated flatware to accessorize a vintage table setting. Though perhaps a little less frantic than it was 10 years ago, the market is still alive and well, and all is good. As collectors/buyers of vintage items, you need to be aware of changing values, whether up or down, and that has definitely been our goal this year. Remember that our prices in no way reflect what you will be paying at garage sales, flea markets or auctions. Our values are well established market retail and generally accepted by seasoned collectors and authorities; most have been checked over before publication by people well versed in their particular fields.

Last season, if you recall, I was a little discouraged about the likelyhood of being able to find good collectibles and antiques at garage sales anymore. Well, not anymore! We've had wonderful luck this year. I think the difference is that instead of shopping in the larger venues where the sales (and competitive buyers) are so concentrated, we've been heading out to small towns and sales scattered through the countryside. (We still love the town-wides, but you can only be first at just so many garage sales!)

Though we go to all the auctions and flea markets within easy driving distance, you can't beat garage sale prices, so they're still our favorite buying venue. Here's a good tip: Sometimes it pays to follow the balloons down unpaved roads to who knows where: less-traveled roads, certainly fewer to compete with for those often-amazing treasures. Here's what we bought at just one of those sales: a yellow ware crown-mark Robinson Ransbottom large mixing bowl, two McCoy mixing bowls with the pink and blue stripes, a dozen Fostoria cobalt blue water goblets in the Argus pattern, Hall range shakers, some vintage jewelry, a Marshal Studios vase, a hand-painted Fenton vase, and some Pfaltzgraff that both our daughter and granddaughter collect. Granted, it wasn't a typical sale. We had to 'kiss a lot frogs' in between, but it certainly wasn't the only great sale we found this summer. Again, way out in the countryside, we bought an assorted lot of wonderful collectibles including a large Fenton milk glass

Hobnail bowl (I paid $7.00, it booked for $85.00 and sold in the mall for $65.00 after the dealer discount); a matching butter dish; a painted toleware chandelier; a Noritake place setting in a popular pattern, unused and in its original box (price: $5.00); an Arthur Court aluminum chip and dip plate (original box, $2.00); an oval Indian Sandwich vegetable bowl; a small Dragon Ware vase; and half a dozen lovely handkerchiefs that had never been used. All was in wonderful condition and I had no trouble selling most of it right away. What fun! Great floral handkerchiefs are easy to find for 50¢ to $1.00 and most sell at a minimum of $5.00.

Some of my better buys this season were in jewelry. In a little zipper bag full of odds and ends that I purchased at a town-wide for $3.00 was an old Masonic badge dated 1944. As I was listing it for eBay, describing the enamel work and the bright cutting, I began to recognize the quality of the workmanship I was looking at decided I would have my jeweler look at it. Though it wasn't marked, it did test positive for gold. EBay bidding was brisk, and it sold at a very good price. Besides the badge, there was an old 10k Masonic ring, two sterling bracelets, and a wide pewter bride's bracelet from the nineteenth century. (If you do town-wides you know there's no time to waste between sales, and I was drawn to the bag in the first place by an old rhinestone brooch that was more bling than buck! In my defense, the bag and contents were originally priced at $5.00. I asked if she would sell me just the brooch, and the lady said 'take the whole bag for $3.00.') The second great jewelry buy was at a country garage sale where three 20-somethings were selling grandma's nicknacks. While all my attention was riveted on trying to inspect Lefton figurines for chips in the early morning gray light (remember, 'go early'), Bob picked up a rather grimy plateau mirror rounded up with beaded 'junk' necklaces. 'How much for all this? If she has to go through it piece by piece we'll be here all day!' (He can sometimes get impatient if I shop one sale too long.) 'A dollar' was the answer; so it went in the back seat with the old books, the absolutely mint ironstone coffeepot, the Garfield pressed glass historical bread plate, loads of figurines, some milk bottles from a defunct local dairy, and odds and ends of glassware. We dumped it out when we got back home and were stunned to find among the junk three wonderful costume jewerly brooches (two marked Kramer) and a great silver and turquoise bracelet signed by the artist. Grandma had style!

We've never been especially drawn to auctions, but since we've had the mall booth, we've been going to all that are nearby. Sometimes things do go high; we've learned if that's the case, we leave. We find we do much better at the smaller, less publicized auctions, as they usually have fewer bidders and therefore less competition. If you're tuned into a wide variety of collectibles, you'll always find something worthwhile at auction that you can buy underpriced, either for yourself or to sell at a profit — cookware (Visions, Corning Ware, and Guardian Ware, for example); linens (printed tablecloths, feed sacks, aprons, handkerchiefs, embroidered pillow cases, chenille bedspreads); glassware (of course, Depression, Indiana or Imperial carnival, Early American Prescut or Wexford items, Fenton, some elegant glassware now and then); dinnerware; old sheet music; jewelry; ceramics (Lefton items, Josef Originals, Occupied Japan, Holt Howard, Enesco, etc.); pottery; silverware; Christmas items; vintage

3

purses (Enid Collins, Lucite, tooled leather); salt and pepper shakers — the list could go on and on.

The key is to be able to recognize a 'good' item when one presents itself, and then to know how much you should pay for it. We try to go prepared. We not only study sale bills and the photos that are sometimes posted on the auctioneer's website, but we usually go with books on the subjects we expect to encounter at the sale. We always take a current *Garage Sale and Flea Market Annual* with us, as well as *Schroeder's Antiques Price Guide* and *Flea Market Trader*. Even though we've personally edited these books for more than 25 years, I still need to have them on hand; they're indispensable whenever and wherever I shop for antiques and collectibles.

The market is constantly changing. Gene Florence has always influenced the glassware market with his books on Depression glass, Elegant glass, kitchen glass, and the post-depression glassware of the '40s, '50s, and '60s. He has recently expanded his glassware research and writing to include Hazel-Atlas, Fire-King, and Anchor Hocking. It's the better, more modern collectible glassware of this type that we see so much of at estate sales today, and if you're schooled to recognize the more valuable examples, you'll be ahead of the vast majority of competetive buyers. Even Pyrex pie plates in the non-standard sizes sell very well in good condition. This summer we sold four of the fluted 7" pie plates on eBay to the same buyer at $70.00. We paid $12.00 for the box of miscellaneous old kitchen items they were hiding in, so it was well worth the two hours we had to wait for them to sell.

We've found the biggest drawback at auctions is bidding against someone who simply hasn't kept current with market prices, which as we said are much softer than they were five years ago. I often wonder if some of those dealers will even recover their initial investment. To buy for resale, you obviously have to know your market. My mall booth and eBay are my only outlets, so I make knowing my bidding limits a priority. Of course, if you're buying something for yourself just because you love it, you'll decide what it's worth from that perspective.

Few weekends have passed this season but what we have bought an amazing amount of 'goodies' to pack away to sell later. Here's a list of buys we made at an auction we attended this summer: a seven-piece berry set of American Sweetheart Monax for $2.50 (I had to ask the auction worker, 'What did I just buy'? — I was amazed); six footed water tumblers in American Fostoria at $25.00 for the lot; several vintage tablecloths in great condition for $5.00, among them one printed in Fiesta dinnerware colors of '40s that I expect will sell for a minimum of $60.00; a Reader's Digest book of favorite oldies music for $3.00 (worth $20.00 on eBay); and six

Moss Rose demitasse cups and saucers for $6.00. At my estimation, the $41.50 I spent represents a potential of $270.00 — certainly not bad for a pleasant day's work; and I know that the things I bought will sell quickly. Anyone willing to spend time in studying a variety of collectibles can do as well. If you know what you're doing, you're well ahead of 90% of the other buyers, many of whom are buying 'pretty,' 'interesting,' or simply useful items and have no idea of their actual worth.

The only flea market we do is local, within 45 minutes of our house, and it's only once a month. We look forward to it, and though it's small, we've found some wonderful items there as well: a 12" Heisey Plantation torte plate and console bowl for only $15.00 (they book at a total of $175.00 in Florence's current *Collectible Glassware from the '40s, '50s, and '60s*); a Blue Garland vegetable bowl for $2.00 (book is $35.00); 10k gold Masonic cuff links in their original box for $20.00 (probably a $75.00 value); a great 4-strand turquoise and sterling silver turquoise heishi necklace ($25.00!); several small pieces of Starburst Franciscan, cheap (which I think should probably bring about $65.00); and I could list much more. The marketplace is varied — you never know what you'll run into. But in order to take advantage of the 'sleepers,' you need to be informed.

In this edition, we've included several new categories where we've seen indications of emerging interest. Many narratives have references to books you'll want to read for even more information. The vast majority of our listings zero in on items from the 1940s on, since that's where the market's activity is strongest today. We list websites, clubs, tradepapers, and newsletters related to many specific areas; we recommend them all. Besides pleasant social interaction, collector clubs are a great way to garner knowledge, simply by networking with collectors whose interests are similar to yours.

An exclusive feature of this book is the section called Directory of Contributors and Special Interests. It contains the addresses of authors, collectors, and dealers sorted by specific collectible categories. Under most circumstances, they'll be willing to help you with questions that remain after you've made a honest attempt at your own research. Just remember if you do write one of our people, you will have to include an SASE for their response. And if you call, please consider the differences in time zones. But first, please read the text. Then go to your library; you should be able to find most of the books we reference. Check them out for study — they're all wonderful. Buy the ones you find particularly helpful or interesting. Good books soon pay for themselves many times over.

As another feature of this book, we'll give you some advice on how to hold your own garage sale. And we'll give you some timely pointers on how to set up at your first flea market.

How to Hold Your Own Garage Sale

Just as we promised we would, here are our suggestions for holding your own garage sale. If you're toying with the idea of getting involved in the business of buying and selling antiques and collectibles but find yourself short of any extra cash to back your venture, this is the way we always recommend you get started. Everyone has items they no longer use; get rid of them! Use them to your advantage. Here's how.

Get Organized. Gather up your merchandise. Though there's not a lot of money in selling clothing, this is the perfect time to

unload things you're not using. Kids' clothing does best, since it's usually outgrown before it's worn out, and there's lots of budget-minded parents who realize this and think it makes good sense to invest as little as possible in their own children's wardrobes. Everything should of course be clean and relatively unwrinkled to sell at all, and try to get the better items on hangers.

Leave no stone unturned. Clean out the attic, the basement, the garage — then your parent's attic, basement, and garage. If you're really into it, bake cookies, make some crafts. Divide your house plants; pot the starts in attractive little containers — ladies love 'em. Discarded and outgrown toys sell well. Framed prints and silk flower arrangements you no longer use, recipe books and paperbacks, tapes, records, and that kitchen appliance that's more trouble to store than it's worth can be turned into cash to get you off and running!

After you've gathered up your merchandise, you'll need to price it. Realistically, clothing will bring at the most about 15% to 25% of what you had to pay for it, if it's still in excellent, ready-to-wear shape and basically still in style. There's tons of used clothing out there, and no one is going to buy much of anything with buttons missing or otherwise showing signs of wear. If you have good brand-name clothing that has been worn very little, you would probably do better by taking it to a resale or consignment shop. They normally price things at about one-third of retail, with their cut being 30% of that. Not much difference money-wise, but the garage-sale shopper that passes up that $150.00 suit you're asking $25.00 for will probably give $50.00 for it at the consignment shop, simply because like department stores, many have dressing rooms with mirrors so you can try things on before you buy. Even at $25.00, the suit is no bargain if it doesn't fit when you get it home.

Remember that garage-sale buyers expect to find low prices. Depending on how long you plan on staying open, you'll have one day, possibly two to move everything. If you start out too high, you'll probably be stuck with lots of leftover merchandise, most of which you've already decided is worthless to you. The majority of your better buyers will hit early on; make prices attractive to them and you'll do all right. If you come up with some 'low-end' collectibles — fast-food toys, character glasses, played-with action figures, etc. — don't expect to get much out of them at a garage sale. Your competition down the block may underprice you. But if you have a few things you think have good resale potential, offer them at about half of 'book' price. If they don't sell at your garage sale, take them to a flea market or a consignment shop. You'll probably find they sell better on that level, since people expect to find prices higher there than at garage sales.

You can use pressure-sensitive labels or masking tape for price tags on many items. But *please* do not use either of these on things where damage is likely to occur when they're removed. For instance (as one reader pointed out), on boxes containing toys, board games, puzzles, etc.; on record labels or album covers; or on ceramics or glass with gold trim or unfired, painted decoration. Unless a friend

or a neighbor is going in on the sale with you, price tags won't have to be removed; the profit will all be yours. Of course, you'll have to keep tabs if others are involved. You can use a sheet of paper divided into columns, one for each of you, and write the amount of each sale down under the appropriate person's name, or remove the tags and restick them on a piece of poster board, one for each seller. I've even seen people use straight pins to attach small paper price tags which they remove and separate into plastic butter tubs. When several go together to have a sale, the extra help is nice, but don't let things get out of hand. Your sale can get *too* big. Things become congested, and it's hard to display so much merchandise to good advantage.

Advertise. Place your ad in your local paper or on your town's cable TV information channel. It's important to make your ad interesting and upbeat. Though most sales usually start early on Friday or Saturday mornings, some people are now holding their sales in the early evening, and they seem to be having good crowds. This gives people with day jobs an opportunity to attend. You *might* want to hold your sale for two days, but you'll do 90% of your selling during the first two or three hours, and a two-day sale can really drag on. Make signs — smaller ones for street corners near your home to help direct passers-by and a large one for your yard. You might even want to make another saying 'Clothing ½-Price after 12:00.' (It'll cut way down on leftovers that you'll otherwise have to dispose of yourself.) Be sure that you use a wide-tipped felt marker and print in letters big enough that the signs can be read from the street. Put the smaller signs up a few days in advance unless you're expecting rain. (If you are, you might want to include a rain date in your advertising unless your sale will be held under roof.) Make sure you have lots of boxes and bags and plenty of change. If you price your items in increments of 25¢, you won't need anything but a few rolls of quarters, maybe ten or fifteen ones, and a few five-dollar bills. Then on the day of the sale, put the large sign up in a prominent place out front with some balloons to attract the crowd. Take a deep breath, brace yourself, and raise the garage door!

What to Do With What's Left. After the sale, pack up any good collectibles that didn't sell. Think about that consignment shop or setting up at a flea market. (We'll talk about that later on.) Sort out the better items of clothing for Goodwill or a similar charity, unless your city has someone who will take your leftovers and sell them on consignment. This is a fairly new concept, but some of the larger cities have such 'bargain centers.'

Learning to Become a Successful Bargain Hunter

Let me assure you, anyone who takes the time to become an informed, experienced bargain hunter will be successful. There is enough good merchandise out there to make it well worthwhile, at all levels. Once you learn what to look for, what has good resale potential, and what price these items will probably bring for you, you'll be equipped and ready for any hunting trip. You'll be the one to find treasures. They are out there!

Garage sales are absolutely wonderful for finding bargains. But you'll have to get up early! Even non-collectors can spot quality merchandise, and at those low garage sale prices (low unless of course held by an owner who's done his homework) those items will be the first to move.

In order for you to be a successful garage sale shopper, you have to get yourself organized. It's important to conserve your time. The sales you hit during the first early-morning hour will prove to be the best nine times out of 10, so you must have a plan before you ever leave home. Plot your course. Your local paper will have a section on garage sale ads, and local cable TV channels may also carry garage sale advertising. Most people hold their sales on the weekend, but some may start earlier in the week, so be sure to turn to the 'Garage Sales' ads daily. Write them down and try to organize them by areas — northwest, northeast, etc. At first, you'll probably need your city map, but you'll be surprised at how quickly the streets will become familiar to you. Upper middle-class neighborhoods generally have the best sales and the best merchandise, so concentrate on those areas, though sales in older areas may offer older items. (Here's where you have to interpret those sale ads.) And don't forget the sales in the country; these are often very productive as well. When you've decided where you want to start, 'go early'! If the ad says 8:00, be there at 7:00 (unless it specifically states 'no early sales'). You can pull this off without being rude or pushy. Many times it will make the difference between finding great items or so-so items. And chances are when you get there an hour early, you'll not be their first customer. If they're obviously not ready for business, just politely inquire if you may look. If you're charming and their nerves aren't completely frayed from trying to get things ready, chances are they won't mind.

In town, competition can be fierce during those important early-morning hours. Learn to scan the tables quickly, then move to the area that looks the most promising. Don't be afraid to ask for a better price if you feel it's too high, but most people have already priced garage sale merchandise so that it will sell. Keep a notebook to jot down items you didn't buy the first time around but think you might be interested in if the price were reduced later on. After going through dozens of sales (I've done as many as 30 or so in one morning), you won't remember where you saw what! Often by noon, at least by mid-afternoon, veteran garage sale buyers are finished with their rounds and attendance becomes very thin. Owners are usually much more receptive to the idea of lowering their prices, so it may pay you to make a second pass. In fact, some people find it advantageous to go to the better sales on the last day as well as the first. They'll make an offer for everything that's left, and since most of the time the owner is about ready to *pay* someone to take it at that point, they can usually name their price. Although most of the collectibles will be gone at this point, there are nearly always some useable household items and several pieces of good, serviceable clothing left. The household items will sell at flea markets or consignment shops, and if there are worthwhile clothing items, take them to a resale boutique. They'll either charge the 30% commission fee or buy the items outright for about half of the amount they feel they can ask, a new practice some resale shops are beginning to follow. Because they want only clothing that is in style, in season, and like new, their prices may be a little higher than others shops, so half of that asking price is a good deal.

Tag sales are common in the larger cities. They are normally held in lieu of an auction, when estates are being dispersed, or when families are moving. Sometimes only a few buyers are admitted at one time, and as one leaves another is allowed to take his place. So just as is true with garage sales, the early bird gets the goodies. Really serious shoppers begin to arrive as much as an hour or two before the scheduled opening time. I know of one who will spend the night in his van and camp on the 'doorstep' if he thinks the sale is especially promising. And he can tell you fantastic success stories! But since it's customary to have tag sale items appraised before values are set, be prepared to pay higher prices. That's not to say, though, that you won't find bargains here. (I once bought a Wavecrest ferner for $20.00, because the seller thought it should have had a lid.) If you think an item is overpriced, leave a bid. Just don't forget to follow through on it, since if it doesn't sell at their asking price, they may end up holding it for you.

Auctions can go either way. Depending on the crowd and what items are for sale, you can sometimes spend all day and never be able to buy anything. Better items often go high. On the other hand, there are often 'sleepers' that can be bought cheaply enough to resell at a good profit. Toys, dolls, Hummels, Royal Doultons, banks, cut glass, and other 'high-profile' collectibles usually sell well, but white ironstone, dinnerware sets from the '20s through the '70s, kitchen glassware, and linens, for instance, often pass relatively unnoticed by the majority of the buyers.

If there is a consignment auction house in your area, check it out. These are usually operated by local auctioneers, and the sales they hold in-house often involve low-income estates. You won't find something every time, so try to investigate the merchandise ahead of schedule to see if it's going to be worth your time to attend. Competition is probably less at one of these than in any of the other types of sales we've mentioned, and wonderful buys have been made from time to time.

Flea markets are often wonderful places to find bargains. I don't like the small ones — not that I don't find anything there, but I've learned to move through them so fast (to get ahead of the crowd), I don't get my 'fix'; I just leave wanting more. If you've never been to a large flea market, you don't know what you're missing. Even if you're not a born-again collector, I guarantee you will love it. And they're excellent places to study the market. You'll be able to see where the buying activity is; you can check and compare prices, talk with dealers and collectors, and do hands-on inspections. I've found that if I first study a particular subject by reading a book or a magazine article, this type of exposure really 'locks in' what I have learned.

Because there are many types of flea market dealers, there are plenty of bargains. The casual, once-in-a-while dealer may not always keep up with changing market values. Some of them simply price their items by what they themselves had to pay for it. Just as being early at garage sales is important, here it's a must. If you've ever been in line waiting for a flea market to open, you know that cars are often backed up for several blocks, and people will be standing in line waiting to be admitted hours before the gate opens. Browsers? Window shoppers? Not likely. Competition! So if you're going to have a chance at all, you'd better be in line yourself. Take a partner and split up on the first pass so that you can cover the grounds more quickly. It's a common sight to see the serious buyers conversing with their partners via cell phones, and if you like to discuss possible purchases with each other before you actually buy, this is a good way to do it.

Learn to bargain with dealers. Their prices are usually negotiable, and most will come down by 10% to 20%. Be polite and fair, and you can expect the same treatment in return. Unpriced items are harder to deal for. I have no problem offering to give $8.00 if an item is marked $10.00, but it's difficult for me to have to ask the price and then make a counter offer. So I'll just say 'This isn't marked. Will you take...?' I'm not an aggressive barterer, so this works for me.

There are so many reproductions on the flea market level (and at malls and co-ops), that you need to be suspicious of anything that looks too new! Some fields of collecting have been especially hard hit. Whenever a collectible becomes so much in demand that prices are high, reproductions are bound to make an appearance. For instance, Black Americana, Nippon, Roseville, banks, toys of all types, teddy bears, lamps, glassware, doorstops, cookie jars, prints, advertising items, and many other fields have been especially vulnerable. Learn to check for telltale signs — paint that is too bright, joints that don't fit, variations in sizes or colors, creases in paper that you can see but not feel, and so on. Remember that zip codes have been used only since 1963, and this can sometimes help you date an item in question. Check glassware for areas of wavy irregularities often seen in new glass.

Antique malls and co-ops should be visited on a regular basis. Many mall dealers restock day after day, and traffic and buying competition is usually fierce. As a rule, you won't often find great bargains here; what you do save on is time. And if time is what you're short of, you'll be able to see lots of good merchandise under one roof, on display by people who've already done the leg work and invested *their* time, hence the higher prices. But there are always underpriced items as well, and if you've taken the time to do your homework, you'll be able to spot them right away.

Unless the dealer who rents the booth happens to be there, though, mall and co-op prices are usually firm. But often times they'll run sales — '20% off everything in booth #101.' If you have a dealer's license, and you really should get one, most will give you a courtesy 10% to 20% discount on items over $20.00, unless you want to pay with a credit card.

Antique shows are exciting to visit, but obviously if a dealer is paying several hundred dollars to set up for a three-day show, he's going to be asking top price to offset expenses. So even though bar-

gains will be few, the merchandise is usually superior, and you may be able to find that special item you've been looking for.

Goodwill stores and resale shops are usually listed in the telephone book. When you travel, it will pay you to check them out. If there's one in your area, visit it often. You never know what may turn up there.

The internet is, of course, at the hub of most of the buying/selling activity today. Set-price online malls are expanding as many dealers find that auction prices are very often too soft to accept, and scores of long-time antiques and collectibles dealers now have wonderful websites. Buyers often voice the opinion that they are more confident when trading with these well established sellers than they are some of the part-time vendors more often encountered on eBay and similar sites. Still, there is no doubt that there are many bargains to be had on eBay, and it continues to be a big factor in the marketplace. But where you could basically sell anything via eBay a couple of years ago, now to attract a buyer, you may very often have to relist your item, and you'll find some things won't sell at all. The look of eBay is constantly changing; where once it was basically an online auction, now many items start out with a 'buy it now' or 'best offer' price line. Reserve-price sales often go by without a single bid, as buyers look for low starting prices and the possibility of getting a bargain.

What's Hot on Today's Market

Whether you're a collector or buying to resell, here's a look at some collectible categories that may be helpful as you shop at the garage sale and flea market levels. Even though you'll seldom find items old enough to be classified as 'antique,' there are always good buys on items made during the 1940s through the 1970s and beyond, and those are the years this publication covers. Though in general, the market is soft, there are still good opportunities to buy and sell at a fair profit, if you're willing to take the necessary time to do your research. From the collector's viewpoint, there's never been a better time to add to your collection. Rationally, we have to expect that lower buying/selling prices will entice new collectors. When that happens, values may start back up as demand and supply come back into balance. Some dealers believe that the pre-eBay market was over inflated and due for an adjustment. Today, many feel that in time the market will level out.

In particular, look at the new categories we add each year. Our staff works with auction prices, eBay auctions, LiveAuctioneers.com; we talk with members of our huge advisory board on a regular basis; and we follow the market on a personal level. As soon as we see new spurts of interest, we do a workup so we can include information on that subject.

In addition to at-home study, you would be wise to attend shows and talk to dealers and fellow collectors. Read tradepapers and magazines and check out the 'antiques and collectibles' aisles of your bookstore. Watch for new books on any subject. Sometimes that's all it takes to get a potential collectible off and running.

Here is a list of various collectibles you're most apt to find as you make your garage sale rounds. (It's simply alphabetized, not in any particular order of importance.)

Cast iron items: Doorstops, bookends, door knockers, trivets, and bottle openers. Subject matter, the absence or presence of

a trademark, rarity, and, of course, condition of the paint are the important worth-assessing factors here. Compared to an example in excellent paint, one with considerable wear may be worth as much as 75% less. Common pieces that are lacking paint are worth very little. Beware, reproductions are everywhere! Be suspicious of paint that seems too bright and joints that do not fit well together. Trivets are worth very little if they are not marked and/or dated.

Ceramics: Among the top-selling figural ceramics are head vases and salt and pepper shakers. Wall pocket values are down, but those with good designs and made well still find a ready market.

Among the top-selling American producers of ceramic/pottery figurines are Rosemeade, Stangl, Hagen-Renaker, Ceramic Arts Studio, and Kay Finch. You would be well advised to prioritize your study time to include all of these. Though most examples will be marked, some (Rosemeade, for instance) originally carried labels which may have been removed over the years. Royal Haeger made some wonderful figural pieces as well — many of them very large, but Haeger figurals are relatively harder to find (though I have picked up several in the Bennington Brown Foam glaze). All of these topics are covered in this guide; time spent on becoming familiar with these wares can really pay off.

Holt Howard in general is doing well, though prices have softened to some extent over the past few years. The Pixies, however, continue to be very popular and for the most part are holding their own.

Prices for Lefton figurines are stronger — especially Kewpies, birthday angels, unusual subject matter (mermaids, for example), lovely ladies with their names on their bases, matched pairs (Pinky and Boy for instance), and the larger examples. Miss Priss, Blue Birds, and Christmas items are always good. Besides the figural pieces, tea and coffee sets are also selling well.

Enesco, another importing company, marketed wonderful figural items too, and some of these are bringing good prices on eBay and at our mall. They made lovely head vases and several lines geared specifically toward collectors: Cherished Teddies, David Winter Cottages, and My Little Kitchen Fairies among them. Mother in the Kitchen (or Kitchen Prayer Ladies, as they are often called) have been popular with collectors for several years.

Nearly any well done, marked ceramic figurine has value. Other marks to look for are Royal Copley, Shawnee, Regal, Treasure Craft, Will-George, Hedi Schoop, Brayton Laguna, Twin Winton, Josef Originals, Gilner, and Weilware. Though many of these are worth in the $25.00 to $75.00 range, every company made some that bring much higher prices — keep those in mind. You never know what you may encounter.

Children's things: Especially glassware, china, sewing items, records, and books from the 1940s (and earlier) through the 1970s.

Cameras: Be careful to buy only quality items that show little wear. Values depend on quality and availability of parts, batteries, and accessories. Box cameras from the 1930s and before are very collectible as are Rangefinders (especially of German and Japanese manufacture). Most common Poloroids and movie cameras have little investment potential.

Christmas, Halloween, and other holiday collectibles: These are the kind of things that tend to be passed down in the family and reused again and again. At some point in this progression, they often fall into the hands of someone who prefers the new to the traditional, and if you're watching for them, you'll find they often turn up in the most unexpected places. Look for figural bulbs, ornaments, and candy containers; die-cut witches and black cats; holiday postcards; and aluminum Christmas trees.

Clothing: Anything vintage; things from the '40s through the '70s are hot! Look for accessories like ladies' platform shoes and the Lucite shoes from the '50s, Hawaiian shirts (those with Hawaiian labels are best), and watch for good designer labels.

Decorative items and discontinued 'party plan' wares: Coppercraft Guild, Homco framed prints and figurines (especially the Masterpiece Collection and Denim Days lines), Longaberger baskets and pottery, Princess House glassware, Syroco mirrors and wall plaques, and paint-by-number pictures.

Dinnerware: High on many collectors' want lists are the mid-century high-style lines by designers such as Zeisel, Schreckengost, and Russel Wright, but more traditional lines by chinaware companies like Hall and Homer Laughlin are not far behind. Don't pass up attractive lines by Franciscan (in Desert Rose look for the older marks; it has been reproduced), Harker, Red Wing, Stangl, Syracuse, Weil, Winfield, and Vernon Kilns — all are discontinued, and the secondary market is the only source left for replacement pieces. We're seeing some of the post-'86 Fiesta on the secondary market, and the discontinued colors are starting to attract nearly as many buyers as the vintage line.

Dolls: Vintage Barbie prices barely trail some of the high-end French fashion dolls. If you're tempted to buy Holiday Barbie dolls (their are so many on eBay that values are steadily falling), be sure that the even the box is in at least near mint condition, if you want to be sure of selling it at a good price. Sometimes the difference between a doll in a mint box and the same doll in a box with crumpled corners or torn flaps can be as much as 50%. Liddle Kiddles that are still mint in the original box find a ready market. Also watch for Mattel talkers (Chatty Cathy in particular), Dawn and Ideal dolls, and celebrity dolls. Strawberry Shortcake is doing very well, especially the earlier editions. Steiff animals with their original identification tags often sell for hundreds of dollars.

Furniture: Depending on individual taste, several styles of furniture are hot right now. Arts & Crafts, for instance, Fifties Modern, painted pine pieces, and accessories such as clocks, lighting fixtures, and lamps needed to complete the look sell quickly.

Fishing tackle: Lures with good original paint and hardware, reels, rods, decoys, and advertising ephemera.

Glassware: Crackle glass, Elegant glass, Fenton, Fire-King/Anchor Hocking, Hazel-Atlas, Depression glass, and glassware from the '40s, '50s, and '60s. Take this book along, as we cover all of these fields, and be sure to study the books on these topics by Gene and Cathy Florence. Of all our 'what's hot' collectibles, good glassware is easiest to find at garage sales and flea markets. You'll find that Fenton pieces turn up often, and, of course, the '40s, '50s, and '60s glassware is plentiful at this point in time.

Jewelry: Look for maker's marks — Marcia Brown has several wonderful books with very good information on many of the top manufacturers (Trifari, Hattie Carnegie, Napier, Coro, Kramer, Haskell, and Lisner, to name but a few). Though signed pieces are preferred, anything well made and in good condition is collectible, as long as it is attractive and stylish. Rhinestones and aurora borealis (especially in color) have been popular with collectors for some time, and good Bakelite pieces command very high prices. In vintage costume jewelry, the bigger and bolder, the better!

Kitchen items from the '30s through the '60s: Egg timers, string holders, Texas-ware and similar Melmac pieces (especially in the brighter colors), and Guardian cookware. Those items sell well; but Kromex canister sets, flour sifters, rolling pins and other kitchen gadgets, crocheted hot pads, and vintage appliances also have collector appeal.

Lamps: Especially unusual TV lamps, some vintage lava lamps, motion lamps, Moss lamps, and Aladdin oil and electric lamps.

Linens: Vintage aprons, brightly patterned tablecloths, handkerchiefs, tea towels, embroidered pillow cases, barkcloth draperies, feed sacks, aprons, and quilts. Nice handkerchiefs can often be bought for very little at garage sales — colorful printed hankies often start at $5.00 and go up from there, according to the pattern. Table cloths with vibrant flowers and fruits, states themes, Mexican motifs, and those signed by a well known illustrator/designer often sell in the $50.00 to $80.00 range. Aprons that have been handmade and commercially made aprons with original tags are among the best.

Pottery: Aside from the vases and flowerpots obviously made for the florist trade, virtually any marked piece of American-made pottery is worth considering. Though prices have softened to a large extent, interest will always be there for quality pieces, and as supply evens out with demand, you can expect to see a resurgence in prices. Be sure to check carefully for chips, excessive crazing, and hairlines, as they can be overlooked in haste. Though Roseville prices are down from their high of a few years ago, a good piece is still a treasure to be found. As is true of pottery from almost every major company, some pieces will be unmarked. Become familiar with their production lines if you want to be able to identify those unmarked items that are not so quickly snatched up by the competition.

Purses and handbags: Look for designer labels here! Enid Collins, Coach, Louis Vuitton, Guess, Prada, Kate Spade, Vera Bradley, Gucci, and many others; but watch for fakes — they're everywhere. For info on imposter handbags, go to fakefendihandbags. com, knockoffs.com, and PurseForum.com. Vintage Lucite, beaded, and good tooled-leather purses are quick to sell.

Toys: In general, doing very well. Vehicles of all kinds, especially Matchboxes and Hot Wheels; battery-operated toys; coloring books; guns; Star Wars; Western character collectibles; and model kits are very sought after, and prices seem to be steady for the most part. Again, it's condition that's the most powerful force relative to value.

Other things to watch for:
American Indian relics
Automobilia
Bottles: painted-label soda bottles and milk bottles
Black Americana
Breweriana
Cookbooks
Compacts and ladies' purse accessories
Corning ware and Visions cookware in good condition
Fountain pens
Golf collectibles
Graniteware
John Deere collectibles
Lunch boxes
Marbles
Paintings and prints
Perfume bottles: made in Czechoslovakia or those from famous perfume makers
Pocketknives
Racing collectibles: Indy 500, NASCAR
Radios: character and novelty, transistor, Bakelite
Rock 'n roll memorabilia
Sewing collectibles and buttons
Sports memorabilia
Soda pop memorabilia: especially vintage Coca-Cola, Hires, Pepsi-Cola, unusual brands
Sports collectibles
Toothpick holders

How to Evaluate Your Holdings

When viewed in its entirety, granted, the antiques and collectibles market can be overwhelming. But in each line of glassware, any type of pottery or toys, or any other field I could mention, there are examples that are more desirable than others, and these are the ones you need to be able to recognize. If you're a novice, it will probably be best at first to choose a few areas that you find most interesting and learn just what particular examples or types of items are most in demand within that field. Concentrate on the top 25%. This is where you'll do 75% of your business. Do your homework. Quality sells. Obviously no one can be an expert in everything, but gradually you can begin to broaden your knowledge. As an added feature of our guide, information on clubs and newsletters, always a wonderful source of up-to-date information on any subject, is contained in each category when available. (Advisor's names are listed as well. We highly recommend that you exhaust all other resources before you contact them with your inquiries. Their role is simply to check over our data before we go to press to make sure it is as accurate as we and they can possibly make it for you; they do not agree to answer readers' questions, though some may. If you do write, you must send them an SASE. If you call, please take the time zones into consideration. Some of our advisors are professionals and may charge an appraisal fee, so be sure to ask. Please, do *not* be offended if they do not respond to your contacts, they are under no obligation to do so.)

There are many fields other than those we've already mentioned that are strong and have been for a long time. It's impossible to list them all. But we've left very little out of this book; at least we've tried to represent each category to some extent and where at all possible to refer you to a source of further information. It's up to you to read, observe the market, and become acquainted with it to the point that you feel confident enough to become a part of today's antiques and collectibles industry.

The thousands of current values found in this book will increase your awareness of today's wonderful world of buying, selling, and collecting antiques and collectibles. Use it to educate yourself to the point that you'll be the one with the foresight to know what and how to buy as well as where and how to turn those sleepers into cold, hard cash.

In addition to this one, there are several other very fine price guides on the market. One of the best is *Schroeder's Antiques Price Guide*; another is *Flea Market Trader*. Both are published by Collector Books. *The Antique Trader Antiques and Collectibles Price Guide, Warman's Antiques and Their Prices,* and *Kovel's Antiques and Collectibles Price List* are others. You may want to invest in a copy of each. Where you decide to sell will have a direct bearing on how you price your merchandise, and nothing will affect an item's worth more than condition.

If you're not familiar with using a price guide, here's a few tips that may help you. When convenient and reasonable, antiques will be sorted by manufacturer. This is especially true of pottery and most glassware. If you don't find the item you're looking for under manufacturer, look under a broader heading, for instance, cat collectibles, napkin dolls, cookie jars, etc. And don't forget to use the index. Most guides of this type have very comprehensive indexes — a real boon to the novice collector. If you don't find the exact item you're trying to price, look for something similar. For instance, if it's a McCoy rabbit planter you're researching, go through the McCoy section and see what price range other animal planters are in. (There are exceptions, however, and if an item is especially rare and desirable, this will not apply. Here's where you need a comprehensive McCoy book.) Or if you have a frame-tray puzzle with Snow White and the Seven Dwarfs, see what other Disney frame-trays are priced at. Just be careful not to compare apples to oranges. Age is important as well. You can judge the value of a 7" Roseville Magnolia vase that's not listed in any of your guides; just look at the price given for one a little larger or smaller and adjust it up or down. Pricing collectibles is certainly not a science; the bottom line is simply where the buyer and the seller finally agree to do business. Circumstances dictate sale price, and we can only make suggestions, which we base on current sales, market observations, and the expert opinions of our advisors.

Once you've found 'book' price, decide how much less you can take for it. 'Book' price represents a high average retail. A collectible will often change hands many times, and obviously it will not always be sold at book price. How quickly do you want to realize a profit? Will you be patient enough to hold out for top dollar, or would you rather price your merchandise lower so it will turn over more quickly? Just as there are both types of dealers, there are two types of collectors. Many are bargain hunters. They shop around — do the legwork themselves. On the other hand, there are those who are willing to pay whatever the asking price is to avoid spending precious time searching out pieces they especially want, but they represent the minority. You'll often see tradepaper ads listing good merchandise (from that top 25% we mentioned before) at prices well above book value. This is a good example of a dealer who knows that his merchandise is good enough to entice the buyer who is able to pay a little more and doesn't mind waiting for him (or her) to come along, and that's his prerogative.

Don't neglect to access the condition of the item you want to sell. This is especially important in online and mail order selling. Most people, especially inexperienced buyers and sellers, have a tendency to overlook some flaws and to overrate merchandise. Mint condition means that an item is complete and undamaged — in effect, just as it looked the day it was made. Glassware, china, and pottery may often be found today in wonderful mint condition. Check for signs of wear, though, since even wear will downgrade value. (Looking 'good considering its age' is like coming close

in horseshoes — it doesn't really count!) Remember that when a buyer doesn't have the option of seeing for himself, your written description is all he has to go by. Save yourself the hassle of costly and time-consuming returns by making sure the condition of your merchandise is accurately and completely described. Unless a toy is still in its original box and has never been played with, you seldom see one in mint condition. Paper collectibles are almost never found without some deterioration or damage. Most price guides will list values that apply to glass and ceramics that are mint (unless another condition is specifically indicated within some descriptions). Other items are usually evaluated on the assumption that they are in the best as-found condition common to that area of collecting, for instance magazines are simply never found in mint condition. Grade your merchandise as though you were the buyer, not the seller. You'll be building a reputation that will go a long way toward contributing to your success. If it's glassware or pottery you're assessing, an item in less than excellent condition will be mighty hard to sell at any price. Just as a guideline (a basis to begin your evaluation, though other things will factor in), use a scale of one to five with good being a one, excellent being a three, and mint being a five. As an example, a beer tray worth $250.00 in mint condition would then be worth $150.00 if excellent and $50.00 if only good. Remember, the first rule of buying (for resale or investment) is 'Don't put your money in damaged goods.' And the second rule should be be, 'If you do sell damaged items, indicate 'as is' on the price tag, and don't price the item as though it were mint.' The Golden Rule applies just as well to us as antique dealers as it does to any other interaction. Some shops and co-ops have poor lighting, and damage can be easily missed by a perspective buyer — your honesty will be greatly appreciated. If you include identification on your tags as well, be sure it's accurate. If you're not positive, say so. Better yet, let the buyer decide.

Deciding Where to Best Sell Your Merchandise

Personal transactions are just one of many options. Overhead and expenses will vary with each and must be factored into your final pricing. If you have some especially nice items and can contact a collector willing to pay top dollar, that's obviously the best of the lot. Or you may decide to sell to a dealer who may be willing to pay you only half of book. Either way, your expenses won't amount to much more than a little gas or a phone call.

Internet auctions may be your preferred venue. Look at completed auctions for sales results of similar items to decide. Unless you have a digital camera, factor in the cost of photography (sales of items with no photograph suffer), image hosting, and listing fees. Remember that the cost of boxes and bubble wrap must also be considered, not to mention the time spent actually listing the item, answering e-mail questions, contacting the buyer with the winning bid, leaving feedback, etc.

Internet selling works. In fact, I know some dealers who have quit doing shows and simply work out of their home. No more unpacking, travel expenses, or inconvenience of any kind to endure. You may sell through a set-price online mall or an auction. If you choose the auction (eBay is the most widely used right now), you can put a 'reserve' on everything you sell, a safeguard that protects the

seller and prevents an item from going at an unreasonably low figure should there be few bidders.

Classified ads are another way to get a good price for your more valuable merchandise without investing much money or time. Place a 'for sale' ad or run a mail bid in one of the collector magazines or newsletters, several of which are listed in the back of this book. Many people have had excellent results this way. If you have several items and the cost of listing them all is prohibitive, simply place an ad saying (for instance) 'Several pieces of Royal Copley (or whatever) for sale, send SASE for list.' Be sure to give your correct address and phone number.

When you're making out your list or talking with a prospective buyer by phone or by email, try to draw a picture with words. Describe any damage in full; it's much better than having a disgruntled customer to deal with later, and you'll be on your way to establishing yourself as a reputable dealer. Better yet, send photographs. Seeing the item exactly as it is will often help the prospective buyer make up his or her mind. If you use regular mail, send an SASE along and ask that your photos be returned to you, so that you can send them out again, if need be. A less expensive alternative is to have your item photocopied. This works great for many smaller items, not just flat shapes but things with some dimension as well. It's wonderful for hard-to-describe dinnerware patterns or for showing their trademarks. Of course, the easiest way to communicate and send photos is through email, and digital cameras make the process so convenient. If at all possible, invest in one!

If you've made that 'buy of a lifetime' or an item you've hung onto for a few years has turned out to be a scarce, highly sought collectible, you should be able to get top dollar for your prize. If you decide to take it online, you'll want to start your auction with a high but reasonable reserve. Should the item fail to meet reserve, relist it with one that is lower than the original. The final bid the first time around will give you a good idea of where it may go the second time.

Be sure to let your buyer know what form of payment you prefer. Some dealers will not ship merchandise until personal checks have cleared. This delay may make the buyer a bit unhappy. So you may want to request a money order or a cashier's check. Nowadays there are several hassle-free ways to make transactions online, and though Pay Pal is by far the most familiar, there are are other alternatives. Check them out through your favorite search engine.

Be very careful about how you pack your merchandise for shipment. Breakables need to be well protected. There are several things you can use. Plastic bubble wrap is excellent and adds very little weight to your packages. Or use scraps of foam rubber such as carpet padding (check with a carpet-laying service or confiscate some from family and friends who are getting new carpet installed). I've received items wrapped in pieces of egg-crate type mattress pads (watch for these at garage sales!). If there is a computer business near you, check their dumpsters for discarded foam wrapping and other protective packaging. It's best not to let newspaper come in direct contact with your merchandise, since the newsprint may stain certain surfaces. After you've wrapped them well, you'll need boxes. Find smaller boxes (one or several, whatever best fits your needs) that you can fit into a larger one with several inches of space between them. First pack your well-wrapped items snugly into the smaller box, using crushed newspaper to keep them from shifting. Place it into the larger box, using more crushed paper underneath and along the sides, so that it will not move during transit. Remember, if it arrives broken, it's still your merchandise, even though you have received payment. You may want to insure the shipment; check with your carrier. Some have automatic insurance up to a specified amount.

After you've mailed your box, it's good to follow it up with a phone call or an e-mail after a few days. Make sure it arrived in good condition and that your customer is pleased with the merchandise. Most people who sell by mail or the internet allow a 10-day return privilege, providing their original price tag is still intact. For this purpose, you can simply initial a gummed label or use one of those pre-printed return address labels that most of us have around the house.

For very large or heavy items such as furniture or slot machines, ask your buyer for his preferred method of shipment. If the distance involved is not too great, he may even want to pick it up himself.

Flea market selling can either be lots of fun, or it can turn out to be one of the worst experiences of your life. Obviously you will have to deal with whatever weather conditions prevail, so be sure to listen to weather reports so that you can dress accordingly. You'll see some inventive shelters you might want to copy. Even a simple patio umbrella will offer respite from the blazing sun or a sudden downpour. I've recently been seeing stands catering just to the needs of the flea market dealer — how's that for being enterprising! Not only do they carry specific items the dealers might want, but they've even had framework and tarpaulins, and they'll erect shelters right on the spot!

Be sure to have plastic table covering in case of rain and some large clips to hold it down if there's much wind. The type of clip you'll need depends on how your table is made, so be sure to try them out before you actually get caught in a storm. Glass can blow over, paper items can be ruined, and very quickly your career as a flea market dealer may be cut short for lack of merchandise!

Price your things, allowing yourself a little bargaining room. Unless you want to collect tax separately on each sale (for this you'd need lots of small change), mentally calculate the amount and add this on as well. Sell the item 'tax included.' Everybody does.

Take snacks, drinks, paper bags, plenty of change, and somebody who can relieve you occasionally. Collectors are some of the nicest people around. I guarantee that you'll enjoy this chance to meet and talk them, and often you can make valuable contacts that may help you locate items you're especially looking for yourself.

Auction houses are listed in the back of this book. If you have an item you feel might be worth selling at auction, be sure to contact one of them. Many have appraisal services; some are free while others charge a fee, dependent on number of items and time spent. We suggest you first make a telephone inquiry before you send in a formal request.

In Summation

Whatever your purpose — whether you buy to sell or for your own pleasure — you need basic knowledge of the market. Even if you've been buying and selling antiques for years, chances are you may not be well versed in the more modern collectible fields. We would encourage you to familiarize yourself with emerging trends, as we've found that the new collectors tend to be the most active buyers and often prefer mid-century collectibles. Knowlege is the key, and the time you invest in gaining it will be rewarding. Keep an open mind and develop good instincts. Read, attend shows, and talk with experienced collectors. By doing so you will be prepared to enjoy the hunt for today's collectibles, tomorrow's antiques!

Abbreviations

dia — diameter
ea — each
EX — excellent
G — good condition
gal — gallon
H — high
L — long, length
lg — large
M — mint condition
med — medium
MIB — mint in (original) box
MIP — mint in package
MOC — mint on card
NM — near mint
NRFB — never removed from box
oz — ounce
pc — piece
pr — pair
pt — pint
qt — quart
sm — small
sq — square
VG — very good
w/ — with
(+) — has been reproduced

Note: When no condition is noted within our description lines, assume that the value we give is for mint condition items.

Abingdon

You may find smaller pieces of Abingdon around, but it's not common to find many larger items. This company operated in Abingdon, Illinois, from 1934 until 1950, making not only nice vases and figural pieces but some kitchen items as well. Their cookie jars are very well done and popular with collectors. They sometimes used floral decals and gold to decorate their wares, and a highly decorated item is worth a minimum of 25% more than the same shape with no decoration. Some of their glazes also add extra value. If you find a piece in black, bronze, or red, you can add 25% to those as well.

For more information we recommend *Abingdon Pottery Artware, 1934 – 50, Stepchild of the Great Depression,* by Joe Paradis (Schiffer).

See also Cookie Jars.

Club: Abingdon Pottery Collectors Club
Elaine Westover, Membership and Treasurer
210 Knox Hwy. 5, Abingdon, IL 61410; 309-462-3267

Ashtray, 8-sided, #551, 7"......................................$20.00
Bookends, Russian, #321, 6½".............................$285.00
Bookends, Trojan Head, #499, 7½"......................$175.00
Bowl, Bulb, #543, 5½"..$12.50
Bowl, Fern Leaf, #425, 10½"..................................$95.00
Bowl, La Fleur, #155, 10"..$10.00
Box, Trista, #354, 2x3"..$20.00
Candleholder, Aladdin Lamp, #579, ea..................$85.00
Candleholders, Triple Chain, #404, 3x8½", pr.......$50.00
Cornucopia, #303, 7½"...$40.00
Flowerpot, Egg & Dart, #366, 5¼"..........................$15.00
Lamp base, sq standard, #256, 22½".......................$90.00
Leftover container, #RE6, 6" dia.............................$50.00
Planter, Drape, #710, 7" L..$38.00
Planter, Fawn, #672, 5"..$38.00
Tea tile, Coolie, #401, 5x5"......................................$75.00
Vase, Athenian, #315, 9"..$35.00
Vase, Bali, #521, 9"...$80.00
Vase, Classic, #116, 10"...$32.50
Vase, Delta, #112, 6"...$25.00
Vase, Dutch Boy, #459, 8".......................................$50.00
Vase, Floral, #180, 10"..$55.00
Vase, Laurel, #442, 5½"...$45.00

Vase, Laurel, #443, 8", $145.00.

Vase, Tulip, #504D, 6"...$60.00
Vase, Wreath, #457, 8"...$65.00

Wall pocket, butterfly, #601, 8½x8½", from $75.00 to $100.00.

Wall vase, book form, #676D, 6½"......................................$85.00

Adams, Matthew

In the 1950s a trading post located in Alaska contacted Sascha Brastoff to design a line of decorative ceramics with depictions of Eskimos, Alaskan scenes, or animals indigenous to that area. These items were intended to target the tourist trade.

Brastoff selected Matthew Adams as the designer. These earlier examples have the Sascha B mark on the front, and the pattern number often appears on the back.

After the Alaska series became successful, Matthew Adams left Brastoff's studio and opened his own. (In all, Mr. Adams was employed by Brastoff for three years.) Pieces made in his studio are all signed Matthew Adams in script on the front. Some carry the word Alaska as well.

Mr. Adams was born in 1915. Presently his studio is located in Los Angeles, but he is no longer working.

Advisor: Marty Webster (See Directory, California Pottery)

Bowl, walrus on ice floe, bright cobalt sky with golden 'aurora borealis' streaks, 3x10" diameter, $85.00. (Photo courtesy flatbaycuriosities)

Ashtray, hooded; Walrus on black, 5½"...............................$65.00
Ashtray, Husky, 13x10"..$65.00
Ashtray, Walrus, star shape, 10x12"....................................$95.00
Ashtray, Walrus on green, boomerang shape, 6x11"............$65.00

Bowl, Husky, 6" $20.00
Bowl, Igloo & Dog, boat shape, #138, 9½" $50.00
Bowl, Polar Bear on green, free-form, 7½" L........$40.00
Bowl, salad; Ram & Mountain Top, 13¼x15", +6 bowls ...$235.00
Bowl, Seal, oval, 9" $50.00
Bowl, Seal on black, free-form, w/lid, #145, 7½".....$55.00
Box, Glacier on blue, 12" $95.00
Charger, Caribou on dark blue, 18" $150.00
Cigarette lighter, Cabin on Stilts, 5x5" $50.00
Cookie jar, Cabin, elliptical shape, #023, 7x5" ...$100.00
Creamer, Seal, #144, 5x5¼" $20.00
Cup & saucer, Sled on blue..................................$25.00
Dish, Log Cabin, w/lid, #145, 4x7½x5" $35.00
Jar, Eskimo on ice blue, w/lid, 6" $35.00
Mug, Husky, #112a, 4½x4¾"................................$25.00
Pitcher, Eskimo Mother & Child, 13", +6 5½" mugs........$265.00
Plate, Igloo & Northern Lights, #162, 7½" $36.00
Platter, Polar Bears (2) on ice, 12x10"..................$75.00
Shakers, Rams on green, 4", pr $40.00
Tankard, Eskimo Man on Brown, 19", +6 mugs, from $250 to..$285.00
Teapot, Walrus on ice blue, 6½" $75.00
Tray, Polar Bear & Iceberg, #910, 13x9¾" $75.00
Vase, Eskimo Mother & Child on teal, cylindrical, 17" $165.00
Vase, Iceberg on gray, 7" $50.00
Vase, Reindeer, 4½"..$45.00
Vase, Seal & Glacier on brown, free-form, #911, 11" $95.00

Advertising Character Collectibles

The advertising field holds a special fascination for many of today's collectors. It's vast and varied, so its appeal is universal; but the characters of the ad world are its stars right now. Nearly every fast-food restaurant and manufacturer of a consumer product has a character logo. Keep your eyes open on your garage sale outings; it's not at all uncommon to find the cloth and plush dolls, plastic banks and mugs, bendies, etc., such as we've listed here. Unless noted otherwise, our values are for items in near mint to mint condition.

See also Breweriana; Bubble Bath Containers; Character Clocks and Watches; Character and Promotional Drinking Glasses; Coca-Cola Collectibles; Novelty Radios; Novelty Telephones; PEZ Candy Containers; Pin-Back Buttons; Salt and Pepper Shakers; Soda Pop Memorabilia.

Aunt Jemima

One of the most widely recognized ad characters of them all, Aunt Jemima has decorated bags and boxes of pancake flour for more than 90 years. In fact, the original milling company carried her name, but by 1926 it had become part of the Quaker Oats Company. She and Uncle Mose were produced in plastic by the F&F Mold and Die Works in the 1950s, and the salt and pepper shakers, syrup pitchers, cookie jars, etc., they made are perhaps the most sought-after of the hundreds of items available today. (Watch for reproductions.) Age is a big worth-assessing factor for memorabilia such as we've listed below, of course, but so is condition. In the following listings, when no condition is noted, all values are for examples in excellent condition, except glass and ceramic items, in which case values are for mint condition items. Watch for very chipped or worn paint on the F&F products, and avoid buying soiled cloth dolls.

Advisor: Judy Posner (See Directory, Advertising)

Box, Aunt Jemima Ready-Mix Pancakes, smiling face on red, unopened, holds 1-lb & 4-oz, 6¾x4x2⅛" $70.00
Button, Aunt Jemima Breakfast Club, clips to pencil, ⅞".....$18.00
Cookie jar, Aunt Jemima figural, plastic, F&F, from $400 to.. $450.00
Magazine ad, Aunt Jemima Pancakes & Log Cabin Syrup, black & white, Haddon Sunblom art, 1948, 5x8".......................$8.00

Pancake grill, Model No PG 706B, metal with plastic knobs, NM, from $1,500.00 to $2,000.00. (Photo courtesy Collector's Auction Services)

Paper plate, Aunt Jemima Days, 9¾" $30.00
Paper plate, Aunt Jemima Days Are Here Again, 9¼" $25.00
Place mat, Aunt Jemima's Restaurant at Disneyland, paper, 1955, 9¾x13¾" $35.00
Place mat, Story of Aunt Jemima, paper, 14x9¾"................$35.00
Plate, Aunt Jemima's Kitchen, Wellsville China, 1950s-60s, 7" $70.00
Recipe box, hard plastic w/molded face on front, Fosta Products, Made in USA, 3¾x5¼x3" $85.00
Sack, Old Aunt Jemima Hominy Grits, paper litho, 1960s+, 11½" L $22.00
Salt & pepper shakers, Aunt Jemima & Uncle Mose figurals, plastic, F&F, 3½", pr $45.00
Salt & pepper shakers, Aunt Jemima & Uncle Mose figurals, plastic, F&F, 5", pr $75.00
Spice set, 6 Aunt Jemima figural containers, plastic, F&F, in copper rack..$365.00
Syrup container, figural, plastic, F&F, 5½" $75.00
Tin container, Aunt Jemima Cooking & Salad Oil, portrait on all 4 sides, minor scratches, bright colors, 13¾x9¼"..........$295.00

Big Boy and Friends

Bob's Big Boy, home of the nationally famous Big Boy, the original double-deck hamburger, was founded by Robert C. 'Bob' Wian in Glendale, California, in 1938. He'd just graduated from high school, and he had a dream. With the $300.00 realized from the sale of the car he so treasured, he bought a run-down building and enough basic equipment to open his business. Through much hard work and ingenuity, Bob turned his little restaurant into a multimillion-dollar empire. Not only does he have the double-decker two-patty burger to his credit, but car hops and drive-in restaurants were his creations as well.

With business beginning to flourish, Bob felt he needed a symbol — something that people would recognize. One day in walked a chubby lad of six, his sagging trousers held up by reluctant suspenders. Bob took one look at him and named him Big Boy, and that was it! It was a natural name for his double-decker hamburger — descriptive, catchy, and easy to remember. An artist worked out the drawings, and Bob's Pantry was renamed Bob's Big Boy.

The enterprise grew fast, and Bob added location after location. In 1969 when he sold out to the Marriott Corporation, he had 185 restaurants in California, with franchises such as Elias' Big Boy, Frisch's Big Boy, and Shoney's Big Boy in other states. The Big Boy burger and logo was recognized by virtually every man, woman, and child in America, and Bob retired knowing he had made a significant contribution to millions of people everywhere.

Since Big Boy has been in business for over 60 years, you'll find many items and numerous variations. Some, such as the large statues, china, and some menus, have been reproduced. If you're in doubt, consult an experienced collector for help. Many items of jewelry, clothing, and kids promotions were put out over the years, too numerous to itemize separately. Values range from $5.00 up to $1,500.00.

Advisor: Steve Soelberg (See Directory, Advertising)

Nodder, composition, Japan, 1960s, large, EX, $350.00 (NM, minimum value, $450.00). (Photo courtesy LiveAuctioneers.com/Morphy Auctions)

Ashtray, Big Boy figural at side of white tray w/gold trim, 3 rests, Made in Japan, wear to red paint, 3⅝x3¾" **$115.00**
Bank, Big Boy figural, commemorative plaque base, w/pc of concrete foundation & 1949-1992, 8" **$35.00**
Bank, Big Boy figural, hamburger in right hand, Bank printed on front, ceramic, 16" on 6x6" sq base **$680.00**
Comic book, Adventures of Big Boy, #1 .... **$300.00**
Comic book, Adventures of Big Boy, #2-#5, ea **$50.00**
Comic book, Adventures of Big Boy, #6-10, ea **$35.00**
Comic book, Adventures of Big Boy, #11-100, ea **$25.00**
Comic book, Adventures of Big Boy, #101-#250, ea **$20.00**
Crate, Big Boy in white letters on red plastic, 11x13x13" **$45.00**

Menu, We're Happy You Came..., boy holding hamburger, 1960s, 8½x4¼" closed **$46.00**
Nightlight, Big Boy figural, marked at base, 6½" **$30.00**
Nodder, Big Boy figural, plaster/chalkware, Reg US TM, 7" .. **$35.00**
Salt & pepper shakers, Big Boy w/thumbs tucked in suspenders, multicolor on white, ceramic, Japan, 1940s, 4", pr from $150 to **$175.00**
Stationery set, images of 1936 & 1996 versions, w/paper pad & Parker pen, dated 1997, MIB **$37.50**
Wristwatch, Big Boy in center, arms move to note hours & minutes, Swiss Made, brown leather band, w/insert **$35.00**

Campbell Kids

The introduction of the world's first canned soup was announced in 1897. Later improvements in the manufacturing process created an evolutionary condensed soup. The Campbell's® Soup Company is now the primary beneficiary of this early entrepreneurial achievement. Easily identified by their red and white advertising, the company has been built on a tradition of skillful product marketing through five generations of consumers. Now a household name for all ages, Campbell's Soups have grown to dominate 80% of the canned soup market.

The first Campbell's licensed advertising products were character collectibles offered in 1910 — composition dolls with heads made from a combination of glue and sawdust. They were made by the E.I. Horsman Company and sold for $1.00 each. They were the result of a gifted illustrator, their creator, Grace Drayton, who in 1904 gave life to the chubby-faced cherub 'Campbell's Kids.'

In 1994 the Campbell's Soup Kids celebrated their 90th birthday. They have been revised a number of times to maintain a likeness to modern-day children. Over the years hundreds of licensees have been commissioned to produce collectibles and novelty items with the Campbell's logo in a red and white theme.

Licensed advertising reached a peak from 1954 through 1956 with 34 licensed manufacturers. Unusual items included baby carriages, toy vacuums, games, and apparel. Many of the more valuable Campbell's advertising collectibles were made during this period. In 1956 a Campbell's Kid doll was produced from latex rubber. Called 'Magic Skin,' it proved to be the most popular mail-in premium ever produced. Campbell's received more than 560,000 requests for this special girl chef doll.

Doll, composition, six-piece body, Horsman (unmarked), 12", EX, $225.00. (Photo courtesy McMasters Harris Auction Co.)

Beach towel, boy windsurfing, printed cotton, Made in Mexico, 1989, unused, 63x33" $45.00

Book, Rhymes & Recipes, boy holding tomatoes on cover, Campbell Soup Company Ltd, New Toronto...Canada, 26 pages ..$60.00

Cookie jar, All Aboard Special Edition, Kids on train engine, multicolor, ceramic, 9x10x6" $45.00

Chuck Wagon, Amsco, small, NMIB, $125.00. (Photo courtesy LiveAuctioneers.com/Morphy Auctions)

Doll, porcelain, Miss Campbell w/ribbon across chest & gold trophy, PS Loveless, 1998, NRFB $45.00

Dolls, porcelain & cloth, Dancing Chef/Miss Sniffle, Danbury Mint, 1995/1996, 10" $40.00

Dolls, porcelain w/cloth torso, she in red, he in tux, 100th Anniversary, Ashton Drake, 2004, 10", pr $75.00

Dolls, vinyl, boy & girl in colonial costumes, 10", pr, MIB ..$45.00

Dolls, vinyl, boy & girl in red & white outfits, 1960s-70s, 10", pr, MI(Christmas)B...$60.00

Lunch box, Kids in various scenes w/blue border, tin, 1959, no thermos, G...$48.00

Memo holder, Kid holds note pad & pencil, painted chalkware, wire hanger, 1940s, 9½x5" $185.00

Paperweight, A Tempting Idea Right Now, girl w/braids picking vegetables, sealed in glass, 1954 ....$35.00

Thermometer, Kid figural, painted compo, 7½x3¼" $110.00

Toy store, 3-D cardboard litho, punched out & assembled, 9", 1940s, w/original envelope...$135.00

Toy train car, Campbell Kids 100th Anniversary Car, #6-39250, 2004 ....$50.00

Cap'n Crunch

Cap'n Crunch was the creation of Jay Ward, whom you will no doubt remember was also the creator of the Rocky and Bullwinkle show. The Cap'n hails from the '60s and was one of the first heroes of the presweetened cereal crowd. Jean LaFoote was the villain always scheming to steal the Cap'n's cereal.

Animation cel, Cap'n Horatio Crunch battling Crunchberry beast, Jay Ward Productions, 12½x10½" $45.00

Bank, Cap'n figural, plastic, multicolor paint, Niagara Plastics Erie PA, 1974, 7½", from $40 to $45.00

Bank, treasure chest form, plastic, image of Cap'n on lid, skull & crossbones on front & back, 5x6" $45.00

Box, Cap'n Crunch's Choco Crunch, Cap'n w/Choco Creature on front, w/sticker sheet, Quaker, 1983, EX $48.00

Mug, Cap'n Crunch on milk glass w/fired-on red, Anchor Hocking $120.00

Puzzle, Cap'n Crunch, painted wood, Fisher-Price #505......$35.00

Radio, Isis Model 39, from $35.00 to $45.00. (Photo courtesy Bunis and Breed)

Rings, Cap'n's whistle, ship in bottle, pirate puzzle, treasure coin & cutlass, plastic, 1960s, complete set of 5 ....$130.00

T-shirt, Cap'n's portrait on bright blue, Breakfast Not Served Here & flames on back, from Newsboys concert, unused......$50.00

Whistle, red or blue plastic, premium, 1960s, 3" $25.00

Charlie Tuna

Poor Charlie, never quite good enough for the Star-Kist folks to can, though he yearns for them to catch him; but since the early 1970s he's done a terrific job working for them as the company logo. A dapper blue-fin tuna in sunglasses and a beret, he's appeared in magazines, done TV commercials, modeled for items as diverse as lamps and banks, but still they deny him his dream. 'Sorry, Charlie.'

Alarm clock, Charlie's image on face, 2 bells on top, RobertShaws/ Lux Time, 1969 ....$25.00

Bank, Charlie figural, ceramic, 1988, 9½", MIB................$25.00

Bathroom scale, 1972 mail-in, $55.00. (Photo courtesy www.gasolinealleyantiques.com)

Camera, Charlie figural, plastic, uses flash cube, red turn switch advances film, 1971, 9x7" **$50.00**

Cuff links, Charlie figural, gold-plated metal, SKF, Pat 2,974,381 (March 14, 1961), pr **$55.00**

Figure, Charlie in red hat, vinyl, 7½" **$40.00**

Lamp base, Charlie figural, Star Kist, 1970, 12" **$35.00**

Radio, bicycle; Charlie's image on blue, plastic w/metal clip, 1973, 5x3" **$18.00**

Radio, Charlie figural, 9-volt transistor, 1970, 6x3" **$40.00**

Rug, Charlie shape, blue & white w/red details, 40x21" **$25.00**

Telephone, Charlie figural, standing w/hands on hips, 1987 .. **$25.00**

Wacky Wobbler, Charlie figural nodder, pink tongue, Funko, MIB **$18.00**

Wristwatch, Charlie's image on round face, leather band, 25th Anniversary, 1961-68, MIB **$30.00**

Wristwatch, Charlie's image w/Sorry Charlie sign, analog, stainless steel case, leather band, 1973 .... **$40.00**

Colonel Sanders

There's nothing fictional about the Colonel — he was a very real guy, who built an empire on the strength of his fried chicken recipe with 'eleven herbs and spices.' In the 1930s, the Colonel operated a small cafe in Corbin, Kentucky. As the years went by, he developed a chain of restaurants which he sold in the mid-'60s. But even after the sale, the new company continued to use the image of the handsome southern gentlemen as their logo. The Colonel died in 1980.

Ashtray, Colonel's portrait embossed on metal, 4 rests, 4x4".. **$3.00**

Bank, Colonel holding bucket of chicken, plastic, 1977, 7½".. **$18.00**

Bank, Run Starling Plastics Ltd., 12½", from $25.00 to $35.00.

Bobble head, Colonel figural, Our Colonel lettered on base, plastic, Topps, 1967, MIB **$115.00**

Lamp base, resembles cookie jar, 1969 .... **$75.00**

Lapel pin, Colonel's face embossed on gold-tone metal........ **$10.00**

Magazine ad, Jerry Lewis for Muscular Dystrophy, black & white, 1968, full page... **$8.00**

Mask & membership card kit, to punch out of heavy card stock, copyright 1965, 8½x11" sheet **$15.00**

Matchbook, Colonel's portrait on front, front strike, complete w/20 matches, Match Corp of America **$3.00**

Record, Christmas w/Colonel Sanders, RCA Special Products LP, 1967 .... **$12.50**

Salt & pepper shakers, Colonel & Mrs Sanders figurals, white plastic, Margardt Corp, 4", pr.. **$45.00**

Salt & pepper shakers, Colonel figural, white plastic, black base on pepper shaker, Canada, 4⅜", pr **$30.00**

Stamp, Wanted for (Colonel's portrait) Fowl Deeds, 2¾x1¼" .. **$6.50**

Tumbler, Harland Sanders Court & Cafe, blue lettering on clear glass, Libbey, ca 1955... **$22.00**

Wacky Wobbler, Colonel nodder, Funko, retired, MIB, from $20 to **$25.00**

Elsie the Cow and Family

She's the most widely recognized cow in the world; everyone knows Elsie, Borden's mascot. Since the mid-1930s, she's been seen on booklets and posters; modeled for mugs, creamers, dolls, etc.; and appeared on TV, in magazines, and at grocery stores to promote their products. Her husband is Elmer (who once sold Elmer's Glue for the same company) and her twins are best known as Beulah and Beauregard, though they've been renamed in recent years (now they're Bea and Beaumister). Elsie was retired in the 1960s, but due to public demand was soon reinstated to her rightful position and continues today to promote the company's dairy products.

Bank, Elsie (head only), painted chalkware, 1950s, 6⅝" **$325.00**

Charm, Elsie in relief, die-cut metal, Elsie written at base, ¾" dia **$20.00**

Creamer, Elsie full figure, ceramic, shaded brown, 1940s, 6x5" ..**$90.00**

Doll, Elsie, rubber & cloth, in white blouse & blue shirt, 1970s, 11" **$40.00**

Doll, Elsie, rubber face & cloth body, ca 1950s 14" **$70.00**

Lamp, ceramic, with original foil label, 7½", $450.00. (Photo courtesy LiveAuctioneers. com/Morphy Auctions)

Lamp, Elsie w/Beauregard on base, ceramic, multicolor paint, 1950s, 10¼" to top of fixture... **$250.00**

Magazine ad, black & white, for record albums, full page, 1950s. **$5.00**

Milk pail, Elsie wreathed in flower on tin, bail handle, Ohio Art Lithograph Co, 1940s-50s, 5½" **$60.00**

Pin, Elsie portrait, metalized head in yellow enameled flower, 1¾" dia..**$18.00**

Placemat, For Over 125 Years Folks Have Known...Borden's..., printed paper, 11x16½" **$15.00**

Postcard, Elsie & Beauregard in Person, scene in barn, from 1 of Elsie's tours **$15.00**

Ring, Elsie portrait embossed on reticulated metal, adjusts ..**$15.00**

Ring, Elsie transfer on plastic...**$15.00**

Salt & pepper shakers, Beulah & Beauregard, multicolor, pottery, green Japan stamps, 1950s, 3½", pr **$60.00**

Sherbet/sundae, Elsie logo enameled on clear glass w/fluted edge, footed, 4½" **$10.00**

String holder, Elmer the Bull, painted chalkware, 1950s, 7½"...**$350.00**

Toy, Elsie's Dairy, Fisher-Price, 10" long, $440.00. (Photo courtesy LiveAuctioneers.com/Morphy Auctions)

Tumbler, Elsie in white enamel on clear glass, 5x2¼" **$8.00**

Green Giant

The Jolly Green Giant has been a well-known ad fixture since the 1950s (some research indicates an earlier date); he was originally devised to represent a strain of European peas much larger than the average-size peas Americans had been accustomed to. At any rate, when Minnesota Valley Canning changed its name to Green Giant, he was their obvious choice. Rather a terse individual himself, by 1974 he was joined by Little Green Sprout, with the lively eyes and more talkative personality.

In addition to a variety of toys and other memorabilia already on the market, in 1988 Benjamin Medwin put out a line of Little Green Sprout items. Some of these are listed below.

Advertisement, for 48" stuffed Green Giant doll, color scene of girl w/doll, ca 1962, 13⅝x10⅛" **$15.00**

Bank, Little Sprout figural, musical, battery-operated, ceramic, 1985, MIB..**$45.00**

Corn holders, Little Sprout, metal rods w/plastic figural handles, 2 packages of 4 ea **$10.00**

Doll, Green Giant, stuffed/printed cloth, 15¾", MIP.........**$35.00**

Figure, Green Giant, felt-covered foam, button activates talking mechanism that says Ho Ho Ho, 53x25x11", VG+ **$75.00**

Figure, Green Giant, green vinyl, 1970s, 9" **$50.00**

Figure, Green Giant, painted styrofoam, 86" **$175.00**

Figure, Little Sprout, vinyl, 6", from $12 to **$15.00**

Gumball machine, Little Sprout, die-cast metal & green glass, 12x4½", from $30 to **$40.00**

Lamp, Little Sprout holds three light-up balloons, 1985, 14", $25.00. (Photo courtesy Martin and Carolyn Berens)

Patches, Little Sprout, green embroidered cloth, A-B Emblem Corporation, 1½x1", set of 8 ....**$10.00**

Sleeping bag, Green Sprout in varied scenes on yellow, adult size..**$35.00**

Tote bag, Green Giant smiling face on white cotton canvas, Ho Ho Ho in lime green lettering, drawstring top, 15x15".......**$10.00**

Toy, transport truck, Tonka #650, 23" long, VGIB, $400.00. (Photo courtesy LiveAuctioneers.com/Morphy Auctions)

Trash can, Green Giant Niblets Corn can form, tin litho, 13x11", VG..**$22.00**

Joe Camel

Joe Camel, the ultimate 'cool character,' was only on the scene for a few years as a comic character. The all-around Renaissance beast, he dated beautiful women, drove fast motorcycles and cars, lazed on the beach, played pool, hung around with his pals (the Hard Pack), and dressed formally for dinner and the theatre. He was 'done in' by the anti-cigarette lobby because he smoked. Now reduced to a real camel, his comic strip human persona is avidly collected by both women and men, most of whom don't smoke. Prices have been steadily rising as more and more people come to appreciate him as the great icon he is.

Advisors: C.J. Russell and Pamela E. Apkarian-Russell (See Directory, Halloween)

Ashtray, Joe playing pool, heavy plastic, rectangular, 6 rests, 1¼x7½x4½" **$10.00**

Ashtray, Tell 'em Joe Sent You lettered on white center of triangular clear glass dish w/3 rests...**$10.00**

Baseball cap, Joe image on front of blue tie-dyed nylon **$5.00**

Calendar, Week Ends, Joe in hammock on cover, 12 scenes inside, 1993 ....**$7.00**

Can cooler, Joe's head form, 1991 ....**$15.00**

Cigarette pack, Joe at piano **$8.00**

Dartboard, Joe holding dart on 2-part front (opens), arched top, unused, 27x20" **$250.00**

Duffle bag, 14x9x10½" **$28.00**

Golf ball canister, Joe playing golf & 1st Annual Camel Classic on lid, 1994 ....**$4.00**

Jacket, 2 Hard Pack characters on yellow tyvek (feels like paper), zipper front, ca 1992, unused...**$35.00**

Kool pak, Joe Camel on blue, 5½x7½x5½" **$6.00**

Magazine ad, Joe playing pool, 2-page, 1990, 10¾x16"..........**$6.50**

Mug, Joe in beach chair on blue plastic, thermal type, Fridge Cools Like Ice, RJ Reynolds, 1991...**$15.00**

Necktie, Joe playing saxophone, $25.00.
(Photo courtesy Pamela E. Apkarian-Russell)

Playing cards, Hard Pack, single deck, 1991, MIB **$8.50**

Shower curtain **$75.00**

Standee, Joe in leather Jacket w/Camel cash booklet, cardboard, life-size **$125.00**

Tin container, Smokin' Joe's Racing, Joe in triangle on blue, 1994, 7½x4½x2¼" **$8.00**

Wristwatch, Camel Journey, Joe on motorcycle revolves on face...**$100.00**

M & M Candy Men

Everyone recognizes the familiar M&M guy. Today you'll find collectibles of every sort — planters, telephones, dispensers, plush dolls, and scores of other items. Some of the dispensers are harder to find than others, for instance the red skier and the yellow basketball player. In addition to the plain peanut-shaped dispensers, there are others that are more unusual, such as the rock 'n roll cafe and the M&M guys in their recliners. Together they make a darling collection, and the colors are dazzling.

Toppers for M&M packaging first appeared about 1988; since then other M&M items have been introduced that portray the clever antics of these colorful characters. Toppers have been issued for seasonal holidays as well as Olympic events.

Banner, beach scene, plastic, 1995, 26x30" **$12.00**

Bean bag toys, M&M shape, red, green, blue or yellow, 6", ea from $5 to **$10.00**

Calculator, yellow w/different color M&M keys, MIB, from $10 to **$20.00**

Clock, Bed & Breakfast, various characters surround lg house-like structure, Danbury Mint, 18x15x10", MIB...............**$150.00**

Clock, M&M shapes, Yellow swings from pendulum, Red is cuckoo, wall hanger, battery-operated, MIB............................**$110.00**

Cookie cutter, Red (plain) standing w/arms raised, plastic, 3" ..**$4.00**

Cookie jar, M&M cowgirl shape, ceramic, green w/pink bandana, M on white hat (lid), 12x12" **$75.00**

Dispenser, Blue (peanut shape), basketball player, 1997.......**$15.00**

Dispenser, Blue (peanut shape) waving, 3½" **$45.00**

Dispenser, Brown (plain), 1991, sm, from $5 to **$10.00**

Dispenser, Hot Rod, 2 M&M men in blue car **$45.00**

Dispenser, Red (peanut shape), 1992, lg **$20.00**

Dispenser, Red (plain), 1991, lg, from $10 to.....................**$15.00**

Dispenser, Red as baseball pitcher, blue hat, from $15.00 to $20.00.

Dispenser, Yellow (peanut shape) football player, 1995, lg ...**$20.00**

Display figure/dispenser, Yellow (peanut shape) on wheels, 42"..**$100.00**

Doll, Red (plain), plush, 12", from $10 to...........................**$15.00**

Message board magnet, school bus shape, plush, 2" **$8.00**

Tin container, Christmas 1992, dark green w/winter scene..**$12.00**

Tin container, Christmas 1996, Taking a Break at the Diner, rectangular..**$15.00**

Topper, Brown (plain) w/bow & arrow, heart w/arrow on base, 1992 ....**$7.00**

Topper, Red (plain) postman holding pink valentine, 1995 ...**$4.00**

Wristwatch, M&Ms on face, in padded sleeve, 1993 .... **$45.00**
Wristwatch, metallic blue face w/silver M in center, stainless case, metal link band, M in special M&M stainless box........ **$70.00**

Michelin Man (Bibendum or Mr. Bib)

Perhaps one of the oldest character logos around today, Mr. Bib actually originated in the late 1800s, inspired by a stack of tires that one of the company founders thought suggested the figure of a man. Over the years his image has changed considerably, but the Michelin Tire Man continues today to represent his company in many countries around the world.

Ashtray, Mr Bib at side of black Bakelite tray, 5x5" **$100.00**
Bank, Mr Bib, painted cast iron, 2-part mold, Reg 67548 Detroit on back, 6" **$55.00**
Bookends, Mr Bib w/dog & tires, ceramic, blue, white & black, 7" **$140.00**
Compresser, figure stands at side, 110 volts & 3 amps, R Toussaint & Co Paris, professionally restored, 10½x12½x8".... **$2,400.00**
Costume, nylon & metal w/yellow sash **$900.00**
Dice game, white plastic container w/3-D Mr Bib holds 8 dice w/black letters & blue Mr Bib figures, 3½x2½" **$85.00**

Display, standup with easel back, cardboard, 72", EX, $90.00.

Figure, Mr Bib, plastic, adjust to fit on top of truck cab, 1970s-80s, 18" **$140.00**
Figure, Mr Bib, white plastic, Et Cie, 1970s, 12" **$80.00**
Figure, Mr Bib w/hands at waist, ceramic, green, Made in Holland, 1950s, 12½".. **$500.00**
Puzzle, Mr Bib on motorcycle, put together to form figure, MIP **$55.00**
Watch fob, Mr Bib on front, Earth Moving Tires, 1½x1¾"... **$20.00**
Yo-yo, Mr Bib in black outline on white, EX...................... **$10.00**

Mr. Peanut

The trademark character for the Planters Peanuts Company, Mr. Peanut, has been around since 1916. His appearance has changed a little from the original version, becoming more stylized in 1961. Today he's still a common sight on Planters' advertising and product containers.

Mr. Peanut has been modeled as banks, salt and pepper shakers, whistles, and many other novelty items. His image has decorated T-shirts, beach towels, playing cards, sports equipment, etc.

Today Mr. Peanut has his own 'fan club,' Peanut Pals, the collector's organization for those who especially enjoy the Planters Peanuts area of advertising.

Club: Peanut Pals
Ruth Augustine, Membership Chairperson
P.O. Box 113
Nesquehoning, PA 18204
www.peanutpals.org

Cookie jar, Mr Peanut seated figural, hat lid, ceramic, PLC 1990 Made in Taiwan, 12" **$65.00**
Costume, Fiberglas peanut body w/black top hat, ca 1950s+, 56", VG.. **$1,350.00**
Doll, Mr Peanut, stuffed cloth, Chase Bag Company, 1967, 21" **$30.00**
Figure, painted & jointed wood, w/simple wooden cane, 9"... **$155.00**
Golf club, Callaway Mr Peanut Hickory Stick putter, Mr Peanut reserve w/yellow enameling... **$70.00**
Ice bucket, top hat, black plastic w/white lining, Mr Peanut emblem on front, Plexiglas lid, 9x11"...................................... **$45.00**
Jar, Fishbowl, octagon knob lid, no label, 1929, 12½" **$50.00**
Jar, Hexagon, 6-sided w/yellow screened design, peanut finial on lid, 7¼".. **$125.00**
Lamp, Mr Peanut figural, cream on maroon base, hat twists off to insert 7-watt bulb, button switch **$105.00**
Peanut butter maker, Mr Peanut figural, crank handle, Broadway Toys, Nabisco, copyright 1992, MIB **$50.00**

Peanut butter maker, plastic, 1970s, 12½", $30.00. (Photo courtesy B.J. Summers)

Salt & pepper shakers, Mr Peanut figural, orange plastic, pr.. **$110.00**
Scoop, peanut; Planter's Pennant Peanuts/Mr Peanut, tin litho, multicolor, measures 5¢ worth of nuts, 2¾x1⅞" dia **$55.00**
Sign, Planters Nut Department, Serve Yourself Pay Cashier, Mr Peanut at left, cardboard, yellow & black, 1950s, 14x22" **$125.00**
Spoon/pendant, Mr Peanut figural handle, silver, pierced to hang on chain, 2-sided, Sterling, 2¾" **$85.00**
Stein, Mr Peanut figural, ceramic, Taiwan, 8¾", w/certificate of authenticity... **$60.00**

Top, Whip-It, Mr Peanut label, 1940s, 2½", VG $150.00
Toy, Mr Peanut walker, black & yellow plastic w/painted details, key-wind, non-working, ca 1958, 8¼" $85.00
Tray, metal, postcard w/store stamped on bottom, 1950s, 5x7" ..$75.00
Vending Machine, Mr Peanut on front, Tarrson Co of Chicago IL, Hong Kong, 1976, MIB $60.00
Wrapper, Planters Nickel Dessert, 5½x8" $130.00

Old Crow

Old Crow whiskey items are popular with collectors primarily because of the dapper crow dressed in a tuxedo, top hat, spectacles, and cane that was used by the company for promotional purposes from the early 1950s until the early 1970s. Though many collectibles carry only the whiskey's name, in 1985, the 150th anniversary of Old Crow, the realistic crow that had been used prior to 1950 re-emerged.

Chess set, ceramic, 32 decanters in original boxes, ranging in hight from 12-15½", 1960s..................................$345.00
Decanter, Old Crow figural, gold vest, Royal Doulton, 12", from $70 to $95.00
Figure, Old Crow, white plastic w/multicolor details, 9¼" ...$55.00
Figure, Old Crow, white w/multicolor details, blue lettering, plastic, 5½" $25.00
Figure, Old Crow on white base, vinyl, 10" $48.00
Lamp, Old Crow in lantern-like plastic fixture, wall mount, switch in cord, MIB..................................$80.00
Radio, Old Crow figural w/glasses, 8-transistor, 12" $200.00
Sign/thermometer, Old Crow image/Kentucky Bourbon..., tin, 13x9" $48.00

Thermometer, Taste the Greatness..., painted metal: red, white, and black, 1950s, 13x6", $95.00. (Photo courtesy LiveAuctioneers.com/Dirk Soulis Auctions)

Poppin' Fresh (Pillsbury Doughboy) and Family

Who could be more lovable than the chubby blue-eyed Doughboy with the infectious giggle introduced by the Pillsbury Company in 1965. Wearing nothing but a neck scarf and a chef's hat, he single-handedly promoted the company's famous biscuits in a tube until about 1969. It was then that the company changed his name to 'Poppin' Fresh' and soon after presented him with a sweet-faced, bonnet-attired mate named Poppie. Before long, they had created a whole family for him. Many premiums such as dolls, salt and pepper shakers, and cookie jars have been produced over

the years. In 1988 the Benjamin Medwin Co. made several items for Pillsbury; some of these white ceramic Doughboy items are listed below. Also offered in 1988, the Poppin' Fresh Line featured the plump little fellow holding a plate of cookies; trim colors were mauve pink and blue. The Funfetti line was produced in 1992, again featuring Poppin' Fresh, this time alongside a cupcake topped with Funfetti icing (at that time a fairly new Pillsbury product), and again the producer was Benjamin Medwin.

Bank, Poppin' Fresh figural, ceramic, 1988, from $18 to $22.00
Cookbook, Poppin' Fresh Recipes, Doughboy Picks...Favorites on...25th Birthday, softcover, Pillsbury, 1990, 92 pages, VG..............$4.00
Cookie jar, Poppin' Fresh figural, Benjamin Medwin, 1988, 12" ...$25.00
Cookie jar, Poppin' Fresh figural, in blue overalls w/gold trim, 11½" $25.00
Puppet, hand; Poppin' Fresh, plush, Arts Toy, 1997, 16" $20.00
Salt & pepper shakers, Poppin' & Poppie Fresh figurals, white w/colored details, 1974, 4", 3½", pr $35.00
Salt & pepper shakers, Poppin' Fresh figurals, white w/blue & gold trim, 1960s, pr $15.00
Soap dish, Poppin' Fresh stands at corner, Benjamin Medwin, 1988, MIB....................................$27.50
Spoon rest, Poppin' Fresh figural, Benjamin Medwin, 1988, MIB....................................$15.00
Teapot, Poppin' Fresh figural, Benjamin Medwin, 1997.......$45.00
Tool holder, Poppin' Fresh stands before holder, Benjamin Medwin, China, 1988, 7½" $30.00

Utensil holder, Funfetti series, 1992, from $20.00 to $25.00.
(Photo courtesy Lil West)

Reddy Kilowatt

Reddy was developed during the late 1920s and became very well known during the 1950s. His job was to promote electric power companies all over the United States, which he did with aplomb! Reddy memorabilia is highly collectible today. On Reddy's 65th birthday (1992), a special 'one-time-only' line of commemoratives was issued. This line consisted of approximately 30 different items issued in crystal, gold, pewter, and silver. All items were limited editions and quite costly. Because of high collector demand, new merchandise is flooding the market. Watch for items such as a round mirror, a small hand-held game with movable squares, and a ring-toss game marked 'Made in China.'

Cigarette lighter, Reddy enameled on brushed chrome finish, Zippo, 1998, MIB..................................$75.00

Cigarette lighter, Reddy in red enamel on brushed metal case, Zippo, ca 1950s..$315.00

Coaster, printed cardboard, 3½", from $5 to........................$8.00

Coloring book, PA Electric Co (Penelec), 1960s, 14x10½", G....$20.00

Display figure, felt with light-up nose, 17x9", EX, $400.00. (Photo courtesy LiveAuctioneers.com/Morphy Auctions)

Earrings, Reddy figural, red enamel on gold-tone, 1", pr $45.00

Figure, Reddy, hard rubber, 1930s, 3"....................................$8.00

Light bulb, Reddy filament in clear bulb, w/socket-like white stand, ca 1950s..$550.00

Light switch, plastic glow-in-the-dark Reddy, CMCLXI $125.00

Mug, Reddy as chef for utilities company, red pyro on milk glass, Fire-King...$125.00

Nightlight, Panelescent Sylvania, 3" dia, from $35 to..........$40.00

Notepad holder, Reddy image at top, brown Bakelite, Autopoint Memo Case, w/5¢ Rainbow paper tablet, 3x5"...........$185.00

Ovaltine, shake-up cup, Little Orphan Annie & Sandy decal on white plastic w/red lid, Beetleware, 1930s.....................$60.00

Paperweight, Reddy glow-in-the-dark figure atop black Bakelite outlet base, marked MR on 1 ft, R on other...............$140.00

Pencil clip, Reddy running through V, copyright 1942, 1⅝x⅞"..$22.00

Playing cards, double deck, NMIB, from $35.00 to $45.00.

Pocketknife, Reddy in red enameling on brushed chrome finish, cutting blade & nail file, Zippo, 2x1¼" (closed)................$67.50

Postcard, 1¢, Reddy in cowboy hat $8.00

Sign, Another Flameless Home..., Reddy at left on yellow, tin litho, 2-sided, 20x28", VG...$135.00

Sign, No Tresspassing/company name lettered above Reddy, porcelain, red & black on white, 11x16"............................$260.00

Stick pin, Reddy figural, red enamel on metal, 1940s, 1".....$27.50

Tumbler, Reddy, white enamel on clear glass, 3½x3", from $15 to..$20.00

Tumblers, enamel (red, white, blue, or yellow) on clear glass, Reddy scenes in Wyoming & Yellowstone Park, 8-oz, 8 for $50.00

Wacky Wobbler, Reddy figural nodder, Funko, 7½", MIB, from $40 to $50.00

Smokey Bear

The fiftieth anniversary of Smokey Bear, the fire-prevention spokesbear for the State Foresters, Ad Council, and US Forest Service was celebrated in 1994. After ruling out other mascots (including Bambi), by 1944 it had been decided that a bear was best suited for the job, and Smokey was born. When a little cub was rescued from a fire in a New Mexico national forest in 1950, Smokey's role intensified. Over the years his appearance has evolved from one a little more menacing to the lovable bear we know today.

The original act to protect the Smokey Bear image was enacted in 1974. The character name in the 'Smokey Bear Act' is Smokey Bear. Until the early 1960s, when his name appeared on items such as sheet music and Little Golden Books, it was 'Smokey *the* Bear.' Generally, from that time on, he became known as simply Smokey Bear.

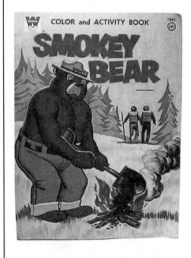

Coloring and Activity Book, Whitman #1662, 1971, some use, VG+, $12.50. (Photo courtesy www.gasolinealleyantiques.com)

Badge, Junior Forest Rangers, Smokey's face in center, gold-tone metal, 1950s-60s, NM..$25.00

Bank, Smokey figural, hard plastic, w/removable shovel, Product Miniatures, 1950s $120.00

Bank, Smokey figural, vinyl, Smokey on belt buckle, brown w/multicolor paint, Artline, 1960s, 14", VG........................$45.00

Bendee, Smokey in yellow hat, blue pants, Official Department of Agriculture seal, Lakeside, 1967, 5¾" $45.00

Book, Smokey Bear & the Campers, S Quentin Hyatt, Mell Crawford illustrator, Golden Press, Little Golden Book, 1961 ....$38.00

Book, Smokey Bear Color & Activity, Whitman #1662, 1971, EX $12.50

Book, Smokey the Bear Golden Stamp Book, Simon & Schuster #P-60, 1958..$35.00

Bookmark/ruler, Smokey die-cut head, Virginia Department of Forestry, 8½x3", from $9 to..$14.00

Bookmark/ruler, Smokey's head die-cut, Please! Only You Can Prevent..., Washington Department of Forestry, 8½x3", EX................$7.50

Brochure, Smokey illustration, Welcome Traveler...Keep Washington Green, late 1950s, 8 pages **$10.00**

Coin, Smokey's image embossed on aluminum, US Department of Agriculture, 1¼" dia **$10.00**

Collar tab, I'm Helping Smokey, tin litho, brown on yellow, unknown maker, 1950s, 2x1¼" **$22.50**

Collar tab, I'm Helping Smokey, tin litho, Green Duck Co, 1950s, 1½" **$15.00**

Coloring book, Smokey Coloring Book, Official License, Abbott #320, 1950s, unused, 12½x11" **$90.00**

Doll, Smokey, hands at sides, yellow hat & blue pants, Dakin, 1970s, scarce size, 4⅝", MIP **$25.00**

Doll, Smokey, vinyl hat, blue jeans w/removable belt, missing shovel, Dakin, 1970s, 8" **$95.00**

Flashlight, hand-held key-chain type, 1950s, NM **$95.00**

Hand puppet, Smokey w/modeled head, printed cloth body, Ideal Toys, ca 1959, scarce **$190.00**

Ink blotter, Smokey & burnt forest, Another 30 Million Acres..., US Government, 6¼x2½", EX **$20.00**

Litter bag, Keep America Green & Clean, Sears & Roebuck, 1960s, 11x8½" **$20.00**

Membership card, Junior Forest Ranger, green on white, Smokey's ABCs, 1971 .... **$18.00**

Mug, coffee; Smokey beside green sapling on milk glass, Smokey Bear Says..., 1960s **$60.00**

Mug, coffee; Smokey's head in brown on milk glass, Help Prevent Forest Fires, 1960s **$45.00**

Patch, arm; Smokey & lettering embroidery on yellow cloth, 3½x3¾" **$20.00**

Pencil, Smokey, Help Prevent Forest Fires on fluorescent pink, M **$3.50**

Photo card, To My Forest Fire Protection Friend..., sepia-tone print of real bear, postcard size **$15.00**

Pin-back button, I'm Smokey's Helper, cartoon of Smokey w/shovel, bird on handle, celluloid, 1970s, 3" **$7.50**

Pin-back button, Join Smokey's Campaign, celluloid, orange & brown, 1950s, 1½" **$24.00**

Pin-back button, Remember Only You Can Prevent Forest Fires, tin litho, black on green, 1½" **$5.00**

Postcard, Be My Guest, But Please..., Smokey w/2 cubs, 1966 .... **$10.00**

Postcard, Only You Can Prevent..., Smokey overlooking deer in field, water & mountains beyond **$10.00**

Postcard booklet, Smokey Bear Color-Grams, Oakland Athletics baseball team, set of 12 photo/12 caricature cards, 1987 .... **$30.00**

Ruler, A Rule To Prevent....Smokey's Friends Don't Play w/Matches, 1960s, 12", EX **$15.00**

Sign, Smokey Says - Let the Burned Stumps Remind You..., Smokey's image at right, 1950s, 11x14" **$45.00**

Soaky, Smokey figural, hard plastic, removable hat, 1960s, EX **$50.00**

Tablecloth, Smokey in jeep, Don't Play w/Matches on bumper, paper, Dennison, 1960s, 54x96", MIP **$50.00**

Toy, Smokey inflatable figure, Jennie Sales Co, 1960s, 30", MIP **$65.00**

View-master, True Story of Smokey Bear, GAF, 1969, 3-reel set, 16-page booklet **$45.00**

Snap!, Crackle!, and Pop!

Bowl, Snap, Crackle & Pop on white plastic, Best to You... along rim, Made in China, 2x6½" **$5.00**

Breakfast set, characters transfer on white plastic, 7½" plate, 5¼" bowl, 12-oz mug **$20.00**

Christmas ornaments, Snap, Crackle & Pop, celluloid w/cloth drum major's hat, gold trim, Japan, 1950s, set of 3 .... **$15.00**

Doll, Crackle, stuffed cloth, fuzzy yellow hair, complete outfit, 7½" .. **$8.00**

Doll, Snap, plastic, multicolor details, 1960s-70s, 7½" **$20.00**

Dolls, Snap, Crackle & Pop, Friendly Folks, wooden w/plastic nose & fabric clothing, 1972, 3", 6 for **$20.00**

Figure, Pop, plastic, multicolor details (some wear), 7" **$12.00**

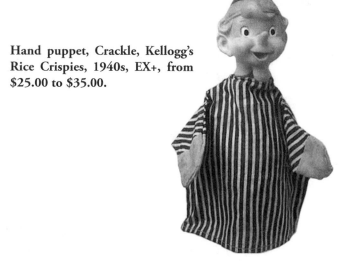

Hand puppet, Crackle, Kellogg's Rice Crispies, 1940s, EX+, from $25.00 to $35.00.

Magazine ad, Snap, Crackle & Pop in school scene, Crisp Every Spoonful!, full color, 1941, 12½x9¾" **$6.00**

Plate, Snap Crackle & Pop in picnic scene on white, tin litho, 1983, 4" **$10.00**

Record, Snap Crackle Pop, 33⅓ rpm, 3 songs ea side, VG+ **$6.00**

Squeak dolls, Snap, Crackle & Pop, vinyl, 1 silent, set of 3 .. **$60.00**

Stencil, faces of Snap, Crackle & Pop, cereal premium, 1970s, 3x5½" **$10.00**

Tony the Tiger

Kellogg's introduced Tony the Tiger in 1953, and since then he's appeared on every box of their Frosted Flakes. In his deep, rich voice, he's convinced us all that they are indeed 'Gr-r-r-eat'!

Baseball, Tony portrait on white leather, promotional item, MIB **$12.50**

Production cel, hand-painted Tony on plain blue background, 5x7" image, 10½x12½" overall **$42.50**

Spoon, Tony figural handle, silver-plate, International Silver, Kellogg, 1965 .... **$8.00**

T-shirt, Tony's portrait & They're GR-R-Reat! on blue cotton, adult lg, EX **$32.00**

Tin container, 12th World Hot Air Balloon Championship in Battlecreek MI, tin litho, limited edition **$30.00**

Wacky Wobbler, Funko, MIB, $25.00.

Wristwatch, Tony on face, black leather band, Swiss movement, Kellogg premium, 1976 ....**$60.00**

Miscellaneous

AC Spark Plugs, doll, AC Man, white & green w/AC on chest, 6", EXIB **$160.00**

AC Spark Plugs, figure, Sparky the Horse, inflatable vinyl, Ideal, 1960s, EXIB **$160.00**

Alka-Seltzer, bank, Speedy figural, vinyl, 5½", EX **$80.00**

Alka-Seltzer, thermometer, Speedy on face, TW O'Connell & Co, 1950s, 12", VG **$175.00**

Alka-Seltzer, Wacky Wobbler, Speedy nodder, Funko, 7", MIB ..**$15.00**

Bazooka Bubble Gum, bubble gum comics & cards, Bazooka Joe & his gang, 165 sm comics & 52 trading cards, 1970s.. **$45.00**

Bumble Bee Tuna, belt buckle, cloisonné image, 3½" long, from $25.00 to $35.00. (Photo courtesy www.gasolinealleyantiques.com)

Burger King, doll, King, stuffed cloth, 1973, 16" **$10.00**

Buster Brown ET Shoes, poster, Buster & ET, Universal City Studios, 15x11", EX+ **$25.00**

Buster Brown Hose Supporter, pin-back button, Buster holding suspenders, celluloid, ⅞", VG **$35.00**

Buster Brown Shoes, pin-back button, Buster & Tige, Brownbilt Club, tin litho, ⅞", VG **$40.00**

Buster Brown Vacation Days Carnival, pocket mirror, Buster & Tige, multicolor on white, 1946, 2¼", VG **$38.00**

Charter Oak Stoves, ashtray, cat's head form, cast iron, 4½x3¾" ...**$120.00**

Dutch Boy Paint, can, Dutch Boy White Lead, Dutch boy waving, orange & black, 2x2¾" dia, VG.........................**$35.00**

Frito-Lay, ad poster, Frito Bandito, Wanted for Theft of Fritos Corn Chips, 1968, 10x13"...**$20.00**

Frito-Lay, cigarette lighter, Frito Bandito enameled on front, I'm a Frito Bandito, multicolor on chrome, unused **$20.00**

Frito-Lay, pencil topper/eraser, Frito Bandito figural, 1960s, unused, 1½", from $20 to **$30.00**

Frito-Lay, pocket protector, Frito Bandito on plastic.............**$4.00**

Frito-Lay, ring, Frito Bandito, plastic premium, multicolor, 1969 ....**$15.00**

Fruit Stripe Gum, bendy man riding motorbike, 1960s, 7½" ..**$75.00**

General Mills, doll, Boo Berry, vinyl squeaker, box premium, 7½" **$55.00**

General Mills, doll, Count Chocula, vinyl squeaker, premium, 8" **$45.00**

General Mills, doll, Fruit Brute, vinyl lion w/striped painted-on shirt, squeaker, 7½" **$75.00**

Gerber, doll, Arrow Rubber & Plastic, 1965 premium, MIB, from $55 to **$65.00**

Hamburger Helper, clock, Helping Hand figural, red & white plastic **$16.50**

Hamburger Helper, doll, Helping Hand, plush glove-like figure w/ facial features on palm, 12x14" **$25.00**

Hamburger Helper, soap, Helping Hand figural, mail-in premium, unused, 2½x3¼" **$8.00**

Hardee's, doll, Gilbert Giddy-Up, stuffed cloth, 1971, EX...**$25.00**

Hawaiian Punch, doll, Punchy, stuffed cloth, 20" **$90.00**

Heinz, baby doll, squeeze vinyl, cloth bib, 1950s, scarce, 9", MIP...**$185.00**

HP Hood Co, doll, Harry Hood, vinyl & cloth premium, 1981, 7½", MIP...**$45.00**

Icee, bank, Icee bear w/drink before him, vinyl, multicolor details, uncut slot in back, 1970s, unused, 7½" **$25.00**

Icee, Pez dispenser, Icee bear figural, older-style head, white plastic..**$14.00**

Jell-O, hand puppet, Mr Wiggle, red vinyl, 1966 ....**$22.00**

Jiffy Lube, nodder, Lube 'n Lou, green figure w/blue nose, MIP..**$40.00**

Jordache Jeans, figure, Jordache Man, Mego, 12", MIB **$30.00**

Jumbo Peanut Butter, doll, Jumbo Elephant, stuffed cloth, 16" ..**$90.00**

Lee Jeans, doll, Buddy Lee, compo, dressed as cowboy, ca 1920-49, 13"...**$310.00**

Lee Jeans, doll, Buddy Lee, compo, dressed as railroad engineer, 1950s, 13" **$385.00**

Lee Jeans, nodder, Buddy Lee in Lee Jeans, 8" **$30.00**

Levi's Jeans, doll, Levi, stuffed, denim w/big E logo, yarn hair, Knickerbocker, 25" **$60.00**

Little Caesar's, doll, Pizza Pizza Man, plush, holding pizza slice, 1990s, 6", MIP **$7.50**

Little Debbie, doll, Little Debbie, vinyl w/cloth outfit, straw hat, 1980s, 11" **$25.00**

McDonald's, action figure, Professor, Remco, 1976, 6"........**$25.00**

Meow Mix, cat figural, vinyl **$35.00**

Mott's Apple Juice, doll, Apple of My Eye Bear, plush, 1988..**$15.00**

Nabisco Fig Newtons, girl figure, plastic, 1980s, 4½" **$10.00**

Ovaltine, cup, Little Orphan Annie, brown plastic, Beetleware, 1930s, 3¾" **$20.00**

Ovaltine, mug, Howdy Doody, decal on red plastic, Copyright Bob Smith, Made in USA, 3⅛" **$110.00**

Proctor & Gamble, figure, Mr Clean, white-painted vinyl, 1961, 8", EX **$150.00**

Schenley's Whiskey, figure, Quaker man, pressed cardboard, 1940s, 20", VG **$42.50**

Snap-On Tools, nodder, mechanic w/lg wrench, composition, MIB **$60.00**

Wrangler Jeans, doll, cowboy, cloth outfit, Ertl, 11½", MIB... **$50.00**

Chateau Quebec, pipe tobacco, G, $23.00. (Photo courtesy B.J. Summers)

7-Up Fresh-Up Freddie, squeeze toy, vinyl, 1959, 9", NM, from $150.00 to $175.00. (Photo courtesy LiveAuctioneers. com/Morphy Auctions)

Advertising Tins

One of the hottest areas of tin collecting today is spice tins, but if those don't appeal to you, consider automotive products, cleaners, cosmetics, guns, medical, fishing, sewing, or sample sizes. Besides the aesthetics factor, condition and age also help determine price. The values suggested below represent what you might pay in an antique store for tins, but what makes this sort of collecting so much fun is that you'll find them much cheaper at garage sales, Goodwill Stores, and flea markets. Values are for examples in condition as coded in each description. For more information we recommend *Modern Collectible Tins* by Linda McPherson (Collector Books).

Ali D'Italia Oil of Peanuts, biplane, multicolor litho, pouring spout on top, rectangular, 10x6x4½", EX **$210.00**

Bell Brand Typewriter Ribbon, JP Bell Company, Lynchburg VA, lg bell graphics on lid, 2½" dia, NM **$90.00**

Bob White Golden Table Syrup, game bird reserve on press-on lid, paper label, 3½x3¼" dia, EX **$68.00**

Capitol Mills Pure Coffee, Capitol building, black & yellow litho, Lincoln, Seyms & Co...Conn, w/lid, 5½x5", VG........ **$275.00**

Chisca Brand Peanut Butter, red & white tin litho label on gold-tone pail, Maury Cole Co, 10-oz, 3"+handle, VG+ **$155.00**

Cook's Potato Chips, Snackin' Good Because..., yellow & blue litho, 14x12" dia, VG **$75.00**

Dixie Peanut Butter, Jackie Cooper portrait on red, pail w/swing handle, sm, 3½x4", VG **$135.00**

Evans Delicious Salt Water Oysters, blue & white litho, VL Evans... MD, slip lid, 5-gal, EX+ **$250.00**

Fairy Queen Marshmallows, lettering on red litho, Kansas MO, 12" dia, VG **$65.00**

Forbes Culture Ripened Coffee, sailing ship scene, multicolor, key-wind lid, 1-lb, NM **$90.00**

Golden Rod Coffee Brand, multicolor on green, pail w/bail handle, Indianapolis Tippecanoe Coffee, 11" **$95.00**

Hard A Port Tobacco, man at ship's wheel, blue & white litho, rectangular, 6x3¾", EX **$250.00**

Harvest Home Coffee, farm scene w/barn & planted acreage, red, cream & black litho, press lid, 4x5¼" dia, VG............. **$90.00**

Hi-Plane Smooth Cut Tobacco, plane on red, rectangular, 4½x3½", NM **$160.00**

Indian Motor Oil, chief facing left, red, white & black litho, minor dents & scratches, 1-qt **$215.00**

Iris Brand Coffee, green & yellow tin litho, ½-lb, 3¼x3¾", VG **$150.00**

Kentucky Windmill Coffee, windmill on red, red & black w/bail handle, w/lid, 12x7⅛" dia................................... **$235.00**

Kibbe Popular Cough Drops, geometric pattern overall, Kibbe Bros & Co, Springfield MA, rectangular, 2⅞", VG............. **$85.00**

Klein Cocoa, parrot on tin, Elizabethtown PA, rectangular sample size, VG+ **$235.00**

Liberty Butter Crackers, eagle on ball, red & yellow litho, press lid, 1930s, 1-lb, 7½" **$90.00**

Little Boy Blue Coffee, boy in blue, Special 5¢ on lid, Lansing Wholesale Gro Co, key-wind lid, 1-lb, EX+ **$210.00**

Little Skipper Coffee, sm sailor beside lg cup of coffee, multicolor litho, key-wind lid, light rust spots **$260.00**

Ocean Brand Mustard, Dayton Biscuit Co, modeled as industrial building, rectangular, VG... **$110.00**

Peter Rabbit Baby Powder, Peter & Mrs Peter put powder on baby bunny, colorful litho, red cap, 3⅝x4¼", EX.............. **$175.00**

Pickaninny Brand Peanut Butter, child at play, red & yellow litho, pail form w/wire bail & slip lid, 1920s, VG.............. **$235.00**

Salt Water Brand Oysters, sailboat scene, blue & white cylinder w/press lid, Distributed by RH Ranagan, Mass, 1-gal, M **$340.00**

Sharp's Home Made Super-Kreem Toffee, Kreemy Kottage, multi-color litho, rectangular w/sloped roof, 1930s, NM **$95.00**

Shedd's Peanut Butter, 6¼", from $15.00 to $25.00. (Photo courtesy Linda McPherson)

Squirrel Brand Fancy Salted Nuts, squirrel on branch, multicolor on mustard yellow, 5-lb, VG **$165.00**

Stork Brand Oysters, stork & baby, Oysters for Health, red, white & blue litho, 1-gal, VG **$150.00**

Tindeco Candy, nursery rhyme scenes on red, Merry Christmas From Santa on lid, rectangular basket w/swing handle, VG **$145.00**

Tindeco Candy, Peter Rabbit theme on blue, rectangular basket w/swing handle, 2½x4½x2¼", EX+ **$150.00**

US Marine Flake Cut Tobacco, yellow lettering on red, US in white letters on blue reserve, upright, pocket size, EX **$220.00**

White Rose Motor Oil, white rose on yellow pail, 5-gal, VG . **$85.00**

Wilbur's Cocoatheta Powdered Chocolate, blue, gold & black litho, rectangular, ½-lb, 5⅛x2¾x1½" **$155.00**

Woodfield's Oysters, sailing ship, orange, green & creamy white litho, Woodfield Fish & Oyster Co, 1-pt **$110.00**

Airline Memorabilia

Even before the Wright brothers' historic flight shortly after the turn of the century, people have been fascinated with flying. What better way to enjoy the evolution and history of this amazing transportation industry than to collect its memorabilia. Today just about any item ever used or made for a commercial (non-military) airline is collectible, especially dishes, glassware, silver serving pieces and flatware, wings and badges worn by the crew, playing cards, and junior wings given to passengers. Advertising items such as timetables and large travel agency plane models are also widely collected. The earlier, the better! Anything pre-war is good; items from before the 1930s are rare and very valuable. Unless noted otherwise, our values are for items in mint condition.

See also Restaurant China.

Advisor: Dick Wallin (See Directory, Airline)

Club/Newsletter: World Airline Historical Society
www.airlinecollectibles.com

Ashtray, Qantas Airlines, plane pictured on white plastic, 2 rests, 4¾x5¾" **$50.00**

Badge, American Airlines stewardess, letter A ea side of golden eagle w/wings up, unmarked, 1¼x1" **$45.00**

Badge, Pan Am stewardess, Pan Am engraved on metal, gold & black enameling, 1959-79, 1⅜" dia. **$300.00**

Badge, Pan Am Traffic & Service Department, globe & gold-filled rings, 1930s-40s, ⅞x1¾" **$200.00**

Badge, Trans World Airlines, TWA red enameled letters on shaft of silver arrow, LGB Sterling, 1940s, ½x3" **$285.00**

Bag, Pan American Airlines, Pan Am logo, Camelot logo, Olympic Games symbol & New Zealand Fern on cloth **$50.00**

Bag, Trans World Airlines, TWA red & white logo on red nylon bag, adjustable strap, 13x11" **$45.00**

Blanket, Trans World Airlines, TWA & stripes in red on dark blue wool, 1st class, Made in Western Germany **$60.00**

Cup and saucer, TWA, Royal Ambassador by Rosenthal, for international first class, 1960s – ca. 1975, from $24.00 to $30.00. (Photo courtesy Barbara Conroy)

Map, Aloha Airlines, Maui, Sheraton Maui advertising, etc, full color, 1960s **$22.00**

Map/pamphlet, United Airlines, full color, shows network of business & vacation area routes, 1962, open: 21x36" **$15.00**

Menu, souvenir; Singapore Airlines, B707 flight from Singapore - Bankok - Hong Kong - Osaka, 1975, 11¼x7½" **$30.00**

Model, Ozark Airlines, metal w/chrome, A/S Fermo Model Factory... Denmark, 7x15", EX **$215.00**

Model, United Airlines B767-300, Boeing Commercial Airplanes, polyurethane, ca 1986, 21¼" L **$135.00**

Paperweight, Alisarda, commemorative of introduction of McDonnell Douglas MD-82 aircraft, print on green glass, 1985 .... **$50.00**

Photo, First Flight of Boeing 747, heavy card stock, 8½x11" .. **$6.00**

Pin-back button, Pan Am 747, speeding cartoon plane, & 1,000,000, blue on white, 2" **$35.00**

Postcard/jigsaw, Braniff Airlines, Braniff BAC 111 in flight, full color, 20-pc, unopened **$50.00**

Poster, Fly BOAC Britannia, The Whispering Giant, plane w/propellers in sky beyond, 1950s, 29½x20", EX **$235.00**

Shot glass, Eastern Airlines, white logo on clear glass, sm foot... **$5.00**

Teaspoon, Pan American embossed on handle, silver plate, International Silver Co, EX **$20.00**

Teaspoon, United & airline logo, silver plate, International Silver Co, EX **$15.00**

Timetable, Eastern Airlines, system-wide schedule for August 1946, shows new DC-4 Silverliner, +baggage sticker **$48.00**

Timetable, Piedmont Airlines, many airlines shown, full schedule for June 1965 .... **$45.00**
Timetable, Western Airlines, Douglass DC-6B, Douglas DC-4, and Convair 240 planes, 1953, EX, +ticket jacket & receipt.. **$42.50**

Timetable holder, Northwest Airlines Inc., metal, logo on three sides, ca. 1930s – 1940s, 6½", EX, $300.00. **(Photo courtesy Wm. Morford Auctions)**

Toy airplane, Northwest 701, tin litho metal, Japan, friction, 6x11", EX **$165.00**
Wings, Air West pilot's, sterling mark, 2 screw posts on back, 3¼" L **$110.00**
Wings, Pan American Airlines, Pan Am Junior Clipper Pilot, blue namel & gold-tone metal, 2¼" **$55.00**
Wings, Panagra Airline Jr Pilot, DC-7 image amid gold stars, gold-tone metal, ¾x2¼", MOC **$275.00**

Akro Agate

The Akro Agate Company operated in West Virginia from 1914 until 1951, and in addition to their famous marbles they made children's dishes as well as many types of novelties — flowerpots, powder jars with Scottie dogs on top, candlesticks, and ashtrays, for instance — in many colors and patterns. Though some of their glassware was made in solid colors, their most popular products were made of the same swirled colors as their marbles. Though many pieces are not marked, you will find some that are marked with their distinctive logo: a crow flying through the letter 'A' holding an Aggie in its beak and one in each claw. Some novelty items may instead carry one of these trademarks: 'JV Co, Inc,' 'Braun & Corwin,' 'NYC Vogue Merc Co USA,' 'Hamilton Match Co,' and 'Mexicali Pickwick Cosmetic Corp.'

Color is a very important worth-assessing factor. Some pieces may be common in one color but rare in others. Occasionally an item will have many exceptionally good colors, and this would make it more valuable than an example with only average color.

For more information we recommend *The Complete Line of the Akro Agate Co.* by our advisors, Roger and Claudia Hardy.

See also marbles.

Advisors: Roger and Claudia Hardy (See Directory, Akro Agate)

Club: Akro Agate Collectors Club
Newsletter: *Clarksburg Crow*
Claudia and Roger Hardy
10 Bailey St., Clarksburg, WV 26301-2524
304-624-7600 (days) or 304-624-4523 (evenings)
www.mkl.com/akro/club

Concentric Rib, cup, purple, 1⁵⁄₁₆" **$60.00**
Concentric Rib, plate, dark green, 3¼" **$3.00**
Concentric Rib, tumbler, white, 2" **$6.00**
Concentric Ring, creamer, ivory or white, 1⅜" **$16.00**
Concentric Ring, cup, blue & white marbleized, 1⁹⁄₁₆" **$75.00**
Concentric Ring, plate, apple or dark green, 4¼" **$20.00**
Concentric Ring, sugar bowl, med or royal blue, 1⅜" **$16.00**
Concentric Ring, teapot lid, blue & white marbleized, 2¹¹⁄₁₆", from $18 to **$20.00**
Interior Panel, creamer, canary yellow, 18 panels, 1⁵⁄₁₆" **$55.00**
Interior Panel, cup, orange, 16 panels, 1½" **$24.00**
Interior Panel, plate, dark green lustre, 16 panels, 4¼" **$16.00**
Interior Panel, sugar bowl, green & white marbleized, 18 panels, 1⁵⁄₁₆" **$32.00**
Interior Panel, teapot lid, ivory, 16 panels, 2¹¹⁄₁₆", from $18 to... **$20.00**
Miss America, creamer, red transparent, 1⁹⁄₁₆", from $150 to.. **$160.00**
Miss America, cup, white, 1⁹⁄₁₆", from $34 to **$38.00**
Miss America, plate, red onyx, 4½" **$60.00**
Miss America, sugar bowl, white w/decal, 3⅝", from $18 to.. **$23.00**
Miss America, sugar bowl lid, white, 2⅝", from $36 to **$40.00**
Miss America, teapot, green transparent, 2½", from $90 to.. **$100.00**
Octagonal, cereal, white or ivory, 3⅜", from $13 to **$15.00**
Octagonal, cup, med or dark blue, 1½", from $10 to **$12.00**

Octagonal, Play Time water set, large, open handles, mixed colors, seven-piece, MIB, $245.00. **(Photo courtesy Margaret and Kenn Whitmyer)**

Octagonal, saucer, canary yellow, 2¾", from $9 to **$10.00**
Octagonal, teapot, orange, closed handle, 3⅝" **$60.00**
Octagonal, teapot, pale blue, open handle, 3⅜", from $30 to.. **$32.00**
Raised Daisy, cup, dark green, 1⁵⁄₁₆" **$32.00**
Raised Daisy, pitcher, dark turquoise or dark blue, 2⅜" **$34.00**
Raised Daisy, sugar bowl, dark turquoise or dark blue, 1⁵⁄₁₆" .. **$85.00**
Raised Daisy, tumbler, Daisy, dark ivory, 2" **$30.00**
Raised Daisy, tumbler, plain, dark turquoise or dark blue, 2" .. **$85.00**
Stacked Disk, cup, dark green, 1⁵⁄₁₆" **$6.00**
Stacked Disk, sugar bowl, dark green, 1⁵⁄₁₆" **$12.00**
Stacked Disk, tumbler, canary yellow, 2" **$8.00**

Stacked Disk & Interior Panel, creamer, green transparent, 1⅜" .. **$50.00**

Stacked Disk & Interior Panel, sugar bowl, blue & white marbleized, 1⅜" **$70.00**

Stacked Disk & Interior Panel, tumbler, ivory or white, 2".. **$50.00**

Stippled Band, creamer, green transparent, 1¼" **$45.00**

Stippled Band, saucer, topaz transparent, 3¾" **$6.00**

Stippled Band, sugar bowl, green transparent, 1½" **$30.00**

Stippled Band, tumbler, topaz transparent, 1¾" **$10.00**

Miscellaneous

Ashtray, orange & white, from $75 to **$90.00**

Basket, #328, w/handles **$30.00**

Bowl, black or marbleized, footed **$600.00**

Candlestick, Short Ribbed, marked, rare, ea **$800.00**

Creamer, pink **$350.00**

Jar, cold cream; black **$55.00**

Jar, powder; #323, solid colors or crystal **$100.00**

Jardiniere, solid colors, bell shape, from $65 to **$85.00**

Pin tray, crystal..**$100.00**

Pitcher, lg, from $1,000 to **$1,200.00**

Puff box, Scottie dog, dark green **$400.00**

Sugar bowl, pink..**$200.00**

Tumbler **$45.00**

Aluminum

The aluminum items which have become today's collectibles range from early brite-cut giftware and old kitchen wares to furniture and hammered aluminum cooking pans. But the most collectible, right now, at least, is the giftware of the 1930s through the 1950s.

There were probably several hundred makers of aluminum accessories and giftware with each developing their preferred method of manufacturing. Some pieces were cast; other products were hammered with patterns created by either an intaglio method or repoussé. Machine embossing was utilized by some makers; many used faux hammering, and lightweight items were often decorated with pressed designs.

As early as the 1940s, collectors began to seek out aluminum, sometimes to add to the few pieces received as wedding gifts. By the late 1970s and early 1980s, aluminum giftware was found in abundance at almost any flea market, and prices of $1.00 or less were normal. As more shoppers became enthralled with the appearance of this lustrous metal and its patterns, prices began to rise and have not yet peaked for the products of some companies. A few highly prized pieces have brought prices of $400 or $500 and occasionally even more.

One of the first to manufacture this type of ware was Wendell August Forge, when during the late 1920s they expanded their line of decorative wrought iron and began to use aluminum, at first making small items as gifts for their customers. Very soon they were involved in a growing industry estimated at one point to be comprised of several hundred companies, among them Arthur Armour, the Continental Silver Company, Everlast, Buenilum, Rodney Kent, and Palmer-Smith. Few of the many original companies survived the WWII scarcity of aluminum.

During the '60s, anodized (colored) aluminum became very popular. It's being bought up today by the younger generations who are attracted to its neon colors and clean lines. Watch for items with strong color and little if any sign of wear — very important factors to consider when assessing value. Because it was prone to scratching and denting, mint condition examples are few and far between.

Prices differ greatly from one region to another, sometimes without regard to quality or condition, so be sure to examine each item carefully before you buy.

Unless otherwise noted, our values are for items in at least near mint condition.

See also Kitchen Collectibles.

Bowl, Arthur Court, Bunny & Grapevine, openwork, 1996, 3¼x12" **$120.00**

Bowl, centerpiece; Arthur Court, monkey handles ea side of banana-leaf bowl, footed, 7x13¾x8", MIB............................**$110.00**

Cake stand, Buenilum, hammered finish, beaded rim, footed, 5x10½" **$65.00**

Candleholders, Bruce Fox, daffodil figural, 2¼x10", pr........**$75.00**

Candleholders, half-ring w/3 holders, hammered finish, pr..**$80.00**

Canoe, Mariposa, beading along top edge, 4x14½x4¾" **$75.00**

Chafing dish, Everlast, Bamboo, base w/lidded dish & glass insert, bamboo detailed handles, 1940s **$50.00**

Cocktail shaker, Buenilum, coiled decoration on finial, tall cylinder, 1940s, 11", EX **$48.00**

Coffee set, Continental, crysanthemum, 15" urn w/electric cord, sugar bowl w/lid, creamer & 19x15" tray, +booklet....**$150.00**

Coffee set, Kensington, Laurel Leaf (wheat pattern w/birds), 1930s, coffeepot, creamer & sugar bowl & lg tray **$125.00**

Console set, Farberware, plate insert marked Triumph American Limoges, engraved foliage, +2 flower-shaped candleholders................**$60.00**

Console set, Wendell August Forge, Pine Cone, 1¾x9½" bowl, +2 candlesticks **$45.00**

Creamer and sugar bowl on tray, Rodney Kent #479, $50.00.

Crumber set, Wendell August Forge, Daisy, 10" crumber & 7¾x5½" tray **$65.00**

Dish, Arthur Court (unmarked), Bunny, w/lid, 1¼x6¾x5"..**$65.00**

Flatware caddy, Arthur Court, embossed flowers & grapes, grapevine handle, MIB **$75.00**

Ice bucket, Continental, Chrysanthemum, applied leaves at handles, #504, 7¼" **$50.00**

Pitcher, Arthur Court, fish figural, applied red stone eyes, fish handle, 1977, 12x6½" **$110.00**

Pitcher, Arthur Court, giraffe figural, 1989, 13⅝x9"...........**$75.00**

Pitcher, Continental, Chrysanthemum, #509, +8 #601 tumblers .. **$135.00**

Pitcher, Nasco Italy, hammered finish, 8x5½", +6 5½x3" tumblers **$50.00**

Salad set, Bali, Bamboo, 10" bowl, wooden salad fork & spoon w/bamboo-patterned aluminum trim on handles **$45.00**

Server, Buenilum, hammered, water in base is heated by electric element, holds 3 1-qt Pyrex bowl w/lids, 17½" **$68.00**

Serving dish, Drumm, embossed foliage on lid, handles, 19x8½" **$95.00**

Skillet, Drumm, embossed rayed pattern on lid, 3x10" dia, 17" L...**$50.00**

Soup tureen, Drumm, heavily embossed foliage, w/lid & ladle, 9x13" (w/handles) **$110.00**

Tidbit tray, Everlast, Bamboo, 3-tier, 5½", 7½", & 10½" plates, 12" overall **$60.00**

Tray, Arthur Armour, Sea Horse, beaded rim, 14x9"" **$60.00**

Tray, Arthur Armour, Shasta Daisy, riveted handles, ¾x20x12¾" ..**$50.00**

Tray, Arthur Court, Bunny, lilies along edge, 1994, 12½" dia.. **$60.00**

Tray, Arthur Court, elephant herd, leopards at handles, rectangular, 1995, 21x9¾" **$50.00**

Tray, Everlast Hand Forged, 2 rectangular rose-embossed tiers, swan handle, 11x75" **$55.00**

Tray, Made in California by Town, Mt Whitney Highest Point in USA, detailed view of mountain, scalloped edge, 11¾"... **$60.00**

Tray, Wendell August Forge, Horse (portrait) & Pine Cones, 8 deep scallops, 17½" dia **$50.00**

Trivet, Arthur Court, Bunny, 1970s, 8" dia **$40.00**

Leaf tray, Bruce Fox, 13" long, $65.00. (Photo courtesy lifeofrileycollectiques.net)

Anodized (Colored)

Bowl, West Bend, purple w/grape clusters, 3x14" **$17.50**

Canisters, Italy, gold lids, spun body, black knobs, 5 for **$15.00**

Canisters, Mirro, copper-pink, wooden knobs, graduated set of 4, +grease jar, bread box & 2 shakers **$70.00**

Cigarette box, Kensington, gold rectangular handle on simple brushed lid, 3-compartment, 1¼x7¼x3¼" **$52.50**

Pitcher, Color Craft, gold, w/ice lip, 7½" **$22.00**

Pitcher, Color Craft, pink, cylindrical, 4¾x2½" **$15.00**

Pitcher, Regal Ware, champagne w/black plastic Deco handle, 8" **$28.00**

Plate, dinner; 3 compartments & center ring for drink, set of 6 in various colors **$90.00**

Sherbet/fruit dish, Bascal, clear ruffled-rim glass inserts, set of 8... **$50.00**

Tallstirs, leaf-shaped long-handled spoons, set of 6, MIB **$45.00**

Tumbler, Permahues Edgerton OH, 5½", set of 8 in metal frame **$65.00**

Water set, Color Craft, 7½" pitcher & 8 5" tumblers w/carrier... **$80.00**

Anchor Hocking/Fire-King

From the 1930s until the 1970s, Anchor Hocking (Lancaster, Ohio), produced a wide and varied assortment of glassware including kitchen ware, restaurant ware, and tableware for the home. Fire-King was their trade name for glassware capable of withstanding high oven temperatures without breakage. So confident were they in the durability of this glassware that they guaranteed it for two years against breakage caused by heat.

Many colors were produced over the years. Blues are always popular with collectors, and Anchor Hocking made two, Turquoise Blue and Azurite (light sky blue). They also made pink, Forest Green, Ruby Red, gold-trimmed lines, and some with fired-on colors. Jade-ite was a soft opaque green glass that was very popular from the 1940s until well into the 1960s. (See the Jade-ite category for more information.) During the late '60s they made Soreno in Avocado Green to tie in with home-decorating trends.

Bubble (made from the '30s through the '60s) was produced in just about every color Anchor Hocking ever made. It is especially collectible in Ruby Red. You may also hear this pattern referred to as Provencial or Bullseye.

Alice was a mid-'40s to '50s line. It was made in Jade-ite as well as white that was sometimes trimmed with blue or red. Cups and saucers were given away in boxes of Mother's Oats, but plates had to be purchased (so they're scarce today).

In the early 1950s they produced a 'laurel leaf' design in peach and 'Gray Laurel' lustres (the gray is scarce), followed later in the decade and into the 1960s with several lines of white glass decorated with decals — Honeysuckle, Fleurette, Primrose, and Game Bird, to name only a few.

One of their most expensive lines of dinnerware today is Philbe in Sapphire Blue, clear glass with a blue tint. It was made during the late 1930s. Values range from about $50.00 for a 6" plate to $1,500.00 for the cookie jar.

If you'd like to learn more about this type of very collectible glassware, we recommend *Anchor Hocking's Fire-King and More* by Gene and Cathy Florence (Collector Books).

Note: Values for Rainbow apply only to items with the color layer in pristine mint condition. Only items identified by pattern names are listed here; for miscellaneous glassware items by Anchor Hocking/Fire-King, see Kitchen Collectibles, Glassware. See also Early American Prescut; Jade-ite.

Alice, cup, Vitrock	**$5.00**
Alice, saucer, Jade-ite...	**$3.00**
Anniversary, bowl, white w/decals, 5"	**$15.00**
Blue Mosaic, bowl, dessert; white w/decals, 4½"	**$8.00**
Blue Mosaic, tray, snack; white w/decals, 7½x10" ...	**$6.00**
Bubble, candlesticks, Forest Green, pr....................	**$110.00**
Bubble, cocktail stem, Forest Green, 4½-oz.............	**$12.00**
Bubble, platter, crystal, oval, 12"	**$12.00**
Bubble, tidbit, Royal Ruby, 2-tier	**$75.00**
Bubble, tumbler, lemonade; crystal, 16-oz	**$12.00**
Classic, chip & dip, crystal....................................	**$38.00**
Classic, vase, Royal Ruby, 10"	**$70.00**
Fish Scale, bowl, soup; ivory w/red, 7½"	**$30.00**
Fish scale, cup, ivory, 8-oz....................................	**$8.00**

Fish Scale, platter, ivory w/blue, 11¾" $75.00
Fleurette, egg plate, white w/decals $175.00
Fleurette, plate, dinner; white w/decals, 9" $5.00
Forest Green, batter bowl..$22.00
Forest Green, pitcher, 22-oz....................................$22.50
Forest Green, tumbler, 14-oz, 5" $7.50
Forget-Me-Not, bowl, dessert; white w/decals, 4½" $8.00
Forget-Me-Not, creamer, white w/decals...................$10.00
Harvest, bowl, vegetable; white w/decals, 8" $16.00
Harvest, saucer, white w/decals, 5¾" $2.00
Hobnail, goblet, tea; Milk White, 13-oz $6.00
Hobnail, jardiniere, coral, green & yellow (fired-on), 5½" ...$12.00
Homestead, cup, white w/decals, 7½-oz.....................$5.00
Homestead, plate, salad; white w/decals, 7½" $15.00
Honeysuckle, mug, white w/decals.........................$50.00
Honeysuckle, relish, 3-part, white w/decals $125.00
Jane Ray, plate, bread & butter; Jade-ite, 6¼" $45.00
Jane Ray, plate, dinner; ivory, 9⅛" $24.00
Jane Ray, platter, Jade-ite, 9x12" $18.00
Lace Edge, bowl, Milk White, footed, 11" $15.00
Lace Edge, sherbet, Milk White, 5¼-oz $3.00
Laurel, bowl, soup; ivory, 7⅝" $15.00
Laurel, plate, salad; Peach Lustre, 7⅜" $9.00
Laurel, sugar, white, footed $10.00
Meadow Green, bowl, vegetable; white w/decals, 8¼".......$12.00
Meadow Green, cake plate, white w/decals, sq, 8" $6.00
Meadow Green, casserole, white w/decals, handles, 12-oz......$3.50
Moonstone, bowl, crystal w/opalescent hobnails, crimped rim, 9½" .$22.00
Moonstone, bowl, dessert; crystal w/opalescent hobnails, crimped rim, 5½" $7.50
Moonstone, creamer, crystal w/opalescent hobnails.............$10.00
Moonstone, cup, crystal w/opalescent hobnails $6.00
Moonstone, vase, bud; crystal w/opalescent hobnails, 5½"...$18.00
Philbe, blue, goblet, 9-oz, 7¼" $250.00
Philbe, green or pink, platter, closed handles, 12".............$125.00
Philbe, plate, grill; crystal, 10½" $40.00
Primrose, compote, white w/decal, Lace Edge, 11" $165.00
Primrose, salt & pepper shakers, white w/decal, pr $275.00

Primrose, tumblers, white with decal: 11-ounce, $25.00; 9½-ounce, $95.00; 5-ounce, $30.00. (Photo courtesy Gene and Cathy Florence)

Rainbow, flowerpot, primary colors, 3¼" $12.00
Rainbow, plate, dinner; pastels, 9¼"...........................$12.00
Rainbow, tumbler, primary colors, footed, 15-oz $15.00
Royal Ruby, bowl, popcorn; 5¼" $12.00

Royal Ruby, creamer, footed....................................$6.00
Royal Ruby, plate, dinner; 9⅛" $9.00
Royal Ruby, plate, sherbet; 6¼" $3.00
Royal Ruby, sherbet..$8.00
Royal Ruby, tumbler, water; 9-oz $3.00

Royal Ruby, vase, 9", $15.00. (Photo courtesy Gene and Cathy Florence)

Sheaves of Wheat, bowl, dessert; crystal, 4½"......................$8.00
Sheaves of Wheat, plate, dinner; Jade-ite, 9" $58.00
Sheaves of Wheat, tumbler, water; crystal, 9-oz.................$18.00
Shell, bowl, cereal; Golden Shell, 6½" $10.00
Shell, creamer, Jade-ite, footed $25.00
Shell, cup, Lustre Shell, 8-oz $5.00
Shell, plate, salad; Aurora Shell, 7¼" $28.00
Shell, platter, Milk White, 11½x15½" $40.00
Soreno, ashtray, Honey Gold, 8" $5.00
Soreno, butter dish, Avocado or Milk White, ¼-lb $6.00
Soreno, pitcher, juice; aquamarine, 28-oz....................$12.00
Soreno, tumbler, iced tea; crystal, 15-oz $4.00
Stars & Stripes, plate, crystal, 8" $12.50
Stars & Stripes, sherbet, crystal $10.00
Stars & Stripes, tumbler, crystal, 5"........................$45.00
Swirl, bowl, flanged soup; Azur-ite, 9¼" $110.00
Swirl, plate, serving; ivory, 11"...........................$22.00
Swirl, saucer, Jade-ite, 5¾" $22.00
Thousand Line, bowl, crystal, handles, 6"...................$8.00
Thousand Line, bowl, vegetable; crystal, 10⅞" $12.00
Thousand Line, fork, crystal $7.50
Thousand Line, relish, crystal, 6-part, 12" $15.00
Three Bands, bowl, vegetable; Jade-ite, 8¼" $85.00
Three Bands, plate, dinner; burgundy, 9⅛".................$325.00
Turquoise Blue, cup $5.00
Turquoise Blue, plate w/cup indent, 9" $6.00
Wheat, casserole, white w/decals, w/knob lid, 1-pt $8.00
Wheat, loaf pan, white w/decals, 5x9" $12.00
Wheat, tray, snack; white w/decals, 6x11".....................$4.00

Angels

Angels, Birthday

Manufactured by many import companies primarily in the 1950s and 1960s, birthday angels are relatively easy to find, although completing a set can be a real challenge. Pricing is determined by the following factors: 1) Condition. 2) Company — Look for Lefton, Napco, Norcrest, and Enesco marks or labels. Unmarked or unknown sets can be of less value. However, if two collectors are looking for the same item to complete their collection prices can go high on the internet. 3) Details — the added touches of flowers, bows, gold trim, 'coconut' trim, rhinestones, etc. More detail means more value. 4) Quality of workmanship involved, detail, and accuracy of painting. 5) Age. 6) As a rule boy angels will usually bring more than girls as far fewer were sold. It is difficult to identify the manufacturer by the design because so many companies used similar designs. In addition to birthday months, angels were made to represent age and days of the week. They often adorned the top of birthday cakes.

Advisors: Jim and Kaye Whitaker (See Directory Josef Originals; no appraisals please)

High Mountain Quality, colored hair, 7", ea from $30 to.... **$32.00**
Japan, J-6736, June bride w/veil & rose bouquet, 5¼"........ **$32.00**
Japan (fine quality), months or days of the week, 4½", ea from $20 to **$25.00**

Japan, #6409, sugar bowl, 4½", from $30.00 to $35.00.

Lefton, #130, Kewpie, 4½", ea from $35 to........................ **$40.00**

Lefton, #489, holding basket of flowers, birthstone on skirt, 4", from $25.00 to $35.00.

Lefton, #556, boy of the month, 5½", ea from $25 to........ **$30.00**

Lefton, #627, day of the week, 3½", ea from $28 to o......... **$32.00**
Lefton, #985, flower of the month, 5", ea from $30 to........ **$35.00**
Lefton, #1411, angel of the month, 4", ea from $28 to **$32.00**
Lefton, #1987J, w/rhinestones, 4½", ea from $30 to **$40.00**
Lefton, #3332, w/basket of flowers, bisque, 4", ea from $25 to ..**$30.00**
Lefton, #4883, in yellow w/January ribbon across white apron, 1985, 3".. **$25.00**
Lefton, #5146, birthstone on skirt, 4½", ea from $22 to **$28.00**
Lefton, #6224, applied flower/birthstone on skirt, 4½", ea from $20 to **$30.00**
Lefton, #6883, day of the week & months in sq frame, 3¼x4", ea from $28 to **$35.00**
Lefton, #6949, day of the week in oval frame, 5", ea from $28 to **$32.00**
Lefton, #8281, day of the week, applied roses, ea from $30 to **$35.00**
Lefton, AR-1987, w/ponytail, 4", ea from $18 to **$22.00**
Mahana Importing, #1194, angel of the month, white hair, 5", ea from $20 to **$22.00**
Mahana Importing, #1294, angel of the month, white hair, 5", ea from $20 to **$22.00**
Mahana Importing, #1600, Pal Angel of the month, boy or girl, 4", ea from $15 to **$20.00**
MBD Inc/Japan, much spaghetti trim, gold ribbon, holds US flag, 7½" **$45.00**
Napco, C1921-1933, boy angel of the month, ea from $20 to **$25.00**
Napco, S1291, day of the week 'Belle,' ea from $22 to........ **$25.00**
Napco, S1361-1372, angel of the month, ea from $20 to....**$25.00**
Napco, S401-413, angel of the month, ea from $20 to........ **$25.00**
Napco, X8371, Christmas angel w/instrument, 3¾", ea......**$26.00**
Norcrest, F-015, angel of the month on round base w/raised pattern on dress, 4", ea from $18 to.................................... **$22.00**
Norcrest, F-120, angel of the month, 4½", ea from $18 to ..**$22.00**
Norcrest, F-210, day of the week, 4½", ea from $18 to **$22.00**
Norcrest, F-535, angel of the month, 4½", ea from $20 to ..**$25.00**
Norcrest, F-755, girl w/mask & jack-o'-lantern pumpkin, 4" ..**$30.00**
Relco, angel of the month, 6", ea from $18 to **$22.00**
Sanmyro, blond girl w/yellow flower, pink streaked gown, March on yellow ribbon, 4" **$23.00**
Schmid, boy sitting w/gift, label, 1950s, 3½" **$29.00**
TMJ, angel of the month w/flower, ea from $20 to **$25.00**
Wales, wearing long white gloves, white hair, Made in Japan, 6⅜", ea from $25 to **$28.00**

Angels, Zodiac

These china figurines were made and imported by the same companies as the birthday angels. Because they were not as popular as birthday angels fewer were made so they are more difficult to find. Examples tend to be more individualized due to each sign having a specific characteristic associated with it.

Josef, holding tablet w/sign written & shown in gold, ea from $30 to **$45.00**
Lefton, K-650, w/applied flowers & gold stars, 4", ea from $40 to **$45.00**

Napco, S-1259, Your Lucky Star Guardian Angel planter series, 4", ea from $30 to $35.00

Semco, w/gold wings, applied roses & pleated ruffle on front edge of dress, 5", ea from $20 to $25.00

Miscellaneous

Japan, nurse w/Red Cross hat, Get Well on base, 3¾" $34.00

Napco, A-1926, September boy w/pencils & schoolbag.......$35.00

Napco, C-6362, boy w/football, 4½" $30.00

Napco, S-1703, girl w/wreath & candy cane, 7¾", from $25 to $35.00

Napco, S-542F, devil boy in red w/long spear looks at sleeping angel, 4" $35.00

Napco, X-6963, Christmas girl w/gold bells.......................$20.00

Norcrest, F-299, w/instrument, all white, plain, 7½" " $12.50

Aprons

America's heartland offers a wide variety of aprons, ranging from those once worn for kitchen duty or general household chores to fancier styles designed for cocktail parties. Today they can be found in an endless array of styles and in fabrics ranging from feed sacks to fine silk with applied rhinestones. Some were embroidered or pieced, some were even constructed of nice handkerchiefs. Aprons were given and received as gifts; often they were cherished and saved. Some of these are now surfacing in today's market. You may find some in unused condition with the original tags still attached.

Condition is important when assessing the value of vintage aprons. Unless very old, pass up those that are stained and torn. Hand-sewn examples are worth more than machine- or commercially-made aprons, and if they retain the tags from their original maker, you can double their price. Some labels themselves are collectible. Children's and young ladies' dress aprons command very high prices, as often they were recycled into quilt patches and dust cloths.

Perhaps no other area of Americana evokes as much nostalgia as vintage aprons. Our advisor's favorite, he says, is a grandmother's that has become stained from cookie baking and worn soft from use. He recommends tying them onto your old caned dining chair or, as he does, to the grandfather clock in his kitchen, giving the impression that the wearer is only temporarily absent.

Advisor: Darrell Thomas (See Directory, Aprons)

Adult's bib type, blue, turquoise & lavender floral print, turquoise rickrack trim, w/pockets.....................................$50.00

Adult's bib type, blue floral cotton print, white trim, XXL size, 1940s $35.00

Adult's bib type, checked cotton w/cotton piping, buttons & ribbon on pockets, 1940s $25.00

Adult's bib type, cotton print, adjustable waist, Carmen Lee tag $25.00

Adult's bib type, floral cotton, patch pocket, pleated flounce sides, white bias-tape trim, sash ties, 1950s $22.00

Adult's bib type, multicolored cottage & garden by river's edge, green piping, 1950s $30.00

Adult's bib type, pale lavender, scalloped top & bottom, white trim...$35.00

Adult's bib type, red & white, bib trimmed as a dickey w/ruffles & flowers, white rickrack trim............................$42.00

Adult's bib type, red flowers printed on white feed sack cotton, red rickrack trim, 1 pocket............................$50.00

Adult's bib type, sheer pink cotton, embroidered flowers, lace ties & trim...$70.00

Adult's bib type, white cotton, embroidered flapper girl w/dog, Love Me Love My Dog, puppies on ea pocket $55.00

Adult's bib type, white cotton w/bright multicolor embroidery, trimmed pocket $22.00

Adult's pinafore type, black printed cotton w/red bias-tape trim, ca 1930s, from $20 to.....................................$28.00

Adult's pinafore type, calico patchwork print, full dress length, 1950s-60s $35.00

Adult's pinafore type, red & white checked cotton, elastic waist, ruffled hem, zipper in back, 1970s....................$25.00

Adult's pinafore type, white cotton, flower-burst eyelet trim, peaked waist seam, early 1900s $50.00

Adult's shoulder type, black w/orange roses & trim, H-strap back..$40.00

Adult's shoulder type, cotton with stenciled and embroidered lady and dog, blanket-stitched edges, ca. 1930s, from $45.00 to $55.00. (Photo courtesy LaRee Johnson Bruton)

Adult's shoulder type, lavender floral feed-sack print, yellow trim, loops over head $35.00

Adult's shoulder type, light green swiss polka-dot organdy w/embroidered front, button back, 1940s...................................$20.00

Adult's shoulder type, sm pink & red floral print, w/pink trim, H-strap back $40.00

Adult's shoulder type, textured aqua fabric, multicolored flowers on white panel at bottom, yellow trim $40.00

Adult's shoulder type, white cotton w/blue bottom ruffle & pocket, 7 embroidered flowers...$40.00

Adult's shoulder type, yellow floral print on white top & pocket, solid yellow flared bottom, pear buttons on back..........$30.00

Adult's smock type, pink cotton w/vertical dark pink stripes on top, horizontal striped waistband & pockets on pink..........$45.00

Adult's smock type, white w/tiny turquoise stripes, lace trim, button back $35.00

Adult's smock type, yellow, lavender, green & gray leaves printed on white, lg pink button on neck & pockets, pink trim..... **$55.00**

Adult's waist type, black & cream gingham w/white embroidery at bottom, 1 pocket **$40.00**

Adult's waist type, blue & green plaid, w/light blue waistband & bottom panel **$23.00**

Adult's waist type, blue gingham w/embroidered flowers & scalloped hemline, w/pockets, 1800s.. **$90.00**

Adult's waist type, bright red w/red & pink carnations on white at waistband & bottom panel **$35.00**

Adult's waist type, California souvenir, multicolored images on white, CALIFORNIA in lg green letters at hem, 1950s............. **$65.00**

Adult's waist type, Isle of Man souvenir, blue w/white dots, red Isle of Man pocket **$28.00**

Adult's waist type, lg blue flowers surrounded by sm red & blue flowers & green leaves, striped red, blue & green trim **$35.00**

Adult's waist type, light brown cotton w/red & pink rose print, ruffled hem, w/pockets **$42.00**

Adult's waist type, orange cotton, lg pockets w/images of black & white poodles, 1950s **$63.00**

Adult's waist type, pink roses w/blue floral print, white rickrack trim.. **$40.00**

Adult's waist type, possibly made from ca. 1940s tablecloth, from $12.00 to $18.00. (Photo courtesy LaRee Johnson Bruton)

Adult's waist type, red, white, & blue floral hankies, w/pockets ..**$40.00**

Adult's waist type, red & yellow flowers on white ribbons print, 1 pocket.. **$20.00**

Adult's waist type, red cotton, To Hell w/Housework above sm devil face, shadow image of lady leaving chores on side........ **$45.00**

Adult's waist type, sheer pink organdy w/appliquéd cotton cabbage roses **$30.00**

Adult's waist type, sheer red nylon w/lg white lace pocket on front, 1950s **$30.00**

Adult's waist type, sheer white organdy w/alternating panels of green kitten print **$40.00**

Adult's waist type, white cotton w/tiny heart print, red rickrack at hem & pocket... **$30.00**

Adult's waist type, white flour sack w/floral embroidery at waist ..**$25.00**

Adult's waist type, white plastic w/lg multicolored flowers, ruffled hem, 1950s **$50.00**

Adult's waist type (cocktail), white rayon w/hand-painted musical notes & martini, fuchsia waistband & ruffle................. **$45.00**

Child's bib type, bunny embroidery on white cotton, blanket stiching, pockets, 1930s-40s................................... **$50.00**

Child's bib type, Dutch kids w/windmill scene, 1940s, from $40 to **$45.00**

Child's bib type, ecru linen w/embroidered butterflies & flowers, striped blue & tan trim, pleated back, 1 pocket........... **$25.00**

Child's bib type, hand crocheted w/ribbon decor................. **$35.00**

Child's pinafore type, cotton muslin w/embroidered boy walking goose, button front **$25.00**

Child's shoulder type, Red Cross, white w/Red Cross on chest & pocket, w/hat, 1940s, EX................................. **$45.00**

Child's waist type, crocheted coral & blue cotton, 1930s..... **$15.00**

Ashtrays

Ashtrays, especially for cigarettes, did not become widely used in the United States much before the turn of the century. The first examples were simply receptacles made to hold ashes for pipes, cigars, and cigarettes. Later, rests were incorporated into the design. Ashtrays were made in a variety of materials. Some were purely functional, while others advertised or entertained, and some stopped just short of being works of art. They were made to accommodate smokers in homes, businesses, or wherever they might be. Today their prices range from a few dollars to hundreds. Since today so many people buy and sell on eBay and other internet auction auction sites, there is much more exposure to ashtray collecting. Also these auction prices must be considered when determining the value of an item. Many of the very fine ashtrays from the turn of the century do not command the same price as they did in the early 1990s unless the maker's name is widely known. And now, in the twenty-first century, many of the old ashtrays are actually antiques. This may contribute to the continued fluctuation of prices in this still new collectibles field.

See also specific glass companies and potteries; Japan Ceramics; Disney; Tire Ashtrays; World's Fairs.

Advertising, Hotel Gibson, Cincinnati OH lettered on cobalt glass, match holder center, 1940s... **$80.00**

Advertising, Johnnie Walker Whiskey, black letters on white, ceramic, James Green & Nephew Ltd, 2¼x4¾x4¾"............... **$65.00**

Advertising, Kool penguins in black w/green lettering on ivory glass, 2 rests, 5½" dia **$30.00**

Advertising, Mobiloil, metal, Deco influence, 5½" long, $235.00. (Photo courtesy B.J. Summers)

Advertising, Monarch Cruise Lines, Monarch Sun, blue lettering on clear glass, 4½" dia **$12.50**

Advertising, Speed Cooking Brand, lady by stove graphics, multi-color on tin, Smoke Stone Co Ltd Japan, 5½" dia **$40.00**

Advertising, Statler Hotel, center match holder on turquoise, Buffalo China, 1940s, 5½" dia...............................**$25.00**

Advertising, The Hostess Room, Wonder Bread (loaf) & Hostess Cake logo in fired-on colors on clear glass, triangular ...**$22.00**

Art Deco, Color King, Tangerine pressed glass, Federal Glass, 1950s, 4", set of 2, MIB............................**$18.00**

Art Deco, nude seated w/knees drawn up, painted metal on frosted glass tray, ca 1970s **$50.00**

Art Deco, sailfish mounted to side of flower-like base, blown glass, white w/brown streaks, 9x8" dia **$35.00**

Art glass, Aries (ram figural), crystal, etched Vannes mark, 4½x6½" **$25.00**

Art glass, turkey intaglio on crystal, Val Saint Lambert, 3 rests, 1¼x6" dia **$55.00**

Decorative, Daisy & Button, vaseline glass, 4-rests, 5½x5½" ..**$35.00**

Decorative, Daisy & Button top hat, clear glass, tricorn top, 2x2¼" dia..**$10.00**

Decorative, green Jade-ite glass, match holder in center, 6-sided, 6 rests...**$38.00**

Decorative, poinsettias on pearl lustre w/gold trim, free-form, Sterling China, Japan **$10.00**

Decorative, seashell in blue glass, 3 shell feet, Cambridge #34, 3" **$15.00**

Decorative, streaky caramel tones on 50s Moderne free-form shape, ceramic, Marcia of Calif #705, 9x7" **$15.00**

Decorative, Tree of Life pattern pressed in clear glass, w/pipe rest at side, 2 cigarette rests, 1⅜x7x5½"...........**$50.00**

Novelty, Amos & Andy stand beside match holder at side of tray w/Ise Regusted on base, painted chalkware, 7½" H...............**$180.00**

Novelty, bear stands at side & gazes at fish in bowl, tan lustre (bear), green (fish) & white, ceramic, unmarked Japan **$24.00**

Novelty, bird perched at edge of birdbath tray, multicolor on white, ceramic, Japan, 4" L...............................**$55.00**

Novelty, Black boy on potty w/sm dove, hand-painted bisque, Japan, 1950s-60s, 3¼x4x2¼"...............................**$80.00**

Novelty, Black man kneeling & shooting craps, Old Dice Shooters Never Die..., painted chalkware, 1954, 6x5", EX..........**$95.00**

Novelty, Charlie Chaplin standing w/top hat, cane & shoes, ceramic w/multicolor paint, Germany, 3x2" **$30.00**

Novelty, Dig That Crazy Hung Jury, court scene w/curvaceous ladies entering jury box, multicolor, ceramic, sq, 3¾".............**$30.00**

Novelty, dog in fireman's hat by hydrant, multicolor cold paint (some wear), ceramic, plastic fire hose, 1930s, 5¼" L ...**$25.00**

Novelty, drunken man hanging on lamppost, multicolor paint, cast iron, marked JULA, 1930s, 5x4x4" **$60.00**

Novelty, duck figural, Pall Mall pattern, clear glass, Duncan Miller, 4¾" L **$27.50**

Novelty, fish form, turquoise fins w/rests, multicolor, ceramic, 8½" L..**$50.00**

Novelty, Good Luck, horse's head in horseshoe, amber glass, 5x5½"...**$20.00**

Novelty, gray mare w/black mane, cold-painted accents, ceramic, Made in Japan, 2½x2½" **$12.50**

Novelty, head of lady in sun-bonnet, Japan, red mark, 3¾" long, from $18.00 to $28.00.
(Photo courtesy Carole Bess White)

Novelty, hollowed log & standing stump w/embedded hatchet, cast metal, 5x7" **$60.00**

Novelty, horse-drawn cart, Century of Progress 1934, colorful details, ceramic, Made in Japan....................**$32.00**

Novelty, lady w/distressed expression, Room for More along over-sized bodice, multicolor details, ceramic, Japan, 5½" ..**$175.00**

Novelty, leaf form, white w/gold trim, ceramic, Maurice of California, 6x8½"..**$12.50**

Novelty, pinup girl w/legs in air (nodder) & fan (also nodder), hand-painted ceramic, Patent TT, 1940s, 5½" L....................**$49.00**

Novelty, skeleton, nodder lower jaw, She's Still Nagging in bowl, ceramic, Japan, 5" L.....................................**$45.00**

Novelty, snail figural, airbrushed w/hand-painted details, ceramic, 1950s, 7½x6" **$20.00**

Novelty, Stetson hat form, blue Delphite glass, Jeannette, 1936, 5½x6½" **$25.00**

Novelty, Tattle Tale!, hillbilly couple & man w/shotgun on leaf shape w/gold rim, ceramic, 1950s, 4" dia **$16.00**

Novelty, 2 kittens w/ball of yarn by rectangular tan lustre tray, ceramic, Japan, 2x2⅝x2⅛" **$16.00**

Autographs

'Philography' is an extremely popular hobby, one that is very diversified. Autographs of sports figures, movie stars, entertainers, and politicians from our lifetime may bring several hundred dollars, depending on rarity and application, while John Adams' simple signature on a document from 1800, for instance, might bring thousands. A signature on a card or cut from a letter or document is the least valuable type of autograph. A handwritten letter is generally the most valuable, since in addition to the signature you get the message as well. Depending upon what it reveals about the personality who penned it, content can be very important and can make a major difference in value.

Many times a polite request accompanied by an SASE to a famous person will result in receipt of a signed photo or a short handwritten note that might in several years be worth a tidy sum!

Obviously as new collectors enter the field, the law of supply and demand will drive the prices for autographs upward, especially when the personality is deceased. There are forgeries around, so before you decide to invest in expensive autographs, get to know your dealers.

Over the years many celebrities in all fields have periodically employed secretaries to sign their letters and photos. They have also sent out photos with preprinted or rubber stamped signatures as time doesn't always permit them to personally respond to fan mail. With today's advanced printing, even many long-time collectors have been fooled with a mechanically produced signature. The letters 'COA' in our descriptions stand for 'certificate of authenticity.'

Astaire, Fred; signed color photo, dancing on set of drums, 8x10" $75.00

Ayres, Lew; signed photo, black & white studio portrait, 1930s, 5x7" $10.00

Bacall, Lauren; signed black & white studio portrait, seated w/ Marilyn Monroe & Betty Grable, ca 1953, 8x10" $130.00

Bach, Barbara; signed color photo, in red swimsuit as Agent Triple X from Bond movie, 8x10" $50.00

Bankhead, Tallulah; signed black & white photo, 1930s, 8x10", +frame $70.00

Barrymore, Drew; signed black & white photo, sexy near-nude pose, ca 1999, COA, 8x10" $65.00

Beach Boys, individual signatures on Capitol LP Christmas Album, +frame $215.00

Blake, Amanda; signature on black & white photo (w/Edgar Buchanan), 1970s, 4x5" $200.00

Cabot, Bruce; inscribed signed photo, hand-tinted sepia, in riding britches, 8x10" $55.00

Cagney, Jimmy; signed & inscribed black & white photo, ca 1930s-40s, 8x10" $275.00

Carson, Johnny; signed color photo, COA, 8x10" $40.00

Cash, Johnny; signed photo of performer on stage, color, 8x10", w/letter from house of Cash verifying signature $240.00

Crosby, Bing; signed black & white photo, ca 1940s, 8x10" .. $95.00

Dangerfield, Rodney; signed color photo in comic pose, 8x10" .. $45.00

Davies, Marion; signed gelatin photo, ca 1930, 8x10" $85.00

Day, Doris; signed black & white close-up photo, 1960s, 5x6" .. $45.00

Denver, John; signed Windsong LP album cover, COA $50.00

Depp, Johnny; signed color photo in jeans & T-shirt, 8x10" .. $85.00

Donlevy, Brian; inscribed signed photo, black & white close-up studio portrait, 5x7" $22.00

Duvall, Robert; signed black & white photo as Western character, 8x10" $85.00

Dylan, Bob; signature on Slow Train Coming album cover .. $68.00

Fawcett, Farrah; signed black & white photo in jeans, ca 1976, 8x10" $55.00

Garcia, J (Jerry); signature on Skeletons from the Closet LP album cover $75.00

Griffith, Andy; signed black & white photo as Andy Taylor, 5x7" $85.00

Haley, Bill; signature on black & white photo, 1950s, 8x10", +frame $150.00

Haley, Jack; signed black & white photo, dated 1932, 8x10" .. $85.00

Hamilton, Margaret; inscribed signed photo, black & white portrait, youthful, 1930s, 5x7" $130.00

Harlow, Jean; inscribed signed photo (likely mother's signature), black & white portrait, 1932, 5x7" $65.00

Hayward, Susan; signed black & white photo as character from Back Street, ca 1961, 8x10" $120.00

Hepburn, Audrey; signed & inscribed photo as character from My Fair Lady, color portrait, 1980s, 8x10" $260.00

Heston, Charlton; signed color photo as character from Planet of the Apes, 8x10" $40.00

Hill, Faith; signed color photo in sexy gown, COA, 8x10" .. $50.00

Jennings, Waylon; signed black & white photo, COA, 8x10" .. $105.00

Johnson, Lyndon B; signed black & white portrait as president, 8x10" $110.00

Karloff, Boris; signed note card, blue ink, 3x5" $100.00

Kelly, De Forest; signed color photo plaque as Dr McCoy, limited edition, COA, 8x10" $100.00

Kerr, Deborah; signed black & white photo from King & I, 8x10" $60.00

Lake, Veronica; signed & inscribed black & white photo, green ink, 8x10" $315.00

Lamour, Dorothy; signed black & white photo, in ornate headdress as character from Road to Bali, 8x10" $55.00

Landon, Michael; signed black & white portrait photo, 8x10". $55.00

Lewis, Jerry; signed black & white photo, dated 1997, 8x10"... $65.00

Madden, John; signed Goal Line Art card, bold signature in silver pen, 4x6" $50.00

Miller, Glen; signed black & white photo, holding trombone, COA, 8x10" $155.00

Mix, Tom; black and white photo, $150.00. (Photo courtesy LiveAuctioneers.com/Morphy Auctions)

Murphy, Audie; signature on card, dated 1948 .... $150.00

Nelson, Willie; signed Always on My Mind LP cover, COA .. $40.00

O'Sullivan, Maureen; signed photo, black & white studio portrait, 1930s, 5x7" $30.00

Oliver, Edna May; inscribed signed photo, black & white studio portrait, 1930s, 5x7" $130.00

Peck, Gregory; signed black & white photo portrait cover of A Tribute to Gregory Peck booklet (45 pages) $60.00

Perry, Steve; signed 3x5" card, w/candid 5x7" photo & COA, 1988...**$150.00**

Powell; Dick; signed black & white photo as young man in 3-pc suit, 7½x9½" **$70.00**

Reeve, Christopher; signed black & white photo w/Jayne Seymour from Somewhere in Time, COA, 8x10"....................**$165.00**

Rigg, Diana; signed black & white photo as Tracy Bond, 8x10"....**$60.00**

Rivers, Joan; signed & inscribed black & white photo, 8x10"... **$45.00**

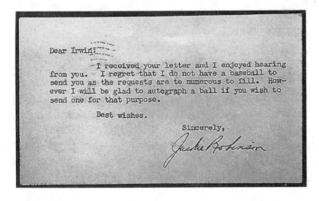

Robinson, Jackie; postcard dated May 23, 1952, $400.00.

Rogers, Roy; signed black & white photo, seated on rearing Trigger, 8x10", +frame **$60.00**

Russell, Jane; signed black & white photo, 5¼x 7¼", +frame .. **$70.00**

Schell, Catherine; signed color photo as character from On Her Majesty's Secret Service, 8x10".................................**$60.00**

Shearer, Norma; boldy signed (black ink) & inscribed 3x5" card, dated 1934 ....**$95.00**

Sheridan, Ann; signed black & white photo, 1930s, 8x7½", mounted on linen-like paper **$85.00**

Smith, Anna Nicole; signed black & white photo, sexy pose on bed, COA, 8x10", +mat & frame **$265.00**

Soo, Jack; signature on 3x5" card, w/black & white 8x10" promo photo **$80.00**

Swanson, Gloria; signed black & white photo, 1920s, 8x10", +mat & frame **$75.00**

Truman, Harry; signed and inscribed black and white photo, 8x10", $250.00. (Photo courtesy LiveAuctioneers.com/Early American History Auctions)

Turner, Tina; signed color photo in white evening gown, 8x10".. **$75.00**

Wayne, John; signed & inscribed wooden plaque w/3x5" sepia-tone photo portrait in Western garb, dated 1961 ....**$100.00**

Whalen, Michael; signed photo, black & white studio portrait, 1930s, 5x7"..**$24.00**

Williams, Hank; signed 3x5" card, matted w/black & white 5x7" portrait photo, 11x14" overall.............................**$85.00**

Woods, Tiger; signed color photo as he swings club, COA, 8x10" **$165.00**

Automobilia

Automobilia remains a specialized field, attracting antique collectors and old car buffs alike. It is a field that encompasses auto-related advertising and accessories like hood ornaments, gear shift and steering wheel knobs, sales brochures, and catalogs. Memorabilia from the high-performance, sporty automobiles of the sixties is very popular with baby boomers. Unusual items have been setting auction records as the market for automobilia heats up. Note: Badges vary according to gold content — 10k or sterling silver examples are higher than average. Dealership booklets (Ford, Chevy, etc.) generally run about $2.00 to $3.00 per page, and because many reproductions are available, very few owner's manuals sell for more than $10.00. Also it should be mentioned here that there are many reproduction clocks and signs out there. Any 'Guard' badges with round Ford logos are fake. Buyers beware. Our values are for items in excellent to near-mint condition unless noted otherwise.

See also License Plates; Tire Ashtrays.

Advisor: Leonard Needham (See Directory, Automobilia)

Blanket, Oldsmobile, bright red fleece w/white logo, 1980s, 60x48" **$46.00**

Book, dealer's; Chevrolet, Chevelle, Chevy II, Corvair, Corvette, etc, lists features, cloth samples, etc, 1966, VG+ **$95.00**

Brochure, Cadillac Sixty Two, 1940, 10x7"..................**$12.00**

Brochure, Oldsmobile, color photos, staple bound, 1938-40, 12 pages, 12x6½"...**$60.00**

Brochure, Oldsmobile Eight, The Completely Modern Car, 1934, 23 pages, 12x9" **$40.00**

Clock, Chevrolet Sales & Service, lighted bubble glass, blue metal case, sq...**$625.00**

Clock, Oldsmobile, neon light, metal with glass face, repainted, 21" diameter, EX, $600.00. (Photo courtesy Collector's Auction Services)

Emblem, radiator; Chrysler Imperial, bird w/wings up, 1960s, 2¼x2¼", MIB...**$40.00**

Emblem, radiator; Dodge Ram, chrome, minor pitting, 7" base.. **$125.00**

Emblem, radiator; Ford Model A flying quail, 3¼" on 2½" cap **$60.00**

Emblem, radiator; Gardner, shape of letter G embossed on metal, 1¾"...**$120.00**

Emblem, radiator; Maxwell on metal shield shape, 2x2⅛" ..**$120.00**

Emblem, radiator; Peerless, detailed honeycomb metal w/blue enameling, 2x2¼"...**$140.00**

Emblem, radiator; Pegasus, bright nickel plate, 4½x6".........**$90.00**

Emblem, wheel cover; Chrysler Imperial, chrome, 1960s, 2-pc, 7⅜" dia, 13⅝" from point to point **$140.00**

Game, Oldsmobile Drivehappy, General Motors, 1974, MIP ..**$38.00**

Lapel pin, There's a Ford in Your Future, hand holding crystal ball, blue & white enameling, ca 1950, ⅝"...........................**$7.50**

License plate, 1959 Brookwood by Chevrolet, red, cream & black painted metal **$110.00**

License plate topper, Drive Safely, lg red eye, Make Sure Your Eyes Are Right, Bausch & Lomb **$80.00**

Pedal car, Ford Mustang convertible, red w/plastic windshield, white steering wheels, AMF, 1965, VG.............................**$300.00**

Pencil, mechanical; Oldsmobile Rockets Ahead, rocketship shape w/4 fins at top, car suspended in liquid, 1950s.............**$40.00**

Postcard, Oldsmobile Dynamic Cruiser Club Sedan, real photo, 1941 ....**$20.00**

Postcard, Oldsmobile Starfire 98 convertible, real color photo, 1957, 5¼x5¼" **$45.00**

Postcard, Pontiac Torpedo, color photo, 1941, unused...........**$7.50**

Postcard/record, clear plastic record over photo of 1956 Ford, Rosemary Clooney & Mitch Miller's Orchestra, VG.....**$12.00**

Promotional car, Chevrolet 2-door sedan, old repaint on plastic, PMC, 8", VG **$55.00**

Promotional car, Oldsmobile Tornado, 1966, 8½"...............**$50.00**

Promotional car, Oldsmobile 98 Hardtop, black w/red interior, wire wheels, Scale Automobile Model Services, 5¼", MIB...**$100.00**

Promotional car/bank, Chevrolet Impala 2-door hardtop, 2-tone green, plastic, 1958, EX+ **$55.00**

Sign, Studebaker Authorized Service Parts, Masonite die cut, 9x13", $525.00. (Photo courtesy Don and R.C. Raycraft)

Watch fob, Buick, multicolor enamel on metal, Schwaabs & S Co Milwaukee on back, 1⅝", G **$5.00**

Autumn Leaf Dinnerware

A familiar dinnerware pattern to just about all of us, Autumn Leaf was designed by Hall China for the Jewel Tea Company who offered it to their customers as premiums. In fact, some people erroneously refer to the pattern as 'Jewel Tea.' First made in 1933, it continued in production until 1978. Pieces with this date in the backstamp are from the overstock that was in the company's warehouse when production was suspended. There are matching tumblers and stemware all made by the Libbey Glass Company, and a set of enameled cookware that came out in 1979. You'll find blankets, tablecloths, metal canisters, clocks, playing cards, and many other items designed around the Autumn Leaf pattern. All are collectible.

Since 1984 the Hall company has been making special items for the National Autumn Leaf Collectors Club. These pieces are designated as such by the 'Club' marking that is accompanied by the date of issue. Limited edition items (also by Hall) are being sold by China Specialties, a company in Ohio; but once you become familiar with the old pieces, these are easy to identify, since the molds have been redesigned or were not previously used for Autumn Leaf production.

For further study, we recommend *The Collector's Encyclopedia of Hall China* by Margaret and Kenn Whitmyer. For information on company products, see Jewel Tea.

Club: National Autumn Leaf Collectors
Newsletter: *Autumn Leaf*
Glen Karlgaard, Editor
13800 Fernando Ave.
Apple Valley, MN 55121; 952-431-1814

Apron, oilcloth, from $600 to..**$1,000.00**

Baker, French, 2-pt..**$175.00**

Baker/souffle, 4½"..**$80.00**

Bean pot, one-handle, from $1,000.00 to $1,200.00. (Photo courtesy Margaret and Kenn Whitmyer)

Blanket, Autumn Leaf color, Vellux, twin size, from $100 to .. **$175.00**

Bowl, cream soup; handles **$40.00**

Bowl, soup; Melmac...**$20.00**

Bowl, vegetable; oval, w/lid, from $50 to **$70.00**

Butter dish, ruffled top, regular, 1-lb....................................**$500.00**

Calendar, 1930s-30s, from $100 to.......................................**$200.00**

Candlesticks, metal, Douglas, pr from $70 to **$100.00**

Casserole, round, w/lid, 2-qt, from $30 to........................**$45.00**

Catalog, Jewel, hardback, from $20 to **$50.00**

Cleanser can, from $750 to..............................$1,500.00
Coffeepot, Jewel's Best, 30-cup $600.00

Coffeepot, Rayed, long spout, from $75.00 to $85.00. (Photo courtesy Margaret and Kenn Whitmyer)

Cooker, waterless, metal, Mary Dunbar, from $50 to $75.00
Creamer & sugar bowl, Rayed, 1930s style $80.00
Fondue set, complete, from $200 to $300.00
Hot pad, round w/metal back, 7¼", from $15 to $25.00
Jug, utility; Rayed; 2½-pt, 6" $25.00
Mug, chocolate; club pc, 1,500 made, 1992, 4-pc set $100.00

Mug, conic, $65.00.

Plate, salad; Melmac, 7" $30.00
Plate, 7¼", from $5 to $10.00
Platter, 11½" L, from $20 to $28.00
Shakers, range; handles, pr from $40 to $45.00
Tablecloth, muslin, 56x81" $300.00
Teapot, Rayed, long spout, 1935..$95.00
Teapot, Solo, club pc, 1,400 made, 1991 ....$100.00
Tumbler, Libbey, frosted, 9-oz, 3¾" $32.00
Vase, bud; regular decal, 6" $350.00
Warmer, oval, from $150 to $225.00

Avon

You'll find Avon bottles everywhere you go! But it's not just the bottles that are collectible — so are items of jewelry, awards, magazine ads, catalogs, and product samples. Of course, the better items are the older ones (they've been called Avon since 1939 — California Perfume Company before that), and if you can find the mint in the box, all the better.

Very popular with today's collectors are the Mrs. Albee figurines. They're remarkably detailed and portray the 'first Avon lady' in elegant period fashions. They're awarded yearly to Avon's most successful representatives.

For more information we recommend *Hastin's Avon Collector's Encyclopedia* by Bud Hastin (Collector Books). See also Cape Cod.

Box, jewelry; Mrs Albee etched on glass lid, wood w/pink 2-compartment liner, 8-sided, representative gift $40.00

Bottles, Gardenia, Sweet Pea, Cotillion, and Trailing Arbutus, set of four glass minis with blue caps, in their miniature hatbox marked 'Fair Lady,' $60.00. (Photo courtesy Monsen & Baer)

Brush, Superman figural, multicolor plastic, 1976, MIB......$28.00
Cake stand, Hummingbird, etched pattern on clear glass, pedestal foot, 3¼x11¾"...$47.50
Clock, church figural, plays 12 Days of Christmas, bell rings on hour, angel twirls in door opening, ca 2000.................$70.00
Cologne, Small World Irish Girl, MIB.................................$35.00
Compact, strawberry form, Strawberry Cream/Fresh Strawberry lip gloss, MIB...$25.00
Figurine, Images of Hollywood, Clark Gable as Rhett Butler, 1984 MGM/Entertainment Company..................................$35.00
Figurine, Images of Hollywood, John Wayne, as in Dark Command, carrying horse saddle, 1985, 7", MIB $22.50
Figurine, Images of Hollywood, Vivien Leigh as Scarlett O'Hara, MIB...$30.00
Figurine, Mrs Albee carrying paisley bag, holding calling card, 1981, from $40 to $45.00
Figurine, Mrs Albee figurine/music box dressed as bride, plays Somewhere My Love...$100.00
Figurine, Mrs Albee holding parasol & sample case, 1978, from $60 to $70.00
Figurine, Mrs Albee standing by umbrella stand, 1993, MIB ..$55.00
Figurine, Mrs Albee standing by white wicker chair, 1990, frm $42 to $48.00
Figurine, Mrs Albee standing by white wicker chair, 1990, MIB, from $55 to $65.00
Figurine, Mrs Albee standing w/fan & satchel, 1994 ....$55.00
Figurine, Mrs Albee standing w/flowers, pedestal at side, 2005, MIB, from $75 to $95.00
Figurine, Mrs Albee standing w/hand to hat, 1996, MIB $40.00
Figurine, Mrs Albee standing w/parasol raised, 1988, from $50 to... $85.00
Figurine, Mrs Albee standing w/sample case by lamppost, 2006, MIB, from $60 to $70.00
Figurine, Mrs Albee standing w/satchel over arm, 1979, from $50 to $75.00
Figurine, Mrs Albee working at desk, 1985........................$40.00
Figurine, Mrs Albee 100th Anniversary commemorative, 1986, MIB...$65.00

Figurine, Nativity, Children in Prayer, white porcelain, 1991, MIB **$35.00**

Figurine, Nativity, Shepherd w/Lamb, white porcelain, 1993, MIB **$47.50**

Figurine, Nativity, Woman w/Water Jar, white porcelain, 6½", MIB **$35.00**

Plate, dinner; Hummingbird, etched pattern on clear glass, MIB .. **$40.00**

Shampoo, Charlie Brown, ca. 1970s, MIB, from $20.00 to $25.00. (Photo courtesy www.whatacharacter.com)

Stein, Endangered Species, Giant Panda, hinged lid, MIB ... **$30.00**

Vanity set, Charisma scented powders, lotions & creams in 7 pcs on 10" tray, all red w/gold trim, 1970s, NM **$66.00**

Barbie® Doll and Her Friends

Barbie was first introduced in 1959, and soon Mattel found themselves producing not only dolls but tiny garments, fashion accessories, houses, cars, horses, books, and games as well. Today's Barbie doll collectors want them all. Though the early Barbie dolls are very hard to find, there are many of her successors still around. The trend today is toward Barbie exclusives — Holiday Barbie dolls and Bob Mackie Barbie dolls are all very 'hot' items. So are special-event Barbie dolls.

When buying the older dolls, you'll need to do lots of studying and comparisons to learn to distinguish one Barbie from another, but this is the key to making sound buys and good investments. Remember, though, collectors are sticklers concerning condition; compared to a doll mint in the box (or package), they'll often give an additional 20% if it has never been opened (or as collectors say 'never removed from box,' indicated in our lines by 'NRFB' or 'NRFP'! As a general rule, a mint-in-the-box doll is worth from 50% to 100% more than one mint, no box. The same doll, played with and in only good condition, is worth half as much (or less than that). If you want a good source for study, refer to one of these fine books: *Barbie Doll Fashion, Vol. I, Vol. II,* and *Vol. III,* by Sarah Sink Eames; *Collector's Encyclopedia of Barbie Doll Exclusives, Collector's Encyclopedia of Barbie Doll Collector's Editions,* and *Barbie Doll Around the World* by J. Michael Augustyniak; *The Barbie Doll Years, 6th Edition,* by Patrick C. and Joyce L. Olds; *Barbie, The First 30 Years, 1959 Through 1989,* by Stefanie Deutsch; and *Schroeder's Collectible Toys, Antique to Modern.* (All are published by Collector Books.)

Dolls

Allan, straight legs, red painted hair, 1964, MIB.............. **$100.00**

Barbie, #2, blond, 1959, MIB, from $5,000 to.............. **$5,250.00**

Barbie, #3, blond or brunette, 1960, MIB, ea from $925 to... **$1,025.00**

Barbie, #6, any color hair, 1962, MIB, ea from $375 to **$425.00**

Barbie, American Girl, redhead, 1965, MIB **$2,000.00**

Barbie, Barbie Celebration, 1987, NRFB............. **$30.00**

Barbie, Brazilian, Dolls of the World, 1990, NRFB........... **$25.00**

Barbie, Carnival Cruise Lines, 1997, NRFB **$30.00**

Barbie, Circus Star, 1995, NRFB............................ **$70.00**

Barbie, Dream Glow, Hispanic, 1986, MIB **$45.00**

Barbie, Enchanted Evening, JC Penney, 1991, NRFB......... **$50.00**

Barbie, Holiday, 1988, NRFB.............................. **$325.00**

Barbie, Knitting Pretty, royal blue, 1965, NRFB.............. **$635.00**

Barbie, Pink & Pretty, 1982, MIB **$50.00**

Barbie, Quick Curl, 1972, MIB, $100.00. (Photo courtesy Sarah Sink Eames)

Barbie, Safari, 1983, Disney, MIB.......................... **$25.00**

Barbie, Standard, any hair color, 1967, MIB................. **$425.00**

Barbie, Swirl Ponytail, redhead, 1964, NRFB **$625.00**

Brad, Talking, 1970, NRFB **$225.00**

Christie, Kissing, 1979, MIB **$50.00**

Christie, Twist 'n Turn, redhead, 1968, MIB **$300.00**

Francie, Malibu, 1971, NRFB **$50.00**

Ken, Army, Black, 1993, NRFB............................ **$35.00**

Ken, Fraternity Meeting, 1964, NRFB **$375.00**

Ken, Ocean Friends, 1996, NRFB **$15.00**

Midge, Cool Times, 1989, NRFB **$15.00**

PJ, Fashion Photo, 1978, MIB............................. **$75.00**

Skipper, Hollywood Hair, 1993, NRFB **$25.00**

Skipper, straight legs, any hair color, 1965, MIB............. **$130.00**

Whitney, Style Magic, 1989, NRFB......................... **$15.00**

Accessories

Case, Barbie Circus Star, FAO Schwarz, 1995, M **$25.00**
Case, Miss Barbie, black patent, 1963, NM+ **$150.00**
Case, Tutti Play Case, blue or pink vinyl w/various scenes, EX ... **$30.00**
Furniture, Barbie Dream Armoire, 1980, NRFB **$35.00**
Furniture, Barbie Dream Kitch-Dinette, #4095, 1964, MIB .. **$600.00**

Furniture, Barbie Fashion Living Room Set, #7404, 1984, NRFB, $30.00. (Photo courtesy Stephanie Deutsch)

Furniture, Living Pretty Cooking Center, 1988, MIB **$25.00**
Gift set, Barbie's Olympic Ski Village, MIB **$75.00**
Gift set, Cinderella, 1992, NRFB **$125.00**
Gift set, Wedding Party Midge, 1990, NRFB **$150.00**
Outfit, Barbie, Bouncy Flouncy, #1805, 1967, NRFP **$300.00**
Outfit, Barbie, City Sparklers, #1457, 1970, NRFP **$125.00**
Outfit, Barbie, Jumpin' Jeans, Pak, 1964, NRFP **$85.00**
Outfit, Barbie, Red Flair, #939, 1962, NRFP **$175.00**
Outfit, Francie, Summer Number, #3454, 1971-72 & 1974, MIP **$175.00**

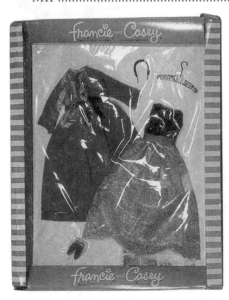

Outfit, Francie and Casey, Two for the Ball, #1232, 1969 – 1970, MIB, $250.00. (Photo courtesy Sarah Sink Eames)

Outfit, Ken, Beach Beat, #3384, 1972, NRFP **$80.00**
Outfit, Ken, Jazz Concert, #1420, 1966, NRFP **$275.00**

Outfit, Midge, Orange Blossom, #987, 1962, NRFP **$75.00**
Outfit, Skipper, Lacy Charmer & Partytimer, #9746, 1977, NRFP **$15.00**
Outfit, Skipper, Skimmy Stripes, #1956, 1968, MIP **$200.00**

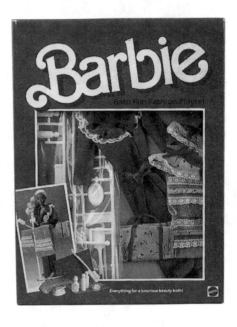

Playset, Barbie Bath Fun Fashion, #9266, 1984, NRFP, $20.00.

Vehicle, Allan's Roadster, aqua, 1964, MIB **$500.00**
Vehicle, Barbie's Silver 'Vette, MIB **$30.00**
Vehicle, Ken's Hot Rod, red, Sears Exclusive, 1964, MIB .. **$3,600.00**
Vehicle, 1957 Chevy Belair, aqua, 1st edition, 1989, MIB. **$150.00**

Miscellaneous

Barbie Ge-Tar, 1965, M **$325.00**
Barbie Shrinky Dinks, 1979, MIB **$30.00**
Game, Barbie 35th Anniversary, Golden, 1994, MIB **$60.00**
Paper Dolls, Midge Cut-Outs, Whitman #1962, uncut, 1963, NM **$150.00**
Quick Curl Miss America Beauty Center, Sears Exclusive, 1976, MIB **$75.00**
Tea set, Barbie 25th Anniversary, 1984, complete, M **$150.00**
Yo-yo, Spectra Star, plastic w/paper sticker, MIP **$5.00**

Barware

Cocktail shakers — the words just conjure up visions of glamour and elegance. Seven hard shakes over your right shoulder and you can travel back in time, back to the glamor of Hollywood movie sets with Fred Astaire and Ginger Rogers and luxurious hotel lounges with gleaming chrome; back to the world of F. Scott Fitzgerald and *The Great Gatsby*; or watch *The Thin Man* movie showing William Powell instruct a bartender on the proper way to shake a martini — the reveries are endless.

An original American art form, cocktail shakers reflect the changing nature of various styles of art, design, and architecture of the era between WWI and WWII. We see the graceful lines of Art Nouveau in the early '20s being replaced by the rage for jagged geometric modern design. The geometric cubism of Picasso that influenced so many designers of the '20s was replaced with the craze for streamline design of '30s. Cocktail shakers of the early '30s were taking the shape of the new deity of American architecture, the skyscraper, thus giving the appearance of movement and speed in a slow economy.

Cocktail shakers served to penetrate the gloom of depression, ready to propel us into the future of prosperity like some Buck Rogers rocket ship — both perfect symbols of generative power, of our perpetration into better times ahead.

Cocktail shakers and architecture took on the aerodynamically sleek industrial design of the automobile and airship. It was as Norman Bel Geddes said: 'a quest for speed.' All sharp edges and corners were rounded off. This trend was the theme of the day, as even the sharp notes of jazz turned into swing.

The sleek streamline cocktail shakers of modern design are valued by collectors of today. Those made by Revere, Chase, and Manning-Bowman have taken the lead in this race. Also commanding high prices are those shakers of unusual design such as penguins, zeppelins, dumbbells, bowling pins, town crier bells, airplanes, even ladies' legs. They're all out there, waiting to be found, waiting to be recalled to life, to hear the clank of ice cubes, and to again become the symbol of elegance.

Advisor: Stephen Visakay (See Directory, Barware)

Museum: The Museum of the American Cocktail
Stephen Visakay, Founding member
visakay@optonline.net
www.museumoftheamericancocktail.org

Shaker, chrome skyscraper style with walnut trim, Manning-Bowman, ca. 1936, from $75.00 to $95.00. (Photo courtesy Stephen Visakay)

Bar set, bowling ball form, marbleized plastic w/gold bowler on top, holds chrome decanter & 6 shots w/colored rings.......**$110.00**
Bottle stopper, ballerina figural, carved & painted wood w/cork at base, attributed to Anri, 6½"..**$90.00**

Cocktail set, pink elephants on clear glass, shaker w/chrome top & 6 shots **$75.00**
Ice bucket, black amethyst w/painted bleeding hearts, gold-tone metal handle, Westmoreland, 1930s...........................**$135.00**
Ice bucket, sea diver's helmet shape, brushed aluminum w/brass plate at base, YSS Gilbey's, 1970s, 9½x9½" **$70.00**
Ice bucket, teakwood w/orange plastic liner, Danish Modern style, Dansk, 15x7½" **$90.00**
Manual, Official Mixer's Manual, Patrick Gavin Duffy, Halcyon House, NY, 1940 2nd edition, hardback, EX w/dust jacket..........**$60.00**

Martini glasses, two men toasting, fired-on red and black, set of six, from $45.00 to $60.00.

Shaker, chrome w/butterscotch Bakelite/Catalin handle, Deco style, Lehman Brothers NY, 13¼".......................................**$85.00**
Shaker, clear glass cylinder w/rooster head top, Heisey, 1930s, NM **$110.00**
Shaker, Masonic Lodge emblem on frosted glass, chrome top, 11¾x4" **$95.00**
Shaker, pink & black elephants on clear glass, chrome screw-on top w/pour spout & separate lid, 1950s-60s......................**$85.00**
Shaker, silver drinking scene overlay on ruby glass, 30-oz, 11", +8 ruby shots w/2 rows of 6 convex circles **$200.00**
Swizzle stick, greyhound dog's head, ruby glass, 5" **$60.00**
Tumblers, decals show hula girl, Spanish dancer, etc, insideview of same girl as nude pinup, 4¾", 6 for **$80.00**

Bauer Pottery

The Bauer Pottery Company is one of the best known of the California pottery companies and is noted for both its artware and its dinnerware. Over the past 10 years, Bauer pottery has become particularly collectible, and prices have risen accordingly. Bauer actually began operations in Kentucky in 1885, but in 1910 they moved to Los Angeles where they continued in business until they closed in 1962. The company produced several popular dinnerware lines, including La Linda, Monterey, and Brusche Al Fresco. Most popular (and most significant) was the Ringware line begun in 1932, which preceded Fiesta as a popular solid-color, everyday dinnerware. The earliest pieces are unmarked, although to collectors they are unmistakable, due in part to their distinctive glazes, which have an almost primitive charm due to their drips, glaze misses, and color variations.

Another dinnerware line popular with collectors is Speckleware, a term that refers to a 1950s-era speckled glaze used on several different kinds of pottery other than dinnerware, including vases, flowerpots, and kitchenware. Though not as popular as Ringware, it holds its value well and is usually available at much lower prices than Ring. Keep an eye out for other flowerpots and mixing bowls, as they are common garage sale items.

Artware by Bauer is not so easy to find any more, but it is worth seeking out because of its high values. So-called oil jars sell for upwards of $1,500.00, and Rebekah vases routinely fetch $400.00 or more. Matt Carlton is one of the most desirable designers of handmade ware.

Colors are particularly important in pricing Bauer pottery, especially Ringware. Burgundy, cobalt blue, delph blue, and ivory are generally higher than other colors. (If no specific color is indicated in the descriptions, our values are mid range.) Black and white glazes on Ringware items are worth as much as twice the prices listed here. Common colors in dinnerware are orange-red, jade green, and Chinese yellow. For more information we recommend *Collector's Encyclopedia of California Pottery* by Jack Chipman (Collector Books).

Caution: A new Bauer line has been produced, using original items as models, with an emphasis on pieces from the 1930s and 1940s.

Art Pottery, #2000 Hi-Fire, and Matt Carlton

Bowl, Half Pumpkin, speckled yellow, Tracy Irwin, 10½" **$85.00**
Bowl, Pumpkin, turquoise matt (aqua) w/airbrushed gold, 4x6" ... **$75.00**

Vase, apricot mottle with black interior, Russel Wright, 8¾", $920.00. (Photo courtesy LiveAuctioneers.com/David Rago Auctions)

Vase, garden; Ring, green, Fred Johnson, #10, 11x12¾" **$140.00**
Vase, Ring, red-brown, 6⅜" **$85.00**
Vase, speckled apricot, pillow form, Russel Wright, 9x10" .. **$510.00**

Brusche

Bowl, covered onion soup; brown, 5½" **$20.00**
Bowl, fruit; burgundy, 5" **$8.00**
Creamer, olive gr, jumbo **$20.00**

Cup, speckled yellow **$8.00**
Plate, dinner; gray, 10" **$15.00**
Plate, lunch/salad; brown, 8" **$8.00**
Platter, 12⅝", from $20 to **$25.00**
Saucer, chartreuse **$3.50**
Tumbler, brown, 8-oz **$15.00**

Cal-Art and Garden Pottery

Ashtray, jade green, Western hat form, Matt Carlton, #132, 2½x4" **$360.00**
Candleholder, jade green, bowl base, w/handle, Matt Carlton, 2¼x4", ea **$55.00**
Figurine, duck preening, white matt, 2½x3¼", minimum value .**$50.00**
Flowerpot, Swirl, olive green or turquoise, 6" **$55.00**
Flowerpot, Swirl, white matt, 3" **$25.00**
Flowerpot, 3-Step, white gloss, 4" **$40.00**
Flowerpot saucer, green, early, unmarked, 7⅜" **$40.00**
Flowerpot saucer, red-brown, unmarked, 6" **$25.00**
Jardiniere, Swirl, white matt, 5" **$40.00**
Jardiniere/flowerpot, speckled pink, #9 ....**$65.00**
Planter, swan form, blue matt, Los Angeles, 5x10" **$70.00**
Snack tray & cup, brown, 2x3¾", 10¼x7" **$25.00**
Spanish pot, speckled green, 4" **$20.00**
Spanish pot, white gloss, 5" **$30.00**
Spanish pot, yellow, 3" **$18.00**
Vase, green matt, floriform, 8½" **$72.00**
Vase, turquoise, cylindrical, Hi-Fire #200, 10x5⅝", NM **$90.00**
Vase, yellow gloss, waisted, Fred Johnson, 5½x3½" **$45.00**
Vase, yellow matt, fan shape w/double radiating ribs, Ray Murray, 6", NM **$60.00**
Vase, yellow w/3-scallop rim, Matt Carlton, mini, 3" **$165.00**

Vases, Cal-Art ware 7½" to 8", $75.00 each. (Photo courtesy Jack Chipman)

Gloss Pastel Kitchenware (aka GPK)

Bowl, batter; yellow, 2-qt **$65.00**
Bowl, mixing; brown, #18, from $35 to **$45.00**
Bowl, mixing; green, #12, 4½x9", NM **$25.00**
Custard cup, all colors **$10.00**
Pitcher, jade green, w/ice lip, 6¼" **$30.00**
Ramekin, light blue **$10.00**
Salt shakers, light brown, 2¼", pr **$20.00**
Teapot, Aladdin, pink, 8-cup, minimum value **$250.00**

La Linda

Bowl, cereal..$25.00
Creamer, 2 styles, ea.......................................$15.00
Cup, gray or pink...$12.50
Cup & saucer, green...$18.00
Plate, bread & butter; green, 6" $10.00
Plate, chop; yellow $75.00
Platter, 10"..$27.50
Tumbler $20.00

Montecito Shape (and Coronado)

Bowl, fruit; 5", from $20 to.............................$30.00
Cake plate, footed, from $200 to....................$300.00
Creamer & sugar bowl, midget, from $40 to.....$60.00
Plate, salad; 7½", from $15 to........................$22.00
Teapot, old style, 6-cup, from $100 to............$150.00

Monterey Moderne and Related Kitchenware

Bowl, chartreuse, 7"..$25.00
Bowl, soup; colors other than black, 5¼", from $15 to........$20.00
Butter dish, pink, round....................................$65.00
Casserole, brown, in copper-plated frame w/wooden handles,
    1-qt $45.00
Casserole, olive green, w/lid, 1½-qt................$40.00
Creamer, burgundy $20.00
Cup, pink..$12.00
Mug, no handle, burgundy, 8-oz......................$20.00
Pitcher, olive green, 6½"...................................$45.00
Platter, brown, 10" $25.00
Sugar bowl, burgundy, no lid $8.00
Tidbit tray, 3-tier...$75.00

Plainware

Ashtray, sq, 3", from $60 to..............................$90.00
Cup & saucer, from $175 to.............................$260.00
Pitcher, pinched spout, 12", from $400 to......$600.00
Sherbet, from $100 to $150.00
Tumble-up, 7" water bottle, minimum value $500.00

Ringware (Ring)

Bowl, mixing; cobalt, double rings, #9.............$250.00
Bowl, mixing; cobalt, double rings, #12...........$180.00
Bowl, mixing; gray, #12 ....$145.00
Bowl, nappy, 7", from $100 to..........................$150.00
Coffee cup & saucer, jade green $55.00
Coffee server, jade green, w/lid, 8-cup.............$140.00
Coffeepot, dripolator, minimum value..............$1,500.00
Creamer, cobalt, restyled $100.00
Custard cup, orange-red......................................$45.00
Gravy boat, gray...$60.00
Pitcher, cobalt, 1½-pt...$125.00
Pitcher, ice lip, turquoise, 7" $100.00

Pitcher, jade green, 2-qt $250.00
Plate, dinner; gray, 9½".....................................$50.00
Plate, relish; from $85 to...................................$125.00
Plate, salad; yellow, 8".......................................$40.00
Punch bowl, chartreuse, footed, scarce, 14" $1,200.00
Saucer, ivory..$15.00
Shaker, dusty burgundy, squat, ea $50.00
Shaker, jade green, squat, ea $25.00
Sugar bowl, flat lid, early, from $250 to...........$375.00
Tea/punch cup, Chinese yellow..........................$60.00
Teapot, orange-red w/yellow lid, 6-cup $95.00

Teapot, red, 7x10", $275.00.

Tumbler, cobalt, 12-oz, from $50 to $60.00
Vase, bud; orange, 6" $500.00

Speckled Kitchenware

Bowl, mixing; white, #36...................................$20.00
Bowl, salad; yellow, low, 7" $25.00
Bowl, salad; yellow, low, 8½".............................$35.00
Buffet server, brown $45.00
Casserole, pink, in brass-plated metal frame, 2½-qt $75.00

Coffeepot, blue, #608, 7", from $50.00 to $65.00. (Photo courtesy Jack Chipman)

Pitcher, beater; pink, 1-qt, EX...........................$35.00
Pitcher, blue, 2-pt, NM......................................$25.00

Pitcher, pink, marked Bauer, 1-pt $30.00
Pitcher, yellow, Brusche style, 1-pt $25.00
Teapot, green, Monterey Modern shape, 6", NM $45.00

Beanie Babies

Ty Beanie Babies were first introduced in 1994. By 1996, they had become widely collected. Crazed collectors swarmed stores for the newest releases, and prices soared for many Beanie Babies through the year 2000, when the hype subsided. However, Beanie Babies continue to be favorites among collectors, and Ty regularly issues new animals. You will still find value in the rare and exclusive Beanies, as well as some of the regular retired issues.

Values given are for Beanie Babies with mint or near-mint condition swing or tush tags. Many counterfiets exist on the market, and it is important to be familiar with swing and tush tags. Removing tags from the more current Beanie Babies or having ripped, creased, or damaged tags decreases the value of the animal. However, most of the rarer 1994, 1995, and 1996 issues are still quite valuable without a swing tag, due to their scarcity. For more information on these tags, see *Ty Beanies & More*, a collector magazine published every other month which contains photos and details on all Beanie Baby tags.

This is just a sampling of the Beanie Babies on the market. Unless otherwise indicated, all Beanie Babies listed are retired and no longer being procuced by Ty, Inc. All current and more common retired Beanie Babies are valued at $3.00 to $6.00, and you will not see them listed here. There are also foreign Beanie Babies produced exclusively in Canada and in Europe that are not listed here; these range in value from $10.00 to $100.00. You'll need to have your Beanie Baby professionally authenticated if you are unsure whether it is one of the rarer, more valuable Beanie Babies listed below. All listings here are for retired Beanies, unless otherwise noted.

Advisor: Amy Sullivan (See Directory, Beanie Babies)

Key: # — style number

Ally the Alligator, #4032...$10.00
Baldy the Eagle, #4074, from $5 to $7.00
Beak the Kiwi, #4211 ....$5.00
Bessie the Cow, #4009, brown $10.00
Blackie the Bear, #4011..$6.00
Blizzard the Tiger, #4163 ....$6.00
Bongo the Monkey, #4067, 2nd issue, tan tail $6.00
Bronty the Brontosaurus, #4085, blue, minimum value.....$150.00
Brownie the Bear, #4010, w/swing tag, minimum value $500.00
Bubbles the Fish, #4078, yellow & black $15.00
Bumble the Bee, #4045, minimum value....................$50.00
Caw the Crow, #4071, minimum value $50.00
Chilly the Polar Bear, #4012, minimum value $125.00
Chops the Lamb, #4019, from $15 to $30.00
Coral the Fish, #4079, tie-dyed................................$15.00
Curly the Bear, #4052, brown, from $5 to..................$7.00
Daisy the Cow, #4006, black & white $10.00
Derby the Horse, #4008, 2nd issue, yarn mane & tail...........$6.00
Digger the Crab, #4027, 1st issue, orange, minimum value ..$60.00

Digger the Crab, #4027, 2nd issue, red, minimum value.....$15.00
Doodle the Rooster, #4171, tie-dyed..........................$6.00
Flashy the Peacock, #4339 ....$8.00
Flip the Cat, #4012, white...$7.00
Floppity the Bunny, lavender, from $4 to....................$7.00
Flutter the Butterfly, #4043, minimum value.............$80.00
Garcia the Bear, #4051, tie-dyed, minimum value $20.00
Glory the Bear, #4188, from $6 to...........................$10.00
Goldie the Goldfish, #4023 ....$10.00
Grunt the Razorback Pig, #4092, red, minimum value....$20.00
Happy the Hippo, #4061, 1st issue, gray, minimum value..$200.00
Happy the Hippo, #4061, 2nd issue, lavender, from $7 to ..$15.00
Holiday Teddy (1997), #4200, from $5 to.....................$8.00
Holiday Teddy (1998), #4204......................................$7.00
Holiday Teddy (1999), #4257......................................$5.00
Holiday Teddy (2000), #4332......................................$5.00
Holiday Teddy (2001), #4395......................................$5.00
Holiday Teddy (2002), #4564......................................$5.00
Hoot the Owl, #4073..$7.00
Hoppity the Bunny, #4117, pink, from $4 to................$7.00
Humphrey the Camel, #4060, minimum value $180.00
Inch the Worm, #4044, felt antennae $15.00
Inch the Worm, #4044, yarn antennae, from $4 to $7.00
Inky the Octopus, #4028, 3rd issue, pink $7.00
Kiwi the Toucan, #4070, minimum value...................$20.00
Lefty the Donkey, #4087, gray...................................$25.00
Libearty the Bear, #4057, minimum value...................$60.00
Lizzy the Lizard, #4033, tie-dyed, minimum value $200.00
Lizzy the Lizard, #4033, 2nd issue, blue $7.00
Lucky the Ladybug, #4040, 1st issue, 7 felt spots $60.00
Lucky the Ladybug, #4040, 3rd issue, 11 spots, from $5 to.$10.00
Magic the Dragon, #4088, from $7 to $10.00
Manny the Manatee, #4081, minimum value $20.00
Millennium the Bear, #4226 ....$5.00
Nectar the Hummingbird, #4361, from $20 to $35.00
Nuts the Squirrel, #4114..$6.00
Patti the Platypus, #4025, 1st issue, magenta, minimum value ...$50.00
Patti the Platypus, #4025, 2nd issue, purple, from $5 to $10.00
Peanut the Elephant, #4062, light blue, from $7 to............$12.00
Peking the Panda Bear, #4013, minimum value................$160.00
Quackers the Duck, #4024, 1st issue, no wings.................$200.00
Quackers the Duck, #4024, 2nd issue, w/wings................$5.00
Radar the Bat, #4019, black, minimum value $15.00
Rex the Tyrannosaurus, #4086, minimum value $160.00
Righty the Elephant, #4085, gray...............................$25.00
Ringo the Raccoon, #4014..$5.00
Rover the Dog, #4101, red..$5.00
Sammy the Bear, #4215, tie-dyed................................$5.00
Seamore the Seal, #4029, white.................................$10.00
Slither the Snake, #4031, minimum value $100.00
Snowball the Snowman, #4201....................................$6.00
Snowgirl the Snowgirl, #4333 ....$5.00
Spangle the Bear, #4245, blue face $7.00
Sparky the Dalmatian, #4100, minimum value...............$12.00
Spooky the Ghost, #4090, orange ribbon $5.00
Spot the Dog, #4000, no spot, minimum value...........$100.00
Sting the Stingray, #4077, tie-dyed $20.00

Tabasco the Bull, #4002, red feet.................................**$20.00**
Tank the Armadillo, #4031, no shell, 7 lines on back, minimum
    value **$15.00**
Teddy Bear, #4050, brown, new face........................**$7.00**
The Beginning Bear, #4267, w/silver stars.................**$5.00**
The End Bear, #4265, black.....................................**$5.00**
Trap the Mouse, #4042, minimum value.................**$300.00**
Tusk the Walrus, #4076, minimum value **$20.00**
Valentino the Bear, #4058, white w/red heart **$5.00**
Velvet the Panther, #4064, minimum value **$6.00**
Web the Spider, #4141, black, minimum value.........**$100.00**

The original nine Beanie Babies shown from back to front: Chocolate the Moose, #4015, $7.00; Squealer the Pig, #4005, $5.00; Splash the Whale, #4022, minimum value $30.00; Spot the Dog, #4000, with spot, $15.00; Cubbie the Bear, #4010, $15.00; Bones the Dog, #4001, brown, $10.00; Flash the Dolphin, #4021, minimum value $30.00; Pinchers the Lobster, #4026, $15.00; and Legs the Frog, #4029, $5.00. (Photo courtesy Amy Sullivan)

Beatles Collectibles

Possibly triggered by John Lennon's death in 1980, Beatles fans (recognizing that their dreams of the band ever reuniting were gone along with him) began to collect vintage memorabilia of all types. Some of the original Beatles material has sold at auction with high-dollar results. Handwritten song lyrics, Lennon's autographed high school textbook, and even the legal agreement that was drafted at the time the group disbanded are among the one-of-a-kind multi-thousand dollar sales recorded.

Unless you plan on attending sales of this caliber, you'll be more apt to find the commercially produced memorabilia that literally flooded the market during the '60s and beyond when the Fab Four from Liverpool made their unprecedented impact on the entertainment world. A word about their 45 rpm records: they sold in such mass quantities that unless the record is a 'promotional' (made to send to radio stations or for jukebox distribution), they have very

little value. Once a record has lost much of its original gloss due to wear and handling, becomes scratched, or has writing on the label, its value is minimal. Even in near-mint condition, $4.00 to $6.00 is plenty to pay for a 45 rpm (much less if it's worn), unless the original picture sleeve is present. (An exception is the white-labeled Swan recording of 'She Loves You/I'll Get You'.) A Beatles' picture sleeve is usually valued at $30.00 to $40.00, except for the rare 'Can't Buy Me Love,' which is worth ten times that amount. (Beware of reproductions!) Albums of any top recording star or group from the '50s and '60s are becoming very collectible, and the Beatles' are among the most popular. Just be very critical of condition! An album must be in at least excellent condition to bring a decent price. Unless another code is given in the descriptions that follow, values are for items in near mint to mint condition.

See also Celebrity Dolls; Magazines; Movie Posters; Records; Sheet Music.

Advisor: Bojo/Bob Gottuso (See Directory, Character and Personality Collectibles)

Newsletter: *Beatlefan*
P.O. Box 33515, Decatur, GA 30033; Send SASE for information
www.beatlefan.com

Apron, heavy white paper w/black graphics, US, 1964, EX..**$500.00**
Ball, black faces w/faux signatures on white oval, 9" dia, EX...**$850.00**
Bobbin' head dolls, 8" car mascots, set of 4, EX................**$600.00**

Bubble gum cards display box, first series, EX, $350.00. (Photo courtesy LiveAuctioneers.com/Morphy Auctions)

Cartoon Colorforms, complete w/instructions, NMIB **$900.00**
Concert book, USA, 1964, 12x12".....................................**$45.00**
Dis-Go case, plastic 45 record holder **$175.00**
Doll, John or George w/instrument, vinyl, Remco, 4", ea..**$125.00**
Doll, Paul or Ringo w/instrument, vinyl, Remco, 4", ea **$75.00**
Dolls, Beatles Forever, Applause, 22", complete set of 4.....**$375.00**
Figural music box, Abbey Road, Franklin Mint, 1993, 5",
    MIB **$150.00**
Figures, Swingers Music Set, set of 4, MOC (sealed) **$125.00**
Game, Flip Your Wig, Milton Bradley, 1964, complete, EX+..**$175.00**
Guitar, Four Pop **$500.00**
Harmonica, Hohner, M in NM box **$175.00**
Lunch box, Yellow Submarine, King Features, 1968, VG...**$275.00**
Lux soap, 2 bars, unopened, 1967, MIB **$450.00**

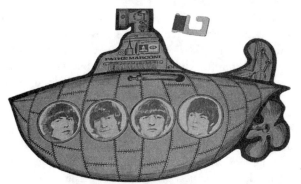

Mobile display, Yellow Submarine, Italy, 1968, from $700.00 to $800.00.
(Photo courtesy Barbara Crawford, Hollis Lamon, and Michael Stern)

Model kit, Paul McCartney figure, Revell, 1964, EXIB $375.00
Money clip, apple cutout, Apple Records..........................$350.00
Notebook, group in doorway of blue brick building, 10½x8"... $75.00
Pennant, We Love You, red on white felt, ca 1964, 29", EX..$120.00
Picture sleeve, I'll Cry Instead, 45 rpm, EX $75.00
Poster, Help!, 1-sheet movie, 1965, 27x41", EX................$600.00
Program, 1965, 6 pages, EX..$50.00
Purse, white vinyl clutch w/leather strap, group photo, EX ..$150.00
Puzzle, Beatles in Pepperland, Jaymar, 650 pcs, complete, 1968,
    EXIB..$125.00
Scrapbook, Beatles Scrapbook Whitman/Nems, 1964, unused,
    EX...$75.00
Sheet music, various songs, 1960s, ea from $15 to..............$25.00
Tie-tac set, NEMS, 1964, MOC (watch for repros)............$75.00
Tumbler, clear class w/black white paint, gold rim, Diary Queen,
    Canadian, 1964, 5", EX...$125.00
Wig, Lowell Toy Mfg, M in EX package..........................$125.00

Beatrix Potter Figures

Since 1902 when *The Tale of Peter Rabbit* was published by Fredrick Warne & Company, generations have enjoyed the adventures of Beatrix Potter's characters. Beswick issued 10 characters in 1947 that included Peter Rabbit, Benjamin Bunny, Squirrel Nutkin, Jemima Puddleduck, Timmy Tiptoes, Tom Kitten, Mrs Tittlemouse, Mrs. Tiggywinkle, Little Pig Robinson, and Samuel Whiskers. The line grew until it included figures from other stories. Duchess (P1355) was issued in 1955 with two feet that were easily broken. Later issues featured the Duchess on a base and holding a pie. This was the first figure to be discontinued in 1967. Color variations on pieces indicate issue dates as do the different backstamps that were used. Backstamps have changed several times since the first figures were issued. There are three basic styles: Beswick brown, Beswick gold, and Royal Albert — with many variations on each of these. Unless stated otherwise, figures listed here are Beswick brown.

Hunca Munca, gold oval mark...$90.00
Johnny Town Mouse, gold oval mark................................$110.00

Little Pig Robinson, BP1 ....$225.00
Little Pig Robinson Spying, 1987 ....$185.00
Miss Moppet, gold mark, G2..$90.00
Mother Ladybird, Royal Albert mark..............................$85.00
Mr Benjamin Bunny, BP2..$220.00
Mr Jackson, rare green color, BP3A $230.00

Mrs. Benjamin Bunny and Peter Rabbit, BP36, 4", $100.00.

Mrs Flopsy Bunny, GP3B $80.00
Mrs Tiggy Winkle, gold mark $95.00
Mrs Tittlemouse, gold oval mark, from $135 to................$185.00

Old Mr. Brown, B3, 3¼", $65.00.

Old Mr Pricklepin, copyright 1983, from $110 to............$125.00
Pigling Bland, maroon, 1st version, BP3..........................$110.00
Pigling Eats His Porridge, copyright 1991 ....$165.00
Ribby, gold mark...$210.00
Sir Isaac Newton, copyright 1973, from $160 to $175.00
Sir Isaac Newton, 1973...$200.00
Susan, 1983..$195.00
Tabitha Twitchit, gold mark...$100.00
Tailor of Gloucester, gold oval mark...............................$92.00
Thomasina Tittlemouse, copyright 1981, from $85 to.......$100.00
Tom Kitten & Butterfly, copyright 1987, from $150 to $165.00

Bellaire, Marc

Marc Bellaire, originally Donald Edmund Fleischman, was born in Toledo, Ohio, in 1925. He studied at the Toledo Museum of Art under Ernest Spring while employed as a designer for the Libbey Glass Company. During World War II while serving in the Navy, he traveled extensively throughout the Pacific, resulting in his enriched sense of design and color.

Marc settled in California in the 1950s where his work attracted the attention of national buyers and agencies who persuaded him to create ceramic lines of his own, employing hand-decorated techniques throughout. As a result, he founded a studio in Culver City. There he produced high quality ceramics often decorated with ultra-modern figures or geometric patterns and executed with a distinctive flair. His most famous pattern was Mardi Gras, decorated with slim dancers on spattered or striped colors of black, blue, pink, and white. Other major patterns were Jamaica, Balinese, Beachcomber, Friendly Island, Cave Painting, Hawaiian, Bird Isle, Oriental, Jungle Dancer, and Kashmir. (Kashmir usually has the name Ingle on the front and Bellaire on the back.)

It is to be noted that Marc was employed by Sascha Brastoff during the '50s. Many believe that he was hired for his creative imagination and style.

During the period 1951 – 1956, Marc was named one of the top ten artware designers by *Giftwares Magazine*. After 1956 he taught and lectured on art, design, and ceramic decorating techniques from coast to coast. Many of his pieces were one of a kind, and his work was commissioned throughout the United States.

During the 1970s he worked from his studio in Marin County, California. He eventually moved to Palm Springs where he set up his final studio/gallery. There he produced large pieces with a Southwest style. Mr. Bellaire died in 1994.

Advisor: Marty Webster (See Directory, California Pottery)

Ashtray, Beachcomber, free-form, 13½" **$65.00**
Bowl, Cave Painting, 5x15x13"....................................... **$70.00**
Box, Jamaican Man w/guitar, free-form, 6x7" **$150.00**
Box, Still Life, fruits & leaves on lid, 2x4½x3½" **$75.00**
Charger, stylized bird on branch, 15".............................. **$165.00**
Dish, Balinese Dancer, 8x10".. **$55.00**
Figurine, buffalo, brown & cream, 10x10" **$90.00**
Figurine, bull, 9"... **$145.00**
Lamp base, lg fighting cock on brown, conical, 9" W at base ...**$125.00**
Platter, Hawaiian figures (3) on orange, 13x7"..................... **$55.00**
Tray, Black Man dancing, triangular, 8½x17" **$75.00**
Vase, Indian on Horseback, #89, 10"............................. **$150.00**
Vase, Jungle Dancer, strong colors, flaring toward bottom, 7x8" **$165.00**
Vase, Polynesian Woman, 9".. **$100.00**

Bells

Bell collectors claim that bells rank second only to the wheel as being useful to mankind. Down through the ages bells have awakened people in the morning, called them to meals and prayers, and readied them to retire at night. We have heard them called rising bells, Angelus Bells (for deaths), noon bells, Town Crier bells (for important announcements), and curfew bells. Souvenir bells are often the first type collected, with interest spreading to other contemporaries, then on to old, more valuable bells. As far as limited edition bells are concerned, the fewer made per bell, the better. (For example a bell made in an edition of 25,000 will not appreciate as much as one from an edition of 5,000.)

Bone china, bright red flowers & green leaves on white w/navy & gold, Crown Staffordshire for Danbury Mint, 5¼".......**$12.50**
Bone china, pink roses on white w/gold, Royal Sutherland, 5½x2½".. **$15.00**
Bone china, Queen Elizabeth II Silver Jubilee 1952-77, Crown Staffordshire England, 5x2¾".................................. **$25.00**
Bone china, San Remo pattern (floral), Coalport, 4" **$45.00**

Brass, Chiantel Fondeur, twentieth century (originally made in Switzerland ca. 1878), 4½", $45.00.

Brass, English coachman, Peerage Made in England, 3¼x1½".. **$60.00**
Brass, goat bell, 2¾x2⅞".. **$15.00**
Brass, hotel type, Nouveau design, side tap, 3¾"............... **$175.00**
Brass, Kewpie figural handle, surface nicks, 5½x2½".......... **$140.00**
Brass, lady in gown w/wide hoop skirt w/ruffles & tiny flowers, ca 1900s, 4x3½"... **$35.00**
Brass, lady w/conical hat, detailed dress, 6".................... **$90.00**
Brass, lady w/tall hat, simple gown, 4".......................... **$70.00**
Brass, Russian Amazon, lady in riding costume & feathered hat, rod-style clapper, 5¾" **$105.00**
Brass, school, turned wood handle, 7x4"........................... **$80.00**
Brass, turtle figural, damascene flamenco dancer & musician on back, press head or tail, Pat 19536/30366, 2x5x2½"..**$200.00**
Bronze, Marie Antoinette, ornate headdress & gown, lost wax casting, 6"... **$70.00**
Cast iron, farm type, CS Bell & Co...No 1 Yoke, ca 1886, 10x14" in 25" yoke **$315.00**
Cast iron, farm type, John Deere Plow Co #2, 16" dia in #12 yoke, rust, 1800s **$300.00**
Cast iron, locomotive, clapper marked Graham White, old paint, 15x12", 46 lbs... **$325.00**

Cast iron, moose head plaque w/bell hanging from neck, 11x8x7" **$215.00**

Cast iron & brass, hotel type, ornate casting, Patented 1876, 4½" **$200.00**

Ceramic, angel figural, holly leaves & red rhinestones on skirt, 5¾" **$15.00**

Ceramic, angel w/candle figural, multicolor, Napco, 4¾" **$15.00**

Ceramic, angels, flowers & plants in relief, multicolor w/gold, Keramos Capodimonte Italy **$20.00**

Ceramic, Atlantic City Convention center scene among blue flowers, Tops in Quality Japan **$12.50**

Ceramic, chambermaid figural, multicolor, Japan, 4½" **$30.00**

Ceramic, clown playing cello, multicolor, Jasco, 4½" **$15.00**

Ceramic, colorful Picasso-like art w/fish-figural handle, Disimone Italy, 4" **$40.00**

Ceramic, Planning Christmas Visits, Norman Rockwell, Gorham, 1982 .... **$12.50**

Ceramic, Scarlett O'Hara in green dress, Enesco, MIB **$100.00**

Ceramic, The Purr-fect Grandma, grandma in rocker w/kitten on lap, Enesco, 1981-88, 5½" **$50.00**

Ceramic, white w/fan finial, Noritake for Danbury Mint, 4" .. **$10.00**

Glass, butterfly cuttings & pinwheels w/sm hobstars, elongated thumbprint cuts, 6-sided serrated finial, ca 1900, 7½" .. **$30.00**

Glass, cobalt w/etched gold florals & scrolls, clear faceted handle & clapper, Czech Republic, 7x3¾" **$45.00**

Glass, cranberry w/Mary Gregory-style child, 1980s, 6x3½" .. **$36.00**

Glass, emerald green w/gold trim, spiral design, clear handle, Czech Republic, 7" **$40.00**

Glass, lovebirds frosted handle (pressed), clear bell, 5x2½" .. **$24.00**

Glass, milk glass w/cobalt handle & blue rim, 9¾" **$135.00**

Glass, Sandwich pattern, blue, 5⅝" **$12.50**

Glass, swan figural handle, clear w/applied pink flowers w/green leaves, 5⅛" **$20.00**

Jasperware, penguins, white on blue, Wedgwood, New Year, 1979, 3x2½" **$30.00**

Metal, counter/desk type, mounted on 3½" sq stepped plinth, 1890s **$130.00**

Metal, cow bell, 4½x5" **$35.00**

Metal, silver-colored w/metal clapper, bone-covered wood handle w/applied snake, 1930s, 6¼" **$40.00**

Porcelain, blond girl in pink nightdown, Schafer & Vater, ca 1920, 4½x2½" **$60.00**

Porcelain, draped goddess figural handle, pale pink w/green bell, gold trim, Benaccio Made in Italy, 6¾" **$60.00**

Porcelain, For Grandmother w/Love & pink roses on white w/gold trim, Russ, 4¾" **$20.00**

Porcelain, Garden Whispers, multicolor cameo, Bradford Editions, 1997 .... **$40.00**

Porcelain, girl w/flowers, multicolor, Jasco, 1978, 4¼x4¼", from $9 to **$12.00**

Porcelain, God Bless Mother & pink rose on white, Designer's Collection, 1970s.. **$16.00**

Porcelain, latticework body, hexagonal, unmarked Lenox, 3x2¾" **$25.00**

Porcelain, Los Ninos, De Grazia, 1st edition, 1980, 8" **$45.00**

Porcelain, Meadowlark, Danbury Mint Songbirds of America series, 5" **$12.50**

Porcelain, Triple Self-Portrait, Norman Rockwell, Danbury Mint, 1979, 7" **$30.00**

Porcelain, Wedding Prayer, dog w/Just Wed sign, Jonathan & David Lic Enesco, 1978 .... **$30.00**

Silver plate, angel w/outstretched wings figural handle, Danbury Mint, 1974, 4½x2¼" **$12.50**

Steel, bent into traditional triangle shape, 6¾x6¾x5½", no ringer **$15.00**

Nickel-plated cast iron, hotel bell, figural knight in armor, Gesch. #103, 7", EX+, $175.00. (Photo courtesy Past Tyme Pleasures)

Black Americana

There are many avenues one might pursue in the broad field of Black Americana and many reasons that might entice one to become a collector. For the more serious, there are documents such as bills of sale for slaves, broadsides, and other historical artifacts. But by and far, most collectors enjoy attractive advertising pieces, novelties and kitchenware items, toys and dolls, and Black celebrity memorabilia.

It's estimated that there are at least 50,000 collectors around the country today that specialize in this field. There are large auctions devoted entirely to the sale of Black Americana. The items they feature may be as common as a homemade pot holder or a magazine or as rare as a Lux Dixie Boy clock or a Mammy cookie jar that might go for several thousand dollars. In fact, many of the cookie jars have become so valuable that they're being reproduced; so are salt and pepper shakers, so beware.

Unless noted otherwise, our values are for items in at least near mint condition.

See also Advertising, Aunt Jemima; Condiment Sets; Cookie Jars; Postcards; Salt and Pepper Shakers; Sheet Music; String Holders.

Advisor: Judy Posner (See Directory, Advertising)

Bank, alligator eating man, multicolor, ceramic, slot on back, Japan, 4x6x2¾" **$37.50**

Bank, boy on pot in misery, painted cast iron, Cry Baby in red on pot, 6" **$35.00**

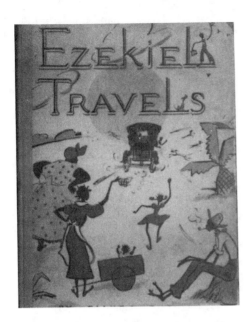

Book, *Ezekiel Travels,* by Elvira Garner, Henry Holt and Company, New York, NY, 1938, from $50.00 to $60.00.

(Photo courtesy P.J. Gibbs)

Book, Little Black Sambo, Kellogg's Story Book of Games #1, cardboard cover, 1931, 8x9¾", EX **$60.00**

Book, Treasury of Steven Foster, Random House, 1946, 1st edition, 224 pages, 9x12", EX **$30.00**

Box, boy hatching from egg, painted porcelain, #19, inscribed #52, 4¼" **$290.00**

Cigarette dispenser, pull lever & man pops up w/cigarette, wood w/inlay, 1940s, 3x4¾x3¾", EX.. **$40.00**

Cigarette holder/match striker, man's face, multicolor, ceramic, Austria, 1930-40s, 2½" **$150.00**

Cookbook, Old Southern Cook Book, Mammy on wooden cover, Culinary Arts Press, 1939, 48 pages, 8x6", EX............. **$38.00**

Figurine, child in broken potty, 2nd child at rim, ceramic, Made in Japan, 3¼" **$37.50**

Figurine, girl seated & eating watermelon, painted chalkware, 13½x6" **$80.00**

Game, Boo Boogy Mans!, puzzle game w/tin boat **$45.00**

Game, Darkies in the Melon Patch, board game w/dice & 4 figures, Hudson Bros, EXIB, from $95 to **$120.00**

Label, fruit crate; Porter Brand Oranges, porter w/orange on tray, California, 1936, 10¾x10" **$45.00**

Lure, Jolly Jigger, caricature face, 5x4", EX on card **$55.00**

Memo board, We Wants Today, Mammy scratching head, list of items w/holes in board & 12 red pegs to mark items, 9x6" **$50.00**

Milk bottle, Sunshine Dairy, I'm Happy Wit' My Sunshine, man's smiling face/Wit' Out My... & sad face on back, ½-pt.. **$35.00**

Photo, Bill Robinson & Lena Horn, black & white, 1943, 8x10" **$40.00**

Plaque, boy w/umbrella, painted chalkware, 1950s, 9" **$20.00**

Plaque, face among leaves & flourishes above 5 coat hooks, cast iron **$45.00**

Plaques, boy & girl w/umbrella, painted chalkware, 1940s, 8", pr **$55.00**

Postcard, He'p Yo'se'f to Grapefruit From Sunny Florida, child holding branch of grapefruit tree, color on linen **$18.00**

Postcard, Hottest Coons in Dixie, elegant couple, early 1900s.. **$48.00**

Recipe box, Aunt Jemima, multicolor on yellow, Fosta Product, Made in USA, 3x5x3½" **$68.00**

Record, Brave Little Sambo, 78 rpm, 1950, in original picture story sleeve, 6¼x6¾" **$55.00**

Salt & pepper shakers, lady w/baskets in ea arm, shakers held in ea basket, ceramic, multicolor, Japan, 1950s, 5¼" **$185.00**

Sheet music, At an Ole Virginia Wedding, Steinberg & Co, TE Harms & Co NY, color cover, 10½x14", VG-, from $75 to **$85.00**

Sheet music, Oh Wouldn't That Jar You!, color cover, Lew Dockstader, ca 1900, EX+ **$75.00**

Sheet music, Sugar Foot Strut, Pierce, Myers & Schwab, caricature cover of figure w/banjo, 1927, EX **$35.00**

Tablecloth, printed figures & varied kitchen utensils along green border on white, 1940s, 45x50"................................ **$95.00**

Teapot, clown face figural, yellow hat forms lid, bail handle, Japan paper label, marked Pat Pending, 5x8½" **$35.00**

Toast rack, ceramic Aunt Jemima face ea end of wire rack, worn paint, Japan, EX.. **$385.00**

Toothbrush holder, comic chef w/bananas & pineapple, multicolor, ceramic, tray at feet, Japan, 4½x2x3" **$95.00**

Toothpaste, Darkie Toothpaste, Haweley & Hazel, black & white tube, unopened, ca 1950, NMIB................................ **$42.50**

Toothpick holder, boy pulling cart, multicolor, ceramic, Made in Japan **$18.00**

Nodder, bisque, 4", $125.00.

(Photo courtesy Morphy Auctions)

Black Cats

Kitchenware, bookends, vases, and many other items designed as black cats were made in Japan during the 1950s and exported to the United States where they were sold by various distributors who often specified certain characteristics they wanted in their own line of cats. Common to all these lines were the red clay used in their production and the medium used in their decoration — their features were applied over the glaze with 'cold (unfired) paint.' The most collectible is a line marked (or labeled) Shafford. Shafford cats are plump and pleasant looking. They have green eyes with black pupils; white eyeliner, eyelashes, and whiskers; and red bow ties. The same design with yellow eyes was marketed by Royal, and another fairly easy-to-find 'breed' is a line by Wales with yellow eyes and gold whiskers. You'll find various other labels as well. Some collectors buy only Shafford, while others like them all.

When you evaluate your black cats, be critical of their paint. Even though no chips or cracks are present, if half of the paint is missing, you have a half-price item (if that). Collectors are very critical. These are readily available on internet auctions, and unless pristine, they realize prices much lower than ours. Remember this when using the following values which are given for cats with near-mint to mint paint.

Advisor: Peggy Way (See Directory Black Cats)

Ashtray, flat face, Shafford, hard-to-find size, 3¾"................**$30.00**
Ashtray, flat face, Shafford, 4¾", from $18 to **$25.00**
Ashtray, head shape, not Shafford, several variants, ea from $15 to...**$20.00**
Ashtray, head shape, Shafford, #109, 3", from $20 to..........**$30.00**
Bank, seated, coin slot in top of head, Shafford, from $125 to...**$150.00**
Bank, upright, Shafford features, marked Tommy, 2-part, minimum value **$100.00**
Biscuit jar, embossed white cat face w/blue eyes, wicker handle, 6", from $30 to **$45.00**
Biscuit jar, embossed yellow-eyed cat, wicker handle, Wales...**$125.00**
Bonbon, flat face, wicker handle, Shafford, scarce, from $50 to..**$75.00**
Cigarette lighter, Shafford, 5½", from $175 to...................**$200.00**
Cigarette lighter, sm cat stands on book by table lamp.........**$30.00**
Condiment set, upright, embossed faces w/yellow eyes, 2 bottles & shakers, pr in wire frame...**$95.00**
Cookie jar, head form, Shafford **$75.00**
Cookie jar, head w/fierce look, yellow eyes, brown-black glaze, red clay, Wales, scarce, lg..**$150.00**
Creamer, Shafford, 5½", from $20 to..................................**$30.00**
Creamer, upraised left paw is spout, yellow eyes, gold trim, 6½x6"..**$25.00**
Creamer & sugar bowl, embossed white cat face w/blue eyes, from $15 to **$20.00**
Creamer & sugar bowl, head lids are shakers, yellow eyes, 5⅜"...**$50.00**
Cruets, O eyes for oil, V eyes for vinegar, Shafford, from $65 to....**$75.00**
Decanter, long cat w/red fish in mouth as stopper **$65.00**
Decanter, upright cat holds bottle w/cork stopper, Shafford, from $50 to **$65.00**
Decanter, upright cat holds bottle w/cork stopper +6 cat-face cups, Shafford, from $95 to **$125.00**
Decanter set, upright, yellow eyes, 6 plain wines..................**$35.00**
Demitasse coffeepot, tail handle, bow finial, Shafford #58/811, 7½", from $100 to **$150.00**
Egg cup, cat face on bowl, pedestal foot, Shafford, from $25 to..**$35.00**
Grease jar, head form, Shafford #58/807, from $125 to.....**$150.00**
Measuring cups, 4 sizes on wood wall rack w/painted cat face, Shafford, rare **$450.00**

Mug, embossed cat face, cat on handle w/cat's head above rim, Shafford, scarce, 3", from $25 to **$50.00**
Mug, embossed cat face, cat on handle w/cat's head below rim, Shafford, rare, 4", from $50 to.....................................**$75.00**
Oil & vinegar set, embossed white cat face w/blue eyes, from $15 to **$20.00**
Oil & vinegar set, 2 cats hugging (1-pc, 2 heads), Royal Sealy or Tico, from $50 to **$60.00**
Paperweight, head on stepped chrome base, open mouth, yellow eyes, rare **$75.00**
Pincushion, cushion on back, tongue measure **$25.00**
Pitcher, squatting cat, pour through mouth, Shafford, rare, cream size, 4½" **$75.00**
Pitcher, squatting cat, pour through mouth, Shafford, very rare, cream size, 5½" **$250.00**
Pitcher, upright cat, pours from ear spout, Shafford, 18-oz or 24-oz, (6" or 6½"), from $130 to **$150.00**
Planter, upright, Shafford, from $25 to...............................**$35.00**
Planter, 2 cats in overturned top hat, 4½x3½x3¾"............**$125.00**
Pot holder caddy, 'teapot' cat, 3 hooks, Shafford #873, minimum value **$150.00**
Salad set, conjoined cruet, shakers pr, fork, spoon & funnel, complete on wall-mount rack, Royal Sealy, from $500 to..**$650.00**
Salt & pepper shakers, embossed white cat face w/blue eyes, pr from $15 to **$20.00**
Salt & pepper shakers, range; upright, Shafford, 5", pr........**$65.00**
Salt & pepper shakers, round-bodied 'teapot' cats, Shafford, pr from $60 to **$75.00**
Salt & pepper shakers, upright, Shafford, 3¾", pr from $22 to...**$28.00**
Shaker, long & crouching (shaker ea end), Shafford, 10", from $30 to **$50.00**

Spice set, triangular, three round tiers (eight in all), in wood wall mount, rare, from $500.00 to $750.00.

Spice set, 4 cat shakers hook onto wireware cat-face wall, rack, Shafford #58-806, from $450 to................................**$600.00**
Spice set, 6 pcs in wood frame, yellow eyes, Wales, from $60 to **$75.00**
Spice set, 6 sq shakers in wood frame, Shafford, from $75 to....**$150.00**
Spice set, 9 pcs in wood frame, yellow eyes, Wales, from $75 to ..**$100.00**
Sugar bowl, Shafford, from $20 to **$30.00**
Teakettle, embossed cat face, yellow eyes, wire handle, Wales, 4x7", from $45 to **$60.00**

Teapot, ball-shaped body, head lid, paw spout, tail handle, Shafford #542, 2-cup, 4"...**$30.00**

Teapot, ball-shaped body, head lid, paw spout, tail handle, Shafford #543, 3-cup, 4½"...**$35.00**

Teapot, ball-shaped body, head lid, paw spout, tail handle, Shafford #545, 5-cup, 6½"...**$45.00**

Teapot, cat face w/double spout, woven rattan handle, scarce, 5", from $150 to **$250.00**

Teapot, embossed white cat face w/blue eyes, kettle style, wire handle...**$40.00**

Teapot, upright, head lid, rare 8", minimum value **$200.00**

Teapot, yellow eyes, from $40.00 to $55.00.

Teapot/teakettle, cat head w/yellow 'straw' hat, blue & white eyes, C superimposed over N (Napco?) mark............................**$30.00**

Thermometer, yellow eyes, red ears, front paws resting on thermometer, 6", from $25 to **$35.00**

Toothpick holder, cat w/arched back beside vase, from $10 to **$12.00**

Utensil set w/cat-shape wall hanger, w/strainer, dipper & funnel, Shafford #5149, from $300 to **$500.00**

Utensil: strainer, dipper or funnel, wood handles, Shafford, ea individual pc **$75.00**

Blenko

The Blenko Glass Company is still operating in Milton, West Virginia, where they began production in 1921 (at that time known as Eureka Art Glass). Though at first they made only stained glass, primarily for making church windows, the depression of the late 1920s and the lack of church construction that resulted caused them to diversify. They hired local workers whom they trained in glassblowing and began producing decorative items for the home — decanters, bowls, candle holders, and the like. The company changed its name to Blenko in 1930. Over the years they have become famous for their brilliant colors, unique forms, and unusual techniques, including crackle glass, bubble glass, Venetian type glass, and mouth-blown cathedral glass from which they made reproductions of Colonial Williamsburg glassware. Most items found today are unmarked, since except for a short time (1950 – 1960) when the ware carried an etched signature, only paper labels were used.

See also Crackle Glass.

Advisors: *Stan and Arlene Weitman (See Directory, Crackle Glass)*

Bottle, cobalt, cylindrical, w/stopper, 1950s, 21" **$315.00**

Bottle, medium blue, Nickerson, #7323, 13½", from $150.00 to $200.00. (Photo courtesy bluecolt.com)

Bottle, olive green, dimpled texture, fluted neck, label, 7¾x3", from $75 to **$100.00**

Bottle, water; deep ruby red, double spout, sq body, 8¼" ..**$210.00**

Bowl, red to clear to blue at bottom, Wayne Husted, 5½x6", from $50 to **$75.00**

Cruet, cranberry-flash crackle, w/crystal 2-ball stopper & handle, 6½", from $55 to **$75.00**

Decanter, amber body, red stopper w/applied flower, 16" ..**$165.00**

Decanter, olive green, Joel Myers, #7054, 33"..................**$325.00**

Decanter, ruby w/golden orange bulbous middle, ruby stopper, 14" **$95.00**

Decanter, Sea Green, tapered body w/6¾" hollow flame-shaped stopper, 22½"...**$120.00**

Decanter, tangerine, w/stopper, Wayne Husted, #59221, 20" **$275.00**

Figurine, penguin, blue w/clear beak, 10½" **$115.00**

Flowerpot, jade green, triangular w/applied button-like plants, 5½" **$165.00**

Goblet, amethyst crackle, very long stem, attributed, 1960s, 13½", from $175 to **$200.00**

Paperweight, 3 owls, crystal, label, 4¼x3½" **$40.00**

Pitcher, cobalt, slim design w/smooth rim, Richard Blenko, 12¾"..**$100.00**

Pitcher, light blue w/dark blue handle, pointed flared spout, 19¼" **$90.00**

Tumbler, amber, pinched, 12-oz..**$8.00**

Vase, amethyst crackle, double neck, late 1940s-50s, 4", from $60 to **$85.00**

Vase, amethyst w/clear band at stem of chalice form, 11x4" ..**$165.00**

Vase, blue, footed bell shape, marked Blenko on base, 9½" ..**$200.00**

Vase, clear crackle w/applied blue serpentine at neck, foil label, 7x5½" **$65.00**

Vase, floor; deep green, slim cylinder neck w/slightly flared body, foil label, 26¾" $195.00

Vase, red w/gold swirl stripes, ruffled top, tapered foot, marked Blenko, 13½" $140.00

Vase, ruby, pinched twice at rim, 4x4" $45.00

Vase, yellow crackle, cylindrical, 1940s-50s, 13½", from $125 to $150.00

Vase, crystal with blue rosettes, ca. 1940s – 1950s, 7", from $110.00 to $150.00. (Photo courtesy Stan and Arlene Weitman)

Block Pottery

Richard Block founded his pottery in Los Angeles, California, sometime around 1940, and during that decade produced figural novelties and decorative items for the home. His product was marked Block Pottery, California, often with a copyright date.

Bank, puppy, white w/blue, green & pink flowers, 4½" $35.00

Flower holder, Betty, lady in blue & white gown, triangular hat, opening at hands, 7¼" $22.00

Flower holder, Boston terrier, white w/bug on side, blue bowl, 4½" $30.00

Flower holders, boy & girl, green & brown tones, she w/basket at elbow, he w/cone-like holder in arms, 7", 6½", pr $40.00

Planter, baby shoe, white, 3x5", from $10 to $12.00

Planter, Bonzo dog, eyes closed, hand-painted flowers, 4x3½x3" $10.00

Planter, dog w/blue eyes, 4", from $22 to $28.00

Planter, Heidi, girl holding basket at side, 6½" $18.00

Planter, spaniel-type dog w/eyes closed, 5" $10.00

Planter, swan, pale pink w/hand-painted flowers, 6¼x8½" ... $15.00

Planter vase, deer & fawn beside tree trunk, hand-painted flowers, 6" $20.00

Polanter, kangaroo, white w/floral decor, 7⅛", EX $26.00

Wall pocket, white disk w/raised blue flowers & green leaves, #2, 5¾" $15.00

Blue Danube

A modern-day interpretation of the early Meissen Blue Onion pattern, Blue Danube is an extensive line of quality dinnerware that has been produced in Japan since the early 1950s and distributed by Lipper International of Wallingford, Connecticut. It is said that the original design was inspired by a pattern created during the Yuan Dynasty (1260 – 1368) in China. This variation is attributed to the German artist Kandleva. The flowers depicted in this blue-on-white dinnerware represent the ancient Chinese symbols of good fortune and happiness. The original design, with some variations, made its way to Eastern Europe where it has been produced for about 200 years. It is regarded today as one of the world's most famous patterns.

At least 125 items have at one time or another been made available by the Lipper company, making it the most complete line of dinnerware now available in the United States. Collectors tend to pay higher prices for items with the earlier banner mark (1951 to 1976), and reticulated (openweave) pieces bring a premium. Unusual serving or decorative items generally command high prices as well. The more common items that are still being produced sell for less than retail on the secondary market.

The banner logo includes the words 'Reg US Pat Off' along with the pattern name. In 1976 the logo was redesigned and the pattern name within a rectangular box with an 'R' in circle to the right of it was adopted. Very similar lines of dinnerware have been produced by other companies, but these two marks are the indication of genuine Lipper Blue Danube. Among the copycats you may encounter are Mascot and Vienna Woods — there are probably others. Some of our listings will indicate the mark, others will have a range. Items with the rectangular mark should be valued at 25% to 40% less than the same item with the banner mark. When our values are ranged, use the lower end to evaluate items with the rectangular mark.

Advisor: Lori Simnioniw (See Directory, Dinnerware)

Bowl, divided vegetable; oval, banner mark, 11x7½", from $65.00 to $85.00. (From the collection of Elaine France)

Ashtray, sq, 7x7", from $25 to $35.00

Ashtray, triangular, rests in ea corner, banner mark, 7" $22.00

Ashtray, 3¾" $8.00

Au gratin, 6½", from $12 to $20.00

Au gratin, 7⅜" dia.......$55.00
Bell, 6", from $20 to.......$25.00
Biscuit jar, 9", from $65 to.......$75.00
Bone dish/side salad, crescent shape, banner mark, 6¾".......$25.00
Bone dish/side salad, crescent shape, banner mark, 9", from $35 to.......$50.00
Bowl, basketweave, scalloped rim, 9".......$60.00
Bowl, cereal; banner mark, 6".......$20.00
Bowl, cereal; rectangular mark, 6".......$12.00
Bowl, cream soup; w/handles, 5" wide (across handles) w/saucer, rectangular mark.......$40.00
Bowl, dessert; banner mark, 5½", from $10 to.......$14.00
Bowl, divided vegetable; oval, rectangular mark, 11x7½", from $35 to.......$48.00
Bowl, heart shape, 2¼x8½".......$65.00
Bowl, lattice edge, banner mark, 8".......$35.00
Bowl, lattice edge, banner mark, 9", from $40 to.......$50.00
Bowl, lattice edge, open handles, oval, 7¾" L, from $35 to.......$45.00
Bowl, low pedestal skirted base, shaped rim, banner mark, 2x9x12", from $65 to.......$70.00
Bowl, onion soup; tab handles, w/lid, 2" H.......$40.00
Bowl, rice; conical, 2x4½", from $25 to.......$30.00
Bowl, rounded diamond shape, ¾" H foot ring, banner mark, 12" L, from $85 to.......$110.00
Bowl, rounded diamond shape, ¾" H foot ring, rectangular mark, 12" L, from $65 to.......$80.00
Bowl, salad; rectangular mark, 3x10".......$50.00
Bowl, soup; banner mark, 8½", from $15 to.......$20.00
Bowl, soup; coupe shape, rectangular mark, 7½".......$15.00
Bowl, spaghetti; 9", rectangular mark, from $20 to.......$30.00
Bowl, spaghetti; 12", from $50 to.......$60.00
Bowl, triangular, 9½".......$42.00
Bowl, vegetable; oval, banner mark, 10" L, from $40 to.......$50.00
Bowl, vegetable; round, banner mark, 9".......$45.00
Bowl, vegetable; round, rectangular mark, 9".......$35.00
Bowl, vegetable; round, w/lid, 5⅝x8", from $100 to.......$125.00
Bowl, vegetable; round w/lid & handles, rectangular mark, 4¾x11x8".......$75.00
Bowl, wedding; w/lid, footed, sq, rectangular mark, 8½x5", from $60 to.......$80.00
Box, white lacquerware, gold label w/rectangular logo, 2¼x4½".......$30.00
Butter dish, banner mark, ¼-lb, from $50 to.......$60.00
Butter dish, rectangular w/handles, 1-lb.......$140.00
Butter dish, round, rectangular mark, 8½", from $55 to.......$65.00
Cache pot, w/handles, 8x8".......$45.00
Cake breaker, long tines.......$30.00
Cake knife, from $20 to.......$30.00
Cake pedestal, lattice edge, rectangular mark, 5x10", from $65 to.......$75.00
Cake pedestal, 4x10".......$55.00
Cake server, ornate semicircular blade, 9x3¼".......$30.00
Candelabrum, 5-light, 12x11".......$225.00
Candleholders, sq base, w/handle, rectangular mark, 2½", pr.......$25.00
Candlesticks, rectangular mark, 6½", pr.......$40.00
Candy dish, open, 8", from $28 to.......$32.00
Candy dish, w/lid, 7½".......$75.00

Candy/nut dish, 3-section w/'Y' handles, rectangular mark, 7x10½".......$40.00
Casserole, French; stick handle, w/lid, banner mark, 7" dia.......$85.00
Casserole, individual; banner mark, 6" across handles, from $25 to.......$30.00
Casserole, individual; rectangle mark, 6" across handles, from $18 to.......$22.00
Casserole, oval, w/lid, banner mark under handle, 9" L.......$55.00
Casserole, round, w/lid, banner mark, 7¼".......$55.00
Casserole, round, w/lid, banner mark, 8¾".......$70.00
Chamber stick, Old Fashioned, 4x6" dia, ea.......$25.00
Cheese board, wooden, w/6" dia tile & glass dome, from $35 to.......$50.00
Cheese knife, 9", from $20 to.......$30.00
Chop plate, banner mark, 12", from $50 to.......$65.00
Chop plate, banner mark, 14", from $60 to.......$70.00
Chop plate, banner mark, 16", from $75 to.......$85.00
Chop plate, rectangular mark, 12".......$45.00
Coasters, 3½", set of 8, from $40 to.......$50.00
Coffee mug, banner mark, 3¼", from $20 to.......$25.00
Coffee mug, rectangular mark, 3¼".......$15.00
Coffee mug, rectangular mark, 4".......$22.00
Coffeepot, 6", from $45 to.......$55.00
Coffeepot, 7½", from $50 to.......$60.00
Coffeepot, 8½", from $60 to.......$70.00
Coffeepot, 10".......$115.00
Compote, 4", from $65 to.......$75.00
Compote, 13", from $85 to.......$100.00
Condiment bowl, 2½" deep, w/saucer, 6¾", from $22 to.......$28.00
Cookie jar, rectangular mark, 8½", from $65 to.......$75.00
Creamer, scroll-decorated spout (like coffeepot), rectangular mark, 2¾x4½".......$18.00
Creamer & sugar bowl, 'Y' handles, bulbous, 4¾", 3½", from $38 to.......$42.00
Cruet, banner mark, 8".......$85.00
Cruets, oil & vinegar, ea 6", on wooden tray w/banner mark.......$75.00
Cup & saucer, 'Y' handle, scalloped rims, rectangular mark.......$6.00
Cup & saucer, demitasse; 2x2⅝", from $15 to.......$18.00
Cup & saucer, Irish coffee; cylindrical cup, banner mark, 3¼".......$12.00
Cutting board, 14x9½", +stainless steel knife.......$45.00
Dish, embossed flowers on bottom, w/handle, no mark, 5¾x4", from $20 to.......$30.00
Dish, lattice rim, braided handles, banner mark, 7½x5".......$40.00
Dish, leaf shape, banner mark, ¾x4".......$25.00
Dish, rim w/5 openweave sections alternating w/5 solid medallions, rectangular mark, 2¼x8".......$38.00
Dish, shell shape, 9x9½".......$45.00
Egg cup, double; rectangular mark, set of 8.......$50.00
Flowerpot, w/undertray, 3½", from $40 to.......$45.00
Fork, serving; 7½".......$35.00
Ginger jar, rectangular mark, 5".......$35.00
Ginger jar, rectangular mark, 7".......$50.00
Goblet, clear glass w/Blue Danube design, 7¼", set of 12, from $80 to.......$100.00
Gravy boat, banner mark, 3¼x5½", w/5½" L undertray.......$70.00
Gravy boat, double spout, w/undertray, rectangular mark, 7" L, from $35 to.......$40.00

Gravy boat, fancy handle, banner mark, 6½x9¾"................$45.00

Gravy boat, w/attached undertray, 3x8" L.........................$40.00

Hurricane lamp, glass mushroom globe........................$75.00

Ice bucket, plastic, from $25 to...................................$30.00

Ice cream scoop, cutting blade, no mark.......................$50.00

Inkstand, 2 lidded inserts, shaped base, banner mark, 9" L ..$300.00

Jam pot, straight sides, w/lid & underplate, rectangular mark,
    4x3"...$40.00

Jar, slender w/flare at rim, w/lid, banner mark, 7"...............$55.00

Jar, slender w/flare at rim, w/lid, banner mark, 9"...............$70.00

Mayonnaise, 5¾x7", from $55.00 to $65.00. (Photo courtesy Elaine France)

Mug, soup; 2⅞x4½", set of 4, from $55 to $70.00

Napkin rack, scalloped back, 3½x6½" L $165.00

Napkin rings, set of 4...$30.00

Napkins, Sunnyweave, set of 4, from $25 to.....................$30.00

Pie plate, 9"..$35.00

Pitcher, milk; 'Y' handle, 5¼", from $25 to.......................$30.00

Pitcher, syrup; tall & slim, banner mark, 5½x5½x3"............$25.00

Pitcher, waisted neck w/wide spout, scroll handle, banner mark,
    6½"...$60.00

Pitcher, waisted neck w/wide spout, scroll handle, rectangular mark,
    5¼", from $18 to..$22.00

Pitcher, water; waisted neck w/lg pouring spout, scroll handle, ban-
    ner mark, 8"...$125.00

Plate, banner mark, 8½", from $10 to $15.00

Plate, banner mark, 10¼", from $15 to $20.00

Plate, bread & butter; 6¾"...$6.00

Plate, collector; from $40 to..$48.00

Plate, cookie; 10", from $38 to.....................................$42.00

Plate, deviled egg; from $80 to.....................................$90.00

Plate, lattice rim, banner mark, 8" $50.00

Plate, lattice rim, banner mark, 10" $60.00

Plate, triangular, 9¾" L $35.00

Platter, banner mark, 12x8½" $65.00

Platter, banner mark, 14x10".......................................$85.00

Platter, banner mark, 16½" L, from $75 to......................$90.00

Platter, banner mark, 18½x13½", from $200 to................$240.00

Platter, rectangular mark, 12x8½", from $40 to................$50.00

Platter, rectangular mark, 14x10", from $50 to..................$65.00

Quiche dish, straight sides, white interior w/sm pattern in center,
    banner mark..$50.00

Reamer, 2-pc, from $35 to...$40.00

Relish, rectangular mark, 7¾", from $25 to......................$35.00

Relish, 2-part, rectangular mark, 7¼", from $25 to.............$35.00

Rolling pin, 16" L, from $75 to......................................$95.00

Salad servers, fork, 11¼", & spoon, 11½", pr $70.00

Salt & pepper shakers, cylindrical, rectangular mark, 3½", pr..$35.00

Salt & pepper shakers, dome top w/bud finial, bulbous bottom, ban-
    ner mark, 5", pr..$40.00

Salt box, wooden lid, 4¾x4¾", from $55 to $65.00

Server, 3-part w/'Y' handle, 11" L..................................$52.00

Snack plate & cup, banner mark, from $25 to...................$30.00

Soap dish, from $10 to..$14.00

Souffle, 7½", from $40 to...$50.00

Soup ladle, Lucky, 10"..$75.00

Spice rack, 8 jars in wooden rack, from $85 to $110.00

Spooner, 4¾x4"...$50.00

Sugar bowl, ovoid, w/lid, rectangular mark, 4x5"...............$22.00

Sugar bowl, w/lid, mini, from $20 to..............................$25.00

Sugar bowl, wide bowl w/'Y' handles, dome lid, banner mark,
    4x8" $50.00

Sugar bowl, wide bowl w/'Y' handles, rectangular mark, scarce,
    5x6" $35.00

Sweetmeat dish, 7½", from $35 to.................................$42.00

Tablecloth, 50x70", +4 napkins, unused $95.00

Tablecloth, 80x62", oval, EX...$50.00

Tablecloth, 100x60", EX...$65.00

Tazza, attached pedestal foot, banner mark, 4½x15", from $85
    to...$95.00

Tazza, lattice edge, ped foot, banner mark, 4x8" $65.00

Tea tile/trivet, 6", from $15 to......................................$20.00

Teakettle, enamel, wooden handle, w/fold-down metal sides,
    9x9½"..$25.00

Teapot, 'Y' handle, rectangular mark, 3⅜".......................$45.00

Teapot, 'Y' handle, rectangular mark, 6½".......................$60.00

Tidbit tray, 1-tier, banner mark, from $25 to....................$30.00

Tidbit tray, 2-tier, banner mark, from $45 to....................$55.00

Tidbit tray, 3-tier, banner mark, from $60 to....................$75.00

Toothbrush holder, from $15 to.....................................$18.00

Tray, oblong, 10¼", from $40 to....................................$45.00

Tray, rectangular, closed handles, slightly scalloped, rectangular
    mark, 14½x7"...$70.00

Tray, rectangular, pierced handles, 14½" $105.00

Tray, sq w/pierced handles, rectangular mark, 10"..............$50.00

Tray, sq w/2 open handles, 2 handle-like closed-in devices on oppos-
    ing sides, banner mark, 12½"......................................$125.00

Tray, sq w/2 open handles, 2 handle-like closed-in devices on oppos-
    ing sides, banner mark, 15½".....................................$225.00

Tray, 5-sided, 12", from $40 to......................................$50.00

Tumbler, china, 3⅜", from $8 to....................................$10.00

Tumbler, glass, 4"...$8.00

Tumbler, glass, 7½", set of 6 ....$60.00

Tureen, w/handles & lid, banner mark, 10x12" L, on 13x9½"
    tray...$200.00

Undertray, for soup tureen, from $50 to $55.00

Vase, bud; 6" **$30.00**
Vase, waisted neck, rectangular mark, 10", from $60 to **$85.00**

Blue Garland

During the 1960s and 1970s, this dinnerware was offered as premiums through grocery stores. Its ornate handles, platinum trim, the scalloped rims on the flat items, and the bases of the hollowware pieces when combined with the 'Haviland' backstamp suggested to most supermarket shoppers that they were getting high quality dinnerware for very little. And indeed the line was of good quality, but the company that produced it had no connection at all to the famous Haviland company of Limoges, France, who produced fine china there for almost 100 years. The mark is Johann Haviland, taken from the name of the founding company that later became Philip Rosenthal and Co. This was a German manufacturer who produced chinaware for export to the United States from the mid-1930s until well into the 1980s. Today's dinnerware collectors find the delicate wreath-like blue flowers and the lovely shapes very appealing.

This line may also be found with the Thailand–Johann Haviland backstamp, a later issue. Our values are for the dinnerware with the Bavarian backstamp. The Thailand line will usually sell for at least 30% less.

Bell, 5½x3¼" **$40.00**
Beverage server/coffeepot, 11", from $45 to **$55.00**
Bowl, coupe soup; 7⅝", from $8 to **$12.00**
Bowl, fruit; 5⅛" **$5.00**
Bowl, oval, scalloped rim, 10¾x7½" **$55.00**
Bowl, oval, 11¼", from $60 to **$75.00**
Bowl, vegetable; round, 8½" **$35.00**
Butter dish, ¼-lb, from $35 to **$50.00**
Butter pat/coaster, 3½" **$5.00**
Candlesticks, 1-light, 4", pr from $35 to **$45.00**
Casserole, metal, stick handle, w/lid, 3-qt, 8¼", from $35 to .. **$50.00**
Casserole, metal, tab handles, w/lid, 3-qt, from $20 to **$28.00**
Casserole, metal, w/lid, 4-qt, 9¾", from $40 to **$50.00**
Casserole, w/lid, 2½-qt, 6x9" **$60.00**
Casserole, 1½-qt, 5x8", from $60 to **$60.00**
Casserole soup tureen, w/lid, 11" wide, from $50 to **$60.00**
Clock plate **$25.00**

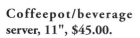

Coffeepot/beverage server, 11", $45.00.

Creamer, 9-oz, 4¼" **$15.00**
Cup & saucer, flat or footed **$5.00**
Fondue pot, w/lid, from $50 to **$65.00**
Goblet, glass, 6¾", set of 6 .... **$40.00**
Gravy boat, w/attached or separate underplate, 10" L, from $20 to **$30.00**
Nut dish, footed, w/handles **$30.00**
Plate, dinner; 10", from $7 to **$10.00**
Roaster, metal, oval, 13", from $50 to **$75.00**
Salt & pepper shakers, 4", pr **$22.00**
Saucepan, metal, w/lid, 1½-qt, 2 styles, ea from $30 to **$40.00**
Skillet, metal, w/lid, 8½", from $35 to **$45.00**
Sugar bowl, w/lid, 5½x7", from $18 to **$22.00**
Teapot, 7¾" **$60.00**
Tray, tidbit; 2-tier **$35.00**
Tray, tidbit; 3-tier **$45.00**

Blue Ridge Dinnerware

Blue Ridge has long been popular with collectors, and prices are already well established, but that's not to say there aren't a few good buys left around. There are! It was made by a company called Southern Potteries, who operated in Erwin, Tennessee, from sometime in the latter '30s until the mid-'50s. They made many hundreds of patterns, all hand decorated. Some collectors prefer to match up patterns, while others like to mix them together for a more eclectic table setting.

One of the patterns most popular with collectors (and one of the most costly) is called French Peasant. It's very much like Quimper with simple depictions of a little peasant man with his staff and a lady. But they also made many lovely floral patterns, and it's around these where most of the buying and selling activity is centered. You'll find roosters, plaids, and simple textured designs, and some vases in addition to the dinnerware.

Very few pieces of dinnerware are marked except for the 'china' or porcelain pieces which usually are. Watch for a similar type of ware often confused with Blue Ridge that is sometimes (though not always) marked Italy.

The values suggested below are for the better patterns. To evaluate the French Peasant line, double these figures; for the simple plaids and textures, deduct 25% to 50%, depending on their appeal.

Advisors: Bill and Betty Newbound (See Directory, Dinnerware)

Newsletter: *National Blue Ridge Newsletter*
Norma Lilly
144 Highland Dr., Blountsville, TN 37617

Baker, divided, 8x13", from $20 to **$25.00**
Basket, aluminum edge, 10" **$25.00**
Bonbon, flat shell, china **$75.00**
Bowl, cereal/soup; Premium, 6" **$20.00**
Bowl, cereal/soup; 6", from $18 to **$25.00**
Bowl, mixing; lg, from $25 to **$30.00**
Bowl, vegetable; oval, 98" **$30.00**
Box, cigarette; sq **$90.00**

Butter dish, Woodcrest..$500.00
Cake tray, Maple Leaf, china....................................$75.00
Carafe, w/lid..$45.00
Child's mug, from $150 to......................................$175.00
Child's plate...$40.00
Coffeepot, ovoid...$175.00

Coffeepot, Williamsburg Bouquet, decorated on both sides, footed, from $150.00 to $225.00. (Photo courtesy Betty and Bill Newbound)

Creamer, Fifties shape, from $15 to.........................$20.00
Creamer, regular...$95.00
Cup & saucer, regular..$20.00
Custard cup, from $18 to...$22.00
Egg cup, Premium...$60.00
Gravy boat...$30.00
Lamp, china, from $125 to.....................................$150.00
Lazy Susan, side pcs..$75.00
Pitcher, Antique, 3½"..$175.00

Pitcher, Chintz, Swirl shape, 6½", from $75.00 to $100.00. (Photo courtesy Betty and Bill Newbound)

Pitcher, Spiral, china, 4¼".....................................$220.00
Pitcher, Spiral, earthenware, 7", from $45 to............$55.00
Plate, Christmas Doorway..$95.00
Plate, dinner; Premium, 10½"..................................$40.00

Plate, Thanksgiving Turkey, from $75 to...................$90.00
Platter, regular, 15"..$55.00
Salt & pepper shakers, Blossom Top, pr....................$85.00
Salt & pepper shakers, Skyline, pr from $35 to...........$40.00
Snack tray, Martha, from $150 to...........................$175.00
Teapot, rope handle..$130.00
Tidbit tray, 3-tier..$55.00
Vase, handle, china..$100.00
Vase, ruffled top, china, 9½", from $95 to................$125.00

Blue Willow Dinnerware and Accessories

Blue Willow dinnerware has been made since the 1700s, first by English potters, then Japanese, and finally American companies as well. Tinware, glassware, even paper 'go-withs' have been produced over the years — some fairly recently, due to on-going demand. It was originally copied from the early blue and white wares made in Nanking and Canton in China. Once in awhile you'll see some pieces in black, pink, red, or even multicolor.

Obviously the most expensive will be the early English wares, easily identified by their backstamps. You'll be most likely to find pieces made by Royal or Homer Laughlin, and even though comparatively recent, they're still collectible, and their prices are very affordable.

For further study we recommend *Gaston's Blue Willow* by Mary Frank Gaston (Collector Books).

See also Royal China.

Advisor: Mary Frank Gaston

Butter dish, English mark, 3x8", from $150.00 to $175.00. (Photo courtesy Mary Frank Gaston)

Ashtray, sq, unmarked Japan, 7½", from $50 to..................$60.00
Bank, kitten figural, unmarked Japan, 9¼" L, from $325 to..$375.00
Biscuit jar, cane handle, octagonal, Gibson, 1912-30, 6½", from $250 to...$275.00
Bonbon, flat shell, from $55 to...$65.00
Bowl, salad; w/salad fork & spoon, unmarked Japan, from $150 to...$175.00
Bowl, soup/cereal; short pedestal foot, Japan, from $30 to...$40.00
Bowl, vegetable; pedestal foot, John Tams Ltd, after 1930, from $150 to...$175.00
Bowl, vegetable; variant center pattern, pictorial border, 10"..$25.00

56

Bowl, vegetable; w/lid, Japan, from $100 to......................$120.00
Butter dish, Buffalo China, after 1964, from $200 to........$250.00
Canisters, barrel shape, Japan, 4-pc set, from $450 to........$550.00
Carafe, w/warmer, Japan, from $250 to $300.00

Coffeepot, Burgess & Leigh, England, ca. 1930s, five-cup, from $40.00 to $50.00. (Photo courtesy Mary Frank Gaston)

Coffeepot, Josiah Wedgwood, 1970s-80s, from $100 to $125.00
Coffeepot, ovoid, from $150 to $175.00
Cup, chili; Japan, 3½x4" $50.00
Cup & saucer, demitasse; Japan, from $14 to $18.00
Egg cup, double, unmarked Japan, 4¼" $30.00
Egg cup, unmarked English, from $40 to $50.00
Ginger jar, porcelain, unmarked Japan, 5", from $50 to $60.00
Jardiniere, John Tams Ltd, after 1930, from $275 to $325.00
Jug, milk; Homer Laughlin, from $125 to $150.00
Match safe, Shenango, from $75 to $85.00
Mug, coffee; unmarked Japan, from $10 to $15.00
Plate, bread & butter; Barlow, 1930s, from $14 to $18.00
Plate, grill; Made in Poland, 10", from $25 to $35.00
Plate, smooth rim, Samuel Radford, 1928-38, 8", from $25 to ..$35.00
Platter, oval, Made in Occupied Japan, 12¼", from $100 to...$120.00
Relish, 5-compartment, Shenango, 9½" dia, from $50 to $60.00
Salt & pepper shakers, jug form, Japan, 3", pr from $40 to .$50.00
Salt & pepper shakers, wood & ceramic, unmarked, ca 1960s, 6", pr
  from $25 to $30.00
Spoon rest, double, Japan, 9", from $40 to $50.00
Tea set, Japan, stacking 2-cup pot+creamer & sugar bowl, from $150
  to $175.00
Teapot, musical base, unmarked Japan, from $130 to........$150.00
Teapot, unmarked Homer Laughlin, from $60 to...............$70.00
Trivet, ceramic in wrought-iron frame, Japan, from $40 to ..$50.00
Tumbler, ceramic, Japan, 3½", from $30 to $35.00
Tumbler, juice; glass, Jeannette, 3½" $12.00
Vase, porcelain, unmarked Japan, 5", from $60 to $70.00

Bookends

You'll find bookends in various types of material and designs. The more inventive their modeling, the higher the price. Also consider the material. Cast-iron examples, especially if in original polychrome paint, are bringing very high prices right now. Brass and copper are good as well, though elements of design may override the factor of materials altogether. If they are signed by the designer or marked by the manufacturer, you can boost the price. Those with a decidedly Art Deco appearance are often good sellers. The consistent volume of common to moderately uncommon bookends that are selling online has given the impression that some are more easily available than once thought. Hence, some examples have not increased in value. See *Collector's Guide to Bookends* by Louis Kuritzky and Charles De Costa (Collector Books) for more information.

Advisor: Louis Kuritzky (See Directory, Bookends)

Club: Bookend Collector Club
Louis Kuritzky
4510 NW 17th Pl. 7
Gainesville, FL 3260; 352-377-3193

Captain (at ship's wheel), iron, unmarked, ca 1925, 5" $125.00
Cupid & Psyche, gray metal, ca 1928, 4½" $125.00
Dancer (Deco) in Wreath, iron, #53, ca 1928, 5" $175.00
End of the Trail, gray metal, LV Aaronson 1925, 4¼" $95.00
Farmer Sowing, bronze, HMH (Austria), ca 1920, 4¼" $850.00
Flicka (horse), gray metal, attributed to Dodge, ca 1935, 6" ..$85.00

Flower Basket, painted cast iron, 7", EX, $500.00. (Photo courtesy LiveAuctioneers.com/Morphy Auctions)

Flyboy (Lindbergh), iron, ca 1928, 6" $175.00
Gazelle Leaping, iron, ca 1930, 5⅜" $90.00
Gnome in Library, gray metal on iron base, Bradley & Hubbard
  shopmark, ca 1924, 5" $195.00
I hear You, cute dog, gray metal, Nuart shopmark, ca 1925, 6" ...$150.00
Liberty Bell, iron, unmarked, ca 1925, 4¾" $40.00
Nude on One Knee, gray metal, Jennings Brothers, ca 1932, 7" .. $275.00
Ox Wagon, iron, red paint, #1849, ca 1931, 4" $65.00
Ready for War, gray metal w/multicolor headdress & decor, attrib-
  uted to Pompeian Bronze, ca 1932, 9½" $275.00
Shakespeare's Library, iron, Bradley & Hubbard shopmark, ca 1925,
  6⅛" $150.00
Shepherd (dog) on Log, gray metal on onyx base, ca 1930, 7"..$175.00

Temple of Saturn, iron, Bradley & Hubbard shopmark, ca 1925, 5½" **$110.00**
Thinker (Doric columns), gray metal, #103, ca 1930, 5½"..**$50.00**
Trumpeting Elephants, gray metal, ca 1930, 8¼"..............**$125.00**
Washington Profile, iron, unmarked, ca 1925, 4¼" **$50.00**
Well-Read Bird (owl on books), bronze-clad, attributed to Pompeian Bronze, ca 1922, 8½"...**$275.00**
Wheat (in shock), gray metal, Jennings Brothers, ca 1930, 6"...**$150.00**
Young Lincoln Profile, iron, EMIG #1568, ca 1925, 5⅞"....**$95.00**

**Nude With Tambourine, cast iron, Gift House, 1926, 5⅛",
$110.00.** (Photo courtesy Louis Kuritzky)

Books

Books have always fueled the imagination. Before television lured us out of the library into the TV room, everyone enjoyed reading the latest novels. Western, horror, and science fiction themes are still popular to this day — especially those by such authors as Louis L'Amour, Steven King, and Ray Bradbury, to name but a few. Edgar Rice Burrough's Tarzan series and L. Frank Baum's Wizard of Oz books are regarded as classics among today's collectors. A first edition of a popular author's first book (especially if it's signed) is avidly sought after, so is a book that 'ties in' with a movie or television program.

Dick and Jane readers are fast becoming collectible. If you went to first grade sometime during the 1930s until the mid-1970s, you probably read about their adventures. These books were used all over the United States and in military base schools over the entire world. They were published here as well as in Canada, the Philippine Islands, Australia, and New Zealand; there were special editions for the Roman Catholic parochial schools and the Seventh Day Adventists', and even today they're in use in some Mennonite and Amish schools.

On the whole, ex-library copies and book club issues (unless they are limited editions) have very low resale values.

Big Little Books

The Whitman Publishing Company started it all in 1933 when they published a book whose format was entirely different than any other. It was very small, easily held in a child's hand, but over an inch in thickness. There was a cartoon-like drawing on the right-hand page, and the text was printed on the left. The idea was so well accepted that very soon other publishers — Saalfield, Van Wiseman, Lynn, World Syndicate, and Goldsmith — cashed in on the idea as well. The first Big Little Book hero was Dick Tracy, but soon every radio cowboy, cartoon character, lawman, and space explorer was immortalized in his own adventure series.

When it became apparent that the pre-teen of the '50s preferred the comic-book format, Big Little Books were finally phased out; but many were saved in boxes and stored in attics, so there's still a wonderful supply of them around. You need to watch condition carefully when you're buying or selling.

Club: Big Little Book Collectors Club of America
Newsletter: *Big Little Times*
Larry Lowery
P.O. Box 1242, Danville, CA 94526
www.biglittlebooks.com

Alice in Wonderland, Featuring Charlotte Henry as Alice, #659, 1933, VG...**$35.00**
Apple Mary & Dennie's Luck Apples, #1403, 1939, VG **$20.00**

Believe It or Not,
**#760, 1931, EX+,
$35.00.**

Blaze Brandon With the Foreign Legion, #1447, 1938, EX ..**$35.00**
Buck Rogers & the Planetoid Plot, #1197, EX+ **$125.00**
Desert Eagle Rides Again, #1458, 1939, EX+ **$35.00**
Donald Duck Lays Down the Law, #1449, 1948, VG+ **$50.00**
Frank Merriwell at Yale, #1121, 1935, EX **$35.00**
Gulliver's Travels, #1172, 1939, VG....................................**$65.00**
Jim Hardy Ace Reporter, #1180, 1940, VG+ **$25.00**
Little Lord Fauntleroy, #1598, 1936, EX **$35.00**
Phantom & the Girl of Mystery, #1416, 1947, VG **$30.00**
Shirley Temple in the Littlest Rebel, #115, 1935, VG..........**$35.00**
Tarzan & the Jewels of Opar, #1495, 1941, VG **$30.00**
Uncle Wiggily's Adventures, #1405, 1946, VG **$30.00**

Children's Miscellaneous Books

Bear's Storytime Favorites, Simon Spotlight, hardcover, 2002, M...**$10.00**
Bertie & the Big Red Ball, Beryl Cook & Edward Lucie-Smith, hardback, 1982, EX+ **$18.00**

Brother & Sister's Vacation, Josephine Lawrence, Julia Green illustrations, Cupples & Leon, 1922, EX w/dust jacket...........**$18.00**

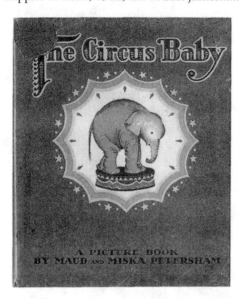

The Circus Baby, **Maud and Miska Petersham, MacMillan, full-page color pictures, hardcover, 1950, $20.00 (with dust jacket, $40.00).** (Photo courtesy Diane McClure Jones and Rosemary Jones)

Cranberry Halloween, Wendy & Harry Devlin, Four Winds Press, hardcover, 1982, EX **$15.00**

Dean's Book of Fairy Tales, Grahame & Johnston, Playmore Inc, hardcover, 1977, EX+ **$18.00**

Ding Dong Dell, Geraldine Clyne, Mother Goose Playhouse Series, pop-ups, paper cover, EX.............................**$25.00**

Donald Duck & His Cat Troubles, Walt Disney Productions, Whitman, hardcover, 1948, 96 pages, VG **$18.00**

Dr Goat, Georgiana & Charles Clement, hardcover, Whitman, 1950, NM **$65.00**

Franklin & Harriet, Paulette Bourgeois & Branda Clark, hardcover, M...**$16.00**

Fuzzy Wuzzy Kitten, **Whitman, oversize square eight-page picture book, EX+, from $20.00 to $25.00.** (Photo courtesy Diane McClure Jones and Rosemary Jones)

Kerry the Fire-Engine Dog, Rand McNally Elf Book, Frank Lewis & Alfred J Corchia, 1951 edition, EX....................**$36.00**

Little Black Sambo, Helen Bannerman, Watty Piper, Platt & Munk, cloth hardcover, 1972, NM............................**$24.00**

Little Black Sambo, Whitman Tell-A-Tale, hardback, copyright 1959, EX **$65.00**

Little Squeegy Bug, Storytelling Time w/Aunt Mary, Bernard H Martin & William I Martin, softcover, 1945, VG.........**$30.00**

Miss Suzy, Miriam Young, Arnold Lobel, Parents Magazine Press, 1964 original edition, NM **$27.50**

Mistress Mary, Geraldine Clyne, Mother Goose Playhouse Series, pop-ups, paper cover, EX.............................**$25.00**

Mother Goose, Rand McNally Junior Elf Book, 1946, EX..**$15.00**

Peter Rabbit, Beatrix Potter, linen-like paper, 1st edition, softcover, 1936, EX+ **$245.00**

Pied Piper of Hamlin, The; Robert Browning, Hope Dunlap illustrations, hardback, 1928, EX **$35.00**

Plant Sitter, Gene Zion, Margaret Bloy Graham, softcover, 1979, G..**$12.50**

Popcorn, A Frank Asch Bear Story; Parents Magazine Original, hardcover, 1979, EX **$15.00**

Private Buck, Clyde Lewis, Rand McNally, 1940s, EX w/dust jacket **$20.00**

Puppy Who Found a Boy, Wonder Book, 1951, VG **$10.00**

Puss in Boots, A Linen-Like Story Book, Artcraft logo, ca 1960s, EX **$38.00**

Pussy Willow, Whitman Tell-A-Tale, hardcover, 1948, EX...**$17.00**

Rag-Doll Jane, Fern Bisel Peat, Saalfield, hardcover, 1935, EX w/ dust jacket **$40.00**

Rufus, Tomi Ungerer, Harper Collins, hardcover, 1961, 1st edition, 31 pages, EX w/dust jacket **$38.00**

Sing a Song of Sixpence, Geraldine Clyne, Mother Goose Playhouse Series, pop-ups, paper cover, VG.....................**$18.00**

Skippy & Others, Mary Macintyre, Georgette Berkmans illustrations, MacMillan, hardcover, 1944, EX **$27.50**

Socks for Supper, Jack Kent, Parent's Magazine Press, hardcover, 1978, NM **$18.00**

Soldier Boy, Tony Sarge, Felicite Lefevre, hardcover, 1926, VG **$15.00**

Their Merry-Go-Round, Ima L Kuykendall & Mona V Kuykendall Harding, Macmillan Co, 1941 1st edition, EX.............**$45.00**

Three Bears, Whitman Big Tell-A-Tale, 1965, EX...............**$20.00**

Three Little Animals, Margaret Wise Brown, Garth Williams illustrations, Harper & Brothers, 1956, VG **$50.00**

Through the Gate, edited by Olive Beaupre Miller, My Book House #4, hardcover, 1960, NM **$14.00**

Tim Tyler in the Jungle, Lyman Young, board book w/pop-ups, Pleasure Books, 1935, VG **$50.00**

Tom Swift & His War Tank, Victor Appleton, Grosset & Dunlap, pictorical cover, 1919, G..**$15.00**

Watermelon Pete, Elizabeth Gordon & Clara Powers Wilson, Rand McNally & Co, hardback, 1937, EX **$30.00**

What Do You See?, Hampton Publishing Co, Chicago, printed cloth, 1965, 5x7½" w/pinked edges **$7.50**

Where the Wild Things Are, M Sendak, Harper Collins, hardcover, 1988, w/dust jacket, NM................................**$10.00**

Wiggles Big Red Car, Grosset & Dunlap, hardcover, 2003, M ...**$10.00**

Juvenile Series Books

Air Service Boys Flying for France, CA Beach, Saalfield reprint, EX..**$10.00**

Air Service Boys Flying for France, Charles Beach, 1919, EX w/dust jacket **$20.00**

Amelia Bedelia, Peggy Parish, Harper & Row, Weekly Reader Book Club, 1963, pictorial hardcover, EX w/dust jacket........**$35.00**

Automobile Girls at Newport, Laura Crane, Altemus, 1910, VG..**$10.00**

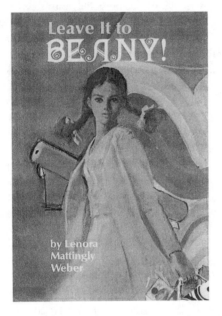

Beanie Malone Series, *Leave It to Beany!,* **Lenora Mattingly Weber, 1950s, first edition with dust jacket, EX+, $225.00; later print with dust jacket, EX+, $25.00.** (Photo courtesy Diane McClure Jones and Rosemary Jones

Beverly Gray on a Treasure Hunt, Grosset & Dunlap, 1938 1st edition, dark green cloth cover, VG **$25.00**

Beverly Gray on a World Cruise, Clair Bank, Grosset, hardcover, EX **$10.00**

Beverly Gray's Island Mystery, Clair Blank, McLoughlin Bros, Grosset & Dunlap, hardcover, 1952, EX **$25.00**

Black Stallion, Walter Farley, Random House, 1941, 1st edition, hardcover, EX w/dust jacket....................................**$25.00**

Bob Flame in Death Valley, Dorr Yeager, cloth-over-board cover, 1937, EX **$20.00**

Boy Troopers on the Trail, Clair W Hayes, AL Burt, ca 1920, cloth-over-board cover, EX...**$15.00**

Camp Fire Girls at Top o' the World, M Sanderson, Reilly & Briton, hardcover, 1916, EX **$20.00**

Cathy & Carl Captured, D Grunbock Johnston, Scripture Press, illustrated hardcover, 1954, EX....................................**$10.00**

Cherry Ames Student Nurse, Helen Wells, Grosset & Dunlap, pictoral cover, 1943, EX...**$10.00**

Daddy Takes Us Hunting Flowers, H Garis, Donohue, paste-on-pictorial cover, 1920s, EX **$35.00**

Eight Cousins, Louisa May Alcott, Junior Deluxe Edition, Doubleday, hardcover, 1948, EX **$10.00**

Flying Wheels Return to Daytona, WE Butterworth, Grosset & Dunlap, pictorial hardcover, 1960s, EX **$15.00**

Henry Huggins, Beverly Cleary, Morrow, hardcover, 1950, EX..**$10.00**

Jack Lightfoot Trapped, Maxwell Stevens, Street & Smith, New Medal Library reprint, EX **$20.00**

Koko King of Arctic Trail, Basil W Miller, Zondervan, hardcover, 1947, EX w/dust jacket..**$15.00**

Little Women, Louisa May Alcott, Orchard House Edition, Little Brown, hardcover, ca 1936, EX w/dust jacket...............**$35.00**

Meg & the Disappearing Diamonds, HB Walker, Whitman, pictorial hardcover, EX **$15.00**

Mysterious Half Cat, Judy Bolton Mystery, Margaret Sutton, Grosset & Dunlap, hardover, 1936, w/dust jacket, EX.............**$35.00**

Nancy Pembroke in New Orleans, M Van Epps, World, hardcover, 1930, EX w/dust jacket..**$30.00**

Our Little Friends of China, Frances Carpenter, 2-color illustrations, hardcover, ca 1931, EX..**$15.00**

Princess Polly at School, Amy Brooks, undated AL Burt reprint, cloth-over-board cover, EX..**$15.00**

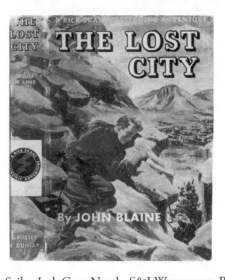

Rick Brant Adventure Series, *The Lost City,* **John Blain, Grosset & Dunlap, 1947, hardcover with early dust jacket (lists itself), EX+, $40.00.** (Photo courtesy Diane McClure Jones and Rosemary Jones)

Sailor Jack Goes North, S&J Wasserman, Benific Press, hardcover, ca 1960, EX **$10.00**

Sandra of the Girl Orchestra, RL Radford, Lise Fomenko illustrations, Whitman, 1946, EX..**$16.00**

Ted Scott Battling the Wind, Franklin Dixon, Grosset & Dunlap, hardcover, EX w/dust jacket..**$25.00**

Three Two Pitch, Bronc Burnett Story; Wilfred McCormick, Grosset & Dunlap, 1958, EX w/dust jacket **$22.00**

Wizard of Oz, L Frank Baum, Whitman Famous Classics, 1957, EX **$17.50**

Wonderful Story of Lincoln, CM Stevens, Inspiration Series of Patriotic Americans, Cupples & Leon, 1917, EX..........**$18.00**

Little Golden Books

Everyone has had a few of these books in their lifetime; some we've read to our own children so many times that we still know them word for word, and today they're appearing in antique malls and shops everywhere. The first were printed in 1942. These are recognizable by their blue paper spines (later ones had gold foil). Until the early 1970s, they were numbered consecutively; after that they were unnumbered.

First editions of the titles having a 25¢ or 29¢ cover price can be identified by either a notation on the first or second pages, or a letter on the bottom right corner of the last page (A for 1, B for 2, etc.). If these are absent, you probably have a first edition.

Condition is extremely important. To qualify as mint, these books must look just as good as they looked the day they were purchased. Naturally, having been used by children, many show signs of wear. If your book is only lightly soiled, the cover has no tears or scrapes, the inside pages have only small creases or folded corners, and the spine is still strong, it will be worth about half as much as one in mint condition. Additional damage would of course lessen the value even more. A missing cover makes it worthless.

A series number containing an 'A' refers to an activity book, while a 'D' number identifies a Disney story.

For more information we recommend *Collecting Little Golden Books* by Steve Santi (who provided us with our narrative material).

Bible Stories of Boys & Girls, retold by Jane Werner, A edition, 1953, EX **$12.50**
Country Mouse & City Mouse, #426, A edition, EX **$16.00**
Deep Blue Sea, A edition, 1958, NM **$16.00**
Frosty the Snow Man, retold by Annie North Bedford, #142, Y edition, 1974 printing, EX **$10.00**
Fury, A edition, 1957, EX...**$16.00**
Good Humor Man, Kathleen N Daly, Tibor Gergely illustrations, #550, A edition, EX......................................**$18.00**
Guess Who Lives Here, Louise Woodcock, Eloise Wilkin illustrations, A edition, 1949, EX **$22.00**
How To Tell Time, #285, A edition, 1957, EX **$24.00**
Howdy Doody & Clarabell, C edition, 1951, EX.................**$20.00**
Huckleberry Hound Builds a House, B edition, 1959, EX ..**$25.00**
Jingle Bells, #553, D edition, 1973, EX...............................**$7.00**
Lively Little Rabbit, Ariane, Tenggren illustrations, #15, E edition, 1943, NM **$30.00**
Lively Little Rabbit, J edition, 1950, VG **$12.00**
Mickey Mouse & Great Lot Plot, D edition, 1974, NM **$9.00**

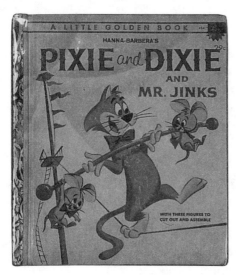

Pixie and Dixie and Mr. Jinks, **EX+, from $12.00 to $18.00.**

Riddles Riddles From A to Z, A edition, 1962, EX.............**$16.00**
Roy Rogers & Cowboy Toby, A edition, 1954, VG+............**$38.00**
Scuffy the Tugboat, Gertrude Crampton, B edition, copyrights 1946 & 1955, EX..**$10.00**
Suprise for Mickey Mouse, A edition, 1971, EX.................**$15.00**

Walt Disney's Paul Revere, copyright 1957, 2nd printing from 1975, EX **$22.00**
Walt Disney's Peter & the Wolf, C edition, copyright dates 1946 & 1947, EX **$30.00**

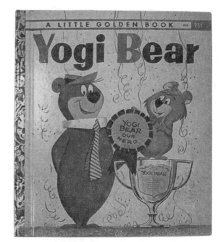

Yogi Bear, **ca. 1960s, from $9.00 to $12.00.**

Movie and TV Tie-Ins

Child Star, Shirley Temple Black, McGraw-Hill, 1988, 1st printing, EX w/dust jacket..**$25.00**
Decision Before Dawn (Call It Treason), George Howe, 20th Century Fox, paperback, EX...**$5.00**

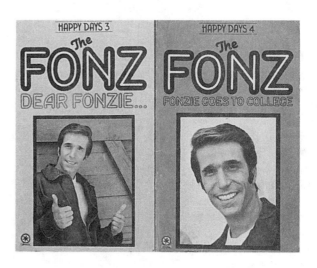

Happy Days The Fonz, **Universal, 1977, #3 and #4 pictured, EX+, from $10.00 to $15.00.** (Photo courtesy Greg Davis and Bill Morgan)

Happy Trails, Story of Roy Rogers & Dale Evans; Carlton Stowers, Guideposts Edition, 1978, EX w/dust jacket **$25.00**
In Starring Roles, Shirley Temple, ca 1934, softcover, 12 pages, 7¾x6½", EX **$45.00**
Joy of a Peanuts Christmas, Hallmark Books, 2000 1st edition, NM...**$48.00**
Little Minister, Katharine Hepburn cover, Engel-van Wiseman Inc, 5 Star Little Book, RKO-Radio Pictures, EX **$25.00**
Marilyn the Classic, Norman Mailer, photo book, hardback, 1st edition, EX w/dust jacket **$45.00**

M*A*S*H, Richard Hooker, Pocket Books, 20th Century Fox, 1970, VG...**$6.00**

Mrs Miniver, Special 1940 Edition w/movie-theme dust jacket, EX+ **$10.00**

One Flew Over the Cuckoo's Nest, Ken Kersey, Movie Edition, Nicholson paperback on cover, EX **$6.00**

Phantom Menace Movie Storybook, Random House, 1999, paperback, EX **$8.00**

Poor Little Rich Girl, Grosset & Dunlap, 20th Century Fox, Shirley Temple softcover, 1936, EX **$36.00**

Star Trek III Search for Spock Storybook, L Weinberg, picture book, 1984 1st edition, EX...................................**$10.00**

Tale of South Pacific, Thana Skouras, Lehmann, NY, 1958, movie theme cover, EX...**$22.00**

This 'n That, Bette Davis; Michael Herskowitz, 1st edition, hardcover, EX **$10.00**

Tony & His Pals (w/chapter by Tom Mix), Junior Press Books, Whitman, 1938 2nd printing, pictorial hardback, EX ..**$49.00**

Walt Disney's Mary Poppins, Walt Disney Productions, 1964, Julie Andrews on softcover, EX **$28.00**

Walt Disney's Souvenir Music Album Book Snow White & 7 Dwarfs, black & white illustrations, for guitar, 1938, EX.........**$195.00**

Bottle Openers

A figural bottle opener is one where the cap lifter is an actual feature of the subject being portrayed — for instance, the bill of a pelican or the mouth of a four-eyed man. Most are made of painted cast iron or aluminum; others were chrome or brass plated. Some of the major bottle-opener producers were Wilton, John Wright, L&L, and Gadzik. They have been reproduced, so beware of any examples with 'new' paint. Condition of the paint is an important consideration when it comes to evaluating a vintage opener.

For more information, read *Figural Bottle Openers, Identification Guide,* by the Figural Bottle Opener Collectors. Several of the examples we list sold recently at a major auction in the East; though they are seldom seen outside mature collections, we've included some of them along with the more common ones. Unless noted otherwise, our values are for examples in excellent original condition.

Club: Figural Bottle Opener Collectors
Newsletter: *Just for Openers*
John Stanley, Editor
P.O. Box 64, Chapel Hill, NC 27514
www.just-for-openers.org

Alligator, painted cast iron, huge jaws (opener), G.............**$150.00**

Amish boy, red shirt, black hat & short trousers w/suspenders, feet wide apart, cast iron, Wilton, NM..............................**$235.00**

Bear head, brown w/red & black details, painted cast iron, F-426, wall mount..**$135.00**

Beer drinker, mustached man in blue suit & white apron that ties in back (opener), cast iron, rare, 5½", NM **$635.00**

Billy goat, painted cast iron, John Wright, 2¾x2¾" **$85.00**

Caddy, brass, F-44 ....**$300.00**

Canadian goose, painted cast iron, Wilton, 1¾x3⅝", G.....**$140.00**

Canvas-back duck, standing, red neck & breast, white body w/blue wings, opener in base, cast iron, 2⅞" **$225.00**

Cat, brass, F-95, 2¼x3" **$40.00**

Cathy Coed, girl stands w/stack of books on ea shoulder, cast iron, L&L Favors, repainted, 4½", G **$345.00**

Cocker spaniel, standing w/right leg raised, black & white, cast iron, John Wright, 3¾" L, G **$150.00**

Cowboy (drunk) by cactus, painted cast iron, John Wright, 3¾x2⅝" **$165.00**

Cowboy w/guitar, painted cast iron, John Wright, 4¾x3⅛"..**$165.00**

Dodo bird, black w/red crest, yellow feathers & lg open beak (opener), painted cast iron, John Wright, 2¼", G **$250.00**

Dragon, cast iron w/green paint, F-195, 5"........................**$225.00**

Duck head, cast iron w/pewter finish, marked Ducky, ca 1920s, 4¾x2¼" **$110.00**

False teeth, painted cast iron, F-420, 3½x2½" **$85.00**

Fish, abolone shells cover body, F-164, 5¾", NM..............**$75.00**

Fish (Flat Fish), green dorsal fin, yellow body shading to red, opener behind lower fin, cast iron, 3¾" L, G **$150.00**

Fish w/tail up, painted cast iron, John Wright, 1¼x4⅝".....**$165.00**

Labrador retriever, painted zinc, Scott Prod Inc, 4x5" **$55.00**

Lady beside lamppost w/rolling pin, painted cast iron, F-7, 4" ...**$40.00**

Minor Kaier's Special Beer, Mahonoy City PA, painted cast iron, F-405 ....**$285.00**

Mr Dry, man w/'pierced' ears, long face, down-turned mouth, in top hat, painted cast iron, Wilton, 5½"............................**$100.00**

Palm tree, painted cast iron, John Wright, 4¼x2¼" **$195.00**

Parrot, brass, F-110, 4¾" **$45.00**

Parrot, plain stand, painted cast iron, John Wright, F-108, 5½"...**$45.00**

Parrot on high perch w/openwork vines (opener), painted cast iron, 4⅝", NM **$635.00**

Parrot w/lg open beak (opener), painted cast iron, Wilton, sm, VG **$35.00**

Patty Pep Cheerleader, painted cast iron, L&L Favors, 4", EX, $700.00. (Photo courtesy LiveAuctioneers.com/Morphy Auctions)

Pelican, white w/huge orange upper beak (opener), green base, painted cast iron, 3⅜", VG **$220.00**

Pretzel, painted cast iron, F-230, 1930-50, 3½" wide **$40.00**

Rooster, painted cast iron, opener in tail feathers, Wilton, VG....**$40.00**

Rooster, very long neck, tail fanned, leafy base (opener), painted cast iron, John Wright, VG.....................**$225.00**

Sailor, painted aluminum, F-18, VG.....................**$235.00**

Sea horse, upright, opener behind, cast iron w/light green paint, John Wright, 4¼".....................**$220.00**

Seagull, painted cast iron, 3¼x2¾".....................**$195.00**

Skull, black & white, cast iron, F-423.....................**$345.00**

Skunk, painted cast iron, 1940s, 2¼x3".....................**$125.00**

Trout fish, painted cast iron, Wilton, 3⅝x4⅞".....................**$280.00**

Washer woman standing by lamppost, metal w/copper patina, 1950s, 4".....................**$120.00**

Woman's shoe, aluminum, F-208, 1982 club pc, M..........**$180.00**

Boyd Crystal Art Glass

After the Degenhart glass studio closed (see the Degenhart section for information), it was bought out by the Boyd family, who added many of their own designs to the molds they acquired from the Degenharts, and other defunct glasshouses. They are located in Cambridge, Ohio, and the glass they've been pressing in more than 350 colors they've developed since they opened in 1978. It is marked with their 'B in diamond' logo. All the work is done by hand, and each piece is made in a selected color in limited amounts — a production run lasts only about 12 weeks or less. Items in satin glass or an exceptional slag are especially collectible, so are those with hand-painted details, commanding as much as 30% more.

Beware: Boyd has recently reissued some of the closed issues, confusing the pricing structure as well as collectors.

Bunny Salt, Bermuda Slag.....................$18.50

Bunny Salt, Columbia Green.....................$16.00

Bunny Salt, English Yew, 1983.....................$25.00

Chick Salt, Candy Swirl, 1st series.....................$68.00

Chick Salt, Firefly (vaseline), 1st series.....................$30.00

Chick Salt, Furr Green, 1st series.....................$30.00

Chick Salt, Impatient, 1st series.....................$35.00

Chick Salt, Snow, 1st series.....................$65.00

Chick Salt, Willow Blue, 1st series.....................$30.00

Child's mug, embossed peacock, blue opalescent, 2½", $15.00.

Duke Scottie Dog, Cobalt Carnival, 2⅜".....................$20.00

Gypsy Pot, Cobalt Blue.....................$17.50

Heart Jewel Box, Apricot, 1979.....................$25.00

Heart Jewel Box, Flame, 1981.....................$32.00

Hen on Nest Covered Dish, Banana Cream.....................$20.00

Hen on Nest Covered Dish, Impatient, #17, 1980.....................$32.00

Hen on Nest Covered Dish, Olde Ivory.....................$30.00

Hen on Nest Covered Dish, Royal Plum Carnival.....................$20.00

JB Scottie Dog, Grape Swirl.....................$22.00

JB Scottie Dog, March Carnival, 2007.....................$22.00

JB Scottie Dog, Nutmeg, #47.....................$15.00

JB Scottie Dog, Sunburst.....................$28.00

Jeremy Frog, Vaseline Carnival, 1978.....................$24.00

Joey Horse, Candy Swirl.....................$20.00

Joey Horse, Cobalt Blue.....................$16.00

Joey Horse, December Swirl Slag, #20, 1982.....................$56.00

Joey Horse, Ebony, #33, 1984.....................$50.00

Joey Horse, Golden Delight, #19, 1982.....................$30.00

Joey Horse, Impatient, #6, 1980.....................$32.00

Joey Horse, Indian Orange, #82, 1985.....................$58.00

Joey Horse, Rubina, #48, 1985.....................$130.00

Joey Horse, Zack Boyd Slag, #7, 1980.....................$30.00

Kitten on Pillow, Apricot, #21, 1979.....................$20.00

Kitten on Pillow, Cobalt Blue, #40, 1981.....................$40.00

Kitten on Pillow, Mardi Gras, #36, 1981.....................$28.00

Kitten on Pillow, Rubina Slag.....................$50.00

Louise Colonial Lady Doll, Christmas Red w/hand-painted decor, 1984.....................$15.00

Louise Colonial Lady Doll, Snow w/hand-painted decor, 1982..$16.00

Owl, Bermuda Red, #67, 1984.....................$15.00

Owl, Black Walnut, #1, 1979.....................$15.00

Owl, Dark Chocolate Slag, #21, 1980.....................$15.00

Owl, December Swirl Slag, #45, 1982.....................$20.00

Owl, Delphinium Blue Slag, #33, 1981.....................$30.00

Owl, Green Applemint Slag, #152.....................$14.00

Owl, Olde Lyme Carnival, #74, 1985.....................$24.00

Owl, Zack Boyd Slag, #28, 1980.....................$15.00

Pooche, Apricot Slag, 328, 1979.....................$30.00

Pooche, Aruba Slag, #128.....................$12.50

Pooche, Columbia Green, #147.....................$14.00

Pooche, Delphinium Blue, #44, 1981.....................$30.00

Pooche, Frosty Blue, #12, 1979.....................$30.00

Pooche, Hokey Pokey, #161.....................$13.00

Pooche, Magic Marble, #37, 1980.....................$30.00

Pooche, Rubina, #21, 1979.....................$30.00

Tramp shoe, Bermuda slag or deep purple, ca. 1985, 3", $15.00 each.

Zack Elephant, Green & White Slag.................................$20.00
Zack Elephant, Indian Orange, #39, 1985.........................$30.00
1963 Corvette Coupe, Nutmeg Carnival, 1999, 3½"..........$22.50
1963 Corvette Coupe, Salmon, 2002, 3½" $20.00

Brastoff, Sascha

Who could have predicted when Sascha Brastoff joined the Army's Air Force in 1942 that he was to become a well-known artist! It was during his service with the Air Force that he became interested in costume and scenery design, performing, creating Christmas displays and murals, and drawing war bond posters.

After Sascha's stint in the Armed Forces, he decided to follow his dream of producing ceramics and in 1947 opened a small operation in West Los Angeles, California. Just six years later, along with Nelson Rockefeller and several other businessmen with extensive knowledge of mass production techniques, he built a pottery on Olympic Boulevard in Los Angeles.

Brastoff designed all the products while supervising approximately 150 people. His talents were so great they enabled him to move with ease from one decade to another and successfully change motifs, mediums, and designs as warranted. Unusual and varying materials were used over the years. He created a Western line that was popular in the 1940s and early 1950s. Just before the poodle craze hit the nation in the 1950s, he had the forsight to introduce his poodle line. The same was true for smoking accessories, and he designed elegant, hand-painted dinnerware as well. He was not modest when it came to his creations. He knew he was talented and was willing to try any new endeavor which was usually a huge success.

Items with the Sascha Brastoff full signature are always popular, and generally they command the highest prices. He modeled obelisks; one with a lid and a full signature would be regarded as a highly desirable example of his work. Though values for his dinnerware are generally lower than for his other productions, it has its own following. The Merbaby design is always high on collectors' lists.

The 1940 Clay Club pieces were signed either with a full signature or 'Sascha.' In 1947 Sascha hired a large group of artists to hand decorate his designs, and 'Sascha B' became the standard mark. Following the opening of his studio in 1953, a chanticleer, the name Sascha Brastoff, the copyright symbol, and a handwritten style number (all in gold) were used on the bottom, with 'Sascha B.' on the front or topside of the item. (Be careful not to confuse this mark with a full signature, California, U.S.A.). Costume designs at 20th Century Fox (1946 – 1947) were signed 'Sascha'; war bonds and posters also carried the signature 'Sascha' and 'Pvt.' or 'Sgt. Brastoff.'

After Brastoff left his company in 1962, the mark became a 'R' in a circle (registered trademark symbol) with a style number, all handwritten. The chanticleer may also accompany this mark. Brastoff died on February 4, 1993. For additional information consult *Collector's Encyclopedia of California Pottery* by Jack Chipman. It is available from Collector Books.

Ashtray, Fancy Peacock, turquoise, gray, white & gold, 2½x5½x5½" $20.00
Ashtray, gold-washed domed shape w/black interior, 3 rests at opening in side, footed, 6½x6" $35.00

Ashtray, Poodle Dog, blue w/gold rhinestones, 2⅜x5½x5¼" ..$35.00
Ashtray, Star Steed, gold & silver on white, free from, 17½x9" ...$40.00

Bowl, ballerina, signed Sascha B, 2¼x10", from $100.00 to $125.00. (Photo courtesy Jack Chipman)

Candleholder, amber resin w/diamond-like geometric carvings, 10", ea $35.00
Candleholder, red resin totem pole w/genie-like face, 10⅛x4x4½", ea $150.00
Candleholder, red resin w/carved diamond-shaped geometrics, 7¾", ea $35.00
Candy/dresser box, exotic bird w/gold plumage on gray to black on lid, black glossy base, 6¾" L $60.00
Cigarette/pin box, Star Steed, gold & silver on white, ¾x9x4¼".$40.00
Creamer, Surf Ballet, turquoise & silver $30.00
Dish, Oriental landscape on white shading to gray to black along rim, #C2, 2x7x5½" $38.00
Dish/bowl, Minos line, textured modernist figure on black matt, 3-footed, 8¾" L $60.00

Figurine, cat, amber resin, 10", $425.00.
(Photo courtesy lifeofrileycollectiques.net)

Figurine, elephant, white w/gold, blue & black decor, Sascha B on backside & SB on tummy, 7x8"................................$215.00
Figurine, owl, blue resin, 7½", from $125 to $140.00

Figurine, owl, blue resin, 14⅝", from $300 to $350.00

Figurine, seal, sea green resin, 7½x9", from $190 to $240.00

Jar, striped egg form w/lid, #044B, 11"............................$125.00

Mugs, colorful leaves on gray to teal green, angular handle, 5", set of 4 ....$50.00

Outlet cover plate, gold & brown stone-like apperance, signed Sascha Brastoff, 1978, set of 4.....................................$150.00

Painting, cherub w/flowers, pastels, signed Sascha Brastoff 60, 24x17", +simple frame...$125.00

Pipe, leaves, multicolor on white to dark gray at rim, ...$25.00

Planter, Prancing Horse, brown & white w/gold trim, #030, 5¼x10x5" $50.00

Planter, vertical bands & stripes, multicolor w/gold fish & squiggles, #030, 5¼x10⅜x4⅞"...$70.00

Plate, abstract design in blue tones w/gold, factory hook on back, 1960s, 11¾"...$60.00

Plate, cowboy/Western symbols, multicolor, signed & inscribed, 11¾"...$65.00

Sugar bowl, Surf Ballet, turquoise & silver, w/lid.................$35.00

Teapot, Surf Ballet, turquoise & silver, 10¼" L, NM...........$30.00

Vase, horizontal stripes, gold, teal & ivory w/crackle, cylindrical, 8½x3¾", NM..$25.00

Vase, Minos line, textured modernist figure on black matt, slim, 19¾"...$170.00

Vase, Rooftops, multicolor on black gloss, 5½x4"..............$100.00

Wall plaque, Sun Face, green painted plaster, 1970s, 6⅜" dia, NM...$85.00

Brayton Laguna

This company's products have proven to be highly collectible for those who appreciate their well-made, diversified items, some bordering on the whimsical. Durlin Brayton founded Brayton Laguna Pottery in 1927. The marriage between Durlin and Ellen (Webb) Webster Grieve a few years later created a partnership that brought together two talented people with vision and knowledge so broad that they were able to create many unique lines. At the height of Brayton's business success, the company employed over 125 workers and 20 designers.

Durlin's personally created items command a high price. Such items are hand-turned, and those that were made from 1927 to 1930 are often incised 'Laguna Pottery' in Durlin's handwriting. These include cups, saucers, plates of assorted sizes, ashtrays, etc., glazed in eggplant, lettuce green, purple, and deep blue as well as other colors. Brayton Laguna's children's series (created by Lietta J. Dodd) has always been favored among collectors. However, many lines such as Calasia (artware), Blackamoors, sculpture, and the Hillbilly line are picking up large followings of their own. The sculptures, Indian and Peruvian pieces including voodoo figures, matadors, and drummers, among others, were designed by Carol Safholm. Andy Anderson created the Hillbilly series, most notably the highly successful shotgun wedding group. He also created the calf, bull, and cow set, which is virtually always found in the purple glaze, though very rarely other colors have been reported as well. Webton Ware is a good line for those who want inexpensive pottery and a Brayton Laguna mark. These pieces depict farmland and country-type themes such as farm-

ers planting, women cooking, etc. Some items — wall pockets, for instance — may be found with only a flower motif; wall hangings of women and men are popular, yet hard to find in this or any of Brayton's lines. Predominantly, the background of Webton Ware is white, and it's decorated with various pastel glazes including yellow, green, pink, and blue.

More than 10 marks plus a paper label were used during Brayton's history. On items too small for a full mark, designers would simply incise their initials. Webb Brayton died in 1948, and Durlin died just three years later. Struggling with and finally succumbing to the effect of the influx of foreign pottery on the American market, Brayton Laguna finally closed in 1968.

For further study, read *Collector's Encyclopedia of California Pottery*, by Jack Chipman (Collector Books).

See also Cookie Jars.

Bowl, 3 native men in draped waistcloths support green bowl, gold trim, stain/chips, 12¾x11½"......................................$150.00

Box, molded fern-like fronds, pink/beige, oval w/knob on lid, 5½" $15.00

Bust, Art Deco lady, black matt, 12", from $250.00 to $265.00.

Creamer & sugar bowl, Gingham Dog & Calico Cat, w/lid ..$30.00

Figurine, Bishop chess piece, signed P Ganine 1947, 13" $75.00

Figurine, Black dice player $55.00

Figurine, blackamoor, in blue & white, w/gold ball in hands, much gold, 13", NM...$85.00

Figurine, Ellen, brown hair, dressed in blue, white & yellow, 7½"..$85.00

Figurine, fawn, brown w/white spots, Disney, 6" $80.00

Figurine, Figaro, playing, 3⅜"..$100.00

Figurine, giraffe w/head turned to side, long curving neck, 11½x10x9½"...$50.00

Figurine, Little Red Riding Hood, 7" $90.00

Figurine, Olga, 7⅛" $50.00

Figurine, peasant lady w/2 baskets, yellow vest, green skirt, 8¾", from $50 to $60.00

Figurine, pirate playing fiddle, multicolor, 5½"...................$50.00

Figurine, Pluto sniffing, 3½x6x3½", from $75 to................$85.00

Figurine, purple cow family, bull, cow & calf, 3-pc set, from $250 to $275.00

Figurine, rabbit from Snow White, yellow, late 1930s, 2½x4¾"...$225.00

Figurine, stylized bird, black w/white trim, twisted neck, #H49, 9½" **$140.00**

Figurine, Victorian couple in nightclothes, 3rd in series of 4, 9" ..**$150.00**

Figurine, 3 men at bar w/spittoon, Gay 90s, 9x6¾x5" **$85.00**

Figurines, George Handy & Lilah Handy, late 1930s, 6", 6¾", pr **$325.00**

Pitcher, turquoise, handmade, marked Durlin, 3½" **$60.00**

Planter, Donna, w/birds, 7" **$25.00**

Planter/vase, Deco-style lady w/2 wolfhounds, blue dress, 11¼"..**$115.00**

Plate, blue, handmade, 9¾" **$70.00**

Salt & pepper shakers, Mammy & Chef, 5¾", pr **$55.00**

Salt & pepper shakers, rooster & hen, multicolor, 5¼", 3½", pr.. **$45.00**

Utensil holder, Sally, blond girl in blue & white, 7"............**$35.00**

Vase, blended greens, fan form w/hand-crimped rim, D Brayton, early, 6"..**$750.00**

Wall pocket, bowl-shaped w/floral decor, Webton-Ware, 3½x6" .. **$35.00**

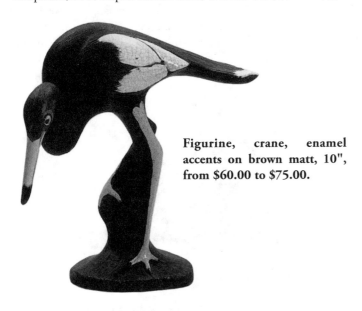

Figurine, crane, enamel accents on brown matt, 10", from $60.00 to $75.00.

Breweriana

Breweriana refers to items produced by breweries which are intended for immediate use and discard, such as beer cans and bottles, as well as countless items designed for long-term use while promoting a particular brand. Desirable collectibles include metal, cardboard, and neon signs; serving trays; glassware; tap handles; mirrors; coasters; and other paper goods.

Breweriana is generally divided into two broad categories: pre- and postprohibition. Preprohibition breweries were numerous and distributed advertising trays, calendars, etched glassware, and other items. Because American breweries were founded by European brewmasters, preprohibition advertising often depicted themes from that region. Brewery scenes, pretty women, and children were also common.

Competition was intense among the breweries that survived prohibition. The introduction of canned beer in 1935, the postwar technology boom, and the advent of television in the late 1940s produced countless new ways to advertise beer. Moving signs, can openers, enameled glasses, and neon are prolific examples of post-prohibition breweriana.

A better understanding of the development of the product as well as advertising practices of companies helps in evaluating the variety of breweriana items that may be found. For example, 'chalks' are figural advertising pieces which were made for display in taverns or wherever beer was sold. Popular in the 1940s and 1950s, they were painted and glazed to resemble carnival prizes. Breweries realized in addition to food shopping, women generally assumed the role of cook — what better way to persuade women to buy a particular beer than a cookbook? Before the advent of the bottle cap in the early 1900s, beer bottles were sealed with a porcelain stopper or cork. Opening a corked bottle required a corkscrew which often had a brewery logo.

Prior to the advent of refrigeration, beer was often served at room temperature. A mug or glass was often half warm beer and half foam. A 1" by 8" flat piece of plastic was used to scrape foam from the glass. These foam scrapers came in various colors and bore the logo of the beer on tap.

Before prohibition, beer logos were applied to glassware by etching the glass with acid. These etched glasses often had ornate designs that included a replica of the actual brewery or a bust of the brewery's founder. After prohibition, enameling became popular and glasses were generally 'painted' with less ornate designs. Mugs featuring beer advertising date back to the 1800s in America; preprohibition versions were generally made of pottery or glass. Ceramic mugs became popular after prohibition and remain widely produced today.

Tap handles are a prominent way to advertise a particular brand wherever tap beer is sold. Unlike today's ornate handles, 'ball knobs' were prominent prior to the 1960s. They were about the size of a billiard ball with a flat face that featured a colorful beer logo.

Unless noted otherwise, values are for items in excellent to near mint condition.

See also Barware.

Club: Beer Can Collectors of America
747 Merus Ct., Fenton, MO 63026
Annual dues: $27; although the club's roots are in beer can collecting, this organization offers a bimonthly breweriana magazine featuring many regional events and sponsors an annual convention www.bcca.com

Ashtray, Hamm's Beer, Born in the Land..., red & blue letters on white ceramic, 6⅝" dia **$15.00**

Beer bottle, Export Beer label w/eagle on keg, brown glass, Grand Rapids Brewing Co, pre-prohibition **$365.00**

Beer can, Altes Lager Beer, Altes Brewing Co, Detroit MI, flat top..**$110.00**

Beer can, Ballantine Beer, Princeton Class of 1940 Reunion, June 9-13, 1965, flat top, full pt **$105.00**

Beer can, Barbarossa, Red Top Brewing, Cincinnati OH, flat top, 1951 ....**$120.00**

Beer can, Club Special, Maier Brewing, Los Angeles CA, pull top..**$115.00**

Beer can, Columbia Ale, Heidelburg Brewing, Tacoma WA, flat top **$120.00**

Beer can, Dawson's Calorie Controlled Lager Beer, Dawson's Brewery, New Bedford MA, flat top, 1950s **$290.00**

Beer can, Grain Belt Friendly Beer, Minneapolis Brewing Co, Minneapolis MN, cone top, 1936, VG......................**$315.00**

Beer can, Heidelburg Brand Pilsner Beer, Valley Brewing Co, Flint MI, cone top...**$315.00**

Beer can, Iron City Beer, Pittsburgh Brewing Co, Pittsburgh PA, red cone top...**$280.00**

Beer can, Old Heidelberg Castle Pilsner, Blatz Brewing, Milwaukee WI, cone top, dated 1938, VG w/original cap...........**$120.00**

Beer can, Old Reading Beer, Old Reading Brewery, Reading PA, 2-sided cone top, 1950s......................................**$315.00**

Beer can, Ranier Beer Jubilee, Sick's Seattle Brewing, flat top, 1950s, unopened, M.......................................**$400.00**

Beer can, Red Ribbon Beer, Mathe-Ruder Brewing Co, Wausau WI, 2-sided cone top, 1950s....................................**$340.00**

Beer can, Schlitz Sunshine Vitamin D Beer, Schlitz Brewing, Milwaukee WI, cone top, 1936 ....**$255.00**

Beer can, Sunshine Extra Light, cone top, Reading, PA, EX, $85.00.

Beer can, Washington XX Pale Beer, eagle, Washington Breweries, Columbus OH, crowntainer **$185.00**

Beer can, Yuengling's Beer, DG Yuengling & Son Brewing, Pottsville PA, low profile cone top **$120.00**

Beer glass, Potosi, red pyro letters on clear glass, 5½", M...**$140.00**

Beer glass, Rhinelander Brewing Co, etched logo on clear glass, gold rim, 3½", M.................................**$270.00**

Belt buckle, Hamm's Beer, solid brass, Lewis Buckles Chicago, 2¼x3½" **$28.00**

Bottle stopper, German man, painted porcelain, Made in Germany US Zone, ca 1945-51, 3½" **$35.00**

Bottle stopper, man holding beer in hand, lever on back causes head to turn, painted wood, 5" **$32.50**

Calendar, Mets & Robin Hood Certified Beer, Earl Moran nude print, full pad, 1937, 24x13½" **$160.00**

Case, Malt City Beer, Riverview Brewing Co, Manitowoc WI, printed letters on wood, ca 1933-37, 10¼x19x12" **$67.50**

Chair, Miller Lite, inflatable orange plastic, MIP **$32.50**

Clock, Storz Beer, curved glass face, 1960s, 14½" dia **$165.00**

Clock, Try Burkhardt Beer Golden Goodness, lights up, 15" dia **$180.00**

Couch, Budweiser, inflatable red plastic, beer holder in ea armrest, storage under cushion for beer & ice, M w/pump **$125.00**

Crate, Budweiser Beer, black & blue stencil on wood, Clydesdales on lid, 14x17¾x13½" **$95.00**

Crate, Oshkosh Brewing Co, Chief Oshkosh, black & red stencil on wood, pre-prohibition.................................**$55.00**

Dinnerware set, Kokanee Beer, melamine, Precidio Inc Precisioncraft, 4 9¾" bowls & 4 7¾" bowls, M **$60.00**

Dispenser, keg top; Kiewel's Beer, 11".................**$120.00**

Display, Miller Beer, revolving, ca. 1950s, NM, $300.00.

(Photo courtesy LiveAuctioneers.com/ Morphy Auctions)

Fan, hand; Mathie Ruder Brewing Co, lady in white hat w/blue ribbon, cardboard litho, 10¾x9¾" **$38.00**

Flag, Shiner Bock Beer, Come & Take It, 22x33", MIP.......**$45.00**

Foam scraper, Hornung's Beer, Jacob Hornung Brewing Co, Philadelphia PA, black lettering on clear plastic **$27.50**

Foam scraper, Scheidt's Rams Head Pale Ale, red lettering on tan plastic, 8¾" **$27.50**

Goblet, National Bohemian Beer, red lettering on clear glass, stemmed, 1950s-60s, M................................**$15.00**

Lamp, Budweiser, Spud Mackenzie (dog) figural, painted plastic, Anheuser-Busch, 1986 ....**$165.00**

Mirror, Budweiser Beer, US Coast Guard Cutter Mackinaw, rope & copper frame, 1 of series of 5, M **$140.00**

Mug, Coors, ceramic, lion in white on maroon, Coors USA, 4¾", M..**$30.00**

Mug, cowboy boot form, clear pressed glass, 8", set of 6, M .**$60.00**

Mug, Lone Star Beer 1882-1982 Centennial, Pi Kappa Epsilon crest, etched on clear glass w/gold rim, 6x3¼", M **$28.00**

Mug, Weiss Beer, etched clear glass, tall & slim, footed, applied handle, 10-oz, M **$75.00**

Opener, Harvard Ale & Lager, painted metal w/printing ea side, Harvard Brewing Co, MA, pre-prohibition, VG........**$195.00**

Opener, Narraganset Lager & Ale, brass w/bronze finish, heavy, 5½", M...**$200.00**

Plaque, Coors Light Beer, wolf head w/cap & red bandana, molded & painted plastic, 14".................................**$65.00**

Refrigerator, Budweiser Can, Sears, 1980s, standard size....**$225.00**

Sign, Falls City Premium Quality Beer, tin litho, cream on red, 9¾x16¾" **$165.00**

Sign, Griesedieck Bros Premium Light Lager Beer, tin litho, 1950s, 14x42" **$325.00**

Sign, Hamm's Beer, panoramic waterfall, light-up motion type, 1965, 12½x40½x4½" **$295.00**

Sign, Pabst Blue Ribbon Beer, die-cut cardboard, 32", VG, $35.00. (Courtesy Buffalo Bay Auction Co.)

Sign, Pabst Brewing Co, A Bottle of Pabst, bottle & lettering on green, cardboard on tin, American Art Works, 7x11" .**$350.00**

Sign, Schlitz on Tap, blinking neon, 1968 ....**$315.00**

Spigot/cask tap, wooden, 8¼" L....................................**$9.00**

Statue, Duke, Have a Duke the Finest Beer in Town, Duquesne Pilsener Beer, painted chalkware, 10¾" **$175.00**

Statue, Hampden Mild Ale, man w/accordion standing on beer keg, painted chalkware, 1950s, 15" **$115.00**

Statue, Heidelberg Beer, Student Prince, painted chalkware, 14" .**$90.00**

Statue, Pfeiffer's Beer, Revolutionary solder w/flute, painted chalkware, 14" **$70.00**

Statue, Ranier Beer anthropomorphic stein man w/tray & towel, painted chalkware, 1955, 10x8x4¾" **$500.00**

Stein, Biker Bob figural, James Lim Biker series limited edition, Made in Germany, 11½", M....................................**$110.00**

Stein, Bud Man figural, ceramic, Ceramart, 1975, M, from $225 to **$275.00**

Stein, Coors, Fly Fisherman, Rocky Mountain series, ceramic, 1993, M..**$25.00**

Stein, cut glass, hunting theme, red to clear, hinged pewter lid, Germany, ca 1960s, 5", M **$50.00**

Stein, Enterprise NCC 1701, embossed & engraved ceramic, Chekov in color scene, 5½", M....................................**$30.00**

Stein, frog figural, ceramic w/metal thumb lift, Germany, #3849, 6", M..**$100.00**

Stein, Hamms Bear w/golf clubs figural, House of Wiebracht, M **$165.00**

Stein, Miller High Life, Birth of a Nation, painted & molded ceramic, 1992, M......................................**$45.00**

Stein, Ruppert Beer, Women's Golf Trophy, lady golfer finial, ceramic, Made in Germany, 22x6", M **$165.00**

Stein, Snow Woodlands Holiday, Ceramarte, Budweiser, 1981, M, from $140 to **$180.00**

Stopper, Kissing Couple, mechanical, carved & painted wood, cork base **$28.00**

Tap handle, Budweiser Bud Man figural, VG.................**$135.00**

Tap handle, Humpback Premium Honey Wheat Bear, humpback whale figural, painted wood (worn), 15"....................**$160.00**

Tap handle, Michelobe Light Beer bottle shape, plastic coated wood w/label **$15.00**

Tap knob, Cremo Beer, red insert on black Bakelite..........**$170.00**

Tap knob, Iroquois Beer Indian head, insert on black Bakelite, Fisher Prod Inc, Syracuse NY **$210.00**

Tap knob, Old Bohemian Extra Dry Beer, Wacker Brewing Co, Lancaster PA, painted metal insert on black Bakelite, M **$260.00**

Tap knob, Old Reading Half & Half, chrome finish, 2½x1½", VG **$230.00**

Thermometer, German Beer Lager, Queen City Brewing, Cumberland MD, 18" dia..**$55.00**

Thermometer, Hamm's, bear thinking of cold beer, in wooden frame, 19x8¼" **$135.00**

Thermometer, Old Export, Cumberland MD, curved glass front, metal back, 6" dia....................................**$40.00**

Tip tray, Enjoy the Good Life w/Miller High Life Beer, wild ducks, rectangular, M..**$12.50**

Tray, Evelyn Nesbitt portrait from film Chinese Honeymoon, Rainier Beer, Seattle WA, sm repaint at rim, ca 1903, 13" dia **$380.00**

Tray, How Good It Feels, Especially Piels, gnome on beer keg w/glass, tin litho, 1934, 13" dia........................**$220.00**

Tray, Leisey the Beer That Satisfies, Chrysanthemum Girl, tin litho, 13¼x10½" **$265.00**

Tray, Liberty Beer in Bottles Only, tin litho, American Brewing Co, Rochester NY, 12" dia **$360.00**

Tray, Olympia Beer, water scene, Olympia Brewing Co, Olympia WA, 12", G..**$315.00**

Tray, Wielands Beer, lady w/roses, tin litho, San Francisco CA, 13¼x10½" **$315.00**

Breyer Horses

Breyer horses have been popular children's playthings since they were introduced in 1952, and you'll see several at any large flea market. Garage sales are good sources as well. The earlier horses had a glossy finish, but after 1968 a matt finish came into use. You'll find smaller domestic animals too. They are evaluated by condition, rarity, and desirability; some of the better examples may be worth a minimum of $150.00. Our values are for average condition; examples in mint condition are worth from 10% to 15% more.

For more information and listings, see *Schroeder's Collectible Toys, Antique to Modern*, and *Breyer Animal Collector's Guide* by Felicia Browell, Kelly Kober-Weimer, and Kelly Kesicki. (Both are published by Collector Books.)

Classic Scale

Andalusian Mare (#3060MA), Classic Andalusian Family, dapple gray w/darker points, socks, 1979-93............................**$11.00**

Arabian Stallion (#3055ST), Classic Arabian Family, brown bay w/black points, diamond star, socks, Sears Book, 1984-85.............. **$18.00**

Bucking Bronco (#190), gray w/darker mane & tail, bald face, stockings, 1961-67...**$43.00**

Ginger (#3040GI), Black Beauty Family, chestnut w/darker mane, tail & hooves, strip & snip, 1980-93 ....**$12.00**

Hobo (#625), Hobo the Mustang of Lazy Heart Ranch, buckskin w/black mane & tail, shading, 1975-80........................ **$32.00**

Lipizzan Stallion (#620), Pegasus, alabaster w/pink hooves, wings fit in slots on back, 1984-87........................**$29.00**

Merrylegs (#3040ML), Black Beauty Family, dapple gray w/white mane & tail, lighter face & lower legs, 1980-83 ....**$12.00**

Might Tango (#3035MT), US Olympic Team Set, bay w/black points, hind socks, Sears Wish Book, 1987..................**$15.00**

Polo Pony (#626), bay w/black points, early, w/socks, molded woodgrain base, 1976-82 ....**$29.00**

Rojo #481, light red dun; light chestnut mane and tail; grayish knees, hocks, and ankles; red striping on legs, Classic scale, from $10.00 to $13.00. (Photo courtesy Carol Karbowiak Gilbert)

Ruffian (#606), dark bay w/black points, star, left hind sock, 1977-90 ....**$16.00**

Swaps (#604), chestnut w/darker mane & tail, star, hind socks & light hoof w/3 dark hooves, 1975-90 ....**$17.00**

Terrang (#605), dark brown w/darker mane & tail, lighter hind leg, 1975-90 ....**$17.00**

Traditional Scale

Action Stock Horse Foal (#235), appaloosa w/black points & hooves, blanket over hind quarters, 1984-88 ....**$13.00**

Balking Mule (#207), bay/chestnut w/darker mane & tail, gray hooves, brown or dark red bridle, 1968-73 ....**$74.00**

Black Stallion (#401), Majestic Arabian Stallion, leopard appaloosa w/black points, brown & black splash spots, 1989-90 ..**$26.00**

Buckshot (#415), Spanish Barb, chestnut pinto w/darker mane, tail & lower front legs, white hind legs, 1988-89.................**$26.00**

Clydesdale Mare (#83), Clydesdale Family Set, red bay w/black mane & tail, white legs & belly, bald face, JC Penney, '83.......**$46.00**

Clydesdale Stallion (#80), no-muscle version, bay w/dark mane & tail, stockings, 1958 (?)-1961 (?)................................**$117.00**

El Pastor (#61), bay w/black points, solid face, left socks, 1987...**$124.00**

Family Arabian Foal (#9), Shah, glossy bay w/black mane & tail, narrow blaze, stockings, black hooves, 1961-66 ....**$12.00**

Fighting Stallion (#31), King, glossy alabaster, gray mane, tail & hooves, pink & gray shaded muzzle, 1961-64..............**$98.00**

Fury Prancer (#P45), woodgrain, may or may not have hat reins, 1960...**$211.00**

Haflinger (#156), sorrel w/flaxen mane & tail, faint socks, gray hooves, Horses Int'l, 1984-85 ....**$27.00**

Indian Pony (#175), alabaster w/light gray mane & tail, red hand print on left haunch, blue sq on left neck, 1970-71 .....**$21.00**

Lady Roxanna (#425), Prancing Arabian Mare, chestnut w/flaxen mane & tail, 3 socks, gray hooves, 1988-89.................**$22.00**

Lying Down Foal (#245), black appaloosa w/bald face, rear blanket, 1969-84 ....**$19.00**

Morgan (#48), black w/bald face, front socks, back stockings, 1965-87 ....**$38.00**

Mustang (#87), Diablo, glossy alabaster w/light gray mane, tail & hooves, black eyes, 1961-66 ....**$129.00**

Pacer (#46), liver chestnut w/slightly darker mane & tail, socks, halter w/gold trim, 1967-87 ....**$27.00**

Pony of the Americas (#155), chestnut leopard appaloosa w/stenciled spots, gray hooves, added shoes, 1976-80 ....**$28.00**

Proud Arabian Foal (#218), Spot, glossy gray appaloosa w/black & dark gray points & hooves, 1956-60............................**$84.00**

Quarter Horse Yearling model #102, Presentation Collection, 1972 – 1973, Traditional scale, from $90.00 to $150.00. (Photo courtesy Carol Karbowiak Gilbert)

Running Mare (#120), woodgrain (light or dark), no markings, black hooves, 1963-65 ....**$132.00**

Saddlebred Weanling (#62), chestnut w/slightly darker mane & tail, 3 socks, 1984 ....**$134.00**

Scratching Foal (#168), liver chestnut w/darker mane & tail, stockings, 1970-71 ....**$64.00**

Shire (#95), dapple gray w/dark gray points, white stockings, 1972-73/1975-76..**$56.00**

Stock Horse Foal (#228), Bay Quarter Horse Stock Foal, bay w/ black points, hind socks, 1983-88..............................**$17.00**

Stock Horse Mare (#227), Sorrel Quarter Horse, flaxen mane & tail, stripe, right hind sock, 1982 .... **$26.00**

Stock Horse Stallion (#226), Bay Quarter Horse, bay w/black points, 1981-88 .... **$25.00**

Stud Spider (#66), black appaloosa w/stenciled blanket pattern over back half, thin star, front sock, 1978-89 .... **$28.00**

Thoroughbred Mare (#3155MA), Pinto Mare & Suckling Foal Set, bay pinto w/black points, socks, Sears Wish Book, 1982-83 .... **$38.00**

Trakehner (#54), bay w/black points, brand on left thigh, 1979-84 .... **$30.00**

Western Horse (#57), glossy palomino, stockings, gray hooves, complete w/saddle, 1956-67 .... **$38.00**

Western Prancing Horse (#110), Cheyenne, glossy black pinto w/bald face, socks, complete saddle, 1961-66 .... **$69.00**

Other Animals

Bear Cub (#308), dark brown w/lighter head, horns & lower legs, darker hooves, 1997-current **$25.00**

Boxer (#1), semigloss woodgrain w/white face stripe, black muzzle, 1959-65 .... **$242.00**

Calf (#347), Brown Swiss, cocoa brown, 1972-73 .... **$31.00**

Charolais Bull (#360), alabaster, 1975-95 .... **$21.00**

Deer (#301BU), buck, tan w/black nose & hooves, w/blue ribbon, 1965-73 .... **$12.00**

Donkey (#81), gray w/stockings, dark mane & tail, pale muzzle or bay variation, 1958-74, ea............................ **$22.00**

Elephant trumpeting (#91), solid gray, 1958-60 .... **$145.00**

German Shepherd (#327), Rin Tin Tin, matt/semigloss brown w/darker back, lighter face & legs, 1958-66 .... **$44.00**

Kitten (#335), Siamese, gray or seal point, blue or green eyes, 1966-71 .... **$64.00**

Polled Hereford Bull (#74), red-brown & white, 1968-current **$26.00**

Poodle (#67), silver-gray, 1968-73 .... **$43.00**

Spanish Fighting Bull (#73), black, white horns w/dark tips, 1970-85 .... **$57.00**

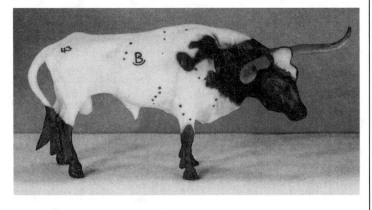

Texas Longhorn Bull, 1996 – current, $22.50. (Photo courtesy Carol Karbowiak Gilbert)

Walking Hereford Bull, glossy, semigloss or matt dark brown to red, brown & white, 1958-81 .... **$37.00**

British Royalty Commemoratives

While seasoned collectors may prefer the older pieces using circa 1840 (Queen Victoria's reign) as their starting point, even present-day souvenirs make a good inexpensive beginning collection. Ceramic items, glassware, metalware, and paper goods have been issued on the occasion of weddings, royal tours, birthdays, christenings, and many other celebrations. Food tins are fairly easy to find, and range in price from about $30.00 to around $75.00 for those made since the 1950s.

We've all seen that items related to Princess Diana have appreciated rapidly since her untimely and tragic demise, and in fact collections are being built exclusively from memorabilia marketed both before and after her death. For more information, we recommend *British Royal Commemoratives* by Audrey Zeder.

Advisor: Audrey Zeder (See Directory, British Royalty Commemoratives)

Mug, Prince Charles and Princess Diana wedding, marked with crown under three feathers, $20.00. (Photo courtesy LiveAuctioneers.com/Metropolitan Galleries at Shaker Square)

Beaker, Elizabeth II jubilee, multicolor, lion-head handles, Caversall **$80.00**

Bell, Prince William birthday/christening, multicolor w/gold, bone china, 6¾" **$60.00**

Book, Royal Souvenirs by Geoffrey Warren, hardback, 1977.. **$45.00**

Booklet, Earl Harewood wedding, Pitkins, 1949 .... **$20.00**

Bookmark, Prince Edward wedding, white leather w/gold decor, 9x1½" **$15.00**

Coin, Princess Diana, 1999 5-pound, special pack, Royal Mint... **$30.00**

Doll, Prince Philip, vinyl, blue uniform, Nisbit, ca 1950, 8½".. **$150.00**

Egg cup, Edward VII, multicolor portrait w/decor, gold rim, footed, 1937 .... **$55.00**

First Day cover, Elizabeth II coronation, w/decorated envelope .. **$20.00**

Illustrated London News Record No, Elizabeth II jubilee, blue cover w/silver decoration, 14x11" **$55.00**

Medal, Victoria coronation, profile & coronation scene, pierced, 2" **$160.00**

Miniature, photo album of 1982 Royal Family, 1¼x2" **$35.00**

Mug, Edward VII coronation, multicolor portrait w/multicolor enamel, gold rim, 2⅛" **$110.00**

Mug, Elizabeth II 80th birthday, multicolor, Chown, LE 25.. **$70.00**

Mug, Princess Beatrice 1988 birthday, white w/gold decor, Wedgwood, 3" **$100.00**

Photograph, Duke of Windsor 1940 radio broadcast, black & white, 5x7" **$45.00**

Photograph, Princess Diana 1987 at London gala, black & white, 6x8" **$50.00**

Plate, Charles/Diana 1981, royal blue, limited edition, Bing & Grondahl, 10½" **$190.00**

Plate, Elizabeth II coronation, profile, sq w/extended handles, 10" **$45.00**

Plate, Princess Elizabeth, Old English, Johnson Brothers, red and gold crown mark, $150.00. (Photo courtesy LiveAuctioneers.com/ Wendlers Auction)

Pressed glass, Prince William 10th birthday, portrait, amber, 3½" **$35.00**

Program, Windsor Castle, town & neighborhood guide, 1934... **$15.00**

Puzzle, Elizabeth II coronation, wood, Valentine, MIB (sealed) .. **$60.00**

Stamp albums, Charles/Diana wedding, 800+ stamps on decorated pages, pr...**$395.00**

Thimble, Elizabeth II 02 jubilee, young queen portrait, multicolor decoration...**$6.00**

Towel, Princess Elizabeth 1952 Trooping Colors, on horse, 9x6" **$75.00**

Brock of California

This was the trade name of the B.J. Brock Company, located in Lawndale, California. They operated from 1947 until 1980, and some of the dinnerware lines they produced have become desirable collectibles. One of the most common themes revolved around country living, farmhouses, barns, chickens, and cows. Patterns were Rooster, California Farmhouse, and California Rustic. Shapes echoed the same concept — there were skillets, milk cans, and flatirons fashioned into sugar bowls, creamers, and salt and pepper shakers. The company marketed a three-piece children's set as well. Also look for their '50s modern line called Manzanita, with pink and charcoal branches on platinum. With the interest in this style of dinnerware on the increase, this should be one to watch.

California Farmhouse, bowl, vegetable; oval, 11" **$18.00**

California Farmhouse, bowl, vegetable; round, w/lid **$40.00**

California Farmhouse, bowl, vegetable; 2-part, oval, 11" **$35.00**

California Farmhouse, coaster, 3½" **$3.00**

California Farmhouse, cup & saucer, yellow border **$10.00**

California Farmhouse, mug, yellow border, 3⅜" **$17.50**

California Farmhouse, mustard jar, milk can shape, w/lid....**$20.00**

California Farmhouse, plate, 10", from $8.00 to $10.00.

California Farmhouse, plate, yellow border, 11"...................**$12.50**

California Rustic, bowl, dessert; turquoise, 5".......................**$7.00**

California Rustic, cup & saucer, turquoise **$10.00**

California Rustic, plate, turquoise, 6½" **$4.00**

California Wildflower, au gratin, coral border, 8⅝".............**$25.00**

California Wildflower, cup & saucer, coral border **$12.50**

California Wildflower, lazy Susan, 5 pcs w/coral border, wooden base **$50.00**

California Wildflower, plate, coral border, 11"....................**$12.00**

Chanticleer, bowl, soup; brown border..............................**$10.00**

Chanticleer, bowl, vegetable; brown border, 9" **$15.00**

Chanticleer, cup & saucer, brown border, from $6 to **$8.00**

Chanticleer, gravy boat, brown border, from $22 to............**$28.00**

Chanticleer, platter, rectangular, brown border, 18" **$50.00**

Chanticleer, snack plate & cup, brown border **$14.00**

Country Lane, coaster, brown border, skillet shape **$2.50**

Country Lane, creamer, brown border, stick handle............**$12.50**

Country Lane, cup & saucer, brown border, from $7 to **$9.00**

Country Lane, gravy boat, brown border, from $22 to **$28.00**

Country Lane, relish jar, brown border, w/lid **$20.00**

Forever Yours, bowl, fruit; aqua border, 5" **$7.00**

Forever Yours, creamer & sugar bowl, aqua border, w/lid.....**$22.50**

Forever Yours, cup & saucer, aqua border, from $9 to..........**$12.00**

Forever Yours, platter, aqua border, 14" L **$30.00**

Harvest, bowl, vegetable; brown border, 9" **$20.00**

Harvest, cup & saucer, brown border, from $9 to................**$12.00**

Harvest, gravy boat, brown border, from $25 to **$28.00**

Harvest, plate, brown border, 10" **$8.00**

Harvest, sugar bowl, brown border, w/lid, from $12 to........**$15.00**

Manzanita, creamer & sugar bowl, pink & coral branches on platinum **$32.00**

Manzanita, cup & saucer, pink & coral branches on platinum, from $18 to **$22.00**

Manzanita, plate, pink & coral branches on platinum, 10", from $20 to **$25.00**

Manzanita, plate, pink & coral branches on platinum, 8" **$8.00**

Forever Yours, plate, 10", from $8.00 to $10.00.

Bubble Bath Containers

Most bubble bath containers were made in the 1960s. The Colgate-Palmolive Company produced the majority of them — they're the ones marked 'Soaky' — and these seem to be the most collectible. Each character's name is right on the bottle. Other companies followed suit; Purex also made a line, so did Avon. Be sure to check for paint loss, and look carefully for cracks in the brittle plastic heads of the Soakies.

For more information, we recommend *Schroeder's Collectible Toys, Antique to Modern* (Collector Books).

Advisors: Matt and Lisa Adams (See Directory, Bubble Bath Containers)

Alvin (Chipmunks) holding microphone, w/contents, Ducair Bioescence, M **$25.00**

Atom Ant, Purex, 1965, NM, from $50 to **$70.00**

Baba Looey, Purex, brown w/blue scarf & green hat, 1960s, NM...**$35.00**

Bambi sitting & smiling, Colgate-Palmolive, NM...............**$25.00**

Beatles, any character, Colgate-Palmolive, EX, ea from $100 to...**$150.00**

Bozo the Clown, cap head, Step Riley, EX **$30.00**

Bugs Bunny, gray, white & orange w/cap ears, Colgate-Palmolive, EX **$30.00**

Cinderella, movable arms, Colgate-Palmolive, 1960s, NM ..**$30.00**

Darth Vader, Omni, 1981, NM...**$20.00**

Dum Dum, white w/pink accents, Purex, 1964, rare, NM, from $75 to **$100.00**

ET, Avon, 1984, NM...**$15.00**

Gumby, M&L Creative Packaging, 1987, NM **$30.00**

Incredible Hulk standing on rock, Benjamin Ansehl, M **$25.00**

Kermit the Frog, Treasure Island outfit, w/tag, Calgon, M.....**$8.00**

Little Orphan Annie, Lander, 1977, NM...........................**$25.00**

Mickey Mouse, Avon, 1969, MIB....................................**$30.00**

Morocco Mole, Purex, 1966, rare, EX..............................**$100.00**

Mummy, Colgate-Palmolive, NM, from $100.00 to $115.00. (Photo courtesy www.whatacharacter.com)

Pebbles & Dino, Pebbles on Dino's back, Cosrich, M............**$6.00**

Pluto, orange w/cap head, Colgate-Palmolive, 1960s, NM ..**$20.00**

Punkin' Puss, orange w/blue outfit, Purex, 1966, VG **$30.00**

Race Car, several variations w/movable wheels, Tidy Toys, NMIB, ea **$40.00**

Robin, Colgate-Palmolive, 1966, EX, from $75 to **$100.00**

Schoolhouse, red, Avon, 1968, MIB **$15.00**

Simba, Kid Care, M..**$6.00**

Smokey Bear, Colgate-Palmolive, 1960s, NM **$25.00**

Snoopy as Flying Ace, Avon, 1969, MIB............................**$20.00**

Snoopy in Tub of Bubbles, Avon, 1971, MIB **$20.00**

Speedy Gonzales, Colgate-Palmolive, 1960s, EX.................**$25.00**

Spouty Whale, blue, original card, Roclar (Purex), M.........**$20.00**

Superman, complete w/cape, Avon, 1978, MIB.................**$35.00**

Sylvester the Cat w/Microphone, Colgate-Palmolive, 1960s, EX.. **$30.00**

Teenage Mutant Ninja Turtles, any character, Kid Care, 1990, ea **$8.00**

Tex Hex (Brave Starr), w/tag, Ducair Bioescence, M...........**$15.00**

Three Little Pigs, any character, Tubby Time, rare, M, ea **$40.00**

Thumper, Colgate-Palmolive, 1960s, EX **$25.00**

Touchè Turtle lying on stomach, green w/pink accents, Purex, EX **$35.00**

Universal Monsters, any character, Colgate-Palmolive, 1960s, NM **$50.00**

Wally Gator, Purex, 1963, rare, NM, from $45 to **$60.00**

Wendy the Witch, Colgate-Palmolive, 1960s, NM **$30.00**

Wolfman, red pants, Colgate-Palmolive, 1963, NM, from $100 to **$125.00**

Woody Woodpecker (Walter Lantz), Colgate-Palmolive, 1960s, NM..$20.00

Yoda (Star Wars), Omni, 1981, NM $20.00

Butter Pats

Butter pats were used extensively in Victorian times, but even up until the 1970s, they were included in commercial table service. Though most were made of vitrified or fine china, a variety of materials — ironstone, sterling, and fine porcelain, for instance — were used as well. You'll find they range from very ornate styles to the very simple. They were made by nearly all major dinnerware manufacturers both here and abroad. Just be careful not to confuse them with small plates intended for other uses, such as nut and sauce dishes, salt dips, coasters, or children's toy dishes.

Blue Rock pattern, bone china, Shelley, 3⅛" dia $37.00

Bluebirds (3), orange-red breasts & blue trim, Japan, ca 1935, 3" dia..$75.00

Bramble pattern, light green w/gold, Alfred Meakin Co England, ca 1890, 3" dia...$21.00

California Poppy, yellow, orange & green on white, Syracuse, 3½" dia..$30.00

Centenary pattern, blue on white china, Baltimore & Ohio Railroad, Lamberton Scammell, 3½" dia......................$30.00

Chang pattern, multicolored transfer, iron red rim, Edge Malkin & Co, 1873-1903, 3" dia, VG..........................$55.00

Chapman pattern, Buffalo China Kniffin & Demarest, ca 1920, 3½" dia..$40.00

Concordia Line, yellow & gold w/metallic gold rim, Concordia Line, Stavangerflit China of Norway, 1955, 4" dia $17.00

Coronation pattern, dark green floral transfer w/gold, DB & Co, ca 1910, NM $20.00

Cries of London pattern, porcelain, Adams, 3¼" dia $27.00

Daisies impressed on white china, gold trim, Suisse Langenthal in gold, 3" dia $7.00

Empire pattern, Great Northern Railway, Syracuse, 3" dia...$21.00

Exotic birds, orange & brown tones on white, Rosenthal Bavaria, 4½" dia $15.00

Floral, orange & yellow flowers w/leaves on white, Rosenthal Bavaria, 3½" dia..$10.00

Floral, purple, yellow & green on white china, gold trim, Sovereign House, 3½" dia..$10.00

Floral-embossed rim, sterling silver, S Kirk & Son, 3¼" dia ..$65.00

Flow blue Argyle pattern, gold trim, marked, 3" dia $35.00

Flow blue Cauldon pattern, gold rim, Cauldon R No 199332 England PF, 3¼" dia...$22.00

Flow blue Cecil pattern, scroll embossing, scalloped edge, 8 rounded sides, Till & Sons, 3" dia $70.00

Flow blue Dainty pattern, gold trim, John Maddock, Royal Vitreous, 3" dia...$29.00

Flow blue floral w/gold, embossed & scalloped rim, 3" dia..$57.00

Flow blue Florida pattern, deeply scalloped rim, Johnson Bros, ca 1900, 2¾" dia...$52.00

Flow blue Grace pattern, gold trim, scalloped rim, WH Grindley & Co, ca 1910, 3½" dia.......................................$50.00

Flow blue Kelvin pattern, Alfred Meakin, 3" dia................$40.00

Flow blue Virginia pattern, Maddock, 3" dia, NM $52.00

Flow blue Wentworth pattern, flowers & wheat w/gold trim, J&G Meakin, 1907, 3" dia..................................$45.00

Fruits, blue & gold border, Richard Ginori Manifattura di Doccia, Florence Italy, 3½" dia $11.00

Geneva, green geometrics on white, attributed to Syracuse, #120, ca 1910, 3½" dia..$80.00

Great Northern Rose pattern, Syracuse China 1-CC on back, 1948, 3½" dia..$39.00

Greek Key Band, green on white porcelain, gold trim, H&Co Bavaria, 3" dia...$15.00

Hans Christian Andersen's house, blue on white porcelain, #15 in 2010 series, Royal Copenhagen, 1965, 3" dia...............$12.00

Indian maid transfer on white ironstone, Coffee Al's on front, ca 1910, 3¼" dia...$35.00

Indian pattern, lavender polychrome transfer, 10 sides, LP&C Ironstone..$23.00

Indian Tree pattern, Copeland Spode, Made in England, 3" dia..$20.00

Island scene, blue, gray, yellow on white, gray rim, Highland Fine Bone China Scotland, 3" dia.................................$6.50

Liberty pattern, red on white, Pennsylvania Railroad, Syracuse, ca 1915, 3½" dia...$30.00

Lilies, white with yellow shading, green leaves, Royal Chelsea, $8.00. (Photo courtesy Marge Geddes)

Little Bohemia in black letters, red & green accent lines, 3½" dia $25.00

Majolica, deep red flower on white, light blue rim, English hallmark, 3" dia...$55.00

Majolica, wild rose pattern on cobalt blue, 3" dia $140.00

Majolica leaf, green, detailed, 3" dia...................................$56.00

Majolica pansy, yellow, blue & purple, Copeland, 3" dia, NM ..$107.00

Melbourne dark gray transfer, pink, blue, cream & yellow details, Victorian Glidea & Walker, 2¾" sq $40.00

Midwinter pattern, multicolored detail, Staffordshire, Made in England $32.00

Montmery pattern on white porcelain, gold rim, Haviland Limoges France, 3" dia...$20.00

Mosebach's Casino, sky blue on white china, Bauscher Brothers, #5, ca 1900, 3¼" dia **$25.00**

Moss Rose pattern on white china, gold trim, Alfred Meakin, ca 1897, 2½" sq **$17.00**

Old Chelsea pattern, pink roses, yellow border w/iron red rim, Whieldon Ware, F Winkle & Co, ca 1915 ....**$15.00**

Old Country Roses pattern, gold trim, Royal Albert, 3" dia...**$45.00**

Old English Countryside pattern, Johnson Brothers, 1¾" dia..**$40.00**

Olde Avesbury pattern, Royal Crown Derby Bone China, A 73 XLIX, 4½" dia **$25.00**

Orange Blossom pattern, multicolored on white, Royal Albert Blossom Time Series, 3¾" dia **$23.00**

Peacock in garden, multicolored on white, blue geometric rim, St Paul & Pacific, 3" dia.......................................**$55.00**

Phi Sigma Kappa Fraternity, gray on white, attributed to Syracuse, ca 1909, 3" dia, EX.......................................**$30.00**

Portrait of a queen wearing crown & Art Nouveau jewelry, gold trim, Haviland Limoges, ca 1888, 2¾" dia **$50.00**

Rosebud Chintz, scalloped edge, Copeland Spode England, 3¼" dia.......................................**$18.50**

Rosedale pattern, 3 groups of gray green flowers on white porcelain, Johnson Bros, 3" dia **$16.00**

Silent Woman Restaurant, Waterville Maine souvenir, fired-on red letters & logo on white, 3½x4".......................................**$67.00**

Southern Pacific Prairie Mountain Wild Flowers, pink, yellow & purple on white, Shenango Pottery Co **$90.00**

St Francis Hotel, light green & tan on white china, Lamberton Scammell, ca 1930, 3½" dia.......................................**$25.00**

Traveler pattern, pink & black on white china, Syracuse, 3" dia.......................................**$30.00**

Violets & Daisies pattern, Shenango China, 4" dia.............**$58.00**

Violets hand painted on thin porcelain, scalloped gold trim, Tressemann & Vogt Limoges France Mark 8, 4" dia **$24.00**

Vista pattern, pink transfer on white ironstone, Mason's, 3" dia..**$35.50**

Western Maryland Railroad, green logo on white, dining car china, 3" dia **$65.00**

Buttons

Collectors refer to buttons made before 1918 as 'old,' those from 1918 on they call 'modern.' Age is an important consideration, but some modern buttons are very collectible too. You might find some still in your grandmother's button jar, and nearly any flea market around will have some interesting examples.

Some things you'll want to look for to determine the age of a button is the material it is made of, the quality of its workmanship, the type of its decoration, and how it was constructed. Early metal buttons were usually made in one piece of steel, copper, or brass. Old glass buttons will have irregularities on the back, while the newer ones will be very smooth. 'Picture' buttons with animals and people as their subjects were popular in the last quarter of the nineteenth century. Many were quite large and very fancy. As a rule, those are the most valuable to collectors.

For more information, refer to *Antique and Collectible Buttons Vol. 1* and *Vol. 2,* by Debra J. Wisniewski. They are published by Collector Books.

Bakelite, brown, lady golfer in concavity, med **$20.00**

Bakelite, carved oval, medium, from $10.00 to $12.00. (Photo courtesy Debra Wisniewski)

Bakelite, green carved flower, oval, med **$11.00**

Bakelite, green ice skater, Sonja Henie, sm **$6.00**

Bakelite w/anchor, yellow on black, med............................**$16.00**

Bakelite/Catalin, fish, realistic carving, metal loop shank, 1" ..**$40.00**

Bone, antler; expertly carved w/fish decor, applied wire shank, 1¼" **$65.00**

Bone, utilitarian, 3- 4- & 5-hole sew-through, 18th or 19th C, ¾", ea **$3.00**

Bone, 2 carved birds w/blue painted eyes, med **$20.00**

Brass, black lacquered owl on branch, med **$15.00**

Brass, Cupid w/umbrella sitting on grapevine on black, lg...**$35.00**

Brass, pierced, iris w/turquoise enamel accents, lg..............**$35.00**

Brass, rampant lion circled by 16 cut steels, lg, 1¾"............**$35.00**

Brass, rooster head on black, lg, 1³⁄₁₆".......................................**$40.00**

Brass, seashore scene enameling, black & gray tones, med ...**$25.00**

Celluloid, Art Deco triangular shape, sew-through, 1"........**$14.00**

Celluloid, bubble-like, striated, self-shank, ¾" **$15.00**

Celluloid, football shape (realistic/detailed), stained for effect, 1½" **$10.00**

Celluloid, light green, floral w/wavy lines, football shape, single shank, lg, 1½x3½" **$18.00**

Celluloid, multicolored duck on black, sm...........................**$8.00**

Ceramic, multicolored butterflies, modern, 1945, med........**$20.00**

Ceramic, multicolored iris w/gold trim, med.......................**$30.00**

Ceramic, white w/blue-green glaze, Ruskin England............**$25.00**

Diminutive, ivory, rose carving, self shank, ¼" **$15.00**

Diminutive, jewel w/rhinestones & black glass, metal shank, ¼" ..**$8.00**

Diminutive, turquoise ball encased in silver wires, ¼"..........**$22.00**

Diminutive, white opaque w/multicolored twisted cane overlay, self-shank, ¼".......................................**$15.00**

Earthenware, bold American Indian decor, sew-through, 1930s-40s, 1½" **$65.00**

Enameled, Deco style, black w/green & gold, rectangular, med..**$22.00**

Enameled dog face, circled by cut steel, sm **$40.00**

Enameled unicorn on blue, modern, ca 1970s, sm.................**$7.00**

Fabric, ribbon woven by JJ Cash, stretched over base, Her Royal Highness Queen Elizabeth II, ¾".......................................**$10.00**

Fabric, silk over metal, Garter, Betty Boop, padded shank, ¾"....**$25.00**

Glass, aqua hat w/3 rhinestones on brim, 1950s, med **$10.00**

Glass, black, castle scene, molded design, med, 1¹⁄₁₆" **$22.00**

Glass, black, girl w/umbrella, impressed design, loop shank, ½" ..**$12.00**

Glass, black, Orientals picking flowers, molded design, 1¼" ..**$75.00**

Glass, black passementerie, cemented to metal framework, 1¼" ..**$18.00**

Glass, black w/clear star center, 2-pc, med **$25.00**

Glass, black w/iridescent flowers in basket, sm....................**$8.00**

Glass, black w/pink foil butterfly paperweight top, sm.........**$33.00**
Glass, black w/silver lustre shell, med....................**$12.50**
Glass, cat face painted on white, lg sew-thru holes for eyes, sm...**$10.00**
Glass, clambroth & blue glass w/embedded foil, sq, ½".........**$6.00**
Glass, clear w/imbedded realistic metal stag head, ¾"..........**$25.00**
Glass, clear w/ocean life painted on reverse, med..............**$15.00**
Glass, fired-on multicolored enamel fly, sm....................**$12.00**
Glass, green, faceted, butterfly shape, lg.....................**$6.00**
Glass, green cat face w/rhinestone eyes, sm....................**$20.00**
Glass, green Christmas tree w/rhinestone lights, med...........**$7.50**
Glass, lacy clear cobalt w/silver lustre, 4-way shank, 1".......**$55.00**
Glass, lady bug (realistic), green & black, self-shank, ¾"......**$10.00**
Glass, lavender, Victorian flower enamel, claw shank, med..**$18.00**
Glass, light blue aurora borealis, sm..........................**$2.50**
Glass, opaque red triangle, ca 1930s, lg.......................**$8.00**
Glass, orange & white striped moonglow, sm....................**$8.00**
Glass, pearl moonglow, sq, med.................................**$10.00**
Glass, pink, faceted, 5-petal flower, sm......................**$4.00**
Glass, resembles crochet over silk, multi-lustre, metal shank, 1"...**$6.00**
Glass, tortoise brown w/silver lustre etching, oblong.........**$4.00**
Glass, w/silver lustre checkerboard, sm.......................**$10.00**
Glass, white opaque, bird (3-D/realistic), painted details, self-shank, ¾"...**$9.00**
Glass, white opaque, molded-in corded & painted design, self-shank, 1"...**$4.00**
Glass, white opaque, Mucha-style head on blue, 4-way shank, 1"...**$40.00**
Glass, white w/6 gold lustre flowers, modern, med.............**$3.00**

Glass with silvered brass bird escutcheon, 1¼", from $15.00 to $20.00. (Photo courtesy Debra Wisniewski)

Lucite, multicolor & clear, carved intaglio design, sq, ¾"......**$9.00**
Pearl, ornate carving, iridescent quality, 3-hole sew-through, 1¼"...**$60.00**
Pewter, swan on lake, lg......................................**$25.00**
Picture type, bird flying, pressed brass applied to steel, ½"....**$4.00**
Picture type, birds under umbrella, brass w/steel back, 1⅜"..**$15.00**
Picture type, boy stealing grapes, pierced brass on velvet, 1"...**$55.00**
Picture type, detailed Cleopatra playing harp, bar shank, LF Depose, 1½"...**$50.00**
Picture type, ducks among cattails, brass, ½"................**$14.00**
Picture type, horse's head w/in horseshoe, pressed metal, ¾".**$10.00**
Picture type, lion's head, brass applied to steel, ½".........**$4.00**
Picture type, pigeon, finely detailed feathers, brass over wood, 1⅜"...**$13.00**

Picture type, Scaramouche w/floral border, brass w/metal liner, 1¼"...**$30.00**
Picture type, Scottie dog's head, pressed metal, ⅞"...........**$40.00**
Picture type, sheperds, flock & fox, brass over wood, 1½"...**$45.00**
Picture type, shepherd w/sheep, floral border, darkened brass, 1¼"...**$26.00**
Picture type, stag in forest, celluloid, stained for effect, self-shank, 2"...**$30.00**
Picture type, terrier head, brass, steel eyes, 1¼".............**$50.00**
Plastic, ladybug (realistic), carved & painted green & black, metal shank, ¾"...**$5.00**
Plastic, laminated to resemble wood, ¾"......................**$4.00**
Plastic, Mah Jongg tile (realistic/incised), metal shank, 1¼"...**$4.00**
Plastic, Mr Bo Jangles w/top hat & bow tie (realistic), metal shank, 1"...**$65.00**
Plastic, plate of realistic fruit, metal shank, 1¼"..........**$10.00**
Plastic, polar bear (realistic/outlined), drilled holes, 1"...**$2.00**
Plastic, realistic penguin, black & white, med...............**$2.00**
Plastic, rolling pin (realistic), drilled holes side to side, ¾".....**$3.00**
Plastic, Scottie dog seated (realistic), black, 1x1"..........**$4.00**
Rhinestones, claw set in silver-plated mounting, snowflake shape, med...**$10.00**
Rubber, anchor design for Navy coat, Goodyear background, 1¾"...**$4.00**
Wood, Alpine hat (carved/realistic), painted, w/tassel, self-shank, ¾"...**$3.00**
Wood, bear standing w/paw raised...............................**$18.00**
Wood, floral urn, ca 1915, med.................................**$15.00**

Picture type, aster on trellis, T.W. & W., Paris Brevete, 1¼", $18.00. (Photo courtesy Debra Wisniewski)

Camark Pottery

Camark Pottery was manufactured in CAMden, ARKansas, from 1927 to the early 1960s. The pottery was founded by Samuel J. 'Jack' Carnes, a native of east-central Ohio familiar with Ohio's fame for pottery production. Camark's first wares were made from Arkansas clays shipped by Carnes to John B. Lessell in Ohio in early to mid-1926. Lessell was one of the associates responsible for early art pottery making. These art wares consisted of Lessell's lustre and iridescent finishes based on similar ideas he pioneered at Weller and other potteries. The variations made for Camark included versions of Weller's Marengo, LaSa, and Lamar. These 1926 pieces were signed only with the 'Lessell' signature. When Camark began operations in the spring of 1927, the company had many talented, experienced workers including Lessell's wife and step-daughter (Lessell himself died unexpectedly in December 1926), the Sebaugh family, Frank Long, Alfred Tetzschner, and Boris Trifonoff. This group produced a wide range of art pottery finished in glazes of many types, including lustre and iridescent (signed LeCamark), Modernistic/Futuristic, crackles, and combination glaze effects such as drips. Art pottery manufacture continued until the early 1930s when emphasis changed to industrial castware (molded wares) with single-color, primarily matt glazes.

In the 1940s Camark introduced its Hand Painted line by Ernst Lechner. This line included the popular Iris, Rose, and Tulip patterns. Concurrent with the Hand Painted Series (which was made until the early 1950s), Camark continued mass production of industrial castware — simple, sometimes nondescript pottery and novelty items with primarily glossy pastel glazes — until the early 1960s.

Some of Camark's designs and glazes are easily confused with those of other companies. For instance, Lessell decorated and signed a line in his lustre and iridescent finishes using porcelain (not pottery) blanks purchased from the Fraunfelter China Company. Camark produced a variety of combination glazes including the popular drip glazes (green over pink and green over mustard/brown) closely resembling Muncie's — but Muncie's clay is generally white while Camark used a cream-colored clay for its drip-glaze pieces. Muncie's are marked with a letter/number combination, and the bottoms are usually smeared with the base color. Camark's bottoms have a more uniform color application.

In the listings that follow, the term '1st block letter' refers to the die-stamped CAMARK mark. These block-style letters were $\frac{3}{16}$" high and were used circa 1928 to the early 1930s, while the '2nd block letter' mark was stamped in $\frac{1}{8}$" letters and used for a brief time in the early to mid-1930s.

Advisor: Tony Freyaldenhoven (See Directory, Camark)

Newsletter: *Camark Pottery News Bulletin*
Colony Publishing, owner: Letitia Landers
P.O. Box 203
Camden, AR 71711
870-836-3022; fax: 870-836-0127

Figurine, razorback hog, maroon, #117, $85.00 to $115.00.

Advertising sign, Camark Pottery on Arkansas shape, green gloss, 6⅜" **$360.00**

Ashtray, yellow w/incurvate scalloped rim & embossed ribs, 1st block letter mark **$15.00**

Ball jug, brown stipple, gold ink stamp, 6½", from $180 to.**$200.00**

Basket, frosted green, 1st block letter mark, 2¼", from $30 to..**$40.00**

Bottle, ear of corn, yellow & green, 1st block letter mark, 7¾", from $80 to **$100.00**

Ewer, Iris, multicolor on cream to pink, slender body, Camark label, 13¾x11" **$48.00**

Figurine, Persian cat, white gloss w/green eyes, 9¾x10" **$360.00**

Flower frog, draped nude, maroon gloss, unmarked, 8¾" ..**$115.00**

Flower frog, egrets (2) on base, turquoise gloss, unmarked, 10¾" **$60.00**

Flower frog, Rose Green Overflow, 1st block letter mark, ¾x3" dia, from $20 to **$30.00**

Humidor, Mirror Black, 1st block letter mark, 7½", from $180 to... **$200.00**

Humidor, Sea Green, 6-sided, unmarked, 6½", from $120 to ..**$140.00**

Pitcher, Orange Green Overflow, unmarked, 11", from $120 to.**$140.00**

Pitcher, Rose Green Overflow, ball form, w/stopper, 6¼" ..**$120.00**

Pitcher, waffle batter; deep yellow w/bird handle, gold ink stamp, 4" **$100.00**

Pitcher, yellow w/green cat handle, Camark Deluxe Artware sticker, #088, 7½" **$90.00**

Planter, covered wagon, green gloss, Camark label, 4½x5" ...**$45.00**

Planter, Orange Green Overflow, multiple plant pockets, 8", from $160 to **$180.00**

Plaque, horse head, burgundy, USA 569, 8½x8½" **$58.00**

Plaque, squirrel, Marshmallow White w/black eyes, Camark USA mark, 9¼" **$65.00**

Vase, blue & white stipple, trumpet neck, 1st block letter mark, 9", from $200 to **$250.00**

Vase, blue mottled, waisted neck, shouldered, 5¾" **$45.00**

Vase, blue stippled jar form w/ring handles, unmarked, 6" ..**$45.00**

Vase, blue-green drip over pink, footed cone w/low handles, stamped mark, 6" **$48.00**

Vase, brown stipple, rim-to-hip handles, 1st block letter mark, 5½", from $250 to **$300.00**

Vase, Celeste Blue, handles, Camark label, 7", from $40 to ..**$50.00**

Vase, Celestial Blue w/black overflow, die stamp, 10¾", from $250 to **$300.00**

Vase, fan; mint green over pink matt, block letters mark, 6x6⅜" **$42.50**

Vase, fan; Uranium Orange, unmarked, 5⅞x6" **$65.00**

Vase, floral embossed on rust, footed, 1st block letter mark, 7", from $60 to **$80.00**

Vase, green drip, angular handles, 5x8" **$100.00**

Vase, ivory crackle, shouldered, gold stamp, 5¾", from $200 to **$250.00**

Vase, Morning Glories embossed on soft spring green, handles, 11½" **$45.00**

Vase, olive green w/light overflow, handles, Camark label, 4½", from $80 to **$100.00**

Vase, Rose Green Overflow, Deco style, 8", from $200 to...**$250.00**

Vase, spade-like leaf on front & back, 2-scallop rim, green gloss, Camark sticker, 10½" **$45.00**

Vase, vining florals embossed on green semi-matt, swollen top, USA 548, Camark label, 7⅜x5" **$180.00**

Vase, Water Lily, integral handles, USA Camark A10K, 7½" .. **$240.00**

Vase, Yellow Green Overflow, 1st block letter mark, 5", from $80 to **$100.00**

Venetian, Venetian Poppy, LeCamark, unmarked, 10", from $500 to **$600.00**

Vase, pink drip over green matt, 6", from $40.00 to $50.00. (Photo courtesy LiveAuctioneers.com/Belhorn Auction Services, LLC)

Cambridge Glass

If you're looking for a 'safe' place to put your investment dollars, Cambridge glass is one of your better options. But as with any commodity, in order to make a good investment, knowledge of the product and its market is required. There are two books we would recommend for your study, *Colors in Cambridge Glass II,* put out by the National Cambridge Collectors Club, and *Elegant Glassware of the Depression Era* by Gene and Cathy Florence.

The Cambridge Glass Company (located in Cambridge, Ohio) made fine quality glassware from just after the turn of the century until 1958. They made thousands of different items in hundreds of various patterns and colors. Values hinge on rarity of shape and color. Of the various marks they used, the 'C in triangle' is the most common. In addition to their tableware, they also produced flower frogs representing ladies and children and models of animals and birds that are very valuable today. To learn more about them, you'll want to read *Glass Animals, Second Edition,* by Dick and Pat Spencer (Collector Books).

See also Glass Animals and Related Items.

Club: National Cambridge Collectors, Inc.
P.O. Box 416
Cambridge, OH 43725-0416
www.cambridgeglass.org

Achilles, crystal, bowl, flared, 4-toed, #3900/62, 12" **$75.00**

Achilles, crystal, cake plate, 2-handled, #3900/35, 13½" **$85.00**

Achilles, crystal, celery/relish dish, 3-part, #3900/126, 12".. **$75.00**

Achilles, crystal, compote, #3900/136, 5½" **$65.00**

Achilles, crystal, mayonnaise, #3900/129 .... **$35.00**

Achilles, crystal, tumbler, footed, #3121, 10-oz **$40.00**

Adonis, crystal, candlestick, double, #399/72, ea **$65.00**

Adonis, crystal, creamer, #3900/41 .... **$25.00**

Adonis, crystal, plate, luncheon; #3500, 8½" **$16.00**

Adonis, crystal, salt & pepper shakers, pr............................ **$85.00**

Adonis, crystal, urn, w/lid, #3500/41, 10" **$395.00**

Apple Blossom, crystal, #3025, 64-oz **$215.00**

Apple Blossom, crystal, bowl, flat, 12" **$55.00**

Apple Blossom, crystal, casserole, #912, 10½" **$195.00**

Apple Blossom, crystal, goblet, cocktail; #3135, 3-oz **$18.00**

Apple Blossom, crystal, plate, dinner; 9½" **$45.00**

Apple Blossom, pink or green, bowl, cereal; 6" **$50.00**

Apple Blossom, pink or green, butter dish, 5½" **$410.00**

Apple Blossom, pink or green, platter, 11½" **$120.00**

Apple Blossom, yellow or amber, ashtray, heavy, 6" **$100.00**

Apple Blossom, yellow or amber, ice bucket....................... **$135.00**

Apple Blossom, yellow or amber, tray, sandwich; center handle, #3400/10, 11" **$50.00**

Candlelight, crystal, bowl, oval, toed, 2-handled, #3900/65, 12".. **$110.00**

Candlelight, crystal, compote, cheese; #3900/135, 5" **$45.00**

Candlelight, crystal, cruet, w/stopper, #3900/100, 6-oz **$175.00**

Candlelight, crystal, goblet, cocktail; #3776, 3-oz............... **$35.00**

Candlelight, crystal, nut cup, 4-footed, #3400/71, 3" **$70.00**

Candlelight, crystal, plate, rolled edge, #3900/166, 14"....... **$85.00**

Candlelight, crystal, plate, salad; #3900/22, 8" **$22.00**

Candlelight, crystal, relish dish, 5-part, #3900-120, 12"...... **$85.00**

Candlelight, crystal, vase, globe form, #1309, 5" **$85.00**

Caprice, blue or pink, ashtray, #216, 5" **$20.00**

Caprice, blue or pink, bowl, pickle; #102, 9" **$55.00**

Caprice, blue or pink, bowl, 4-footed, #49, 8".................... **$115.00**

Caprice, blue or pink, cigarette box, #208, 4½x3½" **$60.00**

Caprice, blue or pink, creamer, individual, #40 .... **$20.00**

Caprice, blue or pink, plate, bread & butter; #21, 6½"........ **$18.00**

Caprice, blue or pink, tumbler, straight sides, #14, 9-oz **$100.00**

Caprice, blue or pink, vase, ball form, #240, 9¼" **$295.00**

Caprice, blue or pink, vase, crimped top, #344, 4½" **$150.00**

Caprice, crystal, bowl, crimped, 4-footed, #53, 10½" **$40.00**

Caprice, crystal, bowl, jelly; 2-handled, #151, 5" **$15.00**

Caprice, crystal, butter dish, #52, ¼-lb **$200.00**

Caprice, crystal, decanter, w/stopper, #187, 35-oz **$195.00**

Caprice, crystal, pitcher, ball shape, #179, 32-ounce, $135.00.

Caprice, crystal, salt & pepper shakers, flat, #96, pr **$35.00**

Caprice, crystal, sherbet, blown, #301, 6-oz....................... **$12.00**

Caprice, crystal, tray, oval, #42, 9" $20.00
Caprice, crystal, vase, rose bowl; footed, #236, 8" $85.00
Cascade, crystal, ashtray, 4½" $5.00
Cascade, crystal, bowl, bonbon; 2-handled, footed, 7" $10.00
Cascade, crystal, bowl, flared rim, 4-footed, 10" $25.00
Cascade, crystal, bowl, fruit; 4½" $6.00
Cascade, crystal, candlestick, 5", ea $10.00
Cascade, crystal, cup $5.00
Cascade, crystal, plate, 4-footed, 11½" $20.00
Cascade, crystal, punch bowl, 15" $110.00
Chantilly, crystal, bowl, flared, 4-footed, 10" $50.00
Chantilly, crystal, candlestick, 5", ea $28.00
Chantilly, crystal, candy box, round $95.00
Chantilly, crystal, cordial, #3625, 1-oz $45.00
Chantilly, crystal, decanter, ball form $250.00
Chantilly, crystal, goblet, wine; #3779, 2½-oz $30.00
Chantilly, crystal, mayonnaise, divided, w/liner & 2 ladles ..$65.00
Chantilly, crystal, pitcher, ball form $195.00
Chantilly, crystal, plate, torte; 14" $45.00
Chantilly, crystal, saucer, #3900/17 ....$3.00
Chantilly, crystal, syrup, Drip-cut top, #1670 ....$250.00
Chantilly, crystal, tumbler, footed, #3775, 5-oz $16.00
Chantilly, crystal, vase, keyhole base, 9" $60.00
Cleo, blue, bowl, vegetable; oval, Decagon, 9½" $135.00
Cleo, blue, compote, tall, #3115, 7" $110.00
Cleo, blue, finger bowl, w/liner, #3077 ....$75.00
Cleo, blue, plate, 2-handled, Decagon, 11" $110.00
Cleo, blue, server, center handle, 12" $70.00
Cleo, pink, green, yellow, or amber, humidor $500.00
Cleo, pink, green, yellow, or amber, tumbler, flat, 12-oz $55.00
Cleo, pink, green, yellow or amber, bowl, cranberry; 3½" $45.00
Cleo, pink, green, yellow or amber, bowl, oval, 11½" $70.00
Cleo, pink, green, yellow or amber, bowl, soup; tab handles, 7½" $32.00
Cleo, pink, green, yellow or amber, gravy boat, w/liner plate, Decagon, #1091 ....$295.00
Daffodil, crystal, basket, 2-handled, low foot, #55, 6" $40.00

Daffodil, crystal: cocktail, $30.00; tumbler, iced tea; #3779, footed, $38.00. (Photo courtesy LiveAuctioneers.com/Jackson's International Auctioneers & Appraisers of Fine Art & Antiques)

Daffodil, crystal, cordial, #1937, 1-oz $100.00
Daffodil, crystal, cup, #11770 ....$25.00
Daffodil, crystal, plate, salad; 8½" $18.00
Daffodil, crystal, salt & pepper shakers, squat, #360, pr $65.00
Daffodil, crystal, sherbet, low, #3779, 6-oz $16.00
Daffodil, crystal, tumbler, footed, #1937, 5-oz $22.00
Daffodil, crystal, vase, footed, #278, 11" $150.00
Decagon, blue, bowl, bouillon; w/liner, #866 ....$35.00
Decagon, blue, bowl, vegetable; #1085, 9" $55.00
Decagon, blue, plate, service; #812, 10" $50.00
Decagon, blue, sugar bowl, footed, #979 ....$20.00
Decagon, blue, tray, service; 2-handled, #1084, 13" $50.00
Decagon, pastel colors, bowl, fruit; belled, #1098, 5½" ...$10.00
Decagon, pastel colors, compote, low foot, #608, 6½" $20.00
Decagon, pastel colors, goblet, cocktail; #3077, 3½" $12.00
Decagon, pastel colors, plate, 7½" $8.00
Decagon, pastel colors, tumbler, footed, #3077, 12-oz $18.00
Diane, crystal, bowl, cream soup; w/liner, #3400 ....$50.00
Diane, crystal, bowl, relish; 2-part, 7" $32.00
Diane, crystal, bowl, 4-footed, 12" $70.00
Diane, crystal, candelabrum, 2-light, keyhole, 6" $40.00
Diane, crystal, goblet, water; #3122, 9-oz $30.00
Diane, crystal, goblet, wine; #1066, 3-oz $30.00
Diane, crystal, lamp, hurricane; candlestick base $195.00
Diane, crystal, pitcher, upright $225.00
Diane, crystal, plate, 8½" $18.00
Diane, crystal, sugar sifter $125.00
Diane, crystal, tumbler, footed, 8-oz $28.00
Diane, crystal, vase, bud; 10" $65.00
Diane, crystal, vase, flower; 13" $165.00
Elaine, crystal, bowl, tab handles, 11" $85.00
Elaine, crystal, candlestick, 3-light, 6", ea $50.00
Elaine, crystal, candy jar, #3500/41, 10" $195.00
Elaine, crystal, goblet, champagne; #7801 ....$125.00
Elaine, crystal, goblet, water; #3104, 9-oz $175.00
Elaine, crystal, ice bucket, w/chrome handle $110.00
Elaine, crystal, parfait, low stem, #3121, 5-oz $35.00
Elaine, crystal, plate, salad; 8" $18.00
Elaine, crystal, salt & pepper shakers, footed, pr $40.00
Elaine, crystal, tumbler, footed, #1402, 9-oz $22.00
Elaine, crystal, vase, keyhole, footed, 9" $135.00
Gloria, crystal, bowl, cereal; sq, 6" $35.00
Gloria, crystal, bowl, oval, 4-footed, 12" $85.00
Gloria, crystal, bowl, pedestal foot, #3400/3, 11" $115.00
Gloria, crystal, cake plate, sq, footed, 11" $110.00
Gloria, crystal, creamer, tall, footed $20.00
Gloria, crystal, goblet, cocktail; #3035, 3½-oz $18.00
Gloria, crystal, sherbet, low, #3120, 6-oz $16.00
Gloria, crystal, tumbler, whiskey; #3400/92, 2-oz $28.00
Gloria, crystal, vase, squared top, 12" $195.00
Gloria, green, pink or yellow, bonbon, 2-handled, 5½" $40.00
Gloria, green, pink or yellow, pitcher, ball form, 80-oz $495.00
Gloria, green, pink or yellow, plate, dinner; 9½" $90.00
Gloria, green, pink or yellow, tray, pickle; tab handles, 9" $70.00
Gloria, green, pink or yellow, tumbler, footed, 5-oz, #3130 .$35.00
Imperial Hunt Scene, colors, bowl, 8" $95.00
Imperial Hunt Scene, colors, goblet, cocktail; #3075, 2½-oz ..$50.00

Imperial Hunt Scene, colors, tumbler, footed, #3085, 2½-oz . **$55.00**

Imperial Hunt Scene, colors or crystal, plate, #810, 9½" **$25.00**

Imperial Hunt Scene, crystal, cordial, #1402, 1-oz.............. **$75.00**

Imperial Hunt Scene, parfait, #3085, 5½-oz **$75.00**

Marjorie, crystal, bowl, nappy, #4111, 4" **$32.00**

Marjorie, crystal, compote, #4011 .... **$90.00**

Marjorie, crystal, creme de menthe, #7606, 2-oz **$100.00**

Marjorie, crystal, cup **$50.00**

Marjorie, crystal, jug, #93, 3-pt **$255.00**

Marjorie, crystal, tumbler, #7606, 5-oz **$15.00**

Marjorie, crystal, tumbler, 1-handled, #8858, 12-oz **$33.00**

Mt Vernon, amber or crystal, ashtray, oval, #71, 6x4½" **$12.00**

Mt Vernon, amber or crystal, bowl, oblong, crimped, #118, 12". **$32.50**

Mt Vernon, amber or crystal, bowl, 2-handled, #39, 10" **$20.00**

Mt Vernon, amber or crystal, candy dish, footed, w/lid, #9, 1-lb **$90.00**

Mt Vernon, amber or crystal, creamer, #86 .... **$10.00**

Mt Vernon, amber or crystal, finger bowl, #23 .... **$10.00**

Mt Vernon, amber or crystal, mug, #84, 14-oz **$30.00**

Mt Vernon, amber or crystal, plate, dinner; #40, 10½" **$30.00**

Mt Vernon, amber or crystal, relish dish, 3-part, #200, 11". **$25.00**

Mt Vernon, amber or crystal, salt & pepper shakers, short, #88, pr **$20.00**

Mt Vernon, amber or crystal, tumbler, footed, #3, 10-oz **$15.00**

Mt Veron, amber or crystal, bottle, scent; w/stopper, #1340, 2 ½-oz.. **$40.00**

Mt Veron, amber or crystal, sugar bowl, footed, #8 .... **$10.00**

No 703, green, bowl, fruit; #928, 5¼" **$12.50**

No 703, green, goblet, cocktail; #3060, 2½-oz.................... **$20.00**

No 703, green, platter, oval, #901, 12½" **$65.00**

No 703, green, tumbler, #3060, 8-oz................................. **$15.00**

No 703, green, tumbler, footed, #3060, 12-oz.................... **$22.50**

No 704, all colors, bowl, 3-footed, 7" **$35.00**

No 704, all colors, candlestick, #227 ½, 2", ea **$20.00**

No 704, all colors, casserole, w/lid, #912, 10½".................. **$175.00**

No 704, all colors, celery tray, #652, 11" **$45.00**

No 704, all colors, compote, #3075, 5" **$30.00**

No 704, all colors, cup, demitasse; #925 .... **$30.00**

No 704, all colors, ice bucket, w/bail, #957 .... **$110.00**

No 704, all colors, plate, cheese; w/lid, #3075 .... **$125.00**

Portia, crystal, basket, upturned sides, 2-handled **$30.00**

Portia, crystal, bowl, flared, 4-footed, 12" **$55.00**

Portia, crystal, bowl, pickle, 7" **$35.00**

Portia, crystal, candlestick, keyhole, #3400/646, 5", ea **$35.00**

Portia, crystal, cocktail shaker, w/glass stopper **$195.00**

Portia, crystal, cordial, #3126, 1-oz................................. **$55.00**

Portia, crystal, cup, footed, sq **$25.00**

Portia, crystal, goblet, brandy; low foot, #3121, 1-oz.......... **$50.00**

Portia, crystal, goblet, water; #3130, 9-oz **$28.00**

Portia, crystal, lamp, hurricane; keyhole base, w/prisms **$250.00**

Portia, crystal, mayonnaise, w/liner & ladle, #3400/11 .... **$55.00**

Portia, crystal, plate, salad; 8".. **$15.00**

Portia, crystal, plate, torte; 14" **$70.00**

Portia, crystal, sherbet, low, #3124, 7-oz **$16.00**

Portia, crystal, tumbler, #3126, 2½-oz **$35.00**

Portia, crystal, tumbler, footed, #3121, 10-oz.................... **$25.00**

Portia, crystal, vase, footed, 8" **$100.00**

Portia, crystal, vase, 13" **$165.00**

Rosalie, amber or crystal, bowl, cranberry; 3½" **$30.00**

Rosalie, amber or crystal, bowl, soup; 8½" **$30.00**

Rosalie, amber or crystal, compote, low foot, 6½" **$30.00**

Rosalie, amber or crystal, gravy dish, double, w/platter, #1147 .. **$100.00**

Rosalie, amber or crystal, nut dish, footed, 2½" **$50.00**

Rosalie, amber or crystal, platter, 15" **$80.00**

Rosalie, amber or crystal, vase, 6" **$55.00**

Rosalie, amber or crystal, wafer tray **$75.00**

Rosalie, blue, pink or green, bowl, Decagon, deep, 14" **$245.00**

Rosalie, blue, pink or green, bowl, 11" **$80.00**

Rosalie, blue, pink or green, cigarette jar, w/lid.................. **$90.00**

Rosalie, blue, pink or green, sugar bowl, footed, #867 .... **$22.00**

Rosalie, blue, pink or green, sugar shaker **$325.00**

Rosalie, blue, pink or green, tumbler, footed, #3077, 8-oz... **$20.00**

Rosalie, pink, blue or green, dressing bottle **$210.00**

Rose Point, crystal, ashtray, sq, #721, 2½" **$30.00**

Rose Point, crystal, basket, 2-handled, #3400/1182, 6" **$35.00**

Rose Point, crystal, bell, dinner; #3121 .... **$135.00**

Rose Point, crystal, bonbon, crimped, #3400/202, 6½" **$75.00**

Rose Point, crystal, bowl, cereal; #3400/10, 6" **$100.00**

Rose Point, crystal, bowl, fancy edge, footed, #3500/19, 11".. **$175.00**

Rose Point, crystal, bowl, fruit; #3500/10, 5" **$75.00**

Rose Point, crystal, bowl, soup; rimmed, #361, 8½" **$250.00**

Rose Point, crystal, candelabrum, 2-light, #3500/94, ea **$150.00**

Rose Point, crystal, candlestick, 2-light, #3900/72, 6", ea.... **$55.00**

Rose Point, crystal, candlesticks, $100.00 for the pair.
(Photo courtesy LiveAuctioneers.com/Homestead Auctions)

Rose Point, crystal, candy box, w/rose finial, 3-footed, #300, 6" ..**$325.00**

Rose Point, crystal, coaster, #1628, 3½" **$50.00**

Rose Point, crystal, compote, scalloped edge, #3900/136, 5½" ...**$65.00**

Rose Point, crystal, creamer, flat, #944............................. **$150.00**

Rose Point, crystal, mayonnaise, 3-pc, #3900/129 .... **$75.00**

Rose Point, crystal, pitcher, w/ice lip, #70, 20-oz............... **$395.00**

Rose Point, crystal, plate, footed, 2-handled, #3500/161, 8" ..**$45.00**

Rose Point, crystal, plate, service; #3900/167, 14" **$80.00**

Rose Point, crystal, punch cup, #488, 5-oz **$40.00**

Rose Point, crystal, relish dish, #3900/123, 7" **$40.00**

Rose Point, crystal, salt & pepper shakers, round, glass base, #1471, lg, pr **$135.00**

Rose Point, crystal, sherbet, tall, #3500, 7-oz......................$22.00

Rose Point, crystal, syrup, w/Drip-cut top, #1670 ....$395.00

Rose Point, crystal, trivet..$110.00

Rose Point, crystal, tumbler, #3400/115, 13-oz $50.00

Rose Point, crystal, tumbler, cone, footed, #3000, 3½-oz...$100.00

Rose Point, crystal, vase, footed, #1620, 9"........................$195.00

Rose Point, crystal, vase, slender, #274, 10" $65.00

Rose Point, crystal, vase, sweet pea; #629..........................$395.00

Tally Ho, amber or crystal, bowl, nappy, 2-handled, 6" $17.50

Tally Ho, amber or crystal, decanter, handled, 34-oz $60.00

Tally Ho, amber or crystal, goblet, wine; high stem, 2½-oz..$20.00

Tally Ho, amber or crystal, plate, luncheon; 9½" $35.00

Tally Ho, amber or crystal, punch bowl, footed, 13" $195.00

Tally Ho, amber or crystal, vase, footed, 12".........................$95.00

Tally Ho, Carmen or Royal, bowl, 2-compartment, 8½" $75.00

Tally Ho, Carmen or Royal, candlestick, 6½", ea $65.00

Tally Ho, Carmen or Royal, goblet, oyster cocktail; #1402..$25.00

Tally Ho, Carmen or Royal, sherbet, tall, 7½-oz $30.00

Tally Ho, Forest Green, bowl, 9" $40.00

Tally Ho, Forest Green, compote, low foot, 7".......................$50.00

Tally Ho, Forest Green, plate, 17½"..$60.00

Tally Ho, Forest Green, punch mug, 6-oz............................$15.00

Tally Ho, Forest Green, tumbler, 5-oz...................................$35.00

Valencia, crystal, ashtray, #3500/128, 4½" dia $16.00

Valencia, crystal, bowl, 2-handled, footed, #3500/115, 9½" $35.00

Valencia, crystal, claret, #1402 ....$35.00

Valencia, crystal, creamer, individual, #3500/15...................$18.00

Valencia, crystal, cup, #3500/1..$15.00

Valencia, crystal, pitcher, Doulton, #3400/141, 80-oz $350.00

Valencia, crystal, plate, sandwich; 2-handled, #1402, 11½"...$28.00

Valencia, crystal, relish dish, 4-compartment, #3500/65, 10" .. $60.00

Valencia, crystal, tumbler, footed, #3500, 16-oz...................$28.00

Valencia, crystal, tumbler, footed, #3500, 2½"......................$22.00

Waverly, candle epergne, four-light, from $125.00 to $140.00.

(Photo courtesy LiveAuctioneers.com/Homestead Auctions)

Wildflower, crystal, bowl, #3900/1185, 10".........................$60.00

Wildflower, crystal, cake plate, #170, 13" $75.00

Wildflower, crystal, cocktail shaker, #3400/175 ....$150.00

Wildflower, crystal, ice bucket, w/chrome handle, #3900/67 .. **$125.00**

Wildflower, crystal, pitcher, ball-form, #3400/38, 80-oz....**$195.00**

Wildflower, crystal, plate, bread & butter; #3900/20, 6½" ..**$10.00**

Wildflower, crystal, sugar bowl, #3400/16 ....**$18.00**

Wildflower, crystal, vase, globular, #3400/102, 5" **$55.00**

Wildflower, crystal, vase, keyhole foot, #1237, 9" **$110.00**

Wilflower, crystal, finger bowl, blown, 4½" **$30.00**

Cameras

Camera collecting as a hobby can provide both enjoyment and potential profit if a careful selection is made. The large number of older cameras that have been offered for sale on the internet continues to create a good buyer's market, and excellent cameras can often be purchased that offer great potential for future increases in value. The faster than expected growth of the digital camera technology and popularity has also strongly affected the film camera market, except for the rare collectible categories. There is currently no 'collectible' market for the digital cameras, and sales of used ones are not good, due to the difficulty of checking out one of these cameras and the complexity of the associated software and computer adapters necessary for their use. The use of digital cameras for first-time photographers is increasing rapidly and will continue to have a drastic effect on the prices of regular film cameras.

Buying at garage sales, flea markets, auctions, or estate sales are ways to add to collections, although it is rare to find an expensive classic camera offered through these outlets. However, buying at such sales to resell to dealers or collectors can be profitable if one is careful to buy quality items, not common cameras that sell for very little at best, especially when they show wear. A very old camera is not necessarily valuable, as value depends on availability and quality. Knowing how to check out a camera or to judge quality will pay off when building a collection or when buying for resale. Another factor to consider on many older film cameras is the growing difficulty in finding the prescribed batteries for them. Many of them used 1.35 volt mercury batteries which are illegal now and no longer available. Conversions to many of the cameras are possible but expensive and often impracticable. Some of the other types of camera batteries are beginning to disapper from the market.

Some very general guidelines follow; but for the serious buyer who intends to concentrate on cameras, there are several reference books that can be obtained. Most are rather expensive, but some provide good descriptions and/or price guidelines.

There are many distinct types of cameras to consider: large format (such as Graflex and large view cameras), medium format, early folding and box styles, 35mm single-lens-reflex (SLR), 35mm range finders, twin-lens-reflex (TLR), miniature or sub-miniature, novelty, and other types — including the more recent 'point-and-shoot' styles, Polaroids, and movie cameras. Though there is a growing interest in certain types, we would caution you against buying common Polaroids and movie cameras for resale, as there is very little market for them at this time. In these categories, buy only those that are like new and still in their original boxes to attract collectors.

Most folding and box-type cameras were produced before the 1930s and today make good collector items. Most have fairly low values because they were made in vast numbers. Many of the more expensive classics were manufactured in the 1930 – 1955 period and include primarily the Rangefinder type of camera and those with the first built-in light meters. The most prized of these are of German or Japanese manufacture, valued because of their innovative designs and great optics. The key to collecting these types of cameras is to find a mint-condition example or one still in the original box. In camera collecting, quality is the most important aspect.

This updated listing includes only a few of the various categories and models of cameras from the many thousands available and gives current average retail prices for working models with average wear. Note that cameras in mint condition or like new with their original boxes may be valued much higher, while very worn examples with defects (scratches, dents, torn covers, poor optics, nonworking meters or rangefinders, torn bellows, corroded battery compartments, etc.) would be valued far less. A dealer, when buying for resale, will pay only a percentage of these values, as he must consider his expenses for refurbishing, cleaning, etc., as well as sales expenses. Again, remember that quality is the key to value, and prices on some cameras vary widely according to condition. Also be aware that many of the great classic cameras, even in very poor condition, are valued for their parts and often have good value if bargains can be found. Look also for camera lenses alone, some of which are very valuable.

Typical collector favorites are old Alpa, Canon, Contax, Nikon, Leica, Rolleiflex, some Zeiss-Ikon models, Exakta, and certain Voigtlander models. For information about these makes as well as models by other manufacturers, please consult the advisor.

Advisor: C.E. Cataldo (See Directory, Cameras)

Agfa, Billy, 1930s	$15.00
Agfa, box type, 1930-50, from $5 to	$20.00
Agfa, Isolette	$20.00
Agfa, Karat-35, 1940	$35.00
Agfa, Optima, 1960s, from $15 to	$35.00
Aires, 35III, 1958, from $15 to	$35.00
Alpa, Standard, 1946-52, Swiss, from $700 to	$1,500.00
Ansco, Cadet	$5.00
Ansco, Folding, Nr 1 to Nr 10, ea from $5 to	$30.00
Ansco, Memar, 1954-58	$20.00
Ansco, Memo, 1927 type, from $60 to	$80.00
Ansco, Speedex, Standard, 1950	$15.00
Argoflex, Seventy-Five, TLR, 1949-58	$7.00
Argus A2F, 1940, from $10 to	$20.00
Argus C3, Black brick type, 1940-50	$8.00
Asahi Pentax, Original, 1957	$200.00
Asahiflex I, 1st Japanese SLR	$500.00
Baldi, by Balda-Werk, 1930s	$30.00
Bell & Howell Dial 35, from $25 to	$40.00
Bell & Howell Foton, 1948, from $500 to	$700.00
Bosley B2	$20.00
Braun Paxette I, 1952, from $20 to	$30.00
Burke & James Cub, 1914	$20.00
Canon A-1, from $50 to	$120.00
Canon AE-IP, from $50 to	$100.00
Canon AE-1, from $40 to	$80.00
Canon F-1, from $150 to	$225.00
Canon IIB, 1949-53	$225.00

Canon IIF Rangefinder, ca 1954, from $175 to	$275.00
Canon III	$250.00
Canon IV SB Rangefinder, w/50/f1.8 lens, 1952-55, from $250 to	$350.00
Canon J, 1939-44, from $3,000 to	$5,000.00

Canon J-11 Rangefinder, 1945, rare, from $4,500.00 to $6,000.00. (Photo courtesy C.E. Cataldo)

Canon L-1, 1956-57	$400.00
Canon P, 1958-61, from $220 to	$350.00
Canon S-II, Seiki-Kogaku, 1946-47, from $500 to	$800.00
Canon S-II, 1947-49	$375.00
Canon T-50, from $30 to	$50.00
Canon TL, from $30 to	$50.00
Canon TX, from $30 to	$40.00
Canon VT, 1956-57, from $200 to	$300.00
Canon 7, 1961-64, from $200 to	$400.00
Canonet QL1, from $25 to	$40.00
Compass Camera, 1938, from $1,000 to	$1,300.00
Conley, 4x5 Folding Plate, 1905, from $90 to	$140.00
Contax II or III, 1936, from $200 to	$400.00
Contessa 35, 1950-55, from $100 to	$150.00
Detrola Model D, Detroit Corp, 1938-40	$20.00
Eastman Folding Brownie Six-20	$12.00
Eastman Kodak Baby Brownie, Bakelite, from $5 to	$10.00
Eastman Kodak Bantam, Art Deco, 1935-38	$35.00

Eastman Kodak Medalist 1, 1941 – 1948, from $150.00 to $200.00. (Photo courtesy C.E. Cataldo)

Eastman Kodak Retina II, from $45 to	$60.00
Eastman Kodak Retina IIa, from $55 to	$75.00

Eastman Kodak Retina IIIC, from $275 to.......................$375.00
Eastman Kodak Retina IIIc, from $90 to.......................$150.00
Eastman Kodak Retinette, various models, ea from $15 to ..$40.00
Eastman Kodak Signet 35...$35.00
Eastman Kodak Signet 80...$50.00
Eastman Kodak 35, 1940-51, from $20 to.......................$40.00
Eastman Premo, many models exist, ea from $30 to.........$200.00
Eastman View Camera, early 1900s, from $100 to...........$200.00
Edinex, by Wirgen...$30.00
Exakta II, 1949-50, from $100 to...............................$130.00
Exakta VX, 1951, from $75 to....................................$85.00
FED 1, USSR, postwar, from $30 to.............................$50.00
FED 1, USSR, prewar, from $70 to.............................$100.00
Fujica AX-3, from $45 to..$75.00
Fujica AX-5..$115.00
Graflex Pacemaker Crown Graphic, various sizes, ea from $80
    to..$150.00
Graflex Speed Graphic, various sizes, ea from $60 to.........$200.00
Hasselblad 1000F, 1952-57, from $300 to......................$500.00
Herbert-George, Donald Duck, 1946................................$25.00
Kodak Jiffy Vest Pocket, 1935-41, from $20 to...................$35.00
Kodak No 2 Folding Pocket Brownie, 1904-07..................$25.00
Konica Autoreflex TC, various models, ea from $40 to........$70.00
Konica FS-1..$50.00
Konica III Rangefinder, 1956-59, from $90 to.................$110.00
Kowa H, 1963-67...$25.00
Leica II, 1963-67, from $200 to..................................$400.00
Leica IID, 1932-38, from $200 to................................$400.00
Leica IIIF, 1950-56, from $200 to...............................$400.00

Leica M3 Rangefinder, double stroke advance, 1954 – 1966, from $700.00 to $1,000.00. (Photo courtesy C.E. Cataldo)

Mamiya-Sekor 500TL, 1966.......................................$20.00
Mamiyaflex TLR, 1951, from $70 to.............................$100.00
Minolta Autocord, TLR, from $75 to............................$100.00
Minolta HiMatic Series, various models, ea from $10 to $25.00
Minolta SR-7..$40.00
Minolta SRT-101, from $40 to.....................................$65.00
Minolta SRT-202, from $50 to.....................................$90.00
Minolta X-700, from $60 to..$125.00
Minolta XD-11, 1977, from $90 to...............................$130.00
Minolta XG-1m XG-7, XG-9, XG-A, ea from $35 to..........$80.00
Minolta 35, early rangefinder models, 1947-50, ea from $250
    to..$400.00

Minolta-16, mini, various models, ea from $15 to...............$30.00
Minox B, spy camera..$125.00
Miranda Automex II, 1963..$70.00
Nikkormat (Nikon), various models, ea from $70 to.........$150.00
Nikon EM, from $45 to..$75.00
Nikon F, various finders & meters, ea from $125 to.........$250.00
Nikon FG..$100.00
Nikon FM..$150.00
Nikon S Rangefinder, 1951-54, from $450 to..................$800.00
Nikon SP Rangefinder, 1958-60, from $1,500 to..........$2,000.00
Nikon S2 Rangefinder, 1954-58, from $700 to.............$1,000.00
Olympus OM-1, from $90 to.......................................$120.00
Olympus OM-10, from $40 to......................................$60.00
Olympus Pen EE, compact half-frame..............................$35.00
Olympus Pen F, compact half-frame SLR, from $100 to....$200.00
Pax M3, 1957...$30.00
Pentax K-1000, from $50 to..$90.00
Pentax ME, from $50 to..$75.00
Pentax Spotmatic, many models, ea from $40 to.............$100.00
Petri FT, FT-1000, FT-EE & similar models, ea from $35 to ..$70.00
Petri-7, 1961..$20.00
Plaubel-Makina II, 1933-39..$200.00
Polaroid, most models, ea from $5 to............................$10.00
Polaroid SX-70, from $20 to..$35.00
Polaroid 110, 110A, 110B, ea from $20 to.......................$40.00
Polaroid 180, 185, 190, 195, ea from $100 to..................$250.00
Praktica FX, 1952-57..$30.00
Praktica Super TL..$40.00
Realist Stereo, 3.5 lens..$80.00
Regula, King, fixed lens, various models, ea......................$25.00
Regula, King, interchangeable lens, various models, ea........$60.00
Ricoh Diacord 1, 1 LR, built-in meter, 1958.....................$65.00
Ricoh Singlex, 1965, from $50 to.................................$70.00
Rollei 35, mini, Germany, 1966-70, from $150 to...........$250.00
Rollei 35, mini, Singapore, from $80 to.........................$150.00
Rolleicord II, 1936-50, from $70 to..............................$90.00
Rolleiflex Automat, 1937 model...................................$125.00
Rolleiflex SL35M, 1978, from $75 to............................$100.00
Rolleiflex 3.5E..$300.00
Samoca 35, 1950s..$25.00
Seroco 4x5, Folding Plate, Sears, 1901, from $90 to.........$135.00
Spartus Press Flash, 1939-50.......................................$10.00
Taron 35, 1955..$25.00
Tessina, mini, from $300 to..$500.00
Topcon Super D, 1963-74...$125.00
Topcon Uni..$35.00
Tower 45, Sears, w/Nickkor lens...................................$200.00
Tower 50, Sears, w/Cassar lens.....................................$20.00
Univex-A, Univ Camera Co, 1933..................................$25.00
Voightlander Vitessa L, 1954, from $150 to....................$200.00
Voightlander Vitessa T, 1957, from $150 to....................$200.00
Voightlander Vito II, 1950..$40.00
Voigtlander Bessa, various folding models, 1931-49, ea from $15
    to..$35.00
Voigtlander Bessa, w/rangefinder, 1936.........................$140.00
Yashica A, TLR..$35.00
Yashica Electro-35, 1966..$25.00

Yashica FX-70 ....**$60.00**

Yashicaflex TLR, Yashikor 80mm lens, from $150.00 to $250.00.
(Photo courtesy C.E. Cataldo)

Yashicamat 124G, TLR, from $100 to..............................**$140.00**
Zeiss Baldur Box Tengor, Frontar lens, 1935, from $35 to.**$150.00**
Zeiss Ikon Juwell, 1927-39 ....**$500.00**
Zeiss Ikon Nettar, Folding Roll Film, various sizes, ea from $25 to **$35.00**
Zeiss Ikon Super Ikonta B, 1937-56 ....**$150.00**
Zenit A, USSR, from $20 to.............................**$35.00**
Zorki, USSR, Rangefinder, 1957-73 ....**$50.00**

Candlewick

This is a beautifully simple, very diverse line of glassware made by the Imperial Glass Company of Bellaire, Ohio, from 1936 to 1982. (The factory closed in 1984.) From all explored written material found so far, it is known that Mr. Earl W. Newton brought back a piece of the French Cannonball pattern upon returning from a trip. The first Candlewick mold was derived using that piece of glass as a reference. As for the name Candlewick, it was introduced at a Wheeling, West Virginia, centennial celebration in August of 1936, appearing on a brochure showing the crafting of 'Candlewick Quilts' and promoting the new Candlewick line.

Imperial did cuttings on Candlewick; several major patterns are Floral, Valley Lily, Starlight, Princess, DuBarry, and Dots. Remember, these are *cuts* and should not be confused with etchings. (Cuts that were left unpolished were called Gray Cut — an example of this is the Dot cut.) The most popular Candlewick etching was Rose of Sharon (Wild Rose). All cutting was done on a wheel, while etching utilized etching paper and acid. Many collectors confuse these two processes. Imperial also used gold, silver, platinum, and hand painting to decorate Candlewick, and they made several items in colors.

With over 740 pieces in all, Imperial's Candlewick line was one of the leading tableware patterns in the country. Due to its popularity with collectors today, it is still number one and has the distinction of being the only single line of glassware ever to have had two books written about it, a national newsletter, and over 15 collector clubs across the USA devoted to it exclusively.

There are reproductions on the market today — some are coming in from foreign countries. Look-alikes are often mistakenly labeled Candlewick, so if you're going to collect this pattern, you need to be well informed. Most collectors use the company mold numbers to help identify all the variations and sizes. The *Imperial Glass Encyclopedia, Vol. 1*, has a very good chapter on Candlewick. Also reference *Candlewick, The Jewel of Imperial*, by Mary Wetzel-Tomalka; *Elegant Glassware of the Depression Era* by Gene and Cathy Florence (Collector Books); and *Candlewick and Decorated Candlewick* by Myrna and Bob Garrison.

Advisor: National Imperial Glass Collectors Society, Inc.

Club: National Imperial Glass Collectors Society, Inc.
P.O. Box 534
Bellaire, Ohio 43906
www.imperialglass.org

Punch bowl set, bowl on 15" tray with 12 cups and ladle, $275.00. (Photo courtesy LiveAuctioneers.com/Auctions By the Bay Inc.)

Ashtray, heart-shaped, #400/174, 6½" **$12.00**
Ashtray, sq, #400/652, 4½".................................**$30.00**
Basket, #400/73/0, 11" **$265.00**
Bell, #400/108, 5" **$95.00**
Bottle, scent; 4-bead, E408 ....**$75.00**
Bowl, belled, #400/106B, 12"..............................**$100.00**
Bowl, cottage cheese; #400/85, 6".......................**$25.00**
Bowl, cream soup; #400/50, 5" **$40.00**
Bowl, crimped, footed, #400/67C, 9" **$185.00**
Bowl, jelly; w/lid, #400/59, 5½" **$75.00**
Bowl, lily, 4-footed, #400/74J, 7" **$80.00**
Bowl, salad; #400/75B, 10½"................................**$40.00**
Bowl, shallow, #400/17F, 12".............................**$47.50**
Bowl, sq, #400/233, 7" **$155.00**
Bowl, vegetable; w/lid, #400/65/1, 8" **$375.00**
Bowl, 3-footed, #400/183, 6" **$60.00**
Butter dish, round, #400/144, 5½" **$35.00**
Cake stand, high foot, #400/103D, 11"...............**$75.00**
Candleholder, tall, 3-bead stems, #400/175, 6½", ea **$175.00**
Candleholder, 2-light, #400/100, ea....................**$24.00**
Candleholder, 3-toed, #400/207, 4½", ea **$120.00**
Candy box, divided, #400/110, 7"........................**$130.00**
Candy box, #400/259, 7" **$150.00**
Claret, #3800, 5-oz..**$75.00**

Coaster, w/spoon rest, #400/226.............................$18.00
Compote, #400/63B, 4½"..$40.00
Compote, fruit; crimped, footed, #40/103C, 10" $225.00
Condiment set, 4-pc, #400/1769.............................$80.00
Creamer, domed foot, #400/18.............................$125.00
Cup, after dinner; #400/77.....................................$20.00
Finger bowl, #3800...$35.00
Goblet, wine; #400/190, 5-oz................................$22.00
Lamp, hurricane; candle base, 2-pc, #400/79.............$135.00
Lamp shade...$85.00
Mayonnaise set, plate, heart bowl, spoon, #400/49.............$40.00
Mirror, standing, round, 4½".................................$165.00
Muddler, #400/19...$15.00
Oil, etched Oil, w/stopper, #400/121 ....$75.00
Parfait, #3400, 6-oz..$60.00
Pitcher, plain, #400/419, 40-oz............................$50.00
Pitcher, short, round, #400/330, 14-oz $210.00
Plate, #400/34, 4½"..$8.00
Plate, bread & butter; #400/1D, 6"...........................$7.00
Plate, crescent salad; #400/120, 8¼"........................$60.00
Plate, crimped, 2-handled, #400/52C, 6¾"...................$30.00
Plate, dinner; #400/10D, 10½"...............................$42.00
Plate, luncheon; #400/7D, 9".................................$15.00
Plate, oval, #400/169, 8".......................................$25.00
Plate, triangular, #400/266, 7½".............................$100.00
Plate, w/indent, #400/50, 8"..................................$12.00
Plate, 2-handled, #400/72D, 10"..............................$35.00
Platter, #400/124D, 13"...$110.00

Relish, five-part, five-handled, 10½", $75.00. (Photo courtesy LiveAuctioneers.com/Dirk Soulis Auctions)

Salt & pepper shakers, straight sides, chrome top, bead foot, #400/247, pr...................................$20.00
Salt dip, #400/19, 2¼"...$10.00
Salt spoon, ribbed bowl, #4000.............................$11.00
Server, deviled egg; center handle, #400/154, 12" $120.00
Snack jar, bead foot, w/lid, #400/139/1 ....$795.00
Teacup, #400/35...$7.00
Tidbit, 2-tier, cupped, #400/2701............................$60.00
Tray, relish; 5-section, #400/102, 13" $65.00
Tray, upturned handles, #400/42E, 5½"......................$25.00

Tumbler, cocktail; footed, #400/19, 3-oz $16.00
Tumbler, footed, #3400, 12-oz.............................$20.00
Tumbler, juice; #400/112, 3½-oz............................$12.00
Tumbler, old-fashioned; #400-19, 7-oz......................$38.00
Vase, flared rim, footed, #400/138B, 6".......................$195.00
Vase, flat, crimped edge, #400/143C, 8".......................$95.00
Vase, sm neck, ball-form, beaded foot, #400/25................$65.00

Salt and pepper shakers, $65.00. (Photo courtesy LiveAuctioneers.com/ Homestead Auctions)

Candy Containers

Most of us can recall buying these glass toys as a child, since they were made well into the 1960s. We were fascinated by the variety of their shapes then, just as collectors are today. Looking back, it couldn't have been we were buying them for the candy, though perhaps as a child those tiny sugary balls flavored more with the coloring agent than anything else were enough to satisfy our 'sweet tooth.'

Glass candy containers have been around since our country's centennial celebration in 1876 when the first two, the Liberty Bell and the Independence Hall, were introduced. Since then they have been made in hundreds of styles, and some of them have become very expensive. The leading manufacturers were in the east — Westmoreland, Victory Glass, J.H. Millstein, Crosetti, L.E. Smith, Jack Stough, T.H. Stough, and West Bros. made perhaps 90% of them — and collectors report finding many in the Pennsylvania area. Most are clear, but you'll find them in various other colors as well.

If you're going to deal in candy containers of either the vintage glass variety or modern plastics, you'll need a book that will show you all the variations available. Vintage candy container buffs will find *Collector's Guide to Candy Containers* by Douglas M. Dezso, J. Leon Poirier, and Rose D. Poirier to be a wonderful source of pictures and information. D&P numbers in our listings refer to that book. Another good reference is *The Compleat American Glass Candy Containers Handbook* by Eilkelberner and Agadjaninian (revised by Adele Bowden).

Because of their popularity and considerable worth, many of the original glass containers have been reproduced. Beware of any questionable glassware that has a slick or oily touch. Among those that have been produced are Amber Pistol, Auto, Carpet Sweeper, Chicken on Nest, Display Case, Dog, Drum Mug, Fire Engine, Independence Hall, Jackie Coogan, Kewpie, Mail Box, Mantel Clock, Mule and Waterwagon, Peter Rabbit, Piano, Rabbit Pushing

Wheelbarrow, Rocking Horse, Safe, Santa, Santa's Boot, Station Wagon, and Uncle Sam's Hat. Others are possible.

Plastic parts were incorporated into candy containers as early as the 1940s, and by 1960 virtually all were made entirely of this inexpensive, colorful, and versatile material. Children were soon clamoring for these new all-plastic containers, many of which seemed as much a toy as a mere candy container. Today most of these are imported from China and Mexico. Shapes vary from vehicles of all sorts to cartoon, movie, and TV characters, TV sets and telephones, to holiday decorations and household items. Collector interest is apparent in shops and malls as well as on the internet.

Our values are given for candy containers that are undamaged, in good original paint, and complete (with all original parts and closure). Repaired or repainted containers are worth much less.

See also Christmas; Easter; Halloween.

Club: Candy Container Collectors of America
Jim Olean, membership chairperson
115 Macbeth Dr.
Lower Burrell, PA 15068-2628
www.candycontainer.org

Vintage, Glass

Airplane, Red Plastic Wing; Musical Toy on cap, D&P 83 .. **$55.00**
Blimp, heavy glass, D&P 88 ....**$200.00**
Camel sitting, Shriner's; clear on amber glass, D&P 4 ....**$35.00**
Car, Station Wagon, JH Millstein, D&P 178 (+) **$40.00**
Cat, Boyd; various colors, D&P 159 ....**$25.00**
Chicken on Sagging Basket, D&P 14 ....**$75.00**
Dog, Little Doggie in the Window; Stough, D&P 30 ....**$30.00**
Elephant, GOP, original paint, DUP 43 ....**$250.00**
Flapper, paper face glued inside, D&P 203 ....**$65.00**
Gun, Stough's 1939 Patent Pending, D&P 400 ....**$25.00**
Horn, Stough's 1953; 3 valve buttons, DUP 453 ....**$40.00**

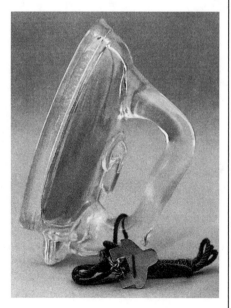

Iron, electric; cardboard closure, Pla-Toy Co., D&P 305, $50.00. (Photo courtesy Poirier, Poirier, and Deszo)

Lamp, Metal Shade; Stough, D&P 335 ....**$50.00**
Lantern, 16-hole, D&P 376 ....**$35.00**

Locomotive, Stough's Musical Toy; D&P 506 ....**$40.00**
Nurser, Plain; rubber nipple, D&P 123 ....**$30.00**
Pipe, Germany, cork closure, D&P 437 ....**$60.00**

Turkey Gobbler, D&P 75, 3½", $175.00.
(Photo courtesy Poirier, Porier, and Dezso)

Miscellaneous

Boy riding pig, movable arms, waving hat, papier-mache & bisque, 4x5" **$360.00**
Bulldog, composition, w/hat, Germany, 4", VG **$130.00**
Donkey w/jack-o'-lantern in mouth, orange plastic w/black details, on wheels, 5½x5½" **$105.00**
Donald Duck sitting on keg, celluloid & cardboard, Made in Japan, Disney, 1930s, 5½" **$425.00**
Dove, composition w/gray paint, pink-painted metal frame, orange glass eyes, 4½x8" **$100.00**

Egg, litho tin with cats, paper lining, 8", EX, $200.00. (Photo courtesy LiveAuctioneers.com/Noel Barrett Antiques & Auctions)

Gas pump, Pump for Candy, red plastic, broken hose, VG ..**$15.00**
George Washington bust, composition, bottom plug, 4-6"...**$150.00**
Happy Hooligan, molded composition, eyes are on metal springs, cardboard bottom marked Germany, ca 1915, 5", EX+ **$425.00**

Horse, papier-maché, head removes, 4½", VG **$155.00**

Jack-o'lantern scarecrow, orange plastic w/black details, Rosen/Rosbro, 1950s, 5" **$80.00**

Jitney Bus, tin, green cab & original green wheels, Westerville Bros, NM.. **$480.00**

Man-in-Moon, cardboard moon face on ea side of cardboard ball that separates, 3½", VG+ **$660.00**

Potato, composition, Germany, 3-4" **$50.00**

Pumpkin man sitting on pumpkin, composition papier-mache, replaced inserts, Germany, pre-1920, 4" **$425.00**

Pumpkin-head chauffeur, painted glass, missing bail handle & cap, 4", G.. **$480.00**

Rooster, compositon, red/white/black paint, metal legs, glass eyes, 9¼" **$250.00**

Snowman, spun cotton, holds sm tree, red hat & buttons, Germany, 9½" **$275.00**

Snowman, white plastic w/red bow tie & black top hat, 1950s... **$15.00**

Train engine, clear plastic w/loop on cowcatcher for hanging, Rosen, unopened, M w/original paper tag **$20.00**

Turkey, composition w/metal feet, head removes, Germany, 5" ...**$100.00**

Turkey, composition w/metal feet, head removes, Germany, 12".. **$425.00**

Turkey, painted wax, fine colors w/EX details, 3½", VG **$30.00**

Turkey, papier-mache w/metal legs, opens at neck, replaced cardboard insert, 11" **$900.00**

Watermelon w/face, molded cardboard w/celluloid body, Austria, 4¼" **$125.00**

Cape Cod by Avon

You can't walk through any flea market or mall now without seeing a good supply of this lovely ruby red glassware. It was made by Wheaton Glass Co. and sold by Avon from 1975 until it was discontinued in 1993. A gradual phasing-out process lasted for approximately two years. The small cruet and tall candlesticks, for instance, were filled originally with one or the other of their fragrances, the wine and water goblets were filled with scented candle wax, and the dessert bowl with guest soap. Many 'campaigns' featured accessory tableware items such as plates, cake stands, and a water pitcher. Though still plentiful, dealers tell us that interest in this glassware is on the increase, and we expect values to climb as supplies diminish.

For more information we recommend *Avon's Cape Cod* by Debbie and Randy Coe.

Advisor: Debbie Coe (See Directory, Cape Cod)

Bell, Hostess; marked Christmas 1979, 6½" **$18.00**

Bowl, dessert; 1979-80, 6½" **$10.00**

Bowl, rimmed soup; 1991, 7½" **$22.00**

Bowl, vegetable; marked Centennial Edition 1886-1986, 8¾"....**$30.00**

Box, trinket; heart-form, w/lid, 1989-90, 4" **$15.00**

Butter dish, 1983-84, ¼-lb, 7" L, from $20 to................. **$22.00**

Cake knife, red plastic handle, wedge-shaped blade, Regent Sheffield, 1981-84, 8" **$18.00**

Cake plate, pedestal foot, 1991, 3½x10¾" dia **$48.00**

Candleholder, hurricane type, clear chimney, 1985, ea......... **$39.50**

Candlesticks, 1983-84, 2½", pr................................ **$9.00**

Candlesticks, 8¾", pr... **$25.00**

Candy dish, 1987-90, 3½x6" **$19.50**

Christmas ornament, 6-sided, marked Christmas 1990, 3¼"...**$12.50**

Creamer, footed, 1981-84, 4" **$10.00**

Cruet, oil; w/stopper, 1957-80, 5-oz......................... **$12.50**

Cup & saucer, 15th Anniversary, marked 1975-90 on cup, 7-oz.. **$20.00**

Cup & saucer, 1990-93, 7-oz................................. **$15.00**

Decanter, 1977, 9¾" **$18.00**

Goblet, claret; 1992, 5-oz, 5¼", from $10 to................. **$14.00**

Goblet, saucer champagne; 1991, 8-oz, 5¼" **$14.00**

Goblet, water; 1976-90, 9-oz................................. **$9.00**

Goblet, wine; 1976-90, 3-oz **$2.00**

Mug, pedestal foot, 1982-84, 5-oz, 5", from $8 to **$12.00**

Napkin ring, 1989-90, 1¾"................................... **$10.00**

Pie plate/server, 1992-93, 10¾" dia, from $20 to............. **$25.00**

Pitcher, water; footed, 1984-85, 60-oz, from $40 to **$45.00**

Plate, bread & butter; 1992-93, 5½"......................... **$8.00**

Plate, cake; pedestal foot, 1991, 3½x10¾" dia **$50.00**

Plate, dessert; 1980-90, 7½"................................. **$7.50**

Plate, dinner; 1982-90, 11", from $20 to..................... **$25.00**

Platter, oval, 1986, 13"..................................... **$48.00**

Relish, rectangular, 2-part, 1985-96, 9½" **$15.00**

Salt & pepper shakers, marked May 1978, pr **$18.00**

Salt & pepper shakers, unmarked, 1978-80, pr................. **$12.00**

Sauceboat, footed, 1988, 8" L............................... **$28.00**

Bell, hostess; unmarked, 1979 – 1980, $17.50.

Cardinal China

This was the name of a distributing company that had its merchandise made to order and sold it through a chain of showrooms and outlet stores in several states from the late 1940s through the 1950s. (Although it made some of its own pottery early on, we have yet to find out just what it produced.) It used its company name to mark cookie jars (some of which were made by the American Bisque Company), novelty wares, and kitchen items, many of which you'll see as you make your flea market rounds. *The Ultimate Collector's Encyclopedia of Cookie Jars* by Fred and Joyce Roerig (Collector

Books) shows a page of its jars, and more can be seen in *American Bisque* by Mary Jane Giacomini (Schiffer).

See also Cookie Jars.

Measuring spoon holder, Measure Boy, with cups and spoons (two missing in photo), if complete, $50.00.

Bowl, lettuce-leaf shape, green, 6¼" **$6.00**
Cake plate, gold-plated, Cardinal China Co Warranted 22 Made in USA, 10¼" **$15.00**
Cake server, gold-plated, Cardinal China Co Warranted 22 Made in USA **$12.00**
Cake stand, I Knew You Were Coming So I Baked a Cake, pink roses & baby's breath, gold trim, w/music box, 4x10¼" dia .. **$30.00**
Candleholder, beehive shape, green, 5x5", ea **$12.00**
Celery dish, celery-stalk form, from $14 to **$17.00**
Cheese dish, cheese wedges (various types) in white, rectangular, 5x3¾" **$8.00**
Corn holder, cornhusks, Corn Husks by Cardinal China, 8¾", 4 for **$24.00**
Corn-serving dish, ear of corn, 11½" **$12.50**
Cracker server, Cracker & Bar Hound, dachshund figural, 10" L **$30.00**
Crock, Stinky Stuff on front, skunk finial, 5" **$20.00**
Crumber set, airbrushed leaves, wood-handled brush w/plastic bristles, 2-pc **$12.50**
Dresser dish, Doxie-dog, from $15 to **$18.00**
Egg dish, rooster decoration, 2 rests in side, 6" **$25.00**
Egg timer, windmill, 4½" **$45.00**
Flower holder, turquoise on white, doughnut shape, 7" **$8.00**
Gravy boat, dark green, double-spout, 2¾x6" dia, 7½" to top of handle **$12.00**
Gravy boat, roses, 2⅝x7¾" **$10.00**
Gravy boat, turquoise, double-spout, single 2" handle, 3 sm feet, embossed mark **$15.00**
Gravy/grease separator, yellow, 7¼" L **$15.00**
Measuring spoon holder, cottage w/peaked roof, 5½" **$50.00**
Measuring spoon holder, flowerpot, plain (not basketweave) base **$10.00**

Measuring spoon holder, flowerpot w/basketweave base, w/spoons .**$12.00**
Measuring spoon holder, Measure Boy **$25.00**
Measuring spoon holder, windowsill-planter shape w/plastic spoons as flowers **$15.00**
Ring holder, elephant figural, shamrock, flat back w/hole for hanging **$12.00**
Scissors holder, nest w/chicken figural **$22.00**
Shrimp boats, 4⅜" L w/cardboard sail on wooden pole, various colors, set of 4, from $65 to **$75.00**
Spoon rest, double sunflower from, 6x5½", from $7 to **$10.00**
Spoon rest, rooster on white, triangular, 1950s **$15.00**
Switch plate, bluebirds, Good Morning/Good Night, 5¼x4". **$22.00**
Teabag holder, single 5-petal flower face **$6.00**
Teapot, Bar-B-Que; 3-D picnic on top w/embossed hamburgers hot dogs etc on side, blue trim on spout & handle, 5x9" **$25.00**

Carnival Chalkware

From about 1910 until sometime in the 1950s, winners of carnival games everywhere in the United States were awarded chalkware figures of Kewpie dolls, the Lone Ranger, Hula girls, comic characters, etc. The assortment was vast and varied. The earliest were made of plaster with a pink cast. They ranged in size from about 5" up to 16".

They were easily chipped, so when it came time for the carnival to pick up and move on, they had to be carefully wrapped and packed away, a time consuming, tedious chore. When stuffed animals became available, concessionists found that they could simply throw them into a box without fear of damage, and so ended an era.

Today the most valuable of these statues are those modeled after Disney characters, movie stars, and comic book heroes.

Our values are for examples in excellent to near-mint condition.

Apache Babe, original marks, 1936-45, 15" **$90.00**
Beach Bather, unmarked, 1940-50, 7½x9" **$60.00**
Boy & dog, marked Pals, 1935-45, 10x9" **$35.00**

Bulldog, marked Illinois State Fair 1939, 16", $75.00. (Photo courtesy LiveAuctioneers.com/Tom Harris Auctions)

Call Me Papa, 1935-45, 14" $15.00

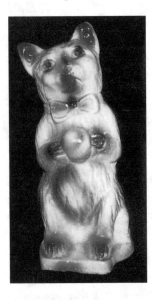

Cat with ball, 7", $25.00. (Photo courtesy Marily Dipboye)

Clown standing w/hand in pockets, ca 1940-50, 9½" $45.00
Colonial lady standing w/dog, 1935-45, 11¼" $55.00
Dead End Kid, ca 1935-45, rare, 15" $165.00
Elephant rearing & wild, ca 1930-45, 9¾" $45.00
Gorilla, King Kong w/fists on chest, flat back, unmarked, ca 1930-40, 6¼" $30.00
Hula girl playing ukulele, ca 1935-45, 12¾" $150.00
Indian chief standing w/arms crossed, 1930-45, 19" $45.00
Kewpie w/both hands on tummy, fat, ca 1935-45, 7½" $20.00
Lady in evening dress, 1935-45, 3½" $75.00
Lion standing & growling, ca 1940-50, 9¼x12" $45.00
Lovebirds kissing, marked Eagle Love, ca 1940-50, 6¼" $30.00
Navy Sailor at ease, ca 1935-45, 12¼" $85.00
Nude bust, lamp, Art Deco style, 1930-40, 8½" $135.00
Pancho, 1940s, 11½" $25.00
Porky Pig, 1940-50, 11" $55.00
Scottie dog w/pointed ears sits w/lady bug on nose, ca 1935-45, 5" $35.00
Shirley Temple standing, holding short skirt, bow on dress & hair, ca 1935-45, 16½" $320.00
Snake coiled, ashtray, 1940s, 5½" $20.00
Snow White standing, holding her dress, 1935-45, 14" $245.00

Soldier Boy, Jenkins, copyright 1944, 9", $45.00.

Uncle Sam rolling up his sleeve, ca 1935-45, 15" $125.00
Westward Ho Cowboy, 1945-50, 10" $35.00
Young girl holding fan, ca 1925-35, 11" $55.00

Cash Family, Clinchfield Artware

Some smaller east Tennessee potteries are beginning to attract collector attention. Clinchfild Artware produced by the Cash family of Erwin is one of them. The pottery was started in 1945 when the family first utilized a small building behind their home where they made three pottery pieces: a rolling-pin planter, a small elephant-shaped pitcher, and a buttermilk jug. Eventually they hired local artists to hand paint their wares. Cash products are sometimes confused with those made by the better-known Blue Ridge Pottery, due to the fact that many of the area's artisans worked first at one local company then another, and as a result, a style emerged that was typical of them all. Molds were passed around as local companies liquidated, adding to the confusion. But Cash's production was limited to specialty and souvenir pieces; the company never made any dinnerware.

Pitcher, violets, 3", $22.00. (Photo courtesy Bill and Betty Newbound)

Ashtray, pink flowers & buds w/green leaves on white free form, rests in center, 2½x9½x6" $22.50
Head vase, Davy Crockett, brown coonskin cap, tail forms handle, 5" $160.00
Jug, Little Brown Jug on white shoulder, brown body, unglazed base, 4¼" $20.00
Piggy bank, purple flowers, wearing hat (unusual), much detail, marked & dated 1945, 6x14" $215.00
Pitcher, Bittersweet, cobalt blue leaves & berries, squat, 5¼" ..$42.50
Pitcher, blue & gray floral design on creamy white, 9" $60.00
Pitcher, blue clovers on white, Jane shape, 7½" $40.00
Pitcher, blue iris & buds, Gaye shape, 6" $25.00
Pitcher, cow scene in blue on white, 7" $30.00
Pitcher, duck figural, green, brown, yellow & white, open mouth forms spout, 9½" $55.00

Pitcher, hunt scene w/deer, dogs & riders, cobalt & white, 8" **$40.00**

Pitcher, orange-brown flowers w/green leaves, Buttermilk shape, 7½" **$45.00**

Pitcher, purple flowers & green leaves on creamy white, Paula-Stein shape, 11⅜" **$38.00**

Pitcher, purple flowers w/olive-green leaves on white, Buttermilk shape, 5" **$25.00**

Planter, canoe, beige w/burnt orange, embossed star & moon, 2½x7½" **$42.50**

Planter, folded baby diaper, blue on creamy white, 2¾x2½x3¾" **$35.00**

Planter, swan, white w/yellow bill & feet, 5" **$42.50**

Turtle, designed to hold air & float in birdbath, brown & green tones, 2x5½" **$70.00**

Vase, bird perched among sunflowers on white, footed, 7x9" .. **$55.00**

Vase, high-button shoe, brown & green flowers, brown buttons & sponging **$28.00**

Vase, lady's high-button shoe, pink & brown flowers & laces on white, 6½x5½" **$40.00**

Wash set, blue violets on white, scalloped rim, 12", 4x16". **$135.00**

Cat Collectibles

Cat collectibles remain popular as cats continue to dominate the world of household pets. Cat memorabilia can be found in almost all categories, and this allows for collections to grow rapidly! Most cat lovers/collectors are attracted to all items and to all breeds, though some do specialize. Popular categories include Siamese, black cats, Kitty Cucumber, Kliban, cookie jars, teapots, books, plates, postcards, and Louis Wain.

Because cats are found throughout the field of collectibles and antiques, there is some 'crossover' competition among collectors. For example: Chessie, the C&O Railroad cat, is collected by railroad and advertising buffs; Felix the Cat, board games, puppets, and Steiff cats are sought by toy collectors. A Weller cat complements a Weller pottery collection just as a Royal Doulton Flambé cat fits into a Flambé porcelain collection.

Since about 1970 the array and quality of cat items have made the hobby explode. And, looking back, the first half of the twentieth century offered a somewhat limited selection of cats — there were those from the later Victorian era, Louis Wain cats, Felix the Cat, the postcard rage, and the kitchen-item black cats of the 1950s. But prior to 1890, cat items were few and far between, so a true antique cat (100-years old or more) is scarce, much sought after, and when found in mint condition, pricey. Examples of such early items would be original fine art, porcelains, and bronzes.

There are several 'cat' books available on today's market; if you want to see great photos representing various aspects of 'cat' collecting, you'll enjoy *Antique Cats for Collectors* by Katharine Morrison McClinton, *American Cat-alogue* by Bruce Johnson, and *The Cat Made Me Buy It* and *The Black Cat Made Me Buy It*, both by Muncaster and Yanow.

See also Black Cats; Character Collectibles; Cookie Jars; Holt Howard; Lefton. Unless otherwise noted, values are for items in mint original condition.

Club: International Cat Collector's Club
Contact: Peggy Way
CatCollectors@earthlink.net
www.CatCollectors.com

Ashtray, cat's face w/lg open mouth, brown stripes on white, ceramic, unmarked Japan, 4x3½" **$30.00**

Book, The Cat That Would Be King, RM Woods, Ethel Hays illustrations, hardback, Saalfield, 1952, VG **$15.00**

Button, cat face, molded glass w/hand-painted details, ⅝x¾" **$6.00**

Cache pot, cat in bib overalls smoking pipe, multicolor paint, ceramic, Japan, 1930s, 6½" **$38.00**

Candy dish, cat sleeping in basket, pink iridescent glass, 7¼" L **$17.50**

Change purse, cat's face, tooled leather w/painted details, snap closure at nose, 3x2¾" **$6.00**

Creamer and sugar bowl, Japan, 4", $25.00.

Egg cup, cat w/cup on back, brown airbrushing on white, green eyes, Japan **$25.00**

Figurine, cat crouching w/tail up, brass, Made in Korea sticker, 15x16" **$75.00**

Figurine, cat Disneykin figure from Fairykins series, Louis Marx, Disney, 1962, 1¼" **$8.00**

Figurine, cat licking paw, Royal Doulton, HN2580, 2x2½" ... **$55.00**

Figurine, cat mama w/2 kittens on chain, brown tones, ceramic, Wales sticker, Made in Japan, 1950s-60s, 6", 1¾" **$20.00**

Figurine, cat seated, brown & white w/green eyes, Norco Fine China Japan, 1950s, 7½x3½" **$15.00**

Figurine, cat seated, brown to white, ceramic, Beswick, 3¾" .. **$55.00**

Figurine, cat seated, cut/faceted crystal w/flexible silver tail, black glass eyes/nose, Swarovski, 1¼" **$30.00**

Figurine, cat seated, looking forward, multicolor, ceramic, Royal Copenhagen, #1803 .... **$75.00**

Figurine, cat seated, on base w/Luck along front, white, ceramic, Duraco Ltd Hanley Sylvan China, 3x2" **$95.00**

Figurine, cat seated, smoky gray glass w/applied eyes, Licio Zanetti, Murano, 9⅛" **$295.00**

Figurine, cat sleeping, fishnet pattern in butterscotch on white, Herend, 1½x2" **$200.00**

Figurine, cat smiling w/slender curled tail, ceramic, multicolor details, Jim Shore, 17½x8¾", MIB **$80.00**

Figurine, cat standing w/tail up, bright red w/black airbrushing, ceramic, unmarked Japan, 1950s, 3¾" **$8.00**

Figurine, cat w/paw raised, brown, orange & white stripes, Napco, 3½" **$15.00**

Figurine, cat w/scared expression & tail up, brown tones, ceramic, Sylvac England, #1046, 6" **$75.00**

Figurine, Siamese cat seated, white w/black points, blue eyes, ceramic, Avon, 1984, 3¼" **$8.00**

Figurine, stylized cat seated, black, ceramic, Royal Dux, 7½x4½" **$48.00**

Figurine, stylized cat seated, white porcelain, Armani, 17" ..**$110.00**

Figurine, stylized cat seated, white porcelain, Armani, 20" ..**$185.00**

Figurine, tabby cat seated, US Statuary, 1980, 7x8½" **$35.00**

Figurine, tabby kitten w/ginger stripes, arched back, Lomonosov Made in Russia, #10, 5½" **$15.00**

Figurines, Siamese cats, airbrushed brown to cream, ceramic, Japan, 8", 7¼", pr..**$50.00**

Magazine rack, cat figural, carved wood, fur-covered sides, opening in back, Witco **$300.00**

Paper dolls, Cat-Snips Paper Doll & Cut-Out Book, Tom Tierney, Tribeca Communications, 1983, unused......................**$20.00**

Pincushion, 2 kittens (china) sit on green velvet cushion, white gloss, Lenwill China Ardalt Japan, 4x3x2½" **$25.00**

Pitchers, figural, mustard w/pink flowers & green leaves, ceramic, Enesco, largest: 6¼", graduated set of 3 ....**$45.00**

Planter, cat reclining, opening in back, white w/painted details, ceramic, Norton, 10" L..**$15.00**

Planter/vase, cat w/arched back, pink gloss, ceramic, Japan, 1940s-50s, 4½x4½" **$50.00**

Plate, Christmas Rose & Cat, blue & white, Royal Copenhagen, 1970 ....**$30.00**

Plate, Persian kitten, Nancy Matthews, gold trim, Franklin Mint Heirloom limited edition **$16.00**

Postcard, alley cat scene, Everything's Swell - Right Up Our Alley!, NM..**$8.00**

Postcard, tabby cat w/cleaning bonnet on head, linen type, CW Hughes & Co, NM **$12.50**

Ring holder, cat on tray, tail up, heavy metal w/bronze finish, ca 1960s, 3½x3¼" **$35.00**

Ring holder, cat standing w/long upswept tail, painted cast metal, Copyright Revere Mfg Made in USA, 4½x2⅞"............**$15.00**

Salt & pepper shakers, black cat in barrel, ceramic, Japan paper label, 4¼", pr **$25.00**

Teapot, black panther figural w/green eyes, ceramic, Omnibus, 8x8" **$165.00**

Teapot, cat w/lg smile, black & orange spots, green eyes, pink ears, tail handle, ceramic, Carlton Ware, 6x8" **$35.00**

Teapot, leopard figural, golden yellow w/black spots, ceramic, Omnibus, 8x8" **$85.00**

Teapot, lion w/full mane, brown tones, ceramic, Albert Kessler & Co...Taiwan, 8x9" **$88.00**

Teapot, white cat w/orange eyes & pink tie collar, ceramic, Goebel W Germany, 9x9" **$38.00**

Toothpick holder, cat seated, opening in back, white gloss, ceramic, 5x4½" **$8.00**

Tray, striped cat in earthy tones, ceramic, Stuart Bass, 8½x5" **$85.00**

Character Cats

Cat in the Hat, bedding set, twin-size comforter & twin sheet set, NM..**$45.00**

Cat in the Hat, blanket, print on blue fleece, striped border, unused, 60x48" **$25.00**

Cat in the Hat, bookends, Cat transfer on painted wood, red, white & black..**$22.00**

Cat in the Hat, ceiling light cover, cats balancing ball decals on milk glass, 14½" dia **$35.00**

Cat in the Hat, comforter, turquoise, red & white, Cat & fish on ball, twin size, MIP **$65.00**

Cat in the hat, fleece fabric, print on orange, 4½-yards, 60" W ..**$50.00**

Cat in the Hat, growth chart, Dr Seuss, laminated front, measures up to 60", 39x8½" **$22.00**

Cat in the Hat, Johnny Lightning diecast car, White Lightning Camaro, white tires, Series 391-10, 1999, MOC........**$140.00**

Cat in the Hat, Johnny Lightning diecast vehicle, White Lightning 1956 Chevy Bus, white bottom & tires, #391-10, MOC..**$50.00**

Cat in the Hat, kaleidoscope, Dr Seuss, 7", MIP **$22.00**

Cat in the hat, lunch box, Cat on 1 side, Horton on reverse, tin litho, Aladdin, 1970, no thermos, EX **$35.00**

Cat in the Hat, pajamas, printed silk, man's, unused............**$75.00**

Cat in the hat, pocket watch, Cat on face, Tick Tocking Time Tickers Dr Seuss limited edition, ArtWatch, 1997........**$25.00**

Cat in the Hat, rocking toy, 1983, $75.00.

Cat in the Hat, scrapbook album, Cat tipping hat on blue striped background, Dr Seuss, unused **$25.00**

Cat in the Hat, standup illustration, printed cardboard, 12⅞x6" ...**$25.00**

Cat in the Hat, step stool, decals on painted wood, 12" **$32.00**

Cat in the Hat, table lamp, hand holding red & white hat, Vandor, 22x10x10" **$60.00**

Cat in the Hat, tie, Cat on red & white stripes, reverses to fish on blue, Dr Seuss, 57½" **$22.00**

Cat in the Hat, wall clock, round blue dial w/characters for numbers, Cat in center, red sq body, requires batteries **$22.50**

Cat in the Hat, wall clock, Thing 1 & Thing 2 pendulum, requires battery, 10½x6½x2" **$50.00**

Cat in the Hat, wall stick-ups, 32½" Cat, boy & girl, 2 blue-haired character faces & fish in bowl **$18.00**

Chessie, ashtray, Chessie asleep in center, white china w/blue border, 4" dia...**$35.00**

Chessie, book, Chessie & Her Kittens, part colored illustrations, pictorial hardback, Veritas, 1937 1st edition, VG+........**$55.00**

Chessie, calendar, Child's Calendar & Appointments...1969, minor stains/etc, 8¼x9¼" **$35.00**

Chessie, child's set, cup, plate & bowl, Chessie for Children, Woodmere China, 1985 ....**$40.00**

Chessie, cup & saucer, demitasse; porcelain, 1983 limited edition, 2³⁄₁₆", 4¼" **$22.50**

Chessie, paperweight, Chessie portrait encased in clear glass, rectangular, recent, 1x4¼x2¾" **$32.00**

Chessie, pin-back button, black & white w/pink, Compliments of Chessie... insert, Whitehead & Hoag, 1½", NM..........**$26.00**

Chessie, plate, Sleep Like a Kitten, C&O Railroad 50th Anniversary, ceramic, 1983, 8¼" **$22.50**

Chessie, playing cards, Chessie System Railroads, MIP (sealed) ..**$26.00**

Chessie, poster, Chessie & Her First Family, Chessie sleeping w/2 kittens, C&O Railway, 1937, 13¾x12⅛" **$40.00**

Chessie, print, Chessie the Cat Goes to War, Charles E Bracker for C&O Railroad, 1944, in 16x13" frame **$150.00**

Felix the Cat, brooch, black Bakelite w/painted details, 1960s-70s, 3½" **$30.00**

Felix the Cat, car mascot, nickel-silver plated metal, mounted to winged radiator cap, 3¾x3½" **$525.00**

Felix the Cat, comic book, Dell Four Color #119, VG **$22.00**

Felix the Cat, doll, mohair, bendable & posable limbs, minor hair loss, 1920s, 12½" **$235.00**

Felix the Cat, halloween noisemaker, cardboard, 1930s, 7", VG **$230.00**

Felix the Cat, hand puppet, Gund, 1960s......................**$50.00**

Felix the Cat, license plate ornament, painted metal, attaches to any license plate frame, unused **$20.00**

Felix the Cat, soaky bath toy, blue plastic, 1960s **$32.00**

Felix the Cat, stuffed toy, green bow tie & felt shorts, Max Hermann & Son, 1950, 8", EX+ **$425.00**

Felix the Cat, toy, Felix on scooter, tin litho, key-wind, rust spots, non-working **$450.00**

Felix the Cat, toy clicker, tin litho, Germany, 1930s-40s, 1½x1".. **$24.00**

Garfield, bank, Garfield in piggy shape w/pink feet, flower decor, ceramic, MIB **$30.00**

Garfield, bobble-head doll, painted resin, Show Me the Coffee, 6", MIB **$28.00**

Garfield, bookends, Garfield & Odie among books, hand-painted, resin, 5½", MIB **$65.00**

Garfield, cake pan, w/insert, Wilton, 1978, NM **$28.00**

Garfield, Christmas plates, Holiday Delights, Finishing Touch, etc, Danbury Mint, set of 8, ea MIB **$65.00**

Garfield, figurine, getting ready to pounce, ceramic, Enesco, 6" L **$32.00**

Garfield, figurine, musical, seated in chair w/Odie at side, Danbury Mint, 8½", MIB **$35.00**

Garfield, film container, plastic, stores 35 mm film, removable head, Agfa, 1997, 3½" **$40.00**

Garfield, golf club cover, Winning Edge Designs **$25.00**

Garfield, latch hook kit, Garfield's Candy Cane, J&P Coates, MIB **$30.00**

Garfield, money box, Garfield playing golf, painted porcelain, 1978, w/tags **$60.00**

Garfield, monopoly game, 25th Anniversy edition, MIB **$40.00**

Garfield, music box, Sittin' on the Dock of the Bay, fishing theme, Danbury Mint, 11x9" dia.................................**$35.00**

Garfield, musical toy, Cupid in Flight, revolving figure w/wings & bow & arrow, Enesco, 1989, M in VG box **$135.00**

Garfield, perpetual calendar, Garfield in bed, In a Perfect World... Mornings Would Start Later in the Day, MIB **$28.00**

Garfield, plate, comicstrip border, porcelain, Enesco, 1981, 7" ...**$28.00**

Garfield, plate, I Composed, Dear Diary series, Danbury Mint, 1990, MIB...**$30.00**

Garfield, plush toy, dressed as Cub scout, 11".................**$28.00**

Garfield, plush toy, leather vest, sings Bad to the Bone & says several phrases, 12", MIP **$35.00**

Garfield, puzzle, wooden frame-tray, 6-pc, Playskool, NM ..**$40.00**

Garfield, shot glass, Best Things in Life Are Edible, I'm in Charge Here, multicolor on clear glass, 2-oz **$24.00**

Garfield, tabletop fountain, w/friends fishing & catching fish, ceramic, battery operated, 7x5"..............................**$32.00**

Felix the Cat, sparkler, large pointed-ear version, Germany, copyright Pat Sullivan, EX, $400.00. (Photo courtesy LiveAuctioneers.com/Morphy Auctions)

Garfield, teapot, crouching, Floyd mouse finial, 6½", $35.00.

Garfield, throw, printed cotton, shown w/Odie, Paws Inc, 65x53",
MIP $23.00
Garfield, toilet seat cover, biker cat, cushioned vinyl, M $25.00
Garfield, trinket box, ceramic, sq, Enesco $26.00
Garfield, trinket box, Wet Paint, ceramic, sq, Enesco..........$27.50

**Kitty Cucumber, cookie jar,
$50.00.** (Photo courtesy Marilyn
Dipboye)

Kitty Cucumber, figurine, Albert painting, ceramic, Schmid, 1985,
3" $65.00
Kitty Cucumber, figurine, Baby Muffin, ceramic, Schmid,
1995... $25.00
Kitty Cucumber, figurine, Back to School, ceramic, Schmid,
MIB.. $16.00
Kitty Cucumber, figurine, Ellie, ceramic, Schmid, 1985 ......$48.00
Kitty Cucumber, figurine, JP Buster & Priscilla square dancing,
ceramic, Schmidt, 1995, 3¼"..$20.00
Kitty Cucumber, figurine, London Bridges, ceramic, Schmid, 1993,
4x6½x4½"...$37.50
Kitty Cucumber, figurine, Miss Fish Hoe Down, ceramic, Schmid,
1995 ....$20.00
Kitty Cucumber, figurine, tabby cat in old-fashioned swimsuit,
w/parasol, ceramic, Schmid, 1987............................$35.00
Kitty Cucumber, music box, Bath Time, plays Tiny Bubbles, ceram-
ic, Schmid, 1988..$37.50
Kitty Cucumber, music box, Slumber Party, plays Thank Heaven for
Little Girls, ceramic, Schmid $55.00
Kitty Cucumber, ornament, Kitty as witch w/jack-o'-lantern, ceram-
ic, Schmid, 1987..$45.00
Kitty Cucumber, ornament, Our First Christmas Together, deco-
rated fireplace, ceramic, Schmid, 1989, 3"...................$25.00
Kitty Cucumber, stuffed toy, Toy Works, 1985, 6" $55.00
Kliban, bank, in red tennis shoes, cold paint on ceramic, B Kliban,
4¾x9"...$45.00
Kliban, beach towel, Cat Paddle, fat cat swimming, NM.....$45.00

Kliban, beach towel, Crazy Cat & cat w/claws extended, 57x35",
NM..$78.00
Kliban, box, Kliban in bathtub, ceramic, Sigma, 4½x7", NM ..$130.00
Kliban, cookie jar, cat in airplane, ceramic, Sigma paper label,
NM $375.00
Kliban, cookie jar, figural mother w/baby in tummy, ceramic, 1970s,
from $200 to $250.00
Kliban, ice bucket, Super Kliban flying w/red cape, red, black &
white, Plexiglas lid, 8x8" $25.00
Kliban, mug, cat head w/bow tie, ceramic, Sigma the Taste Setter,
4" $14.00
Kliban, mug, Sashimi, about to eat w/chopsticks, ceramic, 3½" ..$35.00
Kliban, ornament, cat in car, ceramic, Sigma, 2¾x4" $70.00
Kliban, rubber stamp, Kliban Kat Mail, 2½" $15.00
Kliban, salt & pepepr shakers, cat in red shoes, ceramic, Sigma,
pr $27.50
Kliban, sheet set, cat in red sneakers, Burlington, queen-size flat
sheet & 2 pillowcases, NM $45.00
Kliban, sweatshirt, Adopt a Cat on white cotton, B Kliban Cats
label, unused $52.50
Kliban, sweatshirt, cat on windowsill, San Francisco, blue cotton,
1980s, unused $55.00
Kliban, T-shirt, Bad Cat, printed white cotton, 1980s, unused ...$60.00
Kliban, T-shirt, cat & old-time phonograph on yellow cotton, B
Kliban Crazy Shirt, 1975, unused.............................$55.00
Kliban, T-shirt, cat golfing on blue cotton, Crazy Shirt Hawaii,
w/tags, unused $20.00
Kliban, T-shirt, cat w/computer mouse on gray cotton, Crazy Shirt
Hawaii, unused $30.00

**Kliban, teapot, in tuxedo,
Sigma, 12x11", $175.00.**

Kliban, teapot, spaceship, ceramic, Sigma $350.00
Kliban, trash can, cat in red shoes, Ames RoyalWare, 24" $50.00
Pink Panther, bed set, comforter, 4-pc sheet set & throw pillow, full
size, MIP...$110.00
Pink Panther, bowl, ceramic, Royal Orleans, Japan, 3x7", EXIB..$70.00
Pink Panther, figurine, standing behind The Inspector, ceramic,
Royal Orleans, Japan, w/tag....................................$85.00
Pink Panther, music box, as conductor, Pink Panther collection by
Royal Orleans, 9", w/tag..$115.00

Pink Panther, necktie, printed silk, red, white, blue & pink, 56x3⅜", NM **$30.00**

Pink Panther, ornament, as Santa, Kurt S Adler - Polonaise, 1998, 6½" **$35.00**

Pink Panther, record player, head is cover, working, 1970s, paint wear **$70.00**

Pink Panther, sugar bowl & creamer, ceramic, w/lid, Royal Orleans, Japan **$55.00**

Pink Panther, towel holder, ceramic, Royal Orleans **$80.00**

Pink Panther, transistor radio, Amico, Hong Kong, 1979, MIB .. **$95.00**

Pink Panther, wall mask, face only, ceramic, Royal Orleans, 1981, 8x5½" **$26.00**

Cat-Tail Dinnerware

Cat-Tail was a dinnerware pattern popular during the late '20s until sometime in the '40s. So popular, in fact, that ovenware, glassware, tinware — even a kitchen table was made to coordinate with it. The dinnerware was made primarily by Universal Potteries of Cambridge, Ohio, though a catalog from Hall China circa 1927 shows a three-piece coffee service, and others may have produced it as well. It was sold for years by Sears Roebuck and Company, and some items bear a mark that includes their name.

The pattern is unmistakable: a cluster of red cattails (usually six, sometimes one or two) with black stems on creamy white. Shapes certainly vary; Universal used at least three of their standard mold designs, Camwood, Old Holland, Laurella, and possibly others. Some Cat-Tail pieces are marked Wheelock on the bottom. (Wheelock was a department store in Peoria, Illinois.)

If you're trying to decorate a '40s vintage kitchen, no other design could afford you more to work with. To see many of the pieces that are available and to learn more about the line, read *Collector's Encyclopedia of American Dinnerware* by Jo Cunningham (Collector Books).

Advisors: Barbara and Ken Brooks (See Directory, Dinnerware)

Butter dish, one pound, from $80.00 to $100.00.

Bowl, footed, 9½" **$20.00**
Bowl, mixing; 8" **$23.00**
Bowl, salad; lg **$25.00**
Bowl, sauce; Camwood Ivory, 5¼" **$6.00**

Bowl, soup; flat rim, 7¾" **$15.00**
Bowl, soup; tab handles, 8" **$17.50**
Bowl, straight sides, 6¼" **$12.00**
Bowl, vegetable; oval, 9" **$27.50**
Bowl, vegetable; Universal, 8¾" **$25.00**
Bowl, 3x4" **$15.00**
Bread box, tinware, 12x13½", VG **$50.00**
Butter dish, ¼-lb, 3½x6x3¼", NM **$55.00**
Cake cover & tray, tinware **$35.00**
Cake plate, Mt Vernon **$25.00**
Canister set, tin, 4-pc **$60.00**
Casserole, paneled sides & lid, 6½x8½" **$35.00**
Casserole, w/lid, 4¼x8¼" **$55.00**
Coffeepot, electric, Westinghouse, 13", from $300 to **$350.00**
Coffeepot, 3-pc **$70.00**
Cookie jar, from $75 to **$100.00**
Coookie jar, 8¼" **$175.00**
Cracker jar, barrel shape, 8¼" **$175.00**
Creamer, from $18 to **$25.00**
Creamer & sugar bowl, w/lid, Camwood Ivory, 3¾x5¼" **$45.00**
Cup & saucer, from $6 to **$10.00**
Gravy boat, from $18 to **$25.00**
Jug, ball **$30.00**
Jug, side handle, cork stopper **$38.00**
Jug, water; w/stopper, side handle, EX **$70.00**
Match holder, tinware **$45.00**
Pickle dish/gravy boat liner **$20.00**
Pie plate, from $25 to **$30.00**
Pie server, hole in handle for hanging, marked **$25.00**
Pitcher, batter; shaped like syrup pitcher **$85.00**
Pitcher, ice lip, ball shape, 8", from $45 to **$60.00**
Pitcher, milk; 7½" **$35.00**
Plate, dinner; Laurella shape, from $15 to **$20.00**

Plate, grill; 10", $25.00.

Plate, luncheon; 9", from $7 to **$8.50**
Plate, salad or dessert; round, from $5 to **$6.50**
Plate, tab handles, 11" **$30.00**
Platter, oval, tab handles, Camwood Ivory, 14½" **$35.00**
Platter, oval, tab handles, 13⅜" **$30.00**

Relish tray, Cat-Tail pattern repeated 4 times at rim, oval, 9x5"..**$50.00**
Salad set (fork, spoon & bowl), from $50 to........................**$60.00**
Salt & pepper shakers, footed cylinder w/4 vertical recessed panels,
    4½", pr..**$35.00**
Salt & pepper shakers, Salt or Pepper, glass, 4", pr.............**$35.00**
Salt & pepper shakers, wider ribbed bottom, 4½", pr.........**$50.00**
Scale, metal..**$45.00**
Stack set, 3-pc, w/lid, from $40 to.................................**$50.00**
Sugar bowl, w/lid, from $20 to.......................................**$25.00**
Syrup, red top...**$70.00**
Tablecloth...**$90.00**
Teapot, 7x8"...**$40.00**
Tidbit tray, 2-tier, 6" & 7", from $100 to......................**$120.00**
Tray, for batter set...**$75.00**
Tumbler, juice; glass, 3¾", from $18 to...........................**$25.00**
Waste can, step-on, tinware..**$45.00**

Catalin/Bakelite Napkin Rings

Bakelite (developed in 1910) and Catalin (1930s) are very similar materials — identical, in fact, in chemical composition. Both are phenol resin, and both were made in the same wonderful colors that found favor in American kitchens from the 1930s until the 1950s. In particular, figural napkin rings made of this material have become very collectible. Those most desirable will have an inlaid eye or some other feature of a second color.

Band, lathe-turned, amber, red or green, 1¾", from $8 to ...**$12.00**
Band, plain, amber, red or green, 2", ea from $7 to **$10.00**
Band, plain, green, 1", set of 12...**$85.00**
Bird, no inlaid eyes, green w/brown beak from $40 to.........**$60.00**
Bird, no inlaid eyes (solid color)..**$35.00**
Camel, inlaid eye rod...**$90.00**
Camel, no inlaid eyes...**$70.00**
Chicken, no inlaid eyes..**$30.00**
Chicken, no inlaid eyes, amber w/green beak, from $35 to..**$45.00**
Donald Duck, w/decal, from $120 to...............................**$150.00**
Duck, inlaid eye rod, from $65 to.......................................**$75.00**
Duck, no inlaid eyes..**$30.00**
Elephant, ball on head..**$120.00**
Elephant, inlaid eye rod, from $65 to **$80.00**
Elephant, no inlaid eyes...**$48.00**
Elephant, no inlaid eyes, on wheels...................................**$65.00**
Fish, inlaid eye rod, from $30 to..**$65.00**
Fish, no inlaid eyes..**$40.00**
Mickey Mouse, no decal...**$80.00**
Mickey Mouse, w/decal, from $135 to...............................**$150.00**
Popeye, no decal, no inlaid eyes, from $45 to **$55.00**
Rabbit, inlaid eye rod...**$40.00**
Rabbit, no inlaid eyes...**$30.00**
Rocking horse, inlaid eyes rod..**$50.00**
Rocking horse, no inlaid eyes...**$40.00**
Rooster, inlaid eye rods, from $50 to **$65.00**
Rooster, no inlaid eyes...**$40.00**
Schnauzer sitting, inlaid eye rods **$65.00**
Schnauzer sitting, no inlaid eye rods **$35.00**

Scottie dog, no inlaid eyes, on wheels, $80.00. (Photo courtesy Candace Sten Davis and Patricia J. Baugh)

Scottie sitting, no inlaid eyes, from $40 to..........................**$50.00**
Scottie standing, inlaid eye rods, from $60 to **$70.00**
Squirrel standing over ring, inlaid eyes, rare **$180.00**
8-sided, varied colors, set of 5, MIB..................................**$600.00**

Ceramic Arts Studio

Although most figural ceramic firms of the 1940s and 1950s were located on the west coast, one of the most popular had its base of operations in Madison, Wisconsin. Ceramic Arts Studio was founded in 1940 as a collaboration between entrepreneur Reuben Sand and potter Lawrence Rabbitt. Early ware consisted of hand-thrown pots by Rabbitt, but CAS came into its own with the 1941 arrival of Betty Harrington. A self-taught artist, Harrington served as the studio's principal designer until it closed in 1955. Her imagination and skill quickly brought Ceramic Arts Studio to the forefront of firms specializing in decorative ceramics. During its peak production period in the 1940s, CAS turned out more than 500,000 figurines annually.

Harrington's themes were wide ranging, from ethnic and theatrical subjects, to fantasy characters, animals, and even figural representations of such abstractions as fire and water. While the majority of the studio's designs were by Harrington, CAS also released a limited line of realistic and modernistic animal figures by 'Rebus' (Ulle Cohen). In addition to traditional figurines, the studio responded to market demand with such innovations as salt-and-pepper pairs, head vases, banks, bells, shelf-sitters, and candleholders. Metal display shelves for CAS pieces were produced by Jon-San Creations, a nearby Reuben Sand operation. Most Jon-San designs were produced by Ceramic Art Studio's head decorator Zona Liberace, stepmother of the famed pianist.

Betty Harrington carved her own master molds, so the finished products are remarkably similar to her initial sketches. CAS figurines are prized for their vivid colors, characteristic high-gloss glaze, lifelike poses, detailed decoration, and skill of execution. Unlike many ceramics of the period, CAS pieces today show little evidence of crazing.

Most Ceramic Arts Studio pieces are marked, although in pairs only one piece may have a marking. While there are variants, including early paper stickers, one common base stamp reads 'Ceramic Arts Studio, Madison, Wis.' (The initials 'BH' which appear on many pieces do not indicate that the piece was personally decorated by Betty Harrington. This is simply a design indicator.)

In the absence of a base stamp, a sure indicator of a CAS piece is the decorator 'color marking' found at the drain hole on the base. Each studio decorator had a separate color code for identification purposes, and almost any authentic CAS piece will display these tick marks.

Following the Madison studio's close in 1955, Reuben Sand briefly moved his base of operations to Japan. While perhaps a dozen master molds from Madison were also utilized in Japan, most of the Japanese designs were original ones and do not correlate to those produced in Madison. Additionally, about 20 master molds and copyrights were sold to Mahana Imports, which created its own CAS variations, and a number of molds and copyrights were sold to Coventry Ware for a line of home hobbyware. Pieces produced by these companies have their own individual stampings or labels. While these may incorporate the Ceramic Arts Studio name, the vastly different stylings and skill of execution are readily apparent to even the most casual observer, easily differentiating them from authentic Madison products. When the CAS building was demolished in 1959, all remaining molds were destroyed. Betty Harrington's artistic career continued after the studio's demise; and her later work, including a series of nudes and abstract figurals, are especially prized by collectors. Mrs. Harrington died in 1997. Her last assignment, the limited-edition *M'amselle* series was commissioned for the Ceramic Arts Studio Collectors Association Convention in 1996.

For more information we recommend *Ceramic Arts Studio: The Legacy of Betty Harrington* written by Donald-Brian Johnson (our advisor for this category), Timothy J. Holthaus, and James E. Petzold (Schiffer Publishing, 2003). Mr. Johnson encourages collectors to e-mail him with any new information concerning company history and/or production. See also Directory of Contributors and Special Interests.

Advisor: Donald-Brian Johnson (See Directory, Ceramic Arts Studio)

Club/Newsletter: CAS Collectors
206 Grove St.
Rockton, IL 61072
www.cascollectors.com

Website: www.ceramicartsstudio.org

Banks, Mr & Mrs Blankety Blank, 4½", pr from $240 to .. **$280.00**
Candleholders, Bedtime Boy & Girl, 4¾", pr from $150 to .. **$190.00**
Figurine, Adonis & Aphrodite, 9", 7", pr from $500 to **$700.00**
Figurine, Ballerina Quartet, 4 poses, 6", 3½", 5", from $1,040 to...**$1,120.00**
Figurine, Boy w/Towel, 5", from $300 to **$350.00**
Figurine, Chivalry Suite, St George, Lady Rowena & Dragon, 3 pcs, from $465 to **$550.00**
Figurine, Cinderella & Prince, 6½", pr from $60 to **$80.00**
Figurine, Comedy & Tragedy, 10", pr from $160 to.........**$200.00**
Figurine, Daisy Donkey, 4¾", from $85 to **$110.00**

Figurine, Egyptian Man & Woman, rare, 9½", pr from $1,400 to..**$1,500.00**
Figurine, Gay '90s Man & Woman #2, 6¾", 6½", pr from $110 to **$150.00**
Figurine, Guitar Man on stool, rare, 6½", from $500 to....**$600.00**
Figurine, Harlequin & Columbine w/Masks, 8¾", 8½", pr from $1,800 to **$1,900.00**
Figurine, Leopards A&B, fighting, 3½", 6¼" L, pr from $180 to **$250.00**
Figurine, Lightning & Thunder Stallions, 5¾", pr from $300 to **$350.00**
Figurine, Madonna w/Golden Halo, 9½", from $350 to ...**$450.00**
Figurine, Modern Colt, stylized, 7½", from $225 to.........**$250.00**
Figurine, Monkey Family (Mr, Mrs, Baby), white, 4", 3½", 2", from $300 to **$385.00**
Figurine, Panda w/Hat, 2¾", from $200 to **$225.00**
Figurine, Pioneer Sam & Susie, 5½", 5", pr from $80 to...**$100.00**

Figurine, Praise and Blessing angels, 6¼", 5¾", from $180.00 to $240.00 for the pair.

Figurine, Promenade Man & Woman, 7¾", pr from $200 to ...**$300.00**
Figurine, Shepherd & Shepherdess, 8½", 8", pr from $180 to...**$220.00**
Figurine, Square Dance Boy & Girl, 6½", 6", pr from $200 to.**$250.00**
Figurine, Temple Dance Man & Woman, 7", 6¾", pr from $900 to **$1,000.00**
Figurine, Wee Piggy Boy & Girl, 3¼", 3½", pr from $50 to ..**$70.00**
Head vase, Barbie, 7", from $125 to **$150.00**
Head vase, Bonnie, 7", from $125 to **$150.00**
Miniature, Flying Ducks vase, 2½", from $75 to **$85.00**
Plaque, Harlequin & Columbine, 8¾", 8½", pr from $150 to ..**$240.00**
Shakers, Kangaroo Mother & Joey, snugglers, 4¾", 2½", pr from $130 to **$170.00**
Shakers, Sea Horse & Coral, 3½", 3", pr from $100 to **$140.00**
Shelf sitters, Budgie & Pudgie Parakeets, 6", pr from $100 to **$120.00**
Shelf sitters, Pete & Polly Parrots, 7½", pr from $170 to ...**$250.00**
Shelf sitters, Sitting Boy & Girl w/Puppy & Kitten, 4¼", pr from $150 to **$200.00**
Tray, Kneeling Pixie Girl, 4½", from $125 to....................**$150.00**

Character and Promotional Drinking Glasses

Put out by fast-food restaurant chains or by a company promoting a product, these glasses have for years been commonplace. But now, instead of glass, the giveaways are nearly always plastic. If a glass is offered at all, you'll usually have to pay 99¢ for it.

Some are worth more than others. Among the common ones are Camp Snoopy, B.C. Ice Age, Garfield, McDonald's, Smurfs, and Coca-Cola. The better glasses are those with super heroes, characters from Star Trek and '30s movies such as 'Wizard of Oz,' sports personalities, and cartoon characters by Walter Lantz and Walt Disney. Some of these carry a copyright date, and that's all it is. It's not the date of manufacture.

Many collectors are having a good time looking for these glasses. If you want to learn more about them, we recommend *Tomart's Price Guide to Character and Promotional Drinking Glasses* by Carol Markowski, and *Collectible Drinking Glasses, Identification and Values*, by Mark Chase and Michael Kelly.

There are some terms used in the descriptions that may be confusing. 'Brockway' style refers to a thick, heavy glass that tapers in from top to bottom. 'Federal' style, on the other hand, is thinner, and the top and bottom diameters are the same.

Al Capp, 1975, flat bottom, Daisy Mae, Li'l Abner, Mammy, Pappy, Sadie, ea from $35 to **$50.00**
Al Capp, 1975, flat bottom, Joe Btsfplk, from $35 to..........**$50.00**
Animal Crackers, Chicago Tribune/NY News Syndicate, 1978, Eugene, Gnu, Lana, Lyle Dodo, ea from $7 to **$10.00**
Arby's, Bicentennial Cartoon Character Series, 1976, 10 different, 6", ea from $10 to **$20.00**

Arby's Collector Series, Pac-Man, 1980s, rocks glass, from $2.00 to $4.00. (Photo courtesy www.whatacharacter.com)

Batman Forever, McDonald's, 1995, various embossed glass mugs, ea from $2 to **$4.00**
Beatles, Dairy Queen/Canada, group photos & signatures in white starburst, gold trim, ea from $95 to **$125.00**
Bozo the Clown, Capital Records, 1965, Bozo head image around top w/related character at bottom, ea from $10 to.......**$15.00**

Burger Chef, Friendly Monster Series, 1977, 6 different, ea from $15 to **$25.00**
Cabbage Patch Doll, 1983, plastic, multicolor paint............**$10.00**
California Raisins, Applause, 1989, 32-oz, from $6 to..........**$8.00**
Children's Classics, Libbey Glass Co, Moby Dick, Robin Hood, 3 Musketeers, Treasure Island, ea from $10 to **$15.00**
Disney's All-Star Parade, 1939, 10 different, from $25 to **$50.00**
ET, Pepsi/MCA Home Video, 1988, 6 different, ea from $15 to **$25.00**
Goonies, Godfather's Pizza/Warner Bros, 1985, 4 different, ea from $3 to **$5.00**
Harvey Cartoon Characters, Pepsi, 1970s, action pose, Baby Huey, Hot Stuff, ea from $8 to **$10.00**

Harvey Cartoon Characters, Pepsi, Wendy, action pose, Brockway, 1970s, from $8.00 to $10.00. (Photo courtesy www. whatacharacter.com)

Honey, I Shrunk the Kids, McDonald's, 1989, plastic, 3 different, ea from $1 to **$2.00**
Hopalong Cassidy's Western Series, ea from $25 to **$30.00**
Jungle Book, Disney/Pepsi, 1960s, Bagheera & Shere Kahn, unmarked, ea from $35 to **$60.00**
Little Mermaid, 1991, 3 different sizes, ea from $6 to **$10.00**
Master of the Universe, Mattel, 1986, Battle Cat, He-Man, Man-at-Arms, Orko, Panthor/Skeletor, ea from $3 to **$5.00**
Mickey Mouse, Mickey's Christmas Carol, Coca-Cola, 1982, 3 different, ea from $5 to **$7.00**
Mister Magoo, Polomar Jelly, many different variations & styles, ea from $25 to **$35.00**
PAT Ward, Collector Series, Holy Farms Restaurants, 1975, Boirs, Bullwinkle, Natasha, Rocky, ea from $20 to **$40.00**
Pat Ward, Pepsi, late 1970s, static pose, Bullwinkle (brown lettering/no Pepsi logo), 6", from $15 to....................................**$20.00**
PAT Ward, Pepsi, late 1970s, static pose, Dudley-Do-Right (red lettering/no Pepsi logo), 6", from $10 to **$15.00**
Peanuts Characters, Kraft, 1988, Charlie flying kite, Lucy on swing, Snoopy in pool, Snoopy on surfboard, ea from $20 to ...**$3.00**
Peanuts Characters, Smuckers, 1994, 3 different, ea from $2 to **$4.00**
Pocahontas, Burger King, 1995, 4 different, MIB, ea.............**$3.00**

Popeye, Popey's Famous Fried Chicken/Pepsi, 1982, 10th Anniversary Series, 4 different, ea from $7 to..................................**$10.00**

Ranger Smith Slurpee Cup, 7-11 stores, 1976, 5", $20.00. (Photo courtesy www.gasolinealleyantiques.com)

Sleeping Beauty, American, late 1950s, 6 different, ea from $8 to..**$15.00**
Star Trek: The Motion Picture, Coca-Cola, 1980, 3 different, ea from $10 to **$15.00**
Sunday Funnies, 1976, Brenda Starr, Gasoline Alley, Moon Mullins, etc, ea from $5 to..**$7.00**
Super Heroes, Marvel, 1978, Federal, flat bottom, Spider-Woman, from $100 to **$150.00**
Superman, NPP/M Polanar & Son, 1964, 6 different, various colors, 5¼" or 5¾", ea from $20 to..**$25.00**
Walter Lantz, Pepsi, 1970s, Chilly Willy or Wally Walrus, ea from $25 to **$45.00**
Warner Bros, Arby's, 1988, Adventures Series, footed, Bugs, Daffy, Porky, Sylvester & Tweety, ea from $25 to **$30.00**
Warner Bros, Pepsi, 1976, Interaction, Beaky Buzzard & Cool Cat w/kite, from $8 to..**$10.00**
Wild West Series, Coca-Cola, Buffalo Bill, Calamity Jane, ea from $10 to **$15.00**
Wizard of Oz, Swift's, 1950s-60s, fluted bottom, Emerald City or Flying Monkeys, ea from $8 to **$15.00**
Ziggy, Number Series, 1-8, ea from $4 to **$8.00**

Character Banks

Since the invention of money there have been banks, and having it has always been considered a virtue. What better way to entice children to save than to give them a bank styled after the likeness of one of their favorite characters! Always a popular collectible, mechanical and still banks have been made of nearly any conceivable material. Cast-iron and tin banks are often worth thousands of dollars. The ones listed here were made in the past 50 years or so, when ceramics and plastics were the materials of choice. Still, some of the higher-end examples can be quite pricey!

See also Advertising Character Collectibles; Cowboy Collectibles; Star Wars. Unless otherwise noted, our values are for examples in at least near mint condition.

Alvin (Alvin & the Chipmunks), vinyl, CBS Toys, 1984, 9", $20.00. (Photo courtesy www.whatacharacter.com)

Andy Panda, composition, Crown Toy, 1940s, 5", EX........**$85.00**
Bamm-Bamm, sitting on turtle, plastic, 1960s, 11" **$50.00**

Barney (Flintstones), vinyl, 1994, 6", $15.00. (Photo courtesy www.whatacharacter.com)

Batman, vinyl, Batman Returns, 1991, 9", EX.....................**$10.00**
Betty Boop, red plastic coin sorter w/Betty Boop graphics, drop a coin & she winks, Mag-Nif, 1986, 8", MIB **$18.00**
Bionic Woman in jogging suit running on rocky base, vinyl, Animals Plus, 1976, 10" **$25.00**

Bozo the Clown, plastic, star-shaped base, Star Merchandise, 1960s-70s, 5½", EXIB...$30.00

Bullwinkle standing against tree trunk waving, vinyl, Play Pal Plastics, 1973, 12" $65.00

Cabbage Patch Kid in diaper, hard vinyl, Appalachian Artworks, 1983, 5½x7" $10.00

Daffy Duck, Looney Tunes, Applause, 1980s.......................$25.00

Disney, 2nd National Duck Bank, litho tin building w/Donald as teller & Mickey & Minnie customers, 6½", EX..........$200.00

Dumbo seated upright, vinyl, gray w/orange hat & gray, white & red collar, Play Pal, 1970s, 8".................................$25.00

Flintstones, ceramic, Fred Loves Wilma $100.00

Flintstones, ceramic, Fred stands w/arm behind back & points to himself w/other, Vandor, 1990, 8½", EX $38.00

Grandpa Turtle (Animal Crackers), ceramic, 5" $55.00

Huckleberry Hound, plastic, 1960, 10", EX $20.00

Laurel & Hardy, plastic, Play Pal, 1970s, ea........................$35.00

Lurch of Addams family, ceramic, Koria, 1970s, 8" $200.00

Mickey Mouse, hard plastic, on base, Disney, ca 1970, 19" ..$60.00

Miss Piggy (Muppets), ceramic, Sigma.................................$50.00

Mister Magoo, yellow vinyl w/black & blue trim, Renzi, 1960, 17"...$150.00

Pinocchio, bust w/eyes looking upward, lg bow tie, vinyl, Play Pal, 1970s, 10" $28.00

Quick Draw McGraw, plastic, orange, blue & white, Looney Tunes, 1960s, 10" $35.00

Raggedy Ann and Andy, talking, Bobbs-Merrill, 1977, from $25.00 to $35.00.

Santa Claus, painted composition w/spring-mounted nodder head, 1950s-60s, 6", EX...$50.00

Smurf, molded plastic, Peyo, 1980s....................................$35.00

Snoopy seated, ceramic, white w/red & black details, unmarked, 10" $110.00

Snoopy sitting on bright red strawberry, ceramic, Japan, 1968..$35.00

Underdog, vinyl, Play Pal, 1973, 11" $85.00

Ziggy atop lg red heart, Don't Break My Heart, 6½" $45.00

Character Clocks and Watches

There is a great deal of interest in the comic character clocks and watches produced from about 1930 into the 1950s and beyond. They're in rather short supply simply because they were made for children to wear (and play with). They were cheaply made with pin-lever movements, not worth an expensive repair job, and many were simply thrown away. The original packaging that today may be worth more than the watch itself was usually ripped apart by an excited child and promptly relegated to the wastebasket.

Condition is very important in assessing value. Unless a watch is in like-new condition, it is not mint. Rust, fading, scratching, or wear of any kind will sharply lessen its value, and the same is true of the box itself. Good, excellent, and mint watches can be evaluated on a scale of one to five, with excellent being a three, good a one, and mint a five. In other words, a watch worth $25.00 in good condition would be worth five times that amount if it were mint ($125.00). Beware of dealers who substitute a generic watch box for the original. Remember that these too were designed to appeal to children and (99% of the time) were printed with colorful graphics.

Some of these watches have been reproduced, so be on guard. For more information, we recommend *Schroeder's Collectible Toys, Antique to Modern* (Collector Books). Unless otherwise noted, our values are for working examples in at least near mint condition.

Clocks

Batman & Robin, Talking Alarm & bat on face, molded plastic, Janex, 1975...$120.00

Big Bad Wolf, alarm clock, Ingersoll, EX, $900.00. (Photo courtesy LiveAuctioneers.com/Morphy Auctions)

Howdy Doody, Talking Alarm, molded plastic, Janex, 1977, MIB.. $125.00

Mickey, Donald & Goofy, melody alarm type, plays 4 songs, Lorus, 1988, 5x8", MIB $45.00

Mickey & Minnie Mouse, frosted glass paperweight type w/1½" dia gold quartz clock, Seiko, 1988, 6x4½".........................$60.00

Mickey brass, brass, travel alarm type, 60th Anniversary, Seiko QFD203G, 1988, MIB $125.00

Mickey Mouse & Friends on face, musical & motion dome alarm type, Bradley, 1968, 8" $150.00

Mickey Mouse on face, red base, alarm type, Bradley, Walt Disney Productions, 1960s-70s, 6" $75.00

Mickey Mouse Train Engineer, talking alarm type, Bradley, 1970s, MIB..$195.00

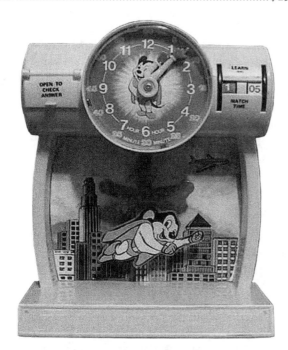

Mighty Mouse, 1970s, 10", $50.00. (Photo courtesy www.whatacharacter.com)

Peter Pan on face, alarm type, Phinney Walker, 1960s, rare...**$90.00**
Smurfs on face, animated action alarm type, Bradley, 1983, MIB...$75.00
Superman, Talking Alarm, molded plastic, Janex, 1975, MIB...**$350.00**
Winnie the Pooh on face, yellow base, alarm type, Bradley, Walt Disney Productions, 1970s, 4".....................................$90.00

Pocket Watches

Betty Boop on face, King Features limited edition w/blond wood display case, 1996, MIB...**$88.00**
Boy Scouts, Be Prepared..., yellow hands, chrome case, Ingersoll, 1937, 2"..$230.00
Don Winslow of the Navy, New Haven, 1938-39, EX....**$1,600.00**
Felix the Cat on face, w/figural holder on wooden pedestal, limited edition, MIB...$115.00
Lone Ranger & Silver, round chrome case, blue strap & silver chain, 1970 ....**$100.00**
Mary Marvel, round chrome case, full figure, red plastic strap, Fawcett, 1948, VG...$125.00
Mickey Mouse, full-figure Mickey on white face, arms move, black strap, Ingersoll, Mickey image on round fob, 1930s, EX $400.00
Popeye, New Haven, 1935, 1¾", from $550 to $1,000.00
Road Runner & Wiley Coyote on face, Warner Bros, Armitron, MIB..$48.00
Superman, yellow numbers on black around image of Superman in flight over city, chrome case, 2" dia, VG $175.00
Wizard of Oz, 4 characters on dial, silver-tone case, Westclock, 1980s, MIB...$75.00

Wristwatches

Dick Tracy on face, red hour & minute hands, gold second hand, pink band, Disney, 1980s **$165.00**
Jetsons, watch & pin set, night sky face, leather band, Hanna-Barbera limited edition, Fossil, 1993, MIB................**$150.00**
Mickey Mouse on face, musical tone, quartz movement, leather band, Disney, Lorus, 1980s...**$165.00**

New Zoo Revue, 1974, from $40.00 to $50.00. (Photo courtesy Greg Davis and Bill Morgan)

Pepe Le Pew & Penelope on face w/lg red rose, leather band, Warner Bros Studio Store, EX **$30.00**
Popeye & characters on face, chrome case, faux leather band, porcelain Pluto display stand, Fossil, 1994, MIB................**$150.00**
Popeye on face, brown leather strap, King Features Syndicate, Swiss Made, 1960s **$60.00**
Reigns of Superman, silver case, leather band, DC Comics, 1993, MIB...**$150.00**
Snoopy dancing on red face, hands indicate hour & minute, Woodstock on second hand, expandable band, Timex, EX **$15.00**
Star Wars, robots in night scene on face, dark blue band, Bradley, 1977, MIB...**$150.00**
Tweety Bird on face, leather band, Warner Bros, Looney Tunes, Armitron, 1998, MIB...**$125.00**
Wicked Witch from Wizard of Oz on face, sun ray dial, chrome case, leather band, Fossil, 2000, MIB...................................**$75.00**

Character Collectibles

Any popular personality, whether factual or fictional, has been promoted through the retail market to some degree. Depending on the extent of their fame, we may be deluged with this merchandise for weeks, months, even years. It's no wonder, then, that the secondary market abounds with these items or that there is such wide-spread collector demand for them today. There are rarities in any field, but for the beginning collector, many nice items are readily available at prices most can afford. Disney characters, Western heroes, TV and movie personalities, super heroes, comic book characters, and sports greats are the most sought after.

For more information we recommend *Schroeder's Collectible Toys, Antique to Modern,* published by Collector Books, which contains an extensive listing of character collectibles with current market values.

See also Advertising Characters; Beatles Collectibles; Bubble Bath Containers; Cat Collectibles; Character and Promotional Drinking Glasses; Character Watches; Coloring Books; Cookie Jars; Cowboy Character Collectibles; Disney Collectibles; Dolls, Celebrity; Elvis Presley Memorabilia; Movie Posters; Paper Dolls; PEZ Candy Containers; Pin-Back Buttons; Rock 'n Roll Memorabilia; Shirley Temple; Star Wars; Toys; Vandor.

**Bugs Bunny, bookends, composition, Holiday Fair, 1970s, 6½",
NM, $50.00 for the pair.** (Photo courtesy www.whatacharacter.com)

Archie, hand puppet, printed vinyl body w/vinyl head, Ideal, 1973, MIP (header reads TV Favorites) $125.00

Babar, ornament, plastic & composition, Babar the elephant driving car w/Christmas package, 4" L, M $6.00

Bamm-Bamm (Flintstones), figure, stuffed cloth, felt hair, hat & outfit, Knickerbocker, 1970s, 8", MIB..........................$45.00

Banana Splits, frame-tray puzzles, Whitman, set of 4, NMIB ...$100.00

Barney (Barney Goodle & Spark Plug), hand puppet, printed cloth body w/name & vinyl head w/cigar, Gund, 1950s, NM+ $100.00

Bart Simpson, doll, vinyl, blue cloth shirt & shorts, blue shoes, holding slingshot, Presents, 1990, 9", M............................$15.00

Bart Simpson, ornament, PVC, figure w/hands at sides, 1990, 4", EX+ $6.00

Batman, Helmet & Cape, plastic, blue helmet w/black face & emblem, vinyl cape, Ideal, 1966, NMIB.....................$450.00

Batman, Shooting Arcade, Ahi/DC Comics, 1977, 8", unused, NMIB..$165.00

Beany (Beany & Cecil), hand puppet, cloth body w/vinyl head, goggle eyes, ca 1950, VG+ $75.00

Beetle Bailey, hand puppet, printed cloth body w/name & vinyl head, Gund, 1960, EX...$100.00

Ben Casey MD, Sweater Guard, chain w/charms, Bing Crosby Products, 1962, MOC..$45.00

Bert (Sesame Street), cake topper, plastic, Bert figure waving on oval base, Wilton, 1980s, 2½", M.............................**$5.00**

Bert (Sesame Street), figure, stuffed cloth, Rag Doll #2601, Knickerbocker, 1975, 10", MIB.............................$35.00

Bert & Ernie (Sesame Street), lamp, ea w/instrument, tin washtub on round wooden base, graphic shade, 1970s, 16", NM.....$35.00

Bert Stacking Toy (Sesame Street), figural, Child Guidance, 1975, 10½", NMIB $25.00

Betty Boop, mug, ceramic bust w/eyes glancing up, 4", 1981, NM $10.00

Big Bird (Sesame Street), figure, PVC, playing guitar, Tara, 1985, 3½", MOC...$10.00

Bob Hope, hand puppet, cloth body w/vinyl head, Zany, 1940s, NM..$125.00

Brady Bunch, Fishing Puzzle & Game, Larami, 1973, MOC..$45.00

Broken Arrow, frame-tray puzzle, Built-Rite #1229, 1957, NM.$55.00

Bugs Bunny, Music Maker, litho tin, Mattel, 1963, VG.......$38.00

Captain Kangaroo, frame-tray puzzle, Whitman #4446, 1960, EX $38.00

Captain Kangaroo, hand puppet, cloth body w/vinyl head, Rushton, 1950s, NM+ $75.00

Captain Kangaroo, mug, plastic figural Captain's head, goggle-eyed, 1950s, 1950s premium, 4", EX............................$15.00

**Captain Marvel, blotter, red on white, 1941, 3x7" long,
VG+, $85.00.** (Photo courtesy LiveAuctioneers.com/Morphy Auctions)

**Chimp on the Farm/Andy Panda, 16mm movie, Castle Films,
$24.00 each.**

Cookie Monster (Sesame Street), figure, stuffed plush, plastic eyes, musical, Knickerbocker, 9", EX+ **$18.00**

Cookie Monster (Sesame Street), hand puppet, bright blue furry plush w/lg plastic eyeballs, Child Horizon, 1970s, NM **$20.00**

Cookie Monster (Sesame Street), squeeze toy, vinyl, sitting w/cookie jar, Child Guidance, 1978, 4", NM **$12.00**

Curious George, figure, stuffed plush, name on red shirt, Gund, 8", 1990, M... **$10.00**

Daffy Duck, figure, stuffed cloth, pillow type w/printed image & name, 1970s, 16", NM **$15.00**

Daisy Mae, Dogpatch U.S.A., plaster, 1968, 8", from $75.00 to $90.00.

Dennis the Menace, doll, stuffed cloth/vinyl, cloth oufit, Mighty Star, 13", MIB **$38.00**

Dennis the Menace, frame-tray puzzle, painting a chair, Whitman, 1960, NM **$45.00**

Dick Tracy, Talking Phone, nonworking, Marx, 1967, NMIB.. **$92.00**

Dick Tracy, Sub Machine Water Gun, plastic, 1950s, MIB, $250.00. (Photo courtesy Dunbar Gallery)

Dr Kildare, jigsaw puzzle, Emergency, Milton Bradley #4318, 1960s, EXIB... **$45.00**

Dukes of Hazzard, paint set, Craft Master #N38001, 1980, scarce, MIB (sealed) **$75.00**

Ernie (Sesame Street), figure, stuffed cloth, vinyl head/hands, striped sweater, print sneakers, Applause, 1985, 12", NM........ **$15.00**

ET, finger light, vinyl finger shape, glows when pressed, battery operated, Knickerbocker, 1982, 5", MOC...................... **$10.00**

Fat Albert, hand puppet, printed vinyl body w/molded head, Ideal, 1973, NM+ **$150.00**

Felix the Cat, figure, standing w/legs together & arms down at sides, vinyl, Eastern Moulded Products, 1962, 6", NM.......... **$45.00**

Flintstones, camera, Fred Flintstone Camera, Hong Kong/Hanna-Barbera, 1960s, MIB.. **$35.00**

Flintstones, Dino figure, swivel head, jointed arms, vinyl, Knixies/Knickerbocker, 1962, 6", EX................................ **$55.00**

Flintstones, frame-tray puzzle, Whitman #4428, 1960, NM .. **$40.00**

Flintstones, iron-on transfer, Fred, Wilma & Pebbles on pink circle outlined in yellow, 1976, 7½x6", M **$18.00**

Flintstones, Fred mug, molded plastic head, F&F Mold Co, 1970s, NM.. **$12.00**

Freddie Kruger (Nightmare on Elm Street), yo-yo, Spectra Star, 1988, MOC.. **$20.00**

G-Men, pencil box, black & white on red, 1930s, 5x8½", EX.... **$85.00**

Ghostbusters, gumball machine, vinyl ghost in red No symbol atop plastic dispenser, Superior Toy, 1986, 7", NM **$12.00**

Green Hornet, Ben Cooper, 1960s, MIB, $60.00.

Green Hornet, Colorforms Cartoon Kit, Greenway Productions, 1966, unused, NM (VG box) **$55.00**

Green Hornet, frame-tray puzzles, Whitman, 1966, set of 4, NMIB... **$125.00**

Green Hornet, Print Putty, Colorforms, 1966, MOC (sealed).. **$80.00**

Gumby, Astronaut Adventure Costume, plastic playset, Lakeside, 1965, MOC.. **$22.00**

Gumby, figure, bendable rubber, Jesco, 6", NM **$8.00**

Gumby, figure, PVC, hand in pocket of brown bomber-type jacket w/white collar, Applause, 1989, 3", NM+...................... **$6.00**

Gumby, paint set, 6 watercolors/paint brush/plastic palette w/image of Gumby & Pokey, Henry Gordy Int'l, 1988, MOC .. **$13.00**

Hansel & Gretel, marionette, Hansel, non-working mouth, Hazelle #813, 14", NMIB... **$125.00**

Hansel & Gretel, marionette, Witch, working mouth, Pelham, 14", NM+IB.. **$135.00**

Harvey Cartoons, hand puppet, Baby Huey, cloth body w/vinyl head, Gund, 1950s, NM...$75.00

Heathcliff, bagatelle games, Heathcliff's Sports Board, 2-pc set w/basketball & tennis, Smethport, 1983, MOC.........................$15.00

Heathcliff, figure, stuffed plush & cloth, printed cowboy outfit w/hat, red velvet vest, Knickerbocker, 1981, 12", EX+ $12.00

Heathcliff, friction toy, plastic, Heathcliff as football player, Talbot Toys, 1982, 8", MIP $12.00

Heckle & Jeckle, hand puppet, black plush bodies w/yellow hands & feet, Rushton Creations, 1950s, ea..................................$75.00

Howdy Doody, bubble pipe, plastic Clarabell figure, Lido Toy, 4½" L, unused, NMOC..$80.00

Howdy Doody, costume, Offical Pl-A-Time Costume, shirt, pants & canvas mask, NMIB...$110.00

Howdy Doody, doll, wood bead type w/compo head, cloth neckerchief, Noma/Cameo, 13", NM+IB $575.00

Howdy Doody, Doodle Slate, Stickless Corp, EX+ $65.00

Howdy Doody, One Man Band, w/4 plastic instruments, Trophy Prod, EXIB $150.00

Howdy Doody, ventriloquist doll, stuffed body w/vinyl head & hands, Goldberger, 1970s, 11", NMIB $65.00

Hulk Hogan, hand puppet, red velvety cloth body w/mechanical black boxing gloves, vinyl head w/headband, 1980s, NM+ $25.00

Incredible Hulk, figure, rubber, 1970s, 5½", EX+.................$20.00

Inspector Gadget, squeeze toy, vinyl, figure in trench coat, Jugasa, 1983, 6½", MIP..$50.00

J Fred Muggs (Today Show), hand puppet, printed cloth body w/vinyl head, Imperial, 1954, NM...$85.00

King Kong, pennant, felt w/multicolored King Kong image atop World Trade Center, New York City down side, 1970s, 25", NM $75.00

Lamb Chop, hand puppet, stocking body w/vinyl head, Tarcher Prod, 1960, NM...$50.00

Laurel and Hardy, figures, vinyl and cloth, 13", $150.00 for the pair.

Laverne & Shirley, Paint-By-Numbers, acrylic paint set, Hasbro, 1981, MIP (sealed) $20.00

Li'l Abner, doll, Li'l Abner, Mammy Yokum or Pappy Yokum, vinyl w/cloth oufit, Baby Barry Toys, 1950s, 14", NM, ea ..$100.00

Little Audrey, doll, vinyl w/cloth dress & hair bow, white vinyl shoes, Juro Novelty, 1950s, 12½", NM+ $175.00

Little Beaver, frame-tray puzzle, Whitman, 1950s, EX+.......$25.00

Little Bill (Fat Albert), doll, stuffed cloth w/vinyl head, Hey Hey Hey! I'm a Cosby Kid, Remco, 1985, 22", MIB $75.00

Little Lulu, figure, stuffed cloth, red cloth dress w/white collar & lace trim, Gund, 1972, 6½", MIB $75.00

Little Red Riding Hood, hand puppet, Little Red Riding Hood, cloth body w/vinyl head, MPI Toys, 1960, NM $85.00

Little Red Riding Hood, marionette, Big Bad Wolf, immobile mouth, Hazelle, 15", NM..$150.00

Looney Tunes, Bugs Bunny Wonder Whiskers (Magnetic) Drawing Set, Henry Gordy Int'l, 1988, MOC $8.00

Lucky Ducky, hand puppet, checked cloth body w/vinyl head, Zany, 1950s, NM $50.00

Mighty Mouse, flashlight, figural, 1970s, 3½", MIP $100.00

Miss Piggy, mirror, ceramic frame w/Miss Piggy figure admiring self in lower corner, Sigma, 1980s, 9", M...........................$75.00

Mr Rogers Neighborhood, hand puppet, King, full cloth body w/weighted base, vinyl head, Ideal, 1976, NM $60.00

Munsters, hand puppet, any character, cloth body w/vinyl head & hands, 1960s, EX, ea..$50.00

Oscar the Grouch (Sesame Street), figure, beanbag plush w/plastic eyes, Knickerbocker, 10", EX+......................................$12.00

Paddington Bear, figure, stuffed cloth, blue cloth shirt w/name, black printed features & ears, Eden Toys, 1975, 13", NM $20.00

Peanuts, music box, Anri, United Features, 1968, plays Take Me Out to the Ball Game, $100.00.

Pebbles (Flintstones), figure, squeeze vinyl, Sanitoy, 1979, 6", NM $25.00

Pink Panter, figure, stuffed pink plush in black satin jacket, plastic eyes, Mighty Star, 1987, 16", NM $25.00

Pink Panther, figure, bendable vinyl, skinny, Amscan, 1970s, 10", NM..$18.00

Pink Panther, windup swimming figure, plastic, Polly Gaz Int'l, 1979, MOC (sealed) $30.00

Planet of the Apes, swimming pool, inflatable vinyl, colorful graphics around rim, Azrak-Hamway, 1970s, 45" dia, EX...$175.00

Porky Pig, figure, squeeze rubber, standing w/head cocked & arms behind back, Sun Rubber, 1940s, 7", NM....................**$50.00**

Rocky & Bullwinkle, frame-tray puzzle, Whitman #4792, 1961, set of 4, M in VG box..**$100.00**

Rocky & Friends, bop bag, Snidley Whiplash, inflatable vinyl, PAT Ward, 1982, M..**$25.00**

Rocky & Friends, Bullwinkle's Double Boomerangs, Larami #3804, 1969, MIP..**$30.00**

Rocky & Friends, Bullwinkle's Electric Quiz Game, Larami, 1971, MIP..**$20.00**

Rocky & Friends, figure, Bullwinkle, stuffed plush, B on orange shirt, Wallace Berry, 1982, 16½", NM+...............**$25.00**

Rocky & Friends, figure, Dudley Do-Right, bendable vinyl, Wham-O, 1972, EX.....................................**$20.00**

Rocky & Friends, figure, Rocky, stuffed plush w/vinyl head, 1966, rare, 9½", VG...**$150.00**

Rocky & Friends, figure, Snidley Whiplash, bendable rubber, black & white w/yellow eyes, Wham-O, 1970s, 5", MOC....**$28.00**

Roy Rogers, frame-tray puzzle, Whitman #4427, VG+........**$40.00**

Scooby Doo, figure, Scooby, stuffed plush, standing on all 4s, Sutton, 1970, 7½"...**$30.00**

Scooby Doo, nightlight, bisque, Scooby, Scrappy & Ghost, 1980s, 7", NM..**$28.00**

Simon (Alvin & the Chipmunks), figure, stuffed cloth, musical, Knickerbocker, 1963, 13", EX..........................**$75.00**

Smurfs, figure, Brainy Smurf, bisque, standing holding book, Wallace Barry, 1982, 4", M..................................**$20.00**

Spider-Man, Crazy Foam, 1970s, MIP.........................**$50.00**

Spider-Man, hand puppet, plastic body w/vinyl head, 1970s, NM+...**$40.00**

Stink (Land of the Lost), pull-string talking figure, 13", $50.00.

Superman, hand puppet, printed cloth body w/name & molded vinyl head, Ideal, 1960s, NM...................................**$100.00**

Superman, Kryptonite Rock, Pro Arts, 1977, MIB...........**$90.00**

Superman, wallet, yellow vinyl w/snap closure, Standard Plastics (Mattel), 1966, unused, M.................................**$88.00**

Tasmanian Devil, figure, rubber, arms over head & bent at elbows, tan & gray, 1980, 5", NM.................................**$10.00**

Theodore (Alvin & the Chipmunks), figure, stuffed plush, talker, red 'T' on long green shirt, CBS Toys, 1983, 19", NM+......**$30.00**

Tom & Jerry, hand puppet, Tom or Jerry, cloth body w/vinyl head, Zany, 1950s, EX, ea.......................................**$75.00**

Tom & Jerry, kaleidoscope, litho metal, Green Monk, 1970s, NM+...**$28.00**

Tom & Jerry, Water Gun, Tom or Jerry figure, vinyl, water squirts out of nose, Marx, 1970s, 6", NMIB, ea....................**$50.00**

Top Cat, frame-tray puzzle, Whitman #4457, 1961, scarce, G...**$20.00**

Tweety Bird, candle, figure w/Happy Birthday on tummy, Wilton, 1979, MIP..**$12.00**

Tweety Bird, pull toy, twirling figure atop wagon, Brice Novelty, 1950s, 9½"..**$125.00**

Uncle Fester (Addams Family), figure, vinyl, standing & holding frog in raised hand, Remco, 1965, 5", EX+..............**$125.00**

Universal Monsters, Famous Monsters Plaster Casting Kit, Creature From the Black Lagoon, Rapco, 1974, MIB.............**$160.00**

Universal Monsters, Magnetic Disguise Set, Wolfman, Imperial, 1987, MOC...**$10.00**

Welcome Back Kotter, record player, portable suitcase type, Teletone, 1976, 12½x10½", NM.......................................**$60.00**

Wonder Woman, figure, jointed arms, standing w/legs together, golden whip, Presents, 1988, 15", NM+.....................**$55.00**

Woody Woodpecker (Walter Lantz), figure, plush & vinyl, California Stuffed Toys, 1980s, NM, ea from $20 to...................**$25.00**

Woody Woodpecker (Walter Lantz), hand puppet, blue & white printed cloth body w/name & vinyl head, 1950s, EX...**$75.00**

Yosemite Sam, figure, PVC, standing w/legs apart & guns raised, Applause, 1989, 2¼", NM+..**$5.00**

Zorro, jigsaw puzzle, Jaymar #2311, 1950s, NM.................**$45.00**

Superman, ring, Secret Chamber, with initial, Ostby & Barton, 1941, VG, $4,000.00. (Photo courtesy LiveAuctioneers.com/ Morphy Auctions)

Cherished Teddies

Cherished Teddies were designed by artist Patricia Hillman. They debuted in 1992 and have proven to be one of the Enesco company's most successful collector-oriented lines. Cherished Teddies are made from cast resin and are highly detailed. On the bottom of each figurine (room permitting), you'll find their name, a saying, and a date.

Advisors: Debbie and Randy Coe (See Directory, Cape Cod)

Figurine, A Mom's Touch Fills the Heart w/Love, #4006418, MIB **$35.00**

Figurine, Abraham, Your Friendship Means the World to Me, signed by Priscilla & Glen Hillman, MIB **$55.00**

Figurine, Alice, 1993, MIB, $100.00.

Figurine, Arthur, Monthly Friends To Cherish (aka Smooth Sailing), 1994 .... **$20.00**

Figurine, Being Nine Is Really Fine, MIB **$45.00**

Figurine, Carolyn, Wishing You All Good Things, 1993-96... **$25.00**

Figurine, Daisy, Friendship Blossoms w/Love, 1992, MIB ... **$85.00**

Figurine, Edna, Leaves of Change Bring Back the Fondest Memories, MIB **$48.00**

Figurine, Edna, September 2001 Event Adoption Center Exclusive, MIB **$40.00**

Figurine, Ernie Banks, Let's Play Two, Chicago Cubs Exclusive Limited Edition, MIB **$150.00**

Figurine, Holding On to Someone Special, Customer Appreciation, 1993, M in VG box **$35.00**

Figurine, Jo & Dee, A Warm Heart Is a Good Home, #789798, MIB **$45.00**

Figurine, Mermaid w/Shell, #854087, 2001, MIB **$55.00**

Figurine, Yellow Brick Road, Dorothy, Tin Man, Lion & Scarecrow on base w/yellow bricks & rainbow, MIB **$50.00**

Figurines, Across the Seas, set of 16 in original wooden display cabinet **$100.00**

Plaque, Heart to Heart, 2 Teddies in heart, retired 1997 ...... **$10.00**

Christmas Collectibles

Christmas is nearly everybody's favorite holiday, and it's a season when we all seem to want to get back to time-honored traditions. The stuffing and fruit cakes are made like Grandma always made them, we go caroling and sing the old songs that were written 200 years ago, and the same Santa that brought gifts to the children in a time long forgotten still comes to our house and yours every Christmas Eve.

So for reasons of nostalgia, there are thousands of collectors interested in Christmas memorabilia. Some early Santa figures are rare and may be very expensive, especially when dressed in a color other than red. Blown glass ornaments and Christmas tree bulbs were made in shapes of fruits and vegetables, houses, Disney characters, animals, and birds. There are Dresden ornaments and candy containers from Germany, some of which were made prior to the 1870s, that have been lovingly preserved and handed down from generation to generation. They were made of cardboard that sparkled with gold and silver trim.

Artificial trees made of feathers were produced as early as 1850 and as late as 1950. Some were white, others blue, though most were green, and some had red berries or clips to hold candles. There were little bottle-brush trees, trees with cellophane needles, and trees from the '60s made of aluminum.

Collectible Christmas items are not necessarily old, expensive, or hard to find. Things produced in your lifetime have value as well. To learn more about this field, we recommend *Pictorial Guide to Christmas Ornaments and Collectibles* by George Johnson (Collector Books).

Values in the listings that follow are for examples in undamaged original condition, unless otherwise noted.

Board game, Rudolph the Red-Nosed Reindeer, Parker Brothers, 1948, complete **$75.00**

Bulb, baby in clown suit, 3¼", from $75 to **$85.00**

Bulb, baseball, embossed stitching, Japan, ca 1950, 2¼" dia.. **$100.00**

Bulb, bell w/Santa face, milk glass, 2¼" **$20.00**

Bulb, candy cane, ca 1950, 2¾" **$55.00**

Bulb, Disney's Snow White, ca 1940, 2¾" **$215.00**

Bulb, frowning dog in basket, ca 1950, 2¾" **$40.00**

Bulb, Kewpie w/red flapper hat, arms at side, Japan, ca 1950, 2¾" **$55.00**

Bulb, pig playing tuba, ca 1950, 2¾" **$185.00**

Bulb, rooster in tub, Japanese, 2¼" **$45.00**

Bulbs, jester, $90.00; Dutch girl, $60.00; snowman on skis, $45.00. (Photo courtesy Margaret and Kenn Whitmyer)

Candelabrum, 8-mini socket white lights on red stair-step candles & base, Royal Electric #782, ca 1954, MIB **$65.00**

Candelabrum, 9-socket Menorah, blue lights w/white tips on white base, center star, Taiwan, ca 1965 .... **$25.00**

Candy container, cornucopia, printed paper, 8" **$12.00**

Candy container, football, painted cardboard, 3¼" **$72.00**

Candy container, Santa, pressed cardboard w/chenille fur trim, Germany, ca 1950, 6½" **$125.00**

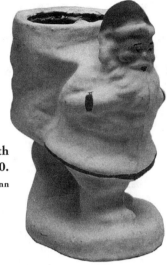

Candy container, Santa with bag, papier-maché, 8", $55.00.
(Photo courtesy Margaret and Kenn Whitmyer)

Candy container, suitcase, pressed paper, 4" **$63.00**

Chain of beads, colored glass, round beads **$15.00**

Decoration, angel child, plastic, late 1940-50s, 1¾x2¼" **$5.00**

Decoration, angel standing w/hands folded, white & gold, clear wings & halo, Levinson Mfg Co, USA, ca 1955, 10" ...**$65.00**

Decoration, Blinko the Snowman, Hy-G Products #603, USA, ca 1957, 8" **$55.00**

Decoration, Cathedral Belfry, Merry Christmas on base, Noma Electric #1507, USA, 1955, 20" **$100.00**

Decoration, Rudolph, nose lights up, musical, marked Raylite Electric Corp New York on base, ca 1950, 7¾x7¾" **$165.00**

Decoration, Santa by street lamp, ceramic, Japan, ca 1960, 6" **$25.00**

Decoration, Santa holding sm tree, white deer on ea side, Merry Christmas on base, Royal Electric #942, ca 1954, 14" W .**$125.00**

Decoration, Santa w/bubble light, Royal Electric, #935, USA, 1950, 7" **$65.00**

Decoration, Santa w/Merry Christmas sign, plastic light-up, Royalite, ca 1955, 7½" **$50.00**

Decoration, snowman holding wreath, hard plastic, black top hat, scarf & mittens, light-up, Royalite, ca 1955, 7½" **$30.00**

Lamp, motion; Santa w/sleigh & reindeer on blue, Lacolite, USA, ca 1965, 11½" H, M..**$300.00**

Lamp, red & green birds, World Wide, 2-pack, Japan, ca 1960, pr, MIB...**$10.00**

Lamp, silvered Christmas tree w/clear glass base, USA, ca 1950, 14"...**$50.00**

Lantern, Christmas Tree Lite, rubber, #1782, battery operated, Hong Kong, ca 1965, MIB...**$20.00**

Light cover, Santa w/hands on stomach, plastic, ca 1950, 4¾"....**$18.00**

Lighting set, Christmas Lamps, #G14, 16-socket, Japan, ca 1950, MIB...**$25.00**

Lighting set, Dealites, Noma Electric Co #110, 8-socket, USA, ca 1927, MIB..**$75.00**

Lighting set, Gen Electric Co #611-B, 8-socket, USA, ca 1950, MIB...**$15.00**

Lighting set, Royal Sparkling Bubble Lamps, Royal Elecric Co #109K, 9-mini socket, USA, ca 1948, MIB.................**$75.00**

Lighting set, Starlites, Pifco #1248, 12-socket, England, ca 1930, MIB..**$50.00**

Lighting set, Triangle Electric Trading Co #D-100, USA, ca 1925, MIB..**$100.00**

Lighting set, Twinkle Star Lites, Hy-G Products Co #TW77, 7-socket, USA, ca 1960, MIB..**$25.00**

Lighting set, Twinkling Star set, set of 10, Japan, ca 1960, MIB ..**$30.00**

Lighting set, Wonder Stars, Matchless Electric Co #475, set of 10, USA, ca 1950, MIB..**$300.00**

Ornament, angel, stamped/embossed aluminum foil, red & white, 1950-60s, 4"...**$8.00**

Ornament, angel bust, glass, gold, silver & red, Germany, ca 1980s, 4" **$175.00**

Ornament, angel standing, silvered plastic, Bradford Plastics, ca 1955, 3¼" **$11.00**

Ornament, baseball w/anchor, glass, 2½" **$200.00**

Ornament, bicycle, beaded glass, Czechoslovakia, ca 1950, 3½" **$35.00**

Ornament, bust of lady w/long wavy hair, embossed roses on chest, glass, Germany, ca 1970, 3¼" **$18.00**

Ornament, cat, free-blown milk glass, Germany, ca 1925, 3" ..**$35.00**

Ornament, chalet house w/elf figure, plastic, West Germany, 2¼"..**$5.00**

Ornament, clear plastic ball w/changing pictures of Santa inside, ca 1950 ....**$18.00**

Ornament, cosmonaut in white by yellow moon, Dresden, ca 1960s, 3½" **$25.00**

Ornament, decorated tree on stand, stamped brass, 2¼" **$12.00**

Ornament, deer standing, glass, in twisted black metal ring, 3" **$45.00**

Ornament, dog in conical hat, glass, 1950s, 4" **$35.00**

Ornament, egg-shaped globe, girl w/umbrella inside, composition, ca 1950s, 4½" **$12.00**

Ornament, elephant, white glow-in-the-dark plastic, Carnival, 4½" **$7.00**

Ornament, filigree bell, bows & holly, plastic, Bradford Plastics, ca 1955-60, med **$1.00**

Ornament, glass ball w/embossed cherries, 2" **$12.00**

Ornament, glass ball w/pink & green stripes, American War Ornaments, ca 1942-43 ....**$3.00**

Ornament, heart, light-reflecting tin-lead alloy, Germany, 4" ..**$75.00**

Ornament, heart w/pansy, bronze, 2¼" **$20.00**

Ornament, Italian oyster shell w/pearl, glass, ca 1950, 2½"..**$82.00**

Ornament, lady's high boot, cardboard covered in pink satin, white lace & gold ribbon accents, ca 1950s, 5½" **$40.00**

Ornament, lady w/porcelain head, fabric body, white dress w/pink ribbon, ca 1975..**$17.00**

Ornament, mushroom & gnome, clay, 3" **$55.00**

Ornament, peasant girl w/lg spoon & carrot in hands, glass, Czechoslovakia, ca 1955, 3½" **$40.00**

Ornament, squirrel, gold w/green nut, glass, Austria, ca 1975, 3" **$22.00**

Ornament, star w/angel on cloud in center, plastic, West Germany, ca 1950, 3" **$8.00**

Ornament, yellow banana, glass, Germany, 3" **$45.00**

Ornament, 2 kittens in a basket, glass, Czechoslovakia, ca 1980s, 2"..$60.00

Santa, bisque head, crepe-paper clothes and bag, metal and celluloid toys, 4½", EX, $350.00. (Photo courtesy LiveAuctioneers.com/Morphy Auctions)

Toy flashlight, figural Santa head w/red handle, battery operated, Hong Kong, ca 1960, MIB...........................$20.00

Tree, Cheer-O-Lite, Noma #615, conical w/pierced ornament shapes, ca 1936, 10" $100.00

Tree, prewired, 9-socket miniature base w/bubble lights, Noma #501G, ca 1948, 18" $125.00

Tree stand, metal, Art Deco style, lights & 4 legs, North Bros MFG Co, Yankee #5A, 14" $55.00

Tree stand, metal, conical, WL Bushnell #100, ca 1950.....$125.00

Tree stand, metal, 6 candelabra base sockets, USA, ca 1950 .$100.00

Tree stand, metal, 6-pointed star, green w/red center, 6 candelabra base sockets, USA, ca 1940, 16" dia $60.00

Tree stand, plastic, red, white & green, 6-sided, Good-Lite Electric Mfg #420, USA, 1955, 13½" W.....................$40.00

Tree topper, angel, composition w/foil-covered cardboard wings, fabric dress, made in USA, ca 1935, 9".........................$20.00

Tree topper, angel, wax & fabric w/white feather wings, Germany, ca 1930, 10"..$175.00

Tree topper, angel w/wand, plastic w/spun-glass hair, lights up, Glolite #536, ca 1945, 7" $15.00

Tree topper, Blinking Pixie (on red bell shape), Thomas Co #169, ca 1965 ....$10.00

Tree topper, Brilliant Bethlehem Star, electric, red, green & white $14.00

Tree topper, Fairy Crown Christmas, Paul Boehland & Co, USA, ca 1935 ....$75.00

Tree topper, Polly Star, Lee Pollock Corp #107, 1937 ....$20.00

Tree topper, Royal Star, 5 socket lights, Royal Electric Co #950A, ca 1949 ....$25.00

Tree topper, Star of Bethleham, Monowatt #120, USA, ca 1927, MIB $100.00

Tree topper, 10-pointed star, picture of Mary & baby Jesus in center, K-B Products #6-26, USA, ca 1960 ....$15.00

Tree topper, 5-point star, foil, double-layered w/socket, National Tinsel Mfg, ca 1940s, 9", NMIB $8.00

Wall hanging, church in winter scene, Buone Feste, West Germany, ca 1955, 9x6¼"..$30.00

Wall hanging, Cresent Moon, white metal frame w/10 orange lights, Majestic Electric Mfg, USA, ca 1940, 11" $100.00

Wall hanging, cross, white frame w/10 blue lights, Majestic #6580, ca 1940, 12" $45.00

Wall hanging, Nativity scene, vinyl, Raylite Electric Corp #364, USA, ca 1954, 19" W....................................$95.00

Wall hanging, Santa walking, vinyl, Noma Electric #98, USA, 1954, 40" H $85.00

Wall hanging, star, cellophane, 10 mini socket lights, ca 1948..$50.00

Wall hanging, Star of Bethlehem, white vinyl w/orange trim, Noma Electric #460, USA, ca 1959, 29" H............................$25.00

Wall hanging, Twin Choir Singers, Noma Electric Co #101, 1954, 18"...$30.00

Wall hanging, 3 bells w/Season's Greetings ribbon, vinyl, LA Goodman #60, USA, ca 1960, 25" W $35.00

Wall hanging, 3 red candles w/halos sitting in greenery, Made in Germany, ca 1945, 9x6½"..$30.00

Wreath, chenille w/Santa face in center, Raylite Electric #6A, ca 1950 ....$30.00

Wreath, orange chenille, 3 candle lights in center, Noma Electric Co #1315, USA, 1930....................................$100.00

Wreath, red leaves w/3 graduated candle lights, Noma #1503, ca 1935 ....$85.00

Tree topper, Heavenly Reflecting Light, with plastic spinner, Bradford Novelty, ca 1955 – 1965, from $15.00 to $20.00. (Photo courtesy George Johnson)

Christmas Pins

Once thought of as mere holiday novelties, Christms pins are now considered tiny prizes among costume jewelry and Christmas collectors. Hollycraft, Weiss, Lisner, and other famous costume jewelry designers created beautiful examples. Rhinestones, colored 'jewels', and lovely enameling make Christmas pins tiny works of art, and what used to be purchased for a few dollars now may command as much as $100.00, especially if signed. Pins are plentiful and prices vary. Buyers should be aware that many fakes and repros are out there. Many 'vintage looking' pins are actually brand new and retail for less than $10.00. Know your dealer, and if you are unsure, let it pass.

Hollycraft, tree, molded balls and rhinestones, from $85.00 to $115.00. (Photo courtesy Jill Gallina)

Anthony Attruia, tree, aurora borealis w/20 blue stones, 3½x2", from $150 to **$200.00**

Anthony Attruia, tree, citrine Austrian crystals w/3 golden snow-flakes, 2½x1½", from $50 to...**$75.00**

Art, tree, metal w/bronze & pewter balls on branches, 2½x1½", from $55 to **$75.00**

Attruia, tree, red crystals, blue baguette candles & gold-tone fireman symbols, 2½x1¾", from $100 to................................**$150.00**

Avante, tree, filigree gold-tone metal w/red & green crystals, 2¼x2¼", from $45 to **$55.00**

Beatrix, tree, silver metal interlocking garlands on metallic red back-ground, green rhinestones, 2⅜x1⅝", from $35 to.........**$50.00**

Benedikt, tree, gold-tone w/tiny clear & red glued-in stones, 2x1¾", from $45 to **$65.00**

Butler & Wilson, tree, thin navettes in pink, green & clear tones, 2x1½", from $95 to **$125.00**

Cadoro, tree, green enameled bird & dangling golden pears, 2¾x2¼", from $60 to **$85.00**

Coventry, tree, brushed silver-tone w/green & red rhinestone balls, 2⅜x1⅜", from $25 to **$35.00**

Dodds, snowflake, brushed gold w/blue stones dotted throughout, 2" dia, from $35 to..**$45.00**

Dominique, tree, miniature red stones, topped w/a clear pear-shaped crystal, 3x2¼", from $100 to **$125.00**

Dorothy Bauer, Have a Ball tree, multicolor stones & rhinestones in gold-tone metal, 2¾x1½"..**$100.00**

Dorothy Bauer, tree, antique silver frame, milk glass stones, rhine-stone at top & covering base, 2¼x2¼"..........................**$97.50**

Dorothy Bauer, tree, gold-toned w/jeweled ornaments, pedestal base, 4x3" **$400.00**

Eisenberg, snowman, pavé set clear, black & red stones, 2¼x1⅜", from $30 to **$40.00**

Eisenberg, tree, gold-tone w/lg cabochon multicolored stones, 3x2⅛", from $30 to **$45.00**

Eisenberg, tree, gold-tone w/round & tiny sq green stones, 2x1½", from $20 to **$35.00**

Hattie Carnegie, tree, green enameled metal w/dangling colored balls, 2½x1½", from $85 to **$110.00**

Hedy, tree, black metal frame w/blue, red, yellow, & gold glued-in rhinestones, 2x1⅝", from $50 to............................**$75.00**

Hobé tree, 7 raspberry-colored balls dangle from antique gold frame, 1¾x1", from $75 to **$125.00**

Hollycraft, tree, antique gold frame, 6 multicolored stones, clear stones form garland, 2¼x1½", from $95 to.................**$150.00**

Hollycraft, tree, gold-tone frame, clear baguette candles & multicol-ored glued-in stones, 2x1½", from $95 to...................**$125.00**

Ian St Gielar, tree, tiny white & blue beads w/3 movable red pear-shaped teardrops, ornament at top, 2x1¾", $140 to ...**$165.00**

Ian St Gielar, tree in gold basket, white flowers w/red, white, green beads & Swarovski crystals, from $190 to...................**$225.00**

JJ, tree, alternating brushed gold & rhinestone branches, 2¾x2", from $45 to **$60.00**

Kirks Folly, Santa head, free-flowing beard, multicolored rhine-stones, limited edition, 3½x2¾"................................**$211.50**

Unsigned, enameled Santa in blue airplane, 1½x1½", from $12 to .**$18.00**

Unsigned, Santa & Mrs Claus, multicolored stones, lg blue stones as eyes, 2¾x1½", from $35 to **$45.00**

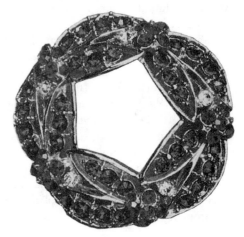

Weiss, wreath, ca. 1970s, from $55.00 to $65.00. (Photo courtesy Jill Gallina)

Wendy Gell, tree, patriotic symbols, sm beads, stones & charms glued on metal frame, 3¼x2½", from $150 to **$175.00**

Cigarette Lighters

Collectors of tobacciana tell us that cigarette lighters are definite-ly hot! Look for novel designs (figurals, Deco styling, and so forth), unusual mechanisms (flint and fuel, flint and gas, battery, etc.), those made by companies now defunct, advertising lighters, and quality lighters made by Dunhill, Evans, Colibri, Zippo, and Ronson.

Newsletter: *On the Lighter Side*
Judith Sanders
P.O. Box 1733
Quitman, TX 75783; 903-763-2795
SASE for information

Advertising, Jim Beam, plastic, bottle shape, Korea, ca 1985, 3x1", from $5 to $10.00

Advertising, Knott's Berry Farm, enamel on chromium, Japan, ca 1965, 1¾x2", from $15 to $25.00

Advertising, Lucky Strike, red painted metal, Japan, ca late 1950s, 4½", from $30 to..$40.00

Advertising, Schweppes, Penguin, Japan, EX, $20.00.
(Photo courtesy www.gasolinealleyantiques.com)

Advertising, Sherwin-Williams, enamel on chromium, Lansing, ca 1975, 1¾x2", from $10 to $20.00

Art Deco, chrome & green enamel, lighter, case & striker, Evans, lighter: 2x1½", case: 2¾x4", from $200 to.................$250.00

Art Deco, chromium & black enamel, Octette, Ronson, ca 1935, 3½x3¾", from $100 to $125.00

Art Deco, lighter/case, chrome & dark brown enamel, Ronson, ca 1939, 3¼x4¾", from $100 to $125.00

Art Deco, lighter/case, chrome & dark green enamel, Evans, ca 1935, 4¼x2½", from $90 to $110.00

Cheesecake, nude woman on front, enamel on brass, Evans, ca 1930s, 2½x1½", from $125 to...................................$150.00

Cheesecake, pinup girl, chrome, Fire-Lite, ca 1950s, 1⅞x1⅝", from $25 to $30.00

Decorative, Aladdin lamp, silver plated, Evans, ca 1950s, 3x4¼", from $30 to $45.00

Decorative, candle table lighter, ceramic and brass, Giv-A-Gift, ca. 1960s, 6", from $20.00 to $35.00. (Photo courtesy James Flanagan)

Decorative, cut crystal, butane, Waterford in Ireland, ca 1975, 3x3½" dia, from $90 to $115.00

Decorative, hand-painted brass, egg shape on footed base, Evans, ca 1955, 2½x3", from $60 to $75.00

Decorative, ivory porcelain w/green & yellow flowers, silver-plated top & base, ca 1952, 3x2¾", from $30 to $50.00

Decorative, knight bust, chromium on tortoise-colored plastic cigarette box, Negbaur, ca 1950, 4⅛x4", from $30 to.........$50.00

Miniature, brass, w/key chain, Pereline, ca 1955, 1¼x1¼", from $5 to $10.00

Miniature, chromium & painted lift arm, Alaska on front, ca 1950s, ⅞x⅝", from $20 to $35.00

Novelty, boot, metal, opens w/lever on back, 1920s, 1¾x2⅝", from $80 to $125.00

Novelty, cigar, plastic, Negbaur, ca 1955, 2½x⅝" dia, from $20 to $30.00

Novelty, dachshund, bronze, tail is striker, Ronson, ca 1940, 4x9", from $175 to $250.00

Novelty, dueling pistol, brass, Dunhill, ca 1930, 4x6¼", from $225 to $300.00

Novelty, elephant, painted metal, Strikalite, ca 1948, 3x3½", from $30 to $40.00

Novelty, golf clubs & bag, brass, Negbaur, ca 1939, 5x1½", from $75 to $100.00

Novelty, horse rearing, chromium, Japan, ca 1988, 7x4½", from $20 to $30.00

Novelty, jockey, chromium, hinged cap operates lighter, ca 1950s, 8½x3", from $175 to $225.00

Novelty, ladybug, metal w/red & black paint, squeeze antennas to reveal lighter, ca 1940s, ¾x1¼", from $30 to...............$50.00

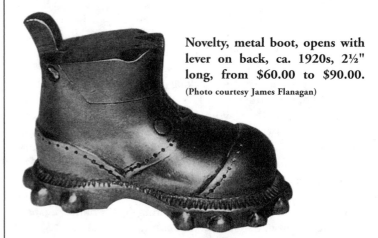

Novelty, metal boot, opens with lever on back, ca. 1920s, 2½" long, from $60.00 to $90.00.
(Photo courtesy James Flanagan)

Novelty, TV, Swank, ca 1963, 2¾x3⅞", from $30 to $50.00

Novelty, wolf (dressed as cowboy), brass striker, ca 1935, 5½x2", from $275 to $325.00

Novelty, wrench, painted metal, butane, German, ca 1990, 2⅞x1¼", from $15 to $25.00

Occupied Japan, birdcage, chromium, ca 1950s, 5½x4", from $200 to $250.00

Occupied Japan, chrome & black enamel w/yellow & green flowers, lighter/case, ca 1940s, 3¾x2¼", from $150 to $200.00

Occupied Japan, chrome w/ceramic base, painted rose on front, ca 1947, 3x2½" dia, from $75 to $100.00

Occupied Japan, fish, detailed brass, ca 1948, 3x3¼", from $125 to **$150.00**

Occupied Japan, football on footed base, chrome, ca 1940s, 2¾x2¾", from $125 to **$175.00**

Occupied Japan, pistol, chrome, ca 1948, 1⅞x2¾", from $75 to **$100.00**

Occupied Japan, silver-plated barrel shape, table, ca 1948, 3⅛x1¾", from $70 to **$100.00**

Pocket, brass, butane, w/gift box, Scripto, ca 1958, 2½x1¼", from $30 to **$50.00**

Pocket, brass & silver-plated basketweave, Evans, ca 1934, 1½x1½", from $40 to **$60.00**

Pocket, chrome w/embossed pilot wings, Evans, ca 1930s, 2x1½", from $50 to **$75.00**

Pocket, chrome w/leather band, lift arm, Superfine, ca 1928, 1⅞x1½", from $70 to **$90.00**

Pocket, chromium, New Method Mfg, ca 1930, w/box, 2x1⅛", from $40 to **$50.00**

Table, ship's wheel, chromium, turn wheel to light, Hamilton, ca. 1930s, 5", from $75.00 to $100.00. (Photo courtesy James Flanagan)

Cleminson Pottery

One of the several small potteries that operated in California during the middle of the century, Cleminson was a family-operated enterprise that made kitchenware, decorative items, and novelties that are beginning to attract a considerable amount of interest. At the height of their productivity, they employed 150 workers, so as you make your rounds, you'll be very likely to see a piece or two offered for sale just about anywhere you go.

They marked their ware fairly consistently with a circular ink stamp that contains the name 'Cleminson.' But even if you find an unmarked piece, with just a little experience you'll easily be able to recognize their very distinctive glaze colors. They're all strong, yet grayed-down, dusty tones. They made a line of bird-shaped tableware items that they marketed as 'Distlefink' and several plaques and wall pockets that are decorated with mottoes and Pennsylvania Dutch-type hearts and flowers.

In Jack Chipman's *Collector's Encyclopedia of California Pottery, Second Edition,* you'll find reference to Cleminson Pottery. Roerigs' *The Ultimate Collector's Encyclopedia of Cookie Jars* has additional information. (Both of these books are published by Collector Books.)

See also Clothes Sprinkler Bottles; Cookie Jars.

Ashtray, stylized flower in center, leaf in ea corner, 6" sq......**$16.00**

Bank, baby in blue diaper w/pink flowers, Bonds for Baby, 7x4". **$30.00**

Bowl, white w/brown floral, Gram's in blue-gray, w/lid, 2½x4" ..**$27.00**

Cheese dish, lady figural, 6½x7½", from $65 to **$80.00**

Coffee, cup, Time's Up, on 8x4" tray, Time Out, w/cigarette rests **$40.00**

Creamer & sugar bowl, Pennsylvania Dutch decor **$18.00**

Cup, jumbo; My Old Man, man sleeping in chair **$20.00**

Darner, little girl, Darn It, original ribbon, 5" **$50.00**

Gravy boat, Distlefink, bird figure, 5¾x6" **$35.00**

Head vase, girl w/curly blond hair & freckles, red lips, 4"....**$50.00**

Jar, clown face, lid is tall conical hat, 6x4x8" **$40.00**

Marmalade, flowerpot w/strawberry finial, from $25 to.......**$30.00**

Mug, Black boy on white, Make Mine Black, polka-dot tie, 3¼" **$32.00**

Pie bird, rooster figural, white w/green, yellow & pink **$50.00**

Pitcher, honey; Queen Bee, 5½", from $75 to **$90.00**

Plaque, Be It Ever So Humble, There's No Place Like Home, wood-like frame, 8¼x10½" **$50.00**

Plaque, Family Tree, flowers hanging from tree w/child, light blue background, from $60 to...**$75.00**

Plaque, 2 applied pink roses, scalloped oval, 6¾x5¾" **$22.00**

Range set, Cherry, 5" grease jar & 6" salt & pepper shakers, 3-pc **$30.00**

Ring holder, dog figure, tail up, peach & white, 3".............**$27.00**

Ring holder, worm in apple..**$60.00**

Salt & pepper shakers, French artist w/palette, 6¼", pr........**$55.00**

Salt & pepper shakers, white w/burgundy pink trim w/green leaf, 6", pr **$13.00**

Soap dish, tray w/star & Soap, 6" L **$24.00**

Spoon rest, white w/musical notes, Whistle While You Work, 8" ..**$35.00**

String holder, winking man's head, wearing hat, 1930s, 5½x5½"...**$80.00**

Sugar bowl, girl figural, top lifts off, 6½", $45.00.

Tea bag holder, teapot shape, 3x4¼" **$15.00**

Wall pocket, black kettle w/heart & verse **$30.00**

Wall pocket, clock, 7x8", from $25.00 to $30.00.

Wall pocket, pink kettle w/heart & verse $40.00
Wall pocket, pitcher & bowl, w/verse, 8x7", from $28 to $35.00
Wall pocket, puppy in basket, 7x7" $28.00
Wall pocket, red long johns...$42.50

Clothes Sprinkler Bottles

In the days before permanent press, the process of getting wrinkles out of laundered clothing involved first sprinkling each piece with water, rolling it tightly to distribute the moisture, and packing it all down in a laundry basket until ironing day. Thank goodness those days are over!

To sprinkle the water, you could simply dip your fingers in a basin and 'fling' the water around, or you could take a plain old bottle with a screw-on cap, pierce the cap a few times, and be in business. Figural ceramic bottles were first introduced in the late 1920s and are found in the forms of a variety of subjects ranging from cute animals to people who actually did the ironing. Maybe these figural bottles were made to add a little cheer to this dreary job. Anyway, since no one irons any more, today they simply represent a little bit of history, and collectors now take an interest in them.

See also Kitchen Prayer Ladies.

Advisor: Larry Pogue (See Directory, Head Vases and String Holders)

Cat, marble eyes, ceramic, American Bisque $400.00
Cat, marble eyes, ceramic, Cardinal USA, 8½" $255.00
Cat, variety of designs & colors, handmade ceramic, from $75 to $125.00
Chinese man, removable head, ceramic, from $250 to.......$400.00
Chinese man, Sprinkle Plenty, white, green & brown, holding iron, ceramic, 8½", from $125 to.................................$175.00
Chinese man, Sprinkle Plenty, yellow & green, ceramic, Cardinal China Co $85.00
Chinese man, towel over arm, ceramic, from $300 to........$350.00
Chinese man, variety of designs & colors, handmade, ceramic, from $50 to $150.00
Chinese man, white & aqua w/paper shirt tag, ceramic, California Cleminsons, from $75 to..................................$100.00
Chinese man w/removable head, ceramic, from $250 to....$400.00

Clothespin, hand decorated, ceramic, from $250 to...........$400.00
Clothespin, red, yellow & green plastic, from $20 to..........$40.00
Clothespin, yellow w/face, ceramic, 1940s-50s, 7¾" $275.00
Dearie Is Weary, ceramic, Enesco, from $350 to $500.00
Dutch boy, green & white, ceramic..................................$275.00
Dutch girl, white w/green & pink trim, wetter-downer, ceramic, from $175 to $250.00
Elephant, pink & gray, ceramic.......................................$165.00
Elephant, trunk forms handle, ceramic, American Bisque, extremely rare, minimum value...$700.00
Emperor, variety of designs & colors, handmade ceramic, from $150 to $200.00
Fireman, California Cleminsons, very rare, 6¼", minimum value $3,000.00
Iron, blue flowers, ceramic, from $100 to $150.00
Iron, green ivy, ceramic, from $95 to $125.00
Iron, green plastic, from $35 to.......................................$75.00
Iron, lady cleaning, ceramic..$125.00
Iron, lady ironing, ceramic..$95.00
Iron, man & woman farmer, ceramic, from $200 to..........$275.00
Iron, souvenir of Aquarena Springs, San Marcos TX, ceramic, from $200 to $300.00
Iron, souvenir of Florida, pink flamingo, ceramic $300.00
Iron, white w/black rooster decoration, black stripe on handle, ceramic w/metal lid, VG Japan sticker, 6½" $100.00
Iron, Wonder Cave - San Marcos TX, white w/green, brown & black scene $300.00
Mammy, ceramic..$450.00
Mary Maid, all colors, plastic, Reliance, from $20 to..........$35.00
Mary Poppins, ceramic, Cleminsons, from $300 to $450.00
Myrtle (Black), ceramic, Pfaltzgraff, from $275 to $375.00
Myrtle (white), ceramic, Pfaltzgraff, from $250 to $350.00
Peasant woman, w/laundry poem on label, ceramic, from $200 to..$300.00
Poodle, gray, pink or white, ceramic, from $200 to............$300.00
Rooster, green, tan & red detailing over white, ceramic, Sierra Vista...$125.00

Clothespin, face with stenciled eyes and airbrushed cheeks, ceramic, marked Cardinal, $400.00. (Photo courtesy Larry Pogue)

Clothing and Accessories

Watch a 'golden oldie' movie, and you can't help admiring the clothes — what style, what glamour, what fun! Due in part to the popularity of old movie classics and great new movies with retro themes, there's a growing fascination with the fabulous styles of the past — and there's no better way to step into the romance and glamour of those eras than with an exciting piece of vintage clothing!

'OOOhhh, it don't mean a thing, if it ain't got that S-W-I-N-G!' In 1935, Benny Goodman, 'king of swing,' ushered in the swing era from Los Angeles's Polmar Ballroom. After playing two standard sets, he switched to swing, and the crowd went crazy! Swing era gals' clothing featured short full or pleated skirts, wide padded shoulders and natural waistlines. Guys, check out those wild, wide ties that were worn with 'gangster-look' zoot suits!

Clothes of the 1940s though the 1970s are not as delicate as their Victorian and Edwardian counterparts; they're easier to find and much more affordable! Remember, the more indicative of its period, the more desirable the item. Look for pieces with glitz and glamour — also young, trendy pieces that were expensive to begin with. Look for designer pieces and designer look-alikes. Although famous designer labels are hard to find, you may be lucky enough to run across one! Be sure to look in skirt seams for labels — that's where many are hidden. American designers like Adrian, Claire McMardell, Charles James, Mainboucher, Hattie Carnegie, Norell, Pauline Trigere, and Mollie Parnis came to the fore during World War II. The '50s were the decade of Christian Dior; others included Balenciaga, Balmain, Chanel, Jacques Heim, Nina Ricci, Ann Fogarty, Oleg Cassini, and Adele Simpson. In the '60s and '70s, Mary Quant, Betsey Johnson, Givenchy, Yves St. Laurent, Oscar de la Renta, Galanos, Pierre Cardin, Rudi Gernreich, Paco Rabanne, Courreges, Arnold Scassi, Geoffrey Beene, Emilio Pucci, Zandra Rhodes, and Jessica McClintock (Gunne Sax) were some of the names that made fashion headlines.

Pucci, Lilli Ann of San Francisco, Eisenberg, and Ceil Chapman designs continue to be especially sought after. Look for lingerie — '30s and '40s lace/hook corsets and '50s pointy 'bullet' bras (like the ones in the Old Maidenform Dream ads). For both men and women, '70s disco platform shoes (the wilder, the better); cowboy shirts and jackets, also fringed 'hippie' items. For men, look for bowling shirts, '50s 'Kramer' shirts, and '40s and '50s wild ties, especially those by Salvadore Dali.

Levi jeans and jackets made circa 1971 and before have a cult following, especially in Japan. Among the most sought-after denim Levi items are jeans with a capitol 'E' on a *red* tab or back pocket. The small 'e' jeans are also collectible; these were made during the late 1960s and until 1970 (with two rows of single stitching inside the back pocket). Worth watching for as well are the 'red line' styles of the '80s (these have double-stitched back pockets). Other characteristics to look for in vintage Levis are visible rivets inside the jeans and single pockets and silver-colored buttons on jackets with vertical pleats. From the same era, Lee, Wrangler, Bluebell, J.C. Penney, Oxhide, Big Yanks, James Dean, Doublewear, and Big Smith denims are collectible as well.

As with any collectible, condition is of the utmost importance. 'Deadstock' is a term that refers to a top-grade item that has never been worn or washed and still has its original tags. Number 1 grade must have no holes larger than a pinhole. A torn belt loop is permissible if no hole is created. There may be a few light stains and light fading. The crotch area must have no visible wear and the crotch seam must have no holes. And lastly, the item must not have been altered. Unless another condition is noted within the lines, values in the listing here are for items in number 1 grade. There are also other grades for items that have more defects.

While some collectors buy with the intent of preserving their clothing and simply enjoy having it, many buy it to wear. If you do wear it, be very careful how you clean it. Fabrics may become fragile with age.

For more information, refer to *Vintage Hats and Bonnets, 1770 – 1970, Identifications and Values,* by Sue Langley; *Vintage Fashions for Women, the 1950s & '60s,* by Kristina Harris (Schiffer); *Clothing and Accessories From the '40s, '50s and '60s,* by Jan Lindenberger (Schiffer); *Vintage Denim* by David Little; *Fashion Footwear, 1800 – 1970,* by Desire Smith; *Plastic Handbags* by Kate E. Dooner; *Fit To Be Tied, Vintage Ties of the '40s and Early '50s,* by Rod Dyer and Ron Spark; and *The Hawaiian Shirt* by H. Thomas Steele. For more information about denim clothing and vintage footwear see *How to Identify Vintage Apparel for Fun and Profit,* available from Flying Deuce Auction & Antiques (see Auction Houses).

Prices are a compilation of shows, shops, and internet auctions. They are retail values and apply to items in excellent condition. Note: Extraordinary items bring extraordinary prices!

Advisors: Ken Weber, Clothing (www.vintagemartini.com); Flying Duce Auctions, Vintage Denim (See Directory, Clothing and Accessories)

1940s Day Wear

Dress, navy and white dotted batiste, navy and white lace trim, no label, $65.00. (Photo courtesy Vintage Martini)

Bloomer shorts, Oriental lantern-print cotton w/elastic gathered waist & legs, dead stock **$35.00**

Blouse, floral on brown rayon, V-neck w/button front, short sleeves, fitted darts, gathers at shoulder line along front **$48.00**

Blouse, red silk crepe, fluted collar, wide shoulder yoke, ¾-raglan sleeves w/gathers at wide cuff...**$45.00**

Dress, blue & white striped bodice w/V-shaped breast pockets, short sleeves, gored skirt w/stitching details **$78.00**

Dress, brown & white check cotton, scoop neck w/ruffles across front, lace trim, short sleeves, full skirt w/flounce **$65.00**

Dress, floral print rayon, crisscross front & back, cap sleeves, panel skirt, covered buttons...**$90.00**

Dress, floral stripes on black silk, V-neck w/bias stand collar, shoulder yoke, short sleeves, 4-panel skirt, side snaps............**$85.00**

Dress, maternity, navy silk crepe, sweetheart neck, princess seams, shoulder ruffles, no sleeves, sash belt ties in back **$85.00**

Dress, printed silk, spread collar, rhinestone buttons, short sleeves, slim skirt w/sm pleats, covered belt **$85.00**

Dress, printed silk w/V-shaped shoulder yoke, draped neck w/sash tie & celluloid slide buckle, short sleeves, slim skirt **$85.00**

Dress, rose boucle knit w/darker rose pattern on bodice, short sleeves, dark rose belt, ribbed skirt w/back slit **$85.00**

Dress, tan boucle knit w/cable design at neck & down front, ¾-sleeves w/cable design at border, neck closure **$78.00**

Shorts, ecru linen w/sombrero applique, multicolor buttons fasten down left side..**$35.00**

Ski suit, blue wool w/reversible red cotton twill jacket, zipper front, long sleeves, string tie closures at ankles.....................**$245.00**

Skirt, black & tan gabardine, wide waist band w/V-shaped hip yoke, ribbon trim, side zipper **$65.00**

Suit, brown wool gabardine, top-stitched collar, button jacket w/pockets, cuffed sleeves, slim skirt, fully lined... **$135.00**

Suit, burgundy wool gabardine, platter collar, princess seams, long raglan sleeves w/sm cuff, sack back, slim skirt.............**$155.00**

Suit, navy wool gabardine, dbl-breasted jacket w/notched lapels, long sleeves, slim skirt w/kick pleat, Saks Fifth Ave.....**$185.00**

Suit, red cotton & rayon twill, spread collar, button front, princess seams, long sleeves, slim skirt.......................................**$125.00**

Sweater, red lamb's wool w/white dots, flat bow at base of neck, short sleeves, ribbed band along waist **$78.00**

Trousers, black gabardine, high waist, pleats down center front, belt loops, inset pockets, stitched detail **$115.00**

1940s Ladies' Coats and Jackets

Jacket, Kelly green wool knit with large brass buttons, fully lined, A. Harris & Co., Dallas, TX, $100.00. (Photo courtesy Vintage Martini)

Jacket, multicolor plaid wool, shoulder pads, pleated yoke & shoulders, front pockets, gathered cuffs **$120.00**

Jacket, plaid wool, Pendleton 49er w/shoulder pads, patch pockets..**$120.00**

Jacket, red-brown sheared sheepskin, swing style w/¾-sleeves, hook & eye closure, rayon lining **$70.00**

Jacket, sueded deerskin leather, 3-button front, notched lapel, fringed sleeves, hem & back yoke, patch pockets **$72.00**

Jacket, white & gold floral jacquard, wide stand collar w/sash ties, long raglan sleeves, fully lined.......................................**$145.00**

1940s Ladies' Evening Wear

Dress, black rayon chiffon, V-neck opening held by collar band & rhinestone buttons, short sleeves, diagonal tucks...........**$85.00**

Dress, black rayon taffeta, off the shoulder with spaghetti straps, pink cabbage roses trim neckline and hem, pink taffeta petticoat exposed behind drapes in skirt, $128.00. (Photo courtesy Vintage Martini)

Dress, black silk crepe, wide scooped neck w/lace ruffle, dart-fitted bodice, no sleeves, A-line skirt w/box pleats..................**$80.00**

Dress, black silk crepe w/plunging V-neck, fluted collar, panels fall over shoulders, ¾-sleeves, Dorothy O'Hara................**$125.00**

Dress, floral on black silk, sq neck, zipper front closure, sash ties from front sides to back **$85.00**

Dress, navy rayon crepe, narrow collar, floral applique on short sleeves, straight skirt w/draped & shirred overskirt........**$85.00**

Dress, printed cotton/rayon, spread collar w/notched lapels, gathers along shoulders, long sleeves, A-line skirt......................**$85.00**

Dress, yellow rayon/silk crepe w/black abstract print, wide shoulder strap on right, spaghetti strap on left w/lg sash **$145.00**

Jumpsuit, black silk w/appliqued felt roosters, sm collar, button front, long sleeves w/cuffs **$165.00**

Jumpsuit, ivory & navy silk crepe, palazzo pants, full sleeves w/navy cuff, velvet ribbon trim, silk lined **$295.00**

1940s Lingerie

Bra, black satin rayon, seamed cups w/no lining or support, ribbon straps, elastic on back strap **$16.00**

Housecoat, floral stripes on black nylon, spread collar, zipper front, elbow-length puffed sleeves $58.00

Lounging robe/dressing gown, peach damask taffeta, padded shoulders, double-breasted w/faux pearl buttons $45.00

Nightgown, floral print cotton, collar & yoke w/lace trim, long sleeves, stretch waist, 51" L..$24.00

Pajamas, pink printed rayon w/lace at collar, short sleeves, elastic waistbands, wide legs $42.00

Robe, tropical print cotton, wrap front w/1 lg button closing waist, short puff sleeves $68.00

1940s Ladies' Accessories

Hat, black felt headband w/black sequined felt petals & black netting $85.00

Hat, black straw skimmer, black satin ribbon trim w/4 trailing tails down back $45.00

Hat, black wool felt fez type w/lg black tassel, wired head ring acts to balance tilt of hat, Adrian LTD $395.00

Hat, black woven straw, wide curved brim w/tall crown, ribbon trim & lg red poppy pinned at back $42.00

Hat, brown felt Glengarry style w/piping, brown rabbit fur covers front & sides, ribbon headband $58.00

Hat, navy felt, shaped crown w/button top, flat bow runs along edge of brim, 22" dia $28.00

Hat, paisley velvet-draped turban, red grosgrain ribbon & soutache trim, Lilly Dache, 21"...$175.00

Hat, shaped buckram fedora, covered in pink feathers, sm brim & tall crown, brown netting..$85.00

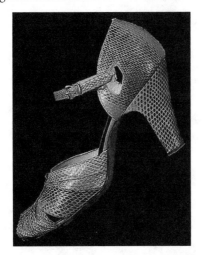

Sandals, snakeskin, Natural Tread Shoes, $65.00. (Photo courtesy Vintage Martini)

Shoes, black leather platform, peep toe w/cutouts on vamp, sling back, 4½" heel $225.00

Shoes, brown & tan snakeskin sandal, open toe, ankle strap w/side buckle, side cutouts, 3" Boulevard heel..$58.00

Shoes, brown crocodile platform, sling back w/side buckle, 4" Cuban heels..$345.00

Shoes, burgundy suede pump w/quilted bow on vamp, 3¼" heel $95.00

Shoes, navy fabric pump, open toe w/high-vamp faille bow, decorative top stitching, 2½" navy Boulevard heel $68.00

Shoes, navy leather platform, open toe, sling back w/side buckle, lg medallion on vamp w/white stitching, 3" sq heel..........$85.00

Shoes, red leather pump, open toe, sq cutout & decorative buckle on vamp, 3" sq cut heel..$78.00

Shoes, silver lamé leather platform sandal, open toe w/crisscross strap across vamp, double ankle strap, 4" heel $95.00

1950s Ladies' Daywear

Blouse, black rayon w/platter-style collar trimmed in beads & pearls, short sleeves, button front..$52.00

Blouse, floral print red cotton, notched collar, button front, ¾-sleeves $32.00

Dress, blue & silver striped knit, black knit collar, ¾-sleeves, peplum, slim skirt..$78.00

Dress, pink, white & black windowpane plaid, sq neck, sleeveless, rhinestone buttons, black belt, 2 lg patch pockets.........$65.00

Dress, purple floral nylon chiffon, scooped neck, pleated cummerbund, full skirt, elbow sleeves..$95.00

Dress, red patterned silk, scoop neck, cap sleeves, button closures, slim skirt w/pockets, w/¾-sleeve jacket $85.00

Dress, white eyelet over yellow nylon, spaghetti straps, bustier bodice, circle skirt, yellow sash..$85.00

Dress, windowpane-patterned cotton, spread collar, button front, short sleeves, rhinestone buttons, matching jacket....$58.00

Dress & coat, watered print silk w/draped bias neck & darted bodice, piped waistline, short sleeves, long blue silk coat ..$175.00

Playsuit, peach printed cotton, halter top w/ties for a lg bow, high-waisted shorts w/side zipper $78.00

Skirt, black cotton twill, pencil style w/kick pleat, zipper.....$35.00

Suit, wool tweed with black faille trim on cuffs, pocket flaps, and collar, Yerlaine Argentina, $150.00. (Photo courtesy Vintage Martini)

Sundress, white pique w/floral border pattern, spaghetti straps, pleated skirt $78.00

Sweather, pink angora, turtle neck w/slide at center front, ¾-sleeves $85.00

1950s Ladies' Coats and Jackets

Coat, black rayon faille, raglan balloon sleeves, rhinestone buttons at lapel & pockets, swing style $40.00

Coat, brown synthetic blend w/brown fur collar, raglan sleeves, 2 slash pockets, knee length **$45.00**

Jacket, black flannel blend w/rayon lining, open front, round collar, long sleeeves, placket pockets **$25.00**

Jacket, black linen, surplice collarless neck, curved dolman sleeves, lg knot buttons, flared, hip length **$52.00**

Jacket, blue wool, round collar, short waist w/4 buttons (appears double-breasted), ¾-sleeves **$38.00**

Jacket, blue wool tweed, sm notched collar, 3-button front w/welt trim, car-coat style w/satin lining **$40.00**

Jacket, brown suede leather, folded-over collar, twist-latch closing, caplet sleeve, sides joined w/leather tabs **$75.00**

Jacket, brown suede leather, sm collar, slash pockets, 6 buttons, sash belt, hip length **$50.00**

1950s Ladies' Cocktail and Evening Wear

Dress, beige silk chiffon, scooped neck w/beige machine lace overlay bodice, aurora borealis sequins & seed pearls **$98.00**

Dress, black damask, rounded neck, 3 lg soutache-covered buttons, elbow-length sleeves, sash tie, full circle skirt **$155.00**

Dress, brown ribbed taffeta with accordion pleated net down left side, Judy Bond, $90.00. (Photo courtesy Vintage Martini)

Dress, lt brown taffeta w/lace-covered bodice, full tiered skirt, strapless w/lace bolero w/elbow-length sleeves **$155.00**

Dress, red floral lace over red taffeta, scooped neck, no sleeves, appliqued bows on full skirt, self belt **$85.00**

Dress, red wool w/silk crepe yoke & sleeves, long princess sleeves, appliques **$78.00**

Dress, yellow crochet lace, scoop beck, fitted bodice, slim skirt, matching jacket w/sm collar, rhinestone buttons **$110.00**

Dress, yellow silk chiffon w/lace-overlay bodice, scoop neck, short sleeves, silk overskirt, back zipper **$85.00**

1950s Lingerie

Bed jacket, blue nylon, cropped, pleated front w/much lace, flutter sleeves, ties at front **$15.00**

Bra, sheer black nylon w/embroidery, satin straps **$12.50**

Crinoline, white net, full skirt, $28.00.

Dressing gown, printed cotton, buttons to waist, hidden metal zipper below, short sleeves w/puffed shoulders **$36.00**

Garter belt, sheer lace front, nylon chiffon sides & back, ruffled trim, metal hooks & tabs **$25.00**

Nightgown, white nylon, gathered fabric straps, sheer lace trim at bust **$30.00**

Pajamas, floral cotton print w/pink piping, short sleves, elastic waist band, tie belt w/fringe **$20.00**

Panty girdle, sheer ivory lace w/garters, sm tummy panel w/blue bow, 4 removable hooks **$45.00**

Robe, quilted peach nylon, double breasted w/silver beading on collar **$35.00**

Slip, pink nylon w/pleats near bust, narrow white lace trim, adjustable satin straps **$26.00**

Slip, white nylon taffeta w/lace strips & shirred tulle at bust, straps adjust **$35.00**

1950s Ladies' Accessories

Shoes, green satin stilettos with metallic gold embroidery, Evins, $78.00. (Photo courtesy La Ree Johnson Bruton)

Gloves, black w/decorative stitching, elbow length..............$12.00

Gloves, brown cotton/Lycra, elastic gathers down side, ¾-length ...$18.00

Gloves, hot pink Nylasuede, gathered & tucked here & there, ¾-length.................$21.00

Hat, cloche w/turned-back rim, pleated back w/bow, black rayon $85.00

Shoes, black faille & silk sandals, wide open toe, sling-back strap w/side buckle, 4" stiletto heel $125.00

Shoes, black silk crepe, sq toe w/lg silk bow on vamp, 2¾" stiletto heels.................$78.00

Shoes, brown silk pump, slightly pointed toes, rosette on vamp, 3½" stiletto heel, Christian Dior $295.00

Shoes, red suede & plastic sandal, open-toe sling-back w/side buckle, 3½" heel.................$68.00

1960s – 1970s Ladies' Day Wear

Dress, geometric printed silk, rounded neck, princess seams, sleeveless, silk lined $68.00

Dress, navy wool knit, stand collar, gold buttons set in military style, short sleeves, silk-lined, mini length.................$95.00

Dress, pink & white gingham check w/scoop neck, lace-trimmed bodice, button front, sleeveless, pleated skirt.................$58.00

Dress, printed cotton shirtwaist w/button front, ¾-sleeves w/wide cuff, sash belt, w/fabric chain-handle purse.................$65.00

Dress, striped cotton shirtdress w/platter collar, button front, short sleeves w/cuffs, gathered skirt.................$58.00

Dress, windowpane wool knit, chest yoke, princess-seamed A-line, no sleeves, w/button-front long sleeve jacket w/collar.......$110.00

Shirt, black silk damask, spread collar w/notched lapels, 2 lg buttons, dropped sleeves, silk-lined slim skirt $135.00

Suit, red cotton, sash-tie collar, 3 lg buttons, ¾-sleeves, sack-back style, fitted skirt w/kick pleat, Neiman Marcus.................$65.00

1960s – 1970s Ladies' Coats and Jackets

Coat, tan plush with curly lamb, tapestry ribbon, and black rickrack trim, ca. 1970, $95.00. (Photo courtesy Vintage Martini)

Blazer, blue polyester knit, princess seams, fold-over notched collar, long sleeves, satin lined $25.00

Cape, windowpane plaid wool, arm openings have cover flaps, slash pockets, fold-over collar, 3 lg buttons, dress length $55.00

Coat, acrylic faux sheared lamb, rabbit collar, double-breasted princess style, knee length $50.00

Coat, black wool, clutch front, wide cape back collar w/wide front lapels, dress length $70.00

Coat, brown & beige windowpane wool plaid, bias sleeves, buton front, matching fringed scarf, satin lining $40.00

Coat, dark gray corduroy w/red piping & trim, raglan ¾-sleeves, knee length $30.00

Coat, floral tapestry, A-line w/wide shawl collar, button front, elbow sleeves, inset pockets, satin lined $165.00

Coat, tan wool w/wide fold-over collar, raglan ¾-sleeves, wood-look buttons, dress length $25.00

Jacket, black rib knit w/raglan long sleeves, tie neck band, 3 lg buttons, hip length.................$35.00

Jacket, red acrylic w/red, white & blue braid trim, 3 buttons, French darts, short.................$30.00

Jacket, striped rayon w/fringed metalic trim, ⅞-sleeves, mandarin collar & cuffs, covered buttons, hip length $25.00

Jacket, wool plaid, pointed collar, gold buttons, long sleeves, Pendleton.................$30.00

Pea coat, navy wool, double-breasted w/gold sailor buttons, wide collar, deep notched lapels, pockets, lined.................$100.00

Poncho jacket, wool blend w/leather trim, clutch front, fully lined, sleeveless $35.00

Ski jacket, quilted nylon taffeta print, convertible collar, princess seaming, White Stag $26.00

Windbreaker jacket, printed nylon taffeta, zipper front, 2 placket pockets, rib knit trim, lined $16.00

1960s – 1970s Ladies' Evening Wear

Shell, tan wool knit with pearls and sequins, silk lining, Made in Hong Kong, $90.00. (Photo courtesy Vintage Martini)

Dress, black crepe w/green silk ribbon & bow, black lace-overlay bodice w/long sleeves, Lilli Diamond.................$145.00

Dress, brown sequins, striped sequin godets along bottom of skirt, sequined straps, full length.................$245.00

Dress, floral pattern w/gold lamé eyelashes scattered all over, sm stand collar, sleeveless, silk lined.................$125.00

Dress, pink paisley silk georgette w/gold lamé brocade, long sleeves, wide cuffs, flounced skirt **$125.00**

Dress, shiny rayon taffeta, boned strapless top w/gathered panel over bust & lg rosette, full skirt w/crinoline **$215.00**

Dress, striped cotton w/cut-out dots in bodice, sleeveless, scooped neck, gathered skirt, sash w/lg slide buckle **$85.00**

Dress, turquoise lame brocade, scoop neck, A-line, sleeveless, sash belt ties at raised waist, Hong Kong...........................**$45.00**

Dress, turquoise silk shiffon w/sequined sleeveless bodice, flowing skirt, matching shoulder scarf **$185.00**

Dress, white twill w/scooped neck, satin ribbon trim at raised waist, long skirt covered in layers of short lace ruffles **$85.00**

Pantsuit, gold lame, platter collar w/gold buttons, patch pockets, long sleeves, genie pants w/gathered waist & ankles......**$45.00**

1960s – 1970s Ladies' Accessories

Bed jacket, ivory polyester w/ruffled lace down front, long puff sleeves w/lace at hem...**$15.00**

Bed jacket, pink cotton w/wide lace strips on yoke, tie front w/2 buttons, low pocket, lace-trimmed sleeves.....................**$15.00**

Boots, blue denim, laces up to knees, red leather cap toes, 2½" chunk heels, Saks Fifth Avenue, w/sm matching purse **$125.00**

Bra, light blue poly-cotton w/polyester fiber lining, embroidery on cups, 2-hook back..**$5.00**

Camisole, black satin w/lace trim, straight neck, 1" non-adjustable straps...**$15.00**

Camisole, white nylon w/lace trim, adjustable straps **$10.00**

Camisole, white shiny nylon w/overlapping lace along neck, wrap bodice, looser along bottom....................................**$15.00**

Gloves, ivory crochet lace w/decorative gauntlets **$28.00**

Half slip, black satin nylon, elastic waist, scalloped bottom, mono-gram **$10.00**

Nightgown, blue & white dotted swiss w/white lace ruffle down front, loose through body, mid-length **$16.00**

Nightgown, pink nylon w/white lace at V-neck, satin ribbon trim, sleeveless **$15.00**

Purse, box style, bright multicolor stripes, white satin lining, 1960s, 4x2½x7", $75.00. (Photo courtesy Vintage Martini)

Robe, floral & geometric polyester print, V-neck, hidden front zipper..**$25.00**

Robe, pink floral printed nylon, button front, tie belt, ¾-length sleeves **$20.00**

Robe, printed nylon tricot, fabric tie, covered buttons, long sleeves **$25.00**

Shoes, brown & white vinyl spectator platform, T-strap w/side buckle, 3½" heel **$48.00**

Shoes, gold vinyl lamé hostess slippers, open toe w/side cutouts, sling back straps w/side buckles, 2½" wedge heel **$45.00**

Slip, white nylon w/lace trim on front & back of bodice, straps adjust **$20.00**

Tennis shoes, red, white & blue suede, rubber sole w/sm heel, decorative topstitching **$38.00**

1940s – 1970s Men's Wear

Boxer shorts, blue & white stripe cotton, snap closures on yoke of waistband, elastic sides, 1950s......................................**$28.00**

Boxer shorts, printed cotton, yoke front, snap closures, elastic waistband...**$28.00**

Dinner jacket, red iridescent silk, shawl collar, single button, patch pockets, 1950s **$165.00**

Jacket, brown suede w/much fringe, notched collar, fully lined, 1950s..**$175.00**

Jacket, gray-green wool w/faint green & rust windowpane, sm collar w/notched lapels, 1-button closure, 1940s **$95.00**

Overcoat, brushed gray wool, spread collar, 3-button front, raglan sleeves w/turned-back cuffs, 1950s................................**$65.00**

Pajamas, blue & white cotton print, V-neck w/inset pocket on chest, button-front pants w/elastic sides, 1950s **$45.00**

Shirt, blue & white plaid dacron-polyester blend, sm spread collar, button front, 2 patch pockets, short sleeves, 1950s.......**$40.00**

Shirt, chartreuse rayon-silk w/navy fleck, notched colalr, button front, 2 lg patch pocket, long sleeves, 1940s **$78.00**

Shirt, Hawaiian batik-style pattern, wide spread collar, button front, set-in short sleeves, Hawaiian label **$65.00**

Shirt, knit polo w/stripes across chest, short sleeves, 4-button front, JC Penney, 1970s..**$48.00**

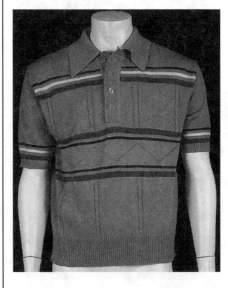

Shirt, light coral with brown and white stripes, J.C. Penney, 1970s, $50.00. (Photo courtesy Vintage Martini)

Shirt, lt green textured nylon, spread collar, button front, 2 patch pockets, short sleeves, 1950s **$65.00**

Shirt, pastel plaid cotton-polyester blend, semi-sheer w/slub texture, oxford style, long sleeves, 1970s......................**$28.00**

Shirt, plaid dacron-polyester blend, spread pointed collar, button front, long sleeves w/button cuffs, 1960s......................**$58.00**

Shirt, striped silk knit, button front, band along bottom, short sleeves, Enrico Felini, 1960s......................**$85.00**

Shirt, white cotton w/lavender stripe, button front, patch pocket, long sleeves w/French cuffs, Lanvin, 1980s......................**$95.00**

Shirt, white cotton w/spread collar, button front, embroidered multicolor dragon on chest, short sleeves, 1960s......................**$62.00**

Shirt, yellow nylon w/windowpane weave, spread collar, button front, 2 patch pockets, short sleeves, 1950s......................**$58.00**

Suit, dark blue silk blend, 2-button front w/pink stitching at collar & pocket flaps, Lanvin Paris, 1981......................**$100.00**

Suit, nubby cotton & wool blend, sm collar w/notched lapels, 3-button, pleated-front pants w/cuffs (2 pr), 1960s....**$145.00**

Swim trunks, beach pattern on blue cotton, drawstring waist, sm pocket w/button flap, 1950s......................**$45.00**

Swim trunks, beige terry knit w/gathered waist & legs, Maut-Mer, 1970s, M in original tube......................**$28.00**

Tuxedo, shawl collar edged in black satin, 1 button, inset pocket, flat front pants w/satin stripe down sides, 1950s......................**$185.00**

Vintage Demim

Jacket, Lee 101J, 1960s, slight soiling, good size......................**$60.00**

Jacket, Levi E, dark blue, lg......................**$50.00**

Jacket, Levi 557XX, near deadstock, early, 1960s, from $210 to..**$250.00**

Jacket, Levi 70505e, single stitch, indigo, 1960s, good size & condition......................**$45.00**

Jeans, indigo denim work style, good color & size, 1940s....**$50.00**

Jeans, Lee Riders, indigo, union made, sanforized, near deadstock, 44x31"......................**$25.00**

Jeans, Lee 101B, med dark blue, 31x31"......................**$200.00**

Jeans, Levi 501, red lines, #6 button, deadstock, 33x30" ...**$300.00**

Jeans, Levi 501, single-stitch red-lines, med color, some hege, 32x32"......................**$210.00**

Jeans, Levi 501, single-stitch red-lines, very dark, 33x32"..**$285.00**

Jeans, Levi 501, single-stitch red-lines, w/patch, 32x33"......**$75.00**

Jeans, Levi 501E, med color, 33x30"......................**$270.00**

Jeans, Levi 501e, single-stitch, good color, slight hege & minor damage, from $150 to......................**$180.00**

Jeans, Levi 501E, very dark, 32x21", from $400 to............**$450.00**

Jeans, Levi 501E (S-type), dark blue, 34x30"......................**$520.00**

Jeans, Levi 501XX, leather patch attached, dark hege, 1940s, 33x32"......................**$1,100.00**

Jeans, Levi 501XX, paper patch attached, med color, slight hege w/good contrast, slight damage......................**$650.00**

Jeans, Levi 501XX, paper patch not attached, good color, slight damage & stains, good size......................**$425.00**

Jeans, Levi 502E, very dark, 32x31"......................**$475.00**

Jeans, Levi 505E, full red-line, good color & contrast, slight damage......................**$310.00**

Jeans, Levi 505e, single-stitch, med to dark blue, grainy effect, EX size......................**$110.00**

Jeans, Levi 517, single stitch, med color, good hege, 33x32" ..**$80.00**

Jeans, Levi 517E, w/flashers, bootcut, deadstock, 1960s **$350.00**

Jeans, Levi 646, bell-bottoms, deadstock......................**$175.00**

Jeans, Levi 646E, good color, some hege, 30x32"..............**$200.00**

Jeans, Wrangler Blue Bell, med dark color, 31x33" **$210.00**

Coca-Cola Collectibles

Coca-Cola was introduced to the public in 1886. Immediately an advertising campaign began that over the years and continuing to the present day has literally saturated our lives with a never-ending variety of items. Some of the earlier calendars and trays have been known to bring prices well into the four figures. Because of these heady prices and the extremely widespread collector demand for good Coke items, reproductions are everywhere, so beware! Some of the items that have been reproduced are pocket mirrors (from 1905, 1906, 1908 – 1911, 1916, and 1920), trays (from 1899, 1910, 1913 – 1914, 1917, 1920, 1923, 1926, 1934, and 1937), tip trays (from 1907, 1909, 1910, 1913 – 1914, 1917, and 1920), knives, cartons, bottles, clocks, and trade cards. In recent years, these items have been produced and marketed: an 8" brass 'button,' a 27" brass bottle-shaped thermometer, cast-iron toys and bottle-shaped door pulls, Yes Girl posters, a 12" 'button' sign (with one round hole), a rectangular paperweight, a 1949-style cooler radio, and there are others. Look for a date line.

In addition to reproductions, 'fantasy' items have also been made, the difference being that a 'fantasy' never existed as an original. Don't be deceived. Belt buckles are 'fantasies.' So are glass doorknobs with an etched trademark, bottle-shaped knives, pocketknives (supposedly from the 1933 World's Fair), a metal letter opener stamped 'Coca-Cola 5¢,' a cardboard sign with the 1911 lady with fur (9" x 11"), and celluloid vanity pieces (a mirror, brush, etc.).

When the company celebrated its 100th anniversary in 1986, many 'centennial' items were issued. They all carry the '100th Anniversary' logo. Many of them are collectible in their own right, and some are already expensive.

If you'd really like to study this subject, we recommend these books: *Goldstein's Coca-Cola Collectibles* by Sheldon Goldstein; *Collector's Guide to Coca-Cola Items, Vols. I* and *II*, by Al Wilson; *Petretti's Coca-Cola Collectibles Price Guide* by Allan Petretti; *Coca-Cola Commemorative Bottles* by Bob and Debra Henrich; *B.J. Summers' Guide to Coca-Cola, B.J. Summers' Pocket Guide to Coca-Cola,* and *Collectible Soda Pop Memorabilia* (all by B.J. Summers).

Advisor: Craig Stifter (See Directory, Soda Pop Memorabilia)

Club: Coca-Cola Collectors Club
PMB 609, 4780 Ashform Dunwoody Rd, Suite A9166
Atlanta, GA 30338
Annual dues: $30
cocacolaclub.org

Ashtray, ceramic, Partners...Coca-Cola, facsimile baseball in red center circle, 1950s, 7¼" sq, EX......................**$160.00**

Ashtray, painted metal, Drink...High in Quick Energy, Low in Calories, exercise scenes in bowl, 1950s, EX................**$30.00**

Bank, metal & plastic, truck, Coca-Cola on dynamic wave logo on side of delivery van, top money drop, EX **$45.00**

Bank, plastic, vending machine, Drink...Play Refreshed, 1950s, EX.................**$165.00**

Blotter, cardboard, Be Prepared Be Refreshed, Boy Scout at cooler holding 2 bottles, 1940s, M.......................**$350.00**

Blotter, Drink Coca-Cola in Bottles...Good!, Sprite boy w/bottle cap hat, 3½x7¼", EX **$35.00**

Book cover, paper, Refresh...Add Zest, planets, space, & rocket, 1960s, EX.................................**$35.00**

Book cover, There's Nothing Like a Coke, crossing guard on front, 1940s, EX...............................**$30.00**

Bottle, Banks County Holiday Festival label, September 1 1986, 10-oz....................................**$28.00**

Bottle, clear glass, hobbleskirt, foreign origin, 10-oz, NM ...**$20.00**

Bottle, display; glass, hobbleskirt, Coca-Cola in script on shoulder, plastic cap, 1960s, 20", EX **$175.00**

Bottle, glass, straight sides, embossed diamond w/embossed bottle & block Coke, 1960s, 10-oz, NM **$70.00**

Bottle, glass, 75th Anniversary clear commemorative, hobbleskirt, anniversary logo on metal cap, 1981, 6½-oz **$75.00**

Bottle, Piggly Wiggly 70th Anniversary label, 1989, 10-oz ..**$15.00**

Bottle protector, paper, Quality Carries on...Drink Coca-Cola, bottle in hand, 1930-40, 6½x3¾", EX...........................**$8.00**

Bottle, 1991 Basketball National Champions, Duke, full, 10-ounce, NM, from $8.00 to $12.00. (Photo courtesy B.J. Summers)

Bottle topper, cardboard, King Size Ice Cold, fold-out for bottle neck, 1960s, M........................**$25.00**

Bumper sticker, vinyl, Max Headroom, Don't Say the P Word, Catch the Wave COKE, 1980s, EX....................**$25.00**

Button, metal, Standard 6 Bottle Carton, w/cardboard 6-pack, 1950s, 16" dia, NM..........................**$425.00**

Calendar, Coke Refreshes You Best, girl w/notepad being handed bottle, double-month, full pad, hanging, 1961, M **$125.00**

Calendar, Drink Coca-Cola, military nurse w/bottle, double-month, hanging, 1943, NM...........................**$585.00**

Calendar, For the Taste You Never Get Tired Of, 5-woman team w/ trophy & Cokes, double-month, hanging, 1967, M **$90.00**

Calendar, Have a Coke & a Smile, Olympic torch, full pad, hanging, 1979, M.................................**$25.00**

Calendar, reference; Puppies, 2 dogs in Christmas stocking, 1960, EX **$35.00**

Calendar, Things Go Better w/Coke, couple w/Cokes by log cabin, double-month display, full pad, hanging, 1965, M.....**$100.00**

Calendar, 1948, paper, two-month display, NM, from $450.00 to $500.00. (Photo courtesy B.J. Summers)

Can, metal, full-length diamond w/bottle in center, 12-oz, EX.................................... **$125.00**

Can, syrup; metal, straight-sided, Coca-Cola circle logo, green/red paper label, 1940s, 1-gal, G **$250.00**

Carrier, aluminum, Drink Coca-Cola... King Size, letters on sides, wire handle, 1950s, holds 6 bottles, EX....................**$145.00**

Carrier, cardboard, Six Bottles...Serve Ice Cold, 1930s, holds 6 bottles, EX................................**$165.00**

Carrier, cardboard, straight-sided box, Drink Coca-Cola, 2 wire handles, 1956, holds 6 bottles, EX...........................**$140.00**

Case, polished aluminum, Coca-Cola, rounded corners, 1940-50s, 24 bottles, EX.............................**$140.00**

Clock, counter; metal & glass, Drink Coca-Cola...Serve Yourself, light-up, 1950s, 9x20", EX.......................**$750.00**

Clock, metal & glass, Drink Coca-Cola in red fishtail logo on white, sq, 1960s, M..............................**$550.00**

Clock, metal & glass, Drink Coca-Cola on red fishtail logo, green background, sq, 1960s, EX........................**$325.00**

Cooler, picnic; stainless steel, Drink Coca-Cola, swing handle lock & removable lid, 1950s, 12x14x9", EX.....................**$225.00**

Cooler, picnic; vinyl, Coke Adds Life to Everything Nice, zip top, 1960-70s, 13x13x9", EX...............................**$45.00**

Cooler, store; metal, Buvez Coca-Cola on fishtail logo, 2 center-hinge top-opening lids, 35x42x27", G **$275.00**

Cooler, store; metal, Ice Cold...Sold Here, floor model, embossed hobbleskirt bottle, lift top, 29x32½x22", VG **$950.00**

Cooler, 6-pack; metal, white Drink Coca-Cola decal on red, zinc liner, 1940s, 9x8", VG **$250.00**

Display, cardboard, Christmas-tree shape, Enjoy Coca-Cola logo in center, 24x14", VG **$55.00**

Display, celluloid, Coca-Cola, round disk w/bottle, 1950s, 9" dia, EX **$295.00**

Display, die-cut cardboard, 3 men holding glasses, So Refreshing, easel back, 1953, 1½x3", VG **$225.00**

Display, metal, Coca-Cola, bottle in hand decal, pilaster shape, no top button, 1940s, 40x16", EX..............$185.00

Display, wood & plastic, Drink Coca-Cola..., fishtail design over courtesy panel, 1960s, 12x15½", VG.........................$145.00

Door push bar, porcelain, Coke Is It!, dynamic wave logo, 1970s, NM..$95.00

Door push bar, porcelain, Refreshing Coca-Cola New Feeling on yellow background, 1950-60s, EX $195.00

Frisbee, white plastic, Coke Adds...Nice in red lettering w/dynamic wave logo, 1960s, EX.................................$15.00

Glass, bell-shaped, 50th anniversary, presented to John W Boucher, 1936, NM $375.00

Glass, water; convention, straight-sided, Springtime in Atlanta 1984, NM...$8.00

Hat, cloth, Drink Coca-Cola in red lettering on yellow, soda jerk cap, EX..$25.00

Ice pick, metal & wood, Coca-Cola in Bottles in red lettering on round handle, 1930-40s, EX........................$40.00

Match safe, porcelain, Compliments of Coca-Cola Bottling Co... Union City TN..., w/striker, 1930s, EX.................$300.00

Matchbook, King Size Coke in red & green lettering on black, 1959, VG...$12.00

Menu board, metal, Drink...Specials To-day, diamond logo at top, chalkboard design, 1931, EX $300.00

Menu sheet, paper, Things Go Better With Coke, plastic holder, 1960s, EX..$55.00

Opener, metal, handheld, Have a Coke, beer-can type, EX....$8.00

Opener, metal, wall-mounted, Drink Coca-Cola (known as bent metal opener), 1950s, EX $25.00

Plate, sandwich; china, Drink Coca...Refresh Yourself, bottle & glass in center, 1930s, 8¼" dia, NM $1,200.00

Postcard, Coke pavilion at 1964 NY World's Fair, 1964, 3½x5½", EX $30.00

Poster, cardboard, Coke...for Hospitality, people at cookout drinking Coke, 1948, 24x36", EX..........................$425.00

Poster, cardboard, Come Over for Coke, hostess at table, 1947, 20x36" $275.00

Poster, cardboard, Mind Reader, bathing beauty being handed bottle of Coke, 1960s, EX $650.00

Rack, display; painted red metal, Drink Coca-Cola panel at top, 1940-50s, 47", EX..$225.00

Radio, plastic, can, Enjoy Coca-Cola, dynamic wave, 1970s, EX $50.00

Radio, plastic, vending machine, Enjoy Coke, vertical dynamic wave logo & push-button selectors, 1970s, EX...................$135.00

Sign, cardboard, hobbleskirt bottle w/no message, Canadian, 33x13", EX $475.00

Sign, countertop; metal, light-up, Lunch With Us..., Price Brothers, 1950s, 8½x19", EX.................................$900.00

Sign, metal, Drink Coca-Cola, w/hobbleskirt bottle, 1950s, 18x54", EX $450.00

Sugar bowl, white w/red & black lettering, Drink Coca..., w/lid, 1930s, M $400.00

Thermometer, metal, Buvez Coca-Cola...La Soif n'a Pasde Saison, silhouette girl at bottom, 1940s, 18x5¾"................$300.00

Thermometer, metal, die-cut bottle, Coca-Cola, 1956, 17x5", NM $160.00

Thermometer, metal, red & white, Drink...Good Taste, 1950s, 30x8", EX...$575.00

Thermometer, metal & glass, Drink Coca-Cola in Bottles, dial type, 1950s, 12" dia, EX......................................$250.00

Thermometer, plastic, Enjoy Coca-Cola, vertical scale w/message panel at bottom, 1960s, 18x7", G.......................$45.00

Thimble, metal, Coca-Cola on red background, 1920s, EX..$95.00

Tray, French version, 1950s, 13x10½", G, $120.00.

Tray, metal, Coca-Cola, cart w/lg basket full of goodies & Coke bottles, 1958, 10½x13¼", EX.....................................$30.00

Tray, metal, Drink Coca-Cola, birdhouse & bottle in center, fishtail logo, 1950s, 13¼x10½", EX $115.00

Tray, metal, Drink...Delicious & Refreshing, girl in swimsuit on spring board w/bottle, 1939, 13x10½", NM...............$425.00

Tray, TV; Duster Girl w/bottle in hand, 1970s, 14½x10¼", EX.$15.00

Coloring and Activity Books

Coloring and activity books representing familiar movie and TV stars of the 1950s and 1960s are fun to collect, though naturally unused examples are hard to find. Condition is very important, of course, so learn to judge their values accordingly. Unused books are worth as much as 50% to 75% more than one only partially colored.

ABC 184 Animals To Color, Merrill, 1941, unused, EX......$20.00

Adventures of Mumbley Super Sleuth Coloring Book, Rand McNally #06440, 1977, some use, scarce, EX.............................$55.00

Alice in Wonderland Coloring Book, Whitman #1001-3, unused, M..$20.00

Amazing Spider-Man Coloring Book, 1981, unused, M......$12.50

Atom Ant Coloring Book, Watkins-Strathmore #1850-F, unused, EX..$55.00

Atom Ant Play Fun, Whitman, some use, VG+IB $85.00

Augie Doggie Coloring Book, Whitman #1186, 1960, some use, EX..$35.00

Barbie & Ken 192-Page Coloring Book, Whitman #1646-59, 1962, unused, EX $25.00

Batman Coloring Book, Whitman #1002, unused, M $25.00

Bewitched Fun & Activity Book, Grossett & Dunlap Treasure Books #8908, 1965, unused, M $30.00

Bionic Woman Adventure Coloring Book, #15011, 1976, unused, NM...$20.00

Bugs Bunny & Elmer Fudd Coloring Book, Watkins-Strathmore, 1963, Bugs w/carrots & Elmer w/stringer of fish, unused, EX $25.00

Bugs Bunny Coloring Book, Whitman #1087, 1972, unused, EX $22.00

Captain Kangaroo, 1960, some use, EX+..................$30.00

Captain Marvel's Fun Book, Fawcett, 1944, unused, EX $95.00

Choo Choo Coloring Book, Watkins-Strathmore #1857, 1961, unused, EX $75.00

Crusader Rabbit A Story Coloring Book, Treasure Books #298, 1957, some use, EX $65.00

Davy Crockett Coloring Book, Whitman, 1955, Davy filling gun-from powder horn on red cover, unused, G $18.00

Disneyland Coloring Book, Whitman, 1959, snow fun scene on cover, unused, M $25.00

Disneyland Coloring Book, Whitman, 1964, unsued, M.....$55.00

Donald Duck Coloring Book, Dell #144, 1957, unused, EX.. $22.00

Donald Duck Coloring Book, Whitman #1183, 1960, unused, EX $65.00

Eve Arden's Coloring Book, Treasure Books, 1958, unused, EX..$18.00

Family Affair Coloring Book, Whitman, 1968, unused, EX..$25.00

Flintstones w/Pebbles & Bamm-Bamm Coloring Book, Whitman #1117, 1963, unused, VG $45.00

Frankenstein Jr Coloring Book, Whitman #1115, 1967, unused, NM+...$75.00

Gene Autry Cowboy Paint Book, Merrill, 1940, some use, NM+ $50.00

Green Hornet Coloring Book, Whitman, 1966, unused, EX ..$55.00

Hanna-Barbera Fun Coloring Book, Watkins-Strathmore, 1963, unused, M $55.00

Have Gun Will Travel Coloring Book, Lowe, 1960, unused, NM $165.00

Hey There It's Yogi Bear! Sticker Fun, Whitman #2190, 1964, unused, NM+ $65.00

Howdy Doody Coloring Book, Whitman #1188, 1956, some use, VG $15.00

Howdy Doody Fun Book, Whitman #2187, 1950s, some use, VG $20.00

Jerry Lewis Coloring Book, Treasure, 1959, unused, EX.....$95.00

Jonny Quest Coloring Book, Whitman, 1965, unused, EX..$115.00

Leave It to Beaver Coloring Book, Saalfield #5338, 1958, unused, EX..$125.00

Liddle Kiddles Coloring Book, Watkins-Strathmore, 1967, unused, M $25.00

Little Lulu, Whitman #1663, 1974, unused, M...................$45.00

Marvel Super Heroes Secret Wars Escape From Doom Coloring Activity Book, w/poster insert, unused, M...................$18.50

Marvel Super Heroes Secret Wars The Tower of Doom Sticker Adventures, 1984, unused, M.............................$18.50

Masks of the Seven Dwarfs & Snow White Punch-Out Book, Whitman #990, 1938, unused, EX+..........................$170.00

Munsters Coloring Book, Whitman, 1965, some use, G $32.00

My Little Margie, Saalfield, 1954, Gale Storm & Charles Farrell pictured on cover, unused, VG+...................................$22.00

Partridge Family Coloring Book, 1971, standing in front of bus w/ kids in windows, some use, EX.............................$20.00

Peter Pan Animated Coloring Book, Derby Foods, 1950s, some use, NM...$30.00

Popeye, Bonnie Books #2945, unused, NM, $65.00. (Photo courtesy www.gasolinealleyantiques.com)

Popeye Coloring Book, Lowe #2834, 1962, unused, EX+....$55.00

Pow! Robin Strikes for Batman Coloring Book, Watkins-Strathmore, 1966, unused, VG $75.00

Prince Valiant Coloring Book, Saalfield #4611, 1957, unused, EX $50.00

QT Hush Private Eye & Shamus Private Nose, A Book To Color, Saalfield #9518-Q, 1962, unused, EX........................$25.00

Ranger Rider Coloring Book, Lowe #2528, unused, M $40.00

Rita Hayworth Dancing Star Coloring Book, Merrill, 1942, EX.. $20.00

Rocky & Bullwinkle Coloring Book, Watkins-Strathmore #1803, 1962, unused, EX $25.00

Rocky Jones Space Ranger Coloring Book, Whitman, 1951, unused, VG..$22.00

Scooby Doo Adventure Paint w/Water, #13369, 1984, unused, M $22.00

Scooby Doo Funtime Paint w/Water, #13368, 1984, unused, M..$22.00

Scooby-Doo Haunted House Paint w/Water, #13371, 1984, unused, M $22.00

Secret Squirrel Coloring Book, Watkins-Strathmore #1850-E, 1967, unused, EX $50.00

Shirley Temple Coloring Book, Saalfield #5353, 1959, unused, NM...$15.00

Six Million Dollar Man Dot-to-Dot, #C2412, 1977, unused, NM+...$35.00

Smokey Coloring Book, Abbott #320, 1950s, unused, M....$75.00

Spike & Tyke Coloring Book, Whitman, 1957, unused, EX..$18.00

Star Trek Punch-Out and Play Album, Saalfield #C2272, 1974, unused, NM, $85.00. (Photo courtesy www.gasolinealleyantiques.com)

Tom Corbett Space Cadet Coloring Book, Saalfield, 1950, Tom standing w/thumbs in belt before spaceships, some use, VG.... **$20.00**
Tom Corbett Space Cadet Push-Outs, Saalfield, 1952, unused, NM...**$100.00**
Tom Mix Draw & Paint, Whitman, 1935, unused, G **$20.00**
Toys To Color Coloring Book, 1958, sand pail, ball & boat on cover, unused, EX **$22.00**
Treasure Island Cut-Out Coloring Book, Whitman/Quaker Oats, 1968, unused, EX+ **$20.00**
TV Roundup of Western Heroes..., Saalfield Artcraft #7819, 1961, unused, NM **$40.00**
Walt Disney's Big Coloring Book, Watkins-Strathmore #1871, 1959, unused, EX **$60.00**
Walter Lantz Woody Woodpecker Sticker Fun w/Activity Pages, Whitman #2180, 1964, some use, EX+ **$25.00**

Yogi Bear Sticker Fun, Whitman #2190, 1964, unused, NM+, $70.00. (Photo courtesy www.gasolinealleyantiques. com)

Comic Books

Though just about everyone can remember having stacks and stacks of comic books as a child, few of us ever saved them for more than a few months. At 10¢ a copy, new ones quickly replaced the old, well-read ones. We'd trade them with our friends, but very soon, out they went. If we didn't throw them away, Mother did. So even though they were printed in huge amounts, few survive, and today they're very desirable collectibles.

Factors that make a comic book valuable are condition (as with all paper collectibles, extremely important), content, and rarity, but not necessarily age. In fact, comics printed between 1950 and the late 1970s are most in demand by collectors who prefer those they had as children to the earlier comics. They look for issues where the hero is first introduced, and they insist on quality. Condition is first and foremost when it comes to assessing worth. Compared to a book in excellent condition, a mint issue might bring six to eight times more, while one in only good condition would be worth less than half the price. We've listed some of the more collectible (and expensive) comics, but many are worth very little. You'll really need to check your bookstore for a good reference book before you actively get involved in the comic book market.

Abbott & Costello, #4, 1948, EX, from $250 to **$350.00**
Adventure Comics, #92, June/July, Last Manhunter Issue, 1944, NM..**$460.00**
Air Fighters Comics Featuring the Black Commander, Hillman Publications #1, November 1941, NM....................**$1,150.00**
Amazing Fantasy (Introducing Spider-Man), #15, from $1,000 to...**$1,400.00**

Amazing Spider-Man, Marvel #5, Dr. Doom, EX, $475.00.

Annie Oakley, Dell #2, 1948, EX+, from $125 to **$150.00**
Anthony & Cleopatra, Ideal #1, 1948, EX+, from $500 to..**$850.00**
Archie Comics, #32, 1948, VG, from $40 to......................**$60.00**

Atomic Thunderbolt, #1, 1946, EX, from $400 to **$500.00**

Avengers, Marvel #100, EX, from $40 to............................**$50.00**

Batman, DC Comics #23, EX, from $1,200 to **$1,500.00**

Batman (Remarkable Ruse of the Riddler), DC Comics #171, 1965, VG, from $50 to.......................................**$65.00**

Beatles Complete Life Stories, Dell Giant #1, 1964, EX+ **$50.00**

Black Cat Mystery, Harvey #41, VG+, from $40 to............**$50.00**

Bouncer (The), Fox Features Syndicate #11, September 1944, NM+...**$690.00**

Brady Bunch, Dell #2, 1970, NM, from $100 to **$115.00**

Buck Rogers (in the 25th Century), Toby Press #151, 1951, EX, from $65 to **$75.00**

Bugs Bunny Finds the Frozen Kingdom, Dell #164, 1947, EX+, from $50 to **$70.00**

Captain Marvel, Fawcett #38, August 1944, NM **$575.00**

Captain Marvel Jr, Fawcett #26, January 1945, NM.........**$345.00**

Captain Midnight, Fawcett #14, November 1944, NM.....**$800.00**

Casper the Friendly Ghost, #7, 1952, VG, from $50 to.......**$65.00**

Challengers of the Unknown, DC Comics #15, 1950s, G, from $40 to **$50.00**

Comics Parade (Li'l Abner in Tree), #21, December 1939, G+ ...**$45.00**

Conan the Barbarian (Curse of the Golden Skull), Marvel #37, NM+, from $35 to...**$45.00**

Crypt of Terror, EC Comics #19, August/September 1950, NM+.**$2,300.00**

Cyclone Comics, #1, June 1940, NM......................**$1,700.00**

Daredevil, #27, 1944, NM, from $950 to **$1,500.00**

Daredevil (The Man Without Fear!), Marvel #1, EX+, from $550 to **$650.00**

Detective Comics (New Feature The Boy Commandos), DC Comics #64, VG, from $550 to....................................**$750.00**

Doll Man Quarterly, #13, 1947, NM+, from $800 to **$1,250.00**

Don Winslow of the Navy, Fawcett #2, 1943, NM+, from $700 to **$1,000.00**

Don Winslow of the Navy, Fawcett #4, June, NM............**$630.00**

Donald Duck in the River of Terror, Dell #108, April 1946, EX+ **$1,380.00**

Famous Funnies (Fighting Buck Rogers), #211, 1954, EX+, from $800 to **$1,100.00**

Famous Gang Book of Comics, Firestone, 1942, EX+, from $600 to **$900.00**

Fantastic Comics, #18, 1941, G+, from $65 to....................**$85.00**

Fantastic Four, Marvel #1, 1961, EX, from $2,500 to **$3,000.00**

Flintstones, Dell #2, NM, from $150 to............................**$175.00**

Flipper, Gold Key #1, 1966, EX+, from $50 to **$60.00**

Gene Autry, Dell #42, 1950, EX+, from $50 to...................**$65.00**

Green Hornet Fights Crime, Harvey #34, 1947, EX+, from $400 to **$500.00**

Hogan's Heroes, Dell #4, 1966, NM, from $50 to **$60.00**

Hopalong Cassidy, Fawcett #3, 1946, NM, from $350 to .**$550.00**

I Love Lucy, Dell #10, 1956, EX, from $45 to **$55.00**

Incredible Hulk (& Now the Wolverine!), Marvel #181, NM, from $750 to **$950.00**

Incredible Hulk (Wolverine Cameo), Marvel #180, 1974, EX, from $35 to **$45.00**

Justice League of America, DC #6, VG, from $55 to...........**$65.00**

Kay Keen Annual, Archie Giant Series #6, 1959-60, EX, from $75 to **$85.00**

KISS, Marvel #1, EX+, $80.00.

Lassie, Dell #8, 1961, EX, from $35 to...............................**$45.00**

Laurel & Hardy, #1, 1949, EX+, from $725 to.............**$1,150.00**

Lone Ranger, Dell #1, 1948, EX+, from $550 to..............**$650.00**

Lone Ranger, Dell #29, 1950, NM+ **$345.00**

Lone Ranger, Dell #125, 1946, EX+, from $40 to..............**$50.00**

Mad (Tales Calculated To Drive You), EC #6, 1953, NM.**$2,000.00**

Man From UNCLE, Gold Key #4, 1960s, EX+, from $40 to.. **$50.00**

Mickey Mouse, Dell #27, 1943, VG, from $165 to...........**$175.00**

Millie the Model, Marvel #3, 1946, NM+, from $550 to ..**$750.00**

New Funnies, Dell #87, 1940s, EX+, from $40 to..............**$50.00**

Partridge Family, Charlton #19, 1973, EX, from $15 to......**$20.00**

Planet of the Apes (w/Rod Serling Interview), Curtis #1, NM, from $35 to **$45.00**

Police Comics, Quality #75, 1948, VG+, from $40 to.........**$60.00**

Rawhide, Dell #1160, 1960, EX, from $45 to **$50.00**

Robin Hood, Dell #1, 1963, NM, from $85 to....................**$95.00**

Roy Rogers Comics, Dell #12, EX, from $35 to..................**$45.00**

Scooby Doo, Marvel #1, 1977, NM+, from $30 to **$35.00**

Sheena Queen of the Jungle, Fiction House #14, 1951, NM+, from $600 to **$800.00**

Silver Surfer, Marvel #1, G, from $40 to............................**$50.00**

Six Million Dollar Man, Charlton #1, 1976, NM, from $20 to **$25.00**

Smash Comics, #49, 1944, NM+, from $600 to............**$1,000.00**

Smilin' Jack, Dell #4, 1942, EX+, from $525 to **$825.00**

Space Squadron, #3, VG, from $60 to **$70.00**

Spotlight Comics, Chesler #1, 1944, NM, from $1,000 to... **$2,000.00**

Star Trek (To Err Is Vulcan!), Gold Key #59, 1978, NM+, from $40 to **$50.00**

Star Wars, Marvel #1, NM..**$1,400.00**

Tales of Suspense (Guest-Starring the Angel), Marvel #49, G, from $45 to **$55.00**

Tarzan, Dell Vol 1 #52, Lex Barker cover, EX, from $55 to ..**$65.00**

Tessie the Typist, #1, 1944, EX, from $450 to **$650.00**

Tex Ritter Western, Fawcett #2, 1954, VG, from $65 to......**$75.00**

Texan, Dell #1027, 1959, EX+, from $40 to **$50.00**

Tom & Jerry, Dell #115, EX, from $20 to $25.00

Tomb of Dracula (Night of the Vampire), Marvel #1, EX+, from $45 to $65.00

Top Cat, Gold Key #5, 1963, EX, from $55 to $65.00

Uncanny X-Men (Wolverine vs Sabertooth), Marvel #213, 1987, NM+, from $40 to...$50.00

Walt Disney's Snow White & the Seven Dwarfs, Dell #49, 1944, EX $350.00

Wambi the Jungle Boy, Fiction House #10, 1950, EX, from $250 to $450.00

Werewolf (by Night), Marvel #32, EX, from $40 to $50.00

Wild Western, Atlas #3, September 1948, NM..................$750.00

Wolverine (Enemy of the State), Marvel #20, NM+, from $25 to $35.00

Wonder Woman in Shamrock Land, AA #14, 1945, G, from $50 to $75.00

Wyatt Earp, Dell #860, EX+, from $75 to $85.00

X-Men, Marvel #12, Guest Starring The Mighty Avengers, EX, $115.00.

Young Allies (Bucky & Toro), Timely Comics #7, April 1943, EX $975.00

Zorro, Golden Key #4, 1966, NM, from $45 to..................$55.00

Compacts

When 'liberated' women entered the work force after WWI, cosmetics, previously frowned upon, became more acceptable, and as a result the market was engulfed with compacts of all types and designs. Some went so far as to incorporate timepieces, cigarette compartments, coin holders, and money clips. All types of materials were used — mother-of-pearl, petit-point, cloisonné, celluloid, and leather among them. There were figural compacts, those with

wonderful Art Deco designs, souvenir compacts, and some with advertising messages.

For further study, we recommend *The Estèe Lauder Solid Perfume Compact Collection* and *Vintage and Contemporary Purse Accessories*, both by Roselyn Gerson (Collector Books).

Newsletter: *The Compacts Collector Chronicle*
Powder Puff
P.O. Box 40
Lynbrook, NY 11563

Babbitt, gold-tone can, moon, stars & floral spray on lid, framed mirror, ¼x2" dia, from $35 to $50.00

Chokin, gold-tone, sloped hexagonal rim, enamel & multicolored metals form intricate geisha, 2¾" dia $23.00

Colgate, black enamel w/engraved floral border on lid, mini #100, framed mirror, 1½" dia, from $65 to $80.00

DeVilbiss, gold-tone w/attached enameled leaves & florets w/rhinestone centers on lid, framed mirror, 2¼x2½" $165.00

Dorothy Gray, brushed gold-tone, raised mask w/incised ribbons & rhinestones on lid, framed mirror, oval, 4", $75 to $90.00

Elegance, gold-tone fan shape w/multicolored padoga scene, slides open to reveal mirror, 2x3", from 22 to $30.00

Elgin American, brown leather designed to look like football, 2x3", from $55 to $75.00

Elgin American, brushed gold-tone, Mother & leaves engraved on lid, 2¼x3", from $60 to..$100.00

Elgin American, brushed gold-tone w/reading lady in black silhouette, bright-cut gold ornate flowers on sides, 2" dia $23.00

Elgin American, gold-tone, etched world map w/compass center on lid, 3½" dia, from $20 to..$25.00

Elgin American, gold-tone w/abstract gray, coral & white enamel lid, framed mirror, 2¾" sq, from $45 to............................$60.00

Elgin American, gold-tone w/multicolored enamel Eastern Star w/ scrolls on lid, framed mirror, 3" dia, from $25 to $40.00

Elizabeth Arden, gold-plated metal, etched flowers w/mounted red crystal flowers on lid, framed mirror, 3" sq $25.00

Estee Lauder, gold-tone & silver-tone basketweave, in original blue box, 4" dia, from $175 to...$225.00

Evans, nickel silver, embossed basket bouquet w/vines & flowers, oval mirror, w/chain, 2½x3", from $25 to $35.00

Evans, silver-tone, black enamel Deco sailboat on metallic beige, framed mirror, w/finger ring, 2" dia, from $20 to........$30.00

Gorham, silver, etched initials on lid, Gorham Sterling 338-0, framed mirror, 3" dia..$25.00

Houbigant, silver-tone, flower basket on white enamel, octagonal, framed mirror, 2" $20.00

House of Tre-Jur, silver-tone, leaping stag on sea foam green enamel lid, wavy concentric circles on bottom, 2" dia..............$30.00

Kigu, gold-tone, bright multicolored abstract design on lid, Made in KIGU England, w/black cloth case, 2½" dia.................$25.00

Kigu, gold-tone, 3 designs engraved on lid, guilloche back, slide clasp, 3" dia $20.00

Lazell, white metal, engine-turned linear lid w/circle monogram, De Meridor logo, framed mirror, 2¼" dia, from $35 to......$50.00

Mary Dunhill, gold-tone & peach enamel, w/pearl-like lid attachment, framed mirror, 2¾x2⅜", from $35 to $50.00

Max Factor, gold-tone, zodiac symbols in relief on lid, push-button stem, 2" dia, from $45 to...$65.00

Norida, hammered white metal, 18th-century lady in relief on lid, revolving powder sifter, framed mirror, 2" dia, $45 to ..$60.00

Parisian Novelty, white metal, lid covered w/hand-painted fabric, framed mirror, 2¼" dia, from $50 to $65.00

Pilcher, copper case w/attached gold-tone rose spray in top corner, framed mirror, 3¼" sq, from $50 to.............................$75.00

Primrose House, gold-tone & black enamel, stylized rising sun & rays on lid, framed mirror, 2¼" sq, from $45 to $60.00

R&G Co, black & white guilloche enamel, rouge pot & crescent mirror in lid, 2", from $30 to..............................$40.00

Revlon, gold-tone w/white champlevé enamel lid, raised wreath & crest, glued mirror, 2⅝" dia, from $15 to......................$20.00

Rex Fifth Avenue, gold-tone with embossed ribboned spray inset with collet-mounted faux emeralds, puff with logo, glued mirror, 4" diameter, $65.00. (Photo courtesy Roselyn Gerson)

Richard Hudnut, gold-tone scrolling on purple enamel lid, framed mirror, 3x2", from $30 to.................................$40.00

Richard Hudnut, gold-tone w/lg embossed flower on lid, lipstick case in lid opening, framed mirror, from $18 to $23.00

Schiaparelli, gold-tone, stick figure silhouette on rose enamel, heart-shaped compartment, 2¼" triangle, from $225 to $250.00

Stratton, gold-tone, floral bouquet in Deco circle on white enamel lid, framed mirror, 2" dia, from $20 to.........................$30.00

Stratton, gold-tone, painted woodland scene w/couple & cherubs, #764125, 3½" dia, from $20 to $25.00

Stratton, red roses w/green & brown leaves on white enamel on lid, framed mirror, 3" dia, from $30 to $35.00

Stratton, silver-tone w/painted jonquil flowers on white enamel, Jonquil March & instructions on label, 2¾" dia $27.00

Sweet Romance, gold-tone, zodiac signs on multicolored enamel, rhinestone center, Sweet Romance USA, 1972, 2½" dia..$25.00

Tre-Jur, white metal, Deco leaping gazelle on green enamel lid, framed mirror, 2" dia, from $45 to...............................$60.00

Unknown, gold-tone w/engraved sun rays, Made in Switzerland, framed mirror, 3⅛" dia, from $35 to $50.00

Unknown, Thai goddess etched on black niello lid, elephants & riders on back, marked Sterling Siam, octagonal, 2½".......$30.00

Unmarked, brushed gold-tone, service emblem centered in Star of David on lid, 2¼x2¾", from $55 to $75.00

Unmarked, red plastic, novelty ladybug shape, from $80 to...**$125.00**

Unmarked, 2-tone wood veneer lid w/Scottie dogs in relief, beaded rim, framed mirror, 3" sq, from $50 to.......................**$65.00**

Vivienne, brushed gold-tone w/painted blue silhouette & banding on lid, framed, 1½" dia, from $75 to..........................**$90.00**

Volupte, gold-tone, rhinestone bar on lid lowers to open, framed mirror, 3" sq **$25.00**

Volupte, gold-tone, sq red jewels in grid, framed mirror, w/care instructions, 2½" sq, from 25 to **$30.00**

Wand Art, gold-tone & black enamel, spangles & brown ribbon borders, glued mirror, 2½x2¾", from $45 to **$50.00**

Webster, hammered silver, engraved floral border & center, Sterling, gold-tone interior, cresent mirror, 2" dia......................**$22.00**

Woodworth, white metal, blue bells w/tendrils engraved on lid, Karess logo, framed mirror, 1¾x2", from $50 to..........**$65.00**

Sterling and enamel with profile of young woman, $65.00.

Cookbooks

Cookbook collecting is not new! Perhaps one of the finest books ever written on the subject goes back to just after the turn of the century when Elizabeth Robins Pennell published *My Cookery Books,* an edition limited to 330 copies; it had tipped-in photographs and was printed on luxurious, uncut paper. Mrs. Pennell, who spent much of her adult life traveling in Europe, wrote a weekly column on food and cooking for the *Pall Mall Gazette,* and as a result, reviewed many books on cookery. Her book was a compilation of titles from her extensive collection which was later donated to the Library of Congress. That this book was reprinted in 1983 is an indication that interest in cookbook collecting is strong and ongoing.

Books on food and beverages, if not bestsellers, are at the least generally popular. Cookbooks published by societies, lodges, churches, and similar organizations offer insight into regional food preferences and contain many recipes not found in other sources. Very early examples are unusually practical, often stressing religious observances and sometimes offering medical advice. Recipes were simple combinations of basic elements. Cookbooks and cooking guides of World Wars I and II stressed conservation of food. In sharp contrast are the more modern cookbooks often authored by doctors, dietitians, cooks, and domestic scientists, calling for more diversified materials and innovative combinations with exotic seasonings. Food manufacturers' cookbooks abound. By comparing early cookbooks to more recent publications, the fascinating evolution in cookery and food preparation is readily apparent.

Because this field is so large and varied, we recommend that you choose the field you find most interesting to you and specialize. Will you collect hardbound or softcover? Some collectors zero in on one particular food company's literature — for instance, Gold Medal Flour and Betty Crocker, the Pillsbury Flour Company's Pillsbury Bake-Offs, and Jell-O. Others look for more general publications on chocolate, spices and extracts, baking powders, or favored appliances. Fund-raising, regional, and political cookbooks are other types to consider.

For more information we recommend *Collector's Guide to Cookbooks* (Collector Books) by Frank Daniels.

Our suggested values are based on cookbooks in near mint condition; remember to adjust prices up or down to evaluate examples in other conditions.

Alice B Toklas Cookbook, AB Toklas, Harper & Bros, 1954 1st edition, hardcover w/jacket, EX.....................**$55.00**

American Frugal Housewife, Mrs Child, Samuel & Wm Wood, 4th edition, 12th printing, green paper boards, 129 pages, EX **$85.00**

Art Culinaire, International Magazine in Good Taste, 8th issue, Spring 1988, hardcover, 80 pages, NM........................**$70.00**

Aunt Jenny's Old Fashioned Christmas Cookies, Lever Bros, 1952, colorful softcover, 22 pages, 7½x5¼", EX....................**$12.50**

Better Homes & Gardens Casserole Cook Book, Meredith Press, 1967, 7th printing, pictorial hardcover, EX **$10.00**

Better Homes & Gardens Salad Book, copyright 1958, Better Homes & Gardens, hardcover, 160 pages, EX **$14.00**

Betty Crocker's Bisquick Cook Book, General Mills, 1956, softcover, 28 pages, EX.........................**$10.00**

Betty Crocker's Dinner in a Dish, Helen Federico, Golden Press, 1965, 1st edition, 1st printing, 152 pages, EX.............**$28.00**

Betty Crocker's Do-Ahead Cookbook, 1962 1st edition, pictorial hardcover, EX **$18.00**

Betty Crocker's Good & Easy Cook Book, Simon & Schuster, 1954 1st edition, spiral-bound hardcover, 256 pages, EX.......**$20.00**

Betty Crocker's New Picture Cook Book, General Mills 1st edition, 5th printing, 1961, hardcover, 455 pages, EX...............**$75.00**

Betty Crocker's Picture Cook Book, General Mills, 1950 1st edition, hardcover, 449 pages, EX.......................**$65.00**

Betty Crocker's Picture Cook Book, 40 color pages, many black & white illustrations, 1956, hard-back binder, EX............**$80.00**

Betty Feezor's Carolina Recipes, B Feezor, 1965 1st edition, 2nd printing, spiral bound, EX...........................**$55.00**

Boston Cooking-School Cook Book, Fannie M Farmer, black & white photos, copyright 1929, hardcover, VG..............**$72.50**

Brown Derby Cookbook, LL Levinson, Doubleday, copyright 1945, 1952 later edition, mission leather cover, 272 pages, EX..............................**$110.00**

Busy Woman's Cook Book, Mabel Claire, 1925, hardcover, 88 pages, VG....................................**$32.00**

Classical Cooking the Modern Way, Eugen Pauli, Culinary Institute of America, 1979, hardback, 625 pages, VG.................**$25.00**

Clementine Paddleford's Cook Young Cookbook, Pocket Books Inc, NY, 1966, softcover, 124 pages, 6x9", EX.....................**$12.50**

Cooking w/Soup, Campbell Soup Co, 1950s, spiral-bound hardcover, EX **$12.00**

Corning's Cook's Choice, Corning Glass Works, 1979, binder style, NM...**$18.00**

Desserts, General Foods, 1935 2nd edition, pictorial softcover, 52 pages, EX **$10.00**

Easy Ways to Good Meals, Ann Marshall, Campbell Soup Co, copyright 1951, softcover, 48 pages........................**$22.00**

Egg-Free, Milk-Free, Wheat-Free Cookbook, Becky Hamrick & SL Wiesenfield MD, Harper & Row, 1982, hardcover, EX..**$25.00**

Elegant Food, Valeria Childs, CLB Publishing Co, 1989, pictorial hardcover, 14½x10", VG................................**$30.00**

Escoffier Cook Book, A Escoffier, 1961, hardcover, 923 pages, NM **$32.00**

Family Harvest, Jane Moss Snow, 1976 1st edition, hardback w/dust jacket, 221 pages, EX.....................................**$7.50**

Farm Journal's Country Cookbook, edited by NB Nichols, Al J Reagan photos, Doubleday & Co, 1959, hardback w/jacket, EX ..**$25.00**

Flavor & Spice & All Things Nice, McCormick, copyright 1929, softcover, 32 pages, EX.............................**$22.00**

Florida's Favorite Foods, Compliments of Zonta Club of Greater Miami, 1961, pictorial cover, NM **$30.00**

Food for Better Living, Irene E McDermotte, illustrated, 1949, 1st edition, hardcover, EX **$32.00**

Frozen Foods Cook Book, Evaporated Milk Association, 1931, softcover, 30 pages, EX..............................**$12.50**

Frugal Gormet, Jeff Smith, 1984, hardcover w/dust jacket, 388 pages, VG **$8.00**

Fun-Filled Butter Cookies Cookbook, Ann Pillsbury, ca 1950 (undated), softcover, 48 pages, EX............................**$22.00**

Gay Cookbook, Chef Lou Rand Hogan, David Costain cartoons, Sherbourne Press, 1965, hardcover, 280 pages, EX **$42.50**

General Federation of Women's Clubs Cook Book - America Cooks, A Seranne, GP Putnams Sons, 1967, hardcover w/ jacket, EX **$60.00**

Grass Roots Cookbook, Jean Anderson, 1977, hardcover w/dust jacket, EX **$6.00**

Great Pumpkin Cookbook, Libby, McNeill & Libby Inc, 1984 1st edition, 1st printing, spiral bound, 128 pages, EX........**$70.00**

Harvest of American Cooking, **Mary Margaret McBride, regional histories and recipes, 1957, $25.00.**

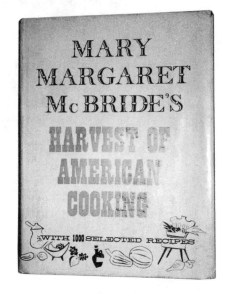

Herbs for the Kitchen, Irma Goodrich Mazza, Little Brown & Co, 1950, Revised Edition, green hardcover, EX **$30.00**

Ideals American Cookbook, Centennial edition of Ideals magazine, copyright 1976, 64 pages, EX **$10.00**

I Hate to Cook Book, The, **Peg Bracken, 1960, $40.00.**
(Photo courtesy Frank Daniels)

Idle Hour Cook Book, Chambers C Model, copyright 1950, softcover, VG **$110.00**

Jack & Marry's Jell-O Recipe Book, 1937 2nd edition, pictorial softcover, EX **$35.00**

Jewel Cook Book, The, **Jewel Tea Co., ad for Autumn Leaf dinnerware, 1950s, 62 pages, $50.00.** **(Photo courtesy Frank Daniels)**

Just Like Mother Made, Ozark Recipes, Louise Henderson, drawings by NS Duell, 1950s, softcover **$15.00**

Let's Cook It Right, Adelle Davis, Harcourt Brace & World Inc, New Revised Edition Copyright 1962, hardcover, NM **$20.00**

Mary Margaret McBride Encyclopedia of Cooking, Homemakers Research Institute, 1963 Deluxe Illustrated Edition, NM.. **$55.00**

McCall's Cook Book, Random House, 1963 1st edition, 1st printing, hardcover w/dust jacket, 876 pages, EX **$85.00**

McCall's Cooking School Cookbook, Fields Publications, 1966, hardback w/dust jacket, EX **$75.00**

New Joys of Jell-O, General Foods, 3rd edition, 13 categories, hardbound, 125 pages, NM **$9.00**

New Magic in the Kitchen, New Magic Sweetened Condensed Milk, 1930, softcover, NM **$12.00**

New York Times Cook Book, Craig Clairborne, Harper & Row, 1976, hardcover, 717 pages, EX **$12.00**

No Time for Cooking, Arlene Francis, Danola Brand Danish Cooked Ham, 1961, hardcover w/dust jacket, 103 pages **$42.00**

Out of Vermont Kitchens, St Paul's Church Burlington VT, 1951, spiral bound, VG **$40.00**

Pillsbury's 4th Grand National Bakeoff Cookbook, Pillsbury Mills Inc, 1953, 1st edition, EX.. **$20.00**

Royal Baker & Pastry Book, Royal Baking Powder Co, copyright 1906, 44 pages, 8x5", VG **$28.00**

Royal Cook Book, Royal Baking Powder Co, 1927, softcover, EX **$16.00**

Sam Houston Schoolhouse Association of Maryville TN, 1980, spiral-bound softcover, 9x7", EX.................................. **$20.00**

Southern Cookbook Fine Old Dixie Recipes, LS Lusting, Culinary Arts Press, 1935 1st edition, softcover, w/wraps, VG+ ... **$135.00**

Southern Living 1988 Annual Recipes, Southern Living Magazine, 1988, hardback, EX **$22.00**

Tex-Mex Cook Book, Sam Huddleston, First National Bank, 1971, softcover, 28 pages, VG.. **$18.00**

Woman's Day Encyclopedia of Cookery, Vols 1 - 12, 1965, hardback, complete set, NM **$48.00**

Woman's Home Companion Cook Book, D Kirk, PF Collier & Son, NY, hardback, 951 pages, EX **$50.00**

Cookie Cutters

In recent years, cookie cutters have come into their own as worthy kitchen collectibles. Prices on many have risen astronomically, but a practiced eye can still sort out a good bargain. Advertising cutters and product premiums, especially in plastic, can still be found without too much effort. Aluminum cutters with painted wood handles are usually worth several dollars each, if in good condition. Red and green are the usual handle colors, but other colors are more highly prized by many. Hallmark plastic cookie cutters, especially those with painted backs, are always worth considering, if in good condition.

Be wary of modern tin cutters being sold for antique. Many present-day tinsmiths chemically antique their cutters, especially if done in a primitive style. These are often sold by others as 'very old.' Look closely because most tinsmiths today sign and date these cutters. Cookie cutters listed here are from the twentieth century, in undamaged original condition unless otherwise noted.

Acrobat, tin, flat back, 6x4" **$74.00**

American flag, red plastic, Tupperware, EXIB **$25.00**

Animal Snacks, miniatures, Hallmark, 1978, MIP, $15.00.
(Photo courtesy Rosemary Henry)

Antlered Deer, tin, flat back, pre-1900, 6x4¾"	$230.00
Betsy McCall, metal, McCall Pub Co 1971 NYC Hong Kong, 8" H, NM	$25.00
Bird in flight, tin, flat back, pre-1900, 2¾x3⅞"	$250.00
Bugs Bunny, red plastic, 1978, 6"	$6.00
Camel, tin, flat back, w/handle, 3¼x2¾"	$60.00
Cat w/tail up, tin, flat back, 2¾x3½"	$45.00
Colonial woman, hand-wrought tin, ¾x11x6"	$110.00
Dove, plastic, Hallmark VKK-47-9, MIP	$15.00
Eagle, tin, flat back, early, 3¾x6"	$50.00
Fish, salmon or trout form, tin, flat back w/handle, 5" L	$25.00
Flower, tin, flat back w/center hole, 4⅜" dia	$28.00
Gingerbread man, copper, flat back, 10x5½"	$16.00
Girl Scout emblem, aluminum, flat back w/handle, Drip-o-lator..., 1950s, 2½x2½"	$20.00
Gumby, green plastic, Domino Sugar, MIP	$25.00
Hatchet, tin, flat black, early, 5x8½"	$75.00
Heart, aluminum, Swan's Down Cake Flour	$15.00
Heart in hand, tin, flat back, pre-1900, 4½" L	$435.00
Hobby horse, tin, flat back, 4½x3¼"	$15.00
Horse, tin, head & tail down, flat back w/handle, early, 5x6"	$100.00
Lady on chamber pot, tin, flat back, pre-1900, 8x5"	$350.00
Leaf, tin, flat back, w/handle, early, 2½x5"	$85.00
Linus (Charlie Brown), red plastic, Hallmark 1971, 5"	$30.00
Man in the Moon, tin, flat back, early, 5¼x3⅝"	$115.00
Mr Peanut, red plastic, flat back w/handle, Made in USA, 1950s, 5"	$17.00
Muffin man, red plastic, HRM	$16.50
Pear w/stem, tin, flat back, 4¼"	$25.00
Penguin, tin, flat back, 3x1¾"	$15.00
Pink Panther head, pink plastic, Ambassador, 1978, 3x4", MIP	$18.00
Rabbit leaping, tin, flat back, early, 4x6½"	$55.00
Raggedy Ann, tin, flat back w/handle, 5"	$35.00
Reddy Kilowatt, red plastic, 3", MIB	$20.00
Rooster, tin, flat back, w/handle, early, 4½x5"	$92.00
Santa, aluminum w/wooden handle	$13.00
Scooby Doo, yellow plastic, Hallmark/Disney, 1970s, 4½x2½"	$40.00
Snoopy, blue plastic, Hallmark, 1971, 4¾"	$30.00

Spade, diamond, heart & club, open backs, 2", 4 for	$40.00
Teddy bear, copper, Nordstrom, 7"	$20.00
Texas, tin, state shape, 4½"	$13.00
Witch riding broom, copper-colored aluminum, 5¼x5"	$15.00

Snowman or gingerbread man, metal, 8", MIB, $10.00.

Cookie Jars

This is an area that for years saw an explosion of interest that resulted in some very high prices. Though the market has drastically cooled off, some of the rare jars still sell for upwards of $1,000. Even a common jar from a good manufacturer will fall into the $40.00 to $100.00 price range. At the top of the list are the Black-theme jars, then come the cartoon characters such as Popeye, Howdy Doody, or the Flintstones — in fact, any kind of a figural jar from an American pottery is collectible.

The American Bisque company was one of the largest producers of these jars from 1930 until the 1970s. Many of their jars have no marks at all; those that do are simply marked 'USA,' sometimes with a mold number. But their airbrushed colors are easy to spot, and collectors look for the molded-in wedge-shaped pads on their bases — these say 'American Bisque' to cookie jar buffs about as clearly as if they were marked.

The Brush Pottery (Ohio, 1946 – 1971) made cookie jars that were decorated with the airbrush in many of the same colors used by American Bisque. These jars tend to hold their values, and the rare ones continue to climb in price. McCoy was probably the leader in cookie jar production. Even some of their very late jars bring high prices. Abingdon, Shawnee, and Red Wing all manufactured cookie jars, and there are lots of wonderful jars by many other companies. Joyce and Fred Roerig's book *The Ultimate Collector's Encyclopedia of Cookie Jars,* covers them all beautifully. It is published by Collector Books.

Warning! The marketplace abounds with reproductions these days. Roger Jensen of Rockwood, Tennessee, is making a line of cookie jars as well as planters, salt and pepper shakers, and many other items which for years he marked McCoy. Because it was believed the 'real' McCoys had never registered their trademark, he was able to receive federal approval to begin using this mark in 1992. Though he added '#93' to some of his pieces, the vast majority of his wares are undated. He used old molds, and novice collectors are being fooled into buying the new for 'old' prices. Here are some of his reproductions that you should be aware of: McCoy Mammy, Mammy With Cauliflower, Clown Bust, Dalmatians, Indian Head, Touring Car, and Rocking Horse; Hull Little Red Riding Hood; Pearl China Mammy; and the Mosaic Tile Mammy. Within the past few years, though, one of the last owners of the McCoy Pottery Company was able to make a successful appeal to end what they regarded as the fradulent use of their mark (it seems that they at last had it registered), so some of the later Jensen reproductions have been marked 'Brush-McCoy' (though this mark was never used on an authentic cookie jar) and 'B.J. Hull.' Besides these forgeries, several Brush jars have been reproduced as well (see the Roerigs' book for more information), and there are others. Some reproductions are being made in Taiwan and China, however there are also jars being reproduced here in the states.

For more information we recommend *Collector's Guide to Don Winton Designs* by our Twin Winton advisor Mike Ellis.

See also Fitz & Floyd; Vandor.

Advisors: Marceyne Scharp and Joyce Higbee (See Directory, Shawnee); Mike Ellis, Twin Winton (See Directory, Twin Winton); Carl Gibbs, Metlox (See Directory, Metlox); George A. Higby, Treasure Craft (See Directory, Treasure Craft)

Newsletter: *Cookie Jarrin' With Joyce*
1501 Maple Ridge Rd.
Walterboro, SC 29488

Abingdon, Bo Peep, #694 ....$235.00
Abingdon, Fat Boy, #495 ....$250.00
Abingdon, Hobby Horse, #602.........................$185.00
Abingdon, Jack-in-the-Box, #611......................$275.00
Abingdon, Little Ol' Lady (Black face), #561, from $300 to... **$375.00**

Abingdon, Miss Muffet, #622, $250.00.

Abingdon, Money Bag, #588 ....**$65.00**
Abingdon, Old Lady, #471, minimum value.............**$250.00**
Abingdon, Three Bears, #696, from $90 to.............**$100.00**
Abingdon, Wigwam, #665 ....**$200.00**
American Bisque, Baby Bear, w/pink bib, unmarked, 1958, from $50 to **$75.00**
American Bisque, Boots, marked USA 742, from $75 to.....**$85.00**
American Bisque, Boy Pig, unmarked, from $90 to...........**$100.00**
American Bisque, Cheerleaders, marked Corner Cookie Jar 802 USA, from $375 to.......................................**$425.00**
American Bisque, Cookie Clock, marked 203, from $30 to.**$40.00**
American Bisque, French Poodle, burgundy, marked USA, from $100 to **$125.00**
American Bisque, Gift Box, marked USA, 1958, from $150 to **$175.00**
American Bisque, Grandma, gold trim, unmarked, from $175 to **$225.00**
American Bisque, Hen w/Chick, multicolored, marked USA, 9", from $150 to **$175.00**
American Bisque, Kitten & Beehive, marked USA, 1958, from $40 to **$50.00**
American Bisque, Little Girl Lamb, marked USA, from $100 to.. **$125.00**
American Bisque, Mug of Hot Chocolate, marked USA, from $60 to **$70.00**
American Bisque, Peasant Girl, marked USA, scarce, from $425 to **$450.00**
American Bisque, Pine Cone Coffeepot, marked USA, from $20 to **$25.00**

American Bisque, Popeye, USA, minimum value, $750.00.
(Photo courtesy LiveAuctioneers.com/ Morphy Auctions)

American Bisque, Recipe Jar, unmarked, from $90 to........**$110.00**
American Bisque, Sack of Cookies, marked USA, from $45 to...**$55.00**
American Bisque, Sadiron, marked USA, from $100 to.....**$125.00**
American Bisque, Sweethearts aka Umbrella Kids, marked USA 739, from $325 to **$350.00**
American Bisque, Toothache Dog, marked USA, from $350 to ..**$375.00**
Brush, Cinderella Pumpkin, #W32 ....**$200.00**
Brush, Cookie House, #W31, from $60 to **$75.00**
Brush, Davy Crockett, no gold, marked USA (+), from $225 to.**$250.00**
Brush, Donkey Cart, ears down, gray, #W33, from $300 to.**$400.00**
Brush, Elephant w/Monkey on Back................**$450.00**

Brush, Gas Lamp, #K1, from $45 to.......................................$65.00

Brush, Granny, pink apron, blue dots on skirt, #W19, from $200 to.......................................$250.00

Brush, Happy Bunny, white, #W25, from $150 to...........$175.00

Brush, Little Angel (+), from $650 to $700.00

Brush, Little Red Riding Hood, gold trim, marked, lg, (+) minimum value...................................$800.00

Brush, Old Clock, #W20, from $75 to........................$100.00

Brush, Peter Pan, no gold, sm, from $425 to $475.00

Brush, Peter Pumkin Eater, #W24, from $200 to $250.00

Brush, Puppy Police, #W8 (+), from $450 to......................$500.00

Brush, Raggedy Ann, #W16, from $400 to $450.00

Brush, Siamese, stylized, #W41, from $375 to..................$425.00

Brush, Squirrel on a Log, #W26, from $60.00 to $80.00.
(Photo courtesy Ermagene Westfall)

Brush, Squirrel w/Top Hat, black coat & hat, #W15, from $225 to $300.00

Brush, Squirrel w/Top Hat, green coat, from $200 to........$225.00

Brush, Teddy Bear, feet together, #014 USA, from $125 to..$175.00

California Originals, Bambi, marked copyright Walt Disney Prod USA 868, minimum value.....................................$1,250.00

California Originals, Crawling Turtle w/Rabbit eating on lid, marked 2728 USA, from $30 to..................................$35.00

California Originals, Duckbilled Platypus, marked 790 USA, from $100 to.....................................$125.00

California Originals, Eeyore, marked 901 c Walt Disney Productions, scarce, from $500 to $600.00

California Originals, Elephant, marked 2643 USA, from $25 to. $30.00

California Originals, Ernie, marked copyright MUPPETS INC 973, from $40 to $50.00

California Originals, Juggling Clown, red suit & hat, marked 876, from $45 to $55.00

California Originals, Lemon, unmarked, from $25 to.........$30.00

California Originals, Sitting Turtle, marked 2635 USA, from $30 to $35.00

California Originals, Small Owl, marked 856 USA, from $28 to $32.00

California Originals, Yellow Cab, unmarked, from $100 to..$125.00

California Originals, Yorkshire Terrier, blue bow, marked 937, from $125 to $150.00

Clay Art, Barnyard Santa, 1993, from $35 to $45.00

Clay Art, Cow Racer, 1994, from $40 to $45.00

Clay Art, Dogbone, 1991, from $35 to..............................$45.00

Clay Art, Midnight Snack, couple in night attire, 1991, from $40 to $50.00

Clay Art, Pig Out, 1991, from $30 to................................$35.00

Clay Art, Sunday Cow, 1992, from $35 to $45.00

De Forest of California, Calorie Sally, 1959, from $40 to....$50.00

De Forest of California, Clown, from $50 to $60.00

De Forest of California, Halo Boy, scarce, 1956, from $700 to..$725.00

De Forest of California, Little King, bib & crown, 1957 ...$800.00

De Forest of California, Monkey, #5516, from $30 to........$40.00

De Forest of California, Pig Head, marked De Forest...Hand-painted, from $40 to.....................................$50.00

De Forest of California, Poodle, marked 19c60...USA, from $40 to $50.00

De Forest of California, Praying Nun, from $250 to $275.00

De Forest of California, Weather House, marked 19c60 De Forest...USA, from $35 to $45.00

Dept 56, Le Chef Cuisine, Japan, from $100 to $125.00

Dept 56, Mrs Kringle, Christmas dress, from $50 to $60.00

Dept 56, Peasant Woman, black dress w/white dots, 1980, from $100 to $125.00

Dept 56, Short-Order Toaster, Japan, from $30 to..............$40.00

Dept 56, Someone's in the Kitchen, red apron w/white dots, Japan, from $100 to $125.00

Disney, Cheshire Cat (Alice in Wonderland).....................$99.00

Disney, Hook, sold through Disney stores, 1990s, from $25.00 to $40.00. (Photo courtesy www.whatacharacter.com)

Disney, Ludwig Von Drake, marked Copyright 1961 Walt...WD-6..................................$220.00

Disney, Micky Mouse Cookie Time Clock, marked WDE-219, glass front..................................$115.00

Disney, Penguin Waiter (Mary Poppins), limited edition ...$175.00

Disney, Pluto Fine Dining, limited edition $90.00

Disney, Three Little Pigs, standing in front of house..........**$120.00**

Disney, Thumper & Flower, by log & flowers, limited edition ...**$90.00**

Disney, 101 Dalmatians, limited edition...........................**$100.00**

Doranne of California, Basket of Lemons, marked J-20 c USA, from $30 to **$40.00**

Doranne of California, Bear, J-7 USA, from $35 to.............**$45.00**

Dorrane of California, Cat, from $30.00 to $40.00.

Doranne of California, Cat w/Bow Tie, marked J-5 USA, from $40 to **$50.00**

Doranne of California, Cow w/Can of Milk, white & pink, marked CJ-106, from $50 to...**$60.00**

Doranne of California, Deer, recumbent w/eyes closed, unmarked, $35 to **$45.00**

Doranne of California, Duck w/Basket of Corn, marked CJ-104, 1984, from $50 to **$60.00**

Doranne of California, Fire Hydrant, red, marked CJ-50, 1984, from $50 to **$60.00**

Doranne of California, Hen, marked CJ-100, from $35 to..**$45.00**

Doranne of California, Hound Dog, marked J-1 USA, from $35 to **$45.00**

Doranne of California, Ice Cream Cone, unmarked, from $25 to...**$30.00**

Doranne of California, Ketchup Bottle, marked CJ-68 USA, 1984, from $30 to **$40.00**

Doranne of California, School Bus, yellow w/black tires, from $150 to **$175.00**

Doranne of California, Snowman, black top hat, marked J-52 USA, from $225 to **$250.00**

Doranne of California, Volkswagen, marked CJ-117 USA c, from $175 to **$200.00**

Enesco, Bear, holding pink COOKIES heart, blue bow tie, Made in China, 1993, from $45 to...**$55.00**

Enesco, Bear Pull-toy, marked...Presents Come & Join the Teddy Bear Parade..., China, 1996, from $50 to **$60.00**

Enesco, Clown Head, marked Enesco Imports Japan E-5835, from $125 to **$150.00**

Hallmark, Ricky Raccoon, Cookie Bandit on yellow shirt, Hallmark Cards, 1981, from $75 to **$95.00**

Helen's Ware, Tat-L-Tale, blue polka-dot dress, from $700 to ...**$750.00**

Hirsch, Beehive, bee finial, from $60 to..............................**$75.00**

Hirsch, Chef, Lot'sa Goodies on front, from $150 to.........**$175.00**

Hirsch, Cow, from $75 to...**$85.00**

Hirsch, Cuckoo Clock, brown, William H Hirsch Mfg, from $100 to...**$125.00**

Hirsch, Treasure Chest, marked WH c '58, from $45 to......**$55.00**

Lefton, Bluebird Love Nest, #7525, 11".........................**$165.00**

Lefton, Chef Boy, #396...**$150.00**

Lefton, Dainty Miss, #040..**$185.00**

Lefton, Miss Priss, #1502...**$135.00**

Lefton, Pear 'n Apple, #4335 ....**$35.00**

Lefton, Scottish Girl, #1173, Japan...................................**$225.00**

Maddux of California, Gigantic Clown, #JA10 USA **$225.00**

Maddux of California, Humpty Dumpty, #2113 ....**$40.00**

McCoy, Animal Crackers **$100.00**

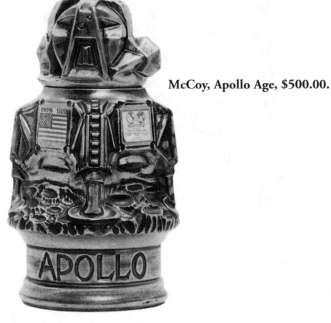

McCoy, Apollo Age, $500.00.

McCoy, Apple, 1950-64...**$50.00**

McCoy, Apples on Basketweave **$70.00**

McCoy, Asparagus..**$50.00**

McCoy, Astronauts...**$500.00**

McCoy, Bananas **$95.00**

McCoy, Barnum's Animals **$150.00**

McCoy, Barrel, Cookies sign on lid......................................**$75.00**

McCoy, Baseball Boy..**$95.00**

McCoy, Basket of Eggs...**$40.00**

McCoy, Basket of Potatoes **$40.00**

McCoy, Bear, cookie in vest, no 'Cookies'............................**$85.00**

McCoy, Betsy Baker (+) **$95.00**

McCoy, Black Kettle, w/immovable bail, hand-painted flowers ..**$40.00**

McCoy, Black Lantern **$65.00**

McCoy, Blue Willow Pitcher..**$55.00**

McCoy, Bobby Baker **$65.00**

McCoy, Bugs Bunny **$125.00**

McCoy, Burlap Bag, red bird on lid **$50.00**

McCoy, Caboose..**$95.00**

McCoy, Cat on Coal Scuttle **$125.00**

McCoy, Chairman of the Board (+) **$550.00**
McCoy, Chef Head **$125.00**
McCoy, Chilly Willy **$65.00**
McCoy, Chipmunk **$125.00**
McCoy, Christmas Tree **$350.00**
McCoy, Churn, 2 bands **$35.00**
McCoy, Circus Horse, black **$150.00**
McCoy, Clown Bust (+) **$75.00**
McCoy, Clown in Barrel, yellow, blue or green **$85.00**
McCoy, Clyde Dog **$95.00**
McCoy, Coalby Cat **$195.00**
McCoy, Coca-Cola Can **$75.00**
McCoy, Coca-Cola Jug **$55.00**
McCoy, Coffee Grinder **$45.00**
McCoy, Coffee Mug **$45.00**
McCoy, Colonial Fireplace **$85.00**
McCoy, Cookie Bank, 1961 .... **$125.00**
McCoy, Cookie Barrel, from $35 to **$45.00**
McCoy, Cookie Boy **$225.00**
McCoy, Cookie Cabin **$80.00**
McCoy, Cookie Jug, double loop **$35.00**
McCoy, Cookie Jug, w/cork stopper, brown & white **$40.00**
McCoy, Cookie Log, squirrel finial **$45.00**
McCoy, Cookie Mug **$45.00**
McCoy, Cookie Pot, 1964 .... **$40.00**
McCoy, Cookie Safe **$45.00**
McCoy, Cookstove, black or white **$35.00**
McCoy, Corn, row of standing ears, yellow or white, 1977 .. **$85.00**
McCoy, Corn, single ear **$150.00**
McCoy, Covered Wagon **$95.00**
McCoy, Cylinder, w/red flowers **$45.00**
McCoy, Dalmatians in Rocking Chair (+) **$150.00**
McCoy, Davy Crockett (+) **$300.00**
McCoy, Dog in Doghouse **$150.00**
McCoy, Dog on Basketweave **$75.00**
McCoy, Drum, red **$90.00**
McCoy, Duck on Basketweave **$75.00**
McCoy, Dutch Boy **$65.00**
McCoy, Dutch Girl, boy on reverse, rare **$250.00**
McCoy, Dutch Treat Barn **$50.00**
McCoy, Eagle on Basket, from $35 to **$50.00**
McCoy, Early American Chest (Chiffoniere) **$65.00**
McCoy, Elephant **$150.00**
McCoy, Elephant w/Split Trunk, rare, minimum value **$200.00**
McCoy, Engine, black **$125.00**
McCoy, Flowerpot, plastic flower on top **$350.00**
McCoy, Football Boy (+) **$125.00**
McCoy, Forbidden Fruit **$90.00**
McCoy, Fortune Cookies **$50.00**
McCoy, Freddy Gleep (+), minimum value **$350.00**
McCoy, Friendship 7 .... **$125.00**
McCoy, Frog on Stump **$75.00**
McCoy, Frontier Family **$55.00**
McCoy, Fruit in Bushel Basket **$65.00**
McCoy, Gingerbread Boy **$75.00**
McCoy, Globe **$195.00**
McCoy, Grandfather Clock **$75.00**

McCoy, Granny **$95.00**
McCoy, Hamm's Bear (+) **$175.00**
McCoy, Happy Face **$80.00**
McCoy, Hen on Nest **$95.00**
McCoy, Hillbilly Bear, rare, minimum value (+) **$900.00**
McCoy, Hobby Horse, brown underglaze (+) **$150.00**
McCoy, Hocus Rabbit **$45.00**
McCoy, Honey Bear, rustic glaze **$80.00**
McCoy, Hot Air Balloon **$40.00**
McCoy, Ice Cream Cone **$45.00**
McCoy, Indian, brown (+) **$250.00**
McCoy, Indian, majolica **$350.00**
McCoy, Jack-O'-Lantern **$400.00**
McCoy, Kangaroo, blue **$250.00**
McCoy, Keebler Tree House **$70.00**
McCoy, Kettle, bronze, 1961 .... **$40.00**
McCoy, Kissing Penguins **$75.00**
McCoy, Kitten on Basketweave **$90.00**
McCoy, Kittens (2) on Low Basket **$600.00**
McCoy, Kittens on Ball of Yarn **$85.00**
McCoy, Koala Bear **$85.00**
McCoy, Kookie Kettle, black **$35.00**
McCoy, Lamb on Basketweave **$90.00**
McCoy, Lemon **$75.00**
McCoy, Leprechaun, minimum value (+) **$1,800.00**
McCoy, Liberty Bell **$75.00**
McCoy, Little Clown **$75.00**
McCoy, Lollipops **$80.00**
McCoy, Mac Dog **$95.00**
McCoy, Mammy, Cookies on base, white w/cold paint (+) .. **$150.00**
McCoy, Mammy w/Cauliflower, G paint, minimum value (+) . **$1,100.00**
McCoy, Milk Can, Spirit of '76 .... **$45.00**
McCoy, Modern **$65.00**
McCoy, Monk **$50.00**
McCoy, Mother Goose **$95.00**
McCoy, Mouse on Clock **$40.00**
McCoy, Mr & Mrs Owl **$90.00**
McCoy, Mushroom on Stump **$55.00**
McCoy, Nursery, decal of Humpty Dumpty, from $70 to **$80.00**
McCoy, Oaken Bucket, from $25 to **$45.00**
McCoy, Orange **$55.00**
McCoy, Owl, brown **$70.00**
McCoy, Pear, 1952 .... **$85.00**
McCoy, Pears on Basketweave **$70.00**
McCoy, Penguin, yellow or aqua **$95.00**
McCoy, Pepper, yellow **$40.00**
McCoy, Picnic Basket **$75.00**
McCoy, Pig, winking **$250.00**
McCoy, Pillsbury Doughboy, from $40 to **$50.00**
McCoy, Pinapple **$80.00**
McCoy, Pine Cones on Basketweave **$70.00**
McCoy, Pineapple Modern **$90.00**
McCoy, Pirate's Chest **$95.00**
McCoy, Popeye, cylinder **$150.00**
McCoy, Potbelly Stove, black **$30.00**
McCoy, Puppy, w/sign **$85.00**
McCoy, Quaker Oats, rare, minimum value **$500.00**

McCoy, Raggedy Ann $110.00

McCoy, Red Barn, cow in door, minimum value, $150.00.

(Photo courtesy Ermagene Westfall)

McCoy, Rooster, white, 1970-74...$60.00
McCoy, Rooster, 1955-57 ....$95.00
McCoy, Round w/hand-painted leaves................................$40.00
McCoy, Sad Clown $85.00
McCoy, Snoopy on Doghouse (+), marked United Features
    Syndicate $125.00
McCoy, Snow Bear..$75.00
McCoy, Spaniel in Doghouse, bird finial $175.00
McCoy, Stagecoach, minimum value..................................$650.00
McCoy, Strawberry, 1955-57 ....$65.00
McCoy, Strawberry, 1971-75 ....$45.00
McCoy, Teapot, 1972...$60.00
McCoy, Tepee, slant top $250.00
McCoy, Tepee, straight top (+)..$200.00
McCoy, Thinking Puppy, #0272 ....$40.00
McCoy, Tilt Pitcher, black w/roses $50.00
McCoy, Timmy Tortoise $45.00
McCoy, Tomato $60.00
McCoy, Touring Car $75.00
McCoy, Traffic Light...$50.00
McCoy, Tudor Cookie House $95.00
McCoy, Tulip on Flowerpot $100.00
McCoy, Turkey, green, rare color.......................................$200.00
McCoy, Turkey, natural colors...$200.00
McCoy, Upside Down Bear, panda $50.00
McCoy, WC Fields...$125.00
McCoy, Wedding Jar..$90.00
McCoy, Windmill $100.00
McCoy, Wishing Well $40.00
McCoy, Woodsy Owl...$150.00
McCoy, Wren House, side lid $125.00
McCoy, Yellow Mouse (head)...$45.00
McCoy, Yosemite Sam, cylinder $125.00
Metlox, Ali Cat $175.00

Metlox, Apple, Red; 3½-qt, 9½" $75.00
Metlox, Bear, Ballerina...$100.00
Metlox, Blue Bird on Stump, glaze decoration $175.00
Metlox, Cookie Bandit, raccoon, bisque $125.00
Metlox, Cookie Girl, color glaze $125.00
Metlox, Dino-Stegosaurus, aqua, French Blue, rose or yellow, ea ..$150.00
Metlox, Downy Woodpecker, on acorn..............................$160.00
Metlox, Ferdinand Calf, minimum value $750.00
Metlox, Humpty Dumpty, no foot, 11", minimum value ..$400.00
Metlox, Katy Cat, white..$85.00
Metlox, Lucy, goose...$125.00
Metlox, Mother Hen Chicken, white $100.00
Metlox, Mouse Mobile, bisque...$75.00
Metlox, Nun, white w/blue trim $100.00
Metlox, Pretty Ann $125.00
Metlox, Salty, pelican..$200.00
Metlox, Scottie Dog, white $250.00
Metlox, Scrub Woman Mammy, minimum value $1,200.00
Metlox, Sir Francis Drake, duck...$50.00
Metlox, Squirrel on Pine Cone, 11" $100.00
Metlox, Teddy Bear, bisque, 3-qt.......................................$40.00
Metlox, Tulip Time, 2-qt...$65.00

Metlox, Uncle Sam Bear, minimum value, $800.00.

Metlox, Yellow Cow, w/white flowers, yellow butterfly &
    bell $425.00
North American Ceramics, Double-decker Bus, red...........$150.00
Omnibus, Buffalo Hunt, from $30 to................................$35.00
Omnibus, Chili Cow, from $30 to.....................................$35.00
Omnibus, German Santa, from $60 to $70.00
Omnibus, Harvest Turkey, c OCI 1990 label, from $30 to..$35.00
Omnibus, Hippo, from $25 to $30.00
Omnibus, Panda, OCI label, from $25 to............................$30.00
Omnibus, Sherlock Hound, yellow coat, OCI label, from $35
    to...$45.00
Red Wing, Bob White, unmarked, from $90 to.................$110.00
Red Wing, Dutch Girl (Katrina), yellow w/brown trim, from $125
    to...$150.00
Red Wing, Jack Frost, unmarked, short, from $550 to $600.00

132

Red Wing, King of Tarts, pink w/blue & black trim, marked, from $750 to **$850.00**

Red Wing, Peasant (design), embossed/painted figures on aqua, short, from $75 to **$90.00**

Red Wing, Pierre (Chef), $150.00. (Photo courtesy Fred and Joyce Roerig)

Shawnee, Basketweave, hand decoration, gold trim, USA, 7½", from $150 to **$175.00**

Shawnee, Dutch Girl (Jill), tulip, USA, from $250 to........**$275.00**

Shawnee, Happy, gold and decals, from $250.00 to $275.00. (Photo courtesy Fred and Joyce Roerig)

Red Wing, Pineapple, yellow...**$100.00**
Regal, Cat, from $425 to **$475.00**
Regal, Churn Boy **$175.00**
Regal, Clown, green collar..**$450.00**
Regal, Davy Crockett **$400.00**
Regal, Diaper Pin Pig..**$350.00**
Regal, Dutch Girl..**$600.00**
Regal, FiFi Poodle, minimum value **$500.00**
Regal, Fisherman, from $650 to **$720.00**
Regal, French Chef, from $475 to..**$525.00**
Regal, Goldilocks (+), from $200 to....................................**$300.00**
Regal, Harpo Marx **$1,080.00**
Regal, Hubert Lion, minimum value **$1,000.00**
Regal, Little Miss Muffet, from $200 to.............................**$275.00**
Regal, Majorette..**$350.00**
Regal, Oriental Lady w/Baskets, from $725 to **$775.00**
Regal, Peek-a-Boo (+), from $925 to..................................**$975.00**
Regal, Quaker Oats...**$95.00**
Regal, Rocking Horse, from $275 to **$325.00**
Regal, Three Bears...**$175.00**
Regal, Toby Cookies, no mark, from $675 to **$725.00**
Regal, Tulip, from $200 to **$225.00**
Regal, Uncle Mistletoe **$765.00**
Robinson Ransbottom, Bud, Army Man, brown, 1942-43, 12", from $125 to **$150.00**
Robinson Ransbottom, Doughgirl Head, thinning paint/stains, from $50 to **$75.00**
Robinson Ransbottom, Frosty the Snowman, from $300 to..**$350.00**
Robinson Ransbottom, Jack, sailor in black, from $150 to...**$175.00**
Robinson Ransbottom, Oscar, pale unglazed face, red hat/lid, from $125 to **$150.00**
Robinson Ransbottom, Peach Bowl, #312 ....**$33.00**
Robinson Ransbottom, Sheriff Pig, gold trim, from $150 to ..**$175.00**
Robinson Ransbottom, Wise Bird, bird w/glasses & book, 12" ..**$30.00**

Shawnee, Jack, blue pants, USA, from $100 to **$125.00**
Shawnee, Jack Tar, cold paint, USA, 12", from $150 to.....**$200.00**
Shawnee, Jumbo, gold & decals, USA, 12", from $950 to..**$1,000.00**
Shawnee, Jumbo Elephant, red or blue bow tie, cold paint, USA, 12", from $200 to **$250.00**
Shawnee, Muggsy, green bow, rare, from $1,600 to **$1,800.00**
Shawnee, Smiley the Pig, shamrock w/gold & decals, USA, from $600 to **$650.00**
Shawnee, Winnie the Pig, peach collar, USA, from $375 to ..**$425.00**
Sierra Vista, Circus Wagon, white w/lion peering through cage, c 1957, from $65 to **$75.00**
Sierra Vista, Clown Head, from $30 to................................**$40.00**
Sierra Vista, Dog on Drum, from $40 to **$50.00**
Sierra Vista, Mushrooms, USA c 1957................................**$40.00**
Sierra Vista, Poodle, gray w/pink bow tie, c 1956, from $100 to **$125.00**
Sierra Vista, Squirrel, red jacket w/green collar, holding nut, from $50 to **$60.00**
Sierra Vista, Stagecoach, marked Sierra Vista Pasadena California..., 1956, from $150 to **$175.00**
Sigma, Chicago Cubs, bear cub in uniform..........................**$50.00**
Sigma, Duck, dressed in pink holding bowl & spoon, 11"...**$25.00**
Sigma, Star Wars, c Lucas Film Ltd, designed by Sigma the Tastesetter, from $100 to **$125.00**
Treasure Craft, Ark, Made in USA, from $40 to **$50.00**
Treasure Craft, Basketball, USA, from $25 to **$35.00**
Treasure Craft, Butterfly Crock, Made in USA, from $20 to..**$25.00**
Treasure Craft, Cat, Auntie Em Collection, Hallmark, from $45 to **$55.00**
Treasure Craft, Chef, Made in USA, from $35 to **$45.00**
Treasure Craft, Cookie Barn, c USA, from $35 to **$45.00**
Treasure Craft, Coyote, white or brown, USA, from $30 to.**$40.00**
Treasure Craft, Dog, wood stain, Made in USA, from $30 to...**$35.00**
Treasure Craft, Dog on Sled, USA, from $35 to **$45.00**

Treasure Craft, Duck, handcrafted stoneware, blue & white, #90222, from $30 to **$40.00**

Treasure Craft, Elmer, elm tree, Rose-Petal Place, minimum.. **$500.00**

Treasure Craft, Fish, pink & lavender, USA, from $30 to **$40.00**

Treasure Craft, Grandma, USA, from $30 to **$40.00**

Treasure Craft, Gumball Machine, USA, from $35 to **$45.00**

Treasure Craft, Hop-A-Long Cactus, USA, from $30 to...... **$35.00**

Treasure Craft, House, yellow, tan & white, Made in USA, from $35 to **$45.00**

Treasure Craft, Kitty, white w/black stripes, c USA, from $35 to **$45.00**

Treasure Craft, Lighthouse, USA, from $30 to.................... **$40.00**

Treasure Craft, Monkey, wood stain, 1968, from $30 to...... **$40.00**

Treasure Craft, Pig Chef, USA, from $35 to **$45.00**

Treasure Craft, Pig w/Rabbit, wearing farmer outfit, c USA, from $35 to **$45.00**

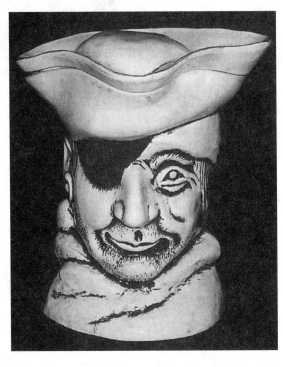

Treasure Craft, Pirate Bust, from $225.00 to $275.00.
(Photo courtesy Fred and Joyce Roerig)

Treasure Craft, Sailor Elephant, unmarked, from $30 to...... **$40.00**

Treasure Craft, Santa, USA, from $35 to **$45.00**

Treasure Craft, Storyteller Bear, white bear wearing Indian blanket & holding 2 sm bears, from $35 to.................................. **$45.00**

Treasure Craft, Tumbles the Hedgehog, Rose-Petal Place, from $350 to **$400.00**

Twin Winton, Barn, Collector's Series, from $90 to........... **$110.00**

Twin Winton, Cookie Elf, signed MAC, from $75 to........ **$100.00**

Twin Winton, Cookie Safe, stamped, from $35 to.............. **$45.00**

Twin Winton, Goose, stamped, from $75 to....................... **$100.00**

Twin Winton, Happy Bull, gray, etched V S, from $50 to... **$60.00**

Twin Winton, Hobby Horse, Collector's Series, from $125 to..**$150.00**

Twin Winton, Little Lamb, red bow & red & blue apron, Collector's Series, stamped, from $90 to.. **$110.00**

Twin Winton, Rabbit, cowboy outfit, stamped, from $75 to.. **$100.00**

Twin Winton, Shaggy Dog, red bow, unmarked, rare, from $150 to **$175.00**

Twin Winton, Tepee, stamped, from $70 to **$90.00**

Warner Bros, Bugs Bunny Baseball, 1993 .... **$30.00**

Warner Bros, Daffy Duck, Hey! Who Ate All the Cookies?, 1997 .... **$52.00**

Warner Bros, Michigan J Frog, wearing top hat **$75.00**

Warner Bros, Pepe & Penelope, in embrace **$50.00**

Warner Bros, Powerpuff Girls.. **$60.00**

Warner Bros., Taz, Applause, 1994, from $65.00 to $75.00.
(Photo courtesy Fred and Joyce Roerig)

Coors Rosebud Dinnerware

Golden, Colorado, was the site for both the Coors Brewing Company and the Coors Porcelain Company, each founded by the same man, Adolph Coors. The pottery's inception was in 1910, and in the early years they manufactured various ceramic products such as industrial needs, dinnerware, vases, and figurines; but their most famous line and the one we want to tell you about is 'Rosebud.'

The Rosebud 'Cook 'n Serve' line was introduced in 1934. It's very easy to spot, and after you've once seen a piece, you'll be able to recognize it instantly. It was made in solid colors — rose, blue, green, yellow, ivory, and orange. The rosebud and leaves are embossed and hand painted in contrasting colors. There are nearly 50 different pieces to collect, and bargains can still be found; but prices are accelerating due to increased collector interest. For more information we recommend *Coors Rosebud Pottery* by Robert Schneider.

Note: Yellow and white tends to craze and stain. Our prices are for pieces with minimal crazing and no staining. To evaluate pieces in blue, add 10% to the prices below; add 15% for items in ivory. Rosebud is prone to have factory flaws, and the color on the rosebuds may be of poor quality. When either of these factors are present, deduct 10%.

Advisor: Rick Spencer (See Directory, Silver-Plated and Sterling Flatware)

Baker, tab handles, 7" **$20.00**

Bean pot, with handles, 5x7", $70.00.

Bowl, batter; sm **$45.00**
Bowl, fruit; lg **$45.00**
Bowl, mixing; 3-pt **$35.00**
Bowl, oatmeal **$22.00**
Honey pot, w/spoon **$300.00**
Pitcher, water; no stopper **$70.00**
Pitcher, water; w/stopper **$120.00**

Plate, dinner; 9¼", $23.00.

Plate, scarce, 8¼" **$25.00**
Platter, 12x9" **$38.00**
Ramekin **$45.00**
Salt & pepper shakers, lg, either style, pr **$45.00**
Salt & pepper shakers, sm, pr **$45.00**

Shirred-egg dish **$25.00**
Sugar shaker **$60.00**
Teapot, 6-cup **$125.00**

Coppercraft

During the 1960s and 1970s, the Coppercraft Guild Company of Taunton, Massachusetts, produced a variety of copper and copper-tone items which were sold through the home party plan. Though copper items such as picture frames, flowerpots, teapots, candle-holders, and trays, were their mainstay, they also made molded wall decorations such as mirror-image pairs of birds on branches and large floral-relief plaques that they finished in metallic copper-tone paint. Some of their pictures were a combination of the copper-tone composition molds mounted on a sheet copper background. When uncompromised by chemical damage or abuse, the finish they used on their copper items has proven remarkably enduring, and many of these pieces still look new today. Collectors are beginning to take notice! Unless otherwise described, the items listed below are made of copper.

Bank, bell shape, slot on side, wooden handle, 8½x3⅛", from $18
to **$20.00**
Bank, owl w/glass eyes, 4" **$15.00**
Basket, 8⅝x8" **$15.00**
Bowl, copper, scalloped w/embossed center, 12x6¾" **$16.00**
Bowl, salad/fruit; footed, 4¾x9" **$55.00**
Bud vase, 8¼" **$12.00**
Butter dish, rectangular w/scalloped base, ¼-lb **$27.50**
Candleholder, brass finger loop, 6½" dia or 4" dia, ea from $10
to **$15.00**
Candleholder, leaf shape, wall hanging, ring at bottom, 13x7",
ea **$15.00**
Clock, face embossed w/acorns & oak leaves **$25.00**

Coffeepot with wooden handle, from $20.00 to $25.00.

Creamer & sugar bowl, 2¾", pr **$15.00**
Fondue pot, w/lid & metal warming stand, 5½" dia, from $25
to **$30.00**

Ice bucket, w/liner, ornate handles, 8", from $25 to **$35.00**

Mirror, copper paint on pressed molded plastic, 22x9½" **$35.00**

Money holder, brass, Cache on lid, 4x3" **$18.00**

Mug, copper w/brass handle, 3½" **$10.00**

Napkin holder, 4¾x7", from $15 to..................................... **$20.00**

Omelet pan, copper clad, 10½" dia...................................... **$30.00**

Piggy bank, all brass, including ears, feet & tail, 5", MIB **$25.00**

Planter, pot hangs from 3 brass chains suspended from simple hanger.. **$18.00**

Platter/tray, hammered surface, 12" dia................................ **$20.00**

Roly poly, 9-oz, 3", 8 for... **$20.00**

Salad servers, 12½", 12¼" **$25.00**

Stein, 5x3¼" **$15.00**

Teapot, copper, side handle, 8x5", from $18 to..................... **$20.00**

Teapot, w/bail handle, Solid Copper Made in USA, 4x5⅛" .. **$20.00**

Tumbler, clear glass w/copper base, 5½", set of 4 .... **$15.00**

Wall decoration, butterflies, copper paint on press-molded plastic, set of 3 .... **$18.00**

Wall decoration, man & hunting dog, copper paint on press-molded plastic, 6½" dia **$10.00**

Wall decoration, owls on limb in relief, copper paint on press-molded plastic, 11x9½".. **$20.00**

Wall decoration, sailing ship, copper paint on press-molded plastic, cMCMLXII, 21x27½"..................................... **$37.50**

Wall plaque, acorns/leaves surround lady w/2 children & dog, copper paint on press-molded plastic, 13" dia, from $20 to........ **$25.00**

Wall plaque, Last Supper, copper paint on press-molded plastic, 9¾x20½" **$25.00**

Corkscrews

When the corkscrew was actually developed remains uncertain (the first patent was issued in 1795), but it most likely evolved from the worm on a ramrod or cleaning rod used to draw wadding from a gun barrel and found to be equally effective in the sometimes difficult task of removing corks from wine bottles. Inventors scurried to develop a better product, and as a result, thousands of variations have been made and marketed. This abundance and diversification invariably attracted collectors, whose ranks are burgeoning. Many of today's collectors concentrate their attention on one particular type — those with advertising, a specific patent, or figural pullers, for instance.

Our advisor has written a very informative book, *Bull's Pocket Guide to Corkscrews* (Schiffer), with hundreds and full-color illustrations and current values.

Advisor: Donald A. Bull (See Directory, Corkscrews)

Advertising, Moerlein on wooden handle, web helix, from $20 to...**$30.00**

All-Ways Handy Combination, AW Stephens, MA, from $20 to **$50.00**

Art, 2-finger pull, figural handle, brass, English, from $15 to .. **$50.00**

Bow, simple folding type w/corkscrew only, from $10 to **$50.00**

Can-opener combination, Vaughan, w/stamped price, from $5 to...**$10.00**

Can-opener combination w/screwdriver, marked Cast Steel, from $40 to..**$50.00**

Direct pull, Walker, w/speed worm & cap lifter, from $150 to .. **$200.00**

Figural, Bar Bum, painted aluminum or bronze finish, from $40 to **$50.00**

Figural, lady's legs, celluloid, mini, 1⅞", from $650 to **$850.00**

Finger pull, 2-finger, direct pull, unmarked, from $20 to.....**$30.00**

Flynut, brass, Edwin Jay Made in Italy, from $15 to............**$30.00**

Frame, brass, 4-column, handle marked Italy, from $70 to ..**$80.00**

Frame, ornate verdigris w/gold-tone finish, roll-over handle, from $80 to **$100.00**

Murphy, dark acorn handle, from $70 to **$100.00**

Peg & worm w/button, faceted or ball end, from $75 to ...**$200.00**

Perpetual, steel, shank moves up and down as handle is turned, from $125.00 to $150.00.
(Photo courtesy Donald A. Bull)

Picnic, brass hex head, machined-in cap lifter, unmarked, from $25 to **$35.00**

Prong puller, Vaughan's Quick & Easy Cork Puller..., from $20 to.. **$30.00**

Roundlet, mottled green celluloid, from $100 to **$125.00**

Sardine key, w/folding fork, from $150 to **$200.00**

Spring type, all steel, unmarked, from $60 to **$100.00**

Spring type, wooden handle, triangular bell, from $30 to **$50.00**

T-handle, metal, clawfoot handle w/bulbed shank, from $100 to **$150.00**

T-handle, wooden, direct pull, from $10 to **$75.00**

Waiter's friend, w/bottle-cap lifter, from $5 to **$25.00**

Wm Rockwell Clough 1876 Patent, 2 pcs of wrapped wire, from $15 to **$50.00**

Corning Ware

Corning Ware was a high-fired glassware capable of going from freezer to oven or range top without fear of breakage. The first to hit the market was the Blue Cornflower line, which was made from 1958 until late in the 1970s in a very extensive range of cooking and serving items, some of which were electric. Lids were made of clear glass, and from 1958 until 1962, the handle was shaped like a bar, tapering on each side. Collectors refer to this type as the 'fin' handle. After 1962 the 'fin' handle was replaced with a simple knob.

Spice O' Life (introduced in 1982 and discontinued in 1987) brought a French flair to the market, as nearly each item carried a French inscription beneath the colorful design of vegetables and herbs. It was the company's second-best seller after Blue Cornflower.

Floral Bouquet (introduced in 1971), Country Festival (1975), Blue Heather (1976), and Wildflower (1977) are just a few of the many other lines of freezer-to-range cookware that were made of this space-age material. To learn more about them, we recommend *The Complete Guide to Corning Ware and Visions Cookware* by Kyle Coroneos (Collector Books). The author urges collectors to be critical of condition. Because the market has been relatively untapped until recently, you should be able to find mint condition examples — possibly even some still unused and in their original boxes.

Avocado Round, Dutch oven, 1968-70, w/matching lid, 4-qt, from $10 to **$12.00**

Black Starburst, percolator, 1959-62, 6-cup, from $15 to **$20.00**

Black Trefoil, party buffet, 1961-65, w/candle warmer & clear knob lid, 1¾-qt, from $8 to **$10.00**

Blue Cornflower, beverage server, 1965, 4-cup, from $12 to ..**$15.00**

Blue Cornflower, cake dish, 1968-71, 8" dia, from $15 to...**$20.00**

Blue Cornflower, deluxe teakettle, 1968-?, bail handle, 7-cup, from $40 to **$45.00**

Blue Cornflower, drip coffeemaker, 1964-71, 8-cup, from $25 to **$30.00**

Blue Cornflower, Dutch oven, 1963-71, w/rack, clear knob on lid, 4-qt, from $15 to **$20.00**

Blue Cornflower, electromatic Dutch oven/skillet combo, 1966-71, 4-qt Dutch oven/10" skillet, from $40 to **$45.00**

Blue Cornflower, loaf dish, 1967-?, 2-qt, from $12 to **$15.00**

Blue Cornflower, Menu-ette covered skillet, 1966 – ?, 6½", $15.00. (Photo courtesy Kyle Coroneos)

Blue Cornflower, open roaster, 1961-75, 13", from $15 to..**$20.00**

Blue Cornflower, petite pan, 1963-1970, w/plastic cover, 1½-cup, from 2 to **$4.00**

Blue Cornflower, pie plate, 1967-?, 9", from $10 to **$12.00**

Blue Cornflower, salt & pepper shakers, pr from $15 to......**$20.00**

Blue Cornflower, saucemaker, 1963-73, 2-spout, 1-qt, from $12 to **$15.00**

Blue Cornflower, saucepan, 1957-71, w/fin or clear knob lid, 1-qt, from $6 to **$8.00**

Blue Cornflower, saucepan, 1959-71, w/clear knob lid, 2½-qt, from $12 to **$15.00**

Blue Cornflower, saucepan w/spout, 1979-?, clear knob on lid, 1½-pt, from $6 to **$8.00**

Blue Cornflower, skillet, 1957-71, w/matching lid, 10", from $15 to **$20.00**

Blue Cornflower, skillet, 1959-71, w/fin or clear knob lid, 7", from $8 to **$10.00**

Butterscotch, Dutch oven, 1969-70, w/clear knob lid, 4-qt, from $10 to **$12.00**

Butterscotch, saucepan, 1969-70, w/matching lid, 2½-qt, from $4 to **$6.00**

Butterscotch, teapot, 1971-?, 6-cup, from $12 to.............**$15.00**

Country Cornflower, casserole, 1988-1993, w/clear knob lid, 2-qt, from $8 to **$10.00**

Country Festival, Menu-ette, 1975-76, w/clear knob lid, 1-pt, from $4 to **$6.00**

Country Festival, skillet, 1975-76, w/clear knob lid, 10", from $15 to **$20.00**

Country Festival, teapot, 1975-76, 6-cup, from $15 to........**$20.00**

Floral Bouquet, baking dish, 1972-74, oblong, 2¾-qt, from $12 to **$15.00**

Floral Bouquet, percolator, 1971-72, 9-cup, from $15 to **$20.00**

Floral Bouquet, saucepan, 1972, w/clear knob lid, 2½-qt, from $8 to **$10.00**

Floral Bouquet, saucepan, 1972-74, w/clear knob lid, 5-qt, from $35 to **$40.00**

Floral Bouquet, skillet, 1972-74, w/clear knob lid, 10", from $12 to **$15.00**

Floral Bouquet, trivet, 1971-74, 6" sq, from $2 to................**$4.00**

French, casserole, bisque, 1982, 2½-qt, from $12 to **$15.00**

French, casserole, white, 1981-?, round, w/plastic lid, 16-oz, from $3 to **$5.00**

French, casserole, white, 1984-?, oval, w/clear knob lid, 4-qt, from $15 to **$20.00**

French, pie/quiche plate, bisque, 1982, 10", from $10 to **$12.00**

Harvest Gold, saucepan, 1971, w/clear knob lid, 1½-qt, from $10 to **$12.00**

Indian Summer, casserole, 1976-77, w/clear knob lid, 2½-qt, from $6 to **$8.00**

Merry Mushroom, saucepan, 1971-?, w/clear knob lid, 8½-qt, from $5 to **$7.00**

Merry Mushroom, teapot, 1971-?, 6-cup, from $12 to........**$15.00**

Nature's Bounty, Brew 'n Serve, 1971, 8-cup, from $20 to ..**$25.00**

Nature's Bounty, loaf dish, 1971, w/plastic lid, 2-qt, from $10 to **$12.00**

Platinum Filigree, Royal Buffet, 1966, w/candle warmer & clear knob lid, 2½-qt, from $10 to **$12.00**

Renaissance, saucepot, 1970, w/serving cradle & clear knob lid, 4-qt, from $20 to **$25.00**

Renaissance, serving tray, 1970, w/serving cradle, 16", from $20 to **$25.00**

Shadow Iris, saucepan, 1988-?, 1½-qt, from $20 to **$25.00**

Spice O' Life, baking dish, 1974-?, w/clear knob lid, 1½-qt, from $6 to **$8.00**

Spice O' Life, covered saucepan, 1972 – 1987, one-quart, from $6.00 to $8.00. (Photo courtesy Klyle Coroneos)

Spice O' Life, open roaster, 1976-?, 10¼x8½", from $12 to..**$15.00**

Spice O' Life, percolator, 1973-76, 10-cup, from $15 to **$20.00**

Spice O' Life, petite pan, 1974-?, w/plastic lid, 1¾-cup, from $2 to **$4.00**

Spice O' Life, saucemaker, 1978-?, 2 spouts, w/clear knob lid, 1-qt, from $12 to **$15.00**

Spice O' Life, saucepan, 1972-87, w/clear knob lid, 1½-qt, from $10 to **$12.00**

Spice O' Life, skillet, 1972-?, w/clear knob lid, 6½", from $5 to...**$7.00**

Symphony, casserole, beige, 1990-93, w/amber knob lid, 1½-qt, from $6 to **$8.00**

Trefoil, electromatic percolator, 1960-65, 10-cup, from $20 to..**$25.00**

Wildflower, rangetop percolator, 1982-84, 6-cup, from $12 to..**$15.00**

Wildflower, skillet, 1977-?, w/clear knob lid, 6½", from $5 to .. **$7.00**

Wildflower, utility dish, 1978-?, 8" sq, from $20 to.............**$25.00**

Cottage Ware

Made by several companies, cottage ware is a line of ceramic table and kitchen accessories, each piece styled as a cozy cottage with a thatched roof. At least four English potteries made the ware, and you'll find pieces marked 'Japan' as well as 'Occupied Japan.' You'll also find pieces styled as windmills and water wheels. The pieces preferred by collectors are marked 'Price Brothers' and 'Occupied Japan.' They're compatible in coloring as well as in styling, and values run about the same. Items marked simply 'Japan' are worth considerably less. Ending prices on eBay indicate how popular this line is in Australia, where collectors often pay up to 50% more than our suggested values.

Bank, double slot, Price Brothers, 4½x3½x5", from $70 to..**$80.00**

Bell, Price Brothers, minimum value....................................**$60.00**

Biscuit/cookie jar, pink, brown & green, sq, Japan, 8½x5½", from $65 to **$75.00**

Biscuit/cookie jar, wicker handle, Maruhon Ware, Occupied Japan, 6½" **$80.00**

Biscuit/cookie jar, windmill, wicker handle, Price Brothers...**$165.00**

Bowl, salad; Price Brothers, 4x9"..**$50.00**

Butter pat, embossed cottage, rectangular, Occupied Japan..**$20.00**

Butter/cheese dish, cottage interior (fireplace), Japan, 6¾x5", from $65 to **$80.00**

Butter/cheese dish, oval, Burlington Ware, 6" **$60.00**

Butter/cheese dish, Price Brothers, from $50 to **$65.00**

Butter/cheese dish, round, Beswick, England, 3½x6" **$75.00**

Butter/cheese dish, sq green base, Old England by Rubian Art Pottery Grimwades, 7½" L..**$85.00**

Butter/cheese dish, Staffordshire Croft Hand Made..., 3¾x7".. **$50.00**

Chocolate pot, Price Brothers, 9½", from $85 to **$135.00**

Condiment set, mustard, salt & pepper, tray, row arrangement, Price Brothers, 6"..**$45.00**

Condiment set, mustard & shakers in row arrangement on tray, Price Brothers, 7¾" **$45.00**

Condiment set, mustard pot, 2½" shakers on 5" handled leaf tray, Price Brothers...**$75.00**

Condiment set, 3-part cottage on shaped tray w/applied bush, Price Brothers, 4½"...**$75.00**

Cookie jar/canister, cylindrical, Price Brothers, 8½x5", from $65 to.**$140.00**

Cookie jar/canister, cylindrical, rare size, 8x3¾".................**$275.00**

Covered dish, Occupied Japan, sm......................................**$35.00**

Creamer, windmill, Occupied Japan, 2⅝" **$25.00**

Creamer & sugar bowl, Price Brothers, 2½x4½" **$40.00**

Cup & saucer, chocolate; straight-sided cup, Price Brothers, 3¾", 5⅜"...**$35.00**

Cup & saucer, Price Brothers, 2½", 4½" **$35.00**

Demitasse pot, Price Brothers, 6x6¼", from $80 to **$110.00**

Egg cup set, Price Brothers, 4 (double) on 5½" sq tray **$65.00**

Egg cup set, Price Brothers, 4 (single) on 6" sq tray.............**$65.00**

Gravy boat & tray, Price Brothers, rare, from $250 to **$275.00**

Grease jar, Occupied Japan...**$30.00**

Hot water pot, Westminster, England, 8¼x4" **$50.00**

Marmalade, Price Brothers, 4" **$45.00**

Marmalade & jelly, 2 conjoined houses, Price Brothers, 5x7" ...**$75.00**

Mug, Price Brothers, 3⅞"..**$55.00**

Pin tray, Price Brothers, 4" dia **$22.00**

Pitcher, embossed cottage, lg flower on handle, Price Brothers, lg, from $100 to **$150.00**

Pitcher, tankard; round, 7 windows on front, Price Brothers, 7½", from $80 to **$120.00**

Plate, 7", from $9 to **$12.00**

Platter, oval, Price Brothers, 11¾x7½" **$60.00**

Reamer, windmill, Japan **$150.00**

Sugar cube box/butter dish, roof as lid, Price Brothers, 4x3x6½" L..**$50.00**

Tea set, child's, Japan, serves 4...**$165.00**

Teapots, 6½": Price Brothers/Kensington, from $50.00 to $65.00; Occupied Japan, from $45.00 to $60.00.

Teapot, Ye Olde Fireside, Occupied Japan, 9x5", from $70 to .. **$85.00**
Toast rack, 3-slot, Price Brothers, 3½" **$75.00**
Toast rack, 4-slot, Price Brothers, 5½" **$70.00**
Tumbler, Occupied Japan, 3½", set of 6.................**$65.00**

Cow Creamers

Cow creamers (and milk pitchers) have been around since before the nineteenth century, but, of course, those are rare. But by the early 1900s, they were becoming quite commonplace. In many of these older ones, the cow was standing on a platform (base) and very often had a lid. Not all cows on platforms are old, however, but it is a good indication of age. Examples from before WWII often were produced in England, Germany, and Japan.

Over the last 50 years there has been a slow revival of interest in these little cream dispensers, including the plastic Moo cows, mad by Whirley Industries, U.S.A, that were used in cafes during the '50s. With the current popularity of anything cow shaped, manufacturers have expanded the concept, and some creamers now are made with matching sugar bowls. If you want to collect only vintage examples, nowadays you'll have to check closely to make sure they're not new.

Coventry Made in USA, black & white w/brown hooves, pink nose
& ears, seated, #5540A, 4¾x5"......................**$55.00**
Crown Devon, blue floral on white, recumbent, 3⅜x7".......**$35.00**

Czechoslovakia, shaded brown, detailed modeling, $40.00.
(Photo courtesy LiveAuctioneers.com/Apple Tree Auction Center)

Delft, sailboat scene w/windmill in cobalt on white, standing tail
handle, 1900, 6¼x9"...................................**$200.00**
France, dainty blue flower sprays on white, tail handle, standing **$10.00**
Germany, cobalt scenery on ea side on white, recumbent, tail handle,
#1891, 3½x7¼" **$80.00**
Germany, gray & white w/white hooves, head up, tail over back,
standing, #6493, 4¾x7"...............................**$145.00**
Goebel, brown & white w/brown hooves, tail curled over back,
standing, blue bee mark (1972-79), 3¾x6" **$75.00**

Goebel, brown & white w/brown hooves, tail curled over back,
standing, blue bee mark (1972-79), 4½x6⅝" **$75.00**
Japan, airbrushed brown to white, painted eye detail, standing,
1950s, 3¼x5½" **$15.00**
Japan, light brown, souvenir of Rawlins WY, standing, ca 1940s,
5x8¼" **$25.00**
Japan, purple, finely muscled, tail curled over back, sm brass bell,
standing, foil sticker: Kennar, 4¼x6" **$27.50**
Japan, purple & white w/black hooves, gold horns, sm brass bell,
standing, 1950s, 4½x5¾"................................**$25.00**
Unmarked, shiny white w/no decor, tail curled over back, standing,
4½x7" **$40.00**

Unmarked Staffordshire, blue floral transfer, $65.00. (Photo
courtesy LiveAuctioneers.com/Clars Auction Gallery)

Unmarked, white w/airbrushed brown, gold horns, tail handle,
standing, 4½x5½" **$20.00**
Unmarked (attributed Germany), Brahma bull, black shading to
browns & grays, recumbent, 9" L **$245.00**

Cowboy Character Memorabilia

When we come across what is now termed cowboy character toys and memorabilia, it rekindles warm memories of childhood days for those of us who once 'rode the range' (often our backyards) with these gallant heroes. Today we can really appreciate them for the positive role models they were. They sat tall in the saddle; reminded us never to tell an un-truth; to respect 'women-folk' as well as our elders, animal life, our flag, our country, and our teachers; to eat all the cereal placed before us in order to build strong bodies; to worship God; and have (above all else) strong values that couldn't be compromised. They were Gene, Roy, and Tex, along with a couple of dozen other names, who rode beautiful steeds such as Champion, Trigger, and White Flash.

They rode into a final sunset on the silver screen only to return and ride into our homes via television in the 1950s. The next decade found us caught up in more western adventures such as Bonanza, Wagon Train, The Rifleman, and many others. These set the stage for a second wave of toys, games, and western outfits.

Annie Oakley was one of only a couple of cowgirls in the corral; Wild Bill Elliott used to drawl, 'I'm a peaceable man'; Ben

Cartwright, Adam, Hoss, and Little Joe provided us with thrills and laughter. Some of the earliest collectibles are represented by Roy's and Gene's 1920s predecessors — Buck Jones, Hoot Gibson, Tom Mix, and Ken Maynard. There were so many others, all of whom were very real to us in the 1930s – 1960s, just as their memories and values remain very real to us today.

Remember that few items of cowboy memorabilia have survived to the present in mint condition. When found, mint or near mint items bring hefty prices, and they continue to escalate every year.

For more information we recommend these books: *Roy Rogers, Singing Cowboy Stars, Silver Screen Cowboys, Hollywood Cowboy Heroes,* and *Western Comics: A Comprehensive Reference,* all by Robert W. Phillips.

See also Toys, Guns; Toys, Rings.

Newsletter: Cowboy Collector Network
Joseph J. Caro, Publisher
P.O. Box 7486
Long Beach, CA 90807
Hoppycnn@aol.com

Club: Hopalong Cassidy Fan Club International
Hopalong Cassidy Newsletter
Laura Bates, Editor
6310 Friendship Dr.
New Concord, OH 43762-9708
www.hopealongcassity.com

Club: The Lone Ranger Fan Club
Newsletter: The Silver Bullet
P.O. Box 9561
Amarillo, TX 79105
theloneranger@sbcglobal.net
www.lonerangerfanclub.com

Gene Autry, gun and holster set, Leslie Henry, EXIB, $450.00.

Annie Oakley, belt, black & white leather embossed w/Annie Oakley & Tag names, silver-tone buckle, 1950s, NM **$60.00**
Cisco Kid, stick horse, vinyl head w/fur-like mane & name, 32" L wooden stick, 1950s, VG **$35.00**
Dale Evans, lamp, plaster figure of Dale on rearing horse, printed shade, 8", EX **$150.00**

Dale Evans, Western Dress-Up Kit, Colorforms/Roy Rogers Ent, 1959, EXIB.. **$50.00**
Davy Crockett, Dart Gun Target, Knickerbocker, unused, MIB **$80.00**
Davy Crockett, Frontier Wagon/Stage, Linemar, 2-pc set, friction toy, ea 3x5" L, NMIB **$650.00**
Davy Crockett, horse, Pied Piper Toys, MIB.................. **$125.00**
Gene Autry, Official Ranch Outfit, G+IB **$75.00**
Gene Autry, wrist cuffs, light brown leather w/silver studs & red rhinestones, VG **$150.00**
Gunsmoke, Wallet Set, vinyl wallet, w/bullet charm & star badge, Marshal misspelled (Marshall) on wallet, 1950s, MOC... **$200.00**
Hopalong Cassidy, bank, Hoppy Savings Club, copper-tone plastic bust figure w/removable hat, 4", 1950s, EX.................. **$50.00**
Hopalong Cassidy, Coloring Outfit, Transogram, 1950s, slight use, NM+IB.. **$85.00**
Hopalong Cassidy, Cowboy Outfit, complete, G+IB **$90.00**
Hopalong Cassidy, Dudin'-Up Kit, w/shampoo, Hair Trainer, comb & 2 trading cards, Fuller Brush, 1950s, unused, MIB **$315.00**
Hopalong Cassidy, handkerchief, white w/Hoppy & Topper embroidery in black on white, 11½x11½", EX+ **$50.00**

Hopalong Cassidy, milk glass with fired-on design, 5", from $25.00 to $35.00.

Hopalong Cassidy, motion lamp, plastic, Roto-Vue/AB Leech, 1950, NM.. **$400.00**
Hopalong Cassidy, pencil case, vinyl w/zipper, black & white image of Toppy w/name & Pencil Case, 5x8", 1950s, EX+ **$95.00**
Hopalong Cassidy, potato chip can, close-up image of Hoppy & Topper on cream, slip lid, 11", 1950s, EX **$175.00**
Hopalong Cassidy, scrapbook, tan vinyl hardcover w/embossed image of Hoppy on Topper, string-bound, 1950s, unused, NM.. **$125.00**
Hopalong Cassidy, shoe caddy, red vinyl w/8 shoe pockets showing various yellow & black scenes, 1950s, EX.................. **$125.00**
Kit Carson, 3-Powered Binocular, 1950s, EXIB................ **$125.00**
Lone Ranger, binoculars, plastic, Harrison, EX+IB **$135.00**
Lone Ranger, horseshoe set, rubber, Gardner, NMIB.......... **$85.00**
Lone Ranger, Punch-Out Set, Lone Ranger, Tonto & Silver w/accessory punch-outs, DeJornette, 1940s, unused, EXIB...... **$85.00**
Lone Ranger, record player, molded plastic image of the Lone Ranger on Silver on front, Mercury, 1950s, VG+...................... **$85.00**

Lone Ranger, record player, wood case, 10x12", Decca/Lone Ranger Inc, EX **$350.00**

Lone Ranger, school bag, canvas w/plastic handle, image of Lone Ranger on side pocket, 1950s, EX **$100.00**

Maverick, Eras-O-Picture Book, Hasbro, 1958, complete, EX ...**$40.00**

Rin-Tin-Tin, outfit, Fighting Blue Devil 101st Cavalry, shirt, leather belt, pouch w/bullets & holster, NMIB **$175.00**

Roy Rogers, Branding Set/Ink Pad, tin container, 2" dia, 1950s, unused, EX **$65.00**

Roy Rogers, Camera w/Telescopic Sight, Herbert George Co, NMIB **$225.00**

Roy Rogers, Crayon Set, Standard Toycraft #940, 1950s, VGIB..**$75.00**

Roy Rogers, game, Lucky Horseshoe, Ohio Art, 1950s, complete, EX **$50.00**

Roy Rogers, guitar, Jefferson, 28" long, EX, from $65.00 to $80.00.

Roy Rogers, hat, taupe felt w/Roy Rogers band, white whipstitching around hat rim, NM+ **$100.00**

Roy Rogers, Paint-by-Number Paint Set, Roy Rogers Ent, 1954, unused, EXIB **$75.00**

Roy Rogers, Trick Lasso, Classy, 1950s, EXIP **$75.00**

Roy Rogers, woodburning set, Burn-Rite, complete, EXIB ..**$175.00**

Roy Rogers flashlight, red & white, w/image & signature, Bantan-Lite, 2 AA cells, 3¼", EX **$45.00**

Tales of Wells Fargo, Paint-by-Number Set, 1959, complete, unused, NMIB **$65.00**

The Texan (Rory Calhoun), hand puppet, full body in white shirt w/ black vest & pants, holster, Tops in Toys, 1960s, NM..**$175.00**

Tom Mix, Shooting Gallery, Parker Bros, c 1930, complete, EXIB **$230.00**

Tonto, soap figure, 4", Kerk Guild, 1939, EXIB (unopened) ..**$50.00**

Wild Bill Hickok, wallet, fastens w/Western buckle, NM+ ..**$75.00**

Zorro, bookends, ceramic, figural w/red Z on white base, glossy w/ red cold paint, Enesco, 1960s, NM **$225.00**

Zorro, key chain/flashlight, c WDP, 1950s, EX+..................**$75.00**

Zorro, ring, black plastic w/Zorro lettered in gold-tone on black stone, M **$75.00**

Cracker Jack

In 1869 Frederick Rueckheim left Hamburg, Germany, bound for Chicago, where he planned to work on a farm for his uncle. But farm life did not appeal to Mr. Rueckheim, and after the Chicago fire, he moved there and helped clear the debris. With another man whose popcorn and confectionary business had been destroyed in the fire, Mr. Rueckheim started a business with one molasses kettle and one hand popper. The following year, Mr. Rueckheim bought out his original partner and sent for his brother, Louis. The two brothers formed Rueckheim & Bro. and quickly prospered as they continued expanding their confectionary line to include new products. It was not until 1896 that the first lot of Cracker Jack was produced — and then only as an adjunct to their growing line. Cracker Jack was sold in bulk form until 1899 when H.G. Eckstein, an old friend, invented the wax-sealed package, which allowed them to ship it further and thus sell it more easily. Demand for Cracker Jack soared, and it quickly became the main product of the factory. Today millions of boxes are produced — each with a prize in every box.

The idea of prizes came along during the time of bulk packaging; it was devised as a method to stimulate sales. Later, as the wax-sealed package was introduced, a prize was given (more or less) with each package. Next, the prize was added into the package, but still not every package received a prize. It was not until the 1920s that 'a prize in every package' became a reality. Initially, the prizes were put in with the confection, but the company feared this might pose a problem, should it inadvertently be mistaken for the popcorn. To avoid this, the prize was put in a separate compartment and, finally, into its own protective wrapper. Thousands of prizes have been used over the years, and it is still true today that there is 'a prize in every package.' Prizes have ranged from the practical girl's bracelet and pencils to tricks, games, disguises, and stick-anywhere patches. To learn more about the subject, you'll want to read *Cracker Jack Toys, The Complete Unofficial Guide for Collectors*, and *Cracker Jack, The Unauthorized Guide to Advertising Collectibles*, both by our advisor, Larry White.

Advisor: Larry White (See Directory, Cracker Jack)

Airplane, plastic, on stand (put-together) **$6.75**

Badge, silver cast metal, 6-point star, multicolored CJ Police, 1931, 1¼" **$45.00**

Bank, tin, 3-D book form, red, green or black, Cracker Jack Bank, early, 2" **$325.00**

Baseball card, paper, 1914, 1 of 144, typical **$75.00**

Baseball players, plastic, 3-D, blue or gray team, 1948, 1½", ea...**$5.25**

Bike sticker, paper, series ID 1380, any **$2.50**

Book, paper, Twigg & Sprigg, Cracker Jack, 1930, mini **$110.00**

Bookmark, dog, rocket, etc, plastic, various colors, ea...........**$4.25**

Breakfast set, agateware in matchbox.................................**$45.00**

Candleholder, metal, single, gold color, ea **$2.50**

Charm, white metal, anchor...**$2.75**

Chicken figure, chenille **$15.00**

Circus wagon, tin, yellow, Cracker Jack Shows, series of 5, ea...**$195.00**

Clicker, tin, Noisy CJ Snapper, pear shape, aluminum, 1949.**$9.50**

Coin, Mystery Club, presidential, any of 22 ....**$3.50**

Comb, plastic, thick, marked, Canadian **$12.50**

Disguise, ears, paper, red (still in carrier), Cracker Jack, 1950, pr...**$22.00**

Eyeglasses, paper w/celluloid insert, Cracker Jack Wherever You Look **$75.00**

Figure, circus, plastic, stands on base, 1 of 12, Nosco, 1951-54...**$3.00**

Flip Action Movie, paper, various subjects, ea $17.50

Frog Chirper, metal, copyright 1946 Cloudcrest $40.00

Game, paper, Drawing Made Easy $27.50

Game, paper, Midget Auto Race, wheel spins, Cracker Jack, 1949, 3⅜" H $9.50

Globe, metal $57.00

Grandfather clock, tin, tall box shape, unmarked, 1947, 1¾"..$65.00

Helicopter, tin, yellow propeller, wood stick, unmarked, 1937, 2⅝" $45.00

License plate, paper, 1954, any of 50, ea $15.00

Lunch box, embossed tin, Cracker Jack, 1970s, 4x7x9" $30.00

Magic game book, paper, erasable slate, Cracker Jack, series of 13, 1946, ea $17.50

Palm puzzle, plastic, ball(s) roll into holes, sq, Cracker Jack, 1920s, ea $25.00

Pencil holder, paper, about 2x4" $90.00

Picture Panorama, any of 14, ea $15.50

Pistol, soft lead cast metal, inked, Cracker Jack on barrel, early, rare, 2⅛" $180.00

Pocket watch, tin, silver or gold, Cracker Jack as numerals, 1931, 1½" $25.00

Prized Pet, paper, any of 12 ....$.50

Sand toy pictures, paper, pours for action, series of 14, 1967, ea..$50.00

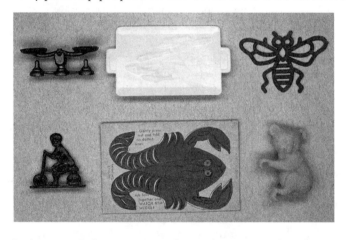

Scales, metal, $75.00; Tray, plastic, $11.00; Outline figure, plastic, $8.00; Stand-up boy on scooter, metal, $27.00; Lobster game, paper, $35.00; Koala bear, plastic, $8.00.
(Photo courtesy Larry White)

Serving tray, plastic, 5 fishes, thick, Canadian $10.00

Slate Fun, paper & plastic, B Series 77, any of 32, ea $2.50

Spinner, metal, You're It, finger pointing $9.50

Spinner, tin, wood stick, Fortune Teller Game, red, white & blue, Cracker Jack, 1½" $90.00

Standup, plastic, Indian, cowboy, etc, NOSCO, ea $2.00

Stickers, glow-in-the-dark, paper, any of 56, ea $1.75

Stud, metal, Cracker Jack Air Corps $24.50

Tennis racquet, metal, Dowst $3.00

Train, engine & tender, lithographed tin, Cracker Jack Line/512 ....$125.00

Train, tin, Lone Eagle Flyer engine, unmarked $95.00

Transfer, paper, iron-on, sports figure or patriotic, unmarked, 1939, ea $6.00

Trick mustache, paper punch-out card $13.50

Truck, lithographed tin, Express $65.00

Crackle Glass

At the height of productivity from the 1930s through the 1970s, nearly 500 companies created crackle glass. As pieces stayed in production for several years, dating an item may be difficult. Some colors, such as ruby red, amberina, cobalt, and cranberry, were more expensive to produce. Smoke gray was made for a short time, and because quantities are scarce, prices tend to be higher than on some of the other colors, amethyst, green, and amber included. Crackle glass is still being produced today by the Blenko Glass Company, and it is being imported from Taiwan and China as well.

See also Blenko.

Advisors: Stan and Arlene Weitman (See Directory, Crackle Glass)

Basket, blue, Kanawha, ca. 1957 – 1987, 3¾", from $55.00 to $85.00. (Photo courtesy Stan and Arlene Weitman)

Basket, clear lustre, braided handle, Westmoreland, 1920-24, 5", from $110 to $150.00

Candy dish, amberina, applied serpentine at bottom, scalloped top, Kanawha, 1957-87, 3", from $55 to $75.00

Cruet, blue, 3 balls on stopper, waisted w/slim neck, w/handle, Rainbow, 1940-60s, 6½", from $85 to........................$100.00

Cruet, orange, bell shaped, pulled-back handle, 2 clear balls on stopper, Rainbow, 1940-60s, 6¾", from $85 to $110.00

Cruet, rose crystal, bulbous, drop-over handle, w/stopper, unknown manufacturer, 4", from $100 to $125.00

Cup, light sea green, wide, low ring drop-over handle, unknown manufacturer, 2½", from $40 to $45.00

Decanter, captain's; ruby, Pilgrim, 1949-69, 8x10", from $250 to...$350.00

Decanter, ruby, flared bottom, flame-shaped stopper, Pilgrim, 1947-67, 15½", from $225 to...$250.00

Decanter, sea green, flame-shaped stopper same length as body, Rainbow, 1940-60s, 12½", from $200 to....................$250.00

Decanter, topaz, bulbous, lg teardrop stopper, Blenko, 1963, 8¾",
from $125 to **$150.00**

Fruit, apple, ruby w/green stem, Viking, 1960-70s, 4¼", from $100
to **$125.00**

Glass, drinking; ruby, pinched, Hamon, 1940-70s, 6", from $85 to.. **$100.00**

Ladle, crystal w/amethyst hook handle, Blenko, 1950s, 15" L, from
$200 to **$300.00**

Pitcher, amberina, slim & high waisted, drop-over handle, Kanawha,
1957-87, 8¼", from $90 to..................................**$110.00**

Pitcher, amethyst, pulled-back handle, waisted, Hamon, 1940-66,
5¼", from $70 to...**$80.00**

Pitcher, blue/green, drop-over handle, hourglass shape, Rainbow,
1950s, 5¼", from $60 to **$65.00**

Pitcher, cream, drop-over handle, waisted, scalloped rim, Rainbow,
1940-60s, 5", from $55 to..................................**$60.00**

Pitcher, crystal w/enameled fish & branches, mold blown, Moser,
1890s, 8", from $500 to **$600.00**

Pitcher, crystal w/pink drop-over handle & rosette, unknown manufacturer, 8", from $150 to.................................**$175.00**

Pitcher, emerald green, waisted w/slim neck, drop-over handle,
unknown manufacturer, 5½", from $45 to **$55.00**

Pitcher, Lemon Lime w/opalescent top, clear drop-over handle,
Pilgrim, 1949-69, 5¼", from $65 to.........................**$70.00**

Pitcher, mini; amberina, pulled-back handle, Kanawha, 1957-87,
3¼", from $45 to...**$55.00**

Pitcher, mini; blue, drop-over handle, Rainbow, 1940-60s, 3", from
$40 to...**$50.00**

Pitcher, mini; cranberry, clear drop-over handle, waisted, Kanawha,
1957-87, 4½", from $75 to..................................**$100.00**

Pitcher, mini; green satin, high-waisted, pulled-back handle,
Kanawha, 1957-87, 4¼", from $60 to **$65.00**

Pitcher, mini; multicolored, drop-over handle, English, 4½", from
$150 to..**$250.00**

Pitcher, mini; tangerine, clear drop-over handle, waisted, Pilgrim,
1949-69, 3¾", from $50 to..................................**$55.00**

Pitcher, mini; topaz, clear shaped handle & frilled top, Pilgrim,
1949-69, 3½", from $50 to..................................**$55.00**

Pitcher, olive green, clear drop-over handle, waisted w/slim neck,
Pilgrim, 1949-69, 5", from $40 to..........................**$50.00**

Pitcher, sea green, pulled-back handle, Stockholms Blasbruk, 4¾",
from $75 to **$100.00**

Pitcher, topaz, flared top, drop-over handle, Bischoff, 1940-63, 11",
from $110 to **$125.00**

Pitcher, water; amber w/blue drop-over handle, blue finial on amber
lid, unknown manufacturer, 12", from $200 to **$300.00**

Pitcher, yellow vaseline, straight sides, drop-over handle, Pilgrim,
1949-69, 7¼", from $80 to..................................**$90.00**

Syrup pitcher, amethyst, pulled-back handle, Kanawha, 1957-87, 6",
from $85 to **$110.00**

Vase, amberina, cylinder shape, unknown manufacturer, 13", from
$125 to..**$150.00**

Vase, amethyst, low waisted, ruffled scalloped rim, Bischoff, 1940-
63, 7½", from $175 to.......................................**$200.00**

Vase, amethyst, waisted w/flared rim, Blenko, 1960s, 4¾", from $85
to **$95.00**

Vase, blue, bulbous, high waist, applied serpentine at short neck,
Rainbow, 1940-60s, 5½", from $65 to.........................**$75.00**

Vase, blue, straight sides, ruffled scalloped top, Bischoff, 1940-63,
10½", from $135 to..**$175.00**

Vase, blue w/applied serpentine at waist, scalloped rim, Pilgrim,
1949-69, 3½", from $50 to...................................**$55.00**

Vase, cranberry, low waisted, scalloped rim, Rainbow, 1940-60s,
5¼", from $80 to..**$85.00**

Vase, crystal, straight sides w/ruffled rim, Bischoff, 5½", from $60
to **$70.00**

Vase, crystal w/applied blue rosettes, flared to top, Blenko, 1940-50s,
7", from $110 to..**$150.00**

Vase, crystal w/green vaseline base, Fry, 1930, 5", from $75 to ..**$100.00**

Vase, green & blue tones, sterling silver rim, waisted, Weiz, 1930,
from $425 to **$525.00**

Vase, lemon lime, applied serpentine at slim neck, Pilgrim, 1949-69,
5", from $65 to...**$75.00**

Vase, orange, ruffled scalloped rim, footed, Blenko, 1940-50s, 7",
from $145 to **$175.00**

Vase, pinched double neck, Blenko, 1947-50s, 4", from $85 to...**$110.00**

Vase, sea green, 2 clear shaped handles, high waisted, Blenko, 1940-
50s, 7½", from $100 to **$115.00**

Vase, smoke gray, Pilgrim, ca. 1949 – 1969, 11", from $100.00 to $125.00. (Photo courtesy Stan and Arlene Weitman)

Cuff Links

Cuff link collecting continues to be one of the fastest growing hobbies. Few collectibles are as affordable, available, and easy to store. Cuff links can often be found at garage sales, thrift shops, and flea markets for reasonable prices.

People collect cuff links for many reasons. Besides being a functional and interesting wearable, cuff links are educational. The design, shape, size, and materials used often relate to events, places, and products, and they typically reflect the period of their manufacture: examples are Art Deco, Victorian, Art Nouveau, and Modern, etc. They offer the chance for the 'big find' which appeals to all collectors. Sometimes pairs purchased for small amounts turn out to be worth substantial sums.

Unless otherwise noted, the following listings apply to cuff links in excellent to mint condition. The higher end of the suggested range of values represents average retail prices asked in antique shops.

Advisor: Gene Klompus (See Directory, Cuff Links)

Club: The National Cuff Link Society
Newsletter: *The Link*
Eugene R. Klompus
P.O. Box 5970
Vernon Hills, IL 60061
Phone: 847-816-0035; fax: 847-816-7466
genek@justcufflinks.com
www.justcufflinks.com

Accordion shape w/round & channel-cut rhinestones on silver-tone, Pell, 1⅜" sq..**$55.00**
Alaska-Yukon-Pacific Exposition of 1909, sterling silver w/multicolored enameling, oval **$100.00**
Art Deco diamond shape, chrome w/red & black enameling in geometric design, Patent 355441, ⅞x½" **$95.00**
Art Deco KUM-A-Part, blue & black enamel, ...Made in USA B&W Co PAT'D 1923, ½" dia **$100.00**
Art Deco ovals, 18k white gold, intricate etching on front, Belais, 5.1 grams, ⅝x½" **$91.00**
Asian lady, ivory resin w/gold-tone finish, dangling hoop earrings, faux pearl under chin, 1½x1" **$105.00**
Baroque gray pearls w/sm diamond centers, 14k white gold, 1x½" **$200.00**
Basket-weave sqs, openwork, 18k yellow gold, 13 grams, ¾". **$265.00**
Black enamel surrounding intricate engraved design, 14k yellow gold, 9.2 grams, ½" dia...**$230.00**
Black onyx w/intricate gold borders, concave center, 14k yellow gold, ½" sq..**$132.00**
Black star sapphire bezel set in center of linen-textured 18k yellow gold, 10.2 grams, ⅞"..**$265.00**
Blue-striped agate stone, silver-tone metal, oval **$93.00**

Boat motors, propellers turn, chromium, Swank, $35.00.

Cameo of Roman soldier, carved lava center, 12k gold-filled body & findings, 1x¾"..**$90.00**

Carved green jade flowers, 10k yellow gold, ⅞" **$90.00**
Carved ivory, long tooth shapes w/14k yellow gold caps, original box, 7.3 grams, ⅞"...**$110.00**

Castles, base metal, 1955, $60.00. (Photo courtesy Gene Klompus)

CBS RADIO Spot Sales, 10k yellow gold, 6.8 grams, ¾x1".**$110.00**
Chinese character & dragon on on reticulated disk, detailed, 14k yellow gold, ⅝" dia **$225.00**
Chinese character for good luck, 14k yellow gold, ¾" sq ...**$210.00**
Circles, decorated w/half-circle reflective sculpted lines, 14k gold, 10.7 grams, ¾"..**$170.00**
Coin, 10k yellow gold, lady's profile, ca 1920-30s, 3.5 grams, ½" dia...**$325.00**
Comedy & Tragedy Masks, 14k yellow gold, 13 grams......**$465.00**
Cylinder shape, 18k yellow gold w/18k yellow gold stripes, Adler, ¾"...**$315.00**
Derringers, detailed hand-carved ivory w/gold-tone accents on front, Swank, ⅞x1¼" **$225.00**
Floral, hand-painted porcelain, gold-leaf frame, 1⅛x⅞" **$70.00**
Folk art, star in center, black, red & white enameling w/gold-tone frame, ½" dia **$50.00**
Football shapes, linen-textured 14k yellow gold, ea w/3 diamonds on white gold bar in center, 9.4 grams, ⅞" **$115.00**
Four-leaf clovers, sterling silver, 925 Denmark, 1" **$175.00**
Gold (14k) circles surrounded by 22 channel cut red garnets, Lucien Piccard, 11 grams, ¾" dia **$255.00**
Golden citrine guilloche enamel, triangular, H-925S, Norway, ¾" **$110.00**
Goldminers, hand-carved ivory w/genuine gold flakes in pans, detailed, gold-tone backings, 1x⅝".............................**$200.00**
Hexagons, 10k yellow gold, engraved circular design, 3.2 grams, ½" dia...**$110.00**
Hexagons, 10k yellow gold w/blue enamel accents, marked F in a shield, 5.1 grams, ½"..**$100.00**
Horse heads, blue stone, silver-tone metal finish, gold-tone bridle accent, 1x½" **$85.00**
Ivory, dragonfly carved in relief w/etching, gold-tone metal, Hong Kong, 1¾x¾" **$85.00**
Mickey Mouse, sterling silver, Walt Disney Productions, 1958 ..**$170.00**
Mint green grid-like enamel, enamel & sterling silver frame, Krementz, ½" sq **$150.00**
Moon-shaped sapphires atop 14k white gold rectangles, Deco style, 13.8 grams, ½x¾" **$148.00**
Mother-of-pearl surrounded by blue enamel, gold accent in center, 18k yellow gold, Deco style, ⅜" dia **$150.00**

Octagons, Deco style, diamond chip in center, 14k white gold...**$90.00**
Octagons, red & gray geometric enameling on gold-tone, #355441, ¾x⅜" ... **$88.00**
Octagons w/scrolling in center, sterling silver, Georg Jensen, Gi-830S Denmark... **$465.00**
Opaque rose-colored stones in sterling silver, Handmade Sterling BrdrBj Denmark, 1" sq ... **$150.00**
Ovals, blue guilloche enamel surrounded by black enamel, Hestenes #925, Norway, ¾x½" ... **$165.00**
Pansies, hand-painted enamel, faux pearl in center, silver-tone, 1⅛" dia... **$80.00**
Peace signs, bright silver-tone, ¾" thick (closed), 1⅛" dia.... **$52.00**
Pentagrams, aqua guilloche enamel on sterling silver, red trim, round ... **$115.00**
Sea horses, hand-painted porcelain w/gold-tone accents on silver, Japan, ⅞x⅝"... **$125.00**
Ship's wheels, compass in center, silver-plated finish, ¾" **$92.00**
Thermometers (working), degrees at top on white background, Made in USA, ⅞" dia ... **$85.00**
Victorian lady, hand-carved ivory set in 14k yellow gold center, gold-plated finding, 1x¾" ... **$115.00**
Western Maryland Railway on rectangles, 14k yellow gold, ⅞x½" ... **$170.00**

Cups and Saucers

Lovely cups and saucers are often available at garage sales and flea markets, and prices are generally quite reasonable. If limited space is a consideration, you might enjoy starting a collection, since they're easy to display en masse on a shelf or one at a time as a romantic accent on a coffee table. English manufacturers have produced endless bone china cups and saucers that are both decorative and functional. American manufactureres were just about as prolific as were the Japanese. Collecting examples from many companies and countries is a wonderful way to study the various ceramic manufacturers. Our advisors have written *Collectible Cups and Saucers, Identification and Values, Books I, II,* and *III* (Collector Books), with hundreds of color photos organized by six collectible categories: cabinet cups, nineteenth and twentiety century dinnerware, English tablewares, miniatures, Japanese, and glass cups and saucers.

Advisors: Jim and Susan Harran (See Directory, Cups and Saucers)

Chocolate, green leaves form band at rim, gold trim, Limoges, 1914-32, from $35 to ... **$45.00**
Coffee, Full Green Vine Wreath pattern w/gilt, swan handle, Meissen, 1930s, 2¾x3¼", 6", from $125 to... **$150.00**
Coffee, gold flowers & scrolls, etched gold band on rim, pedestal cup w/gilt foot, Hutschenreuther, 1920-67, from $55 to..... **$65.00**
Coffee, ornate white & gilt decoration on green, pedestal cup w/gold interior, 2¼x3", 4¾", from $125 to ... **$150.00**
Coffee, ornate white decor on green w/gold, Hutschenreuther, 1920-67, 2¼x3", 4¾", from $125 to... **$150.00**
Coffee, Regency pattern, can cup, Copeland Spode, 1950-60s, 2½", 5", from $75 to... **$95.00**
Coffee, white w/gold trim, lion transfer on straight-sided cup, Germany, 1930-40s, from $25 to ... **$35.00**
Cream soup, much gilt on red, floral transfer inside flared cup, 2 wing-shaped handles, Rosenthal, 1949-54, from $75 to......... **$100.00**
Demitasse, child's, Thousand Faces pattern, can cup w/triangle handle, Takito, 1880-1948, from $60 to... **$70.00**
Demitasse, cobalt blue w/gilt flowers, tapered cup, Bareuther & Co, 1930-50s, from $40 to... **$55.00**
Demitasse, courting scene transfers, flared can cup w/4 gilt curved feet, bird handle, Retch & Co, ca 1953-present... **$55.00**
Demitasse, heavy silver overlay on red, Haviland, 1939-50s, 2½x1¾", 4⅔", from $100 to... **$125.00**
Demitasse, heavy silver overlay on turquoise, footed, Hutschenreuther, 1950s, 1¾x2¾", 4½", from $125 to ... **$150.00**
Demitasse, ivory w/pale floral transfer, tapered cup, Krautheim & Adelberg, ca 1922-45, from $30 to... **$40.00**
Demitasse, mixed floral decor inside & outside, Bute shape cup w/ loop handle, Sarreguemines, 1920s, from $40 to **$55.00**
Demitasse, ornate etched gold inside & out, footed cup, Lenox, 1930-40s, 2½x2¼", 4¾", from $45 to ... **$60.00**
Demitasse, parrot & flowers on white w/gold at rim, straight-sided cup w/ring handle, Scammell China, 1926-54, $40 to .. **$50.00**
Demitasse, purple w/medallion of hand-painted birds, w/gilt, can cup w/sq handle, Vienna Porcelain, 1923-60s, $125 to **$150.00**
Demitasse, Shamrock, Belleek, 1965-80, from $50 to.......... **$60.00**
Miniature coffee, Mandalay pattern, Masons, ca 1970, 1x1⅓", 2½", from $50 to ... **$75.00**
Miniature teacup, brown floral transfer on white, flared cup, Crown Staffordshire, ⅞", 2½", from $100 to... **$125.00**
Miniature teacup, gilt leaves on black, flared cup, Leneige, ca 1930, from $60 to ... **$90.00**
Miniature teacup, Indian Tree pattern, round cup, Coalport, ca 1960-70, from $75 to ... **$100.00**
Teacup, autumn floral transfer, swirled cup, angular handle, Delphine Bone China, 1930-46, from $25 to ... **$30.00**
Teacup, band of gilt filigree design, multicolored flowers inside waisted cup, footed, Tirschenreuth, 1969-present **$42.00**
Teacup, camel scenic on bright orange, Noritake, ca 1911+, from $35 to ... **$45.00**
Teacup, cartouches of roses on robin's egg blue, footed cup, Furstenberg, ca 1950s, from $40 to ... **$50.00**
Teacup, gold on ivory, tapered cup w/ruffled foot & ornate handle, Edelstein Porcelain Factory, 1940s, from $25 to **$30.00**
Teacup, hand-painted magenta flowers w/gilt, footed cup w/wish-bone handle, Herend, ca 1941, from $75 to.............. **$100.00**
Teacup, Imari pattern, slightly flared cup w/fat loop handle, Aynsley, 1930s, from $50 to ... **$75.00**
Teacup, Nouveau poppies, 4-paneled/waisted cup, loop handle, thumb rest, Limoges, 1900-41, from $50 to ... **$60.00**
Teacup, Olde Avesbury pattern in gold, Royal Crown Derby, ca 1969, from $50 to ... **$60.00**
Teacup, Oriental bird design on white w/green floral band, Cauldon, ca 1905-20, from $60 to... **$75.00**
Teacup, red band, floral bouquet w/enamel center, much gold, footed cup, Rosenthal, 1949-55, from $50 to ... **$60.00**
Teacup, Windsor Castle on cobalt blue w/gilt, footed cup, Aynsley, ca 1930s, from $150 to... **$175.00**

Teacup, yellow w/violets inside, 12 flutes, Adderleys Ltd, ca 1962, from $35 to $40.00

Coffee, Deco lady, Goebel, ca. 1935 – 1937, from $75.00 to $85.00. (Photo description Jim and Susan Harran)

Czechoslovakian Glass and Ceramics

Established as a country in 1918, Czechoslovakia is rich in the natural resources needed for production of glassware as well as pottery. Over the years it has produced vast amounts of both. Anywhere you go, from flea markets to fine antique shops, you'll find several examples of their lovely pressed and cut glass scent bottles, Deco vases, lamps, kitchenware, tableware, and figurines.

More than 35 marks have been recorded; some are ink stamped, some etched, and some molded in. Paper labels have also been used.

Club: Czechoslovakian Collectors Guild International
P.O. Box 901395
Kansas City, MO 64190
888-910-0988
cgi@kc.net

Ceramics

Basket, Deco flowers on cream, orange trim at handle & rim, ca 1930s, 4½x6¾x5⅜" $55.00

Candy dish, nude child holds 2 baskets, gold & cobalt trim, 6½x5" $65.00

Creamer, moose head, airbrushed brown on white w/green limb handle, 4½" $42.50

Creamer, nautilus shell, white lustre w/red coral-like handle, 5x6" $40.00

Figurine, draped nude petting fawn, hand-painted details, #14080IV in circle mark, 16½x8" dia..........................$315.00

Flower holder/vase, bird in fork of tree, 2 openings, #45, 5½x3" $65.00

Flower holder/vase, bird on stump, 2 openings, #32, 4¾" ...$50.00

Flower holder/vase, bird on stump w/3 openings, blue & yellow lustre w/purple on sweeping tail, #50, 5¾x2½" $35.00

Flower holder/vase, raven perched on branch of double tree trunk, lattice effect in relief on base, 11¾x8"..........................$265.00

Flower holder/vase, woodpecker on side of stump w/5 openings, #58, 5½x3" $110.00

Lamp base, Deco flowers on orange, slim lathe-turned look w/flared base, 10⅛x5" $45.00

Liquor set, elephant figural, decanter and six glasses inside, 10½", $275.00. (Photo courtesy neatstuffdave)

Pitcher, bird form, orange & black, Deco-style, 9x8"..........$60.00

Pitcher, Deco geometrics in blue & gold on cream, bulbous, 6x7¼" $75.00

Pitcher, geometrics on tan lustre, 3x2⅜" $25.00

Plate, hand-painted pastel flowers on white, Bohemia Ceramic Works, early 1900s, 7"..$30.00

Reamer, Deco floral on cream w/orange trim, 2-pc, #11026, 6½x5½" $95.00

Salt box, Salt in brown letters on white, geometric florals, wooden lid, Karlsbad..., #1688, 6¼x5¾x4½" $42.50

Salt cellars, peach form, stem finial, ⅝", set of 4 ....$45.00

Toby jug, man seated, blue coat, yellow hat, red pants, 5¾"..$45.00

Vase, Deco florals on gourd shape, Amphora mark, 1918-39, 8¼x5½" $245.00

Vase, double-bud; resembles section of fence, white gloss, Robrecht mark, ca 1900..$70.00

Vase, mixed flowers on earthy brown, green embossed cylinder top w/angle handles, some crazing, 6⅞x3⅜" $50.00

Wall pocket, bird perched atop apples among leaves, #5860A $55.00

Wall pocket, bird perched in fork of tree trunk, earthy yellow & brown tones, 5¼" $30.00

Glassware

Candlesticks/bud vases, orange w/varicolored swirls at base & foot, hand blown, 1930s, 10½", pr $50.00

Flower frog, yellow & white variegated w/metal & wire-work top, 5x5" $60.00

Lamp shade, tortoise-shell mottle, globular, 3" fitter, 6" dia. $85.00

Perfume bottle, blue, starburst pattern w/fan-shaped stopper, 4¾x4" $75.00

Perfume bottle, clear with metal filigree overlay accented with green and blue jewels, inner glass stopper with long dauber, 2", $175.00. (Photo courtesy Monsen & Baer)

Perfume bottle, pink, Art Deco-style Rialto form, stopper w/center cutout, 7¼" **$180.00**

Perfume bottle, violet with intaglio abstracts, stopper molded with a dancer, dauber lacking, 4¾", $100.00. (Photo courtesy Monsen & Baer)

Powder jar, blue, pressed pattern, ca 1930, 2¾x3¼" **$30.00**
Vase, birds & flowers painted on orange, black trim at vase & foot, 6½x2⅜" **$50.00**
Vase, blue cased in white, black trim on flat rim, footed, 1930s, 7" **$55.00**
Vase, blue fan form w/yellow threading at top, acid mark, 9⅝x8¼" **$75.00**
Vase, blue opaque w/black serpentine, black trim at ruffled rim, pedestal foot, 9¼x4⅜" **$140.00**
Vase, bud; red cased w/hand-painted flowers & leaves, flared foot w/black trim **$45.00**
Vase, exotic bird on branch, multicolor w/silver & gold on black glass, 13¼" **$225.00**
Vase, green stripes w/silver mica, white cased, black trim on ruffled rim, footed, ca 1920, 9½" **$175.00**
Vase, marbleized pink to white w/blue overlay at base & foot, hand blown, 1950s-60s, 9½x3" **$125.00**

Vase, med gray-brown cased, orange rigaree handles, globular, 6½x7" **$75.00**
Vase, multicolor mottle in autumnal tones, w/silver mica, sm can neck, bulbous body, 4x4½" **$45.00**
Vase, orange & black swirls, cased in white, shaped neck, bulbous body, 10x7" **$125.00**
Vase, orange & black variegated w/3 black buttress feet, ca 1930s, 8⅛" **$95.00**
Vase, orange w/varigated mottle at base, 5 stacked segments in Deco style, footed, ca 1925, 9x4" **$115.00**
Vase, orange w/3 cobalt handles, cobalt rim at top, cylindrical w/bulbous bottom, 7½" **$58.00**

Dakin

Dakin has been in the toy-making business since the 1950s and has made several lines of stuffed and vinyl dolls and animals, and collectors love 'em all. We list a variety of Dakin products below. But the Dakins that garner the most interest are the licensed characters and advertising figures made from 1968 through the 1970s. Originally there were seven Warner Brothers characters, each with a hard plastic body and a soft vinyl head, all under 10" tall. The line was very successful and eventually expanded to include more than 50 cartoon characters and several more that were advertising related. In addition to the figures, there are banks that were made in two sizes. Some Dakins are quite scarce and may sell for over $100.00, though most will be in the $30.00 to $60.00 range. Dakin is now owned by Applause, Inc. Condition is very important, and if you find one still in the original box, add about 50% to its value. Figures in the colorful 'Cartoon Theatre' boxes command higher prices than those that came in a clear plastic bag or package (MIP). For more information we recommend *Schroeder's Collectible Toys, Antique to Modern*, published by Collector Books.

Foghorn Leghorn, 1970s, 8½", $55.00.

Bugs Bunny, stuffed cloth figure, as Uncle Sam, 1976, 11", NM **$25.00**

Bugs Bunny, vinyl, Happy Birthday, Goofy Gram, 1971, 12", NM **$38.00**

Bugs Bunny, vinyl figure, squeeze toy, waving, glancing eyes, orange gloves, 1970s, 7", NM+ **$18.00**

Bullwinkle, stuffed plush figure, B on red sweater, felt antlers, w/tag, 1978, 12", M...**$45.00**

Daffy Duck, vinyl figure, standing w/legs together & feet spread, hand on hip, 1960-70s, 9", NM **$20.00**

Elroy (Jetsons), stuffed cloth figure, printed features, fuzzy yellow hair & beanie, 1986, 12", EX+ **$12.00**

Garfield, stuffed plush figure, hugging-capable hands/feet, Mom Always Liked Me Best, 1980s, 4", NM........................**$12.00**

Hoppy (Flintstones), vinyl figure, jointed, scarce, MIP (The Flintstones on header card) **$150.00**

Laurel & Hardy, either character, vinyl, 1970s, 5½", EX, ea **$30.00**

Laurel & Hardy, vinyl figure, cloth clothing, either character, w/hang tags, 1970s, 8", MIP, ea **$50.00**

Laurel & Hardy, vinyl figure, squeeze toy, either character, 1970s, 5½", EX, ea...**$30.00**

Mighty Mouse, vinyl figure, 1978, MIP (Fun Farm) **$125.00**

Odie, stuffed plush figure, Fun Farm series, 1983, 14", NM+ .. **$12.00**

Olive Oyl, vinyl figure, jointed, 1970s, 7", NRFB (Cartoon Theater box) **$40.00**

Pepe Le Pew, stuffed vinyl figure, You're a Real Stinker on base, 1971, 9", MIP **$75.00**

Pink Panther, vinyl figure, jointed arms, legs together, 2-tone pink, 1971, 8", NM...**$28.00**

Popeye, vinyl figure, jointed head & arms, cloth shirt, holding spinach can, 1970s, 8½", NM+.......................................**$25.00**

Porky Pig, bank, standing w/1 arm bent up & 1 arm down, legs together, 6½", NM **$20.00**

Road Runner, PVC figure, 1970s, 4½", EX **$10.00**

Road Runner, vinyl figure, standing w/legs together, 1968, 9", NM **$25.00**

Rocky the Squirrel, vinyl figure, jointed, 1970s, 6½", MIB (Cartoon Theater box) **$75.00**

Scooby Doo, figure, stuffed ribbed cloth, 1979, 8", NM **$15.00**

Scooby Doo, vinyl figure, jointed, 1980, 6x6", NM+ **$75.00**

Speedy Gonzales, 1968, 7½", $30.00.

Spitballs (Ren & Stempy), soft rubber figure, Ren holding throat as if choking, eyes bulging, 1992, 5", NM+.....................**$12.00**

Tasmanian Devil, bank, standing w/hands clasped in front, closed-mouth smile, 5", NM+ **$75.00**

Tweety Bird, vinyl, swivel head & feet, 1969, 6", NM.........**$25.00**

Tweety Bird, vinyl figure, squeeze toy, standing w/hands on tummy, 1970s, 5", NM **$20.00**

Yosemite Sam, vinyl figure, cloth outfit, red fuzzy beard, black plastic hat, 1968, 7½", NM...**$20.00**

Decanters

The first company to make figural ceramic decanters was the James Beam Distilling Company. Until mid-1992 they produced hundreds of varieties in their own US-based china factory. They first issued their bottles in the mid-'50s, and over the course of the next 25 years, more than 20 other companies followed their example. Among the more prominent of these were Brooks, Hoffman, Lionstone, McCormick, Old Commonwealth, Ski Country, and Wild Turkey. In 1975, Beam introduced the 'Wheel Series,' cars, trains, and fire engines with wheels that actually revolved. The popularity of this series resulted in a heightened interest in decanter collecting.

There are various sizes. The smallest (called miniatures) hold two ounces, and there are some that hold a gallon! A full decanter is worth no more than an empty one, and the absence of the tax stamp doesn't lower its value either. Just be sure that all the labels are intact and that there are no cracks or chips. You might want to empty your decanters as a safety precaution (many collectors do) rather than risk the possibility of the inner glaze breaking down and allowing the contents to leak into the porous ceramic body.

All of the decanters we've listed are fifths unless we've specified 'miniature' within the description.

See also Elvis Presley Collectibles.

Advisor: Roy Willis (See Directory Decanters)

Beam, #3 Telephone, 1928 French Cradle, 1979, $25.00.

ASI, Cadillac, 1903, white, 1979 ....**$72.00**

ASI, Stanley Steamer, 1911, black, 1981 ....**$78.00**

ASI, World's Greatest Hunter, 1979......................$38.00

Beam, Animal, Appaloosa Horse, 1974...................$16.00

Beam, Animal, Armadillo, 1981.............................$18.00

Beam, Animal, Harp Seals, 1986 ....$19.00

Beam, Bird, Bluejay, 1969.....................................$9.00

Beam, Bird, Woodpecker, 1969...............................$9.00

Beam, Chevrolet, 1957 Bel Air Hardtop, Harbor Blue, Pennsylvania, 1987 ....$85.00

Beam, Chevrolet, 1968 Corvette, International Blue, 1992 .$75.00

Beam, Chevrolet, 1969 Camaro, Fathom Green, 1988 ......**$172.00**

Beam, Chevrolet, 1984 Corvette, red, 1988.....................$85.00

Beam, Circus Wagon, 1979....................................$30.00

Beam, Fire Department, Mack 1917 Bulldog Fire Truck, 1982...**$140.00**

Beam, Fish, Bluegill, 1974 ....$28.00

Beam, Fish, Rainbow Trout, 1975..........................$25.00

Beam, Ford, Model A Coupe, olive green, 1980 ....$60.00

Beam, Ford, 1964 Mustang, red, 1985.......................**$125.00**

Beam, General Train, Flat Car, 1988........................$95.00

Beam, Glass, Beatty Burro Race, 1970 ....$10.00

Beam, Glass, Riverside Centennial, 1970 ....$9.00

Beam, Golf, Bing Crosby 29th, 1970.......................$17.00

Beam, Golf, PGA, 1971 ....$17.00

Beam, Grant Train, Passenger Car, 1981 ....$60.00

Beam, People, American Cowboy, 1981 ....$20.00

Beam, People, General Stark, 1972 ....$15.00

Beam, People, Hannah Dustin, 1973.......................$45.00

Beam, People, Thomas Edison, Light Bulb, 1979 ....$16.00

Beam, Police Department, Chevrolet State Trooper Car, white, 1992 ....$50.00

Beam, Sports, Chicago Cubs, Baseball, 1985 ....**$120.00**

Beam, Sports, Indianapolis 500, 1970.....................$12.00

Beam, Sports, Rocky Marciano, Boxing, 1973 ....$35.00

Beam, States, Colorado, 1959 ....$22.00

Beam, States, Michigan, 1967.................................$48.00

Beam, States, Wyoming, 1965 ....$46.00

Beam, Volkswagen, red, 1973 ....$75.00

Brooks, Buffalo Hunter, 1971 ....$9.00

Brooks, Cable Car, green, 1968..............................$7.00

Brooks, Canadian Honker, 1975 ....$21.00

Brooks, Clown Bust #1, Smiley, 1979 ....$32.00

Brooks, Quail, 1970...$12.00

Brooks, Snowmobile, 1972 ....$15.00

Brooks, Telephone, 1971.....................................$18.00

Brooks, VFW, Illinois #1, 1982..............................$24.00

Brooks, White-Tail Deer, 1974 ....$18.00

Brooks, Winston Churchill, 1969 ....$5.00

Cyrus Noble, Bear & Cubs, mini, 1980....................$18.00

Cyrus Noble, Carousel, White Charger, 1979...............$55.00

Cyrus Noble, Gambler, 1974 ....$50.00

Cyrus Noble, Mountain Sheep, mini, 1979 ....$15.00

Cyrus Noble, Music Man, 1977.............................$35.00

Cyrus Noble, Whiskey Drummer, mini, 1977 ....$19.00

Ducks Unlimited, #1, Mallard, 1974 ....$40.00

Ducks Unlimited, #5, Canvasback Drake, 1979 ....$47.00

Ducks Unlimited, #11, Pintail Pair, 1985 ....$65.00

Ducks Unlimited, #21, Harlequin Duck, mini, 1994 ....$49.00

Dugs Nevada, Dollhouse, 1982................................$24.00

Dugs Nevada, Kit Kat Ranch, 1984..........................$135.00

Dugs Nevada, Patrcia's Hacienda, 1981...................$25.00

Dugs Nevada, Valley of the Dolls, 1988....................$50.00

Famous First, Centurion, 1969 ....$28.00

Famous First, Coffee Mill, orange, 1976...................$35.00

Famous First, Corvette, 1963 Stingray, 200 ml, 1979.........$33.00

Famous First, Ferrari, yellow, 1975 ....$50.00

Famous First, Liberty Bell, mini, 1976......................$9.00

Famous First, Phonograph, mini, 1973....................$21.00

Famous First, Spirit of St Louis, gold, 1977 ....**$145.00**

Famous First, Walrus w/Baby, mini, 1981................$35.00

Famoust First, Bear w/Baby, mini, 1981 ....$35.00

Garnier, Cardinal, 1969 ....$15.00

Garnier, Eiffel Tower, 1968 ....$35.00

Garnier, Monmarte, 1960 ....$10.00

Garnier, Woodcocks, 1972 ....$18.00

Garnier, 1911 Renault, 1969 ....$25.00

Granadier, General Robert E Lee, 1976 ....$39.00

Grenadier, African Rifle Corps Soldier, 1970 ....$35.00

Grenadier, American Saddle Bred Horse, 1978 ....$49.00

Grenadier, Count Pulaski, 1978.............................$55.00

Grenadier, Texas Ranger, mini, 1979.......................$15.00

Hoffman, Buffalo Man, 1976 ....$45.00

Hoffman, Cheerleader, topless, 1979 ....$95.00

Hoffman, Civil War Colt Pistol, mini, 1975...............$17.00

Hoffman, Cowboy & Puma, gold, 1978.....................**$300.00**

Hoffman, Golden Eye Decoy, mini, 1978..................$15.00

Hoffman, Johncock #20 Racecar, 1974.....................$65.00

Hoffman, Mallards, Closed Wing, 1982....................$24.00

Hoffman, Mr Lucky, Cobbler, 1973 ....$26.00

Hoffman, Mr Lucky, Sandman, mini, 1974 ....$15.00

Hoffman, Mr Lucky Series #2, Saxophonist, mini, 1975 .....$15.00

Hoffman, Mr Lucky Series #3, Bartender, 1975 ....$36.00

Hoffman, Mr Lucky Series #4, Carpenter, 1979 ....$32.00

Hoffman, Mr. Lucky Series #4, Plumber, 1978, $30.00.

Hoffman, Mr Lucky Series #5, Farmer, 1980......................$29.00

Hoffman, Quarter Horse, mini, 1979 .... $17.00
Hoffman, Shetland Pony, mini, 1979 .... $17.00
Hoffman, Terry Tiger, 50 ml, 1981 .... $15.00
Hoffman, Wolf & Raccoon, mini, 1978 .... $15.00
Kontinental, Dentist, 1978 .... $31.00
Kontinental, Gunsmith, 1977 .... $28.00
Kontinental, Saddle Maker, 1977 .... $28.00
Kontinental, Viking Lief Erickson, 1981 .... $55.00
Lionstone, Bartender, 1969 .... $30.00
Lionstone, Blacksmith, 1973 .... $29.00
Lionstone, Corvette, 1¾-liter, 1984 .... $100.00
Lionstone, Eastern Buebird, 1972 .... $24.00
Lionstone, Fireman, Down Pole, 1975 .... $100.00
Lionstone, Fireman, Red Hat, 1972 .... $98.00

Lionstone, Molly Brown, Old West Series, 1973, $22.00.

Lionstone, Monkey Business Clown, 1978 .... $41.00
Lionstone, Pheasant, 1977 .... $55.00
Lionstone, Riverboat Captain, 1969 .... $25.00
Lionstone, Shamrock, 1983 .... $35.00
Lionstone, Stutz Bearcat, mini, 1978 .... $29.00
Lionstone, Tattooed Lady, 1973 .... $25.00
Lionstone, Timekeeper, 1974 .... $32.00
Lionstone, Woodpecker, 1975 .... $29.00
Lionstone, Woodworker, 1974 .... $25.00
McCormick, Auburn War Eagles, 1972 .... $65.00
McCormick, Bat Masterson, 1972 .... $32.00
McCormick, Ben Franklin, 1975 .... $25.00
McCormick, Betsy Ross, 1975 .... $25.00
McCormick, Cable Car, 1983 .... $29.00
McCormick, California Bears, 1972 .... $65.00
McCormick, Canada Goose, 1984 .... $39.00
McCormick, Cuckoo Clock, 1971 .... $30.00
McCormick, Daniel Boone, 1975 .... $25.00
McCormick, Dune Buggy, 1976 .... $38.00
McCormick, Elvis Bust, 1978 .... $65.00

McCormick, Hank Williams Jr, 1980 .... $95.00
McCormick, Henry Ford, 1977 .... $29.00
McCormick, Hereford Bull, 1972 .... $35.00
McCormick, Jeb Stuart, 1976 .... $62.00
McCormick, Jupiter Train, Locomotive, 1969 .... $29.00
McCormick, King Arthur, 1979 .... $45.00
McCormick, Michigan State Spartans, 1974 .... $46.00
McCormick, Nebraska Football Player, 1972 .... $70.00
McCormick, Ozark Ike, 1979 .... $32.00
McCormick, Queen Anne Chair, 1979 .... $34.00
McCormick, Texas Tech Raiders, 1972 .... $42.00
McCormick, Will Rogers, 1977 .... $29.00
McCormick, Woman Washing Clothes, 1980 .... $35.00
McCormick, Wood Duck, mini, 1984 .... $19.00
Old Commonwealth, Birds of Ireland, 1993 .... $35.00

Old Commonwealth, Fallen Comrade, 1983, $75.00.

Old Commonwealth, Fireman, Black Hat, 1982 .... $66.00
Old Commonwealth, Fireman Nozzleman, 1983 .... $73.00
Old Commonwealth, LSU Tiger, 1979 .... $47.00
Old Commonwealth, Miner, Lunchtime, 1980 .... $40.00
Old Commonewealth, Miner w/Pick, 1976 .... $39.00
Old Commonwealth, Princeton, 1976 .... $23.00
Old Fitzgerald, America's Cup, 1970 .... $21.00
Old Fitzgerald, Birmingham, 1972 .... $44.00
Old Fitzgerald, Diamond, 1961 .... $11.00
Old Fitzgerald, Pheasant, 1972 .... $6.00
Old Fitzgerald, Vermont, 1970 .... $18.00
Old Mr Boston, Bart Star #15 .... $42.00
Old Mr Boston, Deadwood South Dakota, 1975 .... $15.00
Old Mr Boston, Guitar, Music City, 1968 .... $15.00
Old Mr Boston, Rocking Chair, 1965 .... $5.00
Pacesetter, Corvette, black, 1980 .... $73.00
Pacesetter, Corvette Stingray, dark blue, 1975 .... $29.00
Pacesetter, Fire Truck, Mack Pumper $150.00
Pacesetter, Ford Tractor, Big Blue, mini, 1983 .... $45.00
Pacesetter, John Deere Tractor, 1982 .... $149.00
Pacesetter, Z28 Camaro, black, 1982 .... $48.00
Ski Country, African Safari Lions, 1981 .... $65.00
Ski Country, Alaskan Walrus, 1985 .... $63.00

Ski Country, Antelope Dancer, 1982 ....$86.00
Ski Country, Barrel Rider, 1982..$92.00
Ski Country, Blue Wing Teal, 1976 ....$295.00
Ski Country, Bob Cratchit, 1977 ....$62.00
Ski Country, Burrowing Owl, 1981 ....$60.00
Ski Country, Canada Goose, 1973...$115.00
Ski Country, Cardinal, 1979 ....$85.00
Ski Country, Chukar Partridge, 1979....................................$62.00
Ski Country, Cigar Store Indian, 1974..................................$46.00
Ski Country, Circus Lion, 1975 ....$49.00
Ski Country, Eagle on Drum, 1976 ....$138.00
Ski Country, Fire Engine, red & gold, 1981 ....$275.00
Ski Country, Jaguar, 1983 ....$180.00
Ski Country, Labrador w/Pheasant, 1977............................$98.00
Ski Country, Red Tailed Hawk, 1977 ....$82.00
Ski Country, Stone Sheep, 1981...$86.00
Ski Country, Turkey, 1976 ....$38.00
Ski Country, Warrior w/Lance, 1975 ....$161.00
Ski Country, Whooping Crane, 1984 ....$63.00
Wild Turkey, Habitat #1, 1988 ....$110.00
Wild Turkey, Ligget & Myers Turkey, 1971 ....$240.00
Wild Turkey, Series #1, #1 Male, standing, 1971 ....$255.00
Wild Turkey, Series #1, #4 w/Poult, 1974, mini, 1982........$35.00
Wild Turkey, Series #2, #2 Lore, 1980 ....$35.00
Wild Turkey, Series #3, #2 Turkey w/Bobcat, 1983............$139.00
Wild Turkey, Series #3, #9 Turkey & Cubs, 1985 ....$95.00

Wild Turkey, Turkey and Eagle, 1984, $95.00.

DeForest

This family-run company (operated by Jack and Margaret DeForest and sons) was located in California; from the early 1950s until 1970 they produced the type of novelty ceramic kitchenware and giftware items that state has become known for. A favored theme was their onion-head jars, bowls, ashtray, etc., all designed with various comical expressions. Some of their cookie jars were finished in a brown wood-tone glaze and were very similar to many produced by Twin Winton.

See also Cookie Jars.

Ashtray, green boomerang shape, 3 rests, 3-footed, 2x10x10"..$20.00
Ashtray, orange, gold & green free-form, #168 & #8168, 11¼x7¼",
    from $18 to $20.00
Ashtray, red drips on round tray w/3 rests in center, #243, 8½"
    dia $12.00
Bowl, centerpiece; orange coral-like oval in center on shaded green,
    #855, 2x14½x5¾" $25.00
Bowl, pig figural, w/lid, ca 1959, lg $80.00
Bowl, pig figural, w/lid, sm $40.00
Cheese keeper, cheese wedge w/smiling face, 4x5", from $15
    to $18.00
Chip & dip set, pig's head condiment w/Go Ahead Make a Pig... on
    lid, 4 trays form circle on turntable, from $75 to.........$95.00
Cookie jar, pig head, Go Ahead Make a Pig of Your Self $95.00
Creamer, onion head, crying..$60.00
Cruets, Oil & Vinegar; onion heads, pr $135.00
Figure vase, Lizzy, hand up to brim of lg hat, vase behind & to right,
    8½", from $55 to $65.00
Figurine, angel Noel, head bowed, hands clasped, 6¼x3½"..$70.00
Figurine/planter, Lucky elephant, 4¼x5½x2" $20.00
Figurine/planter, Mickey, kitten w/ball under right front paw,
    4" $50.00

Jam jar, $20.00.

Jar, boy's smiling face w/green pickle on forehead, Relish on lid..$32.00
Jar, garlic head, smiling face, 4½", from $20 to....................$25.00
Jar, garlic head w/unhappy face, Mr Garlic Pot at base.........$36.00
Jar, girl's smiling face, May O'Naise on hat lid, 4¾x4", from $55
    to $65.00
Jar, hamburger w/smiling face, olive finial, Relish on top of bun,
    1956, 3½x4¼", from $20 to $22.00
Jar, man's face, Horace Radish on derby hat lid, 5x4" $65.00
Jar, man's face w/lg mustache, Mustard on yellow hat lid $45.00
Jar, man's smiling face, Garlic on derby hat lid....................$50.00
Jar, onion head, tears on cheeks, leaves on lid, from $20 to...$25.00
Jar, Perky (pig's face), black nose & blue bow, Mustard written on
    top, 1956, 3x4½x3", from $35 to $45.00
Jar, Perky (pig's face), Go Ahead Make a Pig of Yourself! on forehead,
    dated 1957, 4", from $35 to $45.00

Jar, Swiss cheese quarter w/smiling face, Cheezy on lid, 4x5x3¼", from $45 to **$55.00**

Jar, wide-eyed boy w/sm mouth, Mustard on yellow hat lid, 4½" ..**$45.00**

Lazy Susan, Perky, from $200.00 to $225.00. (Photo courtesy Fred and Joyce Roerig)

Lazy Susan, 4 shell-like bowls surround center jar w/lid, multicolor pastels, on wooden tray, from $25 to **$35.00**

Nut dish, peanut shape w/squirrel finial, 5x8" **$17.50**

Pitcher, Perky (pig's face), 7½", from $55 to **$65.00**

Planter, caterpillar/inchworm, green w/black top hat, #323 ..**$25.00**

Plaque, fish, pink & purple striped w/gold highlights, 11x8½", from $28 to **$35.00**

Plaque, fish, pink w/gold trim, 5x6½" & 2 babies: 4x3½", set of 3, from $35 to **$45.00**

Salt & pepper shakers, cheese wedge w/smiling face in chef's hat, 3", pr **$28.00**

Salt & pepper shakers, Perky (pig's head), 3", pr.................**$40.00**

Spoon rest, flower on milk-can shape, avocado green, #3278...**$17.50**

Tidbit, 3 gold shell shapes w/touches of olive green & orange, center metal handle, #FL35, from $15 to.............................**$17.50**

Tray, pineapple shape, brown, orange & gold, 1¼x7¼x3½" ..**$12.00**

Tureen, onion head, w/lid & ladle (face in bowl), lg..........**$135.00**

Tureen, rooster figural, w/lid & ladle, 11½x12" **$165.00**

Degenhart Glass

John and Elizabeth Degenhart owned and operated the Crystal Art Glass Factory in Cambridge, Ohio. From 1947 until John died in 1964, they produced some fine glassware. John was well known for his superior paperweights, but the glassware that collectors love today was made after '64, when Elizabeth restructured the company, creating many lovely moulds and scores of colors. She hired Zack Boyd, who had previously worked for Cambridge Glass, and between the two of them, they developed almost 150 unique and original color formulas.

Complying with provisions she had made before her death, close personal friends at Island Mould and Machine Company in Wheeling, West Virginia, took Elizabeth's moulds and removed the familiar 'D in a heart' trademark from them. She had requested that 10 of her moulds be donated to the Degenhart Museum, where they remain today. Zack Boyd eventually bought the Degenhart factory and acquired the remaining moulds. He has added his own logo to them and is continuing to press glass very similar to Mrs. Degenhart's.

For more information, we recommend *Degenhart Glass and Paperweights* by Gene Florence, published by the Degenhart Paperweight and Glass Museum, Inc., Cambridge, Ohio.

Club: Friends of Degenhart
Newsletter: *Heartbeat*
Degenhart Paperweight and Glass Museum
P.O. Box 186, Cambridge, OH 43725
614-432-2626

Pooch, Cambridge Pink, $35.00.

Bird Toothpick Holder, Custard Slag **$25.00**

Bird Toothpick Holder, White **$15.00**

Bird w/Cherry Salt, Autumn...**$15.00**

Buzz Saw Wine, Light Blue...**$20.00**

Candy Dish, Red, footed, w/lid, 5".....................................**$40.00**

Elephant Toothpick Holder, Amber **$25.00**

Elizabeth Degenhart Portrait Plate, Amberina, 5½" **$35.00**

Elizabeth Degenhart Portrait Plate, Ice Blue, 5½"................**$20.00**

Forget-Me-Not Toothpick Holder, Buttercup Slag (very red)...**$30.00**

Forget-Me-Not Toothpick Holder, Pearl Gray......................**$25.00**

Gypsy Pot, Blue Bell **$15.00**

Gypsy Pot, Fawn **$17.50**

Hat, Amethyst Satin...**$18.00**

Heart Jewel Box, Antique Blue, from $25 to........................**$45.00**

Heart Jewel Box, Pink **$20.00**

Heart Toothpick Holder, Gray Tomato **$23.00**

Hen Covered Dish, Custard, 5" **$50.00**

Hen Covered Dish, Heliotrope, 2".......................................**$40.00**

Hen Covered Dish, Mint Green, 2" **$25.00**

Hobo Baby Shoe, Vaseline..**$12.00**

Liberty Bell, Lavender Green...**$20.00**

Liberty Bell, Lemonade..**$15.00**

Owl, Amberina **$35.00**

Owl, Butter Cup **$55.00**

Owl, Chad's Blue **$40.00**

Owl, Crown Tuscan **$30.00**

Owl, Dark Rose Marie	$45.00
Owl, Fog Opaque	$60.00
Owl, Peach Blo	$20.00
Owl, Persimmon	$35.00
Owl, Spiced Brown	$50.00
Owl, Sunset	$40.00
Paperweight, floral bouquet w/5 teardrop bubbles, John Degenhart, 1950s, 3¼"	$250.00
Pooch, Blue Marble Slag	$30.00
Pooch, Canary	$15.00
Pooch, Lemon Opal	$30.00
Pooch, Red	$25.00
Priscilla, Bittersweet Slag	$150.00
Priscilla, Cobalt	$100.00
Robin Covered Dish, Amber, 5"	$30.00
Robin Covered Dish, Dark Amberina, 5"	$70.00
Star & Dewdrop Salt, White Opalescent	$15.00
Texas Boot, Baby Green	$20.00
Tomahawk, Blue Bell	$25.00
Turkey Covered Dish, Custard Slag	$45.00

deLee

Jimmie Lee Adair Kohl founded her company in 1937, and it continued to operate until 1958. She was the inspiration, artist, and owner of the company for the 21 years it was in business. The name deLee means 'of or by Lee' and is taken from the French language. She trained as an artist at the San Diego Art Institute and UCLA where she also earned an art education degree. She taught art and ceramics at Belmont High School in Los Angeles while getting her ceramic business started. On September 9, 1999, at the age of 93, Jimmie Lee died after having lived a long and wonderfully creative life.

The deLee line included children, adults, animals, birds, and specialty items such as cookie jars, banks, wall pockets, and several licensed Walter Lantz characters. Skunks were a favorite subject, and more of her pieces were modeled as skunks than any other single animal. Her figurines are distinctive in their design, charm, and excellent hand painting; when carefully studied, they can be easily recognized. Jimmie Lee modeled almost all the pieces — more than 350 in all.

The beautiful deLee colors were mixed by her and remained essentially the same for 20 years. The same figurine may be found painted in different colors and patterns. Figurines were sold wholesale only. Buyers could select from a catalog or visit the deLee booth in New York and Los Angeles Gift Marts. All figurines left the factory with name and logo stickers. The round Art Deco logo sticker is silver with the words 'deLee Art, California, Hand Decorated.' Many of the figures are incised 'deLee Art' on the bottom.

The factory was located in Los Angeles during its 21 years of production and in Cuernavaca, Mexico, for four years during WWII. Production continued until 1958, when Japanese copies of her figures caused sales to decline. For further study we recommend *deLee Art* by Joanne and Ralph Schaefer and John Humphries.

Advisors: Joanne and Ralph Schaefer (See Directory, deLee)

Figurine, angel girl, blue ribbon in hair, flowers at hem of dress, 7"	$70.00
Figurine, blond girl stands w/hands in muff, round balls as hair curls, 5¼"	$280.00
Figurine, boy sitting cross-legged, resting head on right hand, 1939	$185.00
Figurine, Can-Can lady, ivory, pinks & green w/gold, fine detail, 13½x9½"	$295.00
Figurine, Dapper Dan w/cane & top hat, 7"	$80.00
Figurine, geisha girl, pink & black kimono, 9½"	$40.00
Figurine, Jimmy Aviator, Deco-style sticker, 5½", from $85 to	$100.00
Figurine, June, girl w/black hair holding bouquet in both hands, 4½"	$165.00

Figurine, Lorenzo (pairs with Maria), 10½", from $90.00 to $125.00. (Photo courtesy Joanne and Ralph Schaefer and John Humphries)

Figurine, Siamese cat seated, blue eyes, 12"	$45.00
Figurine, Siamese cat up on back legs, 10"	$35.00
Figurine, Siamese cat w/blue ball of yarn, 6x15"	$85.00
Figurine, Skippy, white dog w/blue collar, sticker, 3½x3½"	$75.00
Figurine, Stinkie & Phew, skunks, 4", 4½", pr	$35.00
Figurine, Topps the giraffe, 7½", from $50 to	$60.00
Figurines, blond twin babies (nude), 3½", pr	$200.00
Figurines, Leilani & Maui (Hawaiian boy & girl), both seated, 9", pr, up to	$500.00
Figurines, Mandy & Moe (Black boy & girl), brown, blue & white, 6", 4½", pr	$350.00
Flower holder, blond boy w/white hat, blue pants, standing before vase	$30.00
Flower holder, blond girl stands by open basket, white w/multicolored flowers on skirt (dainty, sm), 6", from $50 to	$70.00
Flower holder, boy w/vase on shoulder, flowered shirt, white bib pants, 7"	$185.00

Flower holder, Buddy, blond boy holds container on shoulder..**$175.00**

Flower holder, Butch, WWII sailor boy, 5¾", from $75 to ..**$95.00**

Flower holder, Hank, brown hair, plaid vest, blue pants, 7½", from $36 to **$42.00**

Flower holder, Irene, blond girl w/opening in apron, lavender flower trim, 7¼x5" **$35.00**

Flower holder, Johnny, boy w/bouquet, brown jacket, NM, from $60 to **$75.00**

Flower holder, lady in pink floral dress, plumed hat, opening behind, 10" **$165.00**

Flower holder, Lou, girl in pink w/hands up to chin, opening behind, 8x4½" **$85.00**

Flower holder, Mary & her lamb, 6½x3½" **$85.00**

Flower holder, Pedro playing guitar, brown & blue tones, holder behind, 1944, 8" **$120.00**

Flower holder, Sally, blond in peach, green & pink, opening in back, deeLee (sic) mark, 7" **$170.00**

Flower holder, Sis, blond girl w/braids holding jar, peach & green, 1942, 6¾" **$170.00**

Flower holders, boy holding hat (dated 1949), & blond girl w/nosegay in both hands, 7¾", pr **$120.00**

Planter, pony w/pink mane & tail, blue flowers on white body, opening on back, 7½x5½" **$25.00**

Vase, girl leans over edge of flower form, pastels on white, 5x3½"..**$250.00**

Vase, lady w/flowered bonnet (opening there), holds skirt in right hand, flower decoration, 7¾" **$40.00**

Wall hanger, mallard duck, 7x7", from $35 to **$50.00**

Wall pocket, teakettle, black w/cherries & green leaves applied to front, 6¼x6¾" **$30.00**

Figurine, Siamese cat, no mark, 8½", $75.00. (Photo courtesy Jack Chipman)

Delft

Collectors have been in love with the quaint blue and white Delftware for many years. It was originally made in the Dutch city of Delft (hence its name), but eventually it was also produced in England and Germany. Antique Delft can be very expensive, but even items made in the twentieth century are very collectible and much less pricey. Thousands of Delft pieces are being imported every year from the Netherlands, ranging from souvenir grade to excellent quality ware made under the Royal Delft label. All of our examples are from more recent production, such as you might find at garage sales and flea markets. In the listings that follow, items are blue and white unless noted otherwise.

Bowl, floral center, floral sprays along scalloped border w/faint ribs, De Porceleyne Fles, 1952, 8" **$75.00**

Candleholder, windmill scene & flowers, blue-trimmed handle, Delft Blue H Painted, 1950s, 2", ea............................**$85.00**

Canister, Maryland reserve w/crown atop, Delft Made in Holland, 8½x5⅝" **$125.00**

Charger, couple in horse-drawn sled in winter scene, Royal Sphinx Maastricht, 15¾" **$90.00**

Charger, couple riding in carriage, Boch, 15"......................**$85.00**

Charger, floral panels, reserves & borders, signed HW, De Porceleyne Fles, 1951, 16" **$135.00**

Charger, lady w/plumed hat, Boch Delft, 11¼" **$32.50**

Charger, Londen (sic) - Melbourne Race, airplane w/world map as background, October 1934, De Porceleyne Fles..........**$125.00**

Charger, thatched home, windmill, boat & children skating, Boch Belgium, 15¾" **$70.00**

Clock, German, $65.00. (Photo courtesy LiveAuctioneers.com/Skinner Inc. Auctioneers & Appraisers of Antiques & Fine Art)

Cups & saucers, windmills & yachts, Germany, set of 4 ......**$65.00**

Decanter, windmill reserves & flowers, bulbous body, w/stopper, Erven Lucas Bolls, Amsterdam Holland, 7½" **$125.00**

Dresser dish, windmill scene on lid, flower on base, Hand Painted Holland mark, 1950s, 2½x3¼" dia **$25.00**

Egg cup, windmill scene, flared foot, Ter Steege VB Delft Blauw..., 2¾x2" **$32.00**

Ginger jar, flowers & butterflies, octagonal foot, De Porceleyne Fles, 13½" **$100.00**

Ginger jar, lg hand-painted floral, JT (Joust Thooft), #188, 1964, 8x4" **$195.00**

Humidor, smoking man conversing w/man in stocks reserve, van Rossem's Toeback Anno 1750, metal lid, ca 1950s-60s, 6" **$95.00**

Jar, tobacco; Indians and pipes, marked Hand-painted Delft Blue, Holland N, 7", EX, $70.00. (Photo courtesy LiveAuctioneers.com/Dargate Auction Galleries)

Mug, man drives horses pulling wagon of stacked kegs, Heineken, all in reserve among flowers, Delfische Huys..., 5x3" **$15.00**

Mug, windmill and sailboat, Blauw Delfts. SCR/Hand-painted, Made in Holland, 5", $70.00. (Photo courtesy LiveAuctioneers.com/T.W. Conroy, LLC)

Pilgrim flask, floral, flared foot, handles, Royal Porceleyne Fles, 1969, 11½" **$125.00**

Plate, baby & stork, commemorates birth of Catherine Ann Winters, October 18, 1954, Delft Made in Holland, 6¼" **$50.00**

Plate, Commemorative of Holland Liberation, rising sun, Royal Porceleyne Fles, 1945, 9" **$185.00**

Plate, Den Briel (Dutch city), De Porceleyne Fles, 1922, 10¼" **$145.00**

Plate, Euromast building (near harbor) in Rotterdam, De Porceleyne Fles, 1941, 9" **$120.00**

Plate, floral, commemorates tricentenary of Royal Porceleyne Fles factory, 1953, 10" **$85.00**

Plate, floral basket w/bird, ornate border, scalloped, Regina, 1960-70, 8½" **$30.00**

Plate, floral center, simple floral border, De Porceleyne Fles, #189, 1919, 7½" **$130.00**

Plate, homes, lg tree, clouds & bird, fluted shells along scalloped rim, Rosenthal Delft, ca 1905-30, 8½" **$55.00**

Plate, mixed floral center, ornate border, De Porceleyne Fles, 1924, 9" **$70.00**

Plate, Mother's Day 1972, M de Bruijn, Royal Delft, 7", MIB...**$80.00**

Plate, Old Church of Rotterdam, De Porceleyne Fles, 1954, 9"...**$120.00**

Tile, snow-covered church, Christmas 1970, NV Plateelbakkerj Schoonhoven, 6" sq, MIB.. **$20.00**

Vase, floral panels, trumpet neck, flared rim, Royal Sphinx, 12x6" **$85.00**

Vase, windmill scene, flared rim, pedestal base w/sq foot, #160A, Delfts Holland, 6¼"... **$155.00**

Wall pocket, Dutch shoe w/windmill & house, Delft Holland Hangeschilderd, 4x9"... **$27.50**

Department 56 Inc.

In 1976, Department 56 Inc. introduced a line of six handcrafted buildings; this original Snow Village proved to be very successful, and soon the company added not only more buildings but accessories as well. Other villages were added in the 1980s including the Dicken's Series, New England, Alpine, Christmas in the City, and Bethlehem. During that decade they also introduced their popular Snow Babies line; these are very collectible today. Offerings in the '90s included the North Pole, Disney Parks, and Seasons Bay. Dates in our listings indicate the year the item was introduced.

Christmas in the City, Hensley Cadillac and Buick, #59235, retired, from $50.00 to $65.00.

Alpine Village, Altstadter Bierstube, 2000.........................**$100.00**

Alpine Village, Elementary School, #56236, 2006 ....**$75.00**

Alpine Village, Josef Engel Farmhouse, #5952-8, 1987, from $290 to **$340.00**

Christmas in the City, Grand Central Railway Station, #58881, 1996, from $75 to **$100.00**

Christmas in the City, Palace Theater, #59633, 1987, from $160 to **$195.00**

Christmas in the City, St Mark's Cathedral, #3024, 1991, from $600 to **$700.00**

Christmas in the City, Times Tower, #55510, 2000, from $140 to...**$180.00**

Dickens Village, Brightsmith & Sons, Queen's Jewelers, 2001, from $300 to **$450.00**

Dickens Village, Fezziwig's Ballroom Gift Set, from $160 to... **$195.00**

Dickens Village, Margrove Orangery, #58440, 2000............**$95.00**

Dickens Village, Old Royal Observatory, #58453, w/sign, 1999, from $85 to **$100.00**

Dickens Village, Rockingham School, #58479, 2000...........**$65.00**

Dickens Village, St Martin-in-the-Fields Church, #58471, 2000, from $100 to **$135.00**

Dickens Village, Stone Cottage, #65188, 1985, from $100 to..**$125.00**

Dickens Village, Tower Bridge of London, #57805, 2003..**$135.00**

Disney Parks Village, Silversmith, retired in 1998................**$75.00**

Merry Makers, Brewster the Bird Feeder.............................**$75.00**

Merry Makers, Chester the Tester & His Kettle **$115.00**

Merry Makers, Ollie the Optimist **$100.00**

Merry Makers, Porter the Presser at Press & Frederick **$125.00**

New England Village, Mountain View Cabin, #56625 ......**$125.00**

New England Village, Smythe Woolen Mill, #65439, 1987 ..**$350.00**

North Pole, Loading the Sleigh, #52732, 1998 ....**$65.00**

North Pole, Santa's Workshop, #56006, 1990, from $125 to..**$175.00**

Silhouette, Sleighride, #77712, from $85 to **$110.00**

Snow Village, Brownstone, gray roof, #50567, 1980, from $175 to **$225.00**

Snow Village, Champsfield Stadium, #55001, 1999, from $110 to **$135.00**

Snow Village, Country Church (Wayside Chapel), 1976 ...**$165.00**

Snow Village, Elvis Presley's Graceland Gift Set, #55041, 2000 ...**$150.00**

Snow Village, Haunted Mansion, green roof, #45935, 1998, from $175 to **$200.00**

Snow Village, Starbucks Coffee, #54859, 1995, from $140 to..**$165.00**

Snow Village, Stardust Drive-In Theatre, #55064, 2001, from $140 to **$175.00**

Snow Village, Uptown Motors Ford, #55322, 1998, from $90 to..**$140.00**

Snow Village, Victorian House, #50070, 1977 ....**$155.00**

Snow Village Halloween, Black Cat Diner, #55319, from $100 to **$135.00**

Snow Village Halloween, Ghostly Carousel, #55317, 2002, from $150 to **$185.00**

Snow Village Halloween, Haunted Barn, #55060, 2001, from $150 to **$165.00**

Snow Village Halloween, Shipwreck Lighthouse, #55088, 2001..**$110.00**

Snow Village Halloween, Trick-or-Treat Drive, #55393, from $120 to **$140.00**

Snowbabies, Alice in Wonderland, Alice & baby having tea at table, Tea for Two, 2000, 2-pc.............................**$60.00**

Snowbabies, Elmo Loves Santa, MIB, $30.00.

Snowbabies, Finding Fallen Stars, #79855, 1989 ....**$80.00**

Snowbabies, I have a Feeling We're Not in Kansas Anymore, Dorothy standing w/baby, 1998 ....**$65.00**

Snowbabies, Mickey Mouse w/2 babies, A Magical Sleigh Ride..**$45.00**

Snowbabies, Sing Us a Song Santa, MIB...........................**$70.00**

Snowbabies, The Fisherman Three, #69370, 2003..............**$55.00**

Snowbabies, Together We Can Make the Season Bright, #68852, 1998 ....**$65.00**

Depression Glass

Since the early '60s, this has been a very active area of collecting. Interest is still very strong, and although values have long been established, except for some of the rarer items, Depression glass is still relatively inexpensive. Some of the patterns and colors that were entirely avoided by the early wave of collectors are now becoming popular, and it's very easy to reassemble a nice table setting of one of these lines today.

Most of this glass was manufactured during the Depression years. It was inexpensive, mass produced, and available in a wide assortment of colors. The same type of glassware was still being made to some extent during the '50s and '60s, and today the term 'Depression glass' has been expanded to include the later patterns as well.

Some things have been reproduced, and the slight variation in patterns and colors can be very difficult to detect. For instance, the Sharon butter dish has been reissued in original colors of pink and green (as well as others that were not original); and several pieces of Cherry Blossom, Madrid, Avocado, Mayfair, and Miss America have also been reproduced. Some pieces you'll see in antique malls and flea markets today have been recently made in dark uncharacteristic carnival colors, which, of course, are easy to spot.

For further study, Gene and Cathy Florence have written several informative books on the subject, and we recommend them all: *Elegant Glassware of the Depression Era; Glass Candlesticks of the Depression Era, Vols. 1 and 2; Kitchen Glassware of the Depression Years;*

Florences' Glassware Pattern Identification Guides, Vols. I – IV; Pocket Guide to Depression Glass and *Collector's Encyclopedia of Depression Glass.* (Collector Books).

See also Anchor Hocking, Indiana Glass, and other specific companies as some patterns in this category may have also been made in post-Depression colors (Indiana Sandwich, for instance).

American Sweetheart, pink, bowl, cream soup; 4½" $87.50
American Sweetheart, pink, bowl, vegetable; oval, 11" $70.00
American Sweetheart, pink, creamer, footed $14.00
American Sweetheart, pink, plate, dinner; 9¾" $35.00
American Sweetheart, pink, plate, salad; 8" $12.50

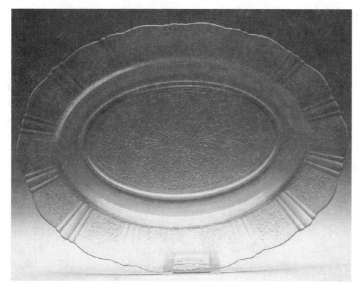

American Sweetheart, pink, platter, 13", $55.00. (Photo courtesy Gene and Cathy Florence)

American Sweetheart, pink, salt & pepper shakers, footed, pr...$595.00
American Sweetheart, pink, tumbler, 9-oz, 4¼" $95.00
Artura, green, cup $8.00
Artura, green, tray, sandwich; ornate center handle.............$35.00
Artura, pink, creamer $12.00
Artura, pink, tumbler, footed $15.00
Aurora, cobalt, bowl, deep, 4½" $68.00
Aurora, cobalt, plate, 6½" $10.00
Aurora, green, saucer $2.50
Aurora, pink, bowl, cereal; 5⅜" $17.00
Aurora, pink, cup $16.00
Beaded Block, amber, bowl, fluted edges, 7½" $30.00
Beaded Block, amber, plate, sq, 7¾" $20.00
Beaded Block, green, bowl, flared, 6¼" $25.00
Beaded Block, pink, bowl, sq, 5½" $20.00
Beaded Block, pink, jelly bowl, stemmed foot, 4½" $28.00
Beaded Block, pink, pitcher, pint jug; 5¼" $110.00
Beaded Block, white opalescent, bowl, celery; 8¼" $60.00
Beaded Block, white opalescent, sugar bowl $55.00
Block Optic, crystal, butter dish, 3x5" $195.00
Block Optic, green, candlesticks, 1¾", pr $110.00
Block Optic, green, goblet, wine; 4½" $45.00
Block Optic, green, pitcher, 54-oz, 8½" $65.00

Block Optic, green, plate, dinner; 9" $25.00
Block Optic, green, salt & pepper shakers, footed, pr $45.00
Block Optic, green, tumbler, flat, 5-oz, 3½" $25.00
Block Optic, green or pink, goblet, wine; 3½", ea.............$525.00
Block Optic, green or pink, plate, sandwich; 10¼", ea........$25.00
Block Optic, pink, bowl, salad; 7¼" $160.00
Block Optic, pink, candy jar, w/lid, 6¼" $165.00
Block Optic, pink, ice bucket...$95.00
Block Optic, pink, plate, dinner; 9" $38.00
Block Optic, pink, saucer w/cup ring, 6⅛" or 5¾", ea $7.00
Block Optic, pink, tumbler, flat, 12-oz, 4⅞" $26.00
Block Optic, pink, tumbler, footed, 10-oz, 6" $38.00
Block Optic, pink, tumbler, 3-oz, 2⅝" $30.00
Block Optic, pink, whiskey, 1-oz, 1⅝" $50.00
Block Optic, yellow, candy jar, w/lid, 2¼" $75.00
Block Optic, yellow, plate, dinner; 9" $50.00
Block Optic, yellow, sherbet, 5½-oz, 3¼" $10.00
Bowknot, green, bowl, cereal; 5½" $38.00
Bowknot, green, plate, salad; 6¾" $16.00
Bowknot, green, sherbet, low foot $23.00
Cameo, crystal w/platinum rim, decanter, w/stopper, 10"..$300.00
Cameo, crystal w/platinum rim, pitcher, water; 56-oz, 8½"..$500.00
Cameo, green, candy jar, w/lid, 6½" $205.00
Cameo, green, cookie jar $65.00
Cameo, green, goblet, wine; 4" $80.00
Cameo, green, pitcher, 20-oz, 5¾" $35.00
Cameo, green, plate, dinner; 9½" $23.00
Cameo, green, plate, grill; 10½" $15.00

Cameo, green, plate, luncheon; 8", $12.00. (Photo courtesy Gene and Cathy Florence)

Cameo, green, tumbler, flat, 11-oz, 5" $35.00
Cameo, green, vase, 5¾" $310.00
Cameo, green, vase, 8" $65.00
Cameo, pink, bowl, berry; lg, 8¼" $175.00
Cameo, pink, cake plate, flat, 10½" $195.00
Cameo, pink, creamer, 4¼" $125.00

Cameo, pink, plate, luncheon; 8" $35.00
Cameo, pink, plate, sandwich; 10" $55.00
Cameo, pink, sugar bowl, 4¼" $125.00
Cameo, pink, tray, domino; no indentation, 7" $275.00
Cameo, pink, tumbler, juice; footed, 3-oz..................$135.00
Cameo, yellow, bowl, vegetable; oval, 10" $45.00
Cameo, yellow, creamer, 3¼" $20.00
Cameo, yellow, pitcher, 20-oz, 5¾".....................$2,000.00
Cameo, yellow, platter, closed handles, 12" $40.00
Cameo, yellow, tumbler, 15-oz, 5¼" $350.00
Cherry Blossom, Delphite, bowl, vegetable; oval, 9" $50.00
Cherry Blossom, Delphite, plate, sherbet; 6" $10.00
Cherry Blossom, Delphite, platter, oval, 11" $45.00
Cherry Blossom, green, bowl, w/handles, 9" $75.00
Cherry Blossom, green, tumbler, flat, pattern at bottom, 12-oz, 5" $85.00
Cherry Blossom, Jadite, plate, grill; 9" $85.00
Cherry Blossom, pink, bowl, soup; flat $110.00
Cherry Blossom, pink, mug, 7-oz $450.00
Cherry Blossom, pink, plate, salad; 7" $27.00
Cherry Blossom, pink, salt & pepper shakers, scalloped bottom, pr $1,300.00
Cherry Blossom, pink or green, creamer $25.00
Cherry Blossom, pink or green, pitcher, pattern at top, footed, 36-oz, 7¾", ea...........$75.00
Cherry Blossom, pink or green, tumbler, pattern at bottom, footed, 9-oz, 4½"..........$38.00
Cherryberry, crystal, butter dish.........................$150.00
Cherryberry, crystal, creamer, lg, 4⅝" $16.00
Cherryberry, pink or green, creamer, sm $22.00
Cherryberry, pink or green, pickle dish, oval, 8¼" $20.00
Circle, green, bowl, flared, 1¾"x5".......................$30.00
Circle, green, goblet, water; 8-oz.........................$11.00
Circle, green, pitcher, 80-oz $40.00
Circle, green, tumbler, flat, 15-oz.......................$30.00
Circle, pink, cup $10.00
Cloverleaf, black, ashtray, match holder in center, 4" $65.00
Cloverleaf, black, salt & pepper shakers, pr..........$100.00
Cloverleaf, green, bowl, 8" $125.00
Cloverleaf, green, sherbet, 3"................................$12.00
Cloverleaf, green, tumbler, flat, 9-oz, 4" $70.00
Cloverleaf, pink or green, saucer $3.00
Cloverleaf, pink or yellow, bowl, dessert; 4" $40.00
Cloverleaf, yellow, creamer, footed, 3⅝" $22.00
Cloverleaf, yellow, sugar bowl, footed, 3⅝" $22.00
Cloverleaf, yellow, tumbler, footed, 10-oz, 5¾"......$45.00
Colonial, crystal, butter dish $42.00
Colonial, crystal, goblet, wine; 2½-oz, 4½" $14.00
Colonial, green, bowl, berry; lg, 9" $32.00
Colonial, green, sugar bowl, 4½" $18.00
Colonial, pink, bowl, soup; low, 7" $75.00
Colonial, pink, plate, dinner; 10" $60.00
Colonial, pink or green, tumbler, iced tea; 12-oz..............$52.00
Colonial, Royal Ruby, tumbler, footed, 10-oz, 5¼"...........$175.00
Colonial Block, crystal, bowl, 7" $12.00
Colonial Block, pink or green, candy jar, w/lid....$42.00
Colonial Block, white, creamer $8.00

Columbia, crystal, bowl, cereal; 5"........................$17.00
Columbia, crystal, bowl, ruffled edge, 10½" $20.00
Columbia, crystal, cup $8.00
Columbia, crystal, plate, chop; 11"........................$18.00
Columbia, crystal, plate, snack.............................$25.00
Columbia, crystal, tumbler, water; 9-oz $32.00
Columbia, pink, cup $25.00
Crow's Foot, black, bowl, footed, 10" $75.00
Crow's Foot, black, compote, 3¼x6¼" $38.00
Crow's Foot, black or Ritz Blue, vase, cupped, 10¼".........$129.00
Crow's Foot, pink, plate, sq, w/handles, 10⅜" $20.00
Crow's Foot, pink or yellow, bowl, console; 11½" $37.50
Crow's Foot, pink or yellow, vase, flared, 11¾" $65.00
Crow's Foot, Ritz Blue, candlestick, sq base, 5¾", ea $30.00
Crow's Foot, Ritz Blue, plate, sq, 8½" $14.00
Crow's Foot, Ritz Blue, sugar bowl, footed............$15.00
Crow's Foot, Ruby Red, bowl, sq, 4⅞" $25.00
Crow's Foot, Ruby Red, cake plate, sq, pedestal foot, 2"......$85.00
Crow's Foot, Ruby Red, gravy boat, pedestal foot.............$135.00
Crow's Foot, Ruby Red, platter, 12".......................$30.00
Crow's Foot, Ruby Red, vase, 4⅝x4⅛" $75.00
Della Robbia, crystal w/ pink lustre, basket, 9" $210.00
Della Robbia, crystal w/pink lustre, creamer, footed $23.00
Della Robbia, crystal w/pink lustre, punch bowl set, 15-pc ..$995.00
Diamond Quilted, amber, bowl, crimped edge, 7"....$25.00
Diamond Quilted, amber, sugar bowl $15.00
Diamond Quilted, amber, vase, fan; dolphin handles..........$75.00
Diamond Quilted, black, cup $17.50
Diamond Quilted, blue, plate, sherbet; 6" $8.00
Diamond Quilted, pink or green, compote, w/lid, 11½" $95.00
Diamond Quilted, pink or green, goblet, champagne; 9-oz, 6" ..$12.00
Diamond Quilted, pink or green, plate, sandwich; 14"........$15.00
Diamond Quilted, pink or green, tumbler, footed, 9-oz $12.50
Diana, amber, plate, bread & butter; 6"..................$2.00
Diana, crystal, bowl, scalloped edge, 12".............$16.00
Diana, crystal, tumbler, 9-oz, 4⅛".......................$35.00
Diana, pink, candy jar, round, w/lid $52.00
Diana, pink, salt & pepper shakers, pr $95.00
Doric, Delphite, pitcher, flat, 32-oz, 5½".............$1,500.00
Doric, green, butter dish.....................................$100.00

Doric, green, pitcher, 36-ounce, $55.00.

Doric, green, salt & pepper shakers, pr $40.00

Doric, pink, bowl, w/handles, 9" $30.00
Doric, pink, cake plate, 3-footed, 10" $30.00
Doric, pink, pitcher, flat, 32-oz, 5½" $50.00
Doric, pink, tray, relish; 4x4" $16.00
Doric, pink, tumbler, footed, 10-oz, 4" $85.00
Doric, pink or green, plate, salad; 7" $25.00
Doric, pink or green, tray, serving; 8x8" $40.00
Ellipse, all colors, bowl, w/handles, 4½" $12.00
Ellipse, all colors, goblet, tea; footed, 14-oz $20.00
Ellipse, all colors, salt & pepper shakers, 3", pr......$35.00
Ellipse, all colors, sherbet $10.00
English Hobnail, green, bowl, nappy; cupped, 8" $30.00
English Hobnail, green, candlestick, round base, 9", ea $45.00
English Hobnail, green, marmalade, w/lid $60.00
English Hobnail, green, pitcher, straight sides, 64-oz.........$300.00
English Hobnail, green, plate, 8½" $15.00
English Hobnail, green, rose bowl, 4" $50.00
English Hobnail, green, sherbet, low, sq foot $12.00
English Hobnail, green, sugar bowl, sq foot $45.00
English Hobnail, green, urn, w/lid, 15" $395.00
English Hobnail, pink, ashtray, sq, 4½" $25.00
English Hobnail, pink, bowl, crimped, shallow, 6" $18.00
English Hobnail, pink, bowl, flared, 10" $40.00
English Hobnail, pink, box, puff; round, w/lid, 6" $50.00
English Hobnail, pink, compote, honey; round, footed, 6"..$30.00
English Hobnail, pink, cup $18.00
English Hobnail, pink, goblet, cocktail; round foot, 3-oz $20.00
English Hobnail, pink, nut dish, footed, individual $20.00
English Hobnail, pink, pickle dish, 8" $30.00
English Hobnail, pink, plate, 8" $12.50
English Hobnail, pink, tumbler, water; 8-oz $22.00
English Hobnail, pink, vase, flared top, 8½" $145.00
English Hobnail, turquoise, bowl, hexagonal foot, w/handles, 8" $165.00
English Hobnail, turquoise, bowl, nappy, 4½" $30.00
English Hobnail, turquoise, bowl, rolled edge, 11" $80.00
English Hobnail, turquoise, box, cigarette; 4½x2½"......$55.00
English Hobnail, turquoise, marmalade, w/lid $85.00
English Hobnail, turquoise, plate, 10" $85.00
English Hobnail, turquoise, salt & pepper shakers, flat, pr ...$250.00
English Hobnail, turquoise, vase, flared top, 8½" $250.00
Floral, green, candlesticks, 4", pr......................$100.00
Floral, green, plate, grill; 9" $325.00
Floral, green, plate, salad; 8" $15.00
Floral, green, relish dish, 2-part oval $22.00
Floral, green, tray, sq, closed handles, 6" $27.50
Floral, green, tumbler, flat, 9-oz, 4½" $185.00
Floral, green, vase, 8-sided, tall, 6⅞" $425.00
Floral, pink, bowl, berry; 4" $22.00
Floral, pink, coaster, 3¼" $12.00
Floral, pink, ice tub, high, oval, 3½" $950.00
Floral, pink, platter, oval, 10¾" $22.50
Floral, pink, salt & pepper shakers, flat, 6" $55.00
Floral, pink, sherbet, ruffled..........................$100.00
Florentine #1, cobalt, cup $85.00
Florentine #1, cobalt, saucer $17.00
Florentine #1, green, bowl, cereal; 6" $25.00

Florentine #1, green, pitcher, footed, 36-oz, 6½" $40.00
Florentine #1, green, sugar bowl, ruffled...............$40.00
Florentine #1, pink, compote, ruffled, 3½" $16.00
Florentine #1, pink, platter, oval, 11½" $28.00
Florentine #1, pink, tumbler, ribbed, 9-oz, 4"..........$22.00
Florentine #1, yellow, butter dish......................$180.00
Florentine #1, yellow, plate, dinner; 10" $28.00
Florentine #1, yellow, tumbler, water; footed, 10-oz, 4¾"....$26.00
Florentine #2, cobalt, compote, ruffled, 3½" $65.00
Florentine #2, cobalt, tumbler, water; 9-oz, 4" $70.00
Florentine #2, green, bowl, 5½" $35.00
Florentine #2, green, candy dish, w/lid $100.00
Florentine #2, green, pitcher, cone foot, 28-oz, 7½" $38.00
Florentine #2, green, plate, dinner; 10" $16.00
Florentine #2, green, plate, grill; w/cream soup ring, 10¼"..$45.00
Florentine #2, green, tumbler, blown, 6-oz, 3½" $18.00
Florentine #2, green, vase or parfait, 6" $30.00
Florentine #2, pink, pitcher, 48-oz, 7½" $135.00
Florentine #2, pink, platter, oval, 11" $16.00
Florentine #2, pink, relish dish, plain, 10" $30.00
Florentine #2, pink, tumbler, juice; 5-oz, 3⅜" $12.00
Florentine #2, yellow, bowl, vegetable; oval, w/lid, 9" $85.00
Florentine #2, yellow, butter dish......................$160.00
Florentine #2, yellow, cup, custard $85.00
Florentine #2, yellow, plate, sherbet; 6" $6.00
Florentine #2, yellow, platter, oval, 11" $25.00
Florentine #2, yellow, sugar bowl $12.00
Florentine #2, yellow, tumbler, footed, 5-oz, 3¼" $20.00
Florentine #2, yellow or green, salt & pepper shakers, pr.....$45.00
Flower Garden w/Butterflies, blue, plate, dinner; 10" $48.00
Flower Garden w/Butterflies, blue, tray, rectangular, 7¾x11¾"...$90.00
Flower Garden w/Butterflies, pink, creamer $70.00
Flower Garden w/Butterflies, pink, tray, sandwich; center handle................................$70.00
Flower Garden w/Butterflies, pink, vase, 10½" $135.00
Fortune, crystal or pink, bowl, w/handles, 4½" $10.00
Fortune, crystal or pink, bowl, 7¾" $28.00
Fortune, crystal or pink, tumbler, water; 9-oz, 4".......$15.00
Fruits, green, bowl, berry; 4½" $40.00
Fruits, green, tumbler, juice; 3½" $80.00
Fruits, green, tumbler, 1-fruit, 4" $20.00
Fruits, green or pink, cup..............................$9.00
Fruits, green or pink, plate, luncheon; 8" $12.00
Fruits, pink, bowl, berry; 8" $55.00
Fruits, pink, saucer....................................$4.00
Fruits, pink, tumbler, combination of fruits, 4" $22.00
Glades, cobalt or ruby, bowl, 7" $25.00
Glades, cobalt or ruby, candlestick, double light, 5", ea $70.00
Glades, cobalt or ruby, plate, 10" $30.00
Glades, cobalt or ruby, tumbler, whiskey; flat, 3-oz.............$25.00
Glades, crystal, bowl, bonbon; tab handles, 6" $15.00
Glades, crystal, bowl, gravy; 7¼" $30.00
Glades, crystal, compote, high, 3½" $27.50
Glades, crystal, creamer, 7-oz $12.50
Glades, crystal, ice tub, 4x6⅜" $75.00
Glades, crystal, plate, serving; 11½" $20.00
Glades, crystal, salt & pepper shakers, round, 2⅛", pr.........$30.00

Glades, crystal, tray, relish; 2-part, w/handles, 12¾" **$40.00**

Glades, crystal, tumbler, tea; 12-oz, 5¼" **$20.00**

Glades, ruby, bowl, cream soup; 4¾" **$25.00**

Grape, all colors, cup **$12.50**

Grape, all colors, goblet, water; 9-oz **$20.00**

Grape, all colors, pitcher, jug; 57-oz................................. **$40.00**

Grape, all colors, plate, luncheon; 8" **$8.00**

Grape, all colors, sugar bowl **$17.50**

Grape, all colors, tumbler, barrel, 9-oz **$20.00**

Grape, all colors, tumbler, 10-oz **$10.00**

Hex Optic, pink or green, bowl, mixing; 10".................... **$30.00**

Hex Optic, pink or green, pitcher, flat, 70-oz, 8".............. **$140.00**

Hex Optic, pink or green, refrigerator dish, 4x4"............... **$18.00**

Hex Optic, pink or green, sherbet, 5-oz.............................. **$7.00**

Hex Optic, pink or green, sugar bowl, 2 styles of handles, ea.. **$7.00**

Hex Optic, pink or green, tumbler, footed, 7-oz, 4¾" **$7.50**

Hobnail, crystal, bowl, crimped, w/handles, 6½" **$17.50**

Hobnail, crystal, decanter, w/stopper, 32-oz...................... **$35.00**

Hobnail, crystal, pitcher, milk; 18-oz **$20.00**

Hobnail, crystal, tumbler, iced tea; 15-oz, 5¼" **$15.00**

Hobnail, crystal, tumbler, juice; footed, 3-oz **$5.00**

Hobnail, pink, plate, luncheon; 8½" **$8.00**

Hobnail, pink, saucer **$4.00**

Hobnail, pink, sugar bowl, footed...................................... **$9.00**

Homespun, pink, butter dish... **$60.00**

Homespun, pink, creamer, footed....................................... **$12.50**

Homespun, pink, plate, dinner; 9¼" **$20.00**

Homespun, pink, sugar bowl, footed **$12.00**

Homespun, pink, tumbler, footed, 5-oz, 4" **$8.00**

Homespun, pink, tumbler, footed, 15-oz, 6⅜"..................... **$30.00**

Homespun, pink, tumbler, water; flared top, 8-oz, 4⅛" **$20.00**

Iris, clear, candy dish and lid, $100.00.

Laced Edge, opalescent blue or green, basket bowl............ **$235.00**

Laced Edge, opalescent blue or green, bowl, oval, 11" **$150.00**

Laced Edge, opalescent blue or green, bowl, 5½".............. **$33.00**

Laced Edge, opalescent blue or green, mayonnaise, 3-pc.... **$135.00**

Laced Edge, opalescent blue or green, plate, bread & butter; 6½".. **$13.00**

Laced Edge, opalescent blue or green, platter, 13".............. **$165.00**

Laced Edge, opalescent blue or green, tidbit, 2-tiered, 8" & 10" plates... **$110.00**

Largo, amber or crystal, ashtray, rectangular, 3" **$16.00**

Largo, amber or crystal, bowl, crimped, 7½"...................... **$22.50**

Largo, amber or crystal, cake plate, pedestal...................... **$35.00**

Largo, amber or crystal, candy dish, 3-part, flat, w/lid **$35.00**

Largo, amber or crystal, creamer, footed............................ **$25.00**

Largo, amber or crystal, plate, cheese; w/indent, 10¾"......... **$20.00**

Largo, amber or crystal, tray, relish; 5-part, 14" **$50.00**

Largo, blue or red, bowl, deep, 6" **$35.00**

Largo, blue or red, bowl, flared rim, 3-footed, 11⅝" **$80.00**

Largo, blue or red, candy dish, 3-part, flat, w/lid **$95.00**

Largo, blue or red, compote, cracker **$25.00**

Largo, blue or red, plate, 6⅝" **$15.00**

Largo, blue or red, sugar bowl, footed................................ **$45.00**

Lincoln Inn, red or blue, bowl, crimped, 9½" **$45.00**

Lincoln Inn, red or blue, bowl, fruit; 5" **$15.00**

Lincoln Inn, red or blue, bowl, olive; w/handles **$18.00**

Lincoln Inn, red or blue, compote **$30.00**

Lincoln Inn, red or blue, finger bowl **$22.00**

Lincoln Inn, red or blue, goblet, wine **$32.00**

Lincoln Inn, red or blue, pitcher, 46-oz, 7¼" **$800.00**

Lincoln Inn, red or blue, plate, 12" **$65.00**

Lincoln Inn, red or blue, salt & pepper shakers, pr............. **$225.00**

Lincoln Inn, red or blue, sugar bowl **$22.50**

Lincoln Inn, red or blue, tumbler, footed, 5-oz.................... **$32.00**

Lincoln Inn, red or blue, vase, footed, 12" **$250.00**

Lincoln Inn, red or blue, vase, 9¾" **$165.00**

Line #555, crystal, bowl, nappy, 6" **$13.00**

Line #555, crystal, bowl, punch.. **$65.00**

Line #555, crystal, candlestick, 1-light, ea........................... **$25.00**

Line #555, crystal, candy dish, pedestal foot, w/lid, 10¼" ... **$35.00**

Line #555, crystal, plate, 8" **$10.00**

Line #555, crystal, punch cup.. **$7.00**

Line #555, crystal, tray, relish; sq, 2-part, 7½" **$14.00**

Line #555, crystal, tray, 9" **$15.00**

Lois, all colors, bowl, salad; flat rim, 10" **$40.00**

Lois, all colors, candy box, w/octagonal lid **$70.00**

Lois, all colors, candy jar, cone shape, w/lid **$60.00**

Lois, all colors, goblet, wine **$30.00**

Lois, all colors, plate, dinner **$40.00**

Lois, all colors, vase, 10" **$85.00**

Lorain, crystal or green, bowl, cereal; 6" **$60.00**

Lorain, crystal or green, plate, dinner; 10¼" **$55.00**

Lorain, crystal or green, tumbler, footed, 9-oz, 4¾" **$26.00**

Lorain, yellow, bowl, salad; 7¼" **$95.00**

Lorain, yellow, creamer, footed.. **$25.00**

Lorain, yellow, plate, salad; 7¾" **$14.00**

Lorain, yellow, platter, 11½" **$45.00**

Lorain, yellow, sugar bowl, footed **$25.00**

Madrid, amber, gravy boat **$1,000.00**

Madrid, amber, pitcher, juice; 36-oz, 5½" **$42.00**

Madrid, amber, salt & pepper shakers, flat, 3½", pr............ **$50.00**

Madrid, amber, tumbler, footed, 10-oz, 5½" **$30.00**

Madrid, amber or green, bowl, soup; 7" **$16.00**

Madrid, amber or green, plate, salad; 7½" **$9.00**

Madrid, green, tumbler, 9-oz, 4¼" $20.00
Madrid, pink, cookie jar...$30.00
Madrid, pink, plate, relish; 10¼" $14.00
Madrid, pink, platter, oval, 11½" $14.00

Mayfair (Open Rose), pink, pitcher, 80-ounce, $125.00.

Monticello, crystal, basket, 10" $22.00
Monticello, crystal, bowl, belled, 6½" $12.50
Monticello, crystal, bowl, lily; 7" $30.00
Monticello, crystal, bowl, shallow, 10" $25.00
Monticello, crystal, cheese dish $75.00
Monticello, crystal, cupsidor $65.00
Monticello, crystal, goblet, cocktail $12.50
Monticello, crystal, plate, 16½".....................................$55.00
Monticello, crystal, tumbler, water; 9-oz $15.00
No 618 (Pineapple & Floral), amber or red, bowl, vegetable; 10"
   L $18.00
No 618 (Pineapple & Floral), amber or red, tumbler, 8-oz,
   4¼" $25.00
No 618 (Pineapple & Floral), crystal, bowl, berry; 4¾" $22.00
No 618 (Pineapple & Floral), crystal, creamer, diamond-
   shaped $9.00
No 618 (Pineapple & Floral), crystal, plate, salad; 8⅜" $8.50
No 618 (Pineapple & Floral), crystal, plate, sandwich;
   11½" $20.00
No 618 (Pineapple & Floral), crystal, sherbet, footed $15.00
No 618 (Pineapple & Floral), crystal, vase, cone-shaped......$55.00
Old Colony, pink, bowl, salad; ribbed, 7¾" $67.50
Old Colony, pink, butter dish.......................................$70.00
Old Colony, pink, compote, 7"......................................$28.00
Old Colony, pink, cup $30.00
Old Colony, pink, plate, luncheon; 8¼" $22.00
Old Colony, pink, platter, 5-part, 12¾".........................$35.00
Old Colony, pink, relish dish, deep, 3-part, 7½".................$88.00
Old Colony, pink, tumbler, flat, 5-oz, 3½" $215.00
Oyster & Pearl, crystal, candleholders, 3½", pr.............$42.00
Oyster & Pearl, pink, bowl, fruit; deep, 10½".............$25.00

Oyster and Pearl, pink: Divided relish, 10½", $18.50; candle-holder, 3½", $26.00 each; bowl, deep, with handles, 6½", $18.00.
(Photo courtesy Gene and Cathy Florence)

Oyster & Pearl, pink, plate, sandwich; 13½" $20.00
Oyster & Pearl, red, bowl, 1-handle, 5½" $22.00
Oyster & Pearl, red, relish dish, oblong, divided, 10½" $20.00
Party Line, amber, cake stand, low foot...............................$30.00
Party Line, amber, creamer, 7-oz...$10.00
Party Line, amber, tumbler, blown, 12-oz $15.00
Party Line, crystal, cocktail shaker, 18-oz............................$65.00
Party Line, crystal, pitcher, w/lid, 32-oz..............................$100.00
Party Line, crystal, plate, 6" $6.00
Party Line, crystal, syrup, 8-oz..$55.00
Party Line, crystal, vase, crimped, 7" $50.00
Party Line, green, bowl, mixing; 8" $25.00
Party Line, green, compote, low foot, 11" $35.00
Party Line, green, marmalade, 12-oz $35.00
Party Line, green, plate, cheese & cracker; w/lid, 10½"........$65.00
Party Line, green, salt & pepper shakers, pr $35.00
Party Line, green, tumbler, wine; 3-oz..................................$12.00
Party Line, green, vase, fan; 6"..$40.00
Peacock & Wild Rose, all colors, bowl, center handle, 10½".....$125.00
Peacock & Wild Rose, all colors, bowl, footed, 8¾"..........$175.00
Peacock & Wild Rose, all colors, cake plate, low foot, 2"...$150.00
Peacock & Wild Rose, all colors, candy dish, w/lid, 7" $250.00
Peacock & Wild Rose, all colors, compote, 6⅜x8"...............$150.00
Peacock & Wild Rose, all colors, creamer, pointed handle, 5" .. $65.00
Peacock & Wild Rose, all colors, ice bucket, 6" $225.00
Peacock & Wild Rose, all colors, pitcher, 5" $395.00
Peacock & Wild Rose, all colors, tray, rectangular, w/handles . $175.00
Peacock & Wild Rose, all colors, vase, elliptical, 8¼"........$395.00
Peacock & Wild Rose, all colors bowl, console; 11"...........$185.00
Petalware, pink, bowl, cream soup; 4½" $17.00
Petalware, pink, plate, salad; 8"..$7.00
Petalware, pink, platter, oval, 13"..$25.00
Petalware, pink, sugar bowl, footed $9.00
Primo, green, bowl, 3-footed, 11" $75.00
Primo, green, coaster/ashtray..$8.00
Primo, green, plate, dinner; 10" $30.00
Primo, green, tray, hostess; w/handles $50.00

Rock Crystal, crystal, bowl, relish; 6-part, 14" $50.00
Rock Crystal, crystal, bowl, salad; scalloped edge, 7" $24.00
Rock Crystal, crystal, candy dish, footed, w/lid, 9¼" $75.00
Rock Crystal, crystal, cruet, oil; 6-oz................................. $115.00
Rock Crystal, crystal, plate, scalloped edge, 9" $18.00
Rock Crystal, crystal, vase, footed, 11" $85.00
Rock Crystal, red, bowl, salad; scalloped edge, 10½" $100.00
Rock Crystal, red, candlesticks, flat, stemmed, pr $150.00
Rock Crystal, red, goblet, wine; 3-oz $55.00
Rock Crystal, red, jelly, scalloped edge, footed, 5" $52.50

**Rock Crystal, red, plate, dinner; large center design, 10½",
$195.00.** (Photo courtesy Gene and Cathy Florence)

Rose Point Band, crystal, bowl, sauce; 3-footed $8.00
Rose Point Band, crystal, butter dish................................... $45.00
Rose Point Band, crystal, pitcher, ½-gal $58.00
Sandwich (Indiana), See Indiana Glass................................ $.09
Sharon, amber, bowl, berry; 5" $8.00
Sharon, amber, cake plate, footed, 11½" $27.50
Sharon, amber, platter, oval, 12½" $17.50
Sharon, pink, butter dish $60.00
Sharon, pink, cup... $12.00
Sharon, pink, plate, dinner; 9½" $18.00
Sharon, pink, sugar bowl... $12.00
Tea Room, green, pitcher, 64-oz... $185.00
Tea Room, green, sundae, ruffled top, footed.................... $135.00
Tea Room, pink, mustard jar.. $175.00
Tea Room, pink, plate, luncheon; 8¼" $50.00
Tea Room, pink, salt & pepper shakers, pr $100.00
Tea Room, pink, vase, straight sides, 11" $165.00
Windsor, crystal, bowl, pointed edge, 8"............................. $18.00
Windsor, crystal, creamer $5.00
Windsor, crystal, tumbler, footed, 4" $8.00
Windsor, pink, bowl, boat shape, 7x11¾"........................... $20.00
Windsor, pink, plate, chop; 13⅝" $40.00
Windsor, pink, tray, 8½x9¾" $15.00

Disney Collectibles

The largest and most popular area in character collectibles is without doubt Disneyana. There are clubs, newsletters, and special shows that are centered around this hobby. Every aspect of the retail market has been thoroughly saturated with Disney-related merchandise over the years, and today collectors are able to find many good examples at garage sales and flea markets.

Disney memorabilia from the late '20s and '30s was marked either 'Walt E. Disney' or 'Walt Disney Enterprises.' After about 1940 the name was changed to 'Walt Disney Productions.' This mark was in use until 1984 when the 'Walt Disney Company' mark was introduced, and this last mark has remained in use up to the present time. Some of the earlier items have become very expensive, though many are still within the reach of the average collector.

During the '30s, Mickey Mouse, Donald Duck, Snow White and the Seven Dwarfs, and the Three Little Pigs (along with all their friends and cohorts) dominated the Disney scene. The last of the '30s characters was Pinocchio, and some 'purists' prefer to stop their collections with him.

The '40s and '50s brought many new characters with them — Alice in Wonderland, Bambi, Dumbo, Lady and the Tramp, and Peter Pan were some of the major personalities featured in Disney's films of this era.

Even today, thanks to the re-releases of many of the old movies and the popularity of Disney's vacation 'kingdoms,' toy stores and department stores alike are full of quality items with the potential of soon becoming collectibles.

If you'd like to learn more about this fascinating field, we recommend *Collecting Disneyana* by David Longest and *Schroeder's Collectible Toys, Antique to Modern*. Both are published by Collector Books.

See also Character and Promotional Drinking Glasses; Character Banks; Character Watches; Cowboy Character Memorabilia; Dolls, Mattel; Enesco; Games; Hagen-Renaker; Pin-Back Buttons; Salt and Pepper Shakers; Toys; Valentines; Wade.

Advisor: Judy Posner (See Directory, Advertising)

Atlantic City, sand pail, 8", VG, $1,150.00. (Photo courtesy LiveAuctioneers.com/ Morphy Auctions)

Aristocats, soap set, Marie, Toulouse & Berlioz soap figures, Avon, 1970s, 2½", MIB **$25.00**

Baloo (Jungle Book), figure, stuffed, rusty brown cloth w/beige felt chest, 2 bottom teeth, 1960s, 6½", NM **$30.00**

Bambi, plaque, painted image on wooden oval w/painted rope-look border, WDP, 1960-70s, 7x6", EX+ **$8.00**

Bambi, push puppet, Kohner, 1960s, M **$65.00**

Bambi, Ride-on-Toy, wood, Bambi figure on colorful rocker base, Gong Bell Toy Co, 1956, 29", EX **$50.00**

Bashful (Snow White), figure, stuffed, felt w/furry beard, looking up, 1960-70s, NM **$25.00**

Captain Hook, figure, vinyl, seated on green base, cloth jacket, hat & scarf, AD Sutton, 1960s, MIB **$75.00**

Cinderella, figure, plush & vinyl, pink & white, Gund, EX+ **$50.00**

Cinderella, hand puppet, full plush body w/vinyl head & slippers, Gund, 1950s, NM+ **$75.00**

Cinderella, marionette, painted features, in evening gown, synthetic hair, Pelham, 1960s, NMIB **$110.00**

Daisy Duck, figure, bisque, playing croquet, WDP, 1970s, 4", M **$28.00**

Disneyland, scrapbook, For Pictures & Clippings, WDP, 1950s, unused, 8½x11", EX+ **$50.00**

Donald Duck, figure, bisque, strutting w/chest out & head up turned, WDE, 1940s, 3½", EX+ **$65.00**

Donald Duck, hand puppet, cloth w/printed body image & name, vinyl head, Walt Disney World, 1970s, VG **$20.00**

Donald Duck, Jack-in-the-Box, composition head w/cloth body, wood box w/push-button action, Spear, 1940s, NM... **$215.00**

Donald Duck, Lenci, 1950s, NM, $600.00. (Photo courtesy LiveAuctioneers.com/ Morphy Auctions)

Donald Duck, pencil sharpener, celluloid figure w/hands on hips, 3", EX+ **$165.00**

Donald Duck, pull toy, Donald Duck Ice Cream Wagon, paper lithograph on wood, Marx, 9", EXIB.......................... **$200.00**

Donald Duck, squeeze toy, Donald holding binoculars, Dell, 1960s, 10½", NM **$50.00**

Donald Duck, Wall Walker, plastic, Kenner/General Mills, 1972, 3½", MOC **$25.00**

Dopey, lamp, ceramic figure, airbrushed details, printed scene on shade, 12", NM **$150.00**

Dopey (Snow White), mug, ceramic w/embossed image & name on banner, pastel colors, Enesco, 1950s, 4", NM+ **$30.00**

Dumbo, figure, inflatable vinyl, seated upright, WDP, 1970s, 18", MIP **$25.00**

Dumbo, hand puppet, printed cloth body w/name on chest, gray vinyl head w/red hat, Gund, 1960s, NM **$50.00**

Dumbo, squeeze toy, Kohner Squeez-Mees, 1960-70s, 3x4", MIP **$40.00**

Eeyore, figure, stuffed, gray corduroy w/black felt features, Gund, 1966, 5", NM+ **$35.00**

Ferdinand the Bull, figure, chalkware, standing, facing forward, flower in mouth, 7x11" L, EX **$75.00**

Ferdinand the Bull, hair bows, rayon w/gold metal center, Stark Productions/WDP, 1938, EXOC **$50.00**

Geppetto (Pinocchio), figure, vinyl, bendable, cloth outfit, Marx, 6", NM+ **$15.00**

Goofy, figure, stuffed, cloth overalls & shirt, Schuco, 1950s, 14", EX **$250.00**

Grumpy (Snow White), figure, stuffed, white furry beard, felt features, vinyl belt, 1960-70s, 7", EX+ **$25.00**

Gus (Cinderella), figure, stuffed plush w/red felt top & green felt shoes, Gund, 15", NM+ **$250.00**

Jiminy Cricket (Pinocchio), push puppet, Kohner, 1960s, NM.. **$45.00**

Jiminy Cricket, wood, 9", EX, $575.00. (Photo courtesy LiveAuctioneers.com/Morphy Auctions)

Lady (Lady & the Tramp), figure, stuffed, seated upright, corduroy-type cloth w/felt ears, WDP, 7", NM **$75.00**

Lady (Lady & the Tramp), squeeze toy, vinyl, seated upright, Lanco, 1960-70s, 2½", M **$12.00**

Lady & the Tramp, tray, lithographed tin w/illustrated spaghetti scene, 13x17", EX **$50.00**

Lucky (101 Dalmatians), hand puppet, white cloth body w/black dots & red trim, vinyl head, Gund, 1960s, NM **$50.00**

Mad Hatter (Alice in Wonderland), marionette, talker, cloth outfit, Peter Puppet Playthings, EX **$100.00**

Maleficent (Sleeping Beauty), hand puppet, cloth body w/vinyl head, Gund, 1950s, NM+..............................$125.00

Mary Poppins, figure, plastic, synthetic hair, yellow cloth dress, Gund/WDP, 1960s, 12", NM $75.00

Mickey & Minnie Mouse, flashlight, Minnie chasing Mickey around tree on handle, EX....................................$150.00

Mickey & Minnie Mouse, Merry Moments Stencil Outfit, Spears, 1930s, complete, EXIB $150.00

Mickey & Minnie Mouse, toy tea set, white ceramic w/decals, gold trim, 8" teapot, French, prewar, NM $400.00

Mickey Mouse, bank, composition, seated on stool, looking & pointing up, WDP, 8", EX..............................$25.00

Mickey Mouse, camera, Mick-A-Matic, Child Guidance #880, 1960s, NMIB $125.00

Mickey Mouse, chalkboard, wood frame w/fold-out legs, top header w/Mickey graphics, Falcon Toys, 37x17", EX+ $180.00

Mickey Mouse, figure, composition, complete cowboy outfit w/2 guns in holster, Knickerbocker, 10", VG+....................$750.00

Mickey Mouse, figure, wood, bead-type body w/pancake hands, chest banner, Fun-E-Flex, 1930s, 5", EX $300.00

Mickey Mouse, game, Mickey Mouse Soldier Set, 8 cardboard Mickey figures, w/cork gun, VGIB $275.00

Mickey Mouse, handkerchief, MIB, from $40.00 to $50.00.
(Photo courtesy Barbara Guggenheim)

Mickey Mouse, lamp, ceramic figure playing mandolin, Mickey figure inside bulb, 12" (no shade), G $300.00

Mickey Mouse, Mystery Art Set, Dixon/WDE, MIB.........$400.00

Mickey Mouse, plastic mechanical toy, Mickey Mouse Scooter-Jockey, windup, figure on 3-wheeled scooter, Mavco, 6", EXIB $150.00

Mickey Mouse, squeeze toy, standing, looking up w/hands behind back, Dell, 1950-60s, 6", EX+ $50.00

Mickey Mouse, telephone, Mickey on candlestick-type phone, NN Hill Brass Co, 1930s, 9", EX $225.00

Mickey Mouse, toothbrush holder, bisque, Mickey washing Pluto's face, 4½", EX....................................$220.00

Mickey Mouse Explorers Outfit, NMIB $250.00

Minnie Mouse, figure, stuffed, pink plush w/white hands & blue feet, blue skirt w/white dots, Woolco, 1960s, 13", G+..$25.00

Minnie Mouse, marionette, composition, cloth outfit, 1941, VG+ $150.00

Peter Pan, figure, plastic, jointed, sleep eyes, cloth outfit & hat, Duchess, 1950s, 9", NM $125.00

Peter Pan, pencil case, cardboard, snap front, sliding drawer, Peter looking into trunk full of pencils, 1950s, 5x9", EX $25.00

Piglet (Winnie the Pooh), figure, stuffed, plush w/black & red striped body, 1966, 7", EX+............................$25.00

Pinocchio, figure, composition, felt outfit & hat, Ideal, 13", EX..$275.00

Pinocchio, figure, wood, bead-type w/name on tummy, felt collar & bow tie, Ideal, 11", G+ $150.00

**Pinocchio, windup walker, Marx, 8½",
EX, $500.00.** (Photo courtesy LiveAuctioneers.
com/Morphy Auctions)

Pluto, figure, rubber, bendable, on all fours, Lakeside/WDP, 1960s, 3x5½", EX $20.00

Pluto, squeeze toy, sitting upright licking his chops, Holland Hall/WDP, 1960s, 6", EX....................................$35.00

Pongo (101 Dalmatians), push puppet, Kohner, 1960s, NM+ . $35.00

Robin Hood, hand puppet, brown & gray cloth body w/white collar, vinyl head w/green felt hat, MPI Toys, 1960s, NM+ ..$125.00

Roo (Winnie the Pooh), figure, stuffed, brown plush w/turquoise felt inner ears & shirt, Sears, 1970s, 10½", NM $18.00

Sleepy (Snow White), pencil holder, painted ceramic, figure on base marked Disneyland, 4", NM $35.00

Snow White, paint box, lithographed tin, WD/MM Ltd, 1930s, unused, 4x9½", EX....................................$50.00

Snow White & the Seven Dwarfs, figure set, bisque, Borgfeldt, 1938, 2½" dwarfs, 3½" Snow White, EXIB..............$275.00

Snow White & the Seven Dwarfs, figure set, composition, cloth outfits, Ideal, 18" Snow White, EX (in individual boxes) $2,400.00

Snow White & the Seven Dwarfs, handkerchief set, 4 different prints, WDE, 1930s, MIB $175.00

Snow White & the Seven Dwarfs, toy dish set, white ceramic w/decals, green trim, Japan, 1930s, 19-pc, EX..............$650.00

Three Little Pigs, figure set, bisque, standing & playing instruments, Borgfeldt, 3½", MIB...$250.00

Tigger (Winnie the Pooh), figure, stuffed, ribbed cloth w/felt features & stripes, long whiskers, Sears, 1960s, 6" L, NM..........$35.00

Tramp (Lady & the Tramp), figure, stuffed, plush 2-color roly-poly body w/vinyl face, musical chimes, Gund, 9", EX+ $40.00

Uncle Scrooge, squeeze toy, standing, gesturing w/finger, Dell, 1960s, 8", NM $60.00

Wendy (Peter Pan), hand puppet, cloth body w/vinyl head, Gund, 1950s, NM $60.00

Winnie-the-Pooh, figure, stuffed, standing & waving, gold plush w/ red top, Gund, 1966, 6½", NM+ $35.00

Winnie-the-Pooh, Magic Slate, Western Publishing, unused, 1965, NM+...$50.00

Winnie the Pooh, phonograph, Lionel, EX, $180.00. (Photo courtesy LiveAuctioneers.com/Philip Weiss Auctions)

101 Dalmatians, Colorforms Cartoon Kit, 1961, NMIB.....$25.00

Dog Collectibles

Dog lovers appreciate the many items, old and new, that are modeled after or decorated with their favorite breeds. They pursue, some avidly, all with dedication, specific items for a particular accumulation or a range of objects, from matchbook covers to bronzes.

The Scottish terrier is one of the most highly sought-out breeds of dogs among collectors; at any rate, Scottie devotees are more organized than most. Both the Aberdeen and West Highland terriers were used commercially; often the two are found together in things such as magnets, Black & White Scotch Whiskey advertisements, jewelry, and playing cards, for instance. They became a favorite of the advertising world in the 1930s and 1940s, partly as a result of the public popularity of President Roosevelt's dog, Fala.

Poodles were the breed of the 1950s, and today items from those years are cherished collectibles. Trendsetter teeny-boppers wore poodle skirts, and the 5-&-10¢ stores were full of pink poodle figurines with 'coleslaw' fur. For a look back at these years, we recommend *Poodle Collectibles of the '50s and '60s* by Elaine Butler (L-W Books).

Many of the earlier collectibles are especially prized, making them expensive and difficult to find. Prices listed here may vary as they are dependent on supply and demand, location, and dealer assessment.

Club: Heart of America Scottish Terrier Club
scollyjake@aol.com

Afghan hound, figurine, creramic, brown matt, EX details, unmarked, 5x5¾x2"..$30.00

Airedale, figurine, painted metal, unmarked, 6¼" $35.00

Basset hound, figurine, ceramic, beige gloss, Giftcraft, Japan, 5½x7½x3"..$24.00

Basset hound, figurine, ceramic, brown to white paint, Japan, C6741, 3x5½" $10.00

Beagle puppy, figurine, ceramic, laying in basket, black & brown on white, Enesco, 1960s, 1x2" $5.00

Bonzo, egg cup, ceramic, white w/black & red details, Made in Japan, 2⅝" $55.00

Borzoi, brooch, sterling, 3", from $125.00 to $175.00.
(Photo courtesy Ann Mitchell Pitman/Laurel Ladd Ciotti collection)

Borzoi, figurine, white porcelain w/gold accents, Japan, 4½x6½"..$35.00

Borzoi, paperweight, painted cast iron, Hubley, 4½x3¼" $42.50

Borzoi pr, figurine, painted porcelain, on base, Karl ENS, #4461, 7½x10x4½" $285.00

Boxer, figurine, painted porcelain, free-standing, Rosenthal, 7x7¾" $225.00

Boxer, planter, ceramic, brown tones w/black details, unmarked, 8x12⅞x4½"..$40.00

Boxer, plate, 4 Boxers, Simon Mendez, Danbury Mint, 8¼", MIB..$85.00

Bulldog, ice bucket, aluminum, head form, Arthur Court, 1979, 9¼x8¾x7½"..$125.00

Cocker spaniel, ashtray, metal figural, flap on back opens to hold ashes, painted details, Made in Austria, 3½x6½"..........$70.00

Cocker spaniel, figurine, black & white, ceramic, Gaylan Studio, 1980s, 5¾x8" $65.00

Cocker spaniel, figurine, bronze, rich coppery patina, unmarked, 8x11" $85.00

Cocker spaniel, figurine, porcelain, brown & white, Made in Japan, 4x6" $15.00

Cocker spaniel, figurine, porcelain, golden tan w/painted details, Ronzan, Italy, 4x6¼x2¼" $110.00

Cocker spaniel, Lefton #00412, 4½", from $20.00 to $30.00. (Photo courtesy Loretta DeLozier)

Cocker spaniel, pendant, sterling silver, satin finish $55.00
Collie, figurine, dog w/front paws on fence, ceramic, multicolor, Japan, 1930s, 5x6x2½" $25.00

Dachshund, handkerchief, Burmel, from $20.00 to $25.00.
(Photo courtesy Helene Guarnaccia and Barbara Guggenheim)

Dachshund, nodder, brown plastic, Breba, DBGM, 1¾x5"...$65.00
Dachshund puppy, planter, ceramic, brown tones, Napco Japan, #A4066G, 5x5" $20.00
Dalmatian, trinket box, recumbent dog on lid of oval blue porcelain box, Artoria Limoges, 2½x3x2"..................$110.00
Doberman pinscher, figurine, painted porcelain, free-standing, unmarked (Germany), 7½x8" $415.00
English bulldog, paperweight, cast-iron figural, anatomically correct, black paint, 1930s, 2½x4½" $40.00

English pointer, figurine, bronze w/cold paint (minor paint loss), Austria, 1¼x1⅛" $135.00
English setter, postcard, man w/dog photo, 1910s, unused, EX+...$18.00
English setter, salt & pepper shakers, head only, silver-tone cast metal, 1940s, 2¼", pr $25.00
English spaniel, figurine, ceramic, brown tones, Ucagco Japan, 4½" $18.00
German shepherd, bookends, brass seated dog on marble base, 5½x5x2" $90.00
German shepherd, figurine, ceramic, panting tongue, Japan, 1930s-40s, 4¼x3¾" $25.00
German shepherd, figurine, painted china, Lenox green mark, Made in USA, 4¼x8" $175.00
German shepherd, plate, Patience, JL Fitzgerald, Danbury Mint, 8", MIB $55.00
German shepherd puppy, figurine, ceramic, Lenox, 7", MIB.. $125.00
Golden retriever, plate, Great American Sporting Dogs, Jim Killen, Ducks Unlimited, 8¼", MIB $135.00

Great Dane, bookends, gray metal, Made in Canada, 6",
$125.00. (Photo courtesy Louis Kuritzky/Blythe Curry)

Great Dane, planter, dog chewing on pipe, ceramic, brown tones, unmarked, 4¾x7" $15.00
Highland terrier, figurine, Kathy Wise, Enesco Purebed Pet, 1984, 4½x7x3½" $30.00
Hound, paperweight, bronze head, EX details & patina, Newark NJ mark, 4x2¾" $95.00
Irish setter, bookends, head & neck only, brass, 5x4½" $45.00
Irish setter, dresser tray, dog stands at back of ceramic tray w/3 compartments, lg opening behind, Japan, 4¾x7x6"............$15.00
Irish setter, figurine, reddish-brown to white at feet, recumbent, ceramic, Shafford, #141, 6¼x11x5" $32.00
Irish setter, seated, ceramic, reddish-brown tones, Japan, 6"..$25.00
Irish wolfhound, figurine, hand-painted ceramic, Wheaten, 4½x9x4¾" $95.00
Jack Russell terrier, figurine, ceramic, brown & white, Beswick, 2½x3½" $65.00
Pekingese, figurine, ceramic, brown to white, Japan, ca 1940, 4x5½" $40.00
Pekingese, postcard, dog's portrait by M Babington, #301, Alma Publishing, unused..$7.00
Pointer, etching, Elhew Marksman (dog's name), Morgan Dennis (1892-1960), dated 1956, 7½x9" on 12½x13" sheet ..$135.00
Poodle, apron, dogs on hind legs balancing barware on noses, printed cotton, loop at neck, back ties, 1950s-60s $38.00

Poodle, barometer, Mitzi, turns from pink to blue depending on humidity, ceramic, Inarco, 1950s-60s, 4".......................**$55.00**

Poodle, bookends w/pen holders, painted redware, 1950s, 6".. **$35.00**

Poodle, figurine, brass, free-standing, 6¼x7" **$55.00**

Poodle, figurine, ceramic, gray w/brown eyes, seated, Japan, 5x5½x3⅛" **$10.00**

Poodle, figurine, creamic, black w/red collar & tongue, unmarked, 1950s, 11½x12" **$45.00**

Poodle, figurine, playful pose, ceramic, red w/much spaghetti, Japan, 2¾x5x3" **$22.50**

Poodle, figurine, recumbent, ceramic, pink spaghetti, hat w/red bow, rhinestones eyes & collar, 4½x4" **$50.00**

Poodle, lamp, figure on base, porcelain, white w/pink base & details, 1950s, 12" overall **$125.00**

Poodle, sachet holder, ceramic, stand w/basket on back, lavender hat w/sachet, IW Rice/Japan, 1950s, 5x2½x2"....................**$35.00**

Poodle, sewing basket, wicker w/aqua paint & applied poodle (felt), brass-colored knob on lid, 1950s **$60.00**

Poodle, tape measure, fuzzy cloth covering, pull tail for measure, 1950s, 3½x4" **$45.00**

Poodle, wastebasket, tin litho, dogs primping at dressing table, etc, among flowers on light blue, 1950s-60s, 9x10" **$40.00**

Pug, figurine, brass, playing piano, painted details, 5x5"....**$125.00**

Pug, toothpick/match holder, dog by basket, painted bisque, #21, 4¾" **$110.00**

Scottie, bedspread, chenille, multicolor pastels on white, 1940s, crib size, 44x32" **$65.00**

Scottie, book, MacGregor the Scottie, hardcover, 1945, 56 pages, 7¼x9¼" **$115.00**

Scottie, bookends, wooden head on base, Made in Japan, 5¼x4x2⅜" **$65.00**

Scottie, cigarette lighter, Vote (FDR) in 1932, composition dog figural, Made in USA, 2¼x3" **$48.00**

Scottie, figurine, painted cast iron, free-standing, 13"........**$115.00**

Scottie, figurine, painted chalkware, red bow at neck, sm paint chips, 7½x7½x4½" **$50.00**

Scottie, handkerchief, red, white & blue border w/polka dots & dogs, printed cotton, 10½x11" **$20.00**

Scottie, ink blotter, Jade-ite, designed to hold blotter w/metal clips (missing) **$40.00**

Scottie, lamp, 2 dogs 'listening' on base, cast iron w/original crinkle paint, rewired, 9x9" **$80.00**

Scottie, pencil case, vinyl, white on blue, working zipper, 3½x8" **$15.00**

Scottie, pencil holder, painted cast iron, legs on ⅞" ball, very heavy & detailed, 2¼" **$65.00**

Scottie, planter, ceramic, green w/blue eyes & yellow nose, Japan, 4½x8" **$12.50**

Scottie, reamer, Jade-ite w/black fired-on dogs (2), 7"..........**$55.00**

Scottie, salt & pepper shakers, boy pulls cart w/dogs (shakers), painted ceramic, Made in Japan, 3-pc set....................**$110.00**

Scottie, solid perfume, figural, filled w/Tuscany Per Donna, Estee Lauder, 1½", MIB..**$90.00**

Scottie, trinket box, Primrose Scottie & Hearts, Mary Engelbreit, Michel & Co, 2¾x2⅛" **$56.00**

Scottie, tumbler, black on red & black plaid on clear glass, Federal Glass, 4¾" **$8.00**

Scottie, wall pocket, by picket fence, ceramic, multicolor, Japan, 5¼x3½" **$60.00**

Springer spaniel, plate, Kaiser Porcelain, 1st edition, Series of Bird Dogs, John Francis, 7¾" **$185.00**

Terrier, figurine, ceramic, green w/brown collar & bow, #1119, Sylvac, 4" **$45.00**

Terrier, figurine, red bandage around head (toothache?), painted chalkware, 3¼" **$10.00**

Wire-hair fox terrier, figurine, ceramic, brown & white gloss, unmarked, 5x8" **$15.00**

Yorkshire terrier, perfume lamp, ceramic, glass eyes, tan w/red bow, 6½" **$225.00**

Scottie, paperweight, cast iron, Hamilton Foundry, 3½" long, $35.00.

Dollhouse Furniture

Some of the mass-produced dollhouse furniture you're apt to see on the market today was made by Renwal and Acme during the 1940s and Ideal in the 1960s. All three of these companies used hard plastic for their furniture lines and imprinted most pieces with their names. Strombecker furniture was made of wood, and although it was not marked, it has a certain recognizable style to it. Remember that if you're lucky enough to find doll furniture complete in the original box, you'll want to preserve the carton as well. Unless otherwise noted, our values are for items in undamaged original condition.

Advisor: Judith Mosholder (See Directory Dollhouse Furniture)

Acme/Thomas, dog for dogsled, cocker spaniel or dachshund, ea **$8.00**

Acme/Thomas, doll, Dutch girl, flesh-colored, Thomas, 2⅜".. **$5.00**

Acme/Thomas, doll, little brother w/raised hand, Thomas.....**$3.00**

Acme/Thomas, rocker, yellow w/green or yellow w/red, ea **$4.00**

Acme/Thomas, stroller, any color combo, ea..........................**$6.00**

Allied/Pyro, chair, dining; pink, red or white, ea...................**$3.00**

Allied/Pyro, hutch, aqua or red, ea...**$4.00**

Allied/Pyro, piano, black (unmarked) or light blue (Allied), ea.. **$5.00**

Allied/Pyro, radio, floor; yellow, ea.......................................**$8.00**

Allied/Pyro, stove, white, unmarked.......................................**$4.00**

Arcade, bath set (tub, sink, toilet), painted cast iron, white, VG paint $55.00

Arcade, bathroom set, NMIB, $2,200.00.

Arcade, breakfast nook set (Curtis), 3-pc (table & 2 benches), painted cast iron, white..............................$100.00

Arcade, cupboard (Boone), painted cast iron, white, 8" $90.00

Arcade, dresser, arched mirror, 4-drawer, 4-footed, green, 6½"..$220.00

Best, bunk bed, blue or pink, ea...$5.00

Best, cradle, blue $2.00

Blue Box, bed, light brown w/blue spread............................$5.00

Blue Box, hassock, light brown w/blue seat..........................$2.00

Blue Box, piano w/stool $8.00

Blue Box, vanity, w/heart-shaped mirror $4.00

Commonwealth, lamppost w/street sign & mailbox, black or red, ea...$15.00

Commonwealth, lawn mower, any color combo, ea.............$30.00

Commonwealth, watering can, red or white, ea.....................$6.00

Donna Lee, sink, stove or kitchen table, white, ea.................$4.00

Fisher-Price, chair, dining; brown w/tan seat........................$2.00

Fisher-Price, desk set, #261, $6.00. (Photo courtesy Brad Cassidy)

Fisher-Price, dresser w/mirror, white $5.00

Fisher-Price, stove w/hood, yellow..$5.00

Fisher-Price, toilet/vanity, bright green w/white trim $10.00

Ideal, birdbath, marbleized ivory..$18.00

Ideal, chair, chaise lounge; white.......................................$18.00

Ideal, chair, sq back, blue swirl, bright green swirl or med green swirl, all w/brown bases, ea.......................................$15.00

Ideal, china closet, red...$20.00

Ideal, dishwasher, w/lettering $20.00

Ideal, electric ironer, white w/black $18.00

Ideal, highboy, ivory w/blue...$18.00

Ideal, playpen, blue w/pink bottom or pink w/blue bottom, ea..$25.00

Ideal, refrigerator, Deluxe, white w/black, opening door, cardboard backing $30.00

Ideal, shopping cart, blue w/white baskets, white w/red or blue baskets, ea...$40.00

Ideal, sofa, med blue, med green, med green swirl or orange-red swirl, all w/brown bases, ea $22.00

Ideal, television, dog picture, yellow detail $45.00

Ideal, tub, corner; blue w/yellow $18.00

Ideal, vanity stool, ivory w/blue seat....................................$6.00

Ideal, vanity w/mirror, ivory w/blue, mirror good $18.00

Ideal Petite Princess, bed, #4416-4, blue or pink, complete, w/original box, ea...$30.00

Ideal Petite Princess, Buddha, #4437-0, metal....................$15.00

Ideal Petite Princess, candelabra, Fantasia #4438-8, in original box $22.00

Ideal Petite Princess, chair, guest dining; #4414-9, in original box $17.00

Ideal Petite Princess, chair & ottoman, occasional; #4412-3, light brown, w/original box..$22.00

Ideal Petite Princess, hearth place, Regency, #4422-2, complete in original box...$18.00

Ideal Petite Princess, piano & bench, grand; Royal #4425-5...$25.00

Ideal Petite Princess, table set, Heirloom #4428-9, complete, in original box...$27.00

Ideal Petite Princess, tea cart, rolling, #4424-8, complete, in original box...$20.00

Ideal Young Decorator, carpet sweeper, 2 rollers, red w/blue handle..$30.00

Ideal Young Decorator, china closet, dark marbleized maroon ..$25.00

Ideal Young Decorator, table, coffee; dark marbleized maroon..$18.00

Ideal Young Decorator, television, complete.........................$45.00

Irwin, clothes basket, bright yellow, 3" wide $4.00

Irwin, watering can, orange..$10.00

Irwin Interior Decorator, toilet, light green...........................$5.00

Jaydon, bed w/blue spread...$15.00

Jaydon, chair, living room; ivory w/brown base....................$8.00

Jaydon, hamper, red $5.00

Jaydon, refrigerator, ivory w/black......................................$15.00

Jaydon, sink, kitchen; ivory w/black....................................$15.00

Kage, cupboard, china; walnut...$8.00

Kage, table & chairs set, wire legs, red, larger scale $18.00

Kilgore, baby carriage, cast iron, orange w/nickel-plated top, handle & spoke wheels, 5½x5"...$355.00

Marx, curved sofa, hard plastic, ½" scale, bright yellow or red, ea..$15.00

Marx, iron, hard plastic, ¾" scale, white $8.00

Marx Little Hostess, clock, grandfather; red..........................$18.00
Marx Little Hostess, fireplace, ivory.....................................$20.00
Marx Little Hostess, table, tilt-top; black............................$12.00
Marx Little Hostess, wall mirror...**$5.00**
Nancy Forbes, bathroom set, 5-pc medicine cabinet, scale, sink & vanity w/mirror, ivory.....................................$25.00
Plasco, bed, yellow spread & brown headboard.....................**$3.00**
Plasco, chair, living room; w/base, bright green, light green or mauve, ea.....................................$15.00
Plasco, nightstand, brown, med marbleized brown or tan, ea..**$3.00**
Plasco, table, umbrella; blue w/ivory, complete....................$15.00
Plasco, toilet, turquoise w/white..**$8.00**
Reliable, chair, living room; blue w/rust base or red w/rust base, ea.....................................$15.00
Reliable, doll, baby sucking thumb, hard plastic, 2¾"..........**$10.00**
Reliable, table, dining; rust.....................................$20.00
Renwal, baby crib, ivory, Alice, Irene or Mary, ea................$10.00
Renwal, broom, witch's style, metallic blue handle..............$10.00
Renwal, carriage, doll insert, blue, stenciled.........................$35.00
Renwal, chair, club; dark blue base.......................................$15.00
Renwal, clock; ivory or red, ea..$20.00
Renwal, doll, chubby baby, painted diaper............................$45.00
Renwal, doll, painted suit.....................................$10.00
Renwal, garbage can, w/decal, yellow w/red............................**$8.00**
Renwal, highchair, ivory.....................................$30.00
Renwal, playground slide, blue w/red steps or yellow w/blue steps, ea.....................................**$22.00**
Renwal, rocker, yellow w/red...**$8.00**
Renwal, stove, non-opening door, ivory w/black door or turquoise, ea.....................................$12.00
Renwal, telephone, yellow w/red...$22.00
Renwal, vacuum cleaner, yellow w/red decal.........................$25.00
Sounds Like Home, dresser w/music box..............................$12.00
Sounds Like Home, night table w/electric alarm clock...........**$8.00**
Sounds Like Home, tissue box...**$5.00**
Strombecker, sink, bathroom; green w/gold swirl, 1" scale...$20.00
Strombecker, table, dining; walnut, 1930s, 1" scale.............$20.00
Tomy-Smaller Homes, bathtub...$15.00
Tomy-Smaller Homes, cat.....................................$10.00
Tomy-Smaller Homes, range top w/hood.............................$18.00
Tomy-Smaller Homes, stereo cabinet.....................................$15.00
Tomy-Smaller Homes, table lamp..$15.00
Tomy-Smaller Homes, throw rug..**$8.00**
Tootsietoy, buffet, opening drawer, cocoa brown..................$22.00
Tootsietoy, chair, club; blue...**$8.00**
Tootsietoy, chair, tufted look, dark red................................$20.00
Tootsietoy, rocker, wicker style w/cushion, gold or ivory, ea..$20.00
Tootsietoy, table, long, green crackle....................................$22.00

Dolls

Doll collecting is one of the most popular hobbies in the United States. Since many of the antique dolls are so expensive, modern dolls have come into their own and can be had at prices within the range of most budgets. Today's thrift-shop owners know the extent of 'doll mania,' though, so you'll seldom find a bargain there. But if you're willing to spend the time, garage sales can be a good source for your doll buying. Granted most will be in a 'well loved' condition, but as long as they're priced right, many can be re-dressed, rewigged, and cleaned up. Swap meets and flea markets may sometimes yield a good example or two, often at lower-than-book prices.

Modern dolls, those from 1935 to the present, are made of rubber, composition, magic skin, synthetic rubber, and many types of plastic. Most of these materials do not stand up well to age, so be objective when you buy, especially if you're buying with an eye to the future. Doll repair is an art best left to professionals, but if yours is only dirty, you can probably do it yourself. If you need to clean a composition doll, do it very carefully. Use only baby oil and follow up with a soft dry cloth to remove any residue. Most types of wigs can be shampooed with wig shampoo and lukewarm water. Be careful not to matt the hair as you shampoo, and follow up with hair conditioner or fabric softener. Comb gently and set while wet, using small soft rubber or metal curlers. Never use a curling iron or heated rollers.

Modern dolls including Kiddles, Dawn, Chrissy, Tammy, and Tressy, for instance, tend to sell better online, while other dolls such as vintage Barbie and hard plastic dolls seem to do better at shows. Newer collectible dolls fare better at shows as well, since the postage required for online sales has become a major factor for buyers.

In our listings, unless a condition is noted in the descriptions, values are for dolls in excellent condition.

For further study, we recommend these books: *Collector's Guide to Dolls of the 1960s and 1970s* by Cindy Sabulis; *Doll Values, Antique to Modern, 9th Edition,* by Linda Edward; *Horsman Dolls* by Don Jensen; *American Character Dolls* by Judith Izen; and *Collector's Encyclopedia of American Composition Dolls, 1900 – 1950, Vols. I* and *II,* by Ursula R. Mertz. All these references are published by Collector Books.

See also Barbie and Friends; Shirley Temple; Toys (Action Figures and GI Joe).

Magazine: *Doll Castle News*
P.O. Box 247
Washington, NJ 07882
800-752-6607

Newsletter: *Doll News*
United Federation of Doll Clubs
10900 North Pomona Ave.
Kansas City, MO 64153
816-891-7040
www.ufdc.org

Annalees

Barbara 'Annalee' Davis was born in Concord, New Hampshire, on February, 11, 1915. She started dabbling at doll-making at an early age, often giving her creations to friends. She married Charles 'Chip' Thorndike in 1941 and moved to Meredith, New Hampshire, where they started a chicken farm and sold used auto parts. By the early 1950s, with the chicken farm failing, Annalee started crafting her dolls on the kitchen table to help make ends meet. She designed her dolls by looking into the mirror, drawing faces as she saw them, and making the clothes from scraps of material.

The dolls she developed are made of wool felt with 'hand-painted' features and flexible wire frameworks. The earlier dolls from the 1950s had a long white red-embroidered tag with no date. From 1959 to 1964, the tags stayed the same except there was a date in the upper right-hand corner. From 1965 to 1970, this same tag was folded in half and sewn into the seam of the doll. In 1970 a transition period began. The company changed its tag to a satiny white tag with a date preceded by a copyright symbol in the upper right-hand corner. In 1975 they made another change to a long white cotton strip with a copyright date. In 1982 the white tag was folded over, making it shorter. Many people mistake the copyright date as the date the doll was made — not so! It wasn't until 1986 that they finally began to date the tags with the year of manufacture, making it much easier for collectors to identify their dolls. Besides the red-lettered white Annalee tags, numerous others were used in the 1990s, but all reflect the year the doll was actually made.

Annalee's signature can increase a doll's value by as much as $300.00, sometimes more. Annalee died in April 2002, but she had personally signed no dolls for several years. Chuck (her son) and Karen Thorndike are now signing them.

Remember, these dolls are made of wool felt. To protect them, store them with moth balls, and avoid exposing them to too much sunlight, since they will fade. Our advisor has been a collector for almost 20 years and a secondary market dealer since 1988. Most of these dolls have been in her collection at one time or another. She recommends 'If you like it, buy it, love it, treat it with care, and you'll have it to enjoy for many years to come.'

Unless noted otherwise, our values are suggested for dolls in very good to excellent condition, not personally autographed by Annalee herself.

Advisor: Jane Holt (See Directory, Dolls)

Newsletter: *The Club News*
Annalee Doll Society
P.O. Box 1137
50 Reservoir Rd.
Meredith, NH 03253-1137

1963, monk w/white beard, black hooded robe & skullcap, 10". **$85.00**
1963, Santa & Mrs Claus, 7", pr **$60.00**

1970, Country Cousin boy and girl mice, 7", $225.00 for the pair. (Photo courtesy Jane Holt)

1971, boy bunny w/butterfly on nose, yellow, 18"............**$125.00**
1972, duck on sled, 5" **$22.50**
1976, elephant, 18"...**$250.00**
1976, Yankee Doodle Dandy, 18", w/18" horse.................**$250.00**
1977, Jack Frost, 22" **$95.00**
1979, fireman mouse, complete w/ladder............................**$25.00**
1980 only, disco mouse (boy or girl), 7" **$35.00**
1981, mouse in Christmas stocking, 22"..............................**$30.00**
1982, country girl, red pigtails, holds basket, 7" **$30.00**
1982, PJ kid, boy w/black hair, girl w/blond, 18", ea..........**$50.00**
1983, ballooning elves, white, in 10" basket of 2-toned green felt air balloon...**$100.00**
1986, boy bunny w/wheelbarrow, 30"................................**$125.00**
1986, logo kid w/pin, 7"..**$100.00**
1988, bear on sled, 10" **$50.00**
1990, angel, 30"..**$100.00**
1990, artist mouse, 7"...**$20.00**
1990, elf, pink or yellow, 22" **$20.00**
1991, cat, black w/green eyes, 12" **$40.00**
1991, waiter mouse, made for 1 year only, 7" **$40.00**
1993, Christmas girl chicken, 8"...**$40.00**
1993, Flood Relief mouse, 7"...**$30.00**
1993, wizard mouse, 7"..**$25.00**
1994, Hershey kid, dressed in foil-like chocolate kiss, 7" **$40.00**
1997, Happy New Year kid, 7" **$25.00**

Betsy McCall

The tiny 8" Betsy McCall doll was manufactured by the American Character Doll Company from 1957 through 1963. Other companies eventually produced this doll in several different sizes. She was made from high-quality hard plastic with a bisque-like finish and hand-painted features. Betsy came in four hair colors — tosca, red, blond, and brunette. She had blue sleep eyes, molded lashes, a winsome smile, and a fully jointed body with bendable knees. On her back there is an identification circle which reads McCall Corp. The basic doll wore a sheer chemise, white taffeta panties, nylon socks, and Mary Jane-style shoes and could be purchased for $2.25.

There were two different materials used for tiny Betsy's hair. The first was a soft mohair sewn into fine mesh. Later the rubber skullcap was rooted with saran which was more suitable for washing and combing.

Betsy McCall had an extensive wardrobe with nearly 100 outfits, each of which could be purchased separately. They were made from wonderful fabrics such as velvet, taffeta, felt, and even real mink. Each ensemble came with the appropriate footwear and was priced under $3.00. Since none of Betsy's clothing was tagged, it is often difficult to identify other than by its square snap closures (although these were used by other companies as well).

Betsy McCall is a highly collectible doll today but she is getting more difficult to locate in fine condition. Prices continue to rise for this beautiful clotheshorse and her many accessories. For further information we recommend *Betsy McCall, A Collector's Guide,* by Marci Van Ausdall.

Advisor: Marci Van Ausdall (See Directory, Dolls)

Club: Betsy McCall Fan Club
dreams@psin.com

Accessory, Betsy McCall's Pretty Pac, round vinyl hatbox-style case w/strap, graphics on front, accessories inside, NM......**$150.00**

Betsy McCall Fashion Designer Set, unused, M, $125.00.
(Photo courtesy Marci Van Ausdall)

Clothes, Pony Pals, MOC, $95.00. (Photo courtesy Marci Van Ausdall)

Doll, American Character, Linda McCall (Betsy's Cousin), vinyl w/ Betsy face, rooted hair, 1959, 36" **$500.00**
Doll, American Character, vinyl, jointed limbs & waist, rooted hair (made in various colors), original outfit, 1961, 22" **$225.00**
Doll, American Character, vinyl, jointed shoulders & hips, rooted hair, 14", w/trunk & outfits, G, from $400 to............**$500.00**
Doll, American Character, vinyl w/Patti Play Pal-style body, rooted hair, nude, 1959, 36"..**$250.00**
Doll, American Character, vinyl w/rooted hair, flirty eyes, original outfit: Sugar & Spice gown, 20", NM **$350.00**
Doll, Horsman, Betsy McCall's Beauty Box, rigid plastic w/vinyl head, sleep eyes, hairpiece, etc, 1974, 12½", MIB........**$50.00**
Doll, Horsman, rigid plastic teen body w/vinyl head, rooted hair w/ side part, clothes marked BMc, 1974, 29", MIB........**$275.00**

Doll, Ideal, hard palstic body w/rooted hair, nude, played with, 14"..**$45.00**
Doll, Ideal, hard plastic body w/rooted hair, all original, 14" ..**$300.00**
Doll, Uneeda, rigid vinyl body, rooted hair, w/original outfit, 1964, 11½", MIB, minimum value......................................**$125.00**

Celebrity Dolls

Celebrity and character dolls have been widely collected for many years, but they've lately shown a significant increase in demand. Except for rarer examples, most of these dolls are still fairly easy to find at doll shows, toy auctions, and flea markets, and the majority are priced under $100.00. These are the dolls that bring back memories of childhood TV shows, popular songs, favorite movies, and familiar characters. Mego, Mattel, Remco, and Hasbro are among the largest manufacturers.

Condition is a very important worth-assessing factor, and if the doll is still in the original box, so much the better! Should the box be unopened (NRFB), the value is further enhanced. Using mint in box as a standard, deduct 30% to 35% for one that is mint (no box). Increase the price for 'never removed from box' examples by about 40%. Values for dolls in only good or poorer condition drop at a rapid pace.

See also Elvis Presley Memorabilia.

John Travolta, Chemtoy, 1977, 12", from $45.00 to $75.00. (Photo courtesy Cindy Sabulis)

Betty Grable, blond Dynel hair, International Doll Co, 1940s, w/ tag, 1940s, 19", NM, minimum value........................**$400.00**
Brooke Shields, Prom Party, LJN, 1982, rare, 11½", MIB ...**$65.00**
Cher, Growing Hair, Mego, 1976, 12½", MIB..................**$150.00**
Cheryl Ladd, Mattel, 1978, 11½", MIB **$85.00**
Christy Brinkley, Real Model Collection, Matchbox, 1989, 11½", MIB..**$50.00**
Diana Ross, Mego, 1977, 12½", MIB...............................**$150.00**

Diedre Hall (Days of Our Lives), Mattel, 1999, 11½", MIB..**$35.00**

Dolly Parton, black outfit, silver boots, Goldberger, 1990s,12", MIB...**$75.00**

Dorothy Hamill, Olympic Ice Skater, Ideal, 1977, 11½", MIB.**$100.00**

Eleanor Roosevelt, brown dress, Effanbee, 1985, 14½", MIB...**$125.00**

George Burns, black tuxedo, holds cigar, Effanbee, 1996, 17", MIB **$150.00**

Groucho Marx, Julius Henry/Effanbee, 1982, 18", MIB ...**$150.00**

James Dean, sweater & pants, DSI, 1994, 12", MIB **$55.00**

KISS, any member from group, Mego, 1978, 12½", MIB, ea..**$350.00**

Leslie Uggams, light pink dress, Madame Alexander, 1966, 17", MIB...**$350.00**

Margaret O'Brien, Madame Alexander, 18", EX...............**$675.00**

Muhammad Ali, Hasbro, 1997, 12", MIB........................**$45.00**

Patty Duke, marked H on head, 11", from $100.00 to $125.00. (Photo courtesy Cindy Sabulis)

Prince William, as baby, House of Misbet, 1982, 18", MIB ..**$200.00**

Queen Elizabeth, white satin gown, Effanbee, 1980s, 14", MIB..**$75.00**

Selena, red jumpsuit, Arm Enterprise, 1996, 11½", MIB.....**$85.00**

Vanna White, gold dress & purple jumpsuit, HSC, 1990, 11½", MIB...**$55.00**

Chatty Cathy and Other Mattel Talkers

One of the largest manufacturers of modern dolls is the Mattel company, the famous maker of the Barbie doll. But besides Barbie, there are many other types of Mattel's dolls that have their own devotees, and we've tried to list a sampling of several of their more collectible lines.

Next to Barbie, the all-time favorite doll was Mattel's Chatty Cathy. She was first made in the 1960s, in blond and brunette variations, and much of her success can be attributed to that fact that she could talk! By pulling the string on her back, she could respond with eleven different phrases. The line was expanded and soon included Chatty Baby, Tiny Chatty Baby and Tiny Chatty Brother (the twins), Charmin' Chatty, and finally Singing' Chatty. They all sold successfully for five years, and although Mattel reintroduced the line

in 1969 (smaller and with a restyled face), it was not well received.

In 1960 Mattel introduced their first line of talking dolls. They decided to take the talking doll's success even further by introducing a new line — cartoon characters that the young TV viewers were already familiar with.

Below you will find a list of the more popular dolls and animals available. Most MIB (mint-in-box) toys found today are mute, but this should not detract from the listed price. If the doll still talks, you may consider adding a few more dollars to the price. Our values, unless noted otherwise, are for items in excellent condition. For more information we recommend *Collector's Guide to Dolls of the 1960s and 1970s* by our advisor Cindy Sabulis, published by Collector Books.

Advisor: Cindy Sabulis (See Directory, Dolls)

Baby Beans, beanbag w/vinyl head, 1961-75, 12", EX, from $30 to **$40.00**

Baby First Step, battery operated, rooted hair, sleep eyes, pink dress, 1960s, 18", from $120 to **$150.00**

Baby Say 'n See, eyes & lips move while talking, white dress w/pink yoke, 1967-68, 17", from $95 to **$125.00**

Baby Secret, vinyl face & hands, stuffed body, whispers 11 phrases while moving lips, 1966-67, 18", from $75 to..............**$85.00**

Baby Tenderlove, realistic skin, 1967-3, 16", from $25 to....**$35.00**

Buffy, vinyl, holds 6" Mrs Beasley rag doll, 1969-71, 10¾", from $340 to **$360.00**

Buffy and Mrs. Beasley, MIB, $150.00. (Photo courtesy mydollydearest, Sidney Jeffery)

Captain Kangaroo, Sears only, 1967, 19", from $40 to........**$50.00**

Charmin' Chatty, soft vinyl head, long rooted hair, 1963-64, 24", from $150 to **$200.00**

Chatty Baby, red pinafore over romper, 1962-64, 18", from $80 to **$110.00**

Chatty Cathy, blond, pull-string talker, party dress, 1960s, 20", M **$350.00**

Chatty Cathy, vinyl head, hard plastic body, pink & white checked party dress, blond (not pigtails), 1960-63, 20" **$300.00**
Chatty Cathy, 1970 reissue, MIB, from $75 to **$100.00**

Clothing for Chatty Cathy, Sunny Day, #398, very rare, MIP, $225.00. (Photo courtesy mydollydearest, Sidney Jeffery)

Drowsy, vinyl head, sutffed body, dressed in sleeper, 1965-74, 15½", MIB **$200.00**
Herman Munster, cloth, 1965, 21", from $150 to **$175.00**
Shrinkin' Violette, cloth w/yarn hair, eyes close, mouth moves, 1964-65, 16", from $175 to **$200.00**
Singin' Chatty, blond hair, M **$250.00**
Tatters, cloth, wears rag clothes, 1967-67, 19", from $95 to .. **$110.00**
Teachy Keen, vinyl head, cloth body, Sears only, 1966-70, 16", from $20 to **$30.00**
Tiny Chatty Brother, hair parted on side, blue & white suit & cap, 1963-64, 15½", from $85 to **$95.00**

Dawn

Made by Deluxe Topper in the 1970s, this 6" fashion doll and her friends were sold individually as regular or dancing dolls. There were also various series, including modeling agencies, flower fantasies, and majorettes. They're becoming highly collectible, especially when mint in the box. They were issued already dressed in clothes of the highest style, or you could buy additional outfits, many complete with matching shoes and accessories. To evaluate loose dolls in good to very good condition, deduct about 75% to 80% from our NRFB values.

Advisor: Dawn Diaz (See Directory, Dolls)

Doll, Dancing Angie, NRFB **$50.00**
Doll, Dancing Dale, NRFB **$65.00**
Doll, Dancing Glori, NRFB **$50.00**
Doll, Dancing Jessica, NRFB **$50.00**
Doll, Dancing Ron, NRFB **$50.00**
Doll, Dancing Van, NRFB **$80.00**
Doll, Daphne Model Agency, green & silver dress, NRFB. **$100.00**
Doll, Dawn, Head to Toe, silver or pink mini dress, NRFB, from $65 to **$80.00**

Doll, Dawn Majorette, NRFB **$75.00**
Doll, Denise or Dinah Model Agency, NRFB, ea **$100.00**
Doll, Gary or Jessica, NRFB, ea **$50.00**
Doll, Kip Majorette, NRFB **$65.00**
Doll, Longlocks, NRFB **$50.00**
Doll, loose, knees w/green oxidation from metal inside, from $5 to **$15.00**
Doll, Ron, NRFB **$55.00**
Outfit, Bell Bottom Flounce, #0717, NRFB **$25.00**

Doll, Dancing Dawn, 1971, NRFB, $35.00 to $50.00. (Photo courtesy mydollydearest, Sidney Jeffery)

Fisher-Price

Though you're more familiar with the lithographed plastic toys this company has made for years, they also made dolls as well. The earlier dolls that were made in the 1970s had stuffed cloth bodies and vinyl heads, hands, and feet. Some had battery-operated voice boxes. In 1981 they introduced Kermit the Frog and Miss Piggy and a line of clothing for each.

Our values are for dolls in excellent to near mint condition, unless noted otherwise. Outfits are generally priced at $10.00 to $12.00 in excellent conditon.

Joey, #206, jacket and shoes, 1975 – 1976, M, $25.00.
(Photo courtesy Brad Cassidy)

Baby Soft Sounds, #213, MIB **$65.00**
Elizabeth, #205, 1974-75 ....**$25.00**
Jenny, #201, 1974-76, MIB **$55.00**
Mandy, Happy Birthday, #4009, 1985......................**$50.00**
Mikey, #240, 1979-80, EXIB..................................**$45.00**
My Friend Becky, #218, 1982-84, EX.......................**$20.00**
My Friend Jenny, MIB..**$100.00**
My Friend Mandy, #201, 1977-78; #211, 1978-81; or #215, 1982-83, ea **$25.00**
My Friend Mikey, #205, 1982-84 ....**$30.00**
Natalie, #202, 1974-76, MIB **$65.00**

Hasbro

Hasbro is probably best known for their GI Joe dolls, but they made many other lines that are collectible, though on a lesser scale. Among them are the Jem dolls that were introduced in 1985, paralleling the popular Saturday morning TV show. This line consisted of the members of the show's rock band, The Holograms, as well as members of the cast. Their clothes, makeup, and hairdos were wonderfully exotic, and their faces were beautifully modeled. The Jem line was discontinued in 1987. They also made Dolly Darlings, little 4" dolls that came packaged inside round plastic hatbox cases, boxes with celophane fronts, or in a bubble with cardboard backing. Some had rooted hair, while others had hair that was simply molded. Other lines were Flower Darlings, 3½" dolls that came with fragrant pin-on flowers; Storykins, 3½" plastic dolls representing characters such as Mother Hubbard, Cinderella, Snow White, and Pinocchio; World of Love dolls; Leggy dolls (10"); and many others. Unless noted otherwise, our values are for dolls in near mint condition.

Advisor: Cindy Sabulis (See Directory, Dolls)

Pizzazz of the Misfits (Jem), MIB, from $50.00 to $75.00.

Aja (Jem), Hologram, 1st issue, #4210/4005, 12½", from $50 to...**$60.00**
Ashley (Jem), Starlight Girl, no wrist or elbow joints, #4211/4025, 11", from $30 to...............................**$40.00**
Ashley (Jem), Starlight Girl, no wrist or elbow joints, #4211/4025, 11", from $30 to...............................**$40.00**
Dolly Darling, 1965, 4½", from $40 to **$50.00**
Jem, Glitter 'n Gold, #4001, 12½", from $110 to **$125.00**
Jem accessory, Glitter 'n Gold Roadster, NRFB, from $200 to ..**$250.00**
Jem accessory, Star Stage, NRFB, from $40 to **$50.00**
Jem fashion, Encore, #4223/4040, NRFB......................**$35.00**
Jem fashion, Music Is Magic, #4217/4040, NRFB **$30.00**
Jem fashion, Up & Rockin', Flip Side Fashions, #4232/4045, NRFB **$20.00**
Maxie, vinyl, fashion doll, 1987, 11½", from $15 to..........**$20.00**
Shana (Jem), Hologram, 2nd issue, #4203/4005, 12½", from $200 to...**$225.00**
Storykin, Cinderella, Goldilocks, etc, 1967, 3", ea from $40 to..**$50.00**
Sweet Cookie, vinyl, w/cooking accessories, 1972, 18", from $100 to...**$125.00**

Holly Hobbie

In the late 1960s a young homemaker and mother, Holly Hobbie, approached the American Greeting Company with some charming country-styled drawings of children as proposed designs for greeting cards. Her concepts were well received by the company, and since that time thousands of Holly Hobbie items have been produced. Nearly all are marked HH, H. Hobbie, or Holly Hobbie.

Wristwatch, It's Time To Be Happy, Bradley, 1972, MIB, $18.00.
(Photo courtesy LiveAuctioneers.com/Tom Harris Auctions)

Country Fun Holly Hobbie, 16", 1989, NRFB **$20.00**
Grandma Holly, 14", MIB.......................................**$20.00**
Grandma Holly, 24", MIB.......................................**$25.00**
Holly Hobbie, Amy, or Carrie Dream Along, 12", MIB, ea.**$15.00**
Holly Hobbie, Bicentennial, 12", MIB **$25.00**
Holly Hobbie, Day 'n Night, 14", MIB........................**$15.00**
Holly Hobbie, Heather, Amy or Carrie, 6", MIB..............**$5.00**
Holly Hobbie, Heather, Amy or Carrie, 9", MIB, ea **$10.00**

Holly Hobbie, Heather, Amy or Carrie, 16", MIB...............**$20.00**
Holly Hobbie, Heather, Amy or Carrie, 27", MIB, ea **$25.00**
Holly Hobbie, Heather, Amy or Carrie, 33", MIB, ea **$35.00**
Holly Hobbie, scented, clear ornament around neck, 1988, 18",
    NRFB **$30.00**
Holly Hobbie, talker, 4 sayings, 16", MIB **$25.00**
Holly Hobbie, 25th Anniversary, 26", 1994, MIB **$55.00**
Little Girl Holly, 1980, 15", MIB....................................**$20.00**
Robby, 9", MIB **$15.00**
Robby, 16", MIB **$20.00**

Ideal

The Ideal Toy Company made many popular dolls such as Shirley Temple, Betsy Wetsy, Miss Revlon, Toni, and Patti Playpal. Ideal's doll production was so enormous that since 1907 over 700 different dolls have been 'brought to life,' made from materials such as composition, latex rubber, hard plastic, and vinyl.

Since Ideal dolls were mass produced, most are still accessible and affordable. Collectors often find these dolls at garage sales and flea markets. However, some Ideal dolls are highly desirable and command high prices — into the thousands of dollars. These sought-after dolls include the Samantha doll, variations of the Shirley Temple doll, certain dolls in the Patti Playpal family, and some Captain Action dolls.

The listing given here is only a sampling of Ideal dolls made from 1907 to 1989. This listing reports current, realistic selling prices at doll shows and through mail order. Please remember these values are for dolls in excellent condition with original clothing and tags.

For more information please refer to *Collector's Guide to Ideal Dolls* by Judith Izen (Collector Books).

See also Advertising Characters; Shirley Temple; and Dolls' sub-categories: Betsy McCall, Celebrity Dolls, and Tammy.

Club: Ideal Collectors Club
Judith Izen
P.O. Box 623, Lexington, MA 02173
jizen@rcn.com

April Showers, vinyl, battery operated, splashes hands, head turns,
    199, 14", from $35 to..**$40.00**
Baby Pebbles, vinyl head, soft body, rooted hair, painted eyes, leopard print outfit, 1963-64, 14", from $165 to.............**$170.00**
Bamm-Bamm, vinyl, rooted saran hair, leopard skin suit, cap & club,
    1964, 12", from $70 to..**$80.00**
Belly Button Baby (Black), vinyl head, rooted hair, painted eyes,
    1971, 9½", from $40 to...**$45.00**
Belly Button Baby (white), vinyl head, rooted hair, painted eyes,
    1971, 9½", from $30 to...**$40.00**
Bonnie Play Pal, vinyl, saran hair, closed mouth, 1959, 24", from
    $375 to...**$400.00**
Brandi (white), vinyl, rooted growing hair, swivel waist, 1972-73,
    18", from $65 to...**$75.00**
Cinnamon, vinyl head, painted eyes, auburn growing hair, 1972-74,
    13½", from $50 to...**$60.00**
Clarabelle, mask face & cloth body, 1954, 16", from $200 to ..**$225.00**

Cream Puff, vinyl with original clothes, 1958, 21", EX+, from $65.00 to $80.00. (Photo courtesy mydollydearest, Sidney Jeffery)

Daddy's Girl, vinyl & plastic, swivel waist, saran hair, blue sleep eyes,
    1961, 38", from $1,100 to..**$1,200.00**
Dennis the Menace, printed cloth, 1976, 7", from $10 to ...**$15.00**
Joan Palooka, vinyl head, 'Magic Skin' body, jointed arms & legs,
    painted eyes, 1952, 14", from $175 to........................**$200.00**
Judy Splinter, vinylite, ventriloquist doll, open/closed mouth, 1949-
    50, 18", from $200 to...**$225.00**
Miss Curity, hard plastic, saran wig, sleep eyes, black eye shadow,
    1953, 14½", from $300 to...**$350.00**

Revlon, vinyl head with rooted nylon hair, jointed body, VT-18, all original, 18", $345.00. (Photo courtesy McMasters Harris Auction Company)

Saucy Walker Big Sister, hard plastic, flirty blue eyes, crier, saran wig
w/plastic curlers, 1951-55, 14", from $175 to **$200.00**

Tiffany Taylor, vinyl, rooted hair, top of head turns to change color, teenage body, high-heeled, 1974-76, 19", $60 to..........**$70.00**

Toddler, vinyl head, jointed hard plastic body, open/closed mouth w/ teeth, walker, 1953, 11½", from $125 to....................**$150.00**

Liddle Kiddles

These tiny little dolls ranging from ¾" to 4" tall were made by Mattel from 1966 until 1979. They all had poseable bodies and rooted hair that could be restyled, and they came with accessories of many types. Some represented storybook characters, some were flowers in perfume bottles, some were made to be worn as jewelry, and there were even spacemen 'Kiddles.'

Serious collectors prefer examples that are still in their original packaging and for them will often pay a minimum of 30% (to as much as 100%) over the price of a near mint doll with all her original accessories. A doll whose accessories are missing is worth from 65% to 70% less. Unless noted othewise, our values are for dolls in near mint to mint condition and complete with their original accessories. For more information, we recommend *Schroeder's Collectible Toys, Antique to Modern* (Collector Books).

Advisor: Dawn Diaz (See Directory, Dolls)

Alice in Wonderliddle, complete set, $135.00. (Photo courtesy Cindy Sabulis)

Aqua Funny Bunny, #3532	$30.00
Baby Din-Din, #3820	$50.00
Beach Buggy, #5003	$35.00
Calamity Jiddle, #3506, w/high saddle horse	$75.00
Cinderiddle's Palace, plastic window version, #5068	$25.00
Dainty Deer, #3637	$15.00
Flower Charm Bracelet, #3747, MIP	$50.00
Flower Pin Kiddle, #3741, MIP	$50.00
Greta Grape, #3728, from $35 to	$40.00
Heart Pin Kiddle, #3741, MIP	$50.00
Henrietta Horseless Carriage, #3641, from $40 to	$50.00

Honeysuckle Kologne, #3704, MIP	$75.00
Howard Biff Biddle, #3502	$60.00
Jewelry Kiddle, Treasure Box, red, #3735	$25.00
Kiddles & Kars Antique Fair Set, #3806, MIP	$300.00
Kiddles Kologne, #3710 Gardenia, MIP	$75.00
Kleo Kola, #3729, from $35 to	$40.00
Laffy Lemon, #3732, MIP	$85.00
Liddle Biddle Peep, #3544	$150.00
Liddle Kiddles Kabin #3591	$25.00
Liddle Kiddles Kottage, #3534	$25.00
Liddle Kiddles Pop-Up Boutique, #5170	$30.00
Liddle Kiddles Talking Townhouse, #5154, MIB	$50.00
Lilac Locket, #3540, MIP	$75.00
Lois Locket, #3541	$75.00
Lolli-Lemon, #3657, MIP	$75.00
Lou Locket, #3537, MIP	$75.00
Luana Locket, Gold Rush version, #3680, MIP	$85.00
Lucky Locket Jewel Case, #3542	$150.00
Luscious Lime, glitter version, #3733	$50.00
Millie Middle, #3509	$150.00
Olivia Orange Kola Kiddle, #3730, MIP	$80.00
Rapunzel & the Prince, #3783, MIP	$150.00
Romeo & Juliet, #3782, MIP	$150.00
Shirley Strawberry, #3727, from $35 to	$40.00
Sleeping Biddle, #3527, from $150 to	$175.00
Suki Skediddle, #3736	$25.00

Sweet Pea Kiddle Kologne, #3705, original cardboard base and hang tag, $60.00.

Teresa Touring Car, #3644, from $40 to	$50.00
Tiny Tiger, #3636, MIP	$75.00
Tracy Trikediddle, #3769, complete, M	$50.00
Trikey Triddle, #3515	$75.00
Vanilla Lilly, #2819, MIP	$25.00
Violet Kologne, #3713, MIP	$60.00
Windy Fiddle, #3514, complete, M	$85.00
World of the Kiddles Beauty Bazaar, #3586, NRFB	$300.00

Littlechap Family

In 1964 Remco Industries created a family of four fashion dolls that represented an upper-middle class American family. The Littlechaps family consisted of the father, Dr. John Littlechap, his wife, Lisa, and their two children, teenage daughter Judy and pre-teen Libby. Interest in these dolls is on the rise as more and more collectors discover the exceptional quality of these fashion dolls and their clothing.

Advisor: Cindy Sabulis (See Directory, Dolls)

Carrying Case, EX $40.00

Doll, Dr. John, MIB, from $50.00 to $65.00. (Photo courtesy Cindy Sabulis)

Doll, Lisa, MIB...$65.00
Family Room, Bedroom or Doctor John's Office, EX, ea $125.00
Outfit, Doctor John, complete, EX, from $15 to.................$30.00
Outfit, Doctor John, NRFB, from $40 to...........................$50.00
Outfit, Judy, complete, EX, from $25 to.............................$40.00
Outfit, Judy, NRFB, from $35 to $75.00
Outfit, Libby, complete, EX, from $20 to........................$35.00
Outfit, Libby, NRFB, from $35 to......................................$50.00
Outfit, Lisa, complete, EX, from $20 to..........................$35.00
Outfit, Lisa, NRFB, from $35 to......................................$75.00

Madame Alexander

This company was founded in 1923 by Beatrice Alexander. The first doll they produced was Alice in Wonderland, made entirely of cloth with an oil-painted face. With the help of her three sisters, the company prospered, and by the 1960s, there were over 600 employees busy making Madame Alexander dolls. They're still in business today. If you'd like to learn more about these lovely dolls, refer to *Collector's Encyclopedia of Madame Alexander Dolls, 1948 – 1965,* and *Madame Alexander Collector's Dolls Price Guide* by Linda Crowsey. Both are published by Collector Books.

Our values are for perfect dolls. Prices for those made before 1973 will not include the original box; but for those made since that time, the box must be present to warrant the values given below.

Active Miss, hard plastic, Violet/Cissy, 1954 only, 18".......$850.00
Alexander-Kin, basic doll, panties, shoes, socks, 7½-8" $525.00
Baby Madison, vinyl, w/layette, #29750, 1999, 14" $75.00
Black Forest, Wendy Ann, #512, 1989-90, 8"....................$55.00
Cissy Godey Bride, porcelain, #011, 1993 only, 21".........$375.00
Dearest, vinyl baby, 1962-64, 12", from $125 to..............$175.00

Elise Bride, hard plastic with vinyl arms, M, $450.00. (Photo courtesy Cindy Sabulis)

Guinevere, blue dress w/white brocade over dress, #13570, 1999, 8"..$80.00
Irish Lass, #11555, 1995 only, 8".......................................$60.00
Leslie (Black Polly), vinyl, in dress, 1965-71, 18" $275.00
Little Huggums, Jacobsons, 1995..$60.00
Littlest Kitten, lacy dress w/bonnet, 1963, 8", minimum value..$275.00
Mary Cassatt Baby, cloth & vinyl, 1969-70, 14" $175.00
Muffin, cloth, 1966 only, 19"...$100.00
Navajo Boy, Madame Alexander Doll Club Convention, #34480, 2002, 8"..$350.00
Nurse, all white dress, comes w/baby, #429, 1961, 8", minimum value $650.00
Peruvian Boy, hard plastic, bent knees, Wendy Ann, #770, 1966, 8" $350.00
Quiz-Kin, Peter Pan, caracul wig, 1953, 8".....................$850.00
Renoir, hard plastic w/vinyl arms, pink gown, Jacqueline, #2154, 1965, 21"...$700.00
Rusty, cloth & vinyl, 1967-68 only, 20" $300.00

Smarty, plastic & vinyl, #1160, #1136, 1962-63, 12".........**$275.00**

Snow White, Disney Annual Showcase of Dolls, Dancy Drew, 1990, 12"...**$150.00**

Sugar Tears, vinyl baby, Honeybea, 1964 only, 12"............**$100.00**

Trellis Rose Flower Girl, long white dress, #28650, 2001-02, 8"..**$80.00**

Winged Monkey, hard plastic, Maggy, #140501, 1994 only, 8"...**$100.00**

Nancy Ann Storybook

This company was in business as early as 1936, producing painted bisque dolls with mohair wigs and painted eyes. Later they made hard plastic 8" Muffie and Miss Nancy Ann Style Show dolls. Debby (11") and Lori Ann (7½") had vinyl heads and hard plastic bodies. In the 1950s and 1960s, they produced a 10½" Miss Nancy Ann and Little Miss Nancy Ann, both vinyl high-heeled fashion-type dolls.

Our values are for painted bisque dolls, all original and in in near mint to mint condition unless otherwise noted.

Black-Eyed Susan, Flower Girl Series, 1941, 5½", M w/tag..**$185.00**

Bridesmaid, #87, 5½" **$65.00**

The Child That Was Born on the Sabbath, jointed legs, #186, $175.00. (Photo courtesy Elaine M. Pardee and Jackie Robertson)

Christening Baby, Commencement Series, #70, 3½" **$85.00**

Daffy-Down-Dilly, Nursery Rhyme Series, #171, 5½", MIB..**$75.00**

Hush-a-Bye Baby Baby, composition, painted eyes, #210 long dress & cape, 3½", MIB **$380.00**

Judy Ann, Storybook mold, 5"...**$200.00**

Little Bo Peep, Fairyland Series, pudgy tummy, 5½"..........**$130.00**

Little Bo Peep, hard plastic, #153, 5½" **$55.00**

Little Joan, frozen legs, taffeta-trimmed dress, #111, 5", MIB...**$55.00**

Mary Had a Little Lamb, slim body, #152, 1943-47, 5"......**$70.00**

Merry Maid for New Year, #187, 6".....................................**$60.00**

Mexico, International Series, 1942, 5¼" **$175.00**

Miss Checkerboard, Style Show Series, hard plastic, 18"....**$345.00**

Muffie, hard plastic, sleep eyes, in panties & socks, 8", EXIB ...**$250.00**

Pretty Maid, Nursery Rhyme Series, #160, 19402, 5", MIB..**$100.00**

Queen of Hearts, Fairyland Series, brown hair, #157, 5½", MIB **$135.00**

Raggedy Ann and Andy

Raggedy Ann dolls have been made since the early part of the twentieth century, and over the years many companies have produced their own versions. They were created originally by Johnny Gruelle, and though these early dolls are practically nonexistent, they're easily identified by the mark, 'Patented Sept. 7, 1915.' P.F. Volland made them from 1920 to 1934; theirs were very similar in appearance to the originals. The Mollye Doll Outfitters were the first to print the now-familiar red heart on her chest, and they added a black outline around her nose. These dolls carry the handwritten inscription 'Raggedy Ann and Andy Doll/Manufactured by Mollye Doll Outfitters.' Georgene Averill made them ca 1938 to 1950, sewing their label into the seam of the dolls. Knickerbocker dolls (1963 to 1982) also carry a company label. The Applause Toy Company made these dolls for two years in the early 1980s, and they were finally taken over by Hasbro, the current producer, in 1983.

Values apply to examples in conditions noted. Please note: Compared to a near mint condition doll, one in good condition with a few minor flaws (as most are) will be worth approximately 75% less.

Applause, Raggedy Ann & Andy Dance w/Me, elastic straps on hands & feet, 45", M, pr **$225.00**

Georgene, black plastic eyes, all original, 1947, 22", EX....**$165.00**

Georgene, nose outlined in black, all original, 1930s, 19", VG..**$195.00**

Georgene, nose outlined in black, 1940s, 19", EX.............**$365.00**

Georgene, Raggedy Andy, plain nose, black plastic eyes, all original, 1946, 16", VG...**$145.00**

Georgene, Raggedy Ann, button eyes, long nose, 32", G, $150.00.
(Photo courtesy LiveAuctioneers.com/Garth's Auctions Inc.)

Georgene, 2-face (awake & asleep), nose outlined in black, some fading, 1940s, 13½", VG $525.00

Hasbro, in green Christmas dress w/red heart, white pinafore, 1998, 24" $20.00

Knickerbocker, bean-bag type, NMIB..............................$80.00

Knickerbocker, black plastic eyes, bottom lashes, all original, needs minor repairs, 40" $130.00

Knickerbocker, lg plain nose, round black plastic eyes w/bottom lashes, 1971, 31½", MIB $150.00

Knickerbocker, music box inside, windup key in back, 1960s, 15", EX, from $175 to $225.00

Knickerbocker, original blue & green flowered dress w/white pinafore & hanky in pocket, 1963-65, 15", EX..............$110.00

Knickerbocker, style #4109, 1964, 19", MIB......................$90.00

Mollye Goldman, Raggedy Andy, nose outlined in black, orange-red yarn hair, minor stains/sm holes, 1930s, 18", VG.......$275.00

Playskool, Dress Me Raggedy Ann, 14", EX $10.00

Strawberry Shortcake

Strawberry Shortcake came on the market with a bang around 1980. The line included everything to attract small girls — swimsuits, bed linens, blankets, anklets, underclothing, coats, shoes, sleeping bags, dolls and accessories, games, and many other delightful items. Strawberry Shortcake and her friends were short lived, lasting only until the mid-1980s.

Values apply to examples in conditions noted. Please note: Out-of-the-box, played-with dolls should be valued at as much as 75% less than mint-in-box dolls (even less if they show wear).

Online Club: Strawberryland Town Square

Doll, Cherry Cuddler with Gooseberry, $45.00.

Accessory, Berry Cycle, 1983, MIB $38.00

Accessory, Big Berry Trolley, 1982, EX.....................$40.00

Accessory, ice skates, EX.....................$35.00

Accessory, motorized bicycle, NM.....................$100.00

Accessory, sleeping bag, EX.....................$35.00

Accessory, Storybook Playcase, M.....................$35.00

Doll, Almond Tea, 6", MIB $30.00

Doll, Angel Cake & Souffle, 6", NRFB $40.00

Doll, Apple Dumpling, cloth w/yarn yair, 12", EX+ $25.00

Doll, Apple Dumpling & Tea Time Turtle, 6", MIB.....................$75.00

Doll, Apricot, 15", NM $35.00

Doll, Baby Needs a Name, 15", NM $35.00

Doll, Berry Baby Orange Blossom, 6", MIB $35.00

Doll, Butter Cookie, 6", MIB $25.00

Doll, Huckleberry Pie, flat hands, 6", MIB.....................$45.00

Doll, Lemon Meringue, cloth w/yarn hair, 15", EX $25.00

Doll, Lime Chiffon, 6", MIB $45.00

Doll, Mint Tulip, 6", MIB $50.00

Doll, Orange Blossom & Marmalade, MIB $45.00

Doll, Peach Blush & Melonie Belle, 6", MIB.....................$115.00

Doll, Plum Pudding and Elderberry Owl Work at the Blackboard, Strawberryland Miniatures, MIP, $85.00.

Doll, Strawberry Shortcake & Custard, 6", NRFB.............$150.00

Doll, Strawberry Shortcake & Strawberrykin, 6", NRFB...$300.00

Tammy

In 1962 the Ideal Novelty and Toy Company introduced their teenage Tammy doll. Slightly pudgy and not quite as sophisticated-looking as some of the teen fashion dolls on the market at the time, Tammy's innocent charm captivated consumers. Her extensive wardrobe and numerous accessories added to her popularity with children. Tammy had a car, a house, and her own catamaran. In addition, a large number of companies obtained licenses to issue products using the 'Tammy' name. Everything from paper dolls to nurses' kits were made with Tammy's image on them. Her success was not confined to the United States; she was also successful in Canada and several other European countries.

Advisor: Cindy Sabulis (See Directory, Dolls)

Accessory, Pepper's Jukebox, M $65.00
Accessory, Pepper's Pony, MIB $250.00
Accessory, Pepper's Treehouse, MIB....................................... $125.00
Accessory, Tammy Bubble Bath Set, NRFB......................... $75.00
Accessory, Tammy's Car, MIB $75.00
Case, Misty & Tammy, double telephone, green or pink, ea... $25.00
Case, Pepper & Dodi, front opening, blue, EX...................... $30.00
Case, Tammy Evening in Paris, black or red, EX.................. $20.00
Clothes, Afternoon Dress & shoes, #9345-2, NRFP............ $45.00
Clothes, Flower Girl outfit, #99332-8, complete, M........... $50.00
Clothes, Tammy Cutie Coed outfit, #9132-2 or #9932-5, complete,
    M.. $45.00
Doll, Dodi, MIB... $75.00
Doll, Glamour Misty the Miss Clairol Doll, MIB............. $150.00
Doll, Misty, Black, MIB, minimum value $600.00
Doll, Patti, MIB... $200.00
Doll, Pepper, carrot-colored hair, MIB $75.00
Doll, Pepper, trimmer body & smaller face, MIB $75.00
Doll, Pos'n Dodi, M (in plain box) $75.00
Doll, Pos'n Pete, MIB $125.00

**Doll, Tammy, straight legs, marked Ideal Toy Corp., MIB,
$120.00.** (Photo courtesy LiveAuctioneers.com/Philip Weiss Auctions)

Doll, Tammy Grown Up, MIB $85.00
Doll, Tammy's Dad, MIB... $65.00

Tressy

Tressy was American Character's answer to Barbie. This 11½"
fashion doll was made from 1963 to 1967. Tressy had a unique
feature — her hair 'grew' by pushing a button on her stomach.
She and her little sister, Cricket, had numerous fashions and accessories.

Unless otherwise noted, our values are for loose mint condition
items.

Advisor: Cindy Sabulis (See Directory, Dolls)

Accessory, Beauty Salon.. $250.00
Accessory, hair accessory pak, NRFB.................................. $20.00
Accessory, hair dryer.. $25.00
Assessory, outfit, MOC, ea.. $40.00
Assessory, outfit, NRFB, ea minimum value $65.00
Case, Cricket... $30.00
Case, Tressy... $30.00
Doll, American Character Tressy, MIB............................... $100.00

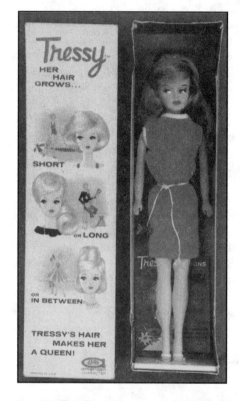

**Doll, American Doll & Toy Corp., 19(copyright)63 on head,
straight legs, 11½", MIB, from $85.00 to $100.00.** (Photo courtesy Cindy Sabulis)

Doll, Pre-Teen Tressy.. $30.00
Doll, Tressy, in Miss America outfit $65.00
Doll, Tressy, Magic-Make-Up Face...................................... $25.00
Doll, Tressy, original dress.. $35.00
Doll, Tressy, original dress, MIB.. $100.00
Doll, Tressy & Her Hi-Fashion Cosmetics, MIB............... $145.00

Uneeda Dolls

The Uneeda Doll Company was located in New York City and
began making composition dolls about 1917. Later a transition was
made to plastics and vinyl. Unless noted otherwise, values are for
dolls in near mint original condition.

Baby Dollikin, hard plastic w/vinyl head, jointed body, drinks &
    wets, 1960, 21", MIB, from $150 to $200.00
Baby Trix, hard plastic & vinyl, 1965, 19", from $18 to...... $25.00
Bareskin Baby, hard plastic & vinyl, 1968, 12½", from $15 to... $20.00
Blabby, hard plastic & vinyl, 1962, 14", from $18 to $25.00
Coquette, hard plastic & vinyl, Black, 1963, 16", from $25 to... $35.00

Coquette, hard plastic & vinyl, 1963, 16", from $15 to **$20.00**

Jennifer, teen body, mod clothes, 1973, 18", from $15 to....**$20.00**

Magic Meg w/Hair That Grows, hard plastic & vinyl, rooted hair, sleep eyes, 16", from $35 to..**$45.00**

Pollyana, made for Disney, 1960, 11", from $25 to **$35.00**

Purty, hard plastic & vinyl, long rooted hair, 1973, 11", from $20 to **$25.00**

Suzette (Carol Brent), hard plastic & vinyl, 12"................**$100.00**

Tiny Teen, 6-pc, hard plastic & vinyl, rooted hair, pierced ears, 1957-59, 10½", from $75 to..**$90.00**

Vogue Dolls, Inc.

Vogue Dolls Incorporated is one of America's most popular manufacturer of dolls. In the early 1920s through the mid-1940s, Vogue imported lovely dolls of bisque and composition, dressing them in the fashionable designs hand sewn by Vogue's founder, Jennie Graves. In the late '40s through the early '50s, they became famous for their hard plastic dolls, most notably the 8" Ginny doll. This adorable toddler doll skyrocketed into nationwide attention in the early '50s as lines of fans stretched around the block during store promotions, and Ginny dolls sold out regularly. A Far-Away-Lands Ginny was added in the late '50s, sold well through the '70s, and is still popular with collectors today. In fact, a modern-day version of Ginny is currently being sold by the Vogue Doll Company, Inc.

Many wonderful dolls followed through the years, including unique hard plastic, vinyl, and soft-body dolls. These dolls include teenage dolls Jill, Jan, and Jeff; Ginnette, the 8" baby doll; Miss Ginny; and the famous vinyl and soft-bodied dolls by noted artist and designer E. Wilkin. It is not uncommon for these highly collectible dolls to turn up at garage sales and flea markets.

Over the years, Vogue developed the well-deserved reputation as 'The Fashion Leaders in Doll Society' based on their fine quality sewing and on the wide variety of outfits designed for their dolls to wear. These outfits included frilly dress-up doll clothes as well as action-oriented sports outfits. The company was among the first in the doll industry to develop the concept of marketing and selling separate outfits for their dolls, many of which were 'matching' for their special doll lines. The very early Vogue outfits are most sought after, and later outfits are highly collectible as well. It is wise for collectors to become aware of Vogue's unique styles, designs, and construction methods in order to spot these authentic Vogue 'prizes' on collecting outings.

Unless noted otherwise, values are for dolls in near mint condition. For further information we recommend *Collectors' Encyclopedia of Vogue Dolls* by Judith Izen and Carol Stover (Collector Books).

Baby Dear, vinyl & cloth, painted eyes, closed mouth, squeaker, 1960-64, 18" **$225.00**

Baby Dear-One, vinyl & cloth, open/closed mind w/2 teeth, sleep eyes, 1962-63, 25" **$25.00**

Brikette, vinyl, swivel waist, elongated swivel neck, flirty sleep eyes, 22"..**$200.00**

Ginnette, vinyl, painted eyes, 1955-56, 1959, 8", M **$150.00**

Ginnette, vinyl, sleep eyes, 1956-69, 8" **$125.00**

Ginny, American Indian, vinyl, jointed arms, straight legs, non-walker, 1965-72, 8", from $100 to **$125.00**

Ginny, Black, strung body, sleep eyes, 1953, minimum value ..**$2,000.00**

Ginny, hard plastic, painted eyes, 1948-50, 8", minimum value **$350.00**

Ginny, hard plastic, sleep eyes, bent-knee walker, 1961, 8"...**$150.00**

Ginny, hard plastic, sleep eyes, bent-knee walker w/turning head, street clothes, 1957-59, 8", from $175 to **$225.00**

Ginny, hard plastic, sleep eyes, molded lashes, straight-leg walker, 1955-56, 8", from $225 to **$350.00**

Ginny, hard plastic head, sleep eyes, original braided hair, 7", NM, dressed in Tiny Miss #42 outfit (1955), MIB, $400.00. (Photo courtesy McMasters Harris Auction Company)

Ginny, hard plastic, sleep eyes, straight-leg walker, 1954, 8" ..**$250.00**

Ginny, hard plastic, strung body, sleep eyes, 1950-53, 8", from $375 to **$450.00**

Ginny, soft vinyl head, hard plastic body, bent-knee walker, 1963-65, 8", minimum value..**$150.00**

Ginny, vinyl, jointed arms & straight legs, non-walker, rooted hair, 1965-72, 8", minimum value....................................**$100.00**

Ginny, vinyl, sleep eyes, rooted hair, 1960, 36", minimum value **$250.00**

Ginny as Davy Crockett, hard plastic, molded lashes, straight-leg walker, 1955, 8"..**$500.00**

Ginny Baby, vinyl, sleep eyes, rooted saran or molded hair, drinks & wets, 1962-63, 20", from $30 to **$45.00**

Ginny Baby, vinyl, sleep eyes, rooted saran or molded hair, drinks & wets, 1971-75, 12", from $20 to **$40.00**

Jeff, vinyl, jointed body, sleep eyes, molded painted hair, 1958-60, 11", MIB **$150.00**

Jill, All New, vinyl, rooted hair, sleep eyes, high-heeled feet, 1962, 10½", from $150 to..**$175.00**

Jill, hard plastic, bent-knee walker, sleep eyes, basic outfit, 1957-60, 10½", minimum value **$150.00**

Jill, History Land, vinyl, various hairdos, 1965, 11", minimum value **$200.00**

Jill, Sweetheart, vinyl, rooted hair, sleep eyes, high-heeled feet, 1963, 10½", from $150 to **$175.00**

Jimmy, vinyl, jointed body, painted eyes, 1958, 8", MIB, from $150 to **$175.00**

Jimmy, vinyl, painted eyes, 1958, 8" **$100.00**

Li'l Imp, vinyl head, hard plastic body, sleep eyes, bent-knee walker, 1959-60, 11" **$150.00**

Li'l Lovable Imp, vinyl, sleep eyes, rooted hair, straight legs, 1964-65, 11" **$65.00**

Littlest Angel, vinyl head, hard plastic body, sleep eyes, bent-knee walker, 1960s, 10½", $65.00.

Miss Ginny, vinyl, sleep eyes, long rooted hair, 1962-64, 16" ..**$80.00**

Miss Ginny Contemporary, vinyl, wide-eyed look, long rooted hair, 1975-80, 15", from $25 to **$45.00**

Nancy, Crib Crowd baby, painted eyes, mohair wig, organdy dress w/lace, knit booties, #830, 1949, from $500 to **$750.00**

Patty, hard plastic, mohair wig, sleep eyes, 14", from $300 to ...**$400.00**

Queen of Hearts Ginny, strung body, sleep eyes, 1950, 8", minimum value **$500.00**

Sunshine Baby, composition, bent legs, molded hair, 1930s to mid-1940s, 8" **$400.00**

Toddles, composition, molded hair, panties attached to dress, 1937-40s, 8", from $250 to **$300.00**

Toddles, Red Riding Hood, composition, Nursery Rhyme Series, 1940s, 8", MIB..**$425.00**

Door Knockers

Though many of the door knockers you'll see on the market today are of the painted cast-iron variety (similar in design to door-stop figures), they're also found in brass and other metals. Most are modeled as people, animals, and birds; and baskets of flowers are common. All items listed are cast iron and in excellent condition unless otherwise noted.

Advisor: Craig Dinner (See Directory, Door Knockers)

Club: Cast Iron Collectors Club
Contact: Dan Morphy Auctions, morphyauctions.com or 717 335-3455

Abe Lincoln profile, Slavery Abolished 1862, brass, 1865, 3" dia **$1,725.00**

Aberdeen Terrier, facing right, brass, 5¼x4" **$100.00**

American eagle sitting on base, wings spread, bronze, ca 1920, 9" **$110.00**

Bust of lady w/hands on heads of 2 lions, bronze, 11x7½"..**$165.00**

Butterfly on sunflower back plate, 3½x4", NM.................**$550.00**

Castle, oval back plate, Hubley, 4" **$700.00**

Castle fortress against embossed woods, CJO, rare, $350.00. (Photo courtesy LiveAuctioneers.com/Morphy Auctions)

Chester Cathedral, bronze, 5¼" **$95.00**

Daffodils in basket, blue bow at top, 4¼x2½"...................**$300.00**

Daisies tied w/bow on oval black plate, 4½x2⅞", VG **$540.00**

Flower basket, multicolor w/lg pink bow at top, Hubley #124 ....**$150.00**

Flowers (mixed) in urn, filigree back plate, 4x2½" **$210.00**

Flowers (mixed) in wicker basket on oval back plate w/rope trim, 4½x3¼" **$175.00**

Fox head, stirrup-form knocker, cast metal, ca 1900, 9x5"..**$120.00**

Genie in turban on oval, CJO, 4½x3" **$120.00**

Lion's head, gilt bronze, ornate scrolling mane, detailed features, 1885-95, 4½x3½" **$240.00**

Lion's head w/in wreath, gilt brass, 9" dia **$210.00**

Lovers kissing w/in pierced circle, brass, Ritter & Sons, 5x3", VG **$42.50**

Neoclassical style, hammer supported by 2 Roman columns, silver on brass, 1800s, 4½x6" **$120.00**

Nude woman flanked by cherubs & pr of dolphins, grotesque mask as back plate, bronze, 14½"...**$840.00**

Oriental woman, bronze, fish-scale base, detailed, 2x3" **$130.00**

Owl on branch, oval back plate, 4x3" **$250.00**

Parrot on leafy perch on oval, 4¾x3" **$150.00**

Roses & mixed flowers in oval, bow at top & bottom, 4¼x2⅝"..**$200.00**
Sailing ship, iron, Hubley, 3½" **$1,200.00**
Scholar reading book, sitting in chair, CJO, 4¼x2⅜".........**$575.00**
Sealyham terrier facing left, brass, English Registry mark, 2½"....**$50.00**
Shakespeare, no paint, ca 1900 ....**$55.00**
Tulip, wide frame, aluminum, 8x5¼"..................................**$165.00**

Rooster, CJO Judd Co., 3¼", $200.00. (Photo courtesy LiveAuctioneers.com/ Morphy Auctions)

Doorstops

There are three important factors to consider when buying doorstops — rarity, desirability, and condition. Desirability is often a more important issue than rarity, especially if the doorstop is well designed and detailed. Subject matter often overlaps into other areas, and if they appeal to collectors of Black Americana and advertising, for instance, this tends to drive prices upward. Most doorstops are made of painted cast iron, and value is directly related to the condition of the paint. If there is little paint left or if the figure has been repainted or is rusty, unless the price has been significantly reduced, pass it by.

Be aware that Hubley, one of the largest doorstop manufacturers, sold many of their molds to the John Wright Company who makes them today. Watch for seams that do not fit properly, grainy texture, and too-bright paint. Watch for reproductions!

The doorstops we've listed here are painted cast iron unless another type of material is referred to in the description. Examples in near mint to mint condition often sell for phenomenal prices at auction. An example in lesser condition than evaluated in the lines that follow should be sharply reduced equivalent to the amount of wear apparent. (Our values are prices realized at a recent online auction.)

Club: Doorstop Collectors of America
Newsletter: *Doorstoppers*
Jeanie Bertoia
2413 Madison Ave.
Vineland, NJ 08361
609-692-4092

Bobby Blake w/teddy bear, Grace Grayton design, Hubley, 9¼",
    EX **$360.00**

Boston terrier w/head turned left, 9x10", VG **$95.00**
Boy w/hands in pockets, full figure, #1276, 11x3½", NM..**$480.00**
Bulldog, facing right, head turned, 9x10", EX **$42.50**
Carmen Miranda, dancing figure in tiered skirt, 11", VG..**$600.00**

Church with stained glass windows, #1250s, rare, 7½x5½", EX, $1,800.00. (Photo courtesy LiveAuctioneers.com/Morphy Auctions)

Clipper ship facing right on base of rolling waves, 8", EX , 8",
    EX.. **$85.00**
Clown w/stooped back, lg ruffled collar, 2-sided, 10½x4¼",
    NM **$900.00**
Cockatoo on stump, strong colors, 14", VG **$325.00**
Colonial lady w/bonnet & purse, overall rust, 10x5¾", G..**$180.00**
Corgi standing w/head erect, orange-brown & white, full figure,
    9¼x7¾", EX **$1,025.00**
Cosmos flowers in vase, Hubley #455, 17¾x10¼", EX...**$1,800.00**
Cottage w/flowers along walls & doorway, Hubley #211, 5¾x7½",
    M...**$325.00**
Dolly, girl holding doll, hand in pocket, Grace Drayton design,
    Hubley, 9¾", M..**$4,800.00**
Ducks (2) on grassy base, Hubley, 8½", EX **$240.00**
Elephant w/trunk raised, facing right, 8x8", G.................**$180.00**
Elephant w/trunk up, standing on rock, 10x10", VG **$135.00**
Flower basket on stepped base, 7x8", VG..........................**$85.00**
Fox terrier, full figure, facing right, Hubley, 8¾x8¼", NM..**$480.00**
Geese (3) on base, Fred Everette, Hubley, 8¼x8" **$720.00**
General George Washington, woodland backdrop, Albany Foundry,
    possible old repair, 9½x5" **$100.00**
Gnome standing, pointed cap, full figure, bright colors, 11x5",
    NM...**$275.00**
Kitten seated, full figure, 7x9¼", EX................................**$120.00**
Lion, full figure, free-standing, 6¾x9½", EX....................**$150.00**
Lion on rocky & grassy base, Copyright 1930, Creations Co #161,
    7⅜x7¼", EX **$120.00**
Little Red Riding Hood, Grace Drayton design, Hubley, 9½x5",
    EX+ **$425.00**

Little Red Riding Hood w/Wolf, Nuydea #860 Pat Pending, 7⅜x9⅝", NM **$1,680.00**

Mammy w/arms akimbo, 13½", G **$480.00**

Monkey's head, 5", VG **$95.00**

Monkey seated in thoughtful pose, 9", VG **$300.00**

Naughty Duck, 13x7", VG **$140.00**

Naughty Puss, girl w/scratch on arm, cat beside, Q Dioughy, Judd, 8⅝x4¼", EX **$2,150.00**

Old Salt, man in yellow slicker & black floppy hat w/fish net, full figure, 11x4⅛", VG+ **$275.00**

Olive Picker w/donkey loaded w/2 full baskets, Hubley #207, 7¾x8¾" **$360.00**

Orange tree, 12x6½", $5,500.00. (Photo courtesy LiveAuctioneers.com/Morphy Auctions)

Owl on books, Eastern Specialty, 9¼x6½", NM **$2,400.00**

Owl on pedestal, B&H #7797, 15½x5", VG **$960.00**

Parrot on perch w/stepped base, Hubley, 10", VG **$110.00**

Penguin, No 1 c 1930 Taylor Cook, 9½x5⅜", NM........**$2,750.00**

Police Boy, baby boy in diaper & police cap directing traffic, 10⅝x7¼", NM **$1,200.00**

Popeye, King Features Syndicate, Hubley, missing pipe, 9x4½", EX **$1,320.00**

Pug dog seated w/ears up & alert expression, 7x8", VG **$120.00**

Rabbit eating carrot, dressed in sweater & facing left, 5x9", VG **$900.00**

Rabbit w/top hat, coat & tail, Albany Foundry, 9⅞x4¾", NM **$275.00**

Rooster crowing, facing left, bright colors, EX **$335.00**

Scottie dog, full figure, 9x10", EX **$155.00**

Scottie dog, seated, embossed red collar, hollow casting, Hubley, 11x15", NM **$1,080.00**

St Bernard standing, full figure, life-like colors, 6⅝x10", EX...**$3,600.00**

Terrior, brown & white spots, 8x9", VG **$360.00**

Unicorn reclining, unmarked, 18x25", G............................**$175.00**

Victorian lady w/bonnet, flower basket in ea hand, 8½", G ..**$42.50**

Windmill on base, National Foundry #10, 7x6⅞", VG........**$60.00**

Dragon Ware

Dragon ware is the name given to Japanese-made ceramics decorated with a fierce slipwork dragon. Sometimes cups have lithophanes in the bottom. It was often sold through gift shops at popular tourist attractions and may be imprinted with names such as Chinatown, San Francisco; Rock City; or Washington D.C. It's still being made, but collectors prefer vintage items, which have much more detail in the dragon. Background color is another clue you can use to determine age. New colors include green, lavender, yellow, pink, blue, pearl, orange, and blue-black. Though some of the same colors may be found in vintage ware, compared to the new, background colors of older pieces are flat rather than glossy.

Club: Dragonware Club
c/o Suzi Hibbard
849 Vintage Ave.
Fairfield, CA 94585
Dragon_Ware@hotmail.com

Ashtray, blue, ¾", from $7.50 to..**$12.50**

Barrel jar, black w/rattan handle, 8½", from $75 to **$125.00**

Biscuit barrel, gray w/gold, simple knob on lid, rattan handle, Hand Painted Japan, 8⅛x8¼" **$95.00**

Casserole, black w/gold handle, w/lid, Made in Japan, 9", from $75 to **$125.00**

Creamer & sugar bowl, gray, w/lid, Nippon black mark **$72.50**

Cup & saucer, blue, geisha lithophane, Hand Painted Occupied Japan, 1⅞x2", 4½" **$55.00**

Cup & saucer, chocolate; Nippon pagoda mark, 2½x2⅝", 5⅛"..**$25.00**

Cup & saucer, demitasse; blue sky, Made in Japan, from $15 to..**$20.00**

Cup & saucer, demitasse; brown cloud, Made in Japan, from $15 to **$30.00**

Cup & saucer, demitasse; goggle eyes, red/black swirl, castle mark, from $30 to **$35.00**

Cup & saucer, demitasse; gray, nude lithophane, from $45 to..**$55.00**

Dish, 3-lobed, 3-footed, w/lid, M-in-wreath Hand Painted Japan mark, 4½x6" **$95.00**

Divided dish, gray traditional pattern, Hand-Painted Made in Japan, Nippon quality, 8½x6", from $75 to **$125.00**

Dutch shoe, gray, from $20 to **$30.00**

Ewer, gray, mini, 3½" **$8.00**

Ice bucket, black traditional pattern, rattan handle, M-over-wreath mark, 8", from $75 to...**$150.00**

Incense burner, gray w/gold handles & finial, ca 1920s-30s, 3¼x3" **$27.50**

Mustard jar, gray traditional pattern, w/spoon, 3½", 3-pc, from $15 to **$45.00**

Nappy, gray, Hand Painted Made in Japan, sq, 5½", from $20 to...**$35.00**

Nappy, gray, scalloped, w/handle, Made in Japan, 1940s, 6¼" dia **$20.00**

Planter, gray traditional pattern, hanging, Hand-Painted Japan, 6", from $75 to **$125.00**

Plate, orange w/thick gold, handles, Japan, 7", 5 for...........**$70.00**

Saki set, blue cloud, w/plate, 7-pc, from $75 to.................**$125.00**

Salt & pepper shakers, black, pr in boat-shaped holder, from $35 to **$45.00**

Salt & pepper shakers, orange, pagoda style, Japan, 4", pr from $15 to **$40.00**

Shakers, gray traditional pattern, Made in Japan, pr from $10 to **$25.00**

Shakers, pink solid, pearlized, Florida souvenir, pr from $5 to .. **$20.00**

Tea set, demitasse; gray traditional pattern, Made in Japan, 24-pc, from $175 to **$275.00**

Tea set, demitasse; white pearl, Japan, 17-pc, from $75 to ..**$125.00**

Tea set, gray traditional pattern, sq, Noritake, Nippon quality, pot+creamer & sugar bowl w/lid, from $75 to...........**$125.00**

Tea/coffee set, green, lithophane, dragon spout, 23-pc, from $175 to **$250.00**

Tea/coffee set, red/brown, Made in Occupied Japan, 23-pc, from $275 to **$350.00**

Tea/dessert set, royal blue w/gold, 2 pots, creamer & sugar bowl, 6 cups & saucers & 6 luncheon dessert plates...............**$325.00**

Teacup & saucer, gray, geisha lithophane, 2x3¾", 5½".........**$50.00**

Teacup & saucer, tan w/black bands, unmarked...................**$28.00**

Teapot, light green solid, unmarked, child size, from $10 to .. **$15.00**

Tureen, soup; gray w/gold trim, w/handles & lid, red Japan mark, 3x10¼" **$95.00**

Vase, blue w/gold, 2⅜", from $10 to...................................**$15.00**

Vase, gray, glass eyes, footed, hand-painted Nippon w/green wreath mark, 4⅜", from $125 to..**$225.00**

Vase, gray, yellow & orange solid, 4¼", set of 3, from $30 to .. **$60.00**

Vase, gray, 3 moriage handles, green M-in-wreath Nippon mark, 6x4" **$150.00**

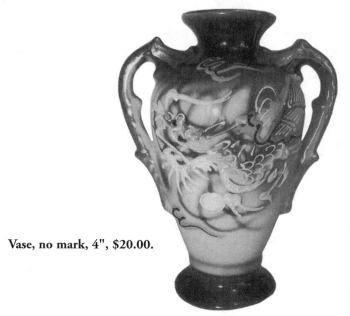

Vase, no mark, 4", $20.00.

Wall pocket, orange, Made in Japan, 9", from $50 to **$75.00**

Duncan and Miller Glassware

Although the roots of the company can be traced back as far as 1865 when George Duncan went into business in Pittsburgh,

Pennsylvania, the majority of the glassware that collectors are interested in was produced during the twentieth century. The firm became known as Duncan and Miller in 1900. They were bought out by the United States Glass Company who continued to produce many of the same designs through a separate operation which they called the Duncan and Miller Division.

In addition to crystal, they made some of their wares in a wide assortment of colors including ruby, milk glass, some opalescent glass, and a black opaque glass they called Ebony. Some of their pieces were decorated by cutting or etching. They also made a line of animals and bird figures. For information on these, see *Glass Animals* by Dick and Pat Spencer (Collector Books).

See also Glass Animals and Related Items.

First Love, crystal, candleholder, Canterbury #115-121, 3", $25.00. (Photo courtesy Gene and Cathy Florence)

Canterbury, crystal, basket, 9¼x10x7¼"............................$55.00
Canterbury, crystal, bowl, crimped, 2¼x8" $20.00
Canterbury, crystal, bowl, oval, flared, 3¼x13x8½".............$35.00
Canterbury, crystal, bowl, w/handles, 2x6" $10.00
Canterbury, crystal, candy dish, w/lid, 6½" $32.50
Canterbury, crystal, cigarette jar, w/lid, 4" $30.00
Canterbury, crystal, decanter w/stopper, 32-oz, 12" $80.00
Canterbury, crystal, goblet, water; 9-oz, 6" $15.00
Canterbury, crystal, pitcher, 16-oz.....................................$55.00
Canterbury, crystal, plate, cake; w/handles, 13½" $40.00
Canterbury, crystal, salt & pepper shakers, pr $22.50
Canterbury, crystal, vase, cloverleaf, 6½"...........................$38.00
Caribbean, blue, bowl, salad; 9"..$75.00
Caribbean, blue, cocktail shaker, 33-oz, 9".......................$300.00
Caribbean, blue, mustard, w/slotted lid, 4" $55.00
Caribbean, blue, plate, luncheon; 8½" $30.00
Caribbean, blue, sugar bowl..$22.00
Caribbean, blue, tumbler, footed, 8½-oz, 5½" $55.00
Caribbean, crystal, bowl, w/handles, 7" $25.00
Caribbean, crystal, candlestick, 1-light, w/blue prisms, 7¼", ea...$65.00
Caribbean, crystal, cruet...$40.00
Caribbean, crystal, server, center handle, 5¾" $13.00

Caribbean, crystal, tray, 12¾" dia..................\$25.00
Caribbean, crystal, vase, straight sides, footed, 8"................\$40.00
First Love, crystal, ashtray, club; #12, 5x3" \$30.00
First Love, crystal, bowl, #111, flared rim, footed, 10x3¾"..\$55.00
First Love, crystal, box, candy; 4¾x6¼" \$55.00
First Love, crystal, candlestick, #115, 3½", ea \$25.00
First Love, crystal, compote, #115, flared rim, 5x5½" \$32.00
First Love, crystal, creamer, #111, 10-oz, 3".........\$18.00
First Love, crystal, ice bucket, #30, 6"................\$110.00
First Love, crystal, plate, #115, 8½"..................\$20.00
First Love, crystal, relish dish, #115, 3-part, w/handles, 8" ..\$25.00
First Love, crystal, rose bowl, #115, 3x5"............\$35.00
First Love, crystal, tumbler, #115, flat, 8-oz........\$25.00
Lily of the Valley, crystal, ashtray, 6" \$35.00
Lily of the Valley, crystal, creamer \$30.00
Lily of the Valley, crystal, plate, cheese & cracker.................\$75.00
Lily of the Valley, crystal, sherbet, high \$25.00
Mardi Gras, crystal, butter dish..................\$75.00
Mardi Gras, crystal, egg cup, footed.................\$45.00
Mardi Gras, crystal, goblet, cocktail \$24.00
Mardi Gras, crystal, oil bottle, w/handle \$40.00
Mardi Gras, crystal, pitcher, syrup; individual..................\$75.00
Mardi Gras, crystal, toothpick holder.................\$45.00
Nautical, blue, bowl, oval, 10" \$225.00
Nautical, blue, decanter..................\$550.00
Nautical, blue, relish dish, 7-part, 12"..............\$75.00
Nautical, blue, tumbler, high-ball...................\$33.00
Nautical, blue, tumbler, whiskey; 8-oz \$30.00
Nautical, crystal, compote, 7" \$110.00
Nautical, crystal, ice bucket..................\$95.00
Nautical, crystal, plate, 10" \$25.00
Nautical, crystal, salt & pepper shakers, w/tray, pr..............\$65.00
Nautical, crystal, tumbler, cocktail \$12.00
Plaza, amber or crystal, bowl, vegetable; 9" L.............\$28.00
Plaza, amber or crystal, cup..................\$5.00
Plaza, amber or crystal, parfait \$10.00
Plaza, amber or crystal, plate, w/handles, 10½".............\$20.00
Plaza, amber or crystal, tumbler, iced tea; footed \$12.00
Plaza, pink or green, bowl, console; flared, 14"............\$75.00
Plaza, pink or green, goblet, wine..................\$22.00
Plaza, pink or green, oil bottle..................\$60.00
Plaza, pink or green, pitcher, flat..................\$100.00
Plaza, pink or green, plate, luncheon; 8½" \$15.00
Puritan, any color, bowl, console; rolled rim, 12" \$55.00
Puritan, any color, bowl, 9¼".....................\$55.00
Puritan, any color, compote \$35.00
Puritan, any color, plate, salad; 7½" \$8.00
Puritan, any color, saucer..................\$2.00
Puritan, any color, sherbet..................\$9.00
Puritan, any color, sugar bowl \$17.50
Puritan, any color, vase..................\$65.00
Puritan, crystal, pitcher \$100.00
Puritan, crystal, vase..................\$50.00
Sandwich, crystal, basket, crimped, w/loop handle, 10".....\$200.00
Sandwich, crystal, bowl, nappy, 2-part, 6" \$14.00
Sandwich, crystal, bowl, nut; 3½" \$10.00
Sandwich, crystal, butter dish, ¼-lb \$50.00

Sandwich, crystal, cake stand, plain pedestal, 13" \$75.00
Sandwich, crystal, candlestick, 3-light, 5", ea......................\$40.00

Sandwich, crystal, candy box, 6", \$395.00. (Photo courtesy Gene and Cathy Florence)

Sandwich, crystal, coaster, 5" \$9.00
Sandwich, crystal, jelly dish, individual, 3" \$8.00
Sandwich, crystal, plate, deviled egg; 12" \$65.00
Sandwich, crystal, tray, oval, 8" \$18.00
Sandwich, crystal, urn, footed, w/lid, 12" \$150.00
Spiral Flutes, amber, green or pink, bowl, bouillon; 3¾"......\$15.00
Spiral Flutes, amber, green or pink, bowl, nappy, w/handles, 6"..\$20.00
Spiral Flutes, amber, green or pink, candy dish, w/lid.........\$45.00
Spiral Flutes, amber, green or pink, mug, 9-oz, 7" \$30.00
Spiral Flutes, amber, green or pink, plate, torte; 13⅝" \$27.50
Spiral Flutes, amber, green or pink, vase, 6½" \$20.00
Tear Drop, crystal, bowl, flower; oval, 8x12" \$50.00
Tear Drop, crystal, bowl, punch; 2½-gal, 15½"..................\$100.00
Tear Drop, crystal, goblet, champagne; 5-oz, 5" \$10.00
Tear Drop, crystal, marmalade, w/lid, 4" \$40.00
Tear Drop, crystal, olive dish, oval, w/handles, 4¼" \$15.00
Tear Drop, crystal, pitcher, milk; 16-oz, 5" \$50.00
Tear Drop, crystal, plate, lemon; w/handles, 7" \$12.50
Tear Drop, crystal, plate, 4 handles, 13" \$35.00
Tear Drop, crystal, relish dish, heart-shaped, 2-part, 7½".....\$20.00
Tear Drop, crystal, tumbler, old-fashioned; flat, 7-oz, 3¼"..\$11.00
Tear Drop, crystal, vase, fan; footed, 9"..................\$30.00
Terrace, amber or crystal, bowl, footed, 9x4½" \$42.00
Terrace, amber or crystal, candleholder, 1-light, 3", ea.........\$25.00
Terrace, amber or crystal, cup \$15.00
Terrace, amber or crystal, goblet, wine; #5111½, 3-oz, 5¼" \$32.50
Terrace, amber or crystal, mayonnaise, crimped, 5½x3½" \$32.00
Terrace, amber or crystal, plate, cracker; w/ring, w/handles, 11" ..\$28.00
Terrace, amber or crystal, plate, sq, 6"..................\$12.00
Terrace, amber or crystal, relish dish, 4-part, 9" \$35.00
Terrace, amber or crystal, saucer, demitasse..................\$5.00
Terrace, amber or crystal, stem, goblet, water; tall, #5111½, 10-oz, 6¾" \$25.00
Terrace, cobalt or red, ashtray, 3½" sq..................\$25.00
Terrace, cobalt or red, candlestick, 1-light, 3", ea................\$95.00

Terrace, cobalt or red, cheese stand, 3x5¼" **$40.00**
Terrace, cobalt or red, finger bowl, #5111½, 4¼" **$65.00**
Terrace, cobalt or red, nappy, w/handles, 6x1¾" **$35.00**
Terrace, cobalt or red, plate, 8½" **$22.00**
Terrace, cobalt or red, relish dish, 4-part, 9" **$100.00**
Terrace, cobalt or red, relish dish, 5-part, w/lid, 12" **$325.00**
Terrace, cobalt or red, tumbler, water; 9-oz, 4" **$65.00**

Tear Drop, crystal, relish, two-part, 7½", $22.50. (Photo courtesy Gene and Cathy Florence)

Early American Prescut

This was a line of inexpensive but good quality glassware made during the 1960s and 1970s by Anchor Hocking. It was marketed through dime-stores and houseware stores, and as is obvious judging from the plentiful supplies available at today's garage sale and flea markets, it sold very well. If you like it, now's the time to buy! For more information, refer to Gene and Cathy Florence's book called *Collectible Glassware from the 40s, 50s, and 60s* (Collector Books).

Serving plate, 13½", $12.50. (Photo courtesy Gene and Cathy Florence)

Ashtray, 5", from $6 to **$8.00**
Bowl, #787, 8¾" **$9.00**
Bowl, paneled, #794, 11¾", from $135 to **$145.00**
Bowl, scalloped rim, 7½" **$16.00**
Bowl, 3-toed, #768, 6¾" **$4.50**
Butter dish, #705, ¼-lb **$6.00**
Cake plate, footed, 13½" plate w/4" stand, 2-pc **$35.00**
Candlestick, double; #784, 7x5⅝", from $25 to **$30.00**

Chip & dip, brass finish holder, #700/733, 10¾" bowl, 5¼".... **$22.00**
Coaster, #700/702 .... **$2.50**
Cruet, w/stopper, #711, 7¾" **$5.00**
Lamp, electric; made from vase, from $25 to **$35.00**
Lazy Susan, #700/713, 9-pc **$35.00**
Oil lamp **$195.00**
Pitcher, #744, 18-oz **$10.00**
Pitcher, #791, 60-oz **$15.00**
Plate, deviled egg/relish; #750, 11¾", from $25 to **$30.00**
Plate, dinner; 11", from $8 to **$10.00**
Plate, no ring, 6¾", from $25 to **$30.00**
Plate, w/ring for 6-oz cup, 6¾" **$30.00**
Plate, 4-part w/swirl dividers, 11", from $100 to **$125.00**
Relish, divided, tab handle, #770, 10" **$18.00**
Sherbet, footed, 6-oz, 3½" **$495.00**
Sugar bowl, w/lid, #753 .... **$4.00**
Tumbler, iced tea; #732, 15-oz, 5", from $15 to **$20.00**
Vase, #742, 10" **$10.00**
Vase, basket/block, #704/205, 6x4½" **$14.00**

Vase, footed, 5", $795.00. (Photo courtesy Gene and Cathy Florence)

Egg Cups

Egg cups were once commonplace kitchen articles that were often put to daily use. These small egg holders were commonly made in a variety of shapes from ceramics, glass, metals, minerals, treen, and plastic. They were used as early as ancient Rome and were very common on Victorian tables. Many were styled like whimsical animals or made in other shapes that would specifically appeal to children. Some were commemorative or sold as souvenirs. Still others were part of extensive china or silver services.

Recent trends in US dietary patterns have caused egg cups to follow butter pats and salt dishes into relative obscurity. Yet today in other parts of the world, especially Europe, many people still eat soft-boiled eggs as part of their daily ritual, so the larger china companies in those locations continue to produce egg cups.

Though many are inexpensive, some are very pricey. Sought-after categories (or cross-collectibles) include Art Deco, Art Pottery,

Black Memorabilia, Chintz, Golliwogs, Majolica, Personalities, Pre-Victorian, Railroad, and Steamship. Single egg cups with pedestal bases are the most common, but shapes vary to include buckets, doubles, figurals, hoops, and sets of many types.

Pocillovists, as egg cup collectors are known, are increasing in numbers every day. For more extensive listings we recommend *Egg Cups: An Illustrated History and Price Guide,* by Brenda C. Blake (Antique Publications), and *Schroeder's Antiques Price Guide* (Collector Books).

Unless noted otherwise, our values are for ceramic egg cups in mint condition.

Advisor: Brenda C. Blake (See Directory, Egg Cups)

Newsletter: *Egg Cup Collector's Corner*
Dr. Joan George, Editor
67 Stevens Ave., Old Bridge, NJ 08857

Double, bright lemon yellow glass, ca 1940s, 4⅛x2¾" **$40.00**
Double, floral, bright multicolor on porcelain, Meito over a crown, Japan, 3½x2⅝" **$45.00**
Double, Red Riding Hood, Columbia China **$18.00**
Double, Rose Chintz, Johnson Bros, England.....................**$40.00**

Figural, boy, Occupied Japan, 2½", from $12.00 to $15.00.

Figural, chick in clown outfit, Foreign, England **$50.00**
Figural, chicken, red & black beak, glass, Vallerysthal..........**$30.00**
Figural, comic policeman (bust only), hat forms salt shaker, Mancer M Made in Italy R57, 5½" **$55.00**
Figural, dog's head, pink & black ceramic, Royal Art Pottery Longton c Made in England **$30.00**
Figural, duck, blue, Fanny Farmer, England, 1930s **$25.00**
Figural, green convertible car, Honiton, England.................**$22.00**
Figural, Pink Panther sitting/holding cup, Royal Orleans, ca 1981 ....**$80.00**
Figural, poodle w/cup on back, ceramic, Japan, 2½"............**$17.50**
Figural, rooster, brown drip glaze, Pfaltzgraff.....................**$32.00**
Figural, sparrow, amethyst pressed glass, 2½x4" **$28.00**
Figural, swan, scalloped rim, glass, Fenton **$25.00**
Single, Blue Dawn, blue, Denby, England **$17.00**
Single, cottage scene, Watcombe Torquay, footed, 2¾" **$36.00**

Single, Oriental scene w/rooster, footed, ca 1935, 2¾" **$12.00**
Single, purple slag, vertical ribs, footed **$70.00**
Single, rabbit & flowers in relief on white, pink interior, ceramic, 2⅝" **$18.00**
Single, vertical stripes, green on white, ceramic, Famus (sic) Brand, Japan, 3⅝" **$8.00**
Single, Victorian violets, Hammersley, England, footed **$15.00**

Single, Lady Carlyle, scalloped gold rim, Royal Albert, $60.00.
(Photo courtesy Helene Guarnaccia)

Egg Timers

Egg timers were largely imported from Japan and Germany during the 1930s and 1940s to help you produce the perfect '3-minute egg.' They were highly functional and consisted of two parts: a little glass tube filled with sand and a figural base to which it was attached. They were made in the likenesses of clowns, Black children, chefs, and animals of every type, and in almost every type of material. Because of their whimsical nature, they are highly sought after by today's collectors!

Because of the very nature of the thin glass tubes that held the sand, they were easily damaged, so many egg timers you find today will be missing the tube. But don't hesitate to buy an otherwise good example for that reason only — tubes can be easily replaced; just buy a new inexpensive egg timer from your local grocery store.

Our values are for complete timers with tubes intact.

Advisor: Larry Pogue, L&J Antiques and Collectibles (See Directory, Head Vases and String Holders)

Amish girl seated on bench before timer, painted cast iron, West Germany, 4" **$15.00**
Baby elephant holds timer in trunk, ceramic, unmarked Japan, 1950s **$135.00**
Bellhop on telephone stands beside timer, ceramic, Made in Japan, 1930s, 3" **$65.00**
Boy carrying pail stands w/timer in right hand, ceramic, unmarked Germany, 1920s, 3⅛" **$110.00**

Boy in short pants stands beside tower-like holder for timer, ceramic, Germany, #2883, 3¾"................................$65.00

Boy on skis stands beside timer, ceramic, Germany.............$75.00

Boy playing accordion, timer at his right, ceramic, multicolor, Germany, 3½"..$85.00

Chef boy holding lg red egg, timer before him, ceramic, Germany 52, #9878, 3½"...$135.00

Chef girl holds timer in raised left hand, ceramic, Germany, #7957, 3"..$75.00

Chicks stand facing ea other, attachment at beaks supports timer, ceramic, Germany, #E230, 2⅝"................................$135.00

Chimney sweep w/ladder holds timer in left hand, ceramic, 3½x3"...$135.00

Clown talking on telephone, ceramic, Germany, 4".............$75.00

Dutch boy stands w/timer in right hand, ceramic, #7510, 3½"...$135.00

Dutch girl stands w/timer before her, ceramic, 1940s, 3½"..$80.00

Flip the Frog, ceramic, 3"...$300.00

Girl in pigtails stands beside timer, ceramic, 3½"................$85.00

Hen & chick in hen house behind timer, rooster at side, pressed cardboard, bright colors, Germany, 9½x6"....................$95.00

Lady on telephone stands beside timer, ceramic, Germany, 3¾"..$45.00

Pixie stands beside timer & recipe card holder, ceramic, Enesco, 5¾x3"...$55.00

Poodle dog w/timer at side, ceramic, black & red, Germany, 3⅛"...$130.00

Spaniel holds timer in mouth, metal, hand painted, hexagonal base, 2½"...$45.00

Welsh lady holds timer w/attachment on left hand, ceramic, GRGM #631 Germany, 4½"...$135.00

Black lady at stove, litho tin, wall mount, 7", G, $85.00. (Photo courtesy Larry Pogue)

Elvis Presley Memorabilia

Since he burst upon the '50s scene wailing 'Heartbreak Hotel,' Elvis has been the undisputed 'king of rock 'n roll.' The fans that stood outside his dressing room for hours on end, screamed themselves hoarse as he sang, or simply danced until they dropped to his music are grown-up collectors today. Many of their children remember his comeback performances, and I'd venture to say that even their grandchildren know Elvis on a first-name basis.

There has never been a promotion in the realm of entertainment to equal the manufacture and sale of Elvis merchandise. By the latter part of 1956, there were already hundreds of items that appeared in every department store, drugstore, specialty shop, and music store in the country. There were bubble gum cards, pinback buttons, handkerchiefs, dolls, guitars, billfolds, photograph albums, and scores of other items. You could even buy sideburns from a coin-operated machine. Look for the mark 'Elvis Presley Enterprises' (along with a 1956 or 1957 copyright date); you'll know you've found a gold mine. Items that carry the 'Boxcar' mark are from 1974 to 1977, when Elvis's legendary manager, Colonel Tom Parker, promoted another line of merchandise to augment their incomes during the declining years. Upon his death in 1977 and until 1981, the trademark became 'Boxcar Enterprises, Inc., Lic. by Factors ETC. Bear, DE.' The 'Elvis Presley Enterprises, Inc.' trademark reverted back to Graceland in 1982, which re-opened to the public in 1983.

Due to the very nature of his career, paper items are usually a large part of any 'Elvis' collection. He appeared on the cover of countless magazines. These along with ticket stubs, movie posters, lobby cards, and photographs of all types are sought after today, especially those from before the mid-'60s.

Though you sometime see Elvis 45s with $10.00 to $15.00 price tags, unless the record is in near mint to mint condition, this is just not realistic, since they sold in such volume. In fact, the picture sleeve itself (if it's in good condition) will be worth more than the record. The exceptions are, of course, the early Sun label records (he cut five in all) that collectors often pay in excess of $500.00 for. In fact, a near-mint copy of 'That's All Right' (his very first Sun recording) realized $2,800.00 at an auction held a couple of years ago! And some of the colored vinyls, promotional records, and EPs and LPs with covers and jackets in excellent condition are certainly worth researching further. For instance, though his *Moody Blue* album with the blue vinyl record can often be had for under $25.00 (depending on condition), if you find one of the rare ones with the black record you can figure on about 10 times that amount! For a thorough listing of his records as well as the sleeves, refer to *Official Price Guide to Elvis Presley Records and Memorabilia* by Jerry Osborne.

For more general information and an emphasis on the early items, refer to *Elvis Collectibles* and *Best of Elvis Collectibles* by Rosalind Cranor, P.O. Box 859, Blacksburg, VA 24063 ($19.95+$1.75 postage each volume). Also available: *Elvis Presley Memorabilia* by Sean O'Neal (Schiffer).

Unless noted otherwise, values are for items in near mint to mint condition. See also Magazines; Movie Posters; Pin-back Buttons; Records.

Advisor: Lee Garmon (See Directory, Elvis Presley Memorabilia)

Apron, Elvis border print, multicolor cotton, gathered at waist, 1960s...$25.00

Belt buckle, Graceland Elvis Memories, silver-tone metal w/red & blue enameling, 2x3"...$25.00

Book, All Elvis, Phil Buckle, Daily Mirror limited edition, copyright 1962, EX **$15.00**

Book, Elvis Remembered: A Three Dimensional Celebration, pop-ups, hardbound, 1997, 11¾x11¾" **$30.00**

Booklet, Memories, RCA promotional, full-color photos, 1977, 16 pages, 5¾x5¾" **$10.00**

Candy tin, Elvis at Christmas tree, Happy Holidays, hinged lid, Russell Stover, 1990, 12x4" **$10.00**

Character jug, Vegas Elvis, Royal Doulton, EP6, 2006 limited edition, lg **$85.00**

Collector's plate, The Legend, Remembering Elvis Series, Bradford Exchange, 1995, 8", MIB **$35.00**

Decanter, McCormick, Aloha Elvis, plays Blue Hawaii, 750 ml, from $100 to **$150.00**

Decanter, McCormick, Elvis '55 Mini, plays Loving You, 50 ml, from $35 to **$45.00**

Decanter, McCormick, Elvis '77, plays 'Love Me Tender,' 750 milliliters, $95.00. (Photo courtesy Lee Garmon)

Decanter, McCormick, Elvis & Rising Sun, plays Green Grass of Home, 750 ml, from $450 to **$475.00**

Decanter, McCormick, Elvis Bust, no music box, 750 ml, from $60 to **$75.00**

Decanter, McCormick, Elvis Designer I Gold, plays Are You Lonesome Tonight, 750 ml, from $175 to **$225.00**

Decanter, McCormick, Elvis Designer I Gold Mini, plays Are You Lonesome Tonight, 50 ml, from $150 to **$175.00**

Decanter, McCormick, Elvis Designer I Silver Mini, plays Are You Lonesome Tonight, 50 ml, from $150 to **$200.00**

Decanter, McCormick, Elvis Designer I White (Joy), plays Are You Lonesome Tonight, 750 ml, from $120 to **$130.00**

Decanter, McCormick, Elvis Designer I White Mini, plays Are You Lonesome Tonight, 50 ml, from $60 to **$75.00**

Decanter, McCormick, Elvis Designer II Gold, plays It's Now or Never, 750 ml, from $200 to **$225.00**

Decanter, McCormick, Elvis Designer II White (Love), plays It's Now or Never, 750 ml, from $75 to **$100.00**

Decanter, McCormick Elvis Designer III Gold, plays Crying in the Chapel, 750 ml, from $200 to **$250.00**

Decanter, McCormick, Elvis Designer III White (Reverence), 750 ml, from $200 to **$225.00**

Decanter, McCormick, Elvis Gold Tribute, plays My Way, 750 ml, from $200 to **$225.00**

Decanter, McCormick, Elvis Gold Tribute Mini, plays My Way, 50 ml, from $100 to **$125.00**

Decanter, McCormick, Elvis Hound Dog, plays Hound Dog, 750 ml, from $500 to **$550.00**

Decanter, McCormick, Elvis Karate Mini, plays Don't Be Cruel, 50 ml, from $100 to **$115.00**

Decanter, McCormick, Elvis Memories, cassette player base, lighted top, very rare, 750 ml, from $650 to **$750.00**

Decanter, McCormick, Elvis on Stage Mini, plays Can't Help Falling in Love, 50 ml (decanter only), from $150 to **$175.00**

Decanter, McCormick, Elvis on Stage Mini (w/separate stage designed to hold decanter), 50 ml, from $400 to **$425.00**

Decanter, McCormick, Elvis Season's Greetings, plays White Christmas, 375 ml, from $175 to **$195.00**

Decanter, McCormick, Elvis Silver, plays How Great Thou Art, 750 ml, from $150 to **$175.00**

Decanter, McCormick, Elvis Teddy Bear, plays Let Me Be Your Teddy Bear, 750 ml, from $600 to **$650.00**

Decanter, McCormick, Elvis 50th Anniversary, plays I Want You, I Need You..., 750 ml, from $485 to **$515.00**

Decanter, McCormick, Elvis 50th Anniversary Mini, plays I Want You, I Need You..., 50 ml, from $200 to **$225.00**

Decanter, McCormick, Elvis '77 Mini, plays Love Me Tender, 50 ml, from $40 to **$50.00**

Decanter, McCormick, Sgt Elvis, plays GI Blues, 750 ml, from $300 to **$325.00**

Decanter, McCormick, St Elvis Mini, plays GI Blues, 50 ml, from $85 to **$115.00**

Decanter, McCormick Elvis '68, plays Can't Help Falling in Love, 750 ml, from $60 to **$80.00**

Doll, '68 Special, black jumpsuit, Hasbro, 1993, 12", MIB, from $35 to **$45.00**

Doll, Aloha From Hawaii jumpsuit, Danbury Mint, 19", on stand, from $60 to **$70.00**

Doll, Army Years, Mattel, 1999 Collector Series (2nd in series), MIB, from $60 to **$75.00**

Doll, Barbie Loves Elvis Gift Set (2 dolls), Mattel, 1996, MIB, from $35 to **$45.00**

Doll, Burning Love, white jumpsuit w/flames, World Doll, 1984, 21", MIB, from $60 to **$70.00**

Doll, gold lame jumpsuit & gold medallion, porcelain w/poseable leather body, World Doll, 1984, 21", MIB, from $100 to **$125.00**

Doll, vinyl 'magic skin,' original clothes, Elvis Presley Enterprises, c 1957, 18", extremely rare, EX, from $900 to **$1,200.00**

Doll, white jumpsuit, poseable arms & head, light on stage base, plays Hound Dog, Franklin Mint, 1987, 18" **$70.00**

Earrings, Loving You..., gold-framed portrait, pierced backs, MIP (watch for repros)...**$225.00**

Figurine, Elvis on motorcycle, ceramic, Westland Giftware, 8x6", MIB...**$35.00**

Guitar, Elvis pick guard & signature decal, acoustic 6-string, EX in hard case...**$100.00**

Lobby card, Love Me Tender, Richard Egan w/arm on Elvis' shoulder, 11x14", EX...**$55.00**

Magazine, Elvis Monthly 1962 Special, photo cover, 60+ pages, EX...**$12.00**

Magazine, Elvis Vs The Beatles, portraits of all on cover, 1965...**$25.00**

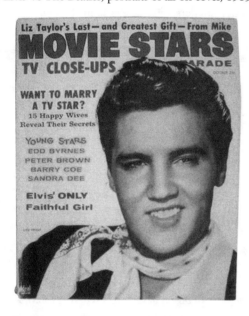

Magazine, Movie Stars, October 1958, EX, $25.00. (Photo courtesy www.gasolinealleyantiques.com)

Mug, Postage Stamp Commemorative, hinged lid, Elvis Presley Enterprises, ca 1998.................................**$28.00**

Music box, Elvis Presley's Graceland, musical front gates, pink Cadillac, plays Love Me Tender, Music Box Collection. **$80.00**

Music box, The Talkies, Elvis in white jumpsuit w/guitar, Nostalgia Collectibles, Elvis Presley Enterprises, 1985, MIB........**$35.00**

Photo, Elvis in blue shirt w/hands in pants pockets, Elvis Presley Enterprises, 1956, 14x11", EX.................................**$25.00**

Pin-back button, portrait/guitar flasher, black & white, 1956, 2½", EX...**$30.00**

Pocket watch, Elvis dancing on case, name on side, Franklin Mint, Graceland 2000, gold-tone chain, in drawstring bag...**$40.00**

Poster, Blue Hawaii, colorful beach scene, 1961, 41x27", EX...**$250.00**

Poster, Kid Galahad, printed on canvas, French version, 61x44", EX...**$55.00**

Poster, Kissing Cousins, figures on white background, fold creases, 1964, 54x78"...**$35.00**

Print, Elvis in white jumpsuit at Hawaii concert on black velvet, ca 1973, 60x36"...**$75.00**

Print, portrait on black velvet, in wood frame, 40x28"........**$85.00**

Sheet music, Love Me Tender, Elvis Presley & Vera Matson, copyright 1956, EX, from $10 to.................................**$15.00**

Snow globe/music box, Graceland, rains musical notes, plays Love Me Tender, Elvis Presley Enterprises..........................**$50.00**

Table lamp, bust in white costume & turquoise scarf, ceramic, 1970s...**$110.00**

Tour book, in white jumpsuit on cover, 1976, EX..............**$30.00**

Wallet, blue vinyl, Elvis Presley Enterprises, dated 1956....**$295.00**

Sheet music, from $25.00 to $40.00 each.

Enesco

Enesco is a company that imports and distributes ceramic novelty items made in Japan. Some of their more popular lines are the Human Beans, Partners in Crime Christmas ornaments, Eggbert, Dutch Kids, and Mother in the Kitchen (also referred to as Kitchen Prayer Ladies, see also that category). Prices are climbing steadily.

See also Cats, Character; Cookie Jars.

Bank, Coca-Cola Airplane, musical, MIB, from $55 to.......**$70.00**

Bank, King Louie & Mowgli, Walt Disney, 1965, 6½x5", NM..**$30.00**

Bank, Snow White at wishing well, Walt Disney, 1960s.......**$50.00**

Bank, Tonka Front End Loader, 2000, 11" L, MIB.............**$30.00**

Doll, Trish, porcelain w/cloth body, #12483, 1984, 7", MIB..**$75.00**

Figurine, angel girl holding wreath, #3117846, 9"..............**$55.00**

Figurine, Black Kewpie stands w/finger to mouth, Jesco, #530808, 1992, 4", MIB, from $85 to.................................**$125.00**

Figurine, Black Kewpie tumbling w/hands on the floor, MIB, from $50 to...**$75.00**

Figurine, black stallion, E-3296, 6x6¾"..........................**$65.00**

Figurine, boy singing carols w/wreath in hand, #119873, 1990, 6¾"...**$40.00**

Figurine, Break Away, football players, E-7277, 7½", MIB..**$37.50**

Figurine, Bumper (North Pole Village), #830909, rare, MIB..**$155.00**

Figurine, Celebrate Spring, gray bunny w/blue bow inside egg which opens, My Blushing Bunnies, 2-pc, 1999, MIB...........**$50.00**

Figurine, Cinderella's Castle of Dreams, Disney Showcase Collection, 12", MIB...**$155.00**

Figurine, Cleopigtra (Miss Piggy as Cleopatra), Famous Femmes du Histoire, 16", MIB...**$150.00**

Figurine, Coca-Cola Doctor Bear, 5"..............................**$110.00**

Figurine, Country Cousin girl in light green dress, apron tied at waist, orange hat, flower in hand, 1981........................**$50.00**

Figurine, Desirae, mermaid from Coral Kingdom, Shimmer Stone beads, #920878, 1995, MIB.................................**$80.00**

Figurine, Happy Holly Days, angel w/scroll, Holly Babes, Morehead, 1984, 3¾"...**$60.00**

Figurine, Helping Hand Fairie, fairy on scrub brush, 2003, MIB..$315.00

Figurine, horse, #4230, 4x4", $40.00.

Figurine, Illumination, angel from Circle of Love series, 14", MIB $62.50

Figurine, Jiggle, North Pole Village, #876887, MIB $75.00

Figurine, Kewpie Bride, #532495, Jesco, 1993, MIB...........$48.00

Figurine, Kewpie by sign, #527939, Jesco, 1991, 4x4½"......$55.00

Figurine, Kewpie Indian w/corn in apron, #602817, Jesco, 1994, MIB..$55.00

Figurine, Kewpiedoodle, dog w/bone in mouth, #117129, Jesco, 1994, 2", MIB $90.00

Figurine, Memories of Yesterday, Every Stitch Is Sewn w/Kindness, Enesco, 1996, 5½"...$60.00

Figurine, painted horse, E-3298, 5½x6½".........................$135.00

Figurine, painted horse, E-4235, 6½x5½"...........................$75.00

Figurine, Ring, girl showing engagement ring to 2nd girl, #953067, 2001, 4"...$40.00

Figurine, Selina, mermaid baby sitting on coral, looking at 2 fish, Shimmer Stone tail, #533092, 1993 ....$50.00

Figurine, Stitch in Time, Calico Kitten series, 1994, 6x4" ...$36.00

Figurine, Tiger Lily, sad-eyed striped cat, 7".....................$35.00

Figurine, Tinkerbell, seated w/feet in air, Walt Disney Productions, 3"..$85.00

Figurine, Under the Mistletoe, Treasured Memories series, 1984, 6½"...$50.00

Figurine, Vatican Nativity Angel, #75135M, 2000, MIB.....$55.00

Figurines, Country Cousins, pilgrim boy & girl praying at table, #438154, 3-pc, MIB.......................................$100.00

Figurines, Snow White & 7 Dwarfs, Walt Disney Productions, 8-pc set, from $65 to $85.00

Figurines, They Followed the Star (3 child-like figures on camels), MIB $95.00

Mug, Calico Kittens, #251798, 1993....................................$45.00

Nightlight, Kewpie w/Santa hat & toys, #301566, Jesco, 1994, 6½", MIB..$70.00

Ornament, Country Cousins, girl on deer, 1988 ....$80.00

Pencil sharpener, kitten w/over-size green eyes by garbage can ..$40.00

Pincushion/tape measure, Betsy Ross sewing flag................$45.00

Planter, gypsy wagon, clothesline & clothes on 1 side, kitten on top, 4x6"...$35.00

Planter, Mary Moo Moo, lights up, holds 4½" pot, #109235, 12" $32.50

Planter, Pinocchio & Jiminy Cricket on storybook, Walt Disney Productions, #WDE-142, 4x5½"...............................$58.00

Salt & pepper shakers, anthropomorphic banana couple dressed as Mexican dancer & bongo player, 4½", 2-pc set.............$25.00

Salt & pepper shakers, cat winking (head only), 3", pr $35.00

Salt & pepper shakers, circus elephant & ball on drum, 2-pc set $20.00

Salt and pepper shakers, devil and dice, from $20.00 to $25.00 for the pair. (Photo courtesy LiveAuctioneers.com/Tom Harris Auctions)

Salt & pepper shakers, Golden Girls, pink w/much gold trim, rhinestones on dresses, 3¾", pr $40.00

Salt & pepper shakers, grill chefs (1 at grill, 2nd w/platter, 4", 2-pc set...$27.50

Salt & pepper shakers, My Little Kitchen Fairies series, fairy on handle of basket holding shakers, #4004848, 3-pc set ..$30.00

Salt & pepper shakers, skewbald painted horse w/black mane, 4x4½", pr..$30.00

Salt & pepper shakers, washtub & bar of Fels soap, 2-pc set ..$35.00

Salt & pepper shakers, 1953 Corvette, 3-pc set, MIB........$200.00

Teapot, Beatrix Potter bunny in watering can, #206911, 1996, 7" $40.00

Teapot, Home Sweet Home, house decorated for Christmas, Mary Engelbreit, 2000, MIB...$20.00

Teapot, It's a Beautiful Day, birds border on white, musical, 8x5x6"...$25.00

Trinket box, Mary Moo Moo Blueberry Pie, You're Berry Special...$18.00

Trinket box, Scarecrow from Wizard of Oz, Turner Entertainment, 4" $20.00

Fans, Electric

Vintage fans can be fascinating collectibles with various complex working parts and styling varying from the very basic to the most wonderful Art Deco designs. Values hinge on age, style, condition, and manufacturer. To qualify as excellent, a fan must retain its original paint (with only a few blemishes). It must be clean and polished, the original cord must be present, and it must be in good working order with no replacement parts.

Century Electric Co, 16" cage, brass blades, 3-speed, red enameling, #3263, 1920s, EX...**$85.00**

Emerson, Northwind, wire cage, 4 brass blades, 14½", EX..**$85.00**

Emerson Jr, 10" wire cage, 4 gold-painted blades, oscillator, on/off switch, EX **$95.00**

Emerson Silver Swan, 4 aluminum blades, oscillator, 3-speed, 18x14"...**$165.00**

General Electric, black painted cage, 3 aluminum propeller-type blades, Deco styling, #89076, 13x10", EX.................**$200.00**

General Electric, Vortalex, 14" cage, 3-blade, floor type, height adjusts to 48", VG+ **$325.00**

General Electric, 12" brass cage w/4 brass blades, ca 1917, EX.....**$200.00**

GE #49X929, black enamel with 4½" black blades, oscillates, ca. 1920s – 1930s, 17x14", EX, $200.00. (Photo courtesy John M. Witt)

Homart Sears, window box fan, 3 blades, 2 speeds, timer dial, original taupe enameling, #4809363-6, 23x26½", EX+ **$155.00**

Menominee, 9½" brass cage w/4 brass blades, circular yoke, oscillator, #15457, 12", EX **$425.00**

Polar Cub, 13" cage, 4 blades, black paint overall, EX **$185.00**

Robbins & Meyers, 13" brass cage, 4 brass blades, #R134031, Pat Oct 9 1906, EX..**$175.00**

Savory Inc, 10" globe cage holds 4 metal paddle blades, 3-speed, #E8555, Pat March 18, 1926, 19", EX......................**$475.00**

Signal, Cool Spot, wire cage, 3 aqua blades, aqua housing w/bullet design, oscillator, sm, EX **$70.00**

Star-Rite, green hexagonal wire cage, 4 brass blades, ca 1940s-50s, 12", EXIB...**$165.00**

Vornado, med olive green w/silver-colored metal interior, 11" blades, 3-speed, #B12D1, 1947, 21", EX+ **$215.00**

Western Electric, 13" brass cage, 6 blades, #S163563A, last patent date: 1914, VG+ **$325.00**

Westinghouse, brass cage, 6 12" brass blades, 3-speed, last patent date: Oct 06, 13" dia, EX........................**$750.00**

Westinghouse, 12" brass cage, 4 5" brass blades, 3-speed, #60677, last patent date December 26 '93, 16½", EX.............**$315.00**

Zero, white wire cage, 4 white blades, white motor housing & base, #1250R, 10" **$110.00**

Fenton Glass

Located in Williamstown, West Virginia, the Fenton company is still producing glassware just as they have since the early part of the century. Nearly all fine department stores and gift shops carry an extensive line of their beautiful products, many of which rival examples of the finest antique glassware. The fact that even some of their fairly recent glassware has collectible value attests to its fine quality.

Over the years they have made many lovely colors in scores of lines, several of which are very extensive. Paper labels were used exclusively until 1970. Since then some pieces have been made with a stamped-in logo.

Numbers in the descriptions correspond with catalog numbers used by the company. Collectors use them as a means of identification as to shape and size. If you'd like to learn more about the subject, we recommend *Fenton Art Glass, 1907 to 1939; Fenton Art Glass Patterns, 1939 to 1980; Fenton Art Glass Colors and Hand-Decorated Patterns, 1939 to 1980; Fenton Art Glass Hobnail Pattern;* all are written by Margaret and Kenn Whitmyer. Other good books are *Fenton Glass Made for Other Companies, 1907 to 1980,* and *Fenton Glass Made for Other Companies, 1970 – 2005, Vol. II,* both by Carrie and Gerald Domitz. These books are all published by Collector Books.

Club: Fenton Art Glass Collectors of America, Inc.
Newsletter: *Butterfly Net*
P.O. Box 384, 702 W. 5th St.
Williamstown, WV 26187

Club: Pacific Northwest Fenton Association
P.O. Box 3901
Hillsboro, OR 79123
www.glasscastle.com/pnwfa.htm

Baskets

Almost Heaven, blue slag, bonbon, #7236, 6½", from $150 to...**$165.00**

Butterfly & Berry, Electric Blue carnival, #9134-BN, from $125 to **$150.00**

Cactus, Red Sunset carnival, double crimped, loop handle, #3436-RN, 7½", from $200 to............................**$225.00**

Coin Dot, Persian Blue opalescent, hat, #1435-XC, 5", from $75 to **$95.00**

Dotted Swiss, Rose Magnolia, #2777, Cracker Barrel, from $75 to **$85.00**

Drapery, aqua opalescent carnival, ribbon-candy edge, #9435-IO, 8½", from $145 to...............................**$165.00**

Emerald Crest, miniature, collector pc, #7567, from $35 to .**$40.00**

Emerald Green, Poinsettia decoration, #7379, from $85 to ..**$95.00**
Hobnail, plum opalescent, #3735-PO, 5½", from $75 to **$95.00**
Hobnail, red satin, #3837-RA, 7", from $75 to **$95.00**
Kittens, Rosalene Carnival, miniature, from $70 to **$80.00**
Love Bouquet, Burmese, #7235-WQ, 5", from $175 to.....**$200.00**

Peach Crest with Tyndale gold rose transfer decoration, #7327, 7", from $90.00 to $110.00. (Photo courtesy Margaret and Kenn Whitmyer)

Persian Medallion, peach opalescent, Coyne's Parade of Gifts, from $120 to **$150.00**
Priscilla, Empress Rose, collector pc, from $55 to **$65.00**
Sheffield, Petal Pink, #6634-PN, from $50 to **$65.00**
Spruce Green, decorated, #6585, Coyne's Parade of Gifts, from $100 to **$125.00**
Swirled Loop, Cameo opalescent, crimped edge, 7", from $100 to **$120.00**
Thumbprint, Sea Mist Green, #9243-LE, from $35 to **$40.00**
Wild Rose & Bowknot, Celestial Blue satin, deep, double crimped, #2834-ES, 7", from $150 to **$175.00**

Bells

Blue topaz decorated w/berries, #1145, Virginia's Gift Shop, from $50 to **$65.00**
Bow & Drape, Dusty Pink, #9268-HK, 7", from $18 to.....**$20.00**
Cobalt blue w/sand-carved butterfly & flowers, collector pc, from $50 to **$65.00**
Daisy & Button, Cameo opalescent, #1967-CO, from $30 to ...**$35.00**
Daisy & Button, Colonial Blue, #1967-CB, from $28 to ...**$32.00**
Daisy & Button, milk glass, #1967-MI, from $22 to...........**$25.00**
Dotted Swiss, Rose Magnolia, Cracker Barrel, #7463, from $40 to **$45.00**
Gracious Touch, Rose Velvet, #8265-VO, 6", from $45 to ..**$55.00**
Hobnail, aqua opalescent carnival, #3645-IO, from $65 to .**$85.00**
Hobnail, glossy vaseline opalescent, fluted, #3667-VO, from $45 to **$65.00**
Hobnail, Persian Blue opalescent, #3645-XC, from $25 to ..**$35.00**

Inverted Strawberry, ruby, 1992 collector pc, from $45 to ...**$55.00**
Love Bouquet, Burmese, petite, #7662-WQ, 4½", from $100 to **$125.00**
Petite Beauty, violet w/rose decoration, #M7778-OE, from $18 to **$22.00**
Sables Arch, light amethyst carnival, #9065-DT, 6", from $50 to **$65.00**
Sheffield, Petal Pink, #6665-PN, from $35 to **$40.00**
Spanish Lace, Persian Pearl, #3567-XV, 6", from $45 to......**$55.00**
Sydenham, green opalescent w/cobalt blue edge, #9063-GK, from $75 to **$85.00**

Threaded Diamond Optic, Colonial Blue, #8465-CB, 1977 – 1979, from $25.00 to $30.00. (Photo courtesy Margaret and Kenn Whitmyer)

Victorian Girl, teal satin, 1989 collector pc, from $75 to.....**$85.00**

Carnival Glass

Note: Carnival glass items listed here were made after 1970.

Bowl, Butterfly & Berry, black, Singleton Bailey, from $100 to .**$125.00**
Bowl, Drapery, deep cranberry opalescent, ribbon-candy edge, #9425-DCO, from $125 to **$150.00**
Bowl, Good Luck, amethyst, #4619-DT, from $75 to.........**$85.00**
Bowl, Grape & Cable, peach opalescent, double crimped, #200-MO, 10", from $200 to...**$220.00**

Bowl, Hearts and Flowers, #8229-CN, 1971 – 1974, from $50.00 to $60.00. (Photo courtesy Margaret and Kenn Whitmyer)

Butter dish, Regency, light amethyst, #8680-DT, from $100 to **$120.00**

Comport, Three Fruits, vaseline opalescent, sq, #8242, 6", from $85 to **$115.00**

Cracker jar, Cactus, Red Sunset, #3480-RN, from $225 to ..**$300.00**

Cruet, Diamond Lattice, Electric Blue, #1768-BN, from $125 to **$150.00**

Cuspidor, Innovation, light amethyst, #4643-DT, from $65 to ..**$75.00**

Decanter, Hobnail, Red Sunset, from $200 to **$225.00**

Pitcher, Cactus, aqua opalescent, #3407-IO, from $300 to ..**$350.00**

Plate, Butterfly & Berry, topaz opalescent, from $175 to ...**$195.00**

Plate, Persian Medallion, Wisteria, #8219, 9½", from $85 to ..**$95.00**

Rose bowl, Drapery, aqua opalescent, #8454-IO, 5", from $85 to **$100.00**

Spittoon, Butterfly & Berry, aqua opalescent carnival, #8240/4, from $85 to **$100.00**

Toothpick holder, Diamond & Panel, light amethyst, #4644-DT, from 24 to **$28.00**

Tumbler, Lincoln Inn, Raven (black), #9003-XB, 4½", from $50 to **$65.00**

Vase, Diamond & Rib, Marigold, swung, #0178, 12-13", from $100 to **$120.00**

Vase, Grape & Cable, blue, cupped 6-point top, footed, from $150 to **$175.00**

Vase, hat; Butterfly & Berry, Electric Blue, #9495-BN, from $65 to **$75.00**

Crests

Peach, jug, #192A, 1942 – 1947, 9", from $70.00 to $90.00. (Photo courtesy Margaret and Kenn Whitmyer)

Apple Blossom, bonbon, #7428-AB, 1960-61, 8", from $40 to .**$50.00**

Apple Blossom, candleholder, #7271-AB, 1960-61, ea from $45 to **$50.00**

Aqua, bowl, double crimped, #192-10½", 1942-43, from $65 to **$70.00**

Aqua, jug, #192, 1942-43, 6", from $55 to **$65.00**

Aqua, top hat, #1923, 1943, 6", from $85 to **$110.00**

Black, plate, #7212, 1960s, 12", from $50 to **$65.00**

Black, tidbit, 2-tier, #7294, 1960s, from $65 to...................**$75.00**

Black Rose, bowl, #7227-BR, 1953-55, from $90 to **$110.00**

Black w/Circle of Love, vase, tulip; smooth or crimped, from $165 to **$185.00**

Blue, cake plate, footed, #7213-BC, 13", from $140 to.....**$160.00**

Blue Ridge, pitcher, #187, from $325 to..........................**$425.00**

Blue Ridge, tumbler, #187, 12-oz, from $65 to **$75.00**

Blue w/Circle of Love, cruet, from $175 to......................**$200.00**

Crystal, bonbon, oval, double crimped, #36, 5½", from $25 to..**$35.00**

Crystal, creamer, w/opal handle, #1924, from $42 to **$47.00**

Crystal, mayonnaise set, #7203-EC, 1953-56, from $75 to ..**$90.00**

Crystal, vase, regular, #192, 9½", from $85 to **$100.00**

Emerald, bowl, dessert; deep, #7221-EC, 1949-56, from $24 to.**$28.00**

Emerald, compote, low foot, #7329-EC, 1954-56, from $50 to..**$55.00**

Emerald, plate, #7210-EC, 1949-54, 10", from $60 to **$90.00**

Emerald, vase, tulip; #711, 1949-52, 6", from $65 to.........**$85.00**

Flame, cake plate, footed, #7213-FC, 13", from $145 to...**$185.00**

Gold, candy jar, w/lid, #192, 1943-44, from $55 to...........**$65.00**

Gold, compote, footed, #7228-GC, 1963-65, from $28 to...**$32.00**

Ivory, plate, #680, 1941-42, 6½", from $12 to **$15.00**

Ivory, top hat, #1922, 1940-41, 8", from $80 to **$100.00**

Peach, candy jar, w/lid, #711, 1949-50, from $100 to.......**$125.00**

Peach, jug, #192, 1942-49, 6", from $35 to.......................**$40.00**

Peach, vase, triangular, #189, 1940-43, 10", from $85 to **$95.00**

Silver, bowl, double crimped, #7224-SC, 1943-71, 10", from $45 to **$55.00**

Silver, planter, 2-tier, #680, 1950-52, from $55 to..............**$60.00**

Silver, punch set, #7306-SC, 1956-63, 15-pc, from $590 to ..**$725.00**

Silver with Violets in the Snow, compote, #7429-DV, 1969 – 1980, from $45.00 to $55.00. (Photo courtesy Margaret and Kenn Whitmyer)

Figurines and Novelties

Owl, Springtime Green carnival, blown, #5178, 6½", from $200 to **$250.00**

Swan, Gracious Touch, custard w/Pretty Pansies decoration, #Q5161-PP, from $25 to **$30.00**

Alley Cat doorstop, purple slag, #5177-PS, 10", from $400 to **$450.00**

Bear, opal satin w/Primrose decoration, #5151-KX, Hallmark, from $45 to **$50.00**

Cat, stylized, Green Burmese, violets & bee decoration, #5065, from $75 to **$85.00**

Cat sitting, rose spongeware, #5165, collector pc, from $45 to...**$50.00**

Doll, opal satin, w/Valentine decoration, #5228, Jillian collector pc, from $75 to **$95.00**

Dolphin, aquamarine, w/Shell decoration, #5087, Lenox, from $55 to..**$60.00**

Donkey, blue opalescent, Duncan Glass collector pc, from $75 to...$85.00

Donkey, opaque blue, #5125-BA, 1972 – 1973, from $150.00 to $175.00; Cart, #5124-BA, from $150.00 to $175.00. (Photo courtesy Margaret and Kenn Whitmyer)

Elephant, sitting, French opalescent, med, collector pc, from $75 to **$95.00**

Fawn, recumbent, Gracious Touch, opal satin w/peach roses, #Q5160-RP, from $40 to...**$45.00**

Frog, Blossoms & Berries, French opalescent, #5274, Cracker Barrel, from $50 to **$65.00**

Giraffe, Rosalene, shiny, collector pc, 1992, from $150 to ..**$200.00**

Happiness Bird, Rosalene, satin, w/floral decoration, Coyne's, from $75 to **$85.00**

Happy Cat, red slag, collector pc, from $65 to **$85.00**

Hen on nest, Federal Blue, #5182-FB, from $50 to............**$65.00**

Kitten slipper, Hobnail, chocolate, #3995-CK, 6", from $25 to **$30.00**

Mouse, ruby marble, from $60 to **$75.00**

Puppy, plum opalescent, #5225, collector pc, from $55 to ..**$65.00**

Snail, topaz opalescent, #5134, from $55 to **$60.00**

Hobnail

Bonbon, blue marble, handled, #3706-MB, 8", from $30 to ..**$35.00**

Bowl, vaseline opalescent, glossy, crimped, #3324-TO, 9", from $100 to **$125.00**

Butter dish, w/lid, round, blue opalescent, #3677-BO, from $100 to **$125.00**

Candy jar, blue opalescent, footed, #3980-BO, from $65 to ..**$75.00**

Comport, topaz opalescent, #3728, from $65 to **$75.00**

Creamer, Colonial Amber, miniature, #3665, from $7 to **$9.00**

Cruet, cranberry opalescent, w/stopper, #3863-CR, from $100 to **$125.00**

Cupsidor, ruby carnival, from $45 to **$55.00**

Decanter, plum opalescent, w/opalescent handle, #3761, from $250 to...**$275.00**

Decanter, Red Sunset carnival, from $200 to **$225.00**

Egg cup, ruby, collector pc, from $25 to **$35.00**

Epergne, pink opalescent, miniature, #3801-UO, from $100 to ..**$125.00**

Pitcher, purple carnival, #3845, 10½", from $200 to **$225.00**

Pitcher, vaseline opalescent, glossy, #3908-TO, 54-oz, from $225 to **$250.00**

Salt & pepper shakers, vaseline opalescent, glossy, footed, #3609-TO, pr from $75 to **$95.00**

Tumbler, vaseline opalescent carnival, #3945, from $40 to ..**$44.00**

Chip 'n Dip, milk glass, #3922, 1970 – 1971, 3¼x12", from $600.00 to $700.00. (Photo courtesy Margaret and Kenn Whitmyer)

Lamps

Table, Bubble Optic, #1306-SB, 1970 – 1978, from $190.00 to $200.00. (Photo courtesy Margaret and Kenn Whitmyer)

Fairy, Coin Dot, cranberry opalescent, #1403-CR, from $200 to **$225.00**

Fairy, Fern Optic, green opalescent, #1803-GO, from $150 to **$175.00**

Fairy, Hobnail, red satin, #3608-RA, from $150 to **$165.00**

Fairy, Persian Medallion, green opalescent w/cobalt edge, #8408-GG, from $125 to **$150.00**

Gone w/the Wind, Hobnail, pink opalescent, #A3308-UO, from $350 to **$400.00**

Gone w/the Wind, Poppy, Electric Blue carnival, #9101-BN, from $225 to **$275.00**

Hurricane, Hobnail, Rose Pastel, #3998-RP, 11", from $90 to ..**$100.00**

Hurricane, Thumbprint, milk glass, #4498, from $50 to.....**$65.00**

Kerosene-style, Poppy, purple carnival, #9105, 18", from $250 to... **$295.00**

Student, Circle of Love, cranberry, 18", from $450 to **$500.00**

Student, Coin Dot, Persian blue opalescent, w/33 hanging prisms, #1413-XC, 22", from $250 to **$300.00**

Student, Dotted Swiss w/Rose Magnolia decoration, Cracker Barrel, 7" shade, from $125 to **$150.00**

Student, Fern Optic, Persian Pearl, #1801-XV, 21", from $325 to.. **$350.00**

Student, Wild Rose & Bowknot, aqua opalescent carnival, #2805-IO, from $250 to **$275.00**

Miscellaneous

Basket, Jack-O'-Lanterns, black, #7379, from $75 to...........**$85.00**

Bowl, Farmyard, Burmese, from $65 to **$85.00**

Bowl, Shell, blue opalescent, #9020, from $125 to **$150.00**

Cup, Dolphin, Purple Stretch, #7581-VY, 5½", from $125 to ..**$145.00**

Pitcher, Spiral Optic, blue opal, #1353, 1939, 9", from $280.00 to $310.00. (Photo courtesy Margaret and Kenn Whitmyer)

Plate, chop; Farmyard, ruby iridescent, 11", from $65 to.....**$85.00**

Rose bowl, Lily of the Valley, marigold over milk glass, from $100 to **$125.00**

Salt & pepper shakers, Vasa Murrhina Swirl, metal tops, pr from $75 to **$85.00**

Vase, Atlantis, Rosalene, from $175 to.............................**$200.00**

Vase, Caprice, Country Cranberry, w/bow, from $100 to ..**$125.00**

Vase, Peacock, ruby marigold, flared neck, from $75 to **$85.00**

Fiesta

Fiesta is a line of solid-color dinnerware made by the Homer Laughlin China Company of Newell, West Virginia. It was introduced in 1936 and was immediately accepted by the American public. The line was varied. There were more than 50 items offered, and the color assortment included red (orange-red), cobalt, light green, and yellow. Within a short time, ivory and turquoise were added. (All these are referred to as 'original colors.')

As tastes changed during the production years, old colors were retired and new ones added. The colors collectors refer to as '50s colors are dark green, rose, chartreuse, and gray, and today these are very desirable. Medium green was introduced in 1959 at a time when some of the old standard shapes were being discontinued. Today, medium green pieces are the most expensive. The majority of pieces are marked. Plates were stamped, and molded pieces usually had an indented mark.

In 1986 Homer Laughlin reintroduced Fiesta, but in colors different than the old line: white, black, cobalt, rose (bright pink), and apricot. Many of the pieces had been restyled, and the only problem collectors have had with the new colors is with the cobalt. But if you'll compare it with the old, you'll see that it is darker. Turquoise, periwinkle blue, yellow, and seamist green were added next, and though the turquoise is close, it is a little greener than the original. Lilac and persimmon were later made for sale exclusively through Bloomingdale's department stores. Production was limited on lilac (not every item was made in it), and once it was discontinued, collectors were clamoring for it, often paying several times the original price. Sapphire blue, a color approximating the old cobalt, was introduced in 1996 — also a Bloomingdale's exclusive, and the selection was limited. Then came Chartreuse (a little more vivid than the chartreuse of the '50s); Gray was next, then Juniper (a rich teal). Several colors have followed: Cinnabar (maroon), a strong yellow called Sunflower; a dark bluish-purple they've aptly named Plum; Shamrock (similar to the coveted medium green); Tangerine (pale orange), Scarlet (described by some as lipstick red), Peacock (a vivid '50s turquoise), and lastly, Evergreen.

Items that have not been restyled are being made from the original molds. This means that you may find pieces with the old mark in the new colors (since the mark is an integral part of the mold). When an item has been restyled, new molds had to be created, and these will have the new mark. So will any piece marked with the ink stamp. The new ink mark is a script 'FIESTA' (all letters upper case), while the old is 'Fiesta.' Compare a few, the difference is obvious. Just don't be fooled into thinking you've found a rare cobalt juice pitcher or individual sugar and creamer set, they just weren't made in the old line. And if you find a piece with a letter H below the mark, you'll know that piece is new.

Because Fiesta is in good supply on eBay, more than ever before, condition has become a major factor in determining value. Unless an item is free from signs of wear, smoothly glazed, and has no distracting manufacturing flaws, it will not bring 'book' price. Use the high end of our ranges only when the item you're evaluating is pristine. Otherwise, the lower end would be more appropriate. EBay prices are erratic. Some items bring good prices, while others do well to reach half of low 'book.' It's a buyer's market!

For more information we recommend *Collector's Encyclopedia of Fiesta, 10th Edition,* by Bob and Sharon Huxford (Collector Books.)

Club: Homer Laughlin China Collector's Association (HLCCA)
P.O. Box 26021
Crystal City, VA 22215-6021
info@hlcca.org

Newsletter: *Fiesta Collector's Quarterly*
China Specialties, Inc.
Box 471, Valley City, OH 44280
www.chinaspecialties.com/books_&_newsletters.htm

Carafe, original colors, from $250.00 to $300.00.

Ashtray, '50s colors, from $55 to...**$75.00**
Ashtray, original colors, from $35 to....................................**$60.00**
Bowl, covered onion soup; red, cobalt or ivory **$600.00**
Bowl, covered onion soup; yellow or light green **$525.00**
Bowl, cream soup; '50s colors, from $60 to **$75.00**
Bowl, cream soup; original colors, from $30 to...................**$60.00**
Bowl, dessert; 6", '50s colors, from $35 to...........................**$45.00**
Bowl, dessert; 6", original colors, from $30 to **$50.00**
Bowl, footed salad; red, cobalt, ivory, or turquoise, from $350 to..**$475.00**
Bowl, footed salad; yellow or light green, from $275 to **$375.00**
Bowl, fruit; 4¾", '50s colors, from $30 to...........................**$35.00**
Bowl, fruit; 4¾", original colors, from $20 to **$30.00**
Bowl, fruit; 5½", '50s colors, from $35 to...........................**$40.00**
Bowl, fruit; 5½", med green, from $65 to.............................**$70.00**
Bowl, fruit; 5½", original colors, from $20 to **$30.00**
Bowl, fruit; 11¾", original colors, from $225 to **$300.00**
Bowl, individual salad; med green, 7½", from $100 to **$120.00**
Bowl, individual salad; red, turquoise, or yellow, 7½", from $80 to **$90.00**
Bowl, mixing; #1, original colors, from $220 to **$300.00**
Bowl, mixing; #2, original colors, from $100 to **$150.00**
Bowl, mixing; #3, original colors, from $110 to **$150.00**
Bowl, mixing; #4, original colors, from $110 to **$185.00**
Bowl, mixing; #5, original colors, from $175 to **$235.00**

Bowl, mixing; #6, original colors, from $230 to **$300.00**
Bowl, mixing; #7, original colors, from $325 to **$500.00**
Bowl, nappy; 8½", '50s colors, from $50 to.........................**$60.00**
Bowl, nappy; 8½", original colors, from $30 to **$50.00**
Bowl, nappy; 9½", original colors, from $55 to **$70.00**
Bowl, Tom & Jerry; ivory w/gold letters, from $250 to......**$260.00**
Bowl, unlisted salad; yellow, from $80 to.........................**$100.00**
Candleholders, bulb; original colors, pr from $80 to **$130.00**
Candleholders, tripod; original colors, pr from $450 to.....**$550.00**
Casserole, French; yellow, from $250 to............................**$300.00**
Casserole, '50s colors, from $250 to..................................**$275.00**
Casserole, original colors, from $150 to............................**$200.00**
Coffeepot, demitasse; original colors other than turquoise, from $350 to **$600.00**
Coffeepot, '50s colors, from $300 to..................................**$350.00**
Coffeepot, original colors, from $180 to............................**$265.00**
Compote, sweets; original colors, from $95 to **$135.00**
Compote, 12", original colors, from $160 to **$200.00**
Creamer, regular; '50s colors, from $35 to **$45.00**
Creamer, regular; original colors, from $20 to....................**$30.00**
Creamer, stick-handled; original colors, from $45 to **$65.00**
Cup & saucer, demitasse; '50s colors, from $325 to...........**$400.00**
Cup & saucer, demitasse; original colors, from $70 to.......**$100.00**
Egg cup, '50s colors, from $140 to **$160.00**
Egg cup, original colors, from $55 to..................................**$70.00**
Marmalade, original colors, from $350 to..........................**$400.00**
Mug, Tom & Jerry; '50s colors, from $80 to........................**$90.00**
Mug, Tom & Jerry; ivory w/gold letters, from $55 to **$65.00**
Mug, Tom & Jerry; original colors, from $50 to **$80.00**
Mustard, original colors, from $240 to **$300.00**
Pitcher, disk juice; Harlequin yellow, from $65 to **$75.00**
Pitcher, disk juice; yellow, from $45 to **$50.00**
Pitcher, disk water; '50s colors, from $200 to **$275.00**
Pitcher, disk water; original colors, from $100 to..............**$175.00**

Pitcher, ice; original colors, from $110.00 to $145.00.

Pitcher, jug, 2-pt; '50s colors, from $120 to......................**$140.00**
Pitcher, jug, 2-pt; original colors, from $70 to **$105.00**
Plate, calendar; 9-10", ea, from $45 to...............................**$55.00**
Plate, chop; 13", '50s colors, from $90 to **$95.00**
Plate, chop; 13", original colors, from $40 to **$55.00**
Plate, chop; 15", '50s colors, from $135 to.......................**$150.00**

Plate, chop; 15", original colors, from $70 to **$100.00**
Plate, compartment; 10½", '50s colors, from $60 to...........**$70.00**
Plate, compartment; 10½", original colors, from $35 to **$45.00**
Plate, compartment; 12", original colors, from $40 to.........**$60.00**
Plate, deep; '50s colors, from $50 to **$55.00**
Plate, deep; med green, from $130 to **$145.00**
Plate, deep; original colors, from $35 to **$60.00**
Plate, 6", '50s colors, from $7 to..................................**$10.00**
Plate, 6", med green, from $30 to.....................................**$45.00**
Plate, 6", original colors, from $4 to.................................**$7.00**
Plate, 7", '50s colors, from $10 to..................................**$12.00**
Plate, 7", med green, from $30 to.....................................**$45.00**
Plate, 7", original colors, from $7 to.................................**$10.00**
Plate, 9", '50s colors, from $20 to..................................**$25.00**
Plate, 9", med green, from $60 to.....................................**$75.00**
Plate, 9", original colors, from $10 to.............................**$20.00**
Plate, 10", '50s colors, from $45 to.................................**$50.00**
Plate, 10", med green, minimum value..............................**$125.00**
Plate, 10", original colors, from $30 to **$45.00**
Platter, '50s colors, from $50 to **$60.00**
Platter, med green, from $175 to **$225.00**
Platter, original colors, from $40 to **$55.00**
Relish tray, gold decor, complete, from $220 to **$250.00**
Relish tray base, original colors, from $80 to **$100.00**
Relish tray center insert, original colors, from $50 to..........**$70.00**
Relish tray side insert, original colors, from $45 to **$60.00**
Salt & pepper shakers, '50s colors, pr from $40 to.............**$45.00**
Salt & pepper shakers, med green, pr from $125 to..........**$150.00**
Salt & pepper shakers, original colors, pr from $22 to.........**$30.00**
Sauce boat, '50s colors, from $60 to **$75.00**
Sauce boat, med green, from $135 to...............................**$185.00**
Sauce boat, original colors, from $40 to............................**$70.00**
Saucer, '50s colors, from $3 to **$5.00**
Saucer, med green, from $10 to **$15.00**
Saucer, original colors, from $2 to....................................**$3.00**
Sugar bowl, individual; turquoise, from $400 to **$500.00**
Sugar bowl, individual; yellow, from $125 to.....................**$175.00**
Sugar bowl, w/lid, '50s colors, 3¼x3½", from $70 to..........**$80.00**
Sugar bowl, w/lid, med green, 3¼x3½", from $150 to......**$200.00**
Sugar bowl, w/lid, original colors, 3¼x3½", from $50 to.....**$75.00**
Syrup, original colors, from $375 to **$425.00**
Teacup, '50s colors, from $35 to **$40.00**
Teacup, med green, from $60 to **$75.00**
Teacup, original colors, from $15 to **$40.00**
Teapot, lg; original colors, from $250 to **$350.00**
Teapot, med; '50s colors, from $250 to.............................**$300.00**
Teapot, med; original colors, from $150 to **$250.00**
Tray, figure-8; cobalt, from $90 to **$100.00**
Tray, figure-8; turquoise, from $350 to **$400.00**
Tray, figure-8; yellow, from $500 to **$600.00**
Tray, utility; original colors, from $40 to.............................**$50.00**
Tumbler, juice; chartreuse or dark green, minimum value..**$750.00**
Tumbler, juice; original colors, from $40 to **$50.00**
Tumbler, juice; rose, from $55 to **$60.00**
Tumbler, water; original colors, from $55 to **$75.00**
Vase, bud; original colors, from $75 to **$125.00**
Vase, 8", original colors, minimum...................................**$400.00**

Vase, 10", original colors, minimum **$550.00**
Vase, 12", red, cobalt, ivory, or turquoise, minimum **$1,000.00**

Kitchen Kraft

Bowl, mixing; 6" **$60.00**
Bowl, mixing; 8" **$80.00**
Bowl, mixing; 10", from $100 to......................................**$110.00**
Cake plate **$35.00**
Cake server, from $100 to...**$135.00**
Casserole, individual; from $150 to **$160.00**
Casserole, 7½"...**$75.00**
Casserole, 8½"...**$85.00**
Covered jar, lg; from $350 to..**$375.00**
Covered jar, med; from $275 to.......................................**$300.00**
Covered jar, sm; from $300 to...**$325.00**

Covered jug, large, from $275.00 to $300.00.

Covered jug, sm, from $300 to **$320.00**
Fork, from $150 to **$160.00**
Metal frame for platter **$15.00**
Pie plate, Spruce Green..**$150.00**
Pie plate, 9" or 10" (other than Spruce Green) **$40.00**
Platter, from $60 to..**$75.00**
Platter, Spruce Green...**$150.00**
Salt & pepper shakers, pr from $120 to **$150.00**
Spoon, from $150 to...**$200.00**
Spoon, ivory, 12", from $400 to **$500.00**
Stacking refrigerator lid, ivory, from $200 to **$225.00**
Stacking refrigerator lid, other than ivory, from $90 to......**$110.00**
Stacking refrigerator unit, ivory, from $200 to...................**$210.00**
Stacking refrigerator unit, other than ivory, from $50 to......**$60.00**

New Fiesta — Post86

Bowl, chili; lilac, 18-oz, from $40 to................................**$50.00**
Bowl, mixing; chartreuse, 44-oz, from $25 to **$30.00**
Bowl, stacking cereal; apricot, 6½", from $15 to.................**$18.00**
Candlestick, pyramid; chartreuse, ea from $28 to **$32.00**
Cup, jumbo; sapphire, 18-oz, from $22 to.........................**$28.00**

Cup & saucer, AD; sapphire, from $22 to $28.00

Five-piece place setting, lilac, MIB, $150.00 to 195.00.
(Photo courtesy LiveAuctioneers.com/Strawser Auction Group)

Hostess set, apricot, 4-pc, from $18 to.................................$22.00
Pie baker, lilac, deep dish, 10¼", from $60 to.....................$75.00
Pitcher, disk; apricot, mini, from $25 to $30.00
Plate, chop; apricot, 11¾", from $25 to $30.00
Plate, chop; chartreuse, 11¾", from $30 to $35.00
Plate, salad; sapphire, 7", from $15 to.................................$22.00
Salt & pepper shakers, apricot, 2¼", pr from $22 to...........$28.00
Sugar caddy, lilac, from $45 to $50.00
Teapot, chartreuse, 2-cup, from $30 to $40.00
Tumbler, sapphire, from $25 to...$30.00
Vase, bud; apricot, 6", from $15 to......................................$20.00

Finch, Kay

Wonderful ceramic figurines signed by sculptor-artist-decorator Kay Finch are among the many that were produced in California during the middle of the last century. She modeled her line of animals and birds with much expression and favored soft color combinations often with vibrant pastel accents. Some of her models were quite large, but generally they range in size from 12" down to a tiny 2". She made several animal 'family groups' and some human subjects as well. After her death a few years ago, prices for her work began to climb.

She used a variety of marks and labels, and though most pieces are marked, some of the smaller animals are not; but you should be able to recognize her work with ease, once you've seen a few marked pieces.

For more information, we recommend *Kay Finch Ceramics, Her Enchanted World*, by Mike Nickel and Cindy Horvath (Schiffer); and *Collector's Encyclopedia of California Pottery, Second Edition*, by Jack Chipman (Collector Books). Please note: Prices below are for near-mint condition items (allowing for moderate crazing, which is normal) decorated in multiple colors, not solid glazes. Chips and cracks drastically reduce values.

Advisors: Mike Nickel and Cindy Horvath (See Directory, Roseville)

Ashtray, Swan, #4958, 4½" $20.00
Bank, Victorian house, 2 chimneys, #4162, 5½"...............$125.00
Candlesticks, turkey figures, #5794, 3¾", pr.......................$95.00
Cat, Jezebel, 6x7"...$100.00
Cup, Kitten Face, Toby, 3" $60.00
Egg box, 9x8" $75.00
Figurine, Afghan angel reclining, blue-tipped wings, 2½x1¾"...$415.00
Figurine, Afghan angel standing, blue-tipped wings, 2½x2½"...$475.00
Figurine, Airedale dog standing, caramel & black, #4832, 5x5"...$180.00
Figurine, Ambrosia cat, professionally restored, 10⅝" $00.00

Figurine, Butch and Biddy, from $135.00 to $165.00 for the pair.

Figurine, Chanticleer, rooster, #129, 11"...........................$175.00
Figurine, Cocker spaniel, black, head up, 3" $200.00
Figurine, Dog Show Maltese, #5833, 2½" $500.00
Figurine, Godey couple, pink w/blue accents, 9¼", 9½", pr....$75.00
Figurine, Grumpy pig, #165, 6x7½" $125.00
Figurine, Guppy, fish, #173, 2½" $50.00
Figurine, Mermaid, #161, 6½"...$150.00

Figurine, Pekingese, #174, $265.00.

Figurine, Pheasant, pink lustre w/gold, #5020, rare, 18" L, pr $200.00
Figurine, Puddin', Yorkshire terrier, #158, 11x12" $1,500.00
Figurine, Scandi boy & girl, #126/#127, 5¼", pr $50.00
Salt & pepper shakers, stallion heads, 5", pr $75.00

Shakers, stallion heads, 5", pr..**$75.00**
Tureen, Turkey, platinum/gray, #5361, 9", w/ladle............**$150.00**
Vase, South Sea Girl, #4912, 8¾"...**$75.00**

Figurine, Yorkie Pups, #170 and #171, $400.00 for the pair.

Fishbowl Ornaments

Prior to World War II, every dime store had its bowl of small goldfish. Nearby were stacks of goldfish bowls — small, medium, and large. Accompanying them were displays of ceramic ornaments for these bowls, many in the shape of Oriental pagodas or European-style castles. The fish died, the owners lost interest, and the glass containers along with their charming ornaments were either thrown out or relegated to the attic. In addition to pagodas and castles, other ornaments included bridges, lighthouses, colonnades, mermaids, and fish. Note that figurals such as mermaids are difficult to find.

Many fishbowl ornaments were produced in Japan between 1921 and 1941, and again after 1947. The older Japanese items often show clean, crisp mold designs with visible detail of the item's features. Others were made in Germany and some by potteries in the United States. Aquarium pieces made in America are not common. Those produced in recent years are usually of Chinese origin and are more crude, less colorful, and less detailed in appearance. In general, the more detail and more colorful, the older the piece. A few more examples are shown in *Collector's Encyclopedia of Made in Japan Ceramics* by Carole Bess White (Collector Books).

Advisor: Carole Bess White (See Directory, Japan Ceramics)

Arch w/lion on top, red, white & blue, 2 bubbler holes, Japan, 3½x3¼x1½"...**$95.00**
Bathing beauty on shell, cinnamon & white lustre, red Japan mark, 3", from $40 to..**$60.00**
Bathing beauty on turtle, multicolor on white, 2½", from $20 to..**$30.00**
Boy riding dolphin on wave, multicolored matt, 3¾", from $20 to..**$40.00**
Bridge, brown & green, arched footbridge style, Japan, 3¼x7x2½"..**$55.00**

Castle, multicolored matt, 4½", from $20.00 to $32.00.
(Photo courtesy Carole Bess White)

Castle towers w/3 arches, tan lustre towers w/red arches on green & white rocks, 5¼"...**$22.00**
Castle w/arch, multicolored, 2½" or 3½", ea.........................**$20.00**
Castle-like tower connected to bridge that reaches wooded hillside, multicolored..**$50.00**
Coral, shiny orange w/shadow of black sea diver, red mark, 3½", from $18 to..**$28.00**
Diver holding dagger, white suit & helmet, blue gloves, brown boots & black airpack, 4¾"...**$22.00**
Diver spearing fish, hole at back of head to attach an air hose, top has blubber hole, Japan, 5½"..**$48.00**
Doorway, stone entry w/open aqua wood-look door, 2".......**$15.00**
Fish, multicolored, black Japan mark, 2½", from $15 to......**$25.00**
Frogs on lily pad before sign: Welcome to Our Pad, multicolored, 3¾x5x3½"..**$16.00**
Houses (2) & tree above sm bridge w/hole for fish to swim through, multicolored, Japan, 3½x2⅜x1⅛"............................**$50.00**
Houses & cave, top has bubbler hole, Japan, 3½".................**$15.00**
Lighthouse, orange, yellow & brown, 2x2½".........................**$16.00**
Lighthouse, tan, black, brown & green, 6½x4"......................**$26.00**
Mermaid, painted bisque, black Japan mark, 4¾", from $45 to..**$65.00**
Mermaid, sitting w/shell in hand, multicolored, unmarked Japan, 4½x4"..**$30.00**
Mermaid on snail, multicolored, Japan, 4", from $45 to......**$65.00**
Mermaid on 2 seashells, multicolored, 3½".........................**$40.00**
Nude on starfish, painted bisque, 4½", from $75 to.........**$125.00**
Octopus, pink & brown, black Japan mark, 4"......................**$35.00**
Pagoda, red, white, blue & green, Japan, 2x2½".................**$25.00**
Pagoda, 3 roof lines, blue, brown & yellow, 4"....................**$27.50**
Pagoda, 6 roof lines, green, yellow & brown, Japan, 6½".....**$50.00**
Ruins among rocks, aqua, green & brown, Japan, 4x4".......**$15.00**
Sailing ship, multicolored, green Japan mark, 4".................**$20.00**
Sand castle, 2 openings for fish to swim through, Japan, 3x3½"..**$18.00**
Sign on tree trunk, No Fishing, brown, black & white, 2¼x4"..**$12.00**
Sunken ship wreckage, pastels, unmarked, 2x8¼x4⅛".........**$50.00**
Thatched house, brown tones, holes for fish to swim through, Hand Decorated Japan, 5x6¾"..**$60.00**
Torii gate, multicolored, 3¾", from $25 to..........................**$35.00**

Towers w/gateway, brown & green, 3 openings, bubbler in roof, from $35 to $45.00

Windmill w/house on mountainside, hole for fish to swim through, multicolored, Japan, 1940s, from $35 to $40.00

Fisher-Price

Probably no other toy manufacture is as well known among kids of today as Fisher-Price. Since the 1930s they've produced wonderful toys made of wood covered with vividly lithographed paper. Plastic parts weren't used until 1949, and this can sometimes help you date your finds. These toys were made for play, so very few older examples have survived in condition good enough to attract collectors. Watch for missing parts and avoid those that are dirty. Edge wear and some paint dulling is normal and to be expected. Our values are for toys with minimum signs of such wear. Mint condition examples will bring considerably higher prices, of course, and if the original box is present, prices skyrocket — often from two to three times our values.

For more information we recommend *Fisher-Price, A Historical, Rarity Value Guide* by John J. Murray and Bruce R. Fox (Books Americana); and *Schroeder's Collectible Toys, Antique to Modern,* published by Collector Books.

Advisor: Brad Cassity (See Directory, Toys)

Club: Fisher-Price Collector's Club
Jacquie Hamblin
38 Main St.
Oneonta, NY 13820-2519

Museum: Toy Town Museum
P.O. Box 238, East Aurora, NY 14052

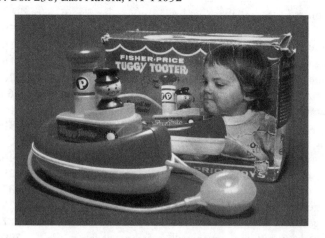

#139, Tuggy Tooter, 1967 – 1973, $30.00. (Photo courtesy Brad Cassity)

#6, Ducky Cart, 1948-49...$50.00
#7, Looky Fire Truck, 1950-53 & Easter 1954 ....$75.00
#11, Ducky Cart, 1940-42...$50.00
#15, Bunny Cart, 1946-48...$50.00
#100, Musical Sweeper, 1950-52, plays Whistle While You Work...$60.00

#109, Lucky Monk, 1932-33...$700.00
#120, Gabby Goose, 1936-37 & Easter 1938 ....$350.00
#125 Uncle Timmy Turtle, 1956-58, red shell $75.00
#136, Play Family Lacing Shoe, 1965-69, complete............$60.00
#140, Coaster Boy, 1941...$700.00
#148, Ducky Daddles, 1942...$225.00
#150, Pop-Up-Pal Chime Phone, 1968-78 ....$15.00
#150, Timmy Turtle, 1953-55 & Easter 1956, green shell...$75.00
#155, Moo-oo Cow, 1958-61 & Easter 1962 ....$75.00
#156, Circus Wagon, 1942-44, bandleader in wagon.........$400.00
#158, Little Boy Blue TV-Radio, 1967, wood & plastic $50.00
#161, Looky Chug-Chug, 1949-52.....................................$175.00
#164, Chubby Cub, 1969-72...$10.00
#166, Bucky Burro, 1955-57 ....$200.00
#169, Snorky Fire Engine, 1961 & Easter 1962, red lithograph..$100.00
#171, Toy Wagon, 1942-47 ....$250.00
#175, Winnie the Pooh TV-Radio, 1971-73, Sears only $50.00
#179, What's in My Pocket Cloth Book, 1972-74, girl's version.. $20.00
#180, Snoopy Sniffer, 1938-55 ....$50.00
#194, Push Pellet, 1971-72 ....$15.00
#20, Animal Cutouts, 1942-46, duck, elephant, pony or Scottie dog, ea $50.00
#234, Nifty Station Wagon, 1960-62 & Easter 1963, removable roof..$250.00
#2500, Little People Main Street, 1986-90 ....$30.00
#2552, McDonald's Restaurant, 1990, 1st version $65.00
#2720, Pick-Up & Peek Wood Puzzle, Little Bo Peep, 1985-88.. $15.00
#303, Bunny Push Cart, 1957 ....$75.00
#304, Running Bunny Cart, 1957 ....$60.00
#305, Walking Duck Cart, 1957-64 ....$40.00
#310, Adventure People Sea Explorer, 1975-80...................$20.00
#314, Husky Boom Crane, 1978-82.....................................$25.00
#325, Adventure People Alpha Probe, 1980-84....................$15.00
#328, Husky Highway Dump Truck, 1980-84 ....$20.00
#339, Husky Power & Light Service Rig, 1983-84 ....$30.00
#355, Adventure People White Water Kayak, 1977-80........$10.00
#375, Adventure People Sky Surfer, 1978 ....$25.00
#401, Push Bunny Cart, 1942 ....$200.00
#415, Super Jet, 1952 & Easter 1953 ....$200.00
#422, Jumbo Jitterbug Pop-Up Kritter, 1940.....................$200.00
#444, Fuzzy Fido, 1941-42 ....$225.00
#444, Queen Busy Bee, 1959, red lithograph $30.00
#447, Woofy Wagger, 1947-48 ....$75.00
#450, Donald Duck Choo-Choo, 1941, 8½" $400.00
#4523, Gravel Hauler, 1985-86 ....$15.00
#4580, Power Tow, 1985-86 ....$20.00
#473, Merry Mutt, 1949-54 & Easter 1955 ....$50.00
#499, Kitty Bell, 1950-51 ....$100.00
#500, Pick-Up & Peek Puzzle, 1972-86..............................$10.00
#505, Bunny Drummer, 1946, bell on front.......................$225.00
#510, Strutter Donald Duck, 1941 ....$250.00
#533, Thumper Bunny, 1942..$500.00
#569, Basic Hardboard Puzzle, Airport, 1975....................$10.00
#625, Playful Puppy, 1961-62 & Easter 1963, w/shoe..........$45.00
#663, Play Family, 1966-70, tan dog, MIP $170.00
#685, Car & Boat, 1968-69, wood & plastic, 5-pc.............$65.00

#694, Suzie Seal, 1979 – 1980, $10.00. (Photo courtesy Brad Cassity)

#695, Pinky Pig, 1956-57, wooden eyes $75.00
#705, Mini Snowmobile, 1971-73 ....$40.00
#724, Ding-Dong Ducky, 1949-50.....................................$200.00
#745, Elsie's Dairy Truck, 1948-49, w/2 bottles.................$600.00
#755, Jumbo Rolo, 1951-52 ....$200.00
#765, Talking Donald Duck, 1955-58.................................$125.00
#788, Rock-A-Bye Bunny Cart, 1940-41..........................$300.00
#854, Animal, 1978-82, plush hand puppet $20.00

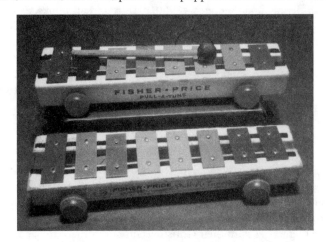

#870, Pull-A-Tune Xylophone, 1957 – 1959, $25.00. (Two styles shown.) (Photo courtesy Brad Cassity)

#904, Beginners Circus, 1965-68..$60.00
#931, Play Family Children's Hospital, 1976-78................$115.00
#933, Play Family Castle, 1974-77, 1st version....................$75.00
#938, Play Family Sesame Street House, 1975-76................$75.00

Fishing Lures

There have been literally thousands of lures made since the turn of the century. Some have bordered on the ridiculous, and some have turned out to be just as good as the manufacturers claimed. In lieu of buying outright from a dealer, try some of the older stores in your area — you just might turn up a good old lure. Go through any old tackle boxes that might be around, and when the water level is low, check out the river banks.

If you have to limit your collection, you might want to concentrate just on wooden lures, or you might decide to try to locate one of every lure made by a particular company. Whatever you decide, try to find examples with good original paint and hardware. Though many lures are still very reasonable, we have included some of the more expensive examples as well to give you an indication of the type you'll want to fully research if you think you've found a similar model. For such information we recommend *Fishing Lure Collectibles, Vol. I,* by Dudley Murphy and Rick Edmisten; *Fishing Lure Collectibles, Vol. II,* by Dudley Murphy and Deanie Murphy; *Modern Fishing Lure Collectibles, Vols. 1 – 4,* all by Russell E. Lewis; *The Pflueger Heritage, Lures and Reels, 1881 – 1952,* by Wayne Ruby; *The Fred Arborgast® Story* by Scott Heston; *Captain John's Fishing Tackle Price Guide* by John A. Kolbeck; and *Spring-Loaded Fish Hook, Traps, and Lures* by William Blauser and Timothy Mierzwa. All are published by Collector Books.

Advisor: Dave Hoover (See Directory, Fishing Lures)

Club: NFLCC Tackle Collectors
Colby Sorrells, secretary
P.O. Box 509
Mansfield, TX 76063
www.nflcc.org

Creek Chub, Gar Minnow, #2900, green, 2 propellers, 3 treble hooks, 1927-53, 5½", from $280 to $350.00
Creek Chub, Husky Pikie, #2300, painted tack eyes & reinforced lip, 3 treble hooks, 1925-78, 6", from $30 to $40.00
Creek Chub, Lucky Mouse, #3600, plastic ears & diving lip, cord tail, 1931-47, from $80 to $90.00
Creek Chub, Salt Spin Darter, #7700, 2 treble hooks, 1955-59, 5½", from $125 to $150.00
Creek Chub, Skipper, #4600, black & white, weighted tail, 2 treble hooks, 1936-51, from $20 to.......................................$30.00
Creek Chub, Spinning Deepster, #9600, #36 Black Sucker color, 2 treble hooks, 1953-55, 2⅛", from $35 to $55.00
Creek Chub, Tarpon Pikie, #4000, yellow w/lg tack eyes, 2 lg single hooks, 1933-61, 6½", from $230 to $275.00
Creek Chub, Tiny Tim, #6400, red, white & black, deep diving lip, 3 treble hooks, 1950-1954, from $40 to.......................$50.00
Heddon, Baby Dowagiac, #20, glassy eyes, propeller, 3 treble hooks, 1952, 2½", from $40 to...$50.00
Heddon, Big Chugg, #9550, white w/red stripes, 1 yellow & red dressed treble hook, 1 plain treble hook, 1970s, 4⅜" $55.00
Heddon, Craw Shrimp, #520, realistic paint, black around eyes, 2 treble hooks, ca 1969, 3", from $30 to $40.00
Heddon, Drop Zara, dressed dropper hook, 1 treble hook, 1980s, 4¼", from $10 to..$15.00
Heddon, Firetail Sonic, #395, yellow, red face & spinning tail, black lightning bolt on sides, ca 1963, 2⅝", $20 to $25.00
Heddon, Giant River-Runt, #7510, white w/red tail & surrounding eyes, 2 treble hooks, 1939-41, 3¼", from $80 to........$100.00
Heddon, Jointed River Runt Spook Floater, #9430, gold & black, 2 treble hooks, 1935-57, 3⅞", from $20 to $25.00

Heddon, Jointed River Runt Spook Sinker, #9110, red & yelow w/ black side stripes, 2 treble hooks, ca 1975, 2½" **$22.50**

Heddon, Migit Digit, #9020, plastic, brown w/black, lg white eyes, 2 treble hooks, 1948-76, 1¾", from $20 to **$30.00**

Heddon, Punkinseed, #730, wood, realistic green paint & yellow eyes, ca 1940, 2⅛", from $70 to **$80.00**

Heddon, Tadpolly Spook, #9000, yellow & black, narrow lip, 2 treble hooks, 1952, from $20 to **$30.00**

Heddon, Tiny Prowler, #7015, black, red & yellow, fish-shaped body, 2 treble hooks, ca 1970s, 2⅝", from $15 to.........**$25.00**

Paw Paw, Aristocat Torpedo, #2400, ivory w/green wavy lines, 2 propellers, 3 treble hooks, ca 1958, 3¾", from $25 to ..**$30.00**

Paw Paw, Crawdad, #500, realistic paint & shape, 1936, 2¾", from $40 to **$50.00**

Paw Paw, Croaker, #71, green paint, 2 side treble hooks, rare, ca 1940, 3", from $300 to..**$350.00**

Paw Paw, Frog Leg Flyrod, #73, mottled green & yellow paint, treble hook, ca 1960, 1¾", from $40 to **$50.00**

Paw Paw, Injured Minnow, #1500, side-mounted eyes, 2 propellers, 2 treble hooks, ca 1940s, 2¾", from $20 to **$25.00**

Paw Paw, Jig-a-Lure, #2700, orange & yellow, lg white painted eyes on sides, 2 treble hooks, 1940-60, 1⅝", $10 to.............**$20.00**

Paw Paw, Mud Minnow Caster, #7000, yellow & black, rounded tail, 1940, 3⅞", from $90 to...**$100.00**

Paw Paw, Musky Wotta-Frog, 3 treble hooks, (1 on body, 1 on ea leg), ca 1941, 5¼", from $500 to.................................**$700.00**

Paw Paw, Old Wounded Minnow, #2500, red, yellow & black, propeller, 2 treble hooks, ca 1940s, 3½", from $20 to........**$30.00**

Paw Paw, Popper, yellow & black, scooped face, 2 treble hooks, ca 1940s, 3", from $20 to **$25.00**

Paw Paw, Shiner Caster, C-1100, realistic paint, sm yellow eyes, 2 treble hooks, ca 1940, 3⅝", from $70 to **$80.00**

Paw Paw, Spinning Torpedo, #9900, green w/white painted eyes, propeller, 2 treble hooks, 1960s, 1⅞", from $10 to.......**$15.00**

Paw Paw, Swimming Mouse, #4600, yellow side-mounted eyes, 2 treble hooks, 1963, from $12 to **$15.00**

Paw Paw, The Bass Seeker, red, yellow & black, scooped face, 2 treble hooks, 4", from $25 to **$30.00**

Pfleuger, Musky Jointed Mustang, orange, 3 treble hooks, ca 1940, 7½", from $200 to...**$225.00**

Pfleuger, Ballerina Minnow, #5400, orange, yellow & black swirl, silver around eyes, 2 treble hooks, ca 1952, 3⅜"...........**$25.00**

Pfleuger, Chum Spoon, #7100, yellow & black, single hook dressed in red, ca 1946, 2¼", from $5 to **$10.00**

Pfleuger, Fan-Tail Squid, plastic, speckled yellow w/red head, slim, dressed single hook, ca 1940, 2¼", $15 to **$20.00**

Pfleuger, Flocked Mouse, ivory w/lg black bead eyes, 1 treble hook, ca 1950, 1⅝", from $180 to **$200.00**

Pfleuger, Frisky Minnow, #6100, gray w/yellow eyes, 2 treble hooks, ca 1952, from $25 to **$30.00**

Pfleuger, Salamo Spoon, #1500, polished finish, dressed treble hook, ca 1948, 4½", from $10 to **$15.00**

Shakespeare, Baby Popper, yellow w/red & black side stripes, overhanging mouth, 2 treble hooks, ca 1940, 2⅛", $35 to **$45.00**

Shakespeare, Egyptian Wobbler, #6636, green w/red head, 3 treble hooks, ca 1940, 5", from $60 to **$75.00**

Shakespeare, Kingfish Wobbler, #6535, yellow w/black stripes, 3 treble hooks, ca 1940, 5", from $60 to **$75.00**

Shakespeare, McKinney Special, slim, 2 propellers, 4 treble hooks, McKinney Sporting Goods, ca 1950, 3¾", $30 to........**$40.00**

Shakespeare, Spinning Mouse, #6380, dark green, lg painted eyes, 2 treble hooks, ca 1950, 2⅛", from $10 to **$15.00**

Shakespeare, Spinning Slim Jim, #6341, orange w/black stripes, 2 propellers, 2 treble hooks, ca 1950, 2¼", $10 to..........**$15.00**

Shakespeare, Spintail, #6303, red & white, 2 treble hooks, ca 1954, 2¼", from $10 to..**$15.00**

South Bend, Be Bop, #903, speckled yellow w/green, 2 treble hooks, 1950-52, 4½", from $15 to...................................**$20.00**

South Bend, Jointed Baby Pike-Oreno, #2956, red & white w/black around eyes, 2 treble hooks, 1941-53, 4", from $15 to..**$20.00**

South Bend, King Bass-Oreno, #977, white w/red accents, scooped face, 2 break-away treble hooks, 1950-52, 4⅝", $30 to.. **$40.00**

South Bend, Li'l Rascal, #955, green w/yellow around eyes, 2 treble hooks, ca 1950-53, 2½", from $10 to..........................**$15.00**

South Bend, Midget Teas-Oreno, #936, thin curved body, 2 treble hooks, ca 1941-50, 2¾", from $20 to......................**$30.00**

South Bend, Nip-I-Diddee, #910, yellow w/red head, 2 propellers, 3 double hooks, 1948-64, 3", from $15 to **$20.00**

South Bend, Spin-Oreno, #967, scooped face, 2 treble hooks, ca 1953-64, 2" **$5.00**

South Bend, Super Snooper, #1960, plastic, 2 treble hooks, ca 1950-52, 2⅞", from $15 to...**$20.00**

South Bend, Surf-Oreno, #963, pressed eyes, 2 propellers, 3 treble hooks, 1950-64, from $20 to..................................**$25.00**

South Bend, Wee-Nippee, #T912, gray, 2 propellers, 2 treble hooks, ca 1952-53, 2⅜", from $10 to **$15.00**

Fitz & Floyd

If you've ever visited a Fitz & Floyd outlet store, you know why collectors find this company's products so exciting. Steven Speilberg has nothing on their designers when it comes to imagination. Much of their production is related to holidays, and they've especially outdone themselves with their Christmas lines. But there are wonderful themes taken from nature featuring foxes, deer, birds, or rabbits, and others that are outrageously and deliberately humorous. Not only is the concept outstanding, so is the quality.

Advisor: Susan Robson (See Directory Fitz & Floyd)

Christmas, cookie jar, Santa's List Rocking Horse, 13".......**$110.00**
Christmas, nativity camel figurine, 11¾" **$110.00**
Christmas Lodge, platter, 15½x20½" **$115.00**
Cookie Thief, cookie jar, 1976, from $50 to **$60.00**
Coq Du Village Rooster, teapot, 7" **$120.00**
Halloween, cookie jar, Haunted House, from $100 to.......**$125.00**
Halloween, cookie jar, witch, 1987, 12"..............................**$100.00**
Halloween, cookie jar, witch w/broom, 1979......................**$95.00**
Halloween, figurine, Dracula, 16½".....................................**$115.00**
Pilgrim's Progress, cranberry bowl **$110.00**
Scarecrow, cookie jar, 1996, 9½x7½" **$100.00**

Snowy Woods, tureen, w/ladle **$125.00**
Thanksgiving Turkey Time, tureen, w/ladle, 1983 .... **$95.00**

Georgian Reindeer, figure, 18x15", $200.00. (Photo courtesy LiveAuctioneers.com/DuMouchelles)

Flashlights

The flashlight was invented in 1898 and has been produced by the Eveready Company for these past 109 years. Eveready dominated the flashlight market for most of this period, but more than 125 other U.S. flashlight companies have come and gone, providing competition along the way. Add to that number more than 35 known foreign flashlight manufacturers, and you end up with over 1,000 different models of flashlights to collect. They come in a wide variety of styles, shapes, and sizes. The flashlight field includes tubular, lanterns, figural, novelty, litho, etc. At present over 45 different categories of flashlights have been identified as collectible. For further information we recommend *Flashlights, Early Flashlight Makers of the First 100 Years of Eveready*, by Bill Utley.

Advisor: Bill Utley (See Directory, Flashlights)

Newsletter: *Flashlight Collectors of America*
Bill Utley
P.O. Box 4095
Tustin, CA 92781
714-730-1252

Bell System, black, angle style, pocket clip, 7½", EX............ **$30.00**
Blaco, Silver Streak, copper body, glass lens, 1947, MIB...... **$42.00**
Brownie/Girl Scout, metal w/bright graphics, Brownie Scout, Made in USA, set of 2, 5½" L, 3" L, MIB............................. **$45.00**
Challenger, copper, Made in USA, VG **$25.00**
Eveready, Little Captain, MIP............................... **$30.00**
Eveready, orange leather covered, narrow boat switch, w/matching cradle, EX **$70.00**
Flasher Is Your Friend, plastic dog figure, tail switch, NM...**$25.00**
Franco #1051, 3 switches & 3 bulbs, beveled glass lens, 1920s, 10", w/3½" dia lens, EX **$35.00**

Fulton Manufacturing, black body, silver on/off switch, bull's eye lens, 2 D cells, NMIB...................... **$35.00**
Lewt Corp Hooks, flashlight/first-aid kit, red w/yellow lettering, rectangular, hangs on belt, 1940s, EX **$55.00**
Niagara Junior Guide, red, 4x3½", EX......................**$25.00**
Ray-o-Vac Rotomatic, fish-eye glass lens, chrome, VG.........**$30.00**
Voit FL3, scuba diving flashlight, 9¾", EX **$45.00**
Winchester, gold-tone, #1511, 2 D cells, 6½", VG **$54.00**
Winchester, lantern type, glass lens, w/6-volt battery, EX.....**$40.00**
Winchester, solid bronze etched on side, 2 C cells, 5⅜".......**$40.00**
Winchester, Sunset Finish Solid-22k-Copper No 0828 etched on side, octagon head, VG **$41.00**

British Ever Ready wooden lanterns, $65.00 each. (Photo courtesy Bill Utley)

Florence Ceramics

During the 1940s Florence Ward began modeling tiny ceramic children as a hobby at her home in Pasadena, California. She was so happy with the results that she expanded, hired decorators, and moved into a larger building where for two decades she produced the lovely line of figurines, wall plaques, busts, etc., that have become so popular today. The 'Florence Collection' featured authentically detailed models of such couples as Louis XV and Madame Pompadour, Pinkie and Blue Boy, and Rhett and Scarlett. Nearly all of the Florence figures have names which are written on their bases.

Many figures are decorated with 22k gold and lace. Real lace was cut to fit, dipped in a liquid material called slip, and fired. During the firing it burned away, leaving only hardened ceramic lace trim. The amount of lace work that was used is one of the factors that needs to be considered when evaluating a 'Florence.' Size is another. Though most of the figures you'll find today are singles, a few were made as groups, and once in a while you'll find a lady seated on a divan. The more complex, the more expensive.

There are Florence figurines that are very rare and unusual, i.e., Mark Anthony, Cleopatra, Story Hour, Grandmother and I, Carmen, Dear Ruth, Spring and Fall Reverie, Clocks, and many others. These may be found with a high price; however, there are bargains still to be had.

Our wide range of values reflects the amounts of detailing and lace work present. If you'd like to learn more about the subject, we recommend *The Complete Book of Florence, A Labor of Love*, by Barbara and Jerry Kline, our advisors for this category, and Margaret

Wehrspaun. (Ordering information may be found in the Directory.) Other references include *Collector's Encyclopedia of California Pottery,* by Jack Chipman; and *The Florence Collectibles, An Era of Elegance,* by Doug Foland.

Advisors: Jerry and Barbara Kline (See Directory, Florence Ceramics)

Club: Florence Ceramics Collectors Club (FCCS)
Jerry Kline
4546 Winslow Drive
Strawberry Plains, TN 37871
865-932-0182
sweetpea@sweetpea.net and florenceceramics@aol.com
www.sweetpea.net

Abigail, beige dress w/red hair, 8", from $170 to **$175.00**
Angel, 7", from $150 to **$175.00**
Ann, pink & white w/gold trim, 6" **$50.00**
Ava, flower holder, 10½", from $300 to **$325.00**
Bea, 7¼", from $50 to **$60.00**
Belle, 8", from $140 to **$150.00**
Birthday Girl, 9", from $2,300 to **$2,500.00**
Catherine, 6¾x7¾" **$700.00**
Charles, 8¾", from $250 to **$275.00**
Colleen, 8", from $275 to **$300.00**

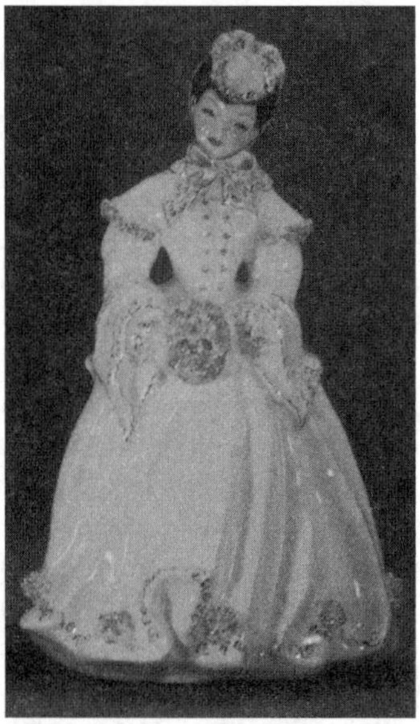

Delia, trimmed in gold and roses, 7¼", from $90.00 to $125.00.

Diana, powder box, 6¼", from $500 to **$550.00**
Edward, 7" **$450.00**
Ellen, from $225 to **$250.00**
Fern, wall pocket, w/gold, 7", from $150 to **$160.00**
Georgette, 10" **$750.00**
Grace, blue, plain, 10", from $200 to **$225.00**
Grace, plain, 7¾", from $225 to **$250.00**
Her Majesty, 7", from $200 to **$250.00**
Jim, child, 6¼", from $125 to **$140.00**
Judy, 9", from $450 to **$500.00**
Kay, fur trim w/gold, 6", from $125 to **$140.00**
Lantern Boy, flower holder, 8¼", from $90 to **$100.00**
Leading Man, 10½" **$475.00**
Madeline, from $400 to **$425.00**
Marsie, 8", from $425 to **$450.00**
Mary, seated, 7½", from $650 to **$700.00**
Matilda, 8½", from $140 to **$160.00**
Patsy, flower holder, 6", from $40 to **$50.00**
Peg, flower holder, 7", from $125 to **$140.00**
Reggie, 7½", from $400 to **$500.00**
Rosemarie, 7", from $400 to **$450.00**
Sally, flower holder, 6¾", from $30 to **$40.00**
Sue, 6", from $60 to **$70.00**
Suzanna, lace trim & gold, 8¾", from $550 to **$600.00**
Toy, 9", from $325 to **$350.00**
Violet, wall pocket, w/gold, 7", from $150 to **$160.00**
Winkyn & Blinkyn, ea 5½", pr from $400 to **$450.00**

Flower Frogs

Flower frogs reached their peak of popularity in the United States in the 1920s and 1930s. During that time nearly every pottery and glass house in the Unted States produced some type of flower frog. At the same time numbers of ceramic flower frogs were being imported from Germany and Japan. Dining tables and sideboards were adorned with flowers sparingly placed around dancing ladies, birds, and aquatic animals in shallow bowls.

In the 1930s garden clubs began holding competitions in cut flower arranging. The pottery and glass flower frogs proved inadequate for the task and a new wave of metal flower frogs entered the market. Some were simple mesh, hairpin, and needle holders; but many were fanciful creations of loops, spirals, and crimped wires.

German and Japanese imports ceased during World War II, and only a very few American pottery and glass companies continued to produce flower frogs into the 1940s and 1950s. Metal flower frog production followed a similar decline; particularly after the water soluble florist foam, Oasis, was invented in 1954. For further information we recommend *Flower Frogs for Collectors* (Schiffer) by our advisor, Bonnie Bull.

Advisor: Bonnie Bull (See Directory, Flower Frogs)

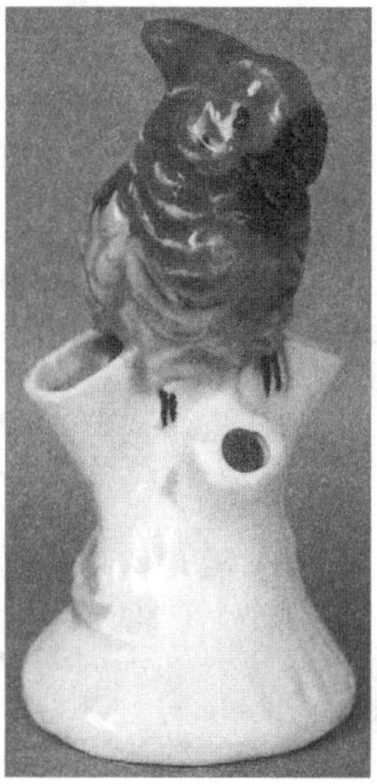

Bird, majolica-style glazes, Japan, 5", from $30.00 to $45.00. (Photo courtesy Carole Bess White)

Butterfly perched on flower w/7 holes in center, bright multicolor, ceramic, unmarked, 2⅛x2¾" **$25.00**

Dancing girls (3) on underplate w/yellow flowers, white porcelain, Hutschenreuther, 8½x9" dia **$330.00**

Double acorn, turquoise & blue, pottery, Van Briggle, 3⅜x4½" **$60.00**

Egyptian lady standing on scarab holding flower, brown glazed pottery, Fulper #295, 7½x2⅜" **$260.00**

Frog on lily pad, turquoise, 11 sm holes, Van Briggle Colorado Springs, 5½" dia **$70.00**

Frogs (3, cobalt) on blue/gray dome, pottery, Van Briggle, 5" dia . **$220.00**

Girl (5") in flowing dress standing in scalloped edge dish, black amethyst glass, 7" dia **$120.00**

Jadite ball-shape, Deco style, on black stepped sq glass base, 6" .. **$115.00**

Lady, Nouveau style, Cowan, 8x5", $225.00.
(Photo courtesy LiveAuctioneers.com/Tom Harris Auctions)

Nude scarf dancer, green pottery, holds 2 candles, leaf-shaped base, Empireware, England, 8x7⅞" **$73.00**

Nude sitting w/elbows on knees & head on hands, lavender satin glass on glass base, abstract style, 2x6¾" dia **$160.00**

Nude stands w/hand back touching foot, pierced bowl-like vase, all white, ceramic, Japan, 6¾" **$55.00**

Parrot, multicolored details, porcelain, Czechoslovakia, 9¾" .. **$110.00**

Pierrot, mottled blue/green tones painted on porcelain, gold lustre base & mandolin, marked MS Sheehan in gold, 6½" ... **$75.00**

Sailboat, glossy white sail & yellow hull, pottery, Haldeman Caliente, #73, Made in California, 5" **$85.00**

Swan, mother-of-pearl lustre, 1930-50s, 7½x9x6" **$25.00**

Thinking mermaid, mauve w/gold trim, Art Nouveau, ball base, 7½" **$140.00**

Turtle, cast iron, 13 holes, 4" L **$130.00**

Turtle, pink glass, detailed w/feet & facial features, 4½" dia ... **$145.00**

Vase, brown, 12 sm holes in shoulder, pottery, marked Aug 4 1941 Pinewood Fairhope Ala, 4x4½" dia **$57.00**

Fostoria

This was one of the major glassware producers of the twentieth century. They were located first in Fostoria, Ohio, but by the 1890s had moved to Moundsville, West Virginia. By the late 1930s they were recognized as the largest producers of handmade glass in the world. Their glassware is plentiful today and, considering its quality, not terribly expensive.

Though the company went out of business in the mid-'80s, the Lancaster Colony Company continues to use some of the old molds — herein is the problem. The ever-popular American and Coin Glass patterns are currently in production, and even experts have trouble distinguishing the old from the new. Before you invest in either line, talk to dealers. Ask them to show you some of their old pieces. Most will be happy to help out a novice collector. Read *Elegant Glassware of the Depression Era* by Gene and Cathy Florence and *The Fostoria Value Guide* by Milbra Long and Emily Seate.

You'll be seeing lots of inferior 'American' at flea markets and (sadly) antique malls. It's often priced as though it is American, but in fact it is not. It's been produced since the 1950s by Indiana Glass who calls it 'Whitehall.' Watch for pitchers with only two mold lines, they're everywhere. (Fostoria's had three.) Remember that Fostoria was handmade, so their pieces were fire polished. This means that if the piece you're examining has sharp, noticeable mold lines, be leery. There are other differences to watch for as well. Fostoria's footed pieces were designed with a 'toe,' while Whitehall feet have a squared peg-like appearance. The rays are sharper and narrower on the genuine Fostoria pieces, and the glass itself has more sparkle and life. And if it weren't complicated enough, the Home Interior Company sells 'American'-like vases, covered bowls, and a footed candy dish that were produced in a foreign country, but at least they've marked theirs.

Coin Glass was originally produced in crystal, red, blue, emerald green, olive green, and amber. It's being reproduced today in crystal, green (darker than the original), blue (a lighter hue), and red. Though the green and blue are 'off' enough to be pretty obvious, the red is very close. Beware. Here are some (probably not all) of the items currently in production: bowl, 8" diameter; bowl, 9" oval; candlesticks, 4½"; candy jar with lid, 6¼"; creamer and sugar bowl; footed comport; wedding bowl, 8¼". Know your dealer!

Numbers included in our descriptions were company-assigned stock numbers that collectors use as a means to distinguish variations in stems and shapes.

See also Glass Animals and Related Items.

Club: Fostoria Glass Society of America

Newsletter: *Facets of Fostoria*
P.O. Box 826, Moundsville, WV 26041
www.fostoriaglass.org

Alexis, crystal, butter dish **$75.00**
Alexis, crystal, goblet, cocktail; 3-oz **$12.50**
Alexis, crystal, pitcher, ice; 64-oz **$85.00**
Alexis, crystal, sugar bowl **$40.00**
Alexis, crystal, tumbler, footed, 10-oz **$20.00**
American, bowl, fruit; 3-footed, 10½" **$40.00**
American, bowl, rolled edge, 11½" **$50.00**
American, crystal, bowl, nappy, regular, 4½" **$12.00**
American, crystal, bowl, vegetable; oval, 9" **$30.00**
American, crystal, bowl, w/handles, 8½" **$74.00**

American, crystal, cake stand, footed, 10" dia $110.00
American, crystal, candlesticks, 3", pr $30.00
American, crystal, candy dish, footed, w/lid $37.50

Camellia, crystal, relish, 3-part, 11⅛" $40.00
Camellia, crystal, vase, footed, 10" $95.00

American, crystal, cookie jar, $275.00. (Photo courtesy LiveAuctioneers.com/Jackson's International Auctioneers & Appraisers of Fine Art & Antiques)

Camellia, crystal with #344 etching, plate, 10½", $30.00.
(Photo courtesy Gene and Cathy Florence)

American, crystal, creamer, 9½-oz $11.00
American, crystal, goblet, water; low $14.00
American, crystal, goblet, wine; hexagonal foot, 4½" $9.00
American, crystal, ice tub, w/liner, 6½" $95.00
American, crystal, jam pot, w/lid $55.00
American, crystal, mustard, w/lid $35.00
American, crystal, pickle dish, oblong, 8" $15.00
American, crystal, pitcher, flat, 1-qt $30.00
American, crystal, plate, dinner; 9½" $18.00
American, crystal, plate, sandwich; sm center, 9" $14.00
American, crystal, salt & pepper shakers, 3", pr $20.00
American, crystal, sauceboat w/underplate $50.00
American, crystal, saucer $3.00
American, crystal, tray, 7½x10½" $70.00
American, crystal, vase, straight sides, 10" $90.00
Baroque, blue, sugar bowl, individual, w/lid $25.00
Baroque, crystal, compote, 6½" $22.00
Baroque, crystal, nut dish, 3-toed, 6" $12.00
Baroque, crystal, platter, oval, 12" $40.00
Baroque, yellow, bowl, salad; 10½" $65.00
Baroque, yellow, ice bucket, chrome handle, w/tongs $55.00
Buttercup, crystal, bowl, salad; 11" $40.00
Buttercup, crystal, dressing bottle $275.00
Buttercup, crystal, plate, sandwich; 11" $25.00
Buttercup, crystal, plate, 7½" $9.00
Buttercup, crystal, tumbler, juice; footed, 4⅝" $12.00
Buttercup, crystal, vase, 10" $110.00
Camellia, crystal, bowl, flared rim, 12" $45.00
Camellia, crystal, ice bucket $60.00
Camellia, crystal, mustard, w/lid & spoon $25.00
Camellia, crystal, plate, luncheon; 8½" $11.00

Century, crystal, ashtray, 2¾" $8.00
Century, crystal, bowl, fruit; 5" $12.00
Century, crystal, bowl, rolled rim, footed, 11" $28.00
Century, crystal, bowl, triangular, 3-footed, 7⅛" $12.00
Century, crystal, creamer, individual $5.00
Century, crystal, oyster cocktail, 3¾" $10.00
Century, crystal, plate, dinner; 9½" $15.00
Century, crystal, platter, 12" $30.00
Century, crystal, tumbler, iced-tea; 12-oz, 5⅞" $16.00
Coin, amber, bowl, nappy, w/handle, 5⅜" $20.00
Coin, amber, candy jar, w/lid, 6¼" $30.00
Coin, amber, crystal or olive, ashtray, 5" $15.00
Coin, amber, crystal or olive, candleholders, 8", pr $50.00

Coin, amber, salver (cake stand), 6½x10", $110.00.

Coin, amber, sugar bowl $35.00
Coin, amber or crystal, bowl, 4" $10.00
Coin, amber or olive, bud vase, 8" $16.00
Coin, blue, bowl, footed, w/lid, 8½" $175.00
Coin, blue, bud vase, 8" $30.00

Coin, blue, candleholders, 8", pr................................$100.00
Coin, blue, cruet, w/stopper, 7-oz............................$125.00
Coin, blue, pitcher, 32-oz, 6¼"...............................$145.00
Coin, blue or ruby, candy jar, w/lid, 6¼" $50.00
Coin, crystal, bowl, footed, w/lid, 8½" $85.00
Coin, crystal, creamer $10.00
Coin, crystal, lamp, coach; oil, 13½"......................$100.00
Coin, crystal, nappy, 4½"...$22.00
Coin, crystal, punch bowl, 1½-gal, 14"...................$110.00
Coin, crystal, punch bowl base................................$140.00
Coin, crystal, punch cup $20.00
Coin, crystal, tumbler, iced-tea/highball; 12-oz, 5⅛" $18.00
Coin, crystal or olive, jelly dish $15.00
Coin, crystal or olive, plate, 8".................................$20.00
Coin, green, bowl, footed, w/lid, 8½".....................$225.00
Coin, green, salt & pepper shakers, w/chrome tops, 3¼", pr..$90.00
Coin, green, sugar bowl, w/lid..................................$65.00
Coin, olive, salt & pepper shakers, w/chrome tops, 3½", pr..$22.00
Coin, ruby, creamer..$20.00
Coin, ruby, plate, 8"...$40.00
Coin, ruby, sherbet, 9-oz, 5¼"....................................$50.00
Colony, crystal, bowl, w/handles, 8½"......................$35.00
Colony, crystal, cheese & cracker $50.00
Colony, crystal, nut dish, 3-toed $18.00
Colony, crystal, pickle dish, 9½"...............................$20.00
Colony, crystal, relish dish, 3-part, 10"....................$22.00
Colony, crystal, tumbler, juice; 3½"..........................$22.00
Colony, crystal, vase, cornucopia; 9¼".....................$80.00
Corsage, crystal, bowl, flared, 12" $45.00
Corsage, crystal, bowl, footed, 4" $22.00
Corsage, crystal, candlestick, duo, ea.......................$35.00
Corsage, crystal, compote, cheese; 3½" $16.00
Corsage, crystal, ice bucket $75.00
Corsage, crystal, plate, torte; 13" $40.00
Corsage, crystal, plate, 7½"..$8.00
Corsage, crystal, relish, 4-part $30.00
Corsage, crystal, sherbet, high; 5⅜" $12.00
Corsage, crystal, vase, footed, 10" $125.00
Cut Rose, crystal, bowl, salad; sm, 2¼" H $16.00
Cut Rose, crystal, cup $10.00
Cut Rose, crystal, pitcher, footed, 53-oz.................$225.00
Cut Rose, crystal, relish, 3-part, 10¾" $20.00
Cut Rose, crystal, salt & pepper shakers, pr $35.00
Cut Rose, crystal, sugar bowl $15.00
Fairfax #2375, amber, ashtray, 4"................................$6.00
Fairfax #2375, amber, bowl, soup; 7"........................$24.00
Fairfax #2375, amber, cake plate, 10" $13.00
Fairfax #2375, amber, plate, grill; 10" $15.00
Fairfax #2375, green or topaz, bowl, cereal; 6"........$15.00
Fairfax #2375, green or topaz, bowl, fruit; 5" $10.00
Fairfax #2375, green or topaz, celery tray, 11½".......$18.00
Fairfax #2375, green or topaz, lemon dish, w/handles, 6½" .$13.00
Fairfax #2375, green or topaz, mayonnaise ladle $20.00
Fairfax #2375, green or topaz, tray, center handle, 11" $18.00
Fairfax #2375, rose, bl or orchid, bowl, cereal; 6" ...$30.00
Fairfax #2375, rose, bl or orchid, dressing bottle.....$210.00
Fairfax #2375, rose, bl or orchid, platter, oval, 15" $100.00

Fuchsia, crystal, bonbon...$33.00
Fuchsia, crystal, candlesticks, 5", pr..........................$90.00
Fuchsia, crystal, compote, low, 6"..............................$35.00
Fuchsia, crystal, plate, bread & butter; 6" $8.00
Fuchsia, crystal, sweetmeat..$30.00
Fuchsia, crystal, tumbler, whiskey; footed, 2½-oz....$30.00
Fuchsia, Wisteria, bowl, 12".....................................$150.00
Fuchsia, Wisteria, compote, low, 6"..........................$100.00
Fuchsia, Wisteria, goblet, wine; 2½-oz.......................$50.00
Fuchsia, Wisteria, oyster cocktail, 4½-oz..................$30.00
Heather, crystal, bowl, fruit; 5" $14.00
Heather, crystal, bowl, salad; 10½" $40.00
Heather, crystal, candlestick, 4½", ea.......................$12.00
Heather, crystal, goblet, parfait; 6-oz, 6⅛" $15.00
Heather, crystal, pitcher, 16-oz, 6⅛" $75.00
Heather, crystal, plate, luncheon; 8½" $10.00
Heather, crystal, platter, 12".....................................$70.00
Heather, crystal, tumbler, iced-tea; 12-oz, 6⅛"........$22.00
Heirloom, any color, basket, 12"...............................$45.00
Heirloom, any color, bowl, crimped, 11" $50.00
Heirloom, any color, bowl, sq, 6" $28.00
Heirloom, any color, bowl, sq, 9" $40.00
Heirloom, any color, bowl, star, 8½" $35.00
Heirloom, any color, bud vase, 6" $18.00
Heirloom, any color, candlesticks, 3½", pr...............$40.00
Heirloom, any color, candlesticks, 6", pr..................$80.00

Heirloom, any color, epergne, 9½x16", $235.00. (Photo courtesy Gene and Cathy Florence)

Heirloom, any color, pitcher vase, 9" $80.00
Heirloom, any color, plate, 11"..................................$45.00
Heirloom, any color, vase, 24"..................................$160.00
Hermitage, amber, gr or topaz, bowl, deep, footed, 8".........$35.00
Hermitage, amber, gr or topaz, oil bottle, 3-oz..........$40.00
Hermitage, amber, gr or topaz, salt & pepper shakers, 3½", pr...$80.00
Hermitage, crystal, decanter, w/stopper, 28-oz.........$35.00
Hermitage, crystal, plate, 9"...................................$12.50
Jamestown, amber or brown, bowl, dessert; 4½".........$6.00
Jamestown, amber or brown, salt & pepper shakers, chrome lids, 3½", pr $20.00
Jamestown, amethyst, crystal or green, creamer, footed, 3½"..$15.00
Jamestown, amethyst, crystal or green, jelly dish, w/lid, 6⅛"..$45.00
Jamestown, blue, pink or ruby, goblet, wine; 4-oz...............$18.00

Jamestown, blue, pink or ruby, pitcher, 48-oz, 7¼".............$150.00
June, blue or rose, bowl, centerpiece; 12"..............$123.00
June, blue or rose, cheese & cracker..............$135.00
June, blue or rose, compote, 6"..............$95.00
June, blue or rose, compote, 7"..............$125.00
June, blue or rose, fan vase, 8½"..............$300.00
June, blue or rose, plate, bread & butter; 6"..............$15.00
June, blue or rose, sugar bowl, footed, w/lid..............$30.00
June, blue or rose, tumbler, 9-oz, 5¼"..............$40.00
June, crystal, ashtray..............$25.00
June, crystal, bowl, cereal; 6½"..............$24.00
June, crystal, bowl, soup; 7"..............$65.00
June, crystal, ice bucket, nickel-plated handle..............$65.00
June, crystal, plate, dinner; 9½..............$15.00
June, crystal, relish dish, 2-part, 8½"..............$35.00
June, crystal, sugar pail, nickel-plated handle..............$70.00
June, topaz, candy dish, w/lid, ½-lb..............$195.00
June, topaz, plate, chop; 13"..............$65.00
Kashmir, blue, bowl, baker, 9"..............$85.00
Kashmir, blue, bowl, cereal; 6"..............$38.00
Kashmir, blue, bowl, soup; 7"..............$95.00
Kashmir, blue, candlesticks, 3", pr..............$65.00
Kashmir, blue, cordial, ¾-oz..............$110.00
Kashmir, blue, ice bucket, nickel-plated handle..............$125.00
Kashmir, blue, plate, luncheon; 9"..............$15.00
Kashmir, blue, plate, salad; sq, 7"..............$7.00
Kashmir, blue, tumbler, footed, 9-oz, 5½"..............$28.00
Kashmir, blue, vase, 8"..............$185.00
Kashmir, green or yellow, bowl, centerpiece; 12"..............$40.00
Kashmir, green or yellow, bowl, fruit; 5"..............$13.00
Kashmir, green or yellow, bowl, soup; 7"..............$35.00
Kashmir, green or yellow, candy dish, w/lid..............$90.00
Kashmir, green or yellow, compote, 6"..............$35.00
Kashmir, green or yellow, pickle dish, 8½"..............$20.00
Kashmir, green or yellow, plate, bread & butter; 6"..............$5.00
Kashmir, green or yellow, plate, luncheon; 9"..............$9.00
Kashmir, green or yellow, plate, salad; round, 8"..............$8.00
Lafayette, amber or crystal, bowl, baker, oval, 10"..............$35.00
Lafayette, amber or crystal, cake plate, oval, 10½"..............$40.00
Lafayette, amber or crystal, mayonnaise, 2-part, 6½"..............$24.00
Lafayette, amber or crystal, pickle dish, 8½"..............$18.00
Lafayette, burgundy, bonbon, handles, 5"..............$30.00
Lafayette, burgundy, Empire Green or Regal Blue, mayonnaise, 2-part, 6½"..............$55.00
Lafayette, burgundy or Empire Green, cake plate, oval, 10½"..$65.00
Lafayette, green, rose or topaz, almond dish, individual.......$15.00
Lafayette, green, rose or topaz, celery dish, 11½"..............$32.00
Lafayette, green, rose or topaz, torte plate, 13"..............$50.00
Lafayette, Regal Blue, torte plate, 13"..............$115.00
Lafayette, Regal Blue or Wisteria, relish dish, 2-part, w/handles..$55.00
Lafayette, Wisteria, bowl, baker, oval, 10"..............$75.00
Lafayette, Wisteria, lemon dish, w/handles, 5"..............$110.00
Lafayette, Wisteria, plate, 9½"..............$40.00
Lafayette, Wisteria, relish dish, 3-part, w/handles..............$90.00
Lido, crystal, bowl, flared rim, 12"..............$35.00
Lido, crystal, bowl, sq, w/handle, 4"..............$12.00
Lido, crystal, compote, cheese; footed, 3¼"..............$18.00

Lido, crystal, plate, dinner; 9½"..............$28.00
Lido, crystal, plate, 6"..............$5.00
Lido, crystal, relish dish, 3-part, 10"..............$22.00
Lido, crystal, tumbler, water; footed, 9-oz, 5½"..............$15.00
Lido, crystal, vase, 5"..............$70.00
Mayflower, crystal, bowl, w/handles, 8½"..............$40.00
Mayflower, crystal, candlestick, 4", ea..............$18.00
Mayflower, crystal, compote, 5½"..............$22.00
Mayflower, crystal, oyster cocktail, 4-oz..............$12.00
Mayflower, crystal, pitcher, footed, 9¾"..............$245.00
Mayflower, crystal, tumbler, water; footed, 5¾"..............$14.00
Meadow Rose, crystal, bowl, flared, 12"..............$50.00
Meadow Rose, crystal, bowl, nappy, 7½"..............$22.00
Meadow Rose, crystal, bowl, tricornered, 4½"..............$12.00
Meadow Rose, crystal, bowl, w/handles, 10½"..............$50.00
Meadow Rose, crystal, candlestick, double, 4½", ea..........$35.00
Meadow Rose, crystal, candy dish, 3-part, w/lid..............$100.00
Meadow Rose, crystal, compote, 4¾"..............$22.00
Meadow Rose, crystal, plate, luncheon; 8½"..............$16.00
Meadow Rose, crystal, plate, 7½"..............$11.00
Meadow Rose, crystal, salt & pepper shakers, footed, 3½", pr..$75.00
Meadow Rose, crystal, sugar bowl, footed, 4½"..............$14.00
Meadow Rose, crystal, tidbit, 3-footed, 8¼"..............$20.00
Navarre, crystal, bowl, serving; footed, w/handles, 8½"........$60.00
Navarre, crystal, candlesticks, 5½", pr..............$70.00
Navarre, crystal, compote, 4½"..............$30.00
Navarre, crystal, cordial, 3⅞"..............$40.00
Navarre, crystal, dinner bell..............$75.00
Navarre, crystal, dressing bottle, 6½"..............$400.00
Navarre, crystal, goblet, cocktail; 3½-oz, 6"..............$18.00

Navarre, crystal, pitcher, footed, 48-ounce, $300.00. (Photo courtesy Gene and Cathy Florence)

Navarre, crystal, plate, dinner; 9½"..............$35.00
Navarre, crystal, plate, luncheon; 8½"..............$15.00
Navarre, crystal, relish dish, 4-part, 10"..............$40.00
Navarre, crystal, sweetmeat, sq, 6"..............$20.00
Navarre, crystal, tumbler, double old-fashioned; flat, 13-oz, 3½"..$100.00
Navarre, crystal, vase, footed, 10"..............$110.00
New Garland, amber or topaz, bowl, soup..............$30.00

New Garland, amber or topaz, compote, 6" $20.00
New Garland, amber or topaz, platter, 12" $35.00
New Garland, amber or topaz, tumbler, footed, 13-oz $15.00
New Garland, rose, bonbon $30.00
New Garland, rose, bowl, baker, 10" $48.00
New Garland, rose, candy jar, w/lid $80.00
New Garland, rose, ice bucket...$120.00
New Garland, rose, plate, 6" $6.00
New Garland, rose, sherbet, high $20.00
Pioneer, amber, crystal or green, bowl, nappy, 9" $17.50
Pioneer, amber, crystal or green, butter dish......................$70.00
Pioneer, amber, crystal or green, celery dish, oval, 11" $20.00
Pioneer, blue, plate, 10" $30.00
Pioneer, blue, sugar bowl, w/lid $30.00
Pioneer, rose or topaz, ashtray, deep, lg $16.00
Pioneer, rose or topaz, egg cup $25.00
Priscilla, amber or green, plate, 8" $8.00

Priscilla, amber or green: tumbler, footed, with handle, $12.00; pitcher, footed, 48-ounce, $110.00. (Photo courtesy LiveAuctioneers.com/ Jackson's International Auctioneers & Appraisers of Fine Art & Antiques)

Priscilla, blue, bowl, cream soup..$20.00
Priscilla, blue, custard, footed, w/handles............................$15.00
Priscilla, blue, pitcher, footed, 48-oz $225.00
Priscilla, blue, plate, 8"..$15.00
Radiance, crystal, bowl, cereal; 5½" $8.00
Radiance, crystal, creamer $7.00
Radiance, crystal, platter, 15" $20.00
Radiance, crystal, salt & pepper shakers, 2½", pr $15.00
Radiance, crystal, tumbler, footed, 5¾"..............................$10.00
Rogene, crystal, bowl, nappy, footed, 5" $17.50
Rogene, crystal, claret...$25.00
Rogene, crystal, compote, 5" or 6" $35.00
Rogene, crystal, cordial $40.00
Rogene, crystal, jug, #2270/7 ....$165.00
Rogene, crystal, marmalade, w/lid.....................................$45.00
Rogene, crystal, oil bottle, cut neck, 5-oz...........................$75.00
Rogene, crystal, parfait...$22.50
Rogene, crystal, plate, 11"...$25.00
Rogene, crystal, salt & pepper shakers, pearl top, pr $55.00

Romance, crystal, bowl, baked apple; 6" $16.00
Romance, crystal, bowl, lily pond; 12" $45.00
Romance, crystal, goblet, 7½"...$16.00
Romance, crystal, plate, 8½"...$11.00
Romance, crystal, relish, 8" $17.00
Romance, crystal, tumbler, footed, 5½" $12.00
Romance, crystal, vase, footed, 7½" $55.00
Royal, amber or green, butter dish $295.00
Royal, amber or green, compote, 7" $25.00
Royal, amber or green, goblet, wine; 2¾" $25.00
Royal, amber or green, platter, 12" $35.00
Royal, amber or green, platter, 15" $40.00
Royal, amber or green, tumbler, flat, 9-oz...........................$20.00
Royal, amber or green, urn, footed.....................................$100.00
Royal, blue, bowl, cereal; 6" $50.00
Royal, blue, ice bucket $130.00
Royal, blue, pickle dish, 9" $40.00
Royal, blue, plate, luncheon; 8½" $16.00
Royal, ebony, bowl, footed, 7" $60.00
Seville, amber, ashtray, 4" $15.00
Seville, amber, bowl, flared, footed, 10½" $25.00
Seville, amber, candy dish, footed, w/lid $100.00
Seville, amber, compote, 8" $27.50
Seville, amber, goblet, wine $20.00
Seville, amber, ice bucket $55.00
Seville, amber, tray, center handle, 11" $27.50
Seville, amber, tumbler, footed, 5-oz $12.00
Seville, crystal, candy dish, flat, 3-part, w/lid $85.00
Seville, green, bowl, footed, 10" $42.50
Seville, green, bowl, fruit; 5½" $12.00
Seville, green, bowl, nappy, 9" $37.50
Seville, green, butter dish $295.00
Seville, green, cheese & cracker, 11"..................................$40.00
Seville, green, plate, chop; 13¾" $35.00
Seville, green, platter, 12" $40.00
Shirley, crystal, bowl, nappy, flared....................................$20.00
Shirley, crystal, cake plate, 10" $35.00
Shirley, crystal, pitcher, footed...$225.00
Shirley, crystal, plate, luncheon; 8¼" $12.50
Shirley, crystal, relish dish, sq, 2-part, 6" $30.00
Shirley, crystal, tumbler, iced tea; footed, 12-oz, 6" $25.00
Sunray, crystal, bowl, rolled edge, 13" $40.00
Sunray, crystal, candy dish, w/lid $55.00
Sunray, crystal, nappy, flared, w/handles $13.00
Sunray, crystal, plate, 9½" $25.00
Sunray, crystal, sugar bowl, footed $10.00
Sunray, crystal, tray, oblong, 10½" $38.00
Sunray, crystal, tumbler, juice; footed, 5-oz.........................$13.00
Sunray, crystal, tumbler, old-fashioned; 6-oz, 3½" $12.00
Trojan, rose, bowl, cereal, 6½" $50.00
Trojan, rose, bowl, fruit; 5" $25.00
Trojan, rose, candlesticks, 3" pr..$27.50
Trojan, rose, plate, 6" $6.00
Trojan, rose, sweetmeat $22.00
Trojan, rose, tumbler, footed, 12-oz, 6" $40.00
Trojan, topaz, bowl, centerpiece; footed, 12" $75.00
Trojan, topaz, bowl, dessert; w/handles, lg $80.00

Trojan, topaz, bowl, grapefruit; 6" $40.00
Trojan, topaz, bowl, soup; 7" $100.00
Trojan, topaz, plate, grill; 10¼" $80.00
Trojan, topaz, tumbler, footed, 2½-oz $40.00
Versailles, blue, mayonnaise, w/plate $75.00
Versailles, blue, platter, 12" $100.00
Versailles, blue, sauceboat $225.00
Versailles, green, bowl, cereal; 6½" $45.00
Versailles, green, bowl, soup; 7" $110.00
Versailles, green, claret, 4-oz, 6" $90.00
Versailles, green, plate, luncheon; 8½" $18.00
Versailles, green, tray, center handle, 11" $50.00

Versailles, pink or yellow: candleholders, $40.00; bowl, centerpiece; scroll, 12" long, $80.00. (Photo courtesy LiveAuctioneers.com/Jackson's International Auctioneers & Appraisers of Fine Art & Antiques)

Versailles, pink or yellow, cheese & cracker $80.00
Versailles, pink or yellow, relish dish, 8½" $38.00
Versailles, pink or yellow, sugar bowl, footed $20.00
Vesper, amber, egg cup $35.00
Vesper, amber, pickle dish $25.00
Vesper, amber, plate, dinner; 10½" $60.00
Vesper, amber or green, ashtray $24.00
Vesper, amber or green, plate, chop; 13¾" $40.00
Vesper, blue, bowl, baker, oval, 10½" $145.00
Vesper, blue, plate, salad; 7½" $18.00
Vesper, blue, sherbet, high $35.00
Vesper, green, candy dish, 3-part, w/lid $125.00
Woodland, crystal, compote, 5" or 6" $15.00
Woodland, crystal, mustard, w/lid $35.00
Woodland, crystal, syrup, nickel-plated top, 8-oz $95.00
Woodland, crystal, torte plate, 11" $14.00
Woodland, crystal, tumbler, #4011½ $10.00

Franciscan Dinnerware

Franciscan is a trade name of Gladding McBean, used on its dinnerware lines from the mid-'30s until it closed its Los Angeles-based plant in 1984. It was the first to market 'starter sets' (four-place settings), a practice that today is commonplace.

Two of the earliest lines were El Patio (simply styled, made in bright solid colors) and Coronado (with swirled borders and pastel glazes). In the late '30s, it made the first of many hand-painted din-

nerware lines. Some of the best known are Apple, Desert Rose, and Ivy. From 1941 to 1977, 'Masterpiece' (true porcelain) china was produced in more than 170 patterns.

Many marks were used, most included the Franciscan name. An 'F' in a square with 'Made in U.S.A.' below it dates from 1938, and a double-line script 'F' was used in more recent years.

For further information, we recommend *Collector's Encyclopedia of California Pottery,* by Jack Chipman.

For other hand-painted patterns not listed below, we recommend the following general guide for comparable pieces (based on current Desert Rose values).

Daisy .... -20%
October .... -20%
Cafe Royal .... Same as Desert Rose
Forget-Me-Not .... Same as Desert Rose
Meadow Rose .... Same as Desert Rose
Strawberry Fair .... Same as Desert Rose
Strawberry Time .... Same as Desert Rose
Fresh Fruit .... Same as Desert Rose
Bountiful .... Same as Desert Rose
Desert Rose .... Base-Line Values
Apple .... +10%
Ivy .... +20%
Poppy .... +50%
Original (small) Fruit .... +50%
Wild Flower .... 200% or more!

Advisor: Shirley Moore (See Directory, Dinnerware)

Coronado

Bowl, cereal; from $10 to $15.00
Bowl, console; w/lid, from $45 to $90.00
Bowl, fruit; from $6 to $12.00
Bowl, onion soup; w/lid, from $25 to $40.00
Cup & saucer, jumbo $32.00
Demitasse pot, from $100 to $150.00

Pitcher, 1½ quart, from $25.00 to $45.00.

Plate, chop; 12½" dia, from $18 to $32.00
Plate, 6½", from $5 to $8.00

Plate, 8½", from $8 to $11.00
Plate, 10½", from $12 to $18.00
Platter, oval, 15½", from $25 to $45.00
Sugar bowl, w/lid, from $10 to $30.00
Vase, 5¼" $65.00

Desert Rose

Ashtray, oval $95.00
Bell, dinner $95.00
Bowl, bouillon; w/lid, from $195 to $295.00
Bowl, fruit $10.00
Bowl, mixing; sm $155.00
Bowl, vegetable; 9" $40.00
Box, heart shape $145.00
Casserole, 1½-qt $75.00
Compote, lg $75.00
Cookie jar $295.00
Cup & saucer, demitasse $35.00
Egg cup $35.00
Gravy boat $38.00
Microwave dish, oblong, 1½-qt $195.00
Mug, cocoa; 10-oz $95.00

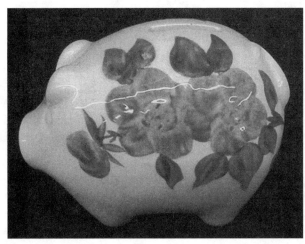

Piggy bank, from $195.00 to $295.00. (Photo courtesy LiveAuctioneers.com/The Auction House)

Pitcher, water; 2½-qt $125.00
Plate, coupe dessert $65.00
Plate, grill; from $75 to $95.00
Plate, 6½" $7.00
Plate, 9½" $20.00
Platter, 12¾" $45.00
Salt shaker & pepper mill, pr from $195 to $295.00
Sherbet $20.00
Tea canister $295.00
Tile, sq $50.00
Tureen, soup; footed, either style............................$695.00

Starburst

Ashtray, oval, lg, from $50 to $75.00

Bowl, oval, 8" $35.00
Bowl, soup/cereal; from $15 to $25.00
Butter dish, from $50 to $65.00
Coffeepot, from $175 to $225.00
Cup & saucer, from $15 to $18.00

Egg cup, from $75.00 to $85.00.

Gravy ladle, from $35 to $45.00
Mug, tall, 5", from $80 to $90.00
Pitcher, 7½", from $70 to $85.00
Plate, dinner; from $15 to $20.00
Platter, 13" $62.00
Relish tray, 3-part, 9", from $75 to $95.00
Salt & pepper shakers, bullet shape, 3½", pr from $50 to $65.00
Sugar bowl, from $30 to $35.00
Tumbler, 6-oz, from $40 to $50.00

Frankoma

John Frank opened a studio pottery in Norman, Oklahoma, in 1933, creating bowls, vases, etc., which bore the ink-stamped marks 'Frank Pottery' or 'Frank Potteries.' At this time, only a few hundred pieces were produced. Within a year, Mr. Frank had incorporated. Though not everything was marked, he continued to use these marks for two years. Items thus marked are not easy to find and command high prices. In 1935 the pot and leopard mark was introduced.

The Frank family moved to Sapulpa, Oklahoma, in 1938. In November of that year, a fire destroyed everything. The pot and leopard mark was never re-created, and today collectors avidly search for items with this mark. The rarest of all Frankoma marks is 'First Kiln a Sapulpa 6-7-38,' which was applied to only about 100 pieces fired on that date.

Grace Lee Frank worked beside her husband, creating many limited edition Madonna plates, Christmas cards, advertising items, birds, etc. She died in 1996.

Clay is important in determining when a piece was made. Ada clay, used through 1954, is creamy beige in color. In 1955 they changed over to a red brick shale from Sapulpa. Today most clay has a pinkish-red cast, though the pinkish cast is sometimes so muted that a novice might mistake it for Ada clay.

Rutile glazes were created early in the pottery's history; these give the ware a two-tone color treatment. However the US government closed the rutile mines in 1970, and Frank found it necessary to buy this material from Australia. The newer rutile produced different results, especially noticeable with their Woodland Moss glaze.

Upon John Frank's death in 1973, their daughter Joniece became president. Though the pottery burned again in 1983, the building was quickly rebuilt. Due to so many setbacks, however, the company found it necessary to file Chapter 11 in order to remain in control and stay in business.

Mr. Richard Bernstein purchased Frankoma in 1991. Sometime in 2001, Mr. Bernstein began to put the word out that Frankoma Pottery Company was for sale. It did not sell and because of declining sales, he closed the doors on December 23, 2004. The company sold July 1, 2005, to another pottery company owned by Det and Crystal Merryman of Las Vegas, Nevada. They took possession the next day and began bringing life back into the Frankoma Pottery once more. Today they are producing pottery from the Frankoma molds as well as their own pottery molds, which goes by the name of 'Merrymac Collection,' a collection of whimsical dogs.

Frank purchased Synar Ceramics of Muskogee, Oklahoma, in 1958; in late 1959, the name was changed to Gracetone Pottery in honor of Grace Lee Frank. Until supplies were exhausted, they continued to produce Synar's white clay line in glazes such as 'Alligator,' 'Woodpine,' White Satin,' 'Ebony,' 'Wintergreen,' and a black and white straw combination. At the Frankoma pottery, an 'F' was added to the stock number on items made at both locations. New glazes were Aqua, Pink Champagne, Cinnamon Toast, and black, known as Gunmetal. Gracetone was sold in 1962 to Mr. Taylor, who had been a long-time family friend and manager of the pottery. Taylor continued operations until 1967. The only dinnerware pattern produced there was 'Orbit,' which is today hard to find. Other Gracetone pieces are becoming scarce as well.

If you'd like to learn more, we recommend *Frankoma Treasures* and *Frankoma and Other Oklahoma Potteries* by Phyllis Bess Boone.

Advisor: Phyllis Bess Boone (See Directory, Frankoma)

Club/Newsletter: Frankoma Family Collectors Association
c/o Nancy Littrell
P.O. Box 32571, Oklahoma City, OK 73123-0771

Ashtray, Prairie Green, ca. 1950, $45.00. (Photo courtesy LiveAuctioneers.com/Luper Auction Galleries)

Ashtray, Prairie Green, Ada clay, #458, 1942 .... $40.00
Ashtray, Tulsamara, Indian's & cowboy's heads on sides, Desert Gold, Sapulpa clay, ca 1957, 7¾" $135.00
Baker, Lazybones, Autumn Yellow, w/candle-warmer base, 3-qt.. $60.00

Bookends, Charger Horse, Desert Gold, Ada clay, $250.00.

Bowl, Jade Green, sq, #30, puma mark, 1934-38 .... $125.00
Bowl, lug soup; Lazybones, Desert Gold, Sapulpa clay, 2-qt, 6½" $10.00
Bowl, Prairie Green, rectangular, #F34, 3½x8x6½" $55.00
Carafe, Desert Gold, Sapulpa clay, 8" $40.00
Chop plate, Wagon Wheel, Desert Gold, Sapulpa clay, 15" .. $65.00
Christmas card, 1949, from $85 to $95.00
Christmas card, 1950-51, from $125 to $150.00
Christmas card, 1952, Donna Frank, from $150 to $200.00
Christmas card, 1952, from $125 to $150.00
Christmas card, 1953, from $90 to $110.00
Christmas card, 1954 .... $110.00
Christmas card, 1957 .... $70.00
Christmas card, 1958-60 .... $65.00
Christmas card, 1969-71 .... $40.00
Christmas card, 1972 .... $35.00
Christmas card, 1973-82, from $25 to $30.00
Flower bowl, Prairie Green, Ada clay, #6, 3¾" $85.00
Honey jug, Prairie Green, Sapulpa clay, ca 1955, 6⅛" $75.00
Honey pitcher, Prairie Green, #8, 1950s, 6¾" $17.50
Honey pot, Prairie Green, Ada clay, bee finial $50.00
Ivy bowl, Red Bud, Ada clay, #27, 1950-57, 6" $75.00
Mug, Donkey, Chocolate Brown, 1979 .... $30.00
Mug, Donkey, Kerry Edwards, red, 2005 .... $15.00
Mug, Elephant, Prairie Green, 1972 .... $30.00
Pitcher, Osage Brown, Ada clay, canteen shape, #554, mini, 2¾" $70.00
Pitcher, Plainsman, Prairie Green, Ada clay, 3-qt $65.00
Planter, pony, Black Onyx, Ada clay, 4½x3½" $260.00
Plate, deviled egg; Woodland Moss, #819, 11½" $50.00
Plate, Wagon Wheel, Prairie Green, Sapulpa clay, #94FL, 10".. $10.00
Salt & pepper shakers, 1st Bank of Tulsa, Prairie Green, pr.. $60.00
Sculpture, Basket Girl, 5-color, Ada clay, #701, 6¼" $70.00
Sculpture, Basket Girl, 6-color, Ada clay, #702, 7½" $130.00
Sculpture, collie's head, deep blue, Sapulpa clay, B Frazier, 7½x3x4" $140.00

Sculpture, colt prancing, brown, Ada clay, 8" **$420.00**
Sculpture, deer group (3), Prairie Green, Ada clay, 1930s, 9½" .. **$2,300.00**
Sculpture, donkey, black, #164, ca 1942, mini, 2¾x2" **$310.00**
Sculpture, Fan Dancer, Rubbed Bisque, pink clay **$60.00**
Sculpture, Ponytail Girl, Desert Sand, Sapulpa clay, #106, 10" .. **$65.00**
Sculpture, puma, Prairie Green, Ada clay, 3" **$82.50**
Sculpture, setter dog, Osage Brown, Ada clay, #163, 3" **$110.00**
Sign, Pottery Show Calif 1987, Prairie Green, limited edition, 9"
    L **$60.00**
Swan dish, Desert Gold, closed tail, #228, 5½x8" **$32.00**

Teapot, Wagon Wheel, Prairie Green, Ada clay, six-cup, $50.00.

Teapot, Westwind, Desert Gold, Sapulpa clay, #6T, 6¼" **$25.00**
Teapot, Westwind, Prairie Green, 1962, 6½" **$55.00**
Tumbler, Plainsman, Prairie Green, 12-oz **$15.00**
Vase, black gloss, cylindrical, w/Deco-style handles, Ada clay, #50,
    1942-52 .... **$200.00**
Vase, collector; V-1, #389, 16", from $125 to **$150.00**
Vase, collector; V-3, 1971 .... **$85.00**
Vase, collector; V-4, hand signed by John Frank, 1972, 13¼x4½" .. **$165.00**
Vase, collector; V-5, 1973, 13" **$85.00**
Vase, collector; V-6, from $80 to **$90.00**
Vase, collector; V-12, 13" **$65.00**
Vase, cornucopia; Desert Gold, Ada clay, #503, 1950-51, mini,
    2" **$60.00**
Vase, Dove Gray, ringed sphere, Ada clay, 2½" **$130.00**
Vase, Jade Green, embossed rings, puma mark, 1936-38, 4¼" .. **$275.00**
Vase, Snail, Red Bud, Ada clay, #31, 6" **$50.00**
Wall masks, Comedy & Tragedy, Flame, pr **$85.00**
Wall plaque, Imp, Dove Gray, 5⅞x4½" **$65.00**
Wall pocket, Phoebe, multicolored, Ada clay, #730, 1948-49,
    NM **$110.00**
Wall vase, ram's head handles, Prairie Green, #193, 6" **$165.00**

Freeman-McFarlin

This California-based company was the result of a union between Gerald McFarlin and Maynard Anthony Freeman, formed in the early 1950s and resulting in the production of a successful line of molded ceramic sculptures (predominately birds and animals, though human figures were also made) as well as decorative items such as vases, flowerpots, and bowls. Anthony was the chief designer, and some of the items you find today bear his name. Glazes ranged from woodtones and solid colors to gold leaf, sometimes in combi-

nation. The most collectible of the Freeman-McFarlin figures were designed by Kay Finch, who sold some of her molds to the company in the early 1960s. The company produced these popular sculptures in their own glazes without Kay's trademark curlicues, making them easy for today's collectors to distinguish from her original work. This line was so successful that in the mid-'60s the company hired Kay herself, and until the late '70s, she designed numerous new and original animal models. Most were larger and more realistically detailed than the work she did in her own studio. She worked for the company until 1980. Her pieces are signed.

In addition to the signatures already mentioned, you may find pieces incised 'Jack White' or 'Hetrick,' both free-lance designers affiliated with the company. Other marks include paper labels and an impressed mark 'F.McF, Calif USA,' often with a date.

Figurines, peafowl, gold leaf, #153, USA Anthony, 13", $80.00 for the pair. (Photo courtesy www.lifeofrileycollectiques.net)

Console set, terra cotta & rust w/swirls, 2 5¾" shouldered vases &
    7½" bowl, 3-pc **$40.00**
Figurine, cat grooming, white glaze, Anthony, #178, 5x8½" .. **$20.00**
Figurine, dog w/floppy ears laying down, gold leaf over red, R
    Hetrick, #466, 5x6" **$25.00**
Figurine, donkey in playful pose, pink & blue pastels w/gold hooves,
    5x3¾" **$20.00**
Figurine, duck, yellow & gray glaze, Anthony, #126, 5x5" ... **$20.00**
Figurine, elephant standing w/trunk up, gold leaf, 5x8" **$30.00**
Figurine, kitten sitting & looking up, gold leaf, 4" **$20.00**
Figurine, kitten sitting & looking up, white glaze, Anthony, #133,
    4" **$30.00**
Figurine, lion, recumbent, flowing mane & tail, dark brown glaze,
    yellow feline eyes, CALIF USA 849 label, 6¾x7½" **$28.00**
Figurine, mouse w/lg ears standing on back feet, gold leaf, Anthony,
    5½" **$30.00**
Figurine, owl on perch, gold leaf over red, Anthony,
    5¼x4x5" **$25.00**
Figurine, pig sitting, gold leaf, 4x6½" **$25.00**
Figurine, pigeons, gold leaf, #838/#839, male: 12½" wingspan,
    female: 10½" L, pr **$50.00**
Figurine, puppy laying on tummy w/tail up, gold leaf over red, R
    Hetrick, #993, 3½x7½" **$30.00**

Figurine, rabbit, pink glaze, lg black & green eyes, Anthony, #115, 6x8" **$30.00**

Figurine, Siamese kitten, head up, blue eyes, 4x4", from $35 to .. **$40.00**

Figurine, squirrel, gold leaf over red, Anthony, dated 1970, 5½x11¼x2¾" **$40.00**

Furniture

A piece of furniture can often be difficult to date, since many seventeenth and eighteenth-century styles have been reproduced. Even a piece made early in the twentieth century now has enough age on it that it may be impossible for a novice to distinguish it from the antique. Sometimes cabinetmakers may have trouble identifying specific types of wood, since so much variation can occur within the same species; so although it is usually helpful to try to determine what kind of wood a piece has been made of, results are sometimes inconclusive. Construction methods are usually the best clues. Watch for evidence of twentieth-century tools — automatic routers, lathes, carvers, and spray guns.

For further information we recommend *Early American Furniture* by John W. Obbard, *Heywood-Wakefield Modern Furniture* by Steve Rouland and Roger Rouland, *Early American Furniture* by John W. Obbard, and *The Marketplace Guide to Oak Furniture* by Peter S. Blundell. All are published by Collector Books. Our values are for items in excellent original condition, unless otherwise described.

Armchair, barrel-back, green velvet, w/down cushion, 1980s.. **$60.00**

Armchair, Chippendale style w/wings, damask upholstery, 43", w/ matching 16" footstool **$400.00**

Armchair, DAR, molded green Fiberglas, 4 peg legs w/metal supports, Eams Modernica, Los Angeles, 30½" **$200.00**

Armchair, faux needlepoint upholstery, upholstered & carved arms, crest rail & base carvings, 1930s, 37x36x36" **$100.00**

Armchair, light blue leather, cabriole legs, 33x29x29", VG ... **$240.00**

Armchair, mahogany Empire style, rectangular top rail, horizontal splat, down-swept arms, upholstered seat, splayed legs ..**$325.00**

Armchair, oak w/pierced back splat, upholstered seat, 39½" .**$250.00**

Armchair, tight-weave rattan, boxy style w/slender legs, natural finish, 34x23x19" **$30.00**

Armchair, upholstered Queen Anne style w/mahogany frame, open arms, pad feet, 36" **$120.00**

Armchair, Windsor style, 9-spindle sack back, distressed black over red paint, 40" **$200.00**

Armoire, cherry, flat cornice w/simple carving, 2 flat-panel doors over drawer, 79x52x24" **$600.00**

Armoire, pine, arched crest, single door, bun feet, access hole in back, 78x41x20" **$300.00**

Baker's rack, scrolled metal frame w/later paint (losses), 3 shelves, 84x37x15" **$180.00**

Baker's rack, 4 tiers of twisted iron, French bow-style w/curled sides & half-circle top, 4 glass shelves, 70x24", VG............. **$150.00**

Bed, Mission-style oak, matching footboard w/vertical spindles, king size **$385.00**

Bed, oak w/Arts & Crafts styling, 7 vertical slats between sq posts, twin size, 44x38" **$215.00**

Bed, oak w/carved crest, headboard probably lowered, refinished, 59x80x57" **$175.00**

Bed, oak w/tall paneled headboard & lower footboard, applied carvings, full size **$600.00**

Bedroom suite, oak bed w/applied carvings, refinished, dressser w/ mirror & wash stand, 3-pc.............................. **$1,800.00**

Bench, chestnut plank top, canted legs, 14½x88" **$75.00**

Bench, pine, applied carvings to crest & aprons, 5-spindle arms, storage under seat, 34½x54x21" **$315.00**

Bench, pine pew style, stripped of finish, ca 1900, 45" L... **$120.00**

Bench, window; Chippendale style w/ball & claw feet, reupholstered top, 17x37x19" **$325.00**

Bookcase, barrister's, dark oak w/4 glass fronts that pull up & slide back, not stacking (free-standing), 58x34x13" **$360.00**

Bookcase, fir w/leaded glass doors, adjustable shelves, early 1900s, 52x38x12" **$350.00**

Bookcase, mahogany, double glass doors, adjustable wooden shelves, claw feet, ca 1920 .... **$480.00**

Bookcase on cabinet, oak, 2 glass doors, adjustable shelves over base w/panel doors, worn finish, 89x50x17" **$215.00**

Cabinet, china; mahogany, straight cornice, glass double doors over drawer over 2 doors, 1940s, 68x35x17" **$135.00**

Cabinet, china; oak cabinet-on-cabinet, sm top separated from lg base by sm vitrine w/sliding glass doors, 66x47x18" **$110.00**

Cabinet, curio; dark oak w/light above 3 glass shelves, canted corners, door in base, recent vintage, 68x23x18½" **$185.00**

Cabinet, oak Hoosier style, 3 doors over 1, side cabinet, wood worktop, 3 drawers/door in base, Kitchen Maid, 70" **$400.00**

Chair, child's, oak, 2-slat back, flat seat, poor finish, 26½" ..**$50.00**

Chair, desk; oak, 5-spindle back w/continuous arms, swivels, w/castors, 33" **$100.00**

Chair, lady's club; Heywood-Wakefield M568-c, ca. 1951 – 1958, 30", minimum value, $900.00. (Photo courtesy Steve Rouland and Roger Rouland)

Chair, side; oak Mission style, 4-slat back, original leather seat (worn), 37", VG **$80.00**

Chair, side; oak w/vase splat, buttocks seat, skirt, cabriole legs, paw feet, worn finish, 34" **$40.00**

Chair, side; pressed oak, vase splat, turned stretchers, cane bottom **$25.00**

Chair, side; walnut w/3-slat back, caned seat, turned stretchers, 35" **$40.00**

Chest-on-chest, tropical hardwoods, curved gallery, 2 short drawers over 3 long, 48x33x19" **$180.00**

Chest-on-chest, walnut Empire style, decorated backsplash, 2 short over 4 long drawers, 55x46x20" **$480.00**

Desk, mahogany kidney shape w/kneehole, 9 drawers, leather inset top, 30x45x24" **$360.00**

Desk, oak C-roll top executive type, tambour front w/2 banks of drawers, fitted interior, wooden handles, 43x66x34" ..**$240.00**

Desk, quartersawn oak, S-roll top, 2 banks of 4 drawers, 31½x50x48¾" **$1,200.00**

Desk, white painted wicker, galleried kidney shape w/drawer, shelf below, 37x36x20", w/aproned armless wicker chair **$400.00**

Dining set, oak & ash sq draw-leaf table w/4 matching chairs, mid-20th C **$300.00**

Dining set, oak rectangular extension table spanning 2 turned columns, 64" w/2 18" leaves, +6 high-back chairs, modern **$500.00**

Dresser, mahogany serpentine front, 4 short drawers over 2 deep & long drawers, worn finish, 35½x42x22" **$135.00**

Dresser, pine, scrolled backsplash, 4 graduated drawers, wooden knobs, worn finish, 39x38x17" **$120.00**

Dresser, tiger oak, curved front w/carving, 2 short drawers over 2 long, brass handles, cabriole legs, stains, 32x47" **$180.00**

Dresser, walnut, sm gallery, 3 graduated drawers, EX original finish, ca 1900, 40x40x19" **$600.00**

Footstool, dark wood w/curved feet, fabric top, fading & wear ...**$55.00**

Footstool, mahogany Empire, tufted top, bun feet, 12x17x17" ..**$150.00**

Footstool, vanity; oval w/upholstered top, 1930s, 18x24x16" ...**$180.00**

Hide-a-bed, Mission style, quartersawn oak w/brown leather upholstery, brass tacks, 34x59x34" **$600.00**

Hide-a-bed, upholstered Biedermeier w/carved oak crest rail & nailhead trim, ebonized ball feet, 50x64" **$215.00**

Magazine rack, Art Deco style w/wire mesh in metal frame & copper tube ends, 15x18x18" **$120.00**

Quilt rack, cherry, barley-twist legs, 34x27x8½", VG **$165.00**

Serving cart, pull-out trays, brass handles, all original, Johnson Furniture, 32x45", VG, $600.00. (Photo courtesy Treadway Gallery)

Side chair, oak w/open arms, Queen Anne-style legs, reupholstered needlework seat, 1920s+ **$65.00**

Sideboard, lacquered with cork-covered center drawers, Paul Frankl for Johnson Furniture, 73" long, $2,400.00.
(Photo courtesy David Rago Auctions)

Stand, cherry Hepplewhite, drawer, delicate legs, repairs, 28½x17x14½" **$240.00**

Stand, cherry Sheraton, dovetailed scratch-beaded drawer, turned legs, clear finish, 27x17x17½" **$425.00**

Stand, fern; carved teakwood w/grapevines, dragons & leaves, soapstone insert on top, 36x20" dia **$325.00**

Stand, painted pine, dovetailed drawer, replaced knob, sm glued repair, 29x17x17" **$200.00**

Stand, pine w/dark finish, painted flower decor & mustard striping, veneered top, drawer, tapered legs, 29x17x17" **$800.00**

Stool, woven splint seat, old red-brown paint on turned legs & rungs, 28" H **$360.00**

Table, coffee; veneered top, ball & claw feet, 27x19x19" ...**$100.00**

Table, dining; antiqued worn wood, curved legs w/claw feet, extends to 100" L **$100.00**

Table, dining; mahogany American Federal style w/carved & painted apron, 2 18" leaves w/apron, 1920s, extends to 105" **$240.00**

Table, dining; mahogany Duncan Phyfe style, legs adjust to lower, can be used as coffee table, opens to 36" W **$180.00**

Table, dining; walnut, turned legs, refinished, no leaves, 1930s, 31x60x45" **$480.00**

Table, dressing; pine American Federal, single drawer, slim turned legs, crazed finish, 34x30x16" **$300.00**

Table, end; mahogany, w/lower shelf, turned & fluted legs, 25x24x15" **$75.00**

Table, hall; carved oak, 2 drawers, low shelf, contemporary, 32x54x17" **$240.00**

Table, side; mahogany Queen Anne style, oval top w/molded edge, skirt w/gadroon carving, tapered legs, 30x30x21" **$350.00**

Table, vanity; mahogany w/lg tilting mirror between scrolling upright, 1 door/1 drawer, +sm velvet-topped bench **$975.00**

Tea cart, mahogany, drop leaves, removable wood-framed glass tray & lower shelf, ca 1940s, 28x28x18" **$150.00**

Tea cart, mahogany, spoke wheels, worn finish, 20th C, 27x28x17", G **$100.00**

Tea cart, white painted wicker, lace under glass inset top, 29x35x17", VG...$300.00

Trunk, camphor wood, brass mounts, case clips, missing lock plate & lid plate, sm cracks, 20x29x20".............................$350.00

Trunk, dovetailed pine, domed top, yellow, red & black graining, minor losses, 10x24x12".............................$1,080.00

Trunk, painted tin & oak, leather handles, fitted inner case, Patented Oct 9, 1895, 22¾x30x14", VG.........................$180.00

Trunk, wood & tin w/textured suede, fitted tray & interior, manufacturer's mark, 27x36x21", G........................$110.00

Washstand, dark-stained hardwood, marble top, single drawer, 2 towel bars, shelf, 36x32x16"...........................$265.00

Washstand, oak, 2 drawers over double doors, original brasses, refinished, replaced brasses, on castors, 35x32x16"............$180.00

Washstand, pine w/tiled backsplash, marble top, frieze drawer & pot cupboard, towel rail ea end........................$150.00

Washstand, walnut, shaped gallery, lower shelf & drawer, 40x30x19".............................$325.00

Games

Games from the 1870s to the 1970s and beyond are fun to collect. Many of the earlier games are beautifully lithographed. Some of their boxes were designed by well-known artists and illustrators, and many times these old games are appreciated more for their artwork than for their entertainment value. Some represent a historical event or a specific era in the social development of our country. Characters from the early days of radio, television, and movies have been featured in hundreds of games designed for children and adults alike.

If you're going to collect games, be sure that they're reasonably clean, free of water damage, and complete. Most have playing instructions printed inside the lid or on a separate piece of paper that include an inventory list. Check the contents and remember that the condition of the box is very important too.

If you'd like to learn more about games, we recommend *Schroeder's Collectible Toys, Antique to Modern* (Collector Books).

Club: Association of Game and Puzzle Collectors
PMB 321, 197 M Boston Post Road West
Marlborough, MA 01752
www.agpc.org

Addams Family, Ideal, 1960s, NMIB.................................$75.00
Amazing Spider-Man, Milton Bradley, 1966, EXIB.............$25.00
Annette's Secret Passage Game, Parker Bros, 1958, EXIB.....$15.00
Annie Oakley Game, Milton Bradley, 1950s, sm, NMIB.....$35.00
As the World Turns, Parker Bros, 1966, NMIB...................$25.00
Bamboozle, Milton Bradley, 1962, NMIB..........................$25.00
Barbie Queen of the Prom, Mattel, 1960s, NMIB..............$75.00
Bash!, Milton Bradley, 1965, NMIB..................................$15.00
Batman, Milton Bradley, 1966, NMIB...............................$35.00
Battlestar Galactica, Parker Bros #58, 1978, NMIB............$20.00
Beetle Bailey The Old Army Game, Milton Bradley, 1963, EXIB..$25.00
Betsy Ross Flag Game, Transogram, 1960s, NMIB.............$40.00
Big Maze, Marx, 1955, MIB...$50.00

Black Beauty, Transogram, 1957, NMIB............................$25.00
Bobbsey Twins, Milton Bradley, 1957, MIB.......................$25.00
Boots & Saddles, Chad Valley, 1960s, EXIB.....................$125.00
Brady Bunch, Whitman, 1973, MIB..................................$75.00
Bullwinkle Hide 'n Seek Game, Milton Bradley, 1961, NMIB...$50.00
Candid Camera, Lowell, 1963, NMIB................................$30.00
Car 54 Where Are You?, Allison, 1963, NMIB...................$75.00
Charlotte's Web, Hasbro, 1974, NMIB..............................$30.00
Cheyenne, Milton Bradley, 1950s, EXIB............................$30.00

CHiPs, Ideal, 1981, from $25.00 to $35.00. (Photo courtesy Greg Davis and Bill Morgan)

Cinderella, Parker Bros, 1964, EXIB................................$25.00
Combat, Ideal, 1963, NMIB...$50.00
Countdown, Lowe, 1967, NMIB.......................................$35.00
Creature From the Black Lagoon, Hasbro, 1963, EXIB.....$175.00
Daniel Boone Wilderness Trail Card Game, Transogram, 1960s, NMIB..$45.00
Davy Crockett Adventures, Gardner, 1950s, EXIB.............$50.00
Deputy Dawg TV Lotto, Ideal, 1960s, EXIB......................$20.00
Dick Tracy the Master Detective, Selchow & Righter, 1960s, EXIB...$35.00
Direct Hit, Northwestern Prod, 1950s, EXIB.....................$165.00
Donnie & Marie Osmond TV Game Show, Mattel, 1977, NMIB..$30.00
Dracula Mystery Game, Hasbro, 1962, EXIB.....................$75.00
Emergency, Milton Bradley, 1970s, NMIB.........................$30.00
Evel Knievel Stunt World, Ideal, 1975, self-contained suitcase unfolds to Coliseum & Snake River, NMIB.................$80.00
F-Troop, Ideal, 1960s, VGIB...$35.00
Fantasy Island, Ideal, 1978, NMIB...................................$45.00
FBI, Transogram, 1950s, EXIB..$45.00
Flintstones Brake Ball, Whitman, 1962, EXIB....................$85.00
Flintstones Stone Age Game Transogram, 1961, NMIB.......$55.00
Formula 1 Car Racing Game, Parker Bros, 1968, NMIB.....$55.00
Fugitive, Ideal, 1964, NMIB..$75.00
Game of Life, Milton Bradley, 1960s, NMIB......................$25.00
Garrison's Gorillas, Ideal, 1967, EXIB...............................$50.00
Gene Autry's Dude Ranch, Built-Rite, 1950s, EXIB............$50.00
Get Smart, Ideal, 1966, NMIB...$35.00
GI Joe Adventure, Hasbro, 1980s, EXIB............................$25.00
Gilligan's Island, Game Gems/T Cohn, 1965, EXIB...........$150.00
Green Ghost Game, Transogram, 1965, NMIB...................$165.00
Groucho Marx TV Quiz, Pressman, 1950s, EXIB...............$45.00
Haunted House Game, Ideal, 1960s, EXIB........................$125.00

Hawaiian Eye, Transogram, 1960s, EXIB............................$50.00

Hogan's Heroes, Transogram, 1960s, VGIB $25.00

Hopalong Cassidy, Milton Bradley, 1950, NMIB $80.00

Hopalong Cassidy Game, Marx, 1950s, EXIB $115.00

Hot Wheels Wipe Out Race Game, Mattel, 1968, NMIB...$40.00

Humpty Dumpty Game, Lowell, 1950s, EXIB...................$30.00

I Spy, Ideal, 1965, EXIB $40.00

I Wanna Be President, JR Mackey, 1983, NMIB $15.00

Ironside, Ideal, 1976, EXIB $50.00

Jack & the Beanstalk Adventure Game, Transogram, 1957, EXIB..$30.00

Jerome Park Steeple Chase, McLoughlin Bros, EXIB $400.00

Jonny Quest, Transogram, 1960s, EXIB............................$225.00

King Kong Game, Ideal, 1970s, EXIB $50.00

Kukla & Ollie - A Game, Parker Bros, 1962, NMIB $30.00

Land of the Giants, Ideal, 1968, NMIB...........................$100.00

Lassie, Game Gems, 1965, EXIB $25.00

Laugh-In's Squeeze Your Bippy, Hasbro, 1960s, VGIB.........$25.00

Lie Detector, Mattel, 1961, NMIB $50.00

Little Rascals Our Gang Clubhouse Bingo, Gabriel, 1958, EXIB..$65.00

M Squad, Bell Toys, 1950s, VGIB $25.00

Magilla Gorilla, Ideal, 1960s, EXIB $50.00

Marvel Comics Super-Heroes Card Game, Milton Bradley, 1970s, MIB (sealed) $75.00

McHale's Navy, Transogram, 1962, NMIB $35.00

Melvin the Moon Man, Remco, 1960s, NMIB...................$75.00

Mickey Mantle's Big League Baseball, Gardner, 1958, VGIB..$100.00

Mighty Comics Super Heroes, Transogram, 1966, NMIB ...$75.00

Monkees Game, Transogram, 1968, NMIB $115.00

Munsters Masquerade Game, Hasbro, 1960s, VGIB..........$175.00

Mushmouth & Punkin Puss, Ideal, 1964, EXIB $50.00

Mystery Date, Milton Bradley, 1965, NMIB $150.00

Nancy Drew Mystery Game, Parker Bros, 1950s, NMIB...$100.00

Nurses, Ideal, 1963, NMIB...$45.00

Oh Magoo, Warren, 1960s, NMIB $25.00

Park & Shop, Milton Bradley, 1960, NMIB $45.00

Peter Gunn Detective Game, Lowell, 1960, NMIB $30.00

Petticoat Junction, Standard Toykraft, 1963, NMIB $75.00

Pirate & Traveler, Milton Bradley, 1953, NMIB $30.00

Pirates of the Caribbean, Parker Bros, 1967, NMIB $35.00

Popeye's Game, Parker Bros, 1948, unused, MIB..............$200.00

Rat Patrol, Transogram, 1966, NMIB $75.00

Rebel, Ideal, 1961, NMIB $80.00

Ricochet Rabbit Game, Ideal, 1965, EXIB $50.00

Rocky & His Friends, Milton Bradley, 1960, EXIB $50.00

Scooby Doo Where Are You?, Milton Bradley, 1973, NMIB ..$25.00

Secret Agent Man, Milton Bradley, 1966, EXIB $30.00

Snake's Alive, Ideal, 1967, NMIB $25.00

Snoopy & the Red Baron, Milton Bradley, 1970, MIB........$40.00

Space Patrol Magnetic Target Game, American Toy, 1950s, EX..$50.00

Spider-Man w/the Fantastic Four, Milton Bradley, 1977, NMIB $35.00

Spy Detector, Mattel, 1960, NMIB $75.00

Star Trek Adventure Game, West End Games, 1985, NMIB..$25.00

Steve Canyon Air Force Game, Lowell, 1950s, NMIB.........$50.00

Surfside 6, Lowell, 1961, unused, EXIB.............................$35.00

That Girl, Remco, 1969, EXIB...$70.00

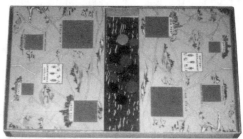

Tiddly Winks Barrage Game, Corey Games, ca. WWII, $125.00. (Photo courtesy Paul Fink)

Time Bomb, Milton Bradley, 1965, NMIB.........................$88.00

Time Tunnel, Ideal, 1966, EXIB.......................................$100.00

Top Cat, Cadaco-Ellis, 1961, NMIB $100.00

Twiggy, Milton Bradley, 1967, EXIB $65.00

Twilight Zone, Ideal, 1964, unused, NMIB........................$180.00

Untouchables Target Game, Marx, 1950s, NM..................$350.00

Wally Gator Game, Transogram, 1963, NMIB $100.00

Which Witch?, Milton Bradley, 1970, EXIB.......................$50.00

Wonder Woman, Hasbro, 1967, NMIB $30.00

Wonderful Game of Oz, Parker Bros, EXIB.......................$200.00

Woody Woodpecker Game, Milton Bradley, 1959, NMIB ..$30.00

Yogi Bear Break a Plate Game, Transogram, 1960s, NMIB..$45.00

77 Sunset Strip, ca. 1960, $95.00. (Photo courtesy www.gasolinealleyantiques.com)

Gas Station Collectibles

Items used and/or sold by gas stations are included in this very specialized area of advertising collectibles. Those with an interest in this field tend to specialize in memorabilia from a specific gas station like Texaco or Signal. This is a very regional market, with items from small companies that are no longer in business bringing the best prices. For instance, memorabilia decorated with Gulf's distinctive 'orange ball' logo may sell more readily in Pittsburgh than in Los Angeles. Gas station giveaways like plastic gas pump salt and pepper sets and license plate attachments are gaining in popularity with collectors. If you're interested in learning more about these types of collectibles, we recommend *Petroleum Collectibles Monthly* (see address below) and *Value Guide to Gas Station Memorabilia* by B.J. Summers and Wayne Priddy (Collector Books).

Unless otherwise noted, our prices are for examples in at least excellent condition.

See also Ashtrays; Automobilia.

Advisor: Scott Benjamin (See Directory Gas Station Collectibles)

Newsletter: *Petroleum Collectibles Monthly*
Scott Benjamin and Wayne Henderson, Publishers
PO Box 556, LaGrange, OH 44050-0556
440-355-6608
www.pcmpublishing.com or www.gasglobes.com

Bank, Shell service station, tin litho, insert quarter, door swings open & attendant emerges, 5¾" L **$180.00**
Bottle, oil; Duraglass, Fill to Line, Mass Oil B Seal, metal spout w/ cap, 1-qt, 14½" **$38.00**
Cap badge, Mobiloil & gargoyle, red, white & blue cloisonne, 1930s, 1⅝"....................................**$320.00**
Clock, Sinclair HC Gasoline, neon, orange second markers, 20" dia..**$390.00**
Clock, Time To Switch to Champion Spark Plugs, lights up, 15½x15½" **$210.00**

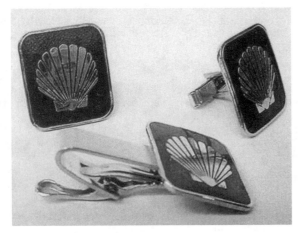

Cuff links and tie bar, Shell, gold-tone with cloisonné, $35.00. (Photo courtesy www.gasolinealleyantiques.com)

Display stand, Pennsylvania Tires, yellow lettering on green, tin litho, 7½x12", VG **$70.00**
Gas globe, Amaco, low-profile metal body, light flaking, VG.. **$480.00**
Gas globe, Cities Service Koolmotor, black & yellow on milk glass clover body, 15" lens **$780.00**

Gas globe, Genoco, three-piece, metal band with glass lens globe, 15", from $400.00 to $500.00. (Photo courtesy B.J. Summers and Wayne Priddy)

Gas globe, Sinclair H-C Gasoline, red & green on milk glass, 16½" **$425.00**
Gas globe, Texaco Sky Chief, red, black & green on milk glass, gill body, some wear.............................**$540.00**
Hat, Esso attendant, blue denim w/black patent leather visor & chinstrap, embroidered emblem patch, plastic frame, 1950s **$95.00**
Hat, Mobil Oil, tan cotton, black leather visor, 1930s, wear & stains.....................................**$120.00**
Hat, Sohio attendant, white cotton w/black patent-leather visor, insignia patch, cardboard frame, discoloration **$45.00**
Hat, Sol Gass attendant, gray-blue wool w/black piping, black leather visor, some wear/moth damage **$85.00**
Hat, Sunoco attendant, navy blue cotton, black patent-leather visor, embroidered patch, bamboo frame, 1940s **$135.00**
Jacket, Gulf mechanic's, blue gabardine w/Gulf emblem, zipper front, 2 breast pockets, rayon lining................**$55.00**
Jar, counter; Sinclair & dinosaur in green enamel on clear glass, green glass lid, 7x6½" dia...........................**$88.00**
Jar, counter; Sunoco etched on clear glass, blue metal lid, 6x5"...**$48.00**
Oil can, Gulflube Motor Oil, tin litho, 11x8", G- **$36.00**
Oil can, Phillips 66 Aviation Gasoline Model Motor Blend, cone top, 1940s-50s, 1-pt, G..............................**$190.00**
Oil can, Phillips 66 Aviation Gasoline Model Motor Oil, red, white & black, 1-pt **$175.00**
Oil can, Signal Outboard Motor Oil, boat motor, multicolor, rectangular, 1-qt **$88.00**
Oil can, Signal Premium Heavy Duty Motor Oil, red, yellow, black & white, full, 1-qt, NM.............................**$150.00**
Oil can, Signal Quality Lubricants, yellow, black & white, 1-lb, G **$32.00**
Oil can, Speedoline Oil, racecar scene, 6½x4¼", G.............**$85.00**
Oil can, Sunoco Motor Oil, blue & yellow litho, 2-gal, 12x8½", G...**$20.00**

Oil can, Valvoline 5-qt Motor Oil, old emblem, green & white, priced at 35¢, 5-qt **$215.00**

Paper sign, Woods' Radiator, Too Hot To Bear, graphics, 30x21" **$1,450.00**

Photo, Magnolia gas station, gravity-feed pumps, Kelly Tire sign, Coca-Cola advertising, 1920s, 8x12", +mat & frame....**$90.00**

Pocketknife, Gulf Oil, inlaid enamel Deco scenes, 3¼", NM . **$550.00**

Poster, Your Map Sir, Shell attendant w/map, minor foxing, 55x40½" **$90.00**

Pump plate, Quaker State Motor Oil, green, black & white, 34x70", G **$450.00**

Pump plate, Texaco Fire-Chief Gasoline, fireman's helmet, multicolor on porcelain 1941, 12x8"....................................**$90.00**

Rack, oil can; Texaco, star logo on red, tin litho w/steel frame, 1950s replica, new, M **$200.00**

Restroom signs, Women/Men, white lettering on blue porcelain, 2½x10", pr, VG **$60.00**

Road map, Sonoco, Michigan, legend records dirt to paved roads, from $5.00 to $15.00. (Photo courtesy B.J. Summers and Wayne Priddy)

Sign, Ask for Gargoyle Mobiloil, black & red on white porcelain, 24x19½", VG..**$50.00**

Sign, Atlantic, red & white on porcelain, some chips & rust, 42x72" **$120.00**

Sign, Authorized Clinton Service Station, red, black & gold on white porcelain, double-sided, 18x24", G.............................**$72.50**

Sign, Exide Batteries Service Station, blue & white porcelain, double-sided, 23x32", G **$250.00**

Sign, Good Gulf, multicolor on porcelain, 8½x11", G **$60.00**

Sign, Gulf Fuel Oil Dealer, multicolor on porcelain, 36" dia, VG...**$1,675.00**

Sign, Imperial Esso Product, red, white & blue on porcelain, oval, ca 1954, 40x58" **$840.00**

Sign, Michelin man on blue, porcelain, double-sided, 23x17"..**$500.00**

Sign, No Free Air, Water or Service, Charge $1.00, red letters on white, double-sided, tin litho, 30x18"..........................**$65.00**

Sign, Pennzoil Ask for It, double-sided, tin litho, minor scratches, 36x24", VG **$30.00**

Sign, Penzoil Motor Oils, text on black, metal w/wooden frame, 14x42" **$180.00**

Sign, Phillips 66, die-cut paper shield, orange & black, double-sided, 30", VG **$300.00**

Sign, Signal, yellow & black w/red trim, metal polymer laminate, 10x36" **$200.00**

Sign, Sinclair Full Service Island, w/dinosaur, red, white & green tin litho, 24x12", NM..**$270.00**

Sign, Socony Mobil, porcelain die-cut Pegasus, red w/white trim, 45x64" **$1,000.00**

Sign, Texaco star, red & white, lights up, 34½" dia...........**$155.00**

Thermometer, Casite Oil Additive, 12" dia, VG **$115.00**

Thermometer, Prestone Anti-freeze, porcelain, 36x9" **$325.00**

Tin container, Marathon Endurance Motor Oil, running man, 5-qt...**$200.00**

Sign, curb; Mobiloil, Property of Socony Vacuum Oil Company Inc. on base, 65", VG+, $400.00.

Gay Fad Glassware

What started out as a home-based 'one-woman' operation in the late 1930s within only a few years had grown into a substantial company requiring much larger facilities and a staff of decorators. The company was founded by Fran Taylor. Originally they decorated kitchenware items but later found instant success with the glassware they created, most of which utilized frosted backgrounds and multicolored designs such as tulips, state themes, and Christmas motifs. Some pieces were decorated with 22-karat gold and sterling silver. In addition to the frosted glass which collectors quickly learn to associate with this company, they also became famous for their 'bentware' — quirky cocktail glasses whose stems were actually bent.

Some of their more collectible lines are Beau Brummel — martini glasses with straight or bent stems featuring a funny-faced drinker wearing a plaid bow tie; Gay Nineties — various designs such as can-can girls and singing bartenders; 48 States — maps with highlighted places of interest; Rich Man, Poor Man (or Beggar Man, Thief, etc.); Bartender (self-explanatory); Currier & Ives — made to coordinate with the line by Royal China; Zombies — extra tall and slim with various designs including roses, giraffes, and flamingos; and the sterling silver- and 22-karat gold-trimmed crystal glassware.

Until you learn to spot it a mile away (which you soon will), look for an interlocking 'G' and 'F' or 'Gay Fad,' the latter mark indicating pieces from the late 1950s to the early 1960s. The frosted glassware itself has the feel of satin and is of very good quality. It can be distinguished from other manufacturers' wares simply by checking the bottom — Gay Fad's are frosted; generally other manufacturers' are not. Hand-painted details are another good clue. (You may find similar glassware signed 'Briard'; this is not Gay Fad.)

This Ohio-based company was sold in 1963 and closed altogether in 1965. Be careful of condition. If the frosting has darkened or the paint is worn or faded, it's best to wait for a better example.

Advisor: Donna S. McGrady (See the Directory, Gay Fad)

Ashtray, Trout Flies, clear **$8.00**
Bent tray, Phoenix Bird, clear, signed Gay Fad, 13¾" dia..... **$20.00**
Bent tray, Stylized Cats, clear, signed Gay Fad, 11½" dia **$30.00**
Beverage set, Apple, frosted, 86-oz ball pitcher+6 13-oz round-bottom tumblers **$120.00**
Beverage set, Colonial Homestead, frosted, 85-oz pitcher & 6 12-oz tumblers **$80.00**
Beverage set, Magnolia, clear, 86-oz pitcher & 6 13-oz tumblers **$75.00**
Canister set, Red Rose, red lids, white interior, 3-pc **$60.00**
Chip 'n dip, Horace the Horse w/cart, knife tail, 3 bowls, double old-fashioned glass as head, signed Gay Fad.................. **$48.00**
Cocktail set, Poodle, metal frame 'body' w/martini mixer, double old-fashioned glass as head & 4 5-oz glasses, signed...... **$60.00**
Cocktail shaker, Ballerina Shoes, red metal screw-top lid, frosted, 32-oz, 7" **$25.00**
Cocktail shaker, full-figure ballerina, frosted, 28-oz, 9" **$40.00**
Cruet set, Oil & Vinegar, Cherry, clear **$14.00**
Decanter set, Gay '90s, Scotch, Rye, Gin & Bourbon, frosted or white inside.. **$85.00**
Goblet, Bow Pete, Hoffman Beer, 16-oz **$15.00**
Ice tub, Gay '90s, frosted **$21.00**
Juice set, Palm, frosted 18-oz jug w/dispenser lid, +6 4-oz tumblers **$45.00**
Juice set, Tommy Tomato, frosted, 36-oz pitcher & 6 4-oz tumblers **$45.00**
Luncheon set, Fantasia Hawaiian flower, 1-place setting (sq plate, cup & saucer) **$20.00**
Martini mixer, 'A Jug of Wine...,' w/glass stirring rod, clear, signed Gay Fad, 10⅝" **$25.00**
Mix-A-Salad set, Ivy, 22-oz shaker w/plastic top, garlic press, measuring spoon, recipe book, MIB **$75.00**
Mug, Notre Dame, frosted, 16-oz **$15.00**
Mug set, minstrels w/different song on ea mug, frosted, 16-oz, 8-pc **$115.00**
Mug set, toasts from a different country on ea mug, frosted, 12-pc **$120.00**
Pilsner set, Gay 90s, portraits: Mama, Papa, Victoria, Rupert, Aunt Aggie, Uncle Bertie, Gramps & Horace, frosted, 8-pc .. **$80.00**
Pitcher, Currier & Ives, blue & white, frosted, 86-oz........... **$90.00**

Pitcher, Ada Orange, frosted, 36-ounce, $20.00. (Photo courtesy Donna McGrady)

Pitcher, martini; cardinal & pine sprig, frosted, w/glass stirrer, 42-oz.. **$38.00**
Pitcher, Musical Notes, frosted, 86-oz................................ **$55.00**
Pitcher, Rosemaling (tulips), white inside, 32-oz................. **$28.00**
Plate, Fruits, lace edge, Hazel-Atlas, 8½" **$17.50**
Punch set, pink veiling, bowl & 8 cups in white metal frame .. **$65.00**
Range set, Rooster, salt, pepper, sugar & flower shakers, frosted w/ red metal lids, 8-oz, 4-pc **$120.00**
Salad set, Fruits, frosted, lg bowl, 2 cruets, salt & pepper shakers, 5-pc **$60.00**
Salad set, Outlined Fruits, lg bowl, 2 cruets, salt & pepper shakers, frosted, 5-pc...................................... **$60.00**
Salt & pepper shakers, Morning Glory, frosted w/red plastic tops, pr **$16.00**
Stem, bent cocktail, Beau Brummel, clear, signed Gay Fad, 3½-oz **$10.00**
Stem, bent cocktail, Souvenir of My Bender, frosted, 3-oz ... **$10.00**
Syrup pitcher, Rosemaling (tulips), frosted, 11½-oz **$20.00**
Tea & toast, Magnolia, sq plate w/cup indent & cup, clear.. **$15.00**
Tom & Jerry set, Christmas bells, milk white, marked GF, bowl & 6 cups **$70.00**
Tumbler, Bob White, brown, turquoise & gold on clear, signed Gay Fad, 10-oz **$12.00**
Tumbler, Christmas Greetings From Gay Fad, frosted, 4-oz. **$17.00**
Tumbler, Hors D'oeuvres, clear, 14-oz **$10.00**
Tumbler, Kentucky state map (1 of 48), pink, yellow or lime, frosted, marked GF, 10-oz **$7.00**
Tumbler, Oregon state map on pink picket fence, clear, marked GF **$8.00**
Tumbler, Pegasus, gold & pink on black, 12-oz **$11.00**
Tumbler, Say When, frosted, 4-oz **$8.00**
Tumbler, Zombie, flamingo, frosted, marked GF, 14-oz....... **$15.00**
Tumbler, Zombie, giraffe, frosted, marked GF, 14-oz.......... **$14.00**
Tumbler, 1948 Derby Winner Citation, frosted, 14-oz **$50.00**
Tumblers, angels preparing for Christmas, frosted, 12-oz, set of 8 .... **$72.00**
Tumblers, Dickens Christmas Carol characters, frosted, 12-oz, set of 8 .... **$54.00**
Tumblers, Famous Fighters (John L Sullivan & the others), frosted, 16-oz, set of 8 .... **$85.00**
Tumblers, French Poodle, clear, 17-oz, set of 8 in original box.. **$96.00**
Tumblers, Game Birds & Animals, clear, 12-oz, set of 8, MIB ... **$65.00**
Tumblers, Ohio Presidents, frosted, 12-oz, set of 8 .... **$55.00**

Tumblers, Rich Man, Poor Man (nursery rhyme), frosted, marked GF, 16-oz, set of 8 ....**$80.00**

Tumblers, Sports Cars, white inside, 12-oz, set of 8 ....**$45.00**

Vanity set, butterflies in meadow, pink inside, 5-pc **$60.00**

Vase, Red Poppy, clear, footed, 10" **$24.00**

Waffle set, Autumn Nocturne, 18-oz waffle batter jug & 11-oz syrup jug, frosted, pr **$65.00**

Waffle set, Blue Willow, 48-oz waffle batter jug & 11-oz syrup jug, frosted, pr **$125.00**

Waffle set, Little Black Sambo, frosted, 48-oz waffle batter jug, 11½-oz syrup jug **$250.00**

Waffle set, Peach Blossoms, 48-oz waffle batter jug & 11½-oz syrup jug, frosted...**$52.00**

Waffle set, Red Poppy, frosted, 48-oz waffle batter jug, 11½-oz syrup jug **$25.00**

Waffle set, Rosemaling: 48-ounce batter jug, $45.00; 11½-ounce syrup, $55.00. (Photo courtesy Donna McGrady)

Wine set, Grapes, decanter & 4 2½-oz stemmed wines, clear, 5-pc.. **$40.00**

Geisha Girl China

The late nineteenth century saw a rise in the popularity of Oriental wares in the US and Europe. Japan rose to meet the demands of this flourishing ceramics marketplace with a flurry of growth in potteries and decorating centers. These created items for export which would appeal to Western tastes and integrate into Western dining and decorating cultures, which were distinct from those of Japan. One example of the wares introduced into this marketplace was Geisha Girl porcelain.

Hundreds of different patterns and manufacturers' marks have been uncovered on Geisha Girl porcelain tea and dinnerware sets, dresser accessories, decorative items, etc., which were produced well into the twentieth century. They all share in common colorful decorations featuring kimono-clad ladies and children involved in everyday activities. These scenes are set against a backdrop of lush flora, distinctive Japanese architecture, and majestic landscapes. Most Geisha Girl porcelain designs were laid on by means of a stencil, generally red or black. This appears as an outline on the ceramic body. Details are then completed by hand-painted washes

in a myriad of colors. A minority of the wares were wholly hand painted.

Most Geisha Girl porcelain has a colorful border or edging with handles, finials, spouts, and feet similarly adorned. The most common border color is red which can range from orange to red-orange to a deep brick red. Among the earliest border colors were red, maroon, cobalt blue, light (apple) green, and Nile green. Pine green, blue-green, and turquoise made their appearance circa 1917, and a light cobalt or Delft blue appeared around 1920. Other colors (e.g. tan, yellow, brown, and gold) can also be found. Borders were often enhanced with gilded lace or floral decoration. The use of gold for this purpose diminished somewhat around 1910 to 1915 when some decorators used economic initiative (fewer firings required) to move the gold to just inside the border or replace the gold with white or yellow enamels. Wares with both border styles continued to be produced into the twentieth century. Exquisite examples with multicolor borders as well as ornate rims decorated with florals and geometrics can also be found.

Due to the number of different producers, the quality of Geisha ware ranges from crude to finely detailed. Geisha Girl porcelain was sold in sets and open stock in outlets ranging from the five-and-ten to fancy department stores. It was creatively used for store premiums, containers for store products, fair souvenirs, and resort memorabilia. The fineness of detailing, amount of gold highlights, border color, scarcity of form and, of course, condition all play a role in establishing the market value of a given item. Some patterns are scarcer than others, but most Geisha ware collectors seem not to focus on particular patterns.

The heyday of Geisha Girl porcelain was from 1910 through the 1930s. Production continued until the World War II era. During the 'Occupied' period, a small amount of wholly hand-painted examples were made, often with a black and gold border. The Oriental import stores and catalogs from the 1960s and 1970s featured some examples of Geisha Girl porcelain, many of which were produced in Hong Kong. These are recognized by the very white porcelain, sparse detail coloring, and lack of gold decoration. The 1990s saw a resurgence of reproductions with a faux Nippon mark. These items are supposed to represent high quality Geisha ware, but in reality they are a blur of Geisha and Satsuma-style characteristics. They are too busy in design, too heavily enameled, and bear a variety of faux Nippon marks. Once you've been introduced to a few of these reproductions, you'll be able to recognize them easily.

Note: Colors mentioned in the following listings refer to borders.

Advisor: Elyce Litts (See Directory, Geisha Girl China)

Ashtray, Temple A, multicolored, spade shape......................**$25.00**

Basket vase, Bamboo Trellis, gold trim, 8½".........................**$75.00**

Biscuit jar, Lady in Rickshaw, melon-ribbed, red-orange w/gold, footed **$55.00**

Bonbon dish, Bamboo Trellis, red w/gold **$15.00**

Bowl, Boat Festival, blue border w/interior gold lacing, handles, Plum Blossom mark, 7½" (handle to handle) **$20.00**

Bowl, Chrysanthemum, Parasol C, red w/gold buds, curled handle, 6"..**$18.00**

Bowl, Dragon Boat, 6-lobed, blue w/gold, 7" **$35.00**

Bowl, Parasol C, floral exterior, red border, fluted rim, Made in Japan, 2¼x6" **$16.00**

Bowl, Picnic A, 6", $48.00. (Photo courtesy Elyce Litts)

Bowl, Samurai Dance, red border w/gold, 3x10" **$38.00**

Box, Mother & Daughter, pink background, gold rim, footed, w/lid, footed, rare, 2x5x4" **$125.00**

Box, trinket; Koto, club shaped.. **$28.00**

Celery dish, Foreign Garden, blue border **$45.00**

Chamberstick, Courtesan Precessional, blue border **$60.00**

Cocoa pot, geishas in reserve, pink & blue flowers, dark orange trim, 9½" **$50.00**

Creamer, Boy w/Scythe, cobalt w/gold................................. **$15.00**

Creamer, Long-Stemmed Peony, slender, fluted, blue w/gold... **$12.00**

Cup & saucer, after dinner; Basket B, dark apple green w/gold, straight sides **$15.00**

Dresser box, Garden Bench B, cobalt w/gold, 6" dia............ **$38.00**

Dresser tray, Garden Bench D, hand-painted green & red w/gold, 10x8" **$55.00**

Ewer, Garden Bench H, red w/gold lacing **$40.00**

Hair receiver, Battledore, grass green, melon-ribbed............ **$24.00**

Hatpin holder, Garden Bench, multicolored border, 4" **$60.00**

Jelly dish, Parasol C, red border w/gold buds, triangular, Made in Japan, 5x5" **$16.00**

Lemonade set, Bellflower, brown w/trim, pitcher & 5 matching mugs **$125.00**

Match holder, Parasol C, red border, Japan, 3¼x2¼" **$26.00**

Nappy, Temple A, hand-fluted edge, single handle, unusual sea green border **$35.00**

Nut dish, Duck Watching A, red w/gold, footed, individual size.. **$8.00**

Plate, Basket, swirl fluted, scalloped edge, dark apple green, 8½" ...**$30.00**

Plate, Child's Play, cobalt w/gold buds, 6½" **$15.00**

Plate, lemon; Child Reaching for Butterfly, blue border w/gold lacing, Japan, 6½x5¾" **$16.00**

Powder jar, Flower Gathering E, red border w/gold lacing, 3½"..**$24.00**

Puff box, Field Laborers, red w/gold **$20.00**

Ring tree, Temple A, Nippon.. **$75.00**

Salt & pepper shakers, Parasol E, blue border, pr **$15.00**

Sauce dish, Meeting B, dark apple green, red & gold border ..**$12.00**

Snack set, Garden Bench D, red & gold border **$35.00**

Teacup & saucer, Garden Bench N, colorful floral surround, Japan **$12.50**

Teacup & saucer, Geisha Band, cobalt border, Made in Japan ..**$16.00**

Teacup & saucer, Origami, cobalt w/gold **$18.00**

Teacup & saucer, Picnic D, multicolored border, unmarked...**$14.00**

Teacup & saucer, Writing B, blue w/gold............................. **$15.00**

Teapot, So Big, hand painted w/multicolored border, 3-footed, Kutani, 5½" **$55.00**

Teapot, Torii, geometric yellow & green border, gold trim, 5", +creamer & sugar bowl.. **$45.00**

Toothpick holder, Circle Dance, cylindrical, red border....... **$15.00**

Vase, Garden Bench F, green & red border w/gold highlights, Kutani mark, 5" **$32.00**

Water jar, Meeting A, red border, mini, 2⅜" **$14.00**

GI Joe

The first GI Joe was introduced by Hasbro in 1964. He was 12" tall, and you could buy him with blond, auburn, black, or brown hair in four basic variations: Action Sailor, Action Marine, Action Soldier, and Action Pilot. There was also a Black doll as well as representatives of many other nations. By 1967 GI Joe could talk, all the better to converse with the female nurse who was first issued that year. The Adventure Team series (1970 – 1976) included Black Adventurer, Talking Astronaut, Sea Adventurer, Talking Team Commander, Land Adventurer, and several variations. At this point, their hands were made of rubber, making it easier for them to grasp the many guns, tools, and other accessories that Hasbro had devised. Playsets, vehicles, and clothing completed the package, and there were kid-size items designed specifically for the kids themselves. The 12" dolls were discontinued by 1976.

Brought out by popular demand, Hasbro's 3¾" GI Joes hit the market in 1982. Needless to say, they were very well accepted. In fact, these smaller GI Joes are thought to be the most successful line of action figures ever made. Loose figures (those removed from the original packaging) are very common, and even if you can locate the accessories that they came out with, most are worth only about $3.00 to $10.00. It's the mint-in-package items that most interest collectors, and they pay a huge premium for the package. There's an extensive line of accessories that goes with the smaller line as well. Many more are listed in *Schroeder's Collectible Toys, Antique to Modern,* published by Collector Books.

12" Figures and Accessories

Accessory, armband, Army Airborne MP, snap connectors (rare), NM.. **$200.00**

Accessory, Astronaut Boots, plastic, VG+, pr...................... **$25.00**

Accessory, Binoculars, Hurricane Spotter, gray, EX **$7.00**

Accessory, Canadian Mountie Set, outfit, rifle, ammunition belt, goggles, radio & mess kit, NM **$290.00**

Accessory, Cobra, Search for the Golden Idol, EX $15.00
Accessory, Diver Belt, 1st issue w/exposed weights & leg strap, EX...$25.00
Accessory, Goggles, Desert Patrol, amber, replaced elastic, EX .. $65.00
Accessory, Grendade Launcher, Action Man, EX $15.00
Accessory, Head Gear, Landing Signal Officer, 1960s, EX ...$60.00
Accessory, Jackhammer, EX+...$275.00
Accessory, radio, Airborne MP, black, marked Hong Kong, G+...$245.00
Accessory, Scuba Gear, orange suit, tanks & fins, NM.......$150.00
Accessory, Shirt & Trousers, Japanese, EX...........................$45.00
Accessory, Space Capsule Collar, inflatable, Sears, EX........$115.00
Figure, Action Marine, Dress Blues Parade Set, #7710, EX..$50.00
Figure, Action Marine, Medic Set, #7719, w/stretcher, MIP..$825.00
Figure, Action Marine, Tank Commander Set, #7731, EX..$350.00
Figure, Action Pilot, Talking, #7890, NM $250.00
Figure, Action Sailor, Deep Freeze, #7623, EX...................$225.00
Figure, Action Sailor, Navy Attack Set, #7607, NM...........$150.00
Figure, Action Sailor, Sea Rescue, #GIHLD-37, EX $200.00
Figure, Action Soldier, Command Post Poncho, 1964, #7519, NM $40.00
Figure, Action Soldier, Heavy Weapons, #7538, EX...........$190.00
Figure, Action Soldier, Mountain Troops Set, #7530, MIP...$365.00
Figure, Action Soldier, Talking, #7590, MIP......................$800.00

Figure, Action Soldier, variation with scar, NMIB, $375.00.
(Photo courtesy LiveAuctioneers.com/Morphy auctions)

Figure, Action Soldier, 30th Anniversary, #81048, 1994, NRFB $100.00
Figure, Adventure Team, Adventurer, Hidden Treasure, #1308-1, EX $20.00
Figure, Adventure Team, Air Adventurer, #7403, EX........$130.00
Figure, Adventure Team, Air Adventurer, Kung Fu Grip, #7823, MIB...$340.00

Figure, Adventure Team, Demolition, #7370, EX..............$25.00
Figure, Adventure Team, Headquarters, #7490, MIP.........$275.00
Figure, Adventure Team, Jungle Survival, #7373, MIP.........$50.00
Figure, Adventure Team, Winter Rescue, #7309-4, NM $80.00
Figure, Adventures of GI Joe, Mysterious Explosion Set, #7021, EX..$70.00
Figure, Australian Jungle Fighter, no equipment, #8205, NM..$250.00
Figure, Japanese Imperial Soldier, w/equipment, #8201, EX..$275.00
Vehicle, Action Pilot, Crash Crew Set, #7820, NM $225.00
Vehicle, Adventure Soldier, Helicopter, #5395, NM $275.00
Vehicle, Adventure Team, Avenger Pursuit Craft, Sears, NM ..$165.00
Vehicle, Adventure Team, Escape Car, #7360, MIP $80.00
Vehicle, Mobile Support Vehicle, EX $250.00
Vehicle, Motorcycle & Sidecar, Cherilea, green, near complete, EX...$50.00
Vehicle, Panther Jet, EX..$400.00
Vehicle, Sea Wolf (submarine), EXIB..................................$100.00

Vehicle, Space Capsule and Space Suit, 13½", EXIB, $165.00.
(Photo courtesy LiveAuctioneers.com/Conestoga Auction Company)

3¾" Figures and Accessories

Accessory, Battlefield Robot Radar Rat, 1989, MIP $25.00
Accessory, HAL Heavy Artillery Laser w/Grand Slam, 1982, #6052, MOC...$110.00
Accessory, Tiger Force Tiger Shark, 1988, MIP....................$30.00
Accessory, Transportable Tactical Battle Platform, 1985, NM..$30.00
Figure, Airborne, 1983, MOC...$65.00
Figure, Barricade, 1992, MOC $8.00
Figure, BAT, 1986, EX...$12.00
Figure, Battle Force 2000 Dodger, 1987, NM $18.00
Figure, Beach Head, 1986, MOC..$35.00
Figure, Blackblast, 1989, MIP..$15.00
Figure, Blaster, 1987, NM..$18.00
Figure, Blocker, 1988, MOC...$30.00
Figure, Breaker, 1982, MOC $80.00
Figure, Cobra Commander, 1984, hooded, NM.................$18.00

Figure, Cobra Officer, 1982, MOC **$130.00**
Figure, Crazylegs, 1987, MOC **$25.00**
Figure, Deep-Six, 1984, NM **$15.00**

Figure, Desert Trooper, 9185, MOC, $300.00. (Photo courtesy www.cloudcity.com)

Figure, Destro, 1983, MOC **$65.00**
Figure, Doc-Medic, 1983, NM **$30.00**
Figure, Eels, 1985, NM...**$28.00**
Figure, Footloose, 1985, MOC **$50.00**
Figure, Gnawgahyde, 1989, MOC **$15.00**
Figure, Gung-Ho, 1983, NM **$35.00**
Figure, Lady Jaye, 1985, MOC **$90.00**
Figure, Mercer, 1991, MOC **$18.50**
Figure, Mutt & Junkyard, 1984, MOC **$60.00**
Figure, Ninja Force Dojo, 1992, MOC **$28.00**
Figure, Psyche-Out, 1987, MOC **$25.00**
Figure, Recondo, 1984, MOC **$70.00**
Figure, Roadblock, 1984, MOC **$60.00**
Figure, Scarlett, 1982, MOC **$140.00**
Figure, Snake Eyes, w/Timber (wolf), 1985, MOC **$160.00**
Figure, Stalker, 1982, MOC......................................**$125.00**
Figure, Tomax & Xamot, 1985, MOC **$180.00**
Vehicle, Cat Crimson Attack Tank, 1985, Sears, MIP........**$110.00**
Vehicle, Crusader Space Shuttle, 1989, MIP.................**$125.00**
Vehicle, LCV Recon Sled, 1986, #6067, EX.....................**$14.00**
Vehicle, Thunderclap, 1989, MIB...............................**$115.00**
Vehicle, USS Flagg Aircraft Carrier, 1986, #6001, EX.......**$160.00**

Gilner

Gilner Potteries was a California company in Culver City. Founded by Beryl Gilner, the company produced decorative items that were marketed across the country to dime stores and gift shops. Their specialty lines included figurines, floral ware, and a number of other items including cookie jars and decorative home accessories. Today their Pixie line continues to be increasingly popular with collectors. Other ceramic items made by Gilner Potters are also gaining in popularity. Gilner Potteries ceased operations in 1957 when competition from imports made it to difficult to continue in business and recover from the effects of a major plant fire.

Nearly all items listed below contain the original company identification names and numbers as found in Gilner Potteries' wholesale catalogs. Original 1950 colors for Pixies include green, chartreuse, maroon, red, and some yellow. Pink and turquoise indicate the 1955+ period of production. Price ranges are for items in very good to excellent condition that are free of chips or stained unglazed parts and have no repairs to re-attach such as broken arms and legs.

In the listings below HP was as an abbreviation for 'Happy People' (boy Pixies) and MM was used for 'Merry Maids' (girl Pixies). Letters after the hyphen refer to poses.

Advisor: Carol Power (See Directory, Gilner Potteries)

Website: wyomingprospector.com/pixiewatch

Ashtray, M-139, red HP108-Q Pixie laying on back on edge of green horseshoe, from $25 to **$30.00**
Box, green heart shape w/green HP-108-H Pixie kneeling on top of lid, 6", from $40 to..**$50.00**
Creamer & sugar bowl, M-128, yellow apples, red HP Pixie as handle of sugar bowl, from $75 to.................................**$80.00**
Figurine, HP-108-C, green Pixie seated w/legs spread & hands touching toes, from $15 to **$20.00**
Figurine, HP-108-P, charteuse Pixie laying on side w/head resting on hand, 4¾", from $30 to **$35.00**
Figurine, HP-109-F, chartreuse Pixie laying on stomach w/head in hands, 2⅜x4½", from $15 to **$20.00**
Figurine, MM-109-B, chartreuse 'Sweetheart' Pixie standing slightly bent at waist, lips puckered, 4¼", from $35 to **$40.00**
Figurine, MM-109-K, red Pixie kneeling w/hands clasped under chin, from $15 to..**$20.00**
Garlic Gus, M-157, red Pixie sitting on garlic bulb, 6½x4½", from $40 to **$45.00**
Planter, M-100, maroon HP Pixie sitting on side of sm chartreuse log, from $15 to...**$20.00**
Planter, M-133, red HP Pixie seated on lg chartreuse 'Happy Shoe,' 4x6", from $25 to...**$30.00**
Planter, M-134, lg green 'Playmate' MM Pixie kneeling beside stump, 6x6", from $30 to **$40.00**
Planter, M-401, green Pixie kneeling in front of fish riding wave (facing right or left), ea from $35 to **$40.00**
Planter, Native ('Happy Cannibal'), boy sitting in yellow & brown canoe, 8½", from $30 to..**$32.00**
Planter, Native ('Happy Cannibal') girl sits on bamboo bench before green bamboo container, 3¾x7¾", from $25 to............**$30.00**
Salt & pepper shakers, M-124, maroon Pixies (1 HP & 1 MM), both standing, pr from $40 to **$45.00**
Shelf sitter, M-108-E, green Pixie w/outstretched arms & open hands, from $35 to **$40.00**
TV lamp/planter, leaf form, pink w/gold trim, #551, 10x11"..**$35.00**

Versatile Happy, M-127, red HP Pixie slotted in rear to fit on rim of drinking glass, from $75 to............$85.00

Wall pocket, Cutie Fruities, M-150, red Pixie w/chef's hat sitting on sm strawberry, 5x5", from $50 to..............$60.00

Wall pocket, Mother's Pets, M-117, red Pixie sitting on large chartreuse grape cluster, 7½x6¼", from $50.00 to $60.00.

Wall pocket, M-412, green clock w/2 chartreuse Pixies kissing, 7x5½x4½", from $55 to...............$60.00

Willie the Waterer, M-161, red, green or chartreuse Pixie on watering can, 6½x3½x2½", from $75 to $85.00

Glass Animals and Related Items

In addition to their dinnerware lines, many important American glass manufacturers — Heisey, Imperial, Cambridge, Fostoria, Paden City, and Tiffin among them — also made many exquisite figurines of animals, birds, fish, and insects. Some were designed as bookends, candleholders, and vases. As these companies went out of business, their molds were often bought by other still-active manufacturers who used them to produce their own products. This can be very confusing to the collector.

See also Fenton; Westmoreland.

Cambridge

Bird on stump, flower frog, green, 5¼", minimum value ...$400.00
Draped Lady, flower frog, green frost, 8½"............$150.00
Eagle, bookend, crystal, 5½x4x4", ea $90.00
Heron, crystal, lg, 12".............$150.00
Swan, Carmen, 6½"............$275.00
Turkey, green, w/lid.............$550.00

Duncan and Miller

Donkey, cart & peon, crystal, 3-pc set $650.00
Duck, ashtray, red, 7" $375.00
Goose, crystal, fat, 6x6" $250.00

Heron, crystal satin, 7" $125.00
Swan, milk glass w/red neck, 10½" $425.00
Swordfish, blue opalescent, rare..............$500.00
Tropical fish, ashtray, pink opalescence, 3½"............$65.00

Fostoria

Bird, candleholder, crystal, 1½", ea $20.00
Cardinal head, Silver Mist, 6½" $200.00
Deer, milk glass, sitting or standing $40.00
Goldfish, crystal, vertical.................$150.00
Lady bug, blue, lemon or olive green, 1¼"............$30.00
Polar Bear, crystal, 4⅝" $55.00
Rebecca at Well, candleholder, crystal frost, ea.............$125.00
Seal, topaz, 3⅞" $75.00

Heisey

Colt, amber, kicking.............$650.00
Dolphin, candlesticks, crystal, #110, pr $400.00
Duck, flower block, Flamingo.............$175.00
Filly, crystal, head backwards.............$1,300.00

Fish, bowl, crystal, 9½", $450.00.

Giraffe, crystal, head to side $275.00
Irish setter, ashtray, crystal...............$30.00
Mallard, crystal, wings up $200.00
Swan, individual nut dish, crystal, #1503.............$20.00

Imperial

Airdale, Ultra Blue $70.00
Bird, Cathay Crystal, scolding.............$175.00
Clydesdale, Salmon $200.00
Colt, Sunshine Yellow, standing $30.00
Elephant, Meadow Green carnival, #674, med..............$75.00
Filly, satin, head forward $75.00
Mallard, caramel slag, wings down $165.00
Owl, jar, caramel slag, 16½"..............$75.00

Rooster, amber $200.00
Wood duck, Ultra Blue satin...$55.00

L.E. Smith

Camel, crystal $50.00
Elephant, crystal...$8.00
Goose Girl, crystal, 6"...$25.00
Horse, bookends, ruby, rearing....................................$100.00
Rooster, butterscotch slag, limited edition, #208..............$100.00
Swan, milk glass w/decoration, 8½" $35.00
Swan, soap dish, crystal..$25.00

New Martinsville

Bear, mama; crystal, 4x6"..$175.00
Gazelle, crystal w/frosted base, leaping, 8¼" $50.00
Piglet, crystal, standing..$175.00
Seal, baby w/ball, crystal $60.00
Ship, bookends, crystal...$130.00
Tiger, crystal frost, head down, 7¼" $200.00

Wolfhound, crystal, 7", $70.00.

Woodsman, crystal, sq base, 7⅜" $90.00

Paden City

Rooster, Barnyard; crystal, 8¾", $110.00.

Bunny, cotton-ball dispenser, crystal frost, ears back $225.00
Dragon swan, crystal, 9¾" L $250.00
Eagle, bookends, crystal $500.00
Polar bear on ice, crystal, 4½" $65.00
Rooster, Barnyard; blue, 8¾" $275.00
Squirrel on curved log, crystal, 5½" $50.00

Tiffin

Cat, Sassy Suzie, black satin w/painted decoration, #9448, 11" ...$175.00
Fawn, flower floater, Citron Green................................$200.00
Fawn, flower floater, Copen Blue $300.00
Fish, crystal, solid, 8¾x9"..$350.00
Frog, candleholders, black satin, pr $225.00
Lovebirds, lamp, orange w/green heads, 10½", from $450 to....$550.00
Owl, lamp, cobalt, 1934-39, minimum value $1,000.00

Viking

Angelfish, amber, 7x7" $100.00
Bird, candy dish, med green, w/lid, 12".........................$50.00
Bird, orange, #1311, 10"..$40.00
Bird, ruby,#1310, 12" $60.00

Cat, sitting; green, 8", $45.00. (Photo courtesy Lee Garmon and Dick Spencer)

Duck, orange, round, footed, 5" $35.00
Duck, vaseline, 5" $60.00
Egret, orange, 12" $50.00
Horse, aqua blue, 11½"..$125.00
Jesus, crystal w/Crystal Mist, flat back, 6x5" $65.00
Rabbit, amber, 6½" $35.00
Rooster, avocado, Viking's Epic Line................................$50.00
Swan, bowl, amber, 6" $25.00

Miscellaneous

American Glass Co, horse, crystal, jumping.........................$40.00
Blenko, owl, paperweight, amber $40.00
Co-Operative Flint Glass, elephant, pink, 4½x7"..............$275.00
Federal, Mopey dog, crystal, 3½" $10.00
Haley, Lady Godiva, bookends, crystal, 1940s $90.00

Indiana, horse head, bookends, milk glass, 6" $65.00

Kemple, horse, milk glass, jumping $75.00

Pilgrim, whale, crystal, #924, w/labels, in 1964 World's Fair box $45.00

Viking for Mirror Images, baby bear, ruby $75.00

Viking for Mirror Images, police dog, ruby $100.00

Glass Knives

Popular during the Depression years, glass knives were made in many of the same colors as the glass dinnerware of the era — pink, green, light blue, crystal, and more rarely, amber or white (originally called opal). Some were hand painted with flowers or fruit. The earliest boxes had poems printed on their tops explaining the knife's qualities in the pre-stainless steel days: 'No metal to tarnish when cutting your fruit, and so it is certain this glass knife will suit.' Eventually, a tissue flyer was packed with each knife, which elaborated even more on the knife's usefulness. 'It is keen as a razor, ideal for slicing tomatoes, oranges, lemons, grapefruit and especially constructed for separating the meaty parts of grapefruit from its rind...' Boxes add interest by helping identify distributors as well as commercial names of the knives.

When originally sold, the blades were ground to a sharp cutting edge, but due to everyday usage, the blades eventually became nicked. Collectors will accept reground, resharpened blades as long as the original shape has been maintained.

Documented US glass companies that made glass knives are the Akro Agate Co., Cameron Glass Corp., Houze Glass Corp., Imperial Glass Corp., Jeannette Glass Co., and Westmoreland Glass Co.

Internet final-bid auction prices indicate what a person is willing to pay to add a new or different piece to a personal collection and may not necessarily reflect any price guide values.

Block, pink, 8¼", from $50 to $55.00

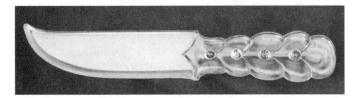

Candlewick, crystal, 8½", $525.00.

Durex 3-Leaf, blue, 9¼", from $35 to $45.00

Durex 3-Leaf, green, 8½", from $35 to $40.00

Durex 3-Leaf, light amber, 9¼", from $225 to $275.00

Durex 3-Leaf, pink, 8½", from $32 to $35.00

Durex 5-Leaf, blue, 8½", from $38 to $45.00

Durex 5-Leaf, green, 9¼", from $30 to $40.00

Pinwheel, crystal, from $6 to $12.00

Plain handle, pink, 9¼", from $60 to $70.00

Rose spray, crystal, 8½", from $80 to $90.00

Rose spray, green, 8½", from $200 to $250.00

Steel-ite, crystal, 7½", from $35 to $40.00

Stonex, amber, 8¼", from $275 to $300.00

Westmoreland, crystal, #1800, ribbed handle, 9¼", from $150 to $175.00

Westmoreland, green, #1801, plain handle, 9¼", from $350 to $395.00

3-Star, blue, 9¼", from $30 to $35.00

3-Star, crystal, 8½", from $10 to $15.00

3-Star, pink, 8½", from $32 to $35.00

Plain handle, green, 8½", from $35.00 to $40.00. (Photo courtesy Gene and Cathy Florence)

Golden Foliage

In 1935 Libbey Glass was purchased by Owens-Illinois but continued to operate under the Libbey Glass name. After World War II, the company turned to making tableware and still does today. Golden Foliage is just one of the many patterns made during the 1950s. It is a line of crystal glassware with a satin band that features a golden maple leaf as well as other varieties. The satin band is trimmed in gold, above and below. Since this gold seems to have easily worn off, be careful to find mint pieces for your collection. This pattern was made in silver as well.

Advisor: Debbie Coe (See Directory, Cape Cod)

Tumbler, water; 10-ounce, $8.50; Goblet, water; 9-ounce, $8.50.

Bowl, 2x3¾" $5.00

Creamer & sugar bowl $12.50

Creamer & sugar bowl, in metal frame $14.50

Decanter, 12" $12.50

Decanter, 12", in metal frame that holds 6 shot glasses $48.00

Goblet, cocktail; 4-oz..$6.00
Goblet, cordial; 1-oz...$8.50
Goblet, pilsner; 11-oz...$9.50
Goblet, sherbet; 6½-oz..$5.00
Ice bucket..$15.00
Ice tub, in metal 3-footed frame.............................$19.50
Pitcher, cocktail; slim, 10½x3", w/glass stir rod...........$45.00
Pitcher, 5¼", w/metal frame....................................$16.50
Salad dressing set, includes 3 bowls (4") & brass-finished
    caddy... $19.50
Tumbler, beverage; 12½-oz......................................$8.50
Tumbler, cooler; tall & slim, 14-oz $9.50
Tumbler, iced tea; flared sides, 15-oz......................$6.50
Tumbler, juice; 6-oz $5.00
Tumbler, old-fashioned; 9-oz................................$6.00
Tumbler, shot glass, 2-oz......................................$6.50
Tumblers, beverage; 12½-oz, set of 8 in metal frame...........$60.00

Graniteware

Though it really wasn't as durable as its name suggests, there's still lots of graniteware around today, though much of it is now in collections. You may even be able to find a bargain. The popularity of the 'country' look in home decorating and the exposure it's had in some of the leading decorating magazines has caused graniteware prices, especially on rare items, to soar in recent years.

It's made from a variety of metals coated with enameling of various colors, some solid, others swirled. It's color, form, and, of course, condition that dictates value. Swirls of cobalt and white, purple and white, green and white, and brown and white are unusual, but even solid gray items such as a hanging salt box or a chamberstick can be expensive because pieces like those are rare. Decorated examples are uncommon — so are children's pieces and salesman's samples.

Unless otherwise noted, our values reflect the worth of items in at least near mint condition. To evaluate items with wear and chipping, be sure to drastically reduce these values in proportion to the amount of damage.

Bean pot, blue and white large swirl, tin lid, M, $285.00; Kettle, emerald green and white large swirl, matching graniteware lid, M, $395.00. (Photo courtesy Helen Greguire)

Ashtray, green, Suporcel Superior...label, rare shape, 3x¾".....$75.00
Baking pan, molded handles, eyelet, lavender-blue & white lg swirl,
    2x9½x8", EX $95.00

Basin, flared sides, blue & white med mottle inside & out, 4½x13",
    EX $70.00
Biscuit cutter, brown & white med mottle, Onyx Ware,
    1¾x1x2¼"..$395.00
Bowl, apple green w/tangerine interior, Vollrath USA, 2½x5¾"..$25.00
Bowl, dough; blue & white fine mottle w/black, Lisk...label,
    5½x14"...$185.00
Bowl, vegetable; red w/black trim, 1⅞x8⅝x6½" $50.00
Bread pan, aqua & white mottle w/cobalt, Granite Steel Ware, 11",
    G+..$295.00
Bucket, berry; cream w/green trim, wire bail, seamless, 5", G+ .. $165.00
Bucket, slop; red & white lg mottle, w/lid, bail handle,
    11¾x9⅝"...$575.00
Bucket, w/lid, green & white lg swirl w/cobalt, 5"............$525.00
Butter dish, white w/cobalt trim, seamless, L&G Mfg, 4¾x8⅞"..$325.00
Candlestick, cobalt & white lg swirl, finger ring, 2¼x4¾", G+,
    ea. $650.00
Candlestick, yellow w/black ring handle & trim, 1¾x5¾", G,
    ea. $65.00
Canister, white w/dark blue trim & lettering, 7½x5" $85.00
Chamber pot, w/lid, blue & white mottle, Lisk, 6½x9½", G+..$240.00

Coffee biggin, blue and white swirl, M, $495.00. (Photo courtesy Helen Greguire)

Coffee biggin, gray lg mottle, 5-pc, 6½x3½", G+..............$375.00
Coffee boiler, green & white relish pattern, cobalt trim, 11¼x8⅝",
    G+ $295.00
Coffeepot, glass Pyrex insert, solid aqua w/black trim & handle,
    white interior, 1930s, 9x5½"...................................$85.00
Coffeepot, seamed body w/welded handle, cream w/green trim,
    8x5½" $95.00
Colander, white, 2½x7½" (w/handles) $60.00
Countertop scale, white, metal trim, Hobart Mfg,
    10x5½x13½"...$145.00
Cream can, seamed body, w/handle, brown & white fine mottle
    inside & out, 8x4½" $140.00
Creamer, dark blue & white med mottle, relish pattern,
    4½x3⅝" $395.00
Cup, white w/black trim & open handle, Lisk...label, 2¼x4¼"...$35.00

Custard cup, cream w/green trim, 2x3½" **$55.00**

Egg plate, white w/black handles & trim, 1x6⅜" dia, G+ **$40.00**

Fry pan, red & white lg swirl inside & out, black trim & handle, 1¼x8" **$185.00**

Fudge pan, lavender, cobalt & white swirl, ¾x6½x9½", G+ .**$195.00**

Funnel, seamless body w/blue & white mottle, gray interior w/fine blue flecks, 5x3" dia, EX..**$165.00**

Grater, red, flat handle, 10x3⅝", G+ **$125.00**

Kettle, seamless, matching lid, gray lg mottle, 6½x9" dia, EX ...**$110.00**

Measure, gray lg mottle, embossed 1 Gal Liquid, Royal...label, 9⅝" **$295.00**

Milk can, gray lg mottle, Nesco-Royal...label, 9x5¼" **$295.00**

Mold, ring; solid yellow w/white interior, 2¼x8", dia, EX ...**$65.00**

Mug, red & white lg swirl w/white interior, red trim, ca 1970, 3x3½" **$30.00**

Mug, seamless w/riveted handle, brown & white lg swirl w/white interior, cobalt trim, 3x4", EX **$155.00**

Pitcher, milk; white w/green trim & handle, 7x5" **$85.00**

Plate, dessert; blue & white lg mottle inside & out, black trim, 1x7" **$75.00**

Platter, fruit & berries on white w/brown, Corona, 16x13" ..**$95.00**

Pudding pan, red, white interior w/black trim, narrow rim, 9¾" dia..**$40.00**

Roaster, seamless, black bottom w/Delft blue lid, 6¼x8½", EX ..**$65.00**

Saucepan, seamless w/wooden handle, red & white lg mottle inside & out, 1960s, 3x4½" dia **$75.00**

Spoon, red w/black handle, 13¼" L **$65.00**

Spoon, solid white w/red trim on handle, 13¼", EX...........**$45.00**

Strainer, gray, 8-sided, w/handle & bottom drain pan........**$345.00**

Strainer, tea; perforated bottom, gray med mottle, 1x4" dia ..**$95.00**

Tart pan, gray lg mottle, 1x6" dia, EX **$45.00**

Teakettle, seamed, solid light pink w/black trim & handle, 7x7½", G+ **$70.00**

Teapot, seamed, red & white lg swirl w/white interior, ca 1950, 8x5" **$195.00**

Toothbrush holder, blue & white lg mottle w/cobalt, ¾x3½x8¾" ..**$325.00**

Tray, gray lg mottle, marked L&G Mfg Co, ½x13½x9½" ..**$155.00**

Trivet, white, fancy cut-out designs, 4 molded feet, 7¾" dia..**$110.00**

Tumbler, brown & white lg swirl w/brown, white interior, 3½x3¼" **$325.00**

Washbowl, dark gray lg mottle, Hoosier...label, 11" dia **$85.00**

Washbowl, white w/gold bands, black trim, brass eyelet, Lisk Warrented No 2... label, 12" dia **$60.00**

Griswold Cast-Iron Cooking Ware

Late in the 1800s, the Griswold company introduced a line of cast-iron cooking ware that was eventually distributed on a large scale nationwide. Today's collectors appreciate the variety of skillets, cornstick pans, Dutch ovens, and griddles available to them, and many still enjoy using them to cook with.

Several marks have been used; most contain the Griswold name, though some were marked simply 'Erie.'

If you intend to use your cast iron, you can clean it safely by using any commercial oven cleaner. (Be sure to re-season it before you cook.)

Our prices are for pieces in excellent condition: having been cleaned, with no rust or pitting, no chips, cracks, warpage, etc. Prices may vary because of variations that may exist in one of the part numbers. Items that are cracked, chipped, pitted, or warped are worth substantially less or nothing at all, depending on rarity.

Note: The letters P/N in the following listings indicate Product Identification Numbers; TM indicates trademark, and FM full writing.

Advisors: Sharon and Charly Harvey (See Directory, Griswald)

Cake mold, rabbit, Griswold Mfg Co, P/Ns 862 & 863, Erie PA (on loop) 1940s-50s (+), from $275 to..............................**$300.00**

Cake mold, Santa, Hello Kiddies...Erie PA, P/Ns 897 & 898, defined tongue/casting flaw lower right, ca, '40s, (+), $450 ......**$500.00**

Cornstick pan, #22, P/N 954, 15 marking variations known, 1880s-1950s, 13⅜x7⅜ & 14½x7½", ea from $40 to............**$150.00**

Cornstick pan, #24 Cornbread Pan; 7-stick, P/N 957, ca 1920s-30s, same size as #21 P/N 961, from $150 to **$200.00**

Cornstick pan, #273, Griswold Crispy...; 7-stick, P/N 930..**$35.00**

Dutch oven, #6, Tite-Top; P/N 2605 base w/lg block EPU TM, P/N 2606 lid marked No 6 Tite-Top..., 1920-50, $300 to.**$400.00**

Dutch oven, #7, Tite-Top; P/N 2603 base w/lg block TM, Pat'd Mar 10 20 2603, lid marked No 7..., 1920-50.....................**$95.00**

Dutch oven, #8, Tite-Top; P/N 1278 base w/lg block EPU TM, P/N 1288 lid marked No 8 Tite-Top, 1920-50 ....**$50.00**

Dutch oven, #9, Flat-Top; P/N 834H base, P/N 838 lid w/nickel-plated steel knob, ca 1905, from $60 to.......................**$75.00**

Gem pan, #100, Heart and Star, P/N A802, cast aluminum, ca. 1920 – 1930, from $700.00 to $900.00. (Note: Priced same as cast iron.)

Golf ball pan, #19, 6-cup, P/N 966, 1923-30s, 1x7¾x4⅝", from $400 to **$500.00**

Griddle, #009, P/N 609, EPU TM, ca 1925-40, from $30 to..**$40.00**

Roaster, #7, P/N 647 base, P/N 648 lid, & P/N 276 trivet, 1920s-40s, 4¾x16¼x11½" **$350.00**

Saucepan, #84, P/N 84, red enamel w/red enamel lid, 1950s, 4x8" dia, from $75 to..**$100.00**

Skillet, #0, P/N 562, Erie USA, 1950s, value depends on handle style (+, usually w/grooved handle), from $60 to **$125.00**

Skillet, #2, P/N 703, block TM, smooth bottom, ca 1930-39, (+), from $350 to **$400.00**

Skillet, #2, P/N 703A, slant TM, smooth bottom, 1939-44, (+), from $500 to **$600.00**

Skillet, #4, P/N 702A, block EPU TM, smooth bottom w/heat ring, ca 1920-20, from $450 to..**$500.00**

Skillet, #4, P/N 702A, block TM, smooth bottom, ca 1920-30, from $60 to...**$80.00**

Skillet, #5, P/N 724, block TM, smooth bottom, ca 1930-39, from $60 to...**$80.00**

Skillet, #5, P/N 724, block TM, smooth bottom w/heat ring, ca 1920-30, from $400 to..**$500.00**

Skillet, #7, P/N 701B, sm block Erie TM, smooth bottom, value depends on handle style, from $10 to............................**$30.00**

Skillet, #8, All-in-One Dinner; P/N 1008, EPU TM, 3 sections, 1932-40, from $450 to...**$600.00**

Skillet, #8, P/N 7009, Victor, FM, ca 1920-35, from $35 to....**$60.00**

Skillet, #9, P/N 710, lg block EPU TM, smooth bottom, ca 1930-39, from $60 to...**$80.00**

Skillet, #10, P/N 716, lg block EPU TM, w/heat ring, ca 1920-30, from $60 to...**$75.00**

Skillet, #11, P/N 717, Erie TM, smoke ring, ca 1905-06, from $150 to...**$200.00**

Skillet, #12, P/N 719, sm block TM, w/self-basting lid, ca 1939-44, from $200 to...**$225.00**

Skillet, #12, P/N 719D, sm block TM, w/heat ring, ca 1939-44, from $50 to...**$75.00**

Skillet, #13, oval, P/N 1012, ca 1940-57, 18¾" L, from $250 to...**$300.00**

Skillet, #14, P/N 718, lg Erie TM, w/heat ring, ca 1920-30, from $100 to...**$150.00**

Skillet, #14, slant TM, w/heat ring, ca 1909-29, from $700 to..**$800.00**

Skillet, #15, oval, P/N 1013, P/N 12013C lid, block TM, ca 1940-1950, (lid is $500 to $600 of total value), from $800 to...**$900.00**

Skillet, #20, 2 handles, P/N 728, block EPU TM, ca 1941-57, from $500 to...**$600.00**

Skillet, Colonial Breakfast; P/N 666, EPU TM, 1940s, 9x9", from $35 to...**$60.00**

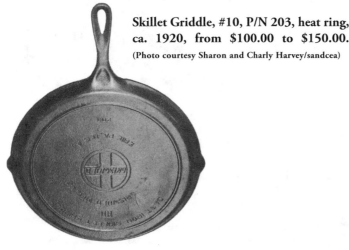

Skillet Griddle, #10, P/N 203, heat ring, ca. 1920, from $100.00 to $150.00.
(Photo courtesy Sharon and Charly Harvey/sandcea)

Skillet Griddle, #109, P/N 202, 1930s, from $100 to........**$125.00**

Skillet lid, #8, Self-Basting Skillet Cover; high dome, plain, 1940s-60s **$35.00**

Skillet lid, #8, Self-Basting Skillet Cover; high dome, raised letters, ca 1931-57..**$35.00**

Skillet lid, #8, Self-Basting Skillet Cover; high dome w/TM, 1940s **$25.00**

Skillet lid, #8, Self-Basting Skillet Cover; low dome, raised letters, ca 1915-35..**$40.00**

Teakettle, #8, Erie spider & web TM on sliding lid, ca 1880-90..**$500.00**

Waffle iron, #06, P/N 305/306/307, unknown circa, 3-pc, from $250 to...**$350.00**

Whole wheat pan, #28, P/N 639, 4 variations made, ca 1925-30, 12⅝x7", from $200 to...**$350.00**

Guardian Ware

The Guardian Service Company was in business from 1935 until 1955. They produced a very successful line of hammered aluminum that's just as popular today as it ever was. (Before 1935 Century Metalcraft made similar ware under the name SilverSeal, you'll occasionally see examples of it as well.) Guardian Service was sold through the home party plan, and special hostess gifts were offered as incentives. Until 1940 metal lids were used, but during the war when the government restricted the supply of available aluminum, glass lids were introduced. The cookware was very versatile, and one of their selling points was top-of-the-stove baking and roasting — 'no need to light the oven.' Many items had more than one use. For instance, their large turkey roaster came with racks and could be used for canning as well. The kettle oven used for stovetop baking also came with canning racks. Their Economy Trio set featured three triangular roasters that fit together on a round tray, making it possible to cook three foods at once on only one burner; for even further fuel economy, the casserole tureen could be stacked on top of that. Projections on the sides of the pans accommodated two styles of handles, a standard detachable utility handle as well as black 'mouse ear' handles for serving.

The company's logo is a knight with crossed weapons, and if you find a piece with a trademark that includes the words 'Patent Pending,' you'll know you have one of the earlier pieces.

In 1955 National Presto purchased the company and tried to convince housewives that the new stainless steel pans were superior to their tried-and-true Guardian aluminum, but the ladies would have none of it. In 1980 Tad and Suzie Kohara bought the rights to the Guardian Service name as well as the original molds. The new company is based in California, and is presently producing eight of the original pieces, canning racks, pressure cooker parts, serving handles, and replacement glass lids. Quoting their literature: 'Due to the age of the GS glass molds, we are unable to provide perfect glass covers. The covers may appear to have cracks or breaks on the surface. They are not breaks but mold marks and should be as durable as the originals.' They go on to say: 'These glass covers are not oven proof.' These mold marks may be a good way to distinguish the old glass lids from the new, and collectors tell us that the original lids have a green hue to the glass. The new company has also reproduced three cookbooks, one that shows the line with the original metal covers. If you want to obtain replacements, see the Directory for Guardian Service Cookware.

Be sure to judge condition when evaluating Guardian Service. Wear, baked-on grease, scratches, and obvious signs of use devaluate its worth. Our prices range from pieces in average to exceptional condition. To be graded exceptional, the interior of the pan must have no pitting and the surface must be bright and clean. An item with a metal lid is worth approximately 25% more than the same piece with a glass lid. To most successfully clean your grungy garage-sale finds, put them in a self-cleaning oven, then wash them in soap and water. Never touch them with anything but a perfectly clean hotpad while they're hot, and make sure they're completely cooled before you put them in water. Abrasive cleansers only scratch the surface.

Advisor: Dennis S. McAdams (See the Directory, Guardian Service Cookware)

Ashtray, glass, w/knight & white stars logo, hostess gift, from $10 to **$15.00**
Bacon fryer, rectangular, 9x13", w/bacon press, from $165 to...**$175.00**
Beverage urn, w/lid (no screen or dripper), common, from $15 to.. **$20.00**
Beverage urn (coffeepot), glass lid, complete w/screen & dripper, 15", from $50 to..**$60.00**
Can of cleaner, unopened..**$15.00**
Casserole, all glass, Alumiglass Ovenware, w/lid, very rare, 3½x8" dia..**$550.00**
Casserole tureen, bottom half, glass lid, 4½x9¾", from $40 to....**$65.00**
Casserole tureen, top half, glass lid, 3⅝x9¾", from $30 to...**$45.00**
Coasters, glass w/knight logo, 6 in upright metal carrier......**$35.00**
Condiment bowl, glass lid, Deco handles, 1 from condiment set, from $40 to **$50.00**
Condiment set, 3 glass-lidded containers in 3-legged wire frame w/ wood knob finial, from $175 to...............................**$225.00**
Cookbook, Century Metal Crafts, 1st edition, metal lids shown.. **$35.00**
Cookbooks, Guardian Ware, metal lids shown, intact, 72 pages, 5½x8½", ea from $25 to...**$35.00**
Dome cooker, Tom Thumb, glass lid, w/handles, 3½x4⅞" dia, from $25 to...**$30.00**
Dome cooker, 1-qt, glass lid, w/handles, 6¾" dia, from $30 to...**$40.00**
Dome cooker, 1-qt, metal lid, w/handles, 6¾" dia, from $45 to.**$50.00**
Dome cooker, 2-qt, glass lid, w/handles, 4½x10½" dia, from $45 to...**$50.00**
Dome cooker, 4-qt, glass lid, w/handles, 6½x10½" dia, from $50 to...**$55.00**
Double boiler, 2 pcs w/handles, glass lid, 12x9¾" overall.....**$75.00**
Fryer, breakfast; glass lid, 10", from $35 to **$50.00**
Fryer, chicken; glass lid, 12", from $60 to............................**$80.00**
Gravy boat, w/undertray, from $25 to....................................**$40.00**
Griddle broiler, octagonal, w/handles, polished center, 16½" dia, from $35 to **$40.00**
Griddle/tray, w/handles, 12½" dia cooking area, 17" wide, from $20 to...**$30.00**
Handle, clamp-on style, from $15 to **$20.00**
Handles, slip-on style, Bakelite, pr from $20 to **$30.00**
Ice bucket, glass lid, liner & tongs, 9", from $50 to............**$60.00**
Ice bucket (silver-tone) & 8 glasses (w/knight & shield), in chrome stand, hostess gift **$75.00**
Kettle oven, glass lid, bail handle, no rack, 8x12" dia, from $85 to **$100.00**
Kettle oven, glass lid, bail handle, w/rack, 6-qt, 11" dia, from $150 to **$185.00**

Kettle oven, glass lid, bail handle, w/rack, 8x12" dia, from $100 to **$125.00**
Lid, glass, triangular, from $20 to **$35.00**
Lid, glass, 7" dia, from $15 to..**$18.00**
Lid, glass, 8½" dia, from $18 to...**$25.00**
Lid, glass, 10" dia, from $30 to..**$35.00**
Lid, glass, 11" dia, DO-241X, from $70 to **$90.00**
Lid, glass, 12" dia, from $70 to..**$95.00**
Omelet pan, hinged in center, black handle on ea half, from $60 to **$75.00**
Pitcher, metal, bulb jug w/recessed disk in ea side, hostess gift, 8x10", minimum value **$275.00**

Pot, triangular, with glass lid, 7" to top of finial, 11" long, from $25.00 to $35.00.

Pot, triangular, w/metal lid, 7" to top of finial, 11" L, from $50 to **$55.00**
Potato ricer, w/wood pestle, complete, 11", from $100 to..**$125.00**
Pressure cooker, minimum value **$100.00**
Roaster, metal lid, 4x12½" L, from $60 to..........................**$80.00**
Roaster, turkey; glass lid, no rack, 16½" L, from $100 to .**$125.00**
Roaster, turkey; glass lid, 4x15" L, from $90 to **$120.00**
Roaster, turkey; metal lid, w/rack, 16½" L, from $150 to ..**$185.00**
Salt & pepper shakers, Dutch boy & girl figures, hostess gift, pr from $50 to **$60.00**
Salt & pepper shakers, metal, chef figures, hostess gift, 3½", pr from $40 to **$50.00**
Service kit, w/3 cleaners, 1 brush, 1 cookbook, 1 clamp-on handle, pr of slip-on handles, steel wool, from $125 to...........**$150.00**
Steak servers, well & tree bottom, oval, set of 4 ....**$60.00**
Travel bar, 4 aluminum tumblers, tray, 2 jiggers & stirrer in fitted carrying case...**$85.00**
Tray, serving; hammered center, w/handles, 13" dia, from $20 to..**$30.00**
Tray, serving; hammered center, w/handles, 15" dia, from $25 to..**$35.00**
Tray/platter, w/handles, hammered surface, also used as roaster cover for stacking, 10x15" L, from $25 to **$35.00**
Trivet, expanding, chrome plated, adjusts from 10⅜" L to 13½x8"...**$80.00**
Trivet, for Economy Trio set, 11¾" dia, from $35 to **$45.00**

Tumblers, glassware, stylized knight & shield in silver, & coasters w/ embossed head of knight, 4 of ea in metal rack............ **$80.00**

Tumblers & ashtray/coasters, glassware w/Guardian logo, white stars & gold trim, hostess gift, 6 of ea, from $275 to.........**$325.00**

Gurley Candle Company

Gurley candles were cute little wax figures designed to celebrate holidays and special occasions. They are all marked Gurley on the bottom. They were made so well and had so much great detail that people decided to keep them year after year to decorate with instead of burning them. Woolworth's and other five-and-dime stores sold them from about 1940 until the 1970s. They're still plentiful today and inexpensive.

Tavern Novelty Candles were actually owned by Gurley. They were similar to the Gurley candles but not quite as detailed. All are marked Tavern on the bottom. Prices listed here are for unburned candles with no fading.

Buyers should note that some of these candles are being reproduced. The Vermont Country Store Fall 2006 catalog has several Halloween, Thanksgiving, and Christmas candles. The listing describes them as reproductions of the 1950s. The candles pictured are witch, ghost, jack-o'-lantern, Indians (two sizes), Pilgrims (two sizes), turkey, angel, Santa, choir boy, and choir girl. At this time it is unknown if these new items are marked.

Advisor: Debbie Coe (See Directory, Cape Cod)

Christmas, snowman, 5x3", $12.00.

Christmas, A Night Before Christmas, boy & girl (2¾") w/sm dog & fireplace (3¼x5"), MIB..**$215.00**

Christmas, angel girl praying, blond hair, blue wings, 3" **$30.00**

Christmas, angel looking down on baby Jesus in manger, star shining above, 6" **$27.50**

Christmas, angel w/gold glitter, 4¾", pr...........................**$15.00**

Christmas, caroler man (Black) w/red clothes, 3"...............**$9.50**

Christmas, caroler man w/red clothes, 7"............................**$8.50**

Christmas, choir boy, maroon, 7", pr.................................**$24.00**

Christmas, choir boy or girl (Black), 2¾", pr **$20.00**

Christmas, evergreen tree, 3¼"...**$6.00**

Christmas, lamppost, 12½", EXIB.....................................**$16.00**

Christmas, man playing violin, lady caroler & street lamp, on starry cardboard scene...**$12.50**

Christmas, Nativity, 2½" Mary, 3" Joseph, 2" Baby Jesus, 2½" lambs & 3½" star, MIP...**$35.00**

Christmas, Rudolph w/red nose, 3" **$3.50**

Christmas, Santa Claus boots, red, 1940s, 3"......................**$6.50**

Christmas, Santa's head (hollow), candle behind lights face..**$20.00**

Christmas, Santa standing, 7½" **$15.00**

Christmas, scenic candle w/lg tree towering at left of snowy scene w/ evergreens & cottage on snow base, MIB.....**$45.00**

Christmas, snowman running w/red hat, 3"..........................**$7.50**

Christmas, snowman w/red pipe & green hat, 5".................**$6.00**

Christmas, spiral candle on pine cone, red & green w/gold glitter, 4"..**$8.00**

Christmas, white church w/choirboy inside, 6"..................**$14.50**

Easter, birdhouse, pink w/yellow bird, 3"............................**$7.50**

Easter, calla lilies, MIB..**$35.00**

Easter, chick, pink or yellow, 3" **$6.00**

Easter, cross, pink on green grassy base, angel & rabbit at foot, 3" **$25.00**

Easter, cross w/lilies on pastel stained-glass window, angel & lamb at base, 5½" **$30.00**

Easter, duck, white w/orange beak & feet, black spot on tail feathers, Socony, 2½", set of 4, MIB............................**$30.00**

Easter, duck, yellow w/purple bow, 5"................................**$9.50**

Easter, egg, pink w/squirrel inside, 3" **$12.00**

Easter, rabbit, pink, winking & holding carrot, 3¼" **$6.00**

Easter, rabbit, pink on green stump w/yellow tulips, MIB ...**$22.00**

Easter, rabbit (yellow) in green basket w/lg draping pink bow...**$25.00**

Easter, rabbit boy & girl: white w/lavender coat & hat, white w/yellow dress, lavender ear tips, 3½", 3¼", pr **$55.00**

Halloween, black cat (4") w/orange candlestick beside it **$22.50**

Halloween, Frankenstein, later issue but harder to find, 6" ..**$24.00**

Halloween, ghost, orange or white, 5", from $18 to **$20.00**

Halloween, ghost in haunted house, 6"...............................**$45.00**

Halloween, ghost w/trick-or-treat bag, 6", MIB..................**$24.00**

Halloween, jack-o'-lantern man, green outfit, brown hat, painted features, 1960s, 3", pr...**$15.00**

Halloween, jack-o'-lantern, orange w/green stem, round eyes & mouth, triangular nose, 3⅜" **$17.50**

Halloween, jack-o'-lantern, orange w/green stem, w/smiling mouth, 3⅝"..**$24.00**

Halloween, owl, black on orange stump, 3½" **$10.00**

Halloween, pumpkin-face scarecrow, 5"..............................**$14.00**

Halloween, skeleton, 8½"...**$45.00**

Halloween, skull, pink w/black, 7" **$28.00**

Halloween, witch, black, 8" **$22.50**

Halloween, witch holding jack-o'-lantern, broom at side, orange & black, 8¾"...**$25.00**

Halloween, witch in cauldron, 6".......................................**$28.00**

Halloween, witch w/black cape, 3½".....................................**$9.50**

Halloween, 4" cut-out orange owl w/7½" black candle behind it ..**$24.00**

Other holidays, birthday boy, marked Tavern, 3" **$5.00**

Other holidays, birthday tugboats, red & blue, set of 4, MIP..**$25.00**

Other holidays, bride & groom, 4½", ea..................**$12.50**
Other holidays, Eskimo & igloo, marked Tavern, 2-pc **$12.50**
Other holidays, St Patrick's Day elf, light green, 1950s, 3½" ..**$24.00**
Other holidays, Western girl or boy, 3", ea..........................**$8.00**
Thanksgiving, acorns & leaves, 3½"...................................**$5.00**
Thanksgiving, gold sailing ship, 7½".................................**$12.50**
Thanksgiving, Indian boy & girl, brown & green clothes, 5", pr...**$24.00**
Thanksgiving, Pilgrim boy & girl, 5¼", 5½", pr..........................**$15.00**
Thanksgiving, Pilgrim girl & boy, 2½", pr.............................**$7.00**
Thanksgiving, Pilgrims (3 boys & 1 girl) & turkey, 3⅜", 3", 3¼x2",
    5-pc set, MIB...**$18.00**
Thanksgiving, sailing ship, orange & yellow-brown, 3½", from $20
    to...**$18.00**
Thanksgiving, turkey, 2½" **$2.50**
Thanksgiving, turkey, 5¾" **$10.00**
Thanksgiving, turkey, 6¼" **$12.00**

Halloween, witch's head, 5½", $24.00.

Hadley, M. A.

Since 1940, the M.A. Hadley Pottery (Louisville, Kentucky) has been producing handmade dinnerware and decorative items painted freehand in a folksy style with barnyard animals, baskets, whales, and sailing ships in a soft pastel palette of predominately blues and greens. Each piece is signed by hand with the first two initials and last name of artist-turned-potter Mary Alice Hadley, who has personally inspired each design. Some items may carry an amusing message in the bottom — for instance, 'Please Fill Me' in a canister or 'The End' in a coffee cup! Examples of this ware are beginning to turn up on the secondary market, and it's being snapped up not only by collectors who have to 'have it all' but by those who enjoy adding a decorative touch to a country-style room with only a few pieces of this unique pottery. Horses and pigs seem to be popular subject matters; unusual pieces and the older, heavier examples command the higher prices.

Advisor: Lisa Sanders (See Directory, Hadley, M.A.)

Ashtray, girl, 8"...**$15.00**
Bean pot, cow & pig, squat pitcher form w/spout, w/lid, 3-qt,
    4½"..**$35.00**
Bean pot, horse ea side, very little blue trim, Whoa! inside bottom,
    w/lid, 7x8"...**$35.00**

Bean pot, pig on front, cow on back, 6", $45.00. (Photo
courtesy Michael Sessman)

Bowl, cereal; bouquet, 5⅝", 4 for.......................................**$40.00**
Bowl, coupe cereal; cat or pig...**$10.00**
Bowl, horse, 8"..**$18.00**
Bowl, salad; farmer & wife, 11" **$32.00**
Bowl, soup; house, cow, horse & rabbit, 2x6½", 4 for........**$40.00**
Butter dish, cow, rectangular, 7¾" L **$25.00**
Butter dish, horse, rectangular, 7¾" L **$25.00**
Cake plate, birthday cake center, A Very Happy Birthday to You
    Today, 1⅜x13"..**$35.00**
Candy dish, snowman shape w/much decoration, 8½x4¼"..**$30.00**
Canister, Goodies, Please Fill Me inside, 7x6½", from $45 to..**$50.00**
Canister, pig, lg...**$50.00**
Casserole, horses, The End inside bowl, w/lid, 11" (including
    handles) **$45.00**
Casserole, pig & cow, w/lid, 7x8", from $30 to **$40.00**
Clock, house, battery-operated, metal hanger on back........**$27.50**
Creamer & sugar bowl, farmer's wife & cow, w/lids, 3½", pr ..**$30.00**
Creamer & sugar bowl, horse, w/lid..................................**$30.00**
Creamer & sugar bowl, skier, w/lid, 2⅝" **$30.00**
Cup & saucer, duck, the End inside, 3x4", 6" **$10.00**
Cup & saucer, pear & grape..**$10.00**
Egg cups, farmer & wife, footed, 4½", pr **$20.00**
Fountain, oval face & bowl, wall mount **$1,200.00**
Honey pot, Sweet to the Sweet, bees, w/lid, 4½" **$20.00**
Hors d'oeuvres, house in center of 7" attached bowl, 15" dia ..**$65.00**
Jar, Cigarettes, w/peaked lid, 6" **$30.00**
Jar, Utensils, flower on back, 5x5"..................................**$25.00**
Ladle, punch bowl..**$25.00**
Mug, cowboy, 4½" **$15.00**
Mug, skier, 4" **$15.00**
Pet dish, Dog & 2 bones, 4x6½".......................................**$20.00**
Pet dish, Kitty, 1½x4¼" **$20.00**
Pie plate, lamb, 9½" **$35.00**

Piggy bank, flowers allover, 4½x9x5" $50.00
Pitcher, bird & flower, light blue vertical stripes, 6¼" $32.00
Pitcher, bouquet, 6¼" $32.00
Pitcher, frog, 2½-qt $35.00
Pitcher, head form, 7" $35.00
Pitcher, pig, 2-qt $40.00
Plate, cow, 9" $12.00
Plate, farmer's wife, 11" $18.00

Pitcher, horse, 5¼", $25.00. (Photo courtesy Michael Sessman)

Plate, house, 7½", 4 for.. $40.00
Plate, house, 8¾", 4 for.. $48.00
Plate, sailing ship, 11" $18.00
Platter, bouquet, 15" dia $30.00
Platter, farmer & wife, 12" dia... $30.00
Platter, farmer & wife, 17x11¼" $40.00
Platter, sailboat, 9x5" $30.00
Platter, sailboat, 19x12" $60.00
Punch bowl, farmer & wife, 6½x15", w/stand, no ladle..... $125.00
Sculpture, bird, mottled brown, 4¼x7", pr $38.00
Sculpture, snowman w/hat & broom, 6" $27.50
Sugar bowl, skier, w/lid, 2⅝".. $10.00
Teapot, bouquet, 6-cup $26.50
Teapot, house, 6⅜" $26.50
Tray, berries, oval, 1¼x9x5¼" $25.00
Tumbler, water; farmer, wife, pig & sheep, 9-oz, 5", 4 for ... $50.00
Water cooler, farmer & wife, brass spout, w/lid, 12"......... $150.00

Hagen-Renaker

This California-based company is one of the few surviving US potteries from the 1940s and 1950s. Hagen-Renaker started out in 1945 in a garage in Culver City, California. In 1946 they moved to Monrovia, California, where they made mostly dishes with hand-painted fruit and animal designs. By 1948 they started producing realistic miniature animals, which are still their bestselling line. In 1952 they introduced Designers Workshop, a line of larger, very life-like animal figurines. The company is particularly famous for their beautiful horses; many of their molds were leased to Breyer, who used them to make their famous plastic horses. In the late 1950s, Hagen-Renaker made gorgeous Disney figurines. Walt Disney was particularly impressed with these pieces, saying that Hagen-Renaker made the finest three-dimensional figurines he had ever seen.

In the late 1950s and early 1960s, Hagen-Renaker produced several new lines in an attempt to compete with cheaply made Japanese imports. Some of the lines they produced during that time were Millesan Drews Pixies, Rock Wall Plaques and Trays decorated with primitive animals similar to cave drawings, a grotesque miniature line called Little Horribles, and Black Bisque animals. They also experimented with cold paint called Aurasperse. This paint was used on miniature animals and a rare group of larger whimsical animals called Zany Zoo. Generally, Aurasperse-painted pieces are more valuable than normally fired items because they were made for such a short time, and the Aurasperse paint tends to wash off. Even with these new lines, the company was forced to shut down for a few months. Shortly after reopening, they moved to San Dimas, California, where they are still operating today.

From 1980 to 1986, Hagen-Renaker operated a second factory that specialized in the larger Designers Workshop figurines. Located in San Marcos, California, it had previously been Freeman-McFarlin. Hagen-Renaker added new designs and colors, but continued to make the Freeman-McFarlin line as well. In some cases it is impossible to tell which of the two companies made a particular piece. Hagen-Renaker also resurrected figurines from its Designers Workshop line of the '50s and '60s. These San Marcos-era pieces are becoming quite desirable, particularly the horses.

In the late '80s Hagen-Renaker introduced new Stoneware and Speciality lines which are generally larger than the miniatures and smaller than the Designer Workshop pieces. The Stoneware line was quickly discontinued, but they still make the Specialty pieces. The current Hagen-Renaker line consists of 50 Specialty pieces and 200 miniatures. In addition, they intermittently release limited edition larger horses. Some are new molds, while others are reissues of the Designers Workshop line. There are currently five of these larger horses available in various colors with more to come. Some of these Designers Workshop horses are only available through the Hagen-Renaker Collector's Club. For more information visit the Hagen-Renaker Online Museum.

Advisors: Ed and Sheri Alcorn (See Directory, Hagen-Renaker)

Newsletter: *The Hagen-Renaker Collector's Club Newsletter*
c/o Debra Kerr
2055 Hammock Moss Drive
Orlando, FL 32820

Bell, duck design, 1946-49, 2½" $75.00
Black Bisque poodle standing, blue-green enamel on black bisque, 1959, 5".. $80.00
Black Bisque quail, white on black bisque, 1959, 3¼" $100.00
Designer's Workshop figurine, Amir, Arab stallion, white, 1959-74, sm, 6" $225.00
Designer's Workshop figurine, Bedouin on horse, 1956-58, 9½", ... $1,200.00
Designer's Workshop figurine, Blue Boy, Weimeraner, 1957-68, 5" $100.00

Designer's Workshop figurine, Canada goose, 1986, 7½".. **$200.00**

Designer's Workshop figurine, Champ, boxer pup crouching, 1956-62, 1½"...**$35.00**

Designer's Workshop figurine, chick seated, yellow, 1961-86, 1⅝".. **$25.00**

Designer's Workshop figurine, chipmunk papa, 1952-53, 2".. **$35.00**

Designer's Workshop figurine, cougar lying, 1957-68, 5x9" ..**$250.00**

Designer's Workshop figurine, Gretchen, goat doe, 1955-67, 4½"...**$125.00**

Designer's Workshop figurine, Herman, German shepherd, 1960-69, 4"..**$85.00**

Designer's Workshop figurine, Kelso, famous racehorse, 196-574, 6½"...**$400.00**

Designer's Workshop figurine, kitten seated, looking up, #133, 1981-86, 4"..**$15.00**

Designer's Workshop figurine, pheasant resting, 1985-86, 4x13"...**$60.00**

Designer's Workshop figurine, Roland, Boston terrier standing, 1955, 4¼"..**$200.00**

Designer's Workshop figurine, Sheba, Arabian mare, white, 1958-70, 7"...**$500.00**

Designer's Workshop figurine, Sherlock, Basset hound seated, 1960-69, 3½"..**$50.00**

Designer's Workshop figurine, Silver, Persian cat, lg version, 1958-81, 12¼"...**$300.00**

Designer's Workshop figurine, Silver, Persian cat, sm version, 1958-68, 9½"..**$75.00**

Designer's Workshop figurine, Son John, lamb, 1955-86, 2¾" ...**$25.00**

Designer's Workshop figurine, Vizsla, 1972, 3"...................**$90.00**

Disney, Dumbo bank, 1956, 5¾" **$300.00**

Disney miniature, Bambi w/butterfly, 1956-60.................**$135.00**

Disney miniature, Cinderella, 1956-57, 2¾"......................**$150.00**

Disney miniature, Jock from Lady & Tramp, 1955-59, 1½" ..**$40.00**

Disney miniature, March Hare from Alice in Wonderland, 1956, 1½"..**$300.00**

Disney miniature, Mickey Mouse bandleader, 1956, 1¾"..**$100.00**

Disney miniature, Unicorn from Fantasia, 1957-58, 2¾" ..**$150.00**

Iris plaque, #651, 1946-49, 4x5" **$35.00**

Little Horribles miniature, Big Foot, 1958, 2¼" **$50.00**

Little Horribles miniature, Coronet Player, 1959, 1⅝" **$150.00**

Little Horribles miniature, High Jumper, 1958, 1½" **$60.00**

Little Horribles miniature, octopus, 1958-59, 1¼" **$80.00**

Miniature, alligator mama, #A-852, 1985-88,⅝" **$15.00**

Miniature, anteater, #A-069, 1966 only, rare, 1¾" **$200.00**

Miniature, Arabian foal standing, white, #A-048, 1959-73, 2" ...**$45.00**

Miniature, Bantie (Bantam) hen, #A-3242, 1997-2000, 1⅝"..**$8.00**

Miniature, Belgian horse, chestnut, #A-3296, 1999-2001, 2½"..**$20.00**

Miniature, bluebird on wire legs, #A-2028, 1988-89, 1½"...**$20.00**

Miniature, boxer puppy w/taped ears, #A-284, 1956-76, 1" .**$10.00**

Miniature, camel w/fez, #A-281, 1950s, 1⅝".....................**$25.00**

Miniature, cat sleeping, gray, #A-313, 1994-99, 1"............**$10.00**

Miniature, cat sucking thumb, tabby or Siamese, #A-367, 1958-87, 1½"..**$20.00**

Miniature, caterpillar papa, w/pipe in mouth, #A-252, 1955-88, 1¼"...**$15.00**

Miniature, collie standing, #A-359, 1957-96, 1½"..............**$10.00**

Miniature, Corgi, #A-3305, 1999 to currrent, 1⅝"............**$7.00**

Miniature, crow baby, 1959-76, ½" **$10.00**

Miniature, donkey walking, #A-22, 1965-81 ....**$20.00**

Miniature, eagle, wings spread, 1983-84, 2" **$10.00**

Miniature, goat doe, brown, #A-3119, 1994-97, 1¾" **$15.00**

Miniature, Hereford calf, #A-291, 1957-65, 1"....................**$25.00**

Miniature, jaguar, 1991-93, #A-2096, 1"............................**$30.00**

Miniature, lamb, ear out, #A-35, early, 1949-51, 1⅝" **$20.00**

Miniature, Lipizzaner on base, Capriole, #A-3169, 1995-97 ..**$30.00**

Miniature, macaw on hoop, #A-2007, 1988-90, 3¼" **$30.00**

Miniature, manatee, #A-3186, 1995-97, ⅞" **$20.00**

Miniature, Mother Goose, flowers on neck, 1958 only, 2"...**$65.00**

Miniature, Old English sheepdog, recumbent, 1993-95, ⅝"..**$15.00**

Miniature, Percheron, white, #A-459, 1959-66, 2¾" **$125.00**

Miniature, puppy seated, #A-12, early, 1949, 1½" **$45.00**

Miniature, Siamese kitten running, #A-057, 1959-70s, 1"..**$15.00**

Miniature, Siamese kitten w/scratching post, 1993 to current, 1⅝" **$5.00**

Miniature, Ski Bears, 1987 – 1988, 2", $15.00 each. (Photo courtesy Ed and Sheri Alcorn)

Miniature, yearling, head up, buckskin, #A-362, 1958-68, 2" ..**$100.00**

Miniature, zebra mama w/head turned, #A-173, 1983-86, 1½" .**$35.00**

Pig toothpick holder, blue w/flowers, rare, 1945-46, 1" **$150.00**

Specialty figurine, angelfish, 1989-91, 2½" **$40.00**

Specialty figurine, Canada goose w/head up, 1989, 1½" **$25.00**

Specialty figurine, fox baby w/thermos, 2000-03, 3"............**$25.00**

Specialty figurine, Grooming Horses on base, 2000 to current, 3" **$20.00**

Specialty figurine, hummingbird on flower, 1988-2001, 3⅛" ..**$35.00**

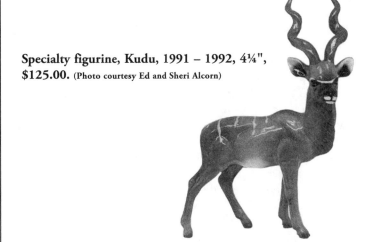

Specialty figurine, Kudu, 1991 – 1992, 4¼", $125.00. (Photo courtesy Ed and Sheri Alcorn)

Specialty figurine, nativity camel, 1st version, 1991-92, 2¾" ..**$50.00**

Specialty figurine, racehorse w/jockey, 1999 to currrent, 4½" ..**$36.00**

Wall plaque, Pompano, 1959-60, 12½x7¾" $100.00
Wall plaque, toucan facing right, 1960, rare, 12x15" $250.00
Zany Zoo yak, Aurasperse finish, 1960 only, 2" $350.00

Hall China Company

Hall China is still in production in East Liverpool, Ohio, where they have been located since around the turn of the century. They have produced literally hundreds of lines of kitchen and dinnerware items for both home and commercial use. Many of these have become very collectible.

They're especially famous for their teapots, some of which were shaped like automobiles, basketballs, doughnuts, etc. Each teapot was made in an assortment of colors, often trimmed in gold. Many were decaled to match their dinnerware lines. Some are quite rare, and collecting them all would be a real challenge.

During the 1950s, Eva Zeisel designed dinnerware shapes with a streamlined, ultra-modern look. Her lines, Classic and Century, were used with various decals as the basis for several of Hall's dinnerware patterns. She also designed kitchenware lines with the same modern styling. They were called Casual Living and Tri-Tone. All her designs are very popular with today's collectors, especially those with an interest in the movement referred to as ''50s modern.'

Although some of the old kitchenware shapes and teapots are being produced today, you'll be able to tell them from the old pieces by the backstamp. To identify these new issues, Hall marks them with the shaped rectangular 'Hall' trademark they've used since the early 1970s.

For more information we recommend *Collector's Encyclopedia of Hall China, Third Edition*, by Margaret and Kenn Whitmyer (Collector Books).

Club/Newsletter: *Hall China Collector's Club newsletter*
P.O. Box 360488, Cleveland, OH 44136

Blue Blossom, baker, rectangular, from $225 to $250.00
Blue Blossom, custard, Thick Rim, from $25 to $28.00
Blue Blossom, syrup, Sundial, from $195 to $225.00
Blue Bouquet, ball jug, #3, from $150 to $170.00
Blue Bouquet, canister, metal, 6" dia, from $20 to $25.00
Blue Bouquet, cup, from $18 to $20.00
Blue Bouquet, plate, 9", from $18 to $22.00
Cactus, batter bowl, Five Band, from $95 to.....................$125.00
Cactus, creamer, New York, from $30 to $35.00
Cactus, sugar bowl, Viking, w/lid, from $40 to $50.00
Cameo Rose, bowl, vegetable; 9", from $20 to $25.00
Cameo Rose, gravy boat & underplate, from $30 to............$35.00
Cameo Rose, platter, 15½" L, from $25 to $30.00
Century Fern, bowl, divided vegetable; from $30 to $35.00
Century Fern, jug, from $30 to.......................................$35.00
Century Fern, ladle, from $18 to $22.00
Century Fern, sugar bowl, w/lid, from $18 to....................$22.00
Christmas Tree, mug, AD coffee; 3-oz, from $40 to $45.00
Christmas Tree, plate, 10", from $35 to $45.00
Christmas Tree, tidbit, 2-tier, from $100 to $125.00

Coffeepot, drip; Jordan shape, from $250 to.....................$300.00
Coffeepot, drip; Medallion, solid color, from $250 to........$300.00
Coffeepot, drip; solid color, #691, from $200 to $220.00
Coffeepot (percolator), Bouquet, from $150 to..................$165.00
Coffeepot (percolator), Seal of Ohio, from $80 to $90.00
Crocus, bowl, fruit; 5½", from $9 to $11.00
Crocus, bowl, Radiance, 9", from $35 to $40.00
Crocus, creamer, New York, from $20 to $22.00
Crocus, leftover, rectangular, from $65 to $95.00
Crocus, plate, 7¼", from $9 to $12.00

Crocus, pretzel jar, from $180.00 to $200.00.

Crocus, soap dispenser, from $110 to $135.00
Crocus, tidbit, 3-tier, from $90 to...................................$100.00
Game Bird, ball jug, #3, from $250 to..............................$300.00
Game Bird, bowl, oval, from $55 to $65.00
Game Bird, casserole, round, #65, 16-oz, from $30 to........$40.00
Game Bird, plate, 10", from $70 to $80.00
Game Bird, sugar bowl, New York, w/lid, from $45 to........$55.00
Heather Rose, bowl, salad; 9", from $16 to.......................$18.00
Heather Rose, creamer, from $9 to...................................$11.00
Heather Rose, teapot, London, from $25 to $30.00
Mums, bowl, flat soup; 8½", from $22 to..........................$25.00

Mums, coffeepot, from 100.00 to $120.00. (Photo courtesy Margaret and Kenn Whitmyer)

Hall China Company

Mums, plate, 9", from $10 to $14.00
Mums, sugar bowl, New York, w/lid, from $30 to $35.00
No 488, bean pot, New England, #3, #4, or #5, from $200 to ...$250.00
No 488, bowl, 9¼", from $50 to $60.00
No 488, casserole, Five Band, from $50 to $75.00
No 488, custard, Radiance, from $20 to......................$25.00
No 488, platter, oval, 13¼", from $50 to....................$55.00
No 488, pretzel jar, from $250 to $300.00
No 488, sugar bowl, Art Deco, w/lid, from $40 to $50.00
Orange Poppy, bowl, fruit; 5½", from $7.50 to $8.50
Orange Poppy, bowl, vegetable; 9¼", from $45 to $55.00
Orange Poppy, cake plate, from $40 to $45.00
Orange Poppy, mustard, w/liner, from $125 to................$145.00
Orange Poppy, platter, 11¼" L, from $30 to..................$35.00
Orange Poppy, teapot, Windshield, from $250 to..............$350.00
Pastel Morning Glory, bowl, 9¼", from $40 to.................$45.00
Pastel Morning Glory, creamer, Modern, from $25 to $27.00
Pastel Morning Glory, drip jar, Radiance, w/lid, from $45 to ..$50.00
Pastel Morning Glory, gravy boat, from $30 to...............$35.00
Pastel Morning Glory, plate, 8¼", from $6 to................$8.50
Pastel Morning Glory, plate, 9", from $10 to................$15.00
Pastel Morning Glory, tea tile, from $90 to.................$120.00
Red Poppy, ball jug, #3, from $110 to $130.00
Red Poppy, bowl, cereal; 5½", from $15 to...................$17.00
Red Poppy, clock, metal teapot shape, from $140 to.........$190.00
Red Poppy, creamer, Daniel, from $22 to $27.00
Red Poppy, drip jar, Radiance, w/lid, from $40 to $45.00
Red Poppy, gravy boat, from $35 to..........................$45.00
Red Poppy, salt & pepper shakers, Teardrop, pr from $36 to..$44.00
Red Poppy, sifter, from $75 to $95.00

Rose White, bowl, Medallion, 8½", $50.00. (Photo courtesy Margaret and Kenn Whitmyer)

Sears' Arlington, bowl, cereal; 6¼", from $6.50 to $7.50
Sears' Arlington, plate, 9¼", from $5 to....................$7.50
Sears' Arlington, platter, 13¼" L, from $18 to..............$22.00
Sears' Monticello, bowl, cream soup; 5", from $80 to.........$90.00
Sears' Monticello, creamer, from $8 to......................$10.00
Sears' Monticello, plate, 6½", from $3 to...................$6.00
Sears' Monticello, platter, 15½" L, from $25 to.............$30.00
Sears' Richmond/Brown-Eyed Susan, bowl, Thick Rim, 8½", from $15 to $18.00
Sears' Richmond/Brown-Eyed Susan, bowl, vegetable; 9", from $22 to $25.00

Sears' Richmond/Brown-Eyed Susan, gravy boat & underplate, from $25 to $30.00
Sears' Richmond/Brown-Eyed Susan, plate, 10", from $7 to..$9.00
Serenade, baker, French; fluted, from $18 to................$20.00
Serenade, bowl, Radiance, 9", from $18 to $20.00
Serenade, cup & saucer, from $9 to $11.00
Serenade, pie baker, from $40 to............................$45.00
Silhouette, bowl, fruit; 5½", from $6.50 to.................$8.00
Silhouette, bowl, salad; 9", from $16 to....................$18.00
Silhouette, bowl, vegetable; 9¼", from $32 to...............$35.00
Silhouette, coffeepot, Five Band, w/glass dripper, from $100 to...$120.00
Silhouette, double boiler, enamel, from $65 to $75.00

Silhouette, platter, 11¼" long, from $18.00 to $22.00.
(Photo courtesy Margaret and Kenn Whitmyer)

Silhouette, salt & pepper shakers, Teardrop, pr from $40 to...$50.00
Silhouette, soap dispenser, from $45 to.....................$55.00
Teapot, Adele, blue, from Deco series, from $200 to $250.00
Teapot, Aladdin, Camellia, standard gold, from $80 to........$90.00
Teapot, Aladdin, silver lustre, from $185 to................$200.00
Teapot, Albany, black w/standard gold, from $50 to..........$60.00
Teapot, Albany, mahogany, w/standard gold, from $45 to ...$55.00
Teapot, Automobile, Dresden, from $400 to $450.00
Teapot, Baltimore, Emerald, from $65 to.....................$75.00
Teapot, Basket, Citrus, from $300 to........................$325.00
Teapot, Boston, Cadet, sm, from $30 to $45.00
Teapot, Boston, Canary, w/standard gold, lg, from $50 to...$55.00
Teapot, Boston, Warm Yellow, w/standard gold, sm, from $45 to $55.00
Teapot, Globe, Camellia, from $50 to........................$60.00
Teapot, Hollywood, stock brown or green, from $30 to.......$40.00
Teapot, Hook Cover, Chinese Red, from $200 to..............$225.00
Teapot, Hook Cover, turquoise, w/standard gold, from $75 to...$85.00
Teapot, Ivory, w/standard gold, from $45 to $55.00
Teapot, Los Angeles, black, w/solid gold, from $45 to $50.00
Teapot, Los Angeles, pink, from $45 to $55.00
Teapot, Marine, Melody shape, from $200 to..................$240.00
Teapot, Melody, Canary, w/standard gold, from $210 to ...$230.00
Teapot, Nautilus, Warm Yellow, from $200 to.................$235.00
Teapot, New York, Addison, w/standard gold, from $35 to...$45.00
Teapot, New York, Chartreuse, from $27 to...................$32.00

Teapot, New York, Emerald, from $40 to $45.00
Teapot, Parade, Warm Yellow, from $60 to $70.00
Teapot, Philadelphia, Blue Willow pattern, from $400 to..$500.00
Teapot, Philadelphia, Delphinium, w/standard gold, from $40 to..$45.00
Teapot, Rose, w/standard gold, from $75 to $85.00
Teapot, Sundial, Marine, from $75 to..................................$85.00
Tomorrow's Classic Arizona, coffeepot, 6-cup, from $90 to..$110.00
Tomorrow's Classic Arizona, plate, 11", from $11 to $13.00
Tomorrow's Classic Arizona, vinegar bottle, from $80 to $85.00
Tomorrow's Classic Bouquet, bowl, cereal; 6", from $10 to .$12.00
Tomorrow's Classic Bouquet, creamer, from $13 to $15.00
Tomorrow's Classic Bouquet, egg cup, from $55 to $60.00
Tomorrow's Classic Bouquet, vase, from $80 to....................$95.00

Tomorrow's Classic Caprice by Eva Zeisel: Plate, dinner; $5.00; Bowl, 9", $10.00; Cup and saucer, $8.00.

Tomorrow's Classic Fantasy, ashtray, from $7 to.....................$9.00
Tomorrow's Classic Fantasy, candlestick, 8", ea from $40 to...$45.00
Tomorrow's Classic Fantasy, platter, 17" L, from $34 to $38.00
Tomorrow's Classic Holiday, bowl, fruit; 5¾", from $8 to ...$10.00
Tomorrow's Classic Holiday, butter dish, from $180 to $210.00
Tomorrow's Classic Holiday, marmite & lid, from $35 to....$40.00
Tomorrow's Classic Holiday, teapot, 6-cup, from $195 to..$225.00
Tomorrow's Classic Peach Blossom, bowl, cereal; 6", from $8 to ..$10.00
Tomorrow's Classic Peach Blossom, butter dish, from $140 to ...$18.00
Tomorrow's Classic Peach Blossom, casserole, 2-qt, from $45 to.$50.00
Tomorrow's Classic Peach Blossom, onion soup, w/lid, from $35 to $37.00
Tulip, bowl, oval, from $32 to $37.00
Tulip, bowl, Thick Rim, 6", from $16 to $18.00
Tulip, casserole, Thick Rim, from $40 to $45.00
Tulip, creamer, Modern, from $18 to...................................$22.00
Tulip, plate, 9", from $11 to $13.00
Tulip, platter, 13¼" L, from $30 to.....................................$35.00
Wildfire, bowl, flat soup; 8½", from $16 to $18.00
Wildfire, bowl, straight sides, 6", from $16 to $18.00
Wildfire, coffeepot, glass dripper, S lid, from $95 to..........$125.00
Wildfire, plate, 9", from $10 to $12.00

Wildfire, teapot, Streamline, from $500 to $600.00
Yellow Rose, coffeepot, Norse, from $75 to $85.00
Yellow Rose, cup & saucer, from $9.50 to............................$12.00
Yellow Rose, platter, 13¼" L, from $30 to $35.00

Hallmark

Since the early 1970s when Hallmark first introduced their glass ball and yarn doll ornaments, many lines and themes have been developed to the delight of collectors. Many early ornaments are now valued at several times their original price. This is especially true of the first one issued in a particular series.

Antique Toy series, Toy Carousel, twirl-about motion, 1st in series, 1978, MIB..$50.00
Baby's First Christmas, satin ball, 1st in series, 1976, MIB ...$185.00
Beatles, group on white stage, 1994, 5-pc gift set, MIB.......$95.00
Classic American Cars, 1957 Corvette, 1st in series, MIB....$60.00

Frosty Friends, first in series, 1980, MIB, from $350.00 to $375.00.

Frosty Friends, Eskimo child & seal pup on ice floe, 1983, MIB, 4th in series, MIB...$150.00
Frosty Friends, Eskimo child and Husky pup in igloo, 2nd in series, 1981, M...$175.00
Frosty Friends, Eskimo child clinging to base of bicycle, 3rd in series, 1982, MIB..$140.00
Here Comes Santa, Santa's Big Rig, 25th (final) in series, 2003, MIB...$60.00
Here Comes Santa, Santa's Express, 2nd in series, 1980, MIB ..$60.00
Here Comes Santa, Santa's Express, 5th in series, 1983, MIB ...$110.00
Here Comes Santa, Santa's Motorcar, 1st in series, 1979, MIB, from $150 to...$195.00
Lighthouse Greetings, Mr & Mrs Claus decorating tree inside, 1st in series, 1997, MIB...$50.00
Lighthouse Greetings, 9th in series, 2005, MIB..................$35.00
Mary's Angels, Bluebell, 2nd in series, 1989, MIB.............$100.00
Mary's Angels, Buttercup, 1st in series, MIB......................$125.00

240

Mary's Angels, Rosebud, 3rd in series, 1990, MIB **$80.00**
Nostalgic Houses, Candy Shoppe, 3rd in series, 1986, MIB, from $65 to **$70.00**
Nostalgic Houses, Victorian house, 1st in series, 1984, M ... **$60.00**
Raggedy Ann, 1975, MIB **$70.00**
Rockin' w/Santa, record player, comes w/3 records, 2005, MIB.. **$75.00**
Rocking Horse, black w/red rockers, 2nd in series, 1982, MIB, from $100 to **$135.00**
Rocking Horse, cream w/red rockers, 1st in series, 1981, MIB, from $265 to **$300.00**
Rocking Horse, red w/green rockers, 3rd in series, 1983, MIB, from $100 to **$140.00**
Santa's Favorite Stop, 1993, MIB **$85.00**
Santas From Around the World, Ireland, holding shamrock, 2004, MIB **$45.00**
Snoopy & Friends, Ice Hockey Holiday, 1st in series, 1979, MIB, from $30 to **$40.00**
Snowflake, sterling silver, Halls Ster 1981, 3x2¾", from $125 to **$165.00**
Star Trek: Starship Enterprise, magic blinking lights, 25th anniversary, 1991, MIB, from $150 to **$165.00**
Tin Locomotive, 1st in series, 1982, MIB, from $145 to... **$175.00**
Tin Locomotive, 4th in series, 1985, MIB **$35.00**
Tin Locomotive, 6th in series, 1987, MIB **$30.00**
Tree-Trimmer, Special Teacher, 1980, MIB **$15.00**
Wizard of Oz, I'm Melting! Melting!, 2004, MIB **$70.00**
Wizard of Oz, Poppy Field, changing lights & scenes in crystal ball, 2001, MIB **$50.00**
Wizard of Oz, The Great Oz, says 3 phrases, MIB **$45.00**
Wizard of Oz, wizard in State Fair balloon, 1996, MIB **$45.00**

Halloween

Halloween is now the second biggest money-making holiday of the year, and more candy is sold at this time than for any other holiday. Folk artists are making new items to satisfy the demands of collectors and celebrators that can't get enough of the old items. Over 100 years of celebrating this magical holiday has built a social history strata by strata, and wonderful and exciting finds can be made from all periods. From one dollar to thousands, there is something to excite collectors in every price range, with new collectibles being born every year. For further information we recommend *Collectible Halloween; More Halloween Collectibles; Halloween: Collectible Decorations & Games; Salem Witchcraft and Souvenirs; Postmarked Yesterday, Art of the Holiday Postcard;* and *The Tastes & Smells of Halloween*; also see *Around Swanzey* and *The Armenians of Worcester* (Arcadia). The author of these books is Pamela E. Apkarian-Russell (Halloween Queen™), a free-lancer who also writes an ephemera column for *Unravel the Gavel.*

Our values are for items in excellent to near mint condition unless noted otherwise.

Advisor: Pamela E. Apkarian-Russell (See Directory, Halloween)

Newsletter: *Trick or Treat Trader*
577 Boggs Run Rd., Benwood, WV 26031-1002

Castle Halloween Museum
halloweenqueen@cheshire.net
http://adam.net/~halloweenqueen/home.html
Subscription: $15 per year in USA ($20 foreign) for 4 issues

Bank, girl dressed as ghost & holding pumpkin, painted cast iron, 6½" **$125.00**
Candy container, devil's head, painted bisque, unmarked Japan, 2¼x2½" **$70.00**

Candy container, separates at neck, 3", EX, $250.00.
(Photo courtesy LiveAuctioneers.com/ Morphy Auctions)

Clicker, tin litho, witch, T Cohn, Made in USA, 3x2" **$30.00**
Costume, Alvin the Chipmunk, Ben Cooper, 1962, MIB.... **$55.00**
Costume, Fairy Princess, Collegeville, 1960s, MIB **$25.00**
Costume, Green Lantern, Ben Cooper, 1960s, MIB **$110.00**
Costume, Mickey Mouse, vinyl & rayon w/hard plastic mask, Ben Cooper, MIB **$25.00**
Costume, Pee Wee Herman, mid-1980s, MIB **$30.00**
Costume, skeleton, white on black cloth, fabric mask, Halco, ca 1930s, VGIB.. **$42.50**
Costume, tiger, hood for head, orange & black felt, Collegeville, NMIB.. **$30.00**
Decoration, black cat, back arched, die-cut cardboard, Made in USA, 18½x11"... **$100.00**
Decoration, black cat sitting on moon, die-cut cardboard, Dennison, USA, 12x10½", VG **$100.00**
Decoration, owl, die-cut cardboard, green eyes, moon behind him, USA, ca 1920s, 18½x12".............................. **$100.00**
Decoration, witch w/jack-o'-lantern, die-cut cardboard, pre-1950s, 23½" **$125.00**
Figurine, cat, cardboard pulp, scuffed legs & ears, 7", VG+ .. **$80.00**
Horn, litho cardboard, cats, skeletons, etc, black on red, Linn Mills Co, 6½", EX **$30.00**
Jack-o'-lantern, papier-mache, paper inserts, 1940s, 5½x6½", VG.. **$95.00**
Lantern, black cat, cardboard w/tissue inside, honeycomb sides, Made in USA, 11x3¾", VG+..................................... **$110.00**

Mask, devil, papier-maché, red & black, 1940s, EX............$52.50

Nodder, devil child in red, ceramic, Japan label, 6"..............$55.00

Noisemaker, tin litho barrel shape w/wooden handle..........$20.00

Noisemaker, tin litho dumbbell shape w/wooden handle, T Cohn $45.00

Noisemaker, tin litho rattle type w/metal handle, Germany ..$20.00

Nut cup, die-cut cardboard, jack-o'-lanterns, black cats etc, 2-sided, Beistle, ca 1940s........................$48.00

Playset, Haunted House, complete, Ideal, 1962, EX (in G box)..$225.00

Postcard, Halloween, anthropomorphic figures waving to witches on brooms, Valentine & Sons, unused $65.00

Postcard, The Adam & Eve Game, Halloween Greetings, 1930s graphics, Gibson Art Co $25.00

Sucker holder, witch on motorcycle, orange plastic w/black paint, Rosbro/Tico Toys, 1940s, 2¾x5" $75.00

Sucker holder, witch riding broom, die-cut cardboard, Rosbro, dated 1948, 4¾x3¾", M..............................$150.00

Tambourine, tin litho, witch & black cats, orange & black, Cohn, 7⅛", VG $75.00

Tambourines: Devil, Kirchhof, ca. 1950s, 6½", NM, $110.00; Great Pumpkin, Chein, 1930s, 7", NM, $325.00; Witch, 1960s, 6", $180.00. (Photo courtesy Pamela Apkarian-Russell)

Toy, witch riding bicycle, orange plastic w/black paint, green wheels, 5x7" $150.00

Tray, tin litho, black w/smiling jack-o'-lantern faces, 2x13" dia, M $15.00

Handkerchiefs

Though ladies no longer carry handkerchiefs as they did in the days before disposable tissues, these mementos of an earlier and perhaps a more genteel era are today being collected by those who find in them a certain charm. Some are delicate works of art with lace and embroidery, while others are souvenirs or represent a particular event or theme. For more information, we recommend *Handkerchiefs, A Collector's Guide, Vol. I* and *Vol. II*, by Helene Guarnaccia and Barbara Guggenheim (Collector Books).

Animal babies playing instruments along yellow border, 8x8" ..$8.00

Appliquéd tulips in white on white linen w/drawn-work hem, 14x14"...$10.00

Appliqués (delicate) in white cotton lawn w/3" scalloped net lace trim..$30.00

Autumn leaves in beautiful colors form scalloped border on white cotton, 12x12"...............................$5.00

Autumn leaves, from $10.00 to $15.00. (Photo courtesy Helene Guarnaccia and Barbara Guggenheim)

Battenburg lace edge on white linen, 10½x10½".................$65.00

Brussels lace in wide border on fine linen, 11½x11½" $195.00

Butterflies & flower border printed on white, Faith Austin, rolled pink edge, 14½x14½" $25.00

Chicken in housedress & apron among trees & flowers printed on white cotton, machine-stitched hem, 12x12"...............$15.00

Children holding balloons printed on white, red machine-stitched edge, sm..$20.00

Cowboy on bucking broncos along green border w/red fence, 1940s-50s...$15.00

Crochet (fine thread, no seams, 2½") on white linen, 14½x14½"..$25.00

Crochet lace edge (pink, 3½") on white linen, 11x11".........$12.50

Crocheted swirled flower in pink on ea corner of white linen, 11¼x12¼"..$12.00

Daisies & forget-me-nots embroidered on white Swiss cotton, 14x14" $10.00

Drawn-work geometric border on silk, 1920s, 11x11".........$24.00

Floral applique (3-dimensional) on white linen, hand-rolled hem, Madeira Portugal, 12x12" $18.00

Flower (oversize, printed) on white, bright colors, machine hemmed, 15¾x15" $20.00

Flowers & ribbons printed on white, pink border, Created by Kimball label, 12x12" $15.00

Grandma & flowers embroidered in corner, lace trim on white cotton, 11x11"..$12.00

Initial in padded satin stitch & rondels, faux pearl accents on white linen w/rolled edge, 13x13" $18.00

Jungle animals in pink & black on white w/geometric pink & black border, 1950s, 8¼x7¾".............................$10.00

Know Your Presidents, Washington to Eisenhower, Franshaw Inc NY, 1954 ....$27.50

Lace (delicate, 1") borders white lawn, early 1900s, 10½x10½" ..$12.50

Magician and horoscope cards, from $20.00 to $25.00.

(Photo courtesy Helene Guarnaccia and Barbara Guggenheim)

Mickey Mouse playing football printed on white w/multicolored leaf border, WDP, 1950s, 8x8" **$25.00**

Mixed bouquet w/pink roses on pale pink cotton w/dark pink hem, 12x12" **$5.00**

Pastel tatting on white cotton, 11½x11½" **$15.00**

Plaid border on white, Peerless, 11x11", set of 3, MIB **$8.00**

Poinsettias embroidered on white cotton, Desco, Made in Switzerland **$15.00**

Puppy w/blocks embroidered on white cotton, yellow border, 8¼x8¼" **$10.00**

Red hearts printed allover on white, lg red heart in ea corner, red scalloped edge, 12½x13½" **$25.00**

Rosebuds embroidered in ea corner on white cotton, blue crocheted edge, 12x12" **$17.50**

Roses printed on black w/gray border, scalloped edge, 12x12".. **$10.00**

Roses printed on pink cotton w/open-weave design **$65.00**

Roses w/shadow work embroidered on white, deeply scalloped, 15½x15½" **$10.00**

Santa & lg wreath, bells & bows embroidered on white, red machine-stitched scalloped edge, 12x12" **$20.00**

Saturday, couple at sock hop printed on white, 12x12" **$15.00**

Shamrocks & Dear Sister embroidered on white rayon blend.. **$15.00**

Shamrocks in green & white printed on white cotton, 12½x13" ... **$17.50**

Southern Bell crocheted in corner, crocheted border, 10½x10½".. **$8.00**

Souvenir of France, American eagle, shield & biplane embroidered on white silk, 12x12" **$65.00**

Teddy bears on a slide printed on white cotton, blue border, 1950s, 8x8" **$25.00**

To My Dear Wife Souvenir de France embroidered on white silk, ca 1912, 13x13" **$25.00**

Tulips in scattered sprays & connecting to form border on white, 13" dia... **$15.00**

Violets in center & ea corner, lavender scalloped edge, Burmel Original, 14½x14½" **$17.50**

Vs & eagles, red, white & blue print on rayon, 9½x9½"...... **$20.00**

White cotton lawn w/3 tiers of delicate lace forming edge, 8x8".. **$22.50**

1959 calendar & good luck symbols, multicolored pastels on silky material, Kreier **$65.00**

Harker Pottery

Harker was one of the oldest potteries in the country. Their history can be traced back to the 1840s. In the '30s, a new plant was built in Chester, West Virginia, and the company began manufacturing kitchen and dinnerware lines, eventually employing as many as 300 workers.

Several of these lines are popular with collectors today. One of the most easily recognized is Cameoware. It is usually found in pink or blue decorated with white silhouettes of flowers, though other designs were made as well. Colonial Lady, Red Apple, Amy, Mallow, and Pansy are some of their better-known lines that are fairly easy to find and reassemble into sets.

If you'd like to learn more about Harker, we recommend *Collector's Encyclopedia of American Dinnerware* by Jo Cunningham, published by Collector Books.

Amy, creamer **$17.50**
Amy, cup & saucer... **$12.50**
Amy, pie lifter/cake slice, 9" **$20.00**
Amy, pitcher, Hi Rise, 9¼" **$55.00**
Cameo Rose, batter jug, blue, w/lid, lg, from $40 to **$60.00**
Cameo Rose, canister, 7x6½" **$50.00**

Cameo Rose, casserole, $38.00; Jug (missing lid), $25.00.

(Photo courtesy Jo Cunningham)

Cameo Rose, pitcher, straight sides, w/lid, 8x7" **$60.00**
Cameo Rose, platter, rectangular, 12x9".............................. **$40.00**
Cameo Rose, syrup jug, blue, w/lid.................................... **$25.00**
Cameo Rose, tidbit, pink, center handle **$14.00**
Country Cottage, rolling pin... **$135.00**
Fruit (apple & pear), bowl, mixing/serving; 3¼x7" **$32.00**
Fruit (apple & pear), canister, 7" **$110.00**
Fruit (apple & pear), custard cup **$22.00**
Fruit (apple & pear), pie lifter & ice cream spoon **$37.50**
Fruit (apple & pear), pitcher, 8x7½x4½" **$55.00**
Fruit (apple & pear), rolling pin, 15" **$80.00**
Fruit (apple & pear), sugar bowl, w/lid.............................. **$60.00**
Honeymoon Cottage, drippings jar, lard, w/lid................... **$65.00**

Honeymoon Cottage, flour shaker, skyscraper shape, 4½" ...**$88.00**
Honeymoon Cottage, salad fork..**$68.00**
Honeymoon Cottage, salt & pepper shakers, pr................**$125.00**
Honeymoon Cottage, teapot, 5¾" **$90.00**
Ivy Wreath, teapot, Gadroon, 6-cup....................................**$55.00**
Mallow, bowl, cereal; 6½" **$18.00**
Mallow, casserole, au gratin; w/lid, 6½" **$65.00**
Mallow, drippings jar, Lard, w/lid **$75.00**
Mallow, rolling pin...**$75.00**
Mallow, stack set, 2 bases w/lid, 3-pc **$55.00**
Mallow, teapot, 6½x9", +hexagonal underplate, from $65 to...**$75.00**
Mallow, tureen, w/lid, 5x7½"...**$40.00**
Modern Tulip, creamer...**$20.00**
Modern Tulip, cup & saucer **$18.00**
Modern Tulip, pie plate, 9¼"...**$42.50**
Modern Tulip, plate, luncheon; 9½" **$10.00**
Monterey, rolling pin, NM **$70.00**
Oriental Poppy, flour shaker, metal top................................**$95.00**
Oriental Poppy, salt & peppers shaker, pr from $65 to **$85.00**
Petit Point, bowl, lug cereal; 6⅞" **$10.00**
Petit Point, bowl, mixing; 9⅛" **$40.00**
Petit Point, cup & saucer **$16.00**
Petit Point, cup & saucer, jumbo **$20.00**
Petit Point, pitcher, water; w/lid, 8¼x8¼"...........................**$50.00**
Petit Point, plate, 9½" **$8.50**
Petit Point, plate, 10¼"..**$14.00**

Petit Point, rolling pin, cork in end, 15" long, $50.00.
(Photo courtesy LiveAuctioneers.com/Dargate Auction Galleries)

Rocaille, creamer & sugar bowl, w/lid...................................**$45.00**
Rocaille, cup & saucer..**$12.50**
Rocaille, plate, bread & butter; 6" **$6.00**
Rocaille, plate, dinner; 10"...**$15.00**
Rockingham, mug, Daniel Boone, 4½"..................................**$35.00**
Rockingham, pitcher, hound handle, 8", from $35 to.........**$45.00**
White Clover, clock, Meadow Green, Russel Wright, General
    Electric..**$35.00**
Wild Rose, bowl, rimmed soup; 8⅜" **$10.00**
Wild Rose, plate, sq, 8½"..**$7.00**
Wild Rose, plate, 10½"...**$12.00**
Wild Rose, platter, 13½" L..**$27.50**

Hartland Plastics, Inc.

The Hartland company was located in Hartland, Wisconsin, where during the '50s and '60s they made several lines of plastic figures: Western and Historic Horsemen, Miniature Western Series, and the Hartland Sport Series of Famous Baseball Stars. Football and bowling figures and religious statues were made as well. The plastic, virgin acetate, was very durable and the figures were hand painted with careful attention to detail. They're often marked.

Though prices have come down from their high of a few years ago, rare figures and horses are still in high demand. Dealers using this guide should take these factors into consideration when pricing their items: values listed here are for the figure, horse (unless they're standing gunfighters), hat, guns, and all other accessories for that particular figure in near mint condition (unless another condition is specified) with no rubs and all original parts. All parts were made exclusively for a special figure, so a hat is not just a hat — each one belongs to a specific figure! Many people do not realize this, and it is important for the collector to be knowledgeable. An excellent source of information is *Hartland Horses and Riders* by Gail Fitch.

In our listings for sports figures, mint to near mint condition values are for figures that are white or near-white in color; excellent values are for those that are off-white or cream-colored. These values are representative of traditional retail prices asked by dealers; internet values for Hartlands, as is so often the case nowadays, seem to be in a constant state of flux. Be aware that Hartland has produced all 18 of the original figures.

See also *Schroeder's Collectible Toys, Antique to Modern* (Collector Books).

Gunfighters

Bat Masterson, NMIB..**$500.00**
Bret Maverick, NM..**$350.00**
Chris Colt, NM **$150.00**
Clay Holister, NM **$200.00**

Dan Troop, NM, from $550.00 to $600.00. (Photo courtesy LiveAuctioneers.com/Morphy Auctions)

Jim Hardy, NM..**$150.00**
Johnny McKay, NM **$800.00**
Paladin, NM **$400.00**
Vint Bonner, NMIB...**$850.00**
Wyatt Earp, NM **$150.00**

Horsemen

Alpine Ike, NM..$150.00

Annie Oakley on rearing palomino, NM, $275.00. (Photo courtesy LiveAuctioneers.com/Morphy Auctions)

Bat Masterson, NM $250.00
Bill Longley, NM...$600.00
Brave Eagle, NM...$200.00
Bret Maverick, miniature series $75.00
Bret Maverick w/coffeedunn horse, NM $500.00
Bret Maverick w/gray horse, rare, NM $600.00
Buffalo Bill, NM..$300.00
Bullet, w/tag, NM...$150.00
Cactus Pete, NM...$150.00
Champ Cowgirl, very rare, NM...$275.00
Cheyenne, miniature series, NM.......................................$190.00
Chief Thunderbird, rare shield, NM.................................$150.00
Cochise, NM $150.00
Commanche Kid, NM..$150.00
Dale Evans, green, NM..$175.00
Dale Evans, purple, NM $250.00
Davy Crockett, NM...$500.00
General Custer, NM $150.00
General Custer, NMIB...$350.00
General George Washington, NMIB..................................$175.00
General Robert E Lee, NMIB $250.00
Gil Favor, semi-rearing, NM $550.00
Hoby Gillman, NM..$250.00
Jim Bowie, w/tag, NM...$250.00
Jim Hardy, EX+ $200.00
Jim Hardy, NMIB..$300.00
Jockey, NM $150.00
Josh Randle, NM $650.00
Lone Ranger, Champ version, w/chaps, black breast collar, NM..$125.00
Lone Ranger, miniature series, NM...................................$75.00

Lone Ranger, NM..$150.00
Lone Ranger, rearing, NMIB $300.00

Matt Dillon, with tag, NM, $250.00. (Photo courtesy LiveAuctioneers.com/Morphy Auctions)

Matt Dillon, w/tag, NMIB $300.00
Paladin, NMIB $350.00
Rebel, miniature series, NM..$125.00
Rebel, NM...$250.00
Rebel, NMIB...$1,200.00
Rifleman, miniature series, EX...$75.00
Rifleman, NMIB..$350.00
Ronald MacKenzie, NM $1,200.00
Roy Rogers, semi-rearing, NMIB......................................$600.00
Roy Rogers, walking, NMIB $300.00
Seth Adams, NM...$275.00
Sgt Lance O'Rourke, NMIB $300.00
Sgt Preston, NM $650.00
Tom Jeffords, NM..$175.00
Tonto, miniature series, NM..$75.00
Tonto, NM...$150.00
Tonto, semi-rearing, rare, NM $650.00
Warpaint Thunderbird, w/shield, NMIB $350.00
Washington, EX+ $200.00
Wyatt Earp, NMIB $250.00

Sports Figures

Babe Ruth, NM, from $175 to $225.00
Bat boy, 25th Anniversary, NM $50.00
Dick Groat, w/bat, NM, minimum value $1,000.00
Dick Groat, 25th Anniversary, MIB, from $30 to.............$40.00
Don Drysdale, EX, from $275 to.......................................$350.00
Duke Snyder, EX+ $360.00

Eddie Matthews, limited edition, 2002, MIB, from $25 to...**$35.00**
Eddie Matthews, NM **$150.00**
Ernie Banks, NM, from $200 to.................................**$250.00**
Ernie Banks, 25th Anniversary, MIB, from $30 to.............**$40.00**
Hank Aaron, EX **$250.00**

Hank Aaron, M, $350.00.
(Photo courtesy LiveAuctioneers.com/ Morphy Auctions)

Hank Aaron, 25th Anniversary, MIB **$35.00**
Harmon Killebrew, NM, from $500 to............................**$600.00**
Harmon Killebrew, 25th Anniversary, MIB, from $30 to **$45.00**
Little Leaguer, 4", EX, from $50 to.................................**$75.00**
Luis Aparicio, NM, from $250 to **$300.00**
Luis Aparicio, 25th Anniversary, MIB.............................**$32.00**
Mickey Mantle, MIB **$535.00**
Mickey Mantle, NM, from $285 to.................................**$320.00**
Mickey Mantle, VG **$150.00**
Mickey Mantle, 25th Anniversary, MIB **$50.00**
Nellie Fox, EX, from $135 to...**$165.00**
Rocky Colavito, NM, from $600 to................................**$700.00**
Roger Maris, NM, from $325 to **$375.00**
Stan Musial, NM **$235.00**
Ted Williams, NM **$300.00**
Ted Williams, VG **$145.00**
Ted Williams, 25th Anniversary, MIP **$50.00**
Warren Spahn, limited edition, 2002, MIB.......................**$25.00**
Washington Redskins, running back, NM, minimum value... **$500.00**
Willie Mays, NM, from $255 to **$285.00**
Willie Mays, 25th Anniversary, MIB..................................**$50.00**
Yogi Berra, no mask, NM, from $100 to **$150.00**
Yogi Berra, w/mask, NM, from $165 to...........................**$200.00**
Yogi Berra, w/mask, 25th Anniversary, M (NM box) **$38.00**

Hazel-Atlas

This company was formed in 1902, the result of a merger between four smaller glass producers: Hazel Glass and Metals, Atlas Glass, Wheeling Metal Plant, and Republic Glass. By the 1930s it had grown to become the largest company in the world making machine-molded glassware, including many patterns of Depression glass, as well as novelty items, children's dishes, and kitchenware in a wide variety of colors that have captured the attention of a goodly number of today's collectors. Though its headquarters were in Wheeling, West Virginia, the company maintained glasshouses throughout the country in states that included New York, Oklahoma, and California. Hazel-Atlas was acquired by the Continental Can Company in 1956. For more information we recommend *The Hazel-Atlas Glass Identification and Value Guide* by Gene and Cathy Florence (Collector Books). See also Kitchen Collectibles, Glassware.

**Moderntone Platonite, Red Willow, salad plate, 7¾",
$18.00.** (Photo courtesy Gene and Cathy Florene)

Apple, bowl, crystal, 4" **$4.00**
Apple, mug, crystal **$5.00**
Apple, plate, crystal, lattice w/cup ring, 8" **$5.00**
Aurora, bowl, cereal; green, 5⅜"......................................**$8.00**
Aurora, bowl, cobalt or pink, 2⅜x4½" **$65.00**
Aurora, bowl, utility; crystal, 2⅜x4½" **$4.00**
Aurora, cup & saucer, green **$10.50**
Aurora, tumbler, cobalt or pink, 10-oz, 4¾" **$26.00**
Beehive, bowl, berry; w/handles, 8⅜"...............................**$12.00**
Beehive, butter dish, 6" **$25.00**
Beehive, creamer, 9½-oz..**$5.00**
Beehive, sherbet, flat, 3¾"...**$6.00**
Beehive, tray, serving; 12¼" **$12.00**
Candy Stripe, bowl, all colors, 4⅞" **$10.00**
Candy Stripe, ice tub, all colors.......................................**$65.00**
Candy Stripe, pitcher, all colors, 80-oz..............................**$95.00**
Candy Stripe, tumbler, all colors, 10-oz, 5⅛"......................**$12.50**
Capri Swirl Colonial, bowl, blue, 5⅜" **$8.00**
Capri Swirl Colonial, plate, salad; blue, 7"............................**$7.00**
Capri Swirl Colonial, sherbet, blue, 6-sided base, 4½" **$7.50**
Cloverleaf, bowl, dessert; green, 4"..................................**$40.00**
Cloverleaf, cup & saucer, pink **$12.00**
Cloverleaf, plate, luncheon; green, 8"..................................**$8.00**
Cloverleaf, tumbler, pink, flat, 10-oz, 3¾" **$30.00**
Colonial Couple, bowl, refrigerator; w/lid, round **$35.00**

Colonial Couple, cup	$15.00
Colonial Couple, plate, dessert	$10.00
Colonial Couple, tumbler, flat, 8-oz	$20.00
Diamond Optic, cup & saucer, pink or green	$10.00
Diamond Optic, tumbler, juice; pink or green, 3"	$7.00
Diamond Optic, tumbler, tea; pink or green, 12-oz	$15.00
Moderntone Platonite, bowl, cream soup; darker colors, 4¾".	$11.00
Moderntone Platonite, bowl, cream soup; pastel colors, 4¾" ..	$5.00
Moderntone Platonite, creamer, darker colors, from $8 to	$11.00
Moderntone Platonite, mug, white w/stripes, 4"	$10.00
Moderntone Platonite, plate, dinner; Deco/Red or Blue Willow, 8⅞"	$20.00
Moderntone Platonite, plate, salad; pastel colors, 7¾"	$3.00
Moderntone Platonite, plate, sandwich; white w/stripes, 10½"	$16.00
Moderntone Platonite, salt & pepper shakers, pastel colors, pr	$14.00
Moderntone Platonite, tumbler, darker colors, from $10 to.	$30.00
Moderntone Platonite, tumbler, pastel colors, 9-oz	$7.00
Newport, bowl, berry; white, 4¾"	$3.00
Newport, bowl, cream soup; fired-on colors, 4¾"	$10.00
Newport, creamer, white	$4.00
Newport, plate, luncheon; fired-on colors, 8½"	$5.00
Newport, plate, sandwich; white, 11½"	$8.00
Newport, tumbler, fired-on colors	$10.00
Ovide, bowl, berry; white w/trim, 4¾"	$3.50
Ovide, bowl, cereal; design on white, deep, 5½"	$11.00
Ovide, creamer, fired-on color	$4.00
Ovide, cup, design on white	$12.50
Ovide, cup, white w/trim	$3.50
Ovide, plate, dinner; fired-on color, 9"	$8.00
Ovide, sugar bowl, white w/trim	$4.50
Ovide, tumbler, design on white	$15.00
Ovide, tumbler, juice; fired-on color, footed	$6.00
Ripple, bowl, berry; any color, shallow, 5"	$15.00
Ripple, creamer, any color	$7.50
Ripple, plate, luncheon; any color, 8⅞"	$6.00
Ripple, saucer, any color, 5⅝"	$1.00
Ripple, tidbit, 3-tier, any color	$35.00
Ships, cocktail mixer, white on cobalt, w/stirrer	$35.00
Ships, pitcher, white on cobalt, ice lip, 82-oz	$65.00
Ships, tumbler, tea; white on cobalt, 15-oz	$40.00
Ships, tumbler, white on cobalt, heavy bottom, 4-oz, 3¼" ...	$28.00

Head Vases

Fun to collect, vases modeled as heads of lovely ladies, delightful children, famous people, clowns — even some animals — were once popular as flower containers. Today they represent a growing area of collector interest. Most of them were imported from Japan, although some American potteries produced a few as well.

If you'd like to learn more about them, we recommend *Collecting Head Vases* by David Barron and *The World of Head Vase Planters* by Mike Posgay and Ian Warner.

Advisor: Larry G. Pogue (See Directory, Head Vases and String Holders)

Newsletter: *Head Hunters Newsletter*
Maddy Gordon
P.O. Box 83H, Scarsdale, NY 10583
914-472-0200

Baby girl w/pink bonnet & bodice, Artmark, 6"	$95.00
Girl w/umbrella, brown hair, multicolor trim, bright red handle, Made in Japan, 5" (8" overall)	$185.00
Girl w/umbrella, brown hair, pink trim, 5" (8" overall)	$145.00
Lady in flat-rimmed hat, bodice w/turned-up collar, Relpo #K1009B, 5½"	$175.00
Lady w/blond hair, blue bodice w/bow at shoulder, pearl earrings, Napcoware #C7293, 5¾"	$165.00
Lady w/blond hair, hand to face, black pierced rim on bonnet, black bodice, #S673B, 4½"	$97.50
Lady w/flat-brimmed hat, white-gloved hands to face, black lashes, #27703, 6½"	$215.00
Lady w/frosted hair, blue-gloved hand to face, daisies on bodice, Napcoware #C6429, 7½"	$245.00
Lady w/frosted hair, white-gloved hand to face, pearls, green bodice, Relpo #K1633, 7¼"	$255.00
Lady w/frosted hair, 2-tone green hat & bodice, pearls, Napcoware #C7498, 10½"	$685.00

Lady with hand up to face, pearls, ring on finger, Relpo, #K1401, 7", $275.00. (Photo courtesy Larry Pogue)

Lady w/white-gloved hand to face, flat-brimmed hat w/flowers, white trim on bodice, Lefton #2359, 7½"	$255.00
Lady w/white-gloved hand to face, ornate hairdo, pearls, Inarco #E779, 1963, 6"	$195.00
Lady w/white-gloved hands crossed under chin, flat-rimmed hat, pearls, Ruben #495, 5½"	$185.00
Newborn baby, blue trim, Hull #92-USA, 5¾"	$65.00
Teen girl, blond hair w/white bow, thick black lashes, flower at white collar, #D3220, 6"	$195.00
Teen girl, flower wreath on blond hair, eyes closed, pearl necklace, Napco #C5676, 6½"	$185.00

Teen girl w/blond updo, hand to face, pearls, Ardco Made in Japan, 7½" **$255.00**

Teen girl w/frosted updo w/green bow, pearls, turtleneck under green jacket, blue eyes, Napcoware #C8497, 7" **$225.00**

Teen girl w/green leaf shape atop blond hair, Velco #6690, 5" ..**$175.00**

Teen girl w/headscarf, thick black lashes, Velco #6686, 5½" .**$175.00**

Teen girl w/light brown hair, thick black lashes, pearl earrings, gold trim, Napcoware #C5939, 6" **$165.00**

Teen girl w/long blond hair, lg green bow, green eyeshadow, green bodice w/white collar, Napcoware #C8493, 6" **$225.00**

Teen girl w/tam, blond frosted hair, pearl earrings, white at throat, Kelvin foil label, 6" **$185.00**

Teen girl w/wide-brimmed bonnet, bow at chin, Napco #C3812A, 1959, 6" **$195.00**

Heisey Glass

From just before the turn of the century until 1957, the Heisey Glass Company of Newark, Ohio, was one of the largest, most successful manufacturers of quality tableware in the world. Though the market is well established, many pieces are still reasonably priced; and if you're drawn to the lovely patterns and colors that Heisey made, you're investment should be sound.

After 1901 much of their glassware was marked with their familiar trademark, the 'Diamond H' (an H in a diamond) or a paper label. Blown pieces are often marked on the stem instead of the bowl or foot.

Numbers in the listings are catalog reference numbers assigned by the company to indicate variations in shape or stem style. Collectors use them, especially when they buy and sell by mail, for the same purpose. Many catalog pages (showing these numbers) are contained in *Heisey Glass, 1896 – 1957*, by Neila and Tom Bredehoft. This book and *Elegant Glassware of the Depression Era* by Gene and Cathy Florence are both excellent references for further study.

See also Glass Animals and Related Items.

Clubs: Heisey Collectors of America
Newsletter: *The Heisey News*
169 W Church St., Newark, OH 43055
740-345-2932

Cabochon, crystal, bonbon, sloped sides, squared handle, 6¼" ...**$24.00**

Cabochon, crystal, bowl, gardenia; low w/irregular cupped edge, 13"..**$18.00**

Cabochon, crystal, butter dish **$30.00**

Cabochon, crystal, creamer **$13.00**

Cabochon, crystal, plate, center handle, 13" **$50.00**

Cabochon, crystal, sherbet, pressed, 6-oz **$6.00**

Charter Oak, Moongleam, compote, low foot, 6"...............**$60.00**

Charter Oak, Moongleam, plate, luncheon; 8" **$20.00**

Chintz, crystal, bowl, vegetable; 10" **$20.00**

Chintz, crystal, plate, dinner; round or sq, 10½" **$40.00**

Chintz, Sahara, bowl, cream soup **$35.00**

Chintz, Sahara, cup..**$25.00**

Chintz, Sahara, salt & pepper shakers, pr..........................**$95.00**

Crystolite, crystal, bowl, gardenia; shallow, 12"................**$65.00**

Crystolite, crystal, bowl, perserve; 5" **$20.00**

Crystolite, crystal, candlestick, 2-light, ea **$35.00**

Crystolite, crystal, creamer, individual...............................**$20.00**

Crystolite, crystal, plate, sandwich; 12"..............................**$45.00**

Crystolite, crystal, punch bowl, 7½-qt **$120.00**

Crystolite, crystal, punch ladle **$35.00**

Crystolite, crystal, vase, footed, 6" **$40.00**

Empress, Flamingo, plate, 6"...**$11.00**

Empress, Flamingo, relish tray, 3-part, 10" **$50.00**

Empress, Flamingo or Sahara, bowl, lemon; w/lid, 6½" L.**$100.00**

Empress, Flamingo or Sahara, cup **$30.00**

Empress, Moongleam, compote, 6".....................................**$100.00**

Empress, Moongleam, mustard, w/lid **$95.00**

Empress, Sahara, plate, 9" **$35.00**

Empress, Sahara, tumbler, ground bottom, 8-oz **$50.00**

Greek Key, crystal, candy dish, 1-lb **$170.00**

Greek Key, crystal, egg cup, 5-oz..**$80.00**

Greek Key, crystal, sherbet, low, 6-oz **$30.00**

Ipswich, crystal, cocktail shaker, w/strainer, #86 stopper, 1-qt ...**$225.00**

Ipswich, crystal, sugar bowl..**$35.00**

Ipswich, Flamingo, pitcher, ½-gal.....................................**$600.00**

Ipswich, Moongleam, tumbler, 10-oz................................**$140.00**

Ipswich, Sahara, goblet, knob in stem, 10-oz **$70.00**

Ipswich, Sahara Yellow, candy jar, $400.00.
(Photo courtesy Gene and Cathy Florence)

Kalonyal, crystal, bowl, crimped, 5"....................................**$35.00**

Kalonyal, crystal, cake plate, footed, 9"............................**$275.00**

Kalonyal, crystal, goblet, wine; 2-oz.................................**$110.00**

Kalonyal, crystal, mug, 8-oz...**$175.00**

Kalonyal, crystal, oil bottle, w/handle, 4-oz **$120.00**

Lariat, crystal, basket, footed, 10" **$185.00**

Lariat, crystal, cheese dish, footed, w/lid, 5" **$45.00**

Lariat, crystal, deviled egg plate, 13" **$225.00**

Lariat, crystal, ice tub..**$75.00**

Lariat, crystal, saucer **$3.00**

Lariat, crystal, tumbler, iced tea; blown, footed, 12-oz........**$25.00**

Lodestar, Dawn, ashtray **$85.00**

Lodestar, Dawn, bowl, shallow, 14" **$130.00**

Lodestar, Dawn, creamer, no handle **$50.00**

Lodestar, Dawn, creamer, w/handle......................................$70.00
Lodestar, Dawn, plate, 8½"...$65.00
Lodestar, Dawn, sugar bowl, w/handles $70.00
Minuet, crystal, mayonnaise, dolphin foot, 5½"................$50.00
Minuet, crystal, plate, salad; 7"..$16.00
Minuet, crystal, saucer champagne, 6-oz..........................$25.00
Minuet, crystal, urn, 6"..$75.00
New Era, crystal, ashtray..$40.00
New Era, crystal, creamer...$37.50
New Era, crystal, goblet, cocktail; high stem, 3½-oz $10.00
New Era, crystal, plate, 9x7"..$25.00
New Era, crystal, tumbler, soda; footed, 14-oz..................$24.00
Octagon, crystal, plate, luncheon; 8" $7.00
Octagon, Flamingo or Moongleam, nut dish, w/handles $25.00
Octagon, Hawthorne, bowl, grapefruit; 6½" $35.00
Octagon, Hawthorne, celery tray, 9"..................................$45.00
Octagon, Moongleam or Sahara, mint dish, 6"..................$25.00
Octagon, Sahara, platter, 12¼" L $30.00
Old Colony, Sahara, bowl, nappy, 8" $40.00
Old Colony, Sahara, cigarette holder.................................$44.00
Old Colony, Sahara, decanter, 1-pt $325.00
Old Colony, Sahara, plate, 7"..$20.00
Old Colony, Sahara, platter, 14" L......................................$55.00
Old Colony, Sahara, saucer $10.00
Old Colony, Sahara, sugar bowl, dolphin foot $45.00
Old Colony, Sahara, tray, center handle, 12" sq.................$50.00
Old Colony, Sahara, tumbler, juice; footed, 5-oz $18.00

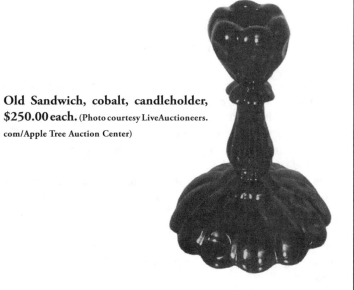

Old Sandwich, cobalt, candleholder, $250.00 each. (Photo courtesy LiveAuctioneers. com/Apple Tree Auction Center)

Old Sandwich, crystal, cup..$40.00
Old Sandwich, crystal, sugar bowl, oval $25.00
Old Sandwich, Flamingo, salt & pepper shakers, pr............$90.00
Old Sandwich, Flamingo or Sahara, bowl, popcorn; cupped rim, footed $110.00
Old Sandwich, Flamingo or Sahara, tumbler, 10-oz............$40.00
Old Sandwich, Moongleam, creamer, oval $50.00
Old Sandwich, Moongleam, goblet, wine; 2½-oz................$55.00
Old Sandwich, Sahara, pilsner, 8-oz...................................$32.00
Orchid, crystal, ashtray, #1435, 3" $30.00

Orchid, crystal, bowl, salad; 7" $60.00
Orchid, crystal, candlestick, 1-light, Queen Ann, w/prisms, ea.$150.00
Orchid, crystal, celery tray, 13"..$60.00
Orchid, crystal, cocktail shaker, #4225, 1-pt.....................$240.00
Orchid, crystal, ice bucket, Waverly, w/handles.................$425.00
Orchid, crystal, plate, dinner; Waverly, 10½" $150.00
Orchid, crystal, salt & pepper shakers, pr $75.00
Orchid, crystal, tumbler, flared, 10-oz...............................$100.00
Plantation, crystal, ashtray, 3½" $35.00
Plantation, crystal, candy dish, w/lid, 7" L.......................$275.00
Plantation, crystal, cup..$40.00
Plantation, crystal, goblet, wine; blown, 3-oz....................$65.00
Plantation, crystal, plate, salad; 8"....................................$35.00
Plantation, crystal, relish dish, 3-part, 11"........................$55.00
Plantation, crystal, sugar bowl, footed..............................$40.00
Plantation, crystal, vase, flared, footed, 9".......................$425.00
Pleat & Panel, crystal, bowl, bouillon; w/handles, 5" $7.00
Pleat & Panel, crystal, marmalade, 4¾" $10.00
Pleat & Panel, crystal, plate, sandwich; 14" $15.00
Pleat & Panel, Flamingo, bowl, vegetable; 9" L..................$35.00
Pleat & Panel, Flamingo, pitcher, 3-pt...............................$140.00

Pleat and Panel, Flamingo, vase, 8", $110.00. (Photo courtesy LiveAuctioneers.com/Phoebus Auction Gallery)

Pleat & Panel, Moongleam, cheese & cracker set, tray w/compote, 10½" $80.00
Pleat & Panel, Moongleam, plate, bread; 7".......................$10.00
Provincial, crystal, bowl, gardenia; 13".............................$40.00
Provincial, crystal, butter dish $80.00
Provincial, crystal, creamer, footed $15.00
Provincial, crystal, mustard $140.00
Provincial, crystal, nut dish, w/handles, 5".......................$15.00
Provincial, crystal, plate, snack; w/handles, 7"..................$25.00
Provincial, crystal, relish dish, 4-part, 10" $30.00
Provincial, crystal, salt & pepper shakers, pr $35.00
Provincial, crystal, tumbler, 8-oz.......................................$12.00
Provincial, crystal, vase, pansy; 4" $35.00
Provincial, Limelight Green, bonbon, upturned sides, w/handles, 7"...$45.00
Provincial, Limelight Green, candy dish, footed, 5½" $450.00

Provincial, Limelight Green, creamer, footed $95.00
Provincial, Limelight Green, nut dish, individual.................$40.00
Provincial, Limelight Green, sugar bowl, footed..................$95.00
Provincial, Limelight Green, tumbler, iced-tea, footed, 12-oz .. $80.00
Ridgeleigh, crystal, bowl, centerpiece; 8" $55.00
Ridgeleigh, crystal, bowl, nappy, scalloped, 4½" $20.00
Ridgeleigh, crystal, candlestick, 1-light, 2".....................$35.00
Ridgeleigh, crystal, coaster $15.00
Ridgeleigh, crystal, plate, hors d'oeuvres; oval $850.00
Ridgeleigh, crystal, punch bowl, 11" $175.00
Ridgeleigh, crystal, punch bowl underplate, 20" $140.00
Ridgeleigh, crystal, punch cup $12.00
Ridgeleigh, crystal, scent bottle, 4-oz $100.00
Ridgeleigh, crystal, torte plate, footed, 13½"....................$45.00
Ridgeleigh, crystal, tumbler, soda; pressed, 8-oz..................$35.00
Ridgeleigh, crystal, vase, #1 individual, cuspidor shape........$40.00
Saturn, crystal, finger bowl......................................$15.00
Saturn, crystal, marmalade $45.00
Saturn, crystal, pitcher, juice $40.00
Saturn, crystal, salt & pepper shakers, pr $35.00
Saturn, crystal, tumbler, 10-oz $20.00
Saturn, crystal, vase, flared, 8½"................................$55.00
Saturn, crytal, compote, 7" $50.00
Saturn, Limelight or Zircon, ashtray $150.00
Saturn, Limelight or Zircon, bowl, salad; 11" $140.00
Saturn, Limelight or Zircon, creamer..............................$180.00
Saturn, Limelight or Zircon, cruet, oil; 3-oz $650.00
Saturn, Limelight or Zircon, plate, luncheon; 8" $50.00
Saturn, Limelight or Zircon, sugar bowl $180.00
Saturn, Limelight or Zircon, tumbler, 10-oz $80.00
Stanhope, crystal, celery tray, w/handles, 12" $55.00
Stanhope, crystal, cigarette box, w/round knob on lid..........$95.00
Stanhope, crystal, claret, #4083, 4-oz............................$25.00
Stanhope, crystal, jelly dish, w/handle...........................$30.00
Stanhope, crystal, mint dish, 2-part, w/handles, 6" $35.00
Stanhope, crystal, torte plate, 15" $65.00
Stanhope, crystal, vase, w/handles, 9" $125.00
Twist, crystal, baker, oval, 9"...................................$25.00
Twist, crystal, cup, w/zigzag handles $10.00
Twist, crystal, pitcher, 3-pt.....................................$95.00
Twist, Flamingo, dressing bottle..................................$100.00
Twist, Flamingo, sugar bowl, footed...............................$30.00
Twist, Flamingo or Marigold, ice bucket w/metal handle...$135.00
Twist, Flamingo or Moonbeam, bowl, w/handles, 6" $20.00
Twist, Marigold, cheese dish, w/handles, 6" $30.00
Twist, Marigold or Moongleam, plate, dinner; 10½" $120.00
Twist, Moongleam, bowl, nasturtium; 8"............................$90.00
Twist, Moongleam, cocktail shaker, metal top.....................$900.00
Twist, Moongleam, tumbler, ground bottom, 8-oz..................$70.00
Yeoman, crystal, bowl, cream soup; w/handles $12.00
Yeoman, crystal, coaster, 4½" $3.00
Yeoman, crystal, compote, low foot, 6" $20.00
Yeoman, crystal, sugar shaker, footed $50.00
Yeoman, Flamingo, bowl, bouillon; footed, w/liner & handles ...$20.00
Yeoman, Flamingo, plate, 10½" $50.00
Yeoman, Flamingo, scent bottle, w/stopper $160.00
Yeoman, Flamingo, tumbler, 10-oz $15.00

Yeoman, Hawthorne, bowl, berry; w/handles, 8½" $35.00
Yeoman, Hawthorne, egg cup $60.00
Yeoman, Hawthorne, vase, #516-2, 6"...............................$75.00
Yeoman, Marigold, baker, 9".......................................$55.00
Yeoman, Marigold, gravy boat, w/underliner $45.00
Yeoman, Marigold, saucer..$10.00
Yeoman, Moongleam, bonbon, w/handle, 6½" $16.00
Yeoman, Moongleam, cruet, oil; 4-oz...............................$85.00
Yeoman, Moongleam, platter, 12" L.................................$26.00
Yeoman, Moongleam, tumbler, whiskey; 2½-oz $40.00
Yeoman, Sahara, creamer...$20.00
Yeoman, Sahara, lemon dish, w/lid, 5"...........................$25.00
Yeoman, Sahara, tray, 12" L.......................................$65.00

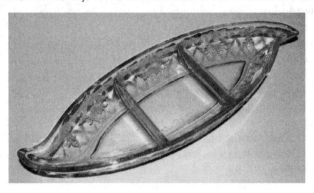

Yeoman, Sahara, three-compartment boat-shaped relish, Empress etching, 13" long, $50.00. (Photo courtesy LiveAuctioneers.com/Apple Tree Auction Center)

Holt Howard

Now's the time to pick up the kitchenware (cruets, salt and peppers, condiments, etc.), novelty banks, ashtrays, and planters marked Holt Howard. They're not only marked but dated as well; you'll find production dates from the 1950s through the 1970s. (Beware of unmarked copycat lines!) There's a wide variety of items and decorative themes; those you're most likely to find will be from the rooster (done in golden brown, yellow, and orange), white cat (called Kozy Kitten), and Christmas lines. Not as easily found, the Pixies are by far the most collectible of all, and in general, Pixie prices continue to climb, particularly for the harder-to-find items. Watch for a new 'generation' of Pixies that are now showing up on eBay. They're marked GHA for Grant Howard associates.

Internet auctions have affected this market with the 'more supply, less demand' principal (more exposure, therefore in some cases lower prices), but all in all, the market has remained sound. Only the very common pieces have suffered.

Our values are for mint condition, factory-first examples. If any flaws are present, you must reduce the price accordingly.

Christmas

Air freshener, girl w/Christmas tree, 1959, 6½" $32.00
Bell, holly & berries, red finial, 3½"....................................$12.50

Candle climbers, elf, pr $25.00
Candleholder, angel, 4", ea from $25 to................................$30.00
Candleholder, boot w/red at top, holly leaves & berries on white, 1963, ea $8.00
Candleholder, boy dressed as 1 of 3 Kings, 1960, ea...........$20.00
Candleholder, Santa in open car, 1959, 3½", from $18 to ...$22.00
Candleholders, elf in igloo, pr, MIB..$30.00
Candleholders, Holly Girls, holly forms body, pr.................$25.00
Candleholders, mouse among greenery, 1958, 2¼", pr $12.00
Candleholders, Santa w/bags, w/label, 1958, pr from $25 to..$30.00
Christmas tree, bottle brush, w/tag $60.00
Figurine, angel w/'spaghetti' trim at bottom of dress, gold details, 1958, 4¼", pr from $25 to $30.00
Head vase, 1959, 4", from $55 to $60.00
Lamp, oil; Holly Girl, unused wick, 7" $40.00
Mug, elf handle, 3½", from $50 to $60.00
Napkin holder, Santa head $30.00
Pitcher, Santa head, 1960, 4¼" $30.00
Planter, elf on boot, 5" $65.00
Planter, Santa Express, Santa riding train, 6x7½"................$30.00
Salt & pepper shakers, angels, 1 w/bell, 2nd w/hands on muff, 1959, 2-pc set $25.00
Salt & pepper shakers, Rudolf & Clarisse heads, #6181, 1950s, 3¾", 3½", 2-pc set..$50.00
Salt & pepper shakers, Santa, Happy New Year on beard, pr..$22.00

Salt and pepper shakers, Santa on gift packages, from $20.00 to $25.00 for the set.
(Photo courtesy Helene Guarnaccia)

Salt & pepper shakers, turkey w/Christmas decoration, pr...$25.00
Tray, Christmas tree shape, 3 compartments, MIB..............$28.00

Kozy Kitten

Ashtray, plaid kitten standing & holding a match in center, sq, 4½", from $100 to $115.00
Butter dish, 2 kittens peek from under lid, 7", from $90 to...$110.00
Cheese crock, Stinky Cheese on side, 2 kissing cats on lid, 1958, from $60 to $70.00
Cookie jar, head form $40.00
Cottage cheese dish, 2 kissing cats atop lid, from $35 to $45.00

Creamer & sugar bowl, stackable, head is sugar bowl, body is creamer w/tail handle, from $125 to $150.00
Grease jar, Keeper of the Grease, figural kitten, 4½" $375.00
Grocery clip, Kitty Catch, 1958, from $125 to.................$150.00
Memo Minder, flat cat w/Memo Minder on collar, 7", from $60 to $75.00
Mug, cat on side, w/squeaker, 8-oz, from $35 to $45.00

Oil and vinegar bottles, 7½", from $200.00 to $235.00 for the pair. (Photo courtesy Pat and Ann Duncan)

Oil bottle, cat sitting, slender, 7½", from $125 to..............$145.00
Pin box, cat on top w/tape-measure tongue, 1958 ....$50.00
Salt & pepper shakers, heads only, blue, green, yellow & pink collars, stacking set of 4 on 6" wooden holder, $125 to..........$150.00
Salt & pepper shakers, heads only, male in cap, pr from $35 to..$55.00
Salt & pepper shakers, kittens in basket, 1 winking, rubber stoppers, 2½", pr from $85 to $95.00
Salt & pepper shakers, 1 w/pink bow tie, 2nd w/blue, noisemaker, 1958, pr...$30.00
Spice set, 4 cat faces hang on vertical wire w/hooks, 11" overall, from $135 to $160.00
Spoon rest/recipe holder, cats on handle w/Hold Recipes here, fish decor on bowl, 1959, 2½x8x3½", from $75 to $85.00
String holder, kitten's face, from $40 to $50.00
Sugar shaker, cat in apron holding sugar can w/cork stopper, 1958..$85.00
Vase, full-bodied cat, male or female, 6½", ea from $65 to ..$85.00
Wall pocket, full-bodied cat w/hook tail, 7x3", from $45 to .$60.00

Pixie Ware

Bottle topper, 300 Proof..$300.00
Candleholder, pixie on handle of teapot, glass chimney, 8", w/tag, ea from $200 to $250.00
Cherries jar, black-haired cross-eyed spoon finial, from $165 to.$225.00
Chile Sauce jar, winking brunette spoon finial, 1959........$595.00
Cocktail Onions jar, green-striped onion spoon finial........$150.00
Honey jar, winking yellow-head spoon finial, rare, from $550 to.$600.00
Hors d'oeuvres, boy w/tall green hat in center, 7½x5¾", from $175 to $200.00

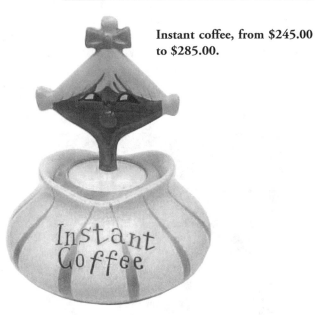

Instant coffee, from $245.00 to $285.00.

Jam 'n Jelly jar, orange-faced pixie spoon finial, from $75 to .. **$85.00**
Ketchup jar, from $60 to **$75.00**
Nut dish, brown pixie w/blond hair forms handle, Nuts on bow at neck, 3½x5" **$265.00**
Oil cruet, blond pixie girl w/cork stopper **$62.50**
Salt & pepper shakers, Salty & Peppy, wooden side handles, pr from $150 to **$175.00**
Serviette, Pixie smiling at side, sm **$265.00**
Spoons, various pixies as handles, set of 4, minimum value .. **$450.00**

Rooster

Bowl, cereal; 6" **$6.00**
Candleholders, figural, 1960, pr from $20 to **$25.00**
Cigarette holder, wooden, 11¾" **$30.00**
Coffeepot, white w/rooster decoration, electric, 1960, from $50 to **$65.00**

Cookie jar, embossed rooster, from $55.00 to $65.00. (Photo courtesy Pat and Ann Duncan)

Creamer, embossed rooster, tail handle, 3½" **$20.00**
Cutting board, 5x8½", from $85 to **$95.00**
Egg cup, double, from $15 to **$20.00**
Jam 'n Jelly jar, embossed rooster, from $30 to **$35.00**
Jam jar, rooster finial, from $25 to **$35.00**
Ketchup jar, embossed rooster, from $50 to **$60.00**
Mug, embossed rooster (3 sizes), ea from $6 to **$9.00**
Napkin holder, 6", from $30 to **$35.00**
Pitcher, embossed rooster, no handle (recessed hand holds) . **$40.00**
Pitcher, milk; embossed rooster, slim, plain handle, 7" **$20.00**
Plate, embossed rooster, 8" **$10.00**
Recipe box, embossed rooster, rectangular **$30.00**
Salt & pepper shakers, figural, 4¾", pr from $20 to **$30.00**
Sugar bowl, white w/red bottom, rooster finial, 1960s, 5x4" dia, from $25 to **$35.00**
Tray, flat rooster form, 4¾x3¾" **$9.00**
Vase, figural, 6¼", from $25 to **$35.00**

Miscellaneous

Tape dispenser, poodle, from $25.00 to $30.00. (Photo courtesy Pat and Ann Duncan)

Candle climbers, ballerinas, 1958, 4 for **$45.00**
Candleholder, girl in yellow dress, 4¼", ea **$28.00**
Candleholder, girl praying, 1960, ea **$10.00**
Candleholders, baby boy & girl beside birthday cakes, in diapers, pr **$32.00**
Candy jar, clown pops up when opened, 1960, 6½" **$40.00**
Cheese crock, Stinky Cheese, mouse & cheese finial **$35.00**
Cherries jar, Butler finial **$110.00**
Jam 'n Jelly jar, crab-apple head finial, 5½" **$55.00**
Olives jar, Butler finial **$45.00**
Planter, jack-o'-lantern w/frightened expression, 5⅜" **$6.00**
Relish jar, crying onion spoon finial **$60.00**
Salt & pepper shakers, anthropomorphic eggs (doctor & chef), 3⅛", 2-pc set **$20.00**
Salt & pepper shakers, beatniks, girl w/peace sign necklace, boy w/ guitar, 2-pc set **$22.00**
Salt & pepper shakers, children w/umbrella on 4 sides, 1964, 4", pr **$18.00**
Salt & pepper shakers, cow & bull heads, 3½", 2-pc set **$18.00**
Salt & pepper shakers, cowboy, 6¼", pr **$20.00**

Salt & pepper shakers, doughnuts, stacking set of 4, w/wooden holder **$12.00**

Salt & pepper shakers, fit together to form apple, 2½", pr...**$22.00**

Salt & pepper shakers, girl hiding behind flower fan, pr **$30.00**

Salt & pepper shakers, Rock 'n Roll, boy & girl heads on coiled wire base, pr from $50 to **$65.00**

Salt & pepper shakers, tomato, 1962, 3x3", pr **$15.00**

Tape dispenser/pencil sharpener, figural duck, 1958 ....**$38.00**

Tea bag holders, teapot shapes, set of 4 in metal caddy **$40.00**

Wall pockets, pheasant on blue cone shape, pr....................**$35.00**

HOMCO Collectibles

Home Interiors & Gifts, Inc. was founded in 1957 by Mary C. Crowley, who began a party plan for women who wanted part-time occupations that would offer a secondary income, while providing modestly priced home-decorating items to women interested in various accent pieces such as figurines, prints, plaques, and mirrors. The company has continued to prosper in much the same fashion, now boasting 2,400 employees. Most popular are the figurines and prints with the HOMCO mark.

Figurine, Autumn Evening, Debbie & Danny by stove, Denim Days, 1985, #1517 ....**$38.00**

Figurine, bear mother w/2 cubs, #1435, 4x5¼x4" **$25.00**

Figurine, cats (family of 3), white w/painted details, #1412, 4x7x3½" **$25.00**

Figurine, chipmunk on limb watching tree snail, 4¾x8¾" ...**$25.00**

Figurine, Danny's Grandma, Danny & grandma w/apples, Denim Days, #1526 ....**$48.00**

Figurine, Francesca, Masterpiece, w/wooden stand, 1997, MIB **$75.00**

Figurine, Harvest Time, boy & girl w/pumpkin, Circle of Friends, 1991, 3½" **$20.00**

Figurine, Helping Mom, Debbie w/mother, Denim Days, #8821 ....**$70.00**

Figurine, I Love Santa, Debbie & Danny w/Santa, Denim Days, 1985 ....**$80.00**

Figurine, Lady Covington, 2003, 9¾"..........................**$42.50**

Figurine, Lady Margaret, Masterpiece #11163-02, 2002, 10¼"..**$45.00**

Figurine, Lion's Pride, male lion, Masterpiece, 2000, 8x10", MIB **$50.00**

Figurine, Milking Time, boy & girl w/cow, Circle of Friends, 1995..**$25.00**

Figurine, Nature's Winged Jewel, Hummingbird w/Datura Flowers, 1990, 9x6x5", MIB...............................**$65.00**

Figurine, Oh Holy Night, Circle of Friends, #54021, 2001, MIB..**$45.00**

Figurine, Promise, dove w/sprig in beak, resting on flowering limb, Masterpiece, #1318-01 ....**$58.00**

Figurine, rabbit mother w/baby, brown tones, Masterpiece, 6x7x3¾" **$15.00**

Figurine, Season of Tranquility, buck deer stands beside doe, Masterpiece, 1996, MIB **$60.00**

Figurine, Sheltering Wings, screech owls, 1993, 9½x8"........**$55.00**

Figurine, Soaring Eagle, 1993, 12", from $50 to.................**$65.00**

Figurine, The Carpenter, Is Not This the Carpenter's Son? Matthew 13:55, 1989 ....**$140.00**

Figurine, white-tail buck on grassy base, Masterpiece Porcelain, 1986, 6½"x7", $35.00.

Figurine, White Washing the Fence, Debbie & Danny at white fence, Denim Days, #15353-01 ....**$62.50**

Figurine, 50th Anniversary Celebration, Debbie & Danny w/family, Denim Days final edition, MIB..................**$120.00**

Figurines, farmer & farmer's wife, both w/apples, wildlife at feet, #1409, 8", pr **$38.00**

Figurines, Halloween Fun, Debbie & Danny in costumes before pumpkins, Denim Days, pr **$40.00**

Plaques, angels in Victorian style, press-moled plastic, antiqued gold, 10½x6", pr....................................**$35.00**

Print, bears in water, autumn trees & mountains beyond, 18½x22½" **$50.00**

Print, flowers in bowl w/southwestern theme, chevron background, pastels, Barbara Mock, 21¾x17¾" **$125.00**

Print, Hothouse Welcome, flower garden scene, 27¾x23¾" ...**$46.00**

Print, May I Play, girl beside lady at piano..........................**$75.00**

Prints, birds on flowered branch (oval gold frame), 1982, 11x89", pr **$35.00**

Prints, Jeweled Falls, waterfall scene & mill scene, retired, 23⅜x16⅜", pr **$75.00**

Homer Laughlin China Co.

In 1873 the city of East Liverpool, Ohio, offered $5,000.00 to Homer and Shakespeare Laughlin for the construction of a whiteware pottery to be located just east of the city. The whiteware the brothers developed was of such high quality that in 1876 at the Philadelphia Centennial, they won numerous awards. In 1877 Shakespeare left the company, and the Laughlin Brothers became the Homer Laughlin China Company. In 1897 Homer Laughlin sold the company to the Aaron and Wells families. It is still owned today by the Wells family and continues to operate as the Homer Laughlin China company.

For further information see we recommended *Homer Laughlin China 1940's and 1950's*, and *Homer Laughlin, A Giant Among Dishes*, both by Jo Cunningham (Schiffer). Another great reference book co-authored by our advisor Darlene Nossaman and Jo Cunningham is *Homer Laughlin China Identification Guide to Shapes and Patterns* (Schiffer). *The Collector's Encyclopedia of Fiesta, Tenth Edition*, by Sharon and Bob Huxford (Collector Books) has photographs and prices of several of the more collectible lines of the company.

See also Fiesta.

Advisor: Darlene Nossaman (See Directory, Dinnerware)

Club/Newsletter: Homer Laughlin China Collector's Association (HLCCA)
P.O. Box 26021
Crystal City, VA 22215-6021
www.hlcca.org

Kwaker

This shape was introduced in 1954; it was popular with Butler Brothers and Sears Roebuck. You'll find it in the following patterns: Neville, Palatial, Rose and Ivory, Rosewood, and Vandemere.

Cup and saucer, from $8.00 to $10.00. (Photo courtesy Darlene Nossaman)

Bowl, fruit; 5", from $4 to	**$6.00**
Casserole, w/lid, from $20 to	**$25.00**
Creamer, from $8 to	**$10.00**
Nappy, 8", from $10 to	**$12.00**
Oatmeal 36's, from $8 to	**$10.00**
Plate, 10", from $8 to	**$10.00**
Platter, 13", from $18 to	**$20.00**
Sauceboat, from $10 to	**$12.00**
Sugar bowl, w/lid, from $10 to	**$14.00**
Teapot, from $35 to	**$40.00**

Marigold

Designed by Frederick Rhead, this shape was introduced in 1934. It was made in the following patterns: Ellen, Old Fashion Garden, Silver Flowers, Rhododendron, and Springtime.

Baker, 7", from $10 to	**$12.00**
Bowl, coupe; 7", from $8 to	**$10.00**
Bowl, 5", from $6 to	**$8.00**
Casserole, w/lid, from $30 to	**$32.00**
Creamer, from $10 to	**$12.00**
Cup, coffee; from $6 to	**$8.00**
Plate, sq, 6", from $10 to	**$12.00**
Plate, 10", from $8 to	**$10.00**
Sauceboat, from $10 to	**$12.00**
Saucer, coffee; from $3 to	**$4.00**
Sugar bowl, w/lid, from $12 to	**$15.00**

Newell

Designed by Frederick Rhead and introduced in 1928, this shape is available in the following patterns: Southern Pride, Hawthorne, Nasturtium, Ramona, and Yellow Glow.

Bowl, 4", from $4 to	**$6.00**
Cake plate, 11", from $18 to	**$22.00**
Casserole, w/lid, from $35 to	**$45.00**
Creamer, from $12 to	**$14.00**
Cup, coffee; from $8 to	**$10.00**
Nappy, 7", from $10 to	**$14.00**
Plate, 7", from $6 to	**$8.00**
Plate, 10", from $8 to	**$10.00**
Platter, 10", from $18 to	**$22.00**
Sauceboat, from $15 to	**$18.00**
Saucer, coffee; from $2 to	**$3.00**
Sugar bowl, w/lid, from $14 to	**$16.00**
Teapot, from $35 to	**$40.00**

Orbit

This shape was designed by art director Vincent Broomhall and introduced in the mid-1960s. It is available in these patterns: Autumn Gold, Maplewood, Orient, Trent, and Vista.

Plate, 10", from $7.00 to $9.00; Saucer, from $2.00 to $30.00. (Photo courtesy Darlene Nossaman)

Bowl, cereal; from $4 to...$6.00
Bowl, dessert; 5½", from $3 to..$5.00
Coffee server, from $20 to..$25.00
Creamer, from $6 to $8.00
Cup, coffee; from $6 to $8.00
Plate, 7", from $7 to..$9.00
Salt & pepper shakers, pr from $12 to $15.00
Sauceboat, from $8 to $10.00
Sugar bowl, w/lid, from $10 to $12.00
Tray, hostess; 12½", from $15 to...$18.00

Virginia Rose

This shape was designed by Frederick Rhead; it was introduced in 1933 and is available in the following patterns: Bouquet, Dixie Rose, Louise, Petit Point, Rose, and Daisy. For pattern JJ59 add 20%.

Bowl, 36's, from $12 to...$18.00
Bowl, 5", from $8 to..$10.00
Casserole, w/lid, from $32 to $35.00
Creamer, from $15 to $18.00
Cup, coffee; from $10 to $12.00
Jug, 24's, w/lid, from $50 to $60.00
Nappy, 7", from $12 to $15.00
Plate, 6", from $6 to $8.00

Plate, 7", from $10.00 to $12.00. (Photo courtesy Darlene Nossaman)

Plate, 10", from $10 to $15.00
Platter, 12"...$14.00
Sauceboat, fast-stand, from $12 to $16.00
Saucer, coffee; from $4 to..$5.00
Sugar bowl, w/lid, from $16 to $20.00

Horton Ceramics

Horton Ceramics was founded by Horace Horton and his wife Geri in 1947 in Mr. Horton's hometown, Eastland, Texas. Geri was the art designer, and Horace was the business manager. The company produced novelty items such as ashtrays, planters, figurines, vases, and patio and kitchen accessories. They marketed their products to grocery stores, gift shops, and department and variety stores all over the United States, but the bulk of their business was with the florist trade. Each piece of Horton is marked with 'horton ceramics' in lower-case letters and a mold number. The Hortons sold their ceramic business in 1961, and it ceased to operate.

Advisor: Darlene Nossaman (See Directory, Horton Ceramics)

Animal planter, chicken, white or yellow, #SC, 5", from $15 to .$18.00
Animal planter, elephant, gray, #E1, 7", from $15 to...........$18.00
Animal planter, lamb, pink & blue, #407, 4x6", from $15 to... $18.00
Animal planter, rabbit, gray & white, #N6, 7", from $15 to ..$18.00
Ashtray, fish, blue & green, #BS120, 5", from $10 to..........$12.00
Ashtray, free-form, blue or turquoise, #212, 5", from $10 to..$12.00
Ashtray, free-form in wrought-iron holder, raspberry, white or green,
    #A10, 7", from $10 to $12.00
Ashtray, horse head, blue, white & brown, #108, 5x7", from $10
    to $12.00
Planter, African violet, purple, #705, 4", from $8 to...........$10.00
Planter, contemporary, gold, pink or black, #807, 4x7", from $10
    to $12.00
Planter, frond shape, green mesh design, #922, 20", from $15
    to $18.00
Planter, lime, burgundy & mustard, round, #406, 7", from $8
    to $10.00
Planter, pedestal bowl, white, pink & green, #AT6, 6", from $8
    to $10.00
Vase, cedar-design bowl, turquoise & white or plum & white, #B63,
    6x3", from $14 to...$16.00

Vase, fluted, pink, white, or turquoise, #V14, 10", from $25.00 to $35.00. (Photo courtesy Darlene Nossaman)

Vase, free-form, coral, pink, green or blue, #BV19, 9x2", from $15
    to $18.00
Vase, fruit, hand-painted natural colors, #KS411, 11" L, from $15
    to $18.00
Vase, Madonna head figure, blue, #M2, 6", from $25 to.....$30.00
Vase, textured bowl, pink, black or green, #C8, 8x7", from $14
    to $16.00

Hull

Hull has a look of its own. Many lines were made in soft, pastel matt glazes and modeled with flowers and ribbons, and as a result, they have a very feminine appeal.

The company operated in Crooksville (near Zanesville), Ohio, from just after the turn of the century until it closed in 1985. From the 1930s until the plant was destroyed by fire in 1950, it producced the soft matt glazes so popular with today's collectors, though a few high gloss lines were made as well. When the plant was rebuilt, modern equipment was installed which it was soon discovered did not lend itself to the duplication of the matt glazes, so Hull began to concentrate on the production of glossy wares, novelties, and figurines.

During the '40s and '50s, it produced a line of kitchenware items modeled after Little Red Riding Hood. Original pieces are expensive today and most are reproduced by companies other than Hull. (See also Little Red Riding Hood.)

Hull's Mirror Brown dinnerware line made from 1960 until the plant closed in 1985 was very successful and was made in large quantities. Its glossy brown glaze was enhanced with a band of ivory foam, and today's collectors are finding its rich colors and basic, strong shapes just as attractive now as they were back then. In addition to table service, there are novelty trays shaped like gingerbread men and fish, canisters and cookie jars, covered casseroles with ducks and hens as lids, vases, ashtrays, and mixing bowls. It's easy to find, and though you may have to pay 'near book' prices at co-ops and antique malls, bargains are out there. It may be marked Hull, Crooksville, O; HPCo; or Crestone. Buyers should be aware that reproductions are being made in both the artware and dinnerware items.

If you'd like to learn more about this subject, we recommend *The Collector's Encyclopedia of Hull Pottery* and *The Collector's Ultimate Encyclopedia of Hull Pottery*, both by Brenda Roberts.

Advisor: Brenda Roberts (See Directory, Hull)

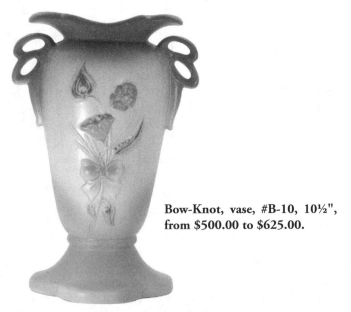

Bow-Knot, vase, #B-10, 10½", from $500.00 to $625.00.

Athena, cornucopia vase, #608, 8½", from $30 to **$40.00**
Blossom Flite, ewer, #T13, 13½", from $165 to **$210.00**
Blossom Flite, honey pot, #T1, 6", from $65 to **$105.00**

Bow-Knot, bowl, console; #B16, 13½", from $375 to **$475.00**
Bow-Knot, vase, #B7, 8½", from $300 to **$365.00**
Butterfly, bonbon dish, #B4, 6½", from $20 to **$25.00**
Butterfly, creamer, #B19, 5", from $65 to **$95.00**
Butterfly, ewer, #B15, 13½", from $165 to **$235.00**
Calla Lily, vase, #501/33, 8", from $185 to **$240.00**
Calla Lily, vase, #502/33, 6½", from $140 to.................... **$165.00**
Camellia, ewer, #105, 7", from $230 to **$275.00**
Camellia, hanging basket, #132, 7", from $260 to............ **$325.00**
Camellia, sugar bowl, #112, 5", from $125 to **$150.00**
Capri, Lion Head urn vase, #50, 9", from $45 to **$60.00**
Capri, swan, #23, 8½", from $50 to **$70.00**
Cinderella Blossom, creamer, #28, 4¼", from $45 to.......... **$70.00**
Cinderella Blossom, shaker, #25, 3½", ea from $20 to......... **$30.00**
Cinderella Bouquet, bowl, sq, brown ink stamp, 9¾", from $100 to **$125.00**
Cinderella Bouquet, pitcher, #29, 32-oz, from $25 to......... **$35.00**
Continental, bud vase, #66, 9½", from $35 to.................... **$50.00**
Continental, ewer, #56, 12½", from $145 to **$225.00**
Coronet, Swan, #213, 6½x10", from $45 to **$60.00**
Crescent, cookie jar, #B8, 9½", from $65 to **$90.00**
Crescent, individual casserole, #B7, 5", from $18 to............ **$25.00**
Debonair, creamer, #014, 3½", from $25 to **$35.00**
Debonair, pitcher, #06, 5", from $35 to.............................. **$45.00**

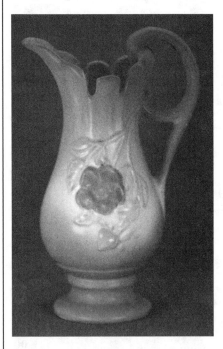

Dogwood, ewer, #505-6½ (actually 8½"), from $245.00 to $300.00.

Dogwood, ewer, #519, 13½", from $675 to....................... **$785.00**
Dogwood, vase, #509, 6½", from $135 to **$155.00**
Ebb Tide, creamer, #E15, 4", from $95 to **$125.00**
Ebb Tide, ewer, #E10, 14", from $210 to **$275.00**
Floral, pitcher, #46, 1-qt, from $40 to.............................. **$55.00**
Floral, shaker, #44, 3½", ea from $15 to **$20.00**
Imperial, candleholder, 1970, #437, 2", ea from $10 to....... **$15.00**
Imperial, vase, #F1, 1961, 4", from $15 to **$20.00**
Iris, candleholder, #411, 5", ea from $125 to.................... **$155.00**
Iris, rose bowl, #412, 7", from $220 to **$275.00**
Iris, vase, #403, 7", from $175 to **$225.00**

Magnolia, ewer, #18, 13½", from $375 to $435.00

Magnolia, vase, #12, 6¼", from $75 to.............................$100.00

Mardi Gras/Granada, candleholder, unmarked, 3¼", ea from $25 to $35.00

Mardi Gras/Granada, ewer, #66, 10", from $125 to $160.00

Mardi Gras/Granada, vase, #216, 9", from $50 to $80.00

New Magnolia, candleholder, #H24, 4", ea from $50 to $65.00

New Magnolia, cornucopia, #H10, 8½", from $115 to $155.00

Novelty, Bandana Duck planter, #75, 7", from $50 to.........$70.00

Novelty, Caladium leaf dish, 1957, 14", from $25 to..........$35.00

Novelty, Flying Goose wall pocket, #67, from $55 to $75.00

Novelty, Jubilee ashtray, #407, 11½", from $30 to..............$45.00

Novelty, Parrot w/Cart planter, #60, 6", from $45 to..........$60.00

Novelty, Swan planter, #413, 10½", from $55 to..................$85.00

Novelty, Twin Deer vase, #62, 1953, 11½", from $60 to $80.00

Orchid, bulb bowl, #312, 7", from $150 to $200.00

Orchid, jardiniere, #310, 6", from $225 to $265.00

Orchid, vase, #304, 10¼", from $350 to $450.00

Poppy, ewer, #610, 4¾", from $165 to $200.00

Poppy, vase, #606, 8½", from $235 to $275.00

Rosella, cornucopia, #R13, 8½", from $125 to $165.00

Rosella, creamer, #R3, 5½", from $45 to.............................$65.00

Rosella, wall pocket, #R10, 6½", from $150 to $175.00

Sun Glow, bowl, mixing; #50, 7½", from $25 to $35.00

Sun Glow, shaker, #54, 2¾", ea from $25 to........................$30.00

Sun Glow Classic, pitcher, ice lip, #55, 7½", from $155 to ..$200.00

Sun Glow Classic, tea bell, rope handle, unmarked, 6¼", from $100 to $125.00

Thistle, vase, #52, 6½", from $90 to.................................$125.00

Tokay/Tuscany, basket, #6, 8", from $75 to $115.00

Tokay/Tuscany, ewer, #3, 8", from $80 to.........................$115.00

Tokay/Tuscany, ewer, #13, 12", from $265 to...................$325.00

Tulip, ewer, #109, 8", from $265 to..................................$300.00

Tulip, vase, #100-33, 6½", from $130 to $150.00

Tulip, vase, #100-33, 10", from $275 to $350.00

Water Lily, basket, #L14, 10½", from $400 to...................$510.00

Water Lily, teapot, #L18, 6", from $245 to $300.00

Water Lily, vase, #L15, 12½", from $475 to $600.00

Wild Flower (# series), double candleholder, #69, 4", ea from $175 to $225.00

Wild Flower (# series), ewer, #57, 4½", from $100 to........$145.00

Wild Flower (# series), vase, #62, 6¼", from $140 to $165.00

Wildflower, basket, #W16, 10½", from $375 to $425.00

Wildflower, candleholder, #W22, 2½", ea from $60 to........$85.00

Wildflower, lamp, non-factory, 12½", from $200 to $250.00

Wildflower, vase, #W4, 6½", from $70 to............................$95.00

Wildflower, vase, #W8, 7½", from $85 to..........................$115.00

Woodland, double cornucopia, #W23, 14", from $235 to.$335.00

Woodland, ewer, #W3, 5½", from $80 to...........................$120.00

Woodland, planter, #W19, 10½", from $175 to..................$235.00

Woodland, vase, double bud; #W15, 8½", from $225 to...$265.00

Various Dinnerware Patterns

Avocado, bowl, salad/soup; 6½", from $4 to $6.00

Avocado, salt & pepper shakers, 3¾", pr from $20 to.........$30.00

Avocado, steak plate, oval, 11¾", from $20 to $25.00

Country Squire, bowl, mixing; 8¼", from $20 to $30.00

Country Squire, mug, soup & sandwich; 5", w/9½" tray, from $20 to $25.00

Country Squire, pitcher, 7½", from $30 to $40.00

Country Squire, plate, dinner; 10¼", from $8 to...............$10.00

Country-Belle, baker, rectangular, 14", from $40 to $60.00

Country-Belle, cheese shaker, 6½", from $20 to $30.00

Country-Belle, mug, clear glaze, no stamp, 5", from $4 to $6.00

Country-Belle, teapot/coffee server, 9", from $65 to...........$95.00

Crestone, bowl, 10", from $20 to $25.00

Crestone, coffee server, 11", from $75 to $125.00

Crestone, sugar bowl, w/lid, 4¼", from $20 to $25.00

Gingerbread Man, coaster/spoon rest, Flint, 5", from $25 to...$35.00

Gingerbread Man, cookie jar, Tawny, 12", from $450 to ...$650.00

Gingerbread man, server, Tawny, 10", from $100 to $125.00

Heartland, bowl, fruit; from $8 to $10.00

Heartland, canister, Sugar, 8", from $75 to $100.00

Heartland, creamer, 4¾", from $25 to $35.00

Heartland, plate, 7¼", from $8 to......................................$10.00

Mirror Almond, creamer, 4½", from $15 to........................$20.00

Mirror Almond, mug, 3¼", from $3 to.................................$4.00

Mirror Almond, plate, dinner; 10¼", from $8 to...............$10.00

Mirror Almond, stein, 5", from $8 to................................$12.00

Mirror Brown, baker, oval, 10", from $20 to $30.00

Mirror Brown, bowl, divided vegetable; 10¾", from $25 to.$35.00

Mirror Brown, bowl, 6½", from $4 to $6.00

Mirror Brown, canister, Coffee, 1978-81, 7", from $100 to ..$125.00

Mirror Brown, chicken casserole, w/lid, 1968-80, 8", from $75 to.$100.00

Mirror Brown, chip and dip tray, 15x11", $20.00. (Photo courtesy Brenda Roberts)

Mirror Brown, duck casserole, w/lid, 1972-85, 8", from $135 to $170.00

Mirror Brown, jug/creamer, 4¼", from $15 to....................$22.00

Mirror Brown, mug, coffee; 3", from $4 to...........................$6.00

Mirror Brown, plate, dinner; 10½", from $8 to $10.00

Mirror Brown, salt & pepper shakers, 3¾", pr from $16 to .$24.00

Mirror Brown, teapot, 6", from $25 to $35.00

Mirror Brown, vase, cylindrical, 9", from $35 to $45.00

Mirror Brown Ringed Ware, pitcher, 9", from $95 to........$135.00

Provincial, chip 'n dip, 15", from $30 to $40.00

Provincial, coffee server, 11", from $50 to.........................$75.00

Provincial, plate, dinner; 10¼", from $7 to $10.00

Provincial, stein, 6", from $10 to **$15.00**
Rainbow, pitcher, 9", from $40 to..............................**$60.00**
Rainbow, plate, luncheon; 8½", from $6 to **$8.00**
Rainbow, soup & sandwich tray & mug, from $20 to **$25.00**
Tangerine, leaf dish, 12", from $45 to..............................**$60.00**
Tangerine, saucer, deep well, 5¾", from $2 to......................**$3.00**
Tangerine, sugar bowl, w/lid, 4", from $20 to.....................**$30.00**

Imperial Glass

Organized in 1901 in Bellaire, Ohio, the Imperial Glass Company made carnival glass, stretch glass, a line called NuCut (made in imitation of cut glass), and a limited amount of art glass within the first decade of the century. In the mid-'30s, they designed one of their most famous patterns (and one of their most popular with today's collectors), Candlewick. Within a few years, milk glass had become their leading product.

During the '50s they reintroduced their NuCut line in crystal as well as colors, marketing it as 'Collector's Crystal.' In the late '50s they bought molds from both Heisey and Cambridge. Most of the glassware they reissued from these old molds was marked 'IG,' one letter superimposed over the other. When Imperial was bought by Lenox in 1973, an 'L' was added to the mark. The ALIG logo was added in 1981 when the company was purchased by Arthur Lorch. In 1982 the factory was sold to Robert Stahl of Minneapolis. Chapter 11 bankruptcy was filled in October that year. A plant resurgence continued production. Many Heisey by Imperial animals done in color were made at this time. A new mark, the NI for New Imperial, was used on a few items. In November of 1984 the plant closed forever and the assets were sold at liquidation. This was the end of the 'Big I.'

Numbers in the listings were assigned by the company and appeared on their catalog pages. They were used to indicate differences in shapes and stems, for instance. Collectors still use them.

For more information on Imperial we recommend *Imperial Glass* by Margaret and Douglas Archer; *Elegant Glassware of the Depression Era* by Gene and Cathy Florence; and *Imperial Glass Encyclopedia, Vol. I, A to Cane; Vol. II, Cane to M; and Vol. III, M to Z*, edited by James Measell.

Note: To determine values for Cape Cod in colors, add 100% to prices suggested for crystal for Ritz Blue and Ruby; Amber, Antique Blue, Azalea, Evergreen, Verde, black, and milk glass are 50% higher than crystal.

See also Candlewick.

Club: National Imperial Glass Collectors' Society, Inc.
P.O. Box 534, Bellaire, OH 43906
www.imperialglass.org

Atterbury Scroll, crystal, basket..............................**$15.00**
Atterbury Scroll, crystal, candy compote, w/lid...................**$22.00**
Atterbury Scroll, crystal, pitcher..............................**$35.00**
Atterbury Scroll, crystal, plate, luncheon..............................**$8.00**
Atterbury Scroll, crystal, sherbet **$6.00**
Atterbury Scroll, crystal, tumbler, water **$10.00**
Big Shots, pitcher, ruby red w/gold at base, Magnum, 9¾x4", + 6
    matching 5" tumblers marked Sure Shot.....................**$295.00**

Cape Cod, crystal, ashtray, 5½"..............................**$17.50**
Cape Cod, crystal, bowl, dessert; tab handles, 4½" **$24.00**
Cape Cod, crystal, cake stand, footed, 10½" **$50.00**
Cape Cod, crystal, cigarette box, 4½" **$45.00**
Cape Cod, crystal, cologne bottle, w/stopper **$60.00**
Cape Cod, crystal, comport, oval, 6½x11¼" **$200.00**

Cape Cod, crystal, cruet, 26-oz., $110.00. (Photo courtesy Gene and Cathy Florence)

Cape Cod, crystal, finger bowl, 5" **$15.00**
Cape Cod, crystal, goblet, 8-oz **$7.00**
Cape Cod, crystal, goblet, 11-oz **$20.00**
Cape Cod, crystal, pitcher, martini; blown, 40-oz..............**$200.00**
Cape Cod, crystal, plate, w/handles, 9½" **$40.00**
Cape Cod, crystal, punch ladle **$25.00**
Cape Cod, crystal, relish, 2-part, w/handles, 8" **$37.50**
Cape Cod, crystal, tray, w/handles, 6"..........................**$30.00**
Cape Cod, crystal, tumbler, juice; flat, 6-oz **$5.00**
Cape Cod, crystal, tumbler, 14-oz..............................**$32.00**
Cape Cod, crystal, vase, footed, 8½"..............................**$45.00**
Cape Cod, crystal, wine carafe, 26-oz **$235.00**
Chroma, all colors, cake stand..............................**$50.00**
Chroma, all colors, compote, w/lid..............................**$50.00**

Chroma, all colors, plate, 8", from $12.00 to $15.00. (Photo courtesy Gene and Cathy Florence)

Chroma, crystal, goblet, tea; 12-oz..............................**$15.00**
Chroma, crystal, sherbet, 6-oz..............................**$8.00**
Chroma, crystal, tumbler, water; 8-oz **$13.00**

Crocheted Crystal, basket, 6" **$25.00**
Crocheted Crystal, bowl, console; 11" **$24.00**
Crocheted Crystal, creamer, flat **$30.00**
Crocheted Crystal, mayonnaise bowl, flat or footed, 5¼" **$10.00**
Crocheted Crystal, plate, 9½" **$10.00**
Crocheted Crystal, punch cup, closed handle **$3.00**
Crocheted Crystal, relish, 4-part, 11½" **$22.00**
Crocheted Crystal, sugar bowl, footed **$15.00**
Crocheted Crystal, vase, 4-footed, 5" **$25.00**
Crocheted Crystal, wine goblet, 4½-oz, 5½" **$20.00**
Free-Hand, flower cuttings in 10 cut panels, crystal w/cobalt rim &
   3 cobalt legs, 1920s, 10½x4⅞" **$450.00**
Free-Hand, vase, blues & greens in marbleized swirl, #3761,
   6" **$415.00**
Free-Hand, vase, caramel slag, tricorner top, 3-footed, 8½"..**$110.00**
Free-Hand, vase, cobalt w/salmon-pink interior, ovoid w/flared rim,
   11¼" **$215.00**
Free-Hand, vase, funeral; Morning Glory, green, 8 ribs, 1950s,
   17" **$280.00**
Free-Hand, vase, Hearts & Vines, blue-white on green w/orange
   interior, 9x2¼" **$525.00**
Free-Hand, vase, Iron Cross, pearl green stretch, 5x5¼" **$98.00**
Iris, candlesticks, Ice stretch, double scroll, #320, 8½", pr...**$265.00**
Slag, basket, Diamond Quilted, red, yellow & white, tall handle, w/
   sticker **$35.00**
Slag, bell, purple, original stickers, 6" **$30.00**
Slag, bowl, Open Rose, red, low foot, 4½x8½" **$38.00**
Slag, bowl, Windmill, caramel, pleated & ruffled rim, 2½x8"... **$45.00**
Slag, candy box, purple, bumble bee finial, 5⅛x5½" **$65.00**
Slag, candy dish, red, scalloped & pleated rim, footed, 6x6½".. **$30.00**
Slag, coffee mug, red, elephant handle **$25.00**
Slag, compote, Heavy Grape, purple, hexagonal, footed, 4x5½".. **$75.00**
Slag, compote, purple, footed, scalloped rim, 6" **$35.00**
Slag, nappy, Grape & Leaf, red, w/handle, 5½" **$55.00**
Slag, pitcher, Windmill, purple, 6½" **$55.00**
Slag, pitcher, Windmill, red, 6" **$50.00**
Slag, toothpick holder, Diamond Quilt, purple **$27.50**

Indiana Glass

In 1971 the Indiana Glass Co. introduced a line of new carnival glass, much of which was embossed with grape clusters and detailed leaves using their Harvest molds. It was first introduced in blue, and later gold and lime green were added. (Prior to 1971 the Harvest molds had been used to produce a snowy white milk glass; blue and green satin or frosted glass; ruby red flashed glass; and plain glass in various shades of blue, amber, and green.) Because this carnival line was mass produced (machine-made), there are still large quantities available to collectors.

They also produced a line of handmade carnival called Heritage, which they made in amethyst and Sunset (amberina). Because it was handmade as opposed to being machine made, production was limited, and it is not as readily available to today's collectors as is the Harvest carnival. There is a significant amount of interest in both lines today. Now that these lines are 30 years old, Grandmother, Mother, and Aunt are leaving a piece or two to the next generation.

The younger generation is off and running to complete Granny's collection via the internet. This has caused a revival of interest in Indiana carnival glass as a collectible.

The company also produced a series of four Bicentennial commemorative plates made in blue and gold carnival: American Eagle, Independence Hall, Liberty Bell, and Spirit of '76. These are valued at $15.00 to $18.00 each (unboxed). A large Liberty Bell cookie jar and a small Liberty Bell bank were also made in gold carnival; today the cookie jars are valued at around $20.00 while the banks generally sell for $10.00 or less.

This glass is a little difficult to evaluate, since you see it in malls and flea markets with such a wide range of 'asking' prices. On one hand, you have sellers who themselves are not exactly sure what it is they have but since it's 'carnival' assume it should be fairly pricey. On the other hand, you have those who just 'cleaned house' and want to get rid of it. They may have bought it new themselves and know it's not very old and wasn't expensive to start with. (The Harvest Princess Punch Set sold for $5.98 in 1971.) So take heart, there are still bargains to be found, though they're becoming fewer with each passing year. The best buys on Indiana carnival glass are found at garage and estate sales.

In addition to the iridescent lines, Indiana Glass produced a line called Ruby Band Diamond Point, a clear, diamond-faceted pattern with a wide ruby-flashed rim band; some items from this line are listed below. Our values are for examples with the ruby flashing in excellent condition.

See also King's Crown; Tiara.

Iridescent Amethyst Carnival Glass (Heritage)

Basket, footed, 9x5x7", from $60 to **$75.00**

Butter dish, 5x7½" diameter, from $50.00 to $65.00.

Candleholders, 5½", pr from $45 to **$60.00**
Center bowl, 4¾x8½", from $50 to **$60.00**
Goblet, 8-oz, from $15 to **$22.00**
Pitcher, 8¼", from $50 to **$70.00**
Punch set, 10" bowl, 8 cups, no pedestal, from $150 to **$185.00**
Punch set, 10" bowl & pedestal, 8 cups, ladle, 11-pc, from
   $200 .... **$235.00**

Swung vase, slender & footed w/irregular rim, 11x3", from $50 to **$60.00**

Iridescent Blue Carnival Glass

Basket, Canterbury, waffled pattern, flared sides drawn in at handle, 11x8x12", from $50 to **$65.00**

Basket, Monticello, allover faceted embossed diamonds, 7x6" sq, from $25 to **$35.00**

Butter dish, Harvest, embossed grapes, ¼-lb, 8" L, from $30 to **$40.00**

Candleholders, Harvest, embossed grapes, compote shape, 4", pr from $20 to **$30.00**

Candy box, embossed ribs, rectangle w/lacy edge, footed, w/lid, 7x7" L, from $30 to **$40.00**

Candy box, Harvest, embossed grapes w/lace edge, footed, w/lid, 6½", from $35 to **$45.00**

Candy box, Princess, diamond-point bands, pointed faceted finial, 6x6" dia, from $18 to **$22.00**

Canister/Candy jar, Harvest, embossed grapes, 7", from $22 to **$35.00**

Canister/Cookie jar, Harvest, embossed grapes, 9", from $125 to **$175.00**

Canister/Snack jar, Harvest, embossed grapes, 8", from $110 to **$135.00**

Center bowl, Harvest, embossed grapes w/paneled sides, 4-footed, common, 4½x8½x12", from $25 to **$35.00**

Compote, Harvest, embossed grapes, scalloped rim on bowl, w/lid, 10", from $30 to **$35.00**

Cooler (iced tea tumbler), Harvest, embossed grapes, 14-oz, 5⅞", from $9 to **$12.00**

Creamer & sugar bowl on tray, Harvest, embossed grapes, 3-pc, from $30 to **$35.00**

Egg/Hors d'oeuvres tray, 12¾", from $32.00 to $42.00.

Goblet, Harvest, embossed grapes, 9-oz, from $9 to **$12.00**

Hen on nest, from $22 to **$30.00**

Pitcher, Harvest, embossed grapes, 10½", common, from $25 to **$30.00**

Plate, Bicentennial; American Eagle, from $12 to **$15.00**

Plate, hostess; Canterbury, allover diamond facets, flared crimped rim, 10", from $18 to **$22.00**

Punch bowl set, Princess, w/ladle & hooks, 26-pc, from $95 to .. **$120.00**

Teardrop (teardrop garland) bowl (compote), paneled w/3 teardrop clusters at rim, 7½x8½" dia, from $15 to **$20.00**

Tidbit, allover embossed diamond points, shallow w/flared sides, 6½" **$12.00**

Wedding bowl (sm compote), Thumbprint, footed, 5x5", from $10 to **$12.00**

Iridescent Gold Carnival Glass

Basket, Canterbury, waffle pattern, flaring sides drawn in at handle terminals, 9½x11x8½", from $35 to **$55.00**

Basket, Monticello, lg faceted allover diamonds, sq, 7x6", from $25 to **$30.00**

Candleholders, Harvest, embossed grapes, compote form, 4x4½", pr **$22.50**

Candy box, Harvest, embossed grapes, lace edge, footed, 6½x5¾", from $20 to **$30.00**

Canister/Candy jar, Harvest, embossed grapes, 7", from $15 to . **$25.00**

Canister/Cookie jar, Harvest, embossed grapes, 9", from $60 to. **$80.00**

Canister/Snack jar, Harvest, embossed grapes, 8", from $40 to... **$50.00**

Center bowl, Harvest, oval w/embossed grapes & paneled sides, 4½x8½x12", from $12 to **$15.00**

Console set, Wild Rose, wide naturalistic petals form sides, 9" bowl w/pr 4½" bowl-type candleholders, 3-pc, $25 to **$30.00**

Cooler (iced tea tumbler), Harvest, embossed grapes, 14-oz, from $8 to **$12.00**

Egg plate, 11", from $25 to **$35.00**

Goblet, Harvest, embossed grapes, 9-oz, from $7 to **$10.00**

Hen on nest, 5½", from $18 to **$25.00**

Pitcher, Harvest, embossed grapes, 10½", from $25 to **$35.00**

Plate, hostess; diamond embossing, shallow w/crimped & flared sides, 10", from $25 to **$30.00**

Punch bowl set, Princess, w/ladle & hooks, 26-pc, from $85 to **$110.00**

Relish tray, Vintage, 6 sections, 9x12¾", from $16 to.......... **$22.00**

Salad set, Vintage, embossed fruit, apple-shaped rim w/applied stem, 13", w/fork & spoon, 3-pc, from $15 to...................... **$20.00**

Snack plate, 8x10", w/2⅞" cup, from $20 to **$25.00**

Tumbler, Harvest, embossed grapes, 4", from $7 to............. **$10.00**

Wedding bowl, Harvest, embossed grapes, pedestal foot, 8½x8", from $20 to **$25.00**

Wedding bowl (sm compote), 5x5", from $9 to................... **$12.00**

Iridescent Lime Carnival Glass

Lime green examples are harder to find than either the gold or the blue.

Candleholders, Harvest, compote shape, 4x4½", pr from $45 to. **$60.00**

Candy box, Harvest, embossed grapes w/lace edge, w/lid, 6½", from $30 to **$38.00**

Canister/Candy jar, Harvest, embossed grapes, 7", from $20 to .**$30.00**

Canister/Cookie jar, Harvest, embossed grapes, 9", from $75 to.**$90.00**

Canister/Snack jar, Harvest, embossed grapes, 8", from $50 to...**$60.00**

Center bowl, Harvest, embossed grapes, paneled sides, 4-footed, 4½x8½x12", from $25 to..**$30.00**

Compote, Harvest, embossed grapes, 7x6", from $15 to......**$20.00**

Compote, tulip, petaled bowl on leafy curving stem, 7½x6¼" .. **$25.00**

Console set, Harvest, embossed grapes, 10" bowl w/compote-shaped candleholders, 3-pc, from $55 to **$75.00**

Cooler (iced tea tumbler), Harvest, embossed grapes, 14-oz, rare, from $22 to **$30.00**

Egg plate, 11", from $35 to **$45.00**

Goblet, Harvest, embossed grapes, 9-oz, from $10 to **$12.00**

Hen on nest, from $30 to **$38.00**

Pitcher, Harvest, embossed grapes, 10½", from $35 to **$45.00**

Plate, hostess; allover diamond points, flared crimped sides, 10", from $15 to **$22.00**

Punch bowl set, Princess, w/ladle & hooks, 26-pc, from $100 to . **$125.00**

Salad set, Vintage, embossed fruit, apple-shaped rim w/applied stem, 13", w/fork & spoon, 3-pc, from $18 to.......................**$25.00**

Snack set, Harvest, embossed grapes, 4 cups & 4 plates, 8-pc, from $80 to **$100.00**

Iridescent Sunset (Amberina) Carnival Glass (Heritage)

Basket, footed, 9x5x7", from $30 to **$45.00**

Basket, 9½x7½" sq, from $40 to **$55.00**

Bowl, crimped, 3¾x10", from $32 to **$40.00**

Bowl, 3½x8½", from $25 to **$30.00**

Butter dish, 5x7½" dia, from $40 to **$50.00**

Center bowl, 4¾x8½", from $30 to **$40.00**

Creamer & sugar bowl, from $30 to **$40.00**

Dessert set, 8½" bowl, 12" plate, 2-pc, from $40 to **$45.00**

Goblet, 8-oz, from $35 to..**$40.00**

Pitcher, Harvest, 10½", from $35.00 to $45.00.

Plate, 12", from $40 to **$50.00**

Plate, 14", from $45 to **$60.00**

Punch set, 10" bowl, pedestal, 8 cups, & ladle, 11-pc, from $125 to **$175.00**

Rose bowl, 4½x6½", from $50 to **$55.00**

Swung vase, slender, footed, w/irregular rim, 11x3", from $50 to..**$60.00**

Tumbler, 3½", from $15 to...**$18.00**

Patterns

Ruby Band Diamond Point: Sugar bowl, $4.00; Compote, 7¼", $12.50; Water goblet, $6.00. (Photo courtesy Gene and Cathy Florence)

Canterbury, basket, waffle pattern, Lime, Sunset, or Horizon Blue, 5½x12", from $35 to **$45.00**

Christmas Candy, bowl, crystal, 5¾" **$3.00**

Christmas Candy, creamer, teal **$22.00**

Christmas Candy, plate, bread & butter; crystal, 6"............**$2.00**

Christmas Candy, plate, sandwich; teal, 11¼".....................**$45.00**

Christmas Candy, tidbit, crystal, 2-tier.................................**$15.00**

Constellation, basket, centerpiece; crystal, 11" **$25.00**

Constellation, bowl, jumbo salad; crystal **$20.00**

Constellation, cake plate, crystal, sq w/pedestal foot **$30.00**

Constellation, cake stand, crystal, round **$30.00**

Constellation, creamer, crystal...**$8.00**

Constellation, plate, buffet; crystal, 18" **$25.00**

Constellation, tumbler, crystal, flat, 8-oz............................**$8.00**

Daisy, bowl, berry; crystal, 4½"..**$3.00**

Daisy, bowl, cereal; green, 6"...**$7.00**

Daisy, bowl, vegetable; red or amber, oval, 10" **$12.00**

Daisy, creamer, crystal, footed **$4.00**

Daisy, plate, dinner; crystal, 9⅜"..**$4.00**

Daisy, plate, dinner; red or amber, 9⅜" **$6.00**

Daisy, plate, salad; green, 7⅜" **$2.00**

Daisy, platter, crystal, 10¾" **$7.00**

Daisy, tumbler, green, footed, 12-oz.....................................**$10.00**

Loganberry, bowl, gold, triangular, 2x7¼", from $12 to **$15.00**

Monticello, basket, lg faceted diamonds overall, Lemon, Lime, Sunset, or Horizon Blue, sq, 7x6", from $25 to............**$35.00**

Monticello, basket, lg faceted diamonds overall, Lemon, Lime, Sunset, or Horizon Blue, 8¾x10½", from $35 to..........**$50.00**

Monticello, candy box, lg faceted overall diamonds, w/lid, Lemon, Lime, Sunset, or Horizon Blue, 5¼x6", from $15 to **$20.00**

Orange Blossom, bowl, dessert; milk white, 5½" **$5.00**

Orange Blossom, creamer, milk white, footed **$5.00**

Orange Blossom, cup & saucer, milk white...........................**$4.00**

Orange Blossom, sugar bowl, milk white, footed **$5.00**

Pretzel, bowl, fruit cup; crystal, 4½" $4.00
Pretzel, celery dish, gold, elongated oval, 10¼" L.................... $8.00
Pretzel, plate, crystal, sq w/indent, 7¼" $9.00
Pretzel, plate, sandwich; crystal, 11½" $11.00
Ruby Band Diamond Point, butter dish, from $20 to......... $25.00
Ruby Band Diamond Point, cake stand, 5x12", from $22 to .. $25.00
Ruby Band Diamond Point, candy dish, footed, w/lid, 12x6", from
    $15 to $18.00
Ruby Band Diamond Point, chip 'n dip set, 13" dia, from $20
    to... $25.00
Ruby Band Diamond Point, compote, w/lid, 16x5½", from $25
    to... $30.00
Ruby Band Diamond Point, cooler (iced tea tumbler), 15-oz, from
    $5 to $8.00
Ruby Band Diamond Point, creamer & sugar bowl, 4½", from $10
    to... $15.00
Ruby Band Diamond Point, creamer & sugar bowl, 4¾", on 6x9"
    tray, from $15 to.. $20.00
Ruby Band Diamond Point, decanter, 24-oz...................... $20.00
Ruby Band Diamond Point, goblet, 12-oz, from $9 to $10.00
Ruby Band Diamond Point, pitcher, 8", from $15 to $20.00
Ruby Band Diamond Point, plate, dinner; 10", from $60 to... $75.00
Ruby Band Diamond Point, plate, hostess; 12", from $18 to .. $25.00
Ruby Band Diamond Point, salt & pepper shakers, 4", pr.. $20.00
Ruby Band Diamond Point, toothpick holder, metal top band,
    3" $35.00
Ruby Band Diamond Point, tumbler, 5¾", from $7 to........ $10.00
Ruby Band Diamond Point, tumbler, on-the-rocks; 9-oz, from $4
    to $6.00
Sandwich, basket, amber or crystal, 10" $30.00
Sandwich, bowl, console; amber or crystal, 11½"................ $15.00
Sandwich, bowl, console; crystal, footed, 9"...................... $14.00
Sandwich, creamer, red... $45.00
Sandwich, cup, amber or crystal...................................... $2.00
Sandwich, goblet, amber or crystal, 9-oz........................... $9.00
Sandwich, plate, teal or blue, oval w/indent for sherbet, 8".... $6.00
Sandwich, sugar bowl, amber or crystal, lg.......................... $8.00
Teardrop, bowl, crystal, 5" $8.00
Teardrop, compote, crystal $12.00
Teardrop, creamer, crystal... $7.50
Teardrop, server, crystal, center handle............................ $15.00
Wild Rose w/Leaves & Berries, bowl, sauce; sprayed & satinized
    colors, handles $7.00
Wild Rose w/Leaves & Berries, candleholder, multicolored, ea.. $25.00
Wild Rose w/Leaves & Berries, sherbet, iridescent, crystal or milk
    glass $4.00
Wild Rose w/Leaves & Berries, tray, sprayed & satinized colors,
    handles... $25.00

Indianapolis 500 Racing Collectibles

You don't have to be a Hoosier to know that unless the weather interfers, this famous 500-mile race is held in Indianapolis every Memorial day and has been since 1911. Collectors of Indy memorabilia have a plethora of race-related items to draw from and can zero in on one area or many, enabling them to build extensive and interesting collections. Some of the special areas of interest they pursue are autographs, photographs, or other memorabilia related to the drivers; pit badges; race programs and yearbooks; books and magazines; decanters and souvenir tumblers; model race cars; and tickets. Unless noted otherwise, our values are for examples in at least near mint condition.

Advisor: Eric Jungnickel (See Directory, Indy 500 Memorabilia)

Badge, bronze, steering wheel shape, Indianapolis Motor Speedway
    1955, Union Made, Bastian Bros..................... $100.00
Badge, bronze-tone metal, movie camera shape, Winning
    1969... $45.00
Badge, pit; silver-tone metal, Champion spark plug, Indianapolis
    Motor Speedway, 1960 .... $98.00
Badge, Ray Harrison (1st winner) portrait embossed on silver-tone
    metal, 2001 .... $25.00
Cuff links, Indy racecar profile, USAC National Champion 1977
    Norton Spirit, gold-tone metal, NMIB..................... $30.00
Film, Glorious 4th, 1977 race, Goodyear Championship Racefilm
    Productions, 16mm w/sound, EX in storage can $65.00
Jacket, blue nylon, w/yellow & white strip down front side, Home
    of 500...Speedway on patch, zipper, 1960s-70s............. $25.00
License plate, Indiana 500 Official Pace Car, 1999 .... $50.00
Lithograph, race scene w/cars nearing curve, phantom racer in sky,
    1985 limited edition, in mat & frame...................... $100.00
Magazine, Saturday Evening Post, Confessions of a Race Driver
    article w/track photos, etc, August 18, 1923, EX.......... $28.00

Model, 1950 Mercury Pace Car, Brooklyn Models, from $100.00 to $120.00. (Photo courtesy LiveAuctioneers.com/Bonhams)

Model car, Bob Estes Special Kurtis Kraft Offical Race Car, diecast
    metal, Carousel 1, 1:18th scale, MIB............................ $90.00
Model car, Wilbur Shaw racer, cast stainless steel, limited produc-
    tion, 9" L... $77.00
Model kit, Indianapolis 500 Racer, Hubley, diecast metal, late 1950s,
    MIB.. $110.00
Model kit, 500 Hall of Fame Set, #63 Watson Roadster, #63 Lotus
    & #74 McLaren cars, MPC, 1:25th scale, 1988, MIB.. $50.00
Music box, Indianapolis Motor Speedway on base, race car & seated
    driver, ceramic, tan w/green highlights, 4½" $20.00
Newspaper, Detroit News, Peter DePaolo Wins...101 Miles Per
    Hour headline, May 31, 1925, EX $30.00

Mug, 1971, last winner listed is Al Unser, 1970, clear shading to rose, from $12.00 to $15.00.
(Photo courtesy B.J. Summers)

Newspaper, Detroit News, Schneider Wins Auto Race headline, May 31, 1931, many photos, EX..**$36.00**

Pin tray, aerial view of track on Melmac, ca 1970s, 5⅞x4⅛", EX **$25.00**

Pin-back, Indianapolis 500 Race Day, May 24, 1998, multicolored enameling, SRE, 1x1½", MIP......................................**$16.50**

Plate, racecar, Indianapolis Motor Speedway on rim, pewter, 1993, 10½" **$30.00**

Postcard, Pat O'Connor in racecar, 1955, oversize, 6x9"......**$25.00**

Poster, Dan Gurney in #48 race car, black & white, 1969, 24x36" **$120.00**

Program, Official; race scene cover, 1993...........................**$17.50**

Program, Official; The 18th 500, red, black & white cover, May 30, 1930 ....**$125.00**

Program, Official; 42nd 500, 1950, 95 pages, VG+.............**$30.00**

Slot car playset, Indianapolis Classic, Marx, #22934, NMIB..**$110.00**

Ticket stub, multicolor race scene, 1947, 5", EX **$45.00**

Toy car, Indianapolis 500 #62 Ferrari racer, tin litho, friction drive, w/driver, Japan, VG+ **$70.00**

Toy car, 2006 C-6 Corvette convertible, track car, diecast metal, 1:18th scale, MIB **$120.00**

Tumbler, lists winners from 1911 to 1971, multicolored enamel, 4x2¾" **$10.00**

Tumblers, lists winners from 1st race through 1966, gold rim, Libbey, set of 6, M in G box...**$25.00**

Yearbook, Official Floyd Cramer's; 1952.............................**$65.00**

Yearbook, US Auto Club, AJ Foyt on color cover, 1964.......**$55.00**

Italian Glass

Throughout the century, the island of Murano has been recognized as one of the major glassmaking centers of the world. Companies including Venini, Barovier, Aureliano Toso, Barvini, Vistosi, AVEM, Canedese, Cappellin, Seguso, and Archimede Seguso have produced very fine art glass, examples of which today often bring several thousand dollars on the secondary market — superior examples much more. Such items are rarely seen at the garage sale and flea market level, but what you will be seeing are the more generic glass clowns, birds, ashtrays, and animals, generally referred to simply as Murano glass. Their values are determined by the techniques used in their making more than size alone. For instance, an item with gold inclusions, controlled bubbles, fused glass patches, or layers of colors is more desirable than one that has none of these elements, even though it may be larger. For more information concerning the specific companies mentioned, see *Schroeder's Antique Price Guide* (Collector Books).

Ashtray, cased pink w/controlled bubble design, gold mica inclusions, 3 rests, Barbini, 2¼x6½" dia **$200.00**

Ashtray, clown figural, multicolored pcs applied to cased green & black body, Murano, 1950s, 10x8" **$90.00**

Ashtray, millefiori and mica in iridescent cobalt, 7", $25.00.

Ashtray, seashell, light blue to turquoise, Murano, very heavy, 1950s, 6¾x6½" **$90.00**

Ashtray, 3 sections cased in red, blue & green, hand blown, Murano, 1960s, 2¾x6½" dia **$125.00**

Bookends, chick, vaseline, high back, 1950s, 7x4"..............**$88.00**

Bookends, pear & apple, plum & blue encased in clear, attributed Seguso, 6¼x3½", 3½x4¼"....................................**$110.00**

Bottle, scent; multicolored millefiori canes, matching ball stopper, 7¾x2⅜" **$185.00**

Bottle, scent; multicolored spatter w/gold mica, swirled neck, gold stopper, Murano, 9¾" **$185.00**

Bottle, scent; purple cased, corseted, 3-sided, matching cone stopper, Venini Murano, 10x2½" **$235.00**

Bowl, amber half-apple shape w/gold aventurine & green inclusions, 2½x6¾x5⅜"...**$65.00**

Bowl, centerpiece; yellow swirled glass w/gold mica cased in clear, triangular w/scalloped edge, clear looped feet.............**$125.00**

Bowl, green & red latticino stripes, flared rim, 6" H............**$90.00**

Bowl, lavender w/deep purple swirls, irregular ruffled rim w/red border, 6x13" **$60.00**

Bowl, multicolored swirls w/much gold mica, sq, Murano, 2¾x6½" **$100.00**

Bowl, red geode cased in clear, Archimede Seguso, 2¾x5½x5½".. **$85.00**

Bowl, shaped like hollowed apple half, red cased w/gold patterned dots, 5" **$36.00**

Decanter, lavender swirl cased in clear, shouldered & slim, matching stopper, Murano, 26½x6" at base..............................**$150.00**

Decanter, Sommerso olive green cased in crystal, controlled bubbles, ca 1950s-60s, 9" **$115.00**

Ewer, swirled multicolored stripes in clear, ruffled rim, green striped arched handle, Bimini, 7¾" **$90.00**

Ewer vase, latticino yellow & white swirled ribbons in clear, 6½" **$60.00**

Lamp base, white w/gold & black banded swirls, attributed to Dino Martens, metal base, 16"..**$132.50**

Paperweight, colorful exotic fish (2) encased in clear 'aquarium' block, controlled bubbles, ca 1950, 6x4x1⅜"..............**$155.00**

Sculpture, bird, sleek stylized form in pink, Venini label, 12x3¾" **$425.00**

Sculpture, clown heads, 8", from $100.00 to $125.00 each.
(Photo courtesy David Barrow)

Sculpture, clown w/accordion, multicolored w/blue hat, millefiori pants, black shoes, Murano, 12" **$125.00**

Sculpture, dolphin on wave, crystal w/gold flecks, Lucetta, 11" ..**$75.00**

Sculpture, dove, orange head & neck fades to clear w/gold aventurine, 4½x3¼x2⅜"..**$60.00**

Sculpture, fish, dark red sommerso & amber cased in clear, Murano, 5½x8x2¼"..**$120.00**

Sculpture, penguin, black & white cased in clear, Murano, 6"..**$72.50**

Sculpture, rooster, multicolored w/clear applied details, curled tail & comb, Murano, 7¾"..**$60.00**

Sculpture, rooster w/tail high, 6-color, ornate tail & comb, 8x5¼", 3½" wingspan **$85.00**

Sculpture, sailboat, green frost w/2 white frosted sails w/multicolored inner veils, Murano, 13½x9½x5¾" **$155.00**

Sculpture, tiger, cased gold w/black stripes, clear applied details, Murano, 6x13½"..**$600.00**

Sculpure, bird, stylized, green cased, clear comb, ca 1950s, 18½x7½" **$75.00**

Vase, black & red lady's torso cased in clear, 17½x7¼" **$240.00**

Vase, blue to clear Corroso w/mica flecks & controlled bubbles, 4-scallop rim, Barovier Seguso, 10"............................**$265.00**

Vase, bud; ruby w/clear controlled bubbles, elongated baluster w/ruffled top, Murano, 12½" **$48.00**

Vase, green cased in clear, applied green jewels, Mid-Century Modern style, 10¾x8"..**$120.00**

Vase, green cased w/much gold mica, ovoid w/flared rim, Murano, 8" **$85.00**

Vase, green cylinder w/4 applied spiraling rods, Made in Italy label, 11¾x7½"..**$215.00**

Vase, handkerchief; latticino ribbons, multicolor in clear, Murano, 5x4½" **$90.00**

Vase, latticino twisted & swirled yellow & white ribbons in clear, clear applied handles, ruffled rim, 4½" **$85.00**

Vase, Lavorazione, cornflower blue cased in white, trumpet neck, ruffled rim, 14x7½" **$25.00**

Vase, multicolored swirls w/gold flecks, 2 sm loop handles, Murano, 8" **$72.50**

Vase, orange-red w/black horizontal bands & gold-leaf trim heavy, 10½x7" **$350.00**

Vase, pink & white filigrana w/applied crystal & gold-flecked rigaree, footed cone form, 8½x5½" **$96.00**

Vase, Sommerso green & bright yellow cased in clear, geode style cylinder, attributed Seguso, 9¼x3¼" **$70.00**

Vase, yellow mottled neck to blue base, applied red opaque serpentine decor, Murano, 9½" **$60.00**

Vase, yellow sphere w/slim amethyst neck, Venini/Italia, 3¾x2¾" **$120.00**

Vase, yellow w/ribbed swirls, shouldered, 9½"....................**$150.00**

Vases, red-violet cased heart form, Salviati, 7½", pr............**$240.00**

Jade-ite Glassware

For the past few years, Jade-ite has been one of the fastest moving types of collectible glassware on the market. It was produced by several companies from the 1940s through 1965. Many of Anchor Hocking's Fire-King lines were available in the soft opaque green Jade-ite, and Jeannette Glass as well as McKee produced their own versions.

It was always very inexpensive glass, and it was made in abundance. Dinnerware for the home as well as restaurants and a vast array of kitchenware items literally flooded the country for many years. Though a few rare pieces have become fairly expensive, most are still reasonably priced, and there are still bargains to be had.

For more information we recommend *Anchor Hocking's Fire-King & More, Kitchen Glassware of the Depression Years,* and *Collectible Glassware from the 40s, 50s, and 60s,* all by Gene and Cathy Florence (Collector Books).

Alice, cup & saucer **$10.00**

Alice, plate, 9½"..**$26.00**

Charm, bowl, soup; 6"..**$35.00**

Charm, creamer **$20.00**

Charm, cup & saucer..**$17.00**

Charm, plate, dinner; 9¼"..**$30.00**

Charm, sugar bowl..**$20.00**

Colonial Kitchen, bowl, mixing; 6", from $70 to **$75.00**

Colonial Kitchen, bowl, mixing; 8¾", from $80 to.............**$90.00**

Restaurant Ware, bowl, flat soup; 9¼"	**$110.00**
Restaurant Ware, cup, narrow rim, 7-oz	**$12.00**
Restaurant Ware, plate, pie/salad; 6¾"	**$10.00**
Restaurant Ware, plate, 10"	**$150.00**
Restaurant Ware, platter, 11½" L	**$35.00**
Restaurant Ware, saucer, 6"	**$6.00**
Sheaves of Wheat, bowl, dessert; 4½"	**$55.00**
Sheaves of Wheat, cup & saucer	**$50.00**
Sheaves of Wheat, plate, dinner; 9"	**$58.00**
Shell, bowl, cereal; 6⅜"	**$25.00**
Shell, bowl, vegetable; 8½"	**$28.00**
Shell, cup, 8-oz	**$10.00**
Shell, plate, dinner; 10"	**$25.00**
Shell, platter, 13" L	**$48.00**
Shell, sugar bowl, footed	**$25.00**
Shell, sugar bowl lid	**$45.00**
Splash Proof, bowl, mixing; flower decal, 2-qt, 7⅝", from $450 to	**$500.00**
Splash Proof, bowl, mixing; no decals, 2-qt, 7⅝", from $60 to	**$65.00**
Three Bands, bowl, vegetable; 8¼"	**$85.00**
Three Bands, plate, dinner; rare, 9⅛"	**$500.00**
1700 Line, bowl, cereal; 5⅞"	**$30.00**
1700 Line, cup, Ransom, 9-oz	**$14.00**
1700 Line, plate, dinner; 9⅛"	**$18.00**

Jane Ray: Plate, dinner; $10.00; Cup and saucer, $15.00. (Photo courtesy Gene and Cathy Florence)

Miscellaneous

Ashtray, sq, 4 rests, 4¼", from $30 to	**$32.00**
Butter dish, rectangular, crystal top, from $100 to	**$110.00**
Candy dish, Sea Shell, sm, from $18 to	**$20.00**
Compote, footed, scalloped rim, 6", from $70 to	**$75.00**
Dessert set, Leaf & Blossom, from $35 to	**$40.00**
Egg cup, double; Breakfast Set, from $40 to	**$45.00**
Jewel box, w/hand-painted flower on lid, sq, from $85 to	**$95.00**
Loaf pan, 5x9", from $45 to	**$50.00**
Mug, Masonic Lodge emblem in gold	**$20.00**
Mug, sides tapered in, very heavy, common, from $8 to	**$10.00**
Pitcher, milk; Breakfast Set, 20-oz, from $80 to	**$90.00**
Plate, 3-compartment, child's size, rare, 7½", from $500 to	**$600.00**
Skillet, 2-spout, 7", from $140 to	**$165.00**
Vase, scalloped rim, 3-bead, application to ea side, 5½", from $20 to	**$22.50**

Vase, tab handles, 7¾", from $85 to	**$95.00**

Japan Ceramics

This category is narrowed down to the inexpensive novelty items produced in Japan from 1921 to 1941 and again from 1947 until the present. Though Japanese ceramics marked Nippon, Noritake, and Occupied Japan have long been collected, some of the newest fun-type collectibles on today's market are the figural ashtrays, pincushions, wall pockets, toothbrush holders, etc., that are marked 'Made in Japan' or simply 'Japan.' In her book *Collector's Encyclopedia of Made in Japan Ceramics,* Carole Bess White explains the pitfalls you will encounter when you try to determine production dates. Collectors refer to anything produced before WWII as 'old' and anything made after 1952 as 'new.' Backstamps are inconsistent as to wording and color, and styles are eclectic. Generally, items with applied devices are old, and they are heavier and thicker. Often they were more colorful than the newer items, since fewer colors mean less expense to the manufacturer. Lustre glazes are usually indicative of older pieces, especially the deep solid colors. When lustre was used after the war, it was often mottled with contrasting hues and was usually thinner.

Imaginative styling and strong colors are what give these Japanese ceramics their charm, and they also are factors to consider when you make your purchases. You'll find all you need to know to be a wise shopper in the book we've recommended. Unless noted otherwise, our values are for items in mint condition.

See also Blue Willow; Cat Collectibles; Condiment Sets; Flower Frogs; Geisha Girl; Holt Howard; Kreiss; Lamps; Lefton; Napkin Dolls; Occupied Japan Collectibles; Powder Jars; Toothbrush Holders; Wall Pockets.

Advisor: Carole Bess White (See Directory, Japan Ceramics)

Newsletter: *Made in Japan Info Letter*
Carole Bess White
2225 NE 33rd
Portland, OR 97212-5116
fax: 503-281-2817
CBESSW@aol.com

Bowl, gold lustre band with fruit basket, Noritake, 7" from $20.00 to $35.00. (Photo courtesy Carole Bess White)

Ashtray, cat figure on canoe, red #1 mark, 1½", from $18 to... **$28.00**

Ashtray, lady figural, multicolored card suit decoration, black mark, 3", set of 4, from $45 to **$65.00**

Basket, red roses on white, 4 gold feet, w/handles, gold mark, 4¼", from $15 to **$20.00**

Biscuit barrel, Moriyama w/reed handle, black & green flowering branch on pale yellow, black mark, 7½", from $60 to **$75.00**

Biscuit jar, multicolored card suits, red mark, from $50 to ..**$80.00**

Bookends, monkey, white w/black accents, #168, 7", pr from $28 to **$48.00**

Bowl, serving; multicolored Art Deco panels, green mark, 9½", from $35 to **$55.00**

Cache pot, dogs in car, 5¾" long, from $15.00 to $25.00.
(Photo courtesy Carole Bess White)

Candleholders, white & black floral on orange, black mark, 5½", pr from $30 to **$40.00**

Cigarette holder, elephant figural, yellow & green, black mark, 4½", from $30 to **$45.00**

Creamer & sugar bowl, multicolored leafy calico, tray, black mark, w/tray, 3-pc set, 8½", from $15 to **$25.00**

Decanter, dog figural, RYE on pink collar, Japan label, 10½", from $15 to...**$25.00**

Egg cup, multicolored flowers on cream, 3½", from $25 to ..**$35.00**

Figurine, batwing lady in green dress w/pink flowers, 10½", from $125 to **$150.00**

Figurine, boy sitting on rock fishing, blue mark, 4¾", from $35 to **$40.00**

Figurine, cat snarling, white glaze on tan clay, from $30 to..**$45.00**

Figurine, football player, bisque, black mark, 5", from $18 to **$28.00**

Figurine, Scottie dog, white w/black accents, detailed, black mark, 10", from $35 to...**$50.00**

Flask, man w/mirror, The Good Fellow Who Drinks With Me, black mark, w/ceramic stopper, 4", from $50 to **$75.00**

Flower frog, nude lady, white, marked Yankoware, 7", from $30 to **$45.00**

Humidor, majolica-style, yellow w/black pipe, dog finial on lid, black mark, 7½", from $35 to....................................**$50.00**

Mayonnaise, multicolored Deco style, black mark, 3-pc, 3¾", from $40 to **$75.00**

Mayonnaise, pink & yellow panels, lotus shape, Goldcastle, red mark, 7", 3-pc, from $15 to...**$25.00**

Napkin ring, boy w/brown hat & pants, ring is body, black mark, 4¼", from $25 to...**$35.00**

Pincushion, dog pulling cart w/cushion, red mark, 3¼", from $18 to **$28.00**

Pincushion, Spanish lady in yellow dress w/cushion in basket, black mark, 4½", from $18 to...**$28.00**

Planter, pink & blue card suits on white, 3", from $15 to ...**$25.00**

Salt & pepper shakers, Gingham Dog & Calico Cat, red mark, 3¼", pr from $15 to **$20.00**

Salt & pepper shakers, Moriyama, black & green flowering branch on pale yellow, sq, 5", pr from $25 to.........................**$45.00**

Salt dip, swan figural, applied pink rose & flowers, red mark, 2¾", from $8 to **$15.00**

Teapot, multicolored Deco triangle design, on tile, red mark, 2-pc, 7¾", from $45 to...**$65.00**

Teapot, Native American face, axe forms handle, black mark, 5½", from $35 to **$55.00**

Toothbrush holder, Dutch boy before container, black mark, 4¾", from $95 to **$135.00**

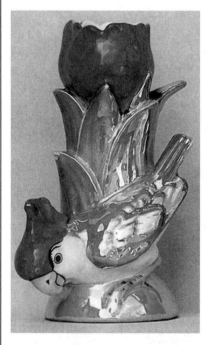

Vase, bird and tulip mold, 7¼", from $40.00 to $65.00. (Photo courtesy Carole Bess White)

Wall plaques, Scottie dogs, multicolored, red mark, 4", pr from $50 to **$75.00**

Wall pocket, pink roses on white, red mark, 8½", from $35 to. **$45.00**

Jewel Tea Company

At the turn of the century, there was stiff competition among door-to-door tea-and-coffee companies, and most of them tried to snag the customer by doling out coupons that could eventually be traded in for premiums. But the thing that set the Jewel Tea people apart from the others was that their premiums were awarded to the customer first, then 'earned' through the purchases that followed. This set the tone of their business dealings which obviously contributed to their success, and very soon in addition to the basic products they started out with, the company entered the food-manufacturing field. They eventually became one of the country's largest retailers. Today their products, containers, premiums, and advertising ephemera are all very collectible. Our values are for undamaged items in at least excellent original condition, unless noted otherwise.

Advisors: Bill and Judy Vroman (See Directory, Jewel Tea)

Baking powder, Jewel, cylindrical tin w/script logo & white lettering, 1950s-60s, 1-lb, from $20 to	**$30.00**
Booklet, Jewel Tea Co Inc Annual Report 1943, EX	**$60.00**
Cake decorator set, late 1940s, from $50 to	**$65.00**
Candy, Jewel Mints, round green tin, 1920s, 1-lb, from $30 to	**$40.00**
Cocoa, Jewel or Jewel Tea, various boxes, ea from $25 to	**$45.00**
Coffee, Jewel Blend, orange & gold w/white lettering & logo, paper label	**$40.00**
Coffee, Jewel Private Blend, brown & white lettering, 1-lb, from $15 to	**$25.00**
Coffee, Royal Jewel, yellow, brown & white, 1-lb, from $20 to	**$35.00**
Coffee, West Coast, orange & brown w/white lettering, bell at top of center, 1960s, 2-lb, from $25 to	**$35.00**
Coffeepot Cleaner, Mary Dunbar, 2 pouches (of 4) in EX box.	**$45.00**
Dishes, Melmac, 8 place settings from $150 to	**$170.00**
Extract, Jewel Imitation Vanilla, in brown box w/orange & white lettering, 1960s, 4-oz	**$20.00**
Garment bag, 1950s, MIP, from $25 to	**$30.00**
Instant Cocoa Mix, brown, yellow & white, 12-oz, 5"	**$32.00**
Laundry, Daybreak Laundry Set, from $15 to	**$20.00**
Malted milk mixer, Jewel-T, from $40 to	**$50.00**
Mixer, Mary Dunbar, hand-held, w/stand, 1940, from $40 to	**$50.00**
Mustard tin, orange, blue & white, Continental Can Co, 4x2¼x2¼", VG	**$45.00**
Napkins, paper w/printed pattern, box of 200	**$25.00**
Pickle fork, Jewel-T, from $20 to	**$25.00**
Recipe booklet, Velveeta the Delicious Cheese Food, 12 recipes, 5½x3"	**$60.00**

Jewelry

Today's costume jewelry collectors may range from nine to ninety and have tastes as varied as their ages, but one thing they all have in common is their love of these distinctive items of jewelry, some originally purchased at the corner five-&-dimes, others from department stores and boutiques.

Costume jewelry became popular, simply because it was easily affordable for all women. Today jewelry made before 1954 is considered to be 'antique,' while the term 'collectible' jewelry generally refers to those pieces made after that time. Costume jewelry was federally recognized as an American art form in 1954, and the copyright law was passed to protect the artists' designs. The copyright mark (c in a circle) found on the back of a piece identifies a post-1954 'collectible.'

Quality should always be the primary consideration when

shopping for these treasures. Remember that pieces with colored rhinestones bring the higher prices. (Note: A 'rhinestone' is a foil-backed, leaded glass crystal, while a 'stone' is not foiled.) A complete set (called a parure) increases in value by 20% over the total of its components. Check for a manufacturer's mark, since a signed piece is worth 20% more than one of comparable quality, but not signed. Some of the best designers are Miriam Haskell, Eisenberg, Weiss, Trifary, Hollycraft, and Joseff.

Early plastic pieces (Lucite, Bakelite, and celluloid, for example) are very collectible. Some Lucite is used in combination with wood, and the figural designs are especially desirable.

There are several excellent reference books available if you'd like more information. Look for *Unsigned Beauties of Costume Jewelry, Signed Beauties of Costume Jewelry, Vol. I* and *II; Coro Jewelry;* and *Rhinestone Jewelry: Figurals, Animals, Whimsicals* by our advisor Marcia Brown. Lillian Baker has written several, including *Fifty Years of Collectible Fashion Jewelry,* and *100 Years of Collectible Jewelry.* Books by other authors include *Collectible Silver Jewelry* and *Costume Jewelry* by Fred Rezazadeh; *Collectible Costume Jewelry* by Cherri Simonds; *Collecting Costume Jewelry 101* and *Collecting Costume Jewelry 202* by Julia C. Carroll; *Inside the Jewelry Box, Vol.1* and *Vol. 2* by Ann Mitchell Pittman; *Brillant Rhinestones* and *20th Century Costume Jewelry, 1900 – 1980,* by Ronna Lee Aikins; and video books *Hidden Treasures Series* by Christie Romero and Marcia Brown. All are available through Collector Books; the videos may be purchased by contacting Marcia Brown.

See also Christmas Tree Pins

Advisor: Marcia Brown (See Directory, Jewelry)

Club/Newsletter: *Vintage Fashion and Costume Jewelry Newsletter and Club*
P.O. Box 265, Glen Oaks, NY 11004
www.lizjewel.com/vf/

Bracelet, gold-plated with tiger eye cabochon framed in mesh, $35.00. (Photo courtesy Marcia Brown)

Bracelet, bangle; carved apricot Bakelite, 1" W, from $55 to	**$75.00**
Bracelet, bangle; carved butterscotch Bakelite, 1935	**$175.00**
Bracelet, bangle; Lea Stein, cellulose acetate laminate, red, white & black w/ellipses, 1960-80	**$275.00**

Bracelet, bangle; maroon Bakelite w/chrome band, 1935...**$125.00**

Bracelet, carved amber Catalin capped w/aluminum balls, 1936-39, from $100 to **$125.00**

Bracelet, Charel, green thermoset plastic links, 1960-70, from $45 to **$55.00**

Bracelet, Danecraft, silver links, dainty, from $50 to............**$85.00**

Bracelet, Hobé, faux jade cabochon w/gold-plated leaves **$85.00**

Bracelet, Monet, tailored, gold-tone links **$45.00**

Bracelet, Renoir, copper 'good health' type...........................**$40.00**

Bracelet, reverse-carved amber Bakelite w/black links, 1930s, from $200 to **$275.00**

Bracelet, unsigned, elastic w/black segments w/clear rhinestone studs **$65.00**

Bracelet, unsigned, pearls & topaz rhinestones in single row ..**$30.00**

Bracelet, white plastic w/aurora borealis rhinestones, hinged, 1960, from $85 to **$125.00**

Brooch, Bakelite, horse's head, metal studs & chain, glass eye, from $250 to **$350.00**

Brooch, Bakelite, yellow with red polka dots, $3,500.00.
(Photo courtesy LiveAuctioneers.com/Morphy Auctions)

Brooch, Barclay, gold-plated anchor w/gold rhinestones & gold-plated rope...**$75.00**

Brooch, Boucher, Skye terrier, gold-tone w/enameled details, 1½" **$60.00**

Brooch, BSK, gold-plated veined leaves w/diamanté pavé center, long & slim...**$50.00**

Brooch, Capri, multicolor rhinestones on cap, green enameling...**$48.00**

Brooch, Eisenberg, diamanté rhinestone ribbon, 3½" **$425.00**

Brooch, Florenza, gold basketweave w/blue baguettes **$80.00**

Brooch, Hattie Carnegie, gold-plated cameo.....................**$110.00**

Brooch, Hollycraft, butterfly, blue/lavender rhinestones, pearls & opalene cabochons **$135.00**

Brooch, JJ, cat, gold-plated w/articulated tail.......................**$20.00**

Brooch, JJ, gold-plated butterfly w/openwork & enameling..**$40.00**

Brooch, Kenneth Jay Lane, dragonfly w/pink & clear rhinestones & enamel wings **$90.00**

Brooch, Lea Stein, cellulose acetate, laminated fox, built up in layers, 1960-80 ....**$175.00**

Brooch, Monet, bee, silver-tone metal w/wire (harp-like) wings..**$55.00**

Brooch, red & black Bakelite w/much carving, 1925, from $150 to **$175.00**

Brooch, Robert Originals, ocean turtle, enameled...............**$80.00**

Brooch, Sandor, white enamel daisy w/green leaves.............**$62.50**

Brooch, Trifary, faux ruby & diamanté rhinestone bouquet..**$325.00**

Brooch, unsigned, chaton rhinestone snowflake, very lg.......**$60.00**

Brooch, unsigned, flower in black & white enamel, 1960s, 1x3½", from $25 to **$45.00**

Brooch, unsigned, silver bug w/rhinestone center **$85.00**

Brooch, Weiss, gold rhinestone sun.....................................**$95.00**

Brooch, Weiss, owl, multicolored enameling.......................**$65.00**

Brooch & earrings, Judy Lee, silver leaves w/aurora borealis rhinestones **$50.00**

Brooch & earrings, Kenneth Jay Lane, gold-plated bow w/pavé diamantè rhinestones **$98.00**

Brooch & earrings, La Roco, purple, pink & aurora borealis rhinestones **$150.00**

Brooch and earrings, red emerald cut and chaton rhinestones, $60.00 for the set. (Photo courtesy Marcia Brown)

Brooch & earrings, Robert Originals, pink pearls, clear & pink rhinestones...**$200.00**

Brooch & earrings, unsigned, orange & gold beaded snowflake, lg...**$80.00**

Buckle, Bakelite & metal, 2-pc, 1935, from $105 to **$125.00**

Earrings, Bakelite, red hoop shapes, 1940s, lg, from $55 to ..**$65.00**

Earrings, carved Bakelite button type, 1935, from $25 to....**$45.00**

Earrings, Coro, lg red rhinestone amid sm pink stones, 1948-55, 1", from $8 to **$12.00**

Earrings, Ledo, green rhinestones form flower, 1" clips, from $20 to **$30.00**

Earrings, Mariam Haskell, turquoise bead w/5 diamanté rhinestone points...**$60.00**

Earrings, orange Bakelite triangular drop, heavy, 1935, from $55 to **$75.00**

Earrings, plastic flower w/rhinestone center, screw-back button, 1960, from $10 to **$20.00**

Earrings, unsigned, aurora borealis rhinestone cluster **$40.00**

Earrings, unsigned, aurora borealis stones on rigid chain **$35.00**

Earrings, unsigned, orange rhinestones dangle from 3 lime green navettes **$25.00**

Fur clip, Boucher, sapphire blue rhinestones on gold plate.**$185.00**

Necklace, Coro, blue glass ribbed stones w/blue rhinestones, 1950s, from $65 to **$75.00**

Necklace, Hattie Carnegie, 20 strands of crystal beads....... **$135.00**

Necklace, Kenneth Jay Lane, faux pearls, 3-strand, initials on clasp **$110.00**

Necklace, Les Bernard, 3 strands of metallic pearls **$65.00**

Necklace, thermoset plastic, turquoise w/wood & painted cork, 1950s, from $35 to **$45.00**

Necklace, unsigned, dark green hand-set chaton rhinestones .. **$60.00**

Necklace, unsigned, gold-tone Nouveau leaves w/faux pearl drops **$65.00**

Necklace, unsigned, sterling silver & abalone shells, 1950s, from $50 to **$85.00**

Necklace, Whiting & Davis, gold mesh fabric bib style **$110.00**

Necklace & bracelet, Hollycraft, blue rhinestones & seed pearls.. **$165.00**

Necklace & earrings, unsigned, glass cabochons w/gold veins & topaz rhinestones **$120.00**

Necklace & earrings, unsigned, silver-tone leaf garland w/blue rhinestones.. **$25.00**

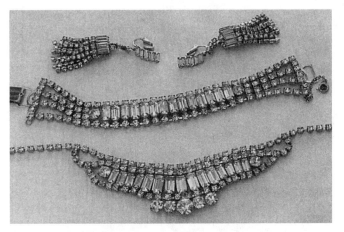

Parure, rhinestone baguettes and chatons, from $95.00 to $115.00 for the set. (Photo courtesy Marcia Brown)

Ring, Ciner, green crystal faceted stone on silver mount, from $45 to **$65.00**

Ring, Sarah Coventry, amethyst-colored stone & sm faux pearls.. **$32.50**

Ring, unsigned, gold-plated twin diamond rhinestone navettes .. **$22.50**

Johnson Bros.

There is a definite renewal of interest in dinnerware collecting right now, and just about any antique shop or mall you visit will offer a few nice examples of the wares made by this Staffordshire company. They've been in business since well before the turn of the century and have targeted the American market to such an extent that during the 1960s and 1970s, as much as 70% of their dinnerware was sold to distributors in this country. They made many scenic patterns as well as florals, and with the interest today's collectors have been demonstrating in Chintz, dealers tell me that Johnson Brothers' Rose Chintz and Chintz (Victorian) sell very well for them, especially the latter. In addition to their polychrome designs, they made several patterns in both blue and pink transferware.

Though some of their lines, Old Britain Castles, Friendly Village, His Majesty, and Rose Chintz, for instance, are still being produced, most are no longer as extensive as they once were, so the secondary market is being tapped to replace broken items that are not available anywhere else.

In her book *Johnson Brothers Dinnerware Pattern Directory and Price Guide* author Mary Finegan breaks pricing down into three groups: Base Price, One Star, and Two Star. About 90% of Johnson Brothers patterns have proven to be popular sellers and have been made in an extensive range of pieces (with the possible exception of buffet plates and 20" turkey platters, which were produced primarily in holiday patterns only). Some of the patterns you are most likely to encounter and are thus included in the Base Price group are Bird of Paradise, Mount Vernon, Castle on the Lake, Old Bradbury, Day in June, Nordic, Devon Sprays, Old Mill (The), Empire Grape, Pastorale, Haddon Hall, Pomona, Harvest Time, Road Home (The), Indian Tree, Vintage (older version), Melody, and Windsor Fruit. (Also included in this value range are any other patterns not mentioned below.)

One-Star patterns include Autumn's Delight, Coaching Scenes, Devonshire, Fish, Friendly Village, Gamebirds, Garden Bouquet, Hearts and Flowers, Heritage Hall, Indies, Millstream, Olde English Countryside, Rose Bouquet, Sheraton, Tulip Time, and Winchester. Two Star patterns include Barnyard King, Century of Progress, Chintz-Victorian, Dorchester, English Chippendale, Harvest Fruit, His Majesty, Historic America, Merry Christmas, Old Britain Castles, Persian Tulip, Rose Chintz, Strawberry Fair, Tally Ho, Twelve Days of Christmas, and Wild Turkeys.

Our prices pertain to older pieces only, usually recognizable by the crown in the backstamp. Newer pieces from the 1990s to the present do not carry this crown and are available in any number of retail and outlet stores today. New prices are much lower — while a complete place setting of Old Britain Castles is normally priced at about $50.00, in some outlets you may be able to purchase it for half of that.

In the listings that follow, values apply only to the patterns in the base price group. One and Two Star patterns are in high demand and hard to find, and so command higher prices. They sell for as much as 20% to 50% over the base values. Not all pieces are available in all patterns. In addition to their company logo, much of the dinnerware is also stamped with the pattern name. Today Johnson Brothers is part of the Wedgwood group.

Bowl, cereal/soup; sq or lug, ea from $10 to **$20.00**

Bowl, soup; round or sq, 7", from $12 to **$25.00**

Bowl, vegetable; oval, from $30 to **$50.00**

Butter dish, from $50 to **$80.00**

Chop/cake plate, from $50 to **$80.00**

Coffee mug, from $20 to **$25.00**

Coffeepot, from $20 to upwards of **$25.00**

Demitasse set, 2-pc, from $20 to **$30.00**

Egg cup, from $15 to... **$30.00**

Pitcher/jug, from $45 to **$55.00**

Plate, dinner; from $14 to.. **$30.00**

Plate, salad; sq or round, from $10 to **$18.00**

Platter, med, 12-14", ea from $45 to **$55.00**
Salt & pepper shakers, pr from $40 to **$48.00**
Sauceboat/gravy, from $40 to...**$48.00**
Sugar bowl, open, from $30 to **$40.00**
Teacup & saucer, from $15 to..**$30.00**
Teapot, from $90 to...**$100.00**
Turkey platter, 20½", from $200 to **$300.00**

Rose Chintz, bowl, soup; round or square, 7", $18.00

Josef Originals

Figurines of lovely ladies, charming girls, and whimsical animals marked Josef Originals were designed by Muriel Joseph George of Arcadia, California, from 1945 to 1985. Until 1960 they were produced in California, but production costs were high, and copies of her work were being made in Japan. To remain competitive, she and her partner, George Good, found a company in Japan to build a factory and produce her designs to her satisfaction. Muriel retired in 1982; however, Mr. Good continued production of her work and made some design changes on some of the figurines. The company was sold in late 1985. The name is currently owned by Dakin/Applause, and a limited number of figurines with the Josef Originals name are being made. Those made during the ownership of Muriel are the most collectible. They can be recognized by these characteristics: the girls have a high-gloss finish, black eyes, and most are signed on the bottom. As of the 1970s a bisque finish was making its way into the lineup, and by 1980 glossy girls were fairly scarce in the product line. Brown-eyed figures date from 1982 through 1985; Applause uses a red-brown eye, although they are starting to release copies of early pieces that are signed Josef Originals by Applause or by Dakin. The animals were nearly always made with a matt finish and bore paper labels only. In the mid-1970s they introduced a line of animals with fuzzy flocked coats and glass eyes. Our advisors, Jim and Kaye Whitaker have three books which we recommend for further study: *Josef Originals, Charming Figurines (Revised Edition); Josef Originals, A Second Look;* and *Josef Originals, Figurines of Muriel Joseph George.* These are all currently available, and each has no repeats of items shown in the other books.

Please note: All figurines have black eyes unless specified otherwise. As with so many collectibles, values have been impacted to a measurable extent since the advent of the internet.

See also Birthday Angels.

Advisors: Jim and Kaye Whitaker (See Directory, Josef Originals; no appraisal requests please)

Angels playing various sports, Sports Angels series, Japan, 2¾", ea..**$35.00**
Belle Series, skirt is bell, 6 in series, Japan, 4", ea.................**$35.00**
Buggy Bugs series, various poses, wire antenna, Japan, 3¼", ea...**$12.00**
Camel baby, recumbent, Japan, 2½" **$35.00**
Christmas angel praying by decorated tree nightlight, 7" **$50.00**
Colonial Days, series of 6 girls doing chores, Japan, 5", ea...**$50.00**
Dalmatian, Kennel Club series, Japan, 3½"........................**$20.00**
Ecology Girls, 1974 debut, 6 in series, Japan, 4", ea **$40.00**
Farmer's Daughter, girl w/hen & basket of eggs, Japan, 5"...**$45.00**
First Date, young lady in green gown holding fan, Japan, 9"..**$95.00**
Girl cutting cake, Japan, 6", from $45 to............................**$50.00**
Happy Home w/Dove Greeting Angel, Japan, 3¾" **$35.00**
Hippo Family, various poses, Japan, 2-2½", ea...................**$14.00**
Hunter, beautiful horse standing, Japan, 6".......................**$25.00**
It's a Wonderful World series, Japan, 3½", ea **$45.00**
Italian Aristocrats, lady & escort, Japan, 7", ea...................**$75.00**
Johnny, w/marbles, Joseph's Children, California, 4¾".........**$85.00**
Lara's Theme music box, Japan, 6"......................................**$60.00**
Lipstick, First Time series, Japan, 4½", from $35 to............**$45.00**
Little Gourmets, girls w/recipes holding food, Japan, 3¾ ", ea.. **$35.00**

Little Internationals (32 countries represented), Japan, 4½", $45.00 each. (Photo courtesy Jim and Kaye Whitaker)

Love Story series, courtship to wedding, 6 in series, Japan, 8", ea..**$95.00**
Make Believe series, Japan, 4½", ea **$40.00**
Mama Ballerina, California, 7" **$80.00**
Mice, Christmas, Japan, 2¾", ea **$9.00**
Miss Mary, Nursery Rhymes series, Japan, 4"......................**$45.00**

Mouse Village, series of mice dressed in various poses, Japan, ½-2", ea **$8.00**

Music box, Happy Anniversary, Japan, 7¼" **$65.00**

Nanette, half-doll w/jewels, several colors, California, 5½" .. **$55.00**

New Home, girl w/key, Special Occasions series, Japan, 4½".. **$35.00**

Nurse, nurse in yellow holding baby, Career Girls series, Japan, 5¾" **$45.00**

Ostriches, adults and two chicks, Japan, from $100.00 to $150.00 for the set. (Photo courtesy Jim and Kaye Whitaker)

Persian cats, various poses, Japan, 2½-4", ea **$18.00**

Pixies, various poses, green trimmed in red & gold, Japan, 2-3¼", ea **$25.00**

Puerto Rico, Little International, Japan, 4" **$40.00**

Rose, girl w/flower hat, Flower Girl series, Japan, 4¼" **$35.00**

Ruby, girl w/'ruby' in crown, Little Jewels series, Japan, 3½".. **$35.00**

Santa, kiss on forehead, Japan, 4¾" **$45.00**

Skunk w/white hair tuft on head, Japan, 2½" **$18.00**

Special Occasions Series, 6 in series, Japan, 4½", ea **$50.00**

Three Kings, Japan, 8½-11", set of 3 .... **$70.00**

Wee Folk, various poses, Japan, 4½", ea **$20.00**

Yorkshire & various other breeds, Kennel Club series, Japan, 3", ea **$20.00**

Kaye of Hollywood

This was one of the smaller pottery studios that operated in California during the 1940s — interesting in that people tend to confuse the name with Kay Finch. Kay (Schueftan) worked for Hedi Schoop before striking out on her own; because her work was so similar to that of her former employer's, a successful lawsuit was brought against her, and it was at this point that the mark was changed from Kaye of Hollywood to Kim Ward.

Figurine, lady dancer, applied lace to full skirt, blond hair, blue base, #301, 10¼" **$40.00**

Flower holder, Black mailman w/pack of letters, Mail on hat, illegible number, 7½" **$70.00**

Flower holder, colonial lady, 1 pot in hands, larger behind, browns & greens, #3118, 10" **$75.00**

Flower holder, colonial man in long blue coat & flowered pants beside lg vase, #105/#3147, 9½" **$60.00**

Flower holder, girl in blue hat, blue open baskets at ea hip, pinks & blues, #3125, 9" **$50.00**

Flower holder, Jack, boy w/lg pot, #3116, 9" **$40.00**

Flower holder, lady with basket, 10", $45.00.

Flower holder, Little Bo Peep w/2 sm pots, #3139, 9" **$50.00**

Flower holder, peasant girl w/lg basket behind her, pink & green, #351, 10x10¾" **$90.00**

Flower holder, Victorian lady, pinks & blues, white hair piled high, #104, 9" **$50.00**

Head vase, curved wide-brim hat, brown hair, rosy cheeks, #3145, 7½" **$65.00**

Wall pocket, lady's head, lg green hat w/applied rose, 7½" ... **$50.00**

Wall pocket, lady w/full skirt, full figure, #201, 9" **$65.00**

Keeler, Brad

California pottery is becoming quite popular among collectors, and Brad Keeler is one of the better known designers. After studying art for a time, he opened his own studio in 1939 where he created naturalistic studies of birds and animals. Sold through giftware stores, the figures were decorated by airbrushing with hand-painted details. Brad Keeler is remembered for his popular flamingo figures and his Chinese Modern Housewares. Keeler died of a heart attack in 1952, and the pottery closed soon thereafter. For more information, we recommend *Collector's Encyclopedia of California Pottery, 2nd Edition*, by Jack Chipman.

Bone dish, fish figure, teal green to tan, #151, 8" **$35.00**

Bowl, Lobster Ware, lettuce leaves, lg red lobster on dome lid, #825, 11" L **$85.00**

Box, duck figure, brown & green w/white band at neck, 4½x5½", from $25 to **$35.00**

Butter dish, Lobster Ware, lobster finial, ladle for melted butter, 6" L, NM **$38.00**

Dish, 2 red radishes resting on green leaf, #863, 7x6½", from $15 to **$20.00**

Figurine, Asian peafowl, 1940s, 6x16x3¼", NM **$195.00**

Figurine, Asian peafowl standing on 1 foot, #22, 7" **$75.00**

Figurine, bird, peach & blue, long scissors-like tail, wings up, #716, 10¾" **$200.00**

Figurine, bird on stump, rose on white, #18, 8¼" **$50.00**

Figurine, bunny scratching, #981, 3" **$30.00**

Figurine, canary, yellow & black on brown stump, 6", from $15 to **$20.00**

Figurine, chipmunk holding acorn, brown & green tones, marked BBK #629, 3" **$35.00**

Figurine, cockatoo, yellow, green & white tones, #35, 8½" .. **$55.00**

Figurine, cockatoo, yellow & green tones, #34, 6x7½", from $35 to **$50.00**

Figurine, cocker spaniel puppy, black & gray, #748, 4½" **$35.00**

Figurine, duck standing on oval base, #50, 4½x6", from $50 to .. **$60.00**

Figurine, eagle w/wings wide, #29, 9½" **$275.00**

Figurine, flamingo in tall grasses, head down, #3, 7½", from $80 to **$90.00**

Figurine, flamingo w/wings half, grassy base, Ceramics by B Keeler, 8½", from $85 to **$100.00**

Figurine, flamingo w/wings up, #813, 7" **$120.00**

Figurine, flamingo w/wings up (wings spanning 4¼"), head up, #47, 10¼" **$140.00**

Figurine, hen w/head up, multicolor, #936, 4½x4¾" **$40.00**

Figurine, peahen, multicolored pastels, head up, 6x7½" **$80.00**

Figurine, pheasant, long plumed tail, #9-38A, 7x11", from $75 to **$100.00**

Figurine, quail pr, 1 bent down, 2nd w/head up, #152 & sticker, 4", 6", pr **$100.00**

Figurine, rooster, black w/green accents, head down, tail up, 8x9½" **$45.00**

Figurine, Siamese, #760, 10" long, from $100.00 to $125.00. (Photo courtesy LiveAuctioneers.com/ Flomaton Antique Auction)

Figurine, Siamese cat on red pillow, #944, 2½x3" **$45.00**

Figurine, Siamese cat playing w/ball of yarn, 6x15", from $140 to **$165.00**

Figurine, Siamese cat standing w/head turned left, 12", from $125 to **$140.00**

Figurine, squirrel, brown tones, #627, 2¼x4x3½" **$15.00**

Figurine, swan w/wings stretched upward, white w/black detail, #705, 14½", from $175 to **$225.00**

Figurines, Siamese kittens (2), 1 about to pounce, 2nd on back, 5", 3", pr **$70.00**

Planter, Santa waving from sled, #909, 7½x8½x4½" **$30.00**

Plate, lobed leaf shape, green, to use w/Lobster Ware, 13" ... **$30.00**

Plate, lobed leaf shape w/tendril handle, green, 8", from $18 to .. **$22.00**

Shelf sitters, Siamese cats, 1 standing & 1 w/paw reaching down, #798/#760, 7", 10", pr **$80.00**

Tray, Lobster Ware, lobster between 2 green leaves, 12x7", from $45 to **$55.00**

Tureen, Lobster Ware, lobster on lettuce leaf lid, #871, 4x8", w/tray & ladle **$90.00**

Tureen, Lobster Ware, lobster on lettuce leaf lid, no #, 4½x5¾", from $35 to **$45.00**

Kentucky Derby Glasses

Since the the late 1930s, every running of the Kentucky Derby has been commemorated with a special glass tumbler. Each year at Churchill Downs on Derby day you can buy them filled with mint juleps. In the early days, this was the only place where these glasses could be purchased. Many collections were started when folks carried the glasses home from the track and then continued to add one for each successive year as they attended the Derby.

The first glass appeared in 1938, but examples from then until 1945 are extremely scarce and are worth thousands — when they can be found. Because of this, many collectors begin with the 1945 glasses. There are three: the tall version, the short regular-size glass, and a jigger. Some years — for instance, 1948, 1956, 1958, 1974, 1986, and 2003 — have slightly different variations, so often there is more than one to collect. To date a glass, simply add one year to the last date on the winner's list found on the back.

Each year many companies put out commemorative Derby glasses. Collectors call them 'bar' glasses (as many bars sold their own versions filled with mint juleps). Because of this, collectors need to be educated as to what the official Kentucky Derby glass looks like.

These prices are for pristine, mint-condition glasses with no chips or flaws. All colors must be bright and show no signs of fading. Lettering must be perfect and intact, even the list of past winners on the back. If gold trim has been used, it must show no wear. If any of these problems exist, reduce our values by 50% to 75%, depending on the glass and the problem. Many more Kentucky Derby shot glasses, jiggers, cordials, boreals, and shooters in various colors and sizes were produced — too many to list here. But be aware that these may present themselves along the collecting trail.

Advisor: Betty L. Hornback (See Directory, Kentucky Derby and Horse Racing)

1940, aluminum **$1,000.00**

1940, French Lick, aluminum **$1,000.00**

1941-1944, plastic Beetleware, ea, from $2,500 to **$4,000.00**

1945, jigger, green horse head, I Have Seen Them All **$1,000.00**

1945, regular, green horse head facing right, horseshoe ... **$1,600.00**

1945, tall, green horse head facing right, horseshoe **$450.00**

1946-47, clear frosted w/frosted bottom, L in circle, ea **$100.00**

1948, clear bottom, green horsehead in horseshoe & horse on other side **$225.00**

1948, frosted bottom, green horse head in horseshoe & horse on other side **$250.00**

1949, He Has Seen Them All, Matt Winn, green on frost.**$225.00**

1950, green horses running on track, Churchill Downs behind. **$450.00**

1951, green winnner's circle, Where Turf Champions Are Crowned **$650.00**

1952, Gold Derby Trophy, Kentucky Derby Gold Cup **$225.00**

1953, black horse facing left, rose garland.......................**$200.00**

1954, green twin spires **$225.00**

1955, green & yellow horses, The Fastest Runners.............**$200.00**

1956, 1 star, 2 tails, brown horses, twin spires **$275.00**

1956, 1 star, 3 tails, brown horses, twin spires **$400.00**

1956, 2 stars, 2 tails, brown horses, twin spires..................**$200.00**

1956, 2 stars, 3 tails, brown horses, twin spires..................**$250.00**

1957, gold & black, horse & jockey facing right...............**$125.00**

1958, Gold Bar, solid gold insignia w/horse, jockey & 1 spire ..**$175.00**

1958, Iron Liege, same as 1957 w/'Iron Leige' added........**$225.00**

1959-60, both black & gold, ea **$100.00**

1961, black horses on track, jockey in red, gold winners....**$110.00**

1962, Churchill Downs, red, gold & black **$70.00**

1963, brown horse, jockey #7, gold lettering **$70.00**

1964, brown horse head, gold lettering...............................**$30.00**

1965, brown twin spires & horses, red lettering..................**$85.00**

1966-68, black, black & blue respectively, ea.....................**$65.00**

1969, green jockey in horseshoe, red lettering....................**$65.00**

1970, green shield, gold lettering **$70.00**

1971, green twin spires, horses at bottom, red lettering **$55.00**

1972, 2 black horses, orange & green print..........................**$55.00**

1973, white, black twin spires, red & green lettering **$60.00**

1974, Federal, regular or mistake, brown & gold, ea..........**$200.00**

1974, mistake (Canonero in 1971 listing on back), Libbey..**$18.00**

1974, regular (Canonero II in 1971 listing on back)............**$16.00**

1975...**$12.00**

1976, plastic tumbler or regular glass, ea...........................**$16.00**

1977...**$14.00**

1978-79, ea...**$16.00**

1980...**$22.00**

1981-82, ea...**$15.00**

1983-85, ea...**$12.00**

1986...**$14.00**

1986 ('85 copy)...**$20.00**

1987-89, ea...**$12.00**

1990-92, ea...**$10.00**

1993-95, ea...**$9.00**

1996-98, ea...**$8.00**

1999-2000, ea...**$6.00**

2001-2002, ea...**$5.00**

2003, mistake...**$6.00**

2003 to 2005 ....**$4.50**

2006-2008 ....**$4.00**

Bluegrass Stakes Glasses, Keeneland, Lexington KY

1996...**$15.00**

1997...**$13.00**

1998-99, ea...**$12.00**

2001-02, ea...**$10.00**

2003...**$8.00**

2004, discontinued at this time

Breeders Cup Glasses

1985, Aqueduct, not many produced.................................**$300.00**

1988, Churchill Downs **$40.00**

1989, Gulfstream Park...**$70.00**

1990, Bellmont Park..**$45.00**

1991, Churchill Downs **$15.00**

1992, Gulfstream Park...**$30.00**

1993, Santa Anita **$35.00**

1993, Santa Anita, 10th Running, gold **$40.00**

1994, Churchill Downs **$15.00**

1995, Belmont Park...**$20.00**

1996, Woodbine, Canada **$30.00**

1997, Hollywood Park..**$20.00**

1998, Churchill Downs **$10.00**

1999, Gulfstream Park...**$10.00**

2000, Churchill Downs **$9.00**

2001, Belmont Park, or 2002, Arlington Park.......................**$8.00**

2003, Santa Anita **$8.00**

2004, Lone Star Park **$8.00**

2005, Belmont Park...**$7.00**

2006, Churchill Downs **$7.00**

2007, Monmouth Park **$7.00**

Festival Glasses

1968, blue on frosted glass, $95.00. (Photo courtesy Betty Hornback/Photographer Dean Langdon)

1984..**$20.00**

1985-86, no glass made..**$.09**

1987-88, ea...**$12.00**

1989-90, ea...**$12.00**

1991-92, ea...**$10.00**

1993, very few produced...**$75.00**

1994-95, ea...**$8.00**

1996-98, ea...**$7.00**

1999-2000, ea...**$7.00**

2001-03, fewer produced, ea...$12.00
2004-2007 ....$10.00

Jim Beam/Spiral Stakes Glasses

1980, 6"...$350.00
1981, 7"...$300.00
1982...$275.00
1983...$50.00
1984...$35.00
1985...$25.00

1986, burgundy, $25.00. (Photo courtesy Betty Hornback/Photographer Dean Langdon)

1987-88, ea...$20.00
1988-90, ea...$16.00
1991-95, ea...$14.00
1996-2000, ea...$12.00
2001-2006, ea...$10.00

Shot Glasses

1987, 1½-ounce, red and gold, $350.00. (Photo courtesy Betty Hornback/ Photographer Dean Langdon)

1987, 3-oz, black/gold lettering $700.00
1987, 3-oz, red & gold $1,500.00
1988, 1½-oz...$45.00
1988, 3-oz...$60.00
1989, 3-oz...$45.00
1989-91, 1½-oz, ea...$35.00
1991, 3-oz...$40.00
1992, 1½-oz...$25.00
1992, 3-oz...$30.00
1993, 1½-oz or 3-oz, ea $20.00
1994, 1½-oz or 3-oz, ea $14.00
1995, 1½-oz or 3-oz, ea $14.00
1996, 1½-oz or 3-oz, ea $12.00
1997, 1½-oz or 3-oz, ea $12.00
1998, 1½-oz or 3-oz, ea $10.00
1999, fluted whiskey, 1½-oz...$10.00
2000-2002, fluted whiskey, 1½-oz, ea $8.00
2003-07, jigger, ea..$7.00

WAMZ Radio KY Derby Bar Glass, Sponsored by Jim Beam

1991...$35.00
1992...$32.00
1993-94, ea...$20.00
1995-96 ....$15.00
1997-99, ea...$12.00
2000...$10.00
2001, discontinued

Kindell, Dorothy

Yet another California artist that worked during the prolific years of the '40s and '50s, Dorothy Kindell produced a variety of household items and giftware, but today she's best known for her sensual nudes. One of her most popular lines consisted of mugs, a pitcher, salt and pepper shakers, a wall pocket, bowls, a creamer and sugar set, and champagne glasses, featuring a lady in various stages of undress, modeled as handles or stems (on the champagnes). In the set of six mugs, she progresses from wearing her glamorous strapless evening gown to ultimately climbing nude, head-first into the last mug. These are relatively common but always marketable. Except for these and the salt and pepper shakers, the other items from the nude line are scarce and rather pricey.

Collectors also vie for her island girls, generally seminude and very sensuous.

Ashtray, Beachcombers, 2 sets of nude legs protrude from under lg sombrero, 6x4½", from $60 to....................................$70.00
Ashtray, Hawaiian hula girl in 7" dia black tray, 4½"........$530.00
Champagne glass, black goblet w/gold nude on side, 6", from $165 to $225.00
Champagne glass, nude at stem, 6", from $125 to............$150.00
Creamer & sugar bowl, nude handles, 3½x3" $300.00
Dresser box, Hawaiian girl finial, 5x4x6½", from $250 to .$325.00
Dresser box, nude seated on jar shaped as stacked disks, 10¾"..$500.00
Dresser box, turtle lying on back, 7x5" $80.00

Figurine, Airdale, seated, marbled glaze, 6" **$45.00**

Figurine, foal, white mane & tail, 5¾" **$45.00**

Figurine, horse, Registered California sticker, 6½" **$45.00**

Figurine, lady dancing in long dark green strapless dress, arms at side, 9" **$295.00**

Figurine, nude w/flowers in hair, legs in air, 9x9", from $175 to..**$235.00**

Figurine, seated nude, red scarf across left arm & behind head, 11½x4½", from $250 to **$300.00**

Head vase, Black native girl, red lips & necklace, 5", from $65 to... **$75.00**

Head vase, Black native girl (bustline as base) w/separate ceramic necklace, red lips & black hair (vase), 6" **$75.00**

Head vase, brunette head & shoulders, green eyeliner & earrings, 5¼" **$80.00**

Head vase, native lady w/beads falling from hat & crossing forehead, 6¼" **$95.00**

Head vase, Oriental lady w/sm green tricorner hat, high-button collar covers cylindrical neck, red lips, 7" **$70.00**

Ice bucket, nude handle on ea side, 11x4½" **$150.00**

Lamp bases (no hardware), kneeling seminude Oriental (man & lady), exotic headgear, 13½", pr **$450.00**

Mug, Boy Scout insignia on bark pattern w/axe handle, 1953, 3½" **$85.00**

Mug, horse head embossed on 1 side w/Pop on other, nude handle, 4⅛", from $30 to **$40.00**

Mug, nude handle, 6 in series, ea from $30 to **$40.00**

Mug, nude w/red ballerina shoes on handle **$175.00**

Pitcher, water; nude handle **$320.00**

Salt & pepper shakers, barrel shape w/nude at side, 3", pr ... **$50.00**

Shelf sitter, nude w/red turban & red towel on lap, 12" **$250.00**

Toby mug, sailor's face, white beard, blue hat, 4", NM **$75.00**

Wall pocket, nude from mug series, rare, from $210.00 to $230.00.

King's Crown, Thumbprint

Back in the late 1800s, this pattern was called Thumbprint. It was first made by the U.S. Glass Company and Tiffin, one of several companies who were a part of the U.S. conglomerate, through the 1940s. U.S. Glass closed in the late '50s, but Tiffin reopened in 1963 and reissued it. Indiana Glass bought the molds, made some minor changes, and during the 1970s, they made this line as well.

Confusing, to say the least! Gene and Cathy Florence's *Collectible Glassware from the 40s, 50s, and 60s,* explains that originally the thumbprints were oval, but at some point Indiana changed theirs to circles. And Tiffin's tumblers were flared at the top, while Indiana's were straight. Our values are for the later issues of both companies, with the ruby flashing in excellent condition.

Bowl, cone, 11¼" **$85.00**

Bowl, crimped rim, 4½x11½" **$145.00**

Bowl, mayonnaise; 5" **$50.00**

Bowl, wedding/candy; footed, 10½x6" **$175.00**

Cake salver, footed, 12½" **$80.00**

Cocktail stem, 2¼-oz **$12.50**

Compote, footed, 6¼" **$25.00**

Creamer **$20.00**

Cup **$8.00**

Goblet, water; nine-ounce, $12.00.

Juice stem, 4-oz... **$7.00**

Mayonnaise, 3-pc set.. **$85.00**

Plate, bread & butter; 5".. **$8.00**

Plate, party; 24".. **$175.00**

Plate, snack; w/indent, 9¾"... **$12.50**

Punch bowl, made in 2 styles, ea...................................... **$775.00**

Relish, 5-part, 14".. **$135.00**

Sugar bowl... **$20.00**

Tumbler, water; 8½-oz **$12.00**

Vase, bud; 9"... **$125.00**

Kitchen Collectibles

If you've never paid much attention to old kitchen appliances, now is the time to do just that. Check in Grandma's basement — or your mother's kitchen cabinets, for that matter. As styles in home decorating changed, so did the styles of appliances. Some have wonderful Art Deco lines, while others border on the primitive. Most of those you'll find still work, and with a thorough cleaning you'll be able to restore them to their original 'like-new' appearance. Missing parts may be impossible to replace, but if it's just a cord that's gone, you can usually find what you need at any hardware store.

Even larger appliances are collectible and are often used to add the finishing touch to a period kitchen.

During the nineteenth century, cast-iron apple peelers, cherry pitters, and food choppers were patented by the hundreds, and because they're practically indestructible, they're still around today. Unless parts are missing, they're still usable and most are very efficient at the task they were designed to perform.

Lots of good vintage kitchen glassware is still around and can generally be bought at reasonable prices. Pieces vary widely from custard cups and refrigerator dishes to canister sets and cookie jars. There are also several books available for further information and study. If this area of collecting interests you, you'll enjoy *300 Years of Kitchen Collectibles* by Linda Campbell and *Hot Kitchen and Home Collectibles of the 30s, 40s, and 50s* by C. Dianne Zweig. Other books include *Kitchen Glassware of the Depression Years* and *Anchor Hocking's Fire-King & More* by Gene and Cathy Florence.

Please note that unless noted otherwise, prices are for appliances and miscellaneous gadgets that are free of rust, pitting, or dents and in excellent working condition. Glassware values are for mint condition examples.

See also Anchor Hocking; Aluminum; Clothes Sprinkler Bottles; Glass Knives; Griswold; Jade-ite; Kitchen Prayer Ladies; Porcelier; Pyrex; Reamers.

Appliances

Blender, Blender Queen, copper-tone base, 6-cup container w/black plastic lid & handle, 3-speed......................................**$120.00**
Blender, Kenmore Model 135.82321, turquoise w/ribbed 5-cup glass canister, 1950s-60s..................................**$48.00**
Blender, Mixi, red & clear plastic, Sibert & Co...NJ, 9x4", MIB...**$70.00**
Blender, Osterizer, pink w/clear plastic canister, black lid, 2-speed...**$50.00**
Blender, Ronson Cook 'n Stir HB-2, 48-oz carafe, hot/cold switch, heats up to 400 degrees.........................**$48.00**
Blender, Vita Mix 3600, Action Dome top, chrome base w/black Bakelite handles, 1670s, 21", w/recipe booklet...........**$100.00**
Blender, Waring, yellow beehive style w/clover-shaped top, 1950s-60s...**$75.00**
Blender, Waring Futura #94, red w/ribbed glass canister, Model 11-159, 1950s-60s, 16".........................**$55.00**
Blender, Waring Futura #950, avocado green, 14 speeds, clover-shaped top...**$56.00**
Blender/juicer, Vita Mix Sidewinder 2200, stainless steel canister, 1978 model #479002..................................**$70.00**
Can opener, Sunbeam, w/scissors sharpener, Patent 1965, 120 volts...**$30.00**
Cooker, Oster Super Pan, heating base, tempura ring, water & blazer pans & lid, 7½x9½", w/recipe booklet, NM.................**$50.00**
Cooker, Presto Cooker-Canner Model 31-B, 21-qt, EX w/instructions...**$80.00**
Crock pot/slow cooker, Rival, Poppy Red, glass lid..............**$45.00**
Deep fryer/cooker, General Electric #1110, chrome body, tempered glass lid, w/basket, 6-qt...**$50.00**

Egg cooker, Blue Onion pattern on crockery, Japan, 5½" **$25.00**
Egg cooker, Hankscraft, orange pottery, aluminum dome lid...**$25.00**
Egg cooker, Sunbeam, metal w/black handles, Deco shape ..**$22.50**
Fryer, Dormeyer #DF2-BU, aluminum w/black base & handles, w/basket & instruction booklet, NM.........................**$20.00**
Grill, PrestoBurger, Thick 'n Thin reversible tray, MIB........**$55.00**
Grill, Sunbeam Party Grill, rectangular, 3-temperature control ...**$38.00**
Hot plate, Dominion Electrical Mfg #1414, M **$25.00**
Hot plate, Star-Rite Samson, black w/chrome legs, NM **$100.00**
Juicer, Champion, Plastaket Mfg #09616............................**$85.00**
Mixer, KitchenAid K5-A, turquoise, complete w/attachments ..**$110.00**
Mixer, KitchenAid 3-B, Hobart Mfg Co, complete w/attachments, MIB...**$480.00**
Mixer, Neupert, Great Northern Product Co, all metal, label decal on top, 3-speed, pre-1938, 10x9x7".........................**$80.00**
Mixer, Stevens, black enameled base, silver-tone canister, 13¼", NM...**$125.00**
Mixer, Sunbeam Mixmaster, copper-tone enameling, hand type..**$30.00**
Mixer, Sunbeam Mixmaster A-9B-b, ivory enamel, complete w/white bowls & attachments, NM.........................**$90.00**
Mixer, Sunbeam Mixmaster 11, black & white, w/white opaque bowls, 10-speed, 1950s...**$80.00**

Mixer, Universal, ca. 1940s, complete, from $65.00 to $75.00. (Photo courtesy C. Dianne Zweig)

Mixer, Vidrio Products Corp, green enamel, motor sits atop green canister, 2-cup...**$32.00**
Mixer/juicer, Sunbeam, Jade-ite juicing bowl & 2 reamers, variable speeds...**$75.00**
Percolator, General Electric, chrome, bulbous, 9x9"............**$35.00**
Percolator, Manning-Bowman, chrome w/black handles, glass top, 11", NM w/instructions...**$55.00**
Percolator, Presto Super Speed CM9, chrome, 1963, MIB...**$45.00**
Percolator, West Bend Flavo-Matic, Color-Glo aluminum, 8-cup, MIB...**$95.00**

Popcorn popper, Dominion, aluminum w/black handles & feet, clear glass lid, EX **$65.00**

Popcorn popper, Mirro Pop-A-Party Set, aluminum w/black legs & handle, complete w/bowls, MIB **$40.00**

Popcorn popper, Mirror, yellow enamel, 4-qt, unused, M w/instructions..**$45.00**

Popcorn popper, West Bend, aluminum w/black handles & feet, 4-qt..**$35.00**

Salad shooter, Presto, w/2 slicing, ripple cutter & shredding cones, funnel guide, MIB **$35.00**

Skillet, Revere Ware, copper-clad stainless steel, black handles, 12", NM...**$100.00**

Skillet, Saladmaster #7817, stainless steel, NM **$120.00**

Skillet, Townecraft, stainless steel, NM w/instructions **$125.00**

Slow cooker, West Bend #4400, burnt-orange pot sits on black base, clear handles, 5 settings, 4-qt, NMIB **$72.50**

Stove/grill, Cromalox enamelware, single burner, 5x12x11" ..**$30.00**

Toaster, Simplex T-211, chrome w/black painted cast-iron base, Patent Dec 8, 1914 ....**$50.00**

Toaster, Sunbeam B, etched Deco pattern, 4½x11½x5" **$50.00**

Toaster, Sunbeam T-35, chrome w/black Bakelite handles, 2-slice, Radiant Control **$15.00**

Toaster, Superior Electrics Ltd, 3-slice, 1920s, VG..............**$45.00**

Toaster, Tost-O-Lator J, chrome w/black Bakelite handles & trim **$90.00**

Vacuum cleaner, Air-Way Sanitizor #55A, canister, blue, complete w/ attachments, 24" **$100.00**

Vacuum cleaner, General Electric AVT-173A, upright w/caddy & attachments, 1947 ....**$175.00**

Vacuum cleaner, Hoover #62, upright, turquoise & tan.....**$225.00**

Vacuum cleaner, Hoover #719 Convertible, upright, blue & cream, refurbished, NM **$155.00**

Vacuum cleaner, Hoover Celebrity QS, canister, mint green, Quadraflex Powermatic head, 1970s **$85.00**

Vacuum cleaner, Hoover Dial-A-Matic #1130, upright, green & cream, 1969-71 ....**$135.00**

Vacuum cleaner, Kenmore PowerMate, cream-colored canister, w/ attachments, NM...**$85.00**

Vacuum cleaner, Kirby #505, upright, no attachments, EX.**$325.00**

Vacuum cleaner, Rainbow E series, complete w/accessories, NMIB **$950.00**

Waffle baker/grill, Sunbeam #CG-1, Radiant Control, makes 9x9" 4-section waffle, 1950s, NM..................................**$50.00**

Waffle iron/grill, General Electric #14G44T, chrome w/black Bakelite handles, NM **$38.00**

Glassware

Batter jug, amber, Paden City #90, from $65 to **$75.00**

Batter jug, clear w/blue lid, Paden City, from $85 to **$95.00**

Batter jug/measure pitcher, custard, McKee, 4-cup, from $55 to .**$60.00**

Beater bowl, green, Jeannette, from $50 to **$65.00**

Bottle, water; Crisscross, green, Hazel-Atlas, 64-oz, from $165 to..**$175.00**

Bottle, water; emerald green, w/top, Hocking, from $75 to.**$95.00**

Bowl, cereal; Skating Dutch, red on white, Hazel-Atlas, 5", from $15 to..**$20.00**

Bowl, green custard, 4½", from $25 to **$30.00**

Bowl, mixing; black, 9⅜", from $65 to **$70.00**

Bowl, mixing; Chalaine Blue, 9", from $125 to.................**$135.00**

Bowl, mixing; Delphite Blue, 7⅜", from $60 to **$75.00**

Bowl, mixing; fired-on colors (yellow, green, red & blue), set of 4, from $30 to..**$38.00**

Bowl, mixing; green, paneled, 11½", from $65 to.............**$75.00**

Bowl, mixing; Jennyware, pink, set of 3, from $200 to......**$225.00**

Bowl, mixing; ruby, set of 3, from $225 to **$250.00**

Bowl, salad; Emerald Glo, w/gold-tone metal base, from $30 to **$35.00**

Bowl, Vitrock w/decal, 9", from $45 to **$50.00**

Butter dish, custard, rectangular, McKee, from $75 to........**$95.00**

Butter dish, green, rectangular, from $55 to......................**$75.00**

Butter dish, pink, rectangular w/bow finial, from $65 to **$75.00**

Canister, caramel, 48-oz, from $250 to **$275.00**

Canister, Dutch boy decal on clear, metal lid, from $18 to ..**$22.00**

Canister, frosted, Owens-Illinois, 40-oz, from $30 to **$35.00**

Canister, green, paper label, w/glass lid, Hocking, 47-oz, from $80 to..**$90.00**

Canister, Jade-ite, black lettering, sq, Jeannette, 48-oz, from $175 to..**$200.00**

Canister, Jade-ite, round, screw-on lid, Jeannette, 40-oz, from $175 to..**$200.00**

Canister, Polka Dot, red on white, round, McKee, 48-oz, from $65 to..**$75.00**

Canister, Sugar, Delphite Blue, 40-oz, from $375 to.........**$425.00**

Canister, Tea, green fired-on color, metal lid, Hocking, from $75 to..**$95.00**

Canister, yellow opaque w/black lettering, screw-on lid, 48-oz, from $225 to **$250.00**

Canisters, Forest Green, Owens-Illinois, from $65.00 to $75.00 each. (Photo courtesy Gene and Cathy Florence)

Casserole, chicken shape, white w/painted details, Glasbake, from $18 to..**$20.00**

Churn, green w/black top, crank handle **$42.50**

Coaster, green custard, from $8 to **$10.00**

Cocktail shaker, green, pinched body, metal top, #151, from $55 to..**$60.00**

Cocktail shaker, ruby, boot shape, from $300 to...............**$350.00**

Cookie jar, black, LE Smith, from $100 to **$125.00**

Cruet, Twist, pink, Heisey, 2½-oz **$140.00**
Decanter, green, pinched body, #102, from $65 to **$75.00**
Decanter, yellow opaque, pinched body, McKee, from $125 to. **$145.00**
Fork & spoon, salad; ruby, from $225 to **$250.00**
Ice bucket, ruby, Hocking, from $40 to **$50.00**
Ice bucket, yellow, Paden City, from $145 to **$155.00**
Ice tub, Emerald Glo, w/gold-tone metal base, w/tongs, from $65 to **$70.00**
Measure pitcher, Jade-ite, Jeannette, 4-cup, from $125 to.. **$135.00**
Measuring cup, green custard, Hocking, 2-cup, from $150 to ..**$175.00**
Measuring cup, Vitrock, w/lid, Hocking, 2-cup, from $65 to.. **$75.00**
Mug, black, from $30 to **$35.00**
Mug, Tom & Jerry, custard, w/gold lettering, from $12 to... **$15.00**
Pitcher, Chalaine Blue, footed, from $100 to **$150.00**
Pitcher, Chesterfield, amber, Imperial's #600, w/lid, from $120 to.. **$125.00**
Pitcher, measure; Delphite Blue, McKee, 4-cup, from $600 to.. **$650.00**

Refrigerator containers, amber: 4½" round, $20.00; 4x4", $18.00; 8x8", $30.00. (Photo courtesy Gene and Cathy Florence)

Refrigerator dish, Chalaine Blue, 4x5", from $60 to **$65.00**
Refrigerator dish, Crisscross, blue, w/lid, Hazel-Atlas, 4x4", from $48 to **$50.00**
Refrigerator dish, green, indented handle, 4x4", from $30 to .. **$35.00**
Refrigerator dish, Vitrock, Hocking, 4x4", from $25 to.......**$30.00**
Refrigerator jar, Hex Optic, green, Jeannette, 4½x5", from $30 to... **$35.00**
Rolling pin, green w/wooden handles, from $450 to **$500.00**
Salt & pepper shakers, blue fired-on color, metal lid, Hocking, pr from $50 to **$55.00**
Shaker, Cinnamon, custard, from $165 to **$175.00**
Soap dish, green custard, from $20 to..................................**$25.00**
Spoon, salad; yellow, from $60 to **$70.00**
Stack set, Hex Optic, pink, Jeannette, 3-pc, +lid, from $75 to.. **$85.00**
Stack set, Skating Dutch, red on white, Hazel-Atlas, 3-pc, from $75 to **$80.00**
Straw holder, Peacock Blue, ca 1950s, from $125 to **$135.00**
Sugar shaker, amber, Paden City, from $200 to..................**$220.00**
Sugar shaker, dark Jade-ite, Jeannette, #2051, from $145 to.. **$175.00**
Sugar shaker, fired-on color, Gemco, from $30 to................**$35.00**
Sundae, green, tulip form, Paden City Line 210, from $18 to.. **$20.00**
Teakettle, Glasbake, clear w/glass handle, from $30 to.........**$35.00**

Teapot, McKee Range-Tec, clear w/embossed rings, black handle, McKee, from $20 to **$25.00**
Tumbler, green, embossed ribs, footed, Paden City, from $18 to **$20.00**
Tumbler, ruby, Reliable Tea Bags label, Hocking, from $10 to.. **$12.00**
Water bottle, ruby, plain or ribbed, Hocking, from $225 to ..**$250.00**

Miscellaneous Gadgets

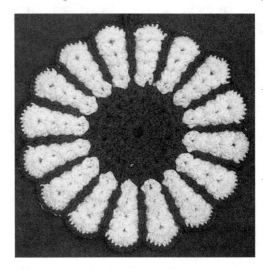

Potholder, red and white crochet, from $6.00 to $8.00.
(Photo courtesy C. Dianne Zweig)

Apple peeler, CE Hudson, Pat Jan 24 82, cast iron w/crank handle **$50.00**
Apple peeler, Goodell Bonanza, original green paint on cast iron, clamps to table..**$275.00**
Apple peeler, Reading, cast iron w/crank handle, ca 1872....**$75.00**
Baster, Pyrex-brand heat-resistant glass, dated 1946, EXIB ..**$35.00**
Cake cutter/server, yellow Bakelite handle, 3¾" tines, 11" **$7.50**
Cake saver/carrier, Scottie & chef on painted tin, wire bail..**$30.00**
Can opener, Joy Kan Kutter, scissors type, 1926 ....**$40.00**
Can opener, Wear-Ever, aluminum **$22.50**
Chopper, Landers Frary & Clark, curly maple handle, 5¾" ..**$65.00**
Chopper, single curved blade, extended wooden handle, 6x7½".. **$60.00**
Churn, Dazey #4, bulbous glass jar, 15", from $150 to **$175.00**
Churn, Dazey #4B-D, electric, steel base **$350.00**
Churn, Dazey #30, flower bottom, rare variations **$400.00**
Churn, Dazey #40, Pat 1922, from $400 to **$250.00**
Churn, Dazey #60, from $150 to **$180.00**
Churn, Dazey #80, from $175 to **$225.00**
Colander, green enamelware w/dark green trim, 4¼x9⅞"+handles... **$27.50**
Crimper, aluminum, spoon shape, 5"....................................**$40.00**
Crimper, brass w/wooden handle, Made in Italy..................**$22.50**
Cutter, vegetable; metal, ruffled, red wooden handle, 7"......**$10.00**
Egg beater, A&J, rotary type, fits atop 4-cup glass bowl, 1923.. **$35.00**
Egg beater, Androck, rotary type, red Bakelite bullet handle...**$40.00**
Egg beater, Broden, metal push-pull top on clear glass jar, dated 1915 ....**$35.00**
Egg beater, Ladd by United Royalties Corp, stainless rotary type, ca 1921 ....**$15.00**

Egg beater, Maynard, crank type w/pink handles, 1950s......**$35.00**

French fry cutter, Ekco, wire grid, lever type, 1950s **$12.00**

Grater, punched tin, half round, 6x3¾" **$25.00**

Grater, wires cross in metal frame, Made in USA, 9x5½"+4" handle **$20.00**

Ice tongs, cast iron, 1930s, 14x13" **$40.00**

Juicer/press, Wear-Ever, aluminum, squeeze type **$50.00**

Meat tenderizer, aluminum block w/pink plastic handle **$15.00**

Meat tenderizer, Rolatender, metal rolling-pin type, 11x3" dia....**$12.00**

Noodle cutter, multiple metal blades, green wooden handle, 7"..**$40.00**

Pastry blender, Androck, arched wires held by red Bakelite handle.. **$12.50**

Pastry blender, Androck, arched wires held by wooden handle . **$12.00**

Potato masher, wire ware w/blue wooden handle **$15.00**

Rolling pin, turned wood w/green wooden handles, 17½"..**$20.00**

Scoop, Androck, metal bowl w/red wooden handle............**$55.00**

Scoop, coffee; Wagner, aluminum, 1-tablespoon, 3⅝" **$28.00**

Sifter, Androck Handi-Sift, flowers on yellow **$30.00**

Sifter, Bromwell, apples on cream, 3-cup **$25.00**

Spatula, Androck, flexible metal w/red Bakelite handle, 10⅛" ..**$18.00**

Spoon, slotted; Androck, metal w/red Bakelite handle, 1940s, 12" **$15.00**

Spoon slotted; Cutco #13, rosewood handle, 1960s, NM **$15.00**

Kitchen Prayer Ladies

The Mother in the Kitchen series (aka Kitchen Prayer Ladies by collectors) was distributed by Enesco in the mid- to late-1950s. It was sold through department stores, gift shops, and dime stores. Most of the items they sold are listed below. The line was made in three colorways: pink and white (the most common), blue and white, and the harder-to-find white with blue trim. The original Kitchen Prayer lady had very dark brown hair; later examples have light brown to strawberry blonde hair. She wears an apron inscribed with a prayer. These are varied and, though commonly written in English, can also be found in other languages.

The ring holder lady holds a crown painted in gold and red. The red paint washes off easily, so you will find that many crowns are now white. Check closely for damage, as the delicate points on the crown break easily. The egg timer was originally held on by a piece of elastic, which over time and through use usually wore out; often a ribbon or a twist tie will have been used to replace it. The scouring pad holder was produced with three different messages in the basket: Scouring Pad, three four-dot flowers, and a gold label that says 'Use my basket for holding soaps, scouring pads, etc.' If there is no message, very likely the label has been washed off. The spoon-storage piece's circular slots for spoons are easily chipped. The cookie jar, instant coffee, and canisters are commonly found with repaired necks and often are chipped on the inside ring from use.

Unless condition is specifically given in the description, use the high end of our range for examples in absolutely mint condition; for items in only very good/excellent condtion, use the low end. For more detailed information, refer to *Mother in the Kitchen and Other Prayer Pieces* by Donna Kopish.

Advisor: Judy Foreman (See Directory, Kitchen Prayer Ladies)

Air freshener, E-5200, 5", from $100 to **$175.00**

Bank, Mother's Pin Money, 5½", from $60 to **$85.00**

Bell, E-1825, 4½", from $65 to **$85.00**

Candleholders, rare, 4", pr from $250 to **$350.00**

Canister, Flour, Sugar, Tea, Coffee; rare, ea from $200 to ..**$350.00**

Cookie jar, blue, 10", from $200 to **$300.00**

Cookie jar, pink, 10", from $100 to....................................**$175.00**

Creamer, pink, 4", from $55 to **$75.00**

Crumb tray & brush, 8½", from $125 to **$175.00**

Egg timer, E-4810, from $50 to..**$70.00**

Jar, Instant Coffee, blue, 6", from $130 to..........................**$165.00**

Jar, Instant Coffee, pink, 6", from $95 to **$115.00**

Mug, blue, rare, 3¾", from $45 to **$75.00**

Napkin holder, blue, E-2826, 6¼", from $15 to **$25.00**

Napkin holder, pink, E-2826, 6¼", from $10 to................**$18.00**

Napkin holder, white, E-2826 6¼", from $20 to **$30.00**

Picture frame, E-4809, 6", NM, minimum value..............**$350.00**

Planter, E-2826, rare, 6¼", from $75 to..............................**$150.00**

Ring holder, E-4247 (red paint on crown often gone, many found w/gold & white crown), 5¾", from $75 to **$110.00**

Salt & pepper shakers, blue, pr from $10 to **$20.00**

Salt & pepper shakers, pink, pr from $10 to......................**$15.00**

Salt & pepper shakers, white, pr from $15 to **$25.00**

Scouring pad/soap dish, blue (tray found in 3 styles), E-4246, 5½", from $50 to **$70.00**

Scouring pad/soap dish, pink (tray found in 3 styles), E-4246, 5½", from $35 to **$55.00**

Spice set, pink ladies, complete, from $130 to **$200.00**

Spoon rest, pink, E-3347, 5¾", from $15 to........................**$25.00**

Spoon storage/holder, pink, upright, E-4811, 6", from $25 to....**$40.00**

String holder, 6", from $85 to..**$125.00**

Sugar bowl, pink, 4", from $55 to **$75.00**

Teapot, blue, 6", from $90 to..**$125.00**

Teapot, pink, 6", from $75 to..**$100.00**

Toothpick holder, blue, E-5199, 4½", from $12 to **$25.00**

Toothpick holder, pink, E-5199, 4½", from $8 to **$15.00**

Toothpick holder, white, E-5199, 4½", from $15 to............**$30.00**

Vase, bud; rare, from $150 to..**$175.00**

Wall plaque, full figure, E-3349, 7½", from $35.00 to $70.00. (Photo courtesy Pat and Ann Duncan)

Kreiss & Co.

Collectors are hot on the trail of figural ceramics, and one area of interest are those unique figurines, napkin dolls, planters, mugs, etc., imported from Japan during the 1950s by the Kreiss company, located in California. Though much of their early production was run of the mill, in the late 1950s, the company introduced unique new lines — all bizarre, off the wall, politically incorrect, and very irreverent — and today it's these items that are attracting the interest of collectors. There are several lines. One is a totally zany group of caricatures called Psycho-Ceramics. There's a Beatnick series, Nudies, and Elegant Heirs (all of which are strange little creatures), as well as some that are very well done and tasteful. Several will be inset with with colored 'jewels.' Many are marked either with an ink stamp or an in-mold trademark (some are dated), so you'll need to start turning likely-looking items over to check for the Kreiss name.

There is a very helpful book on the market. For some great photos and helpful information, we recommend *The World of Kreiss Ceramics* by Pat and Larry Aikins (L-W Book Sales).

Prices are drastically lower than those we saw for Kreiss figures a few years ago, affected no doubt by internet trading which has made them so much more accessible. Our values are based on actual online sales.

See also Napkin Ladies.

Figurine, fat lady on scales, from $50.00 to $65.00. (Photo courtesy gasolinealleyantiques.com)

Ashtray, blue guy w/huge eyes (rhinestone center) holding tray w/ beaded rim $42.50
Ashtray, figure weighed down by lg blue tray on back, rhinestone eyes $27.50
Bank, laughing pig holding package, A Little Money Put Away for Christmas Day, 7½" $36.00
Bank, yellow guy, Put Your Money Where Your Mouth Is, 5½" .$35.00
Bathroom dish, pelican character w/mouth open (for soap), opening for toothpaste tube & toothbrush $30.00

Figurine, Beat Chick, beatnik lady w/long brown hair, arms akimbo, sm black hat..$40.00
Figurine, beatnik, Like Man Lend Me Your Ear, 1960 ....$38.00
Figurine, beatnik man seated w/hands on head, pained expression, 4¾" $22.00
Figurine, beatnik w/lg pink nose, black beard & mustache, sm black hat $36.00
Figurine, blue guy w/lg eyes, Looking for Someone w/a Little Authority $65.00
Figurine, brown guy w/yellow fuzzy forelock, hand out & looking up, puzzled expression, 5" $30.00
Figurine, choir boy, big brown eyes, holds red song book, 5" ..$35.00
Figurine, dinosaur & 2 babies, green rhinestone eyes, attached by chains..$125.00
Figurine, Hawaiian boy sitting on bongo drums & playing ukelele, straw hat & flower lei, 7½" $95.00
Figurine, hobo, Of Course I Belong to Diner's Club, Elegant Heir, 1950s, 6½" $90.00
Figurine, lady in floral dress (lovely), yellow hat, 10⅝" $95.00
Figurine, pink girl w/blond to black to pink hair, pink bow on top, 5¼", w/tag: Is That All You Silly Men Think About $25.00
Figurine, pink guy w/grimace showing many teeth, blue wire hair, series #PF93, 5" $50.00
Figurine, purple guy covered w/stitches, 4⅝", w/tag: Have I Ever Told You About My Operation $20.00
Figurine, Purple People Eater, pink plastic wire hair, 5½" ..$135.00
Figurine, Santa w/sm gift & dark green stocking, #49, 5½" .$25.00
Figurine, yellow guy stands w/Santa Hat, Merry Christmas on tummy, w/tag...$30.00

Mug, green guy with shoe prints, from $50.00 to $65.00. (Photo courtesy gasolinealleyantiques.com)

Salt & pepper shakers, baby bird just hatched from egg, red & blue rhinestones, pr $25.00
Salt & pepper shakers, fox, blue eyes, bushy tail, pr............$30.00
Salt & pepper shakers, He & Haw, donkeys, pr...................$25.00
Salt & pepper shakers, Mr & Mrs Snowman, Christmas attire, blue rhinestone eyes, pr $30.00
Salt & pepper shakers, pups, 1 upright, 2nd recumbent, brown w/ blue rhinestone eyes, pr..$55.00

Lamps

Aladdin Electric Lamps

Aladdin lamps have been made continually since 1908 by the Mantle Lamp Company of America, now Aladdin Mantle Lamp Company in Clarksville, Tennessee. Their famous kerosene lamps are highly collectible, and some are quite valuable. Many were relegated to the storage shelf or thrown away after electric lines came through the country. Today many people keep them on hand for emergency light.

Few know that Aladdin Industries, Inc. was one of the largest manufacturers of electric lamps from 1930 to 1956. They created new designs, colorful glass, and unique paper shades. These are not only collectible but are still used in many homes today. Many Aladdin lamps, kerosene as well as electric, can be found at garage sales, antique shops, and flea markets. You can learn more about them in the books *Aladdin Electric Lamps* and *Aladdin — The Magic Name in Lamps, Revised Edition,* written by J.W. Courter, who also periodically issues updated price guides for both kerosene and electric Aladdins. A free eight-page history of Aladdin lamps is available by writing the author. Our values reflect the worth of undamaged examples unless a specific condition code is noted in the description.

Advisor: J.W. Courter (See Directory, Lamps)

Newsletter: *Mystic Lights of the Aladdin Knights*
J.W. Courter
3935 Kelley Rd., Kevil, KY 42053

Table, G-195, Alacite, lighted base, Whip-O-Lite shade, EX, $100.00. (Photo courtesy Bill and Treva Courter)

Bed, B-45, Whip-o-Lite shade, EX, from $75 to **$100.00**
Bedroom, P-51, ceramic.. **$25.00**
Boudoir, G-42, Allegro, Alacite, from $40 to......................... **$50.00**
Boudoir, G-49, Alacite, from $40 to.. **$50.00**
Figurine, G-234, pheasant... **$275.00**

Floor, #3625, reflector, candle arms, from $175 to **$250.00**
Floor, Model B-293, Antique Ivory lacquer, 1939-42, from $175 to **$225.00**
Foreign Model C, Brazil, C-164, glass font, shelf model, from $100 to **$125.00**
Pinup, G-354, Alacite, from $125 to **$150.00**
Table, G-331, Alacite, illuminated base, from $60 to........... **$80.00**
Table, Model 12 Crystal Vase, Bengel Red, from $500 to .. **$600.00**
Table, W-503, wood & ceramic, from $40 to **$60.00**
TV, MT-520, cherry & brass base, NM, from $400 to **$500.00**

Motion Lamps

Though some were made as early as 1920 and as late as the 1970s, motion lamps were most popular during the 1950s. Most are cylindrical with scenes such as waterfalls and forest fires and attain a sense of motion through the action of an inner cylinder that rotates with the heat of the bulb. Prices below are for lamps with original parts in good condition with no cracks, splits, dents, or holes. Any damage greatly decreases the value. As a rule of thumb, the oval lamps are worth a little more than their round counterparts. **Caution** — some lamps are being reproduced (indicated in our listings by '+'). Currently in production are Antique Autos, Trains, Old Mill, Ships in a Storm, Fish, and three Psychedelic lamps. The color on the scenic lamps is much bluer, and they are in plastic stands with plastic tops. There are quite a few small motion lamps in production that are not copies of the 1950s lamps.

Advisors: Jim and Kaye Whitaker (See Directory, Josef Originals)

Econolite, Old Mill, #765, 11" (+), **$100.00.** (Photo courtesy Jim and Kaye Whitaker)

Advertising, Coor's Beer, wall mount, 1960s, 15" **$55.00**
Advertising, 7-Up, 13" **$75.00**
Econolite, Antique, Car, #768, 11" **$125.00**
Econolite, Butterfly, #7853, 11"... **$150.00**

Econolite, child's lamp, various carousel styles, 10", ea.........**$85.00**
Econolite, Fish (Tropical), 1950s, 11" (+) **$110.00**
Econolite, Fountains of Versailles, #758, 11" **$200.00**
Econolite, Hawaiian Scene, #701, 11" **$175.00**
Econolite, Jet Planes, #774, 11" **$250.00**
Econolite, Miss Liberty, #769, 11" **$225.00**
Econolite, Oriental Garden, 3703, 11" **$165.00**
Econolite, Snow Scene, #766 or #767, 11", ea...................**$115.00**
Econolite, Truck & Bus, 1962, 11" **$150.00**
Elvgren Pinup Girls..**$375.00**
Gritt, Village Blacksmith...**$125.00**
LA Goodman, Davy Crockett...**$150.00**
LA Goodman, Firefighters, 11"..**$150.00**
LA Goodman, fish, flowers, butterflies or geese in bowl, blue, w/top,
   ea **$125.00**
LA Goodman, Oriental Fantasy, 11"................................**$100.00**
LA Goodman, Waterfall-Campfire, 11" **$75.00**
National Co, Off Dartmouth, 13" **$175.00**
Roto-Vue Jr, Econolite, Fountain of Youth, 10" **$95.00**
Roto-Vue Jr, Econolite, Hopalong Cassidy, 2 scenes, 10", ea ..**$245.00**
Roto-Vue Jr, Econolite, Niagara Falls, #NF, 10" **$55.00**
Roto-Vue Jr, Merry-Go-Round, red, yellow or blue, 1949, 10" ..**$90.00**
Scene in Action, Flames, 10"...**$135.00**
Scene in Action, Japanese Twilight, 13" **$150.00**
Scene in Action, Marine Scene, 10" **$150.00**
Scene in Action, Serenader, 13" **$150.00**
Visual Effects Co, Budweiser, 1970, 15" **$45.00**
Visual Effects Co, Op Art Lamp, 1970s, 13" (+) **$50.00**

TV Lamps

By the 1950s, TV was commonplace in just about every home in the country but still fresh enough to have our undivided attention. Families gathered around the set and for the rest of the evening delighted in being entertained by Ed Sullivan or stumped by the $64,000 Question. Pottery producers catered to this scenario by producing TV lamps by the score, and with the popularity of anything from the '50s being what it is today, these lamps are making appearances at flea markets and co-ops everywhere. For more information we recommend *TV Lamps to Light the World* by John A. Shuman III (Collector Books).

See also Maddux of California; Morton Potteries, Royal Haeger.

Bluebirds (2) before fiberglass panel, Lane, 1959, 10½".......**$90.00**
Bulldog w/flock coating, eyes glow, from $60 to..................**$80.00**
Dachshund on wooden base before 2 paper screens,
   10¼x10¼" **$125.00**
Donkey w/planter, wood base, Royal Haeger label, from $95
   to **$105.00**
Duck flying, brown & turquoise, ceramic w/wooden base, from $82
   to **$97.50**
Exotic bird, coral w/gold spray & trim, L-710, 13x12", from $75
   to **$95.00**
Fawn on planter base, Lane, 1959, 12½x14x8"...................**$70.00**
Horse & colt, brown, from $85 to......................................**$90.00**

Horse on rocky planter base, Lane, #P80, 1959, 13½" **$85.00**
Madonna & Child, plaster, bulb lights up faces, from $150
   to **$175.00**
Male ballet dancer, plaster w/Fiberglas shade, American Statuary,
   from $85 to **$95.00**
Monkeys (2), white w/glass eyes, van Res Ceramics, 11x6" ..**$110.00**
Owl, lg, full figure w/light-up eyes, ceramic, Kron, from $45
   to **$65.00**
Panther (black) on rowk-work base, Lane, 13x15", from $90
   to **$110.00**
Panther stalking, tan, brown & cream, cutaway tail for light switch,
   no base, 4x21", from $90 to **$120.00**
Poodle (brown) & pug dog, Kron, 13x12x12", from $90 to . **$110.00**
Poodle (white) & pug dog, Kron, 13x12x12", from $70 to . **$80.00**
Rooster w/rising sun, blue-green mottle, from $125 to......**$140.00**
Sailing ship, 2 masts, ceramic planter on gold-tone metal base, Made
   in CA, #3500-E21855, 11", from $90 to **$110.00**
Siamese cats (3) w/marble eyes, Lane, Made in CA USA, 11", from
   $150 to **$165.00**
Siamese kitten, seated upright, head cocked, 13", from $85
   to **$100.00**
Swordfish leaping, black & white against pink, brass base holder,
   from $75 to **$90.00**

Doves, white with gold spatter, Royal Fleet CA, 10", $45.00.

L.E. Smith

Originating just after the turn of the century, the L.E. Smith company continues to operate in Mt. Pleasant, Pennsylvania, at the present time. In the 1920s they introduced a line of black glass that they are famous for today. Some pieces were decorated with silver overlay or enameling. Using their own original molds, they made a line of bird and animal figures in crystal as well as in colors. The company is currently producing these figures, many in two sizes. They were one of the main producers of the popular Moon and Star pattern which has been featured in their catalogs since the 1960s in a variety of shapes and colors.

For more information we recommend *L.E. Smith Glass Company, the First Hundred Years,* by Tom Felt.

See also Kitchen Collectibles, Glassware; Moon and Star.

Ashtray, black duck, 6½" long, from $8.00 to $12.00.
(Photo courtesy Dick and Pat Spencer)

Ashtray, Daisy & Button, black, kettle form, ca 1953-55, 2⅛x2¼", from $12 to **$18.00**

Basket, Simplicity, Flame (amberina), pulled handle not joined at center, scalloped rim, ca 1960s, 11", from $50 to.........**$75.00**

Bowl, Heritage, blue opalescent, crimped rim, marked SGC, ca 1980, 3¼x8½", from $30 to **$35.00**

Candleholder, star shape, crystal, ca 1941-58, 1⅜x5", ea from $8 to **$10.00**

Candleholder, stepped rings, fired-on orange, ca 1930s-40s, 2⅛x5⅛", ea from $12 to **$15.00**

Candlestick, Rose, Kimberlite (ice blue), made from Imperial mold, 1993-94, 3½x3⅞", ea from $10 to..............................**$15.00**

Candy container, house form, light blue, ca 1915-22, 2⅜x2¾x2⅛", from $300 to **$350.00**

Candy dish, Simplicity, Bittersweet, footed, w/lid, ca 1963-65, 10x5½", from $45 to **$50.00**

Compote, Heritage, milk glass, cupped rim, 8-sided foot, ca 1958-64, 7¼x6⅜", from $25 to **$30.00**

Compote, Heritage, ruby carnival, footed, 1983-98, 5", from $25 to **$30.00**

Covered dish, Conestoga wagon, crystal, 1970s, 5½x6½x2½", from $45 to **$50.00**

Covered dish, Longaberger Pumpkin, caramel, made from old mold for Longaberger, ca 2003, from $35 to **$40.00**

Heart box, diamond-patterned top, ruffled edge, Woodrose Lustre, ca 1982-83, 5", from $20 to **$25.00**

Ivy bowl, Hobnail, milk glass, footed, ca 1934, 1956-68, 2002, 5½x4½", from $20 to **$25.00**

Lamp base, Spanish Dancing Couple, crystal w/fired-on pink, 1940s, 12" (w/shade), from $70 to **$80.00**

Lamp shade, shell motif, crystal w/fired-on blue, 1940s, 5", from $25 to **$35.00**

Plate, Robert E Lee, amethyst carnival, ca 1962-74, 9¼", from $30 to **$35.00**

Powder jar, Elephant Carousel, green satin, 1930s, 5½" dia, from $75 to **$100.00**

Powder jar, Standing Terrier, crystal satin, 1930s, 6" dia, from $85 to **$125.00**

Powder jar, Three Sisters, rose satin, 1930s, 6" dia, from $100 to **$200.00**

Punch set, Broken Column, crystal, ca 1961, 15-pc set, from $150 to **$200.00**

Scroll flask, Colonial Blue, ca 1961-65, 7⅛", from $25 to...**$30.00**

Swan dish, milk glass, 4x7x3", from $25 to **$30.00**

Tidbit tray, Regency, crystal, 2-tiered, ca 1973, 12" dia, from $35 to **$40.00**

Toothpick holder, Daisy & Button, gold carnival, marked SGC, ca 1972-76, 2¼x2", from $10 to **$15.00**

Vase, black w/hand-painted flower, scalloped rim, #1018, ca 1930s, 6¼", from $15 to **$20.00**

Vase, black w/white confetti, crimped top, handles, disk foot, ca 1954-56, 6", from $15 to **$20.00**

Vase, Mount Pleasant, black, ca 1930-33, 7¾x4½", from $15 to...**$25.00**

Lefton China

China, porcelain, and ceramic items with that now familiar mark, Lefton, have been around since the early 1940s and are highly sought after by collectors in the secondary marketplace today. The company was founded by Mr. George Zoltan Lefton, an immigrant from Hungary. In the 1930s he was a designer and manufacturer of sportswear, but eventually his hobby of collecting fine china and porcelain led him to initiate his own ceramic business. When the bombing of Pearl Harbor occurred on December 7, 1941, Mr. Lefton came to the aid of a Japanese-American friend and helped him protect his property from anti-Japanese groups. Later, Mr. Lefton was introduced to a Japanese factory owned by Kowa Koki KK. He contracted with them to produce ceramic items to his specifications, and until 1980 they made thousands of pieces that were marketed by the Lefton company, marked with the initials KW preceding the item number. Figurines and animals plus many of the whimsical pieces such as Bluebirds, Dainty Miss, Miss Priss, Cabbage Cutie, Elf Head, Mr. Toodles, and Dutch Girl are eagerly collected today. As with any antique or collectible, prices vary depending on location, condition, and availability.

See also Birthday Angels.

Box, Green Holly, 6½", from $28.00 to $40.00.

283

Bank, Bluebird, #267, 6½" $40.00

Bank, globe, For My Trip, #1309, 6½" $35.00

Bank, pig, painted flowers, #090, 6½" $38.00

Bank, Uncle Sam, #882, 6⅞" $35.00

Basket, White Holly, Christmas bowl, #7745 ....$30.00

Bell, bride & groom, #3196, 2¾" $8.00

Bell, Green Holly, #6003, 3½" $12.00

Bone dish, Magnolia, #2623, 6½" $18.00

Box, heart shape w/doves on lid, #5597, 4¾" $35.00

Box, Violet Heirloom, footed, #1377, 5" $50.00

Box, White Holly, #6050, 6" dia.....................$35.00

Bread basket, Early American Rooster, #2099, 10" $60.00

Butter dish, Bluebird #437, 6" $85.00

Butter dish, Mr Toodles, #3294, 6¾" $165.00

Candle climber, angel w/musical instrument, #1453, 3¼" ..$15.00

Candleholders, Green Holly, #3620, footed, 7", pr $55.00

Canisters, Sunflower, #147, 4-pc set $15.00

Chip & dip, Rose Chintz, #2282, 10¼" $65.00

Coffeepot, Cuddles, #1448 ....$85.00

Compote, Tiffany Rose, #757 ....$90.00

Creamer, Bluebird, #290 ....$50.00

Creamer & sugar bowl, Dainty Miss, #322, w/lid.......$90.00

Creamer & sugar bowl, Della Robbia, #4135, w/lid $20.00

Creamer & sugar bowl, Elegant Rose, #2930, w/lid.....$65.00

Creamer and sugar bowl, Miss Priss, from $55.00 to $65.00. (Photo courtesy Loretta DeLozier)

Creamer & sugar bowl, Pineapple, #2481, w/lid........$30.00

Cup & saucer, Berry Harvest, #302 ....$32.00

Cup & saucer, Christmas Cardinal, #01248.............$20.00

Egg cup, Miss Priss, #1510 ....$50.00

Egg cup, Mr Toodles, 3¼" $30.00

Figurine, angel, September, #2600 ....$25.00

Figurine, Bloomer Girl, Amelia, #795, 4½" $35.00

Figurine, guardian angel w/2 sm children, #05317 ....$45.00

Figurine, Hereford bull, #750, 6¼" $36.00

Figurine, Jersey cow, #448, 6¾" $32.00

Figurine, leprechaun, #3522, 4" $15.00

Figurine, Lord Bless Our Work, girl sewing, #03457, 4½" ...$22.00

Figurine, Madonna, #10176, 11" $70.00

Figurine, Napoleon, #4213, 8" $75.00

Figurine, Persian cat, #1514, 5" $32.00

Figurine, puppy w/collar, #5221, 12" $95.00

Figurine, roadrunner, #3209, 7" $40.00

Figurine, sheep, Bethlehem Collection, #05609 ....$13.00

Figurines, Golden Pheasants, #6019, 10", pr $200.00

Jam jar, Dainty Miss, #323 ....$80.00

Jam jar, Miss Priss, #1515 ....$60.00

Lamp, hurricane; Green Holly, #4229, 5½" $45.00

Lamp, oil; Brown Heritage Fruit, #4283, 11" $210.00

Mug, Miss Priss, #1503, 4" $65.00

Mug, Washington, #2326, 5½" $40.00

Music box, cardinal, Up Up & Away, #02354, 6" $60.00

Music box, guardian angel w/2 children, Amazing Grace, #06995, 7½" ..$75.00

Napkin holder, Yellow Tulip, #7125 ....$24.00

Nightlight, colonial girl w/umbrella, #8020, 9" $75.00

Pincushion, mouse w/thimble, #2326, 3½" $15.00

Pitcher, Green Holly, #4870, 8¾" $60.00

Pitcher, To a Wild Rose, #2562, 9" $115.00

Pitcher & bowl, Rose Garden, #6627, 6" $58.00

Planter, baby shoe, pink, #4323, 4¼" $15.00

Planter, cocker spaniel, #6974, 6" $35.00

Planter, Green Holly, boot, #5185, 4¾" $22.00

Planter, Humpty Dumpty, #798, 4½" $30.00

Planter, Mr Toodles, #2631 ....$95.00

Planter, pixie on log, #881, 4¾" $16.00

Planter, Rose Chintz, #659, 9" $35.00

Plaque, angel w/lamb, #3206, 5½" $80.00

Plaque, Green Heritage, #045 ....$30.00

Plaque, Madonna w/Baby, #578, 8" $55.00

Plaque, mermaid, #4271, 11½" $45.00

Plaque, witch, #1258, 6" $55.00

Plaques, fish (7") & 2 babies, #60419, 3-pc set......$55.00

Plaques, mermaids, #2346, 5½", pr $55.00

Plate, Christmas Tree, #1096, 8", from $12.00 to $15.00.

Platter, Green Holly, #2048, 9".....................$37.00

Salt & pepper shakers, Cuddles, #1450, pr $20.00

Salt & pepper shakers, Dainty Miss, #439, pr........$12.00

Salt & pepper shakers, Green Holly, shoes, #6035, 3½", pr ..$18.00

Salt & pepper shakers, lobster, #2553, 5", pr $18.00

Salt & pepper shakers, Mr & Mrs Claus in rocking chairs, #8139, pr ..$22.00

Snack set, Golden Wheat, #2769, 9" $13.00

Snack set, Pink Clover, #2603, 8¾" $18.00
Spoon rest, Country Garden, #6301, 7½"..........................$12.00
Sugar bowl, Miss Priss, #1515, w/lid & spoon, 4½" $110.00
Switch plate, gold design, single, 5" $10.00
Teabag holder, Dainty Miss, #648, 3¼" $40.00
Teapot, Bluebirds, #438 ....$300.00
Teapot, Country Garden, #6195..$45.00
Teapot, Cuddles, #1448 ....$185.00
Teapot, Dainty Miss, #3321 ....$150.00
Teapot, Heirloom Elegance, #5394 ....$185.00
Teapot, Miss Priss #1516, 4-cup $135.00
Teapot, Tomato, #3149 ....$95.00
Teapot, White Holly, #6063..$125.00
Toothpick holder, rooster, #541, 6½" $35.00
Tray, To a Wild Rose, 2-tier, #2592 ....$70.00
Tumbler, Golden Laurel, #2403, 4" $12.00
Vase, Brown Heritage Fruit, 1-handle, #3117, 8¾".............$55.00
Vase, bud; Petite Fleurs, #7053, 7"...................................$10.00
Vase, Dainty Miss, #322 ....$30.00
Vase, Dainty Miss, #7797 ....$110.00
Vase, pineapple w/pink roses, #5362, 5" $55.00

Wall plaque, Dainty Miss, #6767, 5", $75.00. (Photo courtesy Loretta DeLozier)

Wall plaques, bluebird & baby, #1957, pr........................$100.00
Wall pocket, apple, #3022, 6"..$20.00
Wall pocket, Dainty Miss..$24.00
Wall pocket, Miss Priss, #1509..$150.00
Wall pocket, Mr & Mrs Bluebird, #283............................$125.00
Wall pocket, violin w/rose, #369 ....$28.00

L.G. Wright

Until closing in mid-1990, the L.G. Wright Glass Company was located in New Martinsville, West Virginia. Mr. Wright started his business as a glass jobber and then began buying molds from defunct glass companies. He never made his own glass, instead many companies pressed his wares, among them Fenton, Imperial, Viking, and Westmoreland. Much of L.G. Wright's glass was reproductions of Colonial and Victorian glass and lamps. Many items were made from the original molds, but the designs of some were slightly changed. His company flourished in the 1960s and 1970s. For more information we recommend *Fenton Glass Made for Other Companies, 1907 – 1980,* by Carrie and Gerald Domitz (Collector Books), and *The L.G. Wright Glass Company* by James Measell and W.C. 'Red' Roetteis (Glass Press).

Barber bottle, amber overlay w/hand-painted floral, bulbous base, from $75 to $85.00
Barber bottle, Hobnail, cranberry opalescent, from $200 to ..$250.00
Barber bottle, Spiral, cranberry opalescent, fluted, from $160 to $180.00
Canoe, Daisy & Button, amber, from $25 to.......................$35.00
Compote, Eye Winker, ruby, w/lid, sm, from $75 to $85.00
Covered dish, bird w/berry, amber, 5", from $25 to.............$30.00

Covered dish, frog on nest, amber, 5", from $30.00 to $45.00. (Photo courtesy Carrie and Gerld Domitz)

Covered dish, hen on nest, amberina, 7", from $40 to.........$45.00
Covered dish, hen on nest, opaque blue & white opal, 5", from $30 to $35.00
Covered dish, hen on nest, purple slag, 7", from $50 to $55.00
Covered dish, horse on nest, amber, 5", from $40 to $45.00
Covered dish, knobby turtle, dark amber, 11", from $100 to....$150.00
Creamer, Moss Rose on custard, tall, from $45 to...............$55.00
Creamer & sugar bowl, Beaded Curtain, green overlay, open, from $75 to $95.00
Cruet, Daisy & Fern, blue opalescent satin, from $150 to.$175.00
Cruet, Stars & Stripes, blue opalescent, from $200 to........$275.00
Cruet, Thumbprint, cranberry, from $75 to.......................$95.00
Epergne, white opalescent w/amethyst crest, 4-lily, from $550 to $650.00
Fairy lamp, Embossed Rose, crystal or amber, round base, 7", from $60 to $75.00
Fairy lamp, Hobnail, amber satin, from $60 to...................$75.00
Flower bowl, Daisy & Button, light blue, from $18 to $20.00
Goblet, Double Wedding Ring, ruby, from $20 to $22.00
Goblet, Priscilla, ruby, from $25 to $30.00

Lamp, banquet; Embossed Rose, rose overlay satin, 36", from $600 to **$650.00**

Lamp, miniature; Beaded Curtain, ruby overlay, from $275 to .. **$300.00**

Lamp, miniature; Daisy and Cube, amberina, from $150.00 to $175.00. (Photo courtesy Carrie and Gerald Domitz)

Pickle castor, Daisy & Button, topaz, from $165 to **$195.00**

Pickle castor, Daisy & Fern, blue opalescent, from $250 to .. **$275.00**

Pitcher, Christmas Snowflake, cranberry, 78-oz, from $300 to .. **$325.00**

Pitcher, Eye Dot, blue opalescent, 9½", from $250 to **$275.00**

Pitcher, Maize, amber overlay, amber handle, 78-oz, from $165 to **$200.00**

Pitcher, milk; Moss Rose on custard, from $75 to **$85.00**

Rose bowl, Embossed Rose, amber overlay, 5½", from $45 to . **$65.00**

Sugar shaker, Maize, pink overlay, metal top, from $85 to .. **$100.00**

Syrup, Thumbprint, ruby overlay, metal hinged top, from $150 to **$175.00**

Tumbler, water; Moss Rose on peachblow, from $50 to **$65.00**

Vase, Beaded Curtain, dark green transparent, from $225 to .. **$275.00**

Vase, Embossed Bird, pink overlay, 14", from $125 to **$145.00**

Wine goblet, Daisy & Button, light blue, from $20 to **$22.00**

Wine goblet, Jersey Swirl, ruby, from $20 to **$25.00**

Liberty Blue

'Take home a piece of American history!,' stated an ad from the 1970s for this dinnerware made in Staffordshire, England. Blue and white depictions of George Washington at Valley Forge, Paul Revere, Independence Hall — 14 historic scenes in all — were offered on different place-setting pieces. The ad goes on to describe this 'unique... truly unusual..museum-quality...future family heirloom.'

For every five dollars spent on groceries you could purchase a basic piece (dinner plate, bread and butter plate, cup, saucer, or dessert dish) for 59¢ on alternate weeks of the promotion. During the promotion, completer pieces could also be purchased. The soup tureen was the most expensive item, originally selling for $24.99. Nineteen completer pieces in all were offered along with a five-year open stock guarantee.

Beware of 18" and 20" platters. These are part of a line of recent imports and are not authentic Liberty Blue. For more information we recommend Jo Cunningham's book, *The Best of Collectible Dinnerware* (Schiffer).

Advisor: Gary Beegle (See Directory, Dinnerware)

Bowl, cereal; 6½" **$10.00**

Bowl, flat soup; 8¾", from $18 to **$20.00**

Bowl, fruit; 5" **$2.50**

Bowl, vegetable; oval, from $30 to **$35.00**

Bowl, vegetable; round **$30.00**

Butter dish, ¼-lb **$45.00**

Casserole, w/lid **$95.00**

Coaster (4 in set, ea w/different scene), ea............................ **$11.00**

Creamer **$14.50**

Creamer & sugar bowl, w/lid, original box **$60.00**

Cup & saucer.. **$3.50**

Gravy boat **$40.00**

Gravy boat liner **$18.00**

Mug.. **$9.50**

Pitcher, 7½", from $85.00 to $95.00.

Plate, bread & butter; 6" **$2.00**

Plate, dinner; 10", from $5 to **$7.00**

Plate, luncheon; scarce, 8¾" **$20.00**

Plate, salad; 7" **$9.00**

Platter, 12", from $35 to **$45.00**

Platter, 14" **$85.00**

Salt & pepper shakers, pr **$35.00**

Soup ladle, plain white, no decal, from $30 to **$35.00**

Soup tureen, w/lid.. **$245.00**

Sugar bowl, no lid **$5.00**

Sugar bowl, w/lid **$24.00**

Teapot, w/lid, from $85 to **$95.00**

License Plates

Some of the early porcelain license plates are valued at more than $500.00. First-year plates are especially desirable. Steel plates with the aluminum 'state seal' attached range in value from $150.00 (for those from 1915 to 1920) down to $20.00 (for those from the early 1940s to 1950). Even some modern plates are desirable to collectors who like those with special graphics and messages.

Our values are given for examples in good condition, unless noted otherwise. For further information see *License Plate Values* distributed by L-W Book Sales.

Advisor: Richard Diehl (See Directory, License Plates)

Club: Automobile License Plate Collectors Association (ALPCA)
ALPCA, Inc.
508 Costal Dr.
Virginia Beach, VA 23451
www.alpca.org

Magazine: *Plates*

Undated, Maryland, shield	$5.50
Undated, Mississippi, wildlife w/deer	$10.00
Undated, Nevada, blue	$3.50

1915, Vermont, white with black letters and numbers, $60.00.

1931, Colorado, truck	$25.00
1932, Nebraska	$20.00

1933, Nevada, unused, NM, $80.00. (Photo courtesy Past Tyme Pleasures)

1942, Alabama	$30.00
1945, Illinois, soybean	$15.50
1957, Rhode Island	$8.50
1960, Wisconsin, metal tabs	$1.00
1961, Kansas	$6.50
1962, Alaska	$15.50

1967, Montana	$7.50
1969, Ohio	$4.00
1970, Michigan	$3.50
1971, Iowa	$4.00
1972, Missouri	$2.50
1972, Oklahoma	$4.50
1975, Hawaii	$8.50
1976, Indiana, Bicentennial	$2.50
1977, Wyoming	$7.50
1981, Michigan	$3.50
1982, Minnesota, graphic	$2.50
1984, Pennsylvania	$3.50
1988, Kentucky	$6.50
1988, North Carolina, First in Flight	$3.50
1989, Florida, Orange State	$3.50
1991, California	$1.50
1991, Idaho, mountains	$2.50
1991, New Mexico, USA	$3.50
1991, Washington	$3.50
1993, Tennessee	$3.50
1994, South Dakota	$3.50
1994, Texas	$1.50
1994, West Virginia	$7.50
1997, Delaware	$6.50
1998, Illinois	$2.50
1998, Utah, arch	$4.50
1999, Georgia	$3.50
1999, Nevada, silver state	$3.50
2002, Arizona	$4.50
2005, Louisiana	$10.50
2006, New Hampshire	$10.50
2006, Vermont	$10.50
2007, Virginia, 400th Anniversary	$5.50

Linens

As early as the 1880s, thrifty farm wives were putting cloth feed sacks to a second use around the home as dishcloths, diapers for the babies, even simple articles of clothing. Soon manufacturers were catering to the ladies by printing the feed sacks in colorful designs better suited for making dresses, curtains, pillowcases, and the like. During the Depression when times were especially hard, literally millions of American ladies and their children were wearing feed sack garments. Besides those with allover designs, some sacks were offered with printed-on patterns for cloth dolls, aprons, or pillowcases. By the late 1940s fabric feed sacks were phased out in favor of those made of heavy paper. Today, these early fabric sacks are coveted collectibles. Especially interesting are those printed with Disney characters, nursery rhyme figures, and those signed by a famous designer.

Tablecloths and dishtowels from the 1940s and 1950s add a cheerful note to any kitchen, and collectors will pay a pretty penny for good examples with vibrant flowers and fruit, classic Dutch boys and girls, sailboats, Mexican motifs, cottages, and the like — all fun types that depict America at a happier, more carefree time. Souvenir linens representing states or particular sites are especially sought after. If they are signed by a well-known illustrator/designer, as is true in other fields of collecting, those signatures serve to drive the prices up even more.

Holiday-related items are hot, but reproductions are out there, buyers beware! Reproduction colors are off and do not show up as much on the back due to less color saturation. They also have plastic-type tags that are sewn in. Old linens feature fabric labels or homemade tags. Close examination of a reproduction shows a looser weave that is less heavy and has fewer details, made by printing rather than the silkscreening process.

When evaluating vintage linens, condition is an important factor — watch for fading, stains, holes, and other signs of wear. Our values are for examples that are in nearly new, very clean, spot-free condition unless noted otherwise.

Advisor: Darrell Thomas

Dishtowel, Scotland plaid, dancers, pipers, horse, and carriage on white cotton, $25.00. (Photo courtesy www.retro-redheads.com)

Dishtowel, embroidered Sunbonnet Girl & days of the week, 31x29½", set of 7...**$35.00**

Dishtowel, printed cornucopia & fruits, fruit along red border on white cotton, 30x15½" **$45.00**

Dishtowel, printed cornucopias w/strawberries & blossoms, multicolor on white cotton, 26x15" **$24.00**

Dishtowel, printed Florida souvenir w/map & palm trees, multicolor on white cotton, 27x15" **$24.00**

Dishtowel, printed gardener at table, vegetable border, multicolor on white cotton, 1940s-50s, 28x16" **$40.00**

Dishtowel, printed housewife hanging up long line of laundry, blue border on white cotton **$55.00**

Dishtowel, printed Mammy & pancakes in kitchen on white cotton blend, Startex, 31½x16½" **$60.00**

Dishtowel, printed Mexican man w/sombrero holds rooster, chevron border, multicolor on white cotton, 26x16"...................**$25.00**

Dishtowel, printed peasant girl & teapot, musical notes along blue border, multicolor on white cotton, 28x17"....................**$36.00**

Dishtowel, printed pinup girl sits below word Tomato, vegetables & red border surround her, white barkcloth, 28x14" .**$28.00**

Dishtowel, printed poodle w/spatula flips burgers at grill, multicolor on white cotton, 1950s, 29x16"....................................**$20.00**

Dishtowel, printed Swiss-style girl selling flowers from cart, flower border, multicolor on white cotton, 28x16"..................**$36.00**

Dishtowel, printed Vermont souvenir, colorful graphics on white cotton, 1940s...**$50.00**

Feed sack, Calypso dancers & musical notes on white cotton, opened, 42x36"...**$40.00**

Feed sack, floral bouquets on pink cotton, opened, 42x36"....**$40.00**

Feed sack, flowers & apples in bright colors on white cotton, opened, 52x38" **$40.00**

Feed sack, girl doing laundry & hanging clothes on clothesline, multicolor on white cotton, opened, 44x36".....................**$45.00**

Feed sack, kites, green, black, white & pink on golden yellow, opened, 42x37"...**$38.00**

Feed sack, pink, rose & gray diamonds on light pink cotton, 1940s, opened, 40x36"...**$38.00**

Feed sack, pink flowers & umbrellas w/green leaves & dots (dainty) on white cotton, opened, 43x37"...............................**$50.00**

Napkins, printed bamboo on green cotton, Wilendur, 16x16", 4 for...**$35.00**

Napkins, printed flamingo, palms, sailboat & dolphin, multicolor w/red border on white cotton, 15x15", 8 for...............**$27.50**

Napkins, printed watermelon slices on green cotton, Vera, 16x16", 6 for...**$38.00**

Placemats & napkins, printed flowers & rope on green, Hermes-Paris, set of 6, MIB..**$130.00**

Tablecloth, embroidered colorful flowers in wide garland on white heavy cotton, 29x40" **$50.00**

Tablecloth, embroidered Mexican dancers, cacti, banana trees, coyotes etc on white cotton, 37x37", +4 9¼" napkins........**$85.00**

Tablecloth, embroidered roses & vines on white cotton, 38x40", +4 matching napkins..**$60.00**

Tablecloth, printed Amish children doing farm chores, green & gold border on white cotton, 50x50"......................**$32.50**

Tablecloth, printed Atlantic City Centennial souvenir, site graphics, multicolor on white cotton, 54x51"..................**$240.00**

Tablecloth, printed Enid Blyton book characters, multicolor on white rayon, ca 1950s, 33x34", VG......................**$110.00**

Tablecloth, printed flower bouquets on wide green trellis, green bows & border on white textured cotton, 59x49"..............**$60.00**

Tablecloth, printed fruits & gourds among pots, turquoise border on white heavy cotton, 40x44"........................**$72.50**

Tablecloth, printed Indian corn among nuts & berries, multicolor on white sailcloth cotton, Wilendur, 54x50"..............**$385.00**

Tablecloth, printed Mammy & family in southern scenes along red floral border on white cotton, Pennicraft, 53x53".......**$175.00**

Tablecloth, printed Mexican scene w/palms, people & pots, multicolor on white, 1940s, 50x50"..................................**$85.00**

Tablecloth, printed pond lilies & cattails forming border, 1940s, 50x50" **$55.00**

Tablecloth, printed red & white geraniums w/teal along border on white cotton, 54x48" **$52.00**

Tablecloth, printed saddles, guns & holsters, cowboy scenes w/cactus border on white cotton, 54x54", +2 dishtowels..........**$180.00**

Tablecloth, printed souvenir of Florida, printed palms & cacti, red, blue & teal on white cotton, 51x49" **$78.00**

Tablecloth, printed souvenir of New York City, allover sites, red scenic border on white cotton, ca 1950s, 50x50" **$125.00**

Tablecloth, printed sunflowers on white cotton, Wilendur, +6 matching napkings, MIB **$155.00**

Tablecloth, printed tennis scenes & courts on white cotton, 50x50" **$145.00**

Tablecloth, printed vegetables & scalloped dark red border on white cotton, 48x52" **$65.00**

Tablecloth, Mexicana colors and theme, ca. 1940s, 49x52", $135.00. (Photo courtesy www.retro-redheads.com)

Little Red Riding Hood

This line of novelty cookie jars, canisters, mugs, teapots, and other kitchenware items was made by both Regal China and Hull. Buyers need to be aware of reproductions in today's market.

The complete line is covered in *The Collector's Ultimate Encyclopedia of Hull Pottery*, by our advisor Brenda Roberts (Collector Books).

Advisor: Brenda Roberts

Bank, standing, 7", from $800 to **$1,000.00**
Butter dish, from $250 to **$350.00**
Canister, cereal **$1,200.00**
Canister, coffee, sugar or flour; ea from $600 to **$700.00**
Canister, salt..................................**$1,100.00**
Canister, tea; from $600 to **$700.00**
Casserole, red w/embossed wolf, Red Riding Hood, Grandma & axe man, 11¾", from $1,800 to **$2,500.00**
Cookie jar, closed basket, from $275 to **$400.00**
Cookie jar, full skirt, from $350 to **$550.00**
Cookie jar, open basket, from $275 to **$400.00**
Cracker jar, unmarked, from $550 to..................**$650.00**
Creamer, top pour, no tab handle, from $275 to **$350.00**
Creamer, top pour, tab handle, from $250 to................**$275.00**
Dresser jar, 8¾", from $450 to..................................**$575.00**
Lamp, from $1,500 to..................................**$2,000.00**
Match holder, wall hanging, from $300 to................**$415.00**

Mustard jar, w/original spoon, from $350 to **$425.00**
Pitcher, 7", from $375 to **$500.00**
Pitcher, 8", from $450 to **$650.00**
Planter, wall hanging, from $300 to..................**$425.00**
Salt & pepper shakers, Pat design 135889, med size, pr from $400 to **$650.00**
Salt & pepper shakers, 3¼", pr from $95 to................**$140.00**
Salt & pepper shakers, 5½", pr from $140 to..................**$200.00**
Spice jar, sq base, ea from $400 to **$600.00**
String holder, from $1,500 to **$1,800.00**
Sugar bowl, crawling, no lid, from $240 to..................**$340.00**
Sugar bowl, standing, no lid, from $150 to..................**$200.00**
Sugar bowl, w/lid, from $175 to **$235.00**
Teapot, from $315 to **$400.00**
Wolf jar, red base, from $750 to..................**$900.00**
Wolf jar, yellow base, from $700 to..................**$800.00**

Creamer, side pour, from $150.00 to $200.00.

Little Tikes

For more than 25 years, this company (a division of Rubbermaid) has produced an extensive line of toys and playtime equipment, all made of heavy-gauge plastic, sturdily built, and able to stand up to the rowdiest children and the most inclement weather. As children usually outgrow these items well before they're worn out, you'll often see them at garage sales, priced at a fraction of their original cost. We've listed a few below, along with what we feel would be a high average for an example in the stated condition. Since there is no established secondary market pricing system, though, you can expect to see a wide range of asking prices.

Big Splash Center Swimimng Pool & Slide, NM, from $200 to .**$250.00**
Castle, built-in slide, NM, from $250 to **$350.00**
Country Cottage Toddler Bed, NM, from $175 to...........**$225.00**
Cozy Cruiser, NM, from $85 to **$150.00**
Endless Adventure Playcenter, NM, from $350 to **$425.00**
Grand Mansion Doll House, w/furniture assortment, NM, from $225 to **$275.00**
Imagine Sounds Playhouse, EX, from $200 to..................**$250.00**

Log Cabin, NM, from $200.00 to $250.00.

Patio Playhouse, NM, from $300 to $350.00
Slam 'n Slide Waterslide, NM, from $250 to $300.00
Super Spiral Inflatable Bouncer, NM, from $350 to $425.00
Thomas the Tank Engine Bed, NM, from $325 to $400.00
Treehouse Player, NM, from $185 to $225.00
Twin Race Car Bed, black, red or blue, 103" L, NM, from $250
   to $300.00
Variety Climber w/Swing Set extension, 2 slides & climbing net, EX,
   from $300 to $350.00
Whirly Rocket Merry-Go-Round, EX, from $175 to.........$200.00
5-in-1 Slid 'n Hide Tower, EX, from $175 to $200.00
5-in-1 Super Sports Bouncer, NM, from $250 to $275.00
8-in Adjustable Playground, NM, from $275 to................$325.00

Lladro Porcelains

Lovely studies of children and animals in subtle colors are characteristic of the Lladro porcelains produced in Labernes Blanques, Spain.
Their retired and limited editions are popular with today's collectors.

Anniversary Dance, #1372, 1987-2004, 12¼" $295.00
Apollo Landing, #6168, 1994-95, 16¼" $375.00
Ballerina, #4559, retired, 14" $350.00
Barrel of Blossoms, #1419, retired, 10½" $415.00
Barrow of Fun, #5460, 1988-91, 8¼", MIB $450.00
Christopher Columbus, #2176, 1987-94, 19¼"................$475.00
Down the Aisle, #5903, 1992-96, 12¼" $275.00
Fallas Queen, #5869, 1992-95, 5¼", MIB.........................$375.00
Fishing w/Gramps, #2351, retired......................................$425.00
Mile of Style, #6507, 1998, 14"..$415.00
Milk for the Lamb, #4926, retired, 10½" $350.00
Moses, #5170, 1982-2000, 16½" $415.00
Mother, #4864, 1974-89, 15x10" $325.00
Out for a Romp, #5761, 1991-95, 8¼", MIB.....................$315.00
Pensive Clown, #5130, 1980-2000, 9¾"............................$300.00
Playing Dogs, #1258, 1974-81, 5¼", minimum value $450.00
Sad Harlequin, #4558, 1969-93, 13¾" $325.00
School Marm, #5209, 1984-90, 13" $325.00

Socialite of the '20s, #5283, 1985-2001, 13¾" $265.00
Summer on the Farm, #5286, 1985-2007, 9½" $325.00
Sunday in the Park, #5365, 1986-96, 8½" $400.00
Suzy & Her Doll, #1378, retired...$325.00
Time for Love, #5992, retired, 10", MIB...........................$415.00
Time for Reflection, #5378, 1986-91 ....$300.00
Touch of Class, #5377, 14½"...$450.00
Voyage of Columbus, #5847, 1992-93, 9½x9" $500.00
Wish for Love, #06562, 1999-2004, 16½", MIB...............$450.00

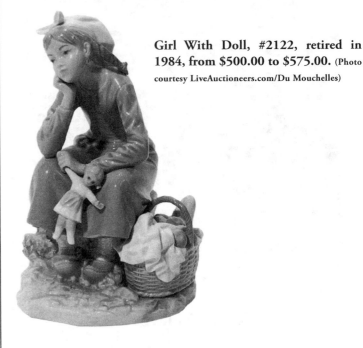

Girl With Doll, #2122, retired in 1984, from $500.00 to $575.00. (Photo courtesy LiveAuctioneers.com/Du Mouchelles)

Longaberger Baskets

In the early 1900s in the small Ohio town of Dresden, John
Wendell ('J.W.') Longaberger developed a love for hand-woven baskets. In 1973 J.W. and his fifth child, Dave, began to teach others
how to weave baskets. J.W. passed away during that year, but the
quality and attention to detail found in his baskets were kept alive
by Dave through the Longaberger Company®.

Each basket is hand woven, using hardwood maple splints.
Since 1978 each basket has been dated and signed by the weaver
upon completion. In 1982 the practice of burning the Longaberger
name and logo into the bottom of each basket began, guaranteeing
its authenticity as a Longaberger Basket®.

New baskets can be obtained only through sales consulants,
usually at a basket home party. Collector and speciality baskets are
available only for a limited time throughout the year. For example,
the 1992 Christmas Collection Basket was offered only from
September through December 1992. After this, the basket was no
longer available from Longaberger®. Once an item is discontinued or
retired, it can only be obtained on the secondary market.

This information is from *The 2006 – 2007 Edition Bentley
Collection Guide*. See the Directory for ordering information or call
1-800-837-4394.

Note: Values are for baskets only, unless accessories such as liners
and protectors are mentioned in the description. Sizes may vary as

much as one-half inch. All dimensions are given in (length) x (width) x (height).

Advisor: Jill S. Rindfuss (See Directory, Longaberger Baskets)

1979-93, Retired Mini Cradle™ (basket only), sm rectangular, no color trim or weave, no handles, wood rockers, $45 to . **$90.00**

1983, JW Collection Medium Market (basket only), from $905.00 to $1,025.00. (Photo courtesy LiveAuctioneers.com/ Homestead Auctions)

1984-90, Booking/Promo Candle™ (basket only), rectangular, no color trim or weave, 1 stationary handle, ⅜" weave, from $30 to **$70.00**

1988-2003, MBA™, Classic stain, no color weave or trim strip, attached lid, given to consultants promoted to Management Bound Associate status, from $55 to **$85.00**

1990, Mother's Day Small Oval™ (basket only), pink weave & trim strip, 2 leather handles, from $51 to **$86.00**

1990-2001, Heartland Bakery™ (basket only), rectangular, Heartland Blue shoestring weave, 2 leather ears, Heartland logo burned on bottom, from $48 to **$55.00**

1990-92, Hostess Remembrance™ (basket only), rectangular, no color trim or weave, 2 swinging handles, woven attached lid, from $125 to **$175.00**

1991, JW Corn® (basket only), round, blue trim & accent weave, 2 leather handles, brass tag: Longaberger — JW Corn, from $200 to **$253.00**

1991, Mother's Day Small Purse™ (basket only), rectangular, pink trim & accent weave, 1 swinging handle, from $67 to.. **$99.00**

1992, All-American Small Market™ (basket only), rectangular, red trim w/red & blue accent weave, 2 swinging handles, from $43 to **$65.00**

1992, Father's Day Paper™ (basket only), rectangular, higher in the back than in the front, Dresden blue & burgundy trim, no handles, from $70 to... **$95.00**

1993, All-Star Trio™ (w/liner & protector), rectangular, red & blue weave & trim, 2 leather ears, from $38 to **$75.00**

1993, Christmas Bayberry™ (basket only), sq, red or green trim & accent weave, ⅜" weave, from $42 to **$69.00**

1993, Crisco® Baking™ (basket only), oval, red & blue weave & trim, 2 leather ears, burned-in Crisco®, from $50 to............ **$107.00**

1994, Father's Day Tall Tissue™ (basket only), Classic stain, burgundy & dark green trim strip, WoodCrafts lid available separately, from $44 to **$60.00**

1994, Holiday Hostess Sleigh Bell™ (basket only), round top, rectangular bottom, red or green trim w/red & green accent weave, 2 swinging handles, from $145 to.............................. **$160.00**

1994, Shades of Autumn Recipe™ (basket only), rectangular w/higher back, green, rust & deep blue weave w/rust trim, Woodcrafts lid, set of recipe cards included, from $54 to **$77.00**

1995-97, Woven Traditions Spring® (basket only), sq, red, blue & green shoestring weave, 1 stationary handle, from $51 to **$65.00**

1996, Sweetheart Bouquet™ (basket only), red weave & trim strip, 1 swinging handle, from $49 to **$75.00**

1997, JW Collection Miniature Waste Basket™ (basket only), blue trim strip, ⅛" blue weave, 2nd in series of reproductions woven by JW Longaberger, brass tag: Longaberger - JW Miniature Waste, available only to Collectors Club members, from $110 to..... **$185.00**

1998, Bee™ (basket only), available to consultants who attended Bee 98, blue & red weave & trim strip, brass tag reads: Join Our Celebration, from $42 to **$50.00**

1998, Perfect Attendance™ (basket only), red weave & trim strip, 1 swinging handle, brass tag/box, given to company employees for perfect attendance July 1, 1997 to June 20, 1998, from $405 to **$425.00**

1999, Collector Club Family Picnic, full set with protector, liner, lid, and three-way divided lift-out, from $225.00 to $300.00. (Photo courtesy LiveAuctioneers.com/Sunflower Auction)

1999, Lots of Luck™ (basket only), sq, green chain-link weave & trim, ⅜" weave, 1 stationary handle, no tag, special burned-in logo, from $50 to.. **$100.00**

1999, May Series Daisy™ (basket only), round, blue weave & trim, 1 swinging handle, ⅜" weave, board bottom, $49 to......... **$93.00**

1999, Traditions® Generosity™ (basket only), oval, green trim & accent weave, 2 swinging handles, no box, brass tag, from $119 to . **$131.00**

2000, Autumn Reflections Small Harvest Blessings™ (basket only), rectangular, sage, brown & burgundy accent weave, 2 leather ears, from $50 to **$79.00**

2000, Cheers™ (basket only), oval, stained, periwinkle & purple double trim, 1 stationary handle, board bottom w/burned-in logo, commemorative silver tag, from $50 to **$71.00**

2000, Frosty™ (basket only), green & red trim strip, works w/ Small Wrought Iron Snowman, same shape & size as Darning Basket, available September 1 to December 31, 2000, from $47 to **$54.00**

2001, Collectors Club Whistle Stop™ (basket only), tall, rectangular, blue trim, red shoestring weave, star-shaped tacks, 1 swinging handle, commemorative tag, Collectors Club logo burned on bottom, w/box **$143.00**

2001, Pumpkin Patch™, shape resembles pumpkin, ⅜" weave in center of basket & ³⁄₁₆" weave at top & woven reinforced bottom, 1 swinging handle, woven from collapsible form, from $90 to **$110.00**

2001, Special Events Inaugural™ (basket only), rectangular, blue trim w/pewter star studs, red shoestring accent weave, 1 swinging handle, from $53 to **$79.00**

2002, Horizon of Hope™ (basket only), classic stain or White-wash w/2-tone pink color weave & trim, round top/sq bottom, 1 swinging handle, ⅜" weave, 8th edition of series, American Cancer Society logo burned into bottom of basket, from $38 to **$79.00**

2002, Small Easter™ (basket only), oval, classic or white-washed stain w/pink, green or yellow trim & accent weave, 1 stationary handle, reinforced board bottom, from $55 to **$68.00**

2002, Tour Golf Basket™ (basket only), classic stain w/dark blue upsplints & trim, 1 swinging handle, woven bottom, brass tag, from $78 to **$110.00**

2003, Entertaining w/Longaberger Book, features 115 recipes, 38 projects, helpful hints for 14 celebrations, includes creative ways to use Longaberger baskets & pottery, full-color photos .. **$30.00**

Miscellaneous

1990, Father Christmas Cookie Mold™ First Casting, brown pottery, inscription on back: Longaberger Pottery - First Casting - Christmas 1990, w/box, from $32 to **$51.00**

1990-91, Roseville Grandma Bonnie's Apple Pie Plate,™ pottery, blue accents, embossing on bottom: Roseville Ohio, w/box, from $35 to **$51.00**

1992-95, Booking/Promo Potpourri Sachet,™ Herbal Garden™ or Garden Splendor™ fabrics, from $13 to **$15.00**

1999, Fruit Medley Pottery - Pitcher,™ Vitrified China, hand-painted fruit designs, logo on bottom, w/box, from $56 to **$80.00**

2002, Pottery Falling Leaves Vase,™ Vitrified China, round opening, butternut color w/sage lip, Longaberger Pottery emblem, w/ box, from $46 to **$75.00**

2002, Pottery Shamrock Ramekin™, Vitrified China, 3-leaf clover shape, Woven Traditions Heritage Green, box **$45.00**

Lu Ray Pastels

This was one of Taylor, Smith, and Taylor's most popular lines of dinnerware. It was made from the late 1930s until sometime in the early 1950s in five pastel colors: Windsor Blue, Persian Cream, Sharon Pink, Surf Green, and Chatham Gray.

Bowl, coupe soup; flat	**$18.00**
Bowl, cream soup	**$70.00**
Bowl, fruit; Chatham Gray, 5"	**$16.00**
Bowl, fruit; 5"	**$6.00**
Bowl, lug soup; tab handled	**$24.00**
Bowl, mixing; 5½", 7", or 8¾", ea	**$125.00**
Bowl, mixing; 10¼"	**$150.00**
Bowl, salad; colors other than yellow	**$65.00**
Bowl, salad; yellow	**$55.00**
Bowl, vegetable; oval, 9½" L	**$25.00**
Bowl, 36s oatmeal	**$60.00**
Bud vase	**$400.00**
Butter dish, Chatham Gray	**$90.00**
Butter dish, w/lid, colors other than Chatham Gray	**$60.00**
Calendar plate, 8", 9", or 10", ea	**$40.00**
Casserole	**$140.00**
Chocolate cup, AD; straight sides	**$80.00**
Chocolate pot, AD; straight sides	**$400.00**
Coaster/nut dish	**$65.00**
Coffee cup, AD	**$22.50**
Coffeepot, AD	**$200.00**
Creamer	**$10.00**
Creamer, AD; from chocolate set, individual	**$92.00**
Creamer, AD; ind	**$40.00**
Egg cup, double	**$30.00**
Epergne	**$125.00**
Jug, water; footed	**$150.00**
Muffin cover	**$140.00**

Muffin cover with 8" underplate, $165.00.

Nappy, vegetable; round, 8½"	**$25.00**
Pickle tray	**$28.00**
Pitcher, bulbous w/flat bottom, colors other than yellow	**$125.00**
Pitcher, bulbous w/flat bottom, yellow	**$95.00**
Pitcher, juice	**$200.00**
Plate, cake	**$70.00**
Plate, chop; 15"	**$38.00**
Plate, grill; 3-compartment	**$35.00**
Plate, 6"	**$3.00**
Plate, 7"	**$12.00**
Plate, 8"	**$25.00**
Plate, 9"	**$10.00**
Plate, 10"	**$25.00**
Platter, 11½"	**$20.00**

Platter, 13"...$24.00
Relish dish, 4-part...$125.00

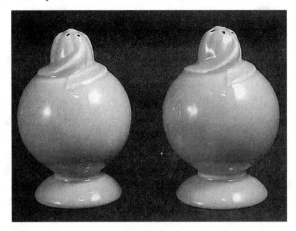

Salt and pepper shakers, $18.00 for the pair.

Sauceboat...$28.00
Sauceboat, fixed stand, yellow............................$27.50
Saucer $2.00
Saucer, coffee; AD...$12.50
Saucer, coffee/chocolate....................................$30.00
Saucer, for cream soup $28.00
Sugar bowl, AD; w/lid...$40.00
Sugar bowl, AD; w/lid, from chocolate set.........$92.00
Sugar bowl, w/lid..$15.00
Teacup..$8.00
Teapot, curved spout...$125.00
Teapot, flat spout $160.00
Tumbler, juice...$50.00
Tumbler, water..$80.00

Lucy and Me

Lucy and Me bears are designed by Seattle artist Lucy Rigg for Enesco. These darling bisque porcelain teddy bears range from 2½" to 3" tall. All feature delightful outfits. The bears are all marked and dated. Besides figurines, there is also matching giftware.

Advisors: Debbie and Randy Coe (See Directory, Cape Cod)

Figurine, Junior Girl Scout, 1995, 3", $15.00. (Photo courtesy Carol Stover)

Figurine, bear dressed as ice-cream sandwich, 1991 ....**$22.50**
Figurine, bride & groom cutting wedding cake (cake is separate pc)..**$35.00**
Figurine, cave man & cave woman, ea w/club, pr **$27.50**
Figurine, Going to Church, he w/cane, she w/Bible, pr **$14.00**
Figurine, mom & dad w/new baby **$16.50**
Figurine, mother & child w/tray of cookies **$17.50**
Music box, bride & groom on top of wedding cake............**$28.00**
Music box, sleeping bear in 4-poster, guardian angel cat beside, Brahm's Lullaby, 4½x2¾"...**$18.00**
Thimble set, bears dressed as vegetables, 1986, 6 for............**$80.00**

Lunch Boxes

Character lunch boxes made of metal have been very collectible for several years, but now even those made of plastic and vinyl are coming into their own.

The first lunch box of this type ever produced featured Hopalong Cassidy. Made by the Aladdin company, it was constructed of steel and decorated with decals. But the first fully lithographed steel lunch box and matching Thermos bottle was made a few years later (in 1953) by American Thermos. Roy Rogers was its featured character. Since then hundreds have been made, and just as is true in other areas of character-related collectibles, the more desirable lunch boxes are those with easily recognizable, well-known subjects — western heroes; TV, Disney, and cartoon characters; and famous entertainers like the Bee Gees and the Beatles.

Learn to grade your lunch boxes carefully. Values hinge on condition. We have given a range of values. Use the low side to evaluate a box in excellent condition, the high side for one mint or nearly so. A grade of 'excellent' for metal boxes means that you will notice only very minor defects and less than normal wear. Plastic boxes may have a few scratches and some minor wear on the sides, but the graphics must be completely undamaged. Vinyls must retain their original shape; brass parts may be tarnished, and the hinge may show signs of beginning splits. If the box you're trying to evaluate is in any worse condition than we've described, to be realistic, you must cut these prices drastically. Values for metal lunch boxes do not include the Thermos; those are listed separately. Prices for vinyl and plastic boxes, however, are for those complete with their original Thermos bottle.

If you would like to learn more, we recommend *Schroeder's Collectible Toys, Antique to Modern*, published by Collector Books.

Note: Watch for reproductions marked 'China.'

Metal

Action Jackson, 1970s, from $550 to **$750.00**
Action Jackson, 1970s, metal bottle, from $100 to **$175.00**
America on Parade, 1970s, from $25 to **$50.00**
America on Parade, 1970s, plastic bottle, from $15 to.........**$25.00**
Annie, 1980s, from $30 to...**$40.00**
Annie, 1980s, plastic bottle, from $5 to.............................**$10.00**
Astronauts, 1960, dome from $85 to **$150.00**
Astronauts, 1960, metal bottle, from $30 to **$50.00**
Atom Ant, 1960s, metal bottle, from $35 to.......................**$65.00**
Atom Ant, 1970s, from $75 to **$175.00**

Battlestar Galactica, 1970s, from $35 to $65.00

Battlestar Galactica, 1970s, plastic bottle, from $15 to $25.00

Berenstein Bears, 1980s, from $50 to.................................$75.00

Berenstein Bears, 1980s, plastic bottle, from $10 to...........$20.00

Black Hole, 1970s, from $30 to..$60.00

Black Hole, 1970s, plastic bottle, from $10 to.....................$20.00

Brave Eagle, 1950s, from $150 to $200.00

Brave Eagle, 1950s, metal bottle, from $50 to $100.00

Buccaneer, 1950s, dome, from $150 to.............................$225.00

Buccaneer, 1950s, metal bottle, from $75 to......................$120.00

Care Bear Cousins, 1980s, from $25 to $50.00

Care Bear Cousins, 1980s, plastic bottle, from $5 to $10.00

Cartoon Zoo Lunch Chest, 1960s, from $200 to $275.00

Cartoon Zoo Lunch Chest, 1960s, metal bottle, from $65 to...$115.00

Chavo, 1970s, from $40 to $90.00

Chavo, 1970s, plastic bottle, from $15 to $25.00

Cyclist, 1970s, from $25 to...$50.00

Cyclist, 1970s, plastic bottle, from $10 to...........................$20.00

Daniel Boone, Aladdin, 1960s, from $125 to.....................$175.00

Daniel Boone, Aladdin, 1960s, metal bottle, from $55 to ...$70.00

Dick Tracy, 1960s, metal bottle, from $25 to......................$50.00

Dick Tracy, 1970s, from $125 to $175.00

Disney's Wonderful World, 1980s, from $15 to...................$30.00

Disney's Wonderful World, 1980s, plastic bottle, from $5 to...$15.00

Dudley Do-Right, 1960s, from $500 to............................$800.00

Dudley Do-Right, 1960s, metal bottle, from $225 to........$325.00

Dukes of Hazzard, 1980s, original Duke boys, from $45 to...$65.00

Dukes of Hazzard, 1980s, plastic bottle, from $10 to $20.00

Dutch Cottage, steel with dome top, 1958, from $250.00 to $400.00. (Photo courtesy LiveAuctioneers.com/Morphy Auctions)

Empire Strikes Back, 1980s, from $35 to.............................$65.00

Empire Strikes Back, 1980s, plastic bottle, from $10 to.......$20.00

ET, 1980s, from $50 to..$75.00

ET, 1980s, plastic bottle, from $10 to.................................$20.00

Flintstones, 1960s, from $125 to $175.00

Flintstones, 1960s, metal bottle, from $30 to......................$60.00

Flipper, 1960s, from $100 to $150.00

Flipper, 1960s, metal bottle, from $20 to............................$40.00

Gentle Ben, 1970s, from $75 to $125.00

Gentle Ben, 1970s, metal bottle, from $20 to......................$40.00

Globe Trotters, 1950s, dome, from $175 to......................$225.00

Globe Trotters, 1950s, metal bottle, from $20 to................$40.00

Gomer Pyle, 1960s, from $100 to....................................$150.00

Gomer Pyle, 1960s, metal bottle, from $20 to.....................$40.00

Gunsmoke, 1959, Marshall, from $200 to.........................$400.00

Gunsmoke, 1959, Marshall, metal bottle, from $50 to......$100.00

Harlem Globetrotters, 1970s, from $30 to...........................$60.00

Harlem Globetrotters, 1970s, metal bottle, from $15 to......$25.00

Heathcliff, 1980s, from $20 to...$30.00

Heathcliff, 1980s, plastic bottle, from $5 to........................$10.00

How the West Was Won, 1970s, from $30 to.......................$50.00

How the West Was Won, 1970s, plastic bottle, from $10 to ..$20.00

Huckleberry Hound & Friends, 1960s, metal bottle, from $20 to..$40.00

Huckleberry Hound & Friends, 1970s, from $100 to........$175.00

Jr Miss, 1960, from $25 to $50.00

Jr Miss, 1970, metal bottle, from $15 to.............................$20.00

Lance Link Secret Chimp, 1970s, from $75 to.................$125.00

Lance Link Secret Chimp, 1970s, metal bottle, from $15 to..$30.00

Lawman, 1960s, from $75 to..$150.00

Lawman, 1960s, metal bottle, from $20 to...........................$40.00

Little House on the Prairie, 1970s, from $50 to................$100.00

Little House on the Prairie, 1970s, plastic bottle, from $20 to..$40.00

Ludwig Von Drake in Disneyland, 1960s, from $125 to ...$175.00

Ludwig Von Drake in Disneyland, 1960s, metal bottle, from $20 to..$40.00

Mer Merlin, 1980s, plastic bottle, from $5 to.....................$15.00

Mork & Mindy, 1970s, from $25 to...................................$50.00

Mork & Mindy, 1970s, plastic bottle, from $5 to...............$15.00

Mr Merlin, 1980s, from $20 to $35.00

Munsters, 1960s, from $150.00 to $300.00. (Photo courtesy LiveAuctioneers.com/Morphy Auctions)

Pac Man, 1980s, from $20 to $35.00

Pac Man, 1980s, plastic bottle, from $5 to.........................$10.00

Pebbles & Bamm Bamm, 1970s, from $40 to.....................$80.00

Pebbles & Bamm Bamm, 1970s, plastic bottle, from $15 to..$30.00

Planet of the Apes, 1970s, from $75 to............................$125.00

Planet of the Apes, 1970s, plastic bottle, from $15 to..........$25.00

Police Patrol, 1970s, from $125 to......................................$175.00
Police Patrol, 1970s, plastic bottle, from $15 to..................$25.00
Porky's Lunch Wagon, 1959, from $450 to........................$550.00
Porky's Lunch Wagon, 1959, metal bottle, from $50 to.......$75.00
Robin Hood, 1970s, from $30 to $60.00
Robin Hood, 1970s, plastic bottle, from $8 to $18.00
Rose Petal Place, 1980s, form $20 to $40.00
Rose Petal Place, 1980s, plastic bottle, from $5 to $15.00
Scooby Doo, 1970s, any, from $50 to...............................$100.00
Scooby Doo, 1970s, plastic bottle, from $22 to..................$38.00
Secret Agent T, 1960s, from $50 to..................................$100.00
Secret Agent T, 1960s, metal bottle, from $25 to................$50.00
Sesame Street, 1970s, from $25 to $50.00
Sesame Street, 1970s, plastic bottle, from $5 to $10.00
Steve Canyon, 1959, from $150 to $250.00
Steve Canyon, 1959, metal bottle, from $55 to $85.00
Thundercats, 1980s, from $25 to......................................$50.00
Thundercats, 1980s, plastic bottle, from $5 to...................$10.00
Underdog, 1970s, from $350 to..$750.00
Underdog, 1970s, metal bottle, from $150 to....................$250.00
V, 1980s, from $75 to..$125.00
V, 1980s, plastic bottle, from $20 to.................................$40.00

Plastic

Values are for boxes complete with their original Thermos, and range from low, indicating excellent condition, to high for a mint example.

A-Team, 1980s, from $15 to $20.00
Astrokids, 1980s, from $15 to..$25.00
Barbie, 1990s, from $10 to $15.00
Benji, 1970s, from $20 to..$30.00

California Raisins, with bottle, from $12.00 to $18.00.
(Photo courtesy L.M. White)

Casper the Friendly Ghost, 1990s, from $8 to.....................$15.00
Crest Toothpaste, 1980s, tubular, from $50 to.....................$75.00
Fat Albert, 1970s, from $20 to...$30.00
Fat Albert, 1970s, from $20 to...$30.00
Hot Wheels, 1990s, from $15 to $20.00
Jurassic Park, 1990s, w/recalled bottle, from $25 to............$30.00

Keebler Cookies, 1980s, from $30 to................................$50.00
Mickey Mouse, 1980s, head form, from $25 to $35.00
Mighty Mouse, 1970s, from $25 to $35.00
Muppet Babies, 1980s, from $15 to $25.00
New Kids on the Block, 1990s, from $15 to........................$25.00
Nosey Bears, 1990s, from $10 to $20.00
Rocky Roughneck, 1970s, from $25 to..............................$35.00
Snoopy & Woodstock, 1970s, dome, from $20 to...............$30.00
SWAT, 1970s, dome, from $30 to $40.00
Yogi bear, 1990s, from $15 to $25.00

Vinyl

Values are for boxes complete with their original Thermos, and range from low, indicating excellent condition, to high for a mint example.

Annie, 1980s, from $50 to...$75.00
Barbarino, 1970s, brunch bag, from $225 to.....................$275.00
Batman, 1990s, from $15 to $25.00
Captain Kangaroo, 1970s, from $350 to............................$450.00
Deputy Dawg, 1960s, from $325 to $375.00
Donnie & Marie, 1970s, brunch bag, from $75 to...........$125.00
Dr Seuss (World of), 1970, from $30 to.............................$60.00
Jr Deb, 1960s, from $100 to...$150.00
Li'l Jodie, 1980s, from $50 to $75.00
Lion in the Van, 1970s, from $50 to.................................$75.00
Mardi Gras, 1970s, from $50 to $110.00

Pebbles and Bamm-Bamm, 1971, with Thermos (not shown), from $165.00 to $325.00. (Photo courtesy L.M. White)

Psychedelic Blue, 1970s, from $40 to.................................$60.00
Soupy Sales, 1960s, from $300 to $375.00
Speedy Turtle, 1970s, drawstring bag, from $15 to $25.00
Tic-Tac-Toe, 1970s, from $50 to $75.00

MAD Collectibles

MAD, a hotly controversial and satirical publication that was first established in 1953, spoofed everything from advertising and politics to the latest movies and TV shoes. Content pivoted around a unique mix of lofty creativity, liberalism, and the ridiculous. A cult-like following has developed over the years. Eagerly sought are items relating to characters that were developed by the comic magazine such as Alfred E. Neuman or Spy Vs Spy. Unless noted otherwise, our values are for items in at least near mint condition.

Book, Mad for Keeps, hardback, 1958, EX w/dust jacket **$35.00**
Bust, Alfred E Neuman, white porcelain on ceramic base, American Ware, 1960s, 6" **$110.00**
Figurine, Alfred E Neuman standing on white base, What Me Worry?, Warner Bros, 14½", MIB................................**$40.00**
Game, Groo: The Game, Sergio Aragones, 1997, MIB (sealed). **$140.00**
Hobby kit, Alfred E Neuman figural, plastic, MIB (sealed). **$200.00**
Key chain, dog-tag type, Alfred E Neuman face, MAD SHOW, ring & 28" chain, 2x1¼" **$95.00**
Long-playing record, Fink Along w/MAD, Bigtop 12-1306, Alfred E Neuman on cover **$35.00**
Magazine, 1952, August..**$130.00**
Magazine, 1957, June...**$80.00**
Magazine, 1959, October..**$80.00**
Model car, Kasey Kahne, 2004 Intrepid #9 Dodge Dealers (Spy vs Spy), 1:24 scale, 2004, MIB..**$40.00**

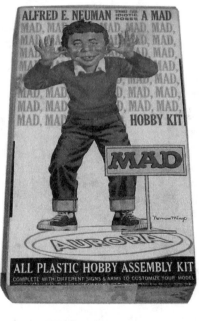

Model kit, Alfred E. Neuman, Aurora, 1965, NRFB (sealed), $225.00.
(Photo courtesy LiveAuctioneers.com/Philip Weiss Auctions)

Press kit, Alfred E Neuman on front cover, holds Mad Money pamphlet, etc, EC Publications, Warner Bros, 1994, 10x13" **$150.00**
T-shirt, Alfred E Neuman & What Me Worry? on front, 100% cotton, size sm **$130.00**

Maddux of California

Founded in Los Angeles in 1938, Maddux not only produced ceramics but imported and distributed them as well. They supplied chain stores nationwide with well-designed figural planters, TV lamps, novelty and giftware items, and during the mid-1960s their merchandise was listed in every major stamp catalog. Because of an increasing amount of foreign imports and an economic slowdown in our own country, the company was forced to sell out in 1976. Under the new management, manufacturing was abandoned, and the company was converted solely to distribution. Collectors have only recently discovered this line, and prices right now are affordable though increasing.

Ashtray, green oval w/3 rests in center along bottom, 1½x10½x4½" **$10.00**
Ashtray, red w/black speckles, swirling free-form shape, #70, 8" L..**$8.00**
Coaster, Aquarius in relief, yellow, 1967, 3⅜" **$20.00**
Figurine, camel, recumbent, golden-tan, #3309 USA, 6½" ..**$18.00**
Figurine, cockatoo on perch, pink to white, 10½" **$45.00**
Figurine, cockatoo w/flower, wings wide, 11¼x10½", from $65 to.. **$75.00**
Figurine, cockatoos on perch, 1 w/wings wide perched high, 2nd w/ closed wings, pink to white, 10½x10"...........................**$75.00**

Figurine, deer, #907, 13", $30.00.
(Photo courtesy LiveAuctioneers.com/Richard D. Hatch & Associates)

Figurine, flamingo, #445, 6x6¼" **$40.00**
Figurine, flamingo standing beak touching S-curve neck, #309, 9½" **$70.00**
Figurine, hen, bright multicolors, 7x6¼x4"..........................**$80.00**
Figurine, rooster, brown w/bright red comb, #982, 15" **$45.00**
Luncheon/bridge set, 6 white shell #3021 bowls & lg covered #3037 bowl **$45.00**
Planter, angelfish (3) rise above base, multicolor pastels, 1959, from $25 to **$35.00**
Planter, bluebird on planter base, #536, 1959.....................**$22.50**
Planter, cockatoo w/crest erect & foot lifted, pink & white, 10¼x8½" **$65.00**
Planter, flamingos back-to-back, pink tones, 5¼x6¾" **$40.00**
Planter, swan, black, 10x7x5"...**$25.00**
Planter, swan w/wings up, pink & white, #510, 11x7½" **$15.00**
Tidbit tray, 3 joined shells white w/center handle, #3042, ca 1940, from $22 to **$28.00**

TV lamp, egret, pearly white, #33509, 10x6x2", from $30 to . **$40.00**

TV lamp, horse, pearly white, 12¼x11x6¼", from $30 to ... **$40.00**

TV lamp, mallard duck w/wings wide over grassy base (no planter), realistic colors, 14x9x9½", from $50 to **$60.00**

TV lamp, 2 birds facing, 1 w/tail up, 2nd w/tail down, 2 planter openings, pink & gray **$50.00**

Vase, horse head, brown woodgrain, #225, 1959, 12½x4½", from $40 to **$48.00**

Vase, swan w/tall feathers forming vase, white, #2321, 12¼", from $35 to **$45.00**

Magazines

There are lots of magazines around today, but unless they're in fine condition (clean, no missing or clipped pages, and very little other damage); have interesting features (cover illustrations, good advertising, or special-interest stories); or deal with sports greats, famous entertainers, or world-renowned personalities, they're worth very little. Issues printed prior to 1950 generally have value, and pre-1900 examples are now considered antique paper. Our values are for magazines in excellent condition. Address labels on the fronts are acceptable, but if your magazine has one, follow these guidelines. Subtract 5% to 10% when the label is not intruding on the face of the cover. Deduct 20% if the label is on the face of an important cover and 30% to 40% if on the face of an important illustrator cover, thus ruining framing quality. For further information see *The Masters Price & Identification Guide to Old Magazines, 5th Edition; Life Magazines, 1898 to 1994; Saturday Evening Post, 1899 – 1965; Old Movie, TV, Radio Magazines, 1st Edition;* and several other up-to-the-minute guides covering specific magazine titles — all by Denis C. Jackson (See Directory, Magazines). We also recommend *Old Magazines* by Richard E. Clear (Collector Books).

See also TV Guides.

Online Publication: *The Illustrator Collector's News*
Denis C. Jackson, Editor
P.O. Box 6433
Kingman, AZ 86401
www.olypen.com/ticn

All-Star Sports, 1968, February, Johnny Unitas & Joe Namath on cover, from $10 to **$15.00**

American Girl, 1946, April, from $2.50 to **$5.00**

American Heritage, 1962, October, Wimar art cover, from $35 to **$45.00**

American Photography, 1966, History of the Nude, from $20 to **$30.00**

American Woman, 1919, July, doughboy w/sweetheart on cover, from $8 to **$10.00**

Argosy, 1949, June, fishing cover, from $3 to **$5.00**

Arizona Highways, 1976, August, from $10 to **$15.00**

Car & Driver, 1963, March, Alsa Romeo feature, from $4 to .. **$6.00**

Child Life, 1947, February, elves making snowflakes on cover, from $8 to **$10.00**

Collier's, 1941, January 25, pinup girl fishing on cover, from $10 to **$15.00**

Collier's, 1942, January 24, comic art on cover, from $15 to.. **$20.00**

Country Living, 1987, April, thatched cottage on cover, from $8 to **$10.00**

Easyriders, 1973, w/centerfold, from $25 to **$30.00**

Ebony, 1950, May, girl in bikini on cover, from $40 to **$50.00**

George, 1995, 1st issue, Cindy Crawford dressed as George Washington on cover, from $40 to.............................. **$45.00**

Good Housekeeping, 1905, June, cowgirl on cover, from $30 to .. **$35.00**

House & Garden, 1964, March, dining room on cover, from $10 to **$12.00**

Jack & Jill, 1961, September, from $8 to **$12.00**

Jack & Jill, 1966, June, Betsy Ross on cover, from $15 to.... **$20.00**

Jet, 1972, November 16, Jackie Robinson on cover, from $30 to .. **$35.00**

Ladies' Home Journal, 1965, Elizabeth Taylor & Richard Burton on cover, from $15 to **$20.00**

Leatherneck, 1949, March, military cover art, from $15 to.. **$20.00**

Liberty, 1940, May, Dionne Quints article, from $15 to **$20.00**

Liberty, 1941, September 13, mother & daughter on cover, from $4 to **$6.00**

Life, 1936, December 14, Archbishop of Canterbury on cover, from $20 to **$25.00**

Life, 1938, August 15, from $10 to **$15.00**

Life, 1938, December 26, from $15 to **$20.00**

Life, 1939, July 31, Diana Barrymore in swimsuit on cover, from $15 to **$20.00**

Life, 1942, March 30, Shirley Temple on cover, from $15 to... **$20.00**

Life, 1945, July 16, Audie Murphy cover, $10.00.

Life, 1955, April 11, Grace Kelly on cover, from $20 to **$25.00**

Life, 1955, February, Shelly Winters in bubble bath on cover, from $15 to **$20.00**

Life, 1957, February 18, Julie London on cover, from $12 to.. **$15.00**

Life, 1957, March 4, Queen Elizabeth & Prince Philip on cover, from $15 to **$20.00**

Life, 1958, September 22, George & Gracie Burns on cover, from $18 to **$22.50**

Life, 1959, April 20, Marilyn Monroe on cover, from $40 to .. **$50.00**

Life, 1959, November 2, Jackie Gleason on cover, from $10 to **$15.00**

Life, 1961, February 3, Queen Elizabeth in India on cover, from $10 to **$15.00**

Life, 1963, JFK Memorial edition, from $15 to **$20.00**

Life, 1964, February, Beatles on cover, from $40 to **$45.00**

Life, 1964, February 28, War in Cypress on cover, from $4 to . **$6.00**

Life, 1964, September 18, Sophia Loren on cover, from $15 to..**$20.00**

Life, 1965, July 30, Mickey Mantle on cover, from $50 to ..**$60.00**

Life, 1966, April 1, Charlie Chaplin & Sophia Loren on cover, from $15 to **$20.00**

Life, 1969, April 18, Mae West on cover, from $15 to.........**$20.00**

Life, 1969, August 8, moon landscape on cover, from $20 to..**$25.00**

Life, 1971, August 20, Princess Anne on cover, from $8 to..**$10.00**

Life, 1971, December 3, Suicide Squad on cover (football), from $5 to **$7.50**

Life, 1971, February 12, Jackie Kennedy Onassis on cover, from $15 to **$20.00**

Life, 1971, October 29, David Cassidy on cover, from $5 to..**$7.50**

Life, 1982, Test Tube Baby on cover, NM, from $5 to.........**$10.00**

Literary Digest, 1931, from $10 to **$15.00**

Living for Young Homemakers, 1961, January, from $8 to..**$10.00**

Look, 1960, May 10, Princess Margaret on cover, from $15 to ..**$20.00**

Look, 1970, August, Ali McGraw on cover, from $6 to **$8.00**

McCall's, 1938, July, from $20 to **$25.00**

McCall's Needlework, 1951-52, Fall & Winter, from $4 to .. **$6.00**

Meet LBJ, 1964, photo cover, from $15 to **$20.00**

Modern Bride, 1964, August-September, preview of fall fashions, from $40 to **$50.00**

Modern Bride, 1981, June-July, from $40 to **$45.00**

Modern Screen, 1955, October, Marilyn Monroe on cover, from $35 to **$40.00**

Modern Teen, 1960, July, Elvis on cover, from $35 to **$50.00**

Movie Life, 1948, November, Frank Sinatra w/family on cover, from $10 to **$15.00**

Movie Stars Parade, 1946, August, Lauren Bacall on cover, from $15 to **$20.00**

Movie Stars Parade, 1948, July, Esther Williams on cover, from $10 to **$15.00**

Movie Story, 1939, September, Joan Crawford, Rosalind Russell & Norma Shearer on cover, from $30 to..........................**$40.00**

Movieland, 1958, Elvis singing on cover, from $45 to.........**$55.00**

Nature Magazine, 1933, November, bird of paradise on cover, from $10 to **$12.00**

Outdoor Life, 1946, January, duck decoy on cover, from $10 to. **$15.00**

People, 1985, March, Madonna on cover, from $40 to........**$50.00**

Photoplay, 1931, October, Joan Crawford (blond hair) on cover, from $50 to **$55.00**

Photoplay, 1937, December, Loretta Young on cover, from $35 to..**$45.00**

Photoplay, 1938, July, Clark Gable on cover **$55.00**

Photoplay, 1938, May, Shirley Temple on cover, from $40 to..**$45.00**

Photoplay, 1948, September, Alan Ladd on cover, from $15 to **$20.00**

Photoplay, 1977, Elvis Presley tribute, from $8 to **$10.00**

Pictorial Review, 1930, April, equestrian cover, from $25 to .**$30.00**

Playboy, 1956, April, Rusty Fisher centerfold, from $30 to..**$40.00**

Playboy, 1964, January, tribute to Marilyn Monroe, from $22 to **$30.00**

Playboy, 1964, June, Mamie Van Doren on cover, from $15 to..**$25.00**

Playboy, 1983, December, Gala Issue w/Joan Collins on cover, from $5 to **$10.00**

Playboy, 1984, 30th Anniversary, from $10 to **$12.00**

Playboy, 1985, September, Madonna on cover, from $20 to...**$25.00**

Popular Mechanics, 1937, October, from $30 to **$35.00**

Popular Mechanics, 1950, May, space related, $10.00. (Photo courtesy LiveAuctioneers. com/Aurora)

Mojo, 1999, November, Jimi Hendrix cover, UK issue, $15.00. (Photo courtesy LiveAuctioneers.com/ Cooper Owen)

Popular Science, 1941, October, military cover, from $10 to..**$15.00**

Popular Science, 1941, September, Building Tomorrow's Navy, from $10 to **$15.00**

Popular Science, 1946, August, from $10 to **$15.00**

Popular Science, 1968, June, astronaut from 2001: A Space Odyssy on cover, from $10 to **$12.00**

Popular Songs, 1953, Alice Faye on cover, from $10 to **$15.00**

Post, 1963, December 14, JFK on cover, from $10 to **$15.00**

Post, 1966, August 27, Beatles on cover, from $20 to **$25.00**

Rolling Stone, 1970, January 21, Disaster at Altamont at Stones concert on cover, from $50 to......................................**$65.00**

Rolling Stone, 1970, June 25, Charles Manson on cover, from $40 to **$50.00**

Rolling Stone, 1981, October 1, Yoko Ono on cover, from $7 to...**$10.00**

Saturday Evening Post, 1906, November 3, cowgirl on cover, from $40 to **$45.00**

Science & Mechanics, 1947, August-September, Detroit Jetway on cover, from $10 to **$12.00**

Screen Album, 1946, Cornel Wilde on cover, from $15 to ..**$20.00**

Screen Album, 1947, Summer, Jeanne Crain on cover, from $15 to **$20.00**

Screen Album, 1964, Elizabeth Taylor on cover, from $15 to..**$20.00**

Screen Stars, 1957, July, Jayne Mansfield on cover, from $40 to **$45.00**

Screen Stories, 1954, November, Marilyn Monroe on cover, from $30 to **$45.00**

Silver Screen, 1932, February, Claudette Colbert on cover, from $40 to **$50.00**

Silver Screen, 1960, April, Elvis in uniform on cover, from $40 to...**$50.00**

Time, 1944, September 11, Planemaker Grumman on cover, Pony edition, from $15 to **$20.00**

Time, 1953, June 15, Mickey Mantle on cover, from $25 to..**$35.00**

Time, 1979, September 24, Pavarotti on cover, from $3 to....**$5.00**

True West, 1965, February, mountain man on cover, from $8 to..**$10.00**

True West, 1965, October, Judge Roy Bean's courthouse on cover, from $8 to **$10.00**

TV People, 1955, Ed Sullivan on cover, from $10 to..........**$12.00**

TV's Top Stars, 1960, special issue, from $15 to.................**$20.00**

TV World, 1956, December, Elvis on cover, from $45 to....**$55.00**

Vogue, 1942, March 1, America's Spring Collection article, from $40 to **$45.00**

Vogue, 1964, November 1, Audrey Hepburn on cover, from $40 to...**$50.00**

Vogue, 1967, August 1, Twiggy on cover, from $40 to.........**$50.00**

Vogue, 1967, December, Special Christmas issue, from $35 to...**$40.00**

Wink, 1947, December, pinup girl on cover, from $40 to...**$50.00**

Woman's Day, 1949, February, farm boy on cover, from $20 to.**$25.00**

Woman's Day, 1949, January, girl & snowman on cover, from $15 to **$20.00**

Woman's Day, 1950, July, children at water's edge on cover, from $20 to...**$25.00**

Woman's Day, 1950, March, baby on cover, from $15 to **$20.00**

Woman's Day, 1974, February, from $5 to...........................**$10.00**

Marbles

There are three broad categories of collectible marbles, the antique variety, machine-made, and contemporary marbles. Under those broad divisions are many classifications. Everett Grist delves into all three categories in his books called *Everett Grist's Big Book of Marbles* and *Antique and Collectible Marbles* (Collector Books).

Sulfide marbles have figures (generally animals or birds) encased in the center. The glass is nearly always clear; a common example in excellent condition may run as low as $100.00, while those with an unusual subject or made of colored glass may go for more than $1,000.00. Many machine-made marbles are very reasonable, but if the colors are especially well placed and selected, good examples sell in excess of $50.00. Peltier comic character marbles often bring prices of $100.00 and up with Betty Boop, Moon Mullins, and Kayo being the rarest and most valuable (in that order). Watch for reproductions. New comic character marbles have the design printed on a large area of plain white glass with color swirled through the back and sides.

No matter where your interests lie, remember that condition is extremely important. From the nature of their use, mint condition marbles are very rare and may be worth as much as three to five times more than one that is near mint. Chipped and cracked marbles may be worth half or less, and some will be worthless. Polishing detracts considerably.

When no size is given, assume our values are for average-size marbles from ½" to 1" in excellent condition.

See also Akro Agate.

Sulfide, crucifix, 1¾", EX+, $750.00. (Photo courtesy LiveAuctioneers.com/Morphy Auctions)

Akro Agate, carnelian oxblood **$175.00**

Akro Agate, lemonade w/oxblood, from $100 to **$120.00**

Akro Agate, limeade corkscrew..**$30.00**

Akro Agate, Moss Agate **$8.00**

Champion Agate, white & clear swirl **$2.00**

Christensen Agate, blue & white flame............................**$150.00**

Christensen Agate, green peewee..**$10.00**

Christensen Agate, guinea, multicolor, from $350 to........**$400.00**

Christensen Agate, orange & yellow striped opaque............**$60.00**

Christensen Agate, submarine, cobalt, white & brown swirls..**$175.00**

Gladding Vitro, caged cat-eye hybrid **$1.00**

Heaton Agate, cat-eye...**$3.00**

Marble King, cub Scout, blue & yellow, shooter size **$4.00**

Marble King, Rainbow, multicolor...**$4.00**
Pelitier, Bimbo **$90.00**
Pelitier, Champion Jr, later variety, ea.........................**$3.00**
Pelitier, Christmas Tree, red, white & green, sm.............**$125.00**
Pelitier, Ketchup & Mustard, red, yellow & white swirls, sm..**$60.00**
Pelitier, Skeezix..**$100.00**
Sulfide, bird (baby eagle?), 1¾"...................................**$350.00**
Sulfide, chicken, 1¾"..**$175.00**
Sulfide, child w/hammer, 1¾"..**$600.00**
Vitro Agate, helmet pattern, from $3 to.........................**$6.00**
Vitro Agate, prominate V in pattern, from $2 to **$10.00**
Vitro Agate, red, white & blue, deep colors **$1.00**

Yellow latticinio swirl, 15x16", NM, $180.00. (Photo courtesy LiveAuctioneers.com/Morphy Auctions)

Mar-crest

The Western Stoneware Company of Monmouth, Illinois, made products for Marshall Burns, a Division of Technicolor (a distributor from Chicago), with the Marshall Burns trademark, 'Mar-Crest.' The most collectible of these wares is a line of old-fashioned oven-proof stoneware finished in the Warm Colorado Brown glaze. The pattern is referred to as Daisy and Dot by collectors, though the motif is called Pennsylvania Dutch on original boxes.

Some of their other lines are collectible a well: Swiss Alpine is a 1960s line with dark blue leaves that alternately radiate with smaller light green leaves around the border of the flat pieces on a white background with turquoise blue trim lines; Nordic Mint is decorated with diamond-shaped radiating leaves at the rims of simple mid-century shapes; and American Heritage features Southern-style mansions, paddlewheelers, spinning wheels, and so forth.

Advisor: Rita Pence (See Directory, Mar-Crest)

Website: www.Mar-Crest.com

American Heritage, cake stand............................**$22.50**
American Heritage, plate, 9½"............................**$5.00**
Daisy & Dot, bean pot, dark brown, individual, 3x4".........**$14.00**

Daisy & Dot, bean pot, dark brown, shouldered, w/handles, 7", from $20 to **$26.00**
Daisy & Dot, bowl, berry; dark brown, scarce, 1¾x5½"......**$18.00**
Daisy & Dot, bowl, dark brown w/green interior, scarce, 6" ..**$70.00**
Daisy & Dot, bowl, divided vegetable; dark brown, 9½".......**$22.00**
Daisy & Dot, bowl, divided vegetable; dark brown, 10"......**$15.00**
Daisy & Dot, bowl, French casserole; dark brown, w/handle, 10-oz..**$8.00**
Daisy & Dot, bowl, lug soup; dark brown, 2¼x3¾"+handle (short & wide, goes w/snack plate).......................**$20.00**
Daisy & Dot, bowl, mixing; dark brown, sq, scarce, 3x6x6" ..**$85.00**
Daisy & Dot, bowl, mixing; dark brown, 9¾"...............**$20.00**
Daisy & Dot, bowl, rare caramel color, 4x9½"..............**$110.00**
Daisy & Dot, bowl, salad; dark brown, 4½x10" **$28.00**
Daisy & Dot, bowl, soup/salad/cereal; dark brown, 14-oz **$8.00**
Daisy & Dot, carafe, dark brown, from $20 to..............**$25.00**
Daisy & Dot, casserole, dark brown, w/lid, 1½-qt **$25.00**
Daisy & Dot, cookie jar, dark brown (came in 6 styles), 7½x6", from $25 to.......................................**$36.00**
Daisy & Dot, creamer, black w/pink interior, scarce, 4" **$33.00**
Daisy & Dot, creamer, dark brown, 8-oz, 4" **$16.00**
Daisy & Dot, creamer & sugar bowl, dark brown, w/lid......**$36.00**
Daisy & Dot, Dutch oven, dark brown, lg..................**$25.00**
Daisy & Dot, Dutch oven, dark brown, sm, scarce.............**$38.00**
Daisy & Dot, grease jar, dark brown, w/lid, 3½x5½", from $30 to...**$35.00**
Daisy & Dot, lazy Susan, dark brown, 3-compartment, on stand, 11" dia, from $80 to................................**$115.00**
Daisy & Dot, lazy Susan stand only, dark brown, cone shaped **$32.00**
Daisy & Dot, mug, dark brown, 3½" **$5.00**
Daisy & Dot, mug/beer stein, dark brown, 18-oz, 5¼" **$8.00**
Daisy & Dot, pie plate, dark brown, 9¾", from $80 to **$94.00**
Daisy & Dot, pitcher, dark brown, barrel shape, scarce, 3-pt, 6¾"..**$65.00**
Daisy & Dot, pitcher, dark brown, jumbo, 2½-qt, 8".........**$30.00**
Daisy & Dot, pitcher, dark brown, med, 36-oz, 6".............**$25.00**
Daisy & Dot, plate, dinner; dark brown, 9½"..............**$12.00**
Daisy & Dot, salt & pepper shakers, dark brown, pr..........**$16.00**
Daisy & dot, skillet casserole, dark brown, scarce, individual size, 4x4"+handle..**$76.00**
Daisy & Dot, skillet casserole, dark brown, sq, scarce, 9x9"+handle..**$110.00**
Daisy & Dot, snack set, dark brown, 9¾" plate w/insert for mug & 3¼x3½" mug **$55.00**
Daisy & Dot, warmer stand, dark brown, stoneware...........**$18.00**
Nordic Mint, butter dish, round........................**$45.00**
Nordic Mint, cup & saucer, from $12 to **$15.00**
Nordic Mint, pie plate, 10"............................**$30.00**
Nordic Mint, plate, dinner; 10", from $8 to **$12.00**
Nordic Mint, plate, salad; 7½".........................**$5.00**
Nordic Mint, platter, 11½" **$40.00**
Nordic Mint, relish, oblong **$20.00**
Ring, bowl, divided vegetable; pastel (blue, white, pink, green, peach or yellow), 3¼x10½x6½" **$25.00**
Ring, coffee mug, pastel (blue, white, pink, green, peach or yellow), 10-oz, 3x3¼" **$15.00**

Ring, pitcher, pastel (blue, white, pink, green, peach or yellow), ice lip, 8" **$40.00**

Ring, teapot, pastel (blue, white, pink, green, peach or yellow), scarce **$55.00**

Swiss Alpine, bowl, coupe soup **$6.00**

Swiss Alpine, bowl, vegetable; 9" **$20.00**

Swiss Alpine, bowl, w/lid, 8⅜" **$20.00**

Swiss Alpine, butter dish, round **$25.00**

Swiss Alpine, casserole, handles, 8¾" **$22.50**

Swiss Alpine, plate, 11½" **$12.00**

Swiss Alpine, platter, 11⅝" **$15.00**

Swiss Alpine, sugar bowl, w/lid **$7.50**

Max, Peter

Born in Germany in 1937, Peter Max came to the United States in 1953 where he later studied art in New York City. His work is colorful and his genre psychedelic. He is a prolific artist, best known for his designs from the '60s and '70s that typified the 'hippie' movement. In addition to his artwork, he has also designed housewares, clothing, toys, linens, etc. In the 1970s, commissioned by Iroquois China, he developed several lines of dinnerware in his own distinctive style. Today, many of those who were the youth of the hippie generation are active collectors of his work.

Ashtray, psychedelic flower design on white, ceramic, Iroquois China, 5" dia, M **$35.00**

Ashtray, stylized lady & Love on yellow circle, white ceramic w/2 rests, Iroquois China, 6½" dia, M, from $60 to **$80.00**

Book, Peace, w/words by Swami Sivananda, Morrow, 1970 printing, EX **$40.00**

Book, Peter Max - Superposter Book, Crown Publishers, 1971, softcover, includes fold-out poster, EX **$80.00**

Book, Peter Max New Age Organic Vegetarian Cook Book, psychedelic cover, 1971, 1st edition, EX **$45.00**

Book, Peter Max Superposter Book, Crown Publishers, 1971, w/pull-out poster, EX **$60.00**

Book jacket, Beautiful Things Happen When You Don't Smoke Cigarettes, American Cancer Society, 1970s, 17x12", EX.. **$30.00**

Brochure, Poinciana Art Gallery, self-portrait, brown & white, 1977, unfolds: 8½x11½", EX **$110.00**

Clock, female figures radiate from center on black, red hands, General Electric #8503, 1960s, 9" dia, EX **$75.00**

Clock, psychedelic flowers, red hands, General Electric #8504, 9" dia, EX **$150.00**

Clock, 7-Up, flower form w/bright yellow numbers, 16½x17", M in worn box **$175.00**

Jigsaw puzzle, Prism Kaleidoscope, octagonal, Springbok, 1967, EXIB **$38.00**

Kaleidoscope, Gemini, NEO Max, 1989, EX **$42.50**

Lithograph, Mime, sexy lady in black & white, signed, dated 1981, 14x9¾", EX **$165.00**

Lithograph, 1979 (title), stylized figure, 28x22", NM **$85.00**

Magazine, Life, Peter Max on cover, September 5, 1969, EX... **$45.00**

Magazine, Peter Max No 2, psychedelic poster still attached, 1970, EX **$36.00**

Needlepoint kit, flowers, 14x16" canvas & various yarns, MIP... **$35.00**

Needlepoint kit, Geometrix III, 14x16", MIP **$40.00**

Pillow, Hello graphics, heavy vinyl blow-up type, 1968, 16x16", NM **$45.00**

Pillow, inflatable, one of 10 different styles, from $50.00 to $75.00. (Photo courtesy Richard Synchef)

Pillow, love, plastic, 15¼x15½", EX **$37.50**

Pin, stylized male profile & flowers on blue, ceramic sq in metal frame, Made in Western Germany, 1970s, 3", M **$100.00**

Place setting, Love graphics, Iroquois China, 10", 7" bowl, & 4¼" mug **$65.00**

Plaque, Fan Dancer, painted porcelain, Franklin Mint, in gold-tone 16½x13" frame **$175.00**

Poster, Bill Clinton Inauguration, An American Reunion, 1993, NM, from $165 to **$200.00**

Poster, butterfly on yellow, 38½x25", NM **$75.00**

Poster, Donovan Leech amid psychedelic imagery, 1967, 36x24", NM **$220.00**

Poster, Earth Summit, multiple scenes, 1992, 34x24", EX .. **$115.00**

Poster, Gloves, removed from Poster Book, 1970, 17x11³⁄₁₆", EX **$32.00**

Poster, Kentucky Oaks 2000, 24x16", EX **$42.50**

Poster, Love, 1970 reprint lithograph, 16x11⅛", NM **$40.00**

Poster, Make Every Day Earth Day!, 1992, 27x24", EX **$110.00**

Poster, My Love Is America, Vote; Lady Liberty, 1976, 38x25", EX **$200.00**

Poster, Top Cat, dark male figure w/butterfly forming bow tie, 36x24", EX **$45.00**

Poster, USA World Cup Soccer, acrylic on canvas, 1994, 36x24" .. **$85.00**

Scarf, Love, silk, rolled hem, 1960s, 26x26", NM, from $60 to . **$90.00**

Scarf, psychedelic running figure & world on black, silk, rolled hem, 14x42" **$85.00**

Scarf, Zodiac signs in circle on rare blue background, acetate, 21x21", NM **$110.00**

Shirt, Beatles, rainbows, etc, pearl button front, long sleeves w/cuffs, EX **$35.00**

Shirt, Different Drummer on pink to blue, orange sleeves, printed cotton, NEO Max label, 1987, M **$55.00**

Shirt, dove print, pink on gray, Van Heusen, long sleeves, 1960s, EX **$140.00**

Shirt, face w/blue over right eye, red & blue sleeves, printed cotton, ¾-sleeves, EX **$45.00**

Shirt, flying man on pocket of star-print cotton, ¾-sleeves, EX...**$36.00**

Swimsuit, colorful splashes on black, Via Objects, Max D-Art, sm child's size **$32.50**

Tablecloth, psychedelic flowers, multicolor earthy tones on heavy white cotton, 52x66" **$75.00**

Toy car, Action 200 Dale Ernhardt #3, diecast Chevy Monte Carlo w/clear windows, 1:24 scale, MIB, from $100 to........**$135.00**

Toy car, Dale Earnhardt #3 Goodwrench Service Plus, Peter Max 2000 Monte Carlo, Action Brand 1:64 diecast, MIB....**$40.00**

Tray, Happy, smiling girl, tin litho, 12½", EX.....................**$35.00**

Tray, Love, tin litho, 12½", EX **$35.00**

Wristwatch, smiling checkerboard-like face, black leather band, Japan, 1988, EX...**$25.00**

McCoy Pottery

This is probably the best known of all American potteries, due to the wide variety of goods they produced from 1910 until the pottery finally closed only a few years ago.

They were located in Roseville, Ohio, the pottery center of the United States. They're most famous for their cookie jars, of which were made several hundred styles and variations. (For a listing of these, see the section entitled Cookie Jars.) McCoy is also well known for their figural planters, novelty kitchenware, and dinnerware.

They used a variety of marks over the years, but with little consistency, since it was a common practice to discontinue an item for awhile and then bring it out again decorated in a manner that would be in sync with current tastes. All of McCoy's marks were 'in the mold.' None were ink stamped, so very often the in-mold mark remained as it was when the mold was originally created. Most marks contain the McCoy name, though some of the early pieces were simply signed 'NM' for Nelson McCoy (Sanitary and Stoneware Company, the company's original title). Early stoneware pieces were sometimes impressed with a shield containing a number. If you have a piece with the Lancaster Colony Company mark (three curved lines — the left one beginning as a vertical and terminating as a horizontal, the other two formed as 'C's contained in the curve of the first), you'll know that your piece was made after the mid-'70s when McCoy was owned by that group. Today even these later pieces are becoming collectible.

If you'd like to learn more about this company, we recommend *McCoy Pottery, Volumes 1, 2,* and *3,* by Bob and Margaret Hanson and Craig Nissen. All are published by Collector Books.

A note regarding cookie jars: Beware of *new* cookie jars marked McCoy. It seems that the original McCoy pottery never registered their trademark, and for several years it was legally used by a small company in Rockwood, Tennessee. Not only did they use the original mark, but they reproduced some of the original jars as well. If you're not an experienced collector, you may have trouble distin-

guishing the new from the old. Some (but not all) are dated #93, the '#' one last attempt to fool the novice, but there are differences to watch for. The new ones are slightly smaller in size, and the finish is often flawed. He has also used the McCoy mark on jars never produced by the original company, such as Little Red Riding Hood and the Luzianne mammy. Only lately did it become known that the last owners of the McCoy pottery actually did register the trademark; so, having to drop McCoy, he has since worked his way through two other marks: Brush-McCoy and and BJ Hull.

See also Cookie Jars.

Advisor: Bob Hanson (See Directory, McCoy)

Newsletter: *NM Xpress*
Carol Seman, Editor
8934 Brecksville Rd., Suite #406
Brecksville, OH 44141-2518
440-526-2094 (voice and fax)
McCjs@aol.com
members.aol.com/nmXpress

Ashtray, Zane's Truce Commemorative, from $50.00 to $60.00. (Photo courtesy Margaret and Bob Hanson and Craig Nissen)

Bank, Metz Premium Beer, barrel form, unmarked, 8¼", from $50 to **$60.00**

Beverage server, Brocade, 1956, on stand, from $60 to........**$80.00**

Bookends, parakeets (2), pastel, NM mark, 1940s, 6", from $175 to **$250.00**

Bowl, embossed 4-petal flowers & diamonds, blue, unmarked, 1930s, 7", from $60 to **$80.00**

Crock, pickling; brown & white stoneware, 1979, 9-qt, from $40 to **$50.00**

Dripolator coffee maker, 3-pc, 1943, 7", from $50 to..........**$60.00**

Ferner, Hobnail, pastel matt, 1940s, 5½", from $25 to........**$35.00**

Flower bowl ornament, peacock, white, 4¾", from $100 to ..**$125.00**

Flower holder, pigeon, yellow or rose, NM mark, 3¼x4", from $100 to **$125.00**

Jardiniere, Basketweave, green or white, NM mark, 7½", from $60
to $75.00
Jardiniere, brown onyx, geometric borders, 1920-30s, 7", from $50
to $60.00
Jardiniere, fish, brown spray, 1958, 7½", from $300 to......$400.00
Jardiniere, Holly, brown onyx, 1930s, 10½", from $100 to ..$150.00
Lamp base, Oriental floral embossed on brown, 1970s, from $50
to $70.00
Pitcher, ball; cobalt gloss, marked, 1940s, 7", from $85 to..$125.00
Planter, baby carriage, blue w/gold trim, marked, 1955, 6x7¾", from
$100 to $125.00

Planter, bird dog, 1954, 8½", from $175.00 to $225.00.
(Photo courtesy Margaret and Bob Hanson and Craig Nissen)

Planter, donkey figural, brown, 1940s, 7", from $40 to.......$50.00
Planter, fawn among foliage, light blue, NM mark, 1940s, 4½x5",
from $50 to $75.00
Planter, football, antiqued finish, 1957, 4½x7", from $75 to..$100.00
Planter, frog w/umbrella, 2-tone green on black, marked, 1954,
6½x7½" $150.00
Planter, rabbit & stump, yellow & purple, from $100 to...$150.00
Planter, shell, yellow or green, 1955, 4x5", from $15 to $20.00
Planter, Wild Rose, lavender, yellow, blue or pink, 1952, 3½x8",
from $40 to $50.00
Plate, dinner; Canyon, brown, sq, 1970s, from $15 to $20.00
Reamer, yellow or white, 1949, 8" L, from $60 to...............$75.00
Sand jar, Sphinx, brown & green matt, 1930s, 16", from $2,000
to $3,000.00
Stretch animal, lion, pastel matt, 1940s, 5½x7½", from $250
to $350.00
Umbrella stand, embossed leaves in panels, light blue matt, cylindri-
cal, unmarked, 19", from $250 to..............................$350.00
Vase, Brown Antique Rose, 1950s-60s, 10", from $30 to.....$45.00
Vase, chrysanthemum, pink or yellow, 1950, 8", from $110 to .$140.00
Vase, ivy, green on yellow, marked, late 1950s, rare, 6", from $300
to $350.00
Vase, Sunburst Gold, conical pedestal foot, 1950s-60s, 6", from $35
to $40.00
Vase, yellow waisted form w/low handles, USA mark, 1940s, 10",
from $90 to $110.00

Wall pocket, bananas, 1950s, 7", from $125.00 to $150.00. (Photo courtesy Margaret and Bob Hanson and Craig Nissen)

Wall pocket, lady w/bonnet, EX/NM cold paint, from $50
to $60.00
Wall pocket, umbrella, Sunburst Gold, mid-1950s, 8¾x6", from $75
to $95.00

Melmac Dinnerware

The postwar era gave way to many new technologies in manufacturing. With the discovery that thermoplastics could be formed
by the interaction of melamine and formaldehyde, Melmac was
born. This colorful and decorative product found an eager market
due to its style and affordability. Another attractive feature was its
resistance to breakage. Who doesn't recall the sound it made as it
bounced off the floor when you'd accidentally drop a piece.

Popularity began to wane: the dinnerware was found to fade
with repeated washings, the edges could chip, and the surfaces could
be scratched, stained, or burned. Melmac fell from favor in the late
'60s and early '70s. At that time, it was restyled to imitate china that
had become popular due to increased imports.

As always, demand and availability determine price. Our values
are for items in mint condition only; pieces with scratches, chips, or
stains have no value. Prices for 'confetti' items are driven by color as
well. Strong or unusual colors are generally worth twice as much as
those that are common or lack appeal. Fifties colors of aqua and pink
are also generally very sought after. As there are many more manufacturers other than those listed, for a more thorough study of the
subject we recommend *Melmac Dinnerware* by Gregory R. Zimmer
and Alvin Daigle Jr.

See also Russel Wright.

Advisor: Gregory R. Zimmer (See Directory, Melmac)
www.notagaingraphics.com/Branchnell/br7.html/

Allied Chemical, Frosted Blue Fall, leaves on white plates, blue &
white cups, bowls & platter, serves 8............................$45.00
Aztec, bowl, fruit/salad; brown w/multicolor confetti, pierced
handles, 3x12" $25.00
Aztec, bowl, fruit/salad; pink w/multicolor confetti, pierced handles,
3x12" $35.00
Boonton, bowl, mixing; light blue w/multicolor confetti, #511CD-
4Q, 5¼x9¾" $22.50

Boonton, bowl, mixing; orange w/multicolor confetti, #511C-4Q, 5⅜x9⅝" **$80.00**

Boonton, bowl, mixing; yellow w/multicolor confetti, 5¼x9½"..**$50.00**

Boonton, bowl, serving; divided, white, w/lid, 8½" **$18.00**

Boonton, bowl & plate, Lassie portrait, 5½", 8" **$27.50**

Boonton, bowls, salad; orange w/multicolor confetti, 1¾x5¼", set of 8 ....**$80.00**

Boonton, butter dish, aqua, rectangular **$12.00**

Boonton, platter, yellow, 14½x10¼" **$20.00**

Boonton, salt & pepper shakers, yellow, pr **$12.00**

Boonton, sherbet, mint green, footed, 4 for **$25.00**

Bopp-Decker, bowl, serving; white w/turquoise speckled base, w/lid, 8⅛" **$18.00**

Bopp-Decker, mugs, roly poly; white w/pink speckled base, 3½", 4 for **$25.00**

Bopp-Decker, tumblers, white w/turquoise speckled base, insulated type, 5x3", 6 for............................**$20.00**

Branchell, bowl, cereal; Color-Flyte, dark green or gray **$5.00**

Branchell, bowl, divided vegetable; Color-Flyte, gray, 2¼x10½x7¾" **$22.50**

Branchell, creamer & sugar bowl, Color-Flyte, lime green, w/lid.**$15.00**

Branchell, plate, Color-Flyte, lime green, 10" **$16.00**

Branchell, plate, Color-Flyte, orange, 10" **$18.00**

Branchell, platter, Color-Flyte, gray, 12x8½" **$12.00**

Branchell, salad tongs, Color-Flyte, lime green, 9", pr **$25.00**

Branchell, salad tongs, Color-Flyte, orange, 9", pr **$27.50**

Brookpark, bowl, mixing; dark red w/multicolor confetti, 5x11½" **$35.00**

Brookpark, bowl, mixing; red w/multicolor confetti, nesting set of 3, largest, 5x11½" **$120.00**

Brookpark, bowl, mixing; white w/multicolor confetti, 5x11½" ..**$40.00**

Brookpark, dinnerware, Only a Rose, pink & white, serves 6, 63-pc set **$32.00**

Brookpark, platter, strawberries & flowers on white, #1521, 21x15" **$25.00**

Brookpark, platter, turkey transfer & harvest border on white, 21x15" **$20.00**

Brookpark, salt & pepper shakers, pink, sq, 2½x2x2", pr.....**$15.00**

Brookpark, sugar bowl, orange, w/lid **$10.00**

Burrite, butter dish, aqua, rectangular **$16.00**

Burrite, butter dish, aqua & yellow, rectangular **$22.50**

Deka, bowl, mixng; yellow w/white leaf-like designs radiating from base, 4x8" **$48.00**

Imperial Ware, coasters, pastel, 6 for **$18.00**

Lenox Ware, platter, cream, 13½" **$10.00**

Libbey, dinnerware, apple green & white, serves 4, 20-pc set, MIB **$42.50**

Mallo-Ware, place setting, solid tangerine, 5-pc, MIB..........**$20.00**

Marimar, bowl, avocado green, 4¾x14¾" **$22.00**

Onieda, dinnerware, Blue Hawaii, serves 8, 45-pc, MIB....**$125.00**

Prolon, bowl, cereal; green w/multicolor confetti, 4 for **$20.00**

Prolon, dinnerware, Beverly, pink & gold leaves on white plates & plain pink, serves 4, 28-pc set, MIB..........................**$32.00**

Prolon Ware, tray, 6-compartment, light gray w/multicolor confetti **$15.00**

Raffia Ware, bowls, cereal; pastel, 4 for **$20.00**

Raffia Ware, mugs, pastels, clear handles, set of 8 ....**$20.00**

Raffia Ware, mugs, various colors w/white interior, clear handles, w/ white lids, 4½", 8 in gold-tone metal carrier................**$45.00**

Raffia Ware, pitcher, water; brown on white, ice lip............**$15.00**

Raffia Ware, tumblers, multicolor, set of 8, on metal 'burlap-look' 17" tray..**$27.50**

Royalon, cups, avocado green w/white interior, 8 for **$16.00**

Royalon, dinnerware, Corsage, lavender & white, 30-pc set.**$25.00**

Sun Valley, dinnerware, autumn leaves on white, plain white saucers, remaining pcs brown, serves 8, 45-pc set **$52.50**

Sun Valley, plate, Disneyland, castle center, scenic border on white, 1950s **$42.50**

Texas Ware, bowl, charcoal gray w/multicolor confetti, 3½x8"....**$38.00**

Texas Ware, bowl, drab gray-green w/multicolor confetti, #118, 10" **$30.00**

Texas Ware, bowl, mixing, light blue w/multicolor confetti, #125, 5x11¼" **$45.00**

Texas Ware, bowl, mixing; pink w/fine confetti, #125, 5x11"..**$85.00**

Texas Ware, bowl, white w/black & multicolor confetti, 4½x10" **$30.00**

Texas Ware, bowl, yellow w/multicolor confetti, 4½x10" **$32.00**

Texas Ware, tray, serving; solid red, rectangular, 15½x10½" ..**$25.00**

Texas Ware type, cherry red w/multicolor fine confetti, 10" ..**$60.00**

Watertown, butter dish, pink, rectangular..........................**$22.50**

Watertown, dinnerware, yellow, 6" & 10" plates & cups, 18-pc set..**$24.00**

Watertown, pitcher, water; pink, w/lid..............................**$12.50**

Pitcher, yellow, with lid, from $20.00 to $25.00. (Photo courtesy Gregory R. Zimmer and Alvin Daigle Jr.)

Metlox Pottery

Founded in the late 1920s in Manhattan Beach, California, this company initially produced tile and commercial advertising signs. By the early '30s, their business in these areas had dwindled, and they began to concentrate their efforts on the manufacture of dinnerware, artware, and kitchenware. Carl Gibbs has authored *Collector's Encyclopedia of Metlox Potteries*, which we recommend for more information.

Carl Romanelli was the designer responsible for modeling many of the figural pieces they made during the late '30s and early

'40s. These items are usually imprinted with his signature and are very collectible today. Coming on strong is their line of Poppets, made from the mid-'60s through the mid-'70s. There were 88 in all, whimsical, comical, sometimes grotesque. They represented characters ranging from the seven-piece Salvation Army Group to royalty, religious figures, policemen, and professionals. Many came with a name tag, some had paper labels, others backstamps. If you have a piece whose label is missing, a good clue to look for is pierced facial features.

Poppytrail and Vernonware were the trade names for their dinnerware lines. Among their more popular patterns were California Ivy, California Provincial, Red Rooster, Homestead Provincial, and the later embossed patterns, Sculptured Grape, Sculptured Zinnia, and Sculptured Daisy.

Some of their lines can be confusing. There are two 'rooster' lines, Red Rooster (red, orange, and brown) and California Provincial (this one is in dark green and burgundy), and three 'homestead' lines, Colonial Homestead (red, orange, and brown like the Red Rooster line) Homestead Provincial (dark green and burgundy like California Provincial), and Provincial Blue.

See also Cookie Jars.

Advisor: Carl Gibbs, Jr. (See Directory, Metlox)

California Aztec, bowl, soup; from $28 to	**$32.00**
California Aztec, coffeepot, from $250 to	**$300.00**
California Aztec, jam & jelly, from $70 to	**$90.00**
California Aztec, platter, 13", from $75 to	**$85.00**
California Ivy, bowl, salad; 11½", from $75 to	**$85.00**
California Ivy, butter dish, from $60 to	**$65.00**

California Ivy: Cup and saucer, six-ounce, from $8.00 to $12.00; Jumbo cup and saucer, rare, from $60.00 to $70.00. (Photo courtesy Carl Gibbs, Jr.)

California Ivy, egg cup, from $30 to	**$35.00**
California Ivy, gravy boat, 12-oz, from $25 to	**$35.00**
California Ivy, salt & pepper shakers, sm, pr from $28 to	**$30.00**
California Ivy, tray, 2-tier, from $50 to	**$55.00**
California Ivy, tumbler, 13-oz, from $30 to	**$35.00**
California Provincial, bowl, cereal; 7¼", from $18 to	**$20.00**
California Provincial, pitcher, milk; 1-qt, from $65 to	**$75.00**
California Provincial, plate, dinner; 10", from $14 to	**$18.00**
California Provincial, sugar bowl, w/lid, 8-oz, from $30 to	**$35.00**

California Provincial, tea canister, from $65 to	**$75.00**
California Strawberry, bowl, fruit; 5⅜", from $10 to	**$12.00**
California Strawberry, buffet server, 13¼" dia, from $45 to	**$55.00**
California Strawberry, cup & saucer, from $8 to	**$10.00**
California Strawberry, pitcher, 1¼-qt, from $40 to	**$50.00**
Colorstax, bowl, fruit; 5½", from $10 to	**$14.00**
Colorstax, bowl, mixing; 16-oz, from $25 to	**$30.00**
Colorstax, buffet plate, coupe; 13", from $30 to	**$40.00**
Colorstax, butter dish, from $40 to	**$50.00**
Colorstax, cup, demitasse; 5-oz, from $18 to	**$22.00**
Colorstax, flowerpot, 6", from $25 to	**$30.00**
Colorstax, plate, salad; 7¾", from $8 to	**$10.00**
Colorstax, teapot, 4½-cup, from $70 to	**$90.00**

Homestead Provincial, mug, 5", from $30.00 to $45.00.
(Photo courtesy LiveAuctioneers.com/The Auction House)

Navajo, bowl, salad; 12", from $70 to	**$80.00**
Navajo, casserole, w/lid, 2-qt, from $75 to	**$85.00**
Navajo, cup & saucer, from $10 to	**$12.00**
Navajo, salt & pepper shakers, pr from $25 to	**$30.00**
Navajo, tumbler, 10-oz, from $30 to	**$35.00**
Provincial Rose, butter dish, from $40 to	**$45.00**
Provincial Rose, coffeepot, from $70 to	**$80.00**
Provincial Rose, cup & saucer, from $8 to	**$10.00**
Provincial Rose, gravy boat, from $25 to	**$30.00**
Provincial Rose, plate, dinner; from $10 to	**$12.00**
Provincial Rose, platter, rectangular, 13", from $30 to	**$35.00**
Provincial Rose, sprinkling can, from $60 to	**$70.00**
Provincial Rose, teapot, from $80 to	**$100.00**
Red Rooster, bowl, salad; 11⅛", from $80 to	**$85.00**
Red Rooster, bowl, soup; 8", from $15 to	**$18.00**
Red Rooster, bowl, vegetable; divided, rectangular, 12", from $45 to	**$55.00**
Red Rooster, butter dish, from $50 to	**$60.00**
Red Rooster, cookie jar, from $100 to	**$110.00**
Red Rooster, creamer, 6-oz, from $20 to	**$25.00**
Red Rooster, cup & saucer, from $10 to	**$12.00**
Red Rooster, kettle casserole, w/lid, 2-qt+12-oz, from $100 to	**$125.00**

Red Rooster, pitcher, 1½-pt, from $40 to $50.00

Sculptured Daisy, creamer, from $15 to $20.00

Sculptured Daisy, cup & saucer, from $10 to.....................$12.00

Sculptured Daisy, oval baker, 11", from $35 to...................$45.00

Sculptured Daisy, plate, luncheon; from $18 to $10.00

Sculptured Daisy, plate, salad; 7½", from $7 to $9.00

Sculptured Daisy, teapot, 7-cup, from $70 to $90.00

Sculptured Zinnia, mug, 8-oz, from $18 to $22.00

Sculptured Zinnia, plate, bread & butter; 6⅝", from $6 to....$8.00

Sculptured Zinnia, plate, dinner; 10½", from $10 to $14.00

Sculptured Zinnia, platter, oval, 12½", from $30 to............$40.00

Sculptured Zinnia, sugar bowl, w/lid, 10-oz, from $25 to ...$30.00

Woodland Gold, bowl, vegetable; w/lid, 2-qt, from $75 to..$85.00

Woodland Gold, plate, salad; 8", from $7 to $9.00

Woodland Gold, platter, oval, 13", from $30 to $40.00

Woodland Gold, salt & pepper shakers, pr from $15 to $25.00

Miscellaneous

Poppet, Casey, policeman, from $45.00 to $55.00.

Beau Line, flower bowl, 4⅜x10½", from $45 to $50.00

Beau Line, jardiniere, 8x6½", from $140 to.......................$155.00

Beau Line, vase, 5x8½", from $50 to $55.00

Celedon, candleholder, 2½x4", ea from $30 to $35.00

Celedon, incense jar, 5¼x5¼", from $75 to $80.00

Celedon, vase, 4½x5½", from $45 to $50.00

Disney, Bambi planter, from $275 to $325.00

Disney, Dumbo, seated, w/bonnet, front legs up, from $200 to ..$225.00

Disney, dwarf (from Snow White), from $200 to...............$225.00

Disney, elephant, Fantasia, from $350 to $425.00

Disney, Lady (Lady & Tramp) sitting, 1¼", from $85 to ..$125.00

Disney, Pinocchio, from $400 to $450.00

Leaves of Enchantment, banana leaf, 10x3", from $20 to $25.00

Leaves of Enchantment, banana leaf, 24x7¼", from $45 to .$50.00

Miniature, duck, 3", from $35 to.......................................$50.00

Miniature, fish, 5½" L, from $125 to................................$175.00

Miniature, goose, 5", from $40 to......................................$60.00

Miniature, Scottie, 4½" L, from $50 to $80.00

Miniature, turtle standing, from $175 to $225.00

Modern Masterpiece, Cowboy, 10¾", minimum value $500.00

Modern Masterpiece, Cowgirl, 9½", from $300 to $375.00

Modern Masterpiece, sailfish vase, 9", from $140 to.........$160.00

Modern Masterpiece, zodiac vase, 8", from $175 to..........$200.00

Nostalgia Line, Chevrolet, from $75 to $85.00

Nostalgia Line, Coachman, from $65 to $70.00

Nostalgia Line, Fire Wagon, from $90 to $100.00

Nostalgia Line, piano & lid, from $75 to $85.00

Nostalgia Line, Santa, from $85 to $90.00

Nostalgia Line, train set, 3-pc, from $150 to $165.00

Owl Line, ashtray, 8", from $30 to $32.00

Owl Line, canister & lid, from $70 to $80.00

Poppet, Babe w/4" bowl, from $70 to................................$80.00

Poppet, Grover, bass drum man, 6¾", from $80 to............$90.00

Poppet, Jenny, seated girl, 8¾", from $45 to $55.00

Poppet, Kitty, little girl, 6⅝", from $40 to $50.00

Poppet, Muriel, bookend girl, 5¾", from $75 to................$85.00

Toppet, Ann, girl w/flowers, from $70 to..........................$80.00

Toppet, Arthur, knight, from $70 to $80.00

Vegetable Line, Corn canister, 2½-qt, from $125 to..........$150.00

Vegetable Line, leaf plate, 11", from $35 to $40.00

Mexican Pottery

Pottery making has long been pursued in many regions of Mexico by native artisans who utilized natural clay and mineral deposits to produce wares ranging from primitive to very sophisticated. Pottery from each area has unique characteristics that can be helpful in determining its origin.

Talavera wares were first produced in Puebla and were inspired by majolica brought into the area by the Spanish settlers. Strict standards were enforced on the potter's guilds to ensure high quality production. Over time, these regulations were modified as local artisans blended the Spanish designs with their own cultural preferences.

Tlaquepaque, Jalisco, is famous for its pottery and glassware. Decorative themes ranged from genre scenes to florals and animals. Colors are vibrant.

These two are perhaps the best known types of Mexican pottery, though there are many others. Both red and white clays were used, though red is the more common type. Various marks may be found — some impressed, others in relief, and some simply painted on by hand. Not all items are marked.

During the last century, tourists brought huge amounts of the brightly colored pottery home as souvenirs, and today collectors are still enjoying the wonderful colored wares that express the culture of our neighbors of the southwest.

Note: In the low-fired redware, minor chipping is very common.

Bowl, armadillos & flowers, blue & green on white, stick handle,
Tlaquepaque, 1940s, 3x7" dia......................................$22.00

Bowl, outline drawing of a flower, scrolling border, white on red w/ green touches, sq, 6½" **$20.00**

Bowl, primitive frog ea side of leafy vegetation, white, green & red on white clay, circular stamped mark, 13", NM............ **$85.00**

Casserole, birds, foliage, & houses, multicolor on red, w/lid, Tlaquepaque style, 1940s, embossed mark, 4x7" **$250.00**

Charger, lg crested bird, leaves & flowers on aqua, EX art, white clay, 24" **$350.00**

Creche, primitive figures, burnished glazes, Tonala, ca 1950s, 3-pc set, Joseph: 7" **$65.00**

Figurine, rabbit, stylized form, sm floral on side, red clay, Tlaquepaque, 1930s, 6" L.. **$32.00**

Hen on basketweave nest, red, blue, green & white on red clay, Tlaquepaque, ca 1930s-40s, 5x4¾", EX........................ **$90.00**

Icon, archangel with three devils, Ocumicho, Michoacan, 13x9", $150.00. (Photo courtesy LiveAuctioneers.com/Allard Auctions Inc.)

Jar, Mexican pottery & cactus, bright colors on aqua, handles, w/lid, 8" **$45.00**

Leaf plate, naturalistic lg flowers, reds, blues, & yellow on green, Tlaquepaque style, 11"... **$65.00**

Pitcher, all-over design: Mexican w/basket on back, cactus, white clay, Tlaquepaque, 8", NM **$115.00**

Plaque, lg cactus, khaki on red, sq, Made in Mexico, 8¼x8½".. **$18.00**

Plate, divided; lg yellow flowers w/red centers & green leaves on red, 9" **$20.00**

Plate, genre scenes on blue, EX art, Tlaquepaque, impressed mark, 9".. **$90.00**

Plate, primitive duck & reeds, white, green & red, stamped mark, 8".. **$20.00**

Relish tray, scenes w/Mexicans working in each of 5 inserts, Tlaquepaque, ca 1940s-50s, on 14" dia base.............. **$200.00**

Salt & pepper shakers, macaw bird, vivid colors, marked, 2¾", pr **$40.00**

Teapot & sugar bowl, Mexican, burro, & flowers on red clay, Tlaquepaque style, 1940s, ea pc: 7½", 1 lid broken, EX. **$125.00**

Tile, Mexican on burrow, lg tree on blue, Tlaquepaque, 4x4".. **$45.00**

Tureen, hen on basketweave nest, multicolor on red clay, ca 1940s, Tlaquepaque style, 12½" L, EX **$75.00**

Turtle bowl w/lid, rows of concentric lappets on body, multicolor on red clay, Tlaquepaque style, 1940s, 14" L, EX **$285.00**

Vase, bands of various simple motifs on light red clay, Tonala style, impressed mark, 9x5"... **$30.00**

Vase, lg primitive flower, pink, blue & green on burnished rose, white clay, stamped mark, 1940s, 5x4", pr................. **$180.00**

Plate, birds and flowers, Tonala, Jalisco, repaired hairline, 20", $135.00. Photo descriptionLiveAuctioneers.com/Allard Auctions Inc.)

Milk Bottles

Between the turn of the century and the 1950s, milk was bought and sold in glass bottles. Until the '20s, the name and location of the dairy was embossed in the glass. After that it became commonplace to pyro-glaze (paint and fire) the lettering onto the surface. Farmers sometimes added a cow or some other graphic that represented the product or related to the name of the dairy.

Because so many of these glass bottles were destroyed when paper and plastic cartons became popular, they've become a scarce commodity, and today's collectors have begun to take notice of them. It's fun to see just how many you can find from your home state — or try getting one from every state in the union!

What makes for a good milk bottle? Collectors normally find the pyro-glaze decorations more desirable, since they're more visual. Bottles from dairies in their home state hold more interest for them, so naturally New Jersey bottles sell better there than they would in California, for instance. Green glass examples are unusual and often go for a premium; so do those with the embossed baby faces. (Watch for reproductions here!) Those with a 'Buy War Bonds' slogan or a patriot message are always popular, and cream-tops are good as well. As the round pyro bottles from the 1930s and 1940s have become rarer and more costly, many newer collectors have turned their attention to the more common and much less expensive square quarts from the 1950s and 1960s.

Some collectors enjoy adding 'go-alongs' to enhance their collections, so the paper pull tops, advertising items that feature dairy bottles, and those old cream-top spoons will also interest them. The spoons usually sell for about $10.00 to $18.00 each.

Club: National Association of Milk Bottle Collectors, Inc.
Newsletter: *The Milk Route*
The Milk Route
18 Pond Place
Cos Cob, CT 06807
milkroute@yahoo.com
www.milkroute.org

Alfalfa Lawn Dairy, Heppner OR, embossed letters, ribbed shoulders, round pt **$35.00**

Allvine Dairy, Kansas City KS, black pyro, Duraglas 1943, round qt **$60.00**

Bell's Milk Co, bell ringing, Homer NY, black pyro, round pt.. **$45.00**

Blachstone's Dairy, Caribou ME, red pyro, round qt **$215.00**

Borden's Dairy, Elsie in daisy, red & yellow pyro, cream top, qt.. **$70.00**

Borden's Dairy Delivery Company & checkerboard design, red & blue pyro, round ½-pt **$55.00**

Burbank Creamery Producer & Distributor of Our Own Milk, Burbank CA, red pyro, rectangular, ½-gal **$65.00**

Capitol Dairy, Capitol Building dome in slug plate, One Pint Liquid, embossed letters, round pt **$58.00**

Chandler Dairy, Petaluma CA, embossed letters, sq ½-pt..... **$35.00**

City View Dairy, Colorado Springs CO, orange & green pyro, round pt **$90.00**

Clardy's Dairy Phone 796, Roswell NM, red pyro, round qt.. **$42.50**

Clover Bloom Dairy, Chrichton AL, embossed letters, round pt **$68.00**

Cornell University Dairy, Cornell insignia on both sides, red pyro, round ½-pt **$42.50**

Dean's Goat Milk, New Castle PA, embossed letters, round qt .. **$190.00**

Driftwood Dairy, Drifty the Cow, orange pyro, sq qt **$42.00**

Dublin Coop Dairies, You Owe It to Your Country — Buy War Bonds, $18.00. (Photo courtesy milkman)

Dutch Maid Dairy & Dutch maid, San Louis Obispo, We Came To Visit Not To Stay..., blue pyro, round qt **$70.00**

E Nelson, Manton MI, embossed letters, round ½-pt **$70.00**

Eaton's Dairy, Chehalis WA, measuring lines on back, orange pyro, round qt **$75.00**

Fairlawn Dairy, Des Moines IA, embossed letters, round pt.. **$75.00**

Frye's Dairy Inc (on both sides), embossed baby face top, $20.00.

(Photo courtesy milkman)

Glen Echo Dairy, Quincy IL, embossed letters, cream top, round qt **$50.00**

Golden Guernsey Products Are Better, Kannapolis-Concord NC, orange pyro, round ½-pt **$45.00**

Green's, York PA, red pyro, cream top, ca 1948, round qt.... **$67.50**

Greenham's Ruddington Farm, Hackettstown NJ, green pyro, round qt **$48.00**

Hershey Dairy Products & poem, Hershey PA, red pyro, round ½-pt **$85.00**

Highland Dairy Company, bagpiper, policeman & boy playing w/ hoop, red pyro, round qt **$35.00**

Highland Park Dairy Co, ice cream cone, Try Our Ice Cream, Hamilton OH, red pyro, round ½-pt **$45.00**

Hunting's Pasteurized Milk the ABC of Health & baby's face, red pyro, round qt **$55.00**

Imperial Farms, We Need Your Help...Buy War Bonds, Uncle Sam, red pyro, round qt **$70.00**

Indian Run Dairy Jos Klein, Danville PA, embossed letters, round pt **$60.00**

Intervale Jersey Farms, WC Arms, Burlington VT, cow's head in circle, red pyro, round qt **$80.00**

Isaly's Milk, red pyro, baby-face cream top, sq qt **$55.00**

J Fred Monro Sanitary Pasteurized Milk, Lock Haven PA, embossed letters, round ½-pt **$100.00**

JF Snyder, S Windsor PA, embossed letters, dated 1928 on base, round pt.. **$180.00**

JM Cunningham, Malden MA, embossed letters on light amethyst, round qt.. **$60.00**

Kelch's Sanitary Dairy, Dwight IL, embossed letters, round qt.. **$80.00**

Klondike Farm, Elkin NC, orange pyro, embossed One Quart Liquid around base, round qt **$60.00**

Lehman's Dairy, Jefferson WI, red pyro, cream top, round qt.. **$65.00**

Lenick's Dairy, baby's portrait, LaPorte IN, orange pyro, round qt... **$40.00**

Liberty Milk Co & Statue of Liberty, Buffalo NY, embossed letters on cobalt, round pt...**$45.00**

Lincoln Dairy Products, Lincoln IL, red pyro, round qt **$60.00**

Macomb Dairy Co, Macomb IL, red pyro, It Whips in red pyro on cream top, round qt...**$75.00**

Mason-MacDonald Co, Haverhill MA, embossed letters, cream top, round qt..**$42.50**

McWilliams Pure Grade A Milk, red pyro, McWilliams Pure Milk... Sheffield Ala embossed on back, round ½-pt **$45.00**

Melville Dairy, Burlington NC, war-era slogan, red pyro, squat qt..**$80.00**

Michigan State College Creamery, embossed letters, original wax seal cardboard top, round qt... **$70.00**

Michigan State College Creamery, green pyro, round qt **$42.50**

Milk Depot, Flagstaff AZ, Phone 2555, embossed letters on slg plate, round qt..**$75.00**

Morlea Brand, red pyro, baby-face cream top, qt **$65.00**

Northeastland Hotel, Presque Isle ME, red pyro, round qt...**$115.00**

One Quart Liquid 7X Dairy Grade A Products Phone 1003, embossed letters, round qt **$60.00**

Peifer's Dairy, Reading PA, embossed letters, round pt.........**$65.00**

Piedmont Dairy Milk, Danville VA, embossed letters, round pt.. **$50.00**

Quality & Service Dairy, Red Lion, PA, recumbent lion, red pyro, cream top, sq qt **$60.00**

Ricker's Dairy, Milo ME, dark red pyro, tall round ½-pt **$40.00**

Riverview Dairy Pasteurized Milk, East Brady PA, orange pyro, round qt...**$52.50**

Rocky Forest Dairy Farm, Laceyville PA, embossed letters, slug plate: Pure Milk, dated 1932, tall round qt **$80.00**

Round Hill Farms (both sides), orange pyro, round pt **$48.00**

RW Heim, Tamaqua PA, embossed letters, embossed ribs at top down to shoulders, round pt..**$65.00**

Sanitary Farms Dairy Inc, Erie PA, coffeepot & cup, red pyro, round pt **$70.00**

Seger-Graham Dairy, Adrian MI, red pyro, cream top, round qt. **$45.00**

Sheshequin Valley Farm, Holstein Milk & cow, black pyro, round qt...**$75.00**

Southern Dairy Farm Phone 778, Tuscaloosa AL, green pyro, round pt **$48.00**

Surry Dairies, Mount Airy NC, red pyro, round 1-gal.......**$180.00**

W Miller Dairy, Upper Sandusky OH, embossed letters, round qt... **$70.00**

Wauregan Dairy, child's poem, red pyro, It Whips in black pyro on cream top, round qt...**$45.00**

Weiser's Dairy, West Des Moines IA, Phone 330, maroon pyro, sq qt...**$135.00**

Miller Studios

Imported chalkware items began appearing in local variety stores in the early '50s. Cheerfully painted hot pad holders, thermometers, wall plaques, and many other items offered a lot of decorator appeal. While not all examples will be marked Miller Studios, good indications of that manufacturer are the holes on the back where stapled-on cardboard packaging has been torn away — thus leaving small holes. There should also be a looped wire hanger on the back, although a missing hanger does not seem to affect price. Copyright dates are often found on the sides. Miller Studios, located in New Philadelphia, Pennsylvania, is the only existing American firm that makes hand-finished wall plaques yet today. Although they had over 300 employees during the 1960s and 1970s, they presently have approximately 75. Because these items are made from material that often tends to chip, our values are suggested for examples in near mint condition. Collectors aware of this, however, generally accept interesting pieces without discounting values to any great extent. If the item you're evaluating is truly mint, you should add from 20% to 30% to our prices.

Bathometer, poodle in tub, 1973 ....**$15.00**

Mirror, white frame w/flower vase & butterfly, gold trim, plastic insert for vase, 1984, 10¼x8"......................................**$12.50**

Plaque, carousel horse, brown, beige & peachy tan, 1966, 8½x9" **$30.00**

Plaque, fish, 6½" long, $18.00. (Photo courtesy Mandi Stewart)

Plaque, Raggedy Andy, 6½x5½"...**$10.00**

Plaque, Recipes on brown box among vegetables & wooden spoon, 1981, 6⅛" L **$17.50**

Plaques, bird (yellow) in relief on black plaque w/gold trim, 1978, 5½" dia, pr...**$25.00**

Plaques, Dutch boy & girl, 1953, 7¼", pr **$50.00**

Plaques, fish, blue w/pink cheeks & red lips, gold sparkles on scales, 1971, 8x8", pr **$45.00**

Plaques, fish, lg blue & 3 sm in pink, blue & green, set of 4, MIB **$20.00**

Plaques, fish w/long tail, pink w/green, 4½x8½", w/2 green bubbles, 1964, 3-pc set...**$34.00**

Plaques, frog couple, she w/red bow, he w/black bow tie, 1977, MIB..**$20.00**

Plaques, Indian heads, brown tones w/red & blue details, 1979, 8x5", pr..**$16.00**

Plaques, owls, brown & yellow tones, 3½x3½", pr..............**$40.00**

Plaques, parrots, bright multicolors, 13", 14", pr **$125.00**

Plaques, Siamese kittens (faces), brown tones, 1954, 3½x4¾", pr **$12.50**

Plaques, swans in oval, pink tail feathers, 1965, 7x3½", pr .. **$45.00**

String holder, apple, red w/green leaves, 8½x7¾x3" **$40.00**

String holder, Little Chef, freckled cheeks, ca 1950 .... **$225.00**

Thermometer, Bless This House, shelves on wall, brown tones, 1975, 6" **$22.50**

Thermometer, fireplace, brown, 7x7" **$25.00**

Model Kits

By far the majority of model kits were vehicular, and though worth collecting, especially when you can find them still mint in the box, the really big news are the figure kits. Most were made by Aurora during the 1960s. Especially hot are the movie monsters, though TV and comic strip character kits are popular with collectors too. As a rule of thumb, assembled kits are valued at about half as much as conservatively priced mint-in-box kits. The condition of the box is just as important as the contents, and top collectors will usually pay an additional 15% (sometimes even more) for a box that retains the factory plastic wrap still intact. *Schroeder's Toys, Antique to Modern* (Collector Books), contains prices and descriptions of hundreds of models by a variety of manufacturers.

Adams, Around the World in 80 Days Balloon, 1960, MIB .. **$325.00**

Addar, Super Scenes, 1975, Jaws in a Bottle, MIB **$60.00**

Addar Planet of the Apes, Stallion & Soldier, 1974, MIB .. **$100.00**

Airfix, Bigfoot, 1978, MIB **$75.00**

AMT, Flintstones, 1974, MIB **$75.00**

AMT, KISS Custom Chevy Van, 1977, MIB **$75.00**

AMT/Ertl, A-Team Van, 1983, MIB **$30.00**

Aurora, Addams Family Haunted House, 1964, MIB **$850.00**

Aurora, Banana Splits, 1969, Banana Buggy, MIB **$525.00**

Aurora, Bride of Frankenstein, 1965, MIB **$750.00**

Aurora, Captain Action, #480-149, 1966, MIB (sealed), $450.00. (Photo courtesy LiveAuctioneers.com/Morphy Auctions)

Aurora, Dick Tracy in Action, 1968, MIB **$350.00**

Aurora, Flying Sub, 1968, NMIB **$200.00**

Aurora, Frankenstein, 1971, glow-in-the-dark, MIB **$150.00**

Aurora, Godzilla's Go-Cart, 1966, assembled, NM **$750.00**

Aurora, Gold Knight of Nice, 1965, MIB **$275.00**

Aurora, Guys & Gals, 1957, Indian Chief, MIB **$125.00**

Aurora, James Bond 007, 1966, MIB **$350.00**

Aurora, Rat Patrol, 1967, MIB **$115.00**

Aurora, Viking, 1959, Famous Fighters, MIB **$250.00**

Bachmann, Animals of the World, 1959, Lion, MIB **$50.00**

Bachmann, Dogs of the World, Mongrel, 1960s, MIB, $70.00.

(Photo courtesy www.gasolinealleyantiques.com)

Bandai, Thunderbird, 1984, MIB **$40.00**

Billiken, She-Creature, 1989, MIB **$175.00**

Geometric Design, Boris Korloff as the Mummy, MIB **$50.00**

Hawk, Bobcat Roadster, 1962, MIB **$30.00**

Hawk, Francis the Foul, 1963, MIB **$60.00**

Hawk, Woodie on a Surfari, 1964, MIB **$100.00**

Horizon, Creature From the Black Lagoon, $115.00. (Photo courtesy www.gasolinealleyantiques.com)

Horizon, Dracula (Bela Lugosi), MIB **$65.00**
Horizon, Invisible Man, NMIB **$50.00**
Horizon, Marvel Universe, 1988, Spider-Man, MIB **$40.00**
Horizon, Robocop, 1989, ED-209, MIB **$70.00**
Imai, Captain Blue, 1982, MIB **$15.00**
Imai, Orguss, 1994, Cable, MIB **$40.00**
ITC, Neanderthal Man, 1959, MIB **$50.00**
Life-Like, Ankylosaureus, 1968, MIB **$35.00**
Lindberg, Flying Saucer, 1952, MIB **$200.00**
Lindberg, Tyrannosaurus, 1987, MIB **$15.00**
Monogram, Bad Machine, 1970s, MIB **$60.00**
Monogram, Buck Rogers, 1970, Marauder, MIB **$70.00**
Monogram, Giraffes, 1961, MIB **$50.00**
Monogram, Space Buggy, 1969, MIB **$100.00**
MPC, Barnabas, 1968, Dark Shadows, MIB **$400.00**
MPC, Beverly Hillbillies Truck, 1968, MIB **$200.00**
MPC, Fonzie & Dream Rod, 1976, NMIB **$40.00**
Pyro, Indian Warrior, 1960s, MIB **$60.00**
Pyro, Restless Gun, 1959, Deputy Sheriff, MIB **$70.00**
Revell, Amazing Moon Mixer, 1970, MIB **$35.00**
Revell, Ariane 4 Rocket, 1985, MIB **$35.00**
Revell, CHiPs, 1980, Helicopter, MIB **$35.00**
Screamin', Friday the 13th's Jason, MIB **$125.00**
Strombecker, Walt Disney's Spaceship, 1958, MIB **$300.00**
Tsukada, Creature From the Black Lagoon, MIB **$150.00**
Tsukuda, Mummy, MIB **$100.00**

Modern Mechanical Banks

The most popular (and expensive) type of bank with today's collectors are the mechanicals, so called because of the antics they perfrom when a coin is deposited. Over 300 models were produced between the Civil War period and the First World War. On some, arms wave, legs kick, or mouths open to swallow up the coin — amusing nonsense intended by the inventor to encourage and reward thriftiness. Some of these original banks have been known to sell for as much as $20,000.00 — well out of the price range most of us can afford! So many opt for some of the modern mechanicals that are available on the collectibles market, including Book of Knowledge and James D. Capron, which are reproductions marked to indicate that they are indeed replicas. But beware — unmarked modern reproductions are common.

Advisor: Dan Iannotti (See Directory, Banks)

Always Did 'Spise a Mule, Boy on Bench, Book of Knowledge, NM **$175.00**
Artillery Bank, Book of Knowledge, NM **$225.00**
Bad Accident, James Capron, M **$700.00**
Boy on Trapeze, Book of Knowledge, NM **$295.00**
Butting Buffalo, Book of Knowledge, M **$250.00**
Cat & Mouse, Book of Knowledge, NM **$200.00**
Clown on Globe, James Capron, M **$650.00**
Cow (kicking), Book of Knowledge, NM **$250.00**
Creedmore Bank, Book of Knowledge, M **$250.00**
Dentist Bank, Book of Knowledge, EX **$125.00**

Eagle & Eaglets, Book of Knowledge, M **$225.00**
Elephant, James Capron, M **$225.00**
Humpty Dumpty, Book of Knowledge, M **$175.00**
Indian & Bear, Book of Knowledge, M **$225.00**
Jonah & the Whale, Book of Knowledge, M **$175.00**
Leap Frog, Book of Knowledge, NM **$225.00**
Lion & Monkeys, James Capron, M **$700.00**
Monkey, James Capron, MIB **$200.00**
Organ Bank (Boy & Girl), Book of Knowledge, NM **$195.00**
Owl (turns head), Book of Knowledge, NM **$175.00**
Paddy & the Pig, Book of Knowledge, NM **$195.00**

Penny Pineapple (Hawaii 50th State), M, $400.00.
(Photo courtesy LiveAuctioneers.com/ The RSL Auction Co.)

Professor Pug Frog's Great Bicycle Feat, James Capron, M. **$850.00**
Punch & Judy, Book of Knowledge, NM **$175.00**
Tammany Bank, Book of Knowledge, NMIB **$200.00**
Teddy & the Bear, Book of Knowledge, NM **$175.00**
Trick Dog, James Capron, NM **$400.00**
Uncle Remus, Book of Knowledge, M **$195.00**
US & Spain, Book of Knowledge, M **$175.00**
William Tell, Book of Knowledge, M **$195.00**

Mood Indigo by Inarco

This line of Japanese-made ceramics probably came out in the 1960s, and enough of it was produced that a considerable amount has reached the secondary market. Because of the interest today's collectors are exhibiting in items from the '60s and '70s, it's beginning to show up in malls and co-ops, and the displays are surprisingly attractive. The color of the glaze is an electric blue, and each piece is modeled as though it were built from stacks of various fruits. It was imported by Inarco (Cleveland, Ohio) and often bears that company's foil label.

Collectors are sticklers for condition (damaged items are worth very little, even if they are rare) and prefer pieces with a deep, rich blue color and dark numbers on the bottom that are very legible. All pieces carry a number, and most collectors use these to keep track of their acquisitions. In addition to the items described and evaluated below, here is a partial listing of other known pieces.

E-2373 — Oblong Pitcher, 3x6"   E-3145 — Pitcher, 6"
E-2374 — Covered candy dish, 9   E-3445 — Plate, 9½"
E-2719 — Relish tray   E-3462 — Pedestal cake plate, 9½"
E-3095 — Fluted vase, 7¾"   E-4011 — Butter dish, 7½"

These pieces can be bought for as little as $5.00 to as much as $75.00. Prices vary widely, and bargains can still be had at many flea markets and garage sales.

Lavabo, two-piece, 11" vase top, half-bowl bottom, from $35.00 to $45.00.

Ashtray, rest in ea corner, E-4283, 9" $25.00
Bell, 5" $15.00
Bowl, fruit; E-3870, 5x11x6½" $30.00
Bud vase, E-3096, 8", from $20 to $22.50
Cake plate, footed, E-3462, 2¾x9⅜" $50.00
Candleholders, goblet shape, 4½", pr................................$28.00
Candleholders, owl figural, E-4612, 6", pr........................$20.00
Candy dish, molded as 2 curved leaves w/fruit to side, 8"....$20.00
Candy jar, cylindrical, footed, w/lid, 9½"..........................$45.00
Centerpiece, stacked-up fruit on ribbed incurvate base, 12x6"..$25.00
Cigarette lighter, E-3100, 3¾" $22.00
Coffee cup, E-2431, 4", from $4 to $6.00
Coffee/teapot, footed, E-2430...$40.00
Cookie jar/canister, E-2374, 8" $18.00
Creamer & sugar bowl, w/lid, from $10 to..........................$12.00

Cruet, E-3098, 7½" $28.00
Decanter, cork stopper, 10", from $15 to...........................$25.00
Dish, footed, w/lid, E-2375, 6"..$15.00
Dish, oval, E-2376, 8½x5¾"..$18.00
Figurine, cat seated, E-2883, rare, 14½" $75.00
Gravy boat, E-2373, 6½"...$15.00
Jam & jelly set, 2 jars w/lids on rectangular tray, E-3322.....$25.00
Jar, cylindrical, w/lid, 6½"...$15.00
Ladle, 9¾"...$25.00
Mug, E-4489, 5"...$12.00
Oil lamp, frosted shade, E-3267, 9½"................................$25.00
Pitcher, E-5240, 4", w/saucer undertray............................$15.00
Pitcher, footed, E-2429, 6½"...$18.00
Pitcher, footed, E-2853, 6"...$15.00
Planter, donkey pulling cart, 6x7¾"..................................$18.00
Planter, hexagonal foot, E-3097, 4½x5" $12.00
Plaque, embossed fruit, E-2432, 10¼", from $25 to $35.00
Plate, hanging; allover fruit, E-2432, 10"...........................$30.00
Platter, 15x10" $45.00
Salt & pepper shakers, E-2371, 3½", pr.............................$12.00
Soap dish, cherub sits on side of shell, E-4656, 4¾" $22.00
Teapot, E-2430, 8"..$22.00
Tray, divided, E-2728, 12x6"..$30.00
Tray, shell shape, 3-compartment, E-4555 ....$40.00
Trivet, 6" dia..$10.00
Tureen/covered dish, E-3379..$30.00

Moon and Star

Moon and Star (originally called Palace) was first produced in the 1880s by John Adams & Company of Pittsburgh. But because the glassware was so heavy to transport, it was made for only a few years. In the 1960s, Joseph Weishar of Wheeling, West Virginia, owner of Island Mould & Machine Company, reproduced some of the original molds and incorporated the pattern into approximately 40 new and different items. Two of the largest distributors of this line were L.E. Smith of Mt. Pleasant, Pennsylvania, who pressed their own glass, and L.G. Wright of New Martinsville, West Virginia, who had theirs pressed by Fostoria and Fenton. Both companies carried a large and varied assortment of shapes and colors. Several other companies were involved in its manufacture as well, especially of the smaller items. All in all, there may be as many as 100 different pieces, plenty to keep you involved and excited as you do your searching.

The glassware is already collectible, even though it is still being made on a limited basis. Colors you'll see most often are amberina (yellow shading to orange-red), green, amber, crystal, light blue, and ruby. Pieces in ruby and light blue are most popular and harder to find than the other colors, which seem to be abundant. Purple, pink, cobalt, amethyst, tan slag, and light green and blue opalescent were made, too, but on a lesser scale.

Current L.E. Smith catalogs contain a dozen or so pieces that are still available in crystal, pink, cobalt (lighter than the old shade), and these colors with an iridized finish. A new color was introduced in 1992, teal green, and the water set in sapphire blue opalescent was pressed in 1993 by Weishar Enterprises. They are now producing limited editions in various colors and shapes, but they are marking their glassware 'Weishar,' to distinguish it from the old line. Cranberry Ice (light transparent pink) was introduced in 1994.

Values are given with a wide range, reflecting not only the color preferences of collectors but also supply and demand. Use the high end to evaluate ruby and light blue; amber and green are represented by the lower end of the range, and amberina values fall near mid-range.

Cigarette lighter, ruby, from $35.00 to $45.00.

Ashtray, allover pattern, moons form scallops along rim, 4 rests, 8" dia, from $16 to...**$25.00**
Ashtray, moons at rim, star in base, 6-sided, 5½", from $18 to...**$28.00**
Ashtray, moons at rim, star in base, 6-sided, 8½", from $24 to...**$32.00**
Banana boat, allover pattern, moons form scallops along rim, 12", from $30 to **$45.00**
Basket, allover pattern, moons form scallops along rim, solid handle, 5", from $30 to...**$45.00**
Basket, allover pattern, moons form scallops along rim, solid handle, 6", from $30 to...**$40.00**
Basket, allover pattern, moons form scallops along rim, solid handle, 9", from $40 to...**$55.00**
Basket, allover pattern, moons form scallops along rim, split handle, 9x6", from $90 to..**$125.00**
Bowl, allover pattern, footed, crimped rim, 7½", from $20 to .. **$30.00**
Bowl, allover pattern, footed, scalloped rim, 3x5", from $18 to **$25.00**
Bowl, allover pattern, footed, scalloped rim, 5x9½", from $30 to...**$45.00**
Bud vase, 6½", from $16 to **$25.00**
Butter dish, allover pattern, stars form scallops along rim of base, star finial, oval, ¼-lb, 8½", from $55 to **$75.00**
Butter/cheese dish, patterned lid, plain base, 7" dia, from $45 to **$65.00**
Cake salver, allover pattern w/scalloped rim, raised foot w/scalloped edge, 5x12" dia, from $50 to **$65.00**
Cake stand, allover pattern, plate removes from standard, 2-pc, 11" dia, from $70 to..**$90.00**
Candle lamp, patterned shade, clear base & cup, 7¾x4½", from $30 to **$45.00**

Candle lamp, patterned shade & base, plain insert, 9", from $45 to **$60.00**
Candleholder, allover pattern, bowl style w/ring handle, 2x5½", ea from $12 to **$18.00**
Candleholders, allover pattern, flared base, 4½", pr from $20 to.. **$35.00**
Candy dish, allover pattern on base & lid, footed ball shape, 6", from $25 to **$45.00**
Canister, allover pattern, 1-lb or 2-lb, from $10 to **$20.00**
Canister, allover pattern, 3½-lb or 5-lb, from $30 to...........**$40.00**
Chandelier, ruffled dome shape w/allover pattern, amber, 10", from $60 to **$70.00**
Cheese dish, patterned base, clear plain lid, 9½", from $50 to. **$65.00**
Compote, allover pattern, raised foot, patterned lid & finial, 7½x6", from $25 to **$35.00**
Compote, allover pattern, raised foot on stem, patterned lid & finial, 10x6", from $45 to **$55.00**
Compote, allover pattern, scalloped foot on stem, patterned lid & finial, 8x4", from $25 to **$38.00**
Compote, allover pattern, scalloped rim, footed, 5x6½", from $10 to **$20.00**
Compote, allover pattern, scalloped rim, footed, 7x10", from $25 to **$40.00**
Console bowl, allover pattern, scalloped rim, flared foot w/flat edge, 8", from $20 to...**$35.00**
Creamer & sugar bowl (open), disk foot, sm, from $15 to .. **$30.00**
Cruet, vinegar; 6¾", from $50 to **$65.00**
Egg plate, from $35 to **$55.00**
Epergne, allover pattern, 2-pc, 9", from $75 to.................**$120.00**
Fairy lamp, cylindrical dome-top shade, 6", from $30 to **$45.00**
Goblet, water; plain rim & foot, 5¾", from $12 to.............**$16.00**
Jardiniere/cracker jar, allover pattern, patterned lid & finial, 7¼", from $60 to **$100.00**
Jelly dish, patterned body w/plain flat rim & disk foot, patterned lid & finial, 6¾x3½", from $25 to **$35.00**
Lamp, miniature; amber, from $100 to...........................**$125.00**
Lamp, miniature; blue, from $165 to................................**$190.00**

Lamp, miniature; ruby, from $175.00 to $225.00.

Lamp, oil or electric; allover pattern, all original, red or light blue, 24", minimum value......................**$300.00**

Lamp, oil; patterned hurricane shade, oval base w/handle, 12", from $45 to **$65.00**

Nappy, allover pattern, crimped rim, 2¾x6", from $18 to ...**$28.00**

Pitcher, straight sides, 1-qt, 7½", from $45 to......................**$85.00**

Plate, patterned body & center, smooth rim, 8", from $30 to .**$60.00**

Relish bowl, 6 lg scallops form allover pattern, 1½x8" L, from $25 to **$40.00**

Relish tray, patterned moons form scalloped rim, star in base, rectangular, 8", from $30 to **$50.00**

Rose bowl, allover pattern, scalloped incurvate rim, 3x4½", from $35 to **$50.00**

Soap dish, allover pattern, oval, 2x6", from $9 to **$12.00**

Spooner, allover pattern, footed, 5½x4", from $60 to **$75.00**

Sugar bowl, allover pattern, straight sides, patterned lid & finial, scalloped foot, 8x4½", from $35 to......................**$50.00**

Sugar/cheese shaker, allover pattern, chrome lid, 4½", from $30 to **$45.00**

Syrup pitcher, allover pattern, metal lid, 4½x3½", from $45 to...**$65.00**

Tumbler, juice; no pattern at rim or on disk foot, 5-oz, 3½", from $10 to **$18.00**

Tumbler, no pattern at rim or on disk foot, 6½", from $20 to. **$28.00**

Vase, pattern near top, ruffled frim, disk foot, 6", from $22 to. **$30.00**

Mortens Studios

During the 1940s, a Swedish sculptor by the name of Oscar Mortens left his native country and moved to the United States, settling in Arizona. Along with his partner, Gunnar Thelin, they founded the Mortens Studios, a firm that specialized in the manufacture of animal figurines. Though he preferred dogs of all breeds, horses, cats, and wild animals were made, too, but on a much smaller scale.

The material he used was a plaster-like composition molded over a wire framework for support and reinforcement. Crazing is common, and our values reflect pieces with a moderate amount, but be sure to check for more serious damage before you buy. Most pieces are marked with either an ink stamp or a paper label.

Collie, seated, 5¾", $55.00.

Boston terrier bulldog puppy, 3¼x4" **$42.50**

Boxer dog down on front legs, brown w/black muzzle, 2½x4".. **$55.00**

Cocker spaniel seated w/head turned right, pink tongue licking coat, Royal Design, 2¼x2" **$42.50**

Collie dog standing, pink tongue showing, 6x6¾" **$45.00**

Dalmatian standing on point, 5½x7¾" **$48.00**

English bulldog sitting, 3x4"......................**$50.00**

Irish terrier puppy sitting, 3"......................**$45.00**

Jack Russell terrier standing, original labels, 5¼x6½" **$85.00**

Maine Coon cat sitting w/head up, 3¾x4½" **$58.00**

Pug puppy seated, 2¼x4" **$45.00**

Wire fox terrier sitting & yawning, 3½x3" **$50.00**

Wirehair fox terrier standing w/tail up, brown & gray tones on white, 5x6" **$60.00**

Morton Pottery

Six different potteries operated in Morton, Illinois, during a period of 99 years. The first pottery, established by six Rapp brothers who had emigrated from Germany in the mid-1870s, was named Morton Pottery Works. It was in operation from 1877 to 1915 when it was reorganized and renamed Morton Earthenware Company. Its operation, 1915 – 1917, was curtailed by World War I. Cliftwood Art Potteries, Inc. was the second pottery to be established. It operated from 1920 until 1940 when it was sold and renamed Midwest Potteries, Inc. In March 1944 the pottery burned and was never rebuilt. Morton Pottery Company was the longest running of Morton's potteries. It was in operation from 1922 until 1976. The last pottery to open was the American Art Potteries. It was in production from 1947 until 1961.

All of Morton's potteries were spin-offs from the original Rapp brothers. Second, third, and fourth generation Rapps followed the tradition of their ancestors to produce a wide variety of pottery. Rockingham and yellow ware to Art Deco, giftwares, and novelties were produced by Morton's potteries.

To learn more about these companies, we recommend *Morton Potteries: 99 Years, Vol. II,* by Doris and Burdell Hall.

Advisors: Doris and Burdell Hall (See Directory, Morton Pottery)

Morton Pottery Works — Morten Earthenware Company, 1877 – 1917

Bowl, mixing; brown, Rockingham, 4½" **$25.00**

Chamber pot, yellow ware, miniature **$70.00**

Cuspidor, brown, 7"......................**$50.00**

Marble, brown, Rockingham, 4¼"......................**$35.00**

Milk jug, brown, Rockingham, 1-pt......................**$55.00**

Miniature, coffee dripolator, brown, Rockingham, 3" **$70.00**

Pie baker, yellow ware, 7"......................**$75.00**

Rice nappy, plain, yellow ware, 13"......................**$85.00**

Rice nappy, yellow ware, fluted, 8" **$80.00**

Stein, yellow ware, 2 blue slip stripes top & bottom **$50.00**

Cliftwood Art Potteries, Inc., 1920 – 1940

Bookends, lion & lioness on Heritage Green bases, 4¼x6¼" .. **$150.00**

Bowl, green/yellow drip over white, sq, w/lid, 6" **$50.00**

Creamer, cow figural, tail forms handle, chocolate drip, 3¼x6½" **$125.00**

Dresser set, apple green, tray, jar, powder box & pr candleholders **$75.00**

Figurine, cat reclining, brown drip, 4½" **$45.00**

Figurine, German shepherd, chocolate drip, 5x8½" **$80.00**

Figurine, lion, gold/brown, miniature, 1¾x4" **$50.00**

Flower frog, Lorelei, blue/Mulberry drip, 6½" **$75.00**

Jar, Pretzels embossed on brown drip, barrel shape, w/lid... **$125.00**

Lamp, pillar base, star-embossed globe, white, Art Deco, #23, 8½" **$40.00**

Reamer, Herbage Green, rare **$55.00**

Vase, Heritage Green, tree-trunk shape, 8x4" **$70.00**

Vase, rectangular w/simulated palm fronds, turq matt, 14".. **$40.00**

Wall pocket, tree trunk w/3 openings, chocolate drip, 8½".. **$80.00**

Midwest Potteries, Inc., 1940 – 1944

Candleholder, Jack-Be-Nimble type, handle, lime green, 7" ..**$24.00**

Creamer, cow figural, brown drip w/yellow handle, 5".........**$24.00**

Figurine, deer, white w/gold decor, 8-point antlers, 12".......**$50.00**

Miniature, camel, brown, 2½" **$18.00**

Miniature, polar bear, white, 1¾" **$12.00**

Planter, deer, recumbent, brown spray, 6½x5½" **$18.00**

Wall mask, man's head caricature, short hair, winking, yellow, 5x3¼" **$35.00**

Morton Pottery Company, 1922 – 1976

Ashtray, hexagonal, Nixon, red, 3¾" **$40.00**

Ashtray, teardrop, Rival Crock Pot, 6" **$40.00**

Bank, church, brown, 3½x4x2" **$30.00**

Bank, pig, wall hanger, blue **$40.00**

Bank, Scottie dog, black, 7" **$30.00**

Bank, shoe, 7x6", $35.00. (Photo courtesy Doris and Burdell Hall)

Cookie jar, circus animals, cylindrical, yellow & orange.......**$45.00**

Cookie jar, Panda, head is lid...**$95.00**

Easter planter, hen w/bonnet, yellow/blue, 4¾" **$20.00**

Figurine, political, donkey, gray, marked Kennedy, 2¼x2¼"..**$125.00**

Grass grower, Christmas tree..**$15.00**

Lamp, teddy bear **$45.00**

Stein, cylindrical, brown Rockingham, embossed advertising.**$28.00**

Water fountain figure, fish, pink **$40.00**

American Art Potteries, 1947 – 1963

Bowl, flat leaf shape, green, #351, 1½x7"............................**$15.00**

Doll parts, head, arms & legs, hand painted, 3½", 6" dia **$72.00**

Figurine, Poland China hog, white w/gray spots, green base, 5½x7½" **$50.00**

Figurine, rooster, gray/black spray, #305, 8".......................**$24.00**

Flower bowl, S shape, yellow/white, 2x10" **$20.00**

Lamp, French poodle, black and pink, 15", $50.00. (Photo courtesy Doris and Burdell Hall)

Nightlight, wall mount, brown/white spray, rare, 6x3x3¼"..**$50.00**

Planter, fish, mauve/pink spray, 4" **$20.00**

Planter, pig, black w/white stripe **$40.00**

TV lamp, conch shell, tan w/green spray, 6½" **$40.00**

Vase, ewer form, pink, 14"..**$20.00**

Vase, 6-sided, pink w/blue interior, 10" **$18.00**

Moss Rose

Though a Moss Rose pattern has been produced by Staffordshire and American pottery companies alike since the mid-1800s, the ware we're dealing with here has a much different appearance. The pattern consists of a pink briar rose with dark green mossy leaves on stark white glaze. Very often it is trimmed in gold. In addition to dinnerware, many accessories and novelties were also made. It was a popular product of Japanese manufacturers from the 1950s on, and even today giftware catalogs show a few Moss Rose items.

Refer to *Schroeder's Antiques Price Guide* (Collector Books) for information on the early Moss Rose pattern. All the items listed below were produced in Japan unless noted otherwise.

Ashtray, $7.00; Smoking set, $18.00.

Ashtrays, fluted rim, rectangular, Japan, 3½x2½", 4 for **$12.00**
Bowl, cereal; Nasco, Japan, 6" **$7.00**
Bowl, fruit/dessert; Japan **$8.00**
Bowl, rimmed soup; Sango, 7½" **$6.00**
Candy dish, divided, w/handles, unmarked Japan, 7½" **$18.00**
Candy/nut dish, Trimont Ware, Japan, 8½x7" **$15.00**
Coffeepot, Ucagco, 3-cup **$27.00**
Compote, footed, rose finial, Japan, 6x4½" **$12.50**
Condiment bowl, w/lid, unmarked Japan, 4¼" **$12.50**
Covered dish, flower finial, Japan, dresser size **$18.00**
Covered dish, ruffled & pleated rim, 4-footed, Japan **$32.00**
Creamer & sugar bowl, w/lid, Royal Sealy Japan, 2½", 3", on 6x3"
    rectangular tray **$15.00**
Cup & saucer, demitasse; footed, Ucagco, 2⅛", from $8 to . **$10.00**
Cup & saucer, footed, Empress, Japan, 2¼" **$8.00**
Cup & saucer, footed bell shape w/ornate handle, unmarked
    Japan **$15.00**
Cup & saucer, Lefton **$18.00**
Dessert set, scalloped plate w/matching cup, gold trim, Japan .. **$15.00**
Egg cup, footed, Japan, 2⅜", from $6 to **$8.00**
Lamp, kerosene; matching shade & base, Japan label, 5¾" .. **$25.00**
Lamp, oil; Aladdin style, clear glass shade, Japan, 7½x5½" .. **$15.00**
Lamp, oil; matching base & globe, Tilso Japan, 10x3½" **$52.50**
Plate, dinner; Royal Sealy, Japan, 10" **$18.00**
Plate, dinner; unmarked Japan, 10¼" **$6.00**
Plate, salad; Japan, 7½", from $5 to **$8.00**
Platter, Empress, Japan, 12" L **$32.00**
Salt & pepper shakers, swirled body, silver trim, silver-tone metal lid,
    Japan, 2½", pr **$20.00**
Sugar bowl, Japan, 3" **$18.00**
Teapot, electric, Japan, 2-cup **$22.00**
Tidbit tray, center handle, Royal Sealy, Japan **$30.00**
Trinket box, gold trim, sq, Japan, 1½x4½x4½" **$22.50**
Vanity mirror, swivel type w/patterned pedestal & foot, Japan, 12" . **$30.00**

Motion Clocks (Electric)

Novelty clocks with some type of motion or animation were popular in spring-powered or wind-up form for hundreds of years.

Today they bring thousands of dollars when sold. Electric-powered or motor-driven clocks first appeared in the late 1930s and were produced until quartz clocks became the standard, with the 1950s being the era during which they reached the height of their production.

Four companies led their field. They were Mastercrafters, United, Haddon, and Spartus in order of productivity. Mastercrafters was the earliest and longest lived, making clocks from the late '40s until the late '80s. (They did, however, drop out of business several times during this long period.) United began making clocks in the early '50s and continued until the early '60s. Haddon followed in the same time frame, and Spartus was in production from the late '50s until the mid-'60s.

These clocks are well represented in the listings that follow; prices are for examples in excellent condition and working. With an average age of 40 years, many now need repair. Dried-out grease and dirt easily cause movements and motions not to function. The other nemesis of many motion clocks is deterioration of the fiber gears. Originally intended to keep the clocks quiet, fiber gears have not held up like their metal counterparts. For fully restored clocks, add $50.00 to $75.00 to our values. (Full restoration includes complete cleaning of motor and movement, repair of same; cleaning and polishing face and bezel; cleaning and polishing case and repairing if necessary; and installing new line cord, plug, and light bulb if needed.) Brown is the most common case color for plastic clocks. Add 10% to 20% or more for cases in onyx (mint green) or any light shade. If any parts noted below are missing, value can drop one-third to one-half. We must stress that 'as is' clocks will not bring these prices. Deteriorated, nonworking clocks may be worth less that half of these values.

Note: When original names are not known, names have been assigned.

Haddon

Based in Chicago, Illinois, Haddon produced an attractive line of clocks. They used composition cases that were hand painted, and sturdy Hansen movements and motions. This is the only clock line for which new replacement motors are still available.

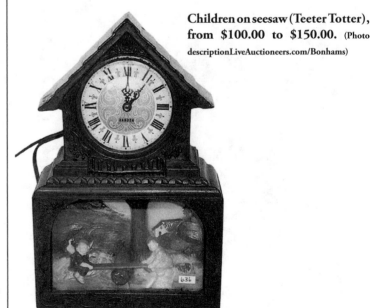

Children on seesaw (Teeter Totter), from $100.00 to $150.00. (Photo description LiveAuctioneers.com/Bonhams)

Cowboy on horse (Ranch-O), composition, 7x12", from $100 to..**$150.00**

Granny rocking on porch (Home Sweet Home), 7½x12½x4", from $75 to **$100.00**

Ship on waves (Ship Ahoy), from $175 to **$225.00**

Lux

This clockmaker was originally called The Lux Clock Company; it was founded 1914 in Waterbury, Pennsylvania. They made a large assortment of novelty clocks including a shoeshine boy, beer drinkers, organ grinder, cat faces, and Li'l Abner's schmoo.

Boy Scout waves semaphore flags, green tent, campfire & pot along edge, 5x4" **$700.00**

Bulldog face, pendulum, brown w/brown glass eyes & green collar, SyrocoWood, 1930s..**$800.00**

Cat face, pendulum causes cat's eyes to roll back and forth, exceptional, clean and working, $400.00. (EX, $150.00). (Photo courtesy LiveAuctioneers.com/Morphy Auctions)

Dixie Boy, blinking eyes, tie pendulum, 8½x4½" **$65.00**

Doghouse w/3 dogs, pendulum causes black dog's head to move side to side, pressed wood, 5½"..**$160.00**

Old Codger, clock in trunk of body, 6¾"..........................**$400.00**

Waiter holding bottle & cloth, painted SyrocoWood, 2" glass dial, ca 1938, 6½"...**$500.00**

Windmill, pressed wood w/painted scene, 1930s, 10¼", EX ..**$145.00**

Mastercrafters

Based in Chicago, Illinois, this company produced many of the most appealing and popular collectible motion clocks on today's market. Cases were made of plastic, with earlier examples being a sturdy urea plastic that imparted quality, depth, and shine to their finishes. Clock movements were relatively simple and often supplied by Sessions Clock Company, who also made many of their own clocks.

Chef on stove, VG **$12.00**

Fireplace w/mantel, marbleized plastic, 10¾", from $60 to..**$90.00**

Golfer practicing putting, from $50 to..............................**$85.00**

Potbelly stove, Model #830, 11½x6½" **$20.00**

Swinging girl (Cottage Swing), from $200 to....................**$250.00**

Toaster, toast pops up & down as clock rotates, Model #362, from $75 to **$125.00**

Spartus

This company made clocks well into the '80s, but most later clocks were not animated. Cases were usually plastic, and most clocks featured animals.

Cat, black, moving eyes & tail, long slender neck, 13" (+8" tail) **$65.00**

Cat & mouse, cat's paw reaching for gray mouse pendulum, white cat in center of blue circle..**$30.00**

Mill w/turning water wheel, plastic, 9x10½", from $45 to...**$50.00**

Panda Bear, eyes move back & forth, from $25 to **$35.00**

Tiger, orange w/black stripes & white cheeks, eyes & tail move, 13" (+8" tail) **$65.00**

United

Based in Brooklyn, New York, United made mostly cast-metal cases finished in gold or bronze. Their movements were somewhat more complex than Mastercrafters'. Some of their clocks contained musical movements, which while pleasing can be annoying when continuously run.

Uncle Sam with Roosevelt portrait, $400.00. (Photo courtesy LiveAuctioneers.com/Early American History Auctions)

Ballerina inside gold-draped case w/clock at side, she turns w/music, wooden, #870, 10x13", from $75 to............................**$85.00**

Children on swing, heart-shaped opening, 12", from $80 to..**$90.00**

Couple watch sailboats move across lake w/lighthouse on side, from $150 to **$200.00**

Cowboy & saddle horse w/clock in between, lasso on clock moves, 11½x20", from $135 to **$185.00**

English horse cab, driver's hand moves w/whip & lamppost lights up, #701, 13x16x4", from $60 to **$70.00**

Fish move in underwater scene, clock in marine steering wheel, 1950s, from $75 to **$100.00**

Horse & carriage, gold-plated brass, wood base, 1934, 9x17x5" **$90.00**

Huck Finn, fishing pole & fish move, from $100 to **$125.00**

Lighthouse w/revolving sailboat scene, 1960s.....................**$110.00**

Owl on branch, eyes move back & forth, 11", from $75 to ..**$90.00**

Pirate ship (The Pirate), 3 pirates & treasure, cast iron, 1930s, 13x12½" **$90.00**

Motorcycle Collectibles

At some point in nearly everyone's life, they've experienced at least a brief love affair with a motorcycle. What could be more exhilarating than the open road — the wind in your hair, the sun on your back, and no thought for the cares of today or what tomorrow might bring. For some, the passion never diminished. For most of us, it's a fond memory. Regardless of which description best fits you personally, you will probably enjoy the old advertising and sales literature, books and magazines, posters, photographs, banners, etc., showing the old Harleys and Indians, and the club pins, dealership jewelry and clothing, and scores of other items of memorabilia such as collectors are now beginning to show considerable interest in. For more information and lots of color photographs, we recommend *Motorcycle Collectibles With Values* by Leila Dunbar.

Unless otherwise noted, our values are for items in excellent to near mint original condition.

See also License Plates.

Advisor: Bob 'Sprocket' Eckardt (See Directory, Motorcycles)

Bag, Indian Motorcycle logo on light brown paper, held sm parts, 3x5¼" **$12.50**

Belt, brown leather, Geo Lawrence Co, 1950s.....................**$32.00**

Belt buckel, Harley-Davidson, man on motorcycle, brass, Lewis Buckles of Chicago, 2¾x4", M **$30.00**

Chaps, black leather, Talon zippers, Scovill snaps, 1950s-60s.**$100.00**

Clock, Harley-Davidson, Bulova, neon lights, $850.00.
(Photo courtesy LiveAuctioneers.com/Clars Auction Gallery)

Fire extinguisher, Harley-Davidson, brass, 9½x2½" cylinder ... **$115.00**

Flag, Harley-Davidson Motor Cycles, black, white & orange, 1980s, 3x5", M **$110.00**

Gauntlet gloves, brown leather, working snaps, WWII era.**$135.00**

Gloves/mitts, black leather, Harley-Davidson, sheepskin lined, ca 1970s **$85.00**

Goggles, Stadium MK4 Silver Cross, leather & safety glass..**$70.00**

Handbook, Harley-Davidson Motorcycle 74 & 80 Twin Models, ca 1934-35 ....**$50.00**

Hat, Harley-Davidson insignia on gray cloth, black visor **$85.00**

Helmet, Arthur Fulmer AF40, black, 1960s.......................**$250.00**

Helmet, black Bell Magnum, Snell Memorial Foundation M80 label **$315.00**

Helmet, flag stripes & stars, no visor, 1970s, VG................**$70.00**

Helmet, red flames w/metallic flakes, 1970s.....................**$150.00**

Jacket, black leather, Harley-Davidson, solid wide leather belt ..**$170.00**

Jacket, black leather, Talon zipper front, zip-up pocket & cuffs, half-waist belt w/buckle, VG...**$85.00**

Jacket, black leather, Taurus, padded shoulders & elbows, zipper front, chin strap, 3 front pockets, 1970s, VG+............**$115.00**

Jacket, black leather, 2 zip-up front pockets, zippered cuffs, action back, nylon quilted lining...**$175.00**

License plate, New Jersey, 1935...**$135.00**

Manual, Triumph 650 CC Twin, EX **$25.00**

Pants, black leather, Bates, zippered pockets, 1960s **$55.00**

Patch, Kiski Valley Motor Club Ramblers, racer & wings embroidered on cloth, 11¾x9¼" **$22.50**

Pin, Indian Motorcycle wings, gold-tone w/red enameling, ¾x2"..**$60.00**

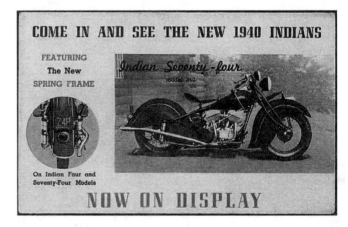

Postcard, advertising 1940 Indian Seventy-Four Model 340, linen, E.B. Thomas publisher, NM, $200.00. (Photo courtesy LiveAuctioneers.com/Lyn Knight Auctions)

Ring, Harley-Davidson Motorcycle emblem enameled on sterling silver **$52.50**

T-shirt, Harley-Davidson Racing, black & white, cotton polyester blend, 1980s, M **$42.50**

T-shirt, Triumph Motorcycles, logo on navy blue, M..........**$15.00**

Trophy, motorcycle & figure in gold-tone metal atop wooden pillar, 1950s, 14¾x8x4" **$40.00**

Visor, Bell Model #520, white w/3 snaps **$40.00**

Wrench, Wakefield, Indian Motorcycles on handle, 6" when closed, opens up to 3" **$40.00**

Movie Posters and Lobby Cards

Although many sizes of movie posters were made and all are collectible, the preferred size today is still the one-sheet, 27" wide and 41" long. Movie-memorabilia collecting is as diverse as films themselves. Popular areas include specific films such as *Gone With the Wind, Wizard of Oz*, and others; specific stars — from the greats to character actors; directors such as Hitchcock, Ford, Speilberg, and others; specific film types such as B-Westerns, all-Black casts, sports related, Noir, '50s teen, '60s beach, musicals, crime, silent, radio characters, cartoons, and serials; specific characters such as Tarzan, Superman, Ellery Queen, Blondie, Ma and Pa Kettle, Whistler, and Nancy Drew; specific artists like Rockwell, Davis, Frazetta, Flagg, and others; specific art themes, for instance, policeman, firemen, horses, attorneys, doctors, or nurses (this list is endless). And some collectors just collect posters they like. In the past 20 years, movie memorabilia has steadily increased in value. Movie memorabilia is a new field for collectors. In the past, only a few people knew where to find posters. Recently, auctions on the east and west coasts have created much publicity, attracting scores of new collectors. Many posters are still moderately priced, and the market is expanding, allowing even new collectors to see the value of their collections increase.

Contra El Imperio Del Crimen, lobby card, from $35.00 to $50.00. (Photo courtesy Harry and Jody Whitworth)

Angels' Wild Women, Ross Hagen, Kent Taylor & Regina Carrol, 1972, 41x27", NM **$30.00**
Angry Sea, John Severson, surfing scene, 14½x8", M **$480.00**
Barbarella, Jane Fonda, John Phillip Law & Marcel Marceau, 1st issue, 1968, 41x27", NM.. **$95.00**
Batman, Adam West, Burt Ward, Lee Meriweither, Cesar Romero & Burgess Merideth, 1966, 61x46½", NM **$240.00**
Beach Blanket Bingo, Frankie Avalon/Annette Funicello, 1965, 60x40", VG **$100.00**
Black Cat, David Manners & Jacqueline Wells, 1934, 27x18", M **$280.00**
Black Sunday, Barbara Steel, lobby card set, 1961, EX....... **$100.00**
Call Northside 777, James Stewart, 1948, 1-sheet, EX....... **$300.00**
Choppers, Arch Hall Jr & Marianne Gaba, 1962, 41x27", NM .. **$145.00**

Citizen Kane, Orson Wells, Joseph Cotton & Agnes Moorehead, 1941, 24½x18½", M.. **$60.00**
Cycle Savages, Bruce Dern, Chris Robinson & Melody Patterson, 1970, 41x27", VG **$50.00**
Giant, Rock Hudson & Elizabeth Taylor, 1956, 1-sheet, NM ..**$500.00**
Goldfinger, Sean Connery, 1964, 1-sheet, EX................... **$650.00**
Hard Ride, Robert Fuller, Sherry Bain & Tony Russel, 1971, 41x27", NM **$75.00**
Horse Soldiers, John Wayne, lobby card, 1959, EX **$75.00**
Hound of Baskervilles, Basil Rathbone, lobby card, 1959, EX..**$325.00**
Jailhouse Rock, Elvis Presley, 1957, 12x8½", EX................. **$45.00**
Lady & the Tramp (Walt Disney), 1955, 28x22", EX......... **$55.00**
Mame, Lucille Ball, 1974, 1-sheet, NM............................ **$35.00**
Mary Poppins, Julie Andrews & Dick Van Dyke, 1964, 41x27", VG **$30.00**
Miracle Worker, Patty Duke & Anne Bancroft, 1962, ½-sheet, VG **$100.00**
Murder on the Orient Express, Amsel artwork, 1974, 1-sheet, EX **$50.00**
Noose Hangs High, Abbott & Costello, 1948, 1-sheet, EX..**$340.00**
Numbered Woman, Sally Blane & Lloyd Hughes, 1938, 39x25½", G **$55.00**
Omega Man, Charleton Heston, 1971, 41x27", EX **$30.00**
On Her Majesty's Secret Service, 1970, 1-sheet, EX........... **$250.00**
Out of Sight, Jonathan Daly & Karen Jensen, 1966, 41x27", NM **$45.00**
Planet Outlaws, Buster Crabbe, 1953, 1-sheet, EX **$360.00**

Saginaw Trail, Gene Autry, 1953, 41x27", EX, $235.00. (Photo courtesy LiveAuctioneers.com/ Morphy Auctions)

Savage Seven, Robert Walker, Larry Bishop & Joanna Frank, 1968, 28x22", EX **$50.00**
Secrets of a Secretary, Claudette Colbert, 1931, 27x21", EX ..**$75.00**
Star Wars, Mark Hamill, Harrison Ford & Carrie Fisher, 1977, 36x24", M **$45.00**
Suddenly Last Summer, Elizabeth Taylor, Katherine Hepburn & Montgomery Clift, 1960, 3-sheet, EX **$200.00**
That Lady in Ermine, Betty Grable & Douglas Fairbanks, restored, 1948, 43x30" **$125.00**

Title card, Peyton Plate, Lana Turner, 1958 ....**$45.00**
Torn Curtain, Paul Newman & Julie Andrews, 1966, 3-sheet, EX **$150.00**
Up Periscope, James Garner, 1958, 22x14", EX...................**$25.00**
Westbound, Randolph Scott & Virginia Mayo, 29½x13", NM ..**$60.00**
Where the Boys Are, Connie Francis & George Hamilton, 1961, 1-sheet, EX...**$75.00**
Window card, Black Scorpion, 1957, NM.........................**$165.00**

Napkin Dolls

Cocktail, luncheon, or dinner..., paper, cotton, or damask..., solid, patterned, or plaid — regardless of size, color, or material, there's always been a place for napkins. In the late 1940s and early 1950s, buffet-style meals were gaining popularity. One accessory common to many of these buffets is now one of today's hot collectibles — the napkin doll. While most of the ceramic and wooden examples found today date from this period, many homemade napkin dolls were produced in ceramic classes of the 1960s and 1970s.

For information on napkin dolls as well as egg timers, string holders, children's whistle cups, baby feeder dishes, razor blade banks, pie birds, laundry sprinkler bottles, and other unique collectibles from the same era, we recommend *Collectibles for the Kitchen, Bath and Beyond*; for ordering information see our advisor's listing in the Directory.

Advisor: Bobbie Zucker Bryson (See Directory, Napkin Dolls)

Betson's, colonial lady in yellow, bell clapper, marked Hand Painted, 9", from $35 to..**$55.00**
Byron Molds, lady in pink & white w/arms crossed holding a bouquet, bow on top of head, 8½", from $55 to **$75.00**
California Ceramic mold, lady in yellow & purple w/candleholder in top of hat, 12½", from $60 to **$75.00**
California Originals, Miss Versatility Cocktail Girl, 13", from $50 to **$75.00**
California Originals, Spanish dancer in pink & white, slits on back only, foil label, 15", from $85 to..............................**$125.00**
Can Can, girl in blue & gold holding skirt open to expose legs, 9½", from $125 to **$150.00**
Enesco, Genie at Your Service, holding lantern, paper label, 8", from $100 to..**$135.00**
German, metal silhouette of Deco woman, black & gold w/wire bottom, marked E Kosta DBGM 1744970, EX, from $75 to...**$135.00**
Goebel, half doll holding a rose on wire frame, marked Goebel, W Germany, ca 1957, 8¼", from $175 to **$250.00**
Hachiya Bros, lady holding yoke w/bucket salt & pepper shakers, hat conceals candleholder, from $125 to...................**$150.00**
Holland Mold, Daisy, No 514, 7¼", from $50 to..............**$75.00**
Holland Mold, lady holding hat behind her back, red & white, 6¾", from $60 to..**$75.00**
Holland Mold, Rebecca No H-265, wearing white dress w/tiers of napkin slits, 10½", from $150 to **$195.00**
Holland Mold, Rosie, No H-132, 10⅞", from $35 to **$55.00**
Holt Howard, pink Sunbonnet Miss, marked Holt Howard, 1958, 5", from $100 to...**$150.00**

Holt Howard, yellow Sunbonnet Miss, marked Holt Howard, 1959, 5", from $100 to..**$150.00**
Holt Howard style, wooden doll w/outstretched arms on wooden base, 11¼", from $20 to **$30.00**
Holt Howard style baker, w/towel & tray of rolls, ceramic & metal, holes at top for toothpicks, #2026, 9", from $95 to ...**$110.00**
Japan, angel, pink, holding flowers, slits in shoulders allow napkins to form wings, 5⅜", from $100 to.............................**$135.00**
Japan, girl in yellow colonial-style dress, brown hair, holds tureen toothpick tray, 9⅞", from $55 to **$75.00**
Japan, lady in blue w/pink umbrella, bell clapper, unmarked, 9", from $50 to..**$75.00**
Japan, lady in pink w/blue shawl & yellow hat, 8½", from $50 to **$75.00**
Japan, Santa, marked Chess, 1957, 6¾", from $95 to........**$135.00**
Kreiss & Co, angel, candleholder in halo, holding a Christmas tree, 11", from $100 to...**$135.00**
Kreiss & Co, green doll w/gold trim holding muff, jeweled eyes, candleholder in hat, marked, 10¼", from $95 to........**$125.00**
Kreiss & Co, green doll w/poodle, jeweled eyes, necklace & ring, candleholder behind hat, marked, 10¾", from $100 to..**$125.00**
Kreiss & Co, lady in yellow w/fan (candleholder behind), marked, 10½", from $40 to..**$65.00**

Kreiss & Co., yellow doll holding muff, yellow with jewels in eyes, candleholder in hat, 10", from $95.00 to $125.00. (Photo courtesy Bobbie Zucker Bryson)

Lefton, white birds w/gold trim, wires in tail for napkins, heads (salt & peppers) lift off, 4⅜", from $20 to **$30.00**
Mallory Ceramics Studio, Christine, blue dress w/purple flower trim, blond hair, 9", from $135 to.............................**$150.00**
Marcia of California, woman w/molded apron, 1 hand holding bowl on her head, blue iridescent finish, 13", from $95 to..**$150.00**
Marybell, Mold P71, Southern lady holding hat, 9¾", from $150 to **$195.00**
Paris Art, Black native, metal w/gold cap, earrings & trim, bold felt bikini-type top, 8", from $75 to **$100.00**
Plastic, half doll w/red hair, green satin decorated bodice, ca 1959, 11", from $30 to...**$50.00**
Rooster, black w/red & yellow trim, slits in sides for napkins, w/ matching salt & pepper shakers, from $30 to **$45.00**

Servy Etta, wood, gray w/marble base, marked USD Patent No 159,005, 11½", from $25 to **$35.00**

Swedish doll, wooden, marked Patent No 113861, 10", from $15 to **$25.00**

Viking Japan, man (bartender), green & white, holding tray w/ candleholder, 8¾", from $85 to **$100.00**

Willoughby Studio, lady in golden yellow w/brown applied trim holding tilted pitcher, 12", from $100 to...................**$125.00**

Wooden, do-do bird w/pointed beak & long neck, slits in body for napkins, 7", from $15 to.......................................**$20.00**

Wooden, doll w/red strawberry toothpick holder on head, 8", from $50 to **$65.00**

Wooden, Jamaican lady, movable arms, paper label: Ave 13 Nov 743, A Sinfonia, Tel 2350 Petropolis, 6", from $35 to **$60.00**

Wooden, umbrella, marked Reg Prop No 382.649, Reproduction Prohibited, Industria Argentina, 8⅜", from $15 to **$30.00**

NASCAR Collectibles

Over the past decade, interest in NASCAR racing has increased to the point that the related collectibles industry has mushroomed into a multi-billion dollar business. Posters, magazines, soda pop bottles, and model kits are only a few examples of hundreds of items produced with the sole intention of attracting racing fans. Also included as a part of this field of collecting are items such as race-worn apparel — even parts from the racing cars themselves — and these, though not devised as such, are the collectibles that command the highest prices!

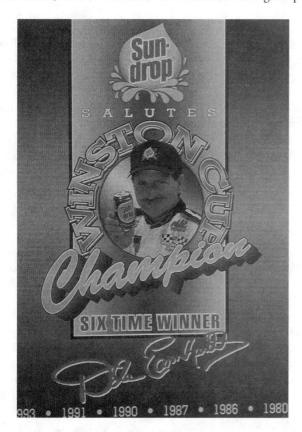

Poster, Dale Ernhardt, 1993 Sun Drop, 28x18", $80.00. (Photo courtesy Racing Collectibles Price Guide)

Book, Nascar International Rule Book, 1957, 6x4", EX **$40.00**

Book, NASCAR Winston Cup, The Official Chronicle..., color photos, hardbound w/jacket, 286-page, 11x9", M **$35.00**

Book, Winston Cup '88, hardcover w/jacket, color photos, 160-page, 1988, NM **$75.00**

Coin, Dale Earnhardt Sr color picture on US mint silver dollar, 2001, 1-oz, M in case **$45.00**

Decals, official NASCAR race decals, 2-pack, w/instructions, 1990, M **$10.00**

Hat, FedEx Racing Team, dark blue w/white 'flames' on sides, unused, M **$12.00**

Photo, Fonty Flock, Red Voght, Bill France & unknown man, black & white, NM..**$35.00**

Photo, Sportsman Division race at Orange Speedway, black & white, 1950s, 10x12", EX **$35.00**

Poster, Team Quaker State, Jeff Gordon, Terry Labonte & Ricky Craven, 22½x30", M **$20.00**

Press kit (8x10" color photo), Shawna Robinson, Polaroid, 1993, M...**$15.00**

Program, Daytona Beach Speed Weeks, softcover, February 1957, NM...**$60.00**

Program, 1st Annual Talladega 500, September 1969, 116-page,11x8½", EX **$50.00**

Program, 3rd Annual Daytona 500, February 1961, EX......**$25.00**

Ticket, Daytona 500, Ernie Irvan winner, February 17, 1991, unused, M **$40.00**

Yearbook, Winston Cup, champion Bill Elliot featured, back issue, hardbound, 167-page, 1985, M **$20.00**

New Martinsville

Located in a West Virginia town by the same name, the New Martinsville Glass Company was founded in 1901 and until it was purchased by Viking in 1944 produced quality tableware in various patterns and colors that collectors admire today. They also made a line of glass animals which Viking continued to produce until they closed in 1986. In 1987 the factory was bought by Mr. Kenneth Dalzell who reopened the company under the title Dalzell-Viking. He used the old molds to reissue his own line of animals, which he marked 'Dalzell' with an acid stamp.

See also Glass Animals and Related Items.

Janice, blue or red, basket, 8x6½" **$135.00**

Janice, blue or red, bonbon, w/handles, 5x7" **$40.00**

Janice, blue or red, bowl, #4551, 12" L...............................**$70.00**

Janice, blue or red, bowl, 10" **$75.00**

Janice, blue or red, creamer, 6-oz **$20.00**

Janice, blue or red, cruet, oil; #4583, w/stopper, 5-oz **$100.00**

Janice, blue or red, plate, torte; rolled edge, 15"...................**$50.00**

Janice, blue or red, plate, 13" **$60.00**

Janice, blue or red, salt & pepper shakers, pr **$85.00**

Janice, blue or red, tumbler, luncheon; #4551/23 ....**$30.00**

Janice, blue or red, vase, footed, 7" **$75.00**

Janice, crystal, basket, 4-toed, 9x6½" **$75.00**

Janice, crystal, bowl, crimped rim, w/handles, 6"................**$33.00**

Janice, crystal, bowl, salad; scalloped rim, 12"....................**$50.00**

Janice, crystal, cup, #4580...$8.00
Janice, crystal, jam jar, #4577, w/lid, 6"................$20.00
Janice, crystal, relish dish, 2-part, w/handles, 6".................$15.00
Janice, crystal, sugar bowl, 6-oz...........................$12.00
Janice, crystal, vase, ball form, 9".......................$55.00
Lions, amber or crystal, candleholder, #37, ea.....................$25.00
Lions, amber or crystal, sugar bowl, #37 ....$15.00
Lions, black, creamer, #34.....................................$35.00
Lions, black, cup, #34...$35.00
Lions, black, plate, cracker; 12" $40.00
Lions, black, sugar bowl, #34................................$35.00
Lions, green or pink, candlestick, #34, ea $35.00
Lions, green or pink, plate, 8"..............................$20.00
Lions, green or pink, saucer, #34...........................$7.50
Lions, green or pink, tray, center handle $45.00
Meadow Wreath, bowl, flat, flared, 10"..................$30.00
Meadow Wreath, cheese & cracker, #42/26, 11"..................$40.00
Meadow Wreath, crystal, bowl, crimped rim, #4220/26, 10" ..$40.00
Meadow Wreath, crystal, creamer, footed, tab handle, #42/26..$12.00
Meadow Wreath, crystal, punch bowl, #4221/26, 5-qt $140.00
Meadow Wreath, crystal, punch ladle, #4226.................$55.00
Meadow Wreath, crystal, vase, crimped rim, #4332/26, 10"...$55.00
Prelude, crystal, bowl, cupped, 7" $25.00

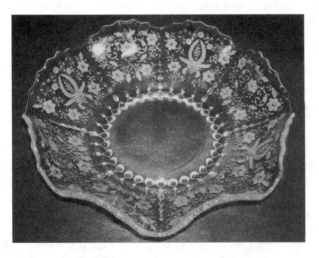

Prelude, crystal, bowl, 12½", $50.00. (Photo courtesy Gene and Cathy Florence)

Prelude, crystal, butter dish, oval, 6½" $37.50
Prelude, crystal, compote, 3x5½" $25.00
Prelude, crystal, mayonnaise, divided, 4-pc............$40.00
Prelude, crystal, plate, 3-footed, 10" $25.00
Prelude, crystal, salt & pepper shakers, 3½", pr $40.00
Prelude, crystal, sherbet, tall, 6-oz.......................$15.00
Prelude, crystal, tumbler, flat, 9-oz......................$18.00
Radiance, amber, bowl, nut; w/handles $12.00
Radiance, amber, bowl, pickle; 7".........................$20.00
Radiance, amber, butter dish.................................$21.00
Radiance, amber, candlesticks, 2-light, pr.............$95.00
Radiance, amber, compote, 6"................................$22.00
Radiance, amber, cup, footed $12.00
Radiance, amber, pitcher, 64-oz $175.00
Radiance, amber, salt & pepper shakers, pr...........$50.00

Radiance, cobalt blue or ice, candlesticks, ruffled, 6", pr....$175.00
Radiance, cobalt blue or ice, punch bowl, 9" $225.00
Radiance, cobalt blue or ice, punch cup............................$15.00
Radiance, cobalt blue or ice, relish, 2-part, 7"....................$35.00
Radiance, cobalt blue or ice, sugar bowl.............................$28.00

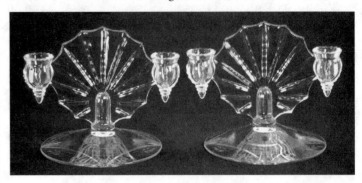

Radiance, crystal, double candleholders, $300.00.

Radiance, red, bowl, flared, 10" $50.00
Radiance, red, candy dish, flat, w/lid $100.00
Radiance, red, condiment set, 4-pc w/tray $325.00
Radiance, red, lamp, 12".....................................$125.00
Radiance, red, saucer...$8.50
Radiance, red, vase, flared, 12"............................$175.00

Nichols, Betty Lou

This California artist/potter is probably best known for her head vases, which display her talents and strict attention to detail to full advantage. Many of her ladies were dressed in stylish clothing and hats that were often decorated with applied lace, ruffles, and bows; the signature long eyelashes are apparent on nearly every model she made. Because these applications are delicate and susceptible to damage, mint-condition examples are rare and very valuable. The few figures she made without applied components generally sell for under $100.00, though some may go higher. Most of her head vases and figurines carry not only her name but the name of the subject as well.

Decanter, English guard, red & white uniform, head-form stopper, 10"...$150.00
Figure planter, Inga, carrying bowl, hair in 2 buns, 5" $65.00
Figure planter, Milicent, long white gown w/pink dots, pink bonnet, 8"...$385.00
Figure vase, B'Lou, hat w/bow draping to shoulder, leg-o-mutton sleeves, wide flaring peplum over long skirt, 7½"........$135.00
Figure vase, Floppsie, bunny in cocked hat holding purse, long lashes, 7"...$125.00
Figurine, boy in Swedish costume, hands on hips, 12".........$80.00
Figurine, Santa, arms out, gesturing, white & gold 'spaghetti' trim on red suit, gold belt, 11½" $100.00
Head vase, Ermyn-Trude, tilted hat covered w/lg flowers, ermine tails at shoulder, 6½"...$275.00
Head vase, Flora Belle, lady in green & yellow plaid, ruffled bodice, thick black lashes, 11", EX..$450.00

Head vase, Judy, blond braids, brown eyes & lashes, green polka-dot dress & green ribbons, 5½"...**$235.00**

Head vase, Linda, platter-style hat, ruffled collar, 5½" **$200.00**

Head vase, Louisa, crimped ribbon, ruffle trim, pink & cream polka-dots on brown dress, thick eyelashes, 6½", NM..........**$300.00**

Head vase, Mary Lou, blond w/hair in long curls, ruffled bodice, 8½" **$400.00**

Head vase, Mary Lou, blond w/thick black lashes, ruffled bodice, 6½" **$250.00**

Head vase, Nancy, 8½", from $575.00 to $650.00. (Photo courtesy Jack Chipman)

Head vase, Nancy Lou, derby-style hat, long curls, ruffled collar extends down left side, 8½" **$295.00**

Head vase, winking man in black top hat, black & white w/multi-colored tie, 5¼" **$65.00**

Plate, lady in full-length profile w/umbrella, reticulated rim, 9½" **$50.00**

Niloak Pottery

The Niloak Pottery company was the continuation of a quarter-century-old family business in Benton, Arkansas. Known as the Eagle Pottery in the early twentieth century, its owner was Charles Dean Hyten who continued in his father's footsteps making utilitarian wares for local and state markets. In 1909 Arthur Dovey, an experienced potter formerly from the Rookwood Pottery of Ohio and the Arkansas-Missouri based Ouachita Pottery companies, came to Benton and created America's most unusual art pottery. Introduced in 1910 as Niloak (kaolin spelled backwards), Dovey and Hyten produced art pottery pieces from swirling clays with a wide range of artificially created colors including red, blue, cream, brown, gray, and later green. Connected to the Arts & Crafts Movement by 1913, the pottery was labeled as Missionware (probably due to its seeming simplicity in the making). Missionware (or swirl) production continued alongside utilitarian ware manufacturing until the

1930s when economic factors led to the making of another type of art pottery and later to (molded) industrial castware. In 1931 Niloak Pottery introduced Hywood Art Pottery (marked as such), consisting of regular glaze techniques including overspray, mottling, and drips of two colors on vases and bowls that were primarily hand thrown. It was short lived and soon replaced with the Hywood by Niloak (or Hywood) line to increase marketing potential through the use of the well-recognized Niloak name. Experienced potters, designers, and ceramists were involved at Niloak; among them were Frank Long, Paul Cox, Stoin M. Stoin, Howard Lewis, and Rudy Ganz. Many local families with long ties to the pottery included the McNeills, Rowlands, and Alleys. Experiencing tremendous financial woes by the mid-1930s, Niloak came under new management which was led by Hardy L. Winburn of Little Rock. To maximize efficiency and stay competetive, they focused primarily on industrial castware such as vases, bowls, figurines, animals, and planters. Niloak survived into the late 1940s when it became known as the Winburn Tile Company of North Little Rock; it still exists today.

Virtually all of Niloak Missionware/swirl pottery is marked with die stamps. The exceptions are generally fan vases, wall pockets, lamp bases, and whiskey jugs. The terms '1st' and '2nd art marks' used in the listings refer to specific die-stamped trademarks. The earlier mark was used from 1910 to 1925, followed by the second, very similar mark used from then until the end of Mission Ware production. Letters with curving raised outlines were characteristic of both; the most obvious difference between the two was that on the first, the final upright line of the 'N' was thin with a solid club-like terminal Be careful when you buy unmarked swirl pottery — it is usually Evans pottery (made in Missouri) which generally has either no interior glaze or is chocolate brown inside. Moreover, Evans made swirl wall pockets, lamp bases, and even hanging baskets that find their way on to today's market and are sold as Niloak. Niloak stickers are often placed on these unmarked Evans pieces — closely examine the condition of the sticker to determine if it is damaged or mutilated from the transfer process.

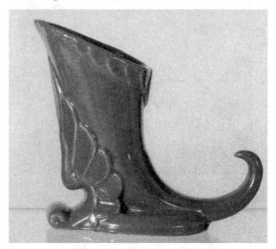

Cornucopia vase, Alley design, 7", $25.00. (Photo courtesy David Edwin Gifford)

Ashtray, Mission, w/penny matchbox holder, 2nd art mark, 6½" **$155.00**

Ashtray/matchbox holder, razorback hog, U of A on base, 6½" dia **$185.00**

Basket, basketweave exterior, braided handle, 7" **$55.00**

Bean pot, Mission, w/handles, lid w/recessed knob, 7" **$385.00**

Bowl, cuspidor form, matt, block letters, 3½" **$30.00**

Bowl, Mission, incurvate rim, attached flower frog, 2nd art mark, 9½" **$165.00**

Candlestick, Mission, flared base, 2nd art mark, 7½", ea from $155 to **$200.00**

Carafe, Mission, slim neck, bulbous body, cork-wrapped stopper, 8" **$485.00**

Compote, Mission, pedestal foot, lid w/knob, 2nd art mark, 6" .. **$790.00**

Creamer, cow figural, tail form handle, high gloss, block letters, 6" L **$85.00**

Ewer, embossed 2½x3" silhouette in frame, 10" **$55.00**

Figurine, French poodle begging, upright w/mouth open, block letters, 5½" **$26.00**

Figurine, razorback hog, matt, U of A side mark **$135.00**

Humidor, Mission, lid w/knob, 2nd art mark, 5½" **$480.00**

Humidor, Mission, predominantly brick red, lid w/knob, 1st art mark, 6" **$550.00**

Jar, mustard; Mission, lid w/knob & slot for spoon, 2nd art mark, 2½" **$300.00**

Jar, strawberry; 4 bud-shaped openings, matt, 11" **$35.00**

Jug, syrup; sm open handle, remnants of original label, block letters, 6" **$45.00**

Letter, on Niloak letterhead promoting products, 1937, 8½x11". **$45.00**

Pitcher, Mission, cylindrical, w/ice lip, 6½" **$320.00**

Pitcher, USA eagle & Missouri mule, high gloss, block letters, 8". **$160.00**

Planter, billy goat, Ozark Blue, foil sticker, 4½" **$60.00**

Planter, dove, Ivory glaze by Lewis, 9", $200.00. (Photo courtesy David Edwin Gifford)

Planter, football w/lacings, high gloss, actual size **$145.00**

Planter, Scottie dog, high gloss, block letters & foil label, 6½" L.. **$55.00**

Planter, teddy bear sitting by bowl, block letters, 3¾" **$85.00**

Smoke set, Mission, 7x10" tray, humidor (w/lid), match holder, w/ striker & ashtray **$1,450.00**

Teapot, Aladdin form, mauve to gray, block letters, 5¼" **$75.00**

Thimble, Mission, ⅞" **$185.00**

Vase, bud; Mission, stick neck w/flared base, 1st art mark, 7½", from $135 to **$160.00**

Vase, Grecian urn form, sm handles, sq base, matt, block letters, 8" **$50.00**

Vase, Mission, high shoulders, no collar, yellow fading to green, FHN, 9⅜" **$175.00**

Vase, Mission, pear shape, 1st art mark w/Riggs Art Store label, 10" **$275.00**

Vase, Mission, squat w/rolled collar, 2nd art mark, 3¾x4½" .. **$270.00**

Vase, Mission, 14x7", $1,100.00. (Photo courtesy Rago Auctions)

Vase, pouter pigeon, matt, block letters, 8¾" **$120.00**

Vase, sea horse w/lg open mouth, block letters, 8" **$45.00**

Vase, Victorian lady, ruffled skirt, matt, 10½" **$55.00**

Wall pocket, cup & saucer, Bouquet, block letters, saucer: 6".. **$55.00**

Noritake

Before the government restricted the use of the Nippon mark in 1921, all porcelain exported from Japan (even that made by the Noritake Company) carried the Nippon mark. The company that became Noritake had its beginning in 1904 and over the years experienced several changes in name and organization. Until 1941 (at the onset of WWII) they continued to export large amounts of their products to America. (During the occupation, when chinaware production was resumed, all imports were to have been marked 'Occupied Japan,' though because of the natural resentment on the part of the Japanese, much of it was not.)

Many variations will be found in their marks, but nearly all contain the Noritake name. Reproductions abound; be very careful.

Club: Noritake Collectors Society
Newsletter: *Noritake News*
David H. Spain
1237 Federal Ave. E, Seattle, WA 98102
206-323-8102
www.noritakecollectors.com

Azalea

The Azalea pattern was produced exclusively for the Larkin Company, who offered it to their customers as premiums from 1916 until the 1930s. It met with much success, and even today locating pieces to fill in your collection is not at all difficult. The earlier pieces carry the Noritake M-in-wreath mark. Later the ware was marked Noritake, Azalea, Hand Painted, Japan.

Bowl, #12, 10"	$38.00
Bowl, cream soup; #363	$135.00
Bowl, fruit; scalloped rim, glass	$95.00
Bowl, vegetable; divided, #439, 9½"	$275.00
Cake plate, #10, 9¾"	$30.00
Coffeepot, demitasse; #182	$595.00
Creamer & sugar shaker, #122, pr	$150.00
Cruet, #190	$180.00
Egg cup, #120	$60.00
Jam jar set, #125, 4-pc	$155.00
Pitcher, milk jug; #100, 1-qt	$175.00
Plate, dinner; #13, 9¾"	$18.00
Platter, turkey; #186, 16"	$425.00
Salt & pepper shakers, bell form, #11, pr	$35.00

Salt and pepper shakers, #126, $28.00 for the pair. (Photo courtesy Linda Williams)

Toothpick holder, #192	$120.00
Tray, celery; #444, w/handles, 10"	$275.00
Vase, bulbous, #452	$1,600.00

Tree in the Meadow

Made by the Noritake China Company during the 1920s and 1930s, this pattern of dinnerware is beginning to show up more and more at the larger flea markets and antique malls. It's easy to spot; the pattern is hand painted, so there are variations, but the color scheme is always browns, gold-yellows, and orange-rust, and the design features a large dark tree in the foreground, growing near a lake. There is usually a cottage in the distance.

Bowl, oatmeal	$25.00
Bowl, soup	$38.00

Butter tub, open, with drainer, $35.00. (Photo courtesy Linda Williams)

Celery dish	$35.00
Compote	$95.00
Cruets, vinegar & oil; conjoined, #319	$210.00
Cup & saucer, breakfast	$18.00
Gravy boat	$35.00
Plate, bread & butter; 6½"	$8.00
Plate, sq, rare, 7½"	$80.00
Snack set (cup & tray), 2-pc	$60.00
Teapot	$75.00

Various Dinnerware Patterns

So many lines of dinnerware have been produced by the Noritake company that to list them all would require a volume in itself. More than 800 patterns have been recorded, and while many had specific names, others simply carried identification numbers. We are listings some of the more popular lines; most were produced from the 1950s through the 1980s.

Maywood #5154, cup, gold edge, 1950s, $12.00. (Photo courtesy Aimee Neff Alden)

Cervantes #7261, coffeepot, 5-cup	$235.00
Cervantes #7261, gravy boat, w/undertray	$125.00
Cervantes #7261, plate, dinner	$27.50
Cervantes #7261, platter, 14" L	$65.00
Colburn #6107, bowl, fruit; 5½"	$12.00

Colburn #6107, cup & saucer.............................$14.00
Colburn #6107, plate, dinner; 10½"..................$18.00
Colburn #6107, sugar bowl, w/lid......................$28.00
Courtney #6520, bowl, lug cereal.......................$12.00
Courtney #6520, bowl, vegetable; oval, 9½"......$27.50
Courtney #6520, cup & saucer............................$17.50
Courtney #6520, plate, bread & butter; 7"..........$8.00
Courtney #6520, sugar bowl, w/lid......................$27.50
Foxboro #4302, creamer, 8-oz............................$125.00
Foxboro #4302, cup & saucer, 3".......................$120.00
Foxboro #4302, plate, dinner.............................$35.00
Foxboro #4302, plate, salad; 8½".......................$40.00
Goldbeam #4786, bowl, rimmed soup..................$25.00
Goldbeam #4786, bowl, vegetable; w/lid............$120.00
Goldbeam #4786, plate, salad; 7½".....................$12.50
Goldbeam #4786, sugar bowl, w/lid....................$30.00
Hailey #4007, bowl, soup; 7½"...........................$30.00
Hailey #4007, creamer, 8-oz...............................$20.00
Hailey #4007, plate, dinner; 10½"......................$12.50
Hailey #4007, platter, 14" L...............................$60.00
Hailey #4007, sugar bowl, w/lid.........................$32.00
Halifax #7729, bowl, vegetable; 8".....................$85.00
Halifax #7729, cup & saucer...............................$22.00
Halifax #7729, plate, dinner; 10½"....................$28.00
Halifax #7729, platter, 13½" L...........................$75.00
Harwood #6312, bowl, cream soup; w/saucer......$22.50
Harwood #6312, creamer, 8-oz...........................$12.50
Harwood #6312, cup & saucer, demitasse............$8.00
Harwood #6312, plate, salad; 8".........................$7.50
Harwood #6312, platter, 14" L...........................$32.00
Lacewood #3803, cheese plate, glass dome.........$28.00
Lacewood #3803, plate, salad; 8".......................$8.00
Lacewood #3803, plate, serving; center handle...$28.00
Lacewood #3803, sugar bowl, w/lid....................$28.00
Laureate #61235, bowl, cereal; 6"......................$12.00
Laureate #61235, bowl, vegetable; oval, 10½"....$28.00
Laureate #61235, bowl, vegetable; w/lid.............$60.00
Laureate #61235, cup & saucer...........................$15.00
Laureate #61235, plate, bread & butter...............$4.00
Laureate #61235, plate, dinner; 10"...................$12.50
Mantigo #8167/W83, bowl, soup.......................$15.00
Mantigo #8167/W83, bowl, vegetable; 10".........$32.00
Mantigo #8167/W83, cup & saucer.....................$15.00
Margarita #5049, bowl, rimmed soup..................$8.00
Margarita #5049, creamer...................................$18.00
Margarita #5049, plate, salad; 7½".....................$7.50
Margarita #5049, platter, 14" L.........................$30.00
Melrose #370, bowl, soup...................................$8.00
Melrose #370, bowl, vegetable; oval, 9½"...........$35.00
Melrose #370, cup & saucer................................$28.00
Melrose #370, plate, luncheon; 9".....................$17.50
Melrose #370, platter, 10" L..............................$38.00
Shahzada #3090, bowl, fruit; 5½".......................$15.00
Shahzada #3090, cup & saucer............................$30.00
Shahzada #3090, platter, 12" L..........................$60.00
Shahzada #3090, sugar bowl, w/lid.....................$42.50
Shahzada #3909, gravy boat w/attached underplate.............$80.00

Valencia #5086, bowl, rimmed soup...................$15.00
Valencia #5086, creamer, 12-oz..........................$25.00
Valencia #5086, cup & saucer, footed.................$22.50
Valencia #5086, plate, dinner; 10".....................$16.00
Valencia #5086, platter, 16½" L.........................$60.00
Whitehall #6115, bowl, lug cereal.......................$15.00
Whitehall #6115, bowl, vegetable; oval, w/handles, 10½"....$35.00
Whitehall #6115, bowl, vegetable; 8½"...............$42.50
Whitehall #6115, plate, dinner...........................$18.00
Whitehall #6115, platter, oval, w/handles, 16"....$75.00

Miscellaneous

Ashtray, cigarette & matches on brown, 4 rests, M-in-wreath mark, 4¼" sq..$90.00
Ashtray, harlequin figure seated at side, multicolor lustre, M-in-wreath mark, 5", $450 to.....................$550.00
Bowl, nappy, floral on white w/gold, 1 pierced gold handle, M-in-wreath mark, 6½".........................$45.00
Bowl, river scenic on yellow, gold handles, M-in-wreath mark, 7".$60.00
Candlesticks, floral on blue mottle w/cobalt & gold, sq, footed, M-in-wreath mark, 9", pr.....................$260.00
Candy jar, river reserve & band on gold lustre, M-in-wreath mark, 6½"..$225.00
Chamberstick, floral band on orange lustre, M-in-wreath mark, 4¾"..$100.00
Condensed milk container, Deco floral w/gold, M-in-wreath mark, 5¼", +tray.......................................$160.00
Egg cup, fruit compote & gold on white, M-in-wreath mark, 3½"... $45.00

Humidor, green mark, 5½", $275.00. (Photo courtesy Joan Van Patten)

Humidor, horse within horseshoe in relief, brown tones, M-in-wreath mark, 7"..$575.00
Jam jar, blue & gold lustre, rose finial, M-in-wreath mark, 5¼", w/ spoon & tray......................................$80.00
Lemon dish, lemons & leaves, tan lustre rim, M-in-wreath mark, 5¾"..$40.00
Mustard jar, floral, blue on white w/gold, M-in-wreath mark, 3½", w/undertray..................................$40.00

Plate, sandwich; river scenic, center handle, M-in-wreath mark, 8" **$65.00**

Spooner, river scenic w/red-roofed cottage, M-in-wreath mark, 8" L **$70.00**

Toast rack, blue lustre w/bird finial, M-in-wreath mark, 5½" L . **$125.00**

Vase, jack-in-pulpit; river scenic, M-in-wreath mark, 7¾" .. **$200.00**

Vase, Wedgwood type, white flowers on blue, w/handles, Komaru mark, 9½" **$475.00**

Wall pocket, musician w/wide ruffled collar on lustre, M-in-wreath mark, 6" **$300.00**

Novelty Radios

Novelty radios come in an unimaginable variety of shapes and sizes from advertising and product shapes to character forms, vehicles, and anything else the manufacturer might dream up. For information on these new, fun collectibles read *Schroeder's Collectible Toys, Antique to Modern* (Collector Books).

Alf, rectangular w/image on front, NMIP **$75.00**

Annie & Sandie, red & white plastic, 1980s, NMIB **$75.00**

Batman, bust figure, 1973, NMIB **$35.00**

Blinking elephant, blue with green and rose ribbon, 6½", form $15.00 to $25.00. (Photo courtesy Bunis and Breed)

Bozo the Clown, 1970s, head & shoulders form, NM, EX .. **$50.00**

Bugs Bunny, w/sing-along microphone, finger points to dial, AM, VG **$50.00**

Bullwinkle, 1969, 12", NM **$150.00**

Cap 'n Crunch, model #39, Isis, NM+ **$45.00**

Charlie Tuna, w/clamp for handlebar, AM, 1970s, EX **$65.00**

Dick Tracy, Creative Creations, 1970s, wristband type, AM, EX **$225.00**

Fonz Jukebox, AM, G **$20.00**

Globe, hard plastic, 6 transistors, Peerless, 1970s, 8½", NM .. **$55.00**

Hopalong Cassidy, red plastic case, lasso antenna, 4½x8x4", NM **$995.00**

Incredible Hulk, Marvel Comics, 1978, 7", M **$75.00**

King Kong, Amico, 1986, 13", M **$35.00**

Masters of the Universe, mouth moves w/music, 5½", EX+ . **$50.00**

McDonald's Big Mac, GE, sm, EX **$60.00**

Mighty Mouse on cheese wedge, Vanity Fair/Viacom International, 1978, 5", M **$150.00**

Mork From Ork Eggship, Concept 2000, 1979, MIB **$35.00**

Pac Man, w/headphones, NM **$50.00**

Popeye, plastic head figure, battery operated, Hong Kong, 1960, 6½", EXIB **$75.00**

Power Rangers, Micro Games of America, 6", NM **$25.00**

Radio Shack, red plastic lettering, AM, Tandy Corporation, 1979, 4x6¾x1¾", EX **$38.00**

Raggedy Ann & Andy, Bobbs-Merrill/Hong Kong, 1975, 8x7", NM+ **$50.00**

Rambo, headband style, ear-phone only unit, Talbot Toys, from $30.00 to $40.00. (Photo courtesy Bunis and Breed)

Rambo, Talbot Toys, w/headphones, EX **$40.00**

Rolls Royce car, side-mounted spare tires are on/off switch & dial, plastic, Hong Kong, EX **$28.00**

R2-D2 Robot, figural, Kenner, AM, MIB **$150.00**

Scooby Doo, brown head w/green collar & red tongue hanging out of his mouth, 1972, NM+ **$30.00**

Sinclair Gas Pump, Dino logo, AM, 1960s, EX **$40.00**

Smurfs, blue & white plastic image of Smurf singing, white tuner w/black musical note, w/belt clip, Nasta, '82, 3x5", EX **$15.00**

Snoopy Doghouse, plastic, Determined, 1970s, 6x4", NMIB . **$55.00**

Snoopy wearing headphones, 3-D, Determined, 1970s, MIB... **$150.00**

Snow White & the Seven Dwarfs, Emerson, 1938, 8x8", VG . **$500.00**

Superman from waist up, transistor, 1970s, EX+ **$50.00**

Yogi Bear, Hanna-Barbera/Markson, NM+ **$125.00**

Zany perfume bottle, AM, Avon, Hong Kong, 1979, EX **$40.00**

Novelty Telephones

Novelty telephones modeled after products or advertising items are popular with collectors — so are those that are character related. For further information we recommend *Schroeder's Collectible Toys, Antique to Modern* (Collector Books).

Alvin (Alvin & the Chipmunks), 1984, MIB......................**$50.00**
Bart Simpson, Columbia Tel-Com, 1990s, MIB.................**$35.00**
Beetle Bailey, plastic figure in dark green fatigues, white rectangular base, Com VUI, 1982, 10", MIB **$65.00**
Cabbage Patch Girl, 1980s, EX, from $65 to.......................**$75.00**
Crest Sparkle, MIB, from $50 to **$75.00**
Ghostbusters, white ghost inside red circle, receiver across center, Remco, 1987, EX **$20.00**
Keebler Elf, NM, from $60 to **$70.00**
Kermit the Frog, AT&T/Henson, 1980s, EXIB................**$100.00**
M&M Candy, talking w/red & green figures sitting by M&M dial, blue figure holds up yellow receiver, MIB **$50.00**
Mickey Mouse, American Telecommunications Corp, 1976, VG+..**$75.00**
Mickey Mouse, Western Electric, 1976, EX......................**$175.00**
Oscar Mayer Weiner, EX..**$65.00**
Power Rangers, NM..**$25.00**
Roy Rogers, plastic wall-type, 1950s, 9x9", EX..................**$50.00**
R2-D2 (Star Wars), top spins when phone rings, 12" **$35.00**

Shoe, ca. 1980s, $30.00.

Snoopy & Woodstock, touch-tone, Am Telephone Corp, 1976, EX..**$100.00**
Strawberry Shortcake, M...**$55.00**
Superman, ATE, 1979, MIB..**$950.00**
Ziggy, 1989, MIB **$75.00**

Occupied Japan Collectibles

Some items produced in Japan during the period from the end of WWII until the occupation ended in 1952 were marked Occupied Japan. No doubt much of the ware from this era was marked sim-ply Japan, since obviously the 'Occupied' term caused considerable resentment among the Japanese people, and they were understandably reluctant to use the mark. So even though you may find identical items marked simply Japan or Made in Japan, only those with the more limited Occupied Japan mark are evaluated here.

Assume that the items described below are ceramic unless another material is mentioned.

Newsletter: *The Upside Down World of an O.J. Collector*
The Occupied Japan Club
c/o Florence Archambault
29 Freeborn St., Newport, RI 02840-1821
Information requires SASE.

Figurine, bird on tree stump, 7⅜", from $35.00 to $40.00. (Photo courtesy Gene and Cathy Florence)

Ashtray, baseball glove, metal **$15.00**
Ashtray, peacock decor in center, metal................................**$10.00**
Bank, elephant trumpeting, white w/floral decor **$35.00**
Bell, chef w/rolling pin, 3" **$35.00**
Book, printed in Occupied Japan, from $25 to....................**$30.00**
Bowl, fruit decor, lattice edge, 5½" **$17.50**
Bowl, soup; Livonia (Dogwood), 8⅞" **$9.00**
Box, dragon (ornate) decor, w/lid, metal, crown mark, 4x7" ..**$27.50**
Box, piano form, silver-tone metal w/red velvet liner **$25.00**
Butter pat, cottage decor, T-in-circle mark **$12.50**
Cigarette box, bobbing bird picks up cigarette, wooden.......**$50.00**
Cigarette lighter, camel sitting, metal, embossed mark on base . **$25.00**
Cookie jar, cottage shape, T-in-circle mark.........................**$75.00**
Creamer, iris decor, sm...**$12.50**
Crumb pan, metal, embossed NY scene, from $10 to.........**$20.00**
Cup & saucer, thatch house by river scene.........................**$17.50**
Cup & saucer, white w/vining floral decor, Merit **$20.00**
Dinnerware, complete set for 12, same as for 4 +3 platters & serving bowl..**$500.00**
Dinnerware, complete set for 6, same as for 4 +gravy boat & plat-ter **$250.00**

Dinnerware set, complete set for 4, w/3 sizes of plates, creamer & sugar bowl, cereal/soup bowls **$200.00**

Dinnerware set, Sango China, floral pattern & rim, serves 4 .. **$200.00**

Doll, baby in snowsuit, celluloid w/painted details, from $45 to **$55.00**

Egg cup, plain white w/gold middle & rim band................**$12.50**

Figurine, angel w/mandolin, 6⅜" **$35.00**

Figurine, ballerina in net dress, 5¾" **$40.00**

Figurine, cat w/tail up over arched back, sm **$6.00**

Figurine, Dutch peasant couple, detailed paint, 8¼", pr **$75.00**

Figurine, girl w/teddy bear in basket, 5⅜"........................**$25.00**

Figurine, Indian maiden standing, 4¼" **$15.00**

Figurine, lion roaring, celluloid..**$20.00**

Figurine, spaniel-type dog, seated, 4⅜", from $20 to **$25.00**

Fish dish, brown & blue, glossy, sm **$12.50**

Incense burner, elephant, white w/gold trim, 2½"..............**$20.00**

Mug, elephant w/trunk forming handle, brown, 4¾" **$20.00**

Pencil holder, dog figure..**$10.00**

Planter, Cupid on sled, bisque, paper label, 5" **$45.00**

Planter, duck w/cart, 3x5", from $6 to..................................**$7.50**

Planter, elf w/tulip pot, sm **$20.00**

Plaque, Dutch boy w/2 baskets, chalkware, 7½" **$25.00**

Salt & pepper shakers, clown on drum, pr...........................**$40.00**

Salt & pepper shakers, penguin, metal, pr...........................**$20.00**

Shelf sitter, boy holding hat, 5¼".......................................**$20.00**

Sugar bowl, windmill shape, w/lid, 3⅞" **$20.00**

Teapot, floral w/draping ivy, gold trim...............................**$40.00**

Teapot, ribbed stoneware ball form w/bamboo handle.........**$30.00**

Tray, lobster in center, 3-part **$40.00**

Vase, urn; embossed grapes, embossed mark **$15.00**

Wall pocket, man & lady in alcoves lower baskets, 7x5", from $40 to **$45.00**

Old MacDonald's Farm

This is a wonderful line of novelty kitchenware items fashioned as the family and the animals that live on Old MacDonald's Farm has been popular with collectors for quite sometime, and prices are astronomical, though they seem to have stabilized, at least for now.

These things were made by the Regal China Company, who also made some of the Little Red Riding Hood items that are so collectible, as well as figural cookie jars, 'hugger' salt and pepper shakers, and decanters.

Butter dish, cow's head..**$135.00**

Canister, cereal, coffee; med, ea, from $225 to..................**$245.00**

Canister, pretzels, peanuts, popcorn, chips, tidbits; lg, ea, from $270 to **$315.00**

Canister, salt, sugar, tea; med, ea from $110 to..................**$135.00**

Canister, soap, cookies; lg, ea from $315 to **$375.00**

Cookie barn **$175.00**

Creamer, rooster, from $65 to..**$75.00**

Grease jar, pig, from $110 to...**$135.00**

Pitcher, milk; from $180 to...**$200.00**

Salt & pepper shakers, boy & girl, pr.................................**$75.00**

Salt & pepper shakers, churn, gold trim, pr **$100.00**

Salt & pepper shakers, feed sack w/sheep, pr from $80 to..**$110.00**

Spice jar, assorted lids, sm, ea from $110 to......................**$135.00**

Sugar bowl, hen **$85.00**

Teapot, duck's head...**$200.00**

Canister, flour; from $225.00 to $245.00.

Paint-By-Numbers Pictures

If you were a child in the 1950s, you probably remember the paint-by-number sets designed to appeal to the the budding artists in all of us. The results were sometimes quite spectacular (if you could tolerate the strong oily smell of the paints long enough to finish your project), and today these 'works of art' are being sought out by those who enjoy the 'retro' look in their home's decor. Large seascapes, mountain scenes, portraits of nudes, and specific breeds of horses and dogs are especially popular. Unless noted othewise, our values are for framed pictures in at least near mint condition.

Bears in autumn scene, snow-capped mountain beyond, eagle soaring above, 12x16" **$70.00**

Blue herons (2) in water scene w/much foliage & water lily, 16x12" **$60.00**

Classical maiden & child embrace, 20x16" **$60.00**

Cockatoo pr among jungle leaves, 18x24" **$100.00**

Collie dog & puppy among grasses w/sky beyond, 16x12" ..**$42.50**

Cowboy on bucking bronco in Western desert scene, 12½x9½"..**$52.50**

Crane & 2 babies in water scene, trees beyond, 17x13" **$65.00**

Emmett Kelly (clown), Craftmaster Oil Painting Set, complete w/2 16x12" paintings, unused 1961, EXIB.......................**$55.00**

Fish caught on line causing huge splash of water, 10x8" **$55.00**

Flowering tree beside lake w/2 swans, dated 1969, 19x11" ..**$48.00**

Goldilocks & 3 bears in bedroom scene, 12x16" **$48.00**

Horse's head, foliage from tree above, 9½x7", pr..................**$75.00**

Incredible Hulk #1, Hasbro, 1982, MIB............................**$70.00**

Lighthouse & beached boat along shore, 11½x17" **$40.00**

Macaws (2) of varied colors on leafy branches, 10x14", pr...**$70.00**

Mexican adobe mission w/figures in foreground & lg interesting tree, 12x16"...**$50.00**

Mona Lisa, 24x18"...**$45.00**

Pansies in bright colors on brown table beside billowing curtain, 15x19"...**$45.00**

Parisian street scene w/street gas lamps burning, much color & activity, 11¾x15¾"...**$40.00**

Parrots (2) perched on limbs of flowering tree w/ocean beyond, 23x19"...**$65.00**

Peacocks in Oriental landscape, 19x23"...........................**$120.00**

Red-pink roses in green vase beside flowing curtain, 20x16"...**$42.50**

Spiderman, 2 8x10" pictures, 6 paints, 1977, MIB (sealed)...**$52.50**

Stallion standing by tree, horse & colt prancing, scenic landscape, 12x16", pr..**$72.50**

Stallions (2) running in rocky landscape, other horses beyond, 18x24"...**$50.00**

Tropical palm trees beside water, mountains beyond, 10x8".....**$35.00**

Tropical scene w/palms, hut, mountains & water, 1960s, 16x12", pr...**$90.00**

Tropical sunset scene w/water, palms, mountains, 14x10", pr..**$55.00**

WWI fighter biplane in sky, 10x11½", pr............................**$48.00**

2 scenes: Asian lady on bridge in landscape; pagoda in landscape, 9x12", pr...**$75.00**

Paper Dolls

One of the earliest producers of paper dolls was Raphael Tuck of England, who distributed many of their dolls in the United States in the late 1800s. Advertising companies used them to promote their products, and some were often included in the pages of leading ladies' magazines.

But over the years, the most common paper dolls have been those printed on the covers of a book containing their clothes on the inside pages. These were initiated during the 1920s and because they were inexpensive, they retained their popularity even during the Depression years. They peaked in the 1940s, but with the advent of television in the 1950s, children began to loose interest. Be sure to check old boxes and trunks in your attic; you just may find some!

But what's really exciting right now are those from more recent years — celebrity dolls from television shows like 'The Brady Bunch' or 'The Waltons,' the skinny English model Twiggy, and movie stars like Rock Hudson and Debbie Reynolds. Unless otherwise noted, our values are for paper dolls in mint, uncut, original condition. Just remember that cut sets (even if all original components are still there) are worth only about half as much. Damaged sets or those with missing pieces should be priced accordingly.

If you'd like to learn more about them, we recommend *20th Century Paper Dolls, Price Guide to Lowe & Whitman Paper Dolls,* and *Price Guide to Saalfield and Merrill Paper Dolls* by Mary Young. Other references: *Schroeder's Collectible Toys, Antique to Modern,* and *Paper Dolls of the 1960s, 1970s, and 1980s* by Carol Nichols.

Advisor: Mary Young (See Directory, Paper Dolls)

Annette, Whitman #1971, 1960.....................................**$75.00**

Annie Oakley, Whitman #2056, 1955.............................**$75.00**

Army Nurse & Doctor, Merrill #3425, 1942, from $100 to..**$125.00**

Baby Beans & Pets, Whitman #1950, 1978.....................**$12.00**

Baby Nancy, Whitman #966, 1935.................................**$75.00**

Betty Bo-Peep/Billy Boy Blue, Lowe #1043, 1942..............**$75.00**

Betty Grable, Whitman #962, 1946.................................**$200.00**

Bionic Woman, Stafford Pemberyton (European), 1978, $25.00. (Photo courtesy Greg Davis and Bill Morgan)

Blondie, Whitman #975, 1943.......................................**$150.00**

Buffy, Whitman #1985, 1969..**$35.00**

Charlie Chaplin & Paulette Goddard, Saalfield #2356, 1941...**$300.00**

Cinderella, Saalfield #2590, 1950.................................**$75.00**

Clothes Crazy, Lowe #1046, 1945.................................**$35.00**

Cowboys & Indians, Lowe #2104, 1961, standups.............**$15.00**

Debbie Reynolds, Whitman #1178, 1953.........................**$125.00**

Doris Day Doll, Whitman #1977, 1957...........................**$100.00**

Dy-Dee Baby Doll, Whitman #969, 1938.........................**$125.00**

Elly May, Watkins-Strathmore #1819A, 1963....................**$50.00**

Fashion Previews, Lowe #1246, 1949.............................**$40.00**

Flying Nun, Saalfield #5121, 1968.................................**$65.00**

Golden Girl, Merrill #1543, 1953...................................**$75.00**

Grace Kelly, Whitman #2049, 1955................................**$125.00**

Gulliver's Travels, Saalfield #1261, 1939.........................**$125.00**

High School Dolls, Merrill #1551, 1948, from $75 to......**$100.00**

Honey Hill Bunch, Whitman #1976-1, 1977, from $10 to..**$18.00**

Joan's Wedding, Whitman #990, 1942.............................**$75.00**

Josie & the Pussycats, Whitman #1982, 1971, EX..............**$30.00**

Laugh-In Party, Saalfield #6045, 1969, from $40 to...........**$65.00**

Linda Darnell, Saalfield #1584, 1953.............................**$100.00**

Little Friends From History, Rand McNally #186, 1936.....**$40.00**

Lucy, Whitman #1963, 1964, from $65 to.........................**$85.00**

Magic Mindy, Whitman #1991, 1970..............................**$15.00**

Mary Poppins, Whitman #1977, 1973, from $25 to **$45.00**
Mother & Daughter, Saalfield #1330, 1962......................... **$25.00**
Movie Starlets, Whitman #960, 1946 .... **$150.00**
My Baby Book, Whitman #1011, 1942.................................. **$50.00**
Nanny & the Professor, Saalfield #1213, 1970..................... **$50.00**
Patty Duke, Whitman #4775, 1965.................................... **$50.00**
Penny's Party, Lowe #4207, 1952.................................... **$40.00**
Pippi Longstockings, Whitman #4390/7409, 1976 .... **$25.00**
Punky Brewster, Golden #1532, 1986, from $5 to **$10.00**
Shari Lewis & Her Puppets, Saalfield #6060, 1960, from $50
    to... **$65.00**
Shirley Temple Dolls & Dresses, Saalfield #2112, 1934.....**$250.00**
Slumber Party, Merrill #4854, 1943, from $65 to............... **$90.00**
Square Dance, Lowe #2707, 1957 .... **$20.00**
Sunshine Family, Whitman #1980, 1977 .... **$12.00**
Sweetie Pie, Lowe #2482, 1958.. **$25.00**
Tammy & Pepper, Whitman #1997, 1965, from $60 to...... **$75.00**
Tender Love 'n Kisses, Whitman #1944-1, 1978 .... **$15.00**
That Girl, Saalfield #1351, 1967, from $45 to **$75.00**
Tony Hair-Do Dress-Up Dolls, Lowe #1251, 1951 .... **$75.00**
Turnabout Dolls, Lowe #1025, 1943 .... **$50.00**
TV Tap Stars, Lowe #990, 1952 .... **$35.00**
Wedding Dolls, Whitman #1953, 1958, from $60 to.......... **$85.00**
Winnie the Pooh, Whitman #1977-24, 1980, from $25 to . **$30.00**

Magic Mary Jane, Milton Bradley #4010-3, 1975, from $10.00 to $25.00. (Photo courtesy Carol Nichols)

Pencil Sharpeners

The whittling process of sharpening pencils with pocketknives was replaced by mechanical means in the 1880s. By the turn of the century, many ingenious desk-type sharpeners had been developed. Small pencil sharpeners designed for the purse or pocket were produced in the 1890s. The typical design consisted of a small steel tube containing a cutting blade which could be adjusted by screws. Mass-produced novelty pencil sharpeners became popular in the late 1920s. The most detailed figurals were made in Germany. These German sharpeners that originally sold for less than a dollar are now considered highly collectible!

Disney and other character pencil sharpeners have been produced in Catalin, plastic, ceramic, and rubber. Novelty battery-operated pencil sharpeners can also be found. For over 50 years pencil sharpeners have been used as advertising giveaways — from Baker's Chocolates and Coca-Cola's metal figurals to the plastic 'Marshmallow Man' distributed by McDonald's. As long as we have pencils, new pencil sharpeners will be produced, much to the delight of collectors.

Advisors: Phil Helley; Martha Hughes (See Directory, Pencil Sharpeners)

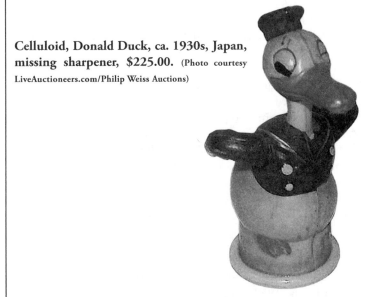

Celluloid, Donald Duck, ca. 1930s, Japan, missing sharpener, $225.00. (Photo courtesy LiveAuctioneers.com/Philip Weiss Auctions)

Aluminum, rocket w/#51 in circle on side, Germany, 5" **$80.00**
Bakelite, Donald Duck decal on butterscotch disk, Walt Disney,
    1" **$75.00**
Bakelite, Dopey decal on butterscotch figural shape, WD Ent,
    1¾" **$70.00**
Bakelite, Dumbo decal on red elephant form....................... **$45.00**
Bakelite, Pete (dog) decal in brass frame on butterscotch octagon,
    1920s **$60.00**
Bakelite, Pinocchio decal on butterscotch figural shape, 2x1" .. **$50.00**
Bakelite, Popeye decal on butterscotch figural shape, King Features
    Syndicate, 1929 .... **$75.00**
Bakelite, Remember Pearl Harbor & battleship decal on marbleized
    disk shape, 1" dia.. **$60.00**
Bakelite, Scottie dog, butterscotch figural shape, 1½x1⅝"....**$25.00**
Bakelite, Scottie dog, green figural shape w/rhinestone eye ..**$35.00**
Bakelite, Snow White decal on red figural shape **$50.00**
Bakelite, US Army Tank decal on green tank shape **$60.00**
Cast iron, elephant holding white sectioned globe, multicolor paint,
    1¾x1½" **$55.00**
Celluloid, elephant on base, white, Made in Japan............. **$165.00**

Celluloid, pelican, white w/orange beak, Made in Japan **$130.00**
Celluloid, penguin on metal base, Made in Japan **$135.00**
Metal, Baker's Chocolate maid serving cocoa, multicolor paint, Reg US Pat Off...**$40.00**
Metal, Great Dane's head, enameled, 1¾" **$55.00**

Metal, old-fashioned car, $10.00. (Photo courtesy LiveAuctioneers. com/O.P.M. Auctions, Ltd.)

Metal, old-time car w/3 windows ea side, Japan, 2" L, VG ..**$40.00**
Metal, potbellied stove, 3½" **$8.00**
Metal, racecar, worn gold paint, Unis France, 1⅞"............**$110.00**
Metal, sadiron, gold-tone paint, Made in Hong Kong, 2⅛".**$24.00**
Plastic, mummy's head, green, ABC products..., NY, 2¾"....**$10.00**
Pot metal, coal-burning stove, dark copper paint, 2¾".........**$17.50**
Pot metal, fireplace hearth, copper paint, Hong Kong, 3x2¼" ..**$12.00**
Pot metal, Golden Eagle slot machine, Hong Kong, 2½x2".**$12.00**
Tin, globe on stand, multicolor litho, Germany, 2" **$40.00**

Pennsbury Pottery

From the 1950s throughout the 1960s, this pottery was sold in gift stores and souvenir shops along the Pennsylvania Turnpike. It was produced in Morrisville, Pennsylvania, by Henry and Lee Below. Much of the ware was hand painted in multicolor on caramel backgrounds, though some pieces were made in blue and white. Most of the time, themes centered around Amish people, barbershop singers, roosters, hex signs, and folksy mottos.

Much of the ware is marked, and if you're in the Pennsylvania/ New Jersey area, you'll find lots of it. It's fairly prevalent in the Midwest as well and can still sometimes be found at bargain prices.

Advisor: Shirley Graff (See Directory, Pennsbury)

Ashtray, Rooster, 4" **$20.00**
Bowl, Dutch Talk, 9" **$85.00**
Bowl, Hex, 9" **$40.00**
Bowl, pretzel; Gay Ninety, 12x8" **$95.00**
Bowl, Rooster, 9" **$45.00**
Bread plate, Sheaves of Wheat, oval or round **$40.00**
Cake stand, Amish, 4½x11½" **$85.00**
Candy dish, Folkart, heart shape..**$25.00**
Canister, Hex, Flour, 7½" **$110.00**

Chip & dip, Folkart..**$80.00**
Coaster, Fisherman, 4½", set of 4................................**$80.00**
Coffeepot, Folkart, 2-cup, 6½" **$25.00**
Cookie jar, Folkart **$100.00**
Cup & saucer, Folkart..**$12.00**
Figurine, Audubon's Warbler, #122, 4" **$160.00**
Figurine, March Wren, #106, 6½" **$120.00**

Figurine, rooster, dark blue and white, 12", $200.00. (Photo courtesy LiveAuctioneers.com/ Morphy Auctions)

Mug, beer; Fisherman **$45.00**
Mug, beverage; Rooster, 5" **$20.00**
Mug, coffee; Amish, 3¼" **$22.00**
Pie plate, Rooster, 9" **$40.00**
Pitcher, Delft Toleware, blue, 5" **$55.00**

Pitcher, E Pluribus Unum, eagle, 6½", from $30.00 to $35.00.

Pitcher, Tulip, 3-qt, 9¾"..**$45.00**
Plaque, boy & girl, 6" **$40.00**

Plaque, Charles W Morgan, ship decoration, 11x8".............**$110.00**
Plaque, eagle, #P214, 22" **$125.00**
Plaque, Iron Horse Ramble, Reading Railroad, 1960, 7¼x5¼" ..**$60.00**
Plaque, Pea Hen, 6" dia **$40.00**
Plaque, river steamboat, 13½x10¼" **$160.00**
Plaque, Walking to Homestead, 6"..**$40.00**
Plate, bread; Give Us This Day Our Daily Bread, 9x6"........**$40.00**
Plate, Neshaminy Woods, 11½" **$120.00**
Plate, Rooster, 8"..**$18.00**
Plate, Treetops Christmas, 1961 ....**$25.00**
Platter, Rooster, 11" **$48.00**
Powder jar, Rooster **$65.00**
Relish tray, Rooster, 14½x11½"..**$85.00**
Sugar bowl, Amish man & lady, 4½"......................................**$20.00**
Tureen, Rooster, w/ladle nook..**$120.00**
Wall pocket, cowboy, from $75 to **$95.00**

Pepsi-Cola

People have been enjoying Pepsi-Cola since before the turn of the century. Various logos have been registered over the years; the familiar oval was first used in the early 1940s. At about the same time, the two 'dots' between the words Pepsi and Cola became one, though more recent items may carry the double-dot logo as well, especially when they're designed to be reminiscent of the old ones. The bottle cap logo came along in 1943 and with variations was used through the early 1960s.

Though there are expensive rarities, most items are still reasonable, since collectors are just now beginning to discover how fascinating this line of advertising memorabilia can be. There are three books in the series called *Pepsi-Cola Collectibles*, written by Bill Vehling and Michael Hunt, which we highly recommend. Another good reference is *Introduction to Pepsi Collecting* by Bob Stoddard. More information can be found in *Antique and Collectible Advertising Memorabilia* and *Collectible Soda Pop Memorabilia*, both by B.J. Summers (Collector Books). In the listings that follow, values are for items in at near mint to mint condition unless noted otherwise.

Advisor: Craig Stifter (See Directory, Soda Pop Memorabilia)

Club: Pepsi-Cola Collectors Club
Newsletter: *Pepsi-Cola Collectors Club Express*
Bob Stoddard, Editor
P.O. Box 817
Claremont, CA 91711
Send SASE for information
www.pepsicolacollectorsclub.com

Bicycle, Columbia, Catch That Spirit, blue, lady's 10-speed w/hand brakes, ca 1970, EX **$175.00**
Bottle opener, cast brass w/Pepsi-Cola impressed in handle, old patina, 5¼" **$48.00**
Bottle opener, metal w/white Bakelite handle, red advertising, 1940s **$6.00**
Button, Pepsi-Cola More Bounce to the Ounce, printed metal, Philadelphia Badge Co, 9" dia, VG...............................**$72.50**

Carton, decaled wood, Buy Pepsi Cola, old-style bottles on ends, zinc trim, ca 1935, 11x8½x6" **$125.00**
Clock, bottle cap in center of dial, concave glass bezel, chrome base, electric tabletop model, 8½", EX **$170.00**
Clock, Say Pepsi Please, electric, streamlined look, lights up, metal frame, rectangular, 16" H **$50.00**
Clock, Say Pepsi Please, lights up, 1960s, 13x13", EX **$360.00**

Clock, Swihart Products, 15" diameter, EX, $425.00. (Photo courtesy LiveAuctioneers.com/Morphy Auctions)

Clock, Think Young - Say Pepsi Please!, bottle cap on yellow, convex glass front, electric, 14½" dia, EX **$575.00**
Cooler, Pepsi-Cola, white logo on turquoise blue, picnic size w/bail handle, G..**$85.00**
License plate, Pepsi-2, New York, VG **$36.00**
Menu board, Have a Pepsi & bottle cap atop blackboard, self-framed tin, 30x19½", EX...**$85.00**
Menu board, Say Pepsi Please, self-framed metal w/blackboard, 30x19½", from $30 to **$50.00**

Menu board, St. Thomas Metals Sign Co., 27x19", EX, $185.00. (Photo courtesy LiveAuctioneers.com/Morphy Auctions)

Pencil, mechanical; floating bottle in center, 1960s..............**$15.00**

Radio, bottle form, repaired base, non-working, 23½x8" **$85.00**

Sign, bottle cap, double-dot logo, celluloid over cardboard, ca 1945, 9", EX...**$175.00**

Sign, bottle cap, painted steel, some rust & oxidation, 18½" dia, G..**$85.00**

Sign, bottle cap, self-framed tin, light surface rust, 31" dia, G...**$300.00**

Sign, bottle cap & bottle, embossed tin, 48x18", EX.........**$395.00**

Sign, Drink & bottle cap on yellow, embossed tin, 1956, 30½x26½", EX **$145.00**

Sign, Drink Pepsi-Cola on metal bottle cap, red neon, 1960s, 30" **$480.00**

Sign, Drink Pepsi-Cola We Deliver, double-dot logo on bottle cap, plastic standup w/easel back, 12x9", EX **$360.00**

Sign, flange; bottle cap, painted steel, 14" dia, EX.............**$395.00**

Sign, girl in red holding bottle glass w/double-dot logo, printed cardboard, Redmond, in gold wood frame, 30" dia, EX.....**$525.00**

Sign, Good! Good! Good!, 5¢ Pepsi-Cola, comic cop w/bottle, double-dot logo, painted steel, 14x10", VG................**$135.00**

Sign, Have a Pepsi & bottle cap, plastic, fits #956 vending machine, ca 1960, 8½x13½", EX..**$45.00**

Sign, Pete & Pepsi (comic cops) w/6 bottles in carton marked 6 Bottles 25¢, cardboard die-cut standup, 14x22" **$120.00**

Sign, Say Pepsi Please, full glass & logo, molded plastic, 8½x12" **$125.00**

Sign, Say Pepsi Please & bottle cap on yellow, embossed tin, 11½x31", EX+ **$150.00**

Sign, Say Pepsi Please & logo on yellow, painted steel, scattered oxidation, 30x26½", G **$85.00**

Sign, Take Home Pepsi & bottle cap, plastic, ca 1950s, 12x15½", EX **$35.00**

Sign, 5¢ Pepsi-Cola 5¢, double-dot logo, red, white & blue, embossed tin, 10x30", EX...**$350.00**

Thermometer, bottle cap at base on yellow-painted tin, Say Pepsi Please, 27x7¼", VG...**$100.00**

Thermometer, Buy Pepsi-Cola, double-dot logo, embossed tin, minor repaint, 27x7¼", VG.......................................**$180.00**

Thermometer, Drink Pepsi-Cola Ice Cold, red, white & blue, Pam, 1950s, 12" dia, EX...**$660.00**

Thermometer, Pepsi-Cola Any Weather, bottle cap on top, white-painted cast iron, weathered, 26x8" **$130.00**

Thermometer, Say Pepsi Please, round dial on pressed tin, sq, 9x9" **$42.50**

Thermometer, Say Pepsi Please on yellow, logo at bottom, embossed tin, 1969, 28x7¼", EX.......................................**$100.00**

Toy truck, Nylint #5500, metal, w/accessories, 16", MIB ..**$600.00**

Tray, Enjoy Pepsi-Cola Hits the Spot, double-dot logo, red, white & blue on tin, 10½x14", EX...**$265.00**

Perfume Bottles

Here's an area of bottle collecting that has come into its own. Commercial bottles, as you can see from our listings, are very popular. Their values are based on several factors. For instance, when you assess a bottle, you'll need to note: is it sealed or full, does it have its original label, and is the original package or box present.

Figural bottles are interesting as well, especially the ceramic ones with tiny regal crowns as their stoppers. Unless otherwise noted, our values are for empty examples in at least near mint condition. See also Czechoslovakia.

Advisor: Monsen & Baer (See Directory, Perfume Bottles)

Club: International Perfume Bottle Association (IPBA)
Susan Arthur, Membership Secretary
295 E. Swedsford Rd. PMB 185
Wayne, PA 19087
Membership: $45 USA or $50 Canada
IPBA_membership@verison.net
www.perfumebottles.org

Houbigant, Chantilly, introduced in 1940, from $45.00 to $60.00. (Photo courtesy Jane Flanagan)

Art Deco atomizer, green coralene w/enameled daisies, missing bulb, nickel-plated brass top, 4¾" **$85.00**

Avon, Hawaiian White Ginger, clear pig w/green ball cap, 1965, 2¼", from $20 to..**$30.00**

Avon, Occur, clear bulbous form w/scalloped foot, frosted stopper, 1963, 3¾x1⅛", from $35 to **$40.00**

Balenciaga, Le Dix, heavy crystal w/mushroom stopper, ca 1956, 3¼x2¼", from $70 to **$90.00**

Berdoues, unknown scene, squat ribbed form w/plastic cap, 1940s-50s, 3¼x1½", from $35 to..**$45.00**

Boucheron, Jaiper, clear form inspired by Nauratan bracelet, blue cap, ca 1994, 3⅞x1½"..**$25.00**

Bourjois, Evening in Paris, cobalt blue w/gold cap, ca 1929, 4½x1¼", from $20 to **$25.00**

Caron, Fete des Roses, clear w/gold enameling in sqs, label on bottom, 4⅛" **$140.00**

Caron, Fleurs de Rocaille, clear w/straight shoulders, ground stopper w/bouquet under glass, 1930s, 2¾", $50 to **$65.00**

Carven, Robe d'un Soir, crystal block form w/gold neck, silver label, ca 1947, 3⅛", M in presentation box, $50 to **$100.00**

Charbert, Breathless, clear heart shape w/decorative lines, fan stopper, 3", in pink & gold box..**$100.00**

Christian Dior, Poison, dark amethyst w/clear stopper, gold lettering, 1985, 3¾x1½", from $50 to **$60.00**

Corday, Zigane, clear violin shape w/gold enameling, 3", M in pink satin-lined box **$245.00**

Coty, Chypre, clear w/sloped shoulders, round gold label near top, frosted stopper, 4½" **$140.00**

D'Orsay, Intoxication, clear pleated star-like shape w/gold label, white cord at neck, 5", NMIB **$75.00**

D'Orsay, Toujours Fidele (Always Faithful), clear octagon w/ball stopper, 2½", NMIB **$115.00**

Des Reg US Patent Office, clear swirling ball form w/embossed waves, fish stopper, 1942, from $75 to **$150.00**

DeVilbiss, amber ginger jar shape w/etched pine needles & gold enameling, atomizer insert, ca 1937, 6¼" **$400.00**

DeVilbiss, clear crystal w/cut florals on 4 sides, w/gold-tone atomizer attachment, 7¼" **$70.00**

DeVilbiss, orange w/black Deco design, black button stopper w/long dauber, 4¾" **$150.00**

DeVilbiss, pink octagon w/gold outlines, pink button stopper w/dauber, 4¼" **$125.00**

Elizabeth Taylor, Passion, amethyst, refillable, 1987, 3⅞", in satin pouch w/mink collar, MIB, from $75 to.....................**$100.00**

Estee Lauder, Cinnabar, white opaque w/black enameled geometric flower, 1978, ¾x1", from $35 to.............................**$50.00**

Evyan, Most Precious, heart-shaped lay-down type w/gold screw-on cap, introduced in 1947, still sold, 2¼", from $25 to **$35.00**

Forvil, Mimosa, clear & frosted cylinder w/stylized daisies, brown patination, R Lalique, 4" **$485.00**

Georgio of Beverly Hills, Giorgio, clear w/gold lettering, 1981, from $50 to **$75.00**

Germaine Monteil, Fleur Savage, clear w/gold lettering, ball stopper, 1953, 2⅞x½", from $60 to **$75.00**

Gourielli, Something Blue, clear w/molded heart-shaped medallion of smiling Cupid in center, 3¼" **$750.00**

Guerlain, Shalimar, clear shouldered form w/gold label, rose-bud stopper, 4½", MIB **$60.00**

Guerlain, Shalimar eau-de-toilet spray, refillable, blue & white print, refillable, late 1960s, 6½", from $25 to......................**$35.00**

Hattie Carnegie, Perfume No 7, head & shoulders, clear glass w/gold, ca 1938, 2½", in grass cloth box **$435.00**

Helen Pessl, Little Lady Toiletries, plastic girl figural w/painted details, ca 1944, 7" **$35.00**

Helena Rubenstein, Barynia, clear hexagonal form w/cube stopper, gold enameling, 3¼", NMIB **$70.00**

Helena Rubenstein, Gala Performance, clear dancer figural, hands aloft, 5¾"..**$400.00**

Houbigant, Le Parfume Ideal, clear w/gold label, sq sides, 3¾", in floral box..**$70.00**

Houbigant, Parfume Presence, clear pleated form w/button stopper, 3½", green moire box **$175.00**

Jacques Griffe, Grilou, clear sq shape w/white enameling, 2½", M in red satin-lined box **$25.00**

Jeanne Lanvin, Arpege, clear bulbous body w/2 gold figures, gold raspberry stopper, 3½" **$250.00**

Jergens, Memories of Paris, paper label on clear Deco form, plastic cap, 1931, 2½x1½", from $20 to **$25.00**

John Robert Powers, Ose, clear shouldered form w/monogram stopper, ca 1959, 3¾x⅞", from $50 to **$100.00**

Jovan, Sculptura, frosted lady's torso, atomizer, 6", MIB....**$100.00**

Lander, Jasmin, frosted lady figural, upper half is stopper w/cork, label on bottom, 4"...**$175.00**

Lander, Spice Bouquet, clear squat form w/Bakelite fan-type cap w/nudes, late 1930s-early 1940s, 3⅞", from $80 to.......**$100.00**

Lazell's, Carnation Pink, clear hexagon w/faceted ball stopper, paper label, 6", NMIB...**$70.00**

Legrain, Promenade a Paris, frosted lady figural, partial label near feet, 8½"...**$200.00**

Lucien LeLong, Opening Night, clear shouldered form, ca 1954, 1⅞x1⅜", from $35 to **$50.00**

Lucky Tiger, Never-Tel, clear shouldered form w/black plastic cap, 1940s-50s, from $15 to **$25.00**

Maison Lalique, Glycines, frosted w/embossed wisteria vines, sq sides, 4¾"..**$375.00**

Marilyn Miglan, Pheromone, green shell shape w/gold top & green tassle, late 1990s, from $20 to **$30.00**

Mary Dunhill, Flowers of Devonshire, clear w/embossed ribs & gold beads, silver label, 2⅜", in floral box.........................**$125.00**

Nanette, Devon Violets, yellow w/embossed tulips, reddish plastic stopper, colorful label, 2⅜" **$215.00**

Neiman Marcus, NM, clear triangular form w/stopper, ca 1950, 2½x1½", from $75 to **$100.00**

Nina Ricci, eau de Coeur Joie, clear canteen shape w/ball stopper, gold label, signed Lalique, 6½" **$105.00**

Prince Alexis N Gagarin, blue w/gold decor, crown & coat of arms, golden double-eagle stopper, 1935, from $150 to.......**$250.00**

Prince Matchabelli, Stradavari, clear & frosted crown w/stopper, 4"...**$150.00**

Prince Matchabelli, Wind Song, miniature, from $25.00 to $40.00.

Prince Obolenski, Creedo, clear sq column w/3 steps at base, gold crown screw-on cap, 1937, 5⅜x1⅞", from $80 to **$150.00**

Saks Fifth Avenue, clear & frosted, 3-sided w/geometrics & gold lining, gold-tone metal atomizer, 7⅜" **$165.00**

Schiaparelli, Sleeping, clear candle figural w/red flame stopper, label at base, 5½" **$300.00**

Suzanne, Secret de Suzanne, clear abstract lady figural (plump), gold label, clear stopper, 5", from $30 to............**$45.00**

Woodbury, unknown scent, clear Deco form w/maker's mark on base, ca 1941, from $35 to **$45.00**

Worth, Je Reviens, smoky blue flattened round form w/turquoise opaque stopper, 3¾", MIB............**$140.00**

Wrisley, Muguet, clear shell form w/white cap, 1940s, from $50 to **$60.00**

Pez Candy Dispensers

Though Pez candy has been around since the late 1920s, the dispensers that we all remember as children weren't introduced until the 1950s. Each had the head of a certain character — a Mexican, a doctor, Santa Claus, an animal, or perhaps a comic book hero. It's hard to determine the age of some of these, but if yours have tabs or 'feet' on the bottom so they can stand up, they were made in the last 10 years. Though early on, collectors focused on this feature to evaluate their finds, now it's simply the character's head that's important to them. Some have variations in color and design, both of which can greatly affect value.

Condition is important; watch out for broken or missing parts. If a Pez is not in mint condition, most are worthless. Original packaging can add to the value, particularly if it is one that came out on a blister card. If the card has special graphics or information, this is especially true. Early figures were sometimes sold in boxes, but these are hard to find. Nowadays you'll see them offered 'mint in package,' sometimes at premium prices. But most intense Pez collectors say that those cellophane bags add very little if any to the value.

For more information, refer to *A Pictorial Guide to Plastic Candy Dispensers Featuring Pez* by David Welch; *Schroeder's Collectible Toys, Antique to Modern* (Collector Books); and *Collecting Toys #10* by Richard O'Brien.

Advisor: Richard Belyski (See Directory, Pez)

Newsletter: *Pez Collector's News*
Richard Belyski, Editor
P.O. Box 14956
Surfside Beach, SC 29587
peznews@juno.com
www.pezcollectorsnews.com

Angel, no feet............**$65.00**
Baloo, w/feet............**$30.00**
Baseball Glove, no feet............**$150.00**
Batman, w/cape, no feet............**$125.00**
Bozo, die-cut, no feet............**$150.00**
Bugs Bunny, no feet............**$15.00**
Captain American, no feet............**$90.00**

Charlie Brown, w/tongue & feet............**$20.00**
Chick in Egg, no feet............**$15.00**
Clown w/Collar, no feet............**$60.00**
Cool Cat, w/feet............**$65.00**

Cow, from $80.00 to $90.00.

Creature From the Black Lagoon, no feet............**$300.00**
Crocodile, no feet............**$95.00**
Daniel Boone, no feet............**$175.00**
Doctor, no feet............**$200.00**
Donald Duck, die-cut, no feet............**$150.00**
Fireman, no feet............**$80.00**
Fisherman, gr, no feet............**$185.00**
Foghorn Leghorn, w/feet............**$65.00**

Giraffe, $125.00.

Girl, yellow hair, w/feet............**$3.00**

Goofy, no feet $15.00
Green Hornet, 1960s, from $200 to $250.00
Hulk, dark green, no feet $40.00
Indian, whistle head, w/feet $20.00
Indian Chief, yellow headdress, no feet $90.00
Jiminy Cricket, no feet $175.00
Joker (Batman), soft head, no feet $175.00
Knight, no feet $250.00
Koala, whistle head, w/feet $40.00
Lamb, whistle head, w/feet $20.00
Mary Poppins, no feet $500.00
Mexican, no feet $200.00
Mowgli, no feet $30.00
Mr Ugly, no feet $45.00
Nurse, no feet $175.00
Olive Oyl, no feet $200.00
Panda, die-cut eyes, no feet $20.00
Parrot, whistle head, w/feet $6.00
Peter Pan, no feet $50.00
Pink Panther, w/feet $5.00
Pirate, no feet $65.00
Policeman, no feet $60.00
Psychedelic Eye, no feet $350.00
Raven, yellow beak, no feet $70.00

Ringmaster, $350.00.

Rooster, whistle head, w/feet $35.00
Rudolph, no feet $50.00
Scrooge McDuck, no feet $35.00
Scrooge McDuck, w/feet $6.00
Smurf or Smurfette, w/feet, ea $5.00
Space Trooper Robot, full body, no feet $300.00
Spaceman, no feet $125.00
Spider-Man, no feet, from $10 to $15.00
Spider-Man, w/feet, from $1 to $3.00
Teenage Mutant Ninja Turtles, 8 different, w/feet, ea from $1
  to $3.00

Thumper, no copyright, w/feet $50.00
Tiger, whistle head, w/feet... $6.00
Tweety Bird, no feet $15.00
Tyke, w/feet $15.00
Uncle Sam, no feet $175.00
Wile E Coyote, w/feet $50.00
Winnie the Pooh, w/feet $75.00
Witch, 3-pc, no feet $15.00
Woodstock, painted feathers, w/feet $15.00

Pfaltzgraff Pottery

Pfaltzgraff has operated in Pennsylvania since the early 1800s making redware at first, then stoneware crocks and jugs, yellow ware and spongeware in the 1920s, artware and kitchenware in the 1930s, and stoneware kitchen items through the hard years of the 1940s. In 1950 they developed their first line of dinnerware, called Gourmet Royale (known in later years as simply Gourmet). It was a high-gloss line of solid color accented at the rims with a band of frothy white, similar to lines made later by McCoy, Hull, Harker, and many other companies. Although it also came in pink, it was the dark brown that became so popular. Today these brown stoneware lines have captured the interest of young collectors as well as the more seasoned, and they all contain more than enough unusual items to make the hunt a bit of a challenge and loads of fun.

The success of Gourmet was just the inspiration that was needed to initiate the production of the many dinnerware lines that have become the backbone of the Pfaltzgraff company.

A giftware line called Muggsy was designed in the late 1940s. It consisted of items such as comic character mugs, ashtrays, bottle stoppers, children's dishes, a pretzel jar, and a cookie jar. All of the characters were given names. It was very successful and continued in production until 1960. The older versions have protruding features, while the later ones were simply painted on.

Village, an almond-glazed line with a folksy, brown stenciled tulip decoration, is now discontinued (though a few pieces are being made now and then for collectors). It's a varied line with many wonderful, useful pieces, and besides the dinnerware itself, the company catalogs carried illustrations of matching glassware, metal items, copper accessories, and linens.

Several dinnerware lines are featured in our listings. To calculate the values of Yorktowne, Heritage, and Folk Art items not listed below, use Village prices.

For further information, we recommend *Pfaltzgraff, America's Potter,* by David A. Walsh and Polly Stetler, published in conjunction with the Historical Society of York County, York, Pennsylvania.

Note: Pfaltzgraff dinnerware prices have been tremendously affected by eBay. Because it is still so readily available on the secondary market, eBay always has hundreds of items up for auction, and many times they are sold at no reserve. This plus the fact that the dinnerware is heavy and shipping charges can mount up fast has caused values to decline, though interest is still evident.

Christmas Heritage, bowl, salad; 1½x8½" $15.00
Christmas Heritage, bowl, soup/cereal; #009, 5½", from $6 to . $8.00
Christmas Heritage, bowl, vegetable; 12-sided oval, 11x8¼" . $18.00

Christmas Heritage, butter tub, from $25 to.........................$35.00
Christmas Heritage, cake plate, pedestal foot, 12" $25.00
Christmas Heritage, casserole, w/lid, 2-qt $40.00

Christmas Heritage, cheese tray, 10½", from $15.00 to $20.00.

Christmas Heritage, coffee carafe, thermal, 13" $22.50
Christmas Heritage, coffee cup, 4".................................$5.00
Christmas Heritage, cookie jar, from $28 to $35.00
Christmas Heritage, dish, oblong w/lobed rim, 8¼x6".........$20.00
Christmas Heritage, gravy boat & undertray........................$20.00
Christmas Heritage, lamp, green shade, 14".......................$30.00
Christmas Heritage, ornament, angel, 1987, MIB, from $22 to.$30.00
Christmas Heritage, pedestal mug, #290, 10-oz....................$5.00
Christmas Heritage, pie plate, 9" $22.00
Christmas Heritage, pitcher, tankard, 7½" $25.00
Christmas Heritage, pitcher, 5¾" $20.00
Christmas Heritage, plate, dinner; #004, 10", from $6 to....$10.00
Christmas Heritage, platter, 16¼x12" $25.00
Christmas Heritage, salt & pepper shakers, lighthouse form, pr..$15.00
Christmas Heritage, star dish, tree & toy train, 1994, 10½",
  MIB..$32.00
Christmas Heritage, teapot, lighthouse shape, 8½" $20.00
Christmas Heritage, tumbler, glass w/red & green decor, 5½", set of
  10, from $25 to...$35.00
Christmas Heritage, 2-tier dish (10" & 8" plates), MIB.......$20.00
Gourmet Royale, ashtray, #69, 10".................................$15.00
Gourmet Royale, ashtray, #321, 7¾", from $9 to..................$12.00
Gourmet Royale, ashtray, #618, 10" $25.00
Gourmet Royale, ashtray, skillet shape, #AT32, 9", from $10 to.$12.00
Gourmet Royale, baker, #323, 9½", from $12 to.................$15.00
Gourmet Royale, baker, oval, #321, 7½", from $8 to...........$10.00
Gourmet Royale, baking dish, 12x7".............................$35.00
Gourmet Royale, bean pot, #11-1, 1-qt, from $10 to $12.00
Gourmet Royale, bean pot, #11-2, 2-qt, from $18 to $22.00
Gourmet Royale, bean pot, #11-3, 3-qt $25.00
Gourmet Royale, bean pot, #11-4, 4-qt $35.00
Gourmet Royale, bean pot, #30, w/lid, lg, from $30 to $40.00
Gourmet Royale, bean-pot warming stand.........................$10.00
Gourmet Royale, bowl, berry; 4⅝".................................$6.00
Gourmet Royale, bowl, cereal; #934SR, 5½" $5.00
Gourmet Royale, bowl, mixing; 6", from $8 to $12.00

Gourmet Royale, bowl, mixing; 8", from $10 to.................$15.00
Gourmet Royale, bowl, mixing; 10", from $20 to...............$25.00
Gourmet Royale, bowl, mixing; 14", from $70 to...............$70.00
Gourmet Royale, bowl, oval, #241, 7x10", from $10 to $12.00
Gourmet Royale, bowl, salad; tapered sides, 10", from $10 to..$14.00
Gourmet Royale, bowl, soup; 2¼x7¼", from $6 to...............$9.00
Gourmet Royale, bowl, spaghetti; shallow, #219, 14", from $15
  to $20.00
Gourmet Royale, bowl, vegetable; divided, #341 ....$14.00
Gourmet Royale, bowl, vegetable; 8⅛"............................$12.50
Gourmet Royale, butter dish, stick type, #394, ¼-lb, from $9
  to $12.00
Gourmet Royale, butter warmer, stick handle, double spout, #301,
  9-oz, w/stand, from $12 to $14.00
Gourmet Royale, candleholders, saucer type w/finger ring, pr .$20.00
Gourmet Royale, candleholders, tall, w/finger ring, 6", pr from $35
  to $45.00
Gourmet Royale, canister set, 4-pc, from $50 to.................$60.00
Gourmet Royale, casserole, hen on nest, 2-qt, from $50 to..$60.00
Gourmet Royale, casserole, stick handle, #399, individual, 12-oz,
  from $7 to $8.50
Gourmet Royale, casserole, stick handle, 1-qt, from $9 to ...$12.00
Gourmet Royale, casserole, stick handle, 2-qt, from $12 to .$15.00
Gourmet Royale, casserole, stick handle, 3-qt, from $15 to .$20.00
Gourmet Royale, casserole, stick handle, 4-qt, from $25 to .$35.00
Gourmet Royale, casserole-warming stand $7.00
Gourmet Royale, chafing dish w/handles, lid & stand, 8x9", from
  $25 to $30.00
Gourmet Royale, cheese shaker, bulbous, 5¾", from $12 to..$15.00
Gourmet Royale, chip 'n dip, #306, 2-pc set, w/stand, from $22
  to $25.00
Gourmet Royale, chip 'n dip, molded in 1 pc, #311, 12" $20.00
Gourmet Royale, coffeepot, 9"...................................$25.00
Gourmet Royale, cookie jar, bean-pot shape w/handles, 6½x7½" ..$40.00
Gourmet Royale, corn dish, 3x8½", from $6 to....................$8.00
Gourmet Royale, creamer, #382...................................$4.00
Gourmet Royale, cruet, coffeepot shape, fill through spout, 4", from
  $12 to $15.00
Gourmet Royale, cup & saucer $5.00
Gourmet Royale, cup & saucer, demitasse $18.00
Gourmet Royale, egg plate, center handle, 8x12"................$20.00
Gourmet Royale, egg/relish tray, 15" L $30.00
Gourmet Royale, goblet, 5¼".....................................$9.00
Gourmet Royale, gravy boat, 2-spout, #426, lg, w/underplate, from
  $9 to $14.00
Gourmet Royale, gravy boat w/stick handle, 2-spout, from $8
  to $12.00
Gourmet Royale, jug, #384, 32-oz, from $18 to $25.00
Gourmet Royale, jug, #385, 48-oz, from $20 to $25.00
Gourmet Royale, jug, ice lip, #386, from $25 to $32.00
Gourmet Royale, ladle, sm, from $12 to $15.00
Gourmet Royale, ladle, 3½" dia bowl, w/11" handle, from $18
  to $20.00
Gourmet Royale, lazy Susan, 3 sections w/center bowl, #308, 14",
  from $22 to $30.00
Gourmet Royale, lazy Susan, 5-part, molded in 1 pc, #220, 11",
  from $15 to $20.00

Gourmet Royale, mug, #286, 18-oz.........................**$20.00**

Gourmet Royale, mug, #391, 12-oz.........................**$7.00**

Gourmet Royale, mug, #392, 16-oz.........................**$12.00**

Gourmet Royale, pie plate, #7016, 9½", from $10 to.........**$15.00**

Gourmet Royale, pitcher (9½") & bowl (3x12")................**$35.00**

Gourmet Royale, plate, bread; #528, 12" L....................**$20.00**

Gourmet Royale, plate, dinner; #88R, from $7 to..............**$10.00**

Gourmet Royale, plate, egg; holds 12 halves, center metal handle, 7¾x12½", from $15 to.........................**$20.00**

Gourmet Royale, plate, Give Us This Day..., 10"................**$45.00**

Gourmet Royale, plate, grill; 3-section, #87, 11", from $9 to..**$12.00**

Gourmet Royale, plate, luncheon; 8½", from $6 to.............**$8.00**

Gourmet Royale, plate, salad; 6¾", from $2 to.................**$4.00**

Gourmet Royale, plate, steak; 12", from $10 to................**$15.00**

Gourmet Royale, platter, #16, 14".............................**$25.00**

Gourmet Royale, platter, #17, 16".............................**$35.00**

Gourmet Royale, platter, #20, 14".............................**$25.00**

Gourmet Royale, rarebit w/lug hdls, oval, #330, 11"...........**$9.00**

Gourmet Royale, relish dish, #265, 5x10", from $12 to........**$15.00**

Gourmet Royale, roaster, oval, #325, 14", from $18 to........**$25.00**

Gourmet Royale, roaster, oval, #326, 16", from $25 to........**$35.00**

Gourmet Royale, salt & pepper shakers, #317/#318, 4½", pr..**$7.00**

Gourmet Royale, salt & pepper shakers, bell shape, pr from $15 to.........................**$20.00**

Gourmet Royale, scoop, any size, from $8 to..................**$12.00**

Gourmet Royale, shirred egg dish, #360, 6", from $7 to......**$10.00**

Gourmet Royale, souffle dish, #393, 5-qt, w/underplate, from $50 to.........................**$60.00**

Gourmet Royale, soup & sandwich, rectangular 12" tray w/cup well & soup cup, from $12 to.........................**$18.00**

Gourmet Royale, sugar bowl, w/handles.......................**$6.00**

Gourmet Royale, teapot, #381, 6-cup, from $18 to............**$22.00**

Gourmet Royale, teapot, #701, 6x10"..........................**$25.00**

Gourmet Royale, toby mug, 6¼", from $30 to..................**$38.00**

Gourmet Royale, tray, serving; round, 4-section, center handle, #397, from $15 to.........................**$18.00**

Gourmet Royale, tray, tidbit; 2-tier, from $10 to.............**$14.00**

Gourmet Royale, tray, 3-part, 15½" L..........................**$20.00**

Heritage, bowl, batter; 3-qt...................................**$24.00**

Heritage, bowl, soup; wide rim, 8½", from $8 to..............**$10.00**

Heritage, butter dish, #002-028..............................**$6.00**

Heritage, butter tub, #065, w/lid, 3x5½".....................**$30.00**

Heritage, cake plate, pedestal, 6½x12½".....................**$75.00**

Heritage, cake/serving plate, #002-529, 11¼" dia............**$9.00**

Heritage, canisters, set of 4, from $55 to....................**$60.00**

Heritage, casserole, straight sides, glass lid, 3-qt, 9¾".......**$28.00**

Heritage, coffee/teapot, 13½"................................**$40.00**

Heritage, condiment server, 3 cups in wood & wire stand...**$30.00**

Heritage, cookie jar, canister shape, 9½"....................**$30.00**

Heritage, corn dish, 8¼" L...................................**$5.00**

Heritage, cup & saucer, #002-002, 9-oz......................**$3.00**

Heritage, fondue pot w/handle, #522H, 7x11½", w/warmer stand.........................**$32.00**

Heritage, gravy boat, w/undertray, from $15 to..............**$20.00**

Heritage, honey pot, w/lid & drizzler........................**$40.00**

Heritage, ice bucket, dome lid, #650.........................**$50.00**

Heritage, lazy Susan, 4-pc, wooden base, from $55 to........**$75.00**

Heritage, mug, footed.......................................**$7.00**

Heritage, napkin rings, set of 4, MIB.........................**$22.00**

Heritage, pitcher, water; 10¼"................................**$35.00**

Heritage, pitcher, 5"...**$17.50**

Heritage, pitcher, 5", w/#772 bowl............................**$25.00**

Heritage, pitcher, water; 10", from $20.00 to $30.00.

Heritage, plate, chop; 12½"...................................**$25.00**

Heritage, plate, dinner; 10¼", from $7 to.....................**$8.00**

Heritage, plate, egg; holds 12 halves, 12½" L, from $40 to..**$50.00**

Heritage, plate, salad; 7", from $3 to.........................**$4.00**

Heritage, platter, 14¼" L.....................................**$16.00**

Heritage, punch bowl, 6 cups & ladle........................**$75.00**

Heritage, quiche dish, 1¾x9".................................**$25.00**

Heritage, salt & pepper shakers w/handle, 5", pr from $20 to.**$30.00**

Heritage, salt crock jar, #560...............................**$35.00**

Heritage, soup tureen, #002-160, 3½-qt, w/ladle & underplate, from $35 to.........................**$45.00**

Heritage, soup tureen, #150, 3½-qt, w/ladle & underplate, from $35 to.........................**$45.00**

Heritage, teapot, lighthouse shape, 8".......................**$32.00**

Heritage, tidbit, 3-tier......................................**$35.00**

Heritage, vase, bud; 6½".....................................**$18.00**

Muggsy, ashtray...**$125.00**

Muggsy, bottle stopper, head, ball shape.....................**$85.00**

Muggsy, canape holder, Carrie, lift-off head pierced for toothpicks, from $125 to.........................**$150.00**

Muggsy, cigarette server.....................................**$95.00**

Muggsy, clothes sprinkler bottle, Myrtle, Black, from $275 to..**$375.00**

Muggsy, clothes sprinkler bottle, Myrtle, white, from $250 to..**$295.00**

Muggsy, cookie jar, character face, minimum value...........**$250.00**

Muggsy, mug, action figure (golfer, fisherman, etc), from $65 to.........................**$85.00**

Muggsy, mug, Black action figure............................**$125.00**

Muggsy, mug, character face.................................**$38.00**

Muggsy, shot mug, character face, ea from $40 to............**$50.00**

Muggsy, tumbler..**$60.00**

Muggsy, utility jar, Handy Harry, hat w/short bill as flat lid.**$150.00**

Planter, donkey, brown drip, common, 10", from $15 to....**$20.00**

Planter, elephant, brown drip, scarce, from $90 to............**$110.00**
Village, baker, oval, #24, 10¼", from $7 to.......................**$10.00**
Village, baker, oval, #240, 7¾", from $6 to.......................**$8.00**
Village, baker, oval, #241, 10"......................................**$10.00**
Village, baker, rectangular, tab handles, #236, 2-qt, from $10 to...**$14.00**
Village, baker, sq, tab handles, #237, 9", from $10 to.........**$14.00**
Village, bean pot, 2½-qt, from $22 to.............................**$28.00**
Village, beverage server, #490, from $18 to......................**$22.00**
Village, bowl, batter; w/spout & handle, 8", from $32 to....**$40.00**
Village, bowl, dough; #462, 8-qt, 7x13", from $40 to.........**$55.00**
Village, bowl, fruit; #008, 5"..**$3.00**
Village, bowl, Kitty..**$45.00**
Village, bowl, mixing; #453, 1-qt, 2-qt, & 3-qt, 3-pc set, from $45 to...**$50.00**
Village, bowl, mixing; enamelware, set of 4 w/lids..............**$50.00**
Village, bowl, onion soup; stick handle..........................**$8.00**
Village, bowl, pasta; 12"...**$50.00**
Village, bowl, rim soup; #012, 8½", from $6 to...................**$8.00**
Village, bowl, serving; #010, 7", from $8 to **$12.00**
Village, bowl, serving; basketweave sides, 2½x9", from $25 to..**$35.00**
Village, bowl, soup/cereal; #009, 6"...............................**$4.00**
Village, bowl, vegetable; #011, 8¾"................................**$12.00**
Village, bowl, vegetable; 2-part, 13x8½"..........................**$25.00**
Village, bowl, vegetable; 3-part, 1½x12x7½".......................**$30.00**
Village, bowl w/handles, 12" L......................................**$26.00**
Village, bread tray, 12"...**$15.00**
Village, butter dish, #028..**$10.00**
Village, candlesticks, pr..**$25.00**
Village, candy dish, rabbit figural..................................**$60.00**
Village, canister, Treats..**$45.00**
Village, canisters, #520, 4-pc set, from $45 to **$55.00**
Village, canisters, wooden w/ceramic oval, sq, set of 4, minimum value..**$200.00**
Village, casserole, #315, w/lid, 2-qt, from $18 to.................**$22.00**
Village, cheese tray, glass dome, round plate, on oval wooden tray, 10x14", from $40 to...**$50.00**
Village, chip & dip set, 2-pc, from $20 to **$30.00**
Village, clock (plate)...**$35.00**
Village, coffee mug, #89F, 10-oz, from $5 to **$8.00**
Village, coffeepot, lighthouse shape, 48-oz, from $20 to......**$25.00**
Village, colander, enamel on metal, footed.......................**$30.00**
Village, cookie jar, #540, 3-qt **$20.00**
Village, cookie jar, glass w/ceramic lid, 10½", from $30 to ..**$35.00**
Village, cooler/drink dispenser, spigot on front, 10x7", from $50 to...**$65.00**
Village, creamer & sugar bowl, #020, from $9 to **$12.00**
Village, cruets, vinegar & oil; pr from $30 to **$40.00**
Village, cup, punch **$5.00**
Village, cup & saucer, #001 & #002................................**$3.50**
Village, flatware, Oneida, service for 4, 20 pcs, from $125 to.**$175.00**
Village, flowerpot, 4½", from $12 to **$15.00**
Village, garlic keeper, 5x4½", from $35 to **$45.00**
Village, gravy boat & saucer, #443, 16-oz, from $12 to.......**$15.00**
Village, ice bucket, metal liner.....................................**$55.00**
Village, ice bucket, wood & copper, 8¾x7½" sq **$50.00**
Village, lazy Susan, 5-pc..**$45.00**

Village, measuring cups, ceramic, 4 on hanging rack **$40.00**
Village, measuring cups, copper, 4 on wooden rack w/pierced copper insert, EX...**$40.00**
Village, mold, heart shape **$42.50**
Village, mug, 10-oz..**$12.00**
Village, onion soup crock, stick handle, #295, sm, from $7 to ..**$9.00**
Village, pedestal mug, #90F, 10-oz..................................**$10.00**
Village, picture frame, 3½x5"...**$38.00**
Village, picture frame w/refrigerator magnet, 2"..................**$15.00**
Village, pie plate, 9½"..**$20.00**
Village, piggy bank..**$25.00**
Village, pitcher, #416, 2-qt, from $20 to **$25.00**
Village, plate, dinner; #004, 10¼", from $3 to **$4.00**
Village, plate, snack; w/indent for cup, 9x12"....................**$15.00**
Village, plate, teddy-bear shape **$55.00**
Village, plate, You Are Special Today, 10½"........................**$70.00**
Village, platter, #016, 14", from $12 to **$18.00**
Village, potpourri jar, 4¾", from $10 to............................**$12.00**
Village, quiche, 9"..**$16.00**
Village, salt & pepper shakers, pr from $10 to **$15.00**
Village, salt box, punched copper w/wooden top **$45.00**

Village, salt crock, from $40.00 to $45.00.

Village, scouring pad holder, high back, 5" W **$32.00**
Village, seafood baker, fish shape, 10½"............................**$45.00**
Village, seafood server, fish shape, w/sauce cup **$50.00**
Village, shell, #243, 3x11x11" w/sm shells, #242, 7-pc set...**$75.00**
Village, soap dish...**$42.00**
Village, soap dispenser, 6"...**$28.00**
Village, soup tureen, #160, w/lid & ladle, 3½-qt, from $40 to .**$45.00**
Village, Sun Tea jar (like drink dispenser w/spigot), glass.....**$35.00**
Village, table light, clear glass chimney on candleholder base, #620, from $12 to...**$14.00**
Village, tape dispenser...**$85.00**
Village, teakettle, 3-qt...**$35.00**
Village, teapot, ball shape w/C handles, 6x11", from $80 to..**$100.00**

Village, teapot, individual, 16-oz..............................$10.00
Village, vase, bud; 5"...$12.00
Village, vase, cylindrical, 7½"...................................$45.00
Village, welcome plaque, oval, 4¾x6¾"...................$30.00

Pie Birds

Pie birds are hollow, china or ceramic kitchen utensils. They date to the 1800s in England, where they were known as pie vents or pie funnels. They are designed to support the upper crust and keep it flaky. They also serve as a steam vent to prevent spill over.

Most have arches on the base and they have one, and *only* one, vent hole on or near the top. There are many new pie birds on both the US and British markets. These are hand painted rather than airbrushed like the older ones.

The Pearl China Co. of East Liverpool, Ohio, first gave pie birds their 'wings.' Prior to the introduction in the late 1920s of an S-neck rooster shape, pie vents were non-figural. They resembled inverted funnels. Funnels which contain certain advertising are the most sought after.

The first bird-shaped pie vent produced in England was designed in 1933 by Clarice Cliff, a blackbird with an orange beak on a white base. The front of the base is imprinted with registry numbers. The bird later carried the name Newport Pottery; more recently it has been marked Midwinter Pottery.

Advisor: Linda Fields (See Directory, Pie Birds)

Newsletter: Pie Birds Unlimited
John LoBello
qps1@earthlink.net
541-994-3007

Donald Duck, identified on side, copyright Walt Disney, $1,000.00.

Aluminum funnel, England $25.00
Bear in green jacket w/hat & shoes, England, 4½".......$55.00

Bird, blue & white on base, Royal Worcester, 2-pc, MIB.....$50.00
Bird, yellow w/pink beak & black eyes, Josef Original, 3", from $35 to $40.00
Bird w/mouth open, arched base, brown, English, 4½".......$88.00
Bird w/thin neck, Scotland, 1972, 4¼", from $75 to..........$90.00
Black cat, red bow & collar, Halloween style, 4¾" $40.00
Black clown holding pie, embossed England on pants, 4½".$45.00
Bugs Bunny, California, 4"....................................$27.00
Chef w/blue coat, white hat, 1930-40s $160.00
Dog in pants & jacket carrying basket, England, 3½".........$50.00
Duck w/long neck, yellow & brown, 1940s-50s, 5"............$75.00
Dutch girl, multipurpose kitchen tool, from $150 to........$195.00

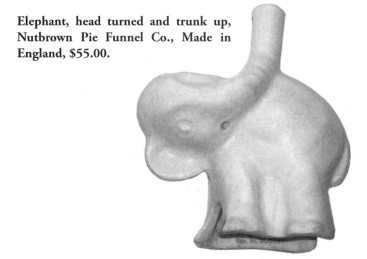

Elephant, head turned and trunk up, Nutbrown Pie Funnel Co., Made in England, $55.00.

Fred the Flower Grater (original hat), dots for eyes, from $65 to $75.00
Funnel, white, unmarked Nutbrown Pie Funnel Co, 1940s, 3"..$25.00
Lilipop Easter bunny, marked Happy Easter CC 95, Cubbard Classic, 4" $55.00
Mammy, red dress, white apron, yellow dots on bandana, Taiwan Import, 4¾" $15.00
Rooster, S-neck, pink, blue & cream, Pearl China, 5¼".......$85.00
Rooster, white w/black, red & yellow details, Marion Drake, 5"...$125.00
Rooster on stump, white, Made in England, 4¾" $45.00
Train engine, black, marked Boyd Special, Boyd Glass, 3½x3¾"...$30.00
Woodpecker on stump, multicolor, California, 6¾"............$36.00
Yankee Blackbird, Made in England, 1950s-60s, 4¼".........$55.00

Pierce, Howard

Howard Pierce studied at the Art Institute of Chicago, California's Pomona College, and the University of Illinois. He married Ellen Van Voorhis of National City, California, who was also to become his business partner. Howard worked alongside William Manker for a short time, and today it is sometimes difficult to tell one artist's work from the other's without first looking at the marks. This is especially true with some of their vases, nut cups, trays, and cups and saucers.

Howard was creative with his designs and selective with his materials. While working as a draftsman at Douglas in Long Beach, California, during World War II, Howard kept his artistic spirit alive by working on weekends in the medium of pewter. The pewter lapel pins he created are considered very desirable by today's collectors and usually sell in the $200.00 to $300.00 range. He dabbled in polyurethane for only a short time as he found he was allergic to it. Today these polyurethane pieces — made nearly exclusively for his immediate family — are scarce and costly. They are extremely lightweight, usually figures of birds on bases. They were hand painted, and many of them have a powdery feel. Howard made a few pieces from aluminum and bronze. Bisque, cement, and Mount St. Helen's ash were also used for a limited number of items. (Be cautious not to confuse Howard's 'textured' items with the Mount St. Helen's ash pieces.) Howard's creativity extended itself to include paper as a workable medium as well, as he often made their own Christmas cards. His love for wildlife was constant throughout his career, and he found porcelain to be the best material to use for wildlife models. As a result, porcelain was used for the vast majority of Pierce's artistic creations.

Howard's earliest mark was probably 'Howard Pierce' in block letters. This was used on metalware (especially the lapel pins), but also can be found on a few very small ceramic animals. After the Pierces moved to Claremont, California, they used this mark: 'Claremont Calif. Howard Pierce,' usually with a stock number. A rubber stamp 'Howard Pierce Porcelains' was used later. Eventually 'Porcelains' was omitted. Not all pieces are marked, especially when part of a two- or three-piece set. As a rule, only the largest item of the set is marked.

In 1992 due to Howard's poor health, he and Ellen destroyed all the molds they had ever created. Later, with his health somewhat improved, he was able to work a few hours a week, creating miniatures of some of his original models and designing new ones as well. These miniatures are marked simply 'Pierce.' Howard Pierce passed away in February 1994.

Advertising dealer's sign, brown, black ink stamp, 2½x6½", from $125 to **$150.00**

Bank, turtle, black w/green shell, black ink stamp, 3x8", from $150 to **$175.00**

Bowl, sunburst, black w/aqua interior, black ink stamp, 2½x7½" **$100.00**

Figurine, arch w/Madonna & Child inside, black ink stamp, 12x3¼" **$160.00**

Figurine, bison, gray w/dark mane & head, unmarked, 9" ..**$175.00**

Figurine, dachshund, brown, black ink stamp, 3¼x10", from $85 to **$100.00**

Figurine, giraffe, gold leaf, unmarked, 14", minimum value ..**$250.00**

Figurine, hippopotamus, blue, black ink stamp, 2½x6½", from $125 to **$150.00**

Figurine, horse, dark brown with speckled mane and tail, 8½x7½", $200.00.
(Photo courtesy Susan Cox)

Figurine, horse standing, white frothy drip over red, 8½x10½" ..**$435.00**

Figurine, male ballet dancer, black ink stamp, 7x3½", from $75 to **$85.00**

Figurine, quail, brown tones, 6x5½" **$35.00**

Figurine, red bird on black rock, black ink stamp, 6x4", from $75 to **$85.00**

Figurine, road runner, speckled brown, green & white, 4¾x12¼x3" **$55.00**

Figurine, skunk, black ink stamp, 5x6", from $80 to **$100.00**

Figurine, Stellar's Jay, blue, white, black & gray, 6½" **$65.00**

Figurine, water bird, white matt over red clay, 13¼", from $60 to **$70.00**

Figurines, llamas, mother & baby, unmarked, 8½x6", 5½x3½", pr **$185.00**

Flowerpot, salmon-colored matt, #81P, 4¼x4¼", from $50 to **$70.00**

Vase, chartreuse high gloss w/bisque fawn & tree, 11½x6", from $85 to **$100.00**

Vase, green w/white fish insert, cornucopia shape, 8x7" **$125.00**

Whistle, bird, black ink stamp, 2¾x2", from $100 to **$125.00**

Pin-Back Buttons

Literally hundreds of thousands of pin-back buttons are available; pick a category and have fun! Most fall into one of three fields —

Figurine, hen and rooster, muted sandstone, 7½", 9½", $120.00 for the pair. (Photo courtesy Jack Chipman)

advertising, political, and personality related, but within these three broad areas are many more specialized groups. Just make sure you buy only those that are undamaged, are still bright and unfaded, and have well-centered designs and properly aligned printing. The older buttons (those from before the 1920s) may be made of celluloid with the paper backing printed with the name of a company or a product.

See also Political.

Advisor: Michael McQuillen (See Directory, Political Memorabilia)

American Legion Baseball Booster, red, white & blue, 1955, 1¾", EX **$135.00**

American Revolution Bicentennial 1776-1976, Liberty Bell, red, white & blue, 3⅜", NM **$12.00**

Batman logo, black on white, 2¼", NM **$6.00**

Champions Cincinnati Reds 1961, red lettering on baseball, 1¾", w/ ribbon, bat & ball on chain, NM **$40.00**

Donald Duck portrait, multicolor, Disneyland, 1960s-70s, 3½", NM..**$10.00**

Ducks Unlimited, 1975, signed Mass, multicolor, 2¼", NM...**$25.00**

Flash, Fastest Man Alive, sent to all who submitted a comic book survey, EX, from $600.00 to $650.00. (Photo courtesy LiveAuctioneers.com/ Morphy Auctions)

Golden Guernsey, black on golden yellow, celluloid, w/insert, EX **$36.00**

Hoffman's Rice Starch, cat licking paw on dark blue, celluloid, ¾", EX **$38.00**

Hopalong Cassidy, black & white portrait on green, ¾", EX..**$35.00**

Hoppy's Favorite Mary Jane Bread, black & white portrait on orange, EX...**$42.50**

I Like Bottled Carbonated Beverages, red & white, 1930s, NM..**$5.00**

It's Christmas Time at Wurzburg, Santa & holly, red, white & green, M...**$22.00**

Live the Triumph Life, red & white, 1960s-70s, 1⅜", NM..**$22.50**

Massey-Harris Co 278, tank in center, red & black on cream, 1¾", VG...**$115.00**

Maxwell in script letters, silver-tone & black, NM..............**$15.00**

Michigan State...Student Tour, Rose Bowl, January 1, 1966, multi-color, 3⅜", EX...**$15.00**

Miller High Life Beer, celluloid, w/Miller girl attachment, 1x3", EX **$65.00**

Milwaukee Braves 1953 Welcome, flags & eagle, red, white & blue, 1⅝", VG **$110.00**

Minnesota Twins, American League Champs 1965, blue lettering over ball scene on white, 3½", EX............................**$130.00**

Popeye, multicolor portrait on white, ⅞", EX **$42.50**

Roger Maris, Yankees, ca. 1960 – 1961, 2⅛", NM, $150.00.
(Photo courtesy LiveAuctioneers.com/Morphy Auctions)

Shoot Peters Shells, shell casing, multicolor on white, FF Pulver, ⅞", VG...**$47.50**

Tom & Jerry Sunbeam, red, white, gray & black, 1950s, 1¼", NM..**$22.50**

Vote for Philip Morris, bellhop calling, multicolor, celluloid, 1", EX **$15.00**

Wear Daisy Rubbers, daisy, multicolor, 1¼", NM...............**$15.00**

Zenith, Marshall-Wells, red, black, gold & white, celluloid, ⅞", EX **$30.00**

7-Up, red, white & green, 3" **$10.00**

Kellogg's Pep Pins

Chances are if you're over 50, you remember them — one in each box of PEP (Kellogg's wheat-flake cereal that was among the first to be vitamin fortified). There were 86 in all, each carrying the full-color image of a character from one of the popular cartoon strips of the day — Maggie and Jiggs, the Winkles, Dagwood and Blondie, Superman, Dick Tracy, and many others. Very few of these cartoons are still in print.

The pins were issued in five sets, the first in 1945, three in 1946, and the last in 1947. They were made in Connecticut by the Crown Bottle Cap Company, and they're marked PEP on the back. You could wear them on your cap, shirt, coat, or the official PEP pin beanie, a orange and white cloth cap made for just that purpose. The Superman pin — he was the only D.C. Comics Inc. character in the group — was included in each set.

Compared to the value of a pin in near mint condition, those that are foxed or faded can be worth as much as 75% less, depending on the extent of the problem.

Andy Gump, EX...**$12.00**

BO Plenty, NM **$30.00**

Corky, NM	$16.00
Dagwood, NM	$30.00
Dick Tracy, NM	$30.00
Don Winslow, MIP	$20.00
Fat Stuff, NM	$15.00
Felix the Cat, NM	$40.00
Flash Gordon, NM	$25.00
Flat Top, NM	$23.00
Goofy, NM	$10.00
Gravel Gertie, NM	$15.00
Harold Teen, NM	$15.00
Inspector, NM	$12.50
Jiggs, NM	$25.00
Judy, NM	$10.00
Kayo, NM	$12.00
Little King, NM	$15.00
Little Moose, NM	$15.00
Maggie, NM	$25.00
Mama de Stross, NM	$30.00
Mama Katzenjammer, NM	$25.00
Mamie, NM	$15.00
Moon Mullins, NM	$10.00
Olive Oyle, NM	$18.00
Orphan Annie, NM	$25.00
Pat Patton, NM	$10.00
Perry Winkle, NM	$15.00
Phantom, NM	$60.00
Pop Jenkins, NM	$15.00
Popeye, NM	$30.00
Rip Winkle, NM	$20.00
Skeezix, NM	$15.00
Smokey Stover, EX	$10.00
Superman, NM	$25.00
Toots, NM	$15.00
Uncle Avery, EX	$20.00
Uncle Walt, NM	$20.00
Uncle Willie, NM	$12.50
Wimpy, NM	$20.00
Winkle Twins, NM	$25.00
Winnie Winkle, NM	$15.00

Pinup Art

Some of the more well-known artists/illustrators in this field are Vargas, Petty, DeVorss, Elvgren, Moran, Ballantyne, Armstrong, and Phillips, and some enthusiasts pick a favorite and concentrate their collections on only his work. From the mid-'30s until well into the '50s, pinup art was extremely popular. As the adage goes, 'Sex sells.' And well it did. You'll find calendars, playing cards, magazines, advertising, and merchandise of all types that depict these unrealistically perfect ladies. Though not all items will be signed, most of these artists have a distinctive, easily identifiable style that you'll soon be able to recognize.

Along with hundreds of other types of collectibles, eBay has lowered the value of pinup art due to flooding the market with online stock. Unless noted otherwise, values listed below are for items in at least near mint condition; consider calendars to be complete with full pads unless noted partial.

Advisor: Denis Jackson (See Directory, Magazines)

Online Newsletter: *The Illustrator Collector's News*
Denis Jackson, Editor
ticn@olypen.com
www.olypen.com/ticn

**Print, Top Partner, Brown and Bigelow, ca. 1950s, 20x16",
$50.00.** (Photo courtesy LiveAuctioneers.com/Michael Ivankovich Antiques & Auction Co., Inc.)

Blotter, girl putting on skates, KO Munson, Brown & Bigelow, late 1940s, 9x4" $20.00
Blotter, Marilyn Monroe w/lg ribbon tied at hip, Earl Moran, lumber company advertising, 1948 calendar, 3½x6" $30.00
Calendar, Artist's Sketch Book, different Fritz Willis girl ea month, spiral bound, 1965, EX $40.00
Calendar, Artist's Sketch Pad, different MacPherson girl ea month, spiral bound, 1940s, 14x9", EX $35.00
Calendar, blond lady in white fur w/ruby necklace & ring, full pad, 1939, 12½x9¼" $60.00
Calendar, different Elvgren girl ea month, Brown & Bigelow, spiral bound, 1967, 9½x7½" $110.00
Calendar, different Petty girl ea month, Esquire, 1955, 11x8⅜", EX w/mailer $70.00
Calendar, different TN Thompson girl ea month, spiral bound, complete, 1953, 11½x8" $35.00
Calendar, different Varga girl ea month, Esquire, 1946, 11⅞x8⅞", EX $70.00
Calendar, different Varga girl ea month, verses by Earl Wilson, 1948, EX $55.00
Calendar, In Reno Nevada It's Harold's Club, nude w/black fan, 1 page remaining on pad, 1944, 17x10¼", in frame $155.00
Calendar, Lady Fair, Deco lady in red & black w/white fur stole, Armstrong, 1942, 22x13", in black & silver Deco frame ..$125.00

344

Calendar, Mariquita, flamenco dancer w/swirling skirt, Eggleston, partial pad, 1935, 15¼x9½", EX....................................**$55.00**

Calendar, Miss Sylvania girl seated on suitcase, Gil Elvgren, partial pad, 1959, 33x16", EX+ **$135.00**

Calendar, Miss Sylvania in blue gown waves, lit Star of David symbol behind her, 1963, 33x16" **$130.00**

Calendar, Miss Sylvania in open carriage, Elvgren, partial pad, 1960, 33x16", EX..**$85.00**

Calendar, Such a Little Lamb, nude w/lamb held by ribbon, DeVorss, 1940, 24x13", EX..**$90.00**

Calendar print, Beat Those Problems, girl seated w/bongo drums, showing top of black nylons, Elvgren, 1950s, 19x16"...**$85.00**

Calendar print, Lets Make a Date, glamorous lady in black & gold gown, Rolf Armstrong, 1940s, 22½x16", EX.............**$75.00**

Calendar print, Take Your Choice, lovely brunette in jeans lays on straw beside yellow chicks, Rolf Armstrong, 13x18" **$45.00**

Cigarette lighter, girl sitting in sm boat, Zippo, 2005 ....**$40.00**

Cigarette lighter, pinup devil girl in red enameling, COOP Zippo Bradford PA, Made in USA N 02, EX.........................**$50.00**

Cigarette lighter, Winter pinup girl, multicolor enameling on chrome finish, Zippo, 2001 ....**$45.00**

Clock, girl in blue swimsuit & heels stands & holds hand tool, Snap On Tools, battery-operated, 23x11".............................**$50.00**

Clock, Sundrop Cola, sexy girl in cup, Refreshing as a Cup of Coffee!, Pam, 1959, 15x15"..**$275.00**

Motion lamp, Elvgren girls on shade, louvered top, tripod base, 1950s, 15½", EX...**$165.00**

Playing cards, Elvgren girl w/Beach Fashions book, Remembrance Playing Cards, 1940s, MIB (sealed) **$85.00**

Playing cards, girl beside pool holding Jaeger pump in her hand, Jaeger Engineered Equipment, 1940s, 53 cards, MIB ...**$70.00**

Playing cards, Naked Truth King Size, ea card w/different nude, 54 cards, EXIB...**$35.00**

Playing cards, pinup backs, Playboy caricature jokers, double deck, 1968, M in case (sealed) **$15.00**

Playing cards, 53 Vargas Girls, 1940s, 52+2 joker cards, MIB...**$100.00**

Poster, Escort Service, girl in shorts walks terrier, Walt Otto, 1950s, 20x16", EX...**$55.00**

Poster, In Reno It's Harolds Club, topless girl in cowboy boots holds cards, dated 1950, 15x10½", EX.................................**$175.00**

Poster, Moonlight Nymph, nude seated by water, Laurette Patten, 1930s, 33½x20" **$50.00**

Poster, seated nude brunette w/demure expression, eyes cast down, McPherson, early 1940s, 10x7", in 10x8" frame...........**$55.00**

Print, blond reclines in filmy black gown, Petty, ca 1950s, in 14¾x19¾", in wood frame...**$40.00**

Print, Carmen, Spanish girl w/red shawl & black lace fan, R Armstrong, 1940s, 9½x7½" in frame **$40.00**

Print, Corral Cuties, cowgirl & horse, Walt Otto, 20x16", EX...**$50.00**

Print, girl in black bathing suit & white heels turned to show back, George Petty, ca 1950s, in 19¾x14¾" frame.................**$60.00**

Print, girl in white shirt holds windblown scarf, bobbed hair, luminous eyes, E Christy, 1920s-30s, in 19x15" frame **$65.00**

Print, Grace, Deco-style girl in filmy costume, Irene Patten, 1930s, 8x6" **$75.00**

Print, Modern Venus, blond nude stands w/hands behind head, Pearson, 1930s, 15x11", in ornate silver gesso frame...**$150.00**

Print, Oh No!, nude sunbathing, pup pulling towel away from her, Gil Elvgren, ca 1969, 9½x7½" **$45.00**

Print, Sincere, brunette portrait on yellow-orange, Rolf Armstrong, 18¼x14"..**$110.00**

Print, Spanish lady draped in red shawl, Marno Brown, 1930s, 19¼x15¼", in gold frame **$95.00**

Print on canvas, girl in striped dress holds terrier, legs up to reveal tops of black hose, Elvgren, 11x8½" **$45.00**

Sign, Mavis Talcum Powder by Vivaudou, nude Petty girl in swing, die-cut cardboard, easel back, 1940s, 12x9½", EX......**$225.00**

Sign, RC Cola, girl in striped swimsuit on chaise lounge w/bottle, cardboard, late 1940s-50s, 13x17", in black frame......**$110.00**

Steering wheel knob, blond in black lingerie under glass, marked Hollywood, ca 1950, EX...**$50.00**

Playing Cards

Here is another collectible that is inexpensive, easy to display (especially single cards), and very diversified. Among the endless variations are backs that are printed with reproductions of famous paintings and pinup art, carry advertising of all types, and picture tourist attractions and world's fair scenes. Early decks are scarce, but those from the '40s on are usually more attractive anyway, so pick an area that interests you most and have fun! Though they're seldom dated, telephone numbers, zip codes, advertising slogans, and patriotic messages are always helpful indications.

For more information, we recommend *Collecting Playing Cards* by Mark Pickvet (Collector Books).

See also Pinup Art.

Club: American Antique Deck Collectors; 52 Plus Joker Club
Newsletter: *Clear the Decks*
Ron Green, Auctioneer
greeneron@msn.com
www.52plusjoker.org

Pearl Beer, $6.00. (Photo courtesy Mark Pickvet)

Adventure, racehorse & dog backs, Elizabeth Bell, full deck, EX (no box) $60.00

American Airlines DC 7 & eagle logo on gold backs, Congress, MIB (sealed)..$50.00

American Red Cross, red & white backs, Arrco, EXIB.........$32.00

Aristocrat #3 Casino, red backs, w/gold seal on wrapper, MIB (sealed) $55.00

Atwater Kent Radio, sailing ship backs, 52 cards+joker & bridge score cards, ca 1920s, EXIB $60.00

Bonnet Girl on green (or yellow) backs, Whitman Publishing, Gallerie Playing Cards, double deck, MIB $48.00

Contentment, Maxfield Parrish art backs, ca 1928, Congress, ca 1928, EXIB...$195.00

Cowboy on horse & cattle w/rainbow scenic backs, Hoyle, double deck, M in plastic case (sealed) $30.00

Cupid backs, Bicycle 8089, US Playing Card Co, pre-1925, 52 cards (no joker), EX in re-issue box $55.00

Deco-style lady w/shawl on black, red border, 52 cards (no joker), EX $35.00

Delaware Lackawanna & Western Railroad, Phoebe Snow crossing Tunkhannock Viaduct, Brown & Bigelow, double deck, EXIB $300.00

Dionne Quintuplets in basket, w/advertising on aces, Nea Service Inc, 1936, EX $30.00

Dopey dressed in red & green, Walt Disney, complete deck, EX+IB $40.00

Flirtation, Gibson girl-style lady in red on backs, Congress 606, ca 1908, EX in torn box...$200.00

France Royale, kings, queens & personages, Piatnik #2142, double deck w/red & blue backs, MIB $80.00

George VI coronation, Universal Playing Card Co, 1930s, MIB $36.00

Grand Hotel, Point Clear Al, red or green backs, double deck, 1930s-40s, MIB...$35.00

Gucci, red & blue backs w/2 jokers, bridge conversion chart & blank card w/ea (2) deck, MIB $62.50

Horse portrait, Duratone, double deck, 104 cards & 2 jokers, MIB $45.00

Jerry's Nugget Casino, Litho in USA, M 4924, complete deck, MIB $100.00

KEM, geometric backs resemble stained glass, double deck, M in case $55.00

Kitten on pink, Arrco, Admiral Playing Cards, 54 cards, MIB.. $35.00

Kitten peeking from bottom corner of card on blue or pink, Claridge Playing Cards, double deck, EXIB $45.00

La Traviata by Erte, ea card is different, Dunhill of London, double deck, MIB..$80.00

Lone Ranger & Tonto (Clayton Moore & Jay Silverheels) portrait backs, double deck, 1989, MIB (sealed)....................$38.00

NFL football players from the early 1960s on card faces, helmets on backs, complete deck, EX $40.00

Northern Pacific Main Street of the Northwest, 52 cards & 2 special jokers, EXIB $35.00

O-So Beverages O-So Good!, blue & white backs, sealed in clear cello wrapper w/tax stamp, MIB $48.00

Panama Canal scenic backs, ea card w/construction info, sites, ships, etc, 52 cards, +joker & 2 score cards, 1935, MIB $40.00

Panama souvenir, photographic backs, US Playing Cards, 1923, M in slip case..$60.00

Ronald Reagan gilt facsimile signature, sketch of jet & words Air Force One, double deck, M in velvet box (sealed).......$235.00

Southern Railway - Serves the South - Look Ahead Look South, double deck, M in green velvet box w/gold logo...........$40.00

Spirit of 76, Richard Nixon gold facsimile signature & presidential seal on backs, bridge size, M (sealed) $55.00

Tulsamara OK 50th Anniversary Celebration, green & red decks, ea w/54 cards, 1957, EXIB..$40.00

USS Forrestal CVA-59 Carrier, black & white backs, Brown & Bigelow, 54 cards, ca 1955-62, EXIB...........................$55.00

White Pass Yukon Route (railroad), red background, 52 cards, +joker & 2 special cards, EX in VG box $30.00

Woody Woodpecker & Chilly Willy backs, Walter Lantz, double deck, MIB...$35.00

1984 Olympics in Los Angeles, Bicycle, red & blue backs, 2 decks, ea MIB (sealed) $120.00

Political Memorabilia

Political collecting is one of today's fastest-growing hobbies. Between campaign buttons, glassware, paper, and other items, collectors are scrambling to acquire these little pieces of history. Before the turn of the century and the advent of the modern political button, candidates produced ribbons, ferrotypes, stickpins, banners, and many household items to promote their cause. In 1896 the first celluloid (or cello) buttons were used. Cello refers to a process where a paper disc carrying a design is crimped under a piece of celluloid (now acetate) and fastened to a metal button back. In the 1920s the use of lithographed (or litho) buttons was introduced.

Campaigns of the 1930s through today have used both types of buttons. In today's media-hyped world, it is amazing that in addition to TV and radio commercials, candidates still use some of their funding to produce buttons. Bumper stickers, flyers, and novelty items also still abound. Reproductions are sometimes encountered by collectors. Practice and experience are the best tools in order to be aware.

One important factor to remember when pricing buttons is that condition is everything. Buttons with any cracks, stains, or other damage will only sell for a fraction of our suggested values. Listed below are some of the items one is likely to find when scrutinizing today's sales.

For more information about this hobby, we recommend you read Michael McQuillen's monthly column 'Political Parade' in *Antique Week* newspaper.

Advisor: Michael McQuillen (See Directory, Political)

Club: A.P.I.C. (American Political Items Collectors) of Indiana
Michael McQuillen
P.O. Box 50022
Indianapolis, IN 46250-0022
michael@politicalparade.com
www.politicalparade.com

Bandanna, Cleveland/Hendricks, portraits, eagle & vignettes on red, 19x20½", EX **$435.00**

Book, Just a Country Lawyer, Sam Ervin, 1974, EX............**$15.00**

Book, Who's in Charge Here?, satire, Pocket Books, 1962, EX...**$15.00**

Booklet, Barry Goldwater Speaks Out on Issues, 1964, 24-page, VG..**$20.00**

Cane, Gerald R Ford for President, SB Outlaw stamped on handle, 35", NM **$45.00**

Coin, FD Roosevelt memorial, gilt on bronze, EX...............**$20.00**

Compact, I Like Ike, telephone dial, 3½" dia, EX..............**$260.00**

I Told You So, JFK & White House, red, white & blue, 1960, 3½", NM..**$22.50**

Lapel pin, Kennedy 60 on bow of gold-tone PT boat, ½x1¾", EX.**$55.00**

License plate topper, I Like Ike & Eisenhower portrait, tin litho, 4¾x10", EX **$60.00**

Nylons, I Like Ike printed near top of ea stocking, 1950s, MIP..**$25.00**

Pennant, Harry Truman for President, purple, 4½x11½", M..**$55.00**

Pin-back button, America's First Lady Jacqueline Kennedy, portrait, red, white & blue background, celluloid, 3½", NM......**$65.00**

Pin-back button, Bush/Quale '88, white or red letters on blue, 1¾", M **$4.00**

Pin-back button, Carter and Mondale, white on green, 1½", $15.00.

Pin-back button, Elect Reagan in '68 for President, blue letters on white, 1¼", M...**$5.00**

Pin-back button, Franklin D Roosevelt color portrait, celluloid, 9", NM...**$60.00**

Pin-back button, Free Angela & All Political Prisoners, Black lady's portrait on red, 1¾", NM **$135.00**

Pin-back button, Hoover portrait, black & white, celluloid oval, 2⅜x3¼", EX **$460.00**

Pin-back button, John Kennedy, blue & white w/portrait, 3", M..**$16.00**

Pin-back button, Mondale/Ferraro, white on blue w/red & white stripes & white star, 1¾", M..**$4.00**

Pin-back button, Mondale/Ferraro color portrait, Steelworkers Together for..., tin litho, 3½", NM **$85.00**

Pin-back button, Parker/Davis, Uncle Sam's White Elephant, Rooseveltism, elephant, multicolor, cello, 1½", EX.....**$190.00**

Pin-back button, Re-elect Hillary's Husband (Clinton), blue & red letters on white, 2¼", M **$2.50**

Pin-back button, Republican for Kennedy, blue letters on white, celluloid, 1¼", EX...**$48.00**

Pin-back button, Teddy Roosevelt, Stand Pat, portrait & hand holding cards, celluloid, 1¼", EX......................................**$265.00**

Pin-back button, Vote for Our Next President Robert F Kennedy, portrait, multicolor, 1968, 1¾", +ribbon **$70.00**

Pin-back button, Vote Truman & Barkley in '48, 2-color, 1", EX **$100.00**

Pin-back button, Willkie Precinct Worker, red, white & blue, St Louis Button Co, 3", EX **$105.00**

Pin-back button, Win w/Wilson & portrait, multicolor, celluloid, 1¼", NM **$52.50**

Pin-back button, Youth for Kennedy, JFK portrait, tin litho, 4", EX **$175.00**

Pocketknife, Elect George Wallace, 2-blade, 1968, 4" (closed), EX **$32.50**

Pocketknife, Jimmy Carter 1980, 2 stainless blades, Case XX USS, M **$25.00**

Postcard, Goldwater cartoon, 1964 campaign, EX **$30.00**

Postcard, Teddy Roosevelt cartoon w/bull moose out of control, EX..**$55.00**

Poster, America Reagan Country, Ronald Reagan in cowboy hat, 10¼x10", M **$40.00**

Poster, Eisenhower for President, portrait, black & white, 1956, 16x11", NM **$60.00**

Poster, Elect Johnson Vote Democrat, color portrait on red, white & blue, 22x14", EX **$15.00**

Poster, Ford & Dole, both men standing together, 1976, 24¾x15", EX **$30.00**

Poster, Jimmy Carter for President, portrait on green, 1977, 21x12", EX **$40.00**

Poster, Keep Him on the Job, Hoover portrait, black & white, 21½x16", EX **$45.00**

Poster, Kennedy, Robert F Kennedy portrait, 1968, 19x12", NM.**$55.00**

Poster, Kennedy for President, Vote Democratic, portrait on red, white & blue background, 1960s, 12¼x9", EX............**$65.00**

Poster, Nixon for President, portrait, black, white & red, 1968, 21½x14", EX **$23.00**

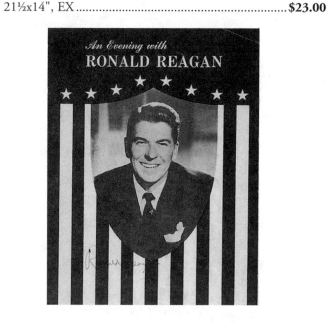

Program, Ronald Regan, Ft. Worth, Texas, 1965, autographed, $225.00. (Photo courtesy LiveAuctioneers.com/Early American History Auctions)

Sign, Vote for Wallace, blue & white litho, 1968, 12¼x24¼", EX ..**$35.00**

T-shirt, Carter for President & peanut character on white, 1970s, M..**$20.00**

Tray, Keep Roosevelt in the White House, White House w/FDR portrait in corner, tin litho, 10½x13", EX.....................**$30.00**

Puzzle, Spiro Agnew, 1970s, 500 pieces, EXIB, $30.00.

Precious Moments

Precious Moments is a line consisting of figurines, picture frames, dolls, plates, and other items, all with inspirational messages. They were created by Samuel J. Butcher and are produced by Enesco Inc. in the Orient. You'll find these in almost every gift store in the country, and some of the earlier, discontinued figurines are becoming very collectible. For more information, we recommend *Collector's Value Guide to Precious Moments by Enesco* (CheckerBee Publishing) and *The Official Precious Moments® Collector's Guide to Figurines* by John and Malinda Bomm (Collector Books).

Always Room for One More, #C-0009, bow & arrow mark ..**$30.00**

Bless This House, E-7164, 1984, MIB...............................**$275.00**

Follow Your Heart, #528080, clef mark, MIB.....................**$25.00**

Friend Is Someone Who Cares, #520632, bow & arrow mark, MIB **$60.00**

From the Beginning, 25th Anniversary limited edition, #110238, crown mark, 6x8", MIB.............................**$140.00**

Fruit of the Spirit Is Love, #52123, butterfly mark **$20.00**

God Blessed Our First Year w/So Much Love & Happiness, E-2854, flower mark...**$35.00**

God Loveth a Cheerful Giver, E-1378, stamped 1977 ....**$350.00**

Growing in Grace, Age 15, #272663, egg mark **$30.00**

His Little Treasure, #PM931, butterfly mark, MIB.............**$30.00**

I Get a Bang Out of You, #12262, heart mark.....................**$45.00**

I Get a Kick Out of You, E-2827, dove mark, MIB.............**$50.00**

I'm Following Jesus, Collectors Club limited edition, #PM-662, 1986, MIB..**$55.00**

In His Time, #PM872, cedar tree mark, MIB.....................**$35.00**

It Is No Secret What God Can Do, Easter Seals limited edition, #531111, 1993, MIB...**$30.00**

Jesus Loves Me, E-1372/G, fish mark **$35.00**

Love One Another, E-1376, dove mark................................**$30.00**

Love One Another, E-13786, sword mark.............................**$45.00**

Loving, #PM932, butterfly mark, MIB................................**$45.00**

Making Spirits Bright, #150118, ship mark.......................**$28.00**

Many Moons in the Same Canoe, Blessum You, flame mark, 1988, from $160.00 to $190.00.

Portrait of Loving, Caring & Sharing, 25th Anniversary Member Exclusive, #108543, crown mark, MIB......................**$315.00**

Seek Ye the Lord, E-9262, cross mark, MIB.........................**$28.00**

September, #110086, flower mark, MIB **$40.00**

Sharing the Good News Together, Members Exclusive, #C0011, MIB..**$25.00**

Spirit Is Willing But the Flesh Is Weak, #100196, vessel mark, MIB..**$60.00**

Tell It to Jesus, #521477, vessel mark, MIB.......................**$30.00**

They Followed the Star, 3 kings on camels, E-5624, dated 1981, tallest: 9", 3-pc set, MIB, from $150 to.....................**$200.00**

We Are All Precious in His Sight, Easter Seals limited edition, 1999, 10", MIB...**$475.00**

Wedding Display, animated bride & groom, plays Wedding March by Meldelsohn, 1996, 18"...**$165.00**

You Are My Happiness, #526185, vessel mark, MIB **$40.00**

You Are Such a Purr-fect Friend, trumpet mark...................**$30.00**

You Are the Rose of His Creation, Easter Seals limited edition, 1994, 9½", MIB **$300.00**

You Are the Type I Love, #523542, vessel mark...................**$30.00**

You Can Always Count on Me, Easter Seals limited edition, #526827, 1995 ....**$25.00**

Princess House Company

The home party plan of Princess House was started in Massachusetts in 1963 by Charlie Collis. His idea was to give women an opportunity to have their own business by being a princess in their house, thus the name for this company. The founder wanted every woman to be able to afford fine glassware. Originally the company purchased glass from other manufacturers; but as they grew, the need developed to make their own. In 1972 they bought the Louis Glass Company of West Virginia.

In 1987 Collis sold his company to Colgate-Palmolive. It became a division of that company but was still allowed to operate under its own name. In 1994 a group of investors bought Princess House from Colgate-Polmolive; they own the company yet today. In order to better focus on the home party plan which had been its primary goal, the company sold the glassmaking division to Glass Works WV in 2000. This company will continue to make glass for Princess House but will also allow the facility to develop a new and greater glass market.

Most Princess House pieces are not marked in the glass — they carry a paper label. The original line of Pets also carries the Princess House label, but animals from the Wonders of the Wild and Crystal Treasures lines are all marked with a PH embossed on the glass itself. This new PH mark will make it easy to identify these pieces on the secondary market.

Heritage is a crystal, cut floral pattern. It was introduced not long after the company started in business. Fantasia is a crystal pressed floral pattern, introduced about 1980. Both lines continue today; new pieces are being added, and old items are continually discontinued.

Advisors: Debbie and Randy Coe (See Directory, Cape Cod)

Animals, Birds, and Fish

Bear, Bernie, Pets collection, #813, 3½", from $20 to.......... **$25.00**
Cat, Pets collection, 3½" **$15.00**
Cougar, Wonders of the Wild, 5¼x6½" **$65.00**
Dolphin, Wonders of the Wild, 6" **$25.00**
Eagle flying, Wonders of the Wild, 7½" **$40.00**
Kitten, Katrina, Pets collection, #811, 3¼" **$12.00**
Lion, Wonders of the Wild, #882, 4½x7", from $40 to **$60.00**
Mouse, Millicent, Pets collection, #882, 3" **$16.00**
Polar bear, Wonders of the Wild, 2¼x2¼" **$42.50**
Puppy, recumbent, Pets collection **$15.00**
Rocking horse, Pets collection, 3x3" **$25.00**
Swan, Pets Collection, 3x4¼" **$20.00**
Trout, Wonders of the Wild, MIB, from $40 to **$48.00**

Fantasia

Baker, #588, 3¼x12¾x8¾", MIB, from $35 to.................... **$45.00**
Baker, w/lid, 4¼x12x8½" **$28.00**
Bowl, salad; #567, 10¾", from $22 to **$25.00**
Butter dish, rectangular, #527, ¼-lb, 8" **$14.50**
Cake plate, domed lid, invert to make punch powl & pedestal... **$85.00**
Casserole, #524, w/lid, 3-qt **$60.00**
Casserole, #5306, w/lid, 6-qt, 6x16x11" **$70.00**
Compote, dessert; footed, #575, 10-oz **$7.00**
Cup & saucer, #515, from $5 to **$6.00**
Deviled egg plate, #591, 10" **$24.00**
Goblet, water; #519, 10½-oz, 7", from $10 to..................... **$15.00**
Mug, #523 .... **$8.00**

Plate, bread & butter; #512, 6", from $4.50 to..................... **$6.00**
Plate, dinner; #511, 10" **$12.00**
Plate, 13" **$20.00**
Tumbler, #545, 12-oz, from $8 to.. **$10.00**

Relish, three-part, #534, 12¼x7", $18.00.

Heritage

Bowl, salad; #441, 5½x10"... **$24.50**
Butter dish, domed lid, #461, 4¾x4½" **$9.50**
Cake plate, domed lid, #076, hostess gift, 8½x9½", from $65 to. **$75.00**
Chip & dip, #41, 11¼".. **$19.50**
Cookie jar **$50.00**
Creamer & sugar bowl, w/lid.. **$25.00**
Decanter **$35.00**
Goblet, bridal flute; #431, 7½-oz, 10", from $10 to **$12.50**
Goblet, cordial; #417, 4⅛"... **$7.00**
Goblet, tulip champagne; #432, 7-oz................................... **$9.50**
Goblet, wine; #420, 6½-oz, from $8.50 to.......................... **$10.00**
Gravy boat, 6½" L **$65.00**
Ice bucket, #522, 5½", MIB **$12.50**
Lamp, ginger jar form w/brass mounts, electric, 13x7", MIB .. **$75.00**
Lamp, hurricane; #428, 2-pc, 11¾", from $20 to **$30.00**
Mayonnaise, 2½x5", w/spoon & 6" underplate.................... **$20.00**
Mug, cappuccino; #580, 14-oz... **$9.50**
Mug, coffee; footed, #504, 10-oz, 5½", from $10 to........... **$12.50**
Mustard jar, w/lid & spoon **$18.00**
Punch bowl set, #584, brandy snifter-shaped bowl, w/12 cups, from
    $55 to.. **$65.00**
Salt & pepper shakers, #471, 4", pr **$10.00**
Straw dispenser, metal lid, 10½", from $55 to **$65.00**
Teapot, #050, hostess gift, from $50 to............................... **$60.00**
Tray, 3-part, 8", 17x8½" **$45.00**
Tumbler, cooler, #4672, 6¼".. **$10.00**
Tumbler, roly poly, 2¼" **$6.00**
Tumbler, 12-oz, 5" **$8.00**
Vase, bud; 4", from $10 to.. **$15.00**
Vase, w/insert, 7½" **$25.00**

Purinton Pottery

With its bold colors, prominent design elements, and unusual shapes, Purinton Pottery is much admired by today's dinnerware collectors.

The company operated in Ohio before it relocated to Pennslvania in 1941. It was founded by Bernard Purington, but it was William H. Blair, brother of Bernard's wife Dorothy, who was responsible for designing most of Purinton's early patterns, in particular Peasant Ware and two of the company's most recognizable patterns, Apple and Intaglio. Peasant Ware was enormously successful; as a result, Purinton was encouraged to expand the pottery. This was accomplished by building a new plant in Shippenville, Pennsylvania. About this time, Bill Blair left Purinton to open his own pottery. Dorothy Purinton assumed the role of designer, and took on the task of training new decorators. However, she was never a paid employee. Once operational in Shippenville, Purinton started full production on their many dinnerware lines.

Purinton's signature pattern was Apple. It features a bold red apple with accents of yellow and brown and two-tone green leaves. Apple (a Blair design) became their bestselling line and was produced throughout the entire life of the pottery. Another top-selling pattern (designed by Dorothy Purinton) was Pennsylvania Dutch featuring stylized hearts and tulips, Other long-term patterns followed, among them the Plaids (Heather — Red, and Normandy — Green) and the Intaglios (Brown, Turquoise, and Caramel). Several short-lived patterns were also produced: Chartreuse, Maywood, Ming Tree, Mountain Rose, Peasant Garden, Petals (made exclusively for Sears, Roebuck & Co.), Provincial Fruit, Saraband, and Tea Rose. One of the most exclusive patterns, Palm Tree, was developed for sale at a Fort Myers, Florida, souvenir store that was owned by a son of Bernard and Dorothy Purinton.

In addition to Purinton's main dinnerware lines, they also produced a line of floral ware such as the planters. Contract work was done for Esmond Industries and RUBEL as well. Both of these companies were distributors based in New York City. Taylor, Smith & Taylor contracted Purinton to make the Howdy Doody cookie jar and bust bank, both of which have become highly collectible.

But today it is the items painted by Dorothy Purinton that are the most collectible. Dorothy made special one-of-a-kind plates for weddings, anniversaries, holidays, and local festivals. She also made Amish- and Pennsylvania Dutch-inspired blessing plates with prayers such as 'Bless this House' and 'Give Us this Day Our Daily Bread.' Dorothy generally signed these special plates on the back. They are avidly sought after by collectors and command premium prices.

The pottery was sold to Taylor, Smith & Taylor in 1958 and closed in 1959, due to heavy competition from foreign imports.

The majority of the dinnerware produced by Purinton was not marked, but its unusual shapes are easily recognized. A small number of items were stamped 'Purinton Slip Ware' in ink, and some of the early Wellsville, Ohio, pieces were signed 'Purinton Pottery.' A limited number of Dorothy's items, including Blessing and Anniversary plates, have been found bearing her signature 'Dorothy Purinton' or 'D. Purinton.' Also several Wellsville, Ohio, items have emerged that were painted by Mr. William H. Blair and are signed on the back with his signature 'Wm. H. Blair' or simply 'Blair.' Such pieces are rare and command premium prices.

Apple, ashtray, center handle, 5½"	$40.00
Apple, bowl, fruit; plain border, 12"	$45.00
Apple, butter dish, 6½"	$150.00
Apple, canister, short, oval, 5", ea.	$55.00

Apple, cruet, w/cork stopper, sm	$38.00
Apple, honey jug, 6¼"	$150.00
Apple, jug, Dutch; 5-pt, 8"	$65.00
Apple, marmalade	$40.00
Apple, plate, breakfast; 8½"	$20.00
Apple, platter, 12"	$45.00
Apple, tumbler, 12-oz, 5"	$20.00
Brown Intaglio, chop plate, 12"	$20.00
Chartreuse, canister, tall, oval, ea.	$60.00
Chartreuse, wall pocket, 3½"	$50.00
Crescent, teapot, 2-cup	$50.00
Fruit, cocktail dish, sea-horse handle, 11¾"	$55.00
Fruit, coffeepot, 8-cup, 11"	$85.00
Fruit, Dorothy Purinton signed plate, 12", minimum value	$650.00
Fruit, plate, lap; 8½"	$30.00
Heather Plaid, beer mug	$20.00
Heather Plaid, chop plate, 12"	$35.00
Heather Plaid, grease jar, 5½"	$60.00
Heather Plaid, salt & pepper shakers, Pour 'n Shake, 4¼", pr.	$60.00

Heather Plaid, teapot, six-cup, 6", $65.00. (Photo courtesy Susan Moris-Snyder)

Intaglio, beer mug, 16-oz, 4¾"	$25.00
Intaglio, butter dish, 6½"	$35.00
Intaglio, gravy pitcher, Taylor Smith & Taylor mold, 3¾"	$65.00
Intaglio, jug, 5-pt, 8"	$75.00
Intaglio, tidbit, 2-tier, metal handle, 10"	$25.00
Ivy (red), biscuit jar, w/lid, 8"	$45.00
Ivy (red), coffeepot, 8-cup	$25.00
Ivy (red), honey jug, 6¼"	$15.00
Ivy (yellow), honey jug, 6¼"	$18.00
Ivy (yellow), jug, Dutch; 2-pt	$20.00
Maywood, baker, 7"	$25.00
Maywood, bowl, vegetable; w/lid	$35.00
Maywood, plate, dinner; 9½"	$30.00
Ming Tree, chop plate, 12"	$125.00
Mountain Rose, jug, Kent; 1-pt, 4½"	$45.00
Mountain Rose, plate, dinner; 9½"	$40.00
Mountain Rose, teapot, 2-cup	$15.00
Normandy Plaid, beer mug, 16-oz, 4¾"	$40.00

Normandy Plaid, bowl, vegetable; open, 8½"......................$20.00
Normandy Plaid, grease jar, w/lid, 5½" $60.00
Normandy Plaid, mug, Kent; 1-pt, 4½" $30.00
Normandy Plaid, tray, roll; 11" $35.00
Palm Tree, plate, dinner; 9¾" $125.00
Palm Tree, salt & pepper shakers, Pour 'n Shake, pr............$75.00
Pennsylvania Dutch, salt & pepper shakers, Pour 'n Shake, pr.. $75.00
Petals, coffeepot, 8-cup, 8" $75.00
Petals, teapot, 8-cup, 8" $75.00
Saraband, bowl, range; w/lid, 5½" $20.00
Saraband, plate, salad; 6¾" $8.00
Saraband, platter, 12" $20.00
Tea Rose, bowl, vegetable; open, 8½" $40.00
Tea Rose, creamer & sugar bowl, w/lid $95.00

Mountain Rose, marmalade, 4½", from $55.00 to $65.00. (Photo courtesy Susan Moris-Snyder)

Purses

By definition a purse is a small bag or pouch for carrying money or personal articles, but collectors know that a lady's purse is so much more! Created in a myriad of wonderful materials reflecting different lifestyles and personalities, purses have become popular collectibles. Lucite examples and those decorated with rhinestones from the 1940s and 1950s are 'hot' items. So are the beautifully jeweled Enid Collins bags of the 1950s and 1960s. Tooled leather is a wonderful look as well as straw, silk, and suede. Look for fine craftsmanship and designer names.

For more information we recommend *100 Years of Purses, 1880s to 1980s,* by Ronna Lee Aikins (Collector Books).

Anne Klein, white ribbed leather, gold tiger logo & 2 gold chains on front, 26" leather strap, 6x12" $30.00
Barlow, Nantucket basket w/ship carving on stained whale bone, whales on hinges & inside cover, wood handle $180.00
Bellstone, crocodile leather, brass hardware & frame, w/change purse, comb & mirror, 4 brass feet, chain handle, 8x11"..........$55.00
Chanel, black leather w/4" quilting at bottom, 2 interior zippered pockets, leather strap woven into chain, 14x17" $190.00
Chanel, lavender leather, silver-tone logo on front flap, leather lined, adjustable leather strap woven into chain, 5x9" $500.00

Chanel, pink nylon w/white leather trim & chrome hardware, white interior, 4 white feet, 2 pink leather straps, 5x13".......$165.00
Chanel, quilted black leather, drawstring, gold-tone hardware, leather lined, w/interior accessory, w/strap, 9x12".......$550.00
Chanel, tote, silvery blue tone-on-tone quilted look, nylon interior, 4 silver feet, w/handles, #8602829............................$365.00
Coach, backpack, black leather, brass hardware, drawstring top, adjustable shoulder straps, 10x7½" $50.00
Coach, bucket, rust-colored leather, adjustable strap, 14" sq w/9" dia bottom..$65.00
Coach, doctor bag, black leather, 4 brass feet, 2 leather handles, #B6E-4410, 7x11x5½" $45.00
Coach, duffle, white leather, nickel hardware, #1452, adjustable strap, 11x11" $235.00
Coach, jaquard w/polished & suede leather, magnetic clasp, full-length zipper, gold-tone hardware, 2 handles, 9x17½" $90.00
Coach, messenger bag, brown leather, gold-tone hardware, #J7C-9927, 10x10½", EX..$40.00
Coach, Soho Hobo, black leather, w/strap, 6½x11x3", #6266SV/BK, w/matching black #6017 wallet..........................$290.00
Coblentz, box type, black leather, gold-tone clasp, hinged, 4 brass feet, center handle, 3½x9½x5½" $22.00
Coblentz, soft black leather, satin lining, w/change purse & mirror, 4 brass feet, gold-tone chain handle, 5½x7½" $25.00
Danieli, red plastic-coated wicker, 4 brass feet & clasp, vinyl lining, w/handle, 7½x10x4" $60.00
Dooney & Burke, blue leather, brown leather 'saddle' trim, 50" brown leather strap, #A7726333, 6½x7", EX...............$20.00
Dooney & Burke, doctor bag, brown on black leather, brass hardware, 2 brown leather handles, 8x11" $40.00
Dooney & Burke, satchel, black leather, messenger style, brass hardware, leather lining, w/19" strap, 7½x10" $65.00
Enid Collins, Beach-Comber, white bird on beach, wood box type, w/white leather latch, 6x11x3"............................$55.00
Enid Collins, Cable Car, jewels in aqua, lime green & brown, gold accents on white, box type, 5½x4x11" $55.00
Enid Collins, Glitter Bugs, 5 jeweled bugs, canvas w/leather trim, 8½x9½" $35.00
Enid Collins, horses decorated w/sequins & stones, bucket style, canvas w/leather trim, handles tied like bridle, 9x6" $40.00
Enid Collins, Hot Air Balloon, Up Up & Away! on side, canvas & leather, wood bottom, 10x12½"...........................$140.00
Enid Collins, Jewel Garden, multicolored glass jewels on cloth, white leather trim & handles, 9x15x4" $60.00
Enid Collins, My Heart Pants 4 You, red applique jewels & raised roses on wood, red leather trim, 6x11x3"......................$85.00
Enid Collins, Sea Garden, teal & green glass jewels on tan canvas, 10x12" $125.00
Enid Collins, Tropicana, glass jeweled pineapple, butterfly, & flowers on white, w/tag, 9x12x4"..$165.00
Enid Collis, Stained Glass, multicolored jewels, black leather & cloth, wood bottom, brass handle rings & clasp, 9x13" $70.00
Gucci, clutch, navy & gray GG fabric w/blue & red stripe, navy leather trim & detachable strap, 7½x10x3" $110.00
Gucci, Doctor's Handbag, brown GG fabric w/red & green stripe, brown leather trim & shoulder strap, 7x11x5".........$200.00

Gucci, Doctor's Handbag, gray & black GG fabric, black leather trim & handles, gold-tone hardware & logo, 7x11x5", EX...**$130.00**

Gucci, portfolio style, tan & brown GG fabric w/tan leather trim & strap, brass locking clasp, w/2 keys, 10½x1½" **$100.00**

Judith Leiber, oblong silver metal box, rows of gold scrolled designs, gold leather lining, silver chain strap, 3x7x2" **$60.00**

Judith Leiber, white leather w/raised brass dots on front & back, gold-tone chain, w/change purse & mirror, 5½x9" **$185.00**

Lesco, red plastic straw, gold-tone hardware, 4 feet, stationary handles, 7x9x4" **$30.00**

Llewellyn, caramel Lucite (tigered accents), floral-carved w/rhinestones, brass hardware, oval, 2 handles, 5x8½" **$700.00**

Louis Vuitton, Bucket, dark brown monogram w/dark brown suede trim, drawstring opening, 12x11x8", EX **$215.00**

Louis Vuitton, light green monogram w/brown leather trim, w/ handle & 32" strap, 10x18" **$70.00**

Louis Vuitton, Shoulder, dark brown w/leather trim, Eclair zipper, 9x13½", EX **$120.00**

MW Handbags, brown Lucite & metal w/engraved flowers on lid, picnic basket shape, 3¼x4" **$165.00**

Patricia of Miami, green Lucite, clear geometric panel on front & as lid, signature clasp, w/4" handle, 5x8" **$200.00**

Plastic Flex, plastic squares connected by leather, ca. 1940s – early 1950s, 14" wide, from $35.00 to $55.00. (Photo courtesy Ronna Lee Aikens)

Rialto, walnut Lucite, turn-style latch, carved zinnias on clear lid, clear stirrup handle (6"), 3½x7x5½" **$370.00**

Roberta di Camerino, black leather & velvet, crocodile skin pattern, velvet covered-leather strap, snap closure, 5x10" **$185.00**

Roberta di Camerino, black leather w/velvet, striped red tones, chunky metal links form handle (21½"), 5x10x3½"....**$225.00**

Unmarked, clear hard plastic, 12 rhinestones on front & 1 lg rhinestone on clasp, hinged frame, 5x7½" **$35.00**

Unmarked, pearl white & clear Lucite & plastic, octagonal, metal hardware, white handle, 5x7½x5" **$155.00**

Unmarked, tote bag, black alligator leather, brass hardware & feet, hinged, 2 shoulder straps, 10x14½" **$200.00**

Wilardy, box type, Lucite embedded w/multicolored stars, 7 built-in accessory compartments, 3½x5¾" **$340.00**

Wilardy, clutch, black Lucite w/Deco-style rhinestones bordering sides & spring-loaded catch, 4½x7x1¾"................**$600.00**

Wilardy, dark tortoise Lucite, filigree on lid & clasp w/aurora borealis rhinestones, kidney shape, 6½x7½" **$315.00**

Wilardy, lunch box shape, clear Lucite, peacock's tail w/1 rhinestone forms latch, 4½x5x3¾" **$135.00**

Unmarked, Lucite, brown with crystal top, double handles, 8½" wide, from $125.00 to $175.00. (Photo courtesy Ronna Lee Aikens)

Pyrex

Though the history of this heat-proof glassware goes back to the early years of the twentieth century, the Pyrex that we tend to remember best is more than likely those mixing bowl sets, casseroles, pie plates, and baking dishes that were so popular in kitchens all across America from the late 1940s right on through the 1960s. Patterned Pyrex became commonplace by the late '50s; if you were a new bride, you could be assured that your bridal shower would produce at least one of the 'Cinderella' bowl sets or an 'Oven, Refrigerator, Freezer' set in whatever pattern happened to be the most popular that year. Among the most recognizable patterns you'll see today are Gooseberry, Snowflake, Daisy, and Butterprint (roosters, the farmer and his wife, and wheat sheaves). There was also a line with various solid colors on the exteriors. You'll seldom if ever find a piece that doesn't carry the familiar logo somewhere. To learn more about Pyrex, we recommend *Kitchen Glassware of the Depression Years,* by Gene and Cathy Florence (Collector Books).

Bottle, clear, w/stopper, 4½" **$12.00**

Bottle, nursing; clear, 8-oz, MIB **$20.00**

Bowl, child's; white w/red Christmas decoration, 8-oz **$30.00**

Bowl, mixing; blue, green, red or yellow fired-on 2½-qt **$12.50**

Bowl, mixing; Balloon-Print Cinderella, 4-qt.....................**$15.00**

Bowl, mixing; blue, green, yellow or red fired-on, 1½-pt **$10.00**

Bowl, mixing; blue, green red or yellow fired-on, 4-qt **$20.00**

Bowl, mixing; Butter-Print Cinderella, 8¼" **$16.00**

Bowl, mixing; Delphite Blue, 8½" **$35.00**

Bowl, mixing; pink, 4-qt..**$35.00**

Butter dish, Butterfly Gold on white, ¼-lb **$12.00**

Butter dish, Spring Blossom on white, #72, ¼-lb...............**$12.00**

Cake dish, clear, round, w/handles, 8⅝" **$12.00**

Cake dish, Tulip-Print, #222, 8½" sq $75.00
Carafe, juice; clear w/yellow lemons, yellow top $15.00
Casserole, clear, windmill & Dutch girl embossed on lid $45.00
Casserole, lime, round, w/lid, 1½-qt $20.00
Custard cups, clear, boxed set of 8 ....$60.00
Divided dish, oval, Daisy-Print Cinderella, w/clear lid, 1½-qt,
    MIB $22.00

Divided server, Cinderella, #963, 1½-quart, with lid, $16.00. (Photo courtesy Gene Florence)

Loaf pan, clear $10.00
Measuring cup, clear, 1-cup $10.00
Measuring cup, dry; clear, no spout, 1-cup $20.00
Measuring cup, red, 2-cup $100.00
Mug, gold eagle w/shield on brown, 10-oz $8.00
Mug, Terra-Print, white interior, 12-oz $5.00
Oven-refrigerator dish, brown, w/clear lid, 1½-cup $10.00
Oven-refrigerator dish, Woodland, white floral on green,
    1½-pt $10.00
Pie plate, clear, fluted rim, 6" $15.00
Pie plate, clear, hexagonal, #1203, 9⅞" $15.00
Ramekin, blue, green, red or yellow, 7-oz $8.00
Refrigerator dish, American Heritage, brown on white, 1½-pt.. $10.00
Refrigerator dish, Butter-Print, w/lid, 1½-qt $18.00
Salt & pepper shakers, Garland, blue on clear, pr $8.00
Salt & pepper shakers, Spring Blossom, green floral on white,
    pr $8.00
Utility dish, Butterfly Gold, 3-qt $18.00

Quilts

Though once primarily considered functional, quilts have always been an avenue though which the designer could find self expression, thus we cannot help but regard them as an art form. Several distinct types define this area of collecting. There are appliquéd quilts, made by stitching small pattern-cut pieces one at a time onto a large one-piece ground fabric or an individual block; pieced quilts, having blocks sewn into intricate patterns with names such as Log Cabin, Dresden Plate, Grandmother's Flower Garden, etc; trapunto quilts with stitched designs that are padded from the back; crazy quilts, random pieces sewn together then embroidered; and album quilts, with each block portraying an event or an item important to the designer or the chosen recipient. Besides condition, quilts are evaluated by the intricacy of their pattern, color effect, and

craftsmanship. Quality quilts have from 10 to 12 stitches to the inch. Values given here are auction results; retail may be somewhat higher. Quilts rated excellent have minor defects, otherwise assume them to be free of any damage, soil, or wear. Also assume that all the stitching is done by hand. Any machine work will be noted. For more information we recommend *Vintage Quilts, Identifying, Collecting, Dating, Preserving & Valuing*, by Bobbie Aug, Sharon Newman, and Gerald Roy (Collector Books).

Appliquéd

Feathers, blue on white, blue binding, tiny patterned quilting,
    1930s, 84x62", EX $600.00
Flowers (6), multicolor on white w/green vining border, all cottons,
    light wear & fading, machine quilted, 75x65" $200.00

Pots of tulips, red in green pots, meandering vine border, 76x75", $1,250.00. (Photo courtesy LiveAuctioneers.com/Garth's Auctions Inc.)

Princess Feather, aqua on white, sawtooth border, fine patterned
    quilting, 1950s, 96x88" $650.00
Ribbons & Roses, multicolor on white, made from kit, 1960s-70s,
    93x82" $450.00
Rose of Sharon, pink & green on white cotton, fine quilting, 1930s,
    95x80", EX $375.00
Sunbonnet Babies, multicolor pastels on white w/pink gridwork &
    borders, fine quilting, 1930s, 84x72", EX $395.00
Yellow roses & green leaves on white cotton, fine patterned quilting,
    made from kit, 1960s, 93x75" $385.00

Pieced

Barn Raising, cotton prints & solid bars, some flour sack printing,
    unbacked, ca 1900, 82x82", EX $425.00
Bear Claw, 16 segments, multicolor w/pink floral gridwork & bor-
    der, fine patterned quilting, 1930s, 82x78" $295.00
Blazing Stars, multicolor cottons on natural ground, sawtooth bind-
    ing, 1950s, 90x90", EX $725.00
Butterflies, multicolor prints & solids on white, embroidered anten-
    nae, 1930s-40s, 88x82" $285.00

Crazy, multicolor silks & velvet, embroidery work, red silk backing, ca 1900s, 56x54", EX **$315.00**

Double Nine Patch, printed & solid cottons, patterned quilting, 78x77", EX..**$375.00**

Double Wedding Ring, multicolor prints & solid cottons on white, white backing w/pink binding, 1930s, 87x87", EX **$245.00**

Dresden Cutter, multicolor on white sqs w/black gridwork, 105x87", EX **$200.00**

Dresden Plate, multicolor cottons on white, patterned quilting, repairs, 82x58", EX..**$125.00**

Fans, multicolor cottons in hot pink & white frames, pink back, hand & machine quilted, 1940s, 94x83", EX..............**$385.00**

Flower Basket, multicolor on white in pink grid, 1940s, 101x84" **$125.00**

Grandma's Flower Garden, bright multicolors & white, top only, 104x80", EX..**$265.00**

Log Cabin, blue, black, browns, blue backing, swag of hearts along border, Amish origin, 1960s, 104x93" **$375.00**

Nine Block Variation, multicolor cottons w/pink borders, king size..**$425.00**

Nine Patch w/Flying Geese, brown calicos & white, white border, rebound, ca 1900, 76x76", EX **$425.00**

Ocean Waves, indigo blue calicos, white triangles & blocks, white back & binding, late 19th C, 81x72", EX **$575.00**

Ocean Waves, multicolor cottons, pink calico backing, fine quilting, 1920s, 78x68"..**$250.00**

Ocean Waves, yellow, blue & white, blue binding, diamond quilting, late 19th C, 83x66", EX **$675.00**

Patchwork/crazy, satin on satin, some bleeding from darker colors, 83x68", VG **$325.00**

Rising Sun, multicolor on white, borders on 2 sides only, ca 1900, 80½x63½", EX **$225.00**

Rob Peter To Pay Paul, burgundy & green cotton & sateen, machined binding, Amish origin, ca 1950, 76x62" **$600.00**

Robbing Peter To Pay Paul, red & white solids, patterned quilting, 1930s, 88x70", EX..**$625.00**

Southern Belle, multicolor pastels on white w/pink grid, embroidered details, 80x60", EX **$150.00**

Starburst, multicolor cottons in white w/bright yellow border, patterned quilting, 84x840", EX......................................**$150.00**

Sunbonnet Sue, red & white, 1970s, 54x52" **$125.00**

Texas Lone Star, pinks & blue on white, fine geometric quilting, 84x82", EX..**$395.00**

Texas Lone Star, red, orange & taupe on ivory ground, red border, 72x72", EX **$265.00**

Tree-like pattern, red & green on white, scalloped edges, solid red border, fine stitching, 88x82", EX..............................**$395.00**

Triple Irish Chain, blue, lavender, pink & cream cottons, feather quilting, 1930-50s, 94x64" **$275.00**

Whirligig, peach & white cottons, double borders, patterned, 1930s, 80x66", EX **$185.00**

Railroadiana

It is estimated that almost 200 different railway companies once operated in this country, so to try to collect just one item represen-

tative of each would be a challenge. Supply and demand is the rule governing all pricing, so naturally an item with a marking from a long-defunct, less prominent railroad generally carries the higher price tag.

Railroadiana is basically divided into two main categories, paper and hardware, with both having many subdivisions. Some collectors tend to specialize in only one area — locks, lanterns, ticket punches, dinnerware, or timetables, for example. Many times estate sales and garage sales are good sources for finding these items, since retired railroad employees often kept such memorabilia as keepsakes. Because many of these items are very unique, you need to get to know as much as possible about railroad artifacts in order to be able to recognize and evaluate a good piece.

Advisor: Lila Shrader (See Directory Railroadiana)

Dinnerware

Platter, Western Pacific, Feather River pattern, marked Shenango Incaware, no railroad stamp, ca. 1940s – 1950s, 7½", from $75.00 to $90.00. (Photo courtesy Barbara Conroy)

Ashtray, GN, Glory of the West, 2 rests, back stamp, 4" dia .**$95.00**

Bowl, oatmeal/salad; GN, Hill, top logo, 6½" **$145.00**

Bowl, UP, Desert Flower, back stamp, Syracuse, 5½" **$30.00**

Bowl, vegetable; IC, Louisane, oval, top logo, no back stamp, 4½x6" **$110.00**

Butter pat, CMStP&P, Peacock pattern, no back stamp, 3", from $32 to **$52.00**

Butter pat, NYH&H, Platinum Blue, top logo, back stamp, 3¼", from $55 to **$80.00**

Butter pat, UP, Portland Rose, no back stamp, 3¼", from $200 to..**$300.00**

Compote, D&RGW, Prospector, pedestal foot, top logo, 2½x6¾" **$345.00**

Creamer, B&O, Centenary, bottom mark, Lamberton, 4".**$180.00**

Creamer, GN, Oriental, handle, no back stamp, individual, 3½" **$130.00**

Cup, bouillon; D&RGW, Prospector, side logo, 2¼" **$60.00**

Cup & saucer, CN, Nova Scotian, side logo, Limoges **$165.00**

Cup & saucer, demitasse; ATSF, Mimbreno, both back stamped, Syracuse **$400.00**

Egg cup, Pullman, Indian Tree, side logo, 3¾" $190.00

Mustard pot, Atlanta & West Point, Montgomery, slotted lid, 3"..$42.00

Plate, GCL, Gulf Coast, top logo, Warwick, 5½" $215.00

Plate, grill; B&O, 3 wells, Scammell's Lamberton, 11½" ...$200.00

Plate, T&P Eagle, top logo, back stamp, 6½" $60.00

Platter, CM&PS, Puget, no back stamp, 13¾x9" $185.00

Platter, PRR, Liberty, keystone top logo & back stamp, 11x8" ...$75.00

Relish dish, SR, Piedmont, back stamp, 7½x3¼" $30.00

Sherbet, UP, Winged Streamliner, Scammell's Trenton, 2½" ..$40.00

Sugar bowl, ATSF, California Poppy, w/lid, no back stamp, 5" ..$275.00

Teapot, KCS, Roxbury, no back stamp, individual, 3½" $65.00

Glassware

Ashtray, B&O, top logo in blue pyro, 2 rests, heavy, 5½" $55.00

Bottle, milk; enamel buzz-saw side logo, Sunnymede Farm, ½-pt $29.00

Bottle, whiskey; IC & Old Forester affixed paper labels, 1½-oz, 3¼" $65.00

Bottle, whiskey; UP The Overland Route Old Forester, paper label.. $36.00

Champagne flute, Amtrak, Silver Service, acid-etched side logo, 7½" $30.00

Cocktail, ATSF, acid-etched script Santa Fe side logo, 4½" ..$55.00

Juice tumbler, WP, white enamel side logo, 3½" $45.00

Martini pitcher, UP, pyro UP shield side logo, 5¼" $22.50

Roly-poly, IC enamel diamond side logo & diesel enamel side logo, 2¾x2¾" $20.00

Shaker, MStP&SSM, hanging banner side logo, silver-tone screw cap, 2¾" $100.00

Shot glass, ATSF, double size, pyro side logo, straight sides, weighted base, 2-oz, 2½" $75.00

Swizzle stick, C of NJ, hollow w/CNJ & distiller's name, 4¾".. $20.00

Tumbler, B&O, white enamel side logo Linking 13 Great States, 5 lines, 5¼" $15.00

Tumbler, Long Island, 125 Years, yellow and black pyro, 4½", $16.00. (Photo courtesy LiveAuctioneers.com/Hassinger & Courtney Auctioneering)

Tumbler, Northern Pacific Yellowstone Park, red & black enamel side logo, 3¾" $60.00

Water goblet, GN interlocking, white enamel, 5¼" $40.00

Wine, B&O, white enamel side logo Linking 13 Great States..., 5½" $20.00

Silver Plate

Bottle opener, CM&StP, Carlton, top mark, Gorham, 5¼" .$60.00

Butter pat, Boston & Albany, bottom mark, Reed & Barton, 3½" $30.00

Crumber, CMStP, The Olympian side logo, 12" L............$90.00

Crumber, Seaboard Air Line RR, top mark & bottom stamp, International, 9" $190.00

Fork, pickle; N&W, Cromwell, bottom mark, International, 6".$40.00

Fork, seafood; NYC&StL, DeSota, full bottom mark, International, 5¾" $55.00

Knife, butter; GN side logo, Zephyr, International, 7" $22.00

Knife, steak; Wabash, Ambassador, top mark, International, 10¼"..$35.00

Menu holder, PRR, applied PRR Keystone side logo, pencil holders, International, 4½x6" $175.00

Mustard, SP, frame w/hinged lid & handle, top logo, Reed & Barton, cobalt glass insert $285.00

Pitcher, syrup; Pere Marquette, hinged lid, attached drip tray, Wallace, side logo, 5" $175.00

Sauceboat, Union News, UNCo side & bottom marks, Reed & Barton, 5½" L.. $35.00

Spoon, serving; N&W, Cromwell, top mark monogram, International, 7".. $40.00

Sugar bowl, Illinois Central side logo & bottom stamp, w/handles, Reed & Barton, 5".. $165.00

Sugar tongs, CMStP, The Olympian, bottom mark, 4½" L..$90.00

Teapot, CCC&StL, bottom mark, Reed & Barton, hinged lid, 5½" $280.00

Teapot, UP System, 6½", EX, from $85.00 to $95.00. (Photo courtesy Studdard's Auctioneers)

Teaspoon, C&NW Ry, Modern Art, bottom mark, 6".........$35.00

Tray, bread; El Paso & South Western RR, top mark, Rogers, 6½x13½" $200.00

Vase, bud; Great Northern side mark, International, weighted base, 7" $245.00

Miscellaneous

Apron, CA Zephyr woven over Pullman logo, white cotton.$22.00

Ashtray/match holder, MP, buzz-saw side logo, cobalt w/gold, Hall China.. $82.00

Badge, hat; KCS, conductor, brass, curved top, 1¾x4" **$160.00**

Book, Cab Forward- SP Articulated Locomotives, Church, 1968, hard cover, 1st edition.................................**$180.00**

Booklet, Fresno, Coalinga & Monterey RR, 1911, 50-page, 10x7" ..**$90.00**

Button, Grand Trunk RR, GTR/Canada, Chanteloup, Montreal, brass, ⅝" **$6.00**

Calendar, ATSF, pocket size, celluloid, 1939, G **$22.00**

Calendar, NYC, colorful scene of streamliner trains, 1954, full pad, 12x19" **$60.00**

Can, kerosene; PRR embossed side mark, swing handle w/grip, hinged top, galvanized, 12" **$23.00**

Cigarette lighter, ATSF, Chico holding SF logo, chrome, Zippo ..**$100.00**

Doorknob, ICRR Co, embossed, brass.............................**$190.00**

Fan, MKT, Bouquet Bluebonnets, Compliments of Katy Line, card-stock, 11" **$30.00**

Handkerchief, C&O, views of Chessie & Peake, unused, original label, 10½" sq **$10.00**

Hanger, clothes; Property of Pullman Co, wood, 8x17", from $7 to **$22.00**

Jacket, porter club car; IC logo & piping in orange on white cotton...**$35.00**

Lantern, switch; Adlake, two red and two blue lenses, from $295.00 to $325.00. (Photo courtesy LiveAuctioneers.com/Tom Harris Auctions)

Luggage sticker, ATSF, Santa Fe/El Capitan, 3" **$6.00**

Magazine, employee; Missouri Pacific Lines, January 1955 ..**$25.00**

Manual, Los Angeles Ry, Car House Organization & Operation, 1926, hardcover, 70-page.........................**$130.00**

Map, wall; D&RGW, wood rods, linen back, hanging eyelets, 30x37" **$145.00**

Menu, breakfast; CB&Q, applied tinted photo, card stock, 1930s, folds to 8½x5½"...**$130.00**

Napkin, DL&W, Lackawanna RR center logo, white on white, 23" sq **$40.00**

Paperweight, NYC, Hudson locomotive on tiered base, metal, 9½" **$155.00**

Pencil clip, MP, old buzz-saw logo, celluloid **$10.00**

Pillowcase, SL&SF, The Frisco Line woven in blue on blue, 19x27" **$5.00**

Pin, lapel; Brotherhood Freight Handlers, screwback, ⅝".....**$20.00**

Poster, ATSF, Land of the Pueblos/Sante Fe, 1960s, 18x24" ..**$610.00**

Sign, MP buzz-saw logo/Eagle, Post Cereal, tin, 1950s, 2½x3½"..**$7.00**

Step stool, Pullman embossed on 2 sides, 18x20" **$200.00**

Timetable, public; FEC, sm map, advertising, 1959, folds to 8x3½" **$12.00**

Towel, hand; CMStP&P, woven top logo on red vertical center stripe, white huck, 13" sq **$15.00**

Wallet, men's; ATSF, black Italian leather, bi-fold w/applied 1" enamel SF logo **$20.00**

Wax sealer, Adams Express, Egg Harbor NJ, brass head, chrome handle, 3" **$190.00**

Razor Blade Banks

Razor blade banks are receptacles designed to safely store used razor blades. While the double-edged disposable razor blades date back to as early as 1904, ceramic and figural razor blade safes most likely were not produced until the early 1940s. The development of the electric razor and the later disposable razors did away with the need for these items, and their production ended in the 1960s.

Shapes include barber chairs, barbers, animals, and barber poles, which were very popular. Listerine produced a white donkey and elephant in 1936 with political overtones. They also made a white ceramic frog. These were used as promotional items for shaving cream. Suggested values are based on availability and apply to items in near mint to excellent condition. Note that regional pricing could vary.

Advisor: Deborah Gillham (See Directory, Razor Blade Banks)

Elephant, Listerine, $30.00; Donkey, Listerine, $25.00; Safe, $50.00; Barber pole, $20.00; Old Blade and Record Shaves, $50.00 each; Dear Old Dad, $50.00. (Photo courtesy LiveAuctioneers.com/Henry Pierce Auctioneers)

Barber, bust only, white shirt w/black sleeves, mustache & hair, unmarked, 5½" **$75.00**

Barber, wood w/Gay Blade bottom, unscrews, Woodcraft, 1950, 6", from $65 to **$75.00**

Barber, wood w/key & metal holders for razor & brush, 9", from $60 to $80.00

Barber chair, sm, from $100 to $125.00

Barber head, different colors on collar, Cleminson, from $25 to .. $35.00

Barber holding pole, marked Blades on back, Occupied Japan, 4", from $65 to $75.00

Barber pole, red & white, w/ or w/out attachments & various titles, from $20 to $25.00

Barber pole, red & white stripes, Royal Copley sticker, 6½".. $30.00

Barber pole w/barber head & derby hat, white, from $40 to .. $60.00

Barber pole w/face, red & white, from $30 to.....................$40.00

Barber standing in blue coat & stroking chin, from $65 to.. $85.00

Barber w/buggy eyes, pudgy full body, Gleason look-alike, from $65 to $75.00

Barbershop quartet, 4 singing barber heads, from $95 to...$125.00

Bell, white w/man shaving, California Cleminsons, 3½"......$25.00

Box w/policeman holding up hand, metal, Used Blades, from $75 to $100.00

Dandy Dans, plastic w/brush holders, from $25 to.............$35.00

Friar Tuck, Razor Blade Holder (on back), Goebel.............$300.00

Frog, green, For Used Blades, from $60 to.........................$70.00

Grinding stone, For Dull Ones, from $80 to $100.00

Half barber pole, hangs on wall, may be personalized w/name, from $40 to $60.00

Half shaving cup, hangs on wall, Gay Blades w/floral design, from $75 to $100.00

Half shaving cup, hangs on wall, Gay Old Blade w/quartet, from $65 to $75.00

Indian head, porcelain, Japan, 4" $25.00

Listerine donkey, from $20 to...$30.00

Listerine elephant, from $25 to...$35.00

Listerine frog, from $15 to..$25.00

Looie, right- or left-hand version, from $85 to $110.00

Man shaving, mushroom shape, Cleminson, from $25 to....$35.00

Man shaving, mushroom shape, Cleminson, personalized, from $45 to $55.00

Razor Bum, from $85 to..$100.00

Safe, green, Blade Safe on front, from $40 to.....................$60.00

Shaving brush, white w/red Blades on front & red bottom, brown bristles, 5½" $40.00

Shaving brush, wide style w/decal, from $45 to $65.00

Souvenir, wood-burned outhouse, For Gay Old Blades, by Crosby, found w/names of several states, from $35 to $45.00

Specialist in Used Blades in bottom of white outhouse, from $75 to $90.00

Tony the Barber, Ceramic Arts Studio, from $85 to............$95.00

Reamers

Reamers were a European invention of the late 1700s, devised as a tool for extracting liquid from citrus fruits, which was often used as a medicinal remedy. Eventually the concept of freshly squeezed juice worked its way across the oceans. Many early U.S. patents (mostly for wood reamers) were filed in the mid-1880s, and thanks to the 1916 Sunkist 'Drink An Orange' advertising campaign, the reamer soon became a permanent fixture in the well-equipped American kitchen. Most of the major U.S. glass companies and pottery manufacturers included juicers as part of their kitchenware lines. However, some of the most beautiful and unique reamers are ceramic figures and hand-painted, elegant china and porcelain examples. The invention of frozen and bottled citrus juice relegated many a reamer to the kitchen shelf. However, the current trend for a healthier diet has garnered renewed interest for the manual juice squeezer.

Most of the German and English reamers listed here can be attributed to the 1920s and 1930s. Most of the Japanese imports are from the 1940s.

Advisor: Bobbie Zucker Bryson (See Directory, See Napkin Dolls)

Club: National Reamer Collectors Association
Pat Carberry
4612 Charles Place
Plano, TX 75093
patcarberry48@yahoo.com
www.reamers.org

Ceramics

Child's face, red w/white reamer top, Made in Japan, 3"....$195.00

Clown, Japan/Sigma, red, orange, and black on white, 6½", $95.00. (Photo courtesy Bobbie Zucker Bryson)

Clown, red, white & black hat, green body w/red & yellow details, T-T...Japan, 1940s, 6", from $75 to...............................$95.00

Clown, red, white & blue cap, green body & collar w/hand-painted details, Hand Painted Made in Japan, 7½", from $85 to...$125.00

Clown, red, white & orange hat, ivory body w/white, blue & orange deails, Mikori Ware, 1940s, 6", from $75 to.................$95.00

Clown, red & blue striped hat, red body w/multicolor details, Japan, 1940s, 5¼", from $75 to $95.00

Clown, white hat w/red stripe, white body w/red & black painted details, Mikori Ware...Japan, 1940s, 7¼", from $85 to...$125.00

Clown face, hat reamer, bright red nose & mouth, multicolor details, Made in Japan, 1940s, 4½", from $60 to.....................$75.00

Clown face, smiling, yellow hat forms reamer, Japan, 1940s, 5¼", from $75 to $95.00

Clown w/teapot-shaped body, orange hat, face & ruffle form reamer top, Japan, 1940s, 6¼", from $75 to.........................$125.00

Duck, blue head w/red beak & yellow topknot, red feet, white reamer top w/red trim, Japan, 2½", from $30 to $45.00

Duck w/reamer on back, white w/orange bill & feet, floral decals on body, Japan, M-in-circle mark, 3x5½", from $30 to **$45.00**

House form, arched doorway, branch handle, airbrushed reamer top, Japan, 5⅛x4½", from $40 to **$55.00**

Jack & Jill in relief, multicolor on white 2-handled pitcher, white reamer top, green Japan mark, 4½", from $50 to.......... **$65.00**

Lemon w/green reamer top, brown twig handle, Hand Painted Made in Japan, 1940s, 4", from $30 to **$45.00**

Lemon w/reamer top, marked Goebel (full bee) Reg 1927, ca 1927, 3½", from $75 to... **$95.00**

Orange w/green leaves, 3-pc, unmarked, 4⅞", from $30 to...**$50.00**

Pear w/leaves & 2 cherries on lid, twig handle, lustreware, Trico... Made in Japan, 3-pc, 5", from $60 to.......................... **$75.00**

Pitcher, Oriental-style floral, multicolor on creamy basket weave, black trim, reamer top, Japan, 5x5¼", from $30 to **$55.00**

Windmill cottage, Japan, from $115.00 to $135.00.
(Photo courtesy Bobbie Zucker Bryson)

Glassware

Amber, ribbed, Federal, loop handle, from $25.00 to $30.00. (Photo courtesy Gene Florence)

Amethyst, sun-colored; 2-pc, Fenton, from $95 to **$110.00**

Amethyst, sun-colored; 2-pc, Westmoreland, from $75 to ...**$95.00**

Blue, 2-pc, Westmoreland, from $245 to **$250.00**

Crystal, embossed ASCO 'Good Morning Orange Juice,' Indian Glass, from $20 to **$25.00**

Crystal, footed, Cambridge, sm, from $20 to.......................**$25.00**

Crystal w/orange decoration, flattened loop handle, Westmoreland, from $40 to **$55.00**

Green, A&J, pitcher & reamer, 4-cup, Hazel-Atlas, from $45 to. **$55.00**

Green, panelled, loop handle, Federal, from $15 to **$25.00**

Green, ribbed, 2-cup pitcher & reamer set, Hocking, from $30 to... **$35.00**

Jadite, dark; embossed, Sunkist, from $60 to **$75.00**

Milk glass with Jack and Jill motif, Fenton, from $75.00 to $90.00. (Photo courtesy LiveAuctioneers.com/Tom Harris Auctions)

Pink, dark; lemon reamer, tab handle, Hazel-Atlas, from $40 to.. **$45.00**

Pink, ribbed, loop handle, Federal, from $40 to...................**$45.00**

Ultra-marine, Jennyware, from $110 to **$125.00**

White, embossed McK, Sunkist, 6", from $10 to.................**$20.00**

White, Sunkist in block letters, from $90 to **$100.00**

White w/red trim, Hazel-Atlas, 4-cup, from $30 to **$45.00**

Records

Records are still plentiful at flea markets and some antique malls, but albums (rock, jazz, and country) from the '50s and '60s are harder to find in collectible condition (very good or better). Garage sales are sometimes a great place to buy old records, since most of what you'll find there have been stored more carefully by their original owners.

There are two schools of thought concerning what is a collectible record. While some collectors prefer the rarities — those made in limited quantities by an unknown who later became famous, or those aimed at a specific segment of music lovers — others like the vintage Top-10 recordings. With the increasing use of internet auctions, which gives amateur sellers access to a world-wide market, many records described as or even believed to be 'scarce' or 'rare' are offered with some frequency. A majority of records offered receive no bids; only truly scarce, unusual, or exceptionally choice records inspire competition. So most records, even if listed in price guides, may be unsaleable, except as garage sale items. Now that they're so often being replaced with CDs, we realize that even though we take them for granted, the possibility of their becoming a thing of the past may be reality tomorrow.

Whatever the slant your collection takes, learn to visually inspect records before you buy them. Condition is one of the most important factors to consider when assessing value. Our values are for records in near mint to mint condition. To be judged as mint, a record may have been played but must have no visual or audible deterioration — no loss of gloss to the finish, no stickers or writing on the label, no holes, no skips when it is played. If any of these are apparent, at best it is considered to be excellent, and its value is up to 90% lower than a mint example. Many records that seem to you to be in wonderful shape would be judged only very good, excellent at the most, by a knowledgeable dealer. Sleeves with no tape, stickers, tears, or obvious damage at best would be excellent; mint condition sleeves are impossible to find unless you've found old store stock.

LPs must be in their jackets, which must be in at least excellent condition. Be on the lookout for colored vinyl or picture discs, as some of these command higher prices; in fact, older Vogue picture discs commonly sell in the $25.00 to $75.00 range, some even higher. It's not too uncommon to find old radio station discards. These records will say either 'Not for Sale' or 'Audition Copy.' These 'DJ copies' may be worth more than their commercial counterparts, especially where records of 'hot' artists such as the Beatles, Elvis Presley, and the Beach Boys are involved.

If you'd like more information, we recommend *American Premium Record Guide* by L.R. Docks.

Advisor: L.R. Docks (See Directory, Records)

45 rpm

Ain't Gonna Tell, Faye Adams, Herald 434, from $5 to **$8.00**
Ain't I'm a Mess, Bart Barton, E&M 1651, from $10 to **$15.00**
Ain't She Sweet, The Beatles, Atco 6308, from $7 to **$10.00**
Anytime, Eddy Arnold, RCA 1224, from $15 to **$20.00**
Baby Come Back, Lee Andrews & The Hearts, Casino 110, from $15 to **$20.00**
Baby Doll, Joe Allison, Dot 15714, from $10 to **$15.00**
Bee Boppin' Daddy, Mack Banks, Fame 580, from $30 to... **$40.00**
Black Land Blues, Charlie Adams, Columbia 21524, from $7 to..**$10.00**
Cadillac Baby, Doug Bowles, Tune 206, from $15 to.......... **$25.00**
City Lights, Bill Anderson, TNT 9015, from $20 to **$30.00**
Clock, Big Bopper, Mercury 71482, from $10 to **$15.00**
Condition Your Heart, The Arabians, Teek 4824, from $15 to...**$25.00**
Crazy Blues, Jimmy Blakeley, Starday 299, from $20 to....... **$30.00**
Cross My Heart, Johnny Ace, Duck 107, from $15 to......... **$20.00**
Dumb Dumb Bunny, Steve Bledsoe, Witch 102, from $20 to ...**$30.00**
Fortune Teller, The Banners, MGM 12862, from $8 to....... **$12.00**
Give Some Love Away, Wes Buchanan, Pep 114, from $30 to.. **$40.00**
Glory of Love, The Angels, Gee 1024, from $10 to **$15.00**
Go Away Mr Blues, Otis Blackwell, Jay-Dee 798, from $8 to .. **$12.00**
Gonna Get My Baby, Ronnie Allen, San 300, from $15 to.. **$20.00**
Hard Hearted Woman, Big Walter & The Thunderbirds, States 145, from $15 to **$20.00**
I'd Rather Be Wrong Than Blue, The Beavers, Brunswick 65026, from $75 to **$100.00**
I Know I Was Wrong, The Barons, Imperial 5359, from $15 to ...**$20.00**
I Want To Be Loved, The Beltones, Jell 188, from $15 to....**$20.00**
If You Were Mine Again, Harold Allen, Mar Vel 1021, from $15 to **$20.00**
Let's Get It On, Herschel Almond, Ace 558, from $15 to....**$20.00**
Lonely Lips, Jeff Barry, RCA 7797, from $7 to................... **$10.00**

Maggie, Andy & The Live Wires, Applause 1249, from $10 to..**$15.00**
Muscle Beach, Al Barkle, Frantic 108, from $8 to.............. **$12.00**
Night Has Gone, Billy Austin & the Hearts, Apollo 444, from $80 to **$100.00**
No Money Down, Chuck Berry, Chess 1615, from $8 to....**$12.00**
No Other Arms, The Arrows, Hugo 11172, from $15 to **$20.00**
Peg Pants, Bill Beach, King 4940, from $25 to **$35.00**
Pinch Me, Jerry Ballard, Skippy 120, from $5 to **$8.00**
Rocking Little Mama, Tony Bassett, Orchid 873, from $15 to...**$20.00**
Shine Again, Adelphis, Rim 2022, from $10 to **$15.00**
Shouldn't I Know, The Cardinals, Atlantic 938, from $80 to.. **$100.00**
Stringin' Along, Chet Atkins, RCA 1236, from $20 to **$30.00**
Swamp Gal, Tommy Bell, Zil 9001, from $25 to................. **$40.00**
Ten Little Indians, The Beach Boys, Pro 4880, from $5 to **$8.00**
Tribute to Buddy Holly, Mike Berry & The Outlaws, Coral 62341, from $10 to **$15.00**
Trying, Laverne Baker, King 4556, from $10 to................... **$15.00**
Turn-A-Bout Date, Denni Alan, Academy 434, from $15 to .. **$20.00**
Wheelin' & Dealin', Charlie Allen, Portrait 107, from $7 to ... **$10.00**
Why, The Beatles, MGM 13227, from $10 to.................... **$15.00**
You Are So Close to Me, The Avons, Hull 726, from $10 to...**$15.00**
You're Getting to Me, American Beetles, Mammoth 102, from $7 to **$10.00**

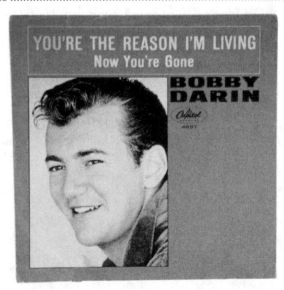

You're the Reason I'm Living, Bobby Darin, Capitol 4897, from $9.00 to $12.00.

Your My Teen Age Baby, The Berry Kids, MGM 12496, from $15 to **$20.00**

78 rpm

A Fine Romance, Fred Astaire, Brunswick 7716, from $7 to..**$10.00**
Ain't You Ashamed?, Arcadia Peacock Orchestra of St Louis, Okeh 40052, from $15 to **$20.00**
Barrel House Blues, Sammy Brown, Gennett 6337, from $200 to **$300.00**
Black Stomp, Atlanta Merrymakers, Madison 1935, from $10 to **$15.00**

Building a Nest for Mary, Al Alberts & His Orchestra, Cameo 9142, from $10 to **$15.00**

Burglar Man, Ruben Burns, Champion 15376, from $10 to... **$15.00**

Dark Holler Blues, Clarence Ashley, Columbia 15489-D, from $40 to **$60.00**

Devil in the Lion's Den, Sam Collins, Gennett 6181, from $200 to **$300.00**

Fare Thee Well Blues, Joe Calicott, Brunswick 7166, from $150 to **$200.00**

Good Time Blues, Jelly Roll Anderson, Gennett 6181, from $200 to **$300.00**

Hot & Anxious, The Baltimore Bellhops, Columbia 2449-D, from $15 to **$20.00**

I'm Done Done Done With You, Charlotte Evans, Domino 3453, from $10 to **$15.00**

I'm Gonna Cry, Connie Boswell, Victor 19639, from $20 to.. **$30.00**

Juke Box Boogie, Big Jeff & The Radio Playboys, Dot 1004, from $10 to **$15.00**

Little Marian Parker, Blind Andy, Okeh 45197, from $5 to... **$8.00**

Military Mike, The Ambassadors, Vocalion 15156, from $8 to **$12.00**

Moonlight Island, Ben Christian & His Texas Cowboys, Four Star 1270, from $7 to **$10.00**

On Top of Old Smoky, Cramer Brothers, Broadway 8071, from $20 to **$30.00**

River Blues, Jesse's String Five, Bluebird 6443, from $7 to... **$10.00**

Roll Down the Line, Allen Brothers, Bluebird 5700, from $10 to **$15.00**

Sweet Miss Stella Blues, Blue Harmony Boys, Paramount 12901, from $75 to **$100.00**

Sweet Sixteen, Walter Davis, Bluebird 5931, from $25 to.... **$40.00**

Sweet Woman Blues, Son Becky, Vocalion 03967, from $20 to **$30.00**

LP Albums

All Aboard the Blue Train, Johnny Cash, Sun 1270, from $30 to **$40.00**

Beyond the Sunset, Elton Britt, ABC Paramount 322, from $15 to **$20.00**

Clovers' Dance Party, The Clovers, Atlantic 8034, from $30 to..**$45.00**

Cowboy Songs of the West, Eddy Arnold, Tops 1612, from $8 to..**$12.00**

Dance Til Quarter to Three, Gary US Bonds, Legrand 3001, from $30 to **$40.00**

Diana, Paul Anka, ABC 420, from $15 to **$20.00**

Favorite Hymns, Roy Acuff, MGM 3707, from $10 to **$15.00**

For Sentimental Reasons, The Cleftones, Gee 707, from $75 to..**$100.00**

Galloping Guitar, Chet Atkins, RCA 3079, from $30 to **$50.00**

Go Champs Go, The Champs, Challenge 601, from $30 to.**$40.00**

Jimmy Bowen, Jimmy Bowen, Roulette 25004, from $30 to.**$50.00**

Jimmy's Happy, Jimmy Clanton, Ace 1007, from $20 to.....**$30.00**

Memorial Album, Johnny Ace, Duke DLP 71, from $50 to.**$75.00**

Miss Rhythm, Ruth Brown, Atlantic 8026, from $30 to......**$40.00**

Mood Music, Charles Brown, Aladdin 809, from $150 to.**$200.00**

Never To Be Forgotten, Eddie Cochran, Liberty 3220, from $40 to **$60.00**

New Orleans House Party, Dave Bartholomew, Imperial 9217, from $20 to **$30.00**

One by One, The Coasters, Atco 123, from $25 to **$35.00**

Patsy Cline, Patsy Cline, Coral 8611, from $20 to...............**$30.00**

Rod Bernard, Rod Bernard & The Twisters, Jin 1007, from $20 to **$30.00**

So Many Ways, Brook Benton & The Sandmen, Mercury 20565, from $15 to **$20.00**

Sweet & Low, The Charioteers, Columbia CL 6014, from $75 to **$100.00**

That's All, Bobby Darin & The Jaybirds, Atco 104, from $15 to **$20.00**

The Best of Rhythm & Blues, Jubilee 1014, from $30 to **$50.00**

The Cadets, The Cadets, Crown CST 370, from $15 to **$25.00**

The Crests Sing All the Biggies, Coed 901, from $50 to......**$75.00**

The Right Time, Nappy Brown, Savoy 14025, from $15 to .**$20.00**

There's Our Song Again, Chantels, End 312, from $20 to...**$30.00**

This Is, Tommy Collins, Capitol 1196, from $15 to............**$20.00**

Tribute to Six, Ray Allen, Blast 6004, from $20 to **$30.00**

Red Wing

For almost a century, Red Wing, Minnesota, was the center of a great pottery industry. In the early 1900s several local companies merged to form the Red Wing Stoneware Company. Until they introduced their dinnerware lines in 1935, most of their production centered around stoneware jugs, crocks, flowerpots, and other utilitarian items. To reflect the changes made in 1935, the name was changed to Red Wing Potteries Inc. In addition to scores of lovely dinnerware lines, they also made vases, planters, flowerpots, etc., some with exceptional shapes and decoration.

Some of their more recognizable lines of dinnerware and those you'll most often find are Bob White (decorated in blue and brown brush strokes with a quail), Tampico (featuring a collage of fruit including watermelon), Random Harvest (simple pink and brown leaves and flowers), and Village Green (or Brown, solid-color pieces introduced in the '50s).

If you'd like to learn more about the subject, we recommend *Red Wing Stoneware*, and *Red Wing Collectibles*, both by Dan DePasquale, Gail Peck, and Larry Peterson. Both are published by Collector Books.

Club: Red Wing Collectors Society, Inc.
Newsletter: *Red Wing Collectors Newsletter*
RWCS
P.O. Box 50
Red Wing, MN 55066
www.redwingcollectors.org.

Artware

Ashtray, gold & brown, sq, #M3005, 11", from $28 to.......**$36.00**

Ashtry, leaf shape, Orchid Fleck, #739, 5", from $20 to **$28.00**

Bowl, blue lustre & coral, flat, sq, #1037, 8", from $38 to ..**$46.00**

Bowl, Gothic; Monarch Line, green w/brown trim, #937, 10", from $40 to **$52.00**

Bowl, Indian Group, rose & aqua, #315, 4½", from $68 to...**$76.00**

Bowl, leaf shape, detailed vein inside bottom, blue & coral lustre, #1251, 12", from $42 to.............**$54.00**

Bowl, Nile Blue Fleck, curled edge, #M1463, 12", from $38 to.**$48.00**

Bowl, Rivera finish, ivory w/matt blue interior, w/handles, #341, 7", from $68 to **$76.00**

Bowl, Yellow Fleck, rectangular, footed, #M1603, 10", from $32 to **$38.00**

Bowl, Zephyr Pink Fleck, spiked rim, #1483, 1957, 18", from $48 to **$60.00**

Candleholders, cinnamon gloss, teardrop shape, #1409, 5", from $30 to **$38.00**

Candleholders, salmon, scalloped rim, #1619, 4½", pr from $32 to **$40.00**

Candleholders, turquoise gloss w/embossed leaves, #1286, 8", from $30 to **$38.00**

Compote, coral w/yellow interior, cherubs on pedestal, #761, 6", from $78 to **$100.00**

Compote, Nile Blue Fleck w/Colonial Buff interior, med pedestal, gold wing label, #5022, 7", from $48 to.............**$60.00**

Cornucopia, Nile Blue Fleck w/Colonial Buff interior, #443, 10", from $52 to **$68.00**

Ewer, white, #1187, 12", from $50.00 to $60.00.
(Photo courtesy LiveAuctioneers. com/Tom Harris Auctions)

Figurine, bird, coral & blue gloss, 5", from $38 to **$46.00**

Figurine, Oriental woman, yellow gloss, #1308, 10", from $100 to **$130.00**

Jardiniere, Cypress Green w/yellow interior, footed, #110, 10", from $58 to.............**$70.00**

Jardiniere, Yellow Fleck gloss, scalloped rim, brass handles, #M1610, 10", from $48 to.............**$62.00**

Planter, aqua gloss, #970, 3½", from $24 to **$36.00**

Planter, baby grand piano, Yellow Fleck, #M1525, 10x9", from $240 to **$350.00**

Planter, shoe shape, white w/light green interior, silver wing label, #651, 6", from $60 to.............**$80.00**

Planter, yellow gloss basket weave w/brown semi-matt interior, rectangular, #431, 10" L, from $24 to **$32.00**

Vase, bud; Coco Brown w/yellow interior, flared top & base, sq, #1621, 8", from $22 to.............**$26.00**

Vase, Egyptian, light green, #154, 12", from $110 to **$135.00**

Vase, English Garden, turquoise & brown wipe w/white interior, #1183, 6", from $56 to.............**$68.00**

Vase, gray, Deco handles, #816, from $120.00 to $145.00.

Vase, Sylvan style, coral gloss w/tan interior, #447, 8", from $65 to **$80.00**

Vase, white w/green interior, bulbous, #1245, 5½", from $42 to.**$56.00**

Wall pocket, Magnolia, ivory w/brown wipe, #1630, 7", from $125 to **$175.00**

Dinnerware

Bob White, pitcher, 12", from $40.00 to $50.00.

Blossom Time, bowl, cereal; 6½" **$8.00**

Blossom Time, gravy boat w/attached underplate.............**$32.00**

Blossom Time, plate, dinner.............**$12.50**

Blossom Time, salt & pepper shakers, pr $20.00
Bob White, bowl, lug soup; 8¼" $30.00
Bob White, bowl, salad; 12¼" $40.00
Bob White, bowl, vegetable; 9½" L $27.50
Bob White, casserole, round, w/lid, 1-qt $40.00
Bob White, cup & saucer $10.00
Bob White, pitcher, 14" $60.00
Bob White, plate, dinner; 11" $15.00
Bob White, plate, salad; 8" $18.00
Bob White, sugar bowl, w/lid $22.00
Capistrano, celery tray $22.00
Capistrano, creamer $22.50
Capistrano, cup & saucer $12.50
Capistrano, gravy boat $30.00
Capistrano, plate, dinner $15.00
Country Garden, bowl, fruit; 5¾" $6.00
Country Garden, cup & saucer $12.50
Country Garden, plate, dinner $22.50
Country Garden, platter, 15" L $50.00
Desert Sun, bowl, vegetable; oval, 8" $22.00
Desert Sun, plate, dinner; 10½" $10.00
Desert Sun, plate, salad; 7¾" $6.00
Desert Sun, sugar bowl, w/lid $18.00
Driftwood, bowl, divided vegetable; 14" $36.00
Driftwood, bowl, soup; 8¼" $12.50
Driftwood, cup & saucer $12.50
Driftwood, platter, 15" L $45.00
Hearthside, bowl, vegetable; 9" $24.00
Hearthside, cup & saucer $10.00
Hearthside, plate, dinner; 10½" $10.00
Hearthside, salt & pepper shakers, pr $18.00
Iris, gravy boat w/attached underplate $42.00
Iris, plate, bread & butter; 6" $6.00
Iris, sugar bowl, w/lid, 1¾" $22.00
Iris, teapot, 2-cup $60.00
Lanterns, bowl, cereal $12.50
Lanterns, casserole, 6½" $75.00
Lanterns, cup & saucer $18.00
Lanterns, sugar bowl, w/lid $27.50
Lexington, bowl, cream soup $20.00
Lexington, bowl, fruit $7.00
Lexington, creamer $11.00
Lexington, cup & saucer $8.00
Lute Song, bowl, divided vegetable; oval $28.00
Lute Song, gravy boat, stick handle, w/lid $42.50
Lute Song, plate, dinner; 10½" $15.00
Lute Song, platter, 13" L $28.00
Lute Song, teapot, 4-cup, from $135 to $150.00
Morning Glory, bowl, fruit; 6" $6.50
Morning Glory, cup & saucer $18.00
Morning Glory, plate, dinner; 10½" $15.00
Morning Glory, platter, 13" L $50.00
Normandy, bowl, vegetable; 9" $38.00
Normandy, creamer $18.00
Normandy, cup & saucer $15.00
Normandy, plate, dinner; 10", from $12 to $15.00
Orleans, plate, dinner; 10" $18.00
Orleans, platter, 14" $50.00
Orleans, teapot, 4-cup $100.00

Pepe, cup and saucer, from $9.00 to $12.00.

Provincial Oomph, baker, 9½" L $50.00
Provincial Oomph, cup & saucer $18.00
Provincial Oomph, pitcher, w/lid $38.00
Provincial Oomph, plate, luncheon; 9½" $8.00
Random Harvest, bowl, soup; 7⅞" $22.00
Random Harvest, plate, dinner; 11" $12.00
Random Harvest, platter, 13" L $25.00
Round-Up, cup & saucer $36.00
Round-Up, pitcher, 11½" $125.00
Round-Up, platter, 13½" L $135.00

Tampico, beverage server, $75.00.

Tampico, bowl, cereal $20.00
Tampico, bowl, salad; 12⅝" $60.00

Tampico, cake plate..**$60.00**
Tampico, pitcher, 64-oz **$75.00**
Tampico, plate, dinner; 10½".......................................**$16.00**
Tampico, sugar bowl, w/lid **$20.00**
Town & Country, bean pot, Rust, w/lid, minimum value..**$400.00**
Town & Country, bowl, soup **$27.50**
Town & Country, coffee mug **$75.00**
Town & Country, pitcher, 2-pt......................................**$95.00**
Town & Country, plate, Forest Green, 10½" **$35.00**
Town & Country, platter, 11x7½" **$55.00**
Town & Country, salt & pepper shakers, Shmoo shape, mixed colors, pr from $100 to **$120.00**
Town & Country, sugar bowl, Peach, w/lid.....................**$55.00**
Town & Country, syrup...**$85.00**
Town & Country, teacup & saucer **$27.50**
Village Green, casserole, w/lid, 9¾" **$55.00**
Village Green, plate, salad; 8¼"....................................**$15.00**
Village Green, sugar bowl, w/lid **$15.00**

Restaurant Ware and Commercial China

Restaurant china, also commonly called diner china, hotelware, or commercial china, is specifically designed for use in commercial food service. In addition to restaurants, it is used on board airplanes, ships, and trains, as well as in the dining areas of hotels, railroad stations, airports, government offices, military facilities, corporations, schools, hospitals, department and drug stores, amusement and sports parks, churches, clubs, and the like. Though most hotelware produced in America before 1900 has a heavy gauge nonvitrified body, vitrified commercial china made post-1900 includes some of the finest quality ware ever produced, far surpassing that of nonvitrified household products. A break- and chip-resistant rolled or welted edge is characteristic of American restaurant ware produced from the 1920s through the 1970s and is still frequently used, though no longer a concern on the very durable high alumina content bodies introduced in the 1960s. In addition, commercial tableware is also made of porcelain, glass-ceramic, glass laminate, glass, melamine, pewter-like metal, and silverplate. Airlines use fine gauge china in first class, due to space and weight factors. And beginning in the late 1970s, fine gauge porcelain and bone china became a popular choice of upscale restaurants, hotels, and country clubs. To reduce loss from wear, most decoration is applied to bisque, then glazed and glaze fired (i.e. underglaze), or to glaze-fired ware, then fired into the glaze (i.e. in-glaze). Until the 1970s many restaurants regularly ordered custom-decorated white, deep tan, blue, or pink-bodied patterns. However, it is estimated that more than 90% of today's commercial ware is plain or embossed white. For decades collectors have searched for railroad and ship china. Interest in airline china is on the rise. (Note: Many airlines discontinued use of china after 9/11.) Attractive standard (stock) patterns are now also sought by many. Western motifs and airbrushed stencil designs are especially treasured. The popularity of high quality American-made Asian designs has increased. Most prefer traditional medium-heavy gauge American vitrified china, though fine china collectors no doubt favor the restaurant china products of Pickard or Royal Doulton. While some find it difficult to pass up any dining concern or transportation system top-marked piece, others seek ware that is decorated with a military logo or department store, casino, or amusement park name. Some collect only creamers, others butters or teapots. Some look for ware made by a particular manufacturer (e.g. Tepco), others specific patterns such as Willow or Indian Tree, or pink, blue, or tan body colors. It is currently considered fashionable to serve home-cooked meals on mismatched top-marked hotelware. Reminiscent of days gone by, restaurant or railroad china made before 1960 brings to mind pre-freeway cross-country vacations by car or rail when dining out was an event, unlike the quick stops at today's fast-food and family-style restaurants.

For a more thorough study of the subject, we recommend *Restaurant China, Identification & Value Guide for Restaurant, Airline, Ship & Railroad Dinnerware, Volume 1* and *Volume 2,* by Barbara Conroy (Collector Books); her website, which has detailed descriptions of her books, contains even more information on additional restaurant china. The URL is listed below.

In the lines that follow, TM indicates top-marked or side-marked with name or logo. Please note: Commercial food service china is neither advertising nor souvenir china, since it is not meant to be removed from the restaurant premises.

See also Railroadiana.

Advisor: Barbara Conroy (See Directory, Dinnerware)

Website: http://restaurantchinacollectors.com

Lobe shape teapot with Syratone underglaze color and gold band, Syracuse, 1960 date code, from $24.00 to $30.00. (Photo courtesy Barbara Conroy)

Aer Lingus Ireland pattern cup & saucer, Aer Lingus & Noritake backstamp, ca 1980s, from $24 to **$30.00**
Alaska Airlines Gold Coast pattern cup & saucer, Alaska Airlines & Racket backstamp, 1980s Gold Coast Service, $18 to..**$22.00**
Alcoa Steamship Co Alcoa Cavalier pattern fruit, Syracuse backstamp, 1960 date code, from $30 to **$40.00**
America West Airlines Desert Cactus bowl, Rego backstamp, late 1980s - 1990s, from $8 to **$12.00**
Bonanza Hotel (Las Vegas casino, NV) 10½" plate, Syracuse backstamp, 1967 date code, from $30 to **$40.00**
Branding Iron - Border pattern sugar bowl w/lid, branding irons spell TEPCO, Tepco backstamp, from $38 to...............**$45.00**

British Airways Coat of Arms pattern butterpat, British Airways & Royal Doulton backstamp, 1972-89 first class, from $12 to.........**$16.00**

Broken Wagon Wheel pattern cup & saucer, Tepco backstamp, from $35 to...**$45.00**

Cartoon Cowboy pattern 10¼" plate, Shenango of California backstamp, 1962 date code, from $25 to.....................**$32.00**

Chesapeake Steamship Co Chesapeake Steamship pattern cake cover, no backstamp, 1930s, from $95 to............................**$110.00**

Chinese Village (Portland OR) 7½" plate, no manufacturer backstamp, from $5 to...**$7.00**

Delta Airlines Delta Dogwood pattern 6" plate, gray floral, Delta Airlines & Mayer backstamp, late 1970s-80s, $9 to......**$12.00**

Far East Cafe (San Francisco & other CA locations) 7" plate, Tepco backstamp, 1950s-60s, from $15 to.....................**$20.00**

George's Gateway Club (Lake Tahoe casino, NV) 6" plate, Tepco backstamp, 1950s, from $70 to...............................**$90.00**

Grace Line Santa Barbara pattern 6" pitcher, Syracuse & Grace Steamship Co backstamp, 1942 date code, from $125 to...................**$160.00**

Horn Blower Dining Yachts (San Francisco Bay) ashtray, no backstamp, 1990s, from $5 to....................................**$6.00**

Liggett's Drug Store (East Coast chain) 7" plate, Warwick, dated 1945, from $30 to.......................................**$40.00**

Mayfair pattern 8" plate, OPCO Mayfair backstamp, 1931 date code, from $16 to...**$22.00**

Nabisco Brands Inc 7" plate, Sterling Lamberton backstamp, 1985 date code, from $15 to...................................**$20.00**

National Airlines Sun King pattern 7" L casserole, Sterling China backstamp, 1974 date code, from $24 to.......................**$30.00**

Nevada Lodge Casino (Lake Tahoe, NV) celery tray, Mayer backstamp, 1964 date code, from $28 to.........................**$35.00**

Norwegian American Cruises Vistafjord pattern ashtray, Pillvyut backstamp, 1981 date code, from $9 to.......................**$12.00**

Pearls Seafood Restaurant (Nashua, NH) mug, 1980s, from $12 to **$15.00**

Pembroke pattern, after-dinner cup and saucer, Mayer, True Ivory backstamp, ca. 1950s, from $20.00 to $25.00.
(Photo courtesy Barbara Conroy)

Peninsular & Occidental Steamship Co Peninsular pattern creamer, Buffalo Old Ivory backstamp, 1930s, from $75 to......**$100.00**

Princess Cruises souvenir mug, no backstamp, 1990s, from $6 to...**$8.00**

Safeway 7¼" plate, Homer Laughlin backstamp, 1972 date code, from $14 to...**$18.00**

San Francisco Giants' stadium restaurant (San Francisco, CA) 7¼" plate, Syracuse backstamp, 1961 date code, $75 to.....**$100.00**

Sears Restaurants mug, Syracuse backstamp, 1973 date code, from $18 to...**$24.00**

Standard Airways Charter pattern 6½" L casserole, Standard Airways & Hall backstamp, 1960s, from $16 to.......................**$20.00**

Sun Line Stella Solaris pattern 6¼" plate, Richard Ginori backstamp, ca 1980s, from $18 to.................................**$22.00**

The China Rose 6" plate, Tatung backstamp, from $6 to......**$8.00**

Tien Hu Crimson pattern 9½" platter, Buffalo backstamp, early 1980s, from $8 to...**$10.00**

Union Oil of California Los Angeles pattern 9" plate, Syracuse Syralite backstamp, 1981 date code, from $40 to.........**$50.00**

United Airlines U Platinum pattern 7" L casserole, United & Wessco backstamp, late 1980s-1992 2st class, from $10 to........**$12.00**

United States Army Medical Department 9" plate, Shenango backstamp, 1956 date code, from $15 to...........................**$20.00**

United States Army Medical Department 10¼" grill plate, Shenango backstamp, 1950 date code, from $20 to....................**$25.00**

United States Coast Guard oatmeal, 13 stars on shield, Shenango backstamp, early 1940s, from $20 to.........................**$25.00**

United States Strike Command 3½" tray, gold rim, D Murphy Co backstamp, from $5 to..**$6.50**

US Navy Captain's Mess 6½" plate, Buffalo backstamp, early 1940s, from $11 to...**$14.00**

Veterans Administration 4½" milk pitcher, Shenango backstamp, 1930s, from $20 to...**$25.00**

Western Airlines Western White pattern, 12½" L plain white tray, Western Airlines & Hall backstamp, 1960s, from $9 to...**$12.00**

Western Sizzlin' Steak House 6¼" plate, Homer Laughlin backstamp, 1988 date code, from $20 to.............................**$25.00**

Western Traveler - Red pattern 6" plate, Tepco backstamp, red on white body (unusual colors), from $28 to....................**$35.00**

Woolworth's (nation-wide variety-store chain) 7¼" plate, OPCO backstamp, 1930 date code, from $38 to.....................**$45.00**

Stock Patterns

Air Canada Gold Scallops pattern 6" plate, Air Canada & Royal backstamp, 1964-70s, from $14 to.............................**$18.00**

Airbrush banded bouillon & saucer, Sterling's Trenton backstamp, 1950s, ea from $5 to.....................................**$7.00**

Ambassador Red pattern cream pitcher, Homer Laughlin, 1982 date code, from $6 to..**$7.50**

Bamboo pattern grapefruit, Tepco backstamp, 1950s-60s, from $18 to **$24.00**

Chardon Rose pattern on tan-bodied cream pitcher, Shenango's Inca Ware backstamp, 1940s, from $15 to.........................**$20.00**

Crest Beige pattern compartment plate, raised Buffalo mark, ca 1960s, from $9 to...**$12.00**

Dogwood pattern 9½" pate, Buffalo China, 1964 date code, from $10 to...**$12.50**

Florama pattern 11½" plate, Walker backstamp, 1960s, from $14 to **$18.00**

Glendale pattern, 8½" L platter, Syracuse, 1926 date code, from $8 to **$10.00**

Green Mill pattern sauceboat, Hutchenreuther Black Knight backstamp, ca 1930s, from $15 to **$20.00**

Indian Tree pattern 9" plate, Warwick backstamp, 1938 date code, from $14 to **$18.00**

Indian Tree pattern 9½" plate, Scammell Lamberton backstamp, 1930s, from $12 to **$16.00**

Malden pattern cup, Mayer's Mayan Ware backstamp, ca 1940s, from $8 to **$10.00**

Marilyn pattern sauceboat, Mayer, 1940s, from $14 to........**$18.00**

Red Lion restaurant, compartment plate, 10", Shenango, Roselyn Castle Grill Plate backstamp, ca. 1960s, from $30.00 to $40.00. (Photo courtesy Barbara Conroy.)

Shanghai pattern 7¼" plate, Syracuse's Old Ivory backstamp, 1936 date code, from $12 to..............................**$15.00**

South Pacific Steamship Lines Morgan Line pattern 8" plate, McNicol & Southern Pacific SS Lines backstamp, from $90 to **$110.00**

Winthrop pattern 9" plate, Wallace's Winthrop pattern backstamp, 1940s-50s, from $10 to **$12.50**

Robinson Ransbottom

A contemporary of McCoy, this company was the result of a union between Frank Ransbottom, one of Roseville, Ohio's, most successful producers of stoneware pots and jars, and the Robinson Clay Products Company, who until the merger in 1920 made mostly brick and tile.

Over the years, they extended their products to include an extensive line of cookie jars, giftware, pet feeders, birdbaths, and gardenware, which collectors are beginning to take note of today. In addition to their cookie jars, some of the more collectible items to watch for are their jardinieres and pedestals, their kitchenware, and their large vases. Though very reminiscent of earlier examples made in the area, the green and brown jardineres, pedestals, floor vases, and flowerpots were made from the 1960s through the 1980s. Many have

been unwittingly purchased for old Roseville pottery, since the mark is 'RRPCO, Roseville, Ohio.' (Just remember, the Roseville Pottery Company was located in nearby Zanesville, Ohio, not Roseville.) Today, though, they're collectible in their own right. The jardinere and pedestal has an embossed wild rose branch and was made from a mold that was purchased from the Weller Pottery when it closed. It was also produced with solid background colors of white, yellow, blue, pink, and green with contrasting flowers. Be sure to watch for their blue-sponged stoneware items, as these are gaining in popularity with those who enjoy the country look in home decor. The things we mention here are those most commonly found at garage sales and flea markets, but today, nearly all their wares are collectible, at least to some extent. For more information we recommend *The Sanford's Guide to the Robinson Ransbottom Pottery Co.,* by Sharon and Larry Skillman (Adelmore Press).

Birdbath insert, boy on fish, green, USA mark, 11" **$30.00**

Bowl, blue & white spongeware, 10", from $35 to **$45.00**

Bowl, mixing; brown bands on yellow ware, #120, 3½x7¼" ..**$20.00**

Bowl, mixing; embossed melon ribs, white w/4 embossed rings along rim, 4¼x8¼" **$20.00**

Bowl, pasta; Wheat, yellow ware w/blue sponging at rim, 3x13½" **$25.00**

Bowl, salad; Williamsburg pattern #303, blue stripes on white, 1¾x6¾", 4 for..**$55.00**

Crock, blue & white spongeware, w/lid, #700, 4-qt, 9½" **$38.00**

Crock, green sponging on tan, low, 2-qt **$18.00**

Dig dish, DOG in brown letters on tan, 3x6¼"..................**$25.00**

Jardiniere and pedestal, embossed wild roses, brown to green blend, #421, 22", from $145.00 to $165.00.

Jardiniere, embossed water lily leaves topped by crisscross vines on white, #126 USA, 6x7"..**$25.00**

Jardiniere/flowerpot, embossed sunbursts on brown shading to green, ca 1970s, 5¾x7¼" **$22.50**

Jardiniere/flowerpot, embossed sunbursts on brown shading to green, ca 1970s, 7x8" **$45.00**

Jug, Wheat, yellow ware w/blue sponging at top, 8½" **$25.00**

Oil jar, bright med blue w/rope design at rim & on handles, #155, 18"...$60.00

Pie dish, Wheat, yellow ware w/blue sponging at rim, 2½x10". **$28.00**

Pitcher, milk; Grecian lady w/harp stands between columns, green, #321, glaze pops **$50.00**

Plate, dinner; yellow ware w/blue sponging, 10⅝" **$30.00**

Vase, blue mottle w/embossed berries & leaves on handles, ca 1938-48, 14x7⅜"...**$75.00**

Vase, burgundy, round shoulders, sm flared rim, #294, 18x9½" .**$58.00**

Vase, dogwood flowers & leaves embossed on brown shading to green, ca 1970s, 18x12"..**$90.00**

Washbowl & pitcher, blue & white spongeware, 3x11¾", 9x8½" **$40.00**

Rock 'n Roll Memorabilia

Ticket stubs and souvenirs issued at rock concerts, posters of artists that have reached celebrity status, and merchandise such as dolls, games, and clothing. that was sold through retail stores during the heights of their careers are just the things that interest collectors of rock 'n roll memorabilia. Some original, one-of-a-kind examples — for instance, their instruments, concert costumes, and personal items — often sell at the large auction galleries in the east where they've realized very high-dollar prices. For more information we recommend *A Price Guide to Rock and Roll Collectibles* by Greg Moore, distributed by L-W Book Sales.

Note: Most posters sell in the range of $5.00 to $10.00; those listed below are the higher-end examples in excellent or better condition.

See also Beatles Collectibles; Elvis Presley Memorabilia; Magazines; Movie Posters; Pin-Back Buttons; Records.

Advisor: Bojo/Bob Gottuso (See Directory, Character and Personality Collectibles)

AC/DC, T-shirt, For Those About To Rock We Salute You, 1982 North American Tour, M...**$95.00**

Aerosmith, harmonica, Rockin' the Joint Tour & wings logo, brown enamel & silver plate, Hohner, 4", M in case **$25.00**

Aerosmith, jersey, Aerosmith Nine Lives Tour, football/hockey style, red, white & black w/embroidered logos, NM.............**$10.00**

Aerosmith, T-shirt, Girls of Summer Tour 2002, long sleeves, NM **$32.00**

Alice Cooper, poster, Welcome to My Nightmare, 1975, 24x24", M...**$30.00**

Alice Cooper, poster, Welcome to My Nightmare, 1975, 60x40", EX **$115.00**

Bay City Rollers, backstage pass, Orpheum, May 11, 1977, EX ..**$15.00**

Bay City Rollers, poster, Bay City Rollers Greatest Hits, closeup portraits, cardboard, center fold, 35¾x35¾", EX.........**$22.50**

Bay City Rollers, T-shirt, decal of group on white cotton, copyright 1976, sm, M **$18.00**

Beastie Boys, T-shirt, Beastie Boys w/Run DMC Together Forever Tour 1987, logo on white, NM **$100.00**

Bee Gees, T-shirt, Spirits Having Flown North American Tour 1979, logo on white, red sleeves, NM..................................**$50.00**

Black Sabbath, T-shirt, Heaven & Hell Tour 1980, yellow on black cotton, M..**$50.00**

Black Sabbath, T-shirt, North American Concert Tour 1975, logo on orange, EX...**$60.00**

Bobby Darin, photo, black & white, w/Sandra Dee, ca 1965, 5x7" **$10.00**

Bruce Springsteen, jacket, Born in the USA Tour, black nylon w/ quilted lining, red, white & blue embroidered logo, EX...**$65.00**

Elton John, belt buckle, Pinball Wizard, Tommy - Pacifica, ca 1976, M..**$75.00**

Eric Clapton, T-shirt, Slowhand Tour 1978, logo on yellow, NM...**$35.00**

Grateful Dead, plate, Dancing Jester by Stanley Mouse, Hamilton Collection, 8¼", M w/certificate of authenticity..........**$65.00**

Grateful Dead, poster, Berkley Community Center, 1984, 23¼x18", NM...**$175.00**

Grateful Dead, wristwatch, Jerry Garcia lazer-engraved signature, Benrus limited edition, MIB..**$75.00**

Grateful Dead/Allman Bros, poster, Watkins Glen, 1978 print to commemorate 5th anniversary of show, 22½x16½", EX......**$135.00**

Grateful Dead/Blues Brothers, poster, Blue Rose, Winterland, 1978, 28x19", EX..**$150.00**

Guns 'n Roses, jean jacket, Appetite for Destruction logo on front, lg logo on back, late 1980s, EX....................................**$80.00**

Ink Spots, record brush, 3½", $15.00.

Iron Maiden, press kit, Somewhere in Time, in black gate-fold sleeve, complete, 1987, EX **$85.00**

Iron Maiden, T-shirt, Piece of Mind Tour 1983, logo on black cotton, EX..**$120.00**

Jefferson Airplane/Junior Wells/Tim Rose, poster, Fillmore Auditorium, 1966, 22¼x14", EX................................**$195.00**

Jimmy Buttett, song book, color portrait cover, copyright 1974, EX..**$55.00**

KISS, bar stool, Destroyer, leaping group on vinyl, swivel top, chrome-plated legs, 29", M..**$60.00**

KISS, costume & mask, Ace Frehley, Collegeville, 1978, EXIB ..**$135.00**

KISS, doll, Ace Frehley, Love Gun, Spencer Gifts, 24", MIB.. **$110.00**

KISS, doll, Paul Stanley - Destroyer, Spencer Gifts, 1998, 24", MIB..**$115.00**

KISS, dolls, Mego, 1977-78, set of 4, EX $400.00

KISS, guitar, 1977, NM, $225.00. (Photo courtesy Bojo/Bob Gottuso)

KISS, necklace, group in gold-tone metal-backed ⅞" sq on gold-tone chain, 1978, EX..**$132.50**
KISS, sleeping bag, group on red & blue, single size, EX...**$150.00**
KISS, tour book, Creatures of the Night 10th Anniversary Tour 1982-83, 20 pages, color photos, 11x14", EX.............**$180.00**
KISS, wastebasket, tin litho, group on black, 19½x10½", EX **$165.00**
Led Zeppelin, program, August 1975 tour, 22 pages, EX...**$150.00**
Madonna, blanket, Confessions Tour 2006, embroidered fleece, 5x50", M **$50.00**
Madonna, jacket, Blond Ambition Tour 1990 crew member, quilted nylon, zipper pocket on sleeve, NM............................**$125.00**
Michael Jackson, jacket, Heal the World Tour 1996, red leather & black suede, NM...**$150.00**
Monkees, concert tour book, Golden Hits of Monkees Show, autographs inside, 1980s, EX...**$110.00**
Monkees, pin-back button, Davy Jones Hair, black lettering on yellow, Guaranteed To Be Authentic by Michael Graber, EX....**$100.00**

Monkees, record case for 45s, Rabert, 1966, from $125.00 to $200.00. (Photo courtesy Greg Davis and Bill Morgan)

Monkees, wallet, group on white vinyl, Raybert Productions Inc, Screen Gems, 1966, 4x4", EX....................................**$100.00**
Motley Crue, T-shirt, Girls Girls Girls Tour 1987, lg, EX....**$65.00**

Pearl Jam, hat, Vote for Change, star in circle on blue cotton, baseball-cap style, 2004, M **$80.00**
Pearl Jam, poster, Soundgarden, Holy Grail, 1992, 35x22", EX...**$150.00**
Pink Floyd, belt buckle, reflective, Pacific Mfg of Los Angeles, Model 12, 1978, EX **$60.00**
Pink Floyd, concert handbill, Pepperland, 1970, 8¼x5¼", EX ..**$100.00**
Pink Floyd, poster, More Than a Movie... (documentary), black on pink, 1972, 41x27", VG..**$85.00**
Prince, tambourine, gold logo on black, Remo limited release celebrating Emancipation album, M **$195.00**
Red Hot Chili Peppers, shorts, black cotton w/purple stars & words Red Hot Chili Peppers, elastic waist w/drawstring, EX ..**$75.00**
Red Hot Chili Peppers, sweatshirt, logo on white cotton/poly blend, EX **$30.00**
Rolling Stones, bobble-head figures, Licks World Tour 2002-03, set of 4, MIB...**$80.00**
Rolling Stones, jacket, Varsity Tour 1994, black, white & red varsity style, wool w/leather sleeves, NM **$100.00**
Rolling Stones, lava lamp, It's Only Rock 'n Roll, red & black, mouth & tongue at base, Vandor, 2006, 16", MIB.......**$60.00**

Rolling Stones, Shmuzzle Puzzle, jigsaw, Musidor, 1983, from $50.00 to $75.00. (Photo courtesy Greg Davis and Bill Morgan)

The Who, poster, Last Tour Ever of the USA 1982, black & tan, 17x11", EX..**$115.00**
Van Halen, T-shirt, 1984 tour, logo on black cotton, NM...**$65.00**
White Zombie, T-shirt, logos on front & back on black cotton, ca 1992, M..**$40.00**
Who, messenger bag, black leather w/magnet closures to hold front flap, strap adjusts, 13½x17½", EX **$200.00**

Rookwood

Although this company was established in 1879, it continued to produce commercial artware until it closed in 1967. Located in Cincinnati, Ohio, Rookwood is recognized today as the largest producer of high-quality art pottery ever to operate in the United States.

Most of the pieces listed here are from the later years of production, but we've included some early pieces as well. With few exceptions, all early Ohio art pottery companies produced an artist-decorated brown-glaze line — Rookwood's was called Standard. Among their other early lines were Sea Green, Iris, Jewel Porcelain, Wax Matt, and Vellum.

Virtually all of Rookwood's pieces are marked. The most familiar mark is the 'reverse R'-P monogram. It was first used in 1886, and until 1900 a flame point was added above it to represent each passing year. After the turn of the century, a Roman numeral below the monogram was used to indicate the current year. In addition to the dating mark, a die-stamped number was used to identify the shape.

Ashtray, #6026, 1919, clown on corner, Sally Toohey, 4x6x6", $475.00. (Photo courtesy LiveAuctioneers.com/Brunk Auctions)

Ashtray, #7223, 1963, Central Life Insurance 100,000 Club, 7½" dia...**$35.00**
Bookend, #2623, 1945, spread-wing eagle, white matt, 6x7" ...**$350.00**
Bookends, #2184, 1939, girl seated on book reading, McDonald mark, EX **$585.00**
Bookends, #2274, 1945, rook, green, X, 6¼" **$360.00**
Bookends, #2502, 1921, 2 boys reading book, tan matt, X, ea..**$360.00**
Bookends, #2635, 1946, owl on book, butterscotch, 6" **$250.00**
Bookends, #2658, 1929, blackbird, green on blue matt, 5½" ..**$1,200.00**
Bookends, #2659, 1931, penguins (2 on ea), 5¾" **$1,100.00**
Bookends, #6022, 1944, Dutch boy (& girl), multicolored, Toohey design, 5¾" **$415.00**
Bookends, #6484, 1964, polar bear, ivory matt **$850.00**
Bookends, #6883, 1945, St Francis, multicolored, 7½" **$575.00**
Bowl, #225, 1931, yellow w/mint green interior, 2½x13"..**$350.00**
Bowl, #2741, 1926, tan matt, handles, 3¾"....................**$185.00**
Figurine, #2906, 1953, Spanish dancer, turquoise dress, 10⅞".**$360.00**
Figurine, #6780, 1940, woodpecker, multicolored, Shirayamadani design, 6" **$235.00**
Figurine, #6786, 1946, jaybird, multicolored, 7"..............**$300.00**
Figurine, #6900, 1959, Madonna w/halo, ivory, 12" **$240.00**
Paperweight, #1855, 1935, geese (2), ivory matt, 4"..........**$480.00**
Paperweight, #2792, 1930, clipper ship, blue matt crystalline, 3¾" **$360.00**
Paperweight, #2797, 1930, elephant, green to brown matt, 3¼" ..**$480.00**

Paperweight, #6030, 1943, rooster, 4-color matt, 5"..........**$550.00**
Paperweight, #6160, 1961, rabbit, yellow-orange gloss......**$500.00**
Paperweight, #6402, 1964, blue matt, 4½"......................**$425.00**
Paperweight, #6661, 1945, playful kitten, blue gloss, 3" L.**$480.00**
Paperweight, #6665, 1945, lamb, white matt, 5" **$195.00**
Paperweight, no #, 1935, book, Commercial Clubs of..., ¾x3½". **$360.00**
Pin tray, #2595, 1948, mottled purple & brown, 1½x4" ...**$350.00**
Planter, #6027, 1929, paneled fan form, footed, green w/pink interior, 7½" **$175.00**
Tile, #3207, 1930, 3 geese, 3-color, 5¾"..........................**$325.00**
Tray, #1084, 1952, owl, brown & white, 4¼"...................**$145.00**
Tray, #1139, 1954, rook, violet gray, Clair de Lune, 4⅜" ..**$2,750.00**
Urn, #5635, 1937, cherub in chariot, ivory matt, 6½" **$140.00**
Vase, #2112, 1938, pink w/embossed decoration, 6½x3"...**$200.00**
Vase, #2154, 1943, rooks on shoulder, squat, 2½" **$230.00**

Vase, #2217, 1934, yellow matt with sunflower motif, 7", $425.00; Vase, #2403, 1921, incised flowers, 7½", $450.00. (Photo courtesy Treadway Gallery Inc.)

Vase, #2414, 1926, blue matt over gray, 9¾" **$385.00**
Vase, #2592, 1946, cattails band, blue, 4¾"........................**$90.00**
Vase, #6053, 1933, blue, 7½" **$125.00**
Vase, #6094, 1940, floral neck band, light ribbing, turquoise matt, 4½" **$235.00**
Vase, #6218, 1932, foliage, blue, 6¼" **$135.00**
Vase, #6254, 1932, green, angle handles, 4⅝" **$170.00**
Vase, #6610, 1937, pink, rim-to-hip handles, 9¾"............**$180.00**
Vase, #6612, 1936, robin's egg blue, porcelain, 8⅜"..........**$130.00**
Vase, #6638, 1937, monkeys in panels, turquoise, 10⅝" ...**$850.00**
Vase, #6833, 1954, lotus blossom, 6¼" **$95.00**
Vase, #7057, 1957, relief floral, ivory matt, 4-sided, 5¾"...**$235.00**
Vase, bud; #2307, 1921, plum-red, 7" **$120.00**

Rooster and Roses

Back in the 1940s, newlyweds might conceivably have received some of this imported Japanese-made kitchenware as a housewarming gift. They'd no doubt be stunned to see the prices it's now bringing! Rooster and Roses (Ucagco called it Early Provincial) is one of those lines of novelty ceramics from the '40s and '50s that are among today's hottest collectibles. Ucagco was only one of several importers whose label you'll find on this pattern; among other are Py, ACSON, Norcrest, and Lefton. The design is easy to spot — there's the rooster, yellow breast with black crosshatching, brown head and, of course, the red crest and waddle, large full-blown roses with green leaves and vines, and a trimming of yellow borders punctuated by groups of brown lines. (You'll find another line having blue flowers among the roses, and one with a rooster with a green head and a green borders. These are not considered Rooster and Roses by purist collectors, though there is a market for them as well.) The line is fun to collect, since shapes are so diversified. Even though there has been relatively little networking among collectors, more than 100 items have been reported and no doubt more will surface.

Advisor: Jacki Elliott (See Directory, Rooster and Roses)

Chamberstick, 3x6" diameter, from $35.00 to $50.00.
(Photo courtesy Jacki Elliott)

Ashtray, rectangular, part of set, 3x2"	**$9.50**
Ashtray, round or sq, sm, from $15 to	**$25.00**
Ashtray, round w/4-lobed well centered by hand-painted rooster, rests between lobes, 6"	**$65.00**
Ashtray, sq, lg, from $35 to	**$45.00**
Basket, flared sides, 6", from $45 to	**$55.00**
Bell, from $45 to	**$75.00**
Bell, rooster & chicken on opposing sides, rare, from $95 to	**$125.00**
Bonbon dish, pedestal base, minimum value	**$55.00**
Bowl, cereal; from $14 to	**$18.00**
Bowl, rice; on saucer, from $25 to	**$35.00**
Bowl, 8", from $45 to	**$55.00**
Box, trinket; w/lid, round, from $25 to	**$35.00**
Box, 4½x3½", from $25 to	**$35.00**
Butter dish, ¼-lb, from $20 to	**$25.00**
Candle warmer (for tea & coffeepots), from $25 to	**$35.00**
Candy dish, flat chicken-shaped tray w/3-dimensional chicken head, made in 3 sizes, from $35 to	**$65.00**
Candy dish, w/3-dimensional leaf handle, from $25 to	**$35.00**
Canister, cylindrical, wooden lid, 7x5", from $160 to	**$195.00**
Canister set, round, 4-pc, from $150 to	**$175.00**

Canister set, sq, 4-pc, from $150 to	**$175.00**
Canister set, stacking, rare, minimum value	**$150.00**
Canister set, tea & coffee stack amid lg sugar & flour, fits in woodem cabinet w/D-curved front, rare, 7x11x3", $275 to	**$300.00**
Carafe, no handle, w/stopper lid, 8", from $65 to	**$85.00**
Carafe, w/handle & stopper lid, 8", from $75 to	**$100.00**
Casserole dish, w/lid, from $65 to	**$85.00**
Castor set in revolving wire rack, 2 cruets, mustard jar & salt & pepper shakers, rare, from $125 to	**$150.00**
Cheese dish, slant lid, from $40 to	**$55.00**
Cigarette box w/2 trays, hard to find, from $60 to	**$70.00**
Coaster, ceramic disk embedded in round wood tray, rare, minimum value	**$45.00**
Coffee grinder, rare, minimum value	**$150.00**
Coffeepot, 'Coffee' in neck band, w/creamer & sugar bowl, both w/ appropriately lettered neck bands, 3 pcs from $75 to	**$85.00**
Coffeepot, new tankard shape, 8"	**$50.00**
Condiment set, 2 cruets, salt & pepper shakers w/mustard jar atop wire & wood holder, 4 spice canisters below, $150 to	**$175.00**
Condiment set, 2 cruets, salt & pepper shakers w/mustard jar on tray, miniature, from $50 to	**$75.00**
Condiment set, 2 sq shakers over 2 cruets, 4 sq shakers on bottom row, in wooden frame	**$60.00**
Cookie jar, ceramic handles, 7x6½", minimum value	**$175.00**
Cookie/cracker jar, cylindrical w/rattan handle, 5x6", from $55 to	**$75.00**
Creamer & sugar bowl, w/lid, 4", from $40 to	**$50.00**
Creamer & sugar bowl on rectangular tray, from $55 to	**$70.00**
Cruets, bottle shape, bulbous bottom, lg handle, pr	**$145.00**
Cruets, cojoined w/twisted necks, sm	**$45.00**
Cruets, oil & vinegar, flared bases, pr, from $50 to	**$60.00**
Cruets, oil & vinegar, sq, lg, pr from $30 to	**$45.00**
Cruets, oil & vinegar, w/salt & pepper shakers in shadow box, from $55 to	**$75.00**
Cup & saucer	**$25.00**
Demitasse pot, elongated ovoid, long handle & spout, 7½", minimum value	**$90.00**
Demitasse pot, w/4 cups & saucer, minimum value	**$150.00**
Demitasse pot, w/6 cups & saucers, minimum value	**$175.00**
Deviled egg plate, 12 indents, patterned center, 10", from $35 to	**$50.00**
Egg cup, from $20 to	**$25.00**
Egg cup on tray, from $35 to	**$45.00**
Flowerpot, buttress handles, 5", from $35 to	**$45.00**
Hamburger press, wood w/embedded ceramic tray, round, minimum value	**$24.00**
Instant coffee jar, no attached spoon holder on side, minimum value	**$55.00**
Instant coffee jar, spoon-holder tube on side, rare	**$45.00**
Jam & jelly containers, conjoined, w/lids & spoons, from $45 to	**$60.00**
Jam & jelly containers, conjoined, w/lids & spoons, w/loop handles & lids, very rare	**$85.00**
Jam jar, attached underplate, from $35 to	**$45.00**
Ketchup or mustard jar, flared cylinder w/lettered label, ea, from $25 to	**$30.00**
Lamp, pinup; made from either a match holder or a salt box, ea, from $75 to	**$100.00**

Lazy Susan on wood pedestal, round covered box at center, 4 sections around outside (2 w/lids), from $150 to **$250.00**

Marmalade, round base w/tab handles, w/lid & spoon, minimum value, from $35 to **$50.00**

Match holder, wall mount, from $50 to..........................**$75.00**

Measuring cup set, 4-pc w/matching ceramic rack, from $45 to.. **$65.00**

Measuring spoons on 8" ceramic spoon-shaped rack, from $40 to... **$55.00**

Mug, rounded bottom, med, from $25 to..........................**$30.00**

Mug, straight upright bar handle, lg, from $25 to...............**$35.00**

Napkin holder, from $30 to **$40.00**

Pipe holder/ashtray, from $30 to **$50.00**

Pitcher, bulbous, 5", from $25 to....................................**$30.00**

Pitcher, lettered Milk on neck band, 8", from $28 to **$35.00**

Pitcher, tankard shape, 3"..**$28.00**

Planter, rolling pin shape, rare, minimum value..................**$50.00**

Plate, bread; from $15 to **$20.00**

Plate, dinner; from $30 to..**$40.00**

Plate, luncheon; from $15 to **$25.00**

Plate, side salad; crescent shape, hard to find, from $50 to ..**$60.00**

Platter, 12", from $50.00 to $60.00. (Photo courtesy Jacki Elliott)

Recipe box, w/salt & pepper shakers; part of shadow-box set, from $40 to **$50.00**

Relish tray, 2 round wells w/center handle, 12", from $35 to .. **$40.00**

Relish tray, 3 wells w/center handle, from $55 to................**$65.00**

Rolling pin, minimum value **$50.00**

Salad fork, spoon, 2 shakers, funnel, oil & vinegar bottles, tea bag jar in wood frame w/4 spice drawers, EX, $65 to...............**$85.00**

Salad fork, spoon & salt & pepper shakers w/wooden handles, on ceramic wall rack, minimum value..............................**$55.00**

Salad fork & spoon w/wooden handles on ceramic wall-mount rack, from $45 to **$65.00**

Salt & pepper shakers, drum shape w/long horizontal ceramic handle, lg, pr from $30 to..**$40.00**

Salt & pepper shakers, w/applied rose, sq, pr **$23.00**

Salt & pepper shakers, w/handle, pr from $15 to................**$20.00**

Salt & pepper shakers, w/lettered neck band, pr **$25.00**

Salt & pepper shakers, wall hanging, 3¾", pr, +2½x6" hanger w/ scalloped top, from $25 to..**$45.00**

Salt & pepper shakers, 4", pr from $15 to **$20.00**

Salt box, wooden lid, from $45 to.......................................**$60.00**

Salt canister, sq, 6x4" **$50.00**

Shaker, cheese or sugar, 4"..**$35.00**

Slipper, 3-dimensional rose on toe, rare, from $85 to **$125.00**

Snack tray w/cup, oval, 2-pc, minimum value....................**$65.00**

Snack tray w/cup, rectangular, 2-pc, from $50 to................**$60.00**

Spice rack, 2 rows of 3 curved-front containers, together forming half-cylinder shape w/flat back, from $75 to.................**$85.00**

Spice rack, 3 rows of 2 curved-front containers, together forming half-cylinder shape w/flat back..................................**$85.00**

Spice set, 9 sq containers in wood frame w/pull-out ceramic tray in base, from $75 to..**$95.00**

Spoon holder, w/lg salt shaker in well on side extension, from $20 to **$25.00**

Stacking tea set, teapot, creamer & sugar bowl...................**$125.00**

Syrup pitcher, w/2 sm graduated pitchers on tray, minimum value **$75.00**

Tazza (footed tray), 3¼x7½" dia, from $45 to.....................**$55.00**

Tazza (footed tray), 3x6" dia **$45.00**

Tea bags jar, bulbous w/lettering, no crosshatching, w/lid, 6" .. **$60.00**

Teapot, 6x9", from $45 to..**$60.00**

Toast holder, rare, minimum value...................................**$75.00**

Tray, closed tab handles ea end, 11", from $25 to...............**$30.00**

Tray, round w/chamberstick-type handle on 1 side, 5½", from $15 to **$20.00**

Tumbler **$18.00**

Vase, round w/flat sides, 6", from $20 to **$30.00**

Wall hanger, teapot shape, pr **$90.00**

Wall pocket, lavabo, 2-pc, mounted on board, from $85 to ..**$125.00**

Wall pocket, scalloped top, bulbous bottom, from $55 to....**$65.00**

Wall pocket, teapots, facing ea other, pr, minimum value **$90.00**

Watering can, from $25 to **$35.00**

Roselane Sparklers

Beginning as a husband and wife operation in the late 1930s, the Roselane Pottery Company of Pasadena, California, expanded their inventory from the figurines they originally sold to local florists to include a complete line of decorative items that eventually were shipped to Alaska, South America, and all parts of the United States.

One of their lines was the Roselane Sparklers. Popular in the '50s, these small animal and bird figures were airbrush decorated and had rhinestone eyes. They're fun to look for, and though prices are rising steadily, they're still not terribly expensive.

If you'd like to learn more, there's a chapter on Roselane in *Collector's Encyclopedia of California Pottery,* by Jack Chipman.

Advisor: Lee Garmon (See Directory, Character and Personality Collectibles; Elvis Presley)

Sparklers

Angelfish, 4½", from $20 to **$25.00**

Basset hound, sitting, 4", from $15 to **$18.00**

Basset hound pup, 2", from $12 to **$15.00**

Basset hound puppies (2), 1 sitting & 1 recumbent, marked #99 & #98, pr..................$50.00

Bulldog, fierce expression, looking up & right, jeweled collar, 3½", from $22 to......................$25.00

Bulldog puppy, blue eyes seated, 1¾"......................$12.00

Cat, recumbent, head turned right, tail & paws tucked under body, from $20 to......................$25.00

Cat, Siamese looking straight ahead, no collar, 5"......$45.00

Cat, Siamese lying down, head turned right & resting on left paw, tail lying over back, jeweled collar, 5½" L..................$45.00

Cat, Siamese sitting, looking straight ahead, jeweled collar, 7", from $40 to......................$50.00

Cat, Siamese sitting, 3⅞""..................$30.00

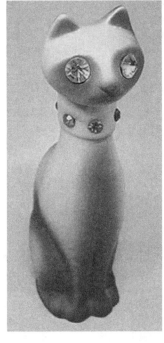

Cat, Siamese sitting, 6½", from $40.00 to $50.00.

Cat, Siamese standing, head turned left, jeweled collar, 4"...$32.00

Cat mama holding babies, 5", from $40 to......................$45.00

Cat sitting, head turned right, tail out behind, from $25 to..$28.00

Cat standing, head turned right, tail arched over back, jeweled collar, 5½", from $25 to......................$30.00

Cats, Siamese mother & 2 babies, blue eyes, 9½", 3¾"........$75.00

Chihuahua sitting, left paw raised, looking straight ahead, 7"..$28.00

Cocker spaniel, 4½", from $15 to......................$20.00

Deer standing, head turned right, looking downward, 5½"..$25.00

Deer w/antlers, standing, jeweled collar, 4½", from $22 to..$28.00

Donkey standing, lg ears, pink eyes......................$35.00

Elephant sitting on hind quarters, 6", from $35 to..............$40.00

Elephant striding, trunk raised, jeweled headpiece, 6", from $35 to......................$40.00

Fawn, legs folded under body, 4x3½"......................$25.00

Fawn, upturned head, 4x3½"......................$20.00

Fawn, 4½x1½"......................$20.00

Kangaroo mama holding babies, 4½", from $40 to..............$45.00

Kitten sitting, 1¾"......................$12.00

Owl, very stylized, lg round eyes, teardrop-shaped body, lg...$25.00

Owl, 3½"......................$15.00

Owl, 5¼"......................$25.00

Owl, 7"......................$30.00

Owl baby, 2¼", from $12 to......................$15.00

Pheasants, 1 (pink, 3¾"), 1 (blue, 5"), looking back, pr from $30 to......................$35.00

Pig, lg......................$25.00

Pouter pigeon, 3½"......................$20.00

Raccoon standing, 4½", from $20 to......................$25.00

Roadrunner, 8½" L, from $30 to......................$45.00

Squirrel eating nut, lg bushy tail, blue & brown highlights, 4"...$30.00

Whippet sitting, 7½", from $25 to......................$28.00

Miscellaneous

Bowl, aqua w/black sqs, #12, 5x11"......................$50.00

Bowl, Chinese Key, sq w/pedestal foot, late 1940s, 2½x6¼"...$25.00

Bowl, Fish, aqua, #25, 14"......................$50.00

Bowl, Fish, aqua, 4 peg feet, #30, 3¼x12¼x6⅜"..................$40.00

Bowl, gray, pink interior w/snowflakes, 9"......................$75.00

Bowl, salad; Fish, aqua, #25, 2¾x12¾", +matching fork & spoon......................$70.00

Candleholder, gray/wine, sq center base w/vertical ribs, #C1, 2½", ea......................$24.00

Carafe, Fish, pink & black, #34, w/lid, 8"......................$80.00

Dealer sign, Roselane in embossed letters, dark aqua, 3x12½"..$350.00

Dresser box, gray sides w/vertical lines, maroon lid, #S3, 6¼".....$27.50

Figurine, Asian female w/lg headpiece, pale green, 8".........$22.50

Figurine, boy w/dog, 5½"......................$25.00

Figurine, deer (2) on base, light green, 5¼"......................$50.00

Figurine, fox, on marked walnut base, 9"......................$180.00

Rosemeade

The Wahpeton Pottery Company of Wahpeton, North Dakota, chose the trade name Rosemeade for a line of bird and animal figurines, novelty salt and pepper shakers, bells, and many other items which were sold from the 1940s to the 1960s through gift stores and souvenir shops in that part of the country. They were marked with either a paper label or an ink stamp; the name Prairie Rose was also used.

Advisor: Bryce Farnsworth (See Directory, Rosemeade)

Club: North Dakota Pottery Collectors Society
Sandy Short, Membership Chairperson
P.O. Box 971
Dickinson, ND 58602
csshortnd@mcn.net
www.ndpcs.org

Ashtray, Campbell Grain Co, elevator on 8-sided base, 4¾", from $100 to......................$150.00

Ashtray, Indian head embossed on green gloss, 5½", from $150 to......................$175.00

Bank, black bear walking, 3¼x5¾", minimum value..........$400.00

Bowl, hand-thrown, pink matt, signed F Lantz, 1¾x6¼", from $125 to......................$150.00

Creamer & sugar bowl, black ducks, from $125 to............**$150.00**

Creamer & sugar bowl, prairie rose carved on pink, 2¾", 2", from $75 to **$100.00**

Figurine, bison, 6½" long, from $150.00 to $180.00.

Figurine, cock pheasant, 9¼x14", from $250 to.................**$400.00**

Figurine, elephant w/trunk up, solid matt color, 2¾", from $100 to **$150.00**

Figurine, lovebird pair on base, 6x2¾", from $60 to............**$80.00**

Flower frog, pheasant, 4¾", from $75.00 to $100.00.

Flower frog, squirrel, upright, marked North Dakota Rosemeade, 4", from $125 to **$150.00**

Mug, ring-necked pheasant decal, 4¾", from $125 to........**$150.00**

Planter, circus horse, matt color, 5x6½", from $75 to **$100.00**

Planter, Ewald Dairy, 2 cow heads in relief, 6", from $125 to. **$150.00**

Plaque, bluegill or brook trout, 3½x6", ea from $225 to....**$275.00**

Shakers, bluegill, 2½x4", pr, minimum value....................**$500.00**

Shakers, brussel sprouts, 1¾", pr from $35 to.....................**$50.00**

Shakers, cock strutting, red & white on green base, 3¾", pr from $75 to **$100.00**

Shakers, coyote pup, 3¼x2½", pr from $300 to **$350.00**

Shakers, dove strutting, yellow gloss, holes form S or P, 3½", pr, minimum value...**$300.00**

Shakers, ear of corn, Trojan on green base, 4½", pr from $350 to **$400.00**

Shakers, ox head, 2¼", pr from $75 to.....................**$100.00**

Shakers, prairie rose, 2½", pr from $35 to.........................**$50.00**

Shakers, red fox, 1 sitting/1 recumbent, largest: 1¾x1¾", pr from $350 to **$400.00**

Spoon rest, horse head, black & blue or black & rose, 5¾", from $125 to **$175.00**

Spoon rest, rooster, head carved in ea end, 7¾x3½", from $100 to **$150.00**

Spoon rest, water lily, rose w/white blossom, 4¾", from $75 to ...**$100.00**

Tea bell, peacock, 5½", from $250 to..............................**$300.00**

Tray, pheasant flying, free-form, no lettering, 4½x6¼", from $65 to **$75.00**

TV lamp, panther looking back, 7x13", minimum value...**$500.00**

Vase, hand-thrown, fluted rim, tapering sides, 3¾", from $50 to **$75.00**

Wall pocket, Egyptian embossed on light blue gloss, 5½", from $200 to **$250.00**

Roseville Pottery

This company took its name from the city in Ohio where they operated for a few years before moving to Zanesville in the late 1890s. They're recognized as one of the giants in the industry, having produced many lines of the finest in art pottery from the beginning to the end of their operations. Even when machinery took over many of the procedures once carefully done by hand, the pottery they produced continued to reflect the artistic merit and high standards of quality the company had always insisted upon.

Several marks were used over the years as well as some paper labels. The very early art lines often carried an applied ceramic seal with the name of the line (Royal, Egypto, Mongol, Mara, or Woodland) under a circle containing the words Rozane Ware. From 1910 until 1928 an Rv mark was used, the 'v' being contained in the upper loop of the 'R.' Paper labels were common from 1914 until 1937. From 1932 until they closed in 1952, the mark was Roseville in script, or R USA. Pieces marked RRP Co Roseville, Ohio, were not made by the Roseville Pottery but by Robinson Ransbottom of Roseville, Ohio. Don't be confused. There are many jardinieres and pedestals in a brown and green blended glaze that are being sold at flea markets and antique malls as Roseville that were actually made by Robinson Ransbottom as late as the 1970s and 1980s. That isn't to say they don't have some worth of their own, but don't buy them for old Roseville.

Most of the listings here are for items produced from the 1930s on — things you'll be more likely to encounter today. If you'd like to learn more about the subject, we recommend *Collector's Encyclopedia of Roseville Pottery, Vols. 1* and *2,* by Sharon and Bob Huxford (revised editions, updated pricing by Mike Nickel) (Collector Books); *A Price Guide to Roseville Pottery by the Numbers* by John Humphries (L&W

Book Sales); *Roseville in All Its Splendor* by Jack and Nancy Bomm (L&W Book Sales); and *Collector's Compendium of Roseville Pottery, Vols. 1* and *2*, by R.B. Monsen (Monsen & Baer).

Advisor: Mike Nickel (See the Directory, Roseville)

Apple Blossom, bowl, pink or green, #326-6, 2½x6½", from $100 to **$125.00**
Artwood, planter, #1055-9, 7x9½", from $75 to **$90.00**
Autumn, shaving mug, 4", from $200 to **$250.00**
Baneda, candleholders, green, #1087, 5½", pr from $450 to .**$500.00**
Bank, beehive, 2½", from $300 to **$350.00**
Bank, buffalo, 3x6½", from $350 to **$400.00**
Bittersweet, bowl vase, #842-7, 7", from $125 to **$150.00**
Bittersweet, wall pocket, #866-7, 7½", from $200 to........**$250.00**
Blackberry, jardiniere, 4", from $250 to **$300.00**
Bleeding Heart, vase, pink or green, #964-6", 6½", from $95 to **$125.00**
Blended Glaze, jardiniere, 5½" base dia, from $100 to......**$125.00**
Blended Glaze, pitcher, Landscape, 7½", from $125 to......**$150.00**
Blended Glaze, tankard, #890, 12", from $100 to **$150.00**
Blue Ware, mug, 6", from $350 to....................................**$400.00**

Bushberry, basket, green, #372, 12", from $300.00 to $400.00.

Bushberry, pitcher, blue, ice lip, #1325, 8½", from $395 to ..**$425.00**
Capri, shell, #C-1120, 13½", from $50 to **$60.00**
Carnelian I, fan vase, 6", from $50 to **$70.00**
Carnelian I, vase, 10", from $125 to **$150.00**
Carnelian II, basket, 4x10", from $200 to **$250.00**
Carnelian II, lamp base, 8", from $500 to **$600.00**
Carnelian II, wall pocket, 7", from $350 to **$375.00**
Carnelian II, wall pocket, 8", from $350 to **$400.00**
Chloron, jardiniere, #487, 5½", from $250 to **$300.00**
Clemana, vase, tan, #756, 9½", from $350 to....................**$400.00**
Clematis, center bowl, green or brown, #458-10, 14", from $100 to **$125.00**
Columbine, cornucopia, blue or tan, #149-6, 5½", from $100 to **$125.00**
Corinthian, jardiniere, #601, 7", from $100 to.................**$125.00**

Cornelian, pitcher & bowl, 12", 15½", from $200 to........**$250.00**
Cornelian, shaving mug, 4", from $50 to............................**$60.00**
Cosmos, flower frog, tan, #39, 3½", from $100 to **$125.00**
Creamware, mug, FOE, 5", from $60 to **$80.00**
Cremona, vase, pink, #361, 12", from $275 to.................**$325.00**
Dahlrose, hanging basket, #343, 7½", from $200 to.........**$250.00**
Dawn, vase, pink or yellow, #833-12, 12", from $350 to ..**$400.00**
Della Robbia, mug, Dutch scene signed FB, 4½", from $400 to **$500.00**
Della Robbia, teapot, sailing ships, 6½", from $1,500 to .**$2,000.00**
Dogwood I, vase, #140, 14½", from $500 to.....................**$600.00**
Dogwood I, wall pocket, 9", from $250 to **$300.00**
Dogwood II, jardiniere, #608, 8", from $200 to................**$250.00**
Donatello, bowl, 3x8", from $75 to **$100.00**
Donatello, plate, 8", from $275 to **$325.00**
Earlam, planter, #89, 5½x10½", from $300 to..................**$350.00**
Earlam, wall pocket, 6½", from $550 to............................**$600.00**
Early Pitcher, goldenrod, 9½", from $150 to **$200.00**
Early Pitcher, poppy, #141, 9", from $200 to **$250.00**
Falline, center bowl, tan, #244, 11", from $250 to **$275.00**
Ferella, bowl/frog, tan, #211, 5", from $375 to **$450.00**
Florane, double bud vase, from $75 to **$100.00**
Florane, vase, 14", from $90 to.......................................**$115.00**
Florentine, hanging basket, #337-7, 9", from $150 to **$175.00**
Florentine, window box, 11½", from $150 to....................**$200.00**
Foxglove, vase, green/pink, #47-8, 8½", from $175 to.......**$200.00**
Freesia, vase, green, #212-8, 8", from $125 to **$175.00**
Fuchsia, vase, brown/tan, #892-6, 6", from $125 to.........**$150.00**
Fuchsia, vase, green, #898-8, 8", from $250 to.................**$275.00**
Futura, vase, #382, 7", from $225 to **$275.00**
Gardenia, vase, #685-10, 10", from $150 to.....................**$175.00**
Imperial I, compote, 6½", from $125 to...........................**$150.00**
Imperial II, bowl, #198, 4½", from $250 to **$275.00**
Imperial II, vase, #473, 7½", from $1,000 to..................**$1,250.00**
Iris, vase, blue, #924-9, 10", from $300 to **$350.00**
Iris, vase, pink or tan, #917-6, 6½", from $100 to............**$125.00**
Ivory II, hanging basket, 7", from $50 to............................**$75.00**
Ivory II, shelf, #8, 5½", from $100 to **$125.00**
Ixia, hanging basket, 7", from $175 to..............................**$200.00**
Jonquil, candlesticks, #1082, 4", pr from $300 to **$350.00**
Juvenile, creamer, Duck w/Hat, 3½", from $75 to............**$100.00**
Juvenile, pitcher, Fat Puppy, 3½", from $350 to **$400.00**
La Rose, jardiniere, #604, 6½", from $125 to **$150.00**
Luffa, vase, 15½", from $1,250 to.................................**$1,500.00**
Magnolia, vase, brown or green, #91-8, 8", from $125 to..**$150.00**
Matt Green, gate, 5x8", from $75 to................................**$100.00**
Matt Green, jardiniere, #456, 5½", from $175 to.............**$200.00**
Matt Green, wall pocket, 15", from $350 to.....................**$400.00**
Mayfair, jardiniere, #1109-4, 4", from $40 to....................**$50.00**
Ming Tree, basket, #509-12, 13", from $200 to **$225.00**
Ming Tree, bookends, #559, 5½", from $125 to................**$150.00**
Mock Orange, pillow vase, #930-8, 7", from $150 to........**$175.00**
Morning Glory, pillow vase, green, #120, 7", from $275 to .**$325.00**
Mostique, compote, 7", from $200 to...............................**$225.00**
Mostique, vase, arrowheads, 6", from $100 to **$125.00**
Novelty Stein, Protection for Infant Industry, 4½", from $150 to **$200.00**

Orian, candleholders, red, #1108, 4½", pr from $200 to ...**$250.00**
Orian, compote, turquoise, #272, 4½x10½", from $150 to .**$200.00**
Peony, bookends, #11, 5½", from $175 to.........................**$225.00**
Persian, jardiniere, 5", from $175 to **$225.00**
Persian, wall pocket, 11", from $350 to **$400.00**
Pine Cone, ashtray, green, #499, 4½", from $100 to.........**$125.00**

Pine Cone, pitcher, blue, #425, 9½", from $800.00 to $900.00.

Pine Cone, vase, brown, #908-8, 8", from $300 to............**$350.00**
Poppy, bowl, gray/green, #336-10, 12", from $150 to.......**$175.00**
Poppy, vase, pink (add 50% for tan), #871-8, 8", from $200
    to **$250.00**
Primrose, vase, blue or pink, #760-6, 7", from $150 to **$175.00**
Raymor, casserole, #183, med, 11", from $75 to **$85.00**
Raymor, gravy boat, #190, 9½", from $30 to.......................**$35.00**
Rosecraft Panel, vase, brown, 10", from $300 to................**$350.00**
Rosecraft Vintage, vase, 12", from $400 to **$450.00**
Rozane Light, mug, floral, Pillsbury, 5", from $200 to **$250.00**
Rozane Light, vase, floral, Pillsbury, 8½", from $350 to **$400.00**
Rozane Pattern, vase, #10-12, 12", from $275 to...............**$325.00**
Russco, vase, crystal-line, #699, 9½", from $175 to...........**$200.00**
Silhouette, double planter, #757-9, 5½", from $100 to......**$150.00**
Snowberry, tray, blue or pink, #1BL-12, 14", from $200 to .**$250.00**
Sunflower, center bowl, 3x12½", from $700 to..................**$800.00**
Sunflower, window box, 3½x11", from $1,000 to...........**$1,200.00**
Teasel, vase, light blue or tan, #881-6, 6", from $100 to....**$125.00**
Thorn Apple, double bud vase, #1119, 5½", from $125 to..**$150.00**
Thorn Apple, wall pocket, #1280-8, 8", from $375 to **$425.00**
Topeo, vase, blue, 9", from $400 to **$450.00**
Topeo, vase, red, 7", from $150 to......................................**$200.00**
Tourmaline, candlesticks, #1089, 5", pr from $125 to.......**$150.00**
Tourmaline, vase, #614, 8", from $125 to **$150.00**
Tuscany, vase, pink, #349, 12", from $250 to **$300.00**
Vermoss, vase, blue, #719, 9½", from $300 to **$350.00**
Vista, basket, 9½", from $600 to **$700.00**

Water Lily, ewer, brown, #12, from $400.00 to $450.00.

Water Lily, vase, rose or green, #78-9, 9", from $175 to **$225.00**
White Rose, vase, #985-8, 8½", from $125 to **$150.00**
Wincraft, ewer, #218-18, 19", from $275 to......................**$325.00**
Windsor, lamp base (factory made), fern rust, #551, 7", from
    $700 to **$800.00**
Wisteria, vase, tan, #682, 10", from $600 to **$650.00**
Zephyr Lily, candleholders, blue, #1162-2, 2", pr from $125
    to **$150.00**

Royal China

Royal China was founded in 1934 by three entrepreneurs: Beatrice L. Miller, John 'Bert' Briggs, and William H. Habenstreit. They chose the former E. H. Sebring Building in Sebring, Ohio, as the location of their new company. During the brunt of the Great Depression, the company began with only $500.00 in cash, six months of free rent, and employees working without pay. In 1969 the company was sold to the Jeannette Glass Corporation. Jeannette continued to operate Royal from the original building until a fire destroyed the plant in February of 1970. After the fire, operations moved to the French Saxon China Company which Royal had previously purchased in 1964. In 1976 the Coca-Cola Bottling Company of New York bought the Jeannette Corporation and continued operations until 1981 when the Jeannette Corporation was sold to the 'J' Corporation, a private investment group. Three years later, Nordic Capital Corporation of New York bought the company. It is interesting to note that 1984 was the fiftieth anniversary of the Nordic Group and the slogan they addopted was 'A New Beginning.' Unfortunately, however, Jeannette filed bankruptcy early in 1986, and in March Royal China shut down completely. The building and its contents were sold during a bankruptcy auction in January of 1987. It is currently being used as a warehouse.

The number of shapes and patterns produced by Royal can boggle the mind of even the most advanced collector. Many lines turn up in unexpected colors: Blue Willow was made not only in blue but black, green, and pink as well. Memory Lane has a border of oak leaves and acorns; Buck County features a Pennsylvania Dutch tulip garland. Fair Oaks has magnolia blossoms. The two most commonly confused patterns are Colonial Homestead and Old Curiosity Shop. Colonial Homestead's border features wooden boards with pegged joints, while Old Curiosity Shop features metal hinges and pulls.

Currier and Ives dinnerware is by far Royal's most popular line and is widely collected. Its familiar scrolled border was designed by Royal's art director, the late Gordon Parker. Our suggested values for Currier and Ives reflect the worth of examples in the blue colorway. The line was also produced in limited quantities in the following colors: pink, brown, black, and green. To evaluate examples in these colors, double the prices for blue.

For further reading on Royal China, we recommend *Royal China Company, Sebring, Ohio* by David J. Folckemer and Deborah G. Folckemer.

Advisor (for Currier and Ives): Mark J. Skrobis (See Directory, Dinnerware, Currier & Ives)

Club: Currier and Ives Dinnerware Collector's Club
c/o Charles Burges, Treasurer
400 Kelly Drive, Brownstown, IN 47220.
www.currierandivesdinnerware.com.

Blue Heaven, bowl, vegetable; 10"	**$22.00**
Blue Willow, ashtray, 5½", from $8 to	**$12.00**
Blue Willow, bowl, cereal; 6¼"	**$15.00**
Blue Willow, bowl, fruit nappy; 5½"	**$6.50**
Blue Willow, bowl, soup; 8¼"	**$15.00**
Blue Willow, bowl, vegetable; 10"	**$28.00**
Blue Willow, butter dish, ¼-lb	**$45.00**
Blue Willow, casserole, w/lid	**$95.00**
Blue Willow, creamer	**$6.00**
Blue Willow, cup & saucer	**$6.00**
Blue Willow, gravy boat, double spout	**$28.00**
Blue Willow, pie plate, 10"	**$30.00**

Blue Willow, pitcher, from $60.00 to $75.00.

Blue Willow, plate, bread & butter; 6¼"	**$3.00**

Blue Willow, plate, dinner; 10"	**$8.00**
Blue Willow, plate, salad; rare, 7¼"	**$7.00**
Blue Willow, platter, oval, 13"	**$32.00**
Blue Willow, platter, serving; tab handles, 10½"	**$20.00**
Blue Willow, salt & pepper shakers, pr	**$25.00**
Blue Willow, sugar bowl, w/lid	**$15.00**
Blue Willow, teapot	**$135.00**
Blue Willow, tray, tidbit; 2-tier	**$95.00**
Colonial Homestead, bowl, cereal; 6¼"	**$15.00**
Colonial Homestead, bowl, fruit nappy; 5½"	**$5.00**
Colonial Homestead, bowl, soup; 8¼"	**$12.00**
Colonial Homestead, bowl, vegetable; 10"	**$24.00**
Colonial Homestead, casserole, angle handles, w/lid	**$75.00**
Colonial Homestead, creamer	**$5.00**
Colonial Homestead, cup & saucer	**$5.00**
Colonial Homestead, gravy boat, double spout	**$15.00**
Colonial Homestead, pie plate	**$25.00**
Colonial Homestead, plate, bread & butter; 6"	**$3.00**
Colonial Homestead, plate, chop; 12"	**$18.00**
Colonial Homestead, plate, dinner; 10"	**$8.00**
Colonial Homestead, plate, salad; rare, 7¼"	**$8.00**
Colonial Homestead, platter, oval, 13"	**$28.00**
Colonial Homestead, platter, serving; tab handles, 10½"	**$15.00**
Colonial Homestead, salt & pepper shakers, pr	**$18.00**
Colonial Homestead, sugar bowl, w/lid	**$15.00**

Colonial Homestead, teapot, from $60.00 to $75.00.

Currier & Ives, ashtray, 5½"	**$15.00**
Currier & Ives, bowl, cereal; round	**$15.00**
Currier & Ives, bowl, dip; from Hostess set, 4⅜"	**$125.00**
Currier & Ives, bowl, fruit nappy; 5½"	**$6.00**
Currier & Ives, bowl, soup; 8½"	**$10.00**
Currier & Ives, bowl, vegetable; deep, 10"	**$30.00**
Currier & Ives, bowl, vegetable; 9"	**$20.00**
Currier & Ives, butter dish, summer scene, ¼-lb	**$45.00**
Currier & Ives, butter dish, winter scene, ¼-lb	**$35.00**
Currier & Ives, cake plate, flat, 10"	**$45.00**
Currier & Ives, cake plate, footed, 10"	**$200.00**
Currier & Ives, casserole, angle handles, w/lid	**$100.00**
Currier & Ives, casserole, angled handles, all white lid	**$175.00**
Currier & Ives, casserole, tab handles, w/lid	**$200.00**
Currier & Ives, clock plate, 10" or 12"	**$1,000.00**
Currier & Ives, creamer, angle handle	**$8.00**

Currier & Ives, creamer, round handle, tall, rare **$50.00**
Currier & Ives, cup & saucer **$6.00**
Currier & Ives, deviled egg tray, from Hostess set **$250.00**
Currier & Ives, gravy boat, double spout **$20.00**
Currier & Ives, gravy boat, tab handles, w/liner (like 7" plate) ..**$150.00**
Currier & Ives, lamp, candle; w/globe.............................. **$375.00**
Currier & Ives, pie baker, from Hostess set, 11" **$60.00**
Currier & Ives, pie baker, 10", (depending on print) from $25 to...**$45.00**
Currier & Ives, plate, bread & butter; 6⅜", from $3 to **$5.00**
Currier & Ives, plate, calendar; ca 1969-86..................... **$20.00**
Currier & Ives, plate, chop; Getting Ice, 11½" **$35.00**
Currier & Ives, plate, chop; Getting Ice, 12½" **$30.00**
Currier & Ives, plate, dinner; 10" **$5.00**
Currier & Ives, plate, luncheon; very rare, 9"..................... **$20.00**
Currier & Ives, plate, salad; rare, 7" **$15.00**
Currier & Ives, plate, snack; 9¼" **$175.00**
Currier & Ives, platter, oval, 13" **$35.00**
Currier & Ives, platter, Rocky Mountains, tab handles, 10½" dia **$20.00**
Currier & Ives, salt & pepper shakers, pr from $30 to........**$35.00**
Currier & Ives, sugar bowl, angle handles, from $15 to **$18.00**
Currier & Ives, sugar bowl, no handles, flared top, w/lid **$50.00**
Currier & Ives, sugar bowl, no handles, straight sides, w/lid...**$35.00**
Currier & Ives, teapot, 8 different styles & stampings, from $125 to **$200.00**
Currier & Ives, tidbit tray, 3-tier (factory-made only) **$75.00**
Currier & Ives, tile & rack, 6x6"....................................... **$150.00**
Currier & Ives, tumbler, iced-tea; glass, 12-oz, 5½" **$15.00**
Currier & Ives, tumbler, juice; glass, 5-oz, 3½"................... **$15.00**
Currier & Ives, tumbler, old-fashioned; glass, 3¼"..............**$15.00**
Currier & Ives, tumbler, water; glass, 4¾"........................... **$15.00**
Currier & Ives, wall plaque, very scarce...........................**$1,000.00**

Memory Lane: Ashtray, from $7.00 to $10.00; cup and saucer, $5.00; plate, dinner; 10½", from $8.00 to $12.00.

Memory Lane, bowl, cereal; 6¼"............................... **$15.00**
Memory Lane, bowl, fruit nappy; 5½"................................. **$6.00**
Memory Lane, bowl, soup; 8½".. **$8.00**

Memory Lane, bowl, vegetable; 10" **$28.00**
Memory Lane, butter dish, ¼-lb **$35.00**
Memory Lane, casserole, w/lid **$85.00**
Memory Lane, creamer **$8.00**
Memory Lane, gravy boat, double spout............................ **$24.00**
Memory Lane, gravy boat liner, from $12 to **$15.00**
Memory Lane, plate, bread & butter; 6⅜" **$3.00**
Memory Lane, plate, chop; 12".. **$25.00**
Memory Lane, plate, chop; 13".. **$35.00**
Memory Lane, plate, luncheon; rare, 9¼" **$18.00**
Memory Lane, plate, salad; rare, 7" **$12.00**
Memory Lane, platter, oval, 13".. **$38.00**
Memory Lane, platter, tab handles, 10½" **$22.00**
Memory Lane, salt & pepper shakers, pr............................. **$25.00**
Memory Lane, sugar bowl, w/lid **$15.00**
Memory Lane, teapot.. **$85.00**
Memory Lane, tumbler, iced tea; glass **$18.00**
Memory Lane, tumbler, juice; glass....................................... **$9.00**
Old Curiosity Shop, ashtray, 5½" dia.................................. **$15.00**
Old Curiosity Shop, bowl, fruit nappy; 5½" **$5.00**
Old Curiosity Shop, bowl, soup/cereal; 6½" **$15.00**
Old Curiosity Shop, bowl, vegetable; 9" **$25.00**
Old Curiosity Shop, bowl, vegetable; 10" **$28.00**
Old Curiosity Shop, butter dish, ¼-lb................................. **$45.00**
Old Curiosity Shop, casserole, w/lid.................................... **$90.00**
Old Curiosity Shop, creamer... **$8.00**
Old Curiosity Shop, cup & saucer **$5.00**
Old Curiosity Shop, pie plate, 10" **$32.00**
Old Curiosity Shop, plate, bread & butter; 6⅜" **$3.00**
Old Curiosity Shop, plate, dinner; 10" **$8.00**
Old Curiosity Shop, plate, luncheon; rare, 9" **$12.00**
Old Curiosity Shop, plate, salad; rare, 7" **$10.00**
Old Curiosity Shop, platter, oval, 13" **$35.00**
Old Curiosity Shop, platter, tab handles, 10½" **$22.00**
Old Curiosity Shop, salt & pepper shakers, pr **$22.00**
Old Curiosity Shop, sugar bowl, w/lid **$15.00**
Old Curiosity Shop, teapot **$115.00**
Old Curiosity Shop, tidbit, 3-tier, center handle, from $35 to.. **$45.00**
Plain (goes w/any pattern), ladle, white.............................. **$50.00**

Royal Copley

This is a line of planters, wall pockets, vases, and other novelty items, most of which are modeled as appealing animals, birds, or human figures. They were made by the Spaulding China Company of Sebring, Ohio, from 1942 until 1957. The decoration is under-glazed and airbrushed, and some pieces are trimmed in gold (which can add 25% to 50% to their values). Not every piece is marked, but they all have a style that is distinctive. Some items are ink stamped; others have (or have had) labels. (In the listings below, 'paper label only' indicates a piece that never was produced with an ink stamp).

Royal Copley is really not hard to find, and unmarked items may sometimes be had at bargain prices. The more common pieces seem to have stabilized, but the rare and hard-to-find examples are showing a steady increase. Your collection can go in several directions; for instance, some people choose a particular animal to collect. If you're a cat lover, they were made in an extensive assortment of styles and sizes. Teddy bears are also popular; you'll find them licking a lollipop, playing a mandolin, or modeled as a bank, and they come in various colors as well. Wildlife lovers can collect deer, pheasants, fish, and gazelles, and there's also a wide array of songbirds.

If you'd like more information, we recommend *Collecting Royal Copley* by Joe Devine.

Advisor: Joe Devine (See Directory, Royal Copley)

Figurine, hen, Royal Windsor, paper label only, brown breast, 7¾", from $100 to **$125.00**
Figurine, hen, 7", from $50 to..**$60.00**
Figurine, mallard hen, Royal Windsor, common, impressed AD Priolo mark, 6¼", from $200 to **$225.00**
Figurine, nuthatch, full bodied, paper label only (+), 4½", from $20 to **$25.00**
Figurine, parrot, full bodied, paper label only, 8", from $50 to ...**$60.00**
Figurine, rooster, black & white w/green base, paper label only, 8", from $110 to **$125.00**
Figurine, rooster, Royal Windsor, white stucco glazing, 7", from $60 to **$75.00**
Figurine, rooster, 6½", from $60 to.....................................**$75.00**

Figurine, spaniel with collar, 6", from $20.00 to $25.00; Planter, cocker spaniel, from $30.00 to $35.00. (Photo courtesy Joe Devine/Glenn Hovinga)

Figurine, swallows, full bodied, tail up, paper label only, 8", from $25 to **$30.00**
Figurine, vireos, 4½", from $15 to **$20.00**
Lamp, birds in the bower, paper label only, 8", from $50 to...**$60.00**
Lamp, lady dancing, metal base, 8", from $150 to.............**$200.00**
Pitcher, Pome Fruit, green stamp, blue, from $65 to............**$75.00**
Planter, angel, made to hang or rest on table, paper label only, blue, from $50 to **$60.00**
Planter, barefooted boy (or girl) wearing hat, paper label only, 7½", from $45 to...**$50.00**
Planter, cockatoo, full bodied, 7¼", from $40 to **$45.00**
Planter, duck & wheelbarrow, common, paper label only, 3¾", from $18 to **$20.00**

Planter, farm boy w/fishing pole, embossed mark, green & rose, 6½", from $30 to **$35.00**
Planter, fighting cock, 6½", from $45 to............................**$50.00**
Planter, Joyce decal, gold stamp, 4", from $12 to.................**$15.00**

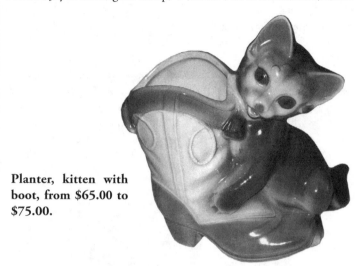

Planter, kitten with boot, from $65.00 to $75.00.

Planter, mallard hen sitting, 5¼", (+), from $50 to **$60.00**
Planter, Oriental boy (or girl) w/lg vase at side, paper label only, from $15 to **$20.00**
Planter, rooster, high tail, common, embossed mark, from $30 to **$35.00**
Planter, rooster, stylized, open beak, embossed mark, white w/rose speckles & lining, 7½x9½", from $40 to **$45.00**
Planter, rooster & wheelbarrow, 8", from $150 to **$175.00**
Plate/planter, fruit, embossed mark, made to hang or rest on table, from $35 to **$40.00**
Vase, Betty decal, gold stamp, 8", from $25 to.....................**$30.00**
Vase, bud; warbler, embossed mark, 5", from $20 to **$25.00**
Vase, Carol's Corsage, green stamp, cobalt, from $25 to **$30.00**
Vase/planter, fish, paper label only, yellow & black w/brown stripe, 6", from $65 to...**$75.00**
Vase/planter, mallard duck on stump, paper label only, 7", from $20 to **$25.00**

Royal Haeger

Many generations of the Haeger family have been associated with the ceramic industry. Starting out as a brickyard in 1871, the Haeger Company (Dundee, Illinois) progressed to include artware in their production as early as 1914. That was only the beginning. In the '30s they began to make a line of commercial artware so successful that as a result a plant was built in Macomb, Illinois, devoted exclusively to its production.

Royal Haeger was their premium line. Its chief designer in the 1940s was Royal Arden Hickman, a talented artist and sculptor who also worked in mediums other than pottery. For Haeger he designed a line of wonderfully stylized animals and birds, high-style vases, and human figures and masks with extremely fine details.

Paper labels were used extensively before the mid-'30s. Royal Haeger ware has an in-mold script mark, and their Flower Ware line (1954 – 1963) is marked 'RG' (Royal Garden).

Club: Haeger Pottery Collectors of America
Lanette Clarke
5021 Toyon Way
Antioch, CA 94509
510-776-7784
www.wisconsinpottery.org/Haeger

Ashtray, Mandarin Orange, #153, 1½x10¾x8", minimum value **$10.00**
Ashtray, orange free-form, #R1755, 14x12" **$20.00**
Bowl, Daisy, gray-white w/lime green interior, #R224, 2¾x12", w/ gray-white fish (flower frog), 11½x5¼" **$135.00**
Bowl, Daisy, green w/blue marbling, 2¾x12", w/sea goddess riding fish (flower frog) in matching glaze, 10¼" **$100.00**
Bowl, Daisy, pink w/blue flowers, #R224, 12", w/sea nymph (flower frog) in matching glaze, 13"............................**$105.00**

Bowl, shell mold, Mauve Agate, #818, 12" long, from $55.00 to $65.00.

Candy dish, green w/yellow lily applied to lid, #R431, 6" dia **$35.00**
Compote/candy dish, smooth matt black w/dark multicolor swirls, footed, w/lid, 11x7½" **$55.00**
Ewer, pink matt, #RG42, 10" **$20.00**
Figurine, dogs (3), brown, #R782, 7x9"............................**$35.00**
Figurine, Harvest Female, dark green, 17" **$42.50**
Figurine, inebriated duck, fallen, #R158, 10" **$50.00**
Figurine, rooster, Chinese Red w/green comb & legs, #R1762, 20" **$125.00**
Figurines, rooster & hen, red w/brown speckles, he, #61: 12", 11", pr **$165.00**
Lamp, Earth Wrap brown, waisted form w/wooden base, 10½", 27" overall **$170.00**
Planter, donkey figural, black w/white marbling, #508, 9¼x8½"...**$38.00**
Planter, fish figural, green agate, 5½x6½".............................**$72.50**
Planter, lady seated between 2 bowls, dark green, w/Haeger sticker, 7½x13" **$45.00**
Planter, Madonna praying, white, 11"..............................**$45.00**

Planter, panther figural, mauve pink, 25¼" L **$125.00**
Planter, panther figural, shiny black, 21" L.......................**$60.00**
Planter, sailfish figural, chartreuse, 9"............................**$40.00**
Planter, swan figural, aqua agate, 7¾x7¼"...........................**$45.00**

Planter, swan, Royal Hickman, 8x6", $45.00. (Photo courtesy www. lifeofrileycollectiques.net)

Shell bowl, blue-pink iridized, #481, 11x9" **$55.00**
Tidbit tray, orange leaves form tiers (2), metal center handle..**$22.50**
Toe Tapper, banjo player, Bennington Brown Foam, 12x3"...**$50.00**
Trinket box, blue-green w/2 metal medallions on top, #R-1688-S, 1½x4½x3½" **$38.00**
TV lamp/planter, Art Deco gazelles, brown w/multicolor marbling, 16½x8¼" **$70.00**
Vase, Art Deco concentric circles, pink agate, 11½x9½" **$90.00**
Vase, Art Deco fan form, pastel green, #3660, 13½x17½" ..**$140.00**
Vase, bird of paradise figural, mottled pink, #186, 12" **$125.00**

Vase, Earth Graphic Wrap, 12¾", from $125.00 to $135.00. (Photo courtesy Cincinnati Art Galleries)

Vase, Earth Wrap brown, cylindrical, 10¾".........................**$35.00**
Vase, Earth Wrap brown, jug form, 11½x10"....................**$60.00**
Vase, Earth Wrap in browns on white, bulbous, short neck w/white rim, 7½x7½" **$65.00**

Vase, green mottle, ovoid w/can neck & flared rim, 12½" ... **$95.00**

Vase, leaves (2 lg) form body of vase, aqua, 9x9½" **$55.00**

Vase, mallard duck figural, deep teal to dark green, 8x8" **$45.00**

Vase, marigold agate, ewer form, 19" **$25.00**

Vase, morning glories (3), green agate, #R452, 16½x9½x5" .. **$150.00**

Vase, orange cylinder w/green & blue bands, earthworm-like decor between bands, 10" **$100.00**

Vase, orange peel, cylindrical, 12x4¾" **$90.00**

Vase, orange peel, ovoid w/can neck, 12¼" **$92.50**

Vase, peacock figural, pink & blue iridescent, 15½" **$65.00**

Vase, shell form, green w/pink interior, #R483, 10¾x10½" ... **$40.00**

Vase, sphere w/3 plumes, pink & blue iridescent, #R281, 10½" .. **$125.00**

Vase, Tall Modern, Cloudy Blue, long slim neck, #R387 (unmarked), 16" **$92.50**

Vase, white w/turquoise interior, petaled top, #491H, 11½" .. **$55.00**

Vase, bud; rose pink, stepped base, #207, 7½" **$25.00**

Vase, creamy white w/blue interior, bulbous, gently curved rim-to-hip handles, 5½x6" **$35.00**

Vase, Dutch Blue w/light blue sponging, trumpet neck w/flared rim, shouldered body, 7½" **$35.00**

Vase, embossed vertical floral design on Pompeian Green, scalloped rim, pedestal foot, 7¼" **$60.00**

Vase, green, curled plume-like handles, #634, 7½x5¼" **$45.00**

Vase, green, ornate embossing & handles, 8" **$42.50**

Vase, green mottle, handles, #256, 6" **$55.00**

Vase, light blue flower form, 12½" **$60.00**

Vase, mauve to blue-green, elephant head handles, 6½" **$85.00**

Vase, seafoam green w/stippled finish, design on neck, #?19, 6¼x3½" **$45.00**

Vase, white matt, ornate handles, footed, #J26, 11½x7" **$95.00**

RumRill

RumRill-marked pottery was actually made by other companies who simply provided the merchandise that George Rumrill marketed from 1933 until his death in 1942. Rumrill designed his own lines, and the potteries who filled the orders were the Red Wing Stoneware Company, Red Wing Potteries, Shawnee (but they were involved for only a few months), Florence, and Gonder. Many of the designs were produced by more than one company. Examples may be marked RumRill or with the name of the specific pottery.

Advisors: Wendy and Leo Frese, Three Rivers Collectibles (See Directory, RumRill)

Bowl, Renaissance Group, ivory with brown wash, #530, 10½", from $45.00 to $60.00. (Photo courtesy B.L. and R.L. Dollen)

Bowl, white w/embossed rim, 3x7" **$40.00**

Candleholders, ivory, flower form, #1619, 1½x4½", pr **$32.00**

Dutch shoe, creamy white, Rumrill Made in USA sticker, 2x5x2¼" **$25.00**

Jug, brilliant orange, ball form, cork lid w/pottery cap, 7½" .. **$45.00**

Salt & pepper shakers, orange & cobalt, S & P on tops, Made for Mammoth Cave by Rumrill stickers, 3", pr **$32.00**

Vase, blue mottle, curved plume-like handles, #634, 7½x5¼" .. **$75.00**

Vase, blue w/light blue sponging, handees, #636, 6¼x6⅝" .. **$75.00**

Vase, blue w/light blue sponging, 3 closed handles, #304, 4½x7¾" **$125.00**

Vase, bright yellow, doves (2) near base, #829, 9" **$42.50**

Russel Wright Designs

One of the country's foremost industrial designers, Russel Wright, was also responsible for several lines of dinnerware, glassware, and spun aluminum that have become very collectible. American Modern, produced by the Steubenville Pottery Company (1939 – 1959) is his best known dinnerware and the most popular today. It had simple, sweeping lines that appealed to tastes of that period, and it was made in a variety of solid colors. Iroquois China made his Casual line, and because it was so serviceable, it's relatively easy to find today. It will be marked with both Wright's signature and 'China by Iroquois.' His spun aluminum is highly valued as well, even though it wasn't so eagerly accepted in its day, due to the fact that it was so easily damaged.

Note: Values are given for solid color dinnerware unless a pattern is specifically mentioned.

American Modern

The most desirable colors are Cantaloupe, Glacier Blue, Bean Brown, and White; add 50% to our values for these colors. Chartreuse is represented by the low end of our range; Cedar, Black Chutney, and Seafoam by the high end; and Coral and Gray near the middle. To evaluate patterned items, deduct 25%.

Casserole, from $30.00 to $40.00; Bowl, vegetable; from $20.00 to $30.00. (Photo courtesy Ann Kerr)

Bowl, baker; from $40 to......................................$50.00
Bowl, salad; from $100 to....................................$115.00
Bowl, vegetable; divided, from $135 to....................$150.00
Coaster, from $15 to..$25.00
Cup, demitasse; from $18 to..................................$22.00
Pitcher, water; tall, from $135 to $150.00
Plate, salad; 8", from $18 to.................................$20.00
Relish, divided, reed handle, from $250 to $300.00
Sugar bowl, stacking, from $15 to...........................$18.00
Teapot, restyled, from $175 to..............................$200.00

Highlight

Bowl, divided vegetable; minimum value......................$100.00
Creamer, from $40 to $55.00
Plate, bread & butter; from $12 to $15.00
Salt & pepper shakers, pr from $100 to.....................$150.00

Iroquois Casual

To price Brick Red, Aqua, and Cantaloupe Casual, double our values; for Avocado, use the low end of the range. Oyster, White, and Charcoal are at the high end.

The high end of the range should be used to evaluate solid-color examples.

Bowl, fruit; 9½-oz, 5½", from $12 to $14.00

Coffeepot, after dinner; from $100.00 to $125.00. (Photo courtesy Ann Kerr)

Coffeepot, from $150 to.......................................$175.00
Creamer, redesigned, from $25 to............................$30.00
Cup & saucer, redesigned, from $25 to.......................$30.00
Gravy boat, 12-oz, 5¼", from $15 to.........................$20.00
Pitcher, 1½-qt, from $150 to.................................$175.00
Plate, dinner; 10", from $12 to..............................$15.00
Salt & pepper shakers, stacking, pr from $30 to $40.00
Teapot, restyled, from $200 to..............................$225.00

Knowles

Centerpiece server, from $150 to $200.00
Cup & saucer, from $12 to....................................$16.00

Plate, bread & butter; 6", from $6 to........................$8.00
Plate, dinner; 10¾", from $15 to $18.00
Platter, 13" L, from $45 to...................................$55.00
Platter, 16" L, from $55 to...................................$75.00
Salt & pepper shakers, pr from $30 to $40.00

Plastic

These values apply to Home Decorator, Residential, and Flair (which is at the high end of the range). Copper Penny and Black Velvet items command 50% more. Meladur items are all hard to find in good condition, and values can be basically computed using the following listings as guidelines (except for the fruit bowl, which in Meladur is slightly higher).

Residential: Divided vegetable bowl, from $20.00 to $25.00; Cup and saucer, from $8.00 to $10.00.

Bowl, lug soup; #706, from $10 to $12.00
Bowl, vegetable; oval, shallow, #708, from $15 to...........$20.00
Plate, bread & butter; #705, from $6 to......................$8.00
Sugar bowl, w/lid, #712, from $12 to $15.00
Tumbler, #715, from $15 to $18.00

Spun Aluminum

Beverage set (pitcher, tray & 6 tumblers), from $450 to $550.00
Casserole, from $150 to......................................$200.00
Cheese knife, from $75 to....................................$100.00

Cheese server, wood insert, 16", $150.00. (Photo courtesy LiveAuctioneers.com/Treadway Gallery Inc.)

Cooking item, from $150 to...............................$200.00
Hot relish server, w/ceramic inserts, from $250 to...........$275.00
Muddler, from $75 to...................................$100.00
Relish rosette, sm....................................$75.00
Spaghetti set, from $500 to............................$600.00
Wastebasket, from $125 to..............................$150.00

Sterling

Bowl, bouillon; 7-oz, from $18 to......................$22.00
Bowl, soup; 6½-oz, from $18 to.........................$22.00
Creamer, individual, 3-oz, from $10 to.................$14.00
Pitcher, water; restyled, from $180 to.................$200.00
Plate, dinner; 10¼", from $10 to.......................$15.00
Plate, service; from $16 to............................$20.00
Relish, divided, 16½", from $65 to.....................$70.00
Sauceboat, 6¼", from $5 to.............................$7.00
Sugar bowl, w/lid, 10-oz, from $22 to..................$25.00
Teapot, 10-oz, from $125 to............................$150.00

White Clover (for Harker)

Ashtray, clover decor, from $40 to.....................$45.00
Bowl, vegetable; open, 7½", from $65 to................$75.00
Bowl, vegetable; w/lid, 8¼", from $75 to...............$100.00
Clock, General Electric, from $75 to...................$85.00
Pitcher, clover decor, w/lid, 2-qt, from $100 to.......$150.00
Plate, chop; clover decor, 11", from $40 to............$50.00
Plate, jumbo; clover decor, 10", from $18 to...........$20.00
Salt & pepper shakers, either size, pr from $30 to.....$35.00

Salt Shakers

Probably the most common type of souvenir shop merchandise from the '20 through the '60s, salt and pepper shakers can be spotted at any antique mall or flea market today by the dozens. Most were made in Japan and imported by various companies, though American manufacturers made their fair share as well. When even new shakers retail for $10.00 and up, don't be surprised to see dealers tagging the better vintage varieties with some hefty prices.

'Miniature shakers' are hard to find, and their prices have risen faster than any others'. They were all made by Arcadia Ceramics (probably an American company). They're usually less than 2" tall, some so small they had no space to accommodate a cork. Instead they came with instructions to 'use Scotch tape to cover the hole.'

Advertising sets and premiums are always good, since they appeal to a cross section of collectors. If you have a chance to buy them on the primary market, do so. Many of these are listed in the Advertising Character Collectibles section of this guide.

Recent sales have shown a rise in price for some shakers that were in the past considered low end. Some attract people who are not really salt shaker collectors but have a connection to the theme or topic that is represented, i.e. doctors will buy medical-related shakers, etc. Fish shakers are on the rise, especially specific breed fish. Some high-end shakers are getting soft. Many of the rare vin-

tage sets are being reproduced and redesigned so collectors can own a set at a more reasonable cost.

To help you stay informed we recommend *Florence's Big Book of Salt & Pepper Shakers* by Gene and Cathy Florence (Collector Books).

See also Advertising Character Collectibles; Breweriana; Condiment Sets; Holt Howard; Occupied Japan; Regal China; Rosemeade; Shawnee; Vandor; and other specific companies.

Note: 'Pr' will indicate sets having both the salt and pepper shaker modeled identically, while '2-pc' will indicate that they are complementary, for instance, Paul Bunyan and Babe the Blue Ox.

Advisor: Judy Posner (See Directory, Advertising)

Club: Novelty Salt and Pepper Shakers Club
c/o Louise Davis, Membership Coordinator
P.O. Box 416
Gladstone, OR 97027-0416
www.saltandpepperclub.com

Advertising

Ballantine Ale beer can, cardboard w/metal lid, 2⅜", pr in carry
    pack...$20.00

Blue Sunoco (brand identity of the Sun Oil Company in the 1950s – 1960s), from $40.00 to $50.00 for the pair.
(Photo courtesy Helene Guarnaccia)

Calvert Daiquiri, whiskey bottle, green glass, white screw-on lid,
    4¼", pr..$20.00
Chicken of the Sea fish, aqua & yellow, pottery, 2x2⅞", pr...$20.00
Gunther Beer bottle, amber glass w/metal top, foil label, 4", pr..$22.00
Homepride's Flour Fred, hard plastic, 4¼", pr..............$25.00
Idaho Potato Spud King, anthropomorphic potato head, Victoria
    Ceramics Made in Japan, 1950s, 3½", pr...............$39.00
Koppitz beer bottle, amber glass w/decal label, metal top, 3⅜",
    pr...$19.00

Lenox Furnace Co's Lennie Lenox, pottery w/front decal (some wear), 195-s, 5", pr **$85.00**

Magic Chef, chef, ceramic, black & white, 1940s, 5", pr **$45.00**

Mason Ball jar, clear glass w/metal screw-on lid, 2⅞", pr **$10.00**

McWilliams (Wine) Moselle monk, ceramic, Japan, 3½", pr..**$45.00**

Nugget Casino's Nugget Sam, ceramic, Japan, 1950s, 4", pr ..**$25.00**

Old Cliff House Restaurant, seal on cliff, pottery, flat unglazed bottom, 3¾", pr **$22.00**

Old Strasburg Railroad conductor & engineer, pottery, Japan label, 1960s, 4¼", 2-pc set **$24.00**

Possom Hollow Whiskey bottle, clear glass w/metal top, 3¾", pr ..**$18.00**

Rosie's Diner, diner (separates), ceramic, 1994, 2½x6¼", 2-pc set **$35.00**

Royal Canadian Whiskey bottle, amber glass w/metal top, 1950s, 4¼", pr **$18.00**

Schlitz beer bottle, amber glass w/decal label, metal top, 4", pr..**$18.00**

Seagram's 7, red 7 w/crown on top, plastic, 1950s, 3½", pr .**$24.00**

Sourdough Jake & burro, multicolor pottery, copyright Kelvin SP-40, 1950s-60s, 4", 2-pc set **$25.00**

Spiller's Homepride Flour's Flower Fred, hard plastic, Airfix, 3⅛", pr **$25.00**

Tastee Freeze Eff & Tee characters, pottery, Japan paper labels, 1960s-70s, 3¾", pr in wicker basket **$20.00**

Utica Club Beer Dooley & Schultz characters, ceramic, tallest: 4¾", 2-pc set **$75.00**

Volkswagen van, pottery, 1990s, 1¼x3¾", pr **$35.00**

Yenems Cigarette pack & book of matches, ceramic, unmarked, 1950s, 3¾", 2⅞", 2-pc set **$19.00**

Animals, Birds, and Fish

Deco dogs, from $15.00 to $18.00. (Photo courtesy Helene Guarnaccia)

Bear, white w/pink & brown trim, ceramic, Bendel, pr........**$75.00**

Bear huggers, brown, Van Tellingen, pr from $25 to...........**$28.00**

Bear huggers, white w/pink & brown trim, Bendel, pr **$75.00**

Bird & birdhouse, ceramic, green Japan mark, 1950s, 3", 2-pc set..**$20.00**

Bull & cow, ceramic, airbrushed mauve w/painted details, PY stamp, Ucagco foil labels, 3½", 2-pc set **$22.00**

Bunny huggers, solid colors, Van Tellingen, pr from, $25 to ..**$28.00**

Bunny huggers, white w/black & pink trim, Bendel, pr.......**$75.00**

Cat seated w/eyes closed, white w/hat & gold bow, Regal, pr....**$150.00**

Chicken & chick emerging from egg, bone china, Hi Style Bone China by Bridge Japan foil labels, 2½", 2-pc set **$18.00**

Circus elephant w/hat, ceramic, realistic, unmarked Japan, 4½", pr **$20.00**

Dinosaur on base, ceramic, unmarked Japan, 1960s-70s, 3⅜", pr..**$30.00**

Dog boy & girl in hats, 1 w/umbrella, 2nd w/cane, ceramic, Japan, 1950s, 4", 2-pc set **$20.00**

Dolphin leaping from water, ceramic, 1970s, 2¾", pr...........**$18.00**

Duck huggers, Van Tellingen, pr from $25 to **$28.00**

Fifi, Regal, pr **$250.00**

Fish, marked C Miller, Regal, 1-pc....................................**$55.00**

Hippopotamus mother & baby, ceramic, attributed to California, 1950s, 2⅜x3½" & smaller, 2-pc set **$20.00**

Iguanodon dinosaurs w/entwined necks, ceramic, Japan paper labels, 4½", pr..**$35.00**

Koala bear, bone china, unmarked Japan, 1960s-70s, 2⅛", pr ..**$20.00**

Oriole bird, ceramic, fine details, Napco foil labels, 1950s, 2½", pr..**$18.00**

Peek-a-Boo (bunny) huggers, red dots, lg, pr (+) from $200 to **$225.00**

Peek-a-Boo (bunny) huggers, red dots, Regal, sm, pr (+) from $100 to **$125.00**

Pheasant cock & hen, ceramic, realistic, Napco, 1950s, 4", 2-pc set..**$18.00**

Pig, pink, marked C Miller, Regal, 1-pc..............................**$75.00**

Pigs, standing mother & recumbent baby, ceramic, attributed to California, 1950s, 2¾", 1⅛", 2-pc set **$22.00**

Pigs kissing, gray w/pink trim, Bendel, lg, pr from $250 to..**$275.00**

Puppy in green vest & maroon bow tie, ceramic, Sunsco Japan foil labels, 1950s, 5¼", pr **$20.00**

Purple cow, ceramic, detailed, applied flowers, Japan mark, 1950s, pr..**$20.00**

Rabbit mother & baby, both w/vests, she w/hat & basket, ceramic, Japan, 1950s, 4", 2¾", 2-pc set..................................**$20.00**

Rooster & chicken, glass w/pottery heads, Made in Czechoslovakia, 3", 2-pc set..**$30.00**

Roosters fighting, ceramic, detailed, Napco, 1950s, 4½", 2-pc set..**$22.00**

Tabby cat, ceramic, Japan stamps on feet, 1950s, 3", pr.......**$20.00**

Teddy bears dressed up, ceramic, stacking, red Japan mark, 4¼", 2-pc set..**$18.00**

Turkey gobbler & hen, ceramic, realistic, Ucagco Ceramics Japan foil labels, 1950s, 3", 2-pc set..**$20.00**

WWII military bears, 1 w/USN hat & life preserver, 2nd w/aviator goggles, ceramic, unmarked, 1940s, 4⅜", 2-pc set **$32.00**

Anthropomorphic

Cat & bee on ball, ceramic, Japan, 1950s, cat: 3", 2-pc set..**$18.00**

Farmer pig, ceramic, Enesco Japan foil labels, 5", pr............**$20.00**

Grape cluster w/face, ceramic, Japan, 1950s, 3⅛", pr...........**$16.00**

Jimmy Carter peanut, ceramic, Made in Japan stickers, #H693, 3½", pr..**$24.00**

Lamb w/glasses on green base, ceramic, Japan, copyright MS, 1950s, 4½", pr **$20.00**

Lion w/monacle & red jacket on green ball, ceramic, Japan, copyright MS, 1950s, 4⅝", pr **$20.00**

Pan and teakettle, PY Japan, from $45.00 to $55.00 for the three-piece set. (Photo courtesy Helene Guarnaccia)

Pear & orange w/faces, ceramic, crudely painted, unmarked Japan, 2½x3¼", joined 1-pc set **$16.00**

Character

Bugs Bunny and Daffy Duck, International Corporation 1993, 5", MIB, $25.00. (Photo courtesy www.whatacharacter.com)

Aladdin & Lamp, ceramic, chartreuse & gold, unmarked USA, 1950s, 2", 2-pc set **$24.00**

Aladdin & Lamp, ceramic, he w/rhinestones & pearls, Made in Japan, ca 1960s, 4¼", 2¾x5¾", 2-pc set **$24.00**

Babar the Elephant, stacking figural, ceramic, Japan, 1950s, 4⅞", 2-pc set **$40.00**

Babar the Elephant & girlfriend, ceramic, dressed in finery, unmarked, 3½", 2-pc set **$35.00**

Bahama policeman, ceramic, 1960s, 4⅜", pr **$18.00**

Betsy Ross & Paul Revere, ceramic, Japan paper labels, 1960s, 4½", 2-pc set **$22.00**

Betty Boop, stacking figural, ceramic, Benjamin Medwin, 1995, 5", 2-pc set, MIB **$18.00**

Billy Sykes & Captain Cuttle (names incised on backs), ceramic, Made in England, 2½", 2-pc set **$22.00**

Bimbo (Betty Boop's dog), ceramic, cold-painted details, marked USA, 1930s, 2½", pr **$65.00**

Bonzo, ceramic, much gold trim, unmarked, 1930s, 3", pr.. **$22.00**

Buddha, ceramic, all white, Japan paper label, 3½", pr **$20.00**

Cat & Fiddle, ceramic, 1950s, 4½", 2-pc set **$24.00**

Charlie McCarthy (bust), ceramic, Japan, 1940s, 3", pr....... **$60.00**

Cinderella's slipper on pillow, stacking, ceramic, Applause, 2⅞x3", 2-pc set **$18.00**

Dogpatch Mammy & Pappy Yokum on sadiron shape, ceramic, Al Capp Enterprises, 1968, pr **$22.00**

Donald Duck, ceramic, Dan Brechner, WD-32 copyright Walt Disney Productions, Japan, 1961, 4⅞", pr **$65.00**

Donald Duck, ceramic, pastel colors, copyright Walt Disney, 1950s, 4", pr **$75.00**

Dudwig Von Drake & Donald Duck, ceramic, Dan Brechnmer Import, Walt Disney Productions, Japan, 1961, 5¼", 2-pc set **$75.00**

Felix the Cat, ceramic, black & white, Benjamin Medwin, 1991, pr, MIB **$18.00**

Gingham Dog & Cat, ceramic, unmarked, 1950s, 4½", 2-pc set **$24.00**

Goose & Golden Egg, ceramic, souvenir of Florida, 1950s, goose: 4", 2-pc set **$22.00**

Humpty Dumpty, ceramic, Regal China, pr **$75.00**

Humpty Dumpty, Regal, pr **$75.00**

Jack & Jill, ceramic, Kreiss, Japan, 1957, 2-pc set **$30.00**

Mammy & Pappy Yokum, ceramic, Made in Japan labels, #2611, 4¼", 2-pc set **$65.00**

Mary and lamb, Van Tellingen, from $40.00 to $50.00.

Miss Muffet & Spider, ceramic, Poinsettia Studio, she: 2½", 2-pc set **$35.00**

Mother Goose, ceramic, Josef Originals foil labels, 3⅝", pr... **$30.00**

Mother Goose drying dishes, ceramic, Fitz & Floyd, ca 1980s, 4¼", pr **$25.00**

Paul Bunyan & Babe, ceramic, souvenir, 1950s, Paul: 5½", 2-pc set **$22.00**

Peter Pumpkin Eater & wife, ceramic, Josef foil labels, 3⅜", 2-pc set **$35.00**

Pinocchio & girlfriend, porcelain, fine painted details, Japan, 1940s, 4⅞", 2-pc set **$65.00**

Pluto, ceramic, cold-painted details, copyright Walt Disney Productions, 1940s, 3¼", pr **$22.00**

Pluto & doghouse, ceramic, Applause, Walt Disney Co, 3¼", 2-pc set **$20.00**

Pooh & Hunny pot, ceramic, New England Collector Society, Disney, ca 1990s, Pooh: 3", 2-pc set **$30.00**

Pooh & Rabbit, ceramic, Walt Disney Productions, Enesco, 1960s, 3½", 4", 2-pc set **$55.00**

Popeye & Olive Oyl, ceramic, hand painted, unmarked, 1960s-70s, 6¼", 2-pc set **$65.00**

Popeye & spinach can, ceramic, 1995, Benjamin Medwin, 5⅜", 2-pc set, MIB **$16.00**

Preacher & Dandy (crows), ceramic, red cold-painted hats, Japan foil labels, 1940s, 3¾", 2-pc set **$55.00**

Queen of Hearts & Jester, pottery, Japan #6440, 4⅜", 2-pc set **$35.00**

Raggedy Ann, ceramic, unmarked vintage import, 4", pr **$30.00**

Robin Hood on rock, ceramic, stacking, Japan, 1950s, 4½", 2-pc set **$22.00**

Rock-a-bye Baby, baby laying on bed, ceramic, stacking, 1950s, 3½", 2-pc set **$22.00**

Royal Canadian Mounted Police, Mountie shaker inserts into horse, ceramic, Japan, 4½", 2-pc set **$30.00**

Rudolf the Red Nose Reindeer, ceramic, #4370, 3", pr **$22.00**

Saggy Baggy Elephant, ceramic, green Japan stamps, 1950s, 2½", pr **$45.00**

Silly Symphony pig (1 w/horn, 2nd w/accordion), ceramic, Japan (unauthorized Disney images), 1930s, 4", pr **$29.00**

Snoopy on doghouse, ceramic, stacking, Benjamin Medwin, 1994, copyright Snoopy 1958 United..., 4⅜", 2-pc set **$25.00**

Tortoise & Hare, ceramic, unmarked USA, 1950s, hare: 3¾", 2-pc set **$25.00**

White Rabbit, ceramic, stacking, red Japan mark, 4", pr......**$45.00**

Holidays and Special Occasions

Christmas carolers, from $12.00 to $18.00 for the pair.

(Photo courtesy Helene Guarnaccia)

Christmas, boy & girl dressed as Santa & his wife, ceramic, unmarked, 4", pr **$22.50**

Christmas, dog & cat w/red caps in top of red boots, ceramic, 2-pc set **$22.50**

Christmas, girl sitting on candy cane, stacking, ceramic, Napco, 1959, 2-pc set **$32.00**

Christmas, Mr & Mrs Christmas mouse, ceramic, Jasco, Hong Kong, 1981, 2-pc set, MIB **$20.00**

Christmas, Santa & bag of toys, ceramic, Lenox, he: 3¼", 2-pc set..**$38.00**

Christmas, Santa & Mrs Claus in teacups, ceramic, Lenox, 3½", 2-pc set **$18.00**

Christmas, Santa head winking, ceramic, Japan, 3¼x3", pr..**$35.00**

Christmas, Santa w/ball, 2nd Santa w/candy cane, ceramic, Japan, 3¼", 2-pc set **$15.00**

Christmas, Santa w/candy cane, Mrs Claus w/candle, ceramic, Japan, 3", 2-pc set..**$16.00**

Christmas, Santa w/candy cane & Mrs Claus w/presents, ceramic, sitting on wooden bench, Japan, 3-pc set **$20.00**

Christmas penguin couple seated on couch made of ice cubes, ceramic, Dept 56, MIB..**$30.00**

Christmas puppies, 1 w/red bow, 2nd w/red bow & green ornament, ceramic, Fitz & Floyd, 4" L, 2-pc set **$28.00**

Christmas Tree (pattern), ceramic, Spode, 3", pr, MIB **$25.00**

Easter bunny (resin) w/basket holding 2 ceramic eggs, 6½", 3-pc set **$15.00**

Easter bunny boy & girl, ceramic, red Japan mark, pr **$12.50**

Easter bunny stands on roots of stump holding lg egg, ceramic, Fitz & Floyd, 1996, 3-pc set..**$30.00**

Snowman & lady, he w/present, tie & hat, she w/holly, purse & hat, ceramic, Napco, 2-pc set..**$18.00**

Thanksgiving, cornucopia, ceramic, hand painted, Tilso Japan stickers, 5½" L, pr..**$10.00**

Thanksgiving, turkey gobbler & hen, ceramic, Japan, 1950s-60s, 3¾", 2⅞", 2-pc set **$18.00**

People

Amish man & woman, ceramic, Japan labels, #H763, 1950s, 4¾", 2-pc set **$18.00**

Babies in diapers, 1 crawling, 2nd sitting up, ceramic, attributed to California, 1940s-50s, tallest: 2½", 2-pc set **$30.00**

Boy & dog huggers, Black, Van Tellingen, pr......................**$75.00**

Boy & dog huggers, white, Van Tellingen, pr......................**$65.00**

Boy & girl kissing, Happiness Springs From Little Things, ceramic, 4¼", 2-pc set..**$24.00**

Boy in spacesuit, ceramic, Japan, 1950s, 3¾", pr **$30.00**

Chef head w/bug, ceramic, green PY mark, 1950s, 3½", pr .**$18.00**

Chef winking (bust), ceramic, Japan paper label, 1950s, 3¼", pr.**$16.00**

Choir boy w/book, ceramic, red Japan mark, 1950s, 4¾", pr ..**$18.00**

Clown, Regal, pr..**$250.00**

Dutch boy & girl, ceramic, Van Tellingen, 2-pc set, from $45 to **$50.00**

Dutch girl, ceramic, Regal, pr from $150 to **$175.00**

Dutch girl & windmill, ceramic, red Japan mark, 4¼", 2-pc set.**$24.00**

Eskimo girl & igloo, ceramic, red Japan mark, 1950s, she: 4½", 2-pc set **$18.00**

Fisherman in boat, ceramic, unmarked Elbee Art, 1950s, 2¾x3", pr **$18.00**

French chef, white w/gold trim, Regal, pr from $150 to **$175.00**

Goebel-type boy & girl, ceramic, Germany, 2⅞", 2-pc set ... **$25.00**

Indian boy & girl, he w/full headress, she w/feather, ceramic, Japan, 1960s, 4⅜", 2-pc set **$22.00**

Jogger in running suit w/hat pulled down, ceramic, Enesco Japan labels, stamped copyright 1978 Enesco, 4⅛", pr **$25.00**

Lyndon B Johnson portrait, ceramic, 2⅜", pr **$16.00**

Maid & chef, she w/spoon & I'm Salt on hat, he w/knife & I'm Pep on hat, ceramic, Japan, 1950s, 3", pr **$20.00**

Man and lady with signs, from $15.00 to $18.00. (Photo courtesy Helene Guarnaccia)

Man & woman, interlocking, ceramic, unmarked, 1950s, 5⅜", 2-pc set **$35.00**

Mexican man w/fruit cart (shakers have fruit tops, fit in cart), ceramic, Made in Japan, 1950s, 3-pc set **$24.00**

Old-fashioned policeman w/bat, ceramic, Japan, 1950s, 3⅞", pr. **$25.00**

Pirate & treasure chest, ceramic, unmarked, 1950s, he: 3½", 2-pc set **$18.00**

Rocket ship & moon man, ceramic, Enesco Japan foil label, 1950s, 4¼", 2-pc set **$40.00**

Sailor & mermaid huggers, Van Tellingen, pr from $100 to .. **$125.00**

Scottish boy & girl, ceramic, Josef Originals & Scotland foil labels, 4½", pr **$28.00**

Serenading Mexican man & woman, ceramic, chartreuse, copyright UC, 1950s, 4¼", 2-pc set **$20.00**

Street sweeper & cart, ceramic, unmarked, 1950s, 4⅜", 2", 2-pc set **$16.00**

Zodiac girl, ceramic, from series, Japan ink stamp, 4½", pr . **$25.00**

Souvenir

Auto, metal w/enameled details, 1¼", w/metal tray embossed Ohio Turnpike, 4¼x3¼", Japan, 3-pc set **$25.00**

Battleship Texas & San Jacinto Monument, ceramic, 1960s-70s, monument: 4", 2-pc set **$24.00**

Bears w/coonskin hats, ceramic, Crystal Lake Cave, Dubuque IA, 1950s, 3¾", pr **$18.00**

Geiser scene on pillar form, ceramic, Spouting Geyser, Saratoga Springs, NY, Staffordshire Royal Winton, 2½", pr **$19.00**

Lobster claw, ceramic, red w/York Beach Maine at base, 4¼", pr . **$20.00**

Mice (kissing) w/sunglasses, souvenir label from Grandy Canada on back of girl, ceramic, Japan, 2⅝", 2-pc set **$18.00**

Washington Monument, metal, 2¾", pr on 4¼x3⅜" chromo litho tray, Japan, 3-pc set **$20.00**

Miscellaneous

Angel & devil, ceramic, unmarked Japan, 1950s, 4¼", 2-pc set.. **$19.00**

Cowgirl leg w/white Western boot, ceramic, unmarked (attributed to California), 1950s, 2¼x3", pr **$16.00**

Flying saucer, ceramic, marked Coventry, 1950s, 1¼x2½x3", pr. **$24.00**

Jack-in-the-box, ceramic, 1950s, 4", pr **$28.00**

Love bug huggers, burgundy, Bendel, lg, pr **$125.00**

Love bug huggers, green, Bendel, sm, pr **$75.00**

Tulip, ceramic, Regal China, pr **$35.00**

Sango Dinnerware

This company is located in Indonesia and has for decades been that country's leading producer of dinnerware. They have successfully marketed their wares through many of this country's larger chain stores. Patterns range from simple solid or two-tone colors to holiday themes, abstracts, and florals. You'll often find nice pieces on your garage sale rounds, and collectors are now searching for items to replace those that have been broken or to add accessories that are no longer available through retail outlets.

Alice Blue, bowl, divided vegetable; 11¼" **$22.50**

Alice Blue, creamer & sugar bowl, w/lid **$24.00**

Alice Blue, cup & saucer **$7.50**

Alice Blue, plate, dinner; 10½" **$12.50**

Alice Blue, plate, salad; 7½" **$5.00**

Boutonniere, bowl, vegetable; w/lid **$50.00**

Boutonniere, cup & saucer **$7.50**

Boutonniere, plate, dinner **$15.00**

Boutonniere, platter, oval, 15¾" **$22.50**

Boutonniere, sugar bowl, w/lid **$12.50**

Calligraphy, bowl, vegetable; 10" **$40.00**

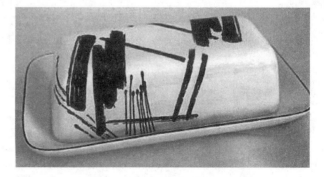

Calligraphy, butter dish, from $25.00 to $35.00.

Calligraphy, creamer **$15.00**

Calligraphy, cup & saucer $12.00
Calligraphy, mug...$25.00
Calligraphy, plate, dinner $20.00
Cotillion - Yellow Rose, bowl, vegetable; 11" L, from $12 to .$18.00
Cotillion - Yellow Rose, creamer $15.00
Cotillion - Yellow Rose, cup & saucer...................................$7.50
Cotillion - Yellow Rose, plate, salad $5.00
Cotillion - Yellow Rose, salt & pepper shakers, pr..............$50.00
Country Cottage, bowl, cereal; 6½" $9.00
Country Cottage, creamer & sugar bowl, w/lid...................$16.00
Country Cottage, cup & saucer, from $9 to........................$12.00
Country Cottage, mug, footed $7.00
Country Cottage, plate, dinner $7.50
Country Cottage, sugar bowl, w/lid $12.00
Country Cottage, tureen, w/lid $65.00
Debutante, bowl, rimmed soup..$8.00
Debutante, cup & saucer, from $8 to....................................$12.00
Debutante, plate, dinner $15.00
Debutante, platter, 16" L..$52.50
Debutante, sugar bowl, w/lid...$22.00
Evening Song, bowl, soup; 6½", from $10 to $12.00
Evening Song, creamer, 16-oz, 4½" $15.00
Evening Song, plate, dinner $12.00
Evening Song, plate, salad $7.50
Fresco, bowl, dessert...$5.00
Fresco, bowl, vegetable; oval $40.00
Fresco, cup & saucer, from $12 to $15.00
Fresco, plate, dinner; 10½"...$15.00
Fresco, platter, 12¼"..$27.50
Home for Christmas, bowl, vegetable; round $32.50
Home for Christmas, butter dish, ¼-lb $22.00
Home for Christmas, chop plate, 12" $36.00
Home for Christmas, cup & saucer...$8.00
Home for Christmas, gravy boat & underplate $37.50
Home for Christmas, mug...$12.50
Home for Christmas, plate, dinner; 11"................................$20.00
Home for Christmas, salt & pepper shakers, pr $22.50
Ming Garden, bowl, rimmed soup..$9.00
Ming Garden, bowl, vegetable; w/lid $55.00
Ming Garden, creamer $15.00
Ming Garden, cup & saucer, footed $8.50
Olivia, bowl, rimmed soup...$9.00
Olivia, mug...$8.00
Olivia, plate, chop; 12"..$32.00
Olivia, plate, salad; 8", from $6 to...$8.00
Pavillion, bowl, vegetable; 9"...$20.00
Pavillion, creamer, from $12 to $15.00
Pavillion, cup & saucer...$7.50
Pavillion, mug..$7.50
Pavillion, plate, chop; 12" $24.00
Pavillion, plate, dinner; 10", from $15 to............................$18.00
Rose Chintz, bowl, cereal; 6½", from $15 to $18.00
Rose Chintz, bowl, vegetable; 9" $28.00
Rose Chintz, creamer, 12-oz, from $15 to............................$18.00
Rose Chintz, cup & saucer..$8.00
Rose Chintz, mug $8.00
Rose Chintz, plate, dinner; from $14 to...............................$18.00

Rose Chintz, plate, salad $8.00
Rose Chintz, salt & pepper shakers, pr $22.00
Spanish Lace, bowl, rimmed soup...$12.00
Spanish Lace, creamer $15.00

Spanish Lace, gravy boat with attached underplate, $60.00.

Spanish Lace, plate, dinner..$25.00
Spanish Lace, plate, salad $12.00
Spanish Lace, platter, 14" L...$45.00
Summersweet, bowl, rimmed soup; 9", from $3 to $5.00
Summersweet, chop plate, 12", from $15 to $18.00
Summersweet, mug, from $3 to...$5.00
Summersweet, plate, salad; 8"..$4.00
Sweet Shoppe, bowl, rimmed soup...$7.50
Sweet Shoppe, bowl, soup; 8", from $20 to $24.00
Sweet Shoppe, bowl, spaghetti..$60.00
Sweet Shoppe, mug, 6", from $7 to $9.00
Sweet Shoppe, plate, dinner $15.00
Sweet Shoppe, plate, salad; from $8 to................................$10.00
Sweet Shoppe, sugar bowl...$18.00
Sweet Shoppe, tureen w/lid...$75.00
Zoey, bowl, vegetable; round, 9"...$15.00
Zoey, cup & saucer $12.00
Zoey, plate, dinner; from $8 to...$12.00
Zoey, sugar bowl, w/lid...$8.00

Schoop, Hedi

One of the most successful California ceramic studios was founded in Hollywood by Hedi Schoop, who had been educated in the arts in Germany. She had studied not only painting but sculpture, architecture, and fashion design as well. Fleeing Nazi Germany with her husband, the famous composer Frederick Holander, Hedi settled in California in 1933 and only a few years later became involved in producing novelty giftware items so popular that they were soon widely copied by other California companies. She designed many animated human figures, some in matched pairs, some that doubled as flower containers. All were hand painted and many were decorated with applied ribbons, sgraffito work, and gold trim. To a lesser extent, she modeled animal figures as well. Until fire leveled the plant in 1958, the business was very productive. Nearly everything she made was marked.

If you'd like to learn more about her work, we recommend *Collector's Encyclopedia of California Pottery,* by Jack Chipman (Collector Books).

Figurine, Chinese flute player from Young China Line, 11", from $70 to **$80.00**

Figurine, Chinese man & woman, ea w/bucket (removable), pink, black & white attire, on black base, 12", pr from $100 to **$130.00**

Figurine, Deco lady walking lg poodle, basket over right arm, 9½x8" **$185.00**

Figurine, Turn-About Cat, male 1 side, female on reverse, gold w/ stylized carving, 16x10¼" **$165.00**

Flower holder, ballerina w/arms up, 1 leg extended, opening on back of tutu, 9½x10½" **$80.00**

Flower holder, lady holds 1 side of skirt wide (opening there), 2nd hand holds pot on head, flowers at waist, NM **$50.00**

Flower holder, Southern belle w/long white dress w/blue trim, slim white basket in ea hand, much detail, 12¼" **$80.00**

Flower holders, Chinese man and woman, he w/2 pots, she w/fan, red-brown & white w/handpainted flowers, 12", 11¼", pr...... **$80.00**

Flower holders, ladies from the Phantasy line, 12", $200.00.

Scouting Collectibles

Collecting scouting memorabilia has long been a popular pastime for many. Through the years, millions of boys and girls have been a part of this worthy organization founded in England in 1907 by retired Major-General Lord Robert Baden-Powell. Scouting has served to establish goals in young people and help them to develop leadership skills, physical strength, and mental alertness. Through scouting, they learn basic fundamentals of survival. The scouting movement came to the United States in 1910, and the first World Scout Jamboree was held in 1911 in England.

Advisor: R.J. Sayers (See Directory, Scouting Collectibles)

Boy Scouts

Bandanna, blue & yellow, Oscar de La Renta for BSA, M ...**$10.00**
Bank, red, white & blue w/logo, lithoed tin, 2¼x2" dia, EX... **$120.00**

Book, Sea Scout Manual, 6th edition, 1949, EX.................**$20.00**

Bookends, logo w/beaver at ea side, marked SP 7 574, 5½x5", EX **$110.00**

Booklet, Cub Scout Guidebook, softcover, 1959 printing, 16 pages, 8x5½", VG.. **$5.00**

Bugle, Official; Rexcraft, brass, ca 1940s, 16½", EXIB **$75.00**

Camera, Imperial #1346-K, 7-pc, EXIB **$45.00**

Charm, Scout figural, gold-plated silver w/enameling, arrow & G logo (Griffith), 1960s-70s, 1⅛", MOC.........................**$10.00**

Cuff links, red & white enamel w/silver buffalo, Sterling, NM. **$95.00**

First aid kit, complete w/intructions/bandages etc, Johnson & Johnson, 1932, tin box, EX.. **$65.00**

Hat, Scout Master Campaingn, Stetson, M (NM in box) **$65.00**

Knife, Camillus commemorative, Men of Tomorrow, single blade & 3 tools, 3⅝", MIB.. **$50.00**

Knife, Tenderfoot emblem on round shield, 3 tools & 1 lg blade, grooved brown imitation slag handle, 1966-76, EX......**$38.00**

Medal, Knot Tying, gold w/blue ribbon, NM **$90.00**

Mess kit, cloth case, early metal cup (later were plastic), Regal, EX.. **$10.00**

Mug, National Scout Jamboree's 75th Anniversary, ceramic, 1985, EX **$5.00**

Neckerchief, National Jamboree at Valley Forge, Washington in prayer, 1957, EX+.. **$15.00**

Neckerchief slide, Cub Scouts, rope knot & wolf's head, blue enameling, 1¼x1½" **$5.00**

Neckerchief slide, sailor's knot & eagle, adjustable back, 1¾x1½", EX **$10.00**

Patch, Camp Sinawa, yellow on blue, turtle & campsite, 1949, EX.. **$10.00**

Patch, National Ecology Workshop, Schiff Scout Reservation, EX **$75.00**

Patch, National Jamboree, embroidered cloth, 1960, 3" dia, EX.. **$15.00**

Patch, National Jamboree, Idaho, 1969, 6", $65.00.

Patch, National Order of the Arrow Conference, 43rd Anniversary, embroidered cloth, shield form, 1958, NM (+) **$75.00**

Patch, National Science Foundation Antarctic Service Square Knot, EX **$65.00**

Patch, Senior Patrol Leader Honors, 2 blue chevrons on white, 1930s, EX **$110.00**

Patch, Service Camp, New York World's Fair, 1940, EX **$45.00**

Patch, Washington Crossing Camporee 1961, embroidered cloth, 3" dia, EX..**$5.00**

Patch, 1969 National Jamboree Idaho, EX..........................**$12.00**

Pennant, Makiling National Park, 1959 World Jamboree, Scout blowing trumpet, 6x12", EX.....................................**$130.00**

Pin badge, Bobcat Cub Scouts BSA, bronze w/bobcat's face in relief, 1950s-60s, ¾" dia, NM **$4.00**

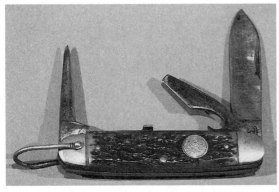

Pocketknife, Remington, 4" long, EX, $35.00. (Photo courtesy LiveAuctioneers.com/Morphy Auctions)

Puzzle, wooden litho camp scene of Scout signaling, 1930s, 154-pc, EX **$115.00**

Ring, eagle & Scouting insignia, red, white & blue enameling, Sterling, EX **$55.00**

Rock & minerals kit, 60 samples w/ID sheet, EXIB **$35.00**

Spoons, Wolf Cub head on handle, Chester EP Co, 4¼", set of 6, EXIB..**$100.00**

Ticket, 5¢ trade at post, 1937 World Jamboree, Good Humor Ice Cream on back, EX..**$8.00**

Tie bar, 15 Year Veteran, LG Balfour, early 1970s, MIB **$27.00**

Uniform, Bear Cub (Cubs BSA), blue, includes twill cap, neckerchief w/slide, belt & shirt, 1940s, NM..................................**$42.50**

Whistle, Acme, brass, 1940-50s, 2½", EX..........................**$25.00**

Woodcarving set, 5 varied chisels, Cattaragus, M in wood box w/ emblem..**$95.00**

Girl Scouts

Brooch, gold-tone with faux pearl, $50.00.

Book, Girl Scout Handbook, green hardcover, 1949, NM...**$15.00**

Book, The Girl Scout Story, Adele DeLeeuw, Garrard Publishing Co, 1965, EX...**$6.00**

Bookends, green leatherette over metal, stamped gold insignia, 5½x5"...**$30.00**

Bracelet, copper w/Art Nouveau look & logo on front, chain links, 1950s, 6½", EX...**$30.00**

Calendar, January shows Debbie Reynolds as troop leader, 1958, M in cover **$12.00**

Camera, Imperial Mark XII, w/flash, EXIB **$40.00**

Catalog, Accessories, 39-page, 1934, EX............................**$35.00**

Coin, Commemorative, Honor the Past-Serve the Future, 1912-1962, NM **$10.00**

Cuff links, trefoils w/embossed GS, #12-171, MIB.............**$70.00**

Doll, Brownie, Effanbee, 1965, 8½", EXIB.........................**$50.00**

Earmuffs, black w/white logos, felt, 28", EX......................**$10.00**

Handbook, Intermediate Program, hardback, 1959, EX **$12.00**

Hat, leader's; green w/black GS, green ribbon w/bow, #2-150, EXIB..**$60.00**

Knife, Kutmaster Utica NY USA on blade, 3 tools, celluloid handle w/insignia, nickel-silver bolsters, green, 3⅜", EX..........**$15.00**

Knife, Ulster #Y-601, 3" blade, bottle opener & screwdriver, VG+ **$75.00**

Paperweight, clear plastic, 1912 Girl Scouts 1972 60th Anniversary, ¾x2½" sq, EX..**$20.00**

Pin, Brownie figural, plastic w/metal clasp, 2", EX **$30.00**

Pin, membership; trefoil w/Brownie, gold-tone metal, 3 stars, EX **$50.00**

Pocketknife, Utica Featherweight, trefoil on handle, 1 blade, EX **$45.00**

Poster, Girl Scout Promise, 22x14", EX **$50.00**

Poster, It's Girl Scout Cookie Time, Scouts hanging banner, 1963, EX **$35.00**

Print, Our America, Learning About the Forest, camp scene, 22x32", EX **$40.00**

Purse, green vinyl, box style, 1950s, 3¼x8x4", EX..............**$15.00**

Ring, insignia, gold-tone w/dark green enameling, EX.........**$45.00**

Songbook, Brownies' Own Songbook, Ann Roos & Alice White, 1968, 48-pg, EX **$8.00**

Tin container, Girl Scout Mixed Nuts, 1950s, 3" dia, EX......**$8.00**

Trivet, 50th Anniversary, 7x7", $100.00.

Umbrella, gold w/green tip & handle, 2 carved daisies, white logo, EX **$15.00**

Uniform, leader's; shirtwaist dress w/long cuffed sleeves, metal side zipper, 1950s, EX...**$75.00**
Wristwatch, logo on face, windup, red leather band, Timex, EX.. **$30.00**
Wristwatch, silver base metal case w/stainless back, green hour markers, green rubber band, Timex, 1950s-60s, NM...........**$60.00**

Sears Kitchen Ware

During the 1970s the Sears Company sold several lines of novelty kitchen ware, including Country Kitchen, Merry Mushrooms, and Neil the Frog. These lines, especially Merry Mushrooms, are coming on strong as the collectibles of tomorrow. There's a lot of it around and unless you're buying it from someone who's already aware of its potential value, you can get it at very low prices. It was made in Japan. Besides the ceramic items, you'll find woodenware, enamelware, linens, and plastics.

Country Kitchen

Bell, 4½", $15.00 for the pair.

Bread box, w/drawers, enamelware, 16x12x18".....................**$75.00**
Butter dish **$15.00**
Canisters, set of 4..**$40.00**
Creamer, 4¼", from $8 to..**$10.00**
Mug, from $6 to **$8.00**
Napkin holder, 4½x5¾"..**$15.00**
Salt & pepper shakers, cylindrical, 4¾", pr **$15.00**
Spoon rest, rectangular, 4 rests, from $10 to **$12.00**

Merry Mushrooms

Ashtray, mushroom shape, rests on side, 6x5" **$85.00**
Blender cover, vinyl, from $10 to.......................................**$15.00**
Bookends **$50.00**
Bowl, salad; w/wooden fork & spoon, rare...........................**$60.00**
Bread box, metal, shelf inside, 10x13x10½'........................**$25.00**

Butter dish, ¼-lb, from $15 to...**$20.00**
Canister set, basketweave background, 4-pc, from $55 to **$65.00**
Canister set, plastic, brown lids, 4-pc **$32.00**
Canister set, smooth background, cylindrical, w/wooden lids, 4-pc, from $50 to **$60.00**
Canister set, textured background, common, 4-pc **$40.00**
Casserole, Corning Ware, glass lid, 1¾-qt **$30.00**
Casserole, Corning Ware, glass lid, 2½-qt, from $40 to **$50.00**
Cheese board, wooden w/round tile insert, MIB.................**$75.00**
Clock, wall mount, battery operated, from $25 to **$30.00**

Coffee mug, plain background, mushrooms on front and back, $10.00.

Coffee mug, textured background, 10-oz **$10.00**
Coffee mug, thermo-plastic, from $12 to............................**$16.00**
Coffee mugs, textured background, 4 on scrolling metal tree... **$45.00**
Coffeepot, 9½", from $25 to..**$35.00**
Cookie jar, frog figural, 12" **$50.00**
Cookie jar, lg canister, from $18 to **$20.00**
Corn dishes, mushroom at end of tray, set of 4, MIB **$60.00**
Creamer & sugar bowl, w/lid...**$35.00**
Curtain valance, 12x66"...**$45.00**
Curtains, 68x24", pr, MIP **$45.00**
Cutlery set consisting of carving knife, filet knife, bread knife & meat fork **$32.50**
Dutch oven, enamelware..**$30.00**
Fondue set, 2-qt, MIB...**$35.00**
Gravy boat, 5½" L, w/7" L undertray **$30.00**
Jar, storage; metal band & flip-down closure, 4½" **$30.00**
Lamp shade, ceiling mount, glass & metal, hexagonal **$60.00**
Lazy Susan canister, 4 units fit together to form lg mushroom, 1 lid covers all, 11½x10½" **$125.00**
Letter holder/mail sorter, painted wood, 3-pocket, wall hanging, 8x6x2", from $20 to **$30.00**
Napkin holder, from $20 to **$25.00**
Napkin ring **$3.00**
Pitchers, mini, 2-3½", set of 4..**$30.00**
Place mats, mushrooms on quilted white fabric w/brown corded edge, set of 4 w/4 orange napkins, from $30 to **$35.00**
Plant mister, smooth background, ball form, rare, 6" to top of pump **$48.00**

Planter, textured background, on brown undertray $35.00
Plaque, mushrooms in relief on oval, 9½x7½" $60.00
Plate, luncheon; 9¼" $10.00
Platter, 8x12" $22.00
Potholders, set of 2 .... $30.00
Salt & pepper shakers, 5", pr from $15 to $20.00
Slow cooker, electric $65.00
Soup mug, hard to find, 3x4¾", from $25 to $30.00
Spice jar, paper label identifies contents, sm $5.00
Spice rack, 2-tier, 2 drawers in base, w/12 spice jars, from $65 to $80.00
Spoon rest, frog lying down at rim of 3 joined lily pads $35.00
Spoon rest, 2 indents at bottom, 7½x5", from $15 to $20.00
Tea bag holder, frog waving from white lily pad, 6¾" center .. $35.00
Tea light holder, mushroom shape, dated 1981, 7¾" $30.00
Teakettle, enamelware $15.00
Teapot, 7" $22.50
Timer, dial in mushroom shape, 1976, 4½" $35.00
Toaster cover, printed cloth $15.00
Toaster cover, vinyl $20.00
Tumblers, decal on clear glass, 3x2¾", set of 4 from $20 to . $25.00
Tureen, w/underplate & ladle, 2½-qt, from $50 to $60.00
Utensil holder, from $20 to $30.00
Wall pocket, pitcher & bowl shape $35.00

Neil the Frog

Bank, frog leaning on elbow, from $35 to $45.00
Bell, frog on yellow lily pad in relief on white, 1978, 4¾", from $60 to $75.00
Bowl, water lily leaves on sides, 2 3-D frogs play at rim, 3¾x7" $60.00
Canister set, enamelware, 4-pc, from $20 to $25.00
Canister set, plastic w/green lids, 4-pc, from $18 to $22.00
Canister set, 4-pc, from $65 to $75.00
Clock, lotus leaf shape, wall mount, battery-operated, 7½x7", from $25 to $35.00
Coffee mug, from $6 to $8.00
Coffee mugs, set of 4 on scrolling metal tree, from $25 to ... $35.00
Cookie jar, frog finial, 10½" $35.00

Creamer, from $10.00 to 12.00.

Creamer & sugar bowl, from $25 to $30.00
Cruets, oil & vinegar, 5", pr $30.00
Figurines, 1 holding yellow flower, 2nd w/umbrella, 1¾", 1⅝", pr from $25 to $30.00
Kitchen towel, frogs playing among mushrooms, 24x15½" $9.00
Mustard jar, slot in lid for spoon (present) $20.00
Napkin holder, frog on lily pad, from $15 to $20.00
Pitcher, frog figural, mouth is spout, 6½", from $45 to $50.00
Place mats, frog on white lily pad, 4 for $25.00
Salt & pepper shakers, frog & lily pad, 2-pc set, from $15 to .. $20.00
Salt & pepper shakers, frog on yellow sunflower, stacking, 2-pc set, from $18 to $22.00
Salt & pepper shakers, much like spice jars, pr from $15 to ... $20.00
Saucepan, enamelware, green lid, 6½" dia $25.00
Skillet, enamelware, 10" $20.00
Spice rack, white painted wood 2-tier shelf w/12 spice shakers ... $85.00
Spoon rest, frog at ea side of 2 lily pads $20.00
Teakettle, enamelware, green lid $45.00
Teapot, 2-cup, 5¾" $95.00
Trivet, cast iron w/ceramic insert, from $20 to $30.00

Sebastians

These tiny figures were first made in 1938 by Preston W. Baston and sold through gift stores, primarily in the New England area. When he retired in 1976, the Lance Corporation chose 100 designs which they continued to produce under Baston's supervision. Since then, the discontinued figures have become very collectible.

Baston died in 1984, but his son, P.W. Baston, Jr., continues the tradition.

The figures are marked with an imprinted signature and a paper label. Early labels (before 1977) were green and silver foil shaped like an artist's palette; these are referred to as 'Marblehead' labels (Marblehead, Massachusetts, being the location of the factory) and figures that carry one of these are becoming hard to find and are highly valued by collectors.

Boston Public Gardens, Copr 1984 .... $25.00
Christmas Sleigh Ride, separate wood base, 8½" L $35.00
Colonial Watchman, Marblehead label $45.00
Coronado & Senora, 1960, 3¼" $25.00
David Copperfield & Wife, Pat Pend, 3" $40.00
Dutchman's Pipe, 1949 .... $55.00
First Cookbook, 1947 .... $55.00
Gathering Tulips, 1949, from $60 to $80.00
George Washington the Mason, 1961, 3½" $32.00
Henry W Longfellow, 2½", NM $95.00
John F Kennedy, 1962 .... $32.00
Marine Memorial, Hampton Beach $55.00
Mr Beacon Hill, Marblehead label, 1947 .... $45.00
Mr Obocell, 1960s $28.00
Mrs Beacon Hill, Marblehead label, 1947 .... $45.00
Nativity, figures & animals covered w/lg green leaves, copr 1954 PV Baston, 1954, 7" $115.00
Parade Rest, 1978, 4½" $25.00
PW Baston Self Portrait, 1984 .... $65.00

Ride to the Hounds $55.00
Skipper, 1966, MIB $48.00

Spirit of '76, $25.00.

SSS Spirit of Massachusetts, 1983, MIB $27.50
Statue of Liberty, 1986, 7" $35.00
Uncle Sam, 1967, 4¼" $35.00

Sewing Collectibles

Ladies whose lot it has been to sew for their families have used a variety of tools — some were strictly utilitarian, while others were whimsical. Seamstresses are few and far between these days, but collectors search for the figural tape measures, sewing baskets, pincushions, and thimbles like grandma once used.

If you're interested in learning more about the subject, we recommend *Sewing Tools & Trinkets, Vols. 1* and *2,* by Helen Lester Thompson (Collector Books). In the listings that follow, unless noted otherwise, values are for examples in at least near mint condition.

Advisor: Kathy Goldsworthy (See Directory, Sewing)

Pincushions, Japan, from $20.00 to $30.00. (Photo courtesy Carole Bess White)

Basket, tan & white wicker, w/tray, cross-stitched flowers on hinged lid, white satin lining, 1930s, 7x13x9½"......................$50.00
Basket, wood, shelf inside, hinged lid opens from both sides, w/ wood handle, footed, 10x10x8" $70.00
Basket, woven cords, sm woven handle in center on lid, silk pad in bottom of lid, 5x6" dia, EX $120.00

Book, Beldings Revised Needle & Hook, 5 color pages, softcover, 82 pages, 9x6", EX..$60.00
Book, pattern; Rag Bag Toys, instructions & patterns, American Thread Co, softcover, 30 pages, 1944 ....$50.00
Book, Singer Sewing Skill Reference, hardcover, 52 pages, 1954, EX...$40.00
Box, attachments; black metal, complete w/attachments, screwdrivers & leaflet, hinged lid, Singer.............................$135.00
Box, light green marble plastic, kittens playing w/yarn on clear lid, divided tray inside, Hommer MFG Co, 3x8x6" $45.00
Darner, clear blue glass, handled egg shape, unmarked Czechoslovakia, 5¼" L..$25.00
Darner, ebony egg w/embossed grapes on silver handle marked Sterling, 6¼"...$70.00
Darner, wooden, handled egg shape, white w/blue & rose swirl paint, 5½" L..$20.00
Embroidery transfer, bluebirds & florals, #7118, Alice Brooks, 1940s, uncut...$35.00
Embroidery transfer for pillow, Pekingese puppy, Laura Wheeler, 1930s, 14x14", uncut $25.00
Emery, suede acorn, feathers carved in sterling silver cap, ⅞" dia.. $75.00
Magazine, Sewing Success, FW Woolworth Co, fully illustrated, 1940, EX+...$8.00
Manual, Lippincott's Home Manuals Clothing for Women, 7 color plates & 262 illustrations, 454 pages, 1921 reprint, EX..$40.00
Manual, Singer Sewing Machine 15-210 & 15-211, 55 pages, 1930s...$10.00
Needle case, brass w/embossed decorations, Favorite Needle Preserver on side, Henry Clark & Co, 2x¼" dia $100.00
Needle case, carved bone, closed parasol form, stanhope of Jerusalem in handle, 5" L................................$90.00
Needle case, metal w/geometric green, white & light blue beading, 3½" $55.00
Needle case, porcelain, hand-painted Limoges-style pink & yellow roses, gilt trim, signed on base, 3½x1½" dia $80.00
Pattern, Butterick #6015 Walk-Away Dress, 1952, cut, complete in envelope, EX...$150.00
Pattern, Vogue #8063, dress or tunic & pants, features cut-out back, 1960s, M in EX package.................................$80.00
Pincushion, beaded w/sequins, heart shape, bird w/flowers on pink, NYS Fair Indian Village, 1950s, 4½x5" $45.00
Pincushion, ceramic, elephant seated in diaper, white w/multicolor details, 5"..$20.00
Pincushion, ceramic, 2 Scottie dogs lay on lace in center of silk cushion, 1920s, 5½" sq, EX.................................$100.00
Pincushion, cloth & leather, American Indian moccasin, multicolor w/brown leather bottom, 1930s.................................$80.00
Pincushion, high heel shoe, pink plastic, burgundy pincushion inside, 1940s, 2¾x3½"..................................$35.00
Pincushion, penguin beside cushion, multicolor, Made in Japan, 3" $32.00
Pincushion, red velvet strawberry, w/cut-out sterling silver cap & hanging loop, silk tassle, 1½x1" $130.00
Pincushion, silk, 10 Oriental figures peer over circumfrence of rim, pink w/multicolor figures, 1950s, 4½".................$40.00
Pincushion, sterling silver, detailed pig w/red cushion on back, England, ⅝x1⅛" $110.00

Pincushion/tape measure, brown puppy w/white tummy & nose, red collar, 'Pull my tongue for tape...' on tag, 1940-50s, 4" .. **$55.00**

Scissors, Art Nouveau floral design on sterling handles, sm ... **$56.00**

Scissors, fancy cut handles, Marshall-Wells, Germany, 4½" .. **$40.00**

Scissors, stork figural, gilded steel, 1930s, 1½" L, EX **$50.00**

Sewing machine, Hoge Mfg. Co., Inc., No. 325 — Popular Model — Little Princess Sewing Machine, metal, ca. 1937, 7x4¼x8¾", $185.00. (Photo courtesy Glenda Thomas)

Tape measure, Bakelite, black cat sitting, pulls out from front paws, 1x1½" **$35.00**

Tape measure, brass, clothes iron, striped stone handle, metric cloth measure, EX **$155.00**

Tape measure, brass, 3-D cat face, green & black glass eyes, knob on back retracts 40" cloth tape, Germany **$110.00**

Tape measure, celluloid, Billiken, tape in base, Florence Pretz, Japan, ca 1930s, 2½" **$75.00**

Tape measure, celluloid, fruit basket, tape pulls out from side, 1¾" dia......... **$30.00**

Tape measure, celluloid, teapot, red w/gold trim, tape pulls out from lid **$170.00**

Tape measure, metal, A Century of Sewing Service 1851-1951, blue, Singer, 1¾" dia......... **$60.00**

Tape measure, metal, owl in frame, glass eyes, Germany, 1920s, 1½" dia......... **$36.00**

Tape measure, metal & brass, windmill, cloth measure retracts w/ windmill blades, Germany, 2" **$190.00**

Tape measure, plastic, horse & chariot, cloth tape extends from red base, 1¾x1" dia......... **$70.00**

Tape measure, sterling silver, sunflower, cloth measure, Webster Co, 1¼" dia **$50.00**

Tape measure, stuffed cloth, dog, red plaid w/white ears & tummy, retractable tape tail, Japan, 1950s, 3x2½" **$45.00**

Tatting shuttle, celluloid, portrait of Lydia Pinkham, Yours for Health...Vegetable Compound, ca 1920, 3" L **$70.00**

Tatting shuttle, sterling silver, floral fabric under clear enamel top, Webster Co **$90.00**

Tattling shuttle, abalone, multicolor, 2½" L......... **$50.00**

Thimble, child's; yellow gold, flower basket in high relief w/surrounding bright cuts **$550.00**

Thimble, china, hand-painted bird w/flowers, signed William Powell, Royal Worcester, 1935, 1" **$455.00**

Thimble, silver, Queen Elizabeth II's Commemoration 1952-53, Henry Griffith & Sons, Sterling, +presentation box.... **$160.00**

Thimble, silver & enamel, Bicentennial 1976 w/image of Betsy Ross sewing flag, 1x½" dia **$130.00**

Thimble, silver w/enameled reindeer in winter ocean landscape, hardstone top, 925 Norway **$485.00**

Thimble, yellow gold, leaves engraved on wide band, raised & deeply carved rim, H Muhr's Sons, ½" dia......... **$75.00**

Thimble, 18k yellow gold, flower decoration on band, 1"... **$100.00**

Thimble holder, shagreen, push-button lock, hinged lid, 1½x1" dia, EX **$110.00**

Thimble holder, silver, hinged lid, Unger Brothers, Sterling, ½-oz, 1x1" dia **$110.00**

Shawnee Pottery

In 1937 a company was formed in Zanesville, Ohio, on the suspected site of a Shawnee Indian village. They took the tribe's name to represent their company, recognizing the Indians to be the first to use the rich clay from the banks of the Muskingum River to make pottery there. Their venture was very successful, and until they closed in 1961, they produced many lines of kitchenware, planters, vases, lamps, and cookie jars that are very collectible today.

They specialized in figural items. There were 'Winnie' and 'Smiley' pig cookie jars and salt and pepper shakers; 'Bo Peep,' 'Puss 'n Boots,' 'Boy Blue,' and 'Charlie Chicken' pitchers; Dutch children; lobsters; and two lines of dinnerware modeled as ears of corn.

Values sometimes hinge on the extent of an item's decoration. Most items will increase by 100% to 200% when heavily decorated with decals and gold trimmed.

Not all of their ware was marked Shawnee; many pieces were simply marked U.S.A. (If periods are not present, it is not Shawnee) with a three- or four-digit mold number. If you'd like to learn more about this subject, we recommend *Shawnee Pottery, The Full Encyclopedia*, by Pam Curran and *The Collector's Guide to Shawnee Pottery* by Duane and Janice Vanderbilt; and *Shawnee Pottery, Identification & Value Guide*, by Jim and Bev Mangus.

See also Cookie Jars.

Advisors: Jim and Beverly Mangus (See Directory, Shawnee)

Club: Shawnee Pottery Collectors' Club
P.O. Box 713
New Smyrna Beach, FL 32170-0713

Corn Ware

Bowl, mixing; King, Shawnee 6, 6½", from $30 to **$35.00**

Butter dish, King or Queen, Shawnee 72, from $50 to........ **$55.00**

Creamer, White Corn, USA, 12-oz, from $25 to **$30.00**

Cup, King, 90, from $27 to **$30.00**

Dish, vegetable; King or Queen, marked Shawnee 95, 9", from $50 to **$55.00**

Jug, King, Shawnee 71, 40-oz, from $65 to **$70.00**

Creamer, #70, from $26.00 to $28.00.

Platter, King or Queen, Shawnee 96, 12", from $50 to	**$55.00**
Popcorn set, King or Queen, from $190 to	**$200.00**
Relish tray, King, Shawnee 79, from $35 to	**$40.00**
Salt & pepper shakers, King or Queen, 5¼", pr from $35 to	**$45.00**
Sugar bowl, King or Queen, Shawnee 78, from $30 to	**$35.00**
Sugar shaker, White, USA, from $65 to	**$75.00**
Teapot, King or Queen, Shawnee 65, individual	**$75.00**
Teapot, King or Queen, Shawnee 65, 10-oz, from $155 to	**$165.00**

Kitchenware

Pitcher, Bo Peep, USA Pat Bo Peep, 40-ounce, from $85.00 to $90.00.

Canister, fruit decal, USA, 2-qt, from $45 to	**$50.00**
Canister, no decoration, USA, 1-qt, from $45 to	**$50.00**
Carafe, patio; Kenwood USA 945, from $75 to	**$80.00**
Creamer, Laurel Wreath, USA, from $20 to	**$22.00**
Creamer, Smiley, all-over gold, Patented Smiley USA, from $375 to	**$400.00**
Creamer, Smiley the Pig w/gold trim & cloverbud, patented Smiley USA, from $150 to	**$165.00**
Creamer, Wave, yellow, USA, from $20 to	**$22.00**

Grease jar, Flower & Fern, from $40 to	**$45.00**
Grease jar, Sahara, Kenwood USA 977, w/lid, from $40 to	**$50.00**
Ice server, elephant, w/black or white collar, marked Shawnee 60 &/or USA Kenwood 60	**$250.00**
Jardiniere, Flower & Fern, 2¼", from $6 to	**$8.00**
Pitcher, Boy Blue, all-over gold, Shawnee 46, 20-oz, from $175 to	**$200.00**
Pitcher, ribbed utility, USA, from $16 to	**$18.00**
Pitcher, Snowflake, ball shape, 2-qt, from $35 to	**$45.00**
Pitcher, Sunflower, ball shape, USA, 48-oz, from $55 to	**$65.00**
Pitcher, Wave, USA, 5½", from $22 to	**$24.00**
Range set, Sahara, salt & pepper shakers & grease jar, MIB, from $120 to	**$30.00**
Salt & pepper shakers, Boy Blue & Bo Peep, sm, pr from $28 to	**$30.00**
Salt & pepper shakers, Dutch Kids, blue & gold, lg, pr from $55 to	**$65.00**
Salt & pepper shakers, Fern, 7-oz, pr from $30 to	**$35.00**
Salt & pepper shakers, flowerpots, white, sm, pr from $40 to	**$50.00**
Salt & pepper shakers, Jack & Jill, no decoration, lg, pr from $40 to	**$45.00**
Salt & pepper shakers, Jumbo the Elephant, sm, pr from $90 to	**$95.00**
Salt & pepper shakers, milk can, pr from $25 to	**$30.00**

Salt and pepper shakers, Muggsy, from $45.00 to $55.00 for the pair.

Salt & pepper shakers, owl, green eyes, sm, pr from $30 to	**$35.00**
Salt & pepper shakers, Sahara, pink or turquoise, lg, pr from $25 to	**$30.00**
Salt & pepper shakers, Swiss Kids, all-over gold, lg, pr from $50 to	**$60.00**
String holder, fruit, unmarked, from $100 to	**$125.00**
Sugar bowl, Fern, 9-oz, from $22 to	**$35.00**
Teapot, Drape, USA, 4-cup, from $30 to	**$35.00**
Teapot, Elite, gold & decals, USA, 4-cup, from $65 to	**$70.00**
Teapot, Fern, octagonal, 6-cup, from $65 to	**$75.00**
Teapot, Laurel Wreath, USA, 5-cup, from $45 to	**$50.00**
Teapot, Tom the Piper's Son, gold trim, Patented Tom the Pipers Son USA, 5-cup, from $150 to	**$160.00**
Tumbler, stars & stripes, USA, 3", from $12 to	**$14.00**
Utility jar, basket, all-over gold, oval, w/lid, USA, from $100 to	**$110.00**

Lobster Ware

Bowl, baker; open, 917, 7", from $35 to **$40.00**
Bowl, batter; w/handle, 928, from $45 to **$50.00**
Butter dish, Kenwood USA 927, from $110 to................. **$120.00**
Casserole, French; charcoal, 904, 2-qt, from $30 to............ **$35.00**
Casserole, French; white (rare color), 904, 2-qt, from $75 to.. **$85.00**
Casserole, French; white (rare color) w/lobster finial, 904, 2-qt, from $125 to **$150.00**
Mug, Kenwood USA 911, 8-oz, from $100 to.................. **$125.00**
Relish, w/lid, Kenwood USA 926, 5½", from $45 to.......... **$50.00**
Salt & pepper shakers, full body, USA, pr from $200 to.... **$225.00**

Valencia

Bowl, fruit..**$10.00**
Bowl, nappy, 8½", from $15 to **$20.00**

Candleholder, bulb style, from $15.00 to $20.00 each. (Photo courtesy Duane and Janice Vanderbilt)

Coffeepot, from $35 to **$40.00**
Covered dish, 8", from $25 to **$30.00**
Creamer, Valencia, from $15 to..**$18.00**
Egg cup, from $12 to **$16.00**
Fork, from $35 to **$40.00**
Pie server...**$45.00**
Pitcher, ice; from $25 to **$30.00**
Plate, 10¾", from $12 to **$14.00**
Punch bowl, 12", from $35 to **$45.00**
Relish tray, from $125 to **$130.00**
Vase, bud; from $14 to **$18.00**
Waffle set, 5 pcs, from $90 to **$100.00**

Miscellaneous

Ashtray, shell form, USA 204, from $20 to..........................**$25.00**
Bowl, console; Flax Blue w/embossed ribs, oval, USA, 4x10", from $18 to **$20.00**
Candleholder, Aladdin's lamp style, USA, 2¼", ea from $14 to **$18.00**
Figurine, Muggsy, w/gold trim, USA 5½" **$80.00**
Flowerpot w/saucer, flared petals, Shawnee USA 466, 5", from $16 to **$18.00**

Lamp base, ballerina figural (sitting on base), unmarked, from $65 to **$75.00**
Miniature, baby buggy, USA, from $18 to..........................**$20.00**
Miniature, swan vase, USA, from $18 to **$20.00**
Planter, baby bottle, embossed flower, USA, from $25 to **$30.00**
Planter, blowfish, USA, from $6 to **$8.00**
Planter, Buddha, USA 524, from $22 to **$24.00**
Planter, canopy bed, Shawnee 734, from $100 to **$125.00**
Planter, cat & sax, USA 729, from $22 to **$25.00**
Planter, covered wagon, USA 514, sm, from $8 to..............**$10.00**
Planter, dog in boat, Shawnee 736, from $18 to **$22.00**
Planter, dove & planting dish, w/gold trim, Shawnee 2025...**$45.00**
Planter, elf & shoe, Shawnee 765, from $12 to **$14.00**
Planter, girl & mandolin, USA 576 ....**$24.00**
Planter, Irish setter, USA, from $8 to **$10.00**
Planter, old mill, w/gold trim, Shawnee 769 ....**$35.00**
Planter, pixie & wheelbarrow, unmarked, from $12 to........**$15.00**
Planter, poodle & carriage, USA 704, from $28 to **$30.00**
Planter, rabbit & cabbage, USA **$10.00**
Planter, rocking horse, USA 526, from $18 to **$20.00**
Vase, bud; swan, USA 725, from $10 to **$12.00**
Vase, geometric, USA, 5", from $12 to **$14.00**
Vase, swirled body, USA, 5", from $12 to **$14.00**
Vase, wheat, USA 1208, 3½", from $12 to **$14.00**
Wall pocket, chef, USA, from $38 to **$42.00**
Wall pocket, red feather **$45.00**
Wall pocket, Scottie dog's head, from $65 to **$75.00**

Sheet Music

Flea markets are a good source for buying old sheet music, and prices are usually very reasonable. Most examples can be bought for less than $5.00. More often than not, it is collected for reasons other than content. Some of the cover art was done by well-known illustrators like Rockwell, Christy, Barbelle, and Starmer, and some collectors like to zero in on their particular favorite, often framing some of the more attractive examples. Black Americana collectors can find many good examples with Black entertainers featured on the covers and the music reflecting an ethnic theme.

You may want to concentrate on music by a particularly renowned composer, for instance George M. Cohan or Irving Berlin. Or you may find you enjoy covers featuring famous entertainers and movie stars from the '40s through the '60s, for instance. At any rate, be critical of condition when you buy or sell sheet music. As is true with any item of paper, tears, dog ears, or soil will greatly reduce its value.

If you'd like a more thorough listing of sheet music and prices, we recommend *The Sheet Music Reference and Price Guide* by Anna Marie Guiheen and Marie-Reine A. Pafik (Collector Books) and *The Collector's Guide to Sheet Music* by Debbie Dillon.

Accent on Youth, Toy Seymour & Vee Lawhurst, Sylvia Sidney & Herbert Marshall photo, 1935 ....**$8.00**
Afraid, Fred Rose, Rex Allen photo, 1949............................**$5.00**
After Sundown, Arthur Freed & Nacio Herb Brown, Movie: Going Hollywood, Bing Crosby & Marion Davies photo, 1933.. **$10.00**

Ah But Is It Love?, EY Harberg & Jay Gorney, 1933 .... **$5.00**

Band of Angels, Sigman & Steiner, Movie: Band of Angels, Clark Gable & Yvonne DeCarlo photo, 1957 .... **$5.00**

Barking Dog, Al Stillman, Crew Cuts photo, 1954 .... **$5.00**

Betty Co-Ed, Sherman & Lewis, 1930 .... **$10.00**

Bluebird's in the Moonlight, Leo Robin & Ralph Rainger, Movie: Gulliver's Travels, 1937 .... **$10.00**

Breakfast at Tiffany's, Henry Mancini, Movie: Breakfast at Tiffany's, Audrey Hepburn photo, 1961 .... **$8.00**

Can't You Just See Yourself, Sammy Cahn & Jules Styne, Musical: High Button Shoes, 1948 .... **$7.00**

Candy Man, Bricusse & Newley, Movie: Willy Wonka & the Chocolate Factory, Gene Wilder & Jack Albertson photo, 1971 .... **$6.00**

Chasing Shadows, Benny Davis & Abner Silver, 1935 .... **$5.00**

Chim Chim Cher-ee, Richard M Sherman & Robert B Sherman, Movie: Mary Poppins (Disney), Andrews & Van Dyke photo, 1963 .... **$10.00**

Close to You, Al Hoffman, Jerry Livingston & Carl G Lampi, Frank Sinatra photo, 1943 .... **$5.00**

Day by Day, Sammy Cahn, Axel Stordahl & Paul Weston, Frank Sinatra photo, 1945 .... **$25.00**

Did You Ever Get Stung? Lorenz Hart & Richard Rodgers, Movie: I Married an Angel, 1938 .... **$10.00**

Enchanted Sea, Frank Metis & Randy Starr, 1959 .... **$5.00**

Exactly Like You, Dorothy Fields & Jimmy McHugh, 1930 .. **$5.00**

Faith Can Move Mountains, Ben Raleigh & Guy Wood, Johnnie Ray photo, 1952 .... **$5.00**

Flight of the Bumble Bee, N Rimsky Korakoff, 1935 .... **$3.00**

Forever & Ever, Malia Roasa & Franz Winkler, Perry Como photo, 1947 .... **$6.00**

Frosty the Snow Man, Steve Nelson & Jack Rollins, 1950 ..... **$3.00**

Full Moon & Empty Arms, Buddy Kaye & Ted Mossman, Eileen Barton photo, 1946 .... **$5.00**

Gee Dear I'm Lonesome, Baldwin, 1931 .... **$5.00**

Get Up You Sleepyhead, Ella Allen, 1933 .... **$3.00**

Girl That I Marry, Irving Berlin, Movie: Annie Get Your Gun (Irving Berlin), 1947 .... **$12.00**

God Bless the Child, Arthur Herzog Jr & Billie Holiday, Billie Holiday photo, 1951 .... **$5.00**

Guitar Boogie, Arthur Smith, Arthur Smith photo, 1946 ...... **$5.00**

Have I Told You Lately That I Love You, Scott Wiseman, Bing Crosby & Andrews Sisters photo, 1946 .... **$10.00**

He's One-A in the Army, Redd Evans, 1941 (WWII) **$10.00**

Heartbreak Hotel, Mae Boren Axton, Tommy Durden & Elvis Presley, Elvis Presley photo, 1956 .... **$38.00**

Hello Dolly, Jerry Herman, Musical: Hello Dolly, 1963 ...... **$10.00**

Here Comes the Sandman, Al Dubin & Harry Warren, 1937... **$5.00**

Home Cookin', Livingston & Evans, Movie: Fancy Pants, Bob Hope & Lucille Ball photo, 1950 .... **$10.00**

How Do I Love Thee, Elizabeth Barrett Browning & Blevins Davis, 1936 .... **$10.00**

Hut-Sut Song, Leo V Killian, Ted McMichel & Jack Owens, The Merry Macs, 1941 .... **$20.00**

I Am Ashamed That Women Are So Simple, Cole Porter, Musical: Kiss Me Kate, 1948 .... **$6.00**

I Beg of You, Elvis Presley, 1957 .... **$20.00**

I Believe in Miracles, Lewis, Wendling & Meyer, Ben Bernie photo, 1934 .... **$5.00**

I Don't See Me in Your Eyes Anymore, Bennie Benjamin & George Weiss, Perry Como photo, 1949 .... **$8.00**

I Heard You Cried Last Night, Ted Grouya & Jerrie Kruger, 1943 .... **$4.00**

I'm Gonna Wash That Man Right Out of My Hair, Richard Rodgers & Oscar Hammerstein II, 1949 .... **$3.00**

I've Got Plenty To Be Thankful For, Irving Berlin, 1942 ..... **$12.00**

I Went to Your Wedding, Jessie Mae Robinson, Patti Page, 1952 .... **$10.00**

Jimmy's Mean Mama Blues, Jimmy Rodgers, Walter O'Neal & Bob Sawyer, 1931 .... **$10.00**

Just a Prayer Away, Charles Tobias & David Kapp, Frankie Carle photo, 1944 .... **$3.00**

Just Because, Skelton & Robin, 1937 .... **$3.00**

Just Forget, Billy Smythe & Art Gillhan, 1930 .... **$3.00**

Just the Way You Are, Billy Joel, 1977 .... **$3.00**

Katinkitschika, George Gershwin, 1931 .... **$5.00**

Keep an Eye on Your Heart, Milton Leeds & Henry Manners, 1940 .... **$3.00**

Kids, Lee Adams & Charles Strouse, Movie: Bye Bye Birdie, 1960 .... **$8.00**

Kiss Me Sweet, Milton Drake, 1959 .... **$7.00**

Lady of Liberty, John W Miller & Paul Wellbaum, 1942 ..... **$10.00**

Last Night on the Back Porch, Lew Brown & Carl Schraubstrader, Cornell College Song Hit, 1950 .... **$3.00**

Lazy Lou'siana Moon, Walter Donaldson, 1930 .... **$6.00**

Let It Snow!, Sammy Cahn and Jule Styne, 1945, $4.00. (Photo courtesy Anna Marie Guiheen and Marie-Reine A. Pafik)

Letter to My Mother, Small & Silver, 1933 .... **$5.00**

Little Bird Told Me, Harvey Q Brooks, Evelyn Knight photo, 1948 .... **$10.00**

Little Boy's Christmas, Claire, Elliott & Hettel, 1959 .... **$5.00**

Little Red Monkey, Stephen Gale & Jack Jordan, Rosemary Clooney photo, 1953 .... **$4.00**

Love Me To-Night, Young, 1932 .... **$5.00**

Make It With You, David Gates, 1970 .... **$3.00**

Managua Nicaragua, Albert Gamse & Irving Fields, Guy Lombardo photo, 1946 .... **$7.00**

Many Tears Ago, Jenny Lou Carson, 1945 .... **$3.00**

Maria, Richard Rodgers & Oscar Hammerstein II, Movie: Sound of Music, Andrews & Plummer photo, 1959 .... **$10.00**

Memory Waltz, Benny Davis & Joe Burke, 1933 .... **$5.00**

Moon River, Johnny Mercer and Henry Mancini, 1961, $14.00.
(Photo courtesy Anna Marie Guiheen and Marie-Reine A. Pafik)

Night Is Young, Oscar Hammerstein II & Sigmund Romberg, 1935 .... **$6.00**

Night We Called It a Day, Tom Adair & Matt Dennis, 1941 ... **$3.00**

Oahu, Carmen Lombardo, 1947 .... **$8.00**

Oh Marie, Howard Johnson & E Di Capua, 1932 .... **$5.00**

Old Lamp-Lighter, Charles Tobias & Nat Simon, Sammy Kaye photo, 1941 .... **$7.00**

On Treasure Island, Leslie & Burke, Gale Storm photo, 1935 .. **$6.00**

Out of Nowhere, Johnny Green, 1931 .... **$5.00**

Painting the Roses Red, Bob Hilliard & Sammy Fain, Movie: Alice in Wonderland (Disney), 1951 .... **$20.00**

Peanut Vendor, L Wolfe Gilbert, Albert Gamse, Moises Simons, 1931 .... **$14.00**

Playmates, Johnny Burke & James V Manaco, 1940 .... **$15.00**

Rags to Riches, Richard Adler and Jerry Ross, Tony Bennett photo, 1953, $10.00.

Rain, Billy Hill & Peter DeRose, Tony Sacco or Loretta Lee photo, 1934 .... **$5.00**

Ramblin' Rose, Noel Sherman & Joe Sherman, Nat King Cole photo, 1962 .... **$4.00**

Ready To Take a Chance, Movie: Foul Play, Chevy Chase & Goldie Hawn photo, 1978 .... **$5.00**

Relax, Johnson, O'Toole & Gill, Movie: Body Double, Melanie Griffith photo, 1984 .... **$3.00**

Riders in the Sky, Stan Jones, Burl Ives photo, 1949 .... **$3.00**

Rosalita, Al Dexter, 1942 .... **$10.00**

Same Old Story, Michael Field & Newt Oliphant, 1940 .... **$4.00**

Santa Claus Express, Abner Silver, Al Sherman & Al Lewis, Uncle Don photo, 1935 .... **$5.00**

Say It With Firecrackers, Irving Berlin, 1942 .... **$10.00**

Say Yes, Erik Satie, 1953 .... **$3.00**

Skaters Waltz, Waldteufel, 1941 .... **$10.00**

Stars in My Eyes, Fields & Kreisler, 1936 .... **$8.00**

Take Me Back to Renfro Valley, John Lair, Rambling Red Foley photo, 1935 .... **$5.00**

Tales From the Vienna Woods, MC Nanderf & Johann Strauss, 1939 .... **$5.00**

Tea on the Terrace, Sam Coslow, 1936 .... **$5.00**

Ten Pretty Girls, Will Grosz & Jimmy Kennedy, 1937, Phil Regan photo **$5.00**

That Old Dream Peddler, Al Stewart & Pepe Delgado, 1947 .. **$5.00**

Thumbelina, Frank Loesser, Movie: Hans Christian Anderson, Danny Kaye photo, 1951 .... **$5.00**

Under Paris Skies, Kim Gannon & Hubert Giraud, Georgia Gibbs photo, 1941 .... **$4.00**

Venus, Ed Marshall, Frankie Avalon, 1959 .... **$3.00**

Very Thought of You, Ray Noble, Fred Waring photo, 1934 . **$9.00**

Volare, Mitchell & Domenico Modugno, McGuire Sisters photo, 1958 .... **$3.00**

Wait Till She Sees You in Your Uniform, Edgar Leslie & John Jacob Loeb, 1940 .... **$10.00**

Wanted, Peter Tinturin & Jack Laurence, 1937 .... **$5.00**

Woodchuck Song, Sid Tepper, Roy Brodsky, Paul Mann & Stephan Weiss, 1946 .... **$5.00**

You Never Miss the Water Till the Well Runs Dry, Paul Secon & Arthur Kent, 1946 .... **$3.00**

Shell Pink

This beautiful soft pink, opaque glassware was made for only a short time in the late 1950s by the Jeannette Glass Company. Though a few pieces are commanding prices of more than $200.00 (the Anniversary cake plate, the cigarette box with the butterfly finial, and the lazy Susan tray with the base), most pieces carry modest price tags, and the ware, though not as easy to find as it was a few years ago, is still available for the collector who is actively searching for it. Refer to *Collectible Glassware from the 40s, 50s, and 60s,* by Gene and Cathy Florence (Collector Books) for photos and more information.

Ashtray, butterfly shape **$15.00**

Base, for lazy Susan, w/ball bearings **$125.00**

Bowl, Florentine, footed, 10" **$22.00**

Bowl, Holiday, footed, 10½" **$35.00**

Bowl, Lombardi, design in center, 4-footed, 11" **$30.00**

Bowl, Pheasant, footed, 8" **$25.00**

Bowl, wedding; w/lid, 6½"................................$15.00
Cake plate, Anniversary................................$295.00
Cake stand, Harp, 10"....................................$33.00
Candleholders, Eagle, 3-footed, pr......................$38.00
Candy dish, Floragold, 4-footed, 5¼"...................$15.00
Candy dish, sq, w/lid, 6½" H............................$22.00
Celery/relish, 3-part, 12½".............................$38.00
Cigarette box, butterfly finial, from $185 to........$160.00
Compote, Windsor, 6"....................................$15.00
Cookie jar, w/lid, 6½"..................................$175.00
Honey jar, beehive shape, notched lid..................$22.00
Powder jar, w/lid, 4¾"..................................$30.00

Punch bowl, $110.00; punch cup (also fits snack tray), $3.00. (Photo courtesy Gene and Cathy Florence)

Relish, Vineyard, octagonal, 4-part, 12"...............$28.00
Stem, water goblet; Thumbprint, 8-oz...................$11.00
Sugar bowl, Baltimore Pear, footed, w/lid..............$12.00
Tray, Harp, w/handles, 12½x9¾".........................$40.00
Tray, lazy Susan, 5-part, 13½".........................$50.00
Tray, Venetian, 6-part, 16½"...........................$22.00
Tray, 5-part, w/handles, 15¾"..........................$45.00
Tumbler, juice; Thumbprint, footed, 5-oz................$8.00
Vase, 7"...$25.00

Shirley Temple

Born April 23, 1928, Shirley Jane Temple danced and smiled her way into the hearts of America in the movie *Stand Up and Cheer*. Many successful roles followed and by the time Shirley was eight years old, she was #1 at box offices around the country. Her picture appeared in publications almost daily, and any news about her was news indeed. Mothers dressed their little daughters in clothing copied after hers and coiffed them with Shirley hairdos.

The extent of her success was mirrored in the unbelievable assortment of merchandise that saturated the retail market. Dolls, coloring books, children's clothing and jewelry, fountain pens, paper dolls, stationery, and playing cards are just a few examples of the hundreds of items that were available. Shirley's face was a common sight on the covers of magazines as well as in the advertisements they contained, and she was the focus of scores of magazine articles.

Though she had been retired from the movies for nearly a decade, she had two successful TV series in the late '50s, *The Shirley Temple Story-Book* and *The Shirley Temple Show*. Her reappearance caused new interest in some of the items that had been so popular during her childhood, and many were reissued.

Always interested in charity and community service, Shirley became actively involved in a political career in the late '60s, serving at both the state and national levels.

If you're interested in learning more about her, we recommend *The Complete Guide to Shirley Temple Dolls and Collectibles* by Tonya Bervaldi-Camaratta and *Shirley in the Magazines* by Gen Jones.

Club: Shirley Temple Collectors by the Sea Club
Newsletter: *Lollipop News*
P.O. Box 6203
Oxnard, CA 93031

Club: The Shirley Temple Club
Newsletter: *The Shirley Temple Collectors News*
8811 Colonial Rd.
Brooklyn, NY 11209

Advertising sheet, Shirley Temple Snowsuit, Shirley modeling, color, NM..$20.00
Book, Films of Shirley Temple, Robert Windeler, 1978, EX...$10.00
Book, Shirley Temple in Heidi, softcover, Saalfield #1771, 1937, EX...$30.00
Book, Shirley Temple Little Star, softcover, Saalfield #1762, 1936, EX...$50.00
Book, Shirley Temple Story Book, hardcover, Saalfield, 1935, EX...$20.00
Book, Shirley Temple Treasury, hardcover, Random House, 1959, EX, from $20 to.................................$40.00
Book, Shirley Temple 21st Birthday Album, softcover, Dell, April 1949, EX.......................................$20.00
Bracelet, fairy-tale charms on gold-tone chain, fine quality, M in signature box..............................$300.00
Candy mold, metal, 2-pc, 1930s, M, minimum value.........$50.00
Cigarette card, Gallery of 1936, 1930s, NM, ea from $5 to..$8.00
Clothing, coat, fuzzy purple cloth, doll size, ca 1958, M w/tag...$15.00
Clothing, school dress, yellow w/embroidered trim on bodice & skirt, w/signature purse, Ideal #9609, for 12" doll, EX...........$60.00
Doll, porcelain, dressed in pink resembling Little Colonel outfit, 1983, 16", M......................................$100.00
Doll, porcelain, Little Bo Peep, Danbury Mint, 1999, 16", M..$125.00
Doll, porcelain, Littlest Grand Marshall, Danbury Mint, 2001, 14"..$100.00
Doll, vinyl, Dutch Girl outfit, light blond braided hair, 1982, 8", MIB..$25.00
Doll, vinyl, Heidi outfit w/felt headband, signature purse, Ideal #9722, 12", M.....................................$175.00
Doll, vinyl, in Fairyland Heroine version of Cinderella's outfit, w/ crown, 1961, 15", M..............................$250.00

Doll, vinyl, in sailor outfit & matching cap, 1950s-60s, 17", MIB..............$325.00

Doll, vinyl, in Wee Willie Winkie outfit (rare red version), 12", MIB..............$250.00

Doll, vinyl, nylon party dress, silver script pin & hangtag, 1959-60, 17", MIB..............$325.00

Doll, vinyl, 1958, 17", NM, $250.00. (Photo courtesy Tonya Bervaldi-Camaratta)

Doll, vinyl baby, sleep eyes, molded hair, pink gown & bonnet, Garfinkle, 30", MIB..............$225.00

Doll patterns, Advance, Wardrobe for Shirley Temple Dolls (official release), EX..............$25.00

Dress, blue cotton print w/white collar & cuffs, Shirley Temple Frock by Cinderella, EX..............$75.00

Dress, white cotton party type, Nannette Shirley Temple, 1950s, EX..............$50.00

Figurine, bronze-painted chalk, Shirley on base, 4", M..............$10.00

Figurine, salt w/painted details, Baby Take a Bow pose, 1930s, 12", EX..............$40.00

Hand fan, printed portrait on card stock w/wooden handle, EX, from $5 to..............$10.00

Magazine, Movie Life, portrait cover, August 1945, EX..............$15.00

Magazine, Movie Mirror, Shirley cover, May 1936, EX..............$35.00

Magnetic Doll w/Jewelry, Gabriel, 1961, MIB..............$60.00

Movie Favorites Embroidery Set, Gabriel 1959, MIB..............$50.00

Mug, portrait on cobalt glass, 1936 (watch for 1970s reproductions valued at $15), M..............$40.00

Paper dolls, Shirley Temple, Saalfield #5160, 1959, uncut...$35.00

Paper dolls, Shirley Temple Dolls & Dresses, Saalfield #2112, 1934, uncut..............$150.00

Paper dolls, Shirley Temple Standing Dolls, Saalfield #1715, 1935, cut & complete..............$40.00

Pen & pencil set, Shirley Temple stamped on barrels, gold clips, Eversharp, 1930s, EX..............$75.00

Photo, hand-colored giveaway, Shirley w/dog, 1930s, NM ..$20.00

Photo, recent reproduction on photo paper or thick card stock, black & white, 8x10", M..............$5.00

Postcard, color portrait, 1930s, EX, ea from $10 to..............$15.00

Purse, plaid cloth, Pyramid, 1930s, EX..............$80.00

Record, Best of Shirley Temple Vol II, 20th Century Fox, 1965, EX..............$15.00

Record, Shirley Temple in the Littlest Rebel, recording from 1940 radio show, 1980 Radio Import release, M..............$20.00

Ring, embossed portrait & blue enameling on silver, marked Sterling, M..............$40.00

Sewing cards, punch-out cards to weave strings through, Saalfield #1721, 1936, MIB..............$100.00

Sheet music, Baby Take a Bow, Shirley on cover, Movietone Music Corporation, 1934, EX..............$20.00

Sheet music, Dreams Are Made for Children, from Shirley Temple Storybook, Shirley on cover, 1950s, EX..............$20.00

Sheet Music, On the Good Ship Lollipop re-release, Movietone Music Corp, 1950s, EX..............$10.00

Sheet music, Someday You'll Find Your Bluebird, Shirley on cover, Robbins Music Corp, 1940, EX..............$30.00

Tiara, gold-tone metal w/glass jewels, M on card..............$250.00

Trading card, black & white photo, 1930s, ea from $5 to......$8.00

Wristwatch, Little Colonel, tin, Shirley on face, Made in Japan, possibly 1930s party favor, EX..............$30.00

Wristwatch, mesh band, came w/Playpal dolls, scarce, EX...$60.00

Outfit, nylon visiting dress, Ideal #9549, for the 12" doll, MIB, $80.00. (Photo courtesy Keith and Loretta McKenzie/Tonya Bervaldi-Camaratta)

Shot Glasses

Shot glasses are small articles of glass that generally hold an ounce or two of liquid; they measure about 2" to 4" in height.

They've been around since the 1830s have been made in nearly every conceivable type of glass.

Shot glass collectors are usually quantity collectors often boasting of hundreds or even a thousand glasses! The most desirable to collectors are whiskey sample or advertising glasses from the Pre-Prohibition era. Most carry etched white lettering that comprises messages relating to a distiller, company, proprietor, or other alcohol-related advertising. Shot glasses like these sell for around $75.00 to $100.00, but recently many rare examples have been auctioned off at prices in excess of $300.00.

These values are only estimates and should be used as a general guide. Many one-of-a-kind items or oddities are a bit harder to classify, especially sample glasses. Often this may depend on the elaborateness of the design as opposed to simple lettering. For more information, we recommend *Shot Glasses* (Schiffer Publishers) and *The Shot Glass Encyclopedia*, both by Mark Pickvet.

Note: Values for shot glasses in good condition are represented by the low end of our ranges, while the high end reflects estimated values for examples in mint condition.

Advisor: Mark Pickvet (See Directory, Shot Glasses)

Barrel shaped, from $5 to	$7.50
Black porcelain replica, from $3 to	$5.00
Carnival colors, plain or fluted, from $100 to	$150.00
Carnival colors, w/patterns, from $125 to	$175.00
Culver 22k gold, from $6 to	$8.00
Depression, colors, from $10 to	$12.50
Depression, colors w/patterns or etching, from $17 to	$25.00
Depression, tall, general designs, from $10 to	$12.50
Depression, tall, tourist, from $5 to	$7.50
European design, rounded w/gold rim, from $4 to	$6.00
Frosted w/gold designs, from $6 to	$8.00
General, advertising, from $4 to	$6.00
General, enameled design, from $3 to	$4.00
General, etched design, from $5 to	$7.50
General, frosted design, from $3 to	$5.00
General, gold design, from $6 to	$8.00
General, porcelain, from $4 to	$6.00
Inside eyes, from $6 to	$8.00
Iridized silver, from $5 to	$7.50
Mary Gregory or Anchor Hocking Ships, from $150 to	$200.00
Nude, from $25 to	$35.00
Plain, w/or w/out flutes, from 50¢ to	$.75
Planet Hollywood/Hard Rock Cafe, from $10 to	$12.50
Pop or soda advertising, from $12 to	$15.00
Ruby flashed, from $35 to	$50.00
Sayings & toasts (1940s & 1950s), from $5 to	$7.50
Sports (Professional Team), from $5 to	$7.50
Square, general, from $6 to	$8.00
Square, w/etching, from $10 to	$12.50
Square, w/pewter, from $12.50 to	$15.00
Square, w/2-tone bronze & pewter, from $15 to	$17.50
Standard glass w/pewter, from $7 to	$10.00
Steuben or Lalique crystal, from $150 to	$200.00
Tiffany, Galle or fancy art, from $600 to	$8.00
Tourist, colored glass, from $4 to	$6.00

Tourist, general, from $3 to	$4.00
Tourist, porcelain, from $3 to	$5.00
Tourist, Taiwan, from $2 to	$3.00
Tourist, turquoise & gold, from $6 to	$8.00
Whiskey or beer advertising, modern, from $5 to	$7.50
Whiskey sample, good condition, from $50 to	$100.00
Whiskey sample, M, from $75 to	$350.00
19th-century cut patterns, from $35 to	$50.00

Railroad, MKT, $9.00.

Silhouette Pictures

These novelty pictures are familiar to everyone. Even today a good number of them are still around, and you'll often see them at flea markets and co-ops. They were very popular in their day and never expensive, and because they were made for so many years (the '20s through the '50s), many variations are available. Though the glass in some is flat, in others it is curved. Backgrounds may be foil, a scenic print, hand tinted, or plain. Sometimes dried flowers were added as accents. But the characteristic common to them all is that the subject matter is reverse painted on the glass. People (even complicated groups), scenes, ships, and animals were popular themes. Though quite often the silhouette was done in solid black to create a look similar to the nineteenth-century cut silhouettes, colors were sometimes used as well.

In the '20s, making tinsel art pictures became a popular pastime. Ladies would paint the outline of their subjects on the back of the glass and use crumpled tinfoil as a background. Sometimes they would tint certain areas of the glass, making the foil appear to be colored. This type is popular with collectors of folk art.

If you'd like to learn more about this subject, we recommend *The Encyclopedia of Silhouette Collectibles on Glass; 1996 – 97 Price Guide for Encyclopedia of Silhouette Collectibles on Glass;* and *Vintage Silhouettes on Glass and Reverse Paintings* (copyright 2000, all new items pictured) by Shirley Mace. These books show examples of Benton Glass pictures with frames made of metal, wood, plaster, and plastic. The metal frames with the stripes are most favored by collectors as long as they are in good condition. Wood frames were actually considered deluxe when silhouettes were originally sold.

Recently some convex glass silhouettes from Canada have been found, nearly identical to the ones made by Benton Glass except for their brown tape frames. Backgrounds seem to be slightly different as well. Among the flat glass silhouettes, the ones signed by Diefenbach are the most expensive. The wildflower pictures, especially ones with fine lines and good detail, are becoming popular with collectors.

The alphanumeric codes in the listings that follow indicate the maker (i.e., FI is Fisher, BG is Benton Glass), the next two numbers indicate the size (68 is 6" x 8"), and the number after the dash is an item number assigned by the author of the book we reference above.

Advisor: Shirley Mace (See Directory, Silhouette Pictures)

Convex Glass

Boy & dog going fishing, colorful scenic background, BA 45-1, Baco Glass Plaque...**$35.00**

Boy flying kite on windy day, BG 3½4½-168, Benton Glass Co..**$35.00**

Boy pushing girl in sled in winter scene, BG 45-151, Benton Glass Co...**$30.00**

Colonial man stands in finery, PW 57-2, Peter Watson's Studio, oval frame...**$30.00**

Couple stand together & hold sheet music, floral border, VG 45-169, Benton Glass Co.................................**$25.00**

Courting couple at table, BG 68-29, Benton Glass Co **$40.00**

Courting couple in autumn landscape, BG 45-58, Benton Glass Co..**$30.00**

Courting couple in winter landscape, BG 68-66, Benton Glass Co...**$40.00**

Girl at window studies 2 birds on branches, advertising at bottom, metal hanger, round, ER 7D-7, CE Erickson Co..........**$22.00**

Horse and rider, BG 68-198, 6x8", $35.00. (Photo courtesy Shirley and Ray Mace)

Lady in finery w/parasol, BI 9D-1, Bilderback's Inc of Detroit, black frame, 9" dia...**$35.00**

Lady in ruffled dress picks flowers in garden, BG 45-21, Benton Glass Co..**$30.00**

Lady seated while child w/string plays w/cat, BG 68-7B, Benton Glass Co..**$60.00**

Lady w/rake & child w/basket, colorful background, BG 45-115, Benton Glass Co...**$30.00**

Lamp, rail, flowers & leaves over courting couple scene, BG-45-131, Benton Glass Co....................................**$18.00**

Man & lady making snowman in winter scene, BG 45-159, Benton Glass Co..**$40.00**

Man in overstuffed chair w/pipe & book, cat on floor beside, BG 45-13, Benton Glass Co.................................**$25.00**

Man pushing lady in swing, colorful autumn background, BG 68-112, Benton Glass Co.................................**$30.00**

Romantic couple, he w/flowers, PW 5D-7, Peter Watson's Studio...**$25.00**

Sailing ship in choppy seas, BG 45-3, Benton Glass Co.......**$25.00**

Scottie dog at fence w/bird perched on post, BG 45-185, Benton Glass Co..**$35.00**

Sleigh & pine trees in colorful winter scene, thermometer insert, advertising, ER 45-3, CE Erickson Co.......................**$30.00**

This Little Piggy, lace & stuffed toy silhouettes overlay baby examining toes, Charlotte Becker, BG 68-100, Benton Glass...**$38.00**

Wonderful Mother, lady & child, colorful background, BG 68-130, Benton Glass Co...**$35.00**

Flat Glass

At the Gate, couple in landscape, gold background, DE 45-26, Deltex Products...**$22.00**

Autumn Bouquet, RE711-40, Reliance................................**$30.00**

Bird on branch, RE 710-23, Reliance **$22.00**

Colonial Girl, head & shoulders portrait, RE 44-61, Reliance..**$20.00**

Couple under willow tree, RE 3 ½ 5-17, Reliance **$18.00**

Courting couple, round black plastic frame w/gold trim, RI 5D-101, Copyright 1937, C&A Richards **$30.00**

Courting couple in landscape, TA 810-7, Tinsel Art............**$25.00**

Courting couple on bridge, FL 410-2, Flowercraft..............**$35.00**

Courtship, couple beneath tree, RE 44-83, Reliance...........**$28.00**

Days of Yore, scene of ladies at fireplace, NE 68-9, Newton...**$28.00**

Deco dancer among Japanese lanterns, reverse painted in red & black on cream, MF 710-1, West Coast Picture Co, 1920 ......**$30.00**

Dutch boy standing among tulips, multicolor, TA 810-8, Tinsel Art **$30.00**

Elfin Music, elfin girl playing violin, RI 57-760, C&A Richards .**$55.00**

Exotic bird on branch, multicolor, TA 1216-26, Tinsel Art .**$25.00**

Hidden Pool, 2 nudes at pool, ½" plaster, BB 68-10, self-framed, unmarked Buckbee-Brehm.......................................**$15.00**

Home From School, children & mother, RE 57-127, Reliance ..**$18.00**

Homeward Bound, sailing ship scene, RE 45-114, Reliance...**$15.00**

John Alden & Priscilla, indoor scene, NE 45-12, Newton ...**$18.00**

Meeting, man presents flower to lady w/parasol, BB 57-24, Buckbee-Brehm...**$20.00**

Sailing ships scenic, butterfly wings background, BW 4½4½-4, Made in London...**$40.00**

Senorita, Spanish lady in archway, silver background, DE-810-7, Deltex Products..**$30.00**

Spanish lady dancing among musicians in outdoor scene, BB 710-26, Buckbee-Brehm **$30.00**

Springtime of Life, Gleam O' Gold Silhouettes, GG 56-3, PF Volland **$35.00**

To My Mother, swans scenic, dried pressed flowers background, FI 4½7-6, Fisher & Flowercraft **$28.00**

Silver-Plated and Sterling Flatware

The secondary market is being tapped more and more as the only source for those replacement pieces needed to augment family heirloom sets, and there are many collectors who admire the vintage flatware simply because they appreciate its beauty, quality, and affordability. Several factors influence pricing. For instance, a popular pattern though plentiful may be more expensive than a scarce one that might be passed over because it very likely would be difficult to collect. When you buy silver plate, condition is very important, since replating can be expensive.

Pieces with no monograms are preferred; in fact, newer monogrammed sterling is very hard to sell. Monograms seem to be better accepted on pieces over 100 years old. To evaluate monogrammed items, deduct 15% from fancy or rare examples; 30% from common, plain items; and 50% to 70% if they are worn.

Interest in silver-plated flatware from the 1950s and 1960s is on the increase as the older patterns are becoming harder to find in excellent condition. As a result, prices are climbing.

Dinner knives range in size from 9⅜" to 10"; dinner forks from 7⅜" to 7¾". Luncheon knives are approximately 8½" to 8¾", while luncheon forks are about 6¾" to 7". Place knives measure 8⅞" to 9¼", and place forks 7⅛" to 7¼".

Our values are given for flatware in excellent condition. Matching services often advertise in various trade papers and can be very helpful in locating the items you're looking for.

If you'd like to learn more about the subject, we recommend *Silverplated Flatware* by Tere Hagan (Collector Books).

Advisor: Rick Spencer (See Directory, Silver-Plated and Sterling Flatware)

Silver Plate

Adoration, dinner knife, French handle, 1847 Rogers, 9¾" ...**$5.50**
Adoration, grill fork, 1847 Rogers, 8½" **$4.50**
Adoration, oval soup spoon, 1847 Rogers, 7¼" **$4.50**
Ancestral, dinner knife, 1847 Rogers, 9¼" **$4.50**
Ancestral, flat butter spreader, 1847 Rogers **$4.00**
Ancestral, salad fork, 1847 Rogers................................**$8.00**
Arbutus, cocktail fork, William Rogers **$12.50**
Arbutus, dinner fork, William Rogers, 7⅜" **$10.00**
Arbutus, master butter knife, William Rogers **$12.00**
Arbutus, strawberry fork, William Rogers **$12.50**
Caprice, dinner fork, Nobility, 7½"................................**$8.00**
Caprice, gravy ladle, Nobility..**$8.00**
Caprice, sugar spoon, Nobility......................................**$3.50**

Caprice, teaspoon, Nobility..**$2.50**
Charter Oak, dinner fork, 1847 Rogers, 7½".................**$6.00**
Charter Oak, luncheon fork, 1847 Rogers, 7" **$13.50**
Charter Oak, table/serving spoon, 1847 Rogers **$20.00**
Coral, cream soup spoon, International, 1892, 6⅛".........**$8.00**
Coral, demitasse spoon, gold-washed bowl, International, 1892..**$8.50**
Coral, dinner fork, International, 1892, 7½" **$6.00**
Coral, grill knife, modern handle, International, 1892, 8½" ..**$5.00**
Coronation, dinner fork, Community................................**$8.00**
Coronation, grill knife, modern handle, Community, 8½" **$4.50**
Coronation, meat fork, Community **$16.00**
Coronation, tablespoon, Community **$8.00**
Daybreak, cereal spoon, Rogers **$6.50**
Daybreak, dinner knife, Rogers, 8½" **$7.50**
Daybreak, salad fork, Rogers, 6" **$7.50**
Eternally Yours, dinner knife, 1847 Rogers, 9½"...................**$11.00**
Eternally Yours, grill knife, 1847 Rogers **$7.00**
Eternally Yours, oval soup spoon, 1847 Rogers **$7.00**
Evening Star, dinner knife, Community, 9¼" **$9.00**
Evening Star, meat fork, Community................................**$12.50**
Evening Star, oval soup spoon, Community....................**$6.50**
Evening Star, salad fork, Community...............................**$7.00**
Floral, bouillon soup spoon, Wallace, 4⅝"......................**$16.50**
Floral, master butter knife, flat handle, Wallace, 7½" **$22.00**
Floral, sauce ladle, Wallace **$29.00**
Grosvenor, dinner fork, Community, 7½"........................**$4.50**
Grosvenor, gravy ladle, Community **$15.00**
Grosvenor, teaspoon, Community....................................**$3.50**
Invitation, cream soup, Gorham, 6¼"..............................**$4.50**
Invitation, master butter knife, Gorham **$5.00**
Invitation, salad fork, Gorham..**$11.00**
Longchamps, grill fork, Prestige.....................................**$6.00**
Longchamps, master butter knife, Prestige.....................**$5.00**
Longchamps, pickle fork, Prestige **$8.00**
Louis XVI, dinner knife, Community, 9½"........................**$7.00**
Louis XVI, gravy ladle, Community **$15.00**
Louis XVI, salad fork, Community....................................**$7.50**
Louis XVI, tablespoon, Community **$10.00**
Marquise, grill knife, modern handle, 1847 Rogers................**$8.00**
Marquise, master butter knife, 1847 Rogers...................**$4.50**
Marquise, teaspoon, 1847 Rogers...................................**$3.75**
Mystic, dinner fork, Rogers, 7½" **$10.00**
Mystic, dinner knife, Rogers, 9½" **$8.00**
Mystic, meat fork, Rogers **$21.00**
Old Colony, cream soup, 1847 Rogers, 7" **$9.00**
Old Colony, dinner fork, 1847 Rogers, 7½" **$5.00**
Patrician, dinner fork, Community, 7¾" **$6.00**
Patrician, gravy ladle, Community **$17.50**
Patrician, lg berry spoon, Community, 9¼" **$22.00**
Patrician, teaspoon, Community......................................**$3.00**
Queen Bess 1946, dinner fork, Oneida, 7½" **$4.50**
Queen Bess 1946, gravy ladle, Oneida **$15.00**
Queen Bess 1946, iced tea spoon, Oneida **$8.00**
Remembrance, grill knife, 1847 Rogers...........................**$6.00**
Remembrance, oval/place soup spoon, 1847 Rogers **$7.50**
Remembrance, tablespoon, 1847 Rogers.........................**$9.00**
Remembrance, teaspoon, 1847 Rogers............................**$4.00**

Royal Rose, cream soup spoon, Nobility, 6¼" $4.50
Royal Rose, master butter knife, Nobility..............................$3.00
Royal Rose, salad fork, Nobility $4.50
Royal Rose, sugar spoon, Nobility......................................$4.00
Sharon, dinner fork, 1847 Rogers, 7¼" $9.50
Sharon, dinner knife, hollow handle, 1847 Rogers, 9¾" $12.50
Sharon, meat fork, 1847 Rogers $16.50
South Seas, gravy ladle, Community...................................$14.00
South Seas, meat fork, Community $11.50
South Seas, salad fork, Community $6.00
South Seas, salad server, flat blade, hollow handle,
　Community $16.00

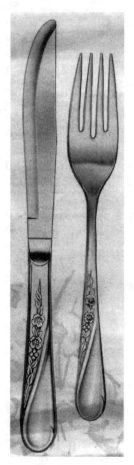

Spring Flower, dinner knife and fork, Wm. Rogers & Son, 1957, from $7.00 to $9.00 each. (Photo courtesy Francis Bones and Lee Roy Fisher)

Tiger Lily, dinner knife, modern handle, Reed & Barton, 9"..$13.00
Tiger Lily, jelly server, Reed & Barton $16.00
Tiger Lily, luncheon fork, Reed & Barton, 7" $10.00
Tiger Lily, meat fork, Reed & Barton..................................$27.50
Victorian Rose, dessert spoon, Rogers $5.75
Victorian Rose, master butter knife.......................................$5.00
Victorian Rose, tablespoon, Rogers $10.00
Victorian Rose, teaspoon, Rogers $3.50
White Orchid, demitasse spoon, Community.........................$6.00
White Orchid, grill set, Community, 4-pc $21.00
White Orchid, sugar spoon, Community................................$6.00
White Orchid, tablespoon, Community $13.00
Wind Song, demitasse spoon, Nobility $7.50
Wind Song, master butter spreader, Nobility $6.00
Wind Song, salad fork, Nobility..$10.00

Wind Song, seafood fork, Nobility..$8.00
Wind Song, tablespoon, Nobility...$13.00

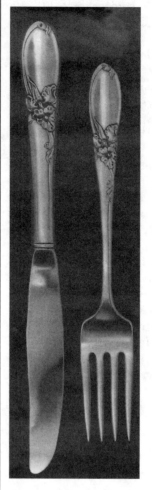

White Orchid, dinner knife and fork, Community, 1950s, from $5.00 to $8.00 each. (Photo courtesy Francis Bones and Lee Roy Fisher)

Sterling

Adante, butter knife, hollow handle, Gorham......................$19.50
Adante, iced tea spoon, Gorham $35.00
Adante, salad fork, Gorham $34.00
Adante, teaspoon, Gorham..$18.50
Bel Chateau, place fork, Lunt, 7⅜" $29.00
Bel Chateau, salad fork, Lunt..$36.00
Bel Chateau, teaspoon, Lunt $25.50
Blithe Spirit, butter spreader, hollow handle, Gorham $8.00
Blithe Spirit, sugar spoon, Gorham....................................$18.50
Blithe Spirit, teaspoon, Gorham...$14.00
Blossomtime, bonbon, International $22.00
Blossomtime, cream soup spoon, International $18.50
Blossomtime, place fork, International, 7¼" $24.00
Blossomtime, teaspoon, International..................................$14.00
Breton Rose, cocktail fork, International..............................$21.00
Breton Rose, cream soup spoon, International $18.50
Breton Rose, salad fork, International $19.50
Breton Rose, tablespoon, International $36.00
Bridal Rose, demitasse spoon, Alvin...................................$23.00
Bridal Rose, gumbo spoon, Alvin.......................................$21.00
Bridal Rose, teaspoon, Alvin, 5¼" $17.50
Brocade, butter spreader, hollow handle, International.........$17.50

Brocade, cream soup spoon, International.............................$18.50

Brocade, place fork, International, 7¼".............................$25.50

Brocade, teaspoon, International.............................$15.00

Cabot, salad fork, Wallace.............................$17.50

Cabot, sugar spoon, Wallace.............................$12.00

Cabot, tablespoon, Wallace.............................$25.50

Cambridge, mustard ladle, gold-washed bowl, Gorham.......$72.50

Cambridge, teaspoon, Gorham, 5¾".............................$10.00

Candlelight, bonbon, Towle.............................$21.00

Candlelight, butter spreader, flat handle, Towle.............$14.00

Candlelight, cream soup spoon, Towle, 6¼".............$23.00

Candlelight, iced tea spoon, Towle.............................$22.00

Candlelight, luncheon fork, Towle, 7¼".............................$24.00

Carolina, dinner fork, Lunt, 7½".............................$25.50

Carolina, gumbo spoon, Lunt, 7".............................$18.50

Carolina, iced tea spoon, Lunt.............................$16.00

Carolina, teaspoon, Lunt, 5¾".............................$10.00

Celeste, butter spreader, hollow handle, Gorham.............$8.00

Celeste, cheese server, Gorham.............................$20.00

Celeste, gravy ladle, Gorham.............................$35.00

Celeste, place spoon, Gorham.............................$21.00

Celeste, sugar spoon, Gorham.............................$15.00

Celeste, tablespoon, Gorham.............................$35.00

Chantilly, butter spreader, modern hollow handle, Gorham..$20.00

Chantilly, iced tea spoon, Gorham.............................$27.50

Chantilly, luncheon fork, Gorham.............................$20.00

Chantilly, mustard ladle, Gorham.............................$80.00

Chapel Bells, bouillon spoon, Alvin.............................$26.50

Chapel Bells, cream soup spoon, Alvin.............................$18.50

Chapel Bells, lemon fork, Alvin.............................$24.00

Chapel Bells, salad serving fork, Alvin.............................$85.00

Chased Diana, butter spreader, flat handle, Towle.............$14.00

Chased Diana, gravy ladle, Towle.............................$35.00

Chased Diana, luncheon fork, Towle, 7¼".............................$24.00

Chased Diana, teaspoon, Towle, 5½".............................$9.00

Chateau, bouillon spoon, Lunt.............................$14.00

Chateau, carving knife, Lunt, 10".............................$32.50

Chateau, dessert spoon, Lunt, 7½".............................$20.00

Chateau, teaspoon, Lunt, 6".............................$12.50

Chelsea Manor, oval soup spoon, Gorham, 6¾".............$31.00

Chelsea Manor, tablespoon, Gorham.............................$40.00

Chelsea Manor, teaspoon, Gorham.............................$15.00

Classic Rose, butter knife, hollow handle, Reed & Barton...$15.00

Classic Rose, casserole, Reed & Barton.............................$125.00

Classic Rose, salad fork, Reed & Barton.............................$29.00

Classic Rose, sugar spoon, Reed & Barton.............................$15.00

Contessina, butter knife, hollow handle, Towle.............$21.00

Contessina, place fork, Towle, 7½".............................$23.00

Contessina, sugar spoon, Towle.............................$21.00

Contessina, teaspoon, Towle.............................$17.50

Damask Rose, casserole spoon, Oneida.............................$50.00

Damask Rose, cocktail fork, Oneida.............................$16.00

Damask Rose, dinner fork, Oneida, 7¾".............................$30.00

Damask Rose, place spoon, Oneida, 6½".............................$30.00

Dawn Star, cold meat fork, Wallace.............................$45.00

Dawn Star, place knife, Wallace, 9¼".............................$17.50

Dawn Star, sugar spoon, Wallace.............................$18.50

English Provincial, cold meat fork, Reed & Barton.............$52.00

English Provincial, pierced tablespoon, Reed & Barton........$45.00

English Provincial, salad fork, Reed & Barton.............$24.00

First Frost, butter spreader, hollow handle, Oneida.............$8.00

First Frost, pickle fork, Oneida.............................$12.50

First Frost, place spoon, Oneida.............................$22.00

First Frost, teaspoon, Oneida.............................$15.00

Foxhall, cream soup spoon, Watson.............................$20.00

Foxhall, luncheon fork, Watson, 7".............................$23.00

Foxhall, salad fork, Watson.............................$26.50

Foxhall, teaspoon, Watson.............................$13.50

Grand Colonial, place fork, Wallace, 7¼".............................$23.00

Grand Colonial, sugar spoon, Wallace.............................$17.50

Grand Colonial, teaspoon, Wallace.............................$12.50

Intaglio, bouillon spoon, Reed & Barton.............................$23.00

Intaglio, cocktail fork, Reed & Barton, 5¾".............................$40.00

Intaglio, teaspoon, Reed & Barton, 5⅞".............................$23.00

Lady Mary, bouillon spoon, Towle.............................$11.00

Lady Mary, iced tea spoon, Towle.............................$23.00

Lady Mary, jelly spoon, Towle.............................$15.00

Lady Mary, teaspoon, Towle, 5⅞".............................$11.00

Lark, cocktail fork, Reed & Barton.............................$25.00

Lark, place spoon, Reed & Barton.............................$35.00

Lark, teaspoon, Reed & Barton.............................$16.00

Louis XIV, cocktail fork, Towle.............................$12.50

Louis XIV, luncheon fork, Towle, 7¼".............................$24.00

Louis XIV, tablespoon, Towle.............................$36.00

Madam Jumel, bouillon spoon, Whiting, 5".............................$16.00

Madam Jumel, dessert spoon, Whiting, 7".............................$30.00

Madam Jumel, teaspoon, Whiting, 8½".............................$9.00

Mansion House, butter knife, flat handle, Oneida.............$15.00

Mansion House, dessert spoon, Oneida.............................$36.50

Mansion House, lemon fork, Oneida.............................$14.00

Mansion House, teaspoon, Oneida.............................$15.00

Meadow Rose, luncheon fork, Watson, 7½".............................$26.50

Meadow Rose, sugar spoon, Watson.............................$20.00

Meadow Rose, teaspoon, Watson.............................$16.00

Modern Victorian, butter knife, hollow handle, Lunt.........$20.00

Modern Victorian, cocktail fork, Lunt.............................$13.00

Modern Victorian, cream soup spoon, Lunt.............................$22.50

Normandie, dinner knife, Wallace, 9½".............................$23.00

Normandie, grapefruit spoon, Wallace.............................$17.50

Normandie, teaspoon, Wallace.............................$13.00

Old English, gravy ladle, Towle.............................$55.00

Old English, salad fork, Towle.............................$36.00

Old English, tablespoon, Towle.............................$27.50

Old English, teaspoon, Towle, 7½".............................$8.50

Overture, cream soup spoon, National.............................$16.50

Overture, sugar spoon, National.............................$12.50

Overture, teaspoon, National.............................$12.50

Paul Revere, dinner knife, Towle, 7¾".............................$29.00

Paul Revere, pastry fork, Towle, 5¾".............................$31.00

Paul Revere, salad fork, gold-washed tines, Towle.............$30.00

Paul Revere, teaspoon, Towle.............................$10.00

Plymouth, beef fork, Gorham.............................$35.00

Plymouth, bouillon, Gorham, 5¼".............................$13.00

Plymouth, cocktail fork, Gorham.............................$13.00

Plymouth, cream ladle, Gorham $24.00
Princess Mary, gumbo spoon, Wallace, &" $22.50
Princess Mary, lemon fork, Wallace $17.50
Princess Mary, luncheon fork, Wallace $22.50
Princess Mary, sugar spoon, Wallace............................$15.00
Repousse, butter spreader, hollow handle, S Kirk & Son $23.00
Repousse, gravy ladle, S Kirk & Son $52.50
Repousse, place fork, S Kirk & Son $29.00
Romantique, cream soup spoon, Alvin $18.00
Romantique, iced tea spoon, Alvin................................$18.50
Romantique, salad fork, Alvin.....................................$18.00
Romantique, teaspoon, Alvin......................................$13.00
Rose Solitaire, cocktail fork, Towle..............................$19.50
Rose Solitaire, salad fork, Towle $26.50
Rose Solitaire, sugar tongs, Towle................................$35.00
Rose Solitaire, teaspoon, Towle $17.50
Rosemary, cocktail fork, Easterling..............................$16.00
Rosemary, cold meat fork, Easterling $42.50
Rosemary, tablespoon, Easterling $30.00
Rosemary, teaspoon, Easterling $12.00
Silver Sculpture, cold meat fork, Reed & Barton $56.00
Silver Sculpture, salad fork, Reed & Barton $25.00
Silver Sculpture, sugar spoon, Reed & Barton....................$18.50
Silver Sculpture, teaspoon, Reed & Barton $16.00
Silver Wheat, butter knife, hollow handle, Reed & Barton ..$13.00
Silver Wheat, place knife, Reed & Barton..........................$16.00
Silver Wheat, salad fork, Reed & Barton.........................$20.00
Stanton Hall, berry spoon, Oneida $92.50
Stanton Hall, cocktail fork, Oneida $18.50
Stanton Hall, dessert spoon, Oneida, 7" $36.00
Stradivari, bonbon, Wallace..$36.00
Stradivari, cocktail fork, Wallace $16.00
Stradivari, iced tea spoon, Wallace................................$24.00
Stradivari, luncheon fork, Wallace $25.50
Valencia, demitasse spoon, International $16.00
Valencia, gravy ladle, International................................$55.00
Valencia, pie server, International.................................$35.00
Valencia, place fork, International.................................$25.50
Virginia Carvel, bouillon spoon, Towle $12.00
Virginia Carvel, jelly spoon, Towle...............................$17.50
Virginia Carvel, tablespoon, Towle................................$26.50
Virginia Carvel, teaspoon, Towle, 6" $14.00
Willow, cold meat fork, Gorham..................................$30.00
Willow, demitasse spoon, Gorham $14.00
Willow, place spoon, Gorham, 7⅛" $27.50
18th Century, cocktail fork, Reed & Barton $30.00
18th Century, place fork, Reed & Barton, 7½".................$29.00
18th Century, place spoon, Reed & Barton $33.50

Skookum Dolls

The Skookums Apple Packers Association of Wenatchee, Washington, had a doll made for their trademark. Skookum figures were designed and registered by a Montana woman, Mary McAboy, in 1917. Although she always made note of the Skookums name, she also used the 'Bully Good' trademark along with other information to inform the buyer that 'Bully Good' translated is 'Skookums.' McAboy had an article published in the March 1920 issue of *Playthings* magazine explaining the history of Skookum dolls. Anyone interested can obtain this information on microfilm from any large library.

In 1920 the Arrow Novelty Company held the contract to make the dolls, but by 1929 the H.H. Tammen Company had taken over their production. Skookums were designed with life-like facial characteristics. The dried apple heads of the earliest dolls did not last, and they were soon replaced with heads made of a composition material. Wool blankets formed the bodies that were then stuffed with dried twigs, leaves, and grass. The remainder of the body was cloth and felt.

Skookum dolls with wooden legs and felt-covered wooden feet were made between 1917 and 1949. After 1949 the legs and feet were made of plastic. The newest dolls have plastic heads. A 'Skookums Bully Good Indians' paper label was placed on one foot of each early doll. Exact dating of a Skookum is very difficult. McAboy designed many different tribes of dolls simply by using different blanket styles, beading, and backboards (for carrying the papoose). The eyes are almost always looking to the right. The store display dolls, 36" and larger, are the most valuable of the Skookums. Prices range from $1,000.00 to $1,500.00 per doll or $2,500.00 to $3,000.00 for the pair. Beware of imitations, they are not not as desirable or valuable as the originals. It should also be noted that condition is critical. Damage, especially to the face, hair, etc., will lower the doll's value significantly.

Advisor: Jo Ann Palmieri (See Directory Skookum Dolls)

Children, plastic legs, from 6" to 8", from $25.00 to $35.00 each.

Child, plastic legs, 8" to 10", from $35 to $50.00
Child, wooden legs, 6½", from $50 to $60.00
Female, wooden legs, 13½", from $150 to.........................$200.00
Female, wooden legs, 16", from $200 to...........................$300.00
Female w/papoose, wooden legs, 8" to 10", from $75 to.....$100.00
Female w/papoose, wooden legs, 10" to 12", from $100 to..$125.00
Female w/papoose, wooden legs, 14" to 16", from $200 to..$225.00
Male, wooden legs, 8" to 10", from $100 to......................$125.00

Male, wooden legs, 10 to 12", from $125 to......................$150.00
Male, wooden legs, 12" to 14", from $150 to....................$175.00
Male, wooden legs, 14" to 16", from $200 to....................$300.00

Smiley Face

The Smiley Face was designed in 1963 by Harvey Ball, a commercial artist that had been commissioned by an insurance company to design a 'happy' logo to use on office supplies and pin-back buttons — seems spirits were low due to unpopular company policies, and the office manager was looking for something that would cheer up employees. 'Operation Smile' was a huge success. Who would have thought that such a simple concept — tiny eyes with a curving line to represent a big smile in black on a bright yellow background — would have become the enduring icon that it did. Mr. Ball was paid a mere $45.00 for his efforts, and no one even bothered to obtain a trademark for Smiley! Over the year, many companies have designed scores of products featuring the happy face. The McCoy Pottery Company was one of them; they made a line of cookie jars, mugs, banks, and planters. No matter if you collect Smiley or McCoy, you'll want to watch for those!

Today, the Smiley face is enjoying renewed popularity. You'll find 'new' examples in nearly any specialty catalog. But if you buy the vintage Smileys, expect to pay several times their original retail price.

Advisor: Pam Speidel (See Directory, Smiley Face)

Cookie jar, McCoy #235, 1970s, 11", from $40.00 to $65.00.

Backpack, black & yellow w/red tongue, vinyl w/Joe Boxer on blue
    straps, NM...$22.50
Bank, black on yellow, pottery, McCoy, 6½".....................$30.00
Bank, pottery, black & red on white, McCoy, 5x4"..............$38.00
Bed in a Bag, faces in black & yellow on red & black plaid, Sears, fits
    full-size bed, NM...$40.00
Brush & comb set, white hard plastic, Made in USA by Tom Field
    Ltd, 1970s, ea 8" L, MIB.....................................$55.00

Coffee mug, green on white glass, Fire-King/Anchor Hocking ...$32.00
Coffee mug, not winking, fired-on yellow, Fire-King/Anchor
    Hocking...$145.00
Coffee mug, winking, fired-on yellow, Fire-King/Anchor
    Hocking... $215.00
Coffee mugs, pottery, McCoy, 4 for $50.00
Material, multicolor faces on black cotton, 45x180"...........$22.50
Material, patriotic theme w/stars & stripes on Smiley faces on blue
    cotton, 45x180"..$22.50
Pin-back button, bloody Smiley Face, Watchmen, DE Comics,
    1986, 1¼"..$32.50
Place setting, black on yellow, pottery, McCoy, plate, bowl & mug,
    3 pcs...$27.50
Planter, yellow & black, pottery, McCoy, #0386, 4½x3"......$18.00
Salt & pepper shakers, ceramic, yellow & black, 3", pr........$27.50
Trinket box, porcelain, PHB - Midwest of Cannon Falls, 1960s,
    sm...$27.50
Tumblers, green & yellow faces on clear glass, 1970s, 4 for .$10.00

Snow Domes

Snow dome collectors buy them all, old and new. The older ones (from the '30s and '40s) are made in two pieces, the round glass globe that sits on a separate base. They were made here as well as in Italy, and today this type is being imported from Austria and the Orient.

During the '50s, plastic snow domes made in West Germany were popular as souvenirs and Christmas toys. Some were half-domes with blue backs; others were made in bottle shapes or simple geometric forms.

There were two styles produced in the '70s. Both were made of plastic. The first were designed as large domes with a plastic figure of an animal, a mermaid, or some other character draped over the top. In the other style, the snow dome itself was made in an unusual shape.

Wile E. Coyote, Feel Better!, 1989, 2¾", $14.00. (Photo courtesy www.whatacharacter.com)

American Household Storage, semi-truck & city skyline, glass on
    brown plastic base, ca 1953......................................$85.00

Barbie Celebrating the Millennium 2000, Barbie seated by globe w/ world inside, musical, Avon, 1999 ....**$25.00**

Betty Boop on unicorn, trailing rainbow, sky & cloud base..**$125.00**

Carlsbad Caverns, cowboy on horse, glass globe on white ceramic base, Made in USA, 3½" **$35.00**

Cinderella figurine w/photo frame & mini snow dome, faux jewels, Princess series (6 in all), Disney, 6x6x3" **$36.00**

Cinderella in globe & other princesses (4) on staircase w/ornate scrollwork, plays Cinderella's theme song, 11", MIB...**$145.00**

Deer & bear on seesaw before plastic mountain scene, Yosemite label at base, encased in clear bottle w/blue cap **$25.00**

Evil Queen portrait on base, apple in globe, battery-operated light, Disney, China, 7" **$42.50**

Finding Nemo, painted resin base, plays Tiny Bubbles, Disneyland, MIB **$115.00**

Girl w/braids holds flowers & offers 1 to teddy bear, plays You've Got a Friend, Gobel, BH 1028, 5½" **$20.00**

Hummingbirds & sunflowers, glass & resin, plays You Are My Sunshine, 5½" **$30.00**

Iguana lizards, painted resin, plays Love Me w/All Your Heart, 5½"..**$27.50**

John Lennon's Imagine, rhino, giraffe & elephant around palm tree, pink & blue snow, revolving lamp, Carter's, MIB.......**$132.00**

Joseph, Mary & Baby Jesus, wooden shooting star atop globe, wooden base, plays Oh Holy Night, San Francisco, 1995.......**$30.00**

Little Mermaid Ariel w/Flounder, blue base w/starfish & mini flowers, globe rests on rocks, Disney, 5x4¾" **$27.50**

Lone Ranger Round-Up, Lone Ranger w/lasso (dexterity game), Driss Co, copyright TLR Inc, 4", from $150 to **$165.00**

Lord of the Rings, Galadriel the Elven Queen, MIB..........**$210.00**

Lord of the Rings, Hobbits in Hiding, MIB **$135.00**

Lord of the Rings, Ringwraiths Servants of Saliron, MIB...**$195.00**

Mickey Mouse in clear globe shaped like ears hat, Mickey dressed as characters all along base, Disney, 1971, 10x8" **$125.00**

New York, Manhattan's skyscrapers, painted resin, plays New York New York, San Francisco Music Box Co, MIB...........**$145.00**

New York City cityscape on black base, musical, Saks Fifth Ave, 7", NMIB..............................**$165.00**

Niagara Falls, Maid of the Mist boat scene, plaster base w/real shells **$125.00**

Nightmare Before Christmas 10th Anniversary, Jack Skellington & characters, Disney, 2003 limited edition, 15½", MIB ..**$150.00**

Panda Bears, painted resin, plays Born Free, 5½" **$27.50**

Pepe Le Pew, clear plastic dome on red base marked Pour L'Amour, 1989, 3", NM **$15.00**

Peter Pan, painted resin, plays You Can Fly, You Can Fly, You Can Fly, Disneyland, MIB..............................**$55.00**

Peter Pan Pirate Ship holds globe containing Peter & children, Plays You Can Fly You Can Fly You Can Fly, MIB..............**$145.00**

Pez Bride & Groom, M&J Variety Co, 4½x3½", MIB.........**$42.50**

Pirate's of the Caribbean Black Pearl, battery-operated cannons on ship holding globe, MIB..............................**$145.00**

Sleeping Beauty & prince, dress changes from pink to blue & back, plays song, painted resin, Disney, 7" **$125.00**

Sleeping Beauty & prince spin in hourglass globe as fairies look on, plays Once Upon a Dream, Disney, MIB **$135.00**

Snow White & dwarf in globe, sm clock w/bird perched atop, behind is door w/tree, painted resin, Disney, 5½" **$75.00**

St Louis Basilica New Orleans, horse & rider before basilica, plastic, Hong Kong, #352, 2¼x2¾" **$35.00**

Superman, Fortress of Solitude, rocket base, DC Comics, 7x4¾", NMIB..............................**$45.00**

Tinkerbell in thoughtful pose on base w/4 sm globes (ea w/Tinkerball in different mood), painted resin, Disney, 12", MIB...**$130.00**

Trylon & Perisphere, Bakelite base, from 1939 World's Fair, 4" **$135.00**

Yellowstone Park decal on front, porcelain cabin inside, glass dome w/hard plastic base, ca 1950s, 4"..............................**$35.00**

Ziggy, You're #1 on base, plastic, oval, 1980s, NM M.........**$10.00**

101 Dalmatians, couple & dogs in globe, puppies & characters on base, plays Cruella De Vil, Disney **$130.00**

Soda-Pop Collectibles

A specialty area of the advertising field, soft-drink memorabilia is a favorite of many collectors. Now that vintage Coca-Cola items have become rather expensive, interest is expanding to include some of the less widely exploited sodas — Grapette, Hires Root Beer, and Dr. Pepper, for instance.

For further information we recommend *Collectible Soda Pop Memorabilia* by B.J. Summers (Collector Books). In the listings that follow, values are given for items in at least near mint condition unless noted otherwise.

See also Coca-Cola; Pepsi-Cola.

Club: National Pop Can Collectors
Newsletter: *Can-O-Gram*
Lance Meade
335 Delwood St. S
Cambridge, MN 55008
www.canogram.com

A&W Root Beer, drinking straw, orange plastic w/bear head, MIP marked the Great Root Bear Straw, 4 for **$12.00**

A&W Root Beer, Mel's A&W Root Beer Stand, pre-assembled plastic, interior lights, O scale, MTH Rail King, MIB........**$85.00**

A&W Root Beer, mug, The Burger Family, orange & brown pyro on milk glass, Fire-King **$85.00**

B-1 Lemon Lime Soda, sign, tin litho, red, white & yellow, 10x28", VG..............................**$30.00**

Bireley's, clock, Bireley's Happifies Thirst, diamond shape, Pam, repainted gold ring, 1950s, 15", EX..............................**$225.00**

Bireley's, crate, painted wood w/divider in center, cut-out handles, 4⅛x15x11¼", EX..............................**$18.00**

Bireley's, sign, embossed tin, The Real Fruit Taste Drink, 4 bottles shown, AAW Coshocton O, 1949, 15x36", EX..........**$375.00**

Bireley's, sign, tin button, Drink Bireley's Non-Carbonated, orange bottle on yellow, 9" dia, EX......................**$245.00**

Bireley's, thermometer, tin, orange bottle on yellow, 1950s, 16x5", EX **$100.00**

Bubble Up, cigarette lighter, Kiss of Lemon - Kiss of Lime, enameling on metal, Penguin High Quality Superlative..., EX........**$48.00**

Bubble Up, sign, embossed tin, Bubble Up...Has Pa-ZAZZ, red, white & blue, 1950s-60s, 12x28" **$235.00**

Canada Dry, bottle opener, metal, wall mount, Starr X Patent, ...87 Made in USA, 2¾x3½x1", EXIB $17.50

Canada Dry, crate, colorful stencil on wood, 12½x16x11½", EX $42.50

Canada Dry, sign, tin, Canada Dry Spur Soda, lg 12-oz bottle, Zip in Every Sip!, 12x3½", VG+ $65.00

Canada Dry, syrup dispenser, glass jug form w/mc label, 1950s, EX $80.00

Dad's Root Beer, bottle, amber w/gold metal cap, brown glass (never held product), Muth Pat Pend Buffalo, mini, 3" $27.50

Dad's Root Beer, clock, bottle cap on yellow, sq wooden frame, EX $88.00

Dad's Root Beer, mug, logo on ceramic barrel shape, licensed by Dad's Old Fashioned Root Beer, heavy, 5x6" $25.00

Dad's Root Beer, sign, tin, ca. 1950s – 1960s, 32x60", VG, $425.00. (Photo courtesy B.J. Summers)

Dad's Root Beer, thermometer, tin litho, Just Right for Dad's..., embossed bottle, 1947, 25x10", EX $215.00

Dad's Root Beer, toy truck, 1951 Ford F-6, w/bottles, diecast metal, First Gear #19-1115, 1993, 4x8", MIB $40.00

Diet Dad's Root Beer, thermometer, tin litho, Less Than 1 Calorie Per Serving, 27x7", M in envelope $120.00

Diet-Rite Cola, bottle carrier, green plastic w/white lettering, holds 6 bottles, center handle, 1966, EX $15.00

Diet-Rite Cola, can, tin litho, blue, white & green, 1970s, 12-oz, unopened $35.00

Diet-Rite Cola, sign, embossed tin, Enjoy Sugar Free..., bottle at left on yellow, 1961, 12x32" $115.00

Diet-Rite Cola, thermometer, Sugar Free... on yellow, #495, Made in USA, 12½" dia $110.00

Dog 'n Suds, menu, dog w/tray & US map, red & yellow on white, 1950s-60s, EX $40.00

Dog 'n Suds, mug, logo on clear glass, 6" $20.00

Dog 'n Suds, poster, What This Country Needs Is a Good Five-Cent Shake..., ca 1970s, 41x28", EX $22.50

Dog 'n Suds Root Beer, flag, printed cloth, dog w/loaded tray, yellow on red cloth, 35x46" $55.00

Double Cola, clock, globe beneath logo, blue numbers on white, 1960s, 12" dia, EX $150.00

Double Cola, clock, red & white, General Electric, 12" dia, EX. $75.00

Double Cola, sign, tin litho, bottle shape, 23½x5¾", EX $35.00

Double Cola, thermometer, tin litho, You'll Like It Better, multicolor on turquoise blue, 17x5", EX $125.00

Dr Pepper, bottle carrier, aluminum, Good for Life, holds 12 bottles, 3½x11½x9", EX $235.00

Dr Pepper, can, flat juice top, Continent Bottlers Inc, Des Moines IA, 1960s, 12-oz $115.00

Dr Pepper, clock, glass face, diamond shape, lights up, Pam, 15" $225.00

Dr Pepper, clock, glass face, Distinctively Different, lights up, sq, 1950s-60s, EX $150.00

Dr Pepper, clock, glass face, Drink Dr Pepper, wooden frame, 1960s-early '70s, 18x14", EX $80.00

Dr Pepper, clock, man in tuxedo on face, pendulum, wooden frame, battery operated, Chapen, 1999, 26x15" $75.00

Dr Pepper, cooler, aluminum can shape, styrofoam liner, 14x9½" dia $62.50

Dr Pepper, cooler, metal chest w/stainless steel lid & handle, green w/embossed white letters, 19x17½x13", EX $200.00

Dr Pepper, crosswalk marker, embossed bronze, Safety First, 10-2-4, 1930s, 3⅞" dia $75.00

Dr Pepper, door push, pressed aluminum, red & white, Stout, modern repro of 1940s item, 4¼x29¾", MIB $55.00

Dr Pepper, sheet music, Texas Ranger Song, full-page ad for Dr Pepper on back, 1936, EX $70.00

Dr Pepper, sign, cardboard, girl in blue work uniform holds bottle, Drink a Bite on the Job, 1940s, 15x26", EX $250.00

Dr Pepper, sign, flange; die-cut steel, double sided, 10-2-4, Deco style, Stout, 1930s, 14x22", EX $225.00

Dr Pepper, sign, printed paper, Frosty, Man - Frosty, lady w/groceries offered bottle, 1960s, 15x25", EX $225.00

Dr Pepper, thermometer, glass front, Pam, 12" dia $350.00

Dr Pepper, thermometer, tin litho, bottle on yellow, 10-2-4, light rust & dents, 25½x9¾", VG $80.00

Dr Pepper, thermometer, tin litho, Drink Dr Pepper Frosty Cold on red & white, Dona 500 1-55, 25", VG+ $165.00

Dr Pepper, thermometer, tin litho, Good for Life, bottle on yellow, 25½x9¾", EX $85.00

Dr Pepper, thermometer, tin litho, Hot or Cold, orange, red & white, round, 1953, EX $75.00

Dr Pepper, thermometer, tin litho, Hot or Cold, red, yellow & white, 1950s-60s, 16x6½" $155.00

Dr Pepper, thermometer, tin litho, Hot or Cold, red & white, 1960, 12x6", EX $115.00

Dr Pepper, train set, K Line, engine, gondola loaded w/Pepsi cartons & caboose, VG $175.00

Dr Pepper, watch fob, embossed metal, 1½", EX $90.00

Dr Pepper, wristwatch, Dr Pepper on face, gold-tone metal, Bulova Accutron, 1977 ....$55.00

Dr Pepper thermometer, glass front, Pam, 12" dia, EX $215.00

Frostie Root Beer, bottle carton, cardboard, No Deposit No Return & elf, 6-pack $10.00

Frostie Root Beer, mug, red & yellow diamond logo on clear glass, 1950s, mini, 3¼" $27.50

Frostie Root Beer, mug, red & yellow elf & lettering on clear glass, 5x3¼", EX $15.00

Frostie Root Beer, sign, paper, elf & lettering, multicolor on white, 1957, 9x18½" $17.50

Frostie Root Beer, sign, plastic, 3-D elf holds sign, 1950s, 12x13", EX $115.00

Frostie Root Beer, sign, tin bottle cap, Drink..., red, white & blue, 22" dia, NM **$335.00**

Frostie Root Beer, thermometer, multicolor logo on white, round..**$90.00**

Grapette, bank, clown-shaped glass jar w/metal top, 7¼", EX .. **$20.00**

Grapette, bank, glass elephant-form jar w/metal lid, EX **$16.00**

Grapette, bottle opener, wall mount, Star X, Brown Mfg Co, Patented in USA, M in VG box..............................**$30.00**

Grapette, crate, stencil on wood, holds 30 bottles, pierced handles, EX **$20.00**

Grapette, crosswalk marker, embossed bronze, Walk Safely, 1930s, 3⅞"...**$55.00**

Grapette, sign, cardboard, lg bottle, Bigger Better, 1940s-50s, 18½x8", EX..**$60.00**

Grapette, thermometer, tin litho, bottle on white, 16x6", VG .. **$70.00**

Gulf Club Dry Lemon Soda, bottle cap, metal w/cork back, Armstrong mark on skirt, EX..............................**$10.00**

Hires Root Beer, clock, glass face, lights up, #4173, 14x14", EX . **$45.00**

Hires Root Beer, cooler, aluminum, logo on front of chest form, 13x22x13", EX..**$95.00**

Hires Root Beer, door push, tin litho, yellow, & white w/black letters, 1930s, 2x18", EX..............................**$45.00**

Hires Root Beer, hand fan, chromolithograph on heavy paper, At the Beach, lady in beach scene, ca 1910, 10½", EX............**$50.00**

Hires Root Beer, sign, embossed tin, ca. 1927, 28x11", NM, $350.00. (Photo courtesy Craig Stifter)

Hires Root Beer, sign, tin litho, It's High Time for..., 1960s, 11½x29⅜" **$90.00**

Hires Root Beer, syrup dispenser, barrel shape, shiny bands & oak tones, complete, 1940s, 21", EX..........................**$325.00**

Hires Root Beer, thermometer, tin litho bottle form, Genuine..., #4145, 28½x7¾", EX **$160.00**

Hires Root Beer, trading card, Bob Friend #24, w/tab, 1958 .. **$160.00**

Hires Root Beer, trading card, Clem Labine, no tab, 1958, EX+ . **$40.00**

Kist, clock, glass face, lady w/bottle, It's Kist Time, lights up, 1950s, 15" dia, EX..**$175.00**

Kist, sign, tin litho, Get Kist Here on red w/bottle, 7½x29½", EX+ **$230.00**

Kist, sign, tin litho bottle cap, red, white & blue, 15", EX .. **$85.00**

Kist Beverages, yo-yo, painted wood, half black, half blue, 2" dia, EX **$15.00**

Lemon Bowl, soda cap, tin litho w/cork back, yellow & green, EX **$25.00**

Mission Orange, sign, flange; bottle cap, orange, black & white, 18⅜", EX..**$220.00**

Mission Orange, thermometer, tin litho, bottle on white, 1950s, 15x5¾", EX..**$85.00**

Mountain Dew, can, tin litho, Sugar-Free, red, white & green, 12-oz..**$80.00**

Mountain Dew, case, painted wood, for 24 bottles, 4x18½x12", EX **$135.00**

Mountain Dew, clock, Mountain Dew, 3, 6, 9 on yellow background, lights up, 1970s, 15x15"..............................**$55.00**

Mountain Dew, doll, Hillbilly Willy, plastic face, foam body, original clothes, poseable, damage/stains, 14", VG **$55.00**

Mountain Dew, sign, embossed metal litho, hillbilly w/jug, bottle, It'll Tickle Yore Innards!, 20x30"..............................**$150.00**

Moxie, cooler, painted tin, red & white, galvanized lining, removable lid hinged in center, 37½x32x22", EX **$300.00**

Moxie, sign, tin litho, horse & car, dated 1933, 18x24", VG.. **$160.00**

Nehi, seltzer bottle, blue glass, Made in Czechoslovakia, 26-oz, w/ metal top, 11x3½" dia..............................**$50.00**

Nehi, sign, paper die-cut, Nehi on lady's knee (legs shown only), bottle on right, Square Deal Service, 1930s, 8x10", EX............**$95.00**

Nesbitt's, patch, Nesbitt's of California, blue embroidery on orange cloth, 1950s-60s, 5x10⅜" **$12.50**

Nesbitt's, recipe leaflet, Recipes w/Nesbitt's, cake & oranges on cover, 27 recipes, EX..............................**$8.00**

Nesbitt's, sign, cardboard, double sided, Open/Closed, red, white & black, 10x12½", EX..............................**$90.00**

Nesbitt's, sign, paper, family outdoor barbecue scene, in 21x29" wooden frame, EX..............................**$105.00**

Nesbitt's, syrup dispenser, glass jug fits on plastic dispensing base, 1960s, EX..**$80.00**

Nesbitt's, thermometer, tin litho, bottle, red, white & blue, 16", EX **$140.00**

Nesbitt's, thermometer, tin litho, bottle cap on yellow, 28x7" ...**$195.00**

NuGrape, bottle opener, embossed metal, ...Imitation Grape Flavor, Over the Top Trademark Made in USA, Vaughn, 3½" L... **$7.50**

NuGrape, clock, glass face, logo in center w/bottle, lights up, round..**$175.00**

NuGrape, clock, glass front, logo & bottle in center, lights up, sq, Swihart Products, EX..............................**$150.00**

NuGrape, sign, tin litho, bottle on yellow, Reg US Pat Office, 36x14", EX..**$55.00**

NuGrape, sign, tin litho bottle cap, purple & yellow, 36" dia, EX **$225.00**

NuGrape, sign, tin litho bottle shape, 17x5", EX..............**$150.00**

NuGrape, thermometer, tin litho, blue & yellow on white, rectangular, EX..**$75.00**

Orange Kist, cooler, painted metal, on legs, removable lid hinged in center, 33x33x24" w/14" deep tank, EX **$80.00**

Orange Kist, sign, paper over Masonite, girl in bonnet picking flowers, 2 bottles on tray, 1950s, 21x14½", EX **$65.00**

Orange-Crush, button, celluloid, with envelope, ca. 1960s, M, $150.00.

Orange-Crush, can, flat top, Crush International, Evanston IL, 12-oz, EX..**$132.50**

Orange-Crush, clock, glass front, lights up, Pam, 1955, 15" dia ..**$275.00**

Orange-Crush, cooler, metal, Crushy & Drink..., chrome handle, holds 6-pack, EX **$85.00**

Orange-Crush, door push, tin litho, Ask for a..., #B-144, Made in USA, 3½x26", EX..**$150.00**

Orange-Crush, sign, tin litho, Ask for a Crush w/Crushy, 1940s, 19½x27½", EX **$295.00**

Orange-Crush, sign, tin litho, Discover..., hand w/bottle, 11½x29¼", EX **$275.00**

Orange-Crush, sign, tin litho, Enjoy Orange Crush, lg bottle, 1960s, 54x18", EX..**$395.00**

Orange-Crush, sign, tin litho, Feel Fresh!, diamond shape, 1930s-40s, 16", EX **$215.00**

Orange-Crush, thermometer, convex glass front w/bottle cap image on face, Pam, 12" dia................................**$250.00**

Orange-Crush, thermometer, tin litho, bottle cap on blue, rectangular, 16", EX **$165.00**

Orange-Crush, thermometer, tin litho, Crushy character at top, Ask for..., 10" L, VG **$125.00**

Orange-Crush, thermometer, tin litho, Thirsty? & bottle cap on green, 1960s, 16x6" **$190.00**

Orange-Crush, thermometer, tin litho bottle form, 28¾x7", EX.. **$175.00**

Royal Crown, cooler, painted steel, red lettering on yellow, Progress Refrigerator Co, VG **$175.00**

Royal Crown, sign, flanged; steel, double-sided, Best by Taste-Test, 11x8", EX **$325.00**

Royal Crown, sign, tin litho, The Big Refreshing Difference, red & white, self-framed, ca 1961, 17x63", EX....................**$115.00**

Royal Crown, thermometer, tin litho, The Fresher Refresher, red & blue on white, 26x10", EX **$85.00**

Royal Crown, thermometer, tin litho, yellow arrow on red, 1950s, rectangular, 26x10", EX.............................**$175.00**

Seven-Up, Boogie bodyboard, 7-Up logo on white, Morey Boogie, ca 1980s, 41x21½", EX **$80.00**

Seven-Up, bottle opener, brass, 1950s, 5⅜", EX **$50.00**

Seven-Up, cigarette lighter, bottle & logo on yellow enamel, penguin, EX **$40.00**

Seven-Up, clock, glass front, metal & plastic frame, lights up, late 1960s, 15½x15½", EX..................................**$125.00**

Seven-Up, cooler, aluminum chest w/hinged lid, Croustroms Mfg, 1950s, VG **$65.00**

Seven-Up, cooler, painted steel chest, logo on white, 13x18x9", EX..**$60.00**

Seven-Up, menu/price board, logo in center, lights up, ca 1970s, 26x20x4½", EX **$55.00**

Seven-Up, sign, flange; tin die-cut, double-sided, logo & bottle, 1954, 18x20"...**$475.00**

Seven-Up, sign, tin litho, First Against Thirst, red, white & green, self-framed, 18¾x27" **$100.00**

Seven-Up, sign, tin litho, Fresh Up!, You Like It, It Likes You, 1955, 12x30", VG **$70.00**

Seven-Up, thermometer, First Against Thirst, glass front, 1966, 12" dia, EX...**$185.00**

Seven-Up, thermometer, glass front, sun rays on white, 1971, 12" dia, VG+ **$70.00**

Seven-Up, thermometer, tin litho, yellow & orange sun rays on white, Barker, Made in USA, 17x5", EX......................**$65.00**

Slice Lemon-Lime Soda, bank, diecast metal truck, Ertl, 3x6¼", NM in EX box **$20.00**

Squirt, bottle opener, metal w/red lettering, wall mount, EX..**$22.50**

Squirt, can, tin, red lettering & sun rays, 12-oz, EX **$30.00**

Squirt, clock, glass front, orange logo & bottle on white, Pam, 1965, 15x15", EX **$250.00**

Squirt, door push, embossed tin litho, Drink... & bottle on blue, 1940s-50s, 4x17½", EX....................................**$165.00**

Squirt, gumball/candy machine, Atlas 5¢, boy opening bottle on yellow, glass top, EX...**$200.00**

Squirt, menu sign, bottle upper left, lined blackboard below, 1958, 28x19", EX **$100.00**

Squirt, sign, embossed tin, AAW USA, 1941, 28x20", G, $125.00.

Squirt, sign, tin bottle cap, red & white, 38" dia, EX **$150.00**

Squirt, thermometer, tin litho, bottle on white, copyright 1971, 13½x", EX **$80.00**

Sun Crest, bottle carrier, printed cardboard, holds 6-pack, EX....**$28.00**

Sun Crest, clock, glass front, Drink... & setting sun, lights up, Swihart, 16x13", EX **$135.00**

Sun Crest, sign, tin litho, blue, white & orange, 10x16", EX ..**$90.00**

Sun Crest, thermometer, tin litho, bottle on yellow & black, 1950s, 16x6½" **$295.00**

Sun-Drop, bottle cap, black lettering on cream, EX.............**$15.00**

Sun-Drop Golden Cola/Mission Orange, case, wood w/stencils, metal bands, 10x16½x10½", EX...................................**$25.00**

Upper 10, sign, tin litho, Picks You Up, multicolor on yellow, 1950s, 12x30", EX **$140.00**

Vernor's Ginger Ale, rack sign, tin litho, yellow & green, 1940s, 9½x13", EX **$50.00**

Vernor's Ginger Ale, tray, tin litho, Say Vernor's - A Case for Home, gold on brown, 1930s, 13x10½", VG+ **$165.00**

Vernor's Ginger Ale, window sign, lovely blond & drink in glass on green, 1950s, matted & framed, EX **$85.00**

Way Up Lemon & Lime, sign, printed cardboard, fruit & blossoms, hot-air balloon, made to attach to bottle, 6½x7", EX ...**$12.50**

Whistle, bottle opener, brass, embossed Whistle ea side, 5½", VG **$100.00**

Whistle, clock/sign, painted Masonite & wood, boy & bottle, Phelps Mfg, Terre Haute IN, #WC6-92, 24x24", EX **$675.00**

Whistle, decal, Refreshing Fruit Flavor & bottle cap, 1940s, 5x5", EX **$10.00**

Whistle, sign, paper die-cut, elf atop bottle, orange, dark blue, green & white, 11⅞x2¾" **$55.00**

Whistle, sign, tin litho, elf w/lg bottle on dolly, 1948, 20x24", EX...**$225.00**

Whistle, sign, tin litho, Thirsty? Just..., black letters on yellow & orange, JV Reed...Louisville KY, 10x28", VG **$150.00**

Wink, bottle cap, Try a Wink, lady winking, Wink Syrup Co, cork lined, unused **$3.50**

Soda Bottles With Painted Labels

The earliest type of soda bottles were made by soda producers and sold in the immediate vicinity of the bottling company. Many had pontil scars, left by a rod that was used to manipulate the bottle as it was blown. They had a flat bottom rather than a 'kick-up,' so for transport, they were laid on their side and arranged in layers. This served to keep the cork moist, which kept it expanded, tight, and in place. Upright the cork would dry out, shrink, and expel itself with a 'pop,' hence the name 'soda pop.'

Until the '30s, the name of the product or the bottler was embossed in the glass or printed on a paper label (sometimes pasted over reused returnable bottles). Though a few paper labels were used as late as the '60s, nearly all bottles produced from the mid-'30s on had painted-on (pyro-glazed) lettering, and logos and pictures were often added. Imaginations ran rampant. Bottlers waged a fierce competition to make their soda logos eye catching and sales inspiring. Anything went! Girls, airplanes, patriotic designs, slogans proclaiming amazing health benefits, even cowboys and Indians became popular advertising ploys. This is the type you'll encounter

most often today, and collector interest is on the increase. Look for interesting, multicolored labels, rare examples from small-town bottlers, and those made from glass in colors other than clear or green. In the listings that follow, values are for examples in at least near mint condition.

Aces Up, green glass, Sanger Bottling Works, California, 1-qt...**$110.00**

Big Chief, clear glass, red & white label, Brookhaven MS, 12-oz...**$68.00**

Big Chief, clear glass, red & white label, straight sides, Coca-Cola Bottling Co, Richfield UT, ca 1950s, 7½-oz...............**$45.00**

Bubble Up, red and white pyro on green, king size, EX, $6.00. (Photo courtesy B.J. Summers)

Carolina Moon, green glass, orange & yellow label, 12-oz ...**$24.00**

Central Beverages, clear glass, red & white label, Central Bottling Corp, Auburn NY, 7½-oz **$28.00**

Cheer Up, green glass, red & white label, Silver Top Bottling Works, Hanover PA, 24-oz **$30.00**

Circus, clear glass, red & white label, Nesbitt Bottling Co, Mt Clemens MI, 10-oz, 9¼" **$35.00**

Clarion Root Beer, amber glass, 3-color label, 7-oz **$20.00**

Cola Root Beer, clear glass, Indian chief profile, Cola Rootbeer Bottling Co, Santa Ana CA, 12-oz................................**$70.00**

Cow Boy, clear glass, red & white label, Cow Boy Bottling, Phoenix AZ, 6-oz **$30.00**

Donald Duck Cola, clear glass, Donald's face front & back, Commercial Beverage Co, Salem MA, W Disney Productions, 7-oz...**$27.50**

Dr Nut, clear glass, red & white label, Oregon City OR, 7-oz, 8½" **$48.00**

Dr Pepper, clear glass, red & white label, Fairmont MN, 10-oz..**$42.50**

Dr Pepper, green glass, Salutes 1972 World Champions (Dolphins)..$30.00

Dr Swett's Root Beer, clear glass w/embossed ribs, red & yellow label, Desert Bottling Co, Phoenix AZ.....................$22.50

Flip, green glass, yellow & white labels, Division of Dad's Root Beer Co, Chicago Il, 7-oz $22.00

Fox, clear glass, red & white labels w/fox & hunter, Fox Beverages, Freemont OH, 1962, 8½" $20.00

Fudgy, brown glass, labels front & back, Ludlow MA, 6-oz, EX..$85.00

Fufu Berry, clear glass, Metroid Prime Hunters label, Jones Soda Co, unopened, 12-oz $20.00

Holly, clear glass, Betty Boop label, strawberry soda, 1975, unopened..$20.00

Hydrox Club Soda, clear glass, 3-color label, Hydrox Ginger Ale Co, Meriden CT, 12-oz $26.00

Idaho, clear glass, potato label, Kallusky Bros Canyon Bottling Co, Caldwell & Buhl ID, 1950s $16.00

Isaly's Cola, clear glass, red & white labels, Isaly Co, Youngstown OH, ca 1960s, 12-oz $24.00

Kreemo, clear glass, Property of Seven-Up Bottling, Jennings LA, dated 1961...$55.00

Lemmy, clear glass, yellow & green labels, Rapids Beverage Co, Wisconsin Rapids WI, 10-oz $22.50

Lemmy, green glass, yellow label, Tom Collins Jr, Cincinnati OH, dated 1949, 7½" $52.50

Lyons Root Beer, clear glass, red & white label, Lyons Root Beer Bottling Co, Globe AZ, 10-oz $20.00

Mountain Dew, green glass, red & white label, Bottled by Lou & Joann $25.00

Mountain Dew, green glass, Shenley, Keith & Kent, 10-oz..$37.50

Mountain Dew, green glass, Slim & Egbert, 10-oz..............$90.00

Mountain Dew, green glass, Tommy Avent, 10-oz $36.00

Ozark Dew Drop, clear glass, green & white label, 11-oz $40.00

Red Lodge, clear glass, red & white label, Red Lodge MT, 7-oz ..$38.00

Rummy, green glass, red & white label, Rummy on neck, Under License From Wonder Orange Co, Nevada City Bottling, 7-oz...$25.00

SKY, Refrescante, clear glass w/embossed ribs, red & white label, Mexico $24.00

Sno-Maid, clear glass, green & white girl skiing label, Seven-Up bottling Co, Reading Lancaster Pottsville, 12-oz...............$20.00

Sparkeeta Root Beer, clear glass, Owens Glass Co, Sparkletts of Los Angeles CA, 12-oz $45.00

Sunland, clear glass, red & white label, Sunland Bottling Co, Phoenix AZ, 10-oz..$26.00

Texan, green glass, 2-color labels, Cassandra Bottling Works, Cassandra PA, 8" $16.00

Thrill, clear glass, red & white label, Nackard Bottling Co, Flagstaff AZ, 9-oz $20.00

Vegas Vic Beverages, clear glass, blue & white cowboy label, 12-oz $60.00

Waseka, clear glass, red & white label, Waseca Quality Beverages, Waseca MN, 7-oz $20.00

Western, clear glass, 2-color label, Property of the O-So Grape Bottling Co, Albuquerque NM, 8-oz........................$32.50

Whistle, clear glass, blue & white label, Whistle-Vess Bottling Co, Joplin MO, 7-oz $20.00

Sporting Goods

Catalogs and various ephemera distributed by sporting good manufacturers, ammunition boxes, and just about any other item used for hunting and fishing purposes are collectible. In fact, there are auctions devoted entirely to collectors with these interests.

One of the best known companies specializing in merchandise of this kind was the gun manufacturer, The Winchester Repeating Arms Company. After 1931, their mark was changed from Winchester Trademark USA to Winchester-Western. Remington, Ithaca, Peters, and Dupont are other manufacturers whose goods are especially sought after.

In the listings that follow, unless noted otherwise, our values are for examples in at least excellent condition.

Advisor: Kevin R. Bowman (See Directory, Sports Collectibles)

Book, Remington Autoloading & Pump-Action Rifles, E Myszkowski, softcover, 136-page, 9x6" $20.00

Bow, hunting; Kodiak #46, Bear Glass-Powered, right-handed, 1965. 60" L $300.00

Box, cartridge reloading; houses 100 12 bore cases, Erskine #6245, wood, hinged lid $325.00

Box, Kleanbore CB Caps, 100 Rim Fire Cartridges, Remington, empty..$55.00

Box, Monark Skeet Shells, 20-gauge, image of man in red sweater & hat, Aug 8, 1944, empty...............................$145.00

Box, Remington Best Quality Brass Shells, 20-gauge, empty ..$120.00

Box, shotshell; Clinton Cartridge Co., 12 ga. Pointer No. 4, NM, $600.00. (Photo courtesy Lang's Auction)

Broadhead, Black Beauty, ABCC #0218, 1953 ....$75.00

Broadhead, 11/32 Hanson No Plane, vented, 1944, unused ..$90.00

Brush, chamber; 12-gauge, ebony & brass handle...............$40.00

Call, duck; FA Allen, Monmouth IL, VG $32.00

Call, duck; Faulk, Lake Charles LA, ca 1950s $60.00

Call, duck; Henry IL, wood w/2 metal rings, Perdew, 5½" ...$375.00

Call, duck; Ken Martin, wood, w/instructions, MIB $140.00

Call, duck; Weedy's Pinoak, acrylic, vintage **$150.00**

Call, goose; Foiles Showtime #1003, w/cloth case.............**$105.00**

Can, gun oil; spout on top, Winchester #1478035, lead, ca 1923, 3-oz..**$130.00**

Catalog, Fox Traditionally Fine Double Barrel Shotguns, 1941...**$15.00**

Catalog, Garcia Sporting Arms, 1968, 32-page **$15.00**

Catalog, Marble's Outing Equipment, 1930, 31-page, 3½x6" .. **$55.00**

Catalog, Remington Firearms, 1930s, 32-page **$45.00**

Catalog, Savage Arms Repeating Shotgun, 1922 ....**$25.00**

Catalog, Winchester, w/price list & request insert, 1934, M in envelope...**$115.00**

Creel, woven basket type, 2 leather (belt) loops on back, leather hinged lid, ca 1940s, 6x13" **$120.00**

Creel, woven willow basket type, leather trim makes diamond pattern on front & lid, brass buttons, no strap, 7x12".....**$110.00**

Decoy, crow; Gus Nelow, wood, ca 1950s........................**$200.00**

Decoy, duck; hand-painted wood, glass eyes, ca 1920s, 6¼x17x6½" **$140.00**

Fish stringer, Mill Run Cleveland Ohio on slides, holds 8 fish, brass, 72" L **$60.00**

Fishing license, Idaho, #55359, paper, 1920 ....**$70.00**

Magazine, Field & Stream, features game laws, 1931...........**$22.00**

Powder tin, India Rifle Gunpowder, Indian graphics, oval, 6x4"..**$90.00**

Powder tin, Laflin Rand, Orange Extra Sporting in center of logo, oval, 4x3½" **$125.00**

Reel, fly fishing; Hardy Perfect, Iver Johnson Sporting Goods, ca 1945, 4" dia, 2¼" reel foot **$660.00**

Reel, trout; Hardy Ureka, ebonite handles, bar stool release latch, $300.00. (Photo courtesy LiveAuctioneers.com/Lang's Auction)

Rifle barrel, 45/70 to fit US Trapdoor Springfield, 32½" L...**$100.00**

Rifle sight, 3-leaf express, fits ⅜" dovetail, Winchester, complete...**$200.00**

Rod, fly; Heddon Featherweight Blue Waters #10, bamboo, 2-pc, w/ cloth rod bag & aluminum rod tube, 90" **$590.00**

Rod, Regal Rod #9008, Tycoon Tackle Inc, wood, 1938, 83" L **$600.00**

Scale, fish & game; Chatillon, Made in the USA, measures up to 24-lb, brass body, 1920s-30s, 4½" L **$20.00**

Shell scraper, 10-gauge, boxwood & brass.........................**$60.00**

Trap, #4X US Standard, Gibbs & Son Inc Chester PA on pan, Property of US on base, w/chain (+) **$200.00**

Trap, Sargent & Co #0, w/chain **$110.00**

Trap, 415X Triumph, ¾" teeth, 24" L..............................**$225.00**

Weather gauge, Golf Guide, measures barametric pressure, Taylor Instrument Companies, 1955, 4¾" dia.....................**$100.00**

Sports Collectibles

When the baseball card craze began sweeping the country well over a decade ago, memorabilia relating to many types of sports began to interest sports fans. Today ticket stubs, autographed baseballs, sports magazines, and game-used bats and uniforms are prized by baseball fans, and some items, depending on their age or the notoriety of the player or team they represent, may be very valuable. Baseball and golfing seem to be the two sports most collectors prefer, but hockey and auto racing are gaining ground. Game-used equipment is sought out by collectors, and where once they preferred only items used by professionals, now the sports market has expanded, and collectors have taken great interest in the youth equipment endorsed by many star players now enshrined in their respective Hall of Fame. Some youth equipment was given away as advertising premiums and bear that company's name or logo. Such items are now very desirable.

See also Autographs; Indianapolis 500 Memorabilia; Magazines; Motorcycle Memorabilia; Pin-Back Buttons; Puzzles.

Advisors: Don and Anne Kier (See Directory, Sports Collectibles)

Badge, caddie; Bear Hill Golf Club, 44 Class A, white celluloid w/ red letters, metal back, 1921, EX **$25.00**

Badge, membership; Nelson Football Supporters Club, blue & white enamel, metal, 1" dia, EX **$60.00**

Baseball, Jackie Robinson 50th Anniversary, Kemper Funds, 1977, MIB **$45.00**

Baseball, signed by Ted Williams, ca. 1980s, with letter of authenticity, $200.00. (Photo courtesy LiveAuctioneers. com/Morphy Auctions)

Baseball glove, JC Higgens, endorsed by Nellie Fox, 1950s, EX..**$65.00**

Baseball glove, Spalding #127 Roger Maris, brown leather, replaced laces, worn, G-..**$35.00**

Book, Clutch Hitter, Clair Bee, Chip Hilton Story, 1949, 1st ed, EX **$20.00**

Book, Greatest World Series Thrillers, Random House, 1965, NM **$25.00**

Football, Official NFL, Pete Rozelle, Wilson, 1960s, EX **$75.00**

Golf balls, Dino's Brand, Dean Martin image on box, 3-pack, NM **$25.00**

Golf club bag, Titleist, black & white leather grain vinyl, 1970s, 36", EX **$100.00**

Golf shoes, Regal Shoes, brown leather, ca 1955, size 10½, M ..**$280.00**

Marker, (golf) distance; No 18 380 YDS PAR 4 in blue letters on white porcelain, lg, NM.. **$210.00**

Media guide, Baltimore Colts, 1948, 38-page, EX............ **$210.00**

Media guide, New Orleans Saints, 1967, NM **$110.00**

Media guide, Texas A&M Football, 1956, M..................... **$235.00**

Megaphone, NY Giants Yell-A-Phone, plastic & metal, 1960s, NM **$50.00**

Megaphone, UC Berkeley Cal Bears, Beat Stanford label, black & yellow, 1940s, 9", EX... **$130.00**

Mug, Denver Broncos Official 1986 AFC Champions, blue helmet shape, 4x5", M.. **$45.00**

Nodder, Mickey Mantle, Japan, NMIB, from $700.00 to $1,000.00. (Photo courtesy LiveAuctioneers.com/Morphy Auctions)

Patch, jacket; Jack's Surf Shop Huntington Beach, red trim on white diamond shape, 1960s, 2¾x4" **$135.00**

Pennant, Indianapolis Speedway, blue felt, May 31, 1937, 26", M **$1,000.00**

Pennant, Joe DiMaggio in white letters on blue, w/image, 1940s, M **$380.00**

Pennant, NY Giants, red & blue on white, 1950s, EX....... **$125.00**

Press pin, Cubs, bear holding bat, enamel on brass, 1932, NM. **$370.00**

Press pin, 1934 St Louis World Series, red bird, white enamel w/ gold, NM... **$800.00**

Press pin, 1952 All-Star game, bell shape, Martin, NM **$300.00**

Program, LSU Tigers vs Ole Miss Rebels, 10/16/37, EX.... **$370.00**

Program, Super Bowl III, Jets vs Colts, 1/12/69, M.......... **$315.00**

Program, Walter Johnson 20th Anniversary Testimonial, 1927, NM.. **$275.00**

Program, Yankees vs Browns at Sportsman's Park, 8/20/31, EX...**$400.00**

Program, 1938 World Series, Cubs vs Yankees, 12-page, NM...**$260.00**

Program, 1939 World Series, Yankees vs Reds, NM........... **$410.00**

Program, 1946 Rockford Peaches All American Girls Baseball, 14-page, M **$250.00**

Program, 1960 World Series, Pirates vs Yankees, M **$200.00**

Putter, Classic Forged Wilson 8802, copper finish, green & red Head Speed shaft label, leather grip, 1960s, 35½" **$435.00**

Racquet, Ward & Wright model by Wright & Ditson, all wood, EX **$80.00**

Racquet cover, red plaid, AG Spalding & Bros, w/hardwood frame, EX **$20.00**

Schedule, Detroit Tigers, American League Official Schedule, 1950, EX **$22.00**

Score book, Cincinnati Reds, 1973, 40-page, EX **$15.00**

Surfboard, California Semi-Gun, Robert August Precision, single fin, pin tail, Volan style, turquoise, 1970s, 98x20", M......... **$430.00**

Ticket, Illinois vs Michigan, 11/7/53, unused, M **$215.00**

Ticket, Opening Day Rain Check, Yankees, 4/14/1931, M.. **$440.00**

Ticket, World Series, Dodgers vs Yankees, 1953, M.......... **$525.00**

Ticket, 1954 World Series, Game 1, Willie Mays made over the shoulder catch, EX... **$300.00**

Ticket, 1957 NFL World Championship, Lions vs Browns, 12/29/57, NM.. **$200.00**

Wet suit, O' Neill beaver tail, black w/blue striped rubber, O'Neill label bottom front, 1960s-70s, EX............................ **$50.00**

Yearbook, 1950 Phillies, 31 page, NM........................... **$110.00**

Yearbook, 1951 Boston Red Sox, EX **$100.00**

Yearbook, 1954 Brooklyn Dodgers, 48-page, M **$185.00**

Yearbook, 1960 Baltimore Orioles, NM........................... **$70.00**

Yearbook, 1960 Green Bay Packers, NM **$560.00**

Yearbook, 1962 New York Mets, EX............................... **$300.00**

Yearbook, 1962 NY Mets, EX.. **$250.00**

St. Clair Glass

Since 1941, the St. Clair family has operated a small glass-house in Elwood, Indiana. They're most famous for their lamps, though they've also produced many styles of toothpick holders, paperweights, and various miniatures as well. Though the paper-weights are usually stamped and dated, smaller items may not be marked at all. In addition to various colors of iridescent glass, they've also made many articles in slag glass (both caramel and pink) and custard.

At the present, rose weights are in demand, especially the rare pedestal roses; so are sulfides, in particular those with etching or windows. Pieces signed by Ed and Paul are rare, as these brothers signed only items they made during their breaks or lunch time. Sulfides and lamps made by Maude and Bob are in demand as well, and three- and four-ball lamps by Joe are highly sought after by today's collectors. Items signed by Mike Mitchell, who once worked for Bob St. Clair, are scarce and usually bring top prices. For more information, we recommend *St. Clair Glass Collector's Book, Vol. II,* by our advisor, Ted Pruitt.

Advisor: Ted Pruitt (See Directory, St. Clair)

Animal dish, dolphin, blue, Joe St Clair **$175.00**
Apple, from $100 to **$125.00**
Ashtray, bowl shape w/3 rests, browns, from $85 to **$95.00**
Bell, Christmas, from $100 to **$125.00**
Bird, blue & clear, lg, from $75 to **$95.00**
Candleholder, sulfide, multicolor floral, ea from $75 to **$85.00**
Covered dish, robin on nest, from $125 to **$150.00**
Cruet, bulbous w/2 loop handles, blue, w/stopper, from $125
    to **$150.00**
Doll, from $75 to **$85.00**
Doorstop, apple form, signed Mike Mitchell, rare, from $350
    to **$400.00**
Fruit, blueberry, from $140 to **$150.00**
Lemonade glass, from $75 to **$100.00**

**Paperweight, apple, clean with blue interior flowers and
airtraps, 5", $125.00.**

Paperweight, candle form w/lavender & blue flowers, controlled
    bubbles, Maude & Bob, 1983 .... **$35.00**
Paperweight, pear, blue carnival **$100.00**
Paperweight, pitcher form w/red, white & yellow flowers, ribbed
    handle, 3½" **$30.00**
Paperweight, speckled glass, from $90 to **$100.00**
Paperweight, turtle, from $150 to **$175.00**
Ring holder, teapot form, clear w/internal white flowers, 4½" . **$50.00**
Salt cellar, swan, colors other than red or white, ea from $35 to . **$45.00**
Toothpick holder, Bicentennial, cobalt carnival **$25.00**
Toothpick holder, fez hat, from $135 to **$150.00**
Toothpick holder, Indian Head, dark green carnival, Joe St
    Clair **$24.00**
Tumbler, Fan & Feather, white carnival, Joe St Clair, 1960s .. **$45.00**
Tumbler, Fleur-de-Lis, from $40 to **$50.00**
Vase, blown, waisted, from $175 to **$200.00**
Vase, butterfly weighted base, trumpet neck, from $300 to . **$350.00**
Wine goblet, Pinwheel, from $35 to **$45.00**

Stanford Corn

Teapots, cookie jars, salt and pepper shakers, and other kitchen and dinnerware items modeled as ears of yellow corn with green shucks were made by the Stanford company, who marked most of their ware. The Shawnee company made two very similar corn lines; just check the marks to verify the manufacturer.

Butter dish **$45.00**
Casserole, 8" L **$40.00**

**Cookie jar, $75.00; salt and pepper shakers, 4", $25.00 for
the pair.** (Photo courtesy LiveAuctioneers.com/Brunk Auctions)

Corn dish (holds ear) **$22.00**
Creamer & sugar bowl, w/lid **$45.00**
Cup **$15.00**
Grease jar, 6½" **$45.00**
Marmalade jar **$25.00**
Mustard jar **$25.00**
Pitcher, 6½" **$35.00**
Pitcher, 7½" **$45.00**
Plate, 9" L **$25.00**
Relish tray **$35.00**
Salt & pepper shakers, sm, pr **$20.00**
Snack set, cup & plate w/indent, #709 .... **$65.00**
Spoon rest **$25.00**
Sugar bowl **$20.00**
Teapot **$60.00**
Tumbler **$25.00**

Stangl

The Stangl company's roots sprang from the old Sam Hill Pottery (1814), making it one of the longest-existing potteries in the United States. It became known as Fulper ca 1860, when it's output focused mainly on art pottery. Martin Stangl became president in 1928, and although their products began to carry the Stangl name, it was not until 1955 that the name change became official. After Stangl's death in 1972, the firm was purchased by Wheaton

Industries; all operations ceased in 1978. For more information see *Collector's Encyclopedia of Stangl Artware, Lamps, and Birds* by Robert C. Runge, Jr. (Collector Books).

Advisor: Popkorn Antiques (See Directory, Stangl)

Club: Stangl/Fulper Collectors Club
P.O. Box 538
Flemington, NJ 08822
www.stanglpottery.org

Stangl Birds

In 1940, the company introduced a line of ceramic birds in order to fullfill the needs of a market no longer able to access foreign imports, due to the onset of WWII. These bird figures immediately attracted a great deal of attention. At the height of their productivity, 60 decorators were employed to hand paint the birds at the plant, and the overflow was contracted out and decorated in private homes. After WWII, inexpensive imported figurines once again saturated the market, and for the most part, Stangl curtailed their own production, though the birds were made on a very limited basis until as late as 1978.

Nearly all the birds were marked. A four-digit number was used to identify the species, and most pieces were signed by the decorator. An 'F' indicates a bird that was decorated at the Flemington plant.

#3250B, Duck preening, 3¼" $75.00
#3250E, Duck drinking, Terra Rose finish, 1941 only, 2¼", from $60 to $90.00
#3250F, Duck quacking, 3¼" $75.00
#3273, Rooster, solid bottom, 5¾", from $500 to $600.00
#3274, Penquin, 6" $450.00
#3275, Turkey, 3½" $350.00
#3276D, Bluebirds (pr), 8½" $150.00
#3281, Duck, mother, 6", from $500 to $600.00
#3286, Hen, late, 3¼" $50.00
#3400, Lovebird, old version, 4" $100.00
#3400, Lovebird, revised, 4" $50.00
#3402, Oriole, beak down, old style, 3½" $125.00
#3402D, Orioles (pr), revised, w/leaves, 5½" $100.00
#3405, Cockatoo, 6" $50.00
#3406, Kingfisher, teal, 3½" $75.00
#3407, Owl, 4" $300.00
#3408, Bird of Paradise, 5½" $80.00
#3443, Duck flying, gray, 9" $250.00
#3443, Duck flying, teal, 9½x12" $225.00
#3444, Cardinal, female $175.00
#3444, Cardinal, glossy pink, revised, 7" $70.00
#3445, Rooster (med), gray, 10" $225.00
#3446, Hen, yellow, 7" $120.00
#3448, Blue-Headed Vireo, Antique Ivory or turquoise crackle, 1940 only, 4½", from $125 to $175.00
#3448, Blue-Headed Vireo, 4¼" $55.00
#3452, Painted Bunting, 5" $75.00
#3490D, Redstarts (pr), 9" $125.00
#3492, Cock Pheasant $150.00
#3580, Cockatoo, med, 8⅞" $125.00

#3582, Parakeets (pr), green, 7" $175.00
#3582D Parakeets (pr), blue, 7" $250.00
#3584, Cockatoo, signed Jacob, lg, 11⅜" $250.00
#3585, Rufous Hummingbird, 3" $70.00
#3589, Indigo Bunting, 3½" $50.00
#3590, Carolina Wren, 4½" $150.00
#3591, Brewster's Blackbird, 3½" $165.00
#3592, Titmouse, 3" $45.00
#3593, Nuthatch, 2½" $50.00
#3594, Red-Faced Warbler, 3" $100.00
#3595, Bobolink, 4¾" $150.00
#3596, Gray Cardinal, 5" $60.00
#3597, Wilson Warbler, yellow & black, 3" $40.00
#3598, Kentucky Warbler, 3" $45.00
#3599D, Hummingbirds (pr) $250.00
#3627, Rivoli Hummingbird, pink flower, 6" $150.00
#3629, Broadbill Hummingbird, 4½" $125.00
#3634, Allen Hummingbird, 3½" $100.00
#3635, Gold Finches (group) $175.00
#3715, Blue Jay, w/peanut, 10¼" $600.00
#3716, Blue Jay, w/leaf, 10½" $500.00

#3717, Blue Jay, with peanut, 10¼", $600.00. (Photo courtesy David Rago Auctions)

#3747, Canary (left), blue flower, 6¼" $200.00
#3749, Scarlet Tanager, glossy pink, 4¾", from $350 to $425.00

#3749, Western Tanager, 4¾", $350.00. (Photo courtesy David Rago Auctions)

#3749, Western Tanager, yellow & black w/red overglaze, tan flower, 4¾", from $400 to **$425.00**

#3750, Scarlet Tanager, 8½" **$300.00**

#3750D, Western Tanagers (pr), red matt, 8" **$500.00**

#3751, Red-Headed Woodpecker, glossy pink, 6¼"..........**$250.00**

#3751, Red-Headed Woodpecker, red matt, 6¼" **$400.00**

#3751, Red-Headed Woodpecker, red overglaze, 6¼", from $400 to **$475.00**

#3752D, Red-Headed Woodpeckers (pr), glossy pink, 7¼"..**$350.00**

#3754D, White-Wing Crossbills (pr), glossy pink, 9x8" **$450.00**

#3755, Audubon Warbler, pink flower, 4¼" **$300.00**

#3757, Scissor-Tailed Flycatcher, 11" **$650.00**

#3810, Black-Throated Warbler, 3½" **$125.00**

#3811, Chestnut Chickadee, 5" **$125.00**

#3812, Chestnut Warbler, 4½" **$125.00**

#3813, Crested Goldfinch, 5" **$125.00**

#3814, Townsend Warbler, 3" **$150.00**

#3815, Western Bluebird, 7" **$350.00**

#3848, Golden-Crowned Kinglet, 4¼" **$90.00**

#3850, Western Warbler, 4" **$125.00**

#3852, Cliff Swallow, 3½" **$100.00**

#3868, Summer Tanager, 4" **$650.00**

#3924, Yellow Throat, 6" **$500.00**

Stangl Dinnerware

Stangl introduced their first line of dinnerware in the 1920s. By 1954, 90% of their production centered around their dinnerware lines. Until 1942 the clay they used was white. Although most of the dinnerware they made before WWII had solid-color glazes, they also did many hand-painted (but not carved) patterns in the 1930s and early 1940s. In 1942, however, the first of the red-clay lines that have become synonymous with the Stangl name was created. Designs were hand carved into the greenware, then hand painted. More than 100 different patterns have been cataloged. From 1974 until 1978, a few lines previously discontinued on the red clay were reintroduced with a white clay body. Soon after '78, the factory closed.

Della-Ware pitchers, 3¾": Laurita, Festival, $15.00 each.

Amber-Glo #3899, teapot, from $40 to **$50.00**

Americana #2000, bowl, vegetable; oval, 8", from $10 to **$15.00**

Americana #2000, carafe, wooden handle, from $40 to **$50.00**

Bittersweet #5111, mug, stacking; from $20 to....................**$25.00**

Blueberry #3770, bowl, vegetable; divided oval, from $40 to ..**$45.00**

Chicory #3809, bread tray, from $50 to..............................**$60.00**

Chicory #3809, egg cup, from $15 to **$20.00**

Chicory #3809, tidbit, 10", from $10 to **$15.00**

Colonial #1388, cake stand, high, from $20 to **$25.00**

Colonial #1388, cigarette box, from $55 to **$70.00**

Colonial #1388, gravy bowl, from $20 to **$25.00**

Colonial #1388, sugar bowl, bird finial, from $35 to **$45.00**

Country Garden #3943, bowl, soup; from $20 to **$25.00**

Country Garden #3943, pitcher, 1-qt, from $50 to **$60.00**

Festival #5072, relish dish, from $20 to **$30.00**

Fruit #3697, bowl, vegetable; divided oval, from $35 to **$40.00**

Fruit #3697, chop plate, 14½", from $150.00 to $175.00.

(Photo courtesy Robert C. Runge, Jr.)

Fruit #3697, sherbet, from $25 to.......................................**$30.00**

Golden Harvest #3887, coffeepot, 4-cup, from $50 to **$65.00**

Golden Harvest #3887, salt & pepper shakers, pr from $10 to...**$12.00**

Holly #3869, plate, 8", from $20 to **$30.00**

Kiddieware, Indian Campfire, grill plate, 1955, 9", from $200 to...**$250.00**

Magnolia #3870, pitcher, 1-qt, from $40 to **$50.00**

Mediterranean #5186, platter, casual, 13¾", from $55 to **$65.00**

Orchard Song #5110, cake stand, from $10 to **$15.00**

Pink Lily #3888, butter dish, from $25 to **$30.00**

Pink Lily #3888, plate, 11", from $20 to **$25.00**

Pink Lily #3888, warmer, from $20 to.................................**$25.00**

Provincial #3966, plate, picnic; 8", from $8 to **$10.00**

Sculptured Fruit #5179, teapot, plain, 4-cup, from $25 to ..**$30.00**

Star Flower #3864, bread tray, from $20 to **$25.00**

Sunflower #3340, bowl, salad; extra deep, 10", from $75 to...**$85.00**

Sunflower #3340, teapot, from $120 to **$145.00**

Town & Country #5287, dealer sign, blue, from $125 to...**$150.00**

Town & Country #5287, soap dish, brown, from $20 to **$25.00**

Town & Country #5287, teapot, black or crimson, 5-cup, from $75 to **$100.00**

Windfall #3930, butter dish, from $25 to............................**$30.00**

Windfall #3930, cruet, w/stopper, from $20 to....................**$25.00**

Windfall #3930, pickle dish, from $10 to **$15.00**

Windfall #3930, saucer **$5.00**

Yellow Tulip #3637, butter dish, from $40 to **$50.00**

Yellow Tulip #3637, plate, 9", from $15 to **$20.00**

Miscellaneous

Ashtray, Antique Gold, embossed lion border, #4085, 1959-60, 5¼" dia, from $20 to..**$25.00**

Ashtray, bird, Silver Green, #3210, 1938-42, 4", from $50 to .. **$60.00**

Ashtray, ivy leaf form, Terra Rose Blue, #3524, 1941-43, 5¼x4¼", from $15 to..**$20.00**

Basket, hanging; gray matt, #1274, 1930-35, 7x3", from $50 to..**$60.00**

Basket, satin blue, twist handle, #3251, 1939-43, 11x6½", from $30 to..**$40.00**

Basket, satin white, round rope handle, #3560, 1941-43, 11", from $50 to..**$65.00**

Bowl, Blue-of-the-Sky, oval, handles, #1319, 1930-35, 12" L.. **$60.00**

Bowl, scrolled, Satin Blue, 4-sided, #3047, from $35 to......**$50.00**

Candleholders, Silver Green, scalloped, #3108, 1937-40, 3x2", pr **$30.00**

Cigarette box, Tropic Flower (originally Hibiscus), Kay Hackett design, #3791, 1948-52, from $60 to..**$80.00**

Figurine, sailor, Colonial Blue, 1943 only, 9", from $300 to... **$400.00**

Flower holder, figural crane, Apple Green, #1325, 1930-35, 9", from $150 to..**$200.00**

Flower holder, Gazelle, #1320, 6", from $180.00 to $225.00. (Photo courtesy Robert C. Runge, Jr.)

Flower jar, shell, Tangerine, oblong, #2057, from $45 to.....**$55.00**

Flowerpot, Silver Green, pleated, #1213S, 1929-32, 4", from $20 to..**$30.00**

Flowerpot, Terra Rose, embossed leaves on mauve, #2001, 1943-55, 5½", from $35 to..**$45.00**

Jardiniere, rust, #1515, 8", from $35 to..**$40.00**

Jug, Rebecca; stoneware, #6011, 3-4", ea from $60 to.........**$95.00**

Lamp, bird & leaves in relief on dark opaque green, #3070, 1937 only, 8½", from $100 to..**$125.00**

Oyster plate, white (no decoration), 1973-74, 9", from $80 to.. **$100.00**

Pitcher, satin blue, ball form, #3211, 1938-45, 6", from $20 to .. **$30.00**

Rose bowl, Acanthus, turquoise, #1548, from $30 to..........**$40.00**

Salt & pepper shakers, hurricane lamp base & shade, 3½" stacking set, from $40 to..**$50.00**

Shade pull, aqua blue, oval, #3050, from $45 to.................**$55.00**

Strawberry jar, Persian Yellow, #1382, 1931-35, 6", from $45 to..**$6.00**

Tray, hors d'oeuvres; Toastmaster, Silver Green, sq, 1938+, 8", from $5 to..**$6.00**

Vase, bud; Appliqué, white sprigged floral design on blue or green, #4050, 1964-65, 8", from $20 to..**$25.00**

Vase, Caribbean, Phoenician, Kay Hackett design, #5023, 9¾", $30 to..**$35.00**

Vase, figural horse head, solid Terra Rose Green, #3611, 1944-50, 13", from $200 to..**$250.00**

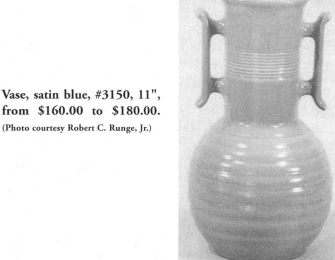

Vase, satin blue, #3150, 11", from $160.00 to $180.00.
(Photo courtesy Robert C. Runge, Jr.)

Vase, satin green, long neck, handles, #3103, 1937-41, 7¼", from $30 to..**$40.00**

Vase, Sunburst, handmade, ball form, #1126, 1929-34, 7½", from $110 to..**$135.00**

Vase, Tangerine, ball form, diagonal cut, #1909, 1935, 8", from $70 to..**$95.00**

Wall pocket, Terra Rose Blue (2-tone), #2091, 1942-50s, 7½", from $50 to..**$60.00**

Star Trek

Trekkies, as fans are often referred to, number nearly 40,000 today, hold national conventions, and compete with each other for choice items of Star Trek memorabilia, some of which may go for hundreds of dollars.

The Star Trek concept was introduced to the public in the mid-1960s through a TV series which continued for many years in syndication. An animated cartoon series (1977), the success of 'Star Trek: The Next Generation' (Fox network, 1987), the great 'Enterprise' series currently being broadcast in syndication, and the release of what now amounts to 10 major motion pictures (1979 through 2002), have all served as a bridge to join two generations of loyal fans.

Its success has resulted in the sale of vast amounts of merchandise, both licensed and unlicensed, such as clothing, promotional items of many sorts, books and comics, toys and games, records and tapes, school supplies, and party goods. Many of these are still available at flea markets around the country. An item that is 'mint in box' is worth at least twice as much as one in excellent condition but without its original packaging. For more information, refer to *Schroeder's Collectible Toys, Antique to Modern* (Collector Books).

Bank, Spock, plastic, Play Pal, 1975, 12", MIB $60.00

Belt buckle, marked 200th Anniversary USS Enterprise on back, 3½", M $15.00

Book, Action Toy Book, Motion Picture, 1976, unpunched, EX.. $30.00

Book, comic; Gold Key #1, 1967, EX.................................. $75.00

Bop Bag, Spock, 1975, MIB $80.00

Colorforms Adventure Set, MIB (sealed) $35.00

Decanter, Mr Spock bust, ceramic, M................................ $40.00

Figure, Galoob, Star Trek Next Generation, Antican, Ferengi, Q, or Selay, MOC, ea... $60.00

Figure, Galoob, Star Trek Next Generation, Data, blue face, MOC $55.00

Figure, Galoob, Star Trek Next Generation, Data, brown face, MOC $35.00

Figure, Galoob, Star Trek Next Generation, Data, flesh face, MOC $22.00

Figure, Galoob, Star Trek Next Generation, Data, spotted face, MOC $15.00

Figure, Galoob, Star Trek Next Generation, LaForge, Lt Worf, Picard, or Riker, MOC, ea... $15.00

Figure, Galoob, Star Trek V, any character, 1989, 7", MIP, ea from $20 to $25.00

Figure, Mego, 3¾", Acturian, Betelgeusian, Klingon, Megarite, Rigelluian, or Zatanite, Series 2, MOC, ea $160.00

Figure, Mego, 3¾", Capt Kirk, Decker, Dr McCoy, Illia, Mr Spock, or Mr Scott, Series 1, MOC, ea $40.00

Figure, Mego, 8", Andorian, 1970s, MOC $650.00

Figure, Mego, 8", Capt Kirk, 1970s, M $30.00

Figure, Mego, 8", Dr McCoy, 1970s, M $45.00

Figure, Mego, 8", Gorn, 1970s, MOC............................... $175.00

Figure, Mego, 8", Klingon, 1970s, MOC $55.00

Figure, Mego, 8", Lt Uhura, 1970s, MOC $135.00

Figure, Mego, 8", Neptunian, 1970s, M $125.00

Figure, Mego, 8", Romulan, 1970s, M $800.00

Figure, Mego, 8", Talos, 1970s, MOC............................... $525.00

Figure, Mego, 8", The Keeper, 1970s, MOC..................... $180.00

Figure, Mego, 12½", Arcturian, 1979, M........................... $65.00

Figure, Mego, 12½", Capt Kirk, 1979, M........................... $40.00

Figure, Mego, 12½", Decker, 1979, M $60.00

Figure, Mego, 12½", Ilia, 1979, MIP.................................. $80.00

Figure, Mego, 12½", Klingon, 1979, MIP $120.00

Figure, Mego, 12½", Mr Spock, 1979, MIP $80.00

Figure, Playmates, DS9, Dr Julian Bashir, 1994, M $12.00

Figure, Playmates, DS9, Dr Julian Bashir, 1994, MIP......... $22.00

Figure, Playmates, First Contact, 5", Borg, Dr Beverly Crusher, Capt Picard, or Lily, 1996, MOC, ea $16.00

Figure, Playmates, First Contact, 5", Data, Deanna Troi, La Forge, Riker, Worf, or Cochrane, 1996, MOC, ea................... $14.00

Figure, Playmates, First Contact, 9", Capt Picard in 21st Century outfit or Cochrane, 1996, MIP..................................... $26.00

Figure, Playmates, First Contact, 9", Data, Capt Picard, or Riker, 1996, MIP, ea $20.00

Figure, Playmates, Insurrection, 9", any character, 1998, MIP, ea from $10 to $15.00

Figure, Playmates, Star Trek Next Generation, 1st Series, Borg, Capt Picard, Riker, Data or Worf, 1992, MOC, ea $22.00

Figure, Playmates, Star Trek Next Generation, first series, Deanna Troi, 1992, MOC, $35.00.

Figure, Playmates, Star Trek Next Generation, 1st Series, Ferengi, Gowron, or Lt Commander La Forge, 1992, MOC, ea .. $30.00

Figure, Playmates, Star Trek Next Generation, 2nd Series, any character, 1993, MOC, ea from $12 to $18.00

Figure, Playmates, Star Trek Next Generation, 3rd Series, Data in red Redemption outfit, 1994, MOC.................................... $325.00

Figure, Playmates, Star Trek Next Generation, 3rd Series, Esoqq, 1994, M.. $40.00

Figure, Playmates, Voyager, 5", Capt Janeway or Lt B'Elanna Torres, M, ea $18.00

Figure, Playmates, Voyager, 5", Capt Janeway or Lt B'Elanna Torres, MOC, ea $30.00

Flashlight gun, plastic, 1968, NM.................................... $50.00

Game, Star Trek, 1967, EXIB, $65.00. (Photo courtesy LiveAuctioneers.com/Sunflower Auctions)

Kite, Spock, Hi-Flyer, 1975, unused, MIP $35.00

Patch, America 1977 Convention, M................................ $40.00

Patch, command insignia, w/instructions for uniform, M....**$25.00**
Phaser Ray Gun, clicking flashlight effect, 1976, MOC.......**$75.00**
Playset, Command Communications Console, Mego, 1976, MIB, from $125 to **$150.00**
Playset, Communications Set, Mego, 1974, MIB **$150.00**
Playset, Telescreen Console, Mego, 1975, MIB..................**$125.00**
Playset, Transporter Room, Mego, 1975, MIB...................**$125.00**
Playset, USS Enterprise Bridge, Mego, 1975, MIB **$130.00**
Starfleet Phaser, Motion Picture, Playmates, MIB **$150.00**
Vehicle, Ferengi Fighter, Star Trek Next Generation, Galoob, 1989, NRFB **$75.00**
Vehicle, Klingon Cruiser, Mego, 1980, 8" L, MIB..............**$70.00**
Vehicle, USS Enterprise, Star Trek II, Corgi, 1982, MOC, from $25 to **$30.00**
Wastebasket, Motion Picture, M **$35.00**

Star Wars

In the late '70s, the movie 'Star Wars' became a box office hit, most notably for its fantastic special effects and its ever-popular theme of space adventure. Two more movies followed, 'The Empire Strikes Back' in 1980 and 'Return of the Jedi' in 1983. After the first movie, an enormous amount of related merchandise was released. A large percentage of these items was action figures, made by the Kenner company who used the logo of the 20th Century Fox studios (under whom they were licensed) on everything they made until 1980. Just before the second movie, Star Wars creator, George Lucas, regained control of the merchandising rights, and items inspired by the last two films can be identified by his own Lucasfilm logo. Since 1987, Lucasfilm Ltd. has operated shops in conjunction with the Star Tours at Disneyland theme park. The most current movies are Episode I through III, and each has spawned a new burst of collector-aimed merchandise.

What to collect? First and foremost, buy what you yourself enjoy. But remember that condition is all important. Look for items still mint in the box or on the card. Using that as a basis, if the packaging is missing, deduct at least half from its mint-in-box value. If a major accessory or part is gone, the item is basically worthless. Learn to recognize the most desirable, most valuable items. There are lots of Star Wars bargains yet to be had!

Original packaging helps date a toy, since the box or card design was updated as each new movie was released. Naturally, items representing the older movies are more valuable than later issues. For more coverage of this subject, refer to *Schroeder's Collectible Toys, Antique to Modern*, and *Star Wars Super Collector's Wish Book* by Geoffery T. Carlton (Collector Books).

Bank, Yoda, Star Wars, Sigma, M...**$90.00**
Book, Return of the Jedi Pop-Up Book, Random House, 1983, hardback, MIB..**$18.00**
Book, Splinter of the Mind's Eye, A Foster, Del Ray Books, hardcover, 1978, NM+...**$12.00**
Bubble bath container, Yoda, Omni, 1981, NM **$15.00**
Doll, Paploo the Ewok, Return of the Jedi, plush, MIB.....**$135.00**
Doll, Wicket the Ewok, Kenner, plush, w/cape, 1983, 15", EX+. **$30.00**
Figure, A-Wing Pilot, Droids, MOC......................................**$150.00**
Figure, Admiral Ackbar, Return of the Jedi, MOC..............**$50.00**

Figure, AT-AT Commander, Empire Strikes Back, MOC **$90.00**
Figure, AT-AT Commander, Return of the Jedi, MOC........**$60.00**
Figure, AT-ST Driver, Power of the Force, MOC.................**$85.00**
Figure, B-Wing Pilot, Return of the Jedi, MOC **$45.00**
Figure, Barada, Power of the Force, M **$60.00**
Figure, Ben (Obi-Wan) Kenobi, Power of the Force, M **$30.00**
Figure, Ben (Obi-Wan) Kenobi, Return of the Jedi, gray or white hair, MOC, ea...**$60.00**
Figure, Bespin Security Guard, Empire Strikes Back, black or white, M...**$15.00**
Figure, Bib Fortuna, Return of the Jedi, M **$15.00**
Figure, Boba Fett, Droids, M...**$25.00**

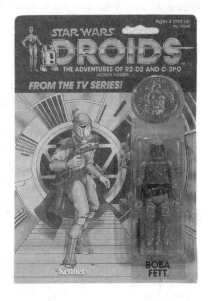

Figure, Boba Fett, Droids, Star Wars, MOC, from $700.00 to $735.00. (Photo courtesy LiveAuctioneers.com/ Morphy Auctions)

Figure, Boba Fett, Empire Strikes Back, 12", M...................**$35.00**
Figure, Boba Fett, Empire Strikes Back, 12", MIB.............**$625.00**
Figure, Bossk, Return of the Jedi, M **$10.00**
Figure, C-3PO, Empire Strikes Back, removable limbs, MOC..**$100.00**
Figure, C-3PO, Star Wars, 12", MIB **$425.00**
Figure, Chewbacca, Star Wars, 12", MIB **$235.00**
Figure, Cloud Car Pilot, Empire Strikes Back, MOC **$130.00**
Figure, Darth Vader, Power of the Force, MOC..................**$160.00**
Figure, Darth Vader, Star Wars, 12", MIB **$270.00**
Figure, Darth Vader (pointing), Return of the Jedi, MOC...**$55.00**
Figure, Death Squad Commander, Star Wars, MOC **$160.00**
Figure, Death Star Droid, Return of the Jedi, MOC...........**$75.00**
Figure, Dengar, Return of the Jedi, MOC............................**$45.00**
Figure, Emperor, Power of the Force, MOC **$85.00**
Figure, Emperor's Royal Guard, Return of the Jedi, MOC...**$55.00**
Figure, Gammorean Guard, Return of the Jedi, MOC **$45.00**
Figure, Greedo, Empire Strikes Back, MOC **$155.00**
Figure, Greedo, Star Wars, MOC...**$295.00**
Figure, Hammerhead, Return of the Jedi, MOC..................**$75.00**
Figure, Han Solo, Power of the Force, Carbonite Chamber, MOC..**$275.00**
Figure, Han Solo, Return of the Jedi, Bespin outfit, MOC..**$75.00**
Figure, Han Solo, Star Wars, lg head, MOC........................**$650.00**
Figure, Han Solo, Star Wars, 12", MIB................................**$595.00**
Figure, IG-88, Return of the Jedi, MOC **$80.00**

Figure, Imperial Commander, Return of the Jedi, MOC $50.00

Figure, Imperial Gunner, M $85.00

Figure, Imperial Storm Trooper, Empire Strikes Back, hot weather gear, MOC $145.00

Figure, Jawa, Return of the Jedi, MOC $50.00

Figure, Jawa, Star Wars, 12", MIB $315.00

Figure, Kea Moll, Droids, MOC $65.00

Figure, Kez-Iban, Droids, MOC $75.00

Figure, Klaatu, Return of the Jedi, Palace outfit, MOC $50.00

Figure, Lady Ugrah Gorneesh, Ewoks, M $10.00

Figure, Lando Cairissian, Empire Strikes Back, MOC $80.00

Figure, Lando Cairissian, Return of the Jedi, MOC $45.00

Figure, Lobot, Return of the Jedi, MOC $45.00

Figure, Luke Skywalker, Empire Strikes Back, X-Wing Pilot, MOC $150.00

Figure, Luke Skywalker, Power of the Force, Stormtrooper outfit, M $165.00

Figure, Luke Skywalker, Return of the Jedi, brown hair, M .. $40.00

Figure, Luke Skywalker, Return of the Jedi, X-Wing Pilot, MOC $65.00

Figure, Luke Skywalker, Star Wars, X-Wing Pilot, MOC ... $250.00

Figure, Luke Skywalker (looking), Empire Strikes Back, Bespin fatigues, blond hair, MOC $150.00

Figure, Luke Skywalker (walking), Empire Strikes Back, Bespin fatigues, brown hair, MOC $250.00

Figure, Luke Skywalker Jedi, Power of the Force, MOC $270.00

Figure, Luke Skywalker Jedi, Return of the Jedi, green light saber, MOC $95.00

Figure, Nien Nunb, Return of the Jedi, M $10.00

Figure, Paploo, Power of the Force, M $34.00

Figure, Power Droid, Empire Strikes Back, MOC $130.00

Figure, Princess Leia, Boushh outfit, MOC $85.00

Figure, Princess Leia, Empire Strikes Back, MOC $295.00

Figure, Princess Leia, Return of the Jedi, combat poncho, MOC .. $50.00

Figure, Princess Leia, Star Wars, 12", MIB $285.00

Figure, Prunface, Return of the Jedi, MOC $40.00

Figure, Rebel Commander, Empire Strikes Back, MOC $140.00

Figure, Rebel Soldier, Empire Strikes Back, MOC $75.00

Figure, R2-D2, Star Wars, 7½", MIB, from $90.00 to $120.00. (Photo courtesy LiveAuctioneers.com/Apple Tree Auction Center)

Figure, Romba, Power of the Force, M $50.00

Figure, R2-D2, Empire Strikes Back, MOC $140.00

Figure, R2-D2, Power of the Force, w/pop-up light saber, M . $120.00

Figure, R2-D2, Star Wars, MOC $280.00

Figure, Sandpeople, Empire Strikes Back, MOC $120.00

Figure, Snaggletooth, Star Wars, MOC $200.00

Figure, Squidhead, Return of the Jedi, MOC $45.00

Figure, Stormtrooper, Empire Strikes Back, MOC $125.00

Figure, Teebo, Power of the Force, MOC $200.00

Figure, TIE Fighter Pilot, Return of the Jedi, MOC $65.00

Figure, Ugnaught, Empire Strikes Back, MOC $100.00

Figure, Walrus Man, Empire Strikes Back, MOC $135.00

Figure, Walrus Man, Return of the Jedi, MOC $65.00

Figure, Weequay, Return of the Jedi, MOC $40.00

Figure, Wicket, Ewocks, MOC $50.00

Figure, Yoda, Return of the Jedi, MOC $175.00

Figure, Zuckuss, Return of the Jedi, MOC $60.00

Game, Empire Strikes Back Yoda Jedi Master, Kenner, 1981, NMIB $75.00

Game, Laser Battle, Star Wars, Kenner, MIB $85.00

Nightlight, Yoda (Return of the Jedi), 1980s, MOC $12.00

Paint kit, Craftmaster, Luke Skywalker or Han Solo, MOC, ea $16.00

Playset, Darth Vader's Star Destroyer, Empire Strikes Back, MIB $245.00

Playset, Droid Factory, Empire Strikes Back, MIB $170.00

Playset, Ewok Village, Return of the Jedi, MIB, from $235.00 to $265.00.

Playset, Imperial Attack Base, Empire Strikes Back, complete, EX $40.00

Playset, Jabba the Hut Dungeon w/Amanaman, Return of the Jedi, complete, EX $135.00

Playset, Land of the Jawas, Star Wars, MIB $185.00

Playset, Turret & Probot, Empire Strikes Back, MIB $160.00

Puzzle, Return of the Jedi Match Blocks, frame-tray, Craftmaster, 1983, MIP (sealed) $12.00

Scissors, Return of the Jedi, MOC $10.00

Soap, Princess Leia embossed on white soap bar, Omni Cosmetics, 1981, 3¾x2½", MIB $10.00

Vehicle, All Terrain Attack Transport, complete, EX $90.00

Vehicle, ATL Interceptor, Droids, complete, EX $25.00

Vehicle, Captivator (Cap-2), Empire Strikes Back, mini-rig, MIB...$35.00

Vehicle, Darth Vader's TIE Fighter, Star Wars, MIB..........$140.00

Vehicle, Desert Sail Skiff, Return of the Jedi, complete, M ..$12.00

Vehicle, Ewok Battle Wagon, Power of the Force, complete, EX..$60.00

Vehicle, Imperial Sniper, Power of the Force, MIB.............$110.00

Vehicle, Interceptor (INT-4), complete, EX $10.00

Vehicle, Landspeeder, Sonic, Star Wars, MIB $620.00

Vehicle, Millennium Falcon, complete, EX $100.00

Vehicle, Millennium Falcon Spaceship, Star Wars, MIB, $375.00.

Vehicle, Mobile Laser Cannon (MLC-3), Empire Strikes Back, mini-rig, MIB...$40.00

Vehicle, Multi-Terrain Vehicle (MTV-7), Empire Strikes Back, mini-rig, MIB...$35.00

Vehicle, One-Man Skimmer, Power of the Force, MIB $100.00

Vehicle, Rebel Transport, Empire Strikes Back, blue background, MIB $190.00

Vehicle, Sandcrawler, radio-controlled, complete, EX........$175.00

Vehicle, Security Scout, Power of the Force, MIB $115.00

Vehicle, Side Gunner, Droids, MIB $85.00

Vehicle, Tatooine Skiff, Power of the Force, complete, EX...$250.00

Vehicle, TIE Fighter, Star Wars, MIB................................$150.00

Vehicle, TIE Fighter (Battle Damage), Return of the Jedi, MIB $135.00

Vehicle, Twin-Pod Cloud Car, Empire Strikes Back, complete, EX $45.00

Vehicle, X-Wing Fighter (Battle Damage), complete, EX $40.00

Vehicle, Y-Wing Fighter, Return of the Jedi, MIB $225.00

Steiff Animals

These stuffed animals originated in Germany around the turn of the century. They were created by Margaret Steiff, whose company continues to operate to the present day. They are identified by the button inside the ear and the identification tag (which often carries the name of the animal) on their chest. Over the years, variations in tags and buttons help collectors determine approximate dates of manufacture.

Teddy bear collectors regard Steiff bears as some of the most valuable on the market. When assessing the worth of a bear, they use some general guidelines as a starting basis, though other features can come into play as well. For instance, bears made prior to 1912 that have long gold mohair fur start at a minimum of $75.00 per inch. If the bear has dark brown or curly white mohair fur instead, that figure may go as high as $135.00. From the 1920s to the 1930s, the rule of thumb would be about $50.00 minimum per inch. A bear (or any other animal) on cast-iron or wooden wheels starts at $75.00 per inch; but if the tires are hard rubber, the value is much lower, more like $27.00 per inch. For more information see Cynthia Powell's *Collector's Guide to Miniature Teddy Bears.*

Club: Toy Stores Steiff Collector's Club
Newsletter: *Collector's Life*
The World's Foremost Publication for Steiff Enthusiasts
Beth Savino, Editor
Westgate Village, 3301 West Central Ave.
Toledo, OH 43606
www.toystore.com

Dog, terrier on wheels, excelsior stuffing, glass eyes, squeaker, 1950s, missing button, 20", $600.00. (Photo courtesy LiveAuctioneers.com/Noel Barrett Antiques & Auctions)

Bear, beige, stitched nose & mouth, button eyes, jointed, 1960s, 6", VG..$350.00

Bear, blond w/red neck bow, stitched nose, mouth & claws, button eyes, felt pads, jointed, 1960s, 8", EX.......................$450.00

Bear, dark brown, black stitched nose, mouth & claws, brown glass eyes, tan felt pads, jointed, 1960s, 13½", VG $200.00

Bear, gold, stitched nose & mouth, glass eyes, no-pad style, jointed, 1950s, 6½", EX...$250.00

Bear, honey gold mohair, glass eyes, partial cloth tag, 1940s-50s, 26", EX+ $2,250.00

Bear, tan, pointy nose, stitched eyes, early, 15", G-............$200.00

Bull Yale Bull Dog, 3 shades of brown, glass eyes, felt 'Y' blanket & red leather collar, 1950s, 10½", EX.............................$525.00

Cow on wheels, brown & white, bell around neck, w/growler, cast-iron wheels, 12", VG $600.00

Dinosaur (Stegosaurus Dinos), multicolored mohair w/yellow underbody, bony backbone, goggle-eyed, 1960s, 12", EX....**$230.00**

Dinosaur (T-Rex Tysus), yellow & tan mohair w/green felt backbone, goggle-eyed, jointed arms, 1960s, 17", VG **$230.00**

Elephant, gray plush, red blanket w/bells, w/tags, 7½", EX..**$75.00**

Horse, gold silky plush, airbrushed facial features, brown eyes & hooves, underscored button, stock tag, 10½", NM **$90.00**

Jocko Monkey, long curly mohair, glass eyes, jointed, raised script button, 1950s, 18", NM..**$300.00**

Koala Bear, cream, gray felt nose, brown eyes, shaved hands & feet, 1960s, 14½", EX..**$225.00**

Lamb, white w/pink felt inner ears, stitched nose & mouth, green eyes, neck ribbon & bell, 1950s, 11½", EX **$175.00**

Lion, long mane & tail, stitched features, amber eyes, 1930s, 20", VG..**$150.00**

Lizzy Lizard, velvet, glass eyes, 1959-61, 12", EX **$385.00**

Llama, cream w/black & brown striping, brown glass eyes, shaved muzzle & lower legs, 1960s, 16½", EX......................**$125.00**

Monkey on handcart, dark brown mohair w/light tan felt face, ears, hands & feet, articulated movement, 10½x9", VG **$150.00**

Moose, button and tag, 9", $210.00. (Photo courtesy LiveAuctioneers.com/Morphy Auctions)

Stick horse, felt head w/mane, harness & rein, wooden stick handle, 1940s, 40", EX+ **$75.00**

Tiger, recumbent, airbrushed details, pink nose, green eyes, paper label, ear tag & button, 1950s, 10", VG **$125.00**

Yuku Gazelle, rare, all ID, 1962-63, 7½", M **$325.00**

Zebra, black airbrushed stripes, glass eyes, ear button, 1950s, 14", VG..**$150.00**

Zotty Bear, curly beige, brown stitched nose, glass eyes, open felt mouth, peach felt pads, 1950s, 16", VG **$175.00**

String Holders

Today we admire string holders for their decorative nature. They are much sought after by collectors. However, in the 1800s, they were strictly utilitarian, serving as dispensers of string used to wrap food and packages. The earliest were made of cast iron. Later, advertising string holders appeared in general stores. They were made of tin or cast iron and were provided by companies pedaling such products as shoes, laundry supplies, and food. These advertising string holders command the highest prices.

These days we take cellophane tape for granted. Before it was invented, string was used to tie up packages. String holders became a staple item in the home kitchen. To add a whimsical touch, in the late 1920s and 1930s, many string holders were presented as human shapes, faces, animals, and fruits. Most of these novelty string holders were made of chalkware (plaster of Paris), ceramics, or wood fiber. If you were lucky, you might have won a plaster of Paris 'Super Hero' or comic character string holder at your local carnival. These prizes were known as 'carnival chalkware.' The Indian string holder was a popular giveaway, so was Betty Boop and Superman.

Our values are for examples in excellent condition.

Advisor: Larry G. Pogue (See Directory, Head Vases and String Holders)

Acorn, painted chalkware, 8½" **$185.00**

Apple w/leaves, painted chalkware, 8".................................**$75.00**

Aunt Jemima (head only), painted chalkware, 1940s-50s, 7¾" ..**$395.00**

Bananas, painted chalkware, 1980s, 5¾"..............................**$85.00**

Black boy eating watermelon in tub, painted chalkware, ATCO, 1940s-50s, 7½" **$645.00**

Black boy on alligator, painted chalkware, Copyright 1948, 9" **$345.00**

Black chef (face only), painted chalkware, 1950s, 6¼".......**$195.00**

Black children (2) eating watermelon slice, painted chalkware, Copyright 1953 USA, 4¾x4¾"...................................**$295.00**

Black girl in her nightie, full figure, painted chalkware, Copyright 1945, 7¾"...**$295.00**

Black Porter (head only), black skin tones, ceramic, Fredericksburg Art Pottery USA, 6½" **$425.00**

Bonzo, full figure, painted chalkware, 6½".........................**$185.00**

Bozo the Clown (head only), painted chalkware, 1950s, 7½"...**$285.00**

Bride, ceramic, Made in Japan, 6¼"...................................**$110.00**

Buddha, sits on countertop, ceramic, Japan, 1940s, 5¾"....**$145.00**

Campbell Soup Kid (head only), ceramic, Copyright Campbell, 1950s, 6¾"..**$395.00**

Carrots, painted chalkware, 1950s, 10"..............................**$225.00**

Cat (face only) w/bow, scissors holder, ceramic, brown & white, 5¾"...**$60.00**

Cat on ball of twin, ceramic, 5½" **$95.00**

Chipmunk (head only), striped bow tie, ceramic, 5⅛".......**$135.00**

Clown (head only), string tied to tooth, painted chalkware, 1950s, 7"..**$250.00**

Coca-Cola Kid (head only), painted chalkware, 1950s, 8" ..**$650.00**

Conovers Chef, painted chalkware, Conovers Original 1945, 6x6" **$245.00**

Corn, multiple ears & green leaves, painted chalkware, 5½"..**$175.00**

Corn (single ear among green shucks), painted chalkware, 1950s, 9"..**$225.00**

Dog (head only) w/collar, scissors holder, ceramic, Arthur Wood, 4½"..**$175.00**

Elmer the Bull (head only), painted chalkware, 1950s, 7½" .**$425.00**

Emmett Kelly Jr (head only), painted chalkware, Copyright Emmet Kelly, Jr, 8" $600.00

Frito Kid (face only), with cowboy hat and neck scarf, painted chalkware, 9", $550.00. (Photo courtesy Larry Pogue)

German Girl (head only) w/ethnic bonnet, painted chalkware, Germany, #054, 8" $195.00

Howdy Doody (face only), painted chalkware, Copyright 195?, 6½" $495.00

Indian brave (head only), w/headband, painted chalkware, 10¼" $285.00

Indian chief (head only) in full headdress, painted chalkware, 8¾" $295.00

Jester (head only), painted chalkware, 1950s, 7½" $245.00

Lady w/scarf (head only), painted chalkware, 9½" $195.00

Lemon w/leaves, painted chalkware, 1950s, 6¾" $145.00

Mammy, A&P advertising, painted chalkware, 1950s, 7½" ..$545.00

Mammy, black skin tones, ceramic, Made in Japan, 6½" ...$235.00

Mammy, full figure, scissors holder, rhinestone eyes, 1940s, 6¾" $325.00

Mammy (big busted), painted chalkware, 1940s, 7¾" $365.00

Mammy (face only), razor blade holder, painted chalkware, Florence Art Co, 6½" $395.00

Marilyn Monroe (head only), painted chalkware, 7" $265.00

Monkey on ball of twine, painted chalkware, 7½" $245.00

Monkey on bananas, painted chalkware, 1950s, 8¼" $295.00

Mrs Mouse, full-figure countertop type, painted composition, 7" $85.00

Mutt dog (head only), painted chalkware, 1950s-60s, 6½"...$185.00

Parrot on flowered branch, painted chalkware, 9½" $225.00

Polka Dot Mammy (face only), 6½" $395.00

Red Riding Hood (head only), painted chalkware, Bello, American Statuary Co, 1941, 9½" $295.00

Rooster (head & neck only), painted chalkware, red comb, 8½" .$225.00

Rooster (slightly turned head only), painted chalkware, #3021, 1950s, 9" $275.00

Rose, red w/green leaves, painted chalkware, 8" $175.00

Sailor boy (head only), painted chalkware, 8" $225.00

Santa Claus (head only), painted chalkware, 1940s-50s, 9" .$245.00

Senor (head only) w/sombrero, painted chalkware, 8¼" $95.00

Senora (head only), painted chalkware, 1940s-50s, 8" $195.00

Shirley Temple (head only), painted chalkware, 1940s-50s, 6¾x6¼" $395.00

Smokey Bear (head only), painted chalkware, Copyright 1957, NM, 5½" $425.00

Speedy Alka Seltzer, painted chalkware, 1950s, 9½"...........$395.00

Strawberry, painted chalkware, 1950s, 6½" $145.00

Strawberry w/blossoms & leaves, painted chalkware, 1950s, 6½" $115.00

Tomato w/face, ceramic, 5½" $125.00

Westie dog (head only), painted chalkware, 9"...................$195.00

Swanky Swigs

These glasses, ranging in size from 3⅛" to 5⅝", were originally distributed by the Kraft company who filled them with their cheese spread. They were introduced in the 1930s and until 1976 were decorated with various colorful designs. Though no one has ever been able to document the actual number of variations available, our advisor tells us that in her own collection, she has cataloged more than 230. Patterns range from sailboats, animals, and flowers to bands, dots, stars, checks, etc.

In 1951 Kraft came out with the first small clear glass with indented designs while still producing the color silkscreen Kraft Cheese Spread Swanky Swig designs such as Bustlin' Betsy, Antique No. 1, Bachelor Button, and Kiddie Kup. Some of the indented patterns were Crystal Petal, Hostess Design, and Coin Design.

By 1976 Kraft had dropped making the color-decorated Swanky Swigs and began using only clear glasses with indented designs — Colonial in 1976 and Petal Star in 1978. (The latter was used for their fiftieth anniversary; these were dated 1933 – 1983 in the glass itself.) Even today, you can buy Kraft Cheese spread in these clear small glasses.

After 27 years, Kraft resumed the production of a few color-decorated Swanky Swigs. There were eight of them, two of which were brought out in 2003 — one with dark blue hearts and red apples, the second with dark blue stars and red hearts. Six more came out in 2004, one with the word Greetings and the image of a passenger car and another with the word Holiday and the image of a train engine. The other four new to the market that year featured NASCAR drivers Mark Martin #6, Matt Kenseth #17, Kurt Busch #97, and Michael Waltrip #15.

In 1999 a few Kraft Swanky Swigs from Australia began to surface. They have been verified as such through Kraft magazine ads. We now have identified Swanky Swigs from three countries: the United States, Canada, and Australia.

Here is a listing of some of the harder-to-find examples: In the small (Canadian) size (about 3¹⁄₁₆" to 3¼") look for Band No. 5 (two red and two black bands); Galleon (two ships on each example, made in five colors — black, blue, green, red, and yellow); Checkers (made in four color combinations — black and red, black and yellow, black and orange, and black and white, all having a top row of black checks); and Fleur-De-Lis (black fleur-de-lis with a bright red filigree motif).

In the regular size (about 3⅜" to 3⅞") look for Dots Forming Diamonds (diamonds made up of small red dots); Lattice and Vine (white lattice with flowers in these combinations — white and blue, white and green, and white and red); Texas Centennial (a cowboy and horse in these colors — black, blue, green, and red); three special issues with dates of 1936, 1938, and 1942; and Tulip No.2 (available in black, blue, green, and red).

In the large (Canadian) size (about 4³⁄₁₆" to 5⅝"), you'll find Circles and Dot (circles with a small dot in the middle, in black, blue, green, and red); Star No. 1 (small scattered stars, made in black, blue, green, and red); Cornflower No. 2 (in dark blue, light blue, red, and yellow); Provencial Crest (made only in red and burgundy with maple leaves).

Even the lids are collectible and are valued at a minimum of $3.00, depending on condition and the advertising message they convey.

For more information we recommend *Swanky Swigs* by Ian Warner; *Swanky Swigs* by Mark Moore; and *Collectible Glassware from the 40s, 50s, and 60s* and *Collector's Encyclopedia of Depression Glass*, both by Gene and Cathy Florence.

Note: In the following listings, all descriptions are for American issues unless noted Canadian.

Advisor: Joyce Jackson (See the Directory, Swanky Swigs)

Antique #1, black, blue, brown, green, orange, or red, 1954, 3¾", $4.00 each. (Photo courtesy Gene and Cathy Florence)

Antique #1, black, blue, brown, green, orange or red, Canadian, 1954, 4¾", ea...$20.00
Antique #1, black, blue, brown, green, orange or red, Canadian, 3¼", ea...$8.00
Antique #2, lime green, deep red, orange, blue or black, Cadadian, 1974, 4⅝", ea...$20.00
Bachelor Button, red, green & white, 1955, 3¾".............$3.00
Bachelor Button, red, white & green, Canadian, 1955, 3¼"..$6.00
Bachelor Button, red, white & green, Canadian, 1955, 4¾"..$15.00
Band #1, red & black, 1933, 3⅜"...................................$3.00
Band #2, black & red, Canadian, 1933, 4¾"..................$20.00
Band #2, black & red, 1933, 3⅜".....................................$3.00
Band #3, white & blue, 1933, 3⅜"...................................$3.00
Band #4, blue, 1933, 3⅜"..$3.00
Bicentennial Tulip, green, red or yellow, 1975, 3¾", ea........$15.00
Blue hearts & red apples, US, 2003 ....$5.00
Blue stars & red hearts, US, 2003 ....$5.00

Blue Tulips, 1937, 4¼"...$20.00
Bustlin' Betty, blue, brown, green, orange, red or yellow, Canadian, 1953, 3¼", ea..$8.00
Bustlin' Betty, blue, brown, green, orange, red or yellow, Canadian, 1953, 4¾", ea..$20.00
Bustlin' Betty, blue, brown, green, orange, red or yellow, 1953, 3¾", ea..$4.00
Carnival, blue, green, red or yellow, 1939, 3½", ea $9.00
Checkerboard, white w/blue, green or red, Canadian, 1936, 4¾", ea...$20.00

Checkerboard, white with blue, green, or red, 1936, 3½", $20.00 each. (Photo courtesy Gene and Cathy Florence)

Circles & Dot, any color, 1934, 3½", ea $7.00
Circles & Dot, black, blue, green or red, Canadian, 1934, 4¾", ea $20.00
Coin, clear & plain w/indented coin decor around base, Canadian, 1968, 3⅛" or 3¼", ea..$2.00
Coin, clear & plain w/indented coin decor around base, 1968, 3¾" $1.00
Colonial, clear w/indented waffle design around middle & base, 1976, 3¾", ea...$.50
Colonial, clear w/indented waffle design around middle & base, 1976, 4⅜", ea...$1.00
Cornflower #1, light blue & green, Canadian, 1941, 4⅝", ea...$20.00
Cornflower #1, light blue & green, Canadian, 3¼", ea $8.00
Cornflower #1, light blue & green, 1941, 3½", ea.................$4.00
Cornflower #2, dark blue, light blue, red or yellow, Canadian, 1947, 3¼", ea..$8.00
Cornflower #2, dark blue, light blue, red or yellow, Canadian, 1947, 4¼", ea...$30.00
Cornflower #2, dark blue, light blue, red or yellow, 1947, 3½", ea...$4.00
Crystal Petal, clear & plain w/fluted base, 1951, 3½", ea.......$2.00
Dots Forming Diamonds, any color, 1935, 3½", ea.............$50.00
Ethnic Series, lime green, royal blue, burgundy, poppy red or yellow, Canadian, 1974, 4⅝", ea.......................................$20.00
Forget-Me-Not, dark blue, light blue, red or yellow, Canadian, 3¼", ea...$8.00
Forget-Me-Not, dark blue, light blue, red or yellow, 1948, 3½", ea...$4.00

Galleon, black, blue, green, red or yellow, Canadian, 1936, 3⅛",
ea **$30.00**

Hostess, clear & plain w/indented grove base, Canadian, 1960, 3⅛"
or 3¼", ea **$2.00**

Hostess, clear & plain w/indented grove base, Canadian, 1960, 5⅝",
ea **$5.00**

Hostess, clear & plain w/indented grove base, 1960, 3¾", ea ... **$1.00**

Jonquil (Posy Pattern), yellow & green, Canadian, 1941, 3¼"... **$8.00**

Jonquil (Posy Pattern), yellow & green, Canadian, 1941, 4⅝",
ea **$20.00**

Jonquil (Posy Pattern), yellow & green, 1941, 3½", ea **$4.00**

Kiddie Kup, black, blue, brown, green, orange or red, Canadian,
1956, 3¼", ea **$6.00**

Kiddie Kup, black, blue, brown, green, orange or red, Canadian,
1956, 4¾", ea **$20.00**

Kiddie Kup, black, blue, brown, green, orange or red, 1956, 3¾",
ea **$3.00**

Lattice & Vine, white w/blue, green or red, 1936, 3½", ea.. **$100.00**

Nascar driver, No 1 Mark Martin #6, No 2 Matt Kinseth #17, US,
2004, ea **$10.00**

Nascar driver, No 3 Kirt Busch #97, No 4 Michael Waltrip #15,
ea **$10.00**

Petal Star, clear, 50th Anniversary of Kraft Cheese Spreads, 1933-
1983, ca 1983, 3¾", ea **$2.00**

Petal Star, clear w/indented star base, Canadian, 1978, 3¼", ea ...**$2.00**

Petal Star, clear w/indented star base, 1978, 3¾", ea .... **$.50**

Plain, clear, like Tulip #1 w/out design, 1940, 3½", ea.......... **$4.00**

Plain, clear, like Tulip #3 w/out design, 1951, 3⅞", ea.......... **$5.00**

Provencial Crest, red & burgundy, Canadian, 1974, 4⅝", ea.. **$25.00**

Sailboat #1, blue, 1936, 3½", ea **$12.00**

Sailboat #2, blue, green, light green or red, 1936, 3½", ea...**$12.00**

Special Issue, Cornflower #1, light blue flowers/green leaves,
Greetings From Kraft, etc, 1941, 3½" **$410.00**

Special Issue, Lewis-Pacific Dairyman's Assoc, Kraft Foods, Sept 13,
1947, Chehalis WA, 3½" **$100.00**

Special Issue, Posy Pattern Tulip, red tulip w/green leaves, Greetings
From Kraft, CA Retail Assoc, etc, 1940, 3½" **$350.00**

Special Issue, Posy Pattern Violet, Greetings From Kraft, CA Retail
Assoc, Grocers Merchants, Del Monte, 1942, 3½" **$350.00**

Special Issue, Sailboat #1, blue, Greetings From Kraft, CA Retail
Assoc, Grocers Merchants, Del Monte, 1936, 3½" **$350.00**

Special Issue, Tulip #1, red, Greetings From Kraft, CA Retail Assoc,
Grocers Merchants, Del Monte, 1938, 3½" **$350.00**

Special Issue, 4-H Club, clear glass w/3 green parallel lines top/bottom,
2 clovers, Farewell Luncheon, 27th National 4-H Club Congress,
Guest of JL Kraft, Dec 2, 1948 .... **$300.00**

Sportsmen Series, red hockey, blue skiing, red football, red baseball
or green soccer, Canadian, 1976, 4⅝", ea **$20.00**

Stars #1, black, blue, green, red or yellow, Canadian, 1934, 4¾",
ea **$20.00**

Stars #1, black, blue, green or red, 1935, 3½", ea **$7.00**

Stars #1, yellow, 1935, 3½", ea.................................. **$25.00**

Stars #2, clear w/orange stars, Canadian, 1971, 4⅝", ea........ **$5.00**

Texas Centennial, black, blue, green or red, 1936, 3½", ea ..**$30.00**

Train, passenger car, Greetings, blue, 2005........................... **$5.00**

Train engine, Holiday, wine, 2004 .... **$5.00**

Tulip (Posy Pattern), red & green, Canadian, 1941, 3¼", ea **$8.00**

Tulip (Posy Pattern), red & green, Canadian, 1941, 4⅝", ea ..**$20.00**

Tulip (Posy Pattern), red & green, 1941, 3½", ea................. **$4.00**

Tulip #1, black, blue, green, red or yellow, Canadian, 3¼", ea.. **$8.00**

Tulip #1, black, blue, green, red or yellow, 1937, 3½", ea...... **$4.00**

Tulip #1, black, blue, green or red, Canadian, 1937, 4⅝", ea ..**$20.00**

Tulip #2, black, blue, green or red, 1938, 3½", ea................ **$25.00**

Tulip #3, dark blue, light blue, red or yellow, Canadian, 1950, 4¾",
ea **$20.00**

Tulip #3, dark blue, light blue, red or yellow, Canadian, 3¼", ea..**$8.00**

Tulip #3, dark blue, light blue, red or yellow, 1950, 3⅞", ea..**$4.00**

Violet (Posy Pattern), blue & green, Canadian, 1941, 3¼", ea.. **$8.00**

Violet (Posy Pattern), blue & green, Canadian, 1941, 4⅝", ea.. **$20.00**

Violet (Posy Pattern), blue & green, 1941, 3½", ea............... **$4.00**

Wildlife Series, black bear, Canadian goose, moose or red fox,
Canadian, 1975, 4⅝", ea.. **$20.00**

Syroco

Syroco Inc. originated in New York in 1890 when a group of European wood carvers banded together to produce original hand carvings for fashionable homes of the area. Their products were also used in public buildings throughout upstate New York, including the state capitol. Demand for those products led to the development of the original Syroco reproduction process that allowed them to copy original carvings with no loss of detail. They later developed exclusive hand-applied color finishes to further enhance the product, which they continued to improve and refine over 90 years.

Syroco's master carvers use tools and skills handed down from father to son through many generations. Woods used, depending on the effect called for, include Swiss pear wood, oak, mahogany, and wormy chestnut. When a design is completed, it is transformed into a metal cast through their molding and tooling process. A compression mold system using wood fiber was employed from the early 1940s to the 1960s. Since 1962 a process has been in use in which pellets of resin are injected into a press, heated to the melting point, and then injected into the mold. Because the resin is liquid, it fills every crevice, thus producing an exact copy of the carver's art. It is then cooled, cleaned, and finished.

Other companies have produced similar items, among them are Multi Products, now of Erie, Pennsylvania. It was incorporated in Chicago in 1941 but in 1976 was purchased by John Hronas. Multi Products hired a staff of artists, made some wood originals and developed a tooling process for forms. They used a styrene-based material, heavily loaded with talc or calcium carbonate. A hydraulic press was used to remove excess material from the forms. Shapes were dried in kilns for 72 hours, then finished and, if the design required it, trimmed in gold. Their products included bears, memo pads, thermometers, brush holders, trays, plaques, nut bowls, napkin holders, etc., which were sold mainly as souvenirs. The large clocks and mirrors were made before the 1940s and may sell for as much as $100.00 and more, depending on condition. Syroco used gold trim, but any other painted decoration you might encounter was very likely done by an outside firm. Some collectors prefer the painted examples and tend to pay a little more to get them. You may also find similar products stamped 'Ornawood,' 'Decor-A-Wood,' and 'Swank'; these are collectible as well.

Ashtray, Indian chief seated at side, glass insert, 1940s, 4¾x6¼" .. **$48.00**
Award, Jiminy Cricket United Campaign 1959, Walt Disney
    Productions, 5¾" **$120.00**
Bookends, DC-3 (?) airplane in relief, ca 1940 .... **$80.00**
Bookends, fireplace w/ship on mantle, pr **$30.00**
Bottle opener, elephant figural, pink **$160.00**
Bottle opener, horse's head, unpainted version, 5¼x5½" **$60.00**
Bottle opener, rooster figural, painted version, 5¾" **$130.00**
Brush holder, Scottie dogs at top, w/brush, 9" **$30.00**

Clock, eight-day, 20", $75.00. (Photo courtesy LiveAuctioneers.com/
Tom Harris Auctions)

Clock, gold sunburst, bubble glass door face, 8-day, jeweled, 22½"
    dia.. **$150.00**
Corkscrew, bartender, painted version, rare **$215.00**
Corkscrew, Scottish terrier, unpainted version, 5½" **$132.00**
Corkscrew, waiter figural, painted version, EX **$50.00**
Figurine, Benjamin Franklin, Great American series, 6" **$345.00**
Figurine, Geppetto, Walt Disney Productions, ca 1940, lg... **$20.00**
Figurine, Jiminy Cricket, Walt Disney Productions, KFS, 1940s,
    4¼" **$42.50**
Figurine, Steve Brodie, Famous American series, ca 1941, 6",
    NM **$185.00**
Figurine, Teddy Roosevelt, Great American series, ca 1941... **$220.00**

**Figurines, peacocks, #13201, 13", 12", from $45.00 to $55.00
for the pair.** (Photo courtesy LiveAuctioneers.com/Dargate Auction Galleries)

Mirror, acanthus leaves crest, scrollwork at bottom of 8-sided
    Italianate-style frame, gold paint, #2049, 1972, 36x17" .. **$80.00**
Mirror, eagle crest atop Federal-style frame, gold paint, convex mir-
    ror, 23x14½" **$75.00**
Mirror, foliate swirls, gold paint, easel back, 20x14" **$55.00**
Mirror, ornate foliate openwork, brown paint, oval, 29x19"... **$55.00**
Plaque, mums, cream & brown paint, 18½x12½" **$20.00**
Plaque, ship, Dart Co, 1962, 21x26" **$25.00**
Plaque, Viking ship, 12x39" **$65.00**
Thermometer, beside Indian chief, 4¾" **$33.00**
Tie holder, Irish setter figure on top, 7x12" **$17.00**
Tie holder, Scottie dog, white paint, red collar & nose, 12" .. **$20.00**
Tray, serving; oak leaves & acorns on rim, 13x7" **$25.00**

Taylor, Smith and Taylor

Though this company is most famous for their pastel dinnerware line, Lu Ray, they made many other patterns, and some of them
are very collectible in their own right. Located in the East Liverpool
area of West Virginia, the 'dinnerware capitol' of the world, their
answer to HLC's very successful Fiesta line was Vistosa. It was made
in four primary colors, and though quite attractive, the line was
never developed to include any more than 20 items.

See also LuRay Pastels; Vistosa.

Cathay, bowl, 9½", from $12.00 to $15.00.

Appalachian Heirloom, bowl, dessert; 5½" **$5.50**
Appalachian Heirloom, cup & saucer **$12.00**
Appalachian Heirloom, plate, dinner; 10" **$12.00**
Appalachian Heirloom, platter, oval, 12" L **$20.00**
Blue Lace, bowl, cereal; 6½" **$5.50**
Blue Lace, creamer **$6.00**
Blue Lace, cup & saucer.. **$7.00**
Blue Lace, plate, bread & butter **$2.00**
Boutonniere, bowl, cereal **$8.50**
Boutonniere, cup & saucer... **$5.50**
Boutonniere, plate, dinner; 10 .... **$6.00**
Boutonniere, platter, 13½" L.. **$12.50**
Bride's Bouquet, bowl, rimmed soup **$10.00**
Bride's Bouquet, cup & saucer **$17.50**
Bride's Bouquet, plate, dinner; 10" **$12.50**

Bride's Bouquet, sugar bowl, w/lid $21.50
Capistrano, butter dish, ¼-lb $27.50
Capistrano, coffeepot $35.00
Capistrano, cup & saucer $15.00
Capistrano, plate, bread & butter $4.00
Capistrano, sugar bowl, w/lid $20.00
Concord, coffeepot, 5-cup $35.00
Concord, cup & saucer $12.00
Concord, plate, dinner; 10½" $8.00
Concord, salt & pepper shakers, pr $16.00
Golden Button, bowl, 9" $30.00
Golden Button, creamer, 8-oz $15.00
Golden Button, plate, bread & butter; 7" $5.00
Golden Button, plate, dinner; 10" $8.00
Golden Button, sugar bowl, w/lid $22.50
Indian Summer, creamer $9.00
Indian Summer, plate, dinner; 10½" $7.50
Indian Summer, platter, 14" L $44.00
Indian Summer, salt & pepper shakers, pr $12.50

King O'Dell, Conversation, platter, 13", from $18.00 to $22.00.

Leaf O' Gold, bowl, vegetable; 9" L $17.50
Leaf O' Gold, creamer, gold trim $7.50
Leaf O' Gold, cup & saucer, gold trim $7.50
Leaf O' Gold, platter, 13½" L $15.00
Matador, creamer $7.50
Matador, cup & saucer $8.00
Matador, gravy boat & underplate $25.00
Matador, platter, 14" L $24.00
Pebbleford, bowl, dessert; from $5 to $7.00
Pebbleford, cup & saucer, from $8 to $10.00
Pebbleford, plate, dinner; 10", from $10 to $12.00
Pebbleford, platter, 11½" L, from $18 to $20.00
Petal Lane, bowl, soup; 8¼" $7.00
Petal Lane, bowl, vegetable; 8½" L $18.00
Petal Lane, plate, dessert; 7" $2.50
Petal Lane, salt & pepper shakers, pr $16.00
Random Leaves, bowl, cereal $7.50
Random Leaves, bowl, vegetable; 9" $27.50
Random Leaves, gravy boat, w/underplate $35.00
Random Leaves, platter, 13½" $18.00

Random Leaves, sugar bowl, w/lid $16.00
Shasta Daisy, bowl, dessert; 5" $7.50
Shasta Daisy, creamer $12.50
Shasta Daisy, plate, salad; 8" $5.00
Shasta Daisy, platter, 11" L $20.00
Twilight Time, bowl, lug cereal $7.00
Twilight Time, bowl, 9" $36.00
Twilight Time, cup & saucer $14.00
Twilight Time, plate, dinner; 10" $7.50
Twilight Time, sugar bowl, w/lid $27.00
Windermere, bowl, soup $7.00
Windermere, cake plate, 11" $22.50
Windermere, cup & saucer $7.50
Windermere, plate, chop; 11½" $15.00
Windermere, sauceboat $22.00
Windermere, sugar bowl, w/lid $15.00
Wood Rose, casserole, oval, w/lid, 1½-qt $36.00
Wood Rose, creamer, 8-oz $12.00
Wood Rose, cup & saucer $7.00
Wood Rose, plate, salad; 8" $5.00
Wood Rose, sauceboat $22.00
Wood Rose, sugar bowl, w/lid $14.00

Tea Bag Holders

Whimsical yet functional, these little trays designed to hold a used tea bag can be found in many shapes. The most common is the teapot, but you'll be amazed at the variety of form and design you may find. They're small, so they take up very little space — a perfect collectible for apartment dwellers or anyone who simply finds them cheerful and fun.

Leaf form, Iniana souvenir, Indiana Toll Road in center, gold trim, loop handle, Made in USA $7.00

Miss Cutie Pie, Napco, $35.00. (Photo courtesy Rosemary Nichols)

Pansy blossom, purple & yellow petals curve to give depth, TEA BAG at top, 4" dia $15.00
Teacup form, I'll Hold Your Bag & smiling face, Japan, 3x4", set of 4 on metal stand $20.00
Teapot form, Florida souvenir, alligator & palm tree, HZ, 3x4" .. $12.00

Teapot form, Florida souvenir, mermaid w/starfish & sea horse, CNI Made in Japan label, 4½".....................................**$10.00**

Teapot form, flying fish scene, souvenir of Catalina Island...**$15.00**

Teapot form, hand-painted peony & leaf on light blue, Genuine Porcelain, Made in China, 3x4"....................................**$12.50**

Teapot form, I Hold the Bag & pink rose, gold trim, Japan, 1950s, 3x4"...**$5.00**

Teapot form, I Hold the Bag & smiling face, Japan, 3x4"....**$12.00**

Teapot form, Let Me Hold the Bag, Cleminson, 3x4½".......**$12.50**

Teapots

The continued popularity of teatime and tea-related items has created a tighter market for collectors on the lookout for teapots. Vintage and finer quality teapots have become harder to find, with those from the 1890s and 1920s reflecting age with three and four digit prices.

Most collectors begin with a general collection of varied tea-pots until they decide upon the specific category that most appeals to them. Collecting categories include miniatures, doll or toy sets, those made by a certain manufacturer, figurals, or a particular style. While teapots made in Japan have waned in collectibility, collectors have begun to realize many detailed and delicate examples are available.

Deco teapot and flowers, Pottery Guild, from $25.00 to $30.00. (Photo courtesy C. Dianne Zweig)

Banquet Tea a Wonderful Flavor Iced Hot, white lettering on brown pottery, 12½", EX.....................................**$100.00**

Birds (yellow) on floral branch, hand painted over transfer outline, green trim, Vista Alegre, 4¼" **$35.00**

Black Bird (aka Chelsea Bird), Copeland Spode, 6x9" **$60.00**

Blue Jasper, 6 classical figures, Wedgwood England, 4½x7"...**$65.00**

Bulbous, white glass, McCormick Tea Baltimore MD, Made in USA, 6¾x9"...**$92.50**

Camel w/howdah, kneeling position, many painted details, rattan handle, ca 1930s, 9" L **$50.00**

Cat figural, dainty flowers on white, paw spout, tail handle, Made in China, 5½" **$15.00**

Cat figural, shiny black w/hand-painted features & bow, Japan, 8½"..**$95.00**

Cat figural, tabby w/green eyes, pink nose, tail handle, cold-painted bow, Japan, 7⅛x7½" **$55.00**

Cat's smiling face, pink & blue w/flower trim, Made in Japan, Chase sticker, 1950s **$110.00**

Cherubs embossed in band, multicolor on blue, white body, Made in Japan, 5x7¼" **$70.00**

Chintz, pink on white w/gold trim, ornate handle, music-box base (Tea for Two), 1940s, 8½x8½" **$40.00**

Chintz floral on white w/green rickrack at rim, Japan, 1940s, 5x6" **$32.50**

Cottage form w/thatched roof & arched doorway, 5½x7½" ..**$25.00**

Cow figural, bird on back forms finial, tail handle, wearing straw bonnet, P&K Made in England **$45.00**

Dragonware, applied dragon on purple, flamingos in reserve, souvenir of Florida, 1950s-60s, 7" **$32.00**

Duck figural, brown gloss w/gold flecks, duck finial, metal handle, Japan, 5x10½" **$40.00**

Duck figural, Delft blue w/hand-painted flowers on white, copper handle, Made in Thailand, Sigma, 4¾x8½" **$55.00**

Embossed ribs on medium green, acorn-like finial, Padre (California), #210, 7½x10½" **$40.00**

Floral chintz w/gold, Wade of England, 5½".......................**$48.00**

Floral medallions painted on shiny brown, Made in Japan, 3¾x6⅞"..**$20.00**

Floral on pale blue w/gold finial, spout & handle, Sadler, 1988, 3¼x3½"...**$25.00**

Floral spray hand-painted on white, embossed ribs & green & gold trim, Japan, 1960s **$30.00**

Flower bouquet in multicolors form lid of pale pink bulbous body, Sadler...**$40.00**

Flowers, ribbons & bows on white basketweave, majolica, Haldon Group 1985 Japan, 6½x9½" **$65.00**

Flowers hand painted on creamy white, canteen shape, unmarked but American made, 1½-cup, 4" **$30.00**

Flowers hand-painted on brown gloss, Japan, 1940s-50s, 7" .**$15.00**

Gingerbread house form, candy-cane handle, Caff Co 1995, 6¾" **$25.00**

Hamilton pattern, lavender flowers & green leaves on white w/gold trim, Price Bros...#2870...............................**$40.00**

Holly leaves & gingerbread men on white, illegible mark, 1989, 7½x10½" **$40.00**

Lotus blossoms on green, Occupied Japan, 2-cup **$45.00**

Mammy face, chef-like hat forms lid, brown skin tones, Hand Painted Japan, ca 1940s, 4¼x5¾" **$285.00**

Memory Lane, bone china, Royal Albert, ca 1965, 5-cup, 6¼" ..**$65.00**

Mickey Mouse playing waiter to Minnie Mouse, multicolor lustres, Walt E Disney Made in Japan **$38.00**

Moriage-style floral & filigree design on brown gloss, redware, Japan, 1940s-50s, 3-cup, 6" **$30.00**

Moriage-type flowers on med green gloss, Made in Japan, 6½" ..**$25.00**

Owl figural, ruffled look at eyes, lustre twig handle, 6½".....**$25.00**

Poppies in panels on white basketweave, Arthur Wood, 1940s, 9x7½" **$30.00**

Rabbit figural, brown airbrushing & hand-painted details, Shafford, 7" **$75.00**

Rose sprays, pink w/gold trim on white, Sadler...Made in England, #2060, 5½x10" **$25.00**

Roses, multicolor w/gold on melon-ribbed body, gold feet, Hand Painted Nippon, 8" **$50.00**

Roses, white on pink, shouldered, curved handle, Noritake Nippon Toki Kaisha, 6¼" **$35.00**

Roses painted on white swirled body w/gold trim, porcelain, Sadler England **$30.00**

Sampan scenic, gold floral band near top, ceramic, Hand Painted Rose Japan mark, lg **$85.00**

Santa figural, ceramic, Lucky Santa Claus Regd No 835842 Made in England, 7x8" **$155.00**

Scenic hand painted on white w/orange lid, spout & handle, Made in Japan **$10.00**

Squash form, ceramic, soft yellow, unmarked American, 1930s-40s, 6x9½" **$40.00**

Tea table, Cardew design, English, 8x10½", $75.00. (Photo courtesy LiveAuctioneers.com/DuMouchelles)

Teapot, celadon green & white bands, ribbed, sm scrolls near top, Porcelier, 5½x9½x6" **$95.00**

Teardrop pattern, green to brown to blue, porcelain, Made in Ireland, Wade, 4¾x7½" **$80.00**

Teddy bear figural, shiny black w/red details, redware, Shafford Japan, 6" **$32.50**

Tomato form, ceramic, bamboo handle, Maruhon Ware, 4½", +4 handleless 3" tumblers **$50.00**

Western Traveler pattern, stagecoach scene, ceramic, Tepco China USA, 2⅞x6½" **$80.00**

Windmill form, multicolor on white, ceramic, Japan, 5" **$30.00**

Witch on broom figural, multicolor on white stoneware, unmarked, 7½" **$50.00**

Tiara Glassware

Tiara Exclusives was the dream of a determined man named Roger Jewett. With much hard work and planning and the involvement of Jim Hooffstetter of Indiana Glass, Tiara home party plan operations were initialized in July of 1970. Tiara Exclusives was a subsidiary of Indiana Glass, which is a division of Lancaster Colony. Tiara did not manufacture the glassware it sold. Several companies were involved in producing the glassware, among them Indiana Glass, Fenton, Fostoria, Dalzell Viking, and L.E. Smith. The Tiara Exclusives direct selling organization closed in 1998.

In 1999 and 2000, Home Interiors offered a small selection of Tiara Sandwich Glass dinnerware in an attractive transparent purple color called Plum. They have also marketed Tiara's square honey box and children's dish set.

Advisor: Mandi Birkinbine (See Directory, Tiara)

Crown Dinnerware

In the mid-1980s Tiara made Crown Dinnerware in Imperial Blue. This is the pattern most collectors know as King's Crown Thumbprint. The color is a rich medium blue, brighter than cobalt.

Bowl, 2⅛x4¼", from $5 to **$7.00**
Bowl, 4x9¼", from $12 to **$15.00**

Candy dish, Imperial Blue, 7½", from $50.00 to $65.00.
(Photo courtesy Carrie and Gerald Domitz)

Cup **$3.00**
Goblet, stemmed, 8-oz, from $3 to **$5.00**
Pitcher, 8¾", from $25 to **$30.00**
Plate, bread; 8" **$5.00**
Plate, dinner; 10" **$7.00**
Saucer **$2.00**

Honey Boxes

One of Tiara's more popular items was the honey box or honey dish. It is square with tiny tab feet and an embossed allover pattern of bees and hives. The dish measures 6" tall with the lid and was made in many different colors, usually ranging in value from $15.00 up to $45.00, depending on the color. Unusual colors may have greater values.

Amber, from $15 to $25.00
Black, from $25 to $35.00
Chantilly (pale) Green, from $25 to....................$40.00
Clear, from $35 to $45.00
Cobalt blue, from $35 to $45.00
Light blue, from $20 to $40.00
Peach, from $35 to $40.00

Spruce (teal) Green, from $15.00 to $25.00. (Photo courtesy Carrie and Gerald Domitz)

Sandwich Pattern

Among the many lovely glass patterns sold by Tiara, the Sandwich pattern was the most popular. Tiara's Sandwich line reintroduced Indiana Glass and Duncan & Miller Glass designs from the 1920s and 1930s alongside items designed specifically for Tiara. Tiara Sandwich Glass has been made in Crystal, Amber, Ruby, Chantilly (light green), Spruce (teal), Peach, and other colors in limited quantities. The dark blue color named Bicentennial Blue was introduced in 1976 in observance of America's Bicentennial. According to the Tiara brochure, Bicentennial Blue Sandwich glass was approved for a production of 15,000 sets. The only Tiara Sandwich items produced in pink were a dinner bell and a 'glo lamp' (fairy lamp). All other pink-toned Tiara Sandwich is actually peach. Because this glass is not rare and is relatively new, collectors tend to purchase only items in perfect condition. Chips or scratches will decrease value significantly.

With most items, the quickest way to tell Anchor Hocking's Sandwich from Tiara and Indiana Sandwich is by looking at the flower in the pattern. The Tiara/Indiana flower is outlined with a single line and has convex petals. Anchor Hocking's flower is made with double lines, so has a more complex appearance, and the convex area in each petal is tiny. Tiara's Chantilly Green Sandwich is a pale green color that resembles the light green glass made by Indiana Glass during the Depression era. Use of a black light can help determine the age of pale green Sandwich Glass. The green Sandwich made by Indiana Glass during the Depression will fluoresce yellow-green under a black light. Tiara's Chantilly Green reflects the purple color of the black light bulb, but does not fluoresce yellow-green. To learn more about the two lines, we recommend *Collectible Glassware*

from the 40s, 50s, and 60s by Gene and Cathy Florence (Collector Books). Also available is *Tiara Exclusives Glass: The Sandwich Pattern* by our advisor, Mandi Birkinbine. (See the Directory for ordering information.)

Ashtray, Amber, 1¼x7½", from $8 to...................$10.00
Basket, Amber, tall & slender, 10¾x4¾", from $40 to........$50.00
Basket, Chantilly Green, 7¾x5x6½", from $50 to $70.00
Basket, Ruby, 10¾x4¾", from $50 to $65.00
Bell, dinner, pink, 6", from $12 to.......................$15.00
Bowl, Amber, slant sides, 1¾x4¾", from $4 to $5.50
Bowl, Amber, 6-sided, 1¼x6¼", from $8 to.........................$12.00
Bowl, console; Amber, footed, flared rim, 3⅞x11", from $25 to $30.00
Bowl, salad; Amber, crimped, 4¾x10", from $15 to $18.00
Bowl, salad; Amber, slant sides, 3x8⅜", from $10 to...........$15.00
Bowl, salad; Chantilly Green, slant sides, 3x8⅜", from $15 to $20.00
Butter dish, Amber, domed lid, 6" H, from $20 to.............$25.00
Butter dish, Bicentennial Blue, domed lid, 6" H, from $25 to.. $35.00
Butter dish, Chantilly Green, domed lid, 6" H, from $20 to... $30.00
Butter dish, Teal Green (dark), domed lid, 6" H, from $25 to.. $35.00
Cake plate, Chantilly Green, footed, 4x10", from $60 to $75.00

Candleholders, Amber, 3¾", from $10.00 to $12.00 for the pair.

Candleholders, Sea Mist (light), 8½", pr from $25 to $35.00
Candy box, Amber, w/lid, 7½", from $65 to $80.00
Canister, Amber, 26-oz, 5⅝", from $12 to $20.00
Canister, Amber, 38-oz, 7½", from $12 to $20.00
Canister, Amber, 52-oz, 8⅞", from $18 to $26.00
Celery tray/oblong relish, Amber, 10⅜x4⅜", from $16 to....$22.00
Celery tray/oblong relish, Bicentennial Blue, 10⅜x4⅜", from $15 to $20.00
Clock, Amber, wall hanging, 12" dia, from $12 to $18.00
Clock, Amber, wall hanging, 16" dia, from $45 to $55.00
Clock, Peach, wall hanging, 12" dia, from $12 to................$18.00
Clock, Spruce, wall hanging, 12" dia, from $12 to $18.00
Coaster, Amber, from $3 to....................................$5.00
Compote, Amber, 8", from $18 to.........................$25.00
Creamer & sugar bowl, Bicentennial Blue, round, flat, pr from $20 to $25.00
Cup, coffee; Amber, 9-oz, from $3 to $4.00
Cup, snack/punch; & saucer, crystal, 2⅝x3⅜", from $3 to $5.00
Cup, snack/punch; Amber, from $2 to................................$3.00

Dish, club, heart, diamond or spade shape, Amber, 4", ea from $3 to **$5.00**

Dish, club, heart, diamond or spade shape, crystal, 4", ea...... **$3.00**

Fairy (Glo) lamp, Amber, egg shape, pedestal foot, 2-pc, 5¾", from $8 to **$12.00**

Fairy (Glo) lamp, Chantilly Green (light), from $20 to **$25.00**

Fairy (Glo) lamp, Horizon (bright) Blue, 2-pc, 5¾", from $15 to **$20.00**

Fairy (Glo) lamp, Peach, 2-pc, 5¾", from $12 to **$15.00**

Fairy (Glo) lamp, Pine Green (dark), from $12 to **$18.00**

Fairy lamp, Hazel Brown (med brown w/purple cast), 2-pc, 5¾", from $12 to **$18.00**

Goblet, table wine; Amber, 8½-oz, 5½", from $6 to **$8.00**

Goblet, water; Amber, 8-oz, 5¼", from $6 to....................... **$8.00**

Goblet, water; Bicentennial Blue, 8-oz, 5¼", from $10 to ... **$12.00**

Goblet, water; crystal, 5¼", from $6 to **$9.00**

Goblet, water; Spruce Green, 8-oz, 5¼", from $5 to.............. **$7.00**

Gravy boat, Amber, 3⅛x7⅜", from $35 to **$45.00**

Mug, Amber, footed, 5½", from $6 to **$8.00**

Napkin holder, Amber, footed fan shape, 4x7½", from $15 to ...**$20.00**

Napkin holder, Spruce Green, footed fan shape, 4x7½", from $30 to **$45.00**

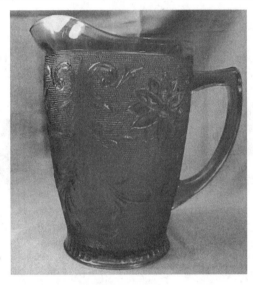

Pitcher, Amber, 8¼", from $25.00 to $35.00. (Photo courtesy Mandi Birkinbine)

Pitcher, Chantilly, straight-sided, 8¼", from $50 to **$75.00**

Pitcher, Peach, footed, 8½", from $20 to **$30.00**

Plate, dinner; Amber, 10", from $9 to................................. **$15.00**

Plate, dinner; Chantilly Green, 10", from $8 to................... **$12.00**

Plate, salad; Amber, 8", from $5 to **$8.00**

Plate, salad; Chantilly Green, 8¼", from $4 to...................... **$8.00**

Platter, Amber, sawtooth rim, 12", from $8.50 to............... **$12.00**

Puff box, Amber, 3⅝" dia, from $10 to................................ **$15.00**

Puff box, Horizon Blue, 3⅝" dia, from $12 to..................... **$15.00**

Salt & pepper shakers, Amber, 4¾", pr from $18 to **$25.00**

Saucer, Amber... **$2.00**

Sherbet, Amber, 3x3⅝".. **$5.00**

Tray, Amber, footed, 1¾x12¾", from $20 to....................... **$35.00**

Tray, Chantilly Green, 3-part, 12", from $12 to................... **$18.00**

Tray, divided relish; Amber, 4-compartment, 10", from $15 to...**$20.00**

Tray, egg; Amber, 12", from $15 to...................................... **$20.00**

Tray, egg; Peach, 12", from $20 to **$35.00**

Tray, egg; Spruce Green, 12", from $15 to **$18.00**

Tray, oval snack; crystal (goes w/punch cup), 8⅜x6¾" **$3.00**

Tray, tidbit; Horizon Blue, center silver-colored metal handle, 8¼" dia, from $12 to... **$15.00**

Tumbler, juice; Amber, footed, 3", from $14 to **$16.00**

Tumbler, juice; Amber, 8-oz, 4", from $12 to **$14.00**

Tumbler, water; Amber, 10-oz, 6½" **$8.00**

Vase, Amber, ruffled, footed, 3¼x6½", from $13 to............ **$15.00**

Vase, bud; Amber, 3⅝", from $15 to.................................... **$20.00**

Wine set, Amber, decanter & tray w/8 goblets, from $30 to .. **$40.00**

Wine set, Chantilly, decanter & tray w/6 goblets, from $45 to...**$65.00**

Wine set, crystal, decanter & tray w/8 goblets, from $45 to..**$60.00**

Tire Ashtrays

Manufacturers of tires issued miniature versions containing ashtray inserts that they usually embossed with advertising messages. Others were used as souvenirs from world's fairs. The earlier styles were made of glass or glass and metal, but by the early 1920s, they were replaced by the more familiar rubber-tired variety. The inserts were often made of clear glass, but colors were also used, and once in awhile you'll find a tin one. The tires themselves were usually black; other colors are rarely found. Hundreds have been produced over the years; in fact, the larger tire companies still issue them occasionally, but you no longer see the details or colors that are evident in the pre-WWII ashtrays. Although the common ones bring modest prices, rare examples sometimes sell for up to several hundred dollars, and eBay has only served to exacerbate this situation. For ladies or non-smokers, some miniature tires were made as pin trays.

For more information we recommend *Tire Ashtray Collector's Guide* by Jeff McVey.

Advisor: Jeff McVey (See Directory, Tire Ashtrays)

Armstrong Rhino-Flex Miracle SD, red & white rhino on clear glass insert.. **$20.00**

Firestone, amber insert embossed w/Century of Progress 1934 World's Fair.. **$55.00**

Firestone, red & black marbleized plastic insert w/3 rests, 1⅞x6" **$15.00**

Firestone GSR Giant Steel Radial, clear glass insert, 6½" **$40.00**

Firestone Made in America 36x10, Firestone Truck Tires Cushion Traction Mileage on aluminum insert......................... **$75.00**

Firestone Max Load 2200 Lbs Keep Inflated to 90 Lbs 36x6HD Gum Dipped & Made in USA (warped), amber glass insert ... **$32.00**

Firestone Super Sports, clear glass insert, 1⅞x5¾"................ **$45.00**

Firestone Super Sports Wide Oval #F-259-0, whitewall tire, clear glass insert, MIB **$50.00**

Firestone Tractor R-1 All Traction Field & Load F 151 Shock Fortified Gum Dipped, clear glass insert, 6" **$38.00**

Firestone Transteel Radial, clear glass insert w/red & white logo, 6½" **$37.50**

Firestone...9.75-18, amber glass insert marked 1933 Century of Progress Chicago 1933, larger version $75.00

General Heavy Duty Cushion 40x12, green glass insert w/2 holes for cigarettes & place for matchbook, 2x4½" $85.00

Good Year Super Torque on tractor tire, clear glass insert w/blue & white logo, 1½x6¼" $34.00

Good Year Farm Tires, clear glass insert w/blue & white logo, 6½" $30.00

Goodrich Silvertown, 6", from $40.00 to $50.00. (Photo courtesy LiveAuctioneers.com/Dirk Soulis Auctions)

Kelly Springfield Heavy Duty Tire, Bell Telephone green glass insert, 6⅜" $35.00

Kelly Springfield Tires Heavy Duty 34x7, embossed lettering on green glass insert, ca 1920s-30s.............................$78.00

Mohawk Rubber Company, Akron Ohio, clear glass insert, 1½x5½" $42.50

Ober-Ramstadt Ordnance Tire Depot 1947, aluminum insert w/2 rests, 6" $30.00

Pennsylvania Rubber Co., CV logo, vaseline glass, $125.00. (Photo courtesy Antiques Cards & Collectibles/Ray Pelly)

Sears & Roebuck Allstate Balloon Tire, green glass insert, 1920s, 1¼x5½" $70.00

Seiberling Sealed-Aire 7.60-15, clear glass insert w/red & yellow logo, 6" $30.00

Super Rock Global 37.25-36 V-524 Yokohama, clear glass insert, 2½x7⅞" $45.00

The 75 Tire 8.25x14 Uniroyal Master..., If It Only Saves You Once..., clear glass insert, 5¾" $35.00

US Royal Tempered Rubber Heavy Duty Six, amber glass insert w/ match holder & cigarette rest, 7⅛" $75.00

Vogue Tyres on white rubber tire & black insert, 3 rests, 2½x6" dia...$85.00

Tobacco Collectibles

Until lately, the tobacco industry spent staggering sums advertising their products, and scores of retail companies turned out many types of smoking accessories such as pipes, humidors, lighters, and ashtrays. Even though the smoking habit isn't particularly popular nowadays, collecting tobacco-related memorabilia is!

Values in the listings that follow are for examples in excellent to near mint condition unless otherwise noted.

See also Advertising Character Collectibles, Joe Camel; Ashtrays; Cigarette Lighters.

Club: Society of Tobacco Jar Collectors
Newsletter: *Tobacco Jar*
1705 Chanticleer Drive
Cherry Hill, NJ 08003
856-489-8363
www.tobaccojarsociety.com

Box, wooden, Piper Heidsieck Plug Tobacco, Victorian lady paper label at top, 3¼x9¼x9¼", VG.....................................$35.00

Carton, Old Gold Cigarettes, $200.00. (Photo courtesy Don and R.C. Raycraft)

Cigar cutter, brass ship's wheel on brass pedestal base, 4⅝" dia $55.00

Cigar cutter, cast-iron pig figural, 8" L on 5½x4" base.......$325.00

Cigar cutter, Financial Times, champagne bottle form, top turns to open & close cutter, 2" $80.00

Cigarette case, hand-chased florals on sterling, gold-washed interior, 3¼x2½" $60.00

Cigarette case, Science Technology & Agriculture, Purdue University & emblem on brown leather, slides apart, 3x2½"..........$65.00

Cigarette dispenser, cast-iron elephant figural, tail rotates inner mechanism for dispensing, ca 1910s?, 6x9" $85.00

Cigarette holder, amber & silver, 3½" $45.00

Cigarette holder, cherry red plastic (not Bakelite) w/red & clear rhinestones, 5" $90.00

Cigarette holder, cherry red translucent Bakelite, Gerard/Redmanol, 6", NM in case $110.00

Display, Prince Albert, easel back, with five small cardboard pocket tins, 1930s, 36x30", MIB, $345.00.

Humidor, blue glass w/hand-painted flowers, silver-plated lid, 6" $160.00

Humidor, cherry wood, fold-down front & hinged lid, presentation plaque on lid (no inscription), 7½x10x7½" $135.00

Humidor, Dunhill, walnut & mahogany, cedar lined, solid brass humidifier, 5¾x13¾x8¾" $300.00

Humidor, Indian chief's head, multicolor, ceramic, unmarked, 7x4½" $100.00

Label, cigar box; Black Hawk Indian, Chief of the Broadleafs... $55.00

Label, crate; The Enchanter, classical couple, stone lithograph, unused $50.00

Lunch box, Worker Cut Plug, tin litho alligator-skin pattern, green & gold, bail handle, 1920s, 5½x7½x4½", VG+ $85.00

Lunch bucket, Duco Smoking & Chewing Tobacco, Wilkes-Barre PA, 6x5½" dia, VG $72.50

Lunch bucket, Great West Cut Plug, tin litho, gold & black lettering on red, bail handle $70.00

Pipe, Barlings Make (block letters) EL 77, marked stem, 5½"... $175.00

Pipe, burl wood, Walt Disney World, wide bowl, 5¾" $155.00

Pipe, Charatan's Wake Special, London England, Made by Hand, lg. $70.00

Pipe, Comoy's Pebble Grain Bulldog, 3-pc C in stem, Made in London England, 5½" $57.50

Pipe, Dunhill Bruyere Billard, sterling band $145.00

Pipe, Dunhill Chestnut Briar 401...Made in England 28, NMIB $200.00

Pipe, Dunhill Red Bark 41QF, ca 1976, 5⅝", MIB $275.00

Pipe, Dunhill Shell Briar Billard, Made in England 7, 5³⁄₁₆", VG $100.00

Pipe, E Andrew, sandblast finish, unmarked silver band, 1984, 5⅝" $65.00

Pipe, Kriswill Bernadott Hand Made Denmark R, 2" bowl, 5¾".. $70.00

Pipe, sultan figural, meerschaum w/carved briar wood inlaid face, cherry wood stem, carved horn ferrule, 16" $215.00

Silk, Wisconsin, baseball pitcher, early 1900s, 7x5" $40.00

Smoking stand, Art Deco chrome w/marble insert, w/light (rewired), Metalcraft Mfg, 1930s-40s, 26x12" dia $165.00

Smoking stand, cast-iron dragon ashtray w/shelf for matches or lighter, attributed to Scroll Art Metal Mfg, 28x8" dia .. $115.00

Smoking stand, Cushman Smoker, dark hardwood w/copper-lined humidor, original ashtray & cigarette holders, 29" $125.00

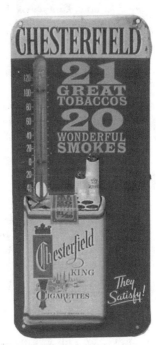

Thermometer, Chesterfield, litho tin, 13½", VG, $150.00. (Photo courtesy LiveAuctioneers.com/Richard Opfer Auctioneering Inc.)

Tin, Admiral Rough Cut, admiral & ship in reserve on black w/gold lettering, 6x4¾", VG+ $85.00

Tin, Buckingham Bright Cut Plug Smoking Tobacco, blossoms, John J Bagley & Co, 4¼x3x1", M (sealed) $130.00

Tin, Bull Dog Smoking Deluxe Mild & Sweet, Won't Bite, dog & 2 pups, cardboard, Lovell & Buffington, 4½x3x1" $245.00

Tin, Chew American Eagle Tobacco, Detroit MI, yellow letters on green, sample size, ½x2½x1½" $82.50

Tin, Hickory Extremely Mild Pipe Mixture on red, John Middleton, Phila PA, 4½x3½" $55.00

Tin, May Queen, draped nude in outdoor scene, JG Flint Jr, Milwaukee WI, sample size, ½x3¾x2¼", VG $78.00

Tin, Model Extra Quality Smoking..., man w/oversize mustache & pipe in reserve on red, marked Complimentary, 4¼".. $100.00

Tin, Union Commander Cut Plug Full Weight, A Cool Sweet Smoke, bail handle, 7x4¼", VG $130.00

Tin, Union Leader, Uncle Sam in reserve on red, Made by P Lorillard Co, 4½x3½x1" $132.00

Tools and Farm Implements

Mass-produced tools have been with us for many years. Some have found their way to the secondary market, as increasing demand for quality tools are a favorite among bargain hunters. Factors important in evaluating tools are scarcity, usefulness, portability, age, and condition. Modern manufactured tools found with the manufacturer's mark are generally worth more than unmarked items. Look for items marked Stanley, Lufkin, Defiance, or Craftsman to name a few.

Country living in the nineteenth century required specialized tools. Though they may seem primitive today, they're appreciated for the inginuity of those early farmers who saw a need and conceived these implements to make their work easier.

Auger, hollow; AA Wood & Sons, fully adjustable, black enameling, ¼-1¼" dia, NM **$150.00**

Auger, hollow; James Swan Co, cylindrical, collar adjustment at base, ¼-1¼" dia, VG **$150.00**

Bit, screwdriver; Stanley #26, Made in USA, ⁵⁄₁₆", M **$10.00**

Brace, Hibbard, Spencer & Bartlet #1908 OVB, cocobolo handle & pad, Universal Jaws, 10" sweep, NM **$65.00**

Brace, Stanley #813G-12, bronze-bushed ball-bearing head, hardwood handle, ca 1940s, 12", EX+ **$65.00**

Brace, Stanley #923-10, cocobolo handle & pad, Universal jaws, Made in USA logo, 10" sweep, VG **$35.00**

Chisel, butt; Keen Kutter, ¼" socket, 3½" blade, replaced handle, 9½", G **$20.00**

Chisel, butt; Stanley #161, 1½" bevel edge, tanged type w/handle & brass ferrule, marked shank, EX **$65.00**

Chisel, flooring; Stanley #210, 2¾" blade, NM **$35.00**

Chisel, socket firmer; Zenith, ¼" bevel-edge, 6" blade, 12½", EX **$35.00**

Chisel, ¾-corner; Lakeside, 8" blade, 15", G **$50.00**

Draw knife, AJ Wilkinson, fruitwood folding handles, Patented July 16 1895 on blade, 8", EX+ **$115.00**

Draw knife, Warranted, Made in USA, beech handles, 6", VG **$42.50**

Drill, breast; Millers Falls #120B, 3-jaw chuck holds up to ½" dia bits, rosewood handles, 2-speed, EX+ **$50.00**

Drill, hand; Keen Kutter, Goodell Pratt Pat Aug 13 1895, 3-jaw chuck, iron 10" frame, brass handle, VG **$50.00**

Drill, hand; Millers Falls, from $15.00 to $20.00.

Drill, hand; North Bros Yankee #1435A, 2-speed, 3-jaw chuck, 1940s, 11", VG **$45.00**

Drill, push; Stanley North Bros Yankee #45, Bakelite handle, nickel plated, NMIB **$50.00**

Gauge, butt; Stearns #85, nickel-plated cast iron, EX **$30.00**

Hammer, claw; Millers Falls #1418, original handle, 7-oz, VG. **$36.00**

Hammer, tack; Capewell, Patented Nov 25 1873, spring-loaded puller, VG **$70.00**

Holder, extension bit; Millers Falls #35, 24", NMIB **$30.00**

Jig, doweling; Stanley #59, set of 6 guides, bit depth stop, NMIB **$65.00**

Jointer, saw; Atkins, levels teeth on rip & crosscut handsaws, VG **$35.00**

Level, Goodell Pratt, sq ends, NM japanning, 6", VG **$120.00**

Level, machinist's; CF Richardson, cast iron, 6", VG **$70.00**

Nippers, Sargent & Co, Bernard's Patent, 6", NM **$25.00**

Plane, jack; Stanley #5, sweetheart cutter, rosewood handle, Made in Canada, NM japanning, EX+ **$85.00**

Plane, jointer; Stanley #7, notched rectangle logo, cocobolo handle, EX japanning **$155.00**

Plane, low-angle block; Millers Falls #57, regular block plane cap, VG japanning, VG+ **$65.00**

Plane, smooth; Stanley #2, notched rectangle logo, nickel-plated cap, rosewood tall knob & handle, EX+ **$375.00**

Plane, smooth; Stanley #4, (18)92 Patent date on cutter, (19) 02 Patent date in bed, rosewood handle, VG **$70.00**

Plane, veneer scraper; Stanley #12, cocobolo handle, mark on cutter, VG **$115.00**

Plumb bob, K&E #6482, long neck, 8-oz, VG **$40.00**

Plumb bob, Warner Tools, nickel plated, w/reel, NM **$70.00**

Pointer, dowel; Stearns #01 (unmarked), fluted pattern on sides, black enameling, points up to ¾", 2½", NM **$40.00**

Pointer, spoke; Millers Falls, depth stop held by thumb screw, points up to 1⅞" dia, VG **$50.00**

Protractor head, LS Starret #12, for combo square, black finish, NM **$18.00**

Rule, brick mason's; Stanley #167, zigzag, 72", EX **$18.00**

Rule, Rabone #1167, boxwood, 4-fold w/round joint, 24", MIB..**$45.00**

Saw, back; Henry Disston & Sons #68, 15 teeth per inch, 8", VG **$55.00**

Saw, back; Richardson, 14 teeth per inch crosscut, applewood handle, 10", VG **$30.00**

Saw, crosscut; Atkins #59, 8 teeth per inch, Special Steel blade, hardwood handle, 26", G **$40.00**

Saw, crosscut; Henry Disston & Sons D-23, 11 teeth per inch, applewood handle w/wheat carving, 1940s, 26", VG....**$65.00**

Saw, crosscut; Spearior, Spear & Jackson Sheffield, 8 teeth per inch, 26", VG **$45.00**

Saw, pruning; Atkins No 13, fruitwood handle, 14" curved blade, VG **$25.00**

Saw vise, Stearns #3, cam-lock 9½" jaws, VG **$40.00**

Scorp, W Bradley, 4½" blade, shallow sweep, 14½", VG......**$65.00**

Screwdriver, offset ratchet; Stanley Yankee #3400, right- or left-handed action, 4", EX+ **$15.00**

Spoke shave, AG Batchelder, cast steel, wood handles w/brass ferrules, VG **$35.00**

Spoke shave, low angle; Stearns, cutter screwed to back, VG. **$70.00**

Spoke shave, Stanley #54, adustable throat, ca 1910, flat bottom, VG **$40.00**

Square, combo; Standard Tool Co, filigreed center head, off-set groove, 12", VG **$45.00**

Square, try & miter; Stanley #1, sweetheart mark on blade, nickel plated, 6", VG **$25.00**

Square, try; Henry Disston & Sons, English & metric graduations, brass-plated roswood handle, VG **$50.00**

Washer cutter, Goodell Pratt #41, EXIB **$30.00**

Wrench, buggy; Diamond Wrench Co, Pat Nov 2 80, minor pitting, 12", G **$35.00**

Wrench, Bullard #0, Pat'd Oct 27 03, nickel plated, 5½", EX **$95.00**

Wrench, Larcoloy Universal, cam-action w/spring, nickel plated, 6", VG+ **$60.00**

Wrench, monkey; Tower & Lyon GEM, 4½", VG **$50.00**

Wrench, pipe; Eaton, Cole & Burnham, Franklin Patent July 6 20 1886, VG **$80.00**

Wrench, pipe; Trojan Wrench, LA Cal, US Pat NO 1968783, quick-adjust, VG **$60.00**

Wrench, spoke; Sevens NY Perfect, 3¾", VG **$30.00**

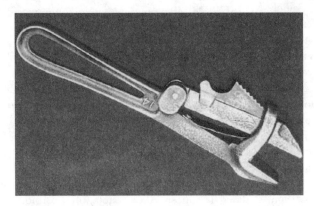

Wrench, Vandegrift #14, 9½" long, $100.00.

Toothbrush Holders

Novelty toothbrush holders have been modeled as animals of all types, in human forms, and in the likenesses of many storybook personalities. Today all are very collectible, especially those representing popular Disney characters. Most of these are made of bisque and are decorated over the glaze. Condition of the paint is an important consideration when trying to arrive at an evaluation.

Bear holds 2 brushes in arms, gray airbrushing, hollow feet, ceramic, 5½" **$100.00**

Bear in checked shirt, holder at shoulder, tray at feet, ceramic, Gold Castle Made in Japan, 5½x3" **$135.00**

Black chef holding bananas & pineapple, tray at feet, ceramic, Made in Japan, 4½x3x2", NM **$95.00**

Bonzo-type dog, holder at arm, tray at feet, ceramic, Japan . **$65.00**

Bonzo-type dog laughing, yellow, orange & black, 3 openings, ceramic, Gold Castle, Made in Japan **$68.00**

Cat, blue lustre, opening at tail, ceramic, Made in Japan, 2¾x4" ... **$25.00**

Clown in red holding black mask, tray at feet, ceramic, Gold Castle **$85.00**

Clown juggling, 3 openings, tray at feet, ceramic, Japan **$95.00**

Clown playing mandolin, openings at hip pocket, lg feet form tray, ceramic, Japan **$125.00**

Cowboy & cactus, openings at hat & lg holsters, tray at feet, ceramic, Made in Japan, 5½" **$155.00**

Cowboy w/gun holster (holds brushes), ceramic, 5⅛" **$225.00**

Dog yawning, yellow & red, ceramic, 2¾" **$25.00**

Donkey, 2 holes, tray at feet, ceramic, Japan, 1940s-50s **$50.00**

Dopey (dwarf) stands & smiles, opening at back, ceramic, Genuine Walt Disney Copyright Foreign, 4" **$250.00**

Duck stands before tray w/3 tubes, ceramic, Made in Japan N&C, 6½x2¾" **$75.00**

Dutch boy stands on washtub to kiss girl, ceramic, Gold Castle Made in Japan, 6¼" **$140.00**

Dutch boy w/hole at ea pocket, ceramic, Weil Ware, 1940s, 6½" **$45.00**

Dutch boy w/openings at pants' pockets, opening in hat, tray at feet, 5" **$75.00**

Girl holding doll, 1920s-style hair & costume, ceramic, Made in Japan **$100.00**

Jockey on horse, multicolor lustre, holder at horse's tail, ceramic, Japan, 1950s **$72.50**

Man in turban seated on base, sq hole in turban, ceramic, Made in Japan, 1930s **$50.00**

Mickey & Minnie Mouse, pie-eyed, painted bisque, #335, C Walt Disney, Made in Japan, 1930s, 3½x3⅞" **$125.00**

Old King Cole, feet form tray, ceramic, Made in Japan, 5¼".. **$110.00**

Peter Pumkin Eater, wife in pumpkin shell, 2 openings, tray at feet, ceramic, Japan, 4⅞x2⅞" **$100.00**

Peter Rabbit, fully dressed, openings at arms, ceramic, Japan, from $85 to **$100.00**

Pinocchio w/donkey's ears, Figaro (cat) at his feet, sq hole at right hand, ceramic, 1940s, 5¼x4" **$160.00**

Pirate w/skull & crossbones on hat, openings at arms & into boots, tray at feet, ceramic, Japan, 5¼x2¼" **$175.00**

Skippy (titled base), right arm jointed, painted bisque, Copyright Percy L Crosby, 1930s, 6" **$65.00**

Sleepy and Dopey, copyright Disney, 1938, some paint wear, $210.00. (Photo courtesy LiveAuctioneers.com/Morphy Auctions)

Soldier boy w/sash, arms hold brushes, tray at feet, ceramic, Souvenir of Richmond VA, Made in Japan, 6", from $130 to ... **$165.00**

Three Bears, brown & white, ceramic, Imperial China Japan, 4x4½" **$130.00**

Three Pigs w/bricks, titled base, painted bisque, Disney, 1930s .. **$55.00**

Toy soldier, holder on left side, tray at feet, ceramic, Made in Japan, 6¾" **$65.00**

Toys

Toy collecting has long been an area of very strong activity, but over the past decade it has literally exploded. Many of the larger auction galleries have cataloged toy auctions, and it isn't uncommon for scarce nineteenth-century toys in good condition go for $5,000.00 to $10,000.00 and up. Toy shows are popular, and there are clubs, newsletters, and magazines that cater only to the needs and wants of toy collectors. Though once buyers ignored toys less than 30 years old, in more recent years, even some toys from the '80s are sought after.

Condition has more bearing on the value of a toy than any other factor. A used toy in good condition with no major flaws will still be worth only about half (in some cases much less) as much as one in mint (like new) condition. Those mint and in their original boxes will be worth considerably more than the same toy without its box.

There are many good toy guides on the market today including: *Schroeder's Collectible Toys, Antique to Modern; Elmer's Price Guide to Toys* by Elmer Duellman; *Occupied Japan Toys With Prices* by David C. Gould and Donna Crevar-Donaldson; and *Collector's Toy Yearbook* by David Longest. More books are listed in the subcategory narratives that follow.

See also Advertising Character Collectibles; Breyer Horses; Bubble Bath Containers; Character Collectibles; Disney Collectibles; Dolls; Fisher-Price; Halloween; Hartland Plastics Inc.; Model Kits; Paper Dolls; Games; Puzzles; Star Wars; Steiff Animals.

Action Figures and Accessories

Back in 1964, Barbie dolls were taking the feminine side of the toy market by storm. Hasbro took a risky step in an attempt to capture the interest of the male segment of the population. Their answer to the Barbie craze was GI Joe. Since no self-respecting boy would admit to playing with dolls, Hasbro called their boy dolls 'action figures,' and to the surprise of many, they were phenomenally successful. Today action figures generate just as much enthusiasm among toy collectors as they ever did among little boys.

Action figures are simply dolls with poseable bodies. Some — the original GI Joes, for instance, were 12" tall, while others were 6" to 9" in height. In recent years, the 3¾" figure has been favored. GI Joe was introduced in the 3¾" size in the '80s and proved to be unprecedented in action figure sales. (See also GI Joe.)

In addition to the figures themselves, each company added a full line of accessories such as clothing, vehicles, play sets, and weapons — all are avidly collected. Be aware of condition! Original packaging is extremely important. In fact, when it comes to the recent issues, loose, played-with examples are seldom worth more than a few dollars.

Best of the West, figure, Chief Cherokee, Marx, MIB, from $175.00 to $215.00.

A-Team, accessory, Command Chopper & Enforcer Van, MIP, from $20 to **$25.00**

A-Team, accessory, Interceptor Jet Bomber (w/Murdock figure), Galoob, MIP, from $50 to **$55.00**

A-Team, accessory, Patrol Boat (w/Hannibal figure), Galoob, MIB, from $25 to **$30.00**

A-Team, figure, Mr T, talking, Galoob, 12", from $65 to **$75.00**

A-Team, figure, Soldiers of Fortune, any character, Galoob, 6½", MOC, ea from $28 to **$38.00**

Action Jackson, accessory, Scramble Cycle, Mego, MIB **$45.00**

Action Jackson, figure, any (except black figure), Mego, MIB, ea from $25 to **$30.00**

Action Jackson, outfit, any, Mego, MIP, ea from $8 to........**$12.00**

Aliens, accessory, Evac Fighter or Hovertread, Kenner, MIP, from $15 to **$20.00**

Aliens, figure, Series 1, Queen Alien, Ripley or Scorpion Alien, Kenner, MOC, ea from $15 to **$20.00**

Aliens, figure set, Series 2, Alien vs Predator, Kenner, MOC, from $28 to **$32.00**

American West, figure, Davy Crockett, Mego, MOC, from $125 to **$135.00**

American West, figure, Sitting Bull, Wild Bill Hickok or Wyatt Earp, MIB, ea from $70 to...**$80.00**

ANTZ, figure, any, Playmates, 1998, MOC, ea from $3 to...**$5.00**

Avengers, figure gift sets, Ant-Man/Giant Man, Hulk, Iron Man, The Wasp or Toy Biz, MOC, ea from $18 to **$22.00**

Banana Splits, figure, any, Sutton, 1970s, MIP, ea from $120 to **$130.00**

Batman (Animated), accessory, Aero Boat, BATV Vehicle, Batcycle or Bat-Signal Jet, Kenner, 1992-95, MIP, ea from $18 to **$32.00**

Batman (Animated), accessory, Batmobile, Kenner, MIP, from $50 to **$60.00**

Batman (Animated), accessory, Robin's Dragster, Kenner, MIP, from $200 to **$230.00**

Batman (Animated), figure, Catwoman, Radar Scope Batman or Rapid Attack Batman, Kenner, MOC, ea from $22 to .**$26.00**

Batman (Animated), figure, Penguin, Kenner, MOC, from $45 to.. **$50.00**

Batman (Crime Squad), accessory, Attack Jet, Kenner, MOC, from $18 to **$22.00**

Batman (Dark Knight), accessory, Batcycle, Kenner, MIP, ea from $35 to **$45.00**

Batman (Dark Knight), accessory, Bola Bullet, Kenner, MIP, from $30 ....**$40.00**

Batman (Dark Knight), figure, Knockout Joker, Kenner, MOC, from $45 to **$55.00**

Batman & Robin, accessory, Leeglow Bathammer, Kenner, MIP, from $45 to **$55.00**

Batman & Robin, figure, Batgirl, Kenner, 5", MIP, from $4 to ...**$6.00**

Batman & Robin, figure, Batman (Ice Blade & Ring), Kenner, 5", MIB, from $6 to...**$10.00**

Batman Forever, figure, Bruce Wayne or The Riddler, Kenner, MOC, ea from $40 to **$45.00**

Battlestar Galactica, accessory, Colonial Steller Probe, Colonial Viper or Cylon Raider, Mattel, MIB, ea from $65 to **$75.00**

Battlestar Galactica, figure, 1st series, Commander Adama or Cylon Centurian, Mattel, 3¾", ea from $38 to **$42.00**

Best of the West, accessory, Covered Wagon, Marx, MIB, from $200 to **$235.00**

Best of the West, figure, Bill Buck, Marx, 1967, NMIB (w/some or all accessories), from $300 to **$350.00**

Best of the West, figure, Johnny West, Marx, 1965, EX (w/some or all accessories), from $25 to **$50.00**

Black Hole, figure, Maximillian, Mego, 3¾", MOC, from $70 to..**$80.00**

Black Hole, figure, Sentry Robot, Mego, 3¾", MOC, from $70 to **$80.00**

Captain Action, accessory, Directional Communicator, Ideal, MIB, from $275 to **$325.00**

Captain Action, accessory, Survival Kit, Ideal, MIB, from $225 to..**$250.00**

Captain Action, figure, Aquaman, Ideal, NM, from $150 to.. **$200.00**

Captain Action, figure, Captain Action, Ideal, NM (photo box), from $275 to **$300.00**

Captain Action, outfit, Lone Ranger, Ideal, NM, from $175 to ..**$225.00**

Charlie's Angels (TV Series), accessory, Adventure Van, Hasbro, MIB, from $70 to **$80.00**

Clash of the Titans, figure, Kraken, Mattel, rare, MOC, from $250 to **$275.00**

Clash of the Titans, figure, Thallo, Mattel, MOC, from $40 to..**$45.00**

Clash of the Titans, horse & figure set, Pegasus & Perseus, Mattel, MIB, from $75 to **$100.00**

Comic Action Heroes, accessory, Exploding Bridge w/Batmobile, Mego, MIP, from $175 to **$225.00**

Comic Action Heroes, figure, Penguin, Shazam or Spider-Man, Mego, MOC, ea from $70 to **$80.00**

Commando (Schwarzenegger), figure, Matrix, Diamond Toymakers, 18", NM to M, from $65 to **$75.00**

Dukes of Hazzard, accessory, Cadillac w/Boss Hogg or Police Car w/Sheriff Rosco figure, 3¾", MIP, ea from $75 to **$85.00**

Dukes of Hazzard, figure, Bo or Luke, Mego, 1981-82, 3¾", MOC, ea from $18 to **$22.00**

Dukes of Hazzard, figure, Coy (Bo) or Vance (Luke), Mego, 8", MOC, ea from $48 to **$52.00**

Flash Gordon, figure, Dale Arden, Mego, MOC, from $80 to **$90.00**

Flash Gordon, figure, Flash Gordon, Mego, MOC, from $100 to..**$115.00**

Happy Days, figure, any, Mego, MOC, ea from $75 to.......**$85.00**

Indiana Jones in Raiders of the Lost Ark, accessory, Map Room, Kenner, MIB, from $75 to...**$85.00**

Indiana Jones in Raiders of the Lost Ark, accessory, Well of the Souls Action Playset, MIB (sealed), from $100 to...............**$125.00**

Indiana Jones in Raiders of the Lost Ark, figure, Belloq (Ceremonial Robe), MOC from $725 to **$750.00**

Inspector Gadget, figure, Galoob, 1983, 11", MIB, from $75 to.**$100.00**

James Bond (Moonraker), figure, Jaws, Mego, 12", MIB, from $450 to..**$475.00**

Johnny Apollo (Astronaut), figure, Johnny Apollo, Marx, MIB, $150 to..**$175.00**

Legend of the Lone Ranger, horse, Scout, Gabriel, MOC, from $18 to **$22.00**

Lone Ranger Rides Again, accessory, Blizzard Adventure, Gabriel, MIB, from $25 to **$30.00**

Lord of the Rings, figure, any, Knickerbocker, 1979, MIP, from $90 to **$100.00**

Love Boat, figure, any, Mego, 1982, 4", MOC, ea from $18 to..**$22.00**

M*A*S*H, accessory, Jeep (w/Hawkeye figure), Tri-Star, MIB, from $35 to **$40.00**

M*A*S*H, figure, Klinger (in dress), Tri-Star, MOC, from $30 to **$35.00**

Mad Monster Series, figure, Horrible Mummy, Mego, 1974, 8", MIB, from $80 to..**$100.00**

Major Matt Mason, accessory, Astro Trac, Mattel, MIB, from $100 to..**$125.00**

Major Matt Mason, figure, Callisto, Mattel, MOC, from $225 to..**$250.00**

Man From UNCLE, figure, Illya Kuryakin or Napoleon Solo, Gilbert, M, ea from $175 to **$20.00**

Marvel Super Heroes, figure, Captain America, Toy Biz, MOC, from $18 to..**$22.00**

Marvel Super Heroes, figure, Dr Doom or Dr Octopus, Toy Biz, MOC, ea from $24 to **$28.00**

Marvel Super Heroes (Secret Wars), figure, Spider-Man (red & blue outfit), Mattel, MOC, from $28 to **$32.00**

Marvel Super Heroes (Talking), figure, any, Toy Biz, MIP, ea from $20 to..**$25.00**

Masters of the Universe, accessory, Mantisaur, Mattel, MIP, from $24 to..**$28.00**

Masters of the Universe, accessory, Screech, Mattel, MIP, from $35 to **$45.00**

Masters of the Universe, figure, Battle Armor Skeletor, Mattel, MOC, ea from $38 to **$42.00**

Masters of the Universe, figure, Blade, Mattel, MOC, from $65 to **$75.00**

Masters of the Universe, figure, Extender, Mattel, MOC, from $40 to **$50.00**

Masters of the Universe, figure, King Randor, Mattel, MOC, from $80 to..**$85.00**

Masters of the Universe, figure, Man-E-Faces, Mattel, MOC, from $60 to..**$70.00**

Masters of the Universe, figure, Prince Adam, Mattel, MOC, from $60 to..**$70.00**

Masters of the Universe, figure, Skeletor, Mattel, MOC, from $175 to **$200.00**

Masters of the Universe, figure, Teela, Mattel, MOC, from $110 to **$120.00**

Micronauts, accessory, Galatic Command Center, MIP, from $40 to **$50.00**

Micronauts, accessory, Mobile Exploration Lab, Mego, MIP, from $30 to **$40.00**

Micronauts, figure, Antron, Mego, MIP, from $90 to........**$100.00**

Micronauts, figure, Phobos Robot, Mego, MIP, from $20 to...**$30.00**

One Million BC, creature, Dimetrodon, Mego, MIB, from $200 to **$225.00**

Planet of the Apes, accessory, Battering Ram, Jail or Dr Zaius' Throne, Mego, 1970s, MIB, ea from $35 to.................**$45.00**

Planet of the Apes, figure, Astronaut, any, Mego, 1970s, 8", MIB, from $225 to **$275.00**

Planet of the Apes, figure, Cornelius, Dr Zaius, Galen or Zira, 1970s, 8", MOC, from $120 to..**$130.00**

Pocket Super Heroes, figure, Batman, Mego, MOC (red card), from $65 to $75.00

Pocket Super Heroes, figure, Incredible Hulk, Mego, MOC (white card), from $38 to.......................................$42.00

Pocket Super Heroes, figure, Wonder Woman, Mego, MOC (white card), from $70 to.......................................$80.00

Rambo, accessory, Defender 6x6 Assault Vehicle, Coleco, MIB, from $28 to $32.00

Rambo, accessory, Skywolf Assault Jet, Coleco, MIB, from $25 to.. $30.00

Rambo, figure, KAT, Mad Dog, Nomad, Rambo or Rambo w/Fire Power, Coleco, MOC, ea from $8 to $15.00

Robin Hood Prince of Thieves, accessory, Sherwood Forest Playset, Kenner, 1991, MIP, from $55 to..................................$65.00

Robin Hood Prince of Thieves, figure, Robin Hood w/Long Bow, Kenner, 1991, MOC, from $12 to $18.00

Robotech, accessory, Veritech Hover Tank or Zentraedi Officer's Battle Pod, Matchbox, MIB, ea from $30 to.................$45.00

Robotech, figure, any, Matchbox, 6", MOC, ea from $18 to . $22.00

Robotech, figure, Corg, Lunk, Max Sterling, Miriya (red) or Rick Hunter, Matchbox, 3¾", MOC, ea from $20 to..........$25.00

She-Ra Princess of Power, accessory, Crystal Castle or Crystal Falls, Mattel, 1984-86, MIP, ea from $55 to.........................$65.00

She-Ra Princess of Power, figure, any creature, Mattel, 1984-86, MIP, ea from $35 to..$45.00

She-Ra Princess of Power, figure, Netossa, Mattel, 1984-86, MOC, from $20 to $30.00

Six Million Dollar Man, accessory, Bionic Transport & Repair Station, Kenner, MIB, from $40 to.............................$50.00

Six Million Dollar Man, figure, Bionic Bigfoot, Kenner, MIB, from $175 to $200.00

Six Million Dollar Man, figure, Steve Austin, Kenner, MIB, from $100 to $125.00

Starsky & Hutch, figure, any, Mego, MOC, from $45.00 to $55.00.

Super Heroes, figure, Batman (painted cowl), Mego, 8", MIB or MOC, from $150 to..$175.00

Super Heroes, figure, Captain America, Mego, 8", MIB, from $400 to $425.00

Super Heroes, figure, Green Arrow, Mego, 8", MIB, from $400.00 to $425.00.

Super Powers, figure, Dr Fate, Kenner, MOC, from $55 to . $65.00

Super Powers, figure, Mantis, Kenner, MOC, from $20 to .. $30.00

Teen Titans, figure, Wondergirl, Mego, MOC, from $500 to. $525.00

Welcome Back Kotter, figure, Epstein, Horshack, Mr Kotter or Washington, Mattel, 1976, 9", MOC, ea from $45 to.. $55.00

WWF, figure, Big John Studd, white skin, LJN, MOC, from $175 to $20.00

WWF, figure, Vince McMann, LJN, Series 5, MOC, from $50 to... $60.00

Zorro (Cartoon Series), figure, Zorro or Amigo, Gabriel, MOC, ea from $25 to $35.00

Battery-Operated Toys

It is estimated that approximately 95% of the battery-operated toys that were so popular from the '40s through the '60s came from Japan. (The remaining 5% were made in the United States.) To market these toys in America, many distributorships were organized. Some of the largest were Cragstan, Linemar, and Rosko. But even American toy makers such as Marx, Ideal, Hubley, and Daisy sold them under their own names, so the trademarks you'll find on Japanese battery-operated toys are not necessarily that of the manufacturer, and it's sometimes just about impossible to determine the specific company that actually did make them. After peaking in the '60s, the Japanese toy industry began a decline, bowing out to competition from the cheaper diecast and plastic toy makers.

Remember that it is rare to find one of these complex toys that has survived in good, collectible condition. Batteries caused corrosion, lubricants dried out, cycles were interrupted and mechanisms ruined, rubber hoses and bellows aged and cracked, so the mortality rate was extremely high. A toy rated good, that is showing signs of wear but well taken care of, is generally worth about half as much as the same toy in mint (like new) condition. Besides condition, battery-operated toys are rated on scarcity, desirability, and the number of 'actions' they perform. A 'major' toy is one that has three or more actions, while one that has only one or two is considered 'minor.' The latter, of course, are worth much less.

Air Control Tower (w/Airplane & Helicopter), Bandai, 1960s, 10½", EXIB..**$250.00**
Animated Squirrel, S&E, 1950s, 9", MIB.....................**$150.00**
Antique Fire Car, TN, 1950s, 10", EXIB....................**$175.00**

Arthur A-Go-Go, Alps, 1960s, 10", NMIB, $450.00. (Photo courtesy Don Hultzman)

Astro Dog, Y, 1960s, remote-controlled, 11", EXIB..........**$125.00**
Automatic Train Station & Rubber Track, Tomiyama/Yonezawa, 8½" L, NMIB...**$190.00**
B-Z Rabbit, MT, 1950s, 7" L, EX **$100.00**
Baby Bertha the Watering Elephant, Mego, 1960s, 9" L, MIB..**$475.00**
Baggage Porter, Cragstan, plush dog pulling 2-wheeled stake cart, 12", EXIB...**$125.00**
Balloon Blowing Monkey w/Lighted Eyes, Alps, 1950s, plush w/ cloth overalls, 12", EXIB..**$130.00**
Barky Puppy, Alps, plush, remote-controlled, 9", EXIB.......**$50.00**
Batman & Robin Batcycle, Hong Kong, NMIB **$615.00**
Bear Target Game, MT, 1950s, tin, 9", NMIB **$300.00**
Beauty Parlor, S&E, 1950s, 9½", EX...............................**$525.00**
Big Dipper, Technofix, 1960s, 3 cars on track, 21" L, EX..**$150.00**
Blinky the Clown, Amico Toy/Japan, remote-controlled, EX+IB **$250.00**
Blushing Frankenstein, Nomura, tin & vinyl, 13", NMIB.**$175.00**
Bongo Monkey (w/Bongo Drums & Lighted Eyes), plastic hat, Alps, 1960s, 10", EXIB...**$175.00**
Bruno Accordion Bear, Y, remote-controlled, 1950s, 10", EXIB **$350.00**
Bubble Blowing Monkey, Alps, 1950s, 11", EXIB **$125.00**
Bubble Blowing Popeye, Linemar, 1950s, 12", EXIB.....**$1,400.00**
Bumper Automatic Control Bus, Bandai, 15", EXIB **$225.00**
Bunny the Magician, plush, Alps, 1950s, 14", VG+IB.......**$325.00**
Busy Housekeeper (Rabbit or Bear), pushing sweeper, plush w/cloth dress, Alps, 1950s, 10", EXIB **$200.00**
Cappy the Happy Baggage Porter, Alps, 1960s, 12", MIB .**$275.00**
Captain Hook, Marusan, 1950s, rare, 11", EX, minimum value **$750.00**

Charlie the Funny Clown, clown in cloth outfit on circus car, 1960s, 10" L, EXIB..**$220.00**
Chee Chee Chihauhua, Mego, 1960s, 8", EX...................**$50.00**
Chippy the Chipmunk, Alps, 1950s, 12", MIB **$125.00**
Circus Queen (Seal), Kosuge, 1950s, rare, 11", MIB **$375.00**
Clown & Lion, clown spins up & down pole as lion roars, MT, 1960s, tin base 13", NMIB...**$325.00**
Comic Choo Choo, Cragstan, 1960s, 10", EX **$65.00**
Coney Island Rocket Ride, Remco, 1950s, 14", EXIB.......**$950.00**
Cragstan Melody Band (Mambo the Jolly Drumming Elephant), 9", EXIB...**$200.00**
Cragstan Playboy, 1960s, 13", EXIB................................**$125.00**
Crowing Rooster, white, yellow & orange, plush, 1950s, 9", EXIB..**$75.00**
Dancing Merry Chimp, Kuramochi, 1960s, 11", NM.......**$150.00**
Dashee the Derby Hat Dachshund, plush w/plastic hat, remote-controlled, Mego, 1970s, MIB....................................**$80.00**
Dilly Dalmatian, plush, remote-controlled, 1950s, 8", VGIB ...**$100.00**
Disney Piston Race Car, Mickey driver, Masudaya, 9", NMIB..**$200.00**
Drinking Licking Cat, tin & plush, TN, 1950s, NMIB.....**$250.00**
Dune Buggy (w/Surf Board), w/driver, TPS, 10", EXIB **$100.00**
Expert Motor Cyclist, tin, MT, 1950s, 12", EX **$375.00**
FBI Godfather Car, Bandai, 1970s, 10", MIB...................**$125.00**
Fighting Bull, Alps, 1950s, 15", MIB **$175.00**
Fire Tricycle, w/driver, tin, TN, 10", EXIB......................**$650.00**
Flexi the Pocket Monkey, Alps, 1960s, 12", MIB.............**$200.00**
Fred Flintstone's Bedrock Band, Alps, 1960s, 10", VGIB...**$350.00**
French Cat, Alps, 1950s, 10" L, MIB **$125.00**
Gino Neapolitan Balloon Blower, Rosko, 1960s, 11", EX+IB..**$175.00**
Good Time Charlie, MT, 1960s, 13", EXIB **$150.00**
Gorilla, white or brown plush, remote-contolled, TN, 1950s, 10", EXIB, ea **$300.00**
Grasshopper, MT, 1950s, 6", M......................................**$350.00**
Hamburger Chef, K, 1960s, 8", MIB **$250.00**
Happy Band Trio, MT, 1970s, 11", NMIB.......................**$500.00**
Happy Naughty Chimp, Daishin, 1960s, 10", EXIB **$100.00**
Happy Singing Bird, MT, 1950s, 3" L, M **$75.00**
Hoopy the Fishing Duck, Alps, 1950s, 10", NMIB...........**$375.00**
Hungry Baby Bear, plush mamma & baby, Y, 1950s, 9", EXIB ..**$150.00**
Ice Cream Baby Bear, MT, 1950s, rare, 10", NM **$475.00**
Johnny Speed Mobile, Remco, 1960s, 15", MIB **$175.00**
Journey Pup, S&E, 1950s, 8" L, M....................................**$50.00**
Jumping Rabbit (Light-Up Eyes), Japan, 1950s, 10", NMIB..**$95.00**
Jungle Trio, Linemar, 8", NMIB **$750.00**
Knight in Armor Target Game, 1950s, 12" figure, NMIB ..**$500.00**
Lady Pup Tending Her Garden, cloth outfit, Cragstan, 1950s, 9", EXIB...**$250.00**
Linemar Music Hall, 6", EXIB..**$150.00**
Little Poochie in Coffee Cup, Alps, 1960s, 9", M...............**$75.00**
Lucky Cement Mixer Truck, MT, 1960s, 12", M **$125.00**
Man From UNCLE Headquarters Transmitter, NMIB......**$200.00**
Marching Bear, drums & cymbals, plush, 1960s, 10", EXIB..**$125.00**
Marvelous Locomotive, TN, 1950s, 10", M **$50.00**
Mew-Mew the Walking Cat, remote-controlled, plush, MT, 1950s, 7", VGIB **$85.00**
Mickey Mouse Locomotive, MT, 1960s, 9", NM **$175.00**
Mickey the Magician, Linemar, 1960s, 10", VG...............**$650.00**

Miss Friday the Typist, TN, 1950s, 8", EXIB **$225.00**

Monkee Mobile, ASC, 1960s, 12", EXIB **$575.00**

Mother Goose, plush, Cragstan, 10", VGIB........................ **$75.00**

Mr Fox the Magician (w/The Magical Disappearing Rabbit), Y, 1960s, 9", NM **$325.00**

Musical Ice Cream Truck, Bandai, 1960s, 11", NM.......... **$150.00**

Musical Marching Bear, Alps, 1950s, 11", EXIB, $400.00.

(Photo courtesy Don Hultzman)

Mystery Plane, TN, 1950s, 10", EXIB.............................. **$250.00**

NBC Television/RCA Victor Truck, Linemar, 9", VG+...... **$500.00**

Overland Stage Coach, MT, 1950s, 15", EXIB **$175.00**

Peppy Puppy w/Bone, Y, 1950s, 7", M **$75.00**

Perky Pup, remote-controlled, plush, 1960s, 8½", MIB....... **$75.00**

Pianist (Jolly Pianist), plush dog at tin piano, Marusan, 1950s, 8½", NMIB.. **$200.00**

Piggy Cook, Y, 1950s, 10", EXIB **$175.00**

Pinocchio Playing Xylophone, Rosco, 9½", EXIB............. **$225.00**

Pistol Pete, Marusan, 1950s, 10", EXIB........................... **$350.00**

Pluto, remote-controlled, plush, Linemar, 1960s, 10", EXIB.. **$65.00**

Pluto Lantern, tin figure w/glass midsection, Linemar, 7", EX+IB **$250.00**

Popcorn Eating Bear, MT, 1950s, EX **$150.00**

Popeye Lantern, litho tin figure w/glass midsection, Linemar, 7½", EXIB... **$550.00**

Professor Owl, Y, 1950s, 8", NMIB **$425.00**

Quick Draw McGraw Target Car w/Baba Looie, EXIB...... **$200.00**

Rembrandt the Monkey Artist, Alps, 1950s, rare, 8", NMIB .. **$35.00**

Robo Tank TR2, TN, 1960s, 6", NM+.............................. **$175.00**

Rocky (Fred Flintstone look-alike), tin, Japan, 4", NMIB.. **$100.00**

Sam the Shaving Man, Plaything Toy Co, 1960s, 12", EXIB.. **$175.00**

Santa in Reindeer Sleigh (Mystery Action), MT, 1950s, 17", EXIB **$300.00**

Shark U-Control Race Car, Remco #610, 1961, 10", MIB.. **$165.00**

Shutter Bug, TN, 1950s, 9", NMIB **$800.00**

Skipping Monkey, jumps rope, TN, 1960s, 10", EXIB........ **$65.00**

Smokey Bill on Old-Fashioned Car, TN, 1960s, 9", MIB.. **$250.00**

Smoking Pa Pa Bear, remote-controlled, SAN, 8", EXIB ... **$100.00**

Smurf Choo Choo w/Headlight, Durham Industries, 1980s, MIB.. **$40.00**

Snappy Puppy, plush, Alps, 1960s, 9", VGIB..................... **$50.00**

Space Traveling Monkey, Yanoman, 1960s, 9", EXIB........ **$125.00**

Strange Explorer, DSK, 1960s, 8", EXIB **$275.00**

Talking Batmobile, Palitoy (Hong Kong)/DC Comics, 1977, 10", NM+IB.. **$175.00**

Teddy Go-Kart, Alps, 1960s, 10", EXIB **$175.00**

Telephone Bear (Ringing & Talking in His Old Rocking Chair), MT, 1950s, 10", EXIB.. **$275.00**

Tin Man Robot (The Wizard of Oz), plastic, Remco, 1969, 21", MIB.. **$200.00**

Tom Tom Indian, Y, 1960s, 11", NMIB **$125.00**

Traveler Bear, remote-controlled, K, 1950s, NMIB.......... **$250.00**

Trumpet Monkey, Alps, 1950s, 10", EXIB....................... **$225.00**

Tumbles the Bear, YM, 1960s, 9", NMIB........................ **$150.00**

Twirly Whirly Rocket Ride, Alps, 13", EXIB, $500.00.

(Photo courtesy Bertoia Auctions)

US Air Force F-105, pilot in open cockpit, 11" L, EX....... **$275.00**

VIP the Busy Boss, S&E, 1950s, 8", EXIB **$200.00**

Waddles Family Car, Y, 1960s, MIB **$100.00**

Walking Donkey, remote-controlled, Linemar, 1950s, 9", VGIB **$150.00**

Wee Little Baby Bear (Reading Bear w/Lighted Eyes), Alps, 10", EXIB... **$375.00**

Yo-Yo Clown, S&E, 1960s, rare, 10", MIB...................... **$425.00**

Guns

One of the bestselling kinds of toys ever made, toy guns were first patented in the late 1850s. Until WWII most were made of cast iron, though other materials were used on a lesser scale. After the war, cast iron became cost prohibitive, and steel and diecast zinc were used. By 1950 most were made of either diecast material or plastic. Hundreds of names can be found embossed on these little guns, a custom which continues to the present time. Because of their tremendous popularity and durability, today's collectors can find a diversity of models and styles, and prices are still fairly affordable.

Army .45 Cap Gun, Hubley, cast iron w/white grips, EX **$50.00**

Atomic Orbetor-X, Italy, plastic, MIB................................. **$75.00**

Automatic Repeater Cap Pistol No 50, steel, Wyandotte, 8", EX+IB..$60.00

Big Game Rifle, Marx, MIB...$125.00

Big Horn Cap Gun, cast iron w/pressed steel revolving cylinder, brown grips, 2nd version, Kilgore, 1940s, 9", VG $250.00

Cheyenne Singin' Saddle Gun, Daisy, 33", NMIB.............$260.00

Cork Shooting Submachine Gun, Marx, 1951, MIB.........$175.00

Cowboy 6-Shooter Water Pistol, Irwin, MIB $75.00

Davy Crockett Cap Pistol, painted plastic w/working metal 'flintlock' hammer & trigger, Marx, 1950s, 10½", NM+......$75.00

Deputy Pistol, nickel plated, Hubley, 10", MIB................$150.00

Derringer w/Dagger, nickel plated w/red plastic push-out dagger, black grips, Hubley, 1960s, 7", NM $90.00

Detective Automatic Repeater Cap Gun, Roth American Inc, 1970s, MOC...$60.00

Fanner-50 Smoking Cap Pistol, revolving cylinder, Mattel, 11", VGIB..$200.00

G-Man Gun/Siren Alarm Pistol, Marx, 9", EXIB $225.00

Hide-A-Mite Secret Holster & Nichols Cap Pistol, Carnell, MOC $45.00

Johnny Seven OMA, Seven Guns in One, plastic, Topper Toys, 1960s, 38", NMIB...$250.00

Kit Carson Pistol, lever opening, profile bust embossed on grips, nickel plated, Kilgore, 9½", NMIB............................$250.00

Long Tom Six Shooter, Kilgore, NMIB............................$800.00

Marshall Revolving Cap Pistol, nickel plated w/black oval on white grips, Leslie-Henry, 10½", EX+.................................$150.00

Mustang 500, Nichols, NMIB $300.00

Pirate Pistol, Hubley, NM+IB $200.00

Private Eye 50 Shot Repeater Cap Pistol #2038, Kilgore, 1960s, M (VG +card)..$30.00

Radar Raider (Cap Shooting Tommy Gun), Arliss/Premier Plastics, 18" L, unused, MIB...$100.00

Ranger Cap Pistol, nickel plated w/dark reddish brown grip, Kilgore, 1940s, 8", EX+ $225.00

Rex Mars Planet Patrol X-92 Sparkling Space Gun, windup, tin & plastic, 21½", NM+IB $300.00

Rifleman Flip Special Rifle, Hubley, NM+IB.....................$450.00

Rocket-2 Sparkling Space Gun, tin & plastic, Marx, NMIB..$400.00

Rodeo Cap Gun, nickel plated w/longhorn steer heads embossed on white grips, Hubley, 1950s, 8", MIB $100.00

Roy Rogers Shootin' Iron, simulated pearl handle, Kilgore, 9", MIB $350.00

Shane Single Gun & Holster Set, marked Alan Ladd, EX gun/NM+ holster $900.00

Shootin' Shell Fanner Cap Pistol, 6 Shootin' Shell cartridges, 12 bullet noses, built-in loader, Mattel, NMIB.....................$150.00

Sixfinger, plastic finger form shoots 6 different projectiles, Topper Toys (De Luxe Reading), 1965, MOC........................$150.00

Space Gun, litho tin, Y, 5", MIB.......................................$75.00

Space Gun, plastic rifle type, black barrel w/brown stock, Pery Nauta, 21", MIB...$50.00

Space Gun S-68 (Space Rocket Pistol), litho tin, battery-operated, Nomura, 10" L, unused, NM+IB $400.00

Space Jet (Space Super Jet Gun), friction, tin & plastic, Yoshiya, 9½", NMIB..$150.00

Space Machine Gun, friction, tin, SY, 1950s, 12½", NMIB..$150.00

Wild Bill Hickok & Jingles Holsters, 1 10" gun, lg medallions on brown & white single holster, NMIB.........................$575.00

Wilma Deering's Gun & Holster (Buck Rogers), NM $500.00

Wyatt Earp (Double) Holster, guns w/black grips, tan & black holsters, Hubley, NM+IB...$550.00

Shootin' Shell Fanner Cap Pistol, Mattel, MIB, $275.00.
(Photo courtesy John Turney)

Ramp Walkers

Though ramp-walking figures were made as early as the 1870s, ours date from about 1935 on. They were made in Czechoslovakia from the '20s through the '40s and in this country during the '50s and '60s by Marx, who made theirs of plastic. John Wilson of Watsontown, Pennsylvania, sold his worldwide. They were known as 'Wilson Walkies' and stood about 4½" high. But the majority has been imported from Hong Kong.

Advisor: Randy Welch (See Directory, Toys)

Ankylosaurus w/Clown $40.00

Astro & George Jetson $75.00

Big Bad Wolf & Mason Pig $50.00

Bird, Czechoslovakian $35.00

Bison w/Native..$40.00

Bull, plastic $20.00

Bunny Pushing Cart..$60.00

Chilly Willy, penguin on sled pulled by parent $25.00

Chipmunks Marching Band w/Drum & Horn, plastic........$35.00

Cow, black and white, Hong Kong (attributed to Marx), VG, $45.00. (Photo courtesy www.gasolinealleyantiques.com)

Dairy Cow, plastic..$20.00
Donald Duck, Wilson..$175.00
Donald Duck Pulling Nephews in Wagon $35.00

Donald Duck Pushing Wheelbarrow, all plastic, $25.00.

(Photo courtesy www.gasolinealleyantiques.com)

Donald's Trio, Huey, Louie & Dewey dressed as Indian Chief, cowboy & 1 carrying flowers, France, NMOC $150.00
Dutch Girl, Czechoslovakian..$60.00
Eskimo, Wilson..$100.00
Figaro the Cat w/Ball...$30.00
Firemen, plastic..$35.00
Fred Flintstone & Barney Rubble $40.00
Fred Flintstone on Dino...$75.00
Goat, plastic...$20.00
Goofy, riding hippo...$45.00
Indian Chief, Wilson..$70.00
Jolly Ollie Orange, Funny Face Kool-Aid, w/plastic coin weight $60.00
Lion w/Clown..$40.00
Mad Hatter w/March Hare..$50.00
Mammy, Wilson..$40.00
Mickey Mouse & Pluto Hunting...$40.00
Mickey Mouse Pushing Lawn Roller.......................................$35.00
Minnie Mouse Pushing Baby Stroller.....................................$35.00
Olive Oyl, Wilson...$175.00
Pig, Wilson $40.00
Policeman, Czechoslovakian...$60.00
Popeye & Wimpy, heads on springs, MIB..................................$85.00
Pumpkin Head Man & Woman, faces on both sides, plastic.$100.00
Rabbit, Wilson $75.00
Santa & Mrs Claus, faces on both sides $50.00
Santa w/white or yellow sack, ea $40.00
Sheriff Facing Outlaw $65.00
Spark Plug..$200.00
Sydney Dinosaur, yellow & purple, Long John Silvers, w/plastic coin weight, 1989 ....$15.00
Teeny Toddler, walking baby girl, plastic, Dolls Inc, lg.........$40.00
Walking Baby, in Canadian Mountie uniform, plastic, lg.....$50.00
Wimpy, Wilson...$175.00
Wiz Walker Milking Cow, plastic, Charmore, lg..................$40.00
Zebra w/Native $40.00

Rings

Toy rings are a fairly new interest in the collecting world. Earlier radio and TV mail-order premiums have been popular for some time but have increased in value considerably over the past few years. Now there is a growing interest in other types of rings as well — those from gumball machines, world's fairs souvenirs, movie and TV show promotions, and any depicting celebrities. They may be metal or plastic; most have adjustable shanks. New rings are already being sought out as future collectibles.

Note: All rings listed here are considered to be in fine to very fine condition. Wear, damage, and missing parts will devaluate them considerably.

Andy Pafko, baseball scorekeeper, EX................................$215.00
Annie, face, EX...$65.00
Annie, initial, EX...$125.00
Babe Ruth, Baseball Club, EX...$165.00
Buck Rogers, birthstone, EX..$565.00
Buck Rogers, Saturn, NM+...$600.00
Capt Marvel, ring/compass, Rocket Raider, 1940s, EX......$350.00
Captain Midnight, Marine Corps, EX $400.00
Captain Midnight, Mystic Sun God, EX...................................$800.00
Captain Midnight, Whirlwind Siren, EX..................................$400.00
Davy Crockett, TV screen flicker action, Karo Syrup, 1955, NM $125.00
Dick Tracy, secret compartment, EX $200.00
Flash Gordon, Post Toasties, MIP.......................................$75.00
Frank Buck, black leopard, bronze, NM $3,200.00
Gabby Hayes, cannon, EX..$250.00
Green Hornet, rubber stamp seal, EX....................................$100.00
Howdy Doody, Clarabelle horn, EX $385.00
Howdy Doody/Poll Parrot, plastic w/raised image of Howdy's head, Poll Parrot incised on sides, open band, EX+ $150.00
Jack Armstrong, Dragon's Eye, glow-in-the-dark plastic, 1940, G $350.00
Lone Ranger, atomic bomb, EX...$215.00
Lone Ranger, flashlight, w/instructions, EX $150.00
Space Patrol, Hydrogen Ray Gun, Wheat Chex, 1950s, EX ..$250.00
Straight Arrow, face, EX...$70.00
Straight Arrow, Nugget Cave w/photo, EX $275.00
Superman, S logo, gold finish, Nestlè, 1978, EX+ $25.00
Terry & the Pirates, gold detector, EX $125.00
Tom Corbett, rocket, w/expansion band, M $475.00
Tom Mix, Look Around, EX...$125.00

Tom Mix, Marlin Guns Target Ring, eagle each side, brass, 1937, EX, from $150.00 to $200.00. (Photo courtesy LiveAuctioneers.com/ Morphy Auctions)

Robots and Space Toys

Japanese toy manufacturers introduced their robots and space toys as early as 1948. Some of the best examples were made in the '50s, during the 'golden age' of battery-operated toys. They became more and more complex, and today some of these in excellent condition may bring well over $1,000.00. By the '60s, more and more plastic was used in their production, and the toys became inferior.

Zabitan, TT, tin windup with vinyl head, 9", Japanese box, NMIB, from $180.00 to $225.00. (Photo courtesy LiveAuctioneers. com/ Morphy Auctions)

Apollo-Z Moon Traveler, battery-operated, tin, Nomura, 12", NMIB..$150.00

Astro Fleet 4-Manned Space Craft w/Launcher Gun, Parks #5055, 1950s, MIB...$30.00

Astronaut Robot, windup, tin, Shudo, 6", MIB................$950.00

Atom Rocket 7, battery-operated, litho tin, MT, 9" L, EXIB..$330.00

Bump 'n Go Space Explorer, crank-operated, tin & plastic, Yoshiya, 6" L, NMIB..$350.00

Busy Cart Robot, construction robot pushing single-wheeled cart, battery-operated, plastic, Horikawa, 11½", NM.........$560.00

Commander (Spaceship), tin w/plastic nose, friction, Yoshiya, 10" L, NMIB...$500.00

Cragstan Astronaut, tin, friction, Yonezawa, 9", EX..........$560.00

Cragstan Mr Robot, battery-operated, tin w/plastic dome head, white w/red version, Yonezawa, 11", VG+.................$428.00

Dino Robot, battery-operated, tin & plastic, Horikawa, 11", NM+IB...$525.00

Electric Robot & Son, plastic, w/son & tools for 'tool chest,' Marx, 1950s, nonworking, NMIB.....................................$200.00

Flying Air Car, battery-operated, aluminum, NMIB.........$275.00

Gyro Space Car, friction, tin, Japan, EX.........................$200.00

Interplanetary Rocket, battery-operated, tin & plastic, Yonezawa, 14", MIB..$200.00

Juniper Robot, windup, tin & plastic, Yoshiya, MIB.........$310.00

King Flying Saucer, battery-operated, tin, KO, 1960s, MIB..$100.00

Luna Expedition, windup, plastic, Technofix, NM............$125.00

Marvelous Mike Tractor, tin & plastic, Saunders-Swadar Toy Co #1000, 13" L, VGIB...$350.00

Moon Explorer (Astronaut), crank-operated, tin, Yoshiya, 7", EX...$150.00

Moon Express (Magic Color), battery-operated, tin & plastic, TPS, NMIB..$250.00

Moon Scout Helicopter, battery-operated, tin & plastic, Marx, 16" L, NMIB..$100.00

Mr LEM, battery-operated, plastic, Hong Kong, scarce, 13", EX. $150.00

Piston-Action Robot ('Pug Robby Robot'), remote-controlled, tin & plastic, Nomura, 9", EX+..$600.00

Planet Robot, windup, tin, Yoshiya, 9", MIB...................$400.00

Regulus (Florida Air Boat), battery-operated, tin, ATC, 8", NMIB..$250.00

Robby Robot Bulldozer, friction, tin, Marusan, 7", EX......$225.00

Robert the Robot (on Bulldozer), remote-controlled, plastic w/rubber treads, Ideal, 9½" L, NMIB..................................$725.00

Robot (Golden), remote-controlled, tin, Linemar, 6½", EX.. $1,000.00

Robot Cosmic Raider Force, battery-operated, plastic, 1970s, 14½", MIB...$138.00

Rotate-O-Matic Super Astronaut, battery-operated, tin, Horikawa, 1960s, NMIB..$225.00

Satellite Explorer Helmet, aluminum, Mirro, NM+IB.......$335.00

Sky Patrol (w/Blinking Jet Engines), battery-operated, tin & plastic, Japan, 13" L, NMIB...$700.00

Sonicon Sonic Control Space Ship, battery-operated, tin, Masudaya, 13" L, NMIB...$900.00

Space Commando, windup, tin & plastic, Nomura, 1956, 8", EX..$285.00

Space Dog, friction, tin, Yoshiya, 7½" L, EX+.................$275.00

Space Drome, tin & plastic, Superior, complete w/accessories, EXIB...$460.00

Space Explorer 11 (Moon Explorer), windup, tin & plastic, Takatoku, NMIB..$175.00

Space Globe, tin, 10", NM..$450.00

Space Man Robot, windup, tin, Yoneya, 8", EXIB.........$1,000.00

Space Patrol/NASA, friction, tin w/plastic astronaut under clear plastic dome, Masudaya, 7" L, NMIB.......................$175.00

Space Radar Scout Pioneer, friction, plastic, Masudaya, 7" L, NMIB..$300.00

Space Scooter, battery-operated, tin & plastic, astronaut figure on scooter, Masudaya, 8" L, NMIB................................$150.00

Space Surveillant X-07, battery-operated, tin, Masudaya, 8½" L, NMIB..$175.00

Space Tank M-41, battery-operated, tin & plastic, Masudaya, 8½" L, NMIB..$275.00

Space Tricycle w/Robot Rider, windup, hollow vinyl robot on litho tin trike w/bell, Frankonia, 1960, 4", EX....................$315.00

Space Vehicle (Lighted) #28905, battery-operated, tin, w/'Floating Satellite,' Masydaya, 8½", NMIB.............................$300.00

Spaceman Toy Sparkler, tin, Arnold, NM......................$112.00

Sparking Robot, windup, tin, Noguchi, 6", MIB..............$250.00

Sparky Robot, windup, tin, Yoshiya, 8", EXIB................$345.00

Super Robot, windup, tin, Noguchi, 5", MIB..................$195.00

Swinging Baby Robot, windup, litho tin, Yone, 6½", NMIB..$400.00

Television Space Robot, battery-operated, tin, Alps, 1959, 14", NM..$300.00

Universe Reconnaissance Boat, battery-operated, tin & plastic, China, 12", NMIB **$100.00**

X-07 Space Surveillant, battery-operated, litho tin, Modern Toys, 8", EX+ **$250.00**

Slot Cars

Slot cars first became popular in the early 1960s. Electric raceways set up in storefront windows were commonplace. Huge commercial tracks with eight and ten lanes were located in hobby stores and raceways throughout the United States. Large corporations such as Aurora, Revell, Monogram, and Cox, many of which were already manufacturing toys and hobby items, jumped on the bandwagon to produce slot cars and race sets. By the end of the early 1970s, people were losing interest in slot racing, and its popularity diminished. Today the same baby boomers that raced slot cars in earlier days are revitalizing the sport. As you would expect, slot cars were generally well used, so finding vintage cars and race sets in like-new or mint condition is difficult. Slot cars replicating the 'muscle' cars from the '60s and '70s are extremely sought after.

Advisor: Gary Pollastro (See Directory, Toys)

Accessory, AMT Service Parts Kit, #2000, VG **$65.00**
Accessory, Aurora AFX Pit Kit, G **$15.00**
Accessory, Aurora Model Motoring Hill Track, 9", EX...........**$8.00**
Accessory, Aurora Model Motoring 4-Way Stop Track, 9", EX ...**$15.00**
Accessory, Strombecker Scale Lap Counter, 1/32 scale, MIB ..**$25.00**
Accessory, Tyoc Trigger Controller, orange, EX **$8.00**
Car, Aurora, Ford Baja Bronco, #1909, red, EX....................**$15.00**
Car, Aurora, Snowmobile, #1485-400, yellow w/blue figure, MIB...**$55.00**
Car, Aurora AFX, Camaro Z-28, #1901, red, white & blue, EX.**$20.00**
Car, Aurora AFX, Dodge Fever Dragster, white & yellow, EX ..**$15.00**
Car, Aurora AFX, Mario Andretti NGK Indy Car, black, M ..**$35.00**
Car, Aurora AFX, Pontiac Firebird #9, white, blue & black, EX.**$25.00**
Car, Aurora AFX, Speed Beamer, red, white & blue stripe, VG ..**$10.00**
Car, Aurora Cigarbox, Dino Ferrari, red, EX **$20.00**
Car, Aurora Cigarbox, Ford J, #6104, yellow & blue w/blue stripe, M (EX+ box) **$25.00**
Car, Aurora G-Plus, Corvette, #1011, red, orange & white, EX.**$15.00**
Car, Aurora Thunderjet, Chaparral 2F #7, #1410, lime & blue, EX..**$25.00**
Car, Aurora Thunderjet, Cobra, #1375, yellow w/black stripe, VG+ **$30.00**
Car, Aurora Thunderjet, Dune Buggy, white w/red striped roof, EX..**$30.00**
Car, Aurora Thunderjet, Ford GT 40, #1374, red w/black stripe, EX **$25.00**
Car, Aurora Vibator, Mercedes, #1542, yellow, EX **$50.00**
Car, TCR, Maintenance Van, red & white, EX....................**$15.00**
Car, Tyco, '40 Ford Coupe, #88534, black w/flames, EX.....**$20.00**
Car, Tyco, '83 Corvette Challenger #33, silver & yellow, EX..**$25.00**
Car, Tyco, Bandit Pickup, black & red, EX...........................**$12.00**
Car, Tyco, Caterpillar #96, black & yellow, EX....................**$20.00**
Car, Tyco, Corvette #12, white & red w/blue stripes, EX **$12.00**
Car, Tyco, Firebird, #6914, cream & red, VG......................**$12.00**

Car, Tyco, Funny Mustang, orange w/yellow flame, EX.......**$25.00**
Car, Tyco, Jam Car, yellow & black, EX **$10.00**
Car, Tyco, Lamborghini, red, VG...**$12.00**
Car, Tyco, Military Police #45, white & blue, EX..............**$30.00**
Car, Tyco, Rokar 240-Z, #7, black, EX................................**$10.00**
Car, Tyco, Turbo Hopper #27, red, EX **$12.00**

Set, Markli Sprint, ca. 1960s, M (in EX box), $265.00.
(Photo courtesy LiveAuctioneers.com/Morphy Auctions)

Vehicles

These are the types of toys that are intensely dear to the heart of many a collector. Having a beautiful car is part of the American dream, and over the past 80 years, just about as many models, makes, and variations have been made as toys for children as the real vehicles for adults. Novices and advanced collectors alike are easily able to find something to suit their tastes as well as their budgets.

One area that is especially volatile includes those '50s and '60s tin scale-model autos by foreign manufacturers — Japan, U.S. Zone Germany, and English toy makers. Since these are relatively modern, you'll still be able to find some at yard sales and flea markets at reasonable prices.

There are several good references for these toys: *Hot Wheels, The Ultimate Redline Guide,* by Jack Clark and Robert P. Wicker; *Collector's Guide to Tonka Trucks, 1947 – 1963,* by Don and Barb deSalle; and *Matchbox Toys, 1947 to 2003; The Other Matchbox Toys;* and *Toy Car Collector's Guide,* all by Dana Johnson.

Newsletter: *Matchbox USA*
Charles Mack
62 Saw Mill Rd., Durham, CT 06422
860-349-1655
MTCHBOXUSA@aol.com
www.charliemackonline.com

Asakusa, Buick Skylark (1966), battery-operated, 2 red & white police lights on front fenders, 11½", NM+IB **$350.00**
Bandai, Cadillac Convertible (1959), friction, 12", EX......**$150.00**
Bandai, Cadillac Sedan (1963), friction, 8", NM+IB **$155.00**
Bandai, Chevy Corvair (1961), friction, 8", NM+IB **$180.00**
Bandai, Ferrari (1960s), friction, 11", NM **$175.00**

Bandai, Ford Fairlane Convertible (1957), friction, trunk opens, 12", NMIB $1,500.00

Bandai, Volkswagen Sedan (King-size), battery-operated, 15", NMIB $250.00

Buddy L, Air Force Searchlight Truck, plastic searchlight, 4-wheeled, 1950s, 15", G $50.00

Buddy L, Ambulance, white w/red cross & 'Ambulance' on cloth canopy, 1950s, 15", EX+ $75.00

Buddy L, Cement Truck, red w/white revolving cement drum, 8-wheeled, 1960s, 15", NM+......................................$225.00

Buddy L, Convertible Coupe, retractable top, 1949, 19", EX+..$375.00

Buddy L, Jr Camaro, 1960s, 9", EX+....................................$20.00

Buddy L, Ladder Truck, #W36, International cab, red w/white ladders, 1930s, 22", EX+ $500.00

Buddy L, Ladder Truck, red w/chrome trim, black wooden wheels, 1940s, EX+ $150.00

Buddy L, Steam Shovel Truck, International, 2-color, rubber tires, 30", VG+ $500.00

Chein, Coal Truck, Hercules series, 20", G+......................$250.00

Chein, Dump Truck, open bench seat, black, Hercules series, 17", G $150.00

Chein, Ice Truck, Hercules series, 20", VG+ $825.00

Chein, Log Truck, 8½", VG+...$150.00

Chien, Dan-Dee Roadster, 9", EXIB.............................$1,000.00

Corgi, Austin Mini Van, #450, from $85 to $110.00

Corgi, Bedford Ambulance, #412, split windscreen, from $125 to..$150.00

Corgi, Capt Marvel's Porche, #262, from $60 to $75.00

Corgi, Chevrolet Stingray, #337, from $60 to......................$80.00

Corgi, Dougal's Car, #807, from $300 to...........................$350.00

Corgi, Jaguar 2.4 Saloon, #208, no suspension, from $120 to..$140.00

Corgi, Land Rover Lepra, #438, from $375 to $425.00

Corgi, Mercedes Benz 220SE, #230, black, from $120 to..$140.00

Corgi, Porsche 924, #321, metallic green, from $60 to........$75.00

Corgi, Vantastic Van, #432, from $30 to $45.00

Dinky, Bedford TK Box Van, #450, Castrol, from $270 to..$295.00

Dinky, Cadillac El Dorado, #175, from $140 to...............$195.00

Dinky, Ferrari, #204, from $115 to....................................$135.00

Dinky, Ford Berth Caravan, #188, from $135 to $175.00

Dinky, Ford Thunderbird, #555, from $265 to $280.00

Dinky, Saab 96, #156, from $150 to...................................$200.00

Dinky, Striker Antitank Vehicle, #691, from $175 to $200.00

Dinky, Volvo 122S, #184, white, from $360 to $400.00

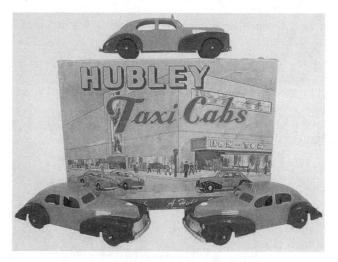

Hubley, Taxi Set, diecast, ca. 1930s, set of three, NMIB, $500.00. (Photo courtesy LiveAuctioneers.com/Morphy Auctions)

Marx, Chevy Impala Taxi Cab, #20, 1965, MIP $25.00

Marx, Cities Service Tow Truck, green & white, tin, 21", NM $225.00

Marx, Delivery Truck/Van, doorless sides, rear doors open, 2-tone, plastic, 10", NM+IB $100.00

Marx, Dodge BP Wreck Truck, #13, 1965, MIP..................$30.00

Marx, Emergency Searchlight Unit Truck, friction, battery-operated roof light & siren, tin, 14", EX................................$125.00

Marx, Lumar Contractors Dump Truck, pressed steel w/litho tin wheels, hand-operated bed, 17", EX $100.00

Marx, US Mail Truck #3, litho tin, 10", VG.....................$400.00

Matchbox, Air Malta A300 Airbus, #SB-027, white, 1981, MIP, from $15 to $20.00

Matchbox, Aston Martin Racer, #19, gray or white driver, 1961, MIP, from $60 to...$80.00

Matchbox, Austin Mk 2 Radio Truck, #68, olive w/black plastic wheels, 1959, MIP, from $70 to $90.00

Matchbox, Baja Dune Buggy, #13, light metallic green w/police shields decal, 1971, MOP from $35 to........................$50.00

Matchbox, Bedford Lomas Ambulance, #14, 1962, MIP.....$50.00

Matchbox, Berkley Cavalier Travel Trailer, #23, lime green, 1956, MIP, from $100 to...$125.00

Matchbox, BMW 3.0 CSL, #45, Superfast wheels, 1975, MIP..$12.00

Matchbox, Cadillac Fire Engine (1933), #Y-61, 1992, MIP, from $25 to $35.00

Matchbox, Caterpillar DB Bulldozer, #18, yellow w/red blade, 1956, MIP, from $80 to...$110.00

Matchbox, Cement Mixer, #3, blue w/gray plastic wheels, 1953, MIP, from $85 to...$100.00

Corgi Junior, #50 Dailey Planet Van, 1976, MOC, $40.00.

(Photo courtesy www.gasolinealleyantiques.com)

Matchbox, Cessna 402, #SB-009, light green & white, 1973, MIP, from $9 to **$12.00**

Matchbox, Corvette ('97), #4, metallic blue, 1997, MIP, from $5 to **$7.00**

Matchbox, Crane Truck, #49, red, 1976, MIP, from $80 to ..**$100.00**

Matchbox, Datsun 280ZX, #24, white w/red & blue Turbo 33 tampo, 1983, MIP, from $6 to....................................**$8.00**

Matchbox, Dennis Refuse Truck, #15, dark blue w/gray container, 1963, MIP, from $45 to...**$60.00**

Matchbox, Dodge Crane Truck, #63, yellow, 1968, M, from $12 to **$16.00**

Matchbox, Eccles Caravan #57, 1970, MIP, $15.00. (Photo courtesy www.serioustoyz.com)

Matchbox, Ergomatic Cab Horse Box, #17, w/2 horses, 1979, from $9 to **$12.00**

Matchbox, Fire Tender, #K009, 1973, MIP, from $12 to.....**$16.00**

Matchbox, Ford Galaxie Police Car, #55, blue dome light, 1966, MIP, fom $50 to **$65.00**

Matchbox, Ford Transit, #66, orange, no towing tab on base, 1977, MIP, from $7 to..**$10.00**

Matchbox, GMC Refrigerator Truck, #44, 1967, MOP, from $12 to **$16.00**

Matchbox, Harley-Davidson Motorcycle, #50, 1980, MIP, from $5 to **$7.00**

Matchbox, Jaguar SS 100 (1936), #Y-1, light yellow w/white-wall tires, England-cast, MIP, from $110 to **$140.00**

Matchbox, Jeep Hot Rod, #2, Superfast wheels, 1972, MIP...**$15.00**

Matchbox, Kenworth Car Transporter, #CY-1, red w/beige ramp, white stripes, 1982, MIP, from $12 to **$16.00**

Matchbox, Lightning, #SB-0212, olive green or silver-gray, 1977, MIP, ea from $8 to...**$12.00**

Matchbox, Log Transport, #K-043, 1981, MOP, from $18 to..**$24.00**

Matchbox, Mack Shovel Transporter, 3CY-32, orange & yellow w/-9-F Shovel Nose tractor, 1992, MIP, from $8 to...........**$12.00**

Matchbox, Mercedes Benz Ambulance, #3, opening rear hatch, 1968, MIP, from $18 to...**$24.00**

Matchbox, Mercedes Truck Stuttgarter (1913), 1988, MIP..**$20.00**

Matchbox, Monteverdi Hai #6, #3, orange w/black base, 1973, MIP, from $18 to **$24.00**

Matchbox, Peterbilt MBTV News Remote Truck, #CY-15, olive w/ Strike Team/LS2009 decal, 1989, MIP, from $20 to.....**$35.00**

Matchbox, Pontiac Grand Prix, #22, Superfast wheels, 1970, MIP **$50.00**

Matchbox, Pony Trailer w/2 Horses, #43, 1968, MIP, from $9 to.**$12.00**

Matchbox, Racing Mini, #26, orange, 1970, MIP, from $12 to ..**$16.00**

Matchbox, Royal Air Force Hawk, #SB-037, red, 1992, MIP, from $7 to **$10.00**

Matchbox, Setra Coach, #12, metallic gold w/tan roof, 1970, MIP, from $25 to **$30.00**

Windup Toys

Windup toys, especially comic character or personality related, are greatly in demand by collectors today. Though most were made through the years of the '30s through the '50s, they carry their own weight against much earlier toys and are considered very worthwhile investments. Mechanisms vary; some are key wound while others depended on lever action to tighten the mainspring and release the action of the toy. Tin and celluloid were used in their manufacture, and although it is sometimes possible to repair a tin windup, experts advise against putting your money into a celluloid toy whose mechanism is not working, since the material may be too fragile to tolerate the repair.

American Circus, Japan, 6", NM **$275.00**

Bar-X Cowboy (cowboy on horse w/lasso), litho tin, Alps, 5", NMIB...**$225.00**

Bear Performing, brown plush bear standing upright holding bar across back of neck, red muzzle, Martin, 8", EX.........**$550.00**

Black Boy Riding Turtle, litho tin, Germany, 5", EX+ **$450.00**

Black Musician (Ringing Bells w/Cymbals on Feet), painted tin, seated in chair, articulated arms & legs, 7"...................**$600.00**

Boat Ride, 3 boats w/passengers on rods swing from tower, litho tin, Unique Art, 9", EX...**$200.00**

Bunny Bell Tricycle, litho tin, Sato, 6", EX......................**$150.00**

Busy Betty, litho tin, Lindstrom, 8", VG.........................**$150.00**

Casper the Friendly Ghost Rollover Tank, litho tin, Linemar, 4" L, EX **$225.00**

Circus Boy, colorful boy ringing bell & waving Circus sign, litho tin, French, 6½", EX+ **$200.00**

Circus Car, blows ball into air, litho tin, KO, 4½" L, EXIB ..**$75.00**

Clown & Trick Dog on 3-wheeled Apparatus, painted tin, 6" L, restored, EX...**$325.00**

Clown Musician (Violinist), tin w/felt outfit, Schuco, 4½", EX.**$225.00**

Clown on Horse w/Jousting Skirt, painted tin w/cloth vest, repainted, 6", EX...**$250.00**

Clown Roller Skater, litho tin figure w/cloth pants, TPS, 6", EX.**$225.00**

Clown w/Spinning Star, painted tin, Germany, 5", VG **$400.00**

Covered Wagon, tin Conastoga wagon w/white cloth top, celluloid mule, Occupied Japan, 9" L, NMIB...........................**$150.00**

Cycling Quacky, litho tin duck on tricycle, Alps, 6", NMIB .**$150.00**

Dodgem Car, litho tin, 4½" L, EXIB.................................**$125.00**

Donald Duck, articulated arms, long bill, celluloid, 3", EX-IB.**$600.00**

Donald Duck Climbing Fireman, litho tin, Linemar, 14", EX.**$400.00**

Donald Duck Waddler, tin & plush, Linemar, 6", NMIB..**$450.00**

Drummer, celluoid figure on wooden base, cloth outfit, Japan, 1930s, 11½", EXIB..**$250.00**

Ducky the Early Bird, litho tin, K Co, 1950s, 4", MIB **$75.00**

Elephant on 3-Wheeled Scooter, litho tin, Gunthermann, 6½", VG+...$300.00

Ferris Wheel, Chein #172, 16", VG (VG box), from $365.00 to $395.00. (Photo courtesy LiveAuctioneers.com/Morphy Auctions)

Finnegan In Again Out Again, litho tin, Unique Art, 13½" L, EXIB...$300.00
Frankenstein Mechanical Monster, plastic, Linemar, 6", MIB. **$725.00**
GI Joe & His Jouncing Jeep, litho tin, Unique Art, 7½", EX. **$200.00**
Good Time Charlie, clown w/cloth outfit & paper hat blows party whistle, Alps, 13", NMIB $200.00
Ham 'n Sam, litho tin, Linemar, 5½", EX $650.00
Hen Pulling Chick on 2-Wheeled Box, litho tin, Hans Eberl, Germany, 9½" L, VG...$350.00
Henry & His Swan, celluloid w/tin cart, Japan/Borgfeldt, 1930s, 6x9", NM $1,800.00
Home Run King, litho tin, Selrite, 6" L, G+.....................$450.00

Ice Cream Scooter, Courtland, 6½" long, NMIB, from $450.00 to $550.00. (Photo courtesy LiveAuctioneers.com/Smith House Toy & Auction Co.)

Indian w/Bow & Arrow Walking, painted tin, 7", EX $450.00
Jazzbo Jim, litho tin, Unique Art, 10", VGIB $350.00
Kiddie Kampers, litho tin, Wolverine, 1930s, 14" L, EXIB ..$450.00
Lincoln Tunnel, litho tin, Unique Art, 24" L, NMIB $375.00
Little Orphan Annie & Sandy, wind Annie & she pulls Sandy, Celluloid & tin, Japan, 6½", EX.................................$700.00
Mama Kangaroo w/Playful Baby, litho tin, TPS, 6½", EX+IB...$100.00
Mickey Mouse (tumbling), cloth-covered, Schuco, 4½", EX .$300.00
Mickey Mouse Circus Train, litho tin w/tent & truck, composition Mickey figure, Lionel/WDE, EXIB.......................$5,500.00

Mickey Mouse Walker, string-jointed celluloid figure, Borgfeldt WDE, 1930s, 7", G $550.00
Mobile Duck (who plays xylophone), litho tin, Sankei, 5½", NMIB...$350.00
Mounted Cavalryman w/Cannon, litho tin w/2 wooden wheels, TPS, 5", NM+IB...$300.00
Musician (Violinist), cloth clothes & top hat, Martin/France, 8", EX+...$450.00
Peacock, litho tin, Ebo/Germany, 9" L, EX.....................$525.00
Pinocchio Musical Carousel, tin carousel w/swings on chains above compostion figure on wood base, France, 14", VG $350.00

Police Motorcycle, Marx, with siren, 8", NM, from $350.00 to $425.00. (Photo courtesy Scott Smiles)

Pool Players, 2 players at ea end of table, litho tin, 14" L, VG+....$300.00
Popeye Tank, turnover action, Linemar, 4", NMIB...........$525.00
Popeye Tumbler, litho tin, Linemar, 4", EX $525.00
Rodeo Joe Crazy Car, litho tin, Unique Art, 7½" L, EXIB ..$400.00
Rubber-Neck Willie the Clown, celluloid figure w/hands in pockets, stretches neck as he wobbles, 8", VG+ $55.00
Sharpshooter, figure w/rifle on belly, celluloid, Alps, 8½" L, NM+IB...$175.00
Sky Rangers, litho tin, Unique Art, 10", EXIB $350.00
Superman M-25 Rollover Tank, litho tin, Linemar, 4" L, EX...$450.00
Three Little Pigs Bank, felt-covered pig standing beating tin drum, Schuco, NM $500.00
Touchdown Chimp, litho tin chimp w/celluloid ball, Technofix, 4½", NMIB $350.00
Traffic Cop, figure in blue uniform w/white gloves, whistle in mouth, litho tin, TN, 6½", EX.................................$100.00
Western Ranger, ranger on horse w/gun drawn, litho tin w/rubber tail, Kokyu, 5", EXIB...$150.00
Zilotone Player, complete w/disks, litho tin, Wolverine, 7½" L, G+...$475.00

Transistor Radios

Introduced during the Christmas shopping season of 1954, transistor radios were at the cutting edge of futuristic design and miniaturization. Among the most desirable is the 1954 four-transistor Regency TR-1 which is valued at a minimum of $750.00 in jade green. Black may go for as much as $300.00, other colors from $350.00 to $400.00. The TR-1 'Mike Todd' version in the 'Around the World in Eighty Days' leather book-look presentation case goes for $4,000.00 and up! Some of the early Toshiba models sell for $250.00 to $350.00, some of the Sonys even higher — their TR-33 books at a minimum of $1,000.00, their TR-55 at $1,500.00 and up! Certain pre-1960 models by Hoffman and Admiral represented the earliest practical use of solar technology and are also highly valued. Early collectible transistor radios all have civil defense triangle markings at 640 and 1240 on the frequency dial and nine or fewer transistors. Very few desirable sets were made after 1963.

Values in our listings are for radios in at least very good condition — not necessarily working, but complete and requiring very little effort to restore them to working order. Cases may show minor wear. All radios are battery-operated unless noted otherwise.

Admiral #Y2091 Imperial 7 Lancer, pearl white plastic, 7 transistors, swing handle, horizontal, AM, 1961, from $20 to........**$30.00**

Admiral #7L12, holiday red, battery or solar power when used w/ Sun Power Pack, horizontal, AM, w/pack & case........**$500.00**

Admiral #742, red leather, clear round dial, lattice grille, crown logo, horizontal, AM, 1959, from $15 to **$20.00**

Aircastle #TR1300, leather, 13 transistors, slide rule dial, horizontal, AM/FM, Japan, 5¾x9⅛x2¼", from $15 to..................**$20.00**

Airline #GEN-1212A, 4 transistors, perforated grille, thumb-wheel knob, M/W logo, AM, horizontal, from $25 to...........**$35.00**

Aladdin, 8 transistors, right front window dial, thumb-wheel tuning, vertical, AM, 1962, from $60 to......................**$70.00**

AristoTone #HT-1244, plastic, 12 transistors, thumb-wheel tuning, vertical, AM, Japan, 4¼", from $20 to..........................**$30.00**

Arvin #8574, white or tan molded case, 6 transistors, front lattice grille, starburst emblem, horizontal, 1958, $40 to........**$50.00**

Bradford #AR-121, 10 transistors, step-back top, 2-band slide-rule dial, lower grille, vertical, AM/FM, 1965, $10 to **$15.00**

Capehart #T6-202 Incomparable, 6 transistors, crown logo, window dial, vertical, AM, 1961, from $100 to **$125.00**

Channel Master, clock combo, black & chrome, 7 transistors, slide-rule dial, 4 knobs, telescoping antenna, AM, 1960 ....**$30.00**

Continental #TFM-1090, 10 transistors, 2-band dial w/thumb-wheel tuning, horizontal, AM/FM, 1964, from $10 to.**$15.00**

Crown #TR-555, 5 transistors, window dial, perforated grille, crown logo, vertical, AM, 1960, from $175 to **$200.00**

Dewald #K-544 Tuckaway, leather, 4 transistors, horseshoe-shaped tuning area, horizontal, AM, 1957, from $50 to...........**$65.00**

Faircrest #2091, 10 transistors, 2-band slide dial, perforated grille, horizontal, AM/FM switch, 1965, from $10 to **$15.00**

General Electric #P766A, metal & leatherette, 6 transistors, metal perforated grille, horizontal, AM, 1968, from $30 to ...**$40.00**

General Electric #P840, brown leatherette, 7 transistors, chrome grille w/cutouts, horizontal, AM, 1961, from $15 to **$20.00**

General Electric S-15, sold as kit, leather, round dial, center grille w/ cutouts, horizontal, AM, 1963, from $10 to..................**$15.00**

Gundig Micro-Boy 201, plastic portable w/speaker box, 6 transistors, horizontal, West Germany, AM, 1961, from $125 to....**$150.00**

Hitachi #KH-915, 9 transistors, window dial, checkered grille, telescoping antenna, horizontal, FM, 1963, from $20 to ...**$25.00**

Hoffman #EP706 Trans Solar, espresso plastic, 6 transistors, metal grille, solar panel, horizontal, AM, 1959, $250 to **$300.00**

Juliette #CLA-1010, lamp combo, plastic, 5 transistors, right clock face, AM, AC, 1968, from $15 to................**$15.00**

Lafayette, #FS-235, 6 transistors, window dial w/thumb-wheel tuning, vertical, AM, 1963, from $25 to..........................**$35.00**

Linmark #T-61, 6 transistors, left front window dial, perforated grille, vertical, AM, 1959, from $35 to **$45.00**

Magnavox AM-62, upper front dial, right side thumb-wheel knob, lower metal grille, vertical, AM, 1963, from $20 to......**$30.00**

Masterwork #M2100TR Galaxy III, 9 transistors, 3-band slide-rule dial, checkered grille, horizontal, AM/FM, 1963, $20 to .**$25.00**

Monacor #RE-3B Deluxe, 8 transistors, 3-band slide-rule dial, telescoping antenna, horizontal, AM, 1964, from $25 to...**$30.00**

Motorola #X16B, blue, 7 transistors, lg grille w/horizontal bars, vertical, AM, 1960, 6⅛", from $20 to **$30.00**

National #T-21, plastic, 7 transistors, 2 front window dials, swing handle, vertical, 4¼", from $20 to **$30.00**

Panasonic #R-111 Tiny Tote, front window dial, side tuning, lower round grille, vertical, AM, 2¾", from $40 to **$50.00**

Panasonic #T-22M, blue plastic, 8 transistors, 2-band dial, lower grille, antenna, horizontal, AM/Marine, from $25 to....**$35.00**

Philco #NT-600BKG, plastic, 6 transistors, window dial, lower left logo, vertical, AM, 3¾", from $10 to...........................**$15.00**

Philco #T-905-124, 9 transistors, 2-band dial, checkered grille, telescoping antenna, horizontal, AM/FM, from $20 to......**$30.00**

Raleigh #805, 8 transistors, thumb-wheel knob, lower oval grille, vertical, AM, 1965, from $20 to................................**$25.00**

RCA #1-T-4J Hawaii, charcoal gray plastic, 8 transistors, center grille, swing handle, vertical, AM, 6⅞", from $25 to **$35.00**

Realistic Hi-Fiver, plastic, dial in wedge-shaped indent, metal grille w/logo, horizontal, AM, Japan, from $60 to.................**$85.00**

Regency #TR-4, ebony or ivory plastic, 4 transistors, round dial knob w/concentric circles, vertical, AM, 1957, $125 to **$150.00**

Satellite #60N63, red plastic, AM, $25.00.
(Photo courtesy Marty and Sue Bunis)

Seminole #600, 6 transistors, horizontal dial, lower grille, vertical, AM, 1962, from $15 to...............................**$20.00**

Siemens #T 2, soft plastic, flip-up door w/2 window dials, horizontal, AM, 1959, from $25 to **$35.00**

Silvertone #2226, 10 transistors, 2-band dial, lower grille, telescoping antenna, handle, horizontal, AM/FM, 1962 .... **$18.00**

Silvertone #9206, black plastic, 6 transistors, double window dial, lower metal grille, swing handle, AM, 1959, $40 to **$50.00**

Sony #TR-63, red, black, green or yellow plastic, 6 transistors, 1st American import, vertical, AM, 1957, from $400 to .. **$500.00**

Sony #TR-818, gray or cream, 8 transistors, horizontal dial, left grille, horizontal, AM, 1963, from $25 to **$35.00**

Star-Lite #MR-777 Star Ruby, plastic, 7 transistors, vertical bars on grille, left side chain w/key ring, sq, AM, $25 to **$35.00**

Sylvania #7P12T, plastic, 7 transistors, lower grille w/logo, swing handle, vertical, AM, 1959, from $35 to **$45.00**

Tonecrest #1051, 10 transistors, 2-band dial, left grille, horizontal, AM/FM, 1965, from $15 to **$20.00**

Toshiba #7TP-352S, plastic, 7 transistors, 2-band dial, metal grille, telescoping antenna, vertical, AM, 1961, $65 to **$75.00**

Trancel #TR 80, plastic, 8 transistors, metal grille w/logo, rear fold-out stand, vertical, AM, from $100 to **$125.00**

Truetone #DC3280, 8 transistors, 2-band dial, lower grille, horizontal, AM, 1962, from $35 to **$45.00**

Valiant Boy's Radio, plastic, 2 transistors, window dial, metal grille, vertical, AM, Japan, from $40 to **$55.00**

Viscount #601, 6 transistors, window dial w/thumb-wheel tuning, horizontal grille bars, strap, AM, 1965, from $5 to **$10.00**

Westinghouse #H-587P7, gray plastic, 7 transistors, checkered grille, horizontal, AM, from $75 to **$85.00**

Westinghouse #H611P5, blue plastic, 5 transistors, checkered grille, horizontal, AM, 1957, from $75 to **$85.00**

Treasure Craft/Pottery Craft

Al Levin commissioned Cope Pottery of Laguna Beach to turn his designs into ceramic novelties in 1947. Their success with 1949's Lucky California Sprites led him to open plants in South Gate and Compton, shifting to wood-stained Latin Dancers, TV lamps, and Barrel kitchenware. Designers Tony Guerrero and Ray Murray (of Bauer fame) created hula dancers, fish, and leaf trays for their new Hawaiian plant in 1959, while wood-textured kitchenware led California production.

Levin's son Bruce transformed designer Robert Maxwell's ideas into Pottery Craft in 1973, the first nationally successful stoneware lines with studio styling. Along with cookie jars by Don Winton and others, these formed the basis for Treasure Craft's 1980s emergence as California's largest (and last) dinnerware maker. Purchased at their 1988 peak by Pfaltzgraff, the vast Compton plants were closed after the 1994 passage of NAFTA. Some molds were sent to Mexico and China; all production ceased a few years later.

For more information we recommend *Treasure Craft Pottery* by our advisor, George A. Higby. See also Cookie Jars.

Advisor: George A. Higby, ISA (See Directory, Treasure Craft)

Dinnerware

Butterfly or Poppy, hermetic canister, from $10 to.............. **$12.00**
Butterfly or Poppy, plate, luncheon or dinner; ea from $12 to.. **$16.00**

Garden Party, candlesticks, pr from $24 to **$26.00**
Garden Party, canisters, set of 4, from $60 to..................... **$80.00**
Mirage of Southwest, butter dish, from $18 to **$22.00**
Mirage of Southwest, chop plate, lg, from $18 to **$22.00**
Saratoga, teapot, teepee, from $29 to **$36.00**
Stitch in Time/Auntie Em, dealer's plaque, from $10 to **$15.00**
Stitch in Time/Auntie Em, quiche pan, from $12 to........... **$15.00**
Taos, teapot, from $25 to.. **$30.00**
Taos, tortilla warmer, from $30 to **$36.00**

Figurines and Novelties

Apple Boy, 1961, 10", from $30 to................................ **$35.00**
Balinese Dancers, airbrushed, 1955, 13", pr from $125 to ... **$150.00**
Calypso Dancers, pr from $100 to **$120.00**
Horse heads (double), TV lamp, from $75 to **$95.00**
Jolly the Clown, 1948 only, w/hang tag, from $50 to **$60.00**
Leprechaun, box/lore, Gardena mark, 1948, from $40 to.... **$50.00**
Santa at hearth, 1950s, 6", from $40 to **$50.00**
Sprite, Lazy, w/lore, 1949, MIB, from $30 to **$35.00**
Sprite, shelf sitter, chartreuse, from $20 to **$24.00**
Sprite, vase, 8½", from $40 to.. **$45.00**

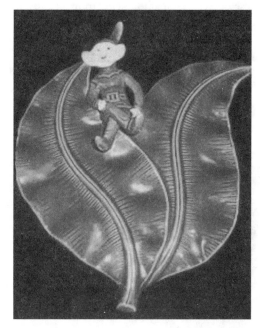

Sprite, wall pocket, 8x6", $20.00.

Wee Wun, planter, stump, from $14 to.............................. **$18.00**

Hawaiian Wares

Bowl, pineapple, low, 9", from $19 to **$25.00**
Drummer boy, 11", from $60 to...................................... **$70.00**
Hula dancer, Royal Hawaiian, grass skirt, from $60 to **$70.00**
Keiki Dancers, girl & boy, 8", pr from $55 to **$65.00**
Menuhine on Oahu chest, tag, 4½", from $20 to **$24.00**
Royal Hawaiian Hula Dancer, 1959, 10", from $60 to........ **$70.00**
Tiki god, Ku, wood stain, 8", from $75 to......................... **$85.00**
Tiki god, Lono, 12", from $110 to **$125.00**

Tray, fish, tapa border, Murray design, from $10 to **$12.00**
Tray, Lei Footprint, Murray design, from $14 to................ **$18.00**
Valet, Elemakule (old man), scarce, 8½", from $110 to **$125.00**

Kitchenware

Butter dish, Lucky Leprechaun line, from $18 to................ **$22.00**
Canisters, Fruit or Fruitwood line, set of 4 from $40 to **$50.00**
Chip & dip, shell, Lime glaze, 1-pc, from $27 to **$30.00**
Deviled egg tray, Cavalier line, lime green, 12", from $14 to.. **$18.00**
Salt & pepper shakers, dog & hydrant, 1940s, 2-pc set, from $18
    to **$22.00**
Salt & pepper shakers, phone & receiver, 1940s, 2-pc set, from $15
    to **$18.00**
Tray, Arches, Raul Coronel design, 1970, 16", from $95 to... **$110.00**
Tray, strawberry, red, 7", from $18 to **$20.00**
Wall pocket, grapes, South Gate mark, from $32 to **$40.00**

Pottery Craft

Botanica vase, intaglio design, 9", from $32 to **$40.00**
Canister, Farm Fresh transfer, from $15 to.......................... **$20.00**
Canister, raised letters, Cinnamon glaze, from $12 to **$15.00**
Carafe/slant cups, Moonstone glaze, from $50 to **$60.00**
Cat, Mitsuo design, Tierra glaze, from $29 to...................... **$35.00**
Clay Menagerie figure (various), sm, ea from $15 to............ **$20.00**
Matsu sprouter, Tierra glaze, from $24 to **$30.00**
Owl, Maxwell design, 11", from $65 to............................... **$75.00**

Vase, earth tones, ca. 1950, $65.00. (Photo courtesy LiveAuctioneers.com/Clars Auction Gallery)

Vase, Masa Mami, corrugated, 15, from $65 to **$75.00**
Vase, Maxwell design, bottle shape, early, 5", from $35 to... **$45.00**
Vase, Maxwell design, hand thrown, overlap glaze, 16", from $50
    to **$60.00**
Vase, Maxwell design, overlap glaze, scarce, 24", from $100 to. **$150.00**

Trolls

The legend of the Troll originated in Scandinavia. Nordic mythology described them as short, intelligent, essentially unpleasant, super-natural creatures who were doomed to forever live underground. During the '70s, a TV cartoon special and movie based on J.R.R. Tolkien's books, *The Hobbit* and *The Lord of the Rings,* caused an increase in Trolls' popularity. As a result, books, puzzles, posters, and dolls of all types were available on the retail market. In the early '80s, Broom Hilda and Irwin Troll were featured in a series of books as well as Saturday morning cartoons. Today trolls are enjoying a strong comeback.

Troll dolls of the '60s are primarily credited to Thomas Dam of Denmark. Many, using Dam molds, were produced in America by Royalty Des. of Florida and Wishnik. In Norway A/S Nyform created a different version. Some were also made in Hong Kong, Japan, and Korea, but those were of inferior plastic and design.

The larger trolls (approximately 12") are rare and very desirable to collectors. Troll animals by Dam, such as the giraffe, horse, cow, donkey, and lion, are bringing premium prices.

Unless otherwise noted, our values are for examples in at least near mint condition and in their original outfits.

Astronaut, red hair, green spiral eyes, w/gold hang cord, Scandia
    House, 2¾"... **$65.00**
Boy (bank) w/long gray & red hair, brown felt hat, blue scarf, yellow
    shirt & brown pants, Thomas Dam 1961, 7" **$68.00**
Boy w/hand in pocket of molded-on bib overalls, glass eyes, gray
    hair, Nyform, 9" **$140.00**
Cave girl, porcelain, Danbury Mint, 1998, 9", MIB........... **$60.00**
Christmas pixie, red hair w/green ornament, blue eyes, red outfit,
    Royalty Designs of Florida, 1968, 2¾" **$40.00**
Clown, purple hair, orange glass eyes, ruffled outfit, Dam Things Est
    1964, 12"... **$65.00**
Cow, blond hair, amber eyes, Dam Things Est 1964, 6½x7½"... **$70.00**
Cow standing, short yellow hair, amber eyes, leather collar w/bell,
    Made in Denmark Dam, 6½x7½" **$55.00**
Devil, blue eyes & purple fur, tail intact, JN Reisler Made in
    Denmark, 1960s **$80.00**
Elephant, pink hair, amber eyes, Made in Denmark Dam Patent,
    1990 limited edition, 6" **$52.50**
Giraffe, gray-white hair, Thomas Dam Denmark, 1960s, 12"... **$52.50**
Girl, apricot hair, amber glass eyes, nude, Dam Things, 3" .. **$65.00**
Girl, blue hair w/black tips, orange eyes, nude, 1965, Scandia House
    heart-shaped tag, 2½" **$80.00**
Girl, blue-gray hair, blue felt dress, Dam Things, 3" **$55.00**
Girl, very long blond hair, rhinestone eyes, yellow & pink felt outfit,
    Dam Things, 1985, 2" **$45.00**
Girl (bank), pink hair w/black tips, purple-pink eyes, nude, Scandia
    House heart-shaped tag, 1965, 2½" **$60.00**
Girl w/lavender hair, orange glass eyes, red felt dress w/green & blue
    sqs on front, 64 Dam, 3".. **$55.00**
Girl w/long blond hair, molded clothing, metal Nyform #703 tag,
    some crazing, 7½"...**$110.00**
Girl w/orange-blond hair, orange eyes, yellow bunny suit w/white
    pom-pom tail, Thomas Dam, 2¾", MIB **$75.00**
Girl w/tail, white hair w/brown streaks, orange eyes, pointed ears,
    hair on tip of tail, nude, Dam Things Est 1965, 7" **$160.00**
Grandpa Claus, white hair & beard, red & white outfit, Dam
    Things, 1970s, 14" **$62.60**
Horse, long orange-blond mane, amber eyes, Dam Things Est 1964,
    2½x2" **$60.00**

Iggy Normous, brown hair, brown glass eyes, felt dress w/plaid blouse & patches, Dam Things 1964, w/tag, 11" **$70.00**

Iggy Normous, orange mohair, amber glass eyes, green outfit & hair bow, Dam Things Est 1964, 12", w/tag...................... **$95.00**

Lion, curly blond mane, orange eyes, unmarked Dam Things, 1960s, 4½".. **$55.00**

Lion, Dam, 1990 limited edition with soft body and less hair than the 1960s version, 5", from $65.00 to $70.00.
(Photo courtesy Pat Peterson)

Man w/toothy grin, black hair & skirt, metal NY #121 tag, 8" ...**$235.00**

Mermaid, bright red hair w/black tips, orange spiral eyes, silver metallic tail, Scandia House, 2¾" **$68.00**

Mod Maude, w/beanie hat, lg tie, print shirt & yellow skirt, red hair, glass eyes, Dam Things Est 1964, 12"........................ **$100.00**

Moon goon, raspberry mohair, amber yellow spiral eyes, nude, L Khem, 1964, 8" **$75.00**

Old lady w/dog & purse, glass eyes, blond hair, molded-on clothes, 9½" **$250.00**

Palace guard, black mohair helmet, Dam Things Est 1965, 8" ...**$40.00**

Pirate (bank), red hair, aqua plastic eyes, w/earrings, Thomas Dam, 7" **$50.00**

Rasta Troll, black & white chenille, black & white necklace w/ Egyptian-look charm, 2½" **$90.00**

Rasta Troll, gray-black chenille hair, ring in bellybutton, eyebrow & nose & 2 in 1 ear, Made in China, 2½"..................... **$110.00**

Robin Goodfellow, hands in pockets, molded-on clothes, balding w/ long white hair, Nyform #210, 21"............................ **$210.00**

Sock-It-To-Me on outfit, pink hair, black 'bug' eyes, Uneeda Wishnik, 6" **$50.00**

Tiny Tim, 3½x5", $65.00. (Photo courtesy LiveAuctioneers.com/
Auction Gallery of the Palm Beaches)

Troll House, vinyl w/3-D interior of bed, fireplace, chair &stool, table & 4 chairs, latch closures, 1960s, 9x12x6", EX **$47.50**

2-headed, black & white hair, orange eyes, w/roller skates, Uneeda, 1965, 2¾", MIP.. **$55.00**

2-headed, white & orange hair, orange eyes, green felt outfit, Uneeda, 1965, 2½" **$60.00**

TV Guides

This publication goes back to the early 1950s, and granted, those early issues are very rare. But what an interesting, very visual way to chronicle the history of TV programming!

Values in our listings are for examples in fine to mint condition; be sure to reduce them significantly when damage of any type is present. For insight into *TV Guide* collecting, we recommend *The TV Guide Catalog* by Jeff Kadet, the *TV Guide* specialist.

Advisor: Jeff Kadet (See Directory, *TV Guides*)

1953, August 7, Ray Milland on cover, $45.00.

1955, January 29-February 4, Martha Raye **$17.00**

1956, June 16-22, Cast of Father Knows Best.................... **$105.00**

1957, January 5-11, Arthur Godfrey................................. **$30.00**

1958, October 18-24, Perry Como **$33.00**

1961, January 7-13, Richard Boone **$45.00**

1961, October 14-20, Red Skelton **$29.00**

1963, January 12-18, Arnold Palmer **$31.00**

1963, October 18-25, Judy Garland **$36.00**

1965, April 3-9, Vince Edwards...................................... **$13.00**

1966, January 1-7, Carol Channing................................. **$12.00**

1967, February 18-24, Dean Martin & Friends.................... **$40.00**

1967, June 17-23, Ed Sullivan **$13.00**

1969, April 5-11, Smothers Brothers **$11.00**

1969, November 8-14, Andy Williams **$19.00**

1971, January 9-15, Andy Griffith................................... **$26.00**

1971, July 3-9, cast of Mod Squad.................................. **$57.00**

1971, November 6-12, William Conrad of Cannon **$10.00**

1973, January 6-12, 1972: How It Looked on Television.....**$16.00**

1973, June 30-July 6, Dennis Weaver of McCloud $12.00

1974, April 20-26, Peter Falk of Columbo..........................$16.00

1974, October 5-11, cast of Sanford & Son.......................$19.00

1975, May 10-16, Muhammad Ali $11.00

1975, October 4-10, Lee Remick as Janine $9.00

1976, November 27, Starsky and Hutch, $30.00. (Photo courtesy Greg Davis and Bill Morgan)

1977, January 1-7, John Travolta $29.00

1977, June 4-10, Alan Alda of M·A·S·H $12.00

1979, January 27-February 2, Katharine Hepburn..............$11.00

1979, September 1-7, Miss America $6.00

1980, May 32-June 6, cast of Vegas $15.00

1981, December 5-11, Lorna Patterson of Private Benjamin...$9.00

1981, January 3-9, cast of Too Close for Comfort $12.00

1983, January 8-14, John Madden.......................................$9.00

1984, December 22-28, cast of Webster...............................$9.00

1984, June 23-29, Connie Selleca $11.00

1985, April 6-12, Richard Chamberlain.............................$12.00

1985, October 26-November 1, network newscasters $6.00

1987, July 4-10, Barbara Walters $9.00

1988, February 13-19, Winter Olympics $11.00

1989, January 14-20, cast of Moonlighting.........................$19.00

1989, November 25-December 1, Victoria Principal $13.00

1990, July 28-August 3, Peter Pan, Rue McClanahan $8.00

1991, August 31-September 6, It's Kirk vs Picard $10.00

1991, January 5-11, Jane Pauley..$8.00

1992, May 16-22, Oprah..$4.00

1993, April 10-16, Ted Danson $12.00

1994, December 24-30, Year in Cheers & Jeers $8.00

1994, July 30- August 5, OJ Simpson..................................$4.00

1995, November 18-24, Beetles '95 ....$25.00

1996, July 6-12, Gillian Anderson of X-Files $20.00

1997, April 26-May 2, Tom Hanks $15.00

1997, August 16-22, Vegas Elvis $10.00

1997, September 20-26, Princess Diana $7.00

1998, July 4-10, Matt Laurer $6.00

1998, September 19-25, Tim Allen $35.00

1999, February 13-29, Rusty Wallace $23.00

1999, July 32-August 6, John F Kennedy Jr........................$15.00

1999, October 2-8, Yankees' Derek Jeeter $11.00

2000, April 2-7, Justin Timberlake of 'N Sync....................$17.00

2000, October 21-27, Santa's Little Helper - Simpsons........$20.00

2000, September 2-8, Dennis Miller.....................................$9.00

2001, October 13-19, Lucy w/nose on fire $15.00

Twin Winton

The genius behind the designs at Twin Winton was sculptor Don Winton. He and his twin, Ross, started the company while sill in high school in the mid-1930s. In 1952 older brother Bruce Winton bought the company from his two younger brothers and directed its development nationwide. They produced animal figures, cookie jars, and matching kitchenware and household items during this time. It is important to note that Bruce was an extremely shrewd business man, and if an order came in for a nonstandard color, he would generally accommodate the buyer — for an additional charge, of course. As a result, you may find a Mopsy (Raggedy Ann) cookie jar, for instance, in a wood stain finish or some other unusual color, even though Mopsy was only offered in the Collector Series in the catalogs. This California company was active until it sold in 1976 to Roger Bowermeister, who continued to use the Twin Winton name. He experimented with different finishes. One of the most common is a light tan with a high gloss glaze. He owned the company only one year until it went bankrupt and was sold at auction. Al Levin of Treasure Craft bought the molds and used some of them in his line. Eventually, the molds were destroyed.

One of Twin Winton's most successful concepts was their Hillbilly line — mugs, pitchers, bowls, lamps, ashtrays, decanters, and novelty items molded after the mountain boys in Paul Webb's cartoon series. Don Winton was the company's only designer, though he free-lanced as well. He designed for Disney, Brush-McCoy, Revell Toys, The Grammy Awards, American Country Music Awards, Ronald Reagan Foundation, and numerous other companies and foundations. Some of Don's more prominent pieces of art are currently registered with the Smithsonian in Washington, D.C. Don Winton passed away in 2007 and will be sorely missed. He was a great artist, husband, father, and friend. His artistic ability has always been appreciated, but only recently has proper recognition been given to the genius he truly possessed.

If you would like more information, read *A Collector's Guide to Don Winton Designs*, written by our advisor Mike Ellis. Other sources of information are *The Ultimate Collector's Encyclopedia of Cookie Jars* (three in the series) by Joyce and Fred Roerig.

See also Cookie Jars.

Advisor: Mike Ellis (See Directory, Twin Winton)

Ashtray, elf reclining, TW-205, 8x8".................................$100.00

Bank, Hotei, TW-411, 8" $50.00

Bank, kitten, TW-415, 8" $50.00

Bank, owl, TW-420, 8" $65.00

Bookends, chipmunk, Expanimal, TW-1237, 7½".............$125.00

Candleholder, Aladdin, TW-510, 6½x9½", ea $45.00

Candleholder, Verdi, long, TW-501L, 9½x4", ea $15.00

Candy jar, train, TW-358, 8x10"..$75.00

Canister, Cookie Bucket, TW-59, 8X9"...............................$60.00

Canister, Flour House, Canisterville, TW-101, 7x11".........$125.00

Canister, Sugar Bucket, TW-61, 6x7" **$40.00**
Creamer & sugar bowl, cow & bull, TW-220, 5x6" **$20.00**
Decanter, Pirate, Rum on base, #432, 11¾" **$50.00**
Figurine, blind mouse, mini, #208, ¾" **$6.00**
Figurine, collie sitting, TW-602, 7½" **$65.00**

Figurine, girl wearing Mickey Mouse ears, T-2, 5½", $150.00.
(Photo courtesy Mike Ellis)

Figurine, Mickey the Sorcerer, 8" **$150.00**
Figurine, Mountain Man, w/hat, #760, 18½" **$85.00**
Figurine, zebra, early, 5" **$45.00**
Flowerpot, gnome on ladder, 5½" **$8.00**
Mug, elephant, 3½x5" **$40.00**
Napkin holder, poodle, TW-474, 7x7" **$75.00**
Napkin holder, rabbit, TW-452, 6x4" **$150.00**
Ornament, Christmas, flying angel w/trumpet, A-130, 3⅜" .. **$4.00**
Plate, dinner; Wood Grain Line, 10" **$40.00**
Salt & pepper shakers, bear, TW-184, pr **$40.00**
Salt & pepper shakers, friar, TW-185, pr **$35.00**
Salt & pepper shakers, pear, TW-136, pr **$50.00**
Salt & pepper shakers, sheriff, TW-155, pr **$50.00**
Spoon rest, Dutch girl, TW-19, 5x10" **$40.00**
Spoon rest, kitten, TW-15, 5x10" **$40.00**
Wall pocket, rabbit (head), TW-302, 5½" **$100.00**

Hillbilly Line

Cigarette box, outhouse, H-109, 7" **$75.00**
Ice bucket, w/jug, TW-33, 14x7½" **$200.00**
Lamp, hillbilly on barrel, H-106, 27" **$300.00**
Mug, H-102, 5" **$30.00**
Pouring spout, H-104, 6½" **$15.00**
Punch bowl, 12", +8 cups **$350.00**

Universal

This pottery incorporated in Cambridge, Ohio, in 1934, the outgrowth of several smaller companies in the area. They produced many lines of dinnerware and kitchenware items, most of which were marked. They're best known for their Ballerina dinnerware (simple modern shapes in a variety of solid colors) and Cat-Tail (see Cat-Tail Dinnerware). The company closed in 1960.

Baby's Breath, bowl, fruit; 5½" **$7.50**
Baby's Breath, bowl, vegetable; 9" **$25.00**
Baby's Breath, cup & saucer **$20.00**
Baby's Breath, plate, bread & butter; 6" **$6.00**
Baby's Breath, sugar bowl **$12.50**
Ballerina, bowl, lug soup **$8.00**
Ballerina, bowl, vegetable; 9" **$28.00**
Ballerina, creamer **$15.00**
Ballerina, cup & saucer **$7.50**
Ballerina, gravy boat **$50.00**
Ballerina, plate, dinner; 10" **$10.00**
Ballerina, plate, luncheon; 9½" **$6.00**
Ballerina, salt & pepper shakers, pr **$18.00**
Bel Air, bowl, dessert; 5½" **$6.00**
Bel Air, creamer, 2½" **$12.50**
Bel Air, cup & saucer **$8.00**
Bel Air, plate, dinner; 10½" **$7.50**
Bel Air, plate, luncheon; 9" **$7.00**
Bittersweet, casserole, round, w/lid, 1¼-qt **$45.00**
Bittersweet, cup & saucer **$12.50**
Bittersweet, drippings jar, w/lid, from $30 to **$35.00**
Bittersweet, pitcher, w/lid **$65.00**
Bittersweet, salt & pepper shakers, egg shape, pr **$25.00**
Bittersweet, salt & pepper shakers, lg, pr **$17.50**
Bittersweet, stack set, 3 pcs w/lid **$50.00**
Calico Fruit, bowl, dessert; 5" **$14.00**
Calico Fruit, bowl, soup; 8" **$22.00**
Calico Fruit, bowl, vegetable; 9" L, from $25 to **$35.00**
Calico Fruit, cup & saucer **$28.00**
Calico Fruit, plate, bread & butter; 6" **$9.00**
Calico Fruit, plate, dinner; 10" **$35.00**
Calico Fruit, platter, 12" L **$35.00**

Calico Fruit, platter, 13", from $18.00 to $22.00.

Calico Fruit, platter, 15" L **$60.00**
Calico Fruit, refrigerator pitcher, w/lid **$85.00**
Harvest, bowl, cereal **$6.00**

Harvest, cake plate $27.50
Harvest, creamer $15.00
Harvest, cup & saucer..$7.50
Harvest, plate, salad $5.00
Iris, bowl, lug cereal $6.00
Iris, bowl, vegetable; 9" L..$25.00
Iris, cake plate, 13"..$28.00
Iris, gravy boat, from $25 to $32.00
Iris, pitcher, 7" $32.50
Iris, plate, luncheon; 9" $10.00
Poppy, creamer $20.00
Poppy, cup & saucer, from $12 to $15.00
Poppy, plate, luncheon; 9" $10.00
Poppy, plate, salad; sq..$7.50
Poppy, platter, 14" L, from $32 to $38.00
Shasta Daisy, bowl, vegetable; round.........................$22.00
Shasta Daisy, creamer $15.00
Shasta Daisy, cup & saucer, from $9 to $12.00
Shasta Daisy, plate, dinner; 10½", from $8 to...........$12.00
Shasta Daisy, platter, 12" L $30.00
Springtime, cake plate, w/handles $25.00
Springtime, cup & saucer...$10.00
Springtime, plate, bread & butter $4.00
Springtime, plate, dinner; 10" $8.00
Thistle, bowl, dessert..$7.00
Thistle, creamer $18.00
Thistle, cup & saucer..$14.00
Thistle, gravy boat & underplate................................$50.00
Thistle, plate, dinner; 10" $12.00
Thistle, sugar bowl, w/lid...$22.50
Woodvine, bowl, mixing; 8½" $30.00
Woodvine, bowl, vegetable; 9" $28.00

Woodvine, pitcher, 7", from $45.00 to $55.00.

Woodvine, plate, bread & butter..............................$4.00

Valentines

Whether you are new to collecting valentine cards or advanced, there are still treasures to be found in this diversified field. As your expertise expands you might want to advance to harder-to-find categories such as period valentine cards, artist-signed cards, or those of the folk art variety. Before investing much money in valentines, it would be wise to research the subject. Knowledge is power in any field of collecting. For more information we recommend *Valentines With Values, One Hundred Years of Valentines,* and *Valentines for the Eclectic Collector,* all by our advisor, Katherine Kreider. Unless noted otherwise, our values are for examples in excellent condition.

Advisor: Katherine Kreider (See Directory, Valentines)

Newsletter: *National Valentine Collectors Bulletin*
Evalene Pulati
P.O. Box 1404
Santa Ana, CA 92702
714-547-1355
www.valentinesdirect.com

Collie attached to doghouse with original chain, Made in Germany, 6¾x6x1½", EX, $50.00. (Photo courtesy Katherine Kreider)

Dimensional, 1D, big-eyed children in front of castle, 1920s, 6x3½x2½"..$20.00
Dimensional, 1D, cannon, accented w/die-cut scraps, Printed in Germany, early 1900s, 5x6x3" $35.00
Dimensional, 1D, Victorian horse-drawn carriage w/honeycomb paper puff, 1930s, 9x10x5"...$35.00
Dimensional, 2D, bluebirds & lily of the valley, Printed in Germany, 1930s, 7½x4x2½" $15.00
Dimensional, 2D, cat sitting on tennis racket, 1 in series, Printed in Germany, early 1900s, 7½x5x1" $20.00
Dimensional, 2D, cherub, Printed in Germany, early 1900s, 2x1x1" $3.00
Dimensional, 3D, holding hands w/forget-me-nots, early 1920s, 8x4x3½" $20.00
Dimensional, 3D, hot air balloon on the ocean, hold-to-light, Made in Germany, 1920s, 10x5x2" $25.00
Dimensional, 3D, Victorian costumed couple surrounded w/Victorian scraps, Printed in Germany, early 1900s, 8½x4x3".........$15.00

Flat, boy in tuxedo & top hat, easel back, Printed in Germany, early 1900s, 2½x1" **$4.00**

Flat, car (sedan), Printed in Germany, early 1900s, 9½x8"...**$35.00**

Flat, children under umbrella, Gibson, JG Scott, 1920s, 3½x2" ..**$4.00**

Flat, Flintstones, 1960s, 4½x3" **$6.00**

Flat, girl ironing, Carrington Co, 1930s, 4½x5½" **$3.00**

Flat, girl playing tambourine, 1920s, 3½x4" **$2.00**

Flat, ice cream soda, 1940s, 4x3" **$3.00**

Flat, Pink Panther, 1960s, 4½x3" **$6.00**

Flat, poodle, flocked, 1950s, 7x3½" **$4.00**

Flat, Raggedy Ann & Andy, Hallmark, 1970s, 5x4" **$6.00**

Flat, Raggedy Ann & Andy, Volland, 1930s, 6x6" **$35.00**

Flat, Rosie the Riveter, USA, 1940s, 4x3½" **$10.00**

Flat, Victorian girl holding tulips, Clappsaddle, early 1900s, 4x2½" **$10.00**

Flat, West Highland White terrier, 1930s, 4x5" **$5.00**

Folded-flat, chef w/rolling pin, 1940s, 4x3½" **$10.00**

Folded-flat, children walking on stilts, USA, 1940s, 3½x3" ...**$2.00**

Folded-flat, roller coaster amusement park ride, 1940s, 3½x4" ..**$2.00**

Greeting card, All My Love satin motif, hand-rolled crepe-paper roses, Paramount, 1950s, 12x10" **$10.00**

Greeting card, angel sitting on throne, unknown maker, early 1900s, 5½x3½" **$3.00**

Greeting card, Baby's 1st Valentine, 1950s, 4x4" **$2.00**

Greeting card, Bathing Beauty series, Whitney, USA, 1940s, 3x3½" **$3.00**

Greeting card, Donald Duck, Hallmark, 1946, 4x3½" **$10.00**

Greeting card, Flower series, Whitney, USA, 1940s, 3x3½" ... **$3.00**

Greeting card, German beer stein, Hallmark, 1950s, 9½x4½" ..**$5.00**

Greeting card, Kewpie, signed Rose O'Neill, ca 1910-20, 6½x4" **$30.00**

Greeting card, pearlized fan, hand colored, USA, Rust Craft, 1930s, 6x8½" **$6.00**

Greeting card, white embossed kitten, chromo litho, early 1900s, 5x3¾" **$3.00**

Honeycomb paper puff, basket, Beistle, 1920s, 5x4x4" **$6.00**

Honeycomb paper puff, big-eyed children having a tea party, air-brushed multicolor, 1920s, 7½x6x3" **$25.00**

Honeycomb paper puff, cherubs netting hearts, Printed in Germany, early 1900s, 5½x4¼x4¼" **$15.00**

Honeycomb paper puff, pedestal w/cherubs, Beistle, 1920s, 8x5x5" **$5.00**

Honeycomb paper puff, sailboat, airbrushed color, unknown maker, 1920s, 9x6x4" **$10.00**

Mechanical-flat, African American farmer, 1940s, 4x2" **$6.00**

Mechanical-flat, big-eyed children on scale, w/side easels, Printed in Germany, 7½x12" **$25.00**

Mechanical-flat, Boy Scout & Native American, Printed in Germany, 1930s, 3¾x5½" **$10.00**

Mechanical-flat, Cleo the Fish, Disney, 1938, USA, 4½x3½" ..**$15.00**

Mechanical-flat, fairy, Germany, 1920s, 4x2" **$6.00**

Mechanical-flat, Felix the Cat, 1930s, 6x6" **$15.00**

Mechanical-flat, Girl Scout riding horse, Printed in Germany, 1920s, 4x2½" **$10.00**

Mechanical-flat, ice cream cone w/child, Made in USA, 1950s, 6½x4¾" **$4.00**

Mechanical-flat, Mexican man in desert, USA, 1940s, 6x5" ..**$5.00**

Mechanical-flat, monkey playing harmonica, Printed in Germany, 1920s, 8x4x4" **$6.00**

Mechanical-flat, motorcycle & roadster car, Printed in Germany, early 1920s, 4½x6½" **$10.00**

Mechanical-flat, pedal car, Printed in Germany, early 1900s, 6x6" **$10.00**

Mechanical-flat, polar bear w/Eskimo, Printed in Germany, 1920s, 4x3½" **$3.00**

Mechanical-flat, Red Cross nurse, trademark G imprinted on back, Printed in Germany, 1940s, 7x5" **$5.00**

Mechanical-flat, Snow White, Disney, USA, 1938, 4½x3½" ..**$25.00**

Novelty, Avon scratch-off message cards, USA, 1977, 4x4"..**$10.00**

Novelty, Chiclets gum w/original boxes attached to card, Art Deco, USA, 1920s, 10x5" **$20.00**

Novelty, Dutch boy w/original stick of gum, JG Scott, Gibson, 1920s, 6½x3½" **$15.00**

Novelty, Jack in the Beanstalk booklet, 1940s, USA, 6½x3½" .. **$10.00**

Novelty, lollipop card w/policeman, Rosen, USA, 6x5" **$6.00**

Novelty, Lov-o-gram, Charles Twelvetrees, 4½x6" **$8.00**

Novelty, plastic sailboat w/lollipop, USA, 5½x6" **$10.00**

Novelty, puzzle, unknown maker, 1930s-40s, 5½x5½" **$10.00**

Penny Dreadful, barber, USA, 1930s, 8x6" **$3.00**

Penny Dreadful, doctor, USA, 1930s, 8x6" **$3.00**

Penny Dreadful, motorcycle cop, USA, 1930s, 8x6" **$3.00**

Wimpy, 1939, NM, $25.00. (Photo courtesy Katherine Kreider)

Vandor

For more than 35 years, Vandor has operated out of Salt Lake City, Utah. They're not actually manufacturers but distributors of novelty ceramic items made overseas. Some pieces will be marked 'Made in Korea,' while others are marked 'Sri Lanka,' 'Taiwan,' or 'Japan.' Many of their best things have been made in the last few years, and already collectors are finding them appealing. They have a line of kitchenware designed around 'Cowmen Mooranda' (an obvious take off on Carmen Miranda), another called 'Crocagator' (a darling crocodile modeled as a teapot, a bank, salt and pepper shakers, etc.), character-related items (Betty Boop and Howdy Doody, among others), and some really wonderful cookie jars reminiscent of '50s radios and jukeboxes.

See also Cat Collectibles; Elvis Presley Memorabilia.

Advisor: Lois Wildman (See Directory, Vandor)

Beatles, Yellow Submarine; musical globe, limited edition, 1999, MIB **$100.00**
Beatles, Yellow Submarine; salt & pepper shakers, submarine, 2-pc set **$18.00**
Betty Boop, cookie jar, she on motorcycle, 2000, 10½x9½" .. **$45.00**

Betty Boop, cookie jar, 1985, $150.00.

Betty Boop, salt & pepper shakers, she & Bimbo in wooden boat, 3-pc set **$18.00**
Betty Boop, salt & pepper shakers, she as salt in Deco headgear; Bimbo in top hat as pepper, MIB **$25.00**
Betty Boop, utensil holder, she (head only) in chef's hat, 1995 ...**$22.00**
Betty Boop, vase, she in sexy pose before rosebush, 1990, 8" **$40.00**
Elvis, cookie jar, EP in pink Cadillac playing guitar, limited edition, MIB **$135.00**
Flintstones, bank, Fred figure, 1990, 8½" **$35.00**
Harley-Davidson, lava lamp, MIB **$125.00**
Harley-Davidson, mini tea set, engine-shaped pot, 2 cups w/logo, on tire-shaped separate base, 1999, MIB **$20.00**
Honeymooners, cookie jar, 4 characters leaning out of New York City bus, limited edition, 1998, MIB **$165.00**
Howdy Doody, salt & pepper shakers, he in open car, 2-pc set...**$50.00**
Howdy Doody, trinket box, he waving from open pink car, 1990, 4½x5" **$20.00**
I Dream of Jeannie, lunch box, metal, TV w/Jeannie show on screen **$20.00**
John Howard Fryman, wall mask, beach scene, 1985, 8" **$18.00**
Koala Bear, teapot, bear as handle of black pot, 1990, 6", EX... **$50.00**
Lowell Herrero, mug, wide-eyed long-haired cat ea side, 1988, 3½" **$35.00**
Lowell Herrero, plate, cat on bathroom scales, 7½" **$32.00**

Lowell Herrero, plate, Neighborhood Watch cats, 7½" **$35.00**
Lowell Herrero, plate, penguins diving from iceberg, 1984, 8" ...**$23.00**
Mona Lisa, salt & pepper shakers, she (bust up) in separate picture frame, 1992, 4x3½x3", 2-pc set **$22.00**
Mona Lisa, teapot, waist up, pours through hand extended palm-side up, 1992 .... **$20.00**
Pink Flamingo, mug, 1985, 4" **$12.00**
Pink Panther, cookie jar, he in pink convertible **$40.00**
Popeye, jewelry box, 1990, 3½x2½x5" **$18.00**

**I Love Lucy, box, 6½",
$30.00.** (Photo courtesy LiveAuctioneers.com/Estate Galleries)

Vernon Kilns

Founded in Vernon, California, in 1931, this company produced many lines of dinnerware, souvenir plates, decorative pottery, and figurines. They employed several well-known artists whose designs no doubt contributed substantially to their success. Among them were Rockwell Kent, Royal Hickman, Don Blanding, and Walt Disney, all of whom were responsible for creating several of the lines most popular with collectors today.

In 1940 they signed a contract with Walt Disney to produce a line of figurines, vases, bowls, and several dinnerware patterns that were inspired by Disney's film *Fantasia*. The Disney items were made for a short time only and are now expensive.

The company closed in 1958, but Metlox purchased some of the molds and continued to produce some of their bestselling dinnerware lines through a specially established 'Vernonware' division.

Most of the ware is marked in some form or another with the company name and in most cases the name or number of the dinnerware pattern.

Advisor: Ray Vlach (See Directory, Dinnerware)

Chatelaine Shape

This designer pattern by Sharon Merrill was made in four color combinations: Topaz, Bronze, Platinum, and Jade.

Bowl, chowder; Topaz or Bronze, 6", from $12 to **$15.00**
Coffee cup, flat base, decorated Platinum or Jade, from $15 to... **$20.00**

Plate, chop; decorated Platinum or Jade, 16", from $65 to ..**$85.00**
Plate, dinner; leaf in 1 corner, Topaz or Bronze, 10½", from $15
   to **$17.00**
Sugar bowl, Topaz or Bronze, w/lid, from $20 to **$30.00**

Lotus and Pan American Lei Shape

Patterns on this shape include Lotus, Chinling, and Vintage. Pan American Lei was a variation with flatware from the San Marino line. To evaluate Lotus, use the low end of our range as the minimum value; the high end of values apply to Pan American Lei.

Ashtray, Pan American Lei only, 5¼" **$35.00**
Butter tray, oblong, w/lid, from $35 to **$60.00**
Plate, coupe; Pan American Lei only, 6" **$12.00**
Tumbler, #5, 14-oz, from $18 to..**$35.00**

Melinda Shape

Patterns found on this shape are Arcadia, Beverly, Blossom Time, Chintz, Cosmos, Dolores, Fruitdale, Hawaii (Lei Lani on Melinda is priced at two to three times base value), May Flower, Monterey, Native California, Philodendron. The more elaborate the pattern, the higher the value.

Monterey, bowl, salad, $75.00. (Photo courtesy Maxine Feek Nelson/ Bob Hutchins)

Bowl, lug chowder; 6", from $12 to.....................................**$16.00**
Butter tray, oblong, w/lid, from $45 to **$75.00**
Egg cup, from $18 to...**$25.00**
Platter, 12" L, from $20 to...**$30.00**
Platter, 14" L, from $35 to...**$50.00**
Salt & pepper shakers, pr from $15 to **$25.00**

Montecito Shape (and Coronado)

This was one of the company's more utilized shapes — well over 200 patterns have been documented. Among the most popular are the solid colors, plaids, the florals, westernware, and the Bird and Turnbull series. Bird, Turnbull, and Winchester 73 (Frontier Days) are two to four times base values. Disney hollow ware is seven to eight times base values. Plaids (except Calico), solid colors, Brown-eyed Susan are represented by the lower range.

Bowl, rim soup; 8½", from $12 to.......................................**$15.00**
Bowl, salad; round or angular, 13", ea from $40 to..............**$65.00**

Coaster/cup warmer, 4½", from $15 to **$25.00**
Jam jar, notched lid, 5", from $65 to **$95.00**
Pepper mill, wood encased, 4½", from $45 to **$55.00**

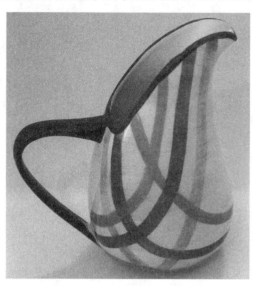

Tam 'O Shanter, pitcher, green and brown plaid, 8¼", from $30.00 to $35.00.

Plate, salad; 7½", from $8 to **$12.00**
Platter, 12" L, from $20 to...**$30.00**
Tumbler, #4, bulbous bottom, 3¾", from $18 to.................**$25.00**

San Clemente (Anytime)

Late research has determined the company name designated for this name was San Clemente, previously named Anytime. Patterns you will find on this shape include Tickled Pink, Heavenly Days, Anytime, Imperial, Sherwood, Frolic, Young in Heart, Rose-A-Day, and Dis 'N Dot.

Bowl, fruit; 5½", from $5 to...**$8.00**
Bowl, vegetable; round, 9", from $12 to **$18.00**
Butter pat, 2½", from $30 to **$40.00**
Butter tray, w/lid, from 425 to **$40.00**
Gravy boat, from $15 to **$20.00**
Mug, 12-oz, from $15 to **$25.00**
Platter, 11" L, from $14 to..**$20.00**
Syrup, Drip-cut top, from $45 to...**$65.00**
Teacup & saucer, from $10 to...**$15.00**
Tumbler, 14-oz, from $12 to...**$25.00**

San Fernando Shape

Known patterns for this shape are Desert Bloom, Early Days, Hibiscus, R.F.D, Vernon's 1860, and Vernon Rose.

Bowl, fruit; 5½", from $8 to...**$12.00**
Bowl, mixing; RFD only, 5", from $15 to **$19.00**
Bowl, mixing; 7", from $22 to **$29.00**
Creamer, regular, from $12 to...**$15.00**

Vernon Rose, plate, dinner; 10½", $18.00; cup and saucer, $18.00. (Photo courtesy Maxine Feek Nelson)

Salt & pepper shakers, pr from $16 to $24.00

San Marino Shape

Known patterns for this shape are Barkwood, Bel Air, California Originals, Casual California, Gayety, Hawaiian Coral, Heyday, Lei Lani (two to three times base values), Mexicana, Pan American Lei (two to three times base values), Raffia, Shadow Leaf, Shantung, Sun Garden, and Trade Winds.

Bowl, mixing; 5", from $15 to $18.00
Bowl, mixing; 9", from $28 to $35.00
Casserole, w/lid, 8" dia, from $35 to $65.00
Cup, jumbo; from $20 to $30.00
Flowerpot, w/saucer, 4", from $35 to $45.00
Plate, bread & butter; 6", from $5 to $8.00
Platter, 9½" L, from $10 to $15.00

Transitional (Year 'Round)

Late research has determined the company name designated for this shape was Transitional; it was previously named Year 'Round. Patterns on this shape include Blueberry Hill, Country Cousin, and Lollipop Tree.

Bowl, soup/cereal; from $8 to $10.00
Bowl, vegetable; 9", from $12 to $17.00
Coffeepot, 6-cup, from $25 to $45.00
Gravy boat, from $18 to $25.00
Mug, 12-oz, from $12 to $20.00
Plate, dinner; 10", from $9 to $13.00
Platter, 11" L, from $12 to $20.00
Teapot, from $25 to $50.00

Ultra Shape

More than 50 patterns were issued on this shape. Nearly all the artist-designed lines (Rockwell Kent, Don Blanding, and Disney) utilized Ultra. The shape was developed by Gale Turnbull, and many of the elaborate flower and fruit patterns can be credited to him as well; use the high end of our range as a minimum value for his work. For Frederick Lunning, use the mid range. For other artist patterns, use these formulas based on the high end: Blanding — 2X (Aquarium 3X); Disney, 5 – 7X; Kent — Moby Dick, 2½X, Our America, 3½X, and Salamina, 5 – 7X.

Bowl, salad; 11", from $45 to **$85.00**
Casserole, w/lid, 8" (inside dia), from $45 to **$95.00**

Hawaii by Blanding, creamer, $25.00; coffeepot, $170.00; sugar bowl, $25.00.

Creamer, individual; open, from $12 to **$20.00**
Egg cup, from $18 to **$25.00**
Plate, chop; 14", from $40 to **$60.00**
Sauceboat, from $20 to **$25.00**
Teapot, 6-cup, from $45 to **$100.00**

Fantasia and Disney Figures

Baby Pegasus, from $250.00 to $300.00. (Photo courtesy LiveAuctioneers.com/Morphy Auctions)

Baby Weems, #37, Disney, from $250 to **$350.00**
Centaurette, #17, Disney, from $600 to **$800.00**
Dumbo, #40 or #41, Disney, ea from $75 to **$150.00**
Elephant, #25, Disney, from $350 to **$400.00**

Goldfish bowl, #121, hand decorated, Disney, from $500 to.. **$600.00**
Hippo, #33, Disney, from $350 to.....................................**$400.00**
Ostrich, #29, Disney, from $1,200 to **$1,500.00**
Pegasus, #21, Disney, from $200 to **$300.00**
Sprite, #12, #10, #9, #7 or #11, Disney, ea from $250 to..**$300.00**
Sprite, #8, Disney, hard to find, from $300 ....**$400.00**
Unicorn sitting, #14, Disney, from $400 to **$500.00**
Winged Pegasus vase, light blue, Disney, 7½x12", from $500
    to **$700.00**

Specialty Wares

Ashtray, city &/or state souvenir, 1-color transfer.................**$20.00**
Cup & saucer, demitasse; souvenir, from $20 to **$30.00**
Pitcher, state seal, Melinda shape, 1½-pt, from $45 to.........**$50.00**
Plate, city &/or state souvenirs, 1-color transfer...................**$20.00**
Plate, French Opera Reproductions, 8½", from $18 to........**$25.00**
Plate, historic places, from $25 to **$45.00**
Plate, Mother Goose **$65.00**
Plate, Music Masters, 8½", from $18 to **$25.00**

**Plate, Noah and the Ark, Gayle Oler, 1953, from $85.00
to $95.00.**

Plate, presidential or armed services, from $35 to **$75.00**
Plate, Race Horse, 10½" **$75.00**
Plate, school or organizations, from $20 to **$35.00**
Plate, Trader Vic, 9½", minimum value **$85.00**
Plate, transportation theme, multicolor, from $65 to...........**$95.00**
Plate, transportation theme, 1-color transfer, from $45 to ...**$60.00**
Plate, Ye Old Times, 10½", from $35 to...............................**$45.00**
Spoon rest, souvenir, minimum value **$35.00**

Vietnam War Collectibles

In 1949 the French had military control over Vietnam. This was
true until they suffered a sound defeat at Dienbienphu in 1954. This
action resulted in the formation of the Geneva Peace Conference

which allowed the French to make peace and withdraw but left
Vietnam divided into North Vietnam and South Vietnam. The
agreement was to reunite the country in 1956 when the general elec-
tions took place. But this didn't happen because of South Vietnam's
political objections. The strife continued and slowly America was
drawn into the conflict from the time of the Eisenhower administration until the Paris Peace Agreement in 1973. The war itself linger-
ed on until 1975 when communist forces invaded Saigon and crushed
the South Vietnamese government there.

Items relating to this conflict from the 1960s and early 1970s
are becoming collectible. Most reflect the unpopularity of this war.
College marches and political unrest headlined the newspapers of
those years. Posters, pin-back buttons, political cartoons, and many
books from that period reflect the anti-war philosophy of the day
and are reminders turbulent times and political policies that cost the
lives of many brave young men. Unless otherwise noted, our values
are for items in excellent to near mint condition.

Belt, ammo; US Army, olive drab cloth, adjustable, holds 10
    shells **$50.00**
Belt, pistol; US Army/Marine Corps, olive drab web, brass fit-
    tings **$55.00**
Beret, green, Van-Thanh label, original issue.....................**$100.00**
Book, Uniforms & Equipment of US Military Advisors in Vietnam,
    PW Miraldi, hardcover, 2000, M w/dust jacket **$60.00**
Book, USS FDR Aircraft Carrier Cruise, 1964 ....**$65.00**
Book, USS Ticonderoga CVA-14 Cruise, 1966-67 ....**$115.00**
Boots, jungle; olive drab canvas & brown leather, double buckle
    closures **$165.00**
Boots, tanker's combat; black leather, straps & buckles........**$90.00**
Bowie knife, Special Forces, Vietnam, Mike Force NCO, Western, in
    brown leather sheath...**$215.00**
Canteen, Army M-1945 w/chain & cap, M-1956 cup & M-1963
    olive-drab cover..**$60.00**
Case, scope; M-14 ART (adjustable ranging telescope) II, ca
    1968 ....**$165.00**
Compass, US Army Magnetic, Union Instrument Corp, dated 1964,
    in olive drab pouch **$60.00**
Compass, US Navy Seal Team, metal w/olive drab nylon wrist band,
    USA WCCo, 2½" dia, in pouch **$65.00**
Field glasses, M19 sniper issue, 7x50, M in EX case **$225.00**
Hat, boonie; camo cloth w/embroidered brim, Combat Infantry
    Badge **$75.00**
Hat, jungle; olive drab cloth, w/insect net..........................**$130.00**
Helmet, MP, black w/red & white stripes, 560th Military Police,
    liner dated 1966, restored **$90.00**
Helmet, Paratrooper M1-C, w/camo cover, some wear to inside
    straps, from $250 to...**$300.00**
Helmet, US Army, painted steel w/jungle camo, w/fabric liner, ca
    1969 ....**$60.00**
Holster, shoulder; US Marine Cor M7, leather, for Colt 45
    M1911A1 pistol, dated 1964 ....**$135.00**
Jacket, field; US Army Airborn Ranger Special Forces, w/all patch-
    es...**$75.00**
Jacket, flight; G-1 style, brown leather, brass zipper, professionally
    restored, dated 1970 ....**$190.00**
Jacket, flight; US Air Force MA-1, Conmar zippers, 1965...**$55.00**

Jacket, jungle; olive drab cotton, button front, rolled-up cuffs, 1967 ....$70.00

Lighter, Zippo, Combat Medic Vietnam, red enameling....$130.00

Lighter, Zippo, Eat Your Heart Out Lifers, sexy couple, 1978 ....$100.00

Lighter, Zippo, 85th Evac Hospital, Vietnam engraved on sides, wear to chrome finish, dated 1966..............................$168.00

Machette, pilot's survival; black Bakelite handle, blackened steel blade, marked Imperial, Prov RI, in A-1 sheath $175.00

Magazine, The Vietnam Grunt, 1968, 48-pg, 10x7".........$140.00

Map, printed silk, Vietnam & Thailand, 25x38" $55.00

Medal, Bronze Star, M in case w/award & citation $60.00

Medal, Vietnam Campaign, map in blue circle, 6-pointed star w/ sunburst behind, 1965 on ribbon, MIB.......................$80.00

Patch, Air Cavalry D Troup 7th Squadron 17th Cavalry Recon insignia w/Snoopy, pre-1973...$75.00

Patch, CCS, $35.00. (Photo courtesy LiveAuctioneers.com/ Livingston's Auctions)

Patch, Special Forces, Grim Reaper Ace of Spades, embroidered cloth...$45.00

Patch, The Deans 120th Aviation Company, embroidered, w/original cheese-cloth backing..$75.00

Pendant, WAR letters in circle, metal w/red enameling......$110.00

Poncho, US Army/Marine Corps, olive drab coated nylon, Mitchell pattern camo straps, dated 1961 ....$65.00

Poncho liner, green camo w/double center, seam, w/tie-down strings, original instruction tag, ca 1969, 76x60" $68.00

Poster, See...Accounts of a Nation Destined..., LBJ lounging amid war scenes, black & white, ca 1969, 37x23" $85.00

Ring, US Marines Viet Nam, raising flag at Iwo Jima scene/Tun Tavern 1775 on sides, 10k gold $315.00

Rucksack, ARVN/Indigenous Ranger Pack, water-resistant cotton, 1969, 16x12", M $150.00

Rucksack frame, radio packboard assembly, complete w/straps, unused, M $200.00

Statuette, Our Sons, Our Brothers, Our Friends, cold-cast polymer, bronze patina, replica of Vietnam War Memorial, 20" ..$150.00

Trousers, OG-107 jungle fatiques, 7-pocket, rip-stop poplin, ca 1968-69...$80.00

Uniform, tiger stripes, button-down shirt w/camp pants, Viet Cong Hunting Club patch $315.00

Wristwatch, Benrus, olive drab finish on stainless steel, w/replaced strap $70.00

Wristwatch, Omega-3 Arrows Sign, stainless steel, Swiss Made, 17-jewel $200.00

Wristwatch, Westclox 75071, General, olive green paint, w/black hand strap, dated 1968...$135.00

Yearbook, US First Infantry Division in Vietnam, 1968 ....$170.00

Viking

Located in the famous glassmaking area of West Virginia, this company has been in business since the 1950s; they're most famous for their glass animals and birds. Their Epic Line (circa 1950s and 1960s) was innovative in design and vibrant in color. Rich tomato-red, amberina, brilliant blues, strong greens, black, amber, and deep amethyst were among the rainbow hues in production at that time. During the 1980s the company's ownership changed hands, and the firm became known as Dalzell-Viking. Viking closed their doors in 1998.

Some of the Epic Line animals were reissued in crystal, crystal frosted, and black.

Ashtray, green crackle, 3 incurvate rests, 7¾" dia $20.00

Bowl, amethyst, 4-footed, w/clear flower frog, 3½x6⅜".......$40.00

Bowl, clear w/etched flowers, 3-toed, incurvate rim, 3½x4½" .. $37.50

Bowl, orange, 3 swirling scallops, 10½" $40.00

Bowl, ruby, 3-footed, 2½x5" $32.50

Bowl, ruby, 6-scallop rim, footed, #1434, 7" $27.50

Bowl, ruby w/silver overlay poinsettias, footed, 8" $30.00

Candlesticks, Hurricane, deep teal blue, 3-arm, ca 1957, 6¼x4¾", pr $65.00

Candy box, violin shape, purple amethyst, 10¼" L.............$42.50

Compote, black w/dolphin standard, ruffled rim, 6x9x6½". $20.00

Compote, Bull's Eye, ruby, with lid, 11½", from $50.00 to $60.00. (Photo courtesy M.R. Miller)

Fairy lamp, cabbage leaf, ruby red, 6½" $35.00

Fairy lamp, Diamond Point, smoke, 7" $22.00

Fairy lamp, owl, amberina, 7" **$80.00**
Fairy lamp, potbellied stove, blue **$55.00**
Paperweight, apple, blue w/green stem, w/label, 4¼" **$42.50**
Paperweight, mushroom, black, w/label, 2½x3½" **$45.00**
Paperweight, mushroom, clear, 2x2½" **$20.00**
Paperweight, strawberry, red w/green stem, 4½" **$35.00**
Paperweights, mushrooms, orange, w/labels, 3½" dia, 2⅝" dia, pr **$60.00**
Trio, Janice, ruby, cup & saucer w/8½" plate **$55.00**
Vase, bud; amberina, footed, pulled rim, 14" **$22.50**
Vase, green, slender w/pulled rim, footed, 17" **$25.00**

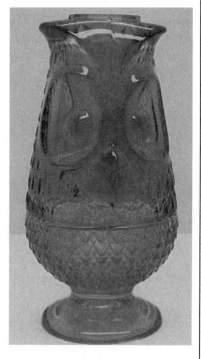

Fairy lamp, owl, amber, 7¼", from $35.00 to $45.00.

Vistosa

Vistosa was produced from about 1938 through the early 1940s. It was Taylor, Smith, and Taylor's answer to the very successful Fiesta line of their nearby competitor, Homer Laughlin. Vistosa was made in four solid colors: mango red, cobalt blue, light green, and deep yellow. 'Pie crust' edges and a dainty five-petal flower molded into handles and lid finials made for a very attractive yet nevertheless commercially unsuccessful product.

Bowl, cereal; 6¾" **$22.00**
Bowl, cream soup; from $30 to **$35.00**
Bowl, fruit **$10.00**
Bowl, salad; footed, rare, 12", minimum value **$200.00**
Bowl, soup; lug handle, from $25 to **$30.00**
Bowl, 3x9¼", from $32 to **$38.00**
Chop plate, 12" **$40.00**
Chop plate, 15", from $40 to **$50.00**
Coffee saucer, AD; from $10 to **$15.00**
Coffeepot, AD; from $80 to **$90.00**
Creamer, from $20 to **$25.00**

Egg cup, footed, from $50 to **$70.00**
Pitcher/water jug, 2-qt, from $90 to **$120.00**
Plate, 6" **$9.00**
Plate, 7", from $12 to **$15.00**
Plate, 9", from $15 to **$20.00**
Plate, 10", from $25 to **$35.00**
Platter, 13" L, from $40 to **$45.00**
Salt & pepper shakers, 3¼", pr from $25 to **$30.00**
Sauceboat, from $175 to **$200.00**
Sugar bowl, w/lid, from $25 to **$30.00**
Teacup & saucer, from $20 to **$30.00**

Teapot, $90.00.

W.S. George

From the turn of the century until the late 1950s, this East Palestine, Ohio, company produced many lines of dinnerware. Some were solid colors, but the vast majority were decaled. Most of the lines were marked. If you'd like more information, we recommend *Collector's Encyclopedia of American Dinnerware* by Jo Cunningham.

Apollo, bowl, vegetable; oval, 9⅝" **$15.00**
Apollo, plate, bread & butter; 6" **$2.50**
Apollo, plate, dinner; 9¾" **$12.00**
Apollo, sugar bowl, w/lid **$16.00**
Basketweave, bowl, vegetable; oval **$18.00**
Basketweave, cup & saucer **$15.00**
Basketweave, plate, luncheon **$7.50**
Basketweave, platter, 11" L **$30.00**
Blossoms, bowl, rimmed cereal **$12.00**
Blossoms, creamer, 10-oz **$25.00**
Blossoms, plate, dinner; 10" **$27.50**
Blossoms, plate, salad; 8" **$9.50**
Blossoms, platter, 11½" L **$28.00**
Blushing Rose, bowl, rimmed soup **$12.50**
Blushing Rose, bowl, vegetable; oval, 9¼" **$27.50**
Blushing Rose, cup & saucer **$15.00**
Blushing Rose, platter, 11½" L **$35.00**
Camellia, bowl, vegetable; round **$27.50**

Camellia, bowl, vegetable; round, w/lid $60.00
Camellia, cup & saucer $12.50
Camellia, plate, bread & butter.....................................$4.00
Cherokee, bowl, rimmed soup $8.00
Cherokee, cup & saucer $7.50
Cherokee, plate, luncheon; 9¼" $7.50
Cherokee, platter, 11½" L...$28.50
Iroquois-Red, bowl, rimmed soup..................................$10.00
Iroquois-Red, creamer $8.00
Iroquois-Red, gravy boat $27.50
Iroquois-Red, plate, salad; 7¼".....................................$6.00
Petalware, bowl, coupe cereal $7.50
Petalware, bowl, vegetable; oval $28.00
Petalware, bowl, vegetable; round $32.00
Petalware, plate, dinner $14.00
Petalware, platter, 11" L...$30.00
Pine Cone, bowl, dessert; 5" $6.00
Pine Cone, bowl, vegetable; oval $15.00
Pine Cone, plate, dinner $12.00
Pine Cone, plate, luncheon $6.00
Pine Cone, platter, 13½" L...$22.00
Priscilla, bowl, vegetable; oval.....................................$18.00
Priscilla, creamer $15.00
Priscilla, cup & saucer...$8.50
Priscilla, platter, 10½" L...$18.00
Rosita, bowl, rimmed soup $7.50
Rosita, gravy boat...$27.50
Rosita, plate, luncheon; 9½" $7.50
Rosita, platter, 13½" L...$20.00
Tango, bowl, coupe soup...$7.50
Tango, cup & saucer $7.50
Tango, plate, dinner $7.50
Tango, plate, salad; 7⅛"...$6.00
Tango, platter, 11" L..$20.00

Wade Porcelain

If you've attended many flea markets, you're already very familiar with the tiny Wade figures, most of which are 2" and under. Wade made several lines of these miniatures, but the most common were made as premiums for the Red Rose Tea Company. Most of these sell for $3.50 to $7.00 or so, with a few exceptions such as the Gingerbread Man. Wade also made a great number of larger figurines as well as tableware and advertising items.

The Wade Potteries began life in 1867 as Wade and Myatt when George Wade and a partner named Myatt opened a pottery in Burslem — the center for potteries in England. In 1882 George Wade bought out his partner, and the name of the pottery was changed to Wade and Sons. In 1919 the pottery underwent yet another change in name to George Wade & Son Ltd. Another Wade Pottery was established in 1891 — J & W Wade & Co., which in turn changed its name to A.J. Wade & Co. in 1927. At this time (1927) Wade Heath & Co. Ltd. was also formed.

These three potteries plus a new Irish pottery named Wade (Ireland) Ltd. were incorporated into one company in 1958 and given the name The Wade Group of Potteries. In 1990 the group was taken over by Beauford PLC and became Wade Ceramics Ltd. It sold again in early 1999 to Wade Management and is now a private company.

If you'd like to learn more, we recommend *The World of Wade, The World of Wade, Book 2; Wade Price Trends — First Edition; The World of Wade — Figurines and Miniatures;* and *The World of Wade, Ireland,* by Ian Warner and Mike Posgay.

Advisor: Ian Warner (See Directory, Wade)

Club: The Official International Wade Collector's Club
Wade Ceramics Ltd.
Royal Victoria Pottery, Westport Rd.
Burslem, Stoke-on-Trent, Staffordshire, ST6 4AG, England, UK
club@wadecollectorsclub.co.uk
www.wadecollectorsclub.co.uk

Animal figurine, Alsatian, glass eyes, ca 1936, 5¼x7½" $350.00
Animal figurine, panther, early to late 1930s, 8½"..........$1,500.00
Animal figurine, Playful Lamb, 1947-53................................$300.00
Animal figurine, single budgerigar, no flowers, 1940s-50s, 7½"...$350.00
Connoisseur's Collection, Goldcrest, 5¼" $400.00

Dinosaurs, Series #1, Jurassic Park, 1993, set of five, $40.00. (Photo courtesy LiveAuctioneers.com/Tom Harris Auctions)

Disney, Mickey Mouse Plate, 1934-late 1950s, 5¾"............$30.00
Disney Hatbox series, Baby Pegasus, 1956-65, 1¾" $90.00
Dogs & Puppies series, Red Setter, 1973-82, 2¼" $30.00
Flower, Anemones, 1930-39, 6" $75.00
Happy Families series, Owl Parent, 1978-86, 1¾" $50.00
Happy Families series, Pig Parent, 1978-86, 1⅛" $50.00
Mabel Lucie Atwell character, Sam, 3⅛" $225.00
Nursery Favourite, Boy Blue, 1974, 2⅞"............................$45.00
Nursery Favourite, Miss Muffet, 1972, 2⅝" $40.00
Nursery Favourite, Old King Cole, 1973, 2½" $55.00
Nursery Rhyme Character, Blynken, no flowers, 1949-58, 2"...$175.00
Nursery Rhyme Character, Goldilocks, 1949-58, 4" $300.00
Nursery Rhyme Character, Soldier, 1949-58, 3" $225.00
Red Rose Tea (Canada), Butterfly, 1967-73, ½x1¾" $7.00
Red Rose Tea (Canada), Fox, 1967-73 ....$6.00
Robertson's Gollies, Saxophone Player, early to mid-1960s,
2⅝" $170.00
Souvenir vase, Nova Scotia, 4½" $14.00

Spirit Containers, Cockatoo, 5" $150.00
Whimsies, Giant Panda, 1953-59, 1¼" $48.00
Whimsies, Golden Eagle, Land series, 1984-88, 1⅛x1¾" $40.00
Whimsies, Hedgehog, 1974, ⅞" $8.00
Whimsies, Lamb, 1971-84, 2⅜x1⅛" $10.00
Whimsies, Polar Bear Blow-Up, ca 1962, 6" $300.00
Whimsies, Rhinoceros, 1955, 1¾" $45.00
Whoppas, Fox, 1976-81, 1¼x2½" $25.00
Whoppas, Otter, 1¼" $25.00
World of Survival series, African Elephant, 1978-82, 6x10" ..$700.00
Zamba Ware Ashtray, sq, 4¼" $12.00

Wall Pockets

A few years ago there were only a handful of avid wall pocket collectors, but today many are finding them intriguing. They were popular well before the turn of the century. Roseville and Weller included at least one and sometimes several in many of their successful lines of art pottery, and other American potteries made them as well. Many were imported from Germany, Czechoslovakia, China, and Japan. By the 1950s, they were passé.

Some of the most popular today are the figurals. Look for the more imaginative and buy the ones you especially like. If you're buying to resell, look for those designed as animals, large exotic birds, children, luscious fruits, or those that are particularly eye catching. Appeal is everything. Examples with a potter's mark are usually more pricey (for instance Roseville, McCoy, Hull, etc.), because of the crossover interest in collecting their products. For more information refer to *Collector's Encyclopedia of Made in Japan Ceramics* by Carole Bess White; and *Collector's Guide to Wall Pockets, Affordable and Others,* by Marvin and Joy Gibson.

Advisor: Carole Bess White (See Directory, Japan Ceramics)

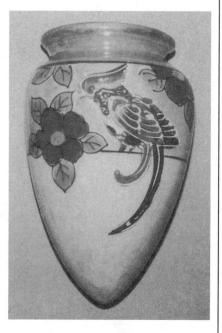

Bird (moriage) and flowers on lustre glazes, 5¼", from $20.00 to $25.00. (Photo courtesy Bill and Betty Newbound)

Angel in pink kneeling in prayer, 6x4" $65.00
Bacchus, aqua, Deco-style, Made in Japan, from $55 to $85.00

Bamboo sticks, green crackle graze, La Miranda California Pottery, ca 1940, 15x3½", pr $140.00
Basket, blue w/white bird & branch on front, majolica style, Japan, 7½", from $20 to $35.00
Basket w/grapes, oval w/embossed basketweave & grape cluster, Made in Japan, 6¾", from $12 to $15.00
Bird, white w/blue crest on flowering branch, Japan, 8", from $65 to $85.00
Bird, yellow w/red wing on flowering blue branch, majolica style, Japan, 8", from $45 to $65.00
Bird & flowers on bulbous vase shape, majolica style, Japan, 6", from $20 to $35.00
Bird mama w/2 babies, Japan, 7¾", from $45 to $65.00
Bird w/teal breast & long tail, majolica style, Japan, 10", from $45 to $65.00
Butterfly, brown body w/yellow & orange wings, silver accents, Germany #3987, 4x3¾" $30.00
Circle w/lg embossed flower & cylindrical vase w/embossed leaves, blue, Made in Japan, 9½", from $55 to $85.00
Clock, It's Later Than You Think on front, HI Co, 1953, 6¾", from $20 to $25.00
Cup & saucer (sq), green leaf decoration, Cherokee China Co, 7½", from $12 to $15.00
Giraffe (figural), recumbent, yellow matt, Mackies California, 15x7" $50.00
Grinder, warm brown, Marcia of California WP-1, 10½", from $20 to $25.00
Hat w/wide brim, white w/red bow & flower, USA, 6", from $10 to $12.00

Horsehead and horseshoe, Japan mark, 8½", from $20.00 to $25.00. (Photo courtesy Bill and Betty Newbound)

Iris, light yellow w/green stem & leaves, Made in Japan, 7½" ..$60.00
Kitten in pink hat holding basket of red roses, #OT6845, 7x5" ..$50.00
Lady's face w/long, thick eyelashes (rectangular) centers sunflower, #S915, 7" $50.00
Nun in blue kneeling in prayer w/white cross behind her, Napco #K1717, 5", from $20 to $30.00
Oriental girl by lg bamboo stalk, Francis Hamilton, 7", from $22 to $25.00
Oriental lady w/basket on back, multicolored semi-matt glazes, Bando ware, Made in Japan, 1922, 9", from $65 to ...$100.00

Owl standing on green branch, Czechoslovakia #6205A, 7½"..**$110.00**

Parrot on horseshoe, muted colors, 7", from $18 to............**$22.00**

Peacock w/teal head, majolica style, Japan, 7", from $20 to.**$35.00**

Pine cone, tan gloss, Corteny, 4¾", from $6 to.................**$8.00**

Rose on stem, pastel pink & green, Czechoslovakia, from $30 to..**$35.00**

Skillet w/lg applied yellow flower, USA, 10", from $12 to...**$15.00**

Swallows, flowers & leaves on short-necked bulbous vase shape (ivory & blue), Made in Japan, 6½x4" **$45.00**

Teacup & saucer, white w/flower & leaf decoration, yellow rim, Japan, 6" dia, from $20 to **$35.00**

Teapot, chef (face) looking at fly, opening in white hat, PY in oval, 7½x5" **$55.00**

Tokanabe style, flowers on bulbous vase shape, Japan, 6", from $20 to **$35.00**

Vase, cone form, Art Deco roses in multicolored glazes, Made in Japan, 8½", from $35 to...**$45.00**

Violin, blue w/gold accents, Goldra E Palestine Ohio, 9", from $12 to **$15.00**

Wallace China

This company operated in California from 1931 until 1964, producing many lines of dinnerware, the most popular of which today are those included in their Westward Ho assortment: Boots and Saddles, Rodeo, and Pioneer Trails. All of these lines were designed by artist Till Goodan, whose signature appears in the design. All are very heavy, their backgrounds are tan, and the designs are done in dark brown. The Rodeo pattern has accents of rust, green, and yellow. When dinnerware with a western theme became so popular a few years ago, Rodeo was reproduced, but the new trademark includes neither 'California' or 'Wallace China.'

Boots & Saddle, bowl, fruit; 5", from $50 to......................**$60.00**

Boots & Saddle, bowl, serving; oval, 12x9¼", from $135 to..**$175.00**

Boots & Saddle, bowl, 9", from $100 to..........................**$125.00**

Boots & Saddle, bowl, 10"...**$250.00**

Boots & Saddle, pitcher, disk type, 7½", from $225 to **$275.00**

Boots & Saddle, plate, bread & butter; 7", from $40 to **$60.00**

Boots & Saddle, plate, dinner; 10½", from $75 to **$100.00**

Boots & Saddle, platter, 15" L, from $200 to **$235.00**

Boots & Saddle, salt & pepper shakers, 3¾", pr.................**$60.00**

Chuck Wagon, bowl, oval, 1½x8", from $65 to.................**$85.00**

Chuck Wagon, plate, cereal; 6", from $30 to **$35.00**

Dahlia, cup & saucer, from $35 to...................................**$40.00**

Dahlia, platter, 11½" L **$40.00**

Dahlia, teapot **$100.00**

El Rancho, bowl, fruit; 5" **$40.00**

El Rancho, cup & saucer **$45.00**

El Rancho, plate, bread & butter; 7" **$37.50**

El Rancho, plate, dinner; 10½", from $70 to.....................**$90.00**

El Rancho, plate, salad; 8¼"...**$45.00**

Hibiscus, bowl, 4½x8¾"...**$90.00**

Hibiscus, cup & saucer **$60.00**

Little Buckaroo, bowl, cereal; 5¾", from $40 to **$50.00**

Little Buckaroo, plate, 9", from $45 to **$55.00**

Longhorn, bowl, lg longhorn, no branding iron, rare, 2x5"..**$165.00**

Longhorn, bowl, mixing; lg..**$295.00**

Longhorn, creamer, footed, 3x6", from $125 to...................**$135.00**

Longhorn, cup & saucer, 6½", from $150 to.....................**$165.00**

Longhorn, disk pitcher, 7½", from $300.00 to $325.00.

Longhorn, plate, bread & butter; 7" **$75.00**

Longhorn, plate, dinner; 10½", from $235 to **$300.00**

Longhorn, platter, oval, 15x13½" **$500.00**

Longhorn, salt & pepper shakers, 5", pr **$135.00**

Longhorn, shot glass, glass w/fired-on longhorn **$75.00**

Madrid, platter, Mexican by campfire, 12x8".....................**$55.00**

Pioneer Trails, ashtray, Kit Carson portrait in center, 4 rests, 5½" dia..**$110.00**

Pioneer Trails, bowl, cereal; 2x6".....................................**$80.00**

Pioneer Trails, bowl, vegetable; oval, 12" L, from $200 to .**$240.00**

Pioneer Trails, cup & saucer, 3", 6".................................**$55.00**

Pioneer Trails, plate, bread & butter; 7", from $50 to..........**$65.00**

Pioneer Trails, sugar bowl, w/lid, 4½x4½" **$135.00**

Rod's Steak House, cup & saucer.....................................**$40.00**

Rod's Steak House, teapot, individual, 4x6½"...................**$195.00**

Rodeo, bowl, fruit; flared rim, 2x5"................................**$60.00**

Rodeo, bowl, salad; 6x14", minimum value.....................**$600.00**

Rodeo, bowl, soup; 14-oz, from $40 to..............................**$50.00**

Rodeo, bowl, vegetable; oval, 12" L, from $160 to **$200.00**

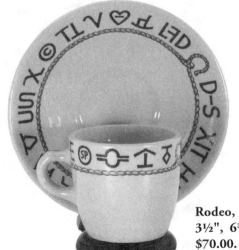

Rodeo, cup and saucer, 3½", 6¾", from $50.00 to $70.00.

Rodeo, cup & saucer, demitasse.............................$40.00
Rodeo, pitcher, disk type, 7x7½", from $195 to...............$225.00
Rodeo, plate, luncheon; trick roper, 9", from $125 to.......$150.00
Rodeo, salt & pepper shakers, 5", pr from $90 to.............$120.00
Rodeo, sugar bowl, open, from $65 to......................$75.00
Shadow Leaf, butter pat, 3", from $20 to...................$25.00
Shadow Leaf, grill plate, 3-compartment, 10¼"...............$40.00
Shadow Leaf, pitcher, 7½", from $125 to...................$140.00
Shadow Leaf, plate, bread & butter; 7⅛"...................$30.00
Shadow Leaf, plate, dinner; 10½", from $65 to..............$80.00
Shadow Leaf, platter, 9" L, from $40 to...................$60.00
Shadow Leaf, teapot..$75.00
Southwest Desert, creamer..................................$65.00
Wild Rose, plate, dinner; 10"...............................$27.50
Ye Olde Mill, plate, dinner; 10½"..........................$20.00

Watt Pottery

The Watt Pottery Company operated in Crooksville, Ohio, from 1922 until sometime in 1935. It appeals to collectors of country antiques, since the body is yellow ware and its decoration rather quaint.

Several patterns were made: Apple, Autumn Foliage, Cherry, Dutch Tulip, Morning-Glory, Pansy, Rooster, Tear Drop, Starflower, and Tulip among them. All were executed in bold brush strokes of primary colors. Some items you'll find will also carry a stenciled advertising message, made for retail companies as premiums for their customers.

For further study, we recommend *Watt Pottery* by Susan Morris-Snyder and Dave Morris.

Advisor: Susan Morris-Snyder (See Directory, Dinnerware)

Club: Watt Collectors Association
Newsletter: *Watt's News*
P.O. Box 253
Sussex, WI 53089-0253
wattcollectorsassociation.com

Apple, bowl, #106, 3½x10¾"..............................$350.00
Apple, bowl, mixing; #9, ribbed, 9".......................$85.00
Apple, canister, #72, 9½x7"...............................$500.00
Apple, coffeepot, #115, 9¾"...........................$3,000.00
Apple, creamer, 4"..$90.00
Apple, ice bucket, w/lid, 7¼x7½"........................$275.00
Apple, mug, #121, 3".......................................$18.50
Apple, pitcher, #17, 8x8½"..............................$275.00
Apple, pitcher, refrigerator; #69, sq, 8½"...............$550.00
Apple, plate, dinner; #101, 10".........................$600.00
Apple, platter, #49, 12" dia.............................$400.00
Apple, teapot, #505, 6"...............................$3,000.00
Autumn Foliage, platter, #31, 15" dia....................$110.00
Autumn Foliage, salt & pepper shakers, hourglass shape, 4½x2½",
    pr..$175.00
Banded (Blue & White), casserole, w/lid, 9"...............$45.00
Banded (Brown), coffeepot, #115, 9¾".....................$850.00

Banded (Brown), plate, salad; #102, 7½"...................$25.00
Banded (Green & White), bowl, mixing; 9".................$25.00
Cherry, bowl, cereal/salad; #23, cherry decoration on inside, 6"...$50.00
Cherry, pitcher, #17, 8x8½"..............................$275.00
Cherry, platter, #31, 15" dia...........................$145.00
Cut-Leaf, pie plate, 9"..................................$150.00
Cut-Leaf (Bull's Eye pattern), plate, 7½"................$55.00
Cut-Leaf (Bull's-Eye pattern), platter, 15" dia..........$110.00

Cut-Leaf Pansy, plate, 7½", $50.00. (Photo courtesy Susan Morris-Snyder)

Cut-Leaf Pansy, saucer, bull's eye pattern w/red swirls, 6½"...$20.00
Dogwood, bread plate, #252...............................$55.00
Dogwood, platter, #31, 15" dia..........................$110.00
Double Apple, bowl, mixing; #4, 2x4"....................$110.00
Double Apple, bowl, mixing; #7, 7".......................$75.00
Dutch Tulip, bowl, #600, ribbed, w/lid, 7¾".............$250.00
Dutch Tulip, pitcher, #15, 5½"..........................$250.00
Dutch Tulip, plate, divided, 10½"......................$800.00
Kitch-N-Queen, pitcher, ice-lip; #17, 8x8½".............$200.00
Morning Glory, cookie jar, #95, 10¾x7½".................$400.00
Raised Pansy, pitcher, refrigerator; w/lid, 5½".........$100.00
Rooster, bean pot, #76, w/handles, 7½"..................$350.00
Rooster, bowl, #5, w/lid, 4x5"..........................$190.00
Rooster, bowl, #73, 9½"..................................$145.00
Rooster, bowl, spaghetti; 3x13".........................$375.00
Rooster, creamer, #62, 4"...............................$250.00
Starflower, bean pot, #76, 6½"..........................$175.00
Starflower, bean server, individual; #75, 2".............$50.00
Starflower, bowl, berry; 1½x5¾"..........................$35.00
Starflower, grease jar, #47, w/lid, 5"..................$250.00
Starflower, mug, #121, 3¾"..............................$275.00
Starflower, pitcher, #16, 6¾"............................$85.00
Starflower, platter, #31, 15"...........................$110.00
Starflower, tumbler, #56, tapered, 4½"..................$325.00
Starflower (Green on Brown), cookie jar, #21, 7½x7".....$125.00
Starflower (Red-on-White), mug, #121, rare, 3¾x3".......$400.00
Starflower (White-on-Red), mug, #121, 3¾"...............$400.00
Starfower (Pink-on-Green), plate, dinner; 10"...........$100.00

Tear Drop, bowl, #66, 7" $45.00
Tear Drop, bowl, #74, 2x5½" $35.00
Tear Drop, cheese crock, #80, 8x8" $375.00
Tear Drop, salt & pepper shakers, barrel shape, 4", pr from $335
   to $350.00
Tulip, cookie jar, #503, 8" $375.00
White Banded, bowl, 2½x5" $25.00
White Daisy, cup & saucer $75.00
Woodgrain, pitcher, #613W, 5¾" $75.00

Rooster, cheese crock, #80, $750.00. (Photo courtesy Susan Morris-Snyder)

Wedding Cake Toppers

For at least the past 100 years, a cake 'topper' featuring a bride and groom, doves, or other matrimonial depiction has dominated the wedding cake. The symbolic bridal couple can be traced back thousands of years to early Greece and Rome. Literature from more recent times cites the writings of a slave in the deep South around the time of the Civil War: 'a bride and groom atop a cake' is all that is given, but it provides an intriguing glimpse into wedding cake traditions of yesteryear.

By the 1890s European bakery chefs had mastered the art of molding marzipan and gum paste into human form. Tiny celluloid doll figures manufactured in Germany were dressed as brides and grooms. Cake-topper fashions of the time reflect brides with upswept hairdos and gowns with necklines that were either high and demure or deeply plunging for very formal or evening weddings. Grooms sported 'handlebar' mustaches, hairstyles with center parts, and long black frock coats.

The early twentieth century saw the introduction of wedding figures in plaster of Paris (chalkware), porcelain, and bisque. Germany and Japan, the two largest exporters to the United States at the time, flooded the market with thousands of miniature bride and groom figures. Illustrations from commercial artists such as Rose O'Neill and Grace Drayton were converted into three-dimensional form and used as toppers. 'Kewpie' and 'Diddums,' angelic and child-like respectively, were very popular as bridal couples. The 'good

luck' horseshoe or an oversized gum-paste bell with letters spelling out the word 'Marriage' were often used as backdrops.

During the 1930s the celluloid 'cutie' and bisque 'googlie' topped the popularity list. Molded curly hair and flirty eyes gave them an appealing look. Each was available in a variety of sizes and could be dressed to personalize any wedding. The first plastic toppers debuted in the 1930s, but their time in the limelight was short-lived, due in part to stepped-up warfare production. Fashions of the period reflected the 'Hollywood' style — elegant lines, cowl necklines, and full-length fitted sleeves. A passing fancy was also noted in the 'pastel' wedding — lilac, lemon, and lime were popular attendants' colors during this period.

During the stark war years of the 1940s, single flower stalks, cardboard, and chalkware replaced extravagant arbors, porcelain, and bisque. Grooms traded tuxedos for military uniforms. Many saltware and spelter toppers were produced during these years. They proved to be an inexpensive, 'no frills' alternative to the ornate toppers of the past.

The 1950s proved to be the 'ceramics era' for cake toppers. Examples from this decade are noted for their bright gold accents. Illuminated cake toppers with concealed batteries, camouflaged wires, and bulbs proved to be a brief fascination. Topper fashions from the 1950s had grooms in white dinner jackets and brides in starched overskirts of lace or satin.

If the 1950s was the ceramics era, the 1960s was the 'plastics' era. The entire topper including flowers and trim was comprised of various forms of plastic.

The 1970s cake toppers saw a return to military uniforms in updated versions as well as uniformed grooms in career fields such as police and firemen. Many toppers were plastic, and a few were chalkware.

'Heirlooms' and 'keepsakes' were all the rage in the 1980s and beyond. Cake toppers followed the trend. A wide range of materials were used to fashion these toppers, including cast resin, china, bisque, and glass, to name but a few.

'Specialty' toppers span the years of cake topper production: 'whimsies' — tiny, delicate china or bisque figures from the late 1800s and early 1900s; wax hands from the 1900s; bridal slippers from the 1930s; crepe-paper and pipe-cleaner figures from the same period; and white doves from the late 1800s and again in the 1970s.

Collectors should learn to determine what type of material a topper is made of (whether it be spelter, saltware, chalkware, celluloid, or gum paste) and should be knowledgeable regarding period bridal fashions. Becoming familiar with all aspects of vintage cake toppers (the cloth flowers, the various types of plastics that were used, netting, lace, how to differentiate between old and modern crepe paper, etc.) will help one avoid the disappointment of purchasing a reproduction.

Values listed below are for cake toppers in very good to excellent condition.

Advisor: Jeannie Greenfield (See Directory, Wedding Cake Toppers)

1890s, porcelain whimsie, 2½" cherub holds gold heart in
   hands $45.00
1900s, gum-paste couple on gum-paste base, bower of cloth flowers
   w/delicately painted centers $150.00

1900s, pair of white wax hands (bride & groom), ea hand approximately 3" L **$75.00**

1915, Kewpie couple (bisque figures) on molded plaster base ...**$135.00**

1920s, bisque couple only, no base or pedestal, marked Germany & 4-digit number, 6" **$85.00**

1920s, gum-paste couple on gum-paste base (bride wears wide collar, popular style for the period) **$120.00**

1930s, bisque 'googlies' standing under 4-poster canopy atop molded cardboard steps, 6" overall **$125.00**

1930s, bisque couple standing atop filigreed chalkware base & pedestal concealing key-wind music box, 11" overall **$75.00**

1930s, celluloid Kewpie-type couple w/crepe-paper clothes, bride wears headband, ea figure 3" **$50.00**

1930s, crepe-paper & pipe-cleaner bridal couple, 5" **$45.00**

1940s, chalkware couple on chalkware base w/silver metal bell hanging from bower **$45.00**

1940s, chalkware military couple stand arm-in-arm, no base or pedestal, 3¾" **$60.00**

1940s, saltware couple, molded in 1 pc, 3½" **$45.00**

1950s, chalkware couple, single mold, no base or pedestal, 4½" .. **$25.00**

1960s, plastic, 2 doves, ea holding a silver metal ring, flank wedding couple, #51 printed on bottom, 9" **$25.00**

1970s, bisque military couple, no base or pedestal, 3½" **$50.00**

1980s, poly-resin, very detailed, 4½", $15.00. (Photo courtesy Jeannie Greenfield)

Related Wedding Memorabilia

Related collectibles are becoming almost as popular as wedding cake toppers themselves. Colorful and picturesque marriage licenses were popular from the mid-1800s to the late 1940s. Their average size was 15x21". The addition of tintypes (early photographs of the couple) increase the value. Bride's books were popular during this time period as well. Early examples are beautifully illustrated and lithographed, offering insight into the personal moments of the bride's engagement and wedding. Most were by 5" x 7" and usually held six to 12 pages for recording guest lists, gifts received, wedding attendants, and other nuptial details.

Favors and novelties abound in the form of commemorative plates, publications on love and marriage, party souvenirs from bridal showers, vases, ornaments, salt and pepper shaker sets, and figural candles, just to name a few.

Paper collectibles include postcards (especially those from the early 1900s to the 1930s featuring matrimonial sentiments), early greeting cards, telegrams or 'wedding wires' from the 1920s to 1940s that include color graphics and theme headers, invitations, and announcements. Prices for examples of paper memorabilia vary from about $5.00 to $100.00, depending on age, condition, and rarity.

Jeannie Greenfield is our advisor for this category. See the Directory for information on her soon-to-be-released book *Wedding Cake Toppers, Memories and More.*

Book, bride's; artwork & poetry on subject of love, hardcover, 1920, 6 pages, 5x7" **$10.00**

Book, bride's; various sections for bride to describe gown, trousseau, etc, hardcover, 1920s, 12 pages, 5x7", unused **$15.00**

Book, The Marriage Altar, JR Miller, hardcover, dated 1893, 33 pages **$5.00**

Card, bridal shower; colorful graphics, 1950s, 4x4" **$1.00**

Card, bridal shower; heavy stock, 1930s, slightly smaller than modern postcard **$5.00**

Card, wedding; bride's bouquet embossed on white paper, silk ribbons hold 2 metal rings, 1960s, 7x3½" **$2.00**

Marriage license, full-color graphics, dated April 24, 1918, 15x20" w/out frame **$40.00**

Napkin, bridal shower; printed paper, ca 1940s-50s **$2.00**

Place card, bridal shower; heavy paper w/silk ribbon, ca 1930s, 6" ..**$35.00**

Place card (seating), handmade ring w/bride's profile in center, colorful graphics w/attached name card, 1930s, 6" **$20.00**

Place cards, cardboard cutouts, ca. 1920s, 4½", $20.00 for the pair. (Photo courtesy Jeannie Greenfield)

Salt & pepper shakers, bride & groom, he in black tux w/striped trousers, Japan sticker, 1950s, 4", 2-pc set **$10.00**

Weeping Gold

In the mid- to late 1950s, many American pottery companies produced lines of 'Weeping Gold.' Such items have a distinctive appearance; most appear to be covered with irregular droplets of lustrous gold, sometimes heavy, sometimes fine. On others the gold is in random swirls, or there may be a definite pattern developed on the surface. In fact, real gold was used; however, there is no known successful way of separating the gold from the pottery. You'll see similar pottery covered in 'Weeping Silver.' Very often, ceramic whiskey decanters made for Beam, McCormick, etc., will be trimmed in 'Weeping Gold.' Among the marks you'll find on these wares are 'McCoy,' 'Kingwood Ceramics,' and 'USA,' but most items are simply stamped '22k (or 24k) gold.'

Planter, fish, 14" long, from $65.00 to $75.00.

Bowl, incurvate scalloped rim, Hand Decorated Weeping Gold... USA, 4x6" **$22.00**
Candy dish, leaf form, incurvate rim, 22k Gold Made in USA, 9½" L **$15.00**
Candy dish, rectangular pagoda shape, 4 sm feet, 4x6x5½" ..**$20.00**
Candy dish/powder box, 6 faint lobes w/stem-like finial, Weeping Bright Gold...USA, 4x6"...**$20.00**
Coffeepot, flared cylinder, McCoy, 7½", from $45 to **$60.00**
Creamer & sugar bowl, w/lid, McCoy **$35.00**
Ewer, bulbous body, gold upper body drips down over black gloss at base, 7"..**$25.00**
Figurine, elephant, Weeping Bright Gold mark, 4" L...........**$35.00**
Figurine, elephant, 8¾x10x3½" **$50.00**
Figurine, pelican w/flower frog base, Hand Decorated Weeping Brilliant Gold, 9"..**$48.00**
Leaf dish, Hand Decorated Weeping Bright Gold USA, 8x7" ..**$25.00**

Planter, horses, 9½x9", from $55.00 to $65.00.

Plate, Hand Decorated Weeping Bright Gold 22k Gold USA, lg..**$20.00**
Salt & pepper shakers, 22k Gold, 3½", pr **$27.50**
Shell dish, Hand Decorated Weeping Bright Gold 22k Gold USA, 8x7"..**$15.00**
Tidbit tray, gold-tone metal center handle, MIB.................**$20.00**
Vase, cornucopia; 24k Gold Made in USA, 5x5½" **$22.50**
Vase, fan form, chevron design at top, flared foot, 6½x6½", from $25 to **$35.00**
Vase, ovoid w/flared rim, Elynor China Made in USA, 6½" ..**$35.00**
Wall pocket, pitcher & bowl, from $40 to **$50.00**
Wall pocket, swan form, 5¾x5" **$30.00**
Wall pockets, sailing ship, 5¾", pr **$110.00**

Weil Ware

Though the Weil company made dinnerware and some kitchenware, their figural pieces are attracting the most collector interest. They were in business from the 1940s until the mid-1950s, another of the small but very successful California companies whose work has become so popular today. They dressed their 'girls' in beautiful gowns of vivid rose, light dusty pink, turquoise blue, and other lovely colors enhanced with enameled 'lace work' and flowers, sgraffito, sometimes even with tiny applied blossoms. Both paper labels and ink stamps were used to mark them, but as you study their features, you'll soon learn to recognize even those that have lost their labels over the years. Four-number codes and decorators' initials are usually written on their bases.

If you want to learn more, we recommend *Collector's Encyclopedia of California Pottery*, by Jack Chipman.

Dinnerware

Malay Bambu, platter, 13", $25.00.

Birchwood, creamer **$15.00**
Birchwood, cup & saucer...**$7.50**
Birchwood, plate, bread & butter..**$6.00**
Birchwood, salt & pepper shakers, pr.................................**$15.00**
Birchwood, sugar bowl, w/lid...**$17.50**
Brentwood, bowl, divided vegetable; from $40 to **$45.00**
Brentwood, cup & saucer...**$15.00**
Brentwood, plate, dinner; from $10 to.................................**$14.00**
Brentwood, plate, salad; from $8 to **$10.00**
Brentwood, sugar bowl, w/lid...**$25.00**

Malay Bambu, bowl, lug cereal $11.50
Malay Bambu, bowl, vegetable; oval.....................................$18.00
Malay Bambu, butter dish, ¼-lb, from $30 to.....................$35.00
Malay Bambu, coffeepot, from $45 to $50.00
Malay Bambu, creamer $12.50
Malay Bambu, cup & saucer $12.00
Malay Bambu, gravy boat w/attached underplate.................$28.00
Malay Bambu, plate, dinner..$10.00
Malay Bambu, plate, salad $6.50
Malay Bambu, sugar bowl, w/lid..$12.50
Malay Blossom, bowl, coupe cereal $8.50
Malay Blossom, bowl, vegetable; oval, 9" $20.00
Malay Blossom, cup & saucer, from $8 to $10.00
Malay Blossom, plate, bread & butter.....................................$3.50
Malay Blossom, plate, dinner $15.00
Mango, bowl, vegetable; oval, from $18 to $22.00
Mango, coffeepot, from $45 to $50.00
Mango, cup & saucer...$12.50
Mango, gravy boat w/attached underplate............................$42.50
Mango, plate, dinner; from $8 to..$10.00
Mango, platter, 13" L...$27.50
Mango, salt & pepper shakers, pr..$17.50
Rose, bowl, dessert; 4½" $7.50
Rose, bowl, vegetable; rectangular, w/lid $58.00
Rose, cup & saucer $14.00
Rose, plate, dinner $15.00
Rose, snack plate & cup, from $12 to $15.00
Rose, tumbler, 4¼" $12.00

Miscellaneous

Flower holder, girl stands w/closed pink umbrella (opening there) in
    left hand, blue flowers on dress, 6½" $22.50
Flower holder, lady holds apron (opening between hands), pink &
    blue w/flowers at hem, sunbonnet hangs behind, 10¼" ..$50.00
Flower holder, lady in pink & green w/much floral decor, opening at
    back of waist, crazing/sm chip, #1733, EX+ $35.00
Flower holder, lady stands beside & rests right arm on tall blue
    planter, floral decoration down bodice & skirt, 9¾" $45.00

**Flower holders, Dutch children, #3040 and #3041, $90.00
for the pair.** (Photo courtesy Jack Chipman)

Flower holders, Oriental boy & girl by stone-look cylinder, yellow w/
    pink trim, #2211/#2210, 6½", pr.................................$55.00
Head vase, lady in blue w/red rose on hat, gold trim, 5¾"...$60.00
Toothbrush holder, Dutch boy stands w/openings at pockets, blue
    cap & shirt, yellow hair & shoes, 6½" $45.00
Vase/planter, conch shell, blue-green pastel w/peachy-pink interior,
    7½x8x6½" $60.00

Weller Pottery

Though the Weller Pottery has been closed since 1948, they
were so prolific that you'll be sure to see several pieces anytime you're
'antiquing.' They were one of the largest of the art pottery giants
that located in the Zanesville, Ohio, area, using locally dug clays to
produce their wares. In the early years, they made hand-decorated
vases, jardinieres, lamps, and other useful and decorative items for
the home, many of which were signed by notable artists such as
Fredrick Rhead, John Lessell, Virginia Adams, Anthony Dunlavy,
Dorothy England, Albert Haubrich, Hester Pillsbury, E.L. Pickens,
and Jacques Sicard, to name only a few. Some of their early lines were
First and Second Dickens, Eocean, Sicardo, Etna, Louwelsa, Turada,
and Aurelian. Portraits of Indians, animals of all types, lady golfers,
nudes, and scenes of Dickens stories were popular themes, and some
items were overlaid with silver filigree. These lines are rather hard to
find at this point in time, and prices are generally high; but there's
plenty of their later production still around, and some pieces are
relatively inexpensive.

If you'd like to learn more, we recommend *Collector's Encyclopedia
of Weller Pottery* by Sharon and Bob Huxford.

Advisor: Hardy Hudson (See Directory, Weller Pottery)

**Coppertone, vase, two
frogs, 8x10", $1,150.00.**
(Photo courtesy David Rago
Auctions)

Alvin, fan vase, 8" $100.00
Alvin, vase, double bud; 6" $95.00
Baldin, bowl, apples on tan, 4" H..$125.00
Barcelona, vase, tumbler shape, 7" $150.00
Blue Drapery, candlestick/lamp base, 9½" $175.00
Bonito, vase, floral, signed HP, 6", from $125 to $175.00
Bouquet, console bowl, B-12, 12½" L $45.00
Burntwood, jardiniere, birds & Deco flowers, 6½" $225.00
Cactus, duck, 4½" $125.00
Cameo, vase, wide body, footed, w/handles, 4", from $35 to...$40.00
Candis, ewer, 11" $90.00
Candis, vase, green & white, 9", from $75 to $85.00

Classic, fan vase, 5" $60.00
Claywood, bowl, floral, 2x3½" $65.00
Coppertone, trumpet vase, 4 frog heads at base, 12" $3,500.00
Cornish, jardiniere, 7", from $125 to $150.00
Darsie, vase, 9½" $100.00
Elberta, cornucopia, 8" $75.00
Elberta, jardiniere, 5½" $100.00
Ethel, vase, 9½" $300.00
Evergreen, vase, 6" $50.00
Florala, wall pocket, 10" $225.00
Florenzo, planter, 4" $50.00
Forest, jardiniere, 4½" $125.00
Forest, vase, 13½" $400.00
Fruitone, vase, 6-panel, 8" $125.00
Gloria, ewer, G-12, 9" $150.00
Gloria, vase, G-22, 8", from $55 to $65.00

Hudson: Vase, birds and fruit, top repaired, 19", $1,550.00; Vase, grapes, signed, 15½", $1,150.00. (Photo courtesy Treadway Galleries)

La Sa, vase, tree scene, 6", from $225 to $300.00
Lavonia, figurine, girl w/skirt held wide, 7½" $300.00
Libo, ewer, 10½" $95.00
Lorbeek, vase, 8" $200.00
Manhattan, vase, 5½" $80.00
Marengo, wall pocket, 8½" $275.00
Marvo, pitcher, 8" $175.00
Mirror Black, vase, 12" $200.00
Oak Leaf, vase, 8½", from $75 to $85.00
Patricia, duck planter, 6½" $175.00
Pumila, vase, 9" $85.00
Roba, vase, rim-to-shoulder handles, 12½" $175.00
Roma, comport, 11" $150.00
Sabrinian, window box, 3½x9" $300.00
Senic, vase, S-8, 9½" $150.00
Sydonia, console bowl, 6x17" $100.00

Sydonia, cornucopia, 8", from $70 to $80.00
Velva, vase, 7½" $275.00
Voile, fan vase, 8x9" $200.00
Warwick, planter, 3-footed, branch handles, 3½" $120.00
Woodcraft, vase, double bud; 8" $150.00

Woodcraft, wall pocket, 15x13", $1,680.00.

Zona, mug, duck, 3" $95.00
Zona, pitcher, red apples on ivory gloss, 6" $125.00

West Coast Pottery

This was a small company operating in the 1940s and 1950s in Burbank, California. The founders were Lee and Bonnie Wollard; they produced decorative pottery such as is listed here. For more information on this company as well as many others, we recommend *Collector's Encyclopedia of California Pottery* by Jack Chipman (Collector Books).

Vase, bowknot, rose and blue blended glaze, #465, 14", from $65.00 to $85.00.

Basket, interwoven leaves form body, celery green, #209, 9¼x6¼x3¼" **$40.00**

Centerpiece/planter, 2 handles (1 upward swirl, 2nd downward swirl), mauve & gray, #217, 5½x12½" L **$32.50**

Figurines, peacocks, ivory, long flowing tails, #474, 7⅞", pr ... **$20.00**

Flower holder, Thelma Kyn, girl w/basket (opening there), #1040D E, 6" **$32.50**

Planter, swirling form resembling angry sea, peachy-pink w/mauve interior, #551, 3½x10x6" **$28.00**

Vase, trumpet flowers w/bow at base, green w/burgundy splashes, #492, 8½" **$60.00**

Wall pocket, lady's bonnet w/pansies on white, #10890B, 9x6½" **$30.00**

Wall pockets, plumes form body, peachy-pink to green, #305 L & #305 R, 8½x6" **$35.00**

Western Collectibles

Although the Wild West era ended over 100 years ago, today cowboy gear is a hot area of collecting. These historic collectibles are not just found out west. Some of the most exceptional pieces have come from the East Coast states and the Midwest. But that should come as no surprise when you consider that the largest manufacturer of bits and spurs was the August Buemann Co. of Newark, New Jersey (1868 – 1926).

Unless otherwise noted, our values are for examples in at least excellent condition.

Bit, cast iron, formed as ladies' bodies, original chin strap, 20th century **$125.00**

Bit, silver overlay w/lg silver rosettes, much engraving, 1940s style, 9" **$70.00**

Boots, black & turquoise leather w/eagle inlay, strong pulls, peg leather soles w/2" stacked leather heels, 1950s, pr **$175.00**

Boots, red leather w/white inlay, classic style, boy's, 1950s, pr ... **$160.00**

Buckle, silver w/engraved roping scene, flower ea corner, Ricardo, Sterling, 2¼x3½" **$230.00**

Bull whip, braided leather w/wooden handle, 60" **$70.00**

Chaps, brown leather, traditional style w/brass studs, ca 1955, 39" **$250.00**

Chaps, brown leather w/decorative stitching, batwing style w/conchos & leather string ties, 36" L, VG **$135.00**

Chaps, gray leather w/nickel-plated fittings, roller buckle, working type, 1940s **$225.00**

Clock, mantel; rider on rearing horse in bronze, horseshoe at side holds clock, Carmody, 1950s, 13x11½" **$140.00**

Figurine, quarter horse stands, saddled & bridled, ceramic, Ace Powell, 7½x9" **$145.00**

Headstall, brown leather w/silver, futurity-style brow band, 2 conchos by bit, rope edging marked Alpaca, Circle Y **$135.00**

Rein spreaders, 14 rings on ea, original harness snaps, flexible .. **$65.00**

Saddle, barrel racing; brown leather, 16" seat, 7¼" gullet, conchos & tie strings, unmarked Simco **$215.00**

Saddle, brown leather, 14" seat, 7" gullet, Heiser, 1920s **$215.00**

Saddle, brown leather, 15" seat, 7" gullet, 12" swells, 25" round skirt, full quarter-horse bars, Tex Tan, 1950s **$255.00**

Saddle, brown leather w/buckstitching, 15" seat, 7" gullet, full quarter-horse bars, 2" cantle, leather stirrups, King **$275.00**

Saddle, brown leather w/fine tooling, padded 15" seat, ca 1950s, child's **$150.00**

Saddle, brown leather w/fine tooling, 14" seat, 7½" gullet, full quarter-horse bars, Simco, 1960s **$150.00**

Saddle, pony; tooled brown leather w/12" seat, 6" tree, brass horn, covered stirrups, EX fleece, child's **$275.00**

Saddle bags, brown leather w/buckles & straps, 1950s, 15½x8x2" **$50.00**

Saddle bags, brown leather w/tooling, 35" from end-to-end, ea 2x9½x8" **$145.00**

Spurs, iron, 1" heel bands, 1½" shanks, 1" rowels, w/leather straps, Renalde era, Crockett, early 1950s, pr **$155.00**

Spurs, iron, 10-point rowels, old leather tooled straps, heel chains, unmarked, 3¼", pr **$195.00**

Spurs, silver plated & chased, 9-point rowels, chap guards, Crockett **$175.00**

Spurs, stainless steel w/silver mounts & conchos, 2" rowels, Menalde **$175.00**

Spurs, 1-pc California style w/heel chains, 10-point rowels, brass jingle bobs, chap guard on chanks, A Buerman, pr **$250.00**

Stirrups, oxbow; rawhide-covered leather, pr **$65.00**

Chaps, tooled latigo belt, German silver conchos, marked Harry HP, 39", $180.00. (Photo courtesy LiveAuctioneers.com/ Allard Auctions Inc.)

Westmoreland Glass

The Westmoreland Specialty Company was founded in 1889 in Grapeville, Pennsylvania. Their mainstay was a line of opalware (later called milk glass) which included such pieces as cream and sugar sets, novel tea jars (i.e., Teddy Roosevelt Bear jar, Oriental tea jars, and Dutch tea jar), as well as a number of covered animal dishes such as hens and roosters on nests. All of these pieces were made as condiment containers and originally held baking soda and Westmoreland's own mustard recipe. By 1900 they had introduced a large variety of pressed tablewares in clear glass and opal, although their condiment containers were still very popular.

By 1910 they were making a large line of opal souvenir novelties with hand-painted decorations of palm trees, Dutch scenes, etc. They also made a variety of decorative vases painted in the fashion of Rookwood Pottery, plus sprayed finishes with decorations of flowers, fruits, animals, and Indians. Westmoreland gained great popularity with their line of painted, hand-decorated wares. They also made many fancy-cut items.

These lines continued in production until 1939, when the Brainard family became full owners of the factory. The Brainards discontinued the majority of patterns made previously under the West management and introduced dinnerware lines, made primarily of milk glass, with limited production of black glass and blue milk glass. Colored glass was not put back into full production until 1964 when Westmoreland introduced Golden Sunset, Avocado, Brandywine Blue, and Ruby.

The company made only limited quantities of carnival glass in the early 1900s and then re-introduced it in 1972 when most of their carnival glass was made in limited editions for the Levay Distributing Company. J.H. Brainard, president of Westmoreland, sold the factory to Dave Grossman in 1981, and he, in turn, closed the factory in 1984. Westmoreland first used the stamped W over G logo in 1949 and continued using it until Dave Grossman bought the factory. Mr. Grossman changed the logo to a W with the word Westmoreland forming a circle around it.

Milk glass was always Westmoreland's main line of production. In the 1950s they became famous for their milk glass tableware in the #1881 'Paneled Grape' pattern. It was designed by Jess Billups, the company's mold maker. The first piece he made was the water goblet. Items were gradually added until a complete dinner service was available. It became their most successful dinnerware line, and today it is highly collectible, primarily because of the excellence of the milk glass itself. No other company has been able to match Westmoreland's milk glass in color, texture, quality, or execution of design and pattern. Collectors need to know which colors were produced by Westmoreland and which were not. If you find a carnival piece be sure to check inside and on the bottom of the base. New carnival reproductions are not carnival on the inside and bottoms. Westmoreland always sprayed the carnival finish on the entire piece.

For more information see *Westmoreland Glass, The Popular Years, 1940 – 1985,* by Lorraine Kovar (Collector Books). See also Depression Glass.

Covered Animal Dishes

Camel, cobalt carnival	**$175.00**
Camel, emerald green carnival	**$175.00**
Camel, lilac mist	**$150.00**
Camel, milk glass	**$100.00**
Cat in boot, black	**$35.00**
Cat on vertically ribbed base, apricot mist (+)	**$75.00**
Cat on vertically ribbed base, milk glass (+)	**$50.00**
Chick on eggpile on basketweave nest, brown, no details, 6¼" (+)	**$85.00**
Chick on egg pile on basketweave nest, milk glass w/allover hand painting (+)	**$175.00**
Chick on oval 2-handled basket, Antique Blue (+)	**$70.00**

Chick on oval 2-handled basket, white carnival (+)	**$35.00**
Dog on vertically ribbed base, Antique Blue, 5½"	**$90.00**
Dog on vertically ribbed base, milk glass, 5½"	**$75.00**
Duck on oval rimmed base, Antique Blue, 8x6"	**$85.00**
Duck on oval rimmed base, white or crystal carnival, 8x6"	**$100.00**
Duck on oval vertically ribbed or basketweave base, black carnival, 5"	**$135.00**
Eagle w/spread wings, Antique Blue, 8x6"	**$150.00**
Eagle w/spread wings, emerald green carnival, 8x6"	**$200.00**

Fox on lacy base, 7½", $125.00. (Photo courtesy Betty and Bill Newbound)

Fox on oval basketweave or lacy base, milk glass, 7½" L	**$125.00**
Fox on oval basketweave or lacy base, ruby marble (both pcs), 1982, 7½" L	**$250.00**
Hen on basketweave nest, black carnival, scarce, 5½" (+)	**$100.00**
Hen on basketweave nest, milk glass, plain or w/hand-painted accents, or olive green, 5½"	**$30.00**
Hen on basketweave nest, milk glass, plain or w/hand-painted accents, 3½"	**$20.00**
Hen on basketweave nest, ruby or black, 3½"	**$40.00**
Hen on nest, Almond w/hand-painted red details, 7½" L (+)	**$100.00**
Lamb on picket-fence base, Antique Blue w/milk glass base, 5½" L	**$85.00**
Lamb on picket-fence base, milk glass (both pcs), 5½" L	**$50.00**
Lamb on picket-fence base, purple marble, 5½" L	**$150.00**
Lion on basketweave base, Antique Blue opaque, 6x8"	**$175.00**
Lion on basketweave base, emerald green carnival, 6x8"	**$225.00**
Lion on basketweave base, milk glass w/hand-painted lion, 6x8"	**$295.00**
Lion on lacy base, milk glass, plain, 6x8"	**$165.00**
Lion on picket-fence base, milk glass w/Antique Blue head, 6x8"	**$135.00**
Lovebirds, almond or mint green, 5¼x6½"	**$85.00**
Lovebirds, Bermuda or Brandywine Blue, 5¼x6½"	**$75.00**
Lovebirds, Golden Sunset, 5¼x6½"	**$55.00**
Lovebirds, olive green mist, 5¼x6½"	**$75.00**
Mother eagle & babies on basketweave base, Antique Blue or milk glass w/hand-painted accents, 8"	**$150.00**
Mother eagle & babies on basketweave base, milk glass, 8"	**$125.00**

Rabbit on diamond base, Electric Blue carnival, limited edition, ca. 1978, from $150.00 to $200.00.

Rabbit on oval vertically ribbed base, black carnival, 5½"....**$80.00**

Rabbit on oval vertically ribbed base, milk glass, 5½" **$50.00**

Rabbit on oval vertically ribbed base, ruby carnival, 5½".....**$75.00**

Rabbit on picket-fence base, Antique Blue, 5½" **$100.00**

Rabbit on picket-fence base, caramel marble carnival or white carnival, 5½" **$145.00**

Rabbit on picket-fence base, milk glass, 5½" **$60.00**

Rabbit w/eggs on oval base, milk glass, 8"...........................**$80.00**

Rabbit w/eggs on oval base, milk glass w/hand-painted accents, 8" **$90.00**

Rabbit w/eggs on oval base, purple slag carnival (150 made), 8"..**$190.00**

Rabbit w/eggs on oval base, ruby marble, 8".....................**$180.00**

Rabbit w/eggs on oval base, white carnival (1,500 made), 8" ..**$160.00**

Robin on twig nest, Almond, Coral, mint green or ruby carnival, 6¼" **$95.00**

Robin on twig nest, Antique Blue, 6¼"...............................**$85.00**

Robin on twig nest, blue pastel, 6¼"....................................**$70.00**

Robin on twig nest, green or light blue mist, olive green or olive green mist, or yellow mist, 6¼".......................................**$70.00**

Robin on twig nest, Laurel Green, 6¼" **$100.00**

Robin on twig nest, milk glass, 6¼".....................................**$50.00**

Robin on twig nest, yellow mist, 6¼"...................................**$75.00**

Rooster on diamond base, Chocolate, 8" **$190.00**

Rooster on diamond base, crystal mist w/hand-painted accents, 8" **$50.00**

Rooster on diamond base, Electric Blue carnival (500 made), emerald green or turquoise carnival, 8"...............................**$225.00**

Rooster on diamond base, milk glass, 8" **$45.00**

Rooster on diamond base, purple marble, 8" **$150.00**

Rooster on diamond base, ruby, 8" **$95.00**

Rooster on lacy base, milk glass, 8" **$45.00**

Rooster on lacy base, milk glass w/hand-painted accents, 8" .**$50.00**

Rooster on lacy base, white carnival (1,500 made), 8" **$100.00**

Rooster on oval vertically ribbed base, purple marble, 5½" ..**$75.00**

Rooster on oval vertically ribbed base, milk glass w/Antique Blue head, 5½" **$65.00**

Rooster standing, Antique Blue, Antique Blue w/milk glass head or black glass w/hand-painted accents, 8½" **$95.00**

Rooster standing, apricot mist, black, Brandywine Blue or Laurel Green, 8½" **$85.00**

Rooster standing, brown marble, purple marble or ruby marble, 8½"...**$95.00**

Rooster standing, brown marble, 8½" **$85.00**

Rooster standing, brown mist or crystal mist, ea w/hand-painted accents, 8½" **$85.00**

Rooster standing, milk glass, 8½" **$30.00**

Rooster standing, milk glass w/hand-painted details, 8½"..**$85.00**

Rooster standing, ruby marble, 8½" **$95.00**

Swan (raised wing) on lacy base, black glass, cobalt carnival or purple marble, 6x9½" **$300.00**

Swan (raised wing) on lacy base, cobalt, 6x9½" **$340.00**

Swan (raised wing) on lacy base, cobalt marble (both pcs), 6x9½" **$400.00**

Swan (raised wing) on lacy base, emerald green, ice blue carnival or turquoise carnival, 6x9½" **$225.00**

Swan (raised wing) on lacy base, light blue or pink mist, 6x9½"..**$150.00**

Swan (raised wing) on lacy base, milk glass, 6x9½"...........**$150.00**

Swan (raised wing) on lacy base, milk glass mother-of-pearl, 6x9½" **$190.00**

Swan on diamond base, black carnival, 5½" **$95.00**

Swan on diamond base, caramel marble carnival, 5½" **$110.00**

Swan on diamond base, milk glass, closed neck, 5½"..........**$70.00**

Swan on diamond base, milk glass, open neck, 5½" **$50.00**

Swan on diamond base, ruby carnival, 5½" **$75.00**

Toy chick on basketweave base, milk glass or milk glass w/red accents, 2"...**$15.00**

Toy chick on basketweave base, milk glass w/any fired-on color, 2" **$20.00**

Figurals and Novelties

Bird ashtray/pipe holder, any color mist..............................**$25.00**

Bird w/feather on head, crystal...**$15.00**

Bulldog, black or black mist, 3½" **$35.00**

Bulldog, brown mist, 3½" **$30.00**

Bulldog doorstop, black or black mist, 7-lb.......................**$550.00**

Bumblebee, crystal, size of a quarter, only shown in 1 undated catalog..**$125.00**

Butterfly (lg), Antique Blue or Antique Blue Mist (w/perch add 25%)..**$40.00**

Butterfly (lg), lilac (w/perch add 25%).................................**$40.00**

Butterfly (lg), pink carnival (w/perch add 25%)...................**$40.00**

Butterfly (lg), purple marble carnival (w/perch add 25%)....**$50.00**

Cardinal, crystal, solid glass..**$15.00**

Cardinal, purple marble, solid glass......................................**$35.00**

Chick & egg pin tray, electric blue opalescent (+) **$65.00**

Chick & egg pin tray, milk glass mother-of-pearl w/hand-painted accents (+)..**$35.00**

Chick egg cup, milk glass w/red hand-painted accents.........**$15.00**

Chick egg cup, milk glass w/yellow & green casing.............**$15.00**

Chick mug, milk glass...**$22.50**

Chick mug, milk glass w/hand-painted accents....................**$35.00**

Chick on oval 2-handled basket, Antique Blue, 4" L (+)......**$70.00**

Doghouse, match holder, black...**$40.00**

Doghouse, match holder, milk glass w/hand-painted accents **$55.00**

Duck salt dip/nut dish, black $30.00
Duck salt dip/nut dish, blue $25.00
Eagle standing, crystal mist, 7½" $350.00
Owl, toothpick holder, milk glass, #62, 3", from $20 to $25.00
Owl on 2 stacked books, apricot or green mist, 3½" $30.00
Owl on 2 stacked books, blue, pink or yellow opaque, 3½" .. $22.50
Owl on 2 stacked books, brown marble, 3½" $30.00
Owl on 2 stacked books, dark or light blue mist, 3½" $22.50
Owl on 2 stacked books, honey amber carnival, 3½" $30.00
Owl standing on tree stump, apricot mist, 5½" $35.00
Owl standing on tree stump, blue or blue mist, 5½" $35.00
Owl standing on tree stump, coral, 5½" $35.00
Owl standing on tree stump, Golden Sunset, 5½" $35.00
Owl standing on tree stump, ruby carnival, 5½" $50.00
Penguin on ice floe, blue & blue mist $125.00
Penguin on ice floe, Brandywine Blue mist, 1970s, 3¾", from $35
    to $45.00
Penguin on ice floe, crystal & crystal mist $110.00
Pouter pigeon, amethyst mist, #9, 2½", from $25 to $35.00
Pouter pigeon, black, 2¾" $42.50
Pouter pigeon, champagne lustre, 2¾" $45.00
Pouter pigeon, light blue mist, 2¾" $32.50
Robin, any mist color or crystal, sm $15.00
Robin, purple carnival, sm $30.00
Starfish candleholders, Almond, 5" wide, pr from $45 to $55.00
Swallow, crystal, wings out, ca 1930s $40.00
Swallow, crystal or green mist, wings down $15.00
Wren, almond or almond mist, w/ or w/o pegs, solid glass .. $35.00
Wren, crystal, w/or w/out pegs, solid glass $20.00
Wren on sq base perch, any color combination $55.00

Lamps

Please note that Americana with any decoration and a scroll base sells for $20.00 more than those items without a scroll base.

Candle, potbellied stove, amberina, $45.00. (Photo courtesy Suellen and Bill Blasdell)

Americana, Country Floral or China Rose, smooth brass base, ca 1981, 13½" $75.00

Americana, green floral or Strawberry, scrolled brass base, ca 1979-80, 13½" $95.00
Americana, pink floral or Antique Fruit, smooth brass base, ca 1981, 13½" $85.00
Boudoir, English Hobnail, orange case w/mist, w/shade, base made from ashtray $65.00
Candle, owl, red or yellow on metal lattice work base, #110, 4¼" $25.00
Candle, owl, yellow, on metal latticework base, #110, 4¼" ... $25.00
Child's electric mini, any child's decoration, wood base $80.00
Colonial, blue floral, electric, scrolled brass base, ca 1977-81, 12¼" $155.00
Colonial, brown Beaded Bouquet, electric, scrolled brass base, ca 1977-81, 12¼" $125.00

Colonial, Pink Rose, ca. 1977, 12", $150.00. (Photo courtesy Lorraine Kovar)

Fairy, Wakefield, crystal w/silver trim, footed $75.00
Gone-w/the-Wind style, milk glass w/pink roses, w/shade, chimney & base $1,500.00
Mini, any mist w/Daisy decor, scrolled brass bottom $50.00
Patterned, American Hobnail, milk glass, electric or oil, footed.. $125.00
Patterned, Beaded Bouquet, any color, electric, brass bottom, mini $70.00
Patterned, Lotus, milk glass, made from oval bowl & sugar bowl, scarce $125.00
Patterned, Lotus, pink, candlestick style, twisted stem, electric, 9" $75.00
Patterned, Old Quilt, milk glass, electric, made from bowl, scarce $125.00
Patterned, Princess Feather, Golden Sunset, from hurricane shade, wood & metal parts, scarce $200.00
Patterned, Roses & Bows, crystal mist w/decoration, electric mini w/scrolled brass bottom $95.00
Patterned, Sawtooth, grandfather's bowl, electric, 9½" W .. $125.00
Patterned, Thousand Eye, crystal, candlestick style, electric, 8½" ... $45.00
Patterned, Thousand Eye, crystal & milk glass, ball form, electric.. $65.00
Tiffa, Almond w/Beaded Bouquet, scrolled brass base, ca 1978-79 .... $140.00
Tiffa, ruby w/hand-painted ruby floral, scrolled brass base, ca 1978-79 .... $195.00
Zodiac, blue mist or cased w/hand-painted accents, cylinder shade $250.00

Modern Giftware

Ashtray, milk glass w/Roses & Bows decoration, sq, 4"........**$22.50**
Ashtray, milk glass w/22k gold, sq, 6½"...............................**$22.50**
Basket, Almond Rose on Almond, 4" W.............................**$55.00**
Basket, any color w/Mary Gregory painting, flat, 4" dia **$45.00**
Bell, Almond Rose on Almond, ruffled rim, 6½" **$55.00**
Bell, brown mist w/Daisy decal, plain rim, 5" **$22.50**
Bell, Cameo, crystal mist w/Roses & Bows decoration........**$30.00**
Bell, crystal w/ruby stain & Mary Gregory painting, plain rim,
  5" **$50.00**
Bell, ruby or ruby stain w/Ruby Floral decoration, plain rim, 5"....**$45.00**
Bell, ruby w/Ruby Floral decoration, ruffled rim **$45.00**
Bell vase, milk glass w/Pastel Fruit decoration, footed, 9" **$95.00**
Bonbon, Beaded Bouquet on milk glass, handles, flat, w/lid...**$50.00**
Bonbon, crystal mist w/Roses & Bows decoration, handles, w/
  lid..**$42.50**
Bonbon, ruby or ruby stain w/Ruby Floral decoration, w/lid...**$40.00**
Bowl, milk glass w/Pastel Fruit decoration, lipped, 9" **$55.00**
Candlesticks, crystal w/ruby lustre, skirted, pr **$50.00**
Candlesticks, milk glass w/forget-me-nots, 4", pr, w/lid......**$55.00**
Chocolate box, any mist w/Daisy decal, oval, w/lid............**$110.00**
Compote, crystal w/ruby lustre, crimped & ruffled, 8½" dia...**$55.00**
Compote, dark blue mist w/Mary Gregory deer, stemmed foot, w/
  lid **$145.00**
Dresser set, milk glass w/gold lines, 4-pc..........................**$475.00**
Flowerpot, Beaded Bouquet on milk glass, w/drip tray **$125.00**

Heart plate, mint green with Beaded Bouquet, $40.00. (Photo courtesy Lorraine Kovar)

Heart trinket box, Almond Rose on Almond **$35.00**
Honey dish, Crystal Velvet, low foot, w/lid, 5" **$40.00**
Jardiniere, any mist w/Daisy decal, straight, footed, 5" **$30.00**
Planter, milk glass w/Roses & Bows decoration, oblong, 5x9" ..**$55.00**
Plate, brown mist w/Mary Gregory painting, Wicket border, 9"..**$45.00**
Plate, milk glass w/Roses & Bows decoration, 11" **$75.00**
Puff box/jelly dish, crystal mist w/Roses & Bows decoration,
  4½" **$45.00**
Server, any mist w/Daisy decal, center handle **$45.00**
Tray, milk glass w/Pastel Fruit decoration, oval, 13½"........**$420.00**
Treasure chest trinket box, milk glass w/Roses & Bows decoration,
  oblong..**$40.00**
Vase, apricot or dark blue mist w/Daisy decal, crimped top, footed,
  tumbler-like **$30.00**
Vase, blue opaque w/Beaded Bouquet decoration, flat bottom,
  10" **$125.00**

Vase, bud; milk glass w/22k gold, scalloped, footed, 11"......**$30.00**
Vase, Crystal Velvet, belled, footed, 8½" **$40.00**
Vase, swung; milk glass w/Pastel Fruit decoration, slender, 14" ...**$45.00**
Wedding bowl, milk glass w/Roses & Bows decoration, w/lid,
  8" **$80.00**

Tableware

American Hobnail, basket, lilac opalescent, crimped & ruffled, 9½"
  W..**$100.00**
American Hobnail, bowl, milk glass, cupped, 8"..................**$40.00**
American Hobnail, cheese dish, milk glass **$35.00**
American Hobnail, compote, milk glass, footed, flared, 4x8" ..**$20.00**
American Hobnail, creamer, lilac opalescent **$17.50**
American Hobnail, egg cup, milk glass, double....................**$17.50**
American Hobnail, goblet, Brandywine Blue, 8-oz..............**$30.00**
American Hobnail, pitcher, milk glass, w/ice lip, applied
  handle **$65.00**
American Hobnail, plate, luncheon; Brandywine Blue, 8½"...**$22.50**
American Hobnail, tumbler, iced tea; crystal, low foot, 11-oz,
  6¼" **$10.00**
American Hobnail, vase, milk glass, cylindrical, 7½" **$27.00**
Asburton, goblet, water; any color, footed, 6¼" **$12.50**
Ashburton, creamer, any color, footed.................................**$20.00**
Ashburton, goblet, iced tea; any color, flat, 5¾" **$17.50**
Beaded Edge, egg cup, milk glass w/red trim, double..........**$30.00**
Beaded Edge, plate, dinner; milk glass, plain, 10½" **$10.00**
Beaded Edge, plate, dinner; milk glass w/hand-painted decora-
  tion..**$30.00**
Beaded Edge, plate, dinner; milk glass w/red trim, 10½".....**$15.00**
Beaded Edge, salt & pepper shakers, milk glass w/hand-painted
  decoration, pr **$90.00**
Beaded Grape, ashtray, Golden Sunset & Bermuda Blue **$30.00**
Beaded Grape, candlesticks, milk glass w/Pastel Fruit decoration, 4",
  pr..**$48.50**
Beaded Grape, cigarette box, Golden Sunset **$55.00**
Beaded Grape, plate, bread & butter; milk glass **$20.00**
Beaded Grape, plate, dinner; milk glass w/hand-painted decoration,
  10½"..**$65.00**
Beaded Grape, plate, torte; milk glass, 15"...........................**$100.00**
Beaded Grape, vase, milk glass, bell rim, footed, 5¾x3¾"....**$55.00**
Cherry, bowl, milk glass, cupped, footed, 8½" **$160.00**
Cherry, cookie jar, almond or mint green, handles...............**$115.00**
Colonial, ashtray, almond or mint green **$20.00**
Colonial, goblet, water; brown or crystal, footed.................**$10.00**
Colonial, pitcher or jug, Bermuda Blue, flat, 8"..................**$90.00**
Colonial, sherbet, moss or olive green **$7.50**
Della Robbia, basket, crystal w/any stain, oval, 12" **$300.00**
Della Robbia, bowl, crystal w/any stain, heart shape, 1-handle,
  8" **$135.00**
Della Robbia, candy dish, crystal mist w/decoration, footed, domed
  lid **$42.50**
Della Robbia, goblet, wine; milk glass, 4⅝" **$18.50**
Della Robbia, plate, luncheon; crystal w/any stain, 9" **$40.00**
Della Robbia, plate, salad; crystal w/any stain, 7½" **$22.00**
Della Robbia, sugar bowl, Antique Blue, footed...................**$17.50**
Della Robbia, tumbler, water; crystal w/any stain, footed, 8-oz...**$28.00**

Della Robbia, tumbler, water; milk glass, footed, 8-oz **$17.50**
English Hobnail, ashtray, crystal or milk glass, hat form, low .. **$15.00**
English Hobnail, basket, blue or pink pastel, 9" **$65.00**
English Hobnail, bowl, crystal or amber, sq, 6" **$10.00**
English Hobnail, bowl, milk glass, oval, crimped, 11½x10" ... **$25.00**
English Hobnail, coaster, green or pink, 3" **$25.00**
English Hobnail, compote, crystal or milk glass, bell form, footed, 5½" **$14.00**

**English Hobnail, console bowl, amber or crystal, 12",
$30.00.** (Photo courtesy Gene and Cathy Florence)

English Hobnail, creamer, crystal or amber, hex shape, footed.. **$8.00**
English Hobnail, goblet, claret; turquoise, footed, 6" **$20.00**
English Hobnail, goblet, cocktail; green or pink (Roselin), footed, 4½" **$20.00**
English Hobnail, goblet, water; black, 6¼" **$40.00**
English Hobnail, pitcher, ruby carnival, 1-qt **$250.00**
English Hobnail, rose bowl, Almond, 6-pointed, 7-8" **$37.50**
English Hobnail, sherbet, crystal w/black trim, footed......... **$17.50**
English Hobnail, tumbler, ginger ale; crystal or amber, flat, 3¾" **$6.00**
English Hobnail, tumbler, iced tea; milk glass, 12½-oz, 6¼".. **$15.00**
English Hobnail, tumbler, water; crystal or amber, round, footed, 9-oz.. **$8.00**
English Hobnail, tumbler, water; green cased, black foot, 7-oz, 4¾" **$15.00**
Lattice Edge, bowl, milk glass, flared rim, footed, 6½x10½".. **$55.00**
Lattice Edge, plate, black opaque, 11" **$25.00**
Lotus, basket, pink opalescent, oval, footed, 8" **$35.00**
Lotus, bell, pink or pink opalescent, umbrella shape, 4" **$25.00**
Lotus, plate, mayonnaise; Bermuda Blue, 7" **$10.00**
Old Quilt, bowl, milk glass, footed, 4½" **$30.00**
Old Quilt, box, milk glass or crystal, sq, 3½" **$32.50**
Old Quilt, creamer, milk glass, 3½" **$15.00**
Old Quilt, honey dish, crystal or milk glass, sq, w/lid, 5" **$20.00**
Old Quilt, mayonnaise, milk glass, footed, 4½" **$25.00**
Old Quilt, plate, salad; milk glass, 8½" **$35.00**
Old Quilt, tumbler, water; lime green, flat, 9-oz **$27.50**
Paneled Grape, banana bowl, milk glass, belled, footed, 12".. **$125.00**
Paneled Grape, candlesticks, milk glass, skirted, 4", pr......... **$25.00**
Paneled Grape, candy dish, milk glass w/22k gold, footed, w/lid, 6½" **$35.00**
Paneled Grape, celery vase, milk glass, belled rim, footed, 6" (+).. **$45.00**
Paneled Grape, jardiniere, milk glass, cupped, footed, 6½" .. **$65.00**

Paneled Grape, pitcher, juuice; crystal or milk glass, footed, 1-pt.. **$125.00**
Paneled Grape, planter, any color mist, 3x8½" **$28.00**
Paneled grape, planter, milk glass, footed, sq, 4½" **$40.00**
Paneled Grape, puff box/jelly bowl, black, w/lid, 4½" **$25.00**
Paneled Grape, sherbet, Golden Sunset, low foot................. **$25.00**
Paneled Grape, sherbet, milk glass, high foot **$40.00**
Paneled Grape, tray/platter, milk glass, 9" L........................ **$65.00**
Paneled Grape, vase, crystal, belled, footed, 9" **$30.00**
Paneled Grape, vase, milk glass, straight, footed, 9½" **$40.00**
Roe & Lattice, basket, Bermude Blue, blue or moss green, oval, crimped rim...**$50.00**
Rose & Lattice, basket, lilac mist, oval, crimped rim............**$50.00**
Rose & Lattice, bowl, Golden Sunset, flat, 11½"................. **$45.00**
Rose & Lattice, candlesticks, milk glass, pr (+) **$45.00**
Rose & Lattice, vase, crystal w/ruby stain, ruffled, handles (+) **$65.00**
Thousand Eye, candlesticks, crystal w/stain, 5", pr **$60.00**
Thousand Eye, goblet, water; crystal, footed, 6½" **$15.00**
Thousand Eye, plate, dinner; crystal w/stain, 10" **$75.00**
Thousand Eye, plate, salad; crystal, 7" **$10.00**
Thousand Eye, plate, torte; crystal, 18"............................. **$95.00**
Thousand Eye, relish, crystal w/stain, 6-part, 10" dia **$25.00**
Thousand Eye, rose bowl, milk glass, 6-part, 5½x7¾" **$75.00**
Thousand Eye, sugar bowl, crystal w/stain, low................... **$30.00**
Thousand Eye, sugar bowl, green or purple marble, flat, w/lid.. **$65.00**
Thousand Eye, tumbler, ginger ale; crystal, 4" **$18.00**
Thousand Eye, tumbler, iced tea; crystal, footed, 6¾".......... **$20.00**
Thousand Eye, tumbler, old-fashioned; crystal, 3½" **$25.00**
Thousand Eye, turtle ashtray, crystal or moss green **$12.50**

**Waterford, plate, dinner; crystal with ruby stain, 10½",
$55.00.** (Photo courtesy Lorraine Kovar)

Wexford

Wexford is a diverse line of glassware that Anchor Hocking has made since 1967. At one time, it was quite extensive, and a few pieces remain in production yet today. It's very likely you'll see it at any flea market you visit, and it's common to see a piece now and then on your garage sale rounds. It's not only very attractive but serviceable — nothing fragile about this heavy-gauge glassware! Right now, it's not only plentiful but inexpensive, so if you like its looks, now's a good time to begin your collection. Gene and Cathy Florence list 75 pieces in their book *Anchor Hocking's Fire-King and More* and say others will no doubt be reported as collectors become more familiar with the market.

Ashtray, 8½" **$6.00**
Bowl, fruit; footed, 10" **$14.00**
Butter dish, ¼-lb **$6.00**
Cake stand **$18.00**
Candy dish, footed, w/lid, 7¼" **$12.00**
Creamer, 8-oz **$2.50**
Cup, 7-oz **$2.00**

Decanter, 32-ounce, $12.00; bowl, 5", $3.00; vase, footed, 10", $12.50. (Photo courtesy Gene and Cathy Florence)

Goblet, cordial, 3½-oz **$3.00**
Goblet, footed, 10-oz **$3.50**
Jar, 34-oz **$6.00**
Lazy Susan, 9-pc, 14" tray+5¼" bowl+6 4x5¾" inserts on swivel rack **$30.00**
Pitcher, footed, 18-oz **$10.00**
Plate, dinner; scalloped rim, 9½" **$20.00**
Plate, snack; w/indent, 9½" **$2.50**
Platter, 14" dia **$5.00**
Punch bowl base, 9¾" **$10.00**
Relish, 3-part, 8½" **$4.00**
Relish tray, 9⅞x5⅛" **$4.00**
Salt & pepper shakers, 8-oz, pr **$3.00**
Sherbet, stemmed, 7¼-oz **$1.50**
Sugar bowl, w/lid, 8-oz **$3.00**
Tray, 5-part, no center ring, 11" **$9.00**
Tumbler, iced tea; 15-oz **$3.50**
Tumbler, rocks, 9½-oz **$3.50**
Vase, bud; 9" **$3.00**

Wheaton

The Wheaton Company of Millville, New Jersey, has produced several series of bottles and flasks which are very collectible today. One of the most popular features portraits of our country's presidents. There was also a series of 21 Christmas bottles produced from 1971 through 1991, and because fewer were produced during the last few years, the newer ones can be hard to find and often bring good prices. Apollo bottles, those that feature movie stars, ink bottles, and bitters bottles are among the other interesting examples. Many colors of glass have been used, including iridescents.

Abraham Lincoln, decanter, amber, 1970s, 8", MIB **$18.00**
Abraham Lincoln, decanter, amber carnival, 8" **$25.00**
Benjamin Franklin, bottle, amber, mini, 3" **$10.00**
Benjamin Franklin, decanter, teal blue, 8" **$15.00**

Clark Gable, brown, from $12.00 to $15.00.

Colonial Lady in long gown carrying basket, figurine, amber, carnival or blue carnival, 5" **$17.50**
Daniel Webster's Recorder INK/American Eagle, bottle, blue carnival, 3" **$18.00**
Dolphin, candy dish, blue, fish finial, 4½x7¼" **$25.00**
Dwight Ike Eisenhower, decanter, green carnival, 8" **$15.00**
Fish, salt & pepper shakers, blue, 4", pr **$22.50**
George Washington, decanter, white frost, 8" **$20.00**
George Washington (head figural), bottle, light blue, First in War, First in Peace, 3½x2½" **$12.50**
Gerald R Ford, decanter, ruby, 8" **$32.00**
Herbert Hoover, decanter, green, star shape, 1968, 8" **$10.00**
Honeycomb, decanter, ruby, 10½x5½" **$25.00**
Jean Harlow, decanter, amber, star shape **$35.00**
Lace Dewdrop, candy dish, blue, footed, w/lid **$17.50**
Liberty Bell, decanter, ruby, 8x4¾" **$20.00**
Pilgrim (man), bottle, amethyst, original cork, ca 1971, 5½" **$7.50**
Plate, Skylab I, May 15 - June 22, 1973, amber carnival, 8" . **$20.00**

Presidential bottles, various colors, late 1972, set of 12 in White House-shaped box...**$85.00**

Southern Belle, figurine, amber carnival or blue carnival, 5¼" .. **$17.50**

Sunburst, flask, green, w/cork, 5½" **$18.00**

Will-George

This is a California-based company that began operations in the 1930. It was headed by two brothers, William and George Climes, both of whom had extensive training in pottery science. They're most famous today for their lovely figurines of animals and birds, though they produced many human figures as well. For more information on this company as well as many others, we recommend *Collector's Encyclopedia of California Pottery* by Jack Chipman (Collector Books).

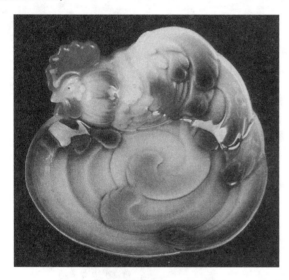

Tray, rooster, small, $75.00. (Photo courtesy Jack Chipman)

Bowl, red onion, green stem finial on lid, 4x4¾" **$30.00**

Candleholders, petal shape, green w/pink interior, 6½", pr ..**$125.00**

Candleholders, upright blade leaves w/1 curled down, turquoise w/ pink interior, 6¼x4¼x2", pr.......................................**$155.00**

Covered dish, reddish pink onion shape w/green top, 4½x4½" ..**$25.00**

Figurine, ballerina, braided auburn hair, holding skirt w/both hands, dress up in back, 9" **$230.00**

Figurine, ballerina girl standing on round base, 5⅜" **$135.00**

Figurine, eagle on rock, white & brown, 10" **$150.00**

Figurine, flamingo, closed-S neck, wings closed, 11½", from $125 to **$145.00**

Figurine, flamingo, head back, wings closed, 10¼", from $175 to...**$200.00**

Figurine, flamingo, head down, wings closed, 6½", from $80 to.. **$100.00**

Figurine, flamingo, head up, wings closed, 10½", from 4150 to... **$165.00**

Figurine, flamingo, head up, wings closed, 12" **$235.00**

Figurine, flamingo, head up, wings up, 8", from $225 to ..**$250.00**

Figurine, flamingo, swimming, head up, wings extended, 3½" ...**$48.00**

Figurine, flamingo in stride/preening, wings extended, round base, 10"...**$200.00**

Figurine, monk, brown bisque, 4½" **$50.00**

Figurine, Oriental boy stands on stool & holds frog, 10"...**$350.00**

Figurine, robin, detailed paint, 3" **$25.00**

Figurine, rooster, multicolor, 4¼".......................................**$50.00**

Figurine, rooster, white w/red comb, 4¼" **$85.00**

Leaf dish w/parrot perched on side, 3¼x14½" **$90.00**

Martini glass, rooster stem w/clear bowl, 5" **$40.00**

Planter, Oriental girl seated on wooden bucket planter, 7½" ..**$85.00**

Planter, Oriental man on knees w/sm basket held on left side of head & lg basket behind, 7½".......................................**$35.00**

Planter, Swiss hiker, flower in left hand, basket on back, 16"..**$50.00**

Planter, ½ red onion shape, 3x11x13" **$45.00**

Plate, luncheon; red onion, 8½" **$15.00**

Tumbler, rooster, formed by tall tail feathers, 4½", from $50 to .**$60.00**

Wilton Cake Pans

You've probably seen several of these as you make your garage sale rounds, but did you know that some are quite collectible? Especially good are the pans that depict cartoon, story book, or movie characters. And, of course, condition is vital — examples with the inserts, instructions, and accessory pieces bring the highest prices.

Wilton started mass merchandising the shaped pans in the early 1960s, and the company has been careful to keep up with trends in pop culture since then. Thus, many of the pans are of limited production which adds to the collectible factor. The company also makes all the items needed for cake decorating, including food dyes, frosting tips, and parchment triangles for making the frosting tubes. In addition, they train instructors in the Wilton method and support the classes in the Wilton method taught at craft stores such as Joann's and Michael's for people who want to learn to decorate. Most of the character and other shaped pans require simple decorating techniques which appeals to amateurs, while the simpler pans (for instance, the heart tiers or the grand piano) can call for more complex decorations, calling for those with professional level decorating skills.

Who knows if there will be a market for Teletubby pans 15 years from now? As with any collectible, future demand is impossible to predict. But since many Wilton pans can be found at garage sales and in thrift stores for $3.00 or less, right now it doesn't take a lot of money to start a collection. Pans without their instructions are worth at least 50% less than if they were present.

Advisor: Cheryl Moody (See Directory, Wilton Cake Pans)

Boba Fett (Star Wars), #502-1852, w/insert, 1983, NM, from $50 to **$70.00**

Bowling a Strike, w/insert, NM, from $10 to **$22.50**

C-3PO (Star Wars), w/insert, 1983, EX............................**$55.00**

Computer/aquarium, #2105-1519, w/insert, 1997, 13½", NM, from $10 to **$20.00**

Cowboy (or girl), #502-3363, 1981, 17", EX, from $16 to ..**$20.00**

Cuddles Cow, #2105-2875, w/insert & instructions, NM, from $10 to **$15.00**

Darth Vader, #502-1409, w/insert, 1980s, EX....................**$60.00**

Football Hero, #2105-4610, w/insert, 1987, NM, from $10 to ..**$25.00**

Frog, #2105-2452, w/insert & instructions, 1979, M, from $20 to **$40.00**

Golf clubs (in bag), #2105-1836, 1987, 16x8½", EX **$15.00**

Grand piano, #502-887, w/attachments, 1973, EX, from $20 to **$40.00**

Little Mermaid, #2105-3400, w/insert, 15x11", NM.......... **$25.00**

Merlin the Wizard, #502-2235, 1984, EX **$42.50**

Mickey Mouse (face), #2105-3603, w/insert & instructions, 2001, M, from $25 to... **$35.00**

Mickey Mouse (full figure), #2105-3601, w/insert & instructions, 1995, NM **$25.00**

Mickey Mouse w/pencil, #502-2987, 1983, EX.................. **$60.00**

Minnie Mouse (full figure), #2105-3602, w/insert & instructions, NM... **$25.00**

Motorcycle, #2105-2025, w/insert & instructions, 1999, M.. **$40.00**

My Little Pony, #2105-2914, w/insert & instructions, 15x11", EX.. **$40.00**

Mystical dragon, #2105-1750, w/insert & instructions, 1984, 15x10½", EX **$70.00**

Pillsbury Dough Boy, 1974, 14x8", EX, from $25 to **$30.00**

Playboy Bunny, #502-2944, w/insert & instructions, EX **$25.00**

R2-D2, #502-1425, w/insert & instructions, 1980, NM..... **$40.00**

Super Heroes (Superman or Batman), with insert, 1981, $20.00. (Photo courtesy whatacharacter.com)

Snoopy the Red Baron, #2105-1319, w/insert & plastic face, EX **$45.00**

Thomas the Tank Engine, #2105-1349, w/insert & instructions, EX, from $15 to **$20.00**

Winnie the Pooh, 3-D, w/core & clips, NM.......................... **$5.00**

Winnie the Pooh #1 Birthday, w/insert & instructions, 19, EX.. **$35.00**

Wonder Woman, #502-7678, w/insert & plastic face, 1978, MIB.. **$60.00**

Winfield

The Winfield pottery first began operations in the late 1920s in Pasadena, California. In 1946 their entire line of artware and giftware items was licensed to the American Ceramic Products Company, who continued to mark their semiporcelain dinnerware with the Winfield name. The original Winfield company changed their trademark to 'Gabriel.' Both companies closed during the early 1960s. For more information see *Collector's Encyclopedia of California Pottery* by Jack Chipman (Collector Books).

Bamboo, bowl, coupe cereal; 6" **$15.00**

Bamboo, bowl, fruit; 5" **$7.50**

Bamboo, bowl, vegetable; sq, 9" **$38.00**

Bamboo, bowl, vegetable; 9" L **$22.00**

Bamboo, cup & saucer.. **$8.00**

Bamboo, sugar bowl, w/lid, 2½" **$17.50**

Bird of Paradise, bowl, divided vegetable; 16" L............... **$16.00**

Bird of Paradise, casserole, w/lid, 2-qt **$24.00**

Bird of Paradise, creamer.. **$7.50**

Bird of Paradise, cup & saucer **$7.50**

Bird of Paradise, gravy boat and tray, from $35.00 to $45.00.

Bird of Paradise, plate, dinner; 10" **$16.00**

Blue Pacific, bowl, divided vegetable; 13" L........................ **$15.00**

Blue Pacific, creamer, 8-oz.. **$12.00**

Blue Pacific, mug **$18.00**

Blue Pacific, plate, dinner; 10" **$18.00**

Desert Dawn, coffeepot... **$38.00**

Desert Dawn, creamer, 12-oz.. **$8.00**

Desert Dawn, cup & saucer **$7.50**

Desert Dawn, gravy boat.. **$24.00**

Desert Dawn, platter, rectangular, 14" L............................ **$18.00**

Desert Dawn, relish, 3-part.. **$25.00**

Dragon Flower, bowl, chowder... **$22.50**

Dragon Flower, bowl, vegetable; 9"................................... **$22.00**

Dragon Flower, plate, chop; sq, 14" **$30.00**

Dragon Flower, plate, dinner.. **$12.00**

Dragon Flower, platter, 12" L **$27.50**

Dragon Flower, sugar bowl, w/lid **$16.00**

Gourmet, bowl, cereal; 6" **$7.50**

Gourmet, bowl, divided vegetable; 13" **$42.50**

Gourmet, creamer, 6-oz **$15.00**

Gourmet, mug **$7.50**

Gourmet, plate, bread & butter **$4.00**

Gourmet, teapot... **$45.00**

Passion Flower, bowl, divided vegetable; oval **$12.00**

Passion Flower, bowl, vegetable; 9" **$22.50**

Passion Flower, creamer.. **$12.00**

Passion Flower, cup & saucer **$7.50**

Passion Flower, gravy boat & underplate............................ **$30.00**

Passion Flower, platter, rectangular, 12" **$22.00**

Passion Flower, salt & pepper shakers, pr........................... **$12.00**

Tiger Iris, bowl, vegetable; 9" L **$30.00**

Tiger Iris, cup & saucer.................................**$7.50**
Tiger Iris, gravy boat **$38.00**
Tiger Iris, plate, dinner **$12.00**
Tiger Iris, platter, rectangular, 14"....................**$32.50**
Tiger Iris, relish, 3-part, lg **$18.00**
Tiger Iris, sugar bowl.......................................**$20.00**

World's Fair Collectibles

Souvenir items have been issued since the mid-1800s for every world's fair and exposition. Few fairgoers have left the grounds without purchasing at least one. Some of the older items were often manufactured right on the fairgrounds by glass or pottery companies who erected working kilns and furnaces just for the duration of the fair. Of course, the older items are usually more valuable, but even souvenirs from the past 50 years are worth hanging on to.

In the following listings, values are given for examples in excellent to near mint condition.

Advisor: Herbert Rolfes (See Directory, World's Fairs and Expositions)

Chicago, 1933

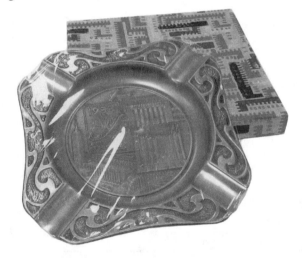

Ashtray, bronzed metal, MIB, $40.00. (Photo courtesy LiveAuctioneers.com/Point Pleasant Galleries)

Ashtray/lighter, metal w/knight standing (lighter in head) on base w/ World's Fair decal, Japan, 7½x6x5"...............**$65.00**
Badge, Century of Progress, 1933, International Exposition, Chicago 1933, nickel plate, Green Duck Co Chi, 2³⁄₁₆x1⅝"......**$155.00**
Badge, radiator grille; Chicago Worlds Fair, I Will 1933, eagle atop brass star shape, Art Forge Inc...1930....................**$110.00**
Bag, Master Marbles, Century of Progress, etc on leather, 4½x3¾" w/drawstring top, +45 assorted solid marbles..............**$135.00**
Book, Chicago & the World's Fair, photos of attractions & architecture, hardcover, 156 pages, 11⅜x8¾"............................**$36.00**
Bottle opener, metal, World's Fair - Chicago - 1933, Kerr Glass Mfg Corp, Sand Springs Okla, 5¼" L **$48.00**

Chef's hat, World's Fair - logo - Chicago 1933 printed on white cloth, some yellowing....................................**$48.00**
Clock, globe novelty, 8-day movement, Gilbert, w/key, 9½" ..**$60.00**
Coasters, embossed fair buildings on brass, 3" dia, set of 6 ..**$30.00**
Compact, celluloid, holds rouge & powder w/2 puffs, beveled mirror, gold & ivory enameling, unused, 3¼x1¾", MN.....**$75.00**
Compact, metal w/embossed Federal Building, Hall of Science, Travel/Transportation Building, green enamel, 2½" L...**$95.00**
Compact, silver-tone metal w/blue enamel, Deco decal, metal mirror, w/powder, rouge & 2 puffs, 1¾x1⅝x⅜", VG **$75.00**
Elongated cent, Chocago World's Fair 1933, embossed........**$36.00**
Fan, hand; romantic riverboat scene printed on heavy paper, Wilson & Co Exhibit, 3-fold, opens to 13" **$45.00**
Lamp, brass w/glass lens, green bulb, World's Fair mark, Chase, 5½x3¼" dia **$120.00**
License plate topper, brass w/eagle atop star, Chicago World's Fair I Will 1933 ....**$70.00**

Match dispenser, metal elephant, 8" long, $225.00.

Money clip, logo embossed on silver, RLB Sterling, 1½x1¼" ..**$32.50**
Pillow cover, fair buildings printed on coral-pink cotton, college pennants on reverse, fringed, 16x17" **$25.00**
Plate, Hall of Science Building, Century of Progress Chicago 1833-1933, china, Pickard, 10½" **$30.00**
Playing cards, 53 fair views, logo backs, NM in EX box **$25.00**
Poster, Deco-style lady stands on globe, seated figures ea side, fair scene beyond, Glen Scheffer, 31½x23¾"+frame **$32.00**
Program, East-West Football, August 24, 20 pages, VG+ **$38.00**
Rug, woven tapestry aerial view of fair, fringed on 2 sides, 50x80" **$65.00**
Souvenir key, Ford Building, Hall of Science Building, embossed metal, 4½" **$30.00**
Thermometer, tower form, silver-tone metal w/blue enameling, Havoline Thermometer Tower...1933 Chicago, 4½x3" ..**$36.00**
Tip tray, glass block building, 1933 Chicago World's Fair A Century of Progress, colored litho on tin **$35.00**
Token, Good Luck, bronze, good luck symbols & fair logo, 1¼" dia..**$50.00**
Toy, GMC Greyhound trailer bus, painted cast iron w/much wear to paint, 14¼" L, G **$135.00**
Toy, Greyhound trailer bus, painted cast iron, Arcade, 5½", VG **$165.00**

Umbrella, red, white & blue paper w/bamboo pole, all spokes in place, working latch, 29x32" dia......................**$55.00**

New York, 1939

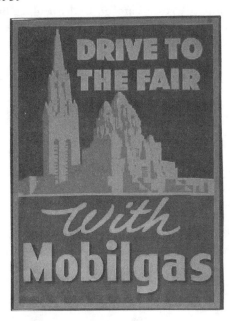

Poster, Mobilgas, scarce, 40x26", NM, $480.00. (Photo courtesy LiveAuctioneers.com/Philip Weiss Auctions)

Ashtray, chrome w/Bakelite base, enameled fair shield, manual tilt lid w/dumping action, 3x3¼" dia........................**$65.00**

Book, World of Tomorrow, Harper & Row NY First Edition, color & black & white photos, hardcover, 240 pages, 1988...**$90.00**

Bottle, Trylon & Perisphere represented in milk glass, embossed 1939 World's Fair 1939 on banner, metal cap, 9x5" **$30.00**

Brooch, arrow, metal w/multicolor enameling, 2⅜" L..........**$28.00**

Butter dish, embossed lettering & Trylon & Perisphere on lid, clear heavy glass, rectangular **$265.00**

Charm bracelet, 6 charms on silver-tone metal chain, Made in USA, 1939, MIP **$35.00**

Compact, Trylon & Perisphere, metal w/rhinestones, attached to leather cover, hinged, mirror, w/powder puff, sq........**$145.00**

Compact, Trylon & Perisphere on mother-of-pearl, mirror, w/puff, 2⅜" dia **$100.00**

Creamer & sugar bowl, Trylon & Perisphere, blue on white ceramic, w/lid, unmarked Porcelier, 3¼x5", 4x5⅜"...................**$175.00**

Frame, Trylon, Perisphere & Helicline in lower left corner, brass, 8x10" **$115.00**

Guide, Official; Unlock the World of Tomorrow, full color, 5½x7" (when folded).......................................**$30.00**

Handkerchief, Trylon & Perisphere embroidered in purple & green on yellow linen, 11½x12" **$24.00**

Kan-O-Seat, chair/cane combination, wood w/fair decal on seat, VG..**$32.50**

Lantern/lamp, brass w/fair illustrations along sides, electric, bail handle..**$110.00**

Magazine, Architectural Forum, spiral bound, 2 color fold-outs, 123 pages, cover wear, VG+ **$55.00**

Map, Sinclair Pictorial Map...Souvenir, includes photo & info about Petroleum Building, G **$24.00**

Paperweight, Trylon & Perisphere, chrome on wood base, 4½" **$28.00**

Pillow, Trylon & Perisphere on satin-like material, warm beige w/ navy & red Deco design, 17x17"+fringe, VG **$55.00**

Plate, Trylon & Perisphere, fair scenes border, blue on white china, Adams of England for Tiffany, 10¼"...........................**$120.00**

Poster, Pond Lily Dill or Sour Pickles..., fair scene, multicolor, 18x12" **$160.00**

Poster, Trylon & Perisphere, The World of Tomorrow, multicolor on navy blue, 36x24" **$27.50**

Scarf, fair scenes & buildings, border of people silhouettes, red, white, blue, yellow & green cloth, 18x20" **$58.00**

Sheet music, Dawn of a New Day, George & Ira Gershwin, copyright 1938, 6-page, glossy Trylon & Perisphere cover....**$55.00**

Teapot, Trylon & Perisphere, gold on cobalt, ceramic, Hall China, 6¼x9¾" **$195.00**

Token, Trylon & Perisphere, brass, 1939, 3" **$42.50**

Token, Trylon & Perisphere embossed on silver-tone metal, marked Official Token **$65.00**

Tray, copper-plated w/orange glass balls along rim, 3½" **$110.00**

Vase, Trylon & Perisphere embossed on white porcelain, Lenox, 5½"...**$300.00**

Seattle, 1962

Ashtray, Monorail scene painted on smoke-colored glass, 4x5" ...**$20.00**

Ashtray, Space Needle in center, metal w/3 rests, 4½" dia....**$24.00**

Bolo tie, silver-tone Space Needle & Monorail medallion w/light green-gray tie **$22.50**

Book, Space Needle USA, Harold Mansfield, photos by G Gulascik, Craftsman Press, softcover, 1962, 10⅞x8⅜", VG **$36.00**

Charm bracelet, gold-tone metal w/10 various fair-related charms, 7"...**$25.00**

Cuff links, fair logo, blue enameling on gold-tone metal, ¾" dia, pr **$27.50**

Dish, clear glass w/silver-overlay Space Needle & flowers, 7½"..**$25.00**

Hobby kit, Space Needle, Century 21, 18", MIB **$55.00**

Lighter, cube-shaped onyx, plaque on side, 3x2½x2½"........**$20.00**

Map, Richfield World's Fair Travel Guide, Space Needle on red & white cover, VG **$17.50**

Mug, Space Needle & monorail embossed on blue-gray stoneware, Pacific Stoneware USA, 4¼x3¼".............................**$35.00**

Necktie, maroon w/Space Needle, Fashion Craft, acetate/rayon blend...**$20.00**

Scarf, multicolor fair scene, silk, 29x29" **$20.00**

Sweatshirt, white logo on green cotton, never worn, sm.......**$47.50**

Toy, telephone, Bell System...Seattle World's Fair, white w/gold lettering, rotary dial, 2x4x2"..**$38.00**

Tumblers, frosted glass w/Space Needle, 6½", set of 4 ....**$20.00**

Wall hanging, goat herder w/goats, hand-carved wood, Ecuador, 6x4" **$20.00**

New York, 1964

Bank, mechanical; Unisphere on US Rocket ship, metal, 11" ...**$165.00**

Banner, Official Red Carpet..., Unisphere, ...Welcomes You, red w/yellow fringe top & bottom, 34x9"..................... **$100.00**

Book, Official Guide; map, ads & exhibits, 312 pages, 8x5".. **$10.00**

Book, Peter & Wendy See the New York World's Fair in Pop-up Action Pictures, Mary Pillsbury, spiral bound, 1963 ..... **$32.50**

Bowl, silver w/bronze insert: NY World's Fair 1964-1965, IBM Electric Typewriter Division..., Cartier, 1⅛x5¼".......... **$75.00**

Bumper sticker, New York World's Fair 1964/65 & Unisphere, M in wrapper.. **$25.00**

Coffee cup, Scout Service Corps, Unisphere, ceramic, USA, 3".. **$30.00**

Doll, inflatable vinyl girl, Alvimar Product, Made in Japan, 1963 New York World's Fair, 14"... **$30.00**

Doll, lady fair guide, cloth, w/hat, purse & camera, 13", mounted on titled stand.. **$75.00**

Encased coin, 1887 Silver dollar, Hall of Education, in acrylic . **$30.00**

Figurine, Unisphere, silver-tone metal................................. **$85.00**

Game, Greyhound Bus Travel Game, board game, complete, NM in VG box... **$30.00**

Incense burner, Oriental scene, hand painted, Hong Kong Pavilion, 4".. **$55.00**

License plate, NY World's Fair 1964-1965, Peace Through Understanding, red, white, blue & black **$100.00**

Matchbook, fair scene, Peace Through Understanding, 6½" L, MIP **$15.00**

Medallion, Pope John XXIII, Vatican Pavilion, gold-plated metal, M in velvet-lined case **$50.00**

Pocketwatch, center black dial rotates, enameled Unisphere logo on silver-tone metal... **$40.00**

Poster, night train scene w/Unisphere, Gateway to the World's Fair..., 12x15", M **$65.00**

Puzzle, jigsaw; Court of Astronauts, Milton Bradley, 750 pcs, EXIB **$15.00**

Souvenir, Unisphere replica, silver, Topping Inc, Elyria OH, Made in USA, copyright 1961, 3½x3" dia, MIB **$38.00**

Stirrer set, plastic holder snaps together, holds 8 gold-tone plastic stirrers, MIB **$60.00**

Tablecloth, various scenes & exhibits printed on white cloth, 52x52", MIP **$95.00**

Tip tray, Unisphere, Peace Through Understanding, litho on stainless steel, 4" dia... **$35.00**

Toy, tire, US Royal Exhibit, plastic, battery-operated, Ideal, 10½", EXIB... **$175.00**

Toy, Unisphere, blue plastic Mold-a-Rama, 3⅝" **$60.00**

Toy, World's Fair Greyhound bus, tin litho, Made in Japan, 12", MIB **$350.00**

Tumblers, frosted glass w/fair scenes, set of 8 .... **$40.00**

Yona

Yona Lippin was a California ceramist who worked for Hedi Schoop in the early 1940s and later opened her own studio. Much of her work is similar to Schoop's. She signed her work with her first name. You'll also find items marked Yona that carry a 'Shafford, Made in Japan' label, suggesting a later affiliation with that importing company. For more information, see *Collector's Encyclopedia of California Pottery* by Jack Chipman (Collector Books).

Christmas ornaments, angels, 1 in orange robe, 2nd in purple robe w/horn, pr... **$30.00**

Cooler, Country Club, red & white stripes w/black letters, brass spigot, 10x8"... **$57.50**

Figurine, clown in tumbling pose, c 1957, 3½x2½" **$25.00**

Figurines, angels, Count Your Blessings..., Always Tell the Truth..., Say Your Prayers, 1956, 5", 3 for **$40.00**

Pill jar, lady w/gray hair, black glasses, Reducing Pills at base... **$32.50**

Salt & pepper shakers, clown tumbling, 4", pr.................... **$22.50**

Auction Houses

Many of the auction galleries we've listed here have allowed us to use their photographs as illustrations in this edition. We're grateful for their co-operation and take this opportunity to extend to them our gratitude. Most of the galleries listed here have appraisal services. Some, though not all, are free of charge. We suggest you contact them first by phone to discuss fees and requirements.

A&B Auctions Inc.
17 Sherman St.
Marboro, MA 01752-3314
508-480-0006
www.aandbauctions.com
English ceramics, flow blue, pottery, and Mason's Ironstone

Allard Auctions Inc.
P.O. Box 1030
419 Flathead St., Ste. 4
Ignatius, MT 59865
406-745-0502
www.allardauctions.com
American Indian collectibles

American Auction Co.
LiveAuctioneers.com

Andre Ammelounx, Stein Auctions
P.O. Box 136
Palatine, IL 60078
847-991-5927
www.garykirsnerauctions.com
Steins; catalogs available

Ant Street Gallery
107 W. Commerce St.
Brenhem, TX 77833
buy@antstreetgallery.com
General antiques and Americana

Apple Tree Auction Center
1616 West Church St.
Newark, OH 43055
www.appletreeauction.com
Glassware, china, jewelry, toys, pottery, and fine art

Aurora
30 Hackmamore Lane, Suite 2
Bell Canyon, CA 91307
818-884-6468
www.auroraauctions.com
Space and aviation memorabilia, automobilia

Bellhorn Auction Services, LLC
Auctioneer and President: Greg Belhorn
P.O. Box 20211
Columbus, OH 43220
614-921-9441
www.belhorn.com

Bertoia Auctions
2141 DeMarco Dr.
Vineland, NJ 08360
856-692-1881 or fax: 856-692-8697
www.bertoiaauctions.com
Online Auctions: Bertoiaonline.com

Antique toys, cast-iron doorstops and door knockers, fine collectibles

Bonhams & Butterfields
220 San Bruno Ave.
San Francisco, CA 94103
415-861-7500
Also: 7601 Sunset Blvd.
Los Angeles, CA 90046
323-850-7500
Also: 595 Madison Ave., 6th Floor
New York, NY 10022
212-644-9001
www.bonhams.com

Brunk Auctions
LiveAuctioneers.com

Buffalo Bay Auction Co.
825 Fox Run Trail
Edmond, OK 74034
405-285-8990
www.buffalobayauction.com
Advertising, tins, and country store items

Calpots.com California Pottery
Michael John Verlangieri
PO Box 844
Cambria, CA 93428
805-927-4428
www.calpots.com

Cerebro
P.O. Box 327
E. Prospect, PA 17317-0327
717-252-2400 or 800-69-LABEL
www.cerebro.com
Antique advertising labels, tobacco ephemera; consignments accepted

Cincinnati Art Galleries
225 E. Sixth St.
Cincinnati, OH 45202
513-381-2128
www.cincinnatiartgalleries.com
American art pottery, American and European fine paintings, watercolors

Clars Auction Galleries
5644 Telegraph Ave.
Oakland, CA 94600
888-339-7600; 510-428-0100
www.clars.com
Fine furniture and antiques, glass, ceramics, Asian arts, fine jewelry, special collections, automobiles

Collector's Auction Services
LiveAuctioneers.com

Conestoga Auction Company
768 Graystone Rd.
Manheim, PA 17545
717-898-7284
www.conestogaauction.com
Antiques, weapons, toys, ephemera, American Indian artifacts, coins

Cooper Owen
74 Station Road
Egham, Sujrrey, TW20 9LF, UK
www.cooperowen.com
Rock 'n roll memorabilia

Craftsman Auctions
109 Main St.
Putnam, CT 06260
860-928-1966
jerry@craftsman-auctions.com
www.craftsman-auctions.com
www.ragoarts.com
Fine pottery, glassware, fifties modern, jewelry, Arts & Crafts; color catalogs available

Dargate Auction Galleries
214 North Lexington
Pittsburgh, PA 15208
412-362-3558
www.gargate.com
Antiques and fine art

David Rago Auctions
Auction hall: 333 N. Main St.
Lambertville, NJ 08530
609-397-9374, fax: 609-397-9377
www.ragoarts.com
info@ragoarts.com
Gallery: 17 S Main St.
Lambertville, NJ 08530
American art pottery and Arts & Crafts

Decoys Unlimited Inc.
Ted and Judy Harmon
P.O. Box 206
2320 Main St.
West Barnstable, MA 02668-0206
www.decoysunlimitedinc.net
Buy, sell, appraise decoys

Dirk Soulis Auctions
P.O. Box 17
Lone Jack, MO 64070
816-697-3830 or 1-800-252-1502
www.dirksoulisauctions.com
Fine art and antiques, furniture, American Indian collectibles, advertising memorabilia, coins, jewelry

Du Mouchelles
409 E. Jefferson Ave.
Detroit, MI 48226-4300
313-963-6255
www.dumouchelle.com
Fine art and antiques, furniture, jewelry

Early American History Auctions
P.O. Box 3507
Rancho Santa Fe, CA 92067
858-759-3290
www.earlyamerican.com
Americana, coins, currency, autographs

Early Auction Co.
123 Main St.
Milford, OH 45150
513-831-4833 or fax: 513-831-1441
www.earlyauctionco.com
Fine art glass, antique furniture, and collectibles

Estate Galleries
LiveAuctioneers.com

Flomaton Antique Auction
207 Palfox St.
Flomaton, AL 36441
251-296-3059
www.flomatonantiqueauction.com
Fine American antiques representing styles in vogue during the nineteenth century

Flying Deuce
14051 W. Chubbuck Rd.
Chubbuck ID 83202
208-237-2002; fax: 208-237-4544
www.flying2.com
flying2@ida.net
Specializing in vintage denim apparel; catalogs $10.00 for upcoming auctions; contact for details on consigning items

Fontaine's Auction Gallery
1485 W. Housatonic St.
Pittsfield, MA 01201
413-448-8922
www.fontaineauction.com
Fine antiques, important twentieth-century lighting, clocks, art glass; color cataogs available

Garth's Auctions Inc.
2690 Stratford Rd.
Box 369, Delaware, OH 43015
740-362-4771
www.garth's.com
Fine art and antiques, primitives, American Indian collectibles, quilts and coverlets, Americana; catalogs available

Glass-Works Auctions
102 Jefferson
East Greenville, PA 18041
215-679-5849
www.glswrk-auction.com
Early American bottles and glass, barbershop memorabilia

Green Valley Auctions Inc.
2259 Green Valley Lane
Mt. Crawford, VA 22841
540-434-4532
www.greenvalleyauctions.com
Southern decorative and folk art, pottery, furniture, carpets, fine art, sculpture, silver, jewelry, glassware, Civil War memorabilia, textiles, toys and dolls, books, Black Americana, ephemera

Hassinger & Courtney Auctioneering
330 Hassinger Way
Richfield, PA 17841
570-658-3536
www.hassingercourtney.com
Real estate, antiques, business liquidations

Henry Pierce Auctioneers
1456 Carson Court
Homewood, IL 60430-4013
708-798-7508
Collectible mechanical and still banks

Homestead Auctions
6825 Wales Ave. N.W. (Rt. 241)
North Canton, OH
330-966-0854
www.homesteadauction.net
Fine art and antiques, Civil War memorabilia, toys

Jackson's International Auctioneers &
    Appraisers of Fine Art & Antiques
2229 Lincoln St.
Cedar Falls, IA 50613
319-277-2256
www.jacksonsauction.com
American and European art pottery and art glass, American and European paintings, decorative arts, toys, and jewelry

James D. Julia Inc.
P.O. Box 830, Rt. 201
Skowhegan Rd.
Fairfield, ME 04937
207-453-7125 or fax: 207-453-2502
www.juliaauctions.com
Fine art and antiques, art glass, lighting, toys, jewelry

John Toomey Gallery
818 N. Blvd.
Oak Park, IL 60301-1302
708-838-5234, fax: 708-383-4828
www.treadwaygallery.com
Furniture and decorative arts of the Arts & Crafts, Art Deco, and Modern Design movements; modern design expert: Richard Wright

Joy Luke Fine Art Brokers and
    Auctioneers
300 E. Grove St.
Bloomington, IL 61701-5290
309-828-5533, fax: 309-829-2266
www.joyluke.com
Antiques, furniture, paintings, Picard china

K. D. Smith Auctions
1901 S. 12th St.
Allentown, PA 18103
610-797-1770
GI Joes, coins, vintage toys

L. R. 'Les' Docks
Box 691035
San Antonio, TX 78269-1035
Providing occasional mail-order record auctions, rarely consigned (the only consignments considered are exceptionally scarce and unusual records)

Lang's Sporting Collectibles Inc.
633 Pleasant Valley Road
Waterville, NY 13480
513-841-4623
www.langsauction.com
Consigns, appraises, auctions antique fishing tackle and memorabilia

Leslie Hindman Auctioneers
122 N. Aberdeen St.
Chicago, IL 60607
3312-280-1212, fax: 312-280-1211
www.lesliehindman.com
Fine arts, antiques, jewelry

Livingston's Auction
4229 Royal Ave., Suite 103
Oklahoma City, OK 75108
405-858-1914
www.LivingstonsAuction.com
Quality items from fine estates, consignments, specialty items, fine and decorative arts

Lloyd Ralston Gallery Inc.
549 Howe Ave.
Shelton, CT 06484
203-924-5804, fax: 203-924-5834
www.lloydralstontoys.com
Toy trains and railroad collectibles, antique toy soldiers, diecast vehicles, antique toys

Luper Auction Galleries
11171 Mill Valley Road
Omaha, NE 68154
www.proxibid.com

Lyn Knight Auctions
P.O. Box 7364
Overland Park, KS 66207
800-243-5211 or 913-338-3379
www.lynknight.com
Coins, currency, postcards

Manion's International Auction House Inc.
P.O. Box 12214
Kansas City, KS 66112
913-299-6692, fax: 913-299-6792
www.manions.com
Militaria, firearms, catalog and internet

McMasters Harris Auction Company
P.O. Box 1755
5855 Glenn Highway
Cambridge, OH 43725-8768
740-432-7400, fax: 740-432-3191;
800-842-3526
www.mcmastersharris.com
Quality antique dolls and toys

Metropolitan Galleries at Shaker Square
13119 Shaker Blvd.
Cleveland, OH 44120
216-491-1111, fax: 26-491-1109
www.metropolitangalleries.com
Fine arts and antiques, silver, carpets, jewelry

Michael Ivankovich Antiques &
    Auction Co. Inc.
P.O. Box 1536
Doylestown, PA 18901
215-345-6094
www.nutting.com
Early hand-colored photography and prints, Wallace Nutting

Monson & Baer, Annual Perfume
    Bottle Auction
Monsen, Randall; and Baer, Rod
Box 529,
Vienna, VA 22183;
703-938-2129, fax: 703-242-1357
Cataloged auctions of perfume bottles; will purchase, sell, and accept consignments; specializing in commercial, Czechoslovakian, Lalique, Baccarat, Victorian, crown top, factices, miniatures

Noel Barrett Antiques & Auctions
P.O. Box 300; 6183 Carversville Rd.
Carversville, PA 18913
215-297-5109, fax: 215-297-0457
www.noelbarrett.com
Antique toys, games, advertising

Norman C. Heckler & Company
79 Bradford Corner Rd.
Woodstock Valley, CT 06282
860-974-1634, fax: 860-974-2003
www.hecklerauction.com
Auctioneers and appraisers of early glass and bottles

O.P.M. Auctions Limited
Robert Baker
790 South Sunrise Hwy.
Bellport, NY 11713
www.opmauctins.com
Fine art, antiques, and collectibles

Past Tyme Pleasures
Steven and Donna Howard
PMB #204
2491 San Ramon Blvd., #1
San Ramon, CA 94583
915-484-4488
www.pasttyme1.com
Offers 2 absentee auction catalogs per year pertaining to old advertising items

Perrault-Rago Gallery
333 N. Main St.
Lambertville, NJ 08530
609-397-9374
www.ragoarts.com
American art pottery, tiles, Arts & Crafts, Moderns, and Bucks County paintings

Philip Weiss Auctions
1 Neil Court
Oceanside, NY 11572
516-594-0731, fax: 516-594-9414
www.philipweissauctions
Collectibles, used and rare books, consultant for many of the country's top auction galleries

Phoebus Auction Gallery
18 E. Mellen St.
Hampton, VA 2363
757-722-9210
www.phoebusauction
Antique furniture, fine and decorative art, jewelry, ceramics, sterling, crystal

Point Pleasant Galleries
626 Ocean Road
Point Pleasant, NJ 08742
732-892-2217, fax 732-892-8304
www.pointpleasantgalleries.com
Estate auctions, collectibles, general line

Premier Auction Center
P.O. Box 537
Post Falls, ID 83877-0537
208-777-8724 or (WA) 509-879-4142
www.premierauctioncenter.com
Quality consignments, eBay Live auctions

R. G. Munn Auction LLC
P.O. Box 705
Cloudcroft, NM 88713
505-687-3767, fax: 505-687-3592
LiveAuctioneers.com
American Indian art and collectibles

R. O. Schmitt Fine Arts
P.O. Box 162
Windham, NH 03087
603-432-2237, fax: 603-432-2271
www.roschmittfinearts.com
Clocks, music boxes, scientific instruments

Randy Inman Auctions Inc.
P.O. Box 726
Waterville, ME 04903
027-872-6900, fax: 207-872-6966
www.inmanauctions.com
Antique toys, advertising, general line

Rich Penn Auctions
P.O. Box 1355
Waterloo, IA 50704
319-291-6688, fax: 319-291-7136
www.richpennauctions.com
Country store memorabilia and antique
advertising

Richard D. Hatch & Associates
913 Upward Road
Flat Rock, NC 28731
828-696-3440, 828-696-0817
www.richardhatchauctions.com
Appraisals, onsite auctions
LiveAuctioneers.com

Richard Opfer Auctioneering, Inc.
1919 Greenspring Dr.
Timonium, MD 21093-4113
410-252-5035, fax: 410-252-5863
www.opferauction.com
info@opferauction.com
Antique dolls, toys, trains, advertising,
collectibles, antique furniture, jewelry,
decorative ceramic, and glassware

RSL Auction Company
1039 Lakemont Dr.
Pittsburgh, PA 15243
1-800-349-8009 or (NJ) 908-439-0064
www.rslauctions.com
Banks, toys, American folk art, Tiffany
lamps, door stops, sculpture

Showplace Antique Center Inc.
40 W. 25th St. (5–6 Aves.)
212-633-6063
www.nyshowplace.com
New York City's best art and antiques
center with over 250 galleries

Skinner, Inc.
The Heritage on the Garden
63 Park Plaza
Boston, MA 02116-3925
617-350-5400, fax: 617-350-5429
Also: 357 Main St.
Bolton, MA 01740
978-779-6241, fax: 978-779-5144
www.skinnerinc.com
Auctioneers and appraisers of antiques
and fine art

Slotin Folk Art
112 E. Shadburn Ave., Buford Hall
Buford, GA 30518
www.slotinfolkart.com
Self-taught art, folk art

Smith & Jones, Inc.
12 Clark Lane
Sudbury, MA 01776
978-443-5517, fax: 978-443-8045
www.smithandjonesauctions.com
Dedham dinnerware, Buffalo china, and
important American art pottery; full-
color catalogs available

Smith House Toy & Auction Co.
P.O. Box 129
Telford, PA 18969
215-721-1389, fax: 215-721-1503
www.smithhousetoys.com
Quality antique toy auctions

Strawser Auction Group
Majolica Auctions
200 N. Main; P.O. Box 332
Wolcottville, IN 46795-0332
260-854-2859, fax: 260-854-3979
www.strawserauctions.com
Issues color catalogs, also specializing in
Fiestaware

Sunflower Auctions
7375 W. 161st St.
Overland Park, KS 66085
www.sunflowerauction.com
Antiques and collectibles, specializing in
eBay Live auctions

Tom Harris Auctions
203 South 18th Ave.
Marshalltown, IA 50158
614-754-4890
www.tomharrisauctions.com
Clocks, watches, high quality antiques
and collectibles, estate and lifetime collections, eBay Live auctions, NAWCC,
NAA, CAI

Treadway Gallery Inc.
2029 Madison Rd.
Cincinnati, OH 45208
513-321-6742, fax: 513-871-7722
www.treadwaygallery.com
info@treadwaygallery.com
Member: National Antique Dealers
Association, American Art Pottery
Association, International Society of
Appraisers, and American Ceramic Arts
Society

TW Conroy, LLC
101 W. Main Street
Elbridge, NY 13060
315-689-3342, fax: 315-638-7039
www.twconroy.com

Antiques, house contents, real estate

Vicki and Bruce Waasdorp
P.O. Box 434
10931 Main St.
Clarence, NY 14031
716-759-2361
www.antiques-stoneware.com
Fine and unusual decorated stoneware,
catalogs available

Willis Henry Auctions Inc.
22 Main St.
Marshfield, MA 02050
781-834-7774, fax: 781-826-3520
www.willishenry.com
Shaker, Americana, decoys, antique
furniture

Wendler's Auction
23811 Washington Ave. C110 #313
Murrieta, CA 92562
951-347-2852
Antique furniture, decorative arts,
bronzes

Wm. Morford
RD #2, Cazenovia, NY 13035
315-662-7625, fax: 315-662-3570
www.morfauction
Antique advertising, Maxfield Parrish
items, comic character toys, political
items, games, shaving mugs, salesman

Contributing Websites

These websites have been the source of photographs as well as information:
www.cloudcity.com
www.gasolinealleyantiques.com
www.lifeofrileycollectiques.net
www.retro-redheads.com
www.rubylane.com
www.SweetlandForemost.com
www.timewasantiques.com
www.whatacharacter.com

Clubs and Newsletters

Several collectors' clubs and newsletters are mentioned throughout this book in their respective categories. There are many more available to collectors today; some are generalized and cover the entire realm of antiques and collectibles, while others are devoted to a specific interest such as toys, coin-operated machines, character collectibles, or railroadiana. We've listed several below. You can obtain a copy of most newsletters simply by requesting one. If you'd like to try placing a 'for sale' ad or a mail bid in one of them, see the introduction for suggestions on how your ad should be composed.

Antique Advertising Association of
    America (AAAA)
P.O. Box 76
Petersburg, IL 62675
Newsletter: *Past Times*

Butter Pat Patter Association
265 Eagle Bend Drive
Bigfork, MT 59911-6235
Newsletter: *The Patter*

International Carnival Glass
    Association, Inc.
Lee Markley, Secretary
Box 306
Mentone, IN 46359

Cast Iron Collector's Club
Contact Dan Murphy Auctions
717-335-3455
morphyauctions.com

Central Florida Insulator Collectors
3557 Nicklaus Dr.
Titusville, FL 32780-5356
407-267-9170
bluebellwt@aol.com

Newsnotes newsletter
Coin-op online newsletter
Ken Durham, Publisher
909 26th St., NW; Suite 502
Washington, DC 20037
www.GameRoomAntiques.com

National Bicycle History Archive
Box 862
Gig Harbor, WA 98335
714-335-9072
Oldbicycle@aol.com
www.nbhaa.com

Newspaper Collectors Society of
    America
517-887-1255
info@historybuff.com
www.historybuff.com

Nutcracker Collectors' Club
Susan Otto, Editor
11204 Fox Run Dr.
Chesterland, OH 44026

Old Stuff
Donna and Ron Miller, Publishers
P.O. Box 1084
McMinnville, OR 97128
www.oldstuffnews.com

Paperweight Collectors Association Inc.
P.O. Box 4153
Emerald Isle, NC 28594
info@paperweight.org

Southern Oregon Antiques and
    Collectibles Club
P.O. Box 508
Talent, OR 97540
www.soacc.com
contact@soacc.com

Statue of Liberty Collectors' Club
Iris November
P.O. Box 535
Chautauqua, NY 14722
www.statueoflibertyclub.com

Thimble Collectors International
Jina Samulka, membership chairperson
membershipVP@thimble.collectors.com
www.thimblecollectors.com

Tiffin Glass Collectors
P.O. Box 554
Tiffin, OH 44883
www.tiffinglass.org

The Wheelmen
Magazine: *Wheelmen Magazine*
Steven Hartson
1135 Portsmuth Ave.
Greenland, NH 03840
www.thewheelmen.org
stephenhartson@verison.net

Directory of Contributors and Special Interests

In this section of the book we have listed dealers/collectors who specialize in many of the fields this price guide covers. Many of them have sent information, photographs, or advised us concerning current values and trends. This is a courtesy listing, and they are under no obligation to field questions from our readers, though some may be willing to do so. If you do write to any of them, don't expect a response unless you include an SASE (stamped self-addressed envelope) with your letter. If you have items to offer them for sale or are seeking information, describe the piece in question thoroughly and mention any marks. You can sometimes do a pencil rubbing to duplicate the mark exactly.
If you write to them, include your phone number as well as your email address, since many people would rather respond with a call or an email than a letter. If you're trying to reach someone by phone, always consider the local time on the other end of your call.

With the exception of the Advertising, Character Collectibles, Dinnerware, and and Toys sections which we've alphabetized by character, pattern/manufacturer or type, our experts are listed alphabetically under bold topics, generally the topic for which they advise us. Recommended reference guides not available from Collector Books may be purchased directly from the authors whose addresses are given in this section.

Advertising
Aunt Jemima
Judy Posner
P.O. Box 2194 SC
Englewood, FL 34295
judyposner@yahoo.com
Also Black Americana, Disney, cookie
jars, novelty salt and pepper shakers;
buy, sell, and trade

Big Boy
Steve Soelberg
29126 Laro Dr.
Agoura Hills, CA 91301
818-889-9909

Airline Memorabilia
Richard Wallin
P.O. Box 22
Rochester, IL 62563
217-498-9279
RRWALLIN@aol.com

Akro Agate
Author of book
Claudia and Roger Hardy
West End Antiques
10 Bailey St.
Clarksburg, WV 26301
304-624-7600 (days)
304-624-4523 (evenings)
Closed Sundays & Mondays; Specializ-
ing in furniture, glass, and Akro authors

of *The Complete Line of Akro Agate Co.;*
Specializing in Akro Agate

Aprons
Darrell Thomas
PO Box 418
New London, WI 54961
woodenclockworks@msn.com

Ashtrays
Tire ashtrays
Author of book ($12.95 postpaid)
Jeff McVey
1810 W State St., #427
Boise, ID 83702

Automobilia
Leonard Needham
P.O. Box 689
Bethel Island, CA 94511
925-684-9674
screensider@sbcgolbal.net

Autumn Leaf
Gwynneth Harrison
11566 River Heights Dr.
Riverside, CA 92505
morgan27@sbcglobal.com

Avon Collectibles
Author of book
Bud Hastin
P.O. Box 11530
Ft. Lauderdale, FL 33339

Banks

Modern mechanical banks
Dan Iannotti
212 W Hickory Grove Rd.
Bloomfield Hills, MI 48302-1127S
248-335-5042
modernbanks@sbcglobal.net

Barware

Author of book
Stephen Visakay
visakay@optonLine.net
Founding member of The Museum of
the American Cocktail
www.MuseumOfTheAmericanCocktail.org

Beanie Babies

Amy Sullivan
c/o Collector Books
P.O. Box 3009
Paducah, KY 42002-3009
amysullivan@collectorbooks.com

Black Cats

*Author of book: Peggy's Mews on Black
Cats*
Peggy Way
Parker, CO
www.catcollectors.com
www.catladyauctions.com
Advanced cat collector specializing in Black
Cats from the 1950s; To order book, email
Glenna Moore at mooremews@hawaiiantel.
net; For identification or evaluation, email
photo and request to Peggy: CatCollectors@
earthlink.net

Black Glass

Author of book
Marlena Toohey
703 S Pratt Pky.
Longmont, CO 80501
303-678-9726

Bookends

Author of book
Louis Kuritzky
4510 NW 17th Pl.
Gainesville, FL 32605
352-377-3193
lkuritzky@aol.com

Boyd's Bears

Christine Cregar
Bearly Believable
218 Elizabeth Drive
Stephens City, VA 22655
Bearlybelievable@msn.com
www.wagglepop.com/stores/bearlybelievablegifts

British Royal Commemoratives

*Author of book, catalogs issued monthly,
$5 each*
Audrey Zeder
1320 SW 10th St
North Bend, WA 98045
Specializing in British Royalty commemoratives from Queen Victoria's
reign through current royalty events

Brush-McCoy Pottery

Authors of book
Steve and Martha Sanford
230 Harrison Ave.
Campbell, CA 95008
408-978-8408
www.sanfords.com

Bubble Bath Containers

Matt and Lisa Adams
Tatonka Toys
8155 Brooks Dr.
Jacksonville, FL 32244
904-772-6911
matadams@bellsouth.net
Also character nodders

California Pottery

Marty Webster
6943 Suncrest Drive
Saline, MI 48176
313-944-1188
Also Orientalia

*Editor of newsletter: The California
Pottery Trader*
Michael John Verlangieri Gallery
Calpots.com
P.O. Box 844
W Cambria, CA 93428-0844
805-927-4428
www.calpots.com
michael@calpots.com
Specializing in fine California pottery;
cataloged auctions (video tapes avail-
able)

Camark

Tony Freyaldenhoven
2200 Ada Ave., Ste. 305
Conway, AR 72034
501-730-3027 or 501-932-0352
tonyfrey@conwaycorp.net

Cameras

Classic, collectible, and usable
C.E. Cataldo
Gene's Cameras
4726 Panorama Dr. SE
Huntsville, AL 35801
256-536-6893
genecams@aol.com

Wooden, detective, and stereo
John A. Hess
P.O. Box 3062
Andover, MA 01810
Also old brass lenses, 19th-century
photography

Candy Containers

Glass
Jeff Bradfield
90 Main St.
Dayton, VA 22821
540-879-9961
Also advertising, cast-iron and tin toys,
postcards, and Coca-Cola

Cape Cod by Avon

Debbie and Randy Coe
Coe's Mercantile
P.O. Box 173
Hillsboro, OR 97123
Also Elegant and Depression glass, art
pottery, Fenton, Golden Foliage by Lib-
bey Glass Company, and Liberty Blue
dinnerware

Cast Iron

*Door knockers, sprinklers, figural paper-
weights, and marked cookware*
Craig Dinner
P.O. Box 131
Warwick NY 10990
ferrouswheel123@aol.com

Cat Collectibles

Peggy Way
International Cat Collectors Club
CatCollectors@earthlink.net
www.CatCollectors.com

Ceramic Arts Studio

*Author of numerous Schiffer Publishing
Ltd. books on collectibles*
Donald-Brian Johnson
3329 South 56th Street, #611
Omaha, NE 68106
donaldbrian@webtv.net
Books include *Ceramic Arts Studio: The
Legacy of Betty Harrington* (in association
with Timothy J. Holthaus and James
E. Petzold), and (with co-author Leslie
Paña), *Higgins: Adventures in Glass;
Higgins: Poetry in Glass; Moss Lamps:
Lighting the '50s; Specs Appeal: Extrava-
gant 1950s and 1960s Eyewear; Whiting
& Davis Purses: The Perfect Mesh; Popular
Purses: It's In the Bag;* and a four-volume
series on the Chase Brass & Copper Co.

Character and Personality Collectibles

Any and all
Terri Ivers
Terri's Toys & Nostalgia
114 Whitworth Ave.
Ponca City, OK 74601
580-762-8697
toylady@cableone.net
Also lunch boxes, Halloween, and
Hartland figures

Batman, Gumby, and Marilyn Monroe
Colleen Garmon Barnes
114 E Locust
Chatham, IL 62629

Beatles
Bojo
Bob Gottuso
P.O. Box 1403
Cranberry Twp., PA 16066-0403
phone or fax: 724-776-0621
bojo@zbzoom.net
www.bojoon.line.com
We do rock 'n roll pricing for all of
Schroeder's guides; specializing in

Beatles, KISS, Monkees, and Elvis
original licensed memorabilia. Beatles
sale catalogs are available 4 times a year
at $3 a copy.

*Disney Western heroes, Gone With the
Wind, character watches ca 1930s to
mid-1950s, premiums, and games*
Ron and Donna Donnelly
Saturday Heroes
15847 Edwardian Dr.
Northport, AL 35475
Buy, sell, trade

Elvis Presley
Lee Garmon
1529 Whittier St.
Springfield, IL 62704

Christmas Collectibles

*Especially from before 1920 and
decorations made in Germany*
J.W. 'Bill' and Treva Courter
3935 Kelley Rd.
Kevil, KY 42053
270-488-2116

Clocks

All types
Bruce A. Austin
1 Hardwood Hill Rd.
Pittsford, NY 14534
716-387-9820
baagll@rit.edu

Clothing and Accessories

Ken Weber
1119 Seminole Trail
Carrollton, TX 75007
cecilimose@aol.com
www.vintagemartini.com

Flying Deuce
1224 Yellowstone
Pocatello, ID 83201
208-237-2002, fax: 208-237-4544
flying2@ida.net

Cookie Jars

Joe Devine
1411 3rd St.
Council Bluffs, IA 51503
712-328-7305
Buy, sell, and trade

Corkscrews

Author of books
Donald Bull
P.O. Box 596
Wirtz, VA 24184
540-721-1128
corkscrew@bullworks.net
www.corkscrewmuseum.com

Cracker Jack Items

Harriet Joyce
415 Soft Shadow Lane
DeBarry, FL 32713-2343

Author of books
Larry White
108 Central St.
Rowley, MA 01969-1317
978-948-8187
larry@larrywhite2.com

Crackle Glass
Authors of book
Stan and Arlene Weitman
101 Cypress St.
Massapequa Park, NY 11758
www.crackleglass.com
scrackled@earthlink.net
Also specializing in Overshot

Cuff Links
Just Cuff Links
Eugene R. Klompus
P.O. Box 5970
Vernon Hills, IL 60061
847-816-0035, fax: 847-816-7466
genek@cufflinksrus.com
www.justcufflinks.com
Also related items

Cups and Saucers
Authors of books
Jim and Susan Harran
208 Hemlock Dr.
Neptune, NJ 07753
www.tias.com/stores/amit

Decanters
Roy Willis
Heartland of Kentucky Decanters and Steins
P.O. Box 428
Lebanon Jct., KY 40150
heartlandky@ka.net.
www.decantersandsteins.com
Huge selection of limited edition decanters and beer steins — open showroom; include large SASE (2 stamps) with correspondence; fee for appraisals

deLee
Authors of book
Joanne and Ralph Schaefer
3182 Williams Rd.
Oroville, CA 95965-8300
530-893-2902 or 530-894-6263
jschaefer@sunset.net

Dinnerware
Blue Danube
Lori Simnioniw
Auburn Main St. Antiques
120 E. Main St.
Auburn, WA 98002
253-804-8041
Specializing in glassware, china, jewelry, and furniture

Blue Ridge
Authors of several books
Bill and Betty Newbound
2206 Nob Hill Dr.

Sanford, NC 27330
Also milk glass, wall pockets, figural planters, collectible china and glass

Currier & Ives Dinnerware
Author of book
Eldon R. Bud Aupperle
29470 Saxon Road
Toulon, IL 61483
309-896-3331, fax: 309-856-6005

Mark J. Skrobis
4016 Jerelin Dr.
Franklin, WI 53132-8727
414-737-4109
mjskrobis@wi.rr.com

Franciscan, LuRay Pastels, Depression Glass, and other American dinnerware
Shirley and Art Moore
4423 E. 31st Street
Tulsa, OK 74135

Fiesta, Franciscan, Bauer, Harlequin, Riviera, Lu Ray, Metlox, and Homer Laughlin
Dishes Old and New
Mick and Lorna Chase
380 Hawkins Crawford Rd.
Cookeville, TN 38501
931-372-8333
www.dishesoldandnew.com

Homer Laughlin China
Author of book
Darlene Nossaman
5419 Lake Charles
Waco, TX 76710

Liberty Blue
Gary Beegle
92 River St.
Montgomery, NY 12549
845-457-3623
Also most lines of collectible modern American dinnerware as well as Depression glass

Restaurant China
Author two restaurant china books
Barbara J. Conroy
http://restaurant-china.home.comcast.net/home.htm
Details contents of *Restaurant China, Volumes 1 & 2*,; information on restaurant china item names, reproductions, manufacturers' marks, related books, and so forth, with links to other restaurant china sites

Royal China
BA Wellman
P.O. Box 673
Westminster, MA 01473-0673
ba@dishinitout.com
Also Ceramic Arts Studio

Russel Wright, Eva Zeisel, Homer Laughlin
Charles Alexander

221 E 34th St.
Indianapolis, IN 46205
317-924-9665
chasalex1848@sbcglobal.net

Vernon Kilns
Ray Vlach
rayvlach@hotmail.com

Dollhouse Furniture and Accessories
Renwal, Ideal, Marx, etc.
Judith A. Mosholder
186 Pine Springs Camp Rd.
Boswell, PA 15531
814-629-9277
jlytwins@floodcity.net

Dolls
Annalee Mobilitee Dolls
Jane's Collectibles
Jane Holt
P.O. Box 115
Derry, NH 03038-0115

Betsy McCall
Marci Van Ausdall
betsymccallfanclub@hotmail.com

Dolls from the 1960s – 1970s, including Liddle Kiddles, Barbie, Tammy, Tressy, etc.
Co-author of several books
Cindy Sabulis
P.O. Box 642
Shelton, CT 06484
203-926-0176
toys4two@snet.net
www.dollsntoys.com
Books include *Collector's Guide to Dolls of the 1960s & 1970s, Volumes I & II; Collector's Guide to Tammy, the Ideal Teen*

Dolls from the 1960s – 1970s, including Liddle Kiddles, Dolly Darlings, Petal People, Tiny Teens, etc.
Author of book on Liddle Kiddles; must send SASE for info
Paris Langford
415 Dodge Ave.
Jefferson, LA 70121
504-733-0667
bbean415@aol.com

Liddle Kiddles and other small dolls from the late '60s and early '70s
Dawn Diaz
20460 Samual Dr.
Saugus, CA 91530-3812
661-263-8697
jamdiaz99@earthlink.net

Egg Cups
Author of book
Brenda Blake
Box 555
York Harbor, ME 03911
301-652-1140
eggcentric@aol.com

Erich Stauffer Figurines
Joan Oates
1107 Deerfield Lane
Marshall, MI 49068
269-781-9791
koates120@earthlink.net
Also Phoenix Bird china

Fishing Collectibles
Publishes fixed-price catalog
Dave Hoover
1023 Skyview Dr.
New Albany, IN 47150
Also miniature boats and motors
lurejockey@aol.com

Fitz and Floyd
Susan Robson
516 Greenridge Drive
Coppell, TX 75019

Flashlights
Author of book; Editor of newsletter
Bill Utley
P.O. Box 4095
Tustin, CA 92781
714-730-1252
flashlight1@cox.net

Florence Ceramics
Jerry Kline
Florence Showcase
4546 Windlow Dr.
Strawberry Plains, TN 37871
865-932-0182
artpotterynants@bellsouth.net

Flower Frogs
Author of book
Bonnie Bull
Flower Frog Gazette Online
www.flowerfrog.com

Frankoma
Author of book
Phyllis Bess Boone
14535 E 13th St.
Tulsa, OK 74108

Fruit Jars
Especially old, odd, or colored jars
John Hathaway
3 Mills Rd.
Bryant Pond, ME 04219
207-665-2124
Also old jar lids and closures

Gas Station Collectibles
Scott Benjamin
Oil Co. Collectibles Inc.
Petroleum Collectibles Monthly Magazine
P.O. Box 556
LaGrange, OH 44050-0556
440-355-6608
Specializing in gas globes, signs, and magazines
www.oilcollectibles.com
www.gasglobes.com

Gay Fad Glassware
Donna S. McGrady
P.O. Box 14, 301 E. Walnut St.
Waynetown, IN 47990
765-234-2187
dmcg@tctc.com

Geisha Girl China
Author of book
Elyce Litts
P.O. Box 394
Morris Plains, NJ 07950
201-707-4241
happy-memories@worldnet.att.net
www.happy-memories.com
Also ladies' compacts

Gilner Potteries
Collector of Gilner Pottery
Carla Chilton
8351 Balboa Blvd #39
Northridge, CA 91325-4078
carlew1@earthlink.net

Carol Power
P.O. Box 528
Columbia, CA 95310
Also Pixie collectibles
PixieWatch@wyoming.com
www.rvingthegoldfields.com/Pixie
Watch/Index.htm

Glass Animals
Authors of book
Dick and Pat Spencer
Glass and More (Shows only)
1203 N. Yale
O'Fallon, IL 62269
618-632-9067
Specializing in Cambridge, Fenton,
Fostoria, Heisey, etc.

Granite Ware
Author of books
Helen Greguire
Helen's Antiques
79 Lake Lyman Hgts.
Lyman, SC 29365
864-848-0408
Also carnival glass and toasters

**Griswold and Wagner Cast-Iron
Cooking Ware**
Sharon and Charly Harvey
14303 Shiloh Way
Laurel, DE 19956-3168
eBay user: sandcea

Guardian Service Cookware
2110 Harmony Woods Road
Owings Mills, MD 21117-1649
410-560-0777
www.members.aol.com/vettelvr93

Hagen-Renaker
Hagen-Renaker Collector's Club
c/o Ed & Sheri Alcorn
14945 Harmon Dr.

Shady Hills, FL 34610
727-856-6762
horsenut@gate.net
www.geocities.com/heartland/7456/
index.html
US subscription rate: $24 a year

Hadley, M.A.
Lisa Sanders
8900 Old State Rd.
Evansville, IN 47711-1326
1dlk@insight.bb.com

Halloween
*Author of books; autographed copies
available from the author*
Pamela E. Apkarian-Russell
The Halloween Queen™
577 Boggs Run Rd.
Benwood, WV 26031-1001
halloweenqueen@castlehalloween.com
www.castlehalloween.com
Lectures and tours available at Castle
Halloween museum. Also interested
in other holidays, postcards, and Joe
Camel

Head Vases and String Holders
Larry G. Pogue
L&J Antiques & Collectibles
8142 Ivan Court
Terrell, TX 75161-6921
972-551-0221
landjantiques@direcway.com
www.landjantiques.com (TIAS.com
member)
Also antique and estate jewelry, egg timers, clothes sprinkler bottles

Horton Ceramics
Darlene Nossaman
5419 Lake Charles
Waco, TX 76710

Indy 500 Memorabilia
Eric Jungnickel
P.O. Box 4674
Naperville, IL 60567-4674
630-983-8339
ericjungnickel@yahoo.com

Insulators
Jacqueline Linscott Barnes
3557 Nicklaus Dr.
Tutusville, FL 32780
bluebellwt@aol.com

Japan Ceramics
Author of books
Carole Bess White
2225 NE 33rd
Portland, OR 97212-5116

Jewel Tea
Products or boxes only; no dishes
Bill & Judy Vroman
739 Eastern Ave.
Fostoria, OH 44830
419-435-5443

Jewelry
Author, lecturer, and appraiser
Marcia Brown (Sparkles)
P.O. Box 2314
White City, OR 97503
541-826-3039, fax: 541-830-5385
Author of *Unsigned Beauties of Costume
Jewelry* and *Signed Beauties of Costume
Jewelry, Vols. I & II*; and *Coro Jewelry*; Co-
author and host of seven *Hidden Treasure*
book-on-tape videos; Antique shows:
Robby/Don Miller appraisal clinics,
Palmer Wirf shows, Calendar shows

Josef Originals
Authors of books
Jim and Kaye Whitaker
Eclectic Antiques
P.O. Box 475, Dept. GS
Lynnwood, WA 98046
eclecticantiques.com
Also motion lamps

Kentucky Derby and Horse Racing
Betty L. Hornback
707 Sunrise Ln.
Elizabethtown, KY 42701
bettysantiques@kvnet.org
Inquiries require a SASE with fee
expected for appraisals and/or identification of glasses. Booklet picturing
Kentucky Derby, Preakness, Belmont,
and other racing glasses available for
$15 ppd.

Kitchen Prayer Ladies
Judy Foreman
JudyForeman@alltel.net

Lamps
Aladdin
Author of books
J.W. Courter
3935 Kelley Rd.
Kevil, KY 42053
502-488-2116

License Plates
Richard Diehl
5965 W Colgate Pl.
Denver, CO 80227

Linens
De Witt & Co.
402-683-2515
402-683-3455 (after hours)
michael@dewittco.com
www.dewittco.com
Carry a wide variety of vintage textiles
and ephemera — fabric, needlework, feed
sacks, sewing patterns; also vintage valentines, road maps, magazines, and postcards

Retro Redheads
www.retro-redheads.com
1-978-8898; on the Web since 1997
An online catalog of vintage linens and
housewares for the Modern Gal and
Dapper Guy

Longaberger Baskets
Editor of collector's guide
Jill S. Rindfuss
597 Sunbury Rd.
Delaware, OH 43015
800-837-4394
infobg@bentleyguide.com
www.bentleyguide.com
The Bently Collection Guide® the most
accurate and reliable reference tool
available for evaluating Longaberger®
products; Full color with individual
photographs of most baskets and
products produced since 1979; Published once a year in June with a free
six-month update being sent in January
to keep the guide current for the entire
year

Magazines
*Issues price guides to illustrators, pinups,
and old magazines of all kinds*
Denis C. Jackson
Illustrator Collector's News
P.O. 6433
Kingman, AZ 86401
ticn@olypen.com

Mar-Crest
Rita Pence
Louisville, KY 40214-1147
OutOfTheBluegrass.com
mail@mar-crest.com
www.mar-crest.com

Match Safes
George Sparacio
P.O. Box 791
Malaga, NJ 08328
856-694-4167, fax: 856-694-4536
mrvesta1@aol.com

Marbles
Author of books
Everett Grist
P.O. Box 91375
Chattanooga, TN 37412-3955
423-510-8052

McCoy Pottery
Author of books
Robert Hanson
P.O. Box 1945
Woodenville, WA 98072

Metlox
Author of book; available from author
Carl Gibbs, Jr.
c/o California Connection
1716 Westheimer Rd.
Houston, TX 77098

Morton Pottery
Authors of books
Doris and Burdell Hall
B&B Antiques
210 W Sassafrass Dr.
Morton, IL 61550-1245

Motorcycles and Motorcycle Memorabilia

Bob 'Sprocket' Eckardt
P.O. Box 172
Saratoga Springs, NY 12866
518-584-2405
sprocketBE@aol.com
Buying and trading; Also literature, posters, toys, trophies, medals, fobs, pennants, FAM – AMA & Gypsy Tour items, programs, photos, jerseys, clocks, advertising items, signs, showroom items, motorcycles, and parts

Napkin Dolls

Co-Author of book
Bobbie Zucker Bryson
634 Cypress Hills Drive
Bluffton, SC 29909
843-705-3820
napkindoll@aol.com
To order a copy of the second edition of *Collectibles for the Kitchen, Bath & Beyond* (featuring 500+ new items & updated pricing on napkin dolls, egg timers, string holders, children's whistle cups and baby feeder dishes, razor blade banks, pie birds, laundry sprinkler bottles, and other unique collectibles from the same era), contact Krause Publications, P.O. Box 5009, Iola, WI 54945-5009
1-800-258-0929

Occupied Japan Collectibles

Florence Archambault
29 Freeborn St.
Newport, RI 03850-1821
florence@aiconnect.com
Publishes *The Upside Down World of an O.J. Collector,* published bimonthly; Information requires SASE

Paper Dolls

Author of books
Mary Young
P.O. Box 9244
Wright Bros. Branch
Dayton, OH 45409-9244

Pencil Sharpeners

Phil Helley
629 Indiana Ave.
Wisconsin Dells, WI 53965
608-254-8659

Pennsbury Pottery

Shirley Graff
4515 Graff Rd.
Brunswick, OH 44212

Perfume Bottles

Especially commercial, Czechoslovakian, Lalique, Baccarat, Victorian, crown top, factices, miniatures; Buy, sell, and accept consignments for auctions
Monsen and Baer
Box 529
Vienna, VA 22183

703-938-2129
Also Roseville, Art Deco

Pez

Richard Belyski
P.O. Box 14956
Surfside Beach, SC 29587
peznews@juno.com
www.pezcollectorsnews.com

Pie Birds

Linda Fields
230 Beech Lane
Buchanan, TN 38222
731-644-2244
Fpiebird@compu.net.
Organizer of pie bird collector's convention and author of *Four & Twenty Blackbirds; Vols. I & II.* Specializing in pie birds, pie funnels, and pie vents

Pixies

Collector of Pixies
Carla Chilton
8351 Balboa Blvd., #39
Northridge, CA 91325-4078
carlew1@earthlink.net

Author of CD for Pixie collectors
Carol Power
P.O. Box 528
Columbia, CA 95310
PixieWatch@wyoming.com
www.rvingthegoldfields.com/Pixie
Watch/Index.htm
Also Gilner pottery in general

Political Memorabilia

Michael and Polly McQuillen
McQuillen's Collectibles
P.O. Box 50022
Indianapolis, IN 46250
317-845-1721
michael@politicalparade.com
www.politicalparade.com
Also Pin-Back Buttons

Pins, banners, ribbons, etc.
Paul Longo Americana
Box 5510
Magnolia, MA 01930
978-525-2290

Puzzles

Wooden jigsaw type from before 1950
Bob Armstrong
Worcester, MA 01609
508-799-0644
raahna@oldpuzzles.com

Radio Premiums

Bill and Anne Campbell
3051 Foxbriar Lane
Cibolo, TX 78108
803-626-1077
captainmarvel11940@satx.rr.com
Also character clocks and watches

Railroadiana

Lila Shrader
Shrader Antiques
2025 Hwy. 199
Crescent City, CA 95531
707-458-3525
Also steamship and other transportation memorabilia; Buffalo, Shelley, Niloak, and Hummels

Razor Blade Banks

Deborah Gillham
47 Midline Ct.
Gaithersburg, MD 20878
301-977-5727

Records

Picture and 78 rpm kiddie records
Peter Muldavin
173 W 78th St. Apt 5-F
New York, NY 10024
212-362-9606
kiddie78s@aol.com
www.members.aol.com/kiddie78s

Especially 78 rpms, author of book
L.R. 'Les' Docks
Box 780218
San Antonio, TX 78278-0218
docks@texas.net (no attachments please!)
www.docks.home.texas.net

Red Wing Artware

Holds cataloged auctions
Wendy and Leo Frese
Three Rivers Collectibles
P.O. Box 551542
Dallas, TX 75355
214-341-5165
Also RumRill pottery

Rooster and Roses

Jacki Elliott
9790 Twin Cities Rd.
Galt, CA 95632
209-745-3860

Rosemeade

NDSU research specialist
Bryce Farnsworth
1334 14½ St. South
Fargo, ND 58103
701-237-3597

Roseville

Author of books
Mike Nickel
P.O. Box 456
Portland, MI, 48875
517-647-7646
mandc@voyager.net
Also Kay Finch, other Ohio art pottery

Royal Copley

Author of books
Joe Devine
1411 3rd St.
Council Bluffs, IA 51503
712-328-7305
Buys & sells; Also pie birds

Scouting Collectibles

R.J. Sayers
P.O. Box 629
Brevard, NC 28712
Certified antiques appraiser; owner of Southeastern Antiques & Collectibles
305 N. Main St.
Hendersonville, NC 28792
rjsayers@citcom.net
Also Pisgah Forest pottery

Sewing

Kathy Goldsworthy
Past Glories
5302 234th St. E
Spanaway, WA 98387
pastglories@comcast.net

Shawnee

Authors of books
Beverly and Jim Mangus
4812 Sherman Church Ave SW
Canton, OH 44706-3958

Marceyne Sharp and Joyce Higbee
22932 Carpenterville Rd.
Brookings, OR 97415
marjoy7@wave.net

Shot Glasses

Author of book
Mark Pickvet
Shot Glass Club of America
5071 Watson Dr.
Flint, MI 48506
Also playing cards

Silhouette Pictures (20th Century)

Author of book
Shirley Mace
Shadow Enterprises
P.O. Box 1602
Mesilla Park, NM 88047
505-524-6717
shadow-ent@zianet.com

Silver-plated and Sterling Flatware

Rick Spencer
Salt Lake City, Utah
801-973-0805
repousse@hotmail.com
Especially grape patterns in silver plate; also Coors, Watt, Regal

Skookum Indian Dolls

Jo Ann Palmieri
27 Pepper Rd.
Towaco, NJ 07082-1357

Smiley Face
Pam Speidel
84475 Hwy. 35
Norfolk, NE 68701
pam@smileycollector.com
www.smileycollector.com

Soda Fountain Collectibles
Harold and Joyce Screen
2804 Munster Rd.
Baltimore, MD 21234
410-661-6765
hscreen@comcast.net

Soda-Pop Memorabilia
Craig Stifter
0062 Elk Mountain Drive
Redstone, CO 81623
cstifter@gmail.com

Sports Collectibles
Kevin R. Bowman
P.O. Box 4500
Joplin, MO 64803
showmequail@joplin.com

Equipment and player-used items
Don and Anne Kier
2022 Marengo St.
Toledo, OH 43614
d.a.k.@worldnet.att.net
Also Royal Bayreuth, Rose O'Neill
Kewpies, autographs

St. Clair Glass
Ted Pruitt
3350 W 700 N
Anderson, IN 46011
Book available ($25)

Stangl
Birds, dinnerware, artware
Popkorn Antiques
Bob and Nancy Perzel
P.O. Box 1057
Flemington, NJ 08822
908-782-9631

Swanky Swigs
Joyce Jackson
817-441-8864
jjpick3@earthlink.net

Tiara Exclusives
Author of Books
Mandi Birkinbine
P.O. Box 121
Meridian, ID 83680-0121
info@shop4antiques.com
www.shop4antiques.com
*Tiara Tiara Exclusives Glass: The
Sandwich Pattern* (pictures and values of
Tiara's Sandwich pattern in over 20 dif-
ferent colors, $39.00+$2.75 postage and
handling in the continental US)

Toys
Hot Wheels
D.W. (Steve) Stephenson
11117 NE 164th Pl.
Bothell, WA 98011-4003
425-488-2603, fax: 425-488-2841

Slot race cars from 1960s – 1970s
Gary T. Pollastro
5047 84th Ave. SE
Mercer Island, WA 98040
206-232-3199

Transformers and Robots
David Kolodny-Nagy
Toy Hell
P.O. Box 75271
Los Angeles, CA 90075
toyhell@yahoo.com
www.toyhell.com

Walkers, ramp-walkers, and windups
Randy Welch
Raven'tiques
27965 Peach Orchard Rd.
Easton, MD 21601-8203
410-822-5441

Treasure Craft
Author of book
George A. Higby, ISA
Sutton Place #205
1221 Minor Ave.
Seattle, WA 98101
206-682-7288
geoahigby@hotmail.com

TV Guides
TV Guide Specialists
Jeff Kadet
P.O. Box 20
Macomb, IL 61455
Giant illustrated 1948 – 1999 TV Guide
Catalog, $3.00; 2000+ catalog, $2.00

Twin Winton
Author of book; now out of print
Mike Ellis
266 Rose Ln.
Costa Mesa, CA 92627
949-646-7112, fax: 949-645-4919
Also Don Winton designs (other than
Twin Winton)

Valentines
*Author of three books on subject; available
from author*
Katherine Kreider
P.O. Box 7957
Lancaster, PA 17604-7957
717-892-3001
Katherinekreider@valentinesdirect.com
www.valentinesdirect.com
Appraisal fee schedule upon request;
Please send a self-addressed stamped
envelope for any replies

Vernon Kilns
Ray Vlach
rayvlach@hotmail.com

Wade
Author of book
Ian Warner
P.O. Box 93022
Brampton, Ontario
Canada L6Y 4V8
idwarner@rogers.com

Wedding Cake Toppers
Author of book
Jeannie Greenfield
310 Parker Rd.
Stoneboro, PA 16153-2810
724-376-2584
dlg3684@yahoo.com
25-year collector of wedding toppers
and memorabilia; author of *Wedding*

Cake Toppers, Memories and More (soon
to be released) with hundreds of color
photos and 76 bibliography sources,
containing a complete history of toppers
and customs; more than 500 toppers
shown in more than 100 photos; tips on
restoration, display, storage, etc.

Weller Pottery
Hardy Hudson
1896 Wingfield Dr.
Longwood, FL 32779
447-404-9009 or 407-963-6093
todiefor@mindspring.com
Also Roseville, Grueby, Newcomb,
Overbeck, Pewabic, Ohr, Teco, Fulper,
Clewell, Tiffany, etc.

Wilton Pans
Cheryl Moody
Hoosier Collectibles
607 N. Lafayette Blvd.
South Bend, IN 46601
www.rubylane.com/shops/hoosiercol
lectibles

World's Fairs and Expositions
Herbert Rolfes
Yesterday's World
P.O. Box 398
Mount Dora, FL 32756
352-735-3947
NY1939@aol.com

Index